MICHIGAN

RULES OF COURT

VOLUME II – FEDERAL

2018

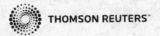
THOMSON REUTERS

Mat #42056312

ISBN 978-0-314-69535-2

PREFACE

Designed for use in the office or courtroom, this pamphlet contains Michigan federal rules.

WHAT'S NEW

Michigan Rules of Court, Volume II – Federal, 2018, includes rules and associated material governing practice before the Michigan federal courts. It is current with amendments received through January 1, 2018.

CONTACT US

For additional information or research assistance, call the reference attorneys at 1-800-REF-ATTY (1-800-733-2889). Contact our U.S. legal editorial department directly with your questions and suggestions by e-mail at editors.us-legal@tr.com.

Thank you for subscribing to this product. Should you have any questions regarding this product please contact Customer Service at 1-800-328-4880 or by fax at 1-800-340-9378. If you would like to inquire about related publications, or to place an order, please contact us at 1-888-728-7677 or visit us at legalsolutions.thomsonreuters.com.

THE PUBLISHER

February 2018

THOMSON REUTERS PROVIEW™

This title is one of many now available on your tablet as an eBook.

Take your research mobile. Powered by the Thomson Reuters ProView™ app, our eBooks deliver the same trusted content as your print resources, but in a compact, on-the-go format.

ProView eBooks are designed for the way you work. You can add your own notes and highlights to the text, and all of your annotations will transfer electronically to every new edition of your eBook.

You can also instantly verify primary authority with built-in links to WestlawNext® and KeyCite®, so you can be confident that you're accessing the most current and accurate information.

To find out more about ProView eBooks and available discounts, call 1-800-344-5009.

TABLE OF CONTENTS

FEDERAL
RULES OF CIVIL PROCEDURE

Including Amendments Effective December 1, 2017

TITLE I. SCOPE OF RULES; FORM OF ACTION

RULE 1. SCOPE AND PURPOSE

These rules govern the procedure in all civil actions and proceedings in the United States district courts, except as stated in Rule 81. They should be construed, administered, and employed by the court and the parties to secure the just, speedy, and inexpensive determination of every action and proceeding.

(Amended December 29, 1948, effective October 20, 1949; February 28, 1966, effective July 1, 1966; April 22, 1993, effective December 1, 1993; April 30, 2007, effective December 1, 2007; April 29, 2015, effective December 1, 2015.)

RULE 2. ONE FORM OF ACTION

There is one form of action—the civil action.

(Amended April 30, 2007, effective December 1, 2007.)

TITLE II. COMMENCING AN ACTION; SERVICE OF PROCESS, PLEADINGS, MOTIONS, AND ORDERS

RULE 3. COMMENCING AN ACTION

A civil action is commenced by filing a complaint with the court.

(Amended April 30, 2007, effective December 1, 2007.)

RULE 4. SUMMONS

(a) Contents; Amendments.

(1) *Contents.* A summons must:

(A) name the court and the parties;

(B) be directed to the defendant;

(C) state the name and address of the plaintiff's attorney or—if unrepresented—of the plaintiff;

(D) state the time within which the defendant must appear and defend;

(E) notify the defendant that a failure to appear and defend will result in a default judgment against the defendant for the relief demanded in the complaint;

(F) be signed by the clerk; and

(G) bear the court's seal.

(2) *Amendments.* The court may permit a summons to be amended.

(b) Issuance. On or after filing the complaint, the plaintiff may present a summons to the clerk for signature and seal. If the summons is properly completed, the clerk must sign, seal, and issue it to the plaintiff for service on the defendant. A summons—or a copy of a summons that is addressed to multiple defendants—must be issued for each defendant to be served.

(c) Service.

(1) *In General.* A summons must be served with a copy of the complaint. The plaintiff is responsible for having the summons and complaint served within the time allowed by Rule 4(m) and must furnish the necessary copies to the person who makes service.

(2) *By Whom.* Any person who is at least 18 years old and not a party may serve a summons and complaint.

(3) *By a Marshal or Someone Specially Appointed.* At the plaintiff's request, the court may order that service be made by a United States marshal or deputy marshal or by a person specially appointed by the court. The court must so order if the plaintiff is authorized to proceed in forma pauperis under 28 U.S.C. § 1915 or as a seaman under 28 U.S.C. § 1916.

(d) Waiving Service.

(1) *Requesting a Waiver.* An individual, corporation, or association that is subject to service under Rule 4(e), (f), or (h) has a duty to avoid unnecessary expenses of serving the summons. The plaintiff may notify such a defendant that an action has been commenced and request that the defendant waive service of a summons. The notice and request must:

(A) be in writing and be addressed:

(i) to the individual defendant; or

(ii) for a defendant subject to service under Rule 4(h), to an officer, a managing or general agent, or any other agent authorized by appointment or by law to receive service of process;

(B) name the court where the complaint was filed;

(C) be accompanied by a copy of the complaint, 2 copies of the waiver form appended to this Rule 4, and a prepaid means for returning the form;

(D) inform the defendant, using the form appended to this Rule 4, of the consequences of waiving and not waiving service;

(E) state the date when the request is sent;

(F) give the defendant a reasonable time of at least 30 days after the request was sent—or at least 60 days if sent to the defendant outside any judicial district of the United States—to return the waiver; and

(G) be sent by first-class mail or other reliable means.

(2) *Failure to Waive.* If a defendant located within the United States fails, without good cause, to sign and return a waiver requested by a plaintiff located within the United States, the court must impose on the defendant:

(A) the expenses later incurred in making service; and

(B) the reasonable expenses, including attorney's fees, of any motion required to collect those service expenses.

(3) *Time to Answer After a Waiver.* A defendant who, before being served with process, timely returns a waiver need not serve an answer to the complaint until 60 days after the request was sent—or until 90 days after it was sent to the defendant outside any judicial district of the United States.

(4) *Results of Filing a Waiver.* When the plaintiff files a waiver, proof of service is not required and these rules apply as if a summons and complaint had been served at the time of filing the waiver.

(5) *Jurisdiction and Venue Not Waived.* Waiving service of a summons does not waive any objection to personal jurisdiction or to venue.

(e) Serving an Individual Within a Judicial District of the United States. Unless federal law provides otherwise, an individual—other than a minor, an incompetent person, or a person whose waiver has been filed—may be served in a judicial district of the United States by:

(1) following state law for serving a summons in an action brought in courts of general jurisdiction in the state where the district court is located or where service is made; or

(2) doing any of the following:

(A) delivering a copy of the summons and of the complaint to the individual personally;

(B) leaving a copy of each at the individual's dwelling or usual place of abode with someone of suitable age and discretion who resides there; or

(C) delivering a copy of each to an agent authorized by appointment or by law to receive service of process.

(f) Serving an Individual in a Foreign Country. Unless federal law provides otherwise, an individual—other than a minor, an incompetent person, or a person whose waiver has been filed—may be served at a place not within any judicial district of the United States:

(1) by any internationally agreed means of service that is reasonably calculated to give notice, such as those authorized by the Hague Convention on the Service Abroad of Judicial and Extrajudicial Documents;

(2) if there is no internationally agreed means, or if an international agreement allows but does not specify other means, by a method that is reasonably calculated to give notice:

(A) as prescribed by the foreign country's law for service in that country in an action in its courts of general jurisdiction;

(B) as the foreign authority directs in response to a letter rogatory or letter of request; or

(C) unless prohibited by the foreign country's law, by:

(i) delivering a copy of the summons and of the complaint to the individual personally; or

(ii) using any form of mail that the clerk addresses and sends to the individual and that requires a signed receipt; or

(3) by other means not prohibited by international agreement, as the court orders.

(g) Serving a Minor or an Incompetent Person. A minor or an incompetent person in a judicial district of the United States must be served by following state law for serving a summons or like process on such a defendant in an action brought in the courts of general jurisdiction of the state where service is made. A minor or an incompetent person who is not within any judicial district of the United States must be served in the manner prescribed by Rule 4(f)(2)(A), (f)(2)(B), or (f)(3).

(h) Serving a Corporation, Partnership, or Association. Unless federal law provides otherwise or the defendant's waiver has been filed, a domestic or foreign corporation, or a partnership or other unincorporated association that is subject to suit under a common name, must be served:

(1) in a judicial district of the United States:

(A) in the manner prescribed by Rule 4(e)(1) for serving an individual; or

(B) by delivering a copy of the summons and of the complaint to an officer, a managing or general agent, or any other agent authorized by appointment or by law to receive service of process and—if the agent is one authorized by statute and the statute so requires—by also mailing a copy of each to the defendant; or

(2) at a place not within any judicial district of the United States, in any manner prescribed by Rule 4(f) for serving an individual, except personal delivery under (f)(2)(C)(i).

(i) Serving the United States and Its Agencies, Corporations, Officers, or Employees.

(1) *United States.* To serve the United States, a party must:

(A)(i) deliver a copy of the summons and of the complaint to the United States attorney for the district where the action is brought—or to an assistant United States attorney or clerical employee whom the United States attorney designates in a writing filed with the court clerk—or

(ii) send a copy of each by registered or certified mail to the civil-process clerk at the United States attorney's office;

(B) send a copy of each by registered or certified mail to the Attorney General of the United States at Washington, D.C.; and

(C) if the action challenges an order of a nonparty agency or officer of the United States, send a copy of each by registered or certified mail to the agency or officer.

(2) *Agency; Corporation; Officer or Employee Sued in an Official Capacity.* To serve a United States agency or corporation, or a United States officer or employee sued only in an official capacity, a party must serve the United States and also send a copy of the summons and of the complaint by registered or certified mail to the agency, corporation, officer, or employee.

(3) *Officer or Employee Sued Individually.* To serve a United States officer or employee sued in an individual capacity for an act or omission occurring in connection with duties performed on the United States' behalf (whether or not the officer or employee is also sued in an official capacity), a party must serve the United States and also serve the officer or employee under Rule 4(e), (f), or (g).

(4) *Extending Time.* The court must allow a party a reasonable time to cure its failure to:

(A) serve a person required to be served under Rule 4(i)(2), if the party has served either the United States attorney or the Attorney General of the United States; or

(B) serve the United States under Rule 4(i)(3), if the party has served the United States officer or employee.

(j) Serving a Foreign, State, or Local Government.

(1) *Foreign State.* A foreign state or its political subdivision, agency, or instrumentality must be served in accordance with 28 U.S.C. § 1608.

(2) *State or Local Government.* A state, a municipal corporation, or any other state-created governmental organization that is subject to suit must be served by:

(A) delivering a copy of the summons and of the complaint to its chief executive officer; or

(B) serving a copy of each in the manner prescribed by that state's law for serving a summons or like process on such a defendant.

(k) Territorial Limits of Effective Service.

(1) *In General.* Serving a summons or filing a waiver of service establishes personal jurisdiction over a defendant:

(A) who is subject to the jurisdiction of a court of general jurisdiction in the state where the district court is located;

(B) who is a party joined under Rule 14 or 19 and is served within a judicial district of the United States and not more than 100 miles from where the summons was issued; or

(C) when authorized by a federal statute.

(2) *Federal Claim Outside State–Court Jurisdiction.* For a claim that arises under federal law, serving a summons or filing a waiver of service establishes personal jurisdiction over a defendant if:

(A) the defendant is not subject to jurisdiction in any state's courts of general jurisdiction; and

(B) exercising jurisdiction is consistent with the United States Constitution and laws.

(*l*) Proving Service.

(1) *Affidavit Required.* Unless service is waived, proof of service must be made to the court. Except for service by a United States marshal or deputy marshal, proof must be by the server's affidavit.

(2) *Service Outside the United States.* Service not within any judicial district of the United States must be proved as follows:

(A) if made under Rule 4(f)(1), as provided in the applicable treaty or convention; or

(B) if made under Rule 4(f)(2) or (f)(3), by a receipt signed by the addressee, or by other evidence satisfying the court that the summons and complaint were delivered to the addressee.

(3) *Validity of Service; Amending Proof.* Failure to prove service does not affect the validity of service. The court may permit proof of service to be amended.

(m) Time Limit for Service. If a defendant is not served within 90 days after the complaint is filed, the court—on motion or on its own after notice to the plaintiff—must dismiss the action without prejudice against that defendant or order that service be made within a specified time. But if the plaintiff shows good cause for the failure, the court must extend the time for service for an appropriate period. This subdivision (m) does not apply to service in a foreign country under Rule 4(f), 4(h)(2), or 4(j)(1), or to service of a notice under Rule 71.1(d)(3)(A).

(n) Asserting Jurisdiction over Property or Assets.

(1) *Federal Law.* The court may assert jurisdiction over property if authorized by a federal statute. Notice to claimants of the property must be given as provided in the statute or by serving a summons under this rule.

(2) *State Law.* On a showing that personal jurisdiction over a defendant cannot be obtained in the district where the action is brought by reasonable efforts to serve a summons under this rule, the court may assert jurisdiction over the defendant's assets found in the district. Jurisdiction is acquired by seizing the assets under the circumstances and in the manner provided by state law in that district.

Rule 4   Notice of a Lawsuit and Request to Waive Service of Summons.

(Caption)

To (*name the defendant or — if the defendant is a corporation, partnership, or association — name an officer or agent authorized to receive service*):

Why are you getting this?

A lawsuit has been filed against you, or the entity you represent, in this court under the number shown above. A copy of the complaint is attached.

This is not a summons, or an official notice from the court. It is a request that, to avoid expenses, you waive formal service of a summons by signing and returning the enclosed waiver. To avoid these expenses, you must return the signed waiver within (*give at least 30 days or at least 60 days if the defendant is outside any judicial district of the United States*) from the date shown below, which is the date this notice was sent. Two copies of the waiver form are enclosed, along with a stamped, self-addressed envelope or other prepaid means for returning one copy. You may keep the other copy.

What happens next?

If you return the signed waiver, I will file it with the court. The action will then proceed as if you had been served on the date the waiver is filed, but no summons will be served on you and you will have 60 days from the date this notice is sent (see the date below) to answer the complaint (or 90 days if this notice is sent to you outside any judicial district of the United States).

If you do not return the signed waiver within the time indicated, I will arrange to have the summons and complaint served on you. And I will ask the court to require you, or the entity you represent, to pay the expenses of making service.

Please read the enclosed statement about the duty to avoid unnecessary expenses.

I certify that this request is being sent to you on the date below.

Date: _____

_____
(Signature of the attorney
or unrepresented party)

_____
(Printed name)

_____
(Address)

_____
(E-mail address)

_____
(Telephone number)

Rule 4   Waiver of the Service of Summons.

(Caption)

To (*name the plaintiff's attorney or the unrepresented plaintiff*):

I have received your request to waive service of a summons in this action along with a copy of the complaint, two copies of this waiver form, and a prepaid means of returning one signed copy of the form to you.

I, or the entity I represent, agree to save the expense of serving a summons and complaint in this case.

I understand that I, or the entity I represent, will keep all defenses or objections to the lawsuit, the court's jurisdiction, and the venue of the action, but that I waive any objections to the absence of a summons or of service.

I also understand that I, or the entity I represent, must file and serve an answer or a motion under Rule 12 within 60 days from_____, the date when this request was sent (or 90 days if it was sent outside the United States). If I fail to do so, a default judgment will be entered against me or the entity I represent.

Date: _____

_____
(Signature of the attorney
or unrepresented party)

_____
(Printed name)

_____
(Address)

_____
(E-mail address)

_____
(Telephone number)

(Attach the following)

Duty to Avoid Unnecessary Expenses of Serving a Summons

Rule 4 of the Federal Rules of Civil Procedure requires certain defendants to cooperate in saving unnecessary expenses of serving a summons and complaint. A defendant who is located in the United States and who fails to return a signed waiver of service requested by a plaintiff located in the United States will be required to pay the expenses of service, unless the defendant shows good cause for the failure.

"Good cause" does not include a belief that the lawsuit is groundless, or that it has been brought in an improper venue, or that the court has no jurisdiction over this matter or over the defendant or the defendant's property.

If the waiver is signed and returned, you can still make these and all other defenses and objections, but you cannot object to the absence of a summons or of service.

If you waive service, then you must, within the time specified on the waiver form, serve an answer or a motion under Rule 12 on the plaintiff and file a copy with the court. By signing and returning the waiver form, you are allowed more time to respond than if a summons had been served.

(Amended January 21, 1963, effective July 1, 1963; February 28, 1966, effective July 1, 1966; April 29, 1980, effective August 1, 1980; amended by Pub.L. 97-462, § 2, January 12, 1983, 96 Stat. 2527, effective 45 days after January 12, 1983; amended March 2, 1987, effective August 1, 1987; April 22, 1993, effective December 1, 1993; April 17, 2000, effective December 1, 2000; April 30, 2007, effective December 1, 2007; April 29, 2015, effective December 1, 2015; April 28, 2016, effective December 1, 2016; April 27, 2017, effective December 1, 2017.)

RULE 4.1. SERVING OTHER PROCESS

(a) In General. Process—other than a summons under Rule 4 or a subpoena under Rule 45—must be served by a United States marshal or deputy marshal or by a person specially appointed for that purpose. It may be served anywhere within the territorial limits of the state where the district court is located and, if authorized by a federal statute, beyond those limits. Proof of service must be made under Rule 4(*l*).

(b) Enforcing Orders: Committing for Civil Contempt. An order committing a person for civil contempt of a decree or injunction issued to enforce federal law may be served and enforced in any district. Any other order in a civil-contempt proceeding may be served only in the state where the issuing court is located or elsewhere in the United States within 100 miles from where the order was issued.

(Adopted April 22, 1993, effective December 1, 1993; amended April 30, 2007, effective December 1, 2007.)

RULE 5. SERVING AND FILING PLEADINGS AND OTHER PAPERS

(a) Service: When Required.

(1) In General. Unless these rules provide otherwise, each of the following papers must be served on every party:

(A) an order stating that service is required;

(B) a pleading filed after the original complaint, unless the court orders otherwise under Rule 5(c) because there are numerous defendants;

(C) a discovery paper required to be served on a party, unless the court orders otherwise;

(D) a written motion, except one that may be heard ex parte; and

(E) a written notice, appearance, demand, or offer of judgment, or any similar paper.

(2) If a Party Fails to Appear. No service is required on a party who is in default for failing to appear. But a pleading that asserts a new claim for relief against such a party must be served on that party under Rule 4.

(3) Seizing Property. If an action is begun by seizing property and no person is or need be named as a defendant, any service required before the filing of an appearance, answer, or claim must be made on the person who had custody or possession of the property when it was seized.

(b) Service: How Made.

(1) Serving an Attorney. If a party is represented by an attorney, service under this rule must be made on the attorney unless the court orders service on the party.

(2) Service in General. A paper is served under this rule by:

(A) handing it to the person;

(B) leaving it:

(i) at the person's office with a clerk or other person in charge or, if no one is in charge, in a conspicuous place in the office; or

(ii) if the person has no office or the office is closed, at the person's dwelling or usual place of abode with someone of suitable age and discretion who resides there;

(C) mailing it to the person's last known address—in which event service is complete upon mailing;

(D) leaving it with the court clerk if the person has no known address;

(E) sending it by electronic means if the person consented in writing—in which event service is complete upon transmission, but is not effective if the serving party learns that it did not reach the person to be served; or

(F) delivering it by any other means that the person consented to in writing—in which event service is complete when the person making service delivers it to the agency designated to make delivery.

(3) Using Court Facilities. If a local rule so authorizes, a party may use the court's transmission facilities to make service under Rule 5(b)(2)(E).

(c) Serving Numerous Defendants.

(1) In General. If an action involves an unusually large number of defendants, the court may, on motion or on its own, order that:

(A) defendants' pleadings and replies to them need not be served on other defendants;

(B) any crossclaim, counterclaim, avoidance, or affirmative defense in those pleadings and replies to them will be treated as denied or avoided by all other parties; and

(C) filing any such pleading and serving it on the plaintiff constitutes notice of the pleading to all parties.

(2) Notifying Parties. A copy of every such order must be served on the parties as the court directs.

(d) Filing.

(1) Required Filings; Certificate of Service. Any paper after the complaint that is required to be served—together with a certificate of service—must be filed within a reasonable time after service. But disclosures under Rule 26(a)(1) or (2) and the following discovery requests and responses must not be filed until they are used in the proceeding or the court orders filing: depositions, interrogatories, requests for documents or tangible things or to permit entry onto land, and requests for admission.

(2) *How Filing Is Made—In General.* A paper is filed by delivering it:

(A) to the clerk; or

(B) to a judge who agrees to accept it for filing, and who must then note the filing date on the paper and promptly send it to the clerk.

(3) *Electronic Filing, Signing, or Verification.* A court may, by local rule, allow papers to be filed, signed, or verified by electronic means that are consistent with any technical standards established by the Judicial Conference of the United States. A local rule may require electronic filing only if reasonable exceptions are allowed. A paper filed electronically in compliance with a local rule is a written paper for purposes of these rules.

(4) *Acceptance by the Clerk.* The clerk must not refuse to file a paper solely because it is not in the form prescribed by these rules or by a local rule or practice.

(Amended January 21, 1963, effective July 1, 1963; March 30, 1970, effective July 1, 1970; April 29, 1980, effective August 1, 1980; March 2, 1987, effective August 1, 1987; April 30, 1991, effective December 1, 1991; April 22, 1993, effective December 1, 1993; April 23, 1996, effective December 1, 1996; April 17, 2000, effective December 1, 2000; April 23, 2001, effective December 1, 2001; April 12, 2006, effective December 1, 2006; April 30, 2007, effective December 1, 2007.)

RULE 5.1. CONSTITUTIONAL CHALLENGE TO A STATUTE—NOTICE, CERTIFICATION, AND INTERVENTION

(a) **Notice by a Party.** A party that files a pleading, written motion, or other paper drawing into question the constitutionality of a federal or state statute must promptly:

(1) file a notice of constitutional question stating the question and identifying the paper that raises it, if:

(A) a federal statute is questioned and the parties do not include the United States, one of its agencies, or one of its officers or employees in an official capacity; or

(B) a state statute is questioned and the parties do not include the state, one of its agencies, or one of its officers or employees in an official capacity; and

(2) serve the notice and paper on the Attorney General of the United States if a federal statute is questioned—or on the state attorney general if a state statute is questioned—either by certified or registered mail or by sending it to an electronic address designated by the attorney general for this purpose.

(b) **Certification by the Court.** The court must, under 28 U.S.C. § 2403, certify to the appropriate attorney general that a statute has been questioned.

(c) **Intervention; Final Decision on the Merits.** Unless the court sets a later time, the attorney general may intervene within 60 days after the notice is filed or after the court

certifies the challenge, whichever is earlier. Before the time to intervene expires, the court may reject the constitutional challenge, but may not enter a final judgment holding the statute unconstitutional.

(d) **No Forfeiture.** A party's failure to file and serve the notice, or the court's failure to certify, does not forfeit a constitutional claim or defense that is otherwise timely asserted.

(Adopted April 12, 2006, effective December 1, 2006; amended April 30, 2007, effective December 1, 2007.)

RULE 5.2. PRIVACY PROTECTION FOR FILINGS MADE WITH THE COURT

(a) **Redacted Filings.** Unless the court orders otherwise, in an electronic or paper filing with the court that contains an individual's social-security number, taxpayer-identification number, or birth date, the name of an individual known to be a minor, or a financial-account number, a party or nonparty making the filing may include only:

(1) the last four digits of the social-security number and taxpayer-identification number;

(2) the year of the individual's birth;

(3) the minor's initials; and

(4) the last four digits of the financial-account number.

(b) **Exemptions from the Redaction Requirement.** The redaction requirement does not apply to the following:

(1) a financial-account number that identifies the property allegedly subject to forfeiture in a forfeiture proceeding;

(2) the record of an administrative or agency proceeding;

(3) the official record of a state-court proceeding;

(4) the record of a court or tribunal, if that record was not subject to the redaction requirement when originally filed;

(5) a filing covered by Rule 5.2(c) or (d); and

(6) a pro se filing in an action brought under 28 U.S.C. §§ 2241, 2254, or 2255.

(c) **Limitations on Remote Access to Electronic Files; Social–Security Appeals and Immigration Cases.** Unless the court orders otherwise, in an action for benefits under the Social Security Act, and in an action or proceeding relating to an order of removal, to relief from removal, or to immigration benefits or detention, access to an electronic file is authorized as follows:

(1) the parties and their attorneys may have remote electronic access to any part of the case file, including the administrative record;

(2) any other person may have electronic access to the full record at the courthouse, but may have remote electronic access only to:

(A) the docket maintained by the court; and

(B) an opinion, order, judgment, or other disposition of the court, but not any other part of the case file or the administrative record.

(d) Filings Made Under Seal. The court may order that a filing be made under seal without redaction. The court may later unseal the filing or order the person who made the filing to file a redacted version for the public record.

(e) Protective Orders. For good cause, the court may by order in a case:

(1) require redaction of additional information; or

(2) limit or prohibit a nonparty's remote electronic access to a document filed with the court.

(f) Option for Additional Unredacted Filing Under Seal. A person making a redacted filing may also file an unredacted copy under seal. The court must retain the unredacted copy as part of the record.

(g) Option for Filing a Reference List. A filing that contains redacted information may be filed together with a reference list that identifies each item of redacted information and specifies an appropriate identifier that uniquely corresponds to each item listed. The list must be filed under seal and may be amended as of right. Any reference in the case to a listed identifier will be construed to refer to the corresponding item of information.

(h) Waiver of Protection of Identifiers. A person waives the protection of Rule 5.2(a) as to the person's own information by filing it without redaction and not under seal.

(Adopted April 30, 2007, effective December 1, 2007.)

RULE 6. COMPUTING AND EXTENDING TIME; TIME FOR MOTION PAPERS

(a) Computing Time. The following rules apply in computing any time period specified in these rules, in any local rule or court order, or in any statute that does not specify a method of computing time.

(1) *Period Stated in Days or a Longer Unit.* When the period is stated in days or a longer unit of time:

(A) exclude the day of the event that triggers the period;

(B) count every day, including intermediate Saturdays, Sundays, and legal holidays; and

(C) include the last day of the period, but if the last day is a Saturday, Sunday, or legal holiday, the period continues to run until the end of the next day that is not a Saturday, Sunday, or legal holiday.

(2) *Period Stated in Hours.* When the period is stated in hours:

(A) begin counting immediately on the occurrence of the event that triggers the period;

(B) count every hour, including hours during intermediate Saturdays, Sundays, and legal holidays; and

(C) if the period would end on a Saturday, Sunday, or legal holiday, the period continues to run until the same time on the next day that is not a Saturday, Sunday, or legal holiday.

(3) *Inaccessibility of the Clerk's Office.* Unless the court orders otherwise, if the clerk's office is inaccessible:

(A) on the last day for filing under Rule 6(a)(1), then the time for filing is extended to the first accessible day that is not a Saturday, Sunday, or legal holiday; or

(B) during the last hour for filing under Rule 6(a)(2), then the time for filing is extended to the same time on the first accessible day that is not a Saturday, Sunday, or legal holiday.

(4) *"Last Day" Defined.* Unless a different time is set by a statute, local rule, or court order, the last day ends:

(A) for electronic filing, at midnight in the court's time zone; and

(B) for filing by other means, when the clerk's office is scheduled to close.

(5) *"Next Day" Defined.* The "next day" is determined by continuing to count forward when the period is measured after an event and backward when measured before an event.

(6) *"Legal Holiday" Defined.* "Legal holiday" means:

(A) the day set aside by statute for observing New Year's Day, Martin Luther King Jr.'s Birthday, Washington's Birthday, Memorial Day, Independence Day, Labor Day, Columbus Day, Veterans' Day, Thanksgiving Day, or Christmas Day;

(B) any day declared a holiday by the President or Congress; and

(C) for periods that are measured after an event, any other day declared a holiday by the state where the district court is located.

(b) Extending Time.

(1) *In General.* When an act may or must be done within a specified time, the court may, for good cause, extend the time:

(A) with or without motion or notice if the court acts, or if a request is made, before the original time or its extension expires; or

(B) on motion made after the time has expired if the party failed to act because of excusable neglect.

(2) *Exceptions.* A court must not extend the time to act under Rules 50(b) and (d), 52(b), 59(b), (d), and (e), and 60(b).

(c) Motions, Notices of Hearing, and Affidavits.

(1) *In General.* A written motion and notice of the hearing must be served at least 14 days before the time specified for the hearing, with the following exceptions:

(A) when the motion may be heard ex parte;

(B) when these rules set a different time; or

(C) when a court order—which a party may, for good cause, apply for ex parte—sets a different time.

(2) *Supporting Affidavit.* Any affidavit supporting a motion must be served with the motion. Except as Rule

59(c) provides otherwise, any opposing affidavit must be served at least 7 days before the hearing, unless the court permits service at another time.

(d) Additional Time After Certain Kinds of Service. When a party may or must act within a specified time after being served and service is made under Rule 5(b)(2)(C) (mail), (D) (leaving with the clerk), or (F) (other means consented to),

3 days are added after the period would otherwise expire under Rule 6(a).

(Amended December 27, 1946, effective March 19, 1948; January 21, 1963, effective July 1, 1963; February 28, 1966, effective July 1, 1966; December 4, 1967, effective July 1, 1968; March 1, 1971, effective July 1, 1971; April 28, 1983, effective August 1, 1983; April 29, 1985, effective August 1, 1985; March 2, 1987, effective August 1, 1987; April 29, 1999, effective December 1, 1999; April 23, 2001, effective December 1, 2001; April 25, 2005, effective December 1, 2005; April 30, 2007, effective December 1, 2007; March 26, 2009, effective December 1, 2009; April 28, 2016, effective December 1, 2016.)

TITLE III. PLEADINGS AND MOTIONS

RULE 7. PLEADINGS ALLOWED; FORM OF MOTIONS AND OTHER PAPERS

(a) Pleadings. Only these pleadings are allowed:

(1) a complaint;

(2) an answer to a complaint;

(3) an answer to a counterclaim designated as a counterclaim;

(4) an answer to a crossclaim;

(5) a third-party complaint;

(6) an answer to a third-party complaint; and

(7) if the court orders one, a reply to an answer.

(b) Motions and Other Papers.

(1) *In General.* A request for a court order must be made by motion. The motion must:

(A) be in writing unless made during a hearing or trial;

(B) state with particularity the grounds for seeking the order; and

(C) state the relief sought.

(2) *Form.* The rules governing captions and other matters of form in pleadings apply to motions and other papers.

(Amended December 27, 1946, effective March 19, 1948; January 21, 1963, effective July 1, 1963; April 28, 1983, effective August 1, 1983; April 30, 2007, effective December 1, 2007.)

RULE 7.1. DISCLOSURE STATEMENT

(a) Who Must File; Contents. A nongovernmental corporate party must file two copies of a disclosure statement that:

(1) identifies any parent corporation and any publicly held corporation owning 10% or more of its stock; or

(2) states that there is no such corporation.

(b) Time to File; Supplemental Filing. A party must:

(1) file the disclosure statement with its first appearance, pleading, petition, motion, response, or other request addressed to the court; and

(2) promptly file a supplemental statement if any required information changes.

(Adopted April 29, 2002, effective December 1, 2002; April 30, 2007, effective December 1, 2007.)

RULE 8. GENERAL RULES OF PLEADING

(a) Claim for Relief. A pleading that states a claim for relief must contain:

(1) a short and plain statement of the grounds for the court's jurisdiction, unless the court already has jurisdiction and the claim needs no new jurisdictional support;

(2) a short and plain statement of the claim showing that the pleader is entitled to relief; and

(3) a demand for the relief sought, which may include relief in the alternative or different types of relief.

(b) Defenses; Admissions and Denials.

(1) *In General.* In responding to a pleading, a party must:

(A) state in short and plain terms its defenses to each claim asserted against it; and

(B) admit or deny the allegations asserted against it by an opposing party.

(2) *Denials—Responding to the Substance.* A denial must fairly respond to the substance of the allegation.

(3) *General and Specific Denials.* A party that intends in good faith to deny all the allegations of a pleading—including the jurisdictional grounds—may do so by a general denial. A party that does not intend to deny all the allegations must either specifically deny designated allegations or generally deny all except those specifically admitted.

(4) *Denying Part of an Allegation.* A party that intends in good faith to deny only part of an allegation must admit the part that is true and deny the rest.

(5) *Lacking Knowledge or Information.* A party that lacks knowledge or information sufficient to form a belief about the truth of an allegation must so state, and the statement has the effect of a denial.

(6) *Effect of Failing to Deny.* An allegation—other than one relating to the amount of damages—is admitted if a responsive pleading is required and the allegation is not denied. If a responsive pleading is not required, an allegation is considered denied or avoided.

(c) Affirmative Defenses.

(1) *In General.* In responding to a pleading, a party must affirmatively state any avoidance or affirmative defense, including:

- accord and satisfaction;
- arbitration and award;
- assumption of risk;
- contributory negligence;
- duress;
- estoppel;
- failure of consideration;
- fraud;
- illegality;
- injury by fellow servant;
- laches;
- license;
- payment;
- release;
- res judicata;
- statute of frauds;
- statute of limitations; and
- waiver.

(2) *Mistaken Designation.* If a party mistakenly designates a defense as a counterclaim, or a counterclaim as a defense, the court must, if justice requires, treat the pleading as though it were correctly designated, and may impose terms for doing so.

(d) **Pleading to Be Concise and Direct; Alternative Statements; Inconsistency.**

(1) *In General.* Each allegation must be simple, concise, and direct. No technical form is required.

(2) *Alternative Statements of a Claim or Defense.* A party may set out 2 or more statements of a claim or defense alternatively or hypothetically, either in a single count or defense or in separate ones. If a party makes alternative statements, the pleading is sufficient if any one of them is sufficient.

(3) *Inconsistent Claims or Defenses.* A party may state as many separate claims or defenses as it has, regardless of consistency.

(e) **Construing Pleadings.** Pleadings must be construed so as to do justice.

(Amended February 28, 1966, effective July 1, 1966; March 2, 1987, effective August 1, 1987; April 30, 2007, effective December 1, 2007; April 28, 2010, effective December 1, 2010.)

RULE 9.　PLEADING SPECIAL MATTERS

(a) **Capacity or Authority to Sue; Legal Existence.**

(1) *In General.* Except when required to show that the court has jurisdiction, a pleading need not allege:

(A) a party's capacity to sue or be sued;

(B) a party's authority to sue or be sued in a representative capacity; or

(C) the legal existence of an organized association of persons that is made a party.

(2) *Raising Those Issues.* To raise any of those issues, a party must do so by a specific denial, which must state any supporting facts that are peculiarly within the party's knowledge.

(b) **Fraud or Mistake; Conditions of Mind.** In alleging fraud or mistake, a party must state with particularity the circumstances constituting fraud or mistake. Malice, intent, knowledge, and other conditions of a person's mind may be alleged generally.

(c) **Conditions Precedent.** In pleading conditions precedent, it suffices to allege generally that all conditions precedent have occurred or been performed. But when denying that a condition precedent has occurred or been performed, a party must do so with particularity.

(d) **Official Document or Act.** In pleading an official document or official act, it suffices to allege that the document was legally issued or the act legally done.

(e) **Judgment.** In pleading a judgment or decision of a domestic or foreign court, a judicial or quasi-judicial tribunal, or a board or officer, it suffices to plead the judgment or decision without showing jurisdiction to render it.

(f) **Time and Place.** An allegation of time or place is material when testing the sufficiency of a pleading.

(g) **Special Damages.** If an item of special damage is claimed, it must be specifically stated.

(h) **Admiralty or Maritime Claim.**

(1) *How Designated.* If a claim for relief is within the admiralty or maritime jurisdiction and also within the court's subject-matter jurisdiction on some other ground, the pleading may designate the claim as an admiralty or maritime claim for purposes of Rules 14(c), 38(e), and 82 and the Supplemental Rules for Admiralty or Maritime Claims and Asset Forfeiture Actions. A claim cognizable only in the admiralty or maritime jurisdiction is an admiralty or maritime claim for those purposes, whether or not so designated.

(2) *Designation for Appeal.* A case that includes an admiralty or maritime claim within this subdivision (h) is an admiralty case within 28 U.S.C. § 1292(a)(3).

(Amended February 28, 1966, effective July 1, 1966; December 4, 1967, effective July 1, 1968; March 30, 1970, effective July 1, 1970; March 2, 1987, effective August 1, 1987; April 11, 1997, effective December 1, 1997; April 12, 2006, effective December 1, 2006; April 30, 2007, effective December 1, 2007.)

RULE 10.　FORM OF PLEADINGS

(a) **Caption; Names of Parties.** Every pleading must have a caption with the court's name, a title, a file number, and a Rule 7(a) designation. The title of the complaint must name all the parties; the title of other pleadings, after naming the first party on each side, may refer generally to other parties.

(b) **Paragraphs; Separate Statements.** A party must state its claims or defenses in numbered paragraphs, each limited as far as practicable to a single set of circumstances. A later pleading may refer by number to a paragraph in an earlier pleading. If doing so would promote clarity, each claim founded on a separate transaction or occurrence—and each defense other than a denial—must be stated in a separate count or defense.

(c) Adoption by Reference; Exhibits. A statement in a pleading may be adopted by reference elsewhere in the same pleading or in any other pleading or motion. A copy of a written instrument that is an exhibit to a pleading is a part of the pleading for all purposes.

(Amended April 30, 2007, effective December 1, 2007.)

RULE 11. SIGNING PLEADINGS, MOTIONS, AND OTHER PAPERS; REPRESENTATIONS TO THE COURT; SANCTIONS

(a) Signature. Every pleading, written motion, and other paper must be signed by at least one attorney of record in the attorney's name—or by a party personally if the party is unrepresented. The paper must state the signer's address, e-mail address, and telephone number. Unless a rule or statute specifically states otherwise, a pleading need not be verified or accompanied by an affidavit. The court must strike an unsigned paper unless the omission is promptly corrected after being called to the attorney's or party's attention.

(b) Representations to the Court. By presenting to the court a pleading, written motion, or other paper—whether by signing, filing, submitting, or later advocating it—an attorney or unrepresented party certifies that to the best of the person's knowledge, information, and belief, formed after an inquiry reasonable under the circumstances:

(1) it is not being presented for any improper purpose, such as to harass, cause unnecessary delay, or needlessly increase the cost of litigation;

(2) the claims, defenses, and other legal contentions are warranted by existing law or by a nonfrivolous argument for extending, modifying, or reversing existing law or for establishing new law;

(3) the factual contentions have evidentiary support or, if specifically so identified, will likely have evidentiary support after a reasonable opportunity for further investigation or discovery; and

(4) the denials of factual contentions are warranted on the evidence or, if specifically so identified, are reasonably based on belief or a lack of information.

(c) Sanctions.

(1) *In General.* If, after notice and a reasonable opportunity to respond, the court determines that Rule 11(b) has been violated, the court may impose an appropriate sanction on any attorney, law firm, or party that violated the rule or is responsible for the violation. Absent exceptional circumstances, a law firm must be held jointly responsible for a violation committed by its partner, associate, or employee.

(2) *Motion for Sanctions.* A motion for sanctions must be made separately from any other motion and must describe the specific conduct that allegedly violates Rule 11(b). The motion must be served under Rule 5, but it must not be filed or be presented to the court if the challenged paper, claim,

defense, contention, or denial is withdrawn or appropriately corrected within 21 days after service or within another time the court sets. If warranted, the court may award to the prevailing party the reasonable expenses, including attorney's fees, incurred for the motion.

(3) *On the Court's Initiative.* On its own, the court may order an attorney, law firm, or party to show cause why conduct specifically described in the order has not violated Rule 11(b).

(4) *Nature of a Sanction.* A sanction imposed under this rule must be limited to what suffices to deter repetition of the conduct or comparable conduct by others similarly situated. The sanction may include nonmonetary directives; an order to pay a penalty into court; or, if imposed on motion and warranted for effective deterrence, an order directing payment to the movant of part or all of the reasonable attorney's fees and other expenses directly resulting from the violation.

(5) *Limitations on Monetary Sanctions.* The court must not impose a monetary sanction:

(A) against a represented party for violating Rule 11(b)(2); or

(B) on its own, unless it issued the show-cause order under Rule 11(c)(3) before voluntary dismissal or settlement of the claims made by or against the party that is, or whose attorneys are, to be sanctioned.

(6) *Requirements for an Order.* An order imposing a sanction must describe the sanctioned conduct and explain the basis for the sanction.

(d) Inapplicability to Discovery. This rule does not apply to disclosures and discovery requests, responses, objections, and motions under Rules 26 through 37.

(Amended April 28, 1983, effective August 1, 1983; March 2, 1987, effective August 1, 1987; April 22, 1993, effective December 1, 1993; April 30, 2007, effective December 1, 2007.)

RULE 12. DEFENSES AND OBJECTIONS: WHEN AND HOW PRESENTED; MOTION FOR JUDGMENT ON THE PLEADINGS; CONSOLIDATING MOTIONS; WAIVING DEFENSES; PRETRIAL HEARING

(a) Time to Serve a Responsive Pleading.

(1) *In General.* Unless another time is specified by this rule or a federal statute, the time for serving a responsive pleading is as follows:

(A) A defendant must serve an answer:

(i) within 21 days after being served with the summons and complaint; or

(ii) if it has timely waived service under Rule 4(d), within 60 days after the request for a waiver was sent, or within 90 days after it was sent to the defendant outside any judicial district of the United States.

(B) A party must serve an answer to a counterclaim or crossclaim within 21 days after being served with the pleading that states the counterclaim or crossclaim.

(C) A party must serve a reply to an answer within 21 days after being served with an order to reply, unless the order specifies a different time.

(2) *United States and Its Agencies, Officers, or Employees Sued in an Official Capacity.* The United States, a United States agency, or a United States officer or employee sued only in an official capacity must serve an answer to a complaint, counterclaim, or crossclaim within 60 days after service on the United States attorney.

(3) *United States Officers or Employees Sued in an Individual Capacity.* A United States officer or employee sued in an individual capacity for an act or omission occurring in connection with duties performed on the United States' behalf must serve an answer to a complaint, counterclaim, or crossclaim within 60 days after service on the officer or employee or service on the United States attorney, whichever is later.

(4) *Effect of a Motion.* Unless the court sets a different time, serving a motion under this rule alters these periods as follows:

(A) if the court denies the motion or postpones its disposition until trial, the responsive pleading must be served within 14 days after notice of the court's action; or

(B) if the court grants a motion for a more definite statement, the responsive pleading must be served within 14 days after the more definite statement is served.

(b) **How to Present Defenses.** Every defense to a claim for relief in any pleading must be asserted in the responsive pleading if one is required. But a party may assert the following defenses by motion:

(1) lack of subject-matter jurisdiction;

(2) lack of personal jurisdiction;

(3) improper venue;

(4) insufficient process;

(5) insufficient service of process;

(6) failure to state a claim upon which relief can be granted; and

(7) failure to join a party under Rule 19.

A motion asserting any of these defenses must be made before pleading if a responsive pleading is allowed. If a pleading sets out a claim for relief that does not require a responsive pleading, an opposing party may assert at trial any defense to that claim. No defense or objection is waived by joining it with one or more other defenses or objections in a responsive pleading or in a motion.

(c) **Motion for Judgment on the Pleadings.** After the pleadings are closed—but early enough not to delay trial—a party may move for judgment on the pleadings.

(d) **Result of Presenting Matters Outside the Pleadings.** If, on a motion under Rule 12(b)(6) or 12(c), matters outside the pleadings are presented to and not excluded by the court, the motion must be treated as one for summary judgment under Rule 56. All parties must be given a reasonable opportunity to present all the material that is pertinent to the motion.

(e) **Motion for a More Definite Statement.** A party may move for a more definite statement of a pleading to which a responsive pleading is allowed but which is so vague or ambiguous that the party cannot reasonably prepare a response. The motion must be made before filing a responsive pleading and must point out the defects complained of and the details desired. If the court orders a more definite statement and the order is not obeyed within 14 days after notice of the order or within the time the court sets, the court may strike the pleading or issue any other appropriate order.

(f) **Motion to Strike.** The court may strike from a pleading an insufficient defense or any redundant, immaterial, impertinent, or scandalous matter. The court may act:

(1) on its own; or

(2) on motion made by a party either before responding to the pleading or, if a response is not allowed, within 21 days after being served with the pleading.

(g) **Joining Motions.**

(1) *Right to Join.* A motion under this rule may be joined with any other motion allowed by this rule.

(2) *Limitation on Further Motions.* Except as provided in Rule 12(h)(2) or (3), a party that makes a motion under this rule must not make another motion under this rule raising a defense or objection that was available to the party but omitted from its earlier motion.

(h) **Waiving and Preserving Certain Defenses.**

(1) *When Some Are Waived.* A party waives any defense listed in Rule 12(b)(2)-(5) by:

(A) omitting it from a motion in the circumstances described in Rule 12(g)(2); or

(B) failing to either:

(i) make it by motion under this rule; or

(ii) include it in a responsive pleading or in an amendment allowed by Rule 15(a)(1) as a matter of course.

(2) *When to Raise Others.* Failure to state a claim upon which relief can be granted, to join a person required by Rule 19(b), or to state a legal defense to a claim may be raised:

(A) in any pleading allowed or ordered under Rule 7(a);

(B) by a motion under Rule 12(c); or

(C) at trial.

(3) *Lack of Subject–Matter Jurisdiction.* If the court determines at any time that it lacks subject-matter jurisdiction, the court must dismiss the action.

(i) **Hearing Before Trial.** If a party so moves, any defense listed in Rule 12(b)(1)-(7)—whether made in a pleading or by motion—and a motion under Rule 12(c) must be heard and decided before trial unless the court orders a deferral until trial.

(Amended December 27, 1946, effective March 19, 1948; January 21, 1963, effective July 1, 1963; February 28, 1966, effective July 1, 1966; March 2, 1987, effective August 1, 1987; April 22, 1993, effective December 1, 1993; April 17, 2000, effective December 1, 2000; April 30, 2007, effective December 1, 2007; March 26, 2009, effective December 1, 2009.)

RULE 13. COUNTERCLAIM AND CROSSCLAIM

(a) Compulsory Counterclaim.

(1) *In General.* A pleading must state as a counterclaim any claim that—at the time of its service—the pleader has against an opposing party if the claim:

    (A) arises out of the transaction or occurrence that is the subject matter of the opposing party's claim; and

    (B) does not require adding another party over whom the court cannot acquire jurisdiction.

(2) *Exceptions.* The pleader need not state the claim if:

    (A) when the action was commenced, the claim was the subject of another pending action; or

    (B) the opposing party sued on its claim by attachment or other process that did not establish personal jurisdiction over the pleader on that claim, and the pleader does not assert any counterclaim under this rule.

(b) Permissive Counterclaim.
A pleading may state as a counterclaim against an opposing party any claim that is not compulsory.

(c) Relief Sought in a Counterclaim.
A counterclaim need not diminish or defeat the recovery sought by the opposing party. It may request relief that exceeds in amount or differs in kind from the relief sought by the opposing party.

(d) Counterclaim Against the United States.
These rules do not expand the right to assert a counterclaim—or to claim a credit—against the United States or a United States officer or agency.

(e) Counterclaim Maturing or Acquired After Pleading.
The court may permit a party to file a supplemental pleading asserting a counterclaim that matured or was acquired by the party after serving an earlier pleading.

(f) [Abrogated]

(g) Crossclaim Against a Coparty.
A pleading may state as a crossclaim any claim by one party against a coparty if the claim arises out of the transaction or occurrence that is the subject matter of the original action or of a counterclaim, or if the claim relates to any property that is the subject matter of the original action. The crossclaim may include a claim that the coparty is or may be liable to the cross-claimant for all or part of a claim asserted in the action against the cross-claimant.

(h) Joining Additional Parties.
Rules 19 and 20 govern the addition of a person as a party to a counterclaim or crossclaim.

(i) Separate Trials; Separate Judgments.
If the court orders separate trials under Rule 42(b), it may enter judgment on a counterclaim or crossclaim under Rule 54(b) when it has jurisdiction to do so, even if the opposing party's claims have been dismissed or otherwise resolved.

(Amended December 27, 1946, effective March 19, 1948; January 21, 1963, effective July 1, 1963; February 28, 1966, effective July 1, 1966; March 2, 1987, effective August 1, 1987; April 30, 2007, effective December 1, 2007; March 26, 2009, effective December 1, 2009.)

RULE 14. THIRD–PARTY PRACTICE

(a) When a Defending Party May Bring in a Third Party.

(1) *Timing of the Summons and Complaint.* A defending party may, as third-party plaintiff, serve a summons and complaint on a nonparty who is or may be liable to it for all or part of the claim against it. But the third-party plaintiff must, by motion, obtain the court's leave if it files the third-party complaint more than 14 days after serving its original answer.

(2) *Third–Party Defendant's Claims and Defenses.* The person served with the summons and third-party complaint—the "third-party defendant":

    (A) must assert any defense against the third-party plaintiff's claim under Rule 12;

    (B) must assert any counterclaim against the third-party plaintiff under Rule 13(a), and may assert any counterclaim against the third-party plaintiff under Rule 13(b) or any crossclaim against another third-party defendant under Rule 13(g);

    (C) may assert against the plaintiff any defense that the third-party plaintiff has to the plaintiff's claim; and

    (D) may also assert against the plaintiff any claim arising out of the transaction or occurrence that is the subject matter of the plaintiff's claim against the third-party plaintiff.

(3) *Plaintiff's Claims Against a Third–Party Defendant.* The plaintiff may assert against the third-party defendant any claim arising out of the transaction or occurrence that is the subject matter of the plaintiff's claim against the third-party plaintiff. The third-party defendant must then assert any defense under Rule 12 and any counterclaim under Rule 13(a), and may assert any counterclaim under Rule 13(b) or any crossclaim under Rule 13(g).

(4) *Motion to Strike, Sever, or Try Separately.* Any party may move to strike the third-party claim, to sever it, or to try it separately.

(5) *Third–Party Defendant's Claim Against a Nonparty.* A third-party defendant may proceed under this rule against a nonparty who is or may be liable to the third-party defendant for all or part of any claim against it.

(6) *Third–Party Complaint In Rem.* If it is within the admiralty or maritime jurisdiction, a third-party complaint may be in rem. In that event, a reference in this rule to the "summons" includes the warrant of arrest, and a reference to the defendant or third-party plaintiff includes, when appropriate, a person who asserts a right under Supplemental Rule C(6)(a)(i) in the property arrested.

(b) When a Plaintiff May Bring in a Third Party.
When a claim is asserted against a plaintiff, the plaintiff may bring in a third party if this rule would allow a defendant to do so.

(c) Admiralty or Maritime Claim.

(1) *Scope of Impleader.* If a plaintiff asserts an admiralty or maritime claim under Rule 9(h), the defendant or a person who asserts a right under Supplemental Rule

C(6)(a)(i) may, as a third-party plaintiff, bring in a third-party defendant who may be wholly or partly liable—either to the plaintiff or to the third-party plaintiff—for remedy over, contribution, or otherwise on account of the same transaction, occurrence, or series of transactions or occurrences.

(2) *Defending Against a Demand for Judgment for the Plaintiff.* The third-party plaintiff may demand judgment in the plaintiff's favor against the third-party defendant. In that event, the third-party defendant must defend under Rule 12 against the plaintiff's claim as well as the third-party plaintiff's claim; and the action proceeds as if the plaintiff had sued both the third-party defendant and the third-party plaintiff.

(Amended December 27, 1946, effective March 19, 1948; January 21, 1963, effective July 1, 1963; February 28, 1966, effective July 1, 1966; March 2, 1987, effective August 1, 1987; April 17, 2000, effective December 1, 2000; April 12, 2006, effective December 1, 2006; April 30, 2007, effective December 1, 2007; March 26, 2009, effective December 1, 2009.)

RULE 15.   AMENDED AND SUPPLEMENTAL PLEADINGS

(a) **Amendments Before Trial.**

(1) *Amending as a Matter of Course.* A party may amend its pleading once as a matter of course within:

(A) 21 days after serving it, or

(B) if the pleading is one to which a responsive pleading is required, 21 days after service of a responsive pleading or 21 days after service of a motion under Rule 12(b), (e), or (f), whichever is earlier.

(2) *Other Amendments.* In all other cases, a party may amend its pleading only with the opposing party's written consent or the court's leave. The court should freely give leave when justice so requires.

(3) *Time to Respond.* Unless the court orders otherwise, any required response to an amended pleading must be made within the time remaining to respond to the original pleading or within 14 days after service of the amended pleading, whichever is later.

(b) **Amendments During and After Trial.**

(1) *Based on an Objection at Trial.* If, at trial, a party objects that evidence is not within the issues raised in the pleadings, the court may permit the pleadings to be amended. The court should freely permit an amendment when doing so will aid in presenting the merits and the objecting party fails to satisfy the court that the evidence would prejudice that party's action or defense on the merits. The court may grant a continuance to enable the objecting party to meet the evidence.

(2) *For Issues Tried by Consent.* When an issue not raised by the pleadings is tried by the parties' express or implied consent, it must be treated in all respects as if raised in the pleadings. A party may move—at any time, even after judgment—to amend the pleadings to conform them to the evidence and to raise an unpleaded issue. But

failure to amend does not affect the result of the trial of that issue.

(c) **Relation Back of Amendments.**

(1) *When an Amendment Relates Back.* An amendment to a pleading relates back to the date of the original pleading when:

(A) the law that provides the applicable statute of limitations allows relation back;

(B) the amendment asserts a claim or defense that arose out of the conduct, transaction, or occurrence set out—or attempted to be set out—in the original pleading; or

(C) the amendment changes the party or the naming of the party against whom a claim is asserted, if Rule 15(c)(1)(B) is satisfied and if, within the period provided by Rule 4(m) for serving the summons and complaint, the party to be brought in by amendment:

(i) received such notice of the action that it will not be prejudiced in defending on the merits; and

(ii) knew or should have known that the action would have been brought against it, but for a mistake concerning the proper party's identity.

(2) *Notice to the United States.* When the United States or a United States officer or agency is added as a defendant by amendment, the notice requirements of Rule 15(c)(1)(C)(i) and (ii) are satisfied if, during the stated period, process was delivered or mailed to the United States attorney or the United States attorney's designee, to the Attorney General of the United States, or to the officer or agency.

(d) **Supplemental Pleadings.** On motion and reasonable notice, the court may, on just terms, permit a party to serve a supplemental pleading setting out any transaction, occurrence, or event that happened after the date of the pleading to be supplemented. The court may permit supplementation even though the original pleading is defective in stating a claim or defense. The court may order that the opposing party plead to the supplemental pleading within a specified time.

(Amended January 21, 1963, effective July 1, 1963; February 28, 1966, effective July 1, 1966; March 2, 1987, effective August 1, 1987; April 30, 1991, effective December 1, 1991; amended by Pub.L. 102–198, § 11, December 9, 1991, 105 Stat. 1626; amended April 22, 1993, effective December 1, 1993; April 30, 2007, effective December 1, 2007; March 26, 2009, effective December 1, 2009.)

RULE 16.   PRETRIAL CONFERENCES; SCHEDULING; MANAGEMENT

(a) **Purposes of a Pretrial Conference.** In any action, the court may order the attorneys and any unrepresented parties to appear for one or more pretrial conferences for such purposes as:

(1) expediting disposition of the action;

(2) establishing early and continuing control so that the case will not be protracted because of lack of management;

(3) discouraging wasteful pretrial activities;

(4) improving the quality of the trial through more thorough preparation; and

(5) facilitating settlement.

(b) Scheduling.

(1) *Scheduling Order.* Except in categories of actions exempted by local rule, the district judge—or a magistrate judge when authorized by local rule—must issue a scheduling order:

(A) after receiving the parties' report under Rule 26(f); or

(B) after consulting with the parties' attorneys and any unrepresented parties at a scheduling conference.

(2) *Time to Issue.* The judge must issue the scheduling order as soon as practicable, but unless the judge finds good cause for delay, the judge must issue it within the earlier of 90 days after any defendant has been served with the complaint or 60 days after any defendant has appeared.

(3) *Contents of the Order.*

(A) *Required Contents.* The scheduling order must limit the time to join other parties, amend the pleadings, complete discovery, and file motions.

(B) *Permitted Contents.* The scheduling order may:

(i) modify the timing of disclosures under Rules 26(a) and 26(e)(1);

(ii) modify the extent of discovery;

(iii) provide for disclosure, discovery, or preservation of electronically stored information;

(iv) include any agreements the parties reach for asserting claims of privilege or of protection as trial-preparation material after information is produced, including agreements reached under Federal Rule of Evidence 502;

(v) direct that before moving for an order relating to discovery, the movant must request a conference with the court;

(vi) set dates for pretrial conferences and for trial; and

(vii) include other appropriate matters.

(4) *Modifying a Schedule.* A schedule may be modified only for good cause and with the judge's consent.

(c) Attendance and Matters for Consideration at a Pretrial Conference.

(1) *Attendance.* A represented party must authorize at least one of its attorneys to make stipulations and admissions about all matters that can reasonably be anticipated for discussion at a pretrial conference. If appropriate, the court may require that a party or its representative be present or reasonably available by other means to consider possible settlement.

(2) *Matters for Consideration.* At any pretrial conference, the court may consider and take appropriate action on the following matters:

(A) formulating and simplifying the issues, and eliminating frivolous claims or defenses;

(B) amending the pleadings if necessary or desirable;

(C) obtaining admissions and stipulations about facts and documents to avoid unnecessary proof, and ruling in advance on the admissibility of evidence;

(D) avoiding unnecessary proof and cumulative evidence, and limiting the use of testimony under Federal Rule of Evidence 702;

(E) determining the appropriateness and timing of summary adjudication under Rule 56;

(F) controlling and scheduling discovery, including orders affecting disclosures and discovery under Rule 26 and Rules 29 through 37;

(G) identifying witnesses and documents, scheduling the filing and exchange of any pretrial briefs, and setting dates for further conferences and for trial;

(H) referring matters to a magistrate judge or a master;

(I) settling the case and using special procedures to assist in resolving the dispute when authorized by statute or local rule;

(J) determining the form and content of the pretrial order;

(K) disposing of pending motions;

(L) adopting special procedures for managing potentially difficult or protracted actions that may involve complex issues, multiple parties, difficult legal questions, or unusual proof problems;

(M) ordering a separate trial under Rule 42(b) of a claim, counterclaim, crossclaim, third-party claim, or particular issue;

(N) ordering the presentation of evidence early in the trial on a manageable issue that might, on the evidence, be the basis for a judgment as a matter of law under Rule 50(a) or a judgment on partial findings under Rule 52(c);

(O) establishing a reasonable limit on the time allowed to present evidence; and

(P) facilitating in other ways the just, speedy, and inexpensive disposition of the action.

(d) Pretrial Orders. After any conference under this rule, the court should issue an order reciting the action taken. This order controls the course of the action unless the court modifies it.

(e) Final Pretrial Conference and Orders. The court may hold a final pretrial conference to formulate a trial plan, including a plan to facilitate the admission of evidence. The conference must be held as close to the start of trial as is reasonable, and must be attended by at least one attorney who will conduct the trial for each party and by any unrepresented party. The court may modify the order issued after a final pretrial conference only to prevent manifest injustice.

(f) Sanctions.

(1) *In General.* On motion or on its own, the court may issue any just orders, including those authorized by Rule 37(b)(2)(A)(ii)-(vii), if a party or its attorney:

(A) fails to appear at a scheduling or other pretrial conference;

(B) is substantially unprepared to participate—or does not participate in good faith—in the conference; or

(C) fails to obey a scheduling or other pretrial order.

(2) *Imposing Fees and Costs.* Instead of or in addition to any other sanction, the court must order the party, its attorney, or both to pay the reasonable expenses—including attorney's fees—incurred because of any noncompliance with this rule, unless the noncompliance was substantially justified or other circumstances make an award of expenses unjust.

(Amended April 28, 1983, effective August 1, 1983; March 2, 1987, effective August 1, 1987; April 22, 1993, effective December 1, 1993; April 12, 2006, effective December 1, 2006; April 30, 2007, effective December 1, 2007; April 29, 2015, effective December 1, 2015.)

TITLE IV. PARTIES

RULE 17. PLAINTIFF AND DEFENDANT; CAPACITY; PUBLIC OFFICERS

(a) Real Party in Interest.

(1) *Designation in General.* An action must be prosecuted in the name of the real party in interest. The following may sue in their own names without joining the person for whose benefit the action is brought:

(A) an executor;

(B) an administrator;

(C) a guardian;

(D) a bailee;

(E) a trustee of an express trust;

(F) a party with whom or in whose name a contract has been made for another's benefit; and

(G) a party authorized by statute.

(2) *Action in the Name of the United States for Another's Use or Benefit.* When a federal statute so provides, an action for another's use or benefit must be brought in the name of the United States.

(3) *Joinder of the Real Party in Interest.* The court may not dismiss an action for failure to prosecute in the name of the real party in interest until, after an objection, a reasonable time has been allowed for the real party in interest to ratify, join, or be substituted into the action. After ratification, joinder, or substitution, the action proceeds as if it had been originally commenced by the real party in interest.

(b) Capacity to Sue or Be Sued. Capacity to sue or be sued is determined as follows:

(1) for an individual who is not acting in a representative capacity, by the law of the individual's domicile;

(2) for a corporation, by the law under which it was organized; and

(3) for all other parties, by the law of the state where the court is located, except that:

(A) a partnership or other unincorporated association with no such capacity under that state's law may sue or be sued in its common name to enforce a substantive right existing under the United States Constitution or laws; and

(B) 28 U.S.C. §§ 754 and 959(a) govern the capacity of a receiver appointed by a United States court to sue or be sued in a United States court.

(c) Minor or Incompetent Person.

(1) *With a Representative.* The following representatives may sue or defend on behalf of a minor or an incompetent person:

(A) a general guardian;

(B) a committee;

(C) a conservator; or

(D) a like fiduciary.

(2) *Without a Representative.* A minor or an incompetent person who does not have a duly appointed representative may sue by a next friend or by a guardian ad litem. The court must appoint a guardian ad litem—or issue another appropriate order—to protect a minor or incompetent person who is unrepresented in an action.

(d) Public Officer's Title and Name. A public officer who sues or is sued in an official capacity may be designated by official title rather than by name, but the court may order that the officer's name be added.

(Amended December 27, 1946, effective March 19, 1948; December 29, 1948, effective October 20, 1949; February 28, 1966, effective July 1, 1966; March 2, 1987, effective August 1, 1987; April 25, 1988, effective August 1, 1988; amended by Pub.L. 100–690, Title VII, § 7049, November 18, 1988, 102 Stat. 4401 (although amendment by Pub.L. 100–690 could not be executed due to prior amendment by Court order which made the same change effective August 1, 1988); April 30, 2007, effective December 1, 2007.)

RULE 18. JOINDER OF CLAIMS

(a) In General. A party asserting a claim, counterclaim, crossclaim, or third-party claim may join, as independent or alternative claims, as many claims as it has against an opposing party.

(b) Joinder of Contingent Claims. A party may join two claims even though one of them is contingent on the disposition of the other; but the court may grant relief only in accordance with the parties' relative substantive rights. In particular, a plaintiff may state a claim for money and a claim to set aside a conveyance that is fraudulent as to that plaintiff, without first obtaining a judgment for the money.

(Amended February 28, 1966, effective July 1, 1966; March 2, 1987, effective August 1, 1987; April 30, 2007, effective December 1, 2007.)

RULE 19. REQUIRED JOINDER OF PARTIES

(a) Persons Required to Be Joined if Feasible.

(1) *Required Party.* A person who is subject to service of process and whose joinder will not deprive the court of subject-matter jurisdiction must be joined as a party if:

(A) in that person's absence, the court cannot accord complete relief among existing parties; or

(B) that person claims an interest relating to the subject of the action and is so situated that disposing of the action in the person's absence may:

(i) as a practical matter impair or impede the person's ability to protect the interest; or

(ii) leave an existing party subject to a substantial risk of incurring double, multiple, or otherwise inconsistent obligations because of the interest.

(2) *Joinder by Court Order.* If a person has not been joined as required, the court must order that the person be made a party. A person who refuses to join as a plaintiff may be made either a defendant or, in a proper case, an involuntary plaintiff.

(3) *Venue.* If a joined party objects to venue and the joinder would make venue improper, the court must dismiss that party.

(b) When Joinder Is Not Feasible. If a person who is required to be joined if feasible cannot be joined, the court must determine whether, in equity and good conscience, the action should proceed among the existing parties or should be dismissed. The factors for the court to consider include:

(1) the extent to which a judgment rendered in the person's absence might prejudice that person or the existing parties;

(2) the extent to which any prejudice could be lessened or avoided by:

(A) protective provisions in the judgment;

(B) shaping the relief; or

(C) other measures;

(3) whether a judgment rendered in the person's absence would be adequate; and

(4) whether the plaintiff would have an adequate remedy if the action were dismissed for nonjoinder.

(c) Pleading the Reasons for Nonjoinder. When asserting a claim for relief, a party must state:

(1) the name, if known, of any person who is required to be joined if feasible but is not joined; and

(2) the reasons for not joining that person.

(d) Exception for Class Actions. This rule is subject to Rule 23.

(Amended February 28, 1966, effective July 1, 1966; March 2, 1987, effective August 1, 1987; April 30, 2007, effective December 1, 2007.)

RULE 20. PERMISSIVE JOINDER OF PARTIES

(a) Persons Who May Join or Be Joined.

(1) *Plaintiffs.* Persons may join in one action as plaintiffs if:

(A) they assert any right to relief jointly, severally, or in the alternative with respect to or arising out of the same transaction, occurrence, or series of transactions or occurrences; and

(B) any question of law or fact common to all plaintiffs will arise in the action.

(2) *Defendants.* Persons—as well as a vessel, cargo, or other property subject to admiralty process in rem—may be joined in one action as defendants if:

(A) any right to relief is asserted against them jointly, severally, or in the alternative with respect to or arising out of the same transaction, occurrence, or series of transactions or occurrences; and

(B) any question of law or fact common to all defendants will arise in the action.

(3) *Extent of Relief.* Neither a plaintiff nor a defendant need be interested in obtaining or defending against all the relief demanded. The court may grant judgment to one or more plaintiffs according to their rights, and against one or more defendants according to their liabilities.

(b) Protective Measures. The court may issue orders—including an order for separate trials—to protect a party against embarrassment, delay, expense, or other prejudice that arises from including a person against whom the party asserts no claim and who asserts no claim against the party.

(Amended February 28, 1966, effective July 1, 1966; March 2, 1987, effective August 1, 1987; April 30, 2007, effective December 1, 2007.)

RULE 21. MISJOINDER AND NONJOINDER OF PARTIES

Misjoinder of parties is not a ground for dismissing an action. On motion or on its own, the court may at any time, on just terms, add or drop a party. The court may also sever any claim against a party.

(Amended April 30, 2007, effective December 1, 2007.)

RULE 22. INTERPLEADER

(a) Grounds.

(1) *By a Plaintiff.* Persons with claims that may expose a plaintiff to double or multiple liability may be joined as defendants and required to interplead. Joinder for interpleader is proper even though:

(A) the claims of the several claimants, or the titles on which their claims depend, lack a common origin or are adverse and independent rather than identical; or

(B) the plaintiff denies liability in whole or in part to any or all of the claimants.

(2) *By a Defendant.* A defendant exposed to similar liability may seek interpleader through a crossclaim or counterclaim.

(b) Relation to Other Rules and Statutes. This rule supplements—and does not limit—the joinder of parties allowed by Rule 20. The remedy this rule provides is in addition to—and does not supersede or limit—the remedy provided by 28 U.S.C. §§ 1335, 1397, and 2361. An action under those statutes must be conducted under these rules.

(Amended December 29, 1948, effective October 20, 1949; March 2, 1987, effective August 1, 1987; April 30, 2007, effective December 1, 2007.)

RULE 23.   CLASS ACTIONS

(a) Prerequisites. One or more members of a class may sue or be sued as representative parties on behalf of all members only if:

(1) the class is so numerous that joinder of all members is impracticable;

(2) there are questions of law or fact common to the class;

(3) the claims or defenses of the representative parties are typical of the claims or defenses of the class; and

(4) the representative parties will fairly and adequately protect the interests of the class.

(b) Types of Class Actions. A class action may be maintained if Rule 23(a) is satisfied and if:

(1) prosecuting separate actions by or against individual class members would create a risk of:

(A) inconsistent or varying adjudications with respect to individual class members that would establish incompatible standards of conduct for the party opposing the class; or

(B) adjudications with respect to individual class members that, as a practical matter, would be dispositive of the interests of the other members not parties to the individual adjudications or would substantially impair or impede their ability to protect their interests;

(2) the party opposing the class has acted or refused to act on grounds that apply generally to the class, so that final injunctive relief or corresponding declaratory relief is appropriate respecting the class as a whole; or

(3) the court finds that the questions of law or fact common to class members predominate over any questions affecting only individual members, and that a class action is superior to other available methods for fairly and efficiently adjudicating the controversy. The matters pertinent to these findings include:

(A) the class members' interests in individually controlling the prosecution or defense of separate actions;

(B) the extent and nature of any litigation concerning the controversy already begun by or against class members;

(C) the desirability or undesirability of concentrating the litigation of the claims in the particular forum; and

(D) the likely difficulties in managing a class action.

(c) Certification Order; Notice to Class Members; Judgment; Issues Classes; Subclasses.

(1) *Certification Order.*

(A) *Time to Issue.* At an early practicable time after a person sues or is sued as a class representative, the court must determine by order whether to certify the action as a class action.

(B) *Defining the Class; Appointing Class Counsel.* An order that certifies a class action must define the class and the class claims, issues, or defenses, and must appoint class counsel under Rule 23(g).

(C) *Altering or Amending the Order.* An order that grants or denies class certification may be altered or amended before final judgment.

(2) *Notice.*

(A) *For (b)(1) or (b)(2) Classes.* For any class certified under Rule 23(b)(1) or (b)(2), the court may direct appropriate notice to the class.

(B) *For (b)(3) Classes.* For any class certified under Rule 23(b)(3), the court must direct to class members the best notice that is practicable under the circumstances, including individual notice to all members who can be identified through reasonable effort. The notice must clearly and concisely state in plain, easily understood language:

(i) the nature of the action;

(ii) the definition of the class certified;

(iii) the class claims, issues, or defenses;

(iv) that a class member may enter an appearance through an attorney if the member so desires;

(v) that the court will exclude from the class any member who requests exclusion;

(vi) the time and manner for requesting exclusion; and

(vii) the binding effect of a class judgment on members under Rule 23(c)(3).

(3) *Judgment.* Whether or not favorable to the class, the judgment in a class action must:

(A) for any class certified under Rule 23(b)(1) or (b)(2), include and describe those whom the court finds to be class members; and

(B) for any class certified under Rule 23(b)(3), include and specify or describe those to whom the Rule 23(c)(2) notice was directed, who have not requested exclusion, and whom the court finds to be class members.

(4) *Particular Issues.* When appropriate, an action may be brought or maintained as a class action with respect to particular issues.

(5) *Subclasses.* When appropriate, a class may be divided into subclasses that are each treated as a class under this rule.

(d) Conducting the Action.

(1) *In General.* In conducting an action under this rule, the court may issue orders that:

(A) determine the course of proceedings or prescribe measures to prevent undue repetition or complication in presenting evidence or argument;

(B) require—to protect class members and fairly conduct the action—giving appropriate notice to some or all class members of:

(i) any step in the action;

(ii) the proposed extent of the judgment; or

(iii) the members' opportunity to signify whether they consider the representation fair and adequate, to intervene and present claims or defenses, or to otherwise come into the action;

(C) impose conditions on the representative parties or on intervenors;

(D) require that the pleadings be amended to eliminate allegations about representation of absent persons and that the action proceed accordingly; or

(E) deal with similar procedural matters.

(2) *Combining and Amending Orders.* An order under Rule 23(d)(1) may be altered or amended from time to time and may be combined with an order under Rule 16.

(e) Settlement, Voluntary Dismissal, or Compromise. The claims, issues, or defenses of a certified class may be settled, voluntarily dismissed, or compromised only with the court's approval. The following procedures apply to a proposed settlement, voluntary dismissal, or compromise:

(1) The court must direct notice in a reasonable manner to all class members who would be bound by the proposal.

(2) If the proposal would bind class members, the court may approve it only after a hearing and on finding that it is fair, reasonable, and adequate.

(3) The parties seeking approval must file a statement identifying any agreement made in connection with the proposal.

(4) If the class action was previously certified under Rule 23(b)(3), the court may refuse to approve a settlement unless it affords a new opportunity to request exclusion to individual class members who had an earlier opportunity to request exclusion but did not do so.

(5) Any class member may object to the proposal if it requires court approval under this subdivision (e); the objection may be withdrawn only with the court's approval.

(f) Appeals. A court of appeals may permit an appeal from an order granting or denying class-action certification under this rule if a petition for permission to appeal is filed with the circuit clerk within 14 days after the order is entered. An appeal does not stay proceedings in the district court unless the district judge or the court of appeals so orders.

(g) Class Counsel.

(1) *Appointing Class Counsel.* Unless a statute provides otherwise, a court that certifies a class must appoint class counsel. In appointing class counsel, the court:

(A) must consider:

(i) the work counsel has done in identifying or investigating potential claims in the action;

(ii) counsel's experience in handling class actions, other complex litigation, and the types of claims asserted in the action;

(iii) counsel's knowledge of the applicable law; and

(iv) the resources that counsel will commit to representing the class;

(B) may consider any other matter pertinent to counsel's ability to fairly and adequately represent the interests of the class;

(C) may order potential class counsel to provide information on any subject pertinent to the appointment and to propose terms for attorney's fees and nontaxable costs;

(D) may include in the appointing order provisions about the award of attorney's fees or nontaxable costs under Rule 23(h); and

(E) may make further orders in connection with the appointment.

(2) *Standard for Appointing Class Counsel.* When one applicant seeks appointment as class counsel, the court may appoint that applicant only if the applicant is adequate under Rule 23(g)(1) and (4). If more than one adequate applicant seeks appointment, the court must appoint the applicant best able to represent the interests of the class.

(3) *Interim Counsel.* The court may designate interim counsel to act on behalf of a putative class before determining whether to certify the action as a class action.

(4) *Duty of Class Counsel.* Class counsel must fairly and adequately represent the interests of the class.

(h) Attorney's Fees and Nontaxable Costs. In a certified class action, the court may award reasonable attorney's fees and nontaxable costs that are authorized by law or by the parties' agreement. The following procedures apply:

(1) A claim for an award must be made by motion under Rule 54(d)(2), subject to the provisions of this subdivision (h), at a time the court sets. Notice of the motion must be served on all parties and, for motions by class counsel, directed to class members in a reasonable manner.

(2) A class member, or a party from whom payment is sought, may object to the motion.

(3) The court may hold a hearing and must find the facts and state its legal conclusions under Rule 52(a).

(4) The court may refer issues related to the amount of the award to a special master or a magistrate judge, as provided in Rule 54(d)(2)(D).

(Amended February 28, 1966, effective July 1, 1966; March 2, 1987, effective August 1, 1987; April 24, 1998, effective December 1, 1998; March 27, 2003, effective December 1, 2003; April 30, 2007, effective December 1, 2007; March 26, 2009, effective December 1, 2009.)

RULE 23.1. DERIVATIVE ACTIONS

(a) Prerequisites. This rule applies when one or more shareholders or members of a corporation or an unincorporated association bring a derivative action to enforce a right that the corporation or association may properly assert but has failed to enforce. The derivative action may not be maintained if it appears that the plaintiff does not fairly and adequately represent the interests of shareholders or members who are similarly situated in enforcing the right of the corporation or association.

(b) Pleading Requirements. The complaint must be verified and must:

    (1) allege that the plaintiff was a shareholder or member at the time of the transaction complained of, or that the plaintiff's share or membership later devolved on it by operation of law;

    (2) allege that the action is not a collusive one to confer jurisdiction that the court would otherwise lack; and

    (3) state with particularity:

        (A) any effort by the plaintiff to obtain the desired action from the directors or comparable authority and, if necessary, from the shareholders or members; and

        (B) the reasons for not obtaining the action or not making the effort.

(c) Settlement, Dismissal, and Compromise. A derivative action may be settled, voluntarily dismissed, or compromised only with the court's approval. Notice of a proposed settlement, voluntary dismissal, or compromise must be given to shareholders or members in the manner that the court orders.

(Adopted February 28, 1966, effective July 1, 1966; amended March 2, 1987, effective August 1, 1987; April 30, 2007, effective December 1, 2007.)

RULE 23.2. ACTIONS RELATING TO UNINCORPORATED ASSOCIATIONS

This rule applies to an action brought by or against the members of an unincorporated association as a class by naming certain members as representative parties. The action may be maintained only if it appears that those parties will fairly and adequately protect the interests of the association and its members. In conducting the action, the court may issue any appropriate orders corresponding with those in Rule 23(d), and the procedure for settlement, voluntary dismissal, or compromise must correspond with the procedure in Rule 23(e).

(Adopted February 28, 1966, effective July 1, 1966; amended April 30, 2007, effective December 1, 2007.)

RULE 24. INTERVENTION

(a) Intervention of Right. On timely motion, the court must permit anyone to intervene who:

    (1) is given an unconditional right to intervene by a federal statute; or

    (2) claims an interest relating to the property or transaction that is the subject of the action, and is so situated that disposing of the action may as a practical matter impair or impede the movant's ability to protect its interest, unless existing parties adequately represent that interest.

(b) Permissive Intervention.

    (1) *In General.* On timely motion, the court may permit anyone to intervene who:

        (A) is given a conditional right to intervene by a federal statute; or

        (B) has a claim or defense that shares with the main action a common question of law or fact.

    (2) *By a Government Officer or Agency.* On timely motion, the court may permit a federal or state governmental officer or agency to intervene if a party's claim or defense is based on:

        (A) a statute or executive order administered by the officer or agency; or

        (B) any regulation, order, requirement, or agreement issued or made under the statute or executive order.

    (3) *Delay or Prejudice.* In exercising its discretion, the court must consider whether the intervention will unduly delay or prejudice the adjudication of the original parties' rights.

(c) Notice and Pleading Required. A motion to intervene must be served on the parties as provided in Rule 5. The motion must state the grounds for intervention and be accompanied by a pleading that sets out the claim or defense for which intervention is sought.

(Amended December 27, 1946, effective March 19, 1948; December 29, 1948, effective October 20, 1949; January 21, 1963, effective July 1, 1963; February 28, 1966, effective July 1, 1966; March 2, 1987, effective August 1, 1987; April 30, 1991, effective December 1, 1991; April 12, 2006, effective December 1, 2006; April 30, 2007, effective December 1, 2007.)

RULE 25. SUBSTITUTION OF PARTIES

(a) Death.

    (1) *Substitution if the Claim Is Not Extinguished.* If a party dies and the claim is not extinguished, the court may order substitution of the proper party. A motion for substitution may be made by any party or by the decedent's successor or representative. If the motion is not made within 90 days after service of a statement noting the death, the action by or against the decedent must be dismissed.

    (2) *Continuation Among the Remaining Parties.* After a party's death, if the right sought to be enforced survives only to or against the remaining parties, the action does not abate, but proceeds in favor of or against the remaining parties. The death should be noted on the record.

    (3) *Service.* A motion to substitute, together with a notice of hearing, must be served on the parties as provided in Rule 5 and on nonparties as provided in Rule 4. A statement noting death must be served in the same manner. Service may be made in any judicial district.

(b) Incompetency. If a party becomes incompetent, the court may, on motion, permit the action to be continued by or against the party's representative. The motion must be served as provided in Rule 25(a)(3).

(c) Transfer of Interest. If an interest is transferred, the action may be continued by or against the original party unless the court, on motion, orders the transferee to be substituted in the action or joined with the original party. The motion must be served as provided in Rule 25(a)(3).

(d) Public Officers; Death or Separation from Office. An action does not abate when a public officer who is a party in an official capacity dies, resigns, or otherwise ceases to hold office while the action is pending. The officer's successor is automatically substituted as a party. Later proceedings should be in the substituted party's name, but any misnomer not affecting the parties' substantial rights must be disregarded. The court may order substitution at any time, but the absence of such an order does not affect the substitution.

(Amended December 29, 1948, effective October 20, 1949; April 17, 1961, effective July 19, 1961; January 21, 1963, effective July 1, 1963; March 2, 1987, effective August 1, 1987; April 30, 2007, effective December 1, 2007.)

TITLE V.   DISCLOSURES AND DISCOVERY

RULE 26.   DUTY TO DISCLOSE; GENERAL PROVISIONS GOVERNING DISCOVERY

(a) Required Disclosures.

(1) *Initial Disclosure.*

(A) *In General.* Except as exempted by Rule 26(a)(1)(B) or as otherwise stipulated or ordered by the court, a party must, without awaiting a discovery request, provide to the other parties:

(i) the name and, if known, the address and telephone number of each individual likely to have discoverable information—along with the subjects of that information—that the disclosing party may use to support its claims or defenses, unless the use would be solely for impeachment;

(ii) a copy—or a description by category and location—of all documents, electronically stored information, and tangible things that the disclosing party has in its possession, custody, or control and may use to support its claims or defenses, unless the use would be solely for impeachment;

(iii) a computation of each category of damages claimed by the disclosing party—who must also make available for inspection and copying as under Rule 34 the documents or other evidentiary material, unless privileged or protected from disclosure, on which each computation is based, including materials bearing on the nature and extent of injuries suffered; and

(iv) for inspection and copying as under Rule 34, any insurance agreement under which an insurance business may be liable to satisfy all or part of a possible judgment in the action or to indemnify or reimburse for payments made to satisfy the judgment.

(B) *Proceedings Exempt from Initial Disclosure.* The following proceedings are exempt from initial disclosure:

(i) an action for review on an administrative record;

(ii) a forfeiture action in rem arising from a federal statute;

(iii) a petition for habeas corpus or any other proceeding to challenge a criminal conviction or sentence;

(iv) an action brought without an attorney by a person in the custody of the United States, a state, or a state subdivision;

(v) an action to enforce or quash an administrative summons or subpoena;

(vi) an action by the United States to recover benefit payments;

(vii) an action by the United States to collect on a student loan guaranteed by the United States;

(viii) a proceeding ancillary to a proceeding in another court; and

(ix) an action to enforce an arbitration award.

(C) *Time for Initial Disclosures—In General.* A party must make the initial disclosures at or within 14 days after the parties' Rule 26(f) conference unless a different time is set by stipulation or court order, or unless a party objects during the conference that initial disclosures are not appropriate in this action and states the objection in the proposed discovery plan. In ruling on the objection, the court must determine what disclosures, if any, are to be made and must set the time for disclosure.

(D) *Time for Initial Disclosures—For Parties Served or Joined Later.* A party that is first served or otherwise joined after the Rule 26(f) conference must make the initial disclosures within 30 days after being served or joined, unless a different time is set by stipulation or court order.

(E) *Basis for Initial Disclosure; Unacceptable Excuses.* A party must make its initial disclosures based on the information then reasonably available to it. A party is not excused from making its disclosures because it has not fully investigated the case or because it challenges the sufficiency of another party's disclosures or because another party has not made its disclosures.

(2) *Disclosure of Expert Testimony.*

(A) *In General.* In addition to the disclosures required by Rule 26(a)(1), a party must disclose to the other parties the identity of any witness it may use at trial to present evidence under Federal Rule of Evidence 702, 703, or 705.

(B) *Witnesses Who Must Provide a Written Report.* Unless otherwise stipulated or ordered by the court, this disclosure must be accompanied by a written report—prepared and signed by the witness—if the witness is one retained or specially employed to provide expert testimony in the case or one whose duties as the party's employee regularly involve giving expert testimony. The report must contain:

(i) a complete statement of all opinions the witness will express and the basis and reasons for them;

(ii) the facts or data considered by the witness in forming them;

(iii) any exhibits that will be used to summarize or support them;

(iv) the witness's qualifications, including a list of all publications authored in the previous 10 years;

(v) a list of all other cases in which, during the previous 4 years, the witness testified as an expert at trial or by deposition; and

(vi) a statement of the compensation to be paid for the study and testimony in the case.

(C) *Witnesses Who Do Not Provide a Written Report.* Unless otherwise stipulated or ordered by the court, if the witness is not required to provide a written report, this disclosure must state:

(i) the subject matter on which the witness is expected to present evidence under Federal Rule of Evidence 702, 703, or 705; and

(ii) a summary of the facts and opinions to which the witness is expected to testify.

(D) *Time to Disclose Expert Testimony.* A party must make these disclosures at the times and in the sequence that the court orders. Absent a stipulation or a court order, the disclosures must be made:

(i) at least 90 days before the date set for trial or for the case to be ready for trial; or

(ii) if the evidence is intended solely to contradict or rebut evidence on the same subject matter identified by another party under Rule 26(a)(2)(B) or (C), within 30 days after the other party's disclosure.

(E) *Supplementing the Disclosure.* The parties must supplement these disclosures when required under Rule 26(e).

(3) *Pretrial Disclosures.*

(A) *In General.* In addition to the disclosures required by Rule 26(a)(1) and (2), a party must provide to the other parties and promptly file the following information about the evidence that it may present at trial other than solely for impeachment:

(i) the name and, if not previously provided, the address and telephone number of each witness—separately identifying those the party expects to present and those it may call if the need arises;

(ii) the designation of those witnesses whose testimony the party expects to present by deposition and, if not taken stenographically, a transcript of the pertinent parts of the deposition; and

(iii) an identification of each document or other exhibit, including summaries of other evidence—separately identifying those items the party expects to offer and those it may offer if the need arises.

(B) *Time for Pretrial Disclosures; Objections.* Unless the court orders otherwise, these disclosures must be made at least 30 days before trial. Within 14 days after they are made, unless the court sets a different time, a party may serve and promptly file a list of the following objections: any objections to the use under Rule 32(a) of a deposition designated by another party under Rule 26(a)(3)(A)(ii); and any objection, together with the grounds for it, that may be made to the admissibility of materials identified under Rule 26(a)(3)(A)(iii). An objection not so made—except for one under Federal Rule of Evidence 402 or 403—is waived unless excused by the court for good cause.

(4) *Form of Disclosures.* Unless the court orders otherwise, all disclosures under Rule 26(a) must be in writing, signed, and served.

(b) Discovery Scope and Limits.

(1) *Scope in General.* Unless otherwise limited by court order, the scope of discovery is as follows: Parties may obtain discovery regarding any nonprivileged matter that is relevant to any party's claim or defense and proportional to the needs of the case, considering the importance of the issues at stake in the action, the amount in controversy, the parties' relative access to relevant information, the parties' resources, the importance of the discovery in resolving the issues, and whether the burden or expense of the proposed discovery outweighs its likely benefit. Information within this scope of discovery need not be admissible in evidence to be discoverable.

(2) *Limitations on Frequency and Extent.*

(A) *When Permitted.* By order, the court may alter the limits in these rules on the number of depositions and interrogatories or on the length of depositions under Rule 30. By order or local rule, the court may also limit the number of requests under Rule 36.

(B) *Specific Limitations on Electronically Stored Information.* A party need not provide discovery of electronically stored information from sources that the party identifies as not reasonably accessible because of undue burden or cost. On motion to compel discovery or for a protective order, the party from whom discovery is sought must show that the information is not reasonably accessible because of undue burden or cost. If that showing is made, the court may nonetheless order discovery from such sources if the requesting party shows good cause, considering the limitations of Rule 26(b)(2)(C). The court may specify conditions for the discovery.

(C) *When Required.* On motion or on its own, the court must limit the frequency or extent of discovery otherwise allowed by these rules or by local rule if it determines that:

(i) the discovery sought is unreasonably cumulative or duplicative, or can be obtained from some other source that is more convenient, less burdensome, or less expensive;

(ii) the party seeking discovery has had ample opportunity to obtain the information by discovery in the action; or

(iii) the proposed discovery is outside the scope permitted by Rule 26(b)(1).

(3) *Trial Preparation: Materials.*

(A) *Documents and Tangible Things.* Ordinarily, a party may not discover documents and tangible things that are prepared in anticipation of litigation or for trial by or for another party or its representative (including the other party's attorney, consultant, surety, indemnitor, insurer, or agent). But, subject to Rule 26(b)(4), those materials may be discovered if:

(i) they are otherwise discoverable under Rule 26(b)(1); and

(ii) the party shows that it has substantial need for the materials to prepare its case and cannot, without undue hardship, obtain their substantial equivalent by other means.

(B) *Protection Against Disclosure.* If the court orders discovery of those materials, it must protect against disclosure of the mental impressions, conclusions, opinions, or legal theories of a party's attorney or other representative concerning the litigation.

(C) *Previous Statement.* Any party or other person may, on request and without the required showing, obtain the person's own previous statement about the action or its subject matter. If the request is refused, the person may move for a court order, and Rule 37(a)(5) applies to the award of expenses. A previous statement is either:

(i) a written statement that the person has signed or otherwise adopted or approved; or

(ii) a contemporaneous stenographic, mechanical, electrical, or other recording—or a transcription of it—that recites substantially verbatim the person's oral statement.

(4) *Trial Preparation: Experts.*

(A) *Deposition of an Expert Who May Testify.* A party may depose any person who has been identified as an expert whose opinions may be presented at trial. If Rule 26(a)(2)(B) requires a report from the expert, the deposition may be conducted only after the report is provided.

(B) *Trial–Preparation Protection for Draft Reports or Disclosures.* Rules 26(b)(3)(A) and (B) protect drafts of any report or disclosure required under Rule 26(a)(2), regardless of the form in which the draft is recorded.

(C) *Trial–Preparation Protection for Communications Between a Party's Attorney and Expert Witnesses.* Rules 26(b)(3)(A) and (B) protect communications between the party's attorney and any witness required to provide a report under Rule 26(a)(2)(B), regardless of the form of the communications, except to the extent that the communications:

(i) relate to compensation for the expert's study or testimony;

(ii) identify facts or data that the party's attorney provided and that the expert considered in forming the opinions to be expressed; or

(iii) identify assumptions that the party's attorney provided and that the expert relied on in forming the opinions to be expressed.

(D) *Expert Employed Only for Trial Preparation.* Ordinarily, a party may not, by interrogatories or deposition, discover facts known or opinions held by an expert who has been retained or specially employed by another party in anticipation of litigation or to prepare for trial and who is not expected to be called as a witness at trial. But a party may do so only:

(i) as provided in Rule 35(b); or

(ii) on showing exceptional circumstances under which it is impracticable for the party to obtain facts or opinions on the same subject by other means.

(E) *Payment.* Unless manifest injustice would result, the court must require that the party seeking discovery:

(i) pay the expert a reasonable fee for time spent in responding to discovery under Rule 26(b)(4)(A) or (D); and

(ii) for discovery under (D), also pay the other party a fair portion of the fees and expenses it reasonably incurred in obtaining the expert's facts and opinions.

(5) *Claiming Privilege or Protecting Trial-Preparation Materials.*

(A) *Information Withheld.* When a party withholds information otherwise discoverable by claiming that the information is privileged or subject to protection as trial-preparation material, the party must:

(i) expressly make the claim; and

(ii) describe the nature of the documents, communications, or tangible things not produced or disclosed—and do so in a manner that, without revealing information itself privileged or protected, will enable other parties to assess the claim.

(B) *Information Produced.* If information produced in discovery is subject to a claim of privilege or of protection as trial-preparation material, the party making the claim may notify any party that received the information of the claim and the basis for it. After being notified, a party must promptly return, sequester, or destroy the specified information and any copies it has; must not use or disclose the information until the claim is resolved; must take reasonable steps to retrieve the information if the party disclosed it before being notified; and may promptly present the information to the court under seal for a determination of the claim. The producing party must preserve the information until the claim is resolved.

(c) **Protective Orders.**

(1) *In General.* A party or any person from whom discovery is sought may move for a protective order in the court where the action is pending — or as an alternative on matters relating to a deposition, in the court for the district where the deposition will be taken. The motion must include a certification that the movant has in good faith conferred or attempted to confer with other affected parties in an effort to resolve the dispute without court action. The court may, for good cause, issue an order to protect a party or person from annoyance, embarrassment, oppression, or undue burden or expense, including one or more of the following:

(A) forbidding the disclosure or discovery;

(B) specifying terms, including time and place or the allocation of expenses, for the disclosure or discovery;

(C) prescribing a discovery method other than the one selected by the party seeking discovery;

(D) forbidding inquiry into certain matters, or limiting the scope of disclosure or discovery to certain matters;

(E) designating the persons who may be present while the discovery is conducted;

(F) requiring that a deposition be sealed and opened only on court order;

(G) requiring that a trade secret or other confidential research, development, or commercial information not be revealed or be revealed only in a specified way; and

(H) requiring that the parties simultaneously file specified documents or information in sealed envelopes, to be opened as the court directs.

(2) *Ordering Discovery.* If a motion for a protective order is wholly or partly denied, the court may, on just terms, order that any party or person provide or permit discovery.

(3) *Awarding Expenses.* Rule 37(a)(5) applies to the award of expenses.

(d) Timing and Sequence of Discovery.

(1) *Timing.* A party may not seek discovery from any source before the parties have conferred as required by Rule 26(f), except in a proceeding exempted from initial disclosure under Rule 26(a)(1)(B), or when authorized by these rules, by stipulation, or by court order.

(2) *Early Rule 34 Requests.*

(A) Time to Deliver. More than 21 days after the summons and complaint are served on a party, a request under Rule 34 may be delivered:

(i) to that party by any other party, and

(ii) by that party to any plaintiff or to any other party that has been served.

(B) *When Considered Served.* The request is considered to have been served at the first Rule 26(f) conference.

(3) *Sequence.* Unless the parties stipulate or the court orders otherwise for the parties' and witnesses' convenience and in the interests of justice:

(A) methods of discovery may be used in any sequence; and

(B) discovery by one party does not require any other party to delay its discovery.

(e) Supplementing Disclosures and Responses.

(1) *In General.* A party who has made a disclosure under Rule 26(a)—or who has responded to an interrogatory, request for production, or request for admission—must supplement or correct its disclosure or response:

(A) in a timely manner if the party learns that in some material respect the disclosure or response is incomplete or incorrect, and if the additional or corrective information has not otherwise been made known to the other parties during the discovery process or in writing; or

(B) as ordered by the court.

(2) *Expert Witness.* For an expert whose report must be disclosed under Rule 26(a)(2)(B), the party's duty to supplement extends both to information included in the report and to information given during the expert's deposition. Any additions or changes to this information must be disclosed by the time the party's pretrial disclosures under Rule 26(a)(3) are due.

(f) Conference of the Parties; Planning for Discovery.

(1) *Conference Timing.* Except in a proceeding exempted from initial disclosure under Rule 26(a)(1)(B) or when the court orders otherwise, the parties must confer as soon as practicable—and in any event at least 21 days before a scheduling conference is to be held or a scheduling order is due under Rule 16(b).

(2) *Conference Content; Parties' Responsibilities.* In conferring, the parties must consider the nature and basis of their claims and defenses and the possibilities for promptly settling or resolving the case; make or arrange for the disclosures required by Rule 26(a)(1); discuss any issues about preserving discoverable information; and develop a proposed discovery plan. The attorneys of record and all unrepresented parties that have appeared in the case are jointly responsible for arranging the conference, for attempting in good faith to agree on the proposed discovery plan, and for submitting to the court within 14 days after the conference a written report outlining the plan. The court may order the parties or attorneys to attend the conference in person.

(3) *Discovery Plan.* A discovery plan must state the parties' views and proposals on:

(A) what changes should be made in the timing, form, or requirement for disclosures under Rule 26(a), including a statement of when initial disclosures were made or will be made;

(B) the subjects on which discovery may be needed, when discovery should be completed, and whether discovery should be conducted in phases or be limited to or focused on particular issues;

(C) any issues about disclosure, discovery, or preservation of electronically stored information, including the form or forms in which it should be produced;

(D) any issues about claims of privilege or of protection as trial-preparation materials, including — if the parties agree on a procedure to assert these claims after production — whether to ask the court to include their agreement in an order under Federal Rule of Evidence 502;

(E) what changes should be made in the limitations on discovery imposed under these rules or by local rule, and what other limitations should be imposed; and

(F) any other orders that the court should issue under Rule 26(c) or under Rule 16(b) and (c).

(4) *Expedited Schedule.* If necessary to comply with its expedited schedule for Rule 16(b) conferences, a court may by local rule:

(A) require the parties' conference to occur less than 21 days before the scheduling conference is held or a scheduling order is due under Rule 16(b); and

(B) require the written report outlining the discovery plan to be filed less than 14 days after the parties' conference, or excuse the parties from submitting a written report and permit them to report orally on their discovery plan at the Rule 16(b) conference.

(g) Signing Disclosures and Discovery Requests, Responses, and Objections.

(1) *Signature Required; Effect of Signature.* Every disclosure under Rule 26(a)(1) or (a)(3) and every discovery request, response, or objection must be signed by at least one attorney of record in the attorney's own name—or by the party personally, if unrepresented—and must state the signer's address, e-mail address, and telephone number. By signing, an attorney or party certifies that to the best of the person's knowledge, information, and belief formed after a reasonable inquiry:

(A) with respect to a disclosure, it is complete and correct as of the time it is made; and

(B) with respect to a discovery request, response, or objection, it is:

(i) consistent with these rules and warranted by existing law or by a nonfrivolous argument for extending, modifying, or reversing existing law, or for establishing new law;

(ii) not interposed for any improper purpose, such as to harass, cause unnecessary delay, or needlessly increase the cost of litigation; and

(iii) neither unreasonable nor unduly burdensome or expensive, considering the needs of the case, prior discovery in the case, the amount in controversy, and the importance of the issues at stake in the action.

(2) *Failure to Sign.* Other parties have no duty to act on an unsigned disclosure, request, response, or objection until it is signed, and the court must strike it unless a signature is promptly supplied after the omission is called to the attorney's or party's attention.

(3) *Sanction for Improper Certification.* If a certification violates this rule without substantial justification, the court, on motion or on its own, must impose an appropriate sanction on the signer, the party on whose behalf the signer was acting, or both. The sanction may include an order to pay the reasonable expenses, including attorney's fees, caused by the violation.

(Amended December 27, 1946, effective March 19, 1948; January 21, 1963, effective July 1, 1963; February 28, 1966, effective July 1, 1966; March 30, 1970, effective July 1, 1970; April 29, 1980, effective August 1, 1980; April 28, 1983, effective August 1, 1983; March 2, 1987, effective August 1, 1987; April 22, 1993, effective December 1, 1993; April 17, 2000, effective December 1, 2000; April 12, 2006, effective December 1, 2006; April 30, 2007, effective December 1, 2007; April 28, 2010, effective December 1, 2010; April 29, 2015, effective December 1, 2015.)

RULE 27. DEPOSITIONS TO PERPETUATE TESTIMONY

(a) Before an Action Is Filed.

(1) *Petition.* A person who wants to perpetuate testimony about any matter cognizable in a United States court may file a verified petition in the district court for the district where any expected adverse party resides. The petition must ask for an order authorizing the petitioner to depose the named persons in order to perpetuate their testimony. The petition must be titled in the petitioner's name and must show:

(A) that the petitioner expects to be a party to an action cognizable in a United States court but cannot presently bring it or cause it to be brought;

(B) the subject matter of the expected action and the petitioner's interest;

(C) the facts that the petitioner wants to establish by the proposed testimony and the reasons to perpetuate it;

(D) the names or a description of the persons whom the petitioner expects to be adverse parties and their addresses, so far as known; and

(E) the name, address, and expected substance of the testimony of each deponent.

(2) *Notice and Service.* At least 21 days before the hearing date, the petitioner must serve each expected adverse party with a copy of the petition and a notice stating the time and place of the hearing. The notice may be served either inside or outside the district or state in the manner provided in Rule 4. If that service cannot be made with reasonable diligence on an expected adverse party, the court may order service by publication or otherwise. The court must appoint an attorney to represent persons not served in the manner provided in Rule 4 and to cross-examine the deponent if an unserved person is not otherwise represented. If any expected adverse party is a minor or is incompetent, Rule 17(c) applies.

(3) *Order and Examination.* If satisfied that perpetuating the testimony may prevent a failure or delay of justice, the court must issue an order that designates or describes the persons whose depositions may be taken, specifies the subject matter of the examinations, and states whether the depositions will be taken orally or by written interrogatories. The depositions may then be taken under these rules, and the court may issue orders like those authorized by Rules 34 and 35. A reference in these rules to the court where an action is pending means, for purposes of this rule, the court where the petition for the deposition was filed.

(4) *Using the Deposition.* A deposition to perpetuate testimony may be used under Rule 32(a) in any later-filed district-court action involving the same subject matter if the deposition either was taken under these rules or, although not so taken, would be admissible in evidence in the courts of the state where it was taken.

(b) Pending Appeal.

(1) *In General.* The court where a judgment has been rendered may, if an appeal has been taken or may still be taken, permit a party to depose witnesses to perpetuate their testimony for use in the event of further proceedings in that court.

(2) *Motion.* The party who wants to perpetuate testimony may move for leave to take the depositions, on the same notice and service as if the action were pending in the district court. The motion must show:

(A) the name, address, and expected substance of the testimony of each deponent; and

(B) the reasons for perpetuating the testimony.

(3) *Court Order.* If the court finds that perpetuating the testimony may prevent a failure or delay of justice, the court may permit the depositions to be taken and may issue orders like those authorized by Rules 34 and 35. The depositions may be taken and used as any other deposition taken in a pending district-court action.

(c) Perpetuation by an Action. This rule does not limit a court's power to entertain an action to perpetuate testimony.

(Amended December 27, 1946, effective March 19, 1948; December 29, 1948, effective October 20, 1949; March 1, 1971, effective July 1, 1971; March 2, 1987, effective August 1, 1987; April 25, 2005, effective December 1, 2005; April 30, 2007, effective December 1, 2007; March 26, 2009, effective December 1, 2009.)

RULE 28.　PERSONS BEFORE WHOM DEPOSITIONS MAY BE TAKEN

(a) Within the United States.

(1) *In General.* Within the United States or a territory or insular possession subject to United States jurisdiction, a deposition must be taken before:

(A) an officer authorized to administer oaths either by federal law or by the law in the place of examination; or

(B) a person appointed by the court where the action is pending to administer oaths and take testimony.

(2) *Definition of "Officer."* The term "officer" in Rules 30, 31, and 32 includes a person appointed by the court under this rule or designated by the parties under Rule 29(a).

(b) In a Foreign Country.

(1) *In General.* A deposition may be taken in a foreign country:

(A) under an applicable treaty or convention;

(B) under a letter of request, whether or not captioned a "letter rogatory";

(C) on notice, before a person authorized to administer oaths either by federal law or by the law in the place of examination; or

(D) before a person commissioned by the court to administer any necessary oath and take testimony.

(2) *Issuing a Letter of Request or a Commission.* A letter of request, a commission, or both may be issued:

(A) on appropriate terms after an application and notice of it; and

(B) without a showing that taking the deposition in another manner is impracticable or inconvenient.

(3) *Form of a Request, Notice, or Commission.* When a letter of request or any other device is used according to a treaty or convention, it must be captioned in the form prescribed by that treaty or convention. A letter of request may be addressed "To the Appropriate Authority in [name of country]." A deposition notice or a commission must designate by name or descriptive title the person before whom the deposition is to be taken.

(4) *Letter of Request—Admitting Evidence.* Evidence obtained in response to a letter of request need not be excluded merely because it is not a verbatim transcript, because the testimony was not taken under oath, or because of any similar departure from the requirements for depositions taken within the United States.

(c) Disqualification. A deposition must not be taken before a person who is any party's relative, employee, or attorney; who is related to or employed by any party's attorney; or who is financially interested in the action.

(Amended December 27, 1946, effective March 19, 1948; January 21, 1963, effective July 1, 1963; April 29, 1980, effective August 1, 1980; March 2, 1987, effective August 1, 1987; April 22, 1993, effective December 1, 1993; April 30, 2007, effective December 1, 2007.)

RULE 29.　STIPULATIONS ABOUT DISCOVERY PROCEDURE

Unless the court orders otherwise, the parties may stipulate that:

(a) a deposition may be taken before any person, at any time or place, on any notice, and in the manner specified—in which event it may be used in the same way as any other deposition; and

(b) other procedures governing or limiting discovery be modified—but a stipulation extending the time for any form of discovery must have court approval if it would interfere with the time set for completing discovery, for hearing a motion, or for trial.

(Amended March 30, 1970, effective July 1, 1970; April 22, 1993, effective December 1, 1993; April 30, 2007, effective December 1, 2007.)

RULE 30. DEPOSITIONS BY ORAL EXAMINATION

(a) When a Deposition May Be Taken.

(1) *Without Leave.* A party may, by oral questions, depose any person, including a party, without leave of court except as provided in Rule 30(a)(2). The deponent's attendance may be compelled by subpoena under Rule 45.

(2) *With Leave.* A party must obtain leave of court, and the court must grant leave to the extent consistent with Rule 26(b)(1) and (2):

(A) if the parties have not stipulated to the deposition and:

(i) the deposition would result in more than 10 depositions being taken under this rule or Rule 31 by the plaintiffs, or by the defendants, or by the third-party defendants;

(ii) the deponent has already been deposed in the case; or

(iii) the party seeks to take the deposition before the time specified in Rule 26(d), unless the party certifies in the notice, with supporting facts, that the deponent is expected to leave the United States and be unavailable for examination in this country after that time; or

(B) if the deponent is confined in prison.

(b) Notice of the Deposition; Other Formal Requirements.

(1) *Notice in General.* A party who wants to depose a person by oral questions must give reasonable written notice to every other party. The notice must state the time and place of the deposition and, if known, the deponent's name and address. If the name is unknown, the notice must provide a general description sufficient to identify the person or the particular class or group to which the person belongs.

(2) *Producing Documents.* If a subpoena duces tecum is to be served on the deponent, the materials designated for production, as set out in the subpoena, must be listed in the notice or in an attachment. The notice to a party deponent may be accompanied by a request under Rule 34 to produce documents and tangible things at the deposition.

(3) *Method of Recording.*

(A) *Method Stated in the Notice.* The party who notices the deposition must state in the notice the method for recording the testimony. Unless the court orders otherwise, testimony may be recorded by audio, audiovisual, or stenographic means. The noticing party bears the recording costs. Any party may arrange to transcribe a deposition.

(B) *Additional Method.* With prior notice to the deponent and other parties, any party may designate another method for recording the testimony in addition to that specified in the original notice. That party bears the expense of the additional record or transcript unless the court orders otherwise.

(4) *By Remote Means.* The parties may stipulate—or the court may on motion order—that a deposition be taken by telephone or other remote means. For the purpose of this rule and Rules 28(a), 37(a)(2), and 37(b)(1), the deposition takes place where the deponent answers the questions.

(5) *Officer's Duties.*

(A) *Before the Deposition.* Unless the parties stipulate otherwise, a deposition must be conducted before an officer appointed or designated under Rule 28. The officer must begin the deposition with an on-the-record statement that includes:

(i) the officer's name and business address;

(ii) the date, time, and place of the deposition;

(iii) the deponent's name;

(iv) the officer's administration of the oath or affirmation to the deponent; and

(v) the identity of all persons present.

(B) *Conducting the Deposition; Avoiding Distortion.* If the deposition is recorded non-stenographically, the officer must repeat the items in Rule 30(b)(5)(A)(i)-(iii) at the beginning of each unit of the recording medium. The deponent's and attorneys' appearance or demeanor must not be distorted through recording techniques.

(C) *After the Deposition.* At the end of a deposition, the officer must state on the record that the deposition is complete and must set out any stipulations made by the attorneys about custody of the transcript or recording and of the exhibits, or about any other pertinent matters.

(6) *Notice or Subpoena Directed to an Organization.* In its notice or subpoena, a party may name as the deponent a public or private corporation, a partnership, an association, a governmental agency, or other entity and must describe with reasonable particularity the matters for examination. The named organization must then designate one or more officers, directors, or managing agents, or designate other persons who consent to testify on its behalf; and it may set out the matters on which each person designated will testify. A subpoena must advise a nonparty organization of its duty to make this designation. The persons designated must testify about information known or reasonably available to the organization. This paragraph (6) does not preclude a deposition by any other procedure allowed by these rules.

(c) Examination and Cross–Examination; Record of the Examination; Objections; Written Questions.

(1) *Examination and Cross–Examination.* The examination and cross-examination of a deponent proceed as they would at trial under the Federal Rules of Evidence, except Rules 103 and 615. After putting the deponent under oath or affirmation, the officer must record the testimony by the method designated under Rule 30(b)(3)(A). The testimony must be recorded by the officer personally or by a person acting in the presence and under the direction of the officer.

(2) *Objections.* An objection at the time of the examination—whether to evidence, to a party's conduct, to the officer's qualifications, to the manner of taking the deposition, or to any other aspect of the deposition—must be noted on the record, but the examination still proceeds; the testimony is taken subject to any objection. An objection must be stated concisely in a nonargumentative and nonsuggestive manner. A person may instruct a deponent not to answer only when necessary to preserve a privilege, to enforce a limitation ordered by the court, or to present a motion under Rule 30(d)(3).

(3) *Participating Through Written Questions.* Instead of participating in the oral examination, a party may serve written questions in a sealed envelope on the party noticing the deposition, who must deliver them to the officer. The officer must ask the deponent those questions and record the answers verbatim.

(d) Duration; Sanction; Motion to Terminate or Limit.

(1) *Duration.* Unless otherwise stipulated or ordered by the court, a deposition is limited to one day of 7 hours. The court must allow additional time consistent with Rule 26(b)(1) and (2) if needed to fairly examine the deponent or if the deponent, another person, or any other circumstance impedes or delays the examination.

(2) *Sanction.* The court may impose an appropriate sanction—including the reasonable expenses and attorney's fees incurred by any party—on a person who impedes, delays, or frustrates the fair examination of the deponent.

(3) *Motion to Terminate or Limit.*

(A) *Grounds.* At any time during a deposition, the deponent or a party may move to terminate or limit it on the ground that it is being conducted in bad faith or in a manner that unreasonably annoys, embarrasses, or oppresses the deponent or party. The motion may be filed in the court where the action is pending or the deposition is being taken. If the objecting deponent or party so demands, the deposition must be suspended for the time necessary to obtain an order.

(B) *Order.* The court may order that the deposition be terminated or may limit its scope and manner as provided in Rule 26(c). If terminated, the deposition may be resumed only by order of the court where the action is pending.

(C) *Award of Expenses.* Rule 37(a)(5) applies to the award of expenses.

(e) Review by the Witness; Changes.

(1) *Review; Statement of Changes.* On request by the deponent or a party before the deposition is completed, the deponent must be allowed 30 days after being notified by the officer that the transcript or recording is available in which:

(A) to review the transcript or recording; and

(B) if there are changes in form or substance, to sign a statement listing the changes and the reasons for making them.

(2) *Changes Indicated in the Officer's Certificate.* The officer must note in the certificate prescribed by Rule 30(f)(1) whether a review was requested and, if so, must attach any changes the deponent makes during the 30–day period.

(f) Certification and Delivery; Exhibits; Copies of the Transcript or Recording; Filing.

(1) *Certification and Delivery.* The officer must certify in writing that the witness was duly sworn and that the deposition accurately records the witness's testimony. The certificate must accompany the record of the deposition. Unless the court orders otherwise, the officer must seal the deposition in an envelope or package bearing the title of the action and marked "Deposition of [witness's name]" and must promptly send it to the attorney who arranged for the transcript or recording. The attorney must store it under conditions that will protect it against loss, destruction, tampering, or deterioration.

(2) *Documents and Tangible Things.*

(A) *Originals and Copies.* Documents and tangible things produced for inspection during a deposition must, on a party's request, be marked for identification and attached to the deposition. Any party may inspect and copy them. But if the person who produced them wants to keep the originals, the person may:

(i) offer copies to be marked, attached to the deposition, and then used as originals—after giving all parties a fair opportunity to verify the copies by comparing them with the originals; or

(ii) give all parties a fair opportunity to inspect and copy the originals after they are marked—in which event the originals may be used as if attached to the deposition.

(B) *Order Regarding the Originals.* Any party may move for an order that the originals be attached to the deposition pending final disposition of the case.

(3) *Copies of the Transcript or Recording.* Unless otherwise stipulated or ordered by the court, the officer must retain the stenographic notes of a deposition taken stenographically or a copy of the recording of a deposition taken by another method. When paid reasonable charges, the officer must furnish a copy of the transcript or recording to any party or the deponent.

(4) *Notice of Filing.* A party who files the deposition must promptly notify all other parties of the filing.

(g) Failure to Attend a Deposition or Serve a Subpoena; Expenses. A party who, expecting a deposition to be taken, attends in person or by an attorney may recover reasonable expenses for attending, including attorney's fees, if the noticing party failed to:

(1) attend and proceed with the deposition; or

(2) serve a subpoena on a nonparty deponent, who consequently did not attend.

(Amended January 21, 1963, effective July 1, 1963; March 30, 1970, effective July 1, 1970; March 1, 1971, effective July 1, 1971; November 20, 1972, effective July 1, 1975; April 29, 1980, effective August 1, 1980; March 2, 1987, effective August 1, 1987; April 22, 1993, effective December 1, 1993; April 17, 2000, effective December 1, 2000; April 30, 2007, effective December 1, 2007; April 29, 2015, effective December 1, 2015.)

RULE 31. DEPOSITIONS BY WRITTEN QUESTIONS

(a) When a Deposition May Be Taken.

(1) *Without Leave.* A party may, by written questions, depose any person, including a party, without leave of court except as provided in Rule 31(a)(2). The deponent's attendance may be compelled by subpoena under Rule 45.

(2) *With Leave.* A party must obtain leave of court, and the court must grant leave to the extent consistent with Rule 26(b)(1) and (2):

(A) if the parties have not stipulated to the deposition and:

(i) the deposition would result in more than 10 depositions being taken under this rule or Rule 30 by the plaintiffs, or by the defendants, or by the third-party defendants;

(ii) the deponent has already been deposed in the case; or

(iii) the party seeks to take a deposition before the time specified in Rule 26(d); or

(B) if the deponent is confined in prison.

(3) *Service; Required Notice.* A party who wants to depose a person by written questions must serve them on every other party, with a notice stating, if known, the deponent's name and address. If the name is unknown, the notice must provide a general description sufficient to identify the person or the particular class or group to which the person belongs. The notice must also state the name or descriptive title and the address of the officer before whom the deposition will be taken.

(4) *Questions Directed to an Organization.* A public or private corporation, a partnership, an association, or a governmental agency may be deposed by written questions in accordance with Rule 30(b)(6).

(5) *Questions from Other Parties.* Any questions to the deponent from other parties must be served on all parties as follows: cross-questions, within 14 days after being served with the notice and direct questions; redirect questions, within 7 days after being served with cross-questions; and recross-questions, within 7 days after being served with redirect questions. The court may, for good cause, extend or shorten these times.

(b) Delivery to the Officer; Officer's Duties. The party who noticed the deposition must deliver to the officer a copy of all the questions served and of the notice. The officer must promptly proceed in the manner provided in Rule 30(c), (e), and (f) to:

(1) take the deponent's testimony in response to the questions;

(2) prepare and certify the deposition; and

(3) send it to the party, attaching a copy of the questions and of the notice.

(c) Notice of Completion or Filing.

(1) *Completion.* The party who noticed the deposition must notify all other parties when it is completed.

(2) *Filing.* A party who files the deposition must promptly notify all other parties of the filing.

(Amended March 30, 1970, effective July 1, 1970; March 2, 1987, effective August 1, 1987; April 22, 1993, effective December 1, 1993; April 30, 2007, effective December 1, 2007; April 29, 2015, effective December 1, 2015.)

RULE 32. USING DEPOSITIONS IN COURT PROCEEDINGS

(a) Using Depositions.

(1) *In General.* At a hearing or trial, all or part of a deposition may be used against a party on these conditions:

(A) the party was present or represented at the taking of the deposition or had reasonable notice of it;

(B) it is used to the extent it would be admissible under the Federal Rules of Evidence if the deponent were present and testifying; and

(C) the use is allowed by Rule 32(a)(2) through (8).

(2) *Impeachment and Other Uses.* Any party may use a deposition to contradict or impeach the testimony given by the deponent as a witness, or for any other purpose allowed by the Federal Rules of Evidence.

(3) *Deposition of Party, Agent, or Designee.* An adverse party may use for any purpose the deposition of a party or anyone who, when deposed, was the party's officer, director, managing agent, or designee under Rule 30(b)(6) or 31(a)(4).

(4) *Unavailable Witness.* A party may use for any purpose the deposition of a witness, whether or not a party, if the court finds:

(A) that the witness is dead;

(B) that the witness is more than 100 miles from the place of hearing or trial or is outside the United States, unless it appears that the witness's absence was procured by the party offering the deposition;

(C) that the witness cannot attend or testify because of age, illness, infirmity, or imprisonment;

(D) that the party offering the deposition could not procure the witness's attendance by subpoena; or

(E) on motion and notice, that exceptional circumstances make it desirable—in the interest of justice and with due regard to the importance of live testimony in open court—to permit the deposition to be used.

(5) *Limitations on Use.*

(A) *Deposition Taken on Short Notice.* A deposition must not be used against a party who, having received less than 14 days' notice of the deposition, promptly moved for a protective order under Rule 26(c)(1)(B) requesting that it not be taken or be taken at a different time or place—and this motion was still pending when the deposition was taken.

(B) *Unavailable Deponent; Party Could Not Obtain an Attorney.* A deposition taken without leave of court under the unavailability provision of Rule 30(a)(2)(A)(iii) must not be used against a party who shows that, when served with the notice, it could not, despite diligent efforts, obtain an attorney to represent it at the deposition.

(6) *Using Part of a Deposition.* If a party offers in evidence only part of a deposition, an adverse party may require the offeror to introduce other parts that in fairness should be considered with the part introduced, and any party may itself introduce any other parts.

(7) *Substituting a Party.* Substituting a party under Rule 25 does not affect the right to use a deposition previously taken.

(8) *Deposition Taken in an Earlier Action.* A deposition lawfully taken and, if required, filed in any federal- or state-court action may be used in a later action involving the same subject matter between the same parties, or their representatives or successors in interest, to the same extent as if taken in the later action. A deposition previously taken may also be used as allowed by the Federal Rules of Evidence.

(b) Objections to Admissibility. Subject to Rules 28(b) and 32(d)(3), an objection may be made at a hearing or trial to the admission of any deposition testimony that would be inadmissible if the witness were present and testifying.

(c) Form of Presentation. Unless the court orders otherwise, a party must provide a transcript of any deposition testimony the party offers, but may provide the court with the testimony in nontranscript form as well. On any party's request, deposition testimony offered in a jury trial for any purpose other than impeachment must be presented in nontranscript form, if available, unless the court for good cause orders otherwise.

(d) Waiver of Objections.

(1) *To the Notice.* An objection to an error or irregularity in a deposition notice is waived unless promptly served in writing on the party giving the notice.

(2) *To the Officer's Qualification.* An objection based on disqualification of the officer before whom a deposition is to be taken is waived if not made:

(A) before the deposition begins; or

(B) promptly after the basis for disqualification becomes known or, with reasonable diligence, could have been known.

(3) *To the Taking of the Deposition.*

(A) *Objection to Competence, Relevance, or Materiality.* An objection to a deponent's competence—or to the competence, relevance, or materiality of testimony—is not waived by a failure to make the objection before or during the deposition, unless the ground for it might have been corrected at that time.

(B) *Objection to an Error or Irregularity.* An objection to an error or irregularity at an oral examination is waived if:

(i) it relates to the manner of taking the deposition, the form of a question or answer, the oath or affirmation, a party's conduct, or other matters that might have been corrected at that time; and

(ii) it is not timely made during the deposition.

(C) *Objection to a Written Question.* An objection to the form of a written question under Rule 31 is waived if not served in writing on the party submitting the question within the time for serving responsive questions or, if the question is a recross-question, within 7 days after being served with it.

(4) *To Completing and Returning the Deposition.* An objection to how the officer transcribed the testimony—or prepared, signed, certified, sealed, endorsed, sent, or otherwise dealt with the deposition—is waived unless a motion to suppress is made promptly after the error or irregularity becomes known or, with reasonable diligence, could have been known.

(Amended March 30, 1970, effective July 1, 1970; November 20, 1972, effective July 1, 1975; April 29, 1980, effective August 1, 1980; March 2, 1987, effective August 1, 1987; April 22, 1993, effective December 1, 1993; April 30, 2007, effective December 1, 2007; March 26, 2009, effective December 1, 2009.)

RULE 33. INTERROGATORIES TO PARTIES

(a) In General.

(1) *Number.* Unless otherwise stipulated or ordered by the court, a party may serve on any other party no more than 25 written interrogatories, including all discrete subparts. Leave to serve additional interrogatories may be granted to the extent consistent with Rule 26(b)(1) and (2).

(2) *Scope.* An interrogatory may relate to any matter that may be inquired into under Rule 26(b). An interrogatory is not objectionable merely because it asks for an opinion or contention that relates to fact or the application of law to fact, but the court may order that the interrogatory need not be answered until designated discovery is complete, or until a pretrial conference or some other time.

(b) Answers and Objections.

(1) *Responding Party.* The interrogatories must be answered:

(A) by the party to whom they are directed; or

(B) if that party is a public or private corporation, a partnership, an association, or a governmental agency, by any officer or agent, who must furnish the information available to the party.

(2) *Time to Respond.* The responding party must serve its answers and any objections within 30 days after being served with the interrogatories. A shorter or longer time may be stipulated to under Rule 29 or be ordered by the court.

(3) *Answering Each Interrogatory.* Each interrogatory must, to the extent it is not objected to, be answered separately and fully in writing under oath.

(4) *Objections.* The grounds for objecting to an interrogatory must be stated with specificity. Any ground not stated in a timely objection is waived unless the court, for good cause, excuses the failure.

(5) *Signature.* The person who makes the answers must sign them, and the attorney who objects must sign any objections.

(c) Use. An answer to an interrogatory may be used to the extent allowed by the Federal Rules of Evidence.

(d) Option to Produce Business Records. If the answer to an interrogatory may be determined by examining, auditing, compiling, abstracting, or summarizing a party's business records (including electronically stored information), and if the burden of deriving or ascertaining the answer will be substantially the same for either party, the responding party may answer by:

(1) specifying the records that must be reviewed, in sufficient detail to enable the interrogating party to locate and identify them as readily as the responding party could; and

(2) giving the interrogating party a reasonable opportunity to examine and audit the records and to make copies, compilations, abstracts, or summaries.

(Amended December 27, 1946, effective March 19, 1948; March 30, 1970, effective July 1, 1970; April 29, 1980, effective August 1, 1980; April 22, 1993, effective December 1, 1993; April 12, 2006, effective December 1, 2006; April 30, 2007, effective December 1, 2007; April 29, 2015, effective December 1, 2015.)

RULE 34. PRODUCING DOCUMENTS, ELECTRONICALLY STORED INFORMATION, AND TANGIBLE THINGS, OR ENTERING ONTO LAND, FOR INSPECTION AND OTHER PURPOSES

(a) In General. A party may serve on any other party a request within the scope of Rule 26(b):

(1) to produce and permit the requesting party or its representative to inspect, copy, test, or sample the following items in the responding party's possession, custody, or control:

(A) any designated documents or electronically stored information—including writings, drawings, graphs, charts, photographs, sound recordings, images, and other data or data compilations—stored in any medium from which information can be obtained either directly or, if necessary, after translation by the responding party into a reasonably usable form; or

(B) any designated tangible things; or

(2) to permit entry onto designated land or other property possessed or controlled by the responding party, so that the requesting party may inspect, measure, survey, photograph, test, or sample the property or any designated object or operation on it.

(b) Procedure.

(1) *Contents of the Request.* The request:

(A) must describe with reasonable particularity each item or category of items to be inspected;

(B) must specify a reasonable time, place, and manner for the inspection and for performing the related acts; and

(C) may specify the form or forms in which electronically stored information is to be produced.

(2) *Responses and Objections.*

(A) *Time to Respond.* The party to whom the request is directed must respond in writing within 30 days after being served or — if the request was delivered under Rule 26(d)(2) — within 30 days after the parties' first Rule 26(f) conference. A shorter or longer time may be stipulated to under Rule 29 or be ordered by the court.

(B) *Responding to Each Item.* For each item or category, the response must either state that inspection and related activities will be permitted as requested or state with specificity the grounds for objecting to the request, including the reasons. The responding party may state that it will produce copies of documents or of electronically stored information instead of permitting inspection. The production must then be completed no later than the time for inspection specified in the request or another reasonable time specified in the response.

(C) *Objections.* An objection must state whether any responsive materials are being withheld on the basis of that objection. An objection to part of a request must specify the part and permit inspection of the rest.

(D) *Responding to a Request for Production of Electronically Stored Information.* The response may state an objection to a requested form for producing electronically stored information. If the responding party objects to a requested form—or if no form was specified in the request—the party must state the form or forms it intends to use.

(E) *Producing the Documents or Electronically Stored Information.* Unless otherwise stipulated or ordered by the court, these procedures apply to producing documents or electronically stored information:

(i) A party must produce documents as they are kept in the usual course of business or must organize and label them to correspond to the categories in the request;

(ii) If a request does not specify a form for producing electronically stored information, a party must produce it in a form or forms in which it is ordinarily maintained or in a reasonably usable form or forms; and

(iii) A party need not produce the same electronically stored information in more than one form.

(c) Nonparties. As provided in Rule 45, a nonparty may be compelled to produce documents and tangible things or to permit an inspection.

(Amended December 27, 1946, effective March 19, 1948; March 30, 1970, effective July 1, 1970; April 29, 1980, effective August 1, 1980; March 2, 1987, effective August 1, 1987; April 30, 1991, effective December 1, 1991; April 22, 1993, effective December 1, 1993; April 12, 2006, effective December 1, 2006; April 30, 2007, effective December 1, 2007; April 29, 2015, effective December 1, 2015.)

RULE 35. PHYSICAL AND MENTAL EXAMINATIONS

(a) Order for an Examination.

(1) *In General.* The court where the action is pending may order a party whose mental or physical condition—including blood group—is in controversy to submit to a physical or mental examination by a suitably licensed or certified examiner. The court has the same authority to order a party to produce for examination a person who is in its custody or under its legal control.

(2) *Motion and Notice; Contents of the Order.* The order:

    (A) may be made only on motion for good cause and on notice to all parties and the person to be examined; and

    (B) must specify the time, place, manner, conditions, and scope of the examination, as well as the person or persons who will perform it.

(b) Examiner's Report.

(1) *Request by the Party or Person Examined.* The party who moved for the examination must, on request, deliver to the requester a copy of the examiner's report, together with like reports of all earlier examinations of the same condition. The request may be made by the party against whom the examination order was issued or by the person examined.

(2) *Contents.* The examiner's report must be in writing and must set out in detail the examiner's findings, including diagnoses, conclusions, and the results of any tests.

(3) *Request by the Moving Party.* After delivering the reports, the party who moved for the examination may request—and is entitled to receive—from the party against whom the examination order was issued like reports of all earlier or later examinations of the same condition. But those reports need not be delivered by the party with custody or control of the person examined if the party shows that it could not obtain them.

(4) *Waiver of Privilege.* By requesting and obtaining the examiner's report, or by deposing the examiner, the party examined waives any privilege it may have—in that action or any other action involving the same controversy—concerning testimony about all examinations of the same condition.

(5) *Failure to Deliver a Report.* The court on motion may order—on just terms—that a party deliver the report of an examination. If the report is not provided, the court may exclude the examiner's testimony at trial.

(6) *Scope.* This subdivision (b) applies also to an examination made by the parties' agreement, unless the agreement states otherwise. This subdivision does not preclude obtaining an examiner's report or deposing an examiner under other rules.

(Amended March 30, 1970, effective July 1, 1970; March 2, 1987, effective August 1, 1987; amended by Pub.L. 100–690, Title VII, § 7047(b), November 18, 1988, 102 Stat. 4401; amended April 30, 1991, effective December 1, 1991; April 30, 2007, effective December 1, 2007.)

RULE 36.   REQUESTS FOR ADMISSION

(a) Scope and Procedure.

(1) *Scope.* A party may serve on any other party a written request to admit, for purposes of the pending action only, the truth of any matters within the scope of Rule 26(b)(1) relating to:

    (A) facts, the application of law to fact, or opinions about either; and

    (B) the genuineness of any described documents.

(2) *Form; Copy of a Document.* Each matter must be separately stated. A request to admit the genuineness of a document must be accompanied by a copy of the document unless it is, or has been, otherwise furnished or made available for inspection and copying.

(3) *Time to Respond; Effect of Not Responding.* A matter is admitted unless, within 30 days after being served, the party to whom the request is directed serves on the requesting party a written answer or objection addressed to the matter and signed by the party or its attorney. A shorter or longer time for responding may be stipulated to under Rule 29 or be ordered by the court.

(4) *Answer.* If a matter is not admitted, the answer must specifically deny it or state in detail why the answering party cannot truthfully admit or deny it. A denial must fairly respond to the substance of the matter; and when good faith requires that a party qualify an answer or deny only a part of a matter, the answer must specify the part admitted and qualify or deny the rest. The answering party may assert lack of knowledge or information as a reason for failing to admit or deny only if the party states that it has made reasonable inquiry and that the information it knows or can readily obtain is insufficient to enable it to admit or deny.

(5) *Objections.* The grounds for objecting to a request must be stated. A party must not object solely on the ground that the request presents a genuine issue for trial.

(6) *Motion Regarding the Sufficiency of an Answer or Objection.* The requesting party may move to determine the sufficiency of an answer or objection. Unless the court finds an objection justified, it must order that an answer be served. On finding that an answer does not comply with this rule, the court may order either that the matter is admitted or that an amended answer be served. The court may defer its final decision until a pretrial conference or a specified time before trial. Rule 37(a)(5) applies to an award of expenses.

(b) Effect of an Admission; Withdrawing or Amending It. A matter admitted under this rule is conclusively established unless the court, on motion, permits the admission to be withdrawn or amended. Subject to Rule 16(e), the court may permit withdrawal or amendment if it would promote the presentation of the merits of the action and if the court is not persuaded that it would prejudice the requesting party in maintaining or defending the action on the merits. An admission under this rule is not an admission for any other purpose and cannot be used against the party in any other proceeding.

(Amended December 27, 1946, effective March 19, 1948; March 30, 1970, effective July 1, 1970; March 2, 1987, effective August 1, 1987; April 22, 1993, effective December 1, 1993; April 30, 2007, effective December 1, 2007.)

RULE 37. FAILURE TO MAKE DISCLOSURES OR TO COOPERATE IN DISCOVERY; SANCTIONS

(a) Motion for an Order Compelling Disclosure or Discovery.

(1) *In General.* On notice to other parties and all affected persons, a party may move for an order compelling disclosure or discovery. The motion must include a certification that the movant has in good faith conferred or attempted to confer with the person or party failing to make disclosure or discovery in an effort to obtain it without court action.

(2) *Appropriate Court.* A motion for an order to a party must be made in the court where the action is pending. A motion for an order to a nonparty must be made in the court where the discovery is or will be taken.

(3) *Specific Motions.*

(A) *To Compel Disclosure.* If a party fails to make a disclosure required by Rule 26(a), any other party may move to compel disclosure and for appropriate sanctions.

(B) *To Compel a Discovery Response.* A party seeking discovery may move for an order compelling an answer, designation, production, or inspection. This motion may be made if:

(i) a deponent fails to answer a question asked under Rule 30 or 31;

(ii) a corporation or other entity fails to make a designation under Rule 30(b)(6) or 31(a)(4);

(iii) a party fails to answer an interrogatory submitted under Rule 33; or

(iv) a party fails to produce documents or fails to respond that inspection will be permitted — or fails to permit inspection — as requested under Rule 34.

(C) *Related to a Deposition.* When taking an oral deposition, the party asking a question may complete or adjourn the examination before moving for an order.

(4) *Evasive or Incomplete Disclosure, Answer, or Response.* For purposes of this subdivision (a), an evasive or incomplete disclosure, answer, or response must be treated as a failure to disclose, answer, or respond.

(5) *Payment of Expenses; Protective Orders.*

(A) *If the Motion Is Granted (or Disclosure or Discovery Is Provided After Filing).* If the motion is granted— or if the disclosure or requested discovery is provided after the motion was filed—the court must, after giving an opportunity to be heard, require the party or deponent whose conduct necessitated the motion, the party or attorney advising that conduct, or both to pay the movant's reasonable expenses incurred in making the motion, including attorney's fees. But the court must not order this payment if:

(i) the movant filed the motion before attempting in good faith to obtain the disclosure or discovery without court action;

(ii) the opposing party's nondisclosure, response, or objection was substantially justified; or

(iii) other circumstances make an award of expenses unjust.

(B) *If the Motion Is Denied.* If the motion is denied, the court may issue any protective order authorized under Rule 26(c) and must, after giving an opportunity to be heard, require the movant, the attorney filing the motion, or both to pay the party or deponent who opposed the motion its reasonable expenses incurred in opposing the motion, including attorney's fees. But the court must not order this payment if the motion was substantially justified or other circumstances make an award of expenses unjust.

(C) *If the Motion Is Granted in Part and Denied in Part.* If the motion is granted in part and denied in part, the court may issue any protective order authorized under Rule 26(c) and may, after giving an opportunity to be heard, apportion the reasonable expenses for the motion.

(b) Failure to Comply with a Court Order.

(1) *Sanctions Sought in the District Where the Deposition Is Taken.* If the court where the discovery is taken orders a deponent to be sworn or to answer a question and the deponent fails to obey, the failure may be treated as contempt of court. If a deposition-related motion is transferred to the court where the action is pending, and that court orders a deponent to be sworn or to answer a question and the deponent fails to obey, the failure may be treated as contempt of either the court where the discovery is taken or the court where the action is pending.

(2) *Sanctions Sought in the District Where the Action Is Pending.*

(A) *For Not Obeying a Discovery Order.* If a party or a party's officer, director, or managing agent—or a witness designated under Rule 30(b)(6) or 31(a)(4)—fails to obey an order to provide or permit discovery, including an order under Rule 26(f), 35, or 37(a), the court where the action is pending may issue further just orders. They may include the following:

(i) directing that the matters embraced in the order or other designated facts be taken as established for purposes of the action, as the prevailing party claims;

(ii) prohibiting the disobedient party from supporting or opposing designated claims or defenses, or from introducing designated matters in evidence;

(iii) striking pleadings in whole or in part;

(iv) staying further proceedings until the order is obeyed;

(v) dismissing the action or proceeding in whole or in part;

(vi) rendering a default judgment against the disobedient party; or

(vii) treating as contempt of court the failure to obey any order except an order to submit to a physical or mental examination.

(B) *For Not Producing a Person for Examination.* If a party fails to comply with an order under Rule 35(a) requiring it to produce another person for examination, the court may issue any of the orders listed in Rule 37(b)(2)(A)(i)-(vi), unless the disobedient party shows that it cannot produce the other person.

(C) *Payment of Expenses.* Instead of or in addition to the orders above, the court must order the disobedient party, the attorney advising that party, or both to pay the reasonable expenses, including attorney's fees, caused by the failure, unless the failure was substantially justified or other circumstances make an award of expenses unjust.

(c) Failure to Disclose, to Supplement an Earlier Response, or to Admit.

(1) *Failure to Disclose or Supplement.* If a party fails to provide information or identify a witness as required by Rule 26(a) or (e), the party is not allowed to use that information or witness to supply evidence on a motion, at a hearing, or at a trial, unless the failure was substantially justified or is harmless. In addition to or instead of this sanction, the court, on motion and after giving an opportunity to be heard:

(A) may order payment of the reasonable expenses, including attorney's fees, caused by the failure;

(B) may inform the jury of the party's failure; and

(C) may impose other appropriate sanctions, including any of the orders listed in Rule 37(b)(2)(A)(i)-(vi).

(2) *Failure to Admit.* If a party fails to admit what is requested under Rule 36 and if the requesting party later proves a document to be genuine or the matter true, the requesting party may move that the party who failed to admit pay the reasonable expenses, including attorney's fees, incurred in making that proof. The court must so order unless:

(A) the request was held objectionable under Rule 36(a);

(B) the admission sought was of no substantial importance;

(C) the party failing to admit had a reasonable ground to believe that it might prevail on the matter; or

(D) there was other good reason for the failure to admit.

(d) Party's Failure to Attend Its Own Deposition, Serve Answers to Interrogatories, or Respond to a Request for Inspection.

(1) *In General.*

(A) *Motion; Grounds for Sanctions.* The court where the action is pending may, on motion, order sanctions if:

(i) a party or a party's officer, director, or managing agent—or a person designated under Rule 30(b)(6) or 31(a)(4)—fails, after being served with proper notice, to appear for that person's deposition; or

(ii) a party, after being properly served with interrogatories under Rule 33 or a request for inspection under Rule 34, fails to serve its answers, objections, or written response.

(B) *Certification.* A motion for sanctions for failing to answer or respond must include a certification that the movant has in good faith conferred or attempted to confer with the party failing to act in an effort to obtain the answer or response without court action.

(2) *Unacceptable Excuse for Failing to Act.* A failure described in Rule 37(d)(1)(A) is not excused on the ground that the discovery sought was objectionable, unless the party failing to act has a pending motion for a protective order under Rule 26(c).

(3) *Types of Sanctions.* Sanctions may include any of the orders listed in Rule 37(b)(2)(A)(i)-(vi). Instead of or in addition to these sanctions, the court must require the party failing to act, the attorney advising that party, or both to pay the reasonable expenses, including attorney's fees, caused by the failure, unless the failure was substantially justified or other circumstances make an award of expenses unjust.

(e) Failure to Preserve Electronically Stored Information. If electronically stored information that should have been preserved in the anticipation or conduct of litigation is lost because a party failed to take reasonable steps to preserve it, and it cannot be restored or replaced through additional discovery, the court:

(1) upon finding prejudice to another party from loss of the information, may order measures no greater than necessary to cure the prejudice; or

(2) only upon finding that the party acted with the intent to deprive another party of the information's use in the litigation may:

(A) presume that the lost information was unfavorable to the party;

(B) instruct the jury that it may or must presume the information was unfavorable to the party; or

(C) dismiss the action or enter a default judgment.

(f) Failure to Participate in Framing a Discovery Plan. If a party or its attorney fails to participate in good faith in developing and submitting a proposed discovery plan as required by Rule 26(f), the court may, after giving an opportunity to be heard, require that party or attorney to pay to any other party the reasonable expenses, including attorney's fees, caused by the failure.

(Amended December 29, 1948, effective October 20, 1949; March 30, 1970, effective July 1, 1970; April 29, 1980, effective August 1, 1980; amended by Pub.L. 96–481, Title II, § 205(a), October 21, 1980, 94 Stat. 2330, effective October 1, 1981; amended March 2, 1987, effective August 1, 1987; April 22, 1993, effective December 1, 1993; April 17, 2000, effective December 1, 2000; April 12, 2006, effective December 1, 2006; April 30, 2007, effective December 1, 2007; April 16, 2013, effective December 1, 2013; April 29, 2015, effective December 1, 2015.)

TITLE VI. TRIALS

RULE 38. RIGHT TO A JURY TRIAL; DEMAND

(a) **Right Preserved.** The right of trial by jury as declared by the Seventh Amendment to the Constitution—or as provided by a federal statute—is preserved to the parties inviolate.

(b) **Demand.** On any issue triable of right by a jury, a party may demand a jury trial by:

(1) serving the other parties with a written demand—which may be included in a pleading—no later than 14 days after the last pleading directed to the issue is served; and

(2) filing the demand in accordance with Rule 5(d).

(c) **Specifying Issues.** In its demand, a party may specify the issues that it wishes to have tried by a jury; otherwise, it is considered to have demanded a jury trial on all the issues so triable. If the party has demanded a jury trial on only some issues, any other party may—within 14 days after being served with the demand or within a shorter time ordered by the court—serve a demand for a jury trial on any other or all factual issues triable by jury.

(d) **Waiver; Withdrawal.** A party waives a jury trial unless its demand is properly served and filed. A proper demand may be withdrawn only if the parties consent.

(e) **Admiralty and Maritime Claims.** These rules do not create a right to a jury trial on issues in a claim that is an admiralty or maritime claim under Rule 9(h).

(Amended February 28, 1966, effective July 1, 1966; March 2, 1987, effective August 1, 1987; April 22, 1993, effective December 1, 1993; April 30, 2007, effective December 1, 2007; March 26, 2009, effective December 1, 2009.)

RULE 39. TRIAL BY JURY OR BY THE COURT

(a) **When a Demand Is Made.** When a jury trial has been demanded under Rule 38, the action must be designated on the docket as a jury action. The trial on all issues so demanded must be by jury unless:

(1) the parties or their attorneys file a stipulation to a nonjury trial or so stipulate on the record; or

(2) the court, on motion or on its own, finds that on some or all of those issues there is no federal right to a jury trial.

(b) **When No Demand Is Made.** Issues on which a jury trial is not properly demanded are to be tried by the court. But the court may, on motion, order a jury trial on any issue for which a jury might have been demanded.

(c) **Advisory Jury; Jury Trial by Consent.** In an action not triable of right by a jury, the court, on motion or on its own:

(1) may try any issue with an advisory jury; or

(2) may, with the parties' consent, try any issue by a jury whose verdict has the same effect as if a jury trial had been a matter of right, unless the action is against the United States and a federal statute provides for a nonjury trial.

(Amended April 30, 2007, effective December 1, 2007.)

RULE 40. SCHEDULING CASES FOR TRIAL

Each court must provide by rule for scheduling trials. The court must give priority to actions entitled to priority by a federal statute.

(Amended April 30, 2007, effective December 1, 2007.)

RULE 41. DISMISSAL OF ACTIONS

(a) **Voluntary Dismissal.**

(1) *By the Plaintiff.*

(A) *Without a Court Order.* Subject to Rules 23(e), 23.1(c), 23.2, and 66 and any applicable federal statute, the plaintiff may dismiss an action without a court order by filing:

(i) a notice of dismissal before the opposing party serves either an answer or a motion for summary judgment; or

(ii) a stipulation of dismissal signed by all parties who have appeared.

(B) *Effect.* Unless the notice or stipulation states otherwise, the dismissal is without prejudice. But if the plaintiff previously dismissed any federal- or state-court action based on or including the same claim, a notice of dismissal operates as an adjudication on the merits.

(2) *By Court Order; Effect.* Except as provided in Rule 41(a)(1), an action may be dismissed at the plaintiff's request only by court order, on terms that the court considers proper. If a defendant has pleaded a counterclaim before being served with the plaintiff's motion to dismiss, the action may be dismissed over the defendant's objection only if the counterclaim can remain pending for independent adjudication. Unless the order states otherwise, a dismissal under this paragraph (2) is without prejudice.

(b) **Involuntary Dismissal; Effect.** If the plaintiff fails to prosecute or to comply with these rules or a court order, a defendant may move to dismiss the action or any claim against it. Unless the dismissal order states otherwise, a dismissal under this subdivision (b) and any dismissal not under this rule—except one for lack of jurisdiction, improper venue, or failure to join a party under Rule 19—operates as an adjudication on the merits.

(c) **Dismissing a Counterclaim, Crossclaim, or Third-Party Claim.** This rule applies to a dismissal of any counterclaim, crossclaim, or third-party claim. A claimant's voluntary dismissal under Rule 41(a)(1)(A)(i) must be made:

(1) before a responsive pleading is served; or

(2) if there is no responsive pleading, before evidence is introduced at a hearing or trial.

(d) **Costs of a Previously Dismissed Action.** If a plaintiff who previously dismissed an action in any court files an action based on or including the same claim against the same defendant, the court:

(1) may order the plaintiff to pay all or part of the costs of that previous action; and

(2) may stay the proceedings until the plaintiff has complied.

(Amended December 27, 1946, effective March 19, 1948; January 21, 1963, effective July 1, 1963; February 28, 1966, effective July 1, 1966; December 4, 1967, effective July 1, 1968; March 2, 1987, effective August 1, 1987; April 30, 1991, effective December 1, 1991; April 30, 2007, effective December 1, 2007.)

RULE 42. CONSOLIDATION; SEPARATE TRIALS

(a) Consolidation. If actions before the court involve a common question of law or fact, the court may:

(1) join for hearing or trial any or all matters at issue in the actions;

(2) consolidate the actions; or

(3) issue any other orders to avoid unnecessary cost or delay.

(b) Separate Trials. For convenience, to avoid prejudice, or to expedite and economize, the court may order a separate trial of one or more separate issues, claims, crossclaims, counterclaims, or third-party claims. When ordering a separate trial, the court must preserve any federal right to a jury trial.

(Amended February 28, 1966, effective July 1, 1966; April 30, 2007, effective December 1, 2007.)

RULE 43. TAKING TESTIMONY

(a) In Open Court. At trial, the witnesses' testimony must be taken in open court unless a federal statute, the Federal Rules of Evidence, these rules, or other rules adopted by the Supreme Court provide otherwise. For good cause in compelling circumstances and with appropriate safeguards, the court may permit testimony in open court by contemporaneous transmission from a different location.

(b) Affirmation Instead of an Oath. When these rules require an oath, a solemn affirmation suffices.

(c) Evidence on a Motion. When a motion relies on facts outside the record, the court may hear the matter on affidavits or may hear it wholly or partly on oral testimony or on depositions.

(d) Interpreter. The court may appoint an interpreter of its choosing; fix reasonable compensation to be paid from funds provided by law or by one or more parties; and tax the compensation as costs.

(Amended February 28, 1966, effective July 1, 1966; November 20, 1972, and December 18, 1972, effective July 1, 1975; March 2, 1987, effective August 1, 1987; April 23, 1996, effective December 1, 1996; April 30, 2007, effective December 1, 2007.)

RULE 44. PROVING AN OFFICIAL RECORD

(a) Means of Proving.

(1) *Domestic Record.* Each of the following evidences an official record—or an entry in it—that is otherwise admissible and is kept within the United States, any state, district, or commonwealth, or any territory subject to the administrative or judicial jurisdiction of the United States:

(A) an official publication of the record; or

(B) a copy attested by the officer with legal custody of the record—or by the officer's deputy—and accompanied by a certificate that the officer has custody. The certificate must be made under seal:

(i) by a judge of a court of record in the district or political subdivision where the record is kept; or

(ii) by any public officer with a seal of office and with official duties in the district or political subdivision where the record is kept.

(2) *Foreign Record.*

(A) *In General.* Each of the following evidences a foreign official record—or an entry in it—that is otherwise admissible:

(i) an official publication of the record; or

(ii) the record—or a copy—that is attested by an authorized person and is accompanied either by a final certification of genuineness or by a certification under a treaty or convention to which the United States and the country where the record is located are parties.

(B) *Final Certification of Genuineness.* A final certification must certify the genuineness of the signature and official position of the attester or of any foreign official whose certificate of genuineness relates to the attestation or is in a chain of certificates of genuineness relating to the attestation. A final certification may be made by a secretary of a United States embassy or legation; by a consul general, vice consul, or consular agent of the United States; or by a diplomatic or consular official of the foreign country assigned or accredited to the United States.

(C) *Other Means of Proof.* If all parties have had a reasonable opportunity to investigate a foreign record's authenticity and accuracy, the court may, for good cause, either:

(i) admit an attested copy without final certification; or

(ii) permit the record to be evidenced by an attested summary with or without a final certification.

(b) Lack of a Record. A written statement that a diligent search of designated records revealed no record or entry of a specified tenor is admissible as evidence that the records contain no such record or entry. For domestic records, the statement must be authenticated under Rule 44(a)(1). For foreign records, the statement must comply with (a)(2)(C)(ii).

(c) Other Proof. A party may prove an official record—or an entry or lack of an entry in it—by any other method authorized by law.

(Amended February 28, 1966, effective July 1, 1966; March 2, 1987, effective August 1, 1987; April 30, 1991, effective December 1, 1991; April 30, 2007, effective December 1, 2007.)

RULE 44.1. DETERMINING FOREIGN LAW

A party who intends to raise an issue about a foreign country's law must give notice by a pleading or other writing. In determining foreign law, the court may consider any relevant material or source, including testimony, whether or not submitted by a party or admissible under the Federal Rules of Evidence. The court's determination must be treated as a ruling on a question of law.

(Adopted February 28, 1966, effective July 1, 1966; amended November 20, 1972, effective July 1, 1975; March 2, 1987, effective August 1, 1987; April 30, 2007, effective December 1, 2007.)

RULE 45. SUBPOENA

(a) In General.

(1) *Form and Contents.*

(A) *Requirements—In General.* Every subpoena must:

(i) state the court from which it issued;

(ii) state the title of the action and its civil-action number;

(iii) command each person to whom it is directed to do the following at a specified time and place: attend and testify; produce designated documents, electronically stored information, or tangible things in that person's possession, custody, or control; or permit the inspection of premises; and

(iv) set out the text of Rule 45(d) and (e).

(B) *Command to Attend a Deposition—Notice of the Recording Method.* A subpoena commanding attendance at a deposition must state the method for recording the testimony.

(C) *Combining or Separating a Command to Produce or to Permit Inspection; Specifying the Form for Electronically Stored Information.* A command to produce documents, electronically stored information, or tangible things or to permit the inspection of premises may be included in a subpoena commanding attendance at a deposition, hearing, or trial, or may be set out in a separate subpoena. A subpoena may specify the form or forms in which electronically stored information is to be produced.

(D) *Command to Produce; Included Obligations.* A command in a subpoena to produce documents, electronically stored information, or tangible things requires the responding person to permit inspection, copying, testing, or sampling of the materials.

(2) *Issuing Court.* A subpoena must issue from the court where the action is pending.

(3) *Issued by Whom.* The clerk must issue a subpoena, signed but otherwise in blank, to a party who requests it. That party must complete it before service. An attorney also may issue and sign a subpoena if the attorney is authorized to practice in the issuing court.

(4) *Notice to Other Parties Before Service.* If the subpoena commands the production of documents, electronically stored information, or tangible things or the inspection of premises before trial, then before it is served on the person to whom it is directed, a notice and a copy of the subpoena must be served on each party.

(b) Service.

(1) *By Whom and How; Tendering Fees.* Any person who is at least 18 years old and not a party may serve a subpoena. Serving a subpoena requires delivering a copy to the named person and, if the subpoena requires that person's attendance, tendering the fees for 1 day's attendance and the mileage allowed by law. Fees and mileage need not be tendered when the subpoena issues on behalf of the United States or any of its officers or agencies.

(2) *Service in the United States.* A subpoena may be served at any place within the United States.

(3) *Service in a Foreign Country.* 28 U.S.C. § 1783 governs issuing and serving a subpoena directed to a United States national or resident who is in a foreign country.

(4) *Proof of Service.* Proving service, when necessary, requires filing with the issuing court a statement showing the date and manner of service and the names of the persons served. The statement must be certified by the server.

(c) Place of Compliance.

(1) *For a Trial, Hearing, or Deposition.* A subpoena may command a person to attend a trial, hearing, or deposition only as follows:

(A) within 100 miles of where the person resides, is employed, or regularly transacts business in person; or

(B) within the state where the person resides, is employed, or regularly transacts business in person, if the person

(i) is a party or a party's officer; or

(ii) is commanded to attend a trial and would not incur substantial expense.

(2) *For Other Discovery.* A subpoena may command:

(A) production of documents, electronically stored information, or tangible things at a place within 100 miles of where the person resides, is employed, or regularly transacts business in person; and

(B) inspection of premises at the premises to be inspected.

(d) Protecting a Person Subject to a Subpoena; Enforcement.

(1) *Avoiding Undue Burden or Expense; Sanctions.* A party or attorney responsible for issuing and serving a subpoena must take reasonable steps to avoid imposing undue burden or expense on a person subject to the subpoena. The court for the district where compliance is required must enforce this duty and impose an appropriate sanction—which may include lost earnings and reasonable attorney's fees—on a party or attorney who fails to comply.

(2) *Command to Produce Materials or Permit Inspection.*

(A) *Appearance Not Required.* A person commanded to produce documents, electronically stored information, or tangible things, or to permit the inspection of premises, need not appear in person at the place of production or inspection unless also commanded to appear for a deposition, hearing, or trial.

(B) *Objections.* A person commanded to produce documents or tangible things or to permit inspection may serve on the party or attorney designated in the subpoena a written objection to inspecting, copying, testing, or sampling any or all of the materials or to inspecting the premises—or to producing electronically stored information in the form or forms requested. The objection must be served before the earlier of the time specified for compliance or 14 days after the subpoena is served. If an objection is made, the following rules apply:

(i) At any time, on notice to the commanded person, the serving party may move the court for the district where compliance is required for an order compelling production or inspection.

(ii) These acts may be required only as directed in the order, and the order must protect a person who is neither a party nor a party's officer from significant expense resulting from compliance.

(3) *Quashing or Modifying a Subpoena.*

(A) *When Required.* On timely motion, the court for the district where compliance is required must quash or modify a subpoena that:

(i) fails to allow a reasonable time to comply;

(ii) requires a person to comply beyond the geographical limits specified in Rule 45(c);

(iii) requires disclosure of privileged or other protected matter, if no exception or waiver applies; or

(iv) subjects a person to undue burden.

(B) *When Permitted.* To protect a person subject to or affected by a subpoena, the court for the district where compliance is required may, on motion, quash or modify the subpoena if it requires:

(i) disclosing a trade secret or other confidential research, development, or commercial information; or

(ii) disclosing an unretained expert's opinion or information that does not describe specific occurrences in dispute and results from the expert's study that was not requested by a party.

(C) *Specifying Conditions as an Alternative.* In the circumstances described in Rule 45(d)(3)(B), the court may, instead of quashing or modifying a subpoena, order appearance or production under specified conditions if the serving party:

(i) shows a substantial need for the testimony or material that cannot be otherwise met without undue hardship; and

(ii) ensures that the subpoenaed person will be reasonably compensated.

(e) Duties in Responding to a Subpoena.

(1) *Producing Documents or Electronically Stored Information.* These procedures apply to producing documents or electronically stored information:

(A) *Documents.* A person responding to a subpoena to produce documents must produce them as they are kept in the ordinary course of business or must organize and label them to correspond to the categories in the demand.

(B) *Form for Producing Electronically Stored Information Not Specified.* If a subpoena does not specify a form for producing electronically stored information, the person responding must produce it in a form or forms in which it is ordinarily maintained or in a reasonably usable form or forms.

(C) *Electronically Stored Information Produced in Only One Form.* The person responding need not produce the same electronically stored information in more than one form.

(D) *Inaccessible Electronically Stored Information.* The person responding need not provide discovery of electronically stored information from sources that the person identifies as not reasonably accessible because of undue burden or cost. On motion to compel discovery or for a protective order, the person responding must show that the information is not reasonably accessible because of undue burden or cost. If that showing is made, the court may nonetheless order discovery from such sources if the requesting party shows good cause, considering the limitations of Rule 26(b)(2)(C). The court may specify conditions for the discovery.

(2) *Claiming Privilege or Protection.*

(A) *Information Withheld.* A person withholding subpoenaed information under a claim that it is privileged or subject to protection as trial-preparation material must:

(i) expressly make the claim; and

(ii) describe the nature of the withheld documents, communications, or tangible things in a manner that, without revealing information itself privileged or protected, will enable the parties to assess the claim.

(B) *Information Produced.* If information produced in response to a subpoena is subject to a claim of privilege or of protection as trial-preparation material, the person making the claim may notify any party that received the information of the claim and the basis for it. After being notified, a party must promptly return, sequester, or destroy the specified information and any copies it has; must not use or disclose the information until the claim is resolved; must take reasonable steps to retrieve the information if the party disclosed it before being notified; and may promptly present the information under seal to the court for the district where compliance is required for a determination of the claim. The person who produced the information must preserve the information until the claim is resolved.

(f) Transferring a Subpoena–Related Motion. When the court where compliance is required did not issue the subpoena, it may transfer a motion under this rule to the issuing court if the person subject to the subpoena consents or if the court finds exceptional circumstances. Then, if the attorney for a person subject to a subpoena is authorized to practice in the court where the motion was made, the attorney may file papers and appear on the motion as an officer of the issuing court. To enforce its order, the issuing court may transfer the order to the court where the motion was made.

(g) Contempt. The court for the district where compliance is required—and also, after a motion is transferred, the issuing court—may hold in contempt a person who, having been served, fails without adequate excuse to obey the subpoena or an order related to it.

(Amended December 27, 1946, effective March 19, 1948; December 29, 1948, effective October 20, 1949; March 30, 1970, effective July 1, 1970; April 29, 1980, effective August 1, 1980; April 29, 1985, effective August 1, 1985; March 2, 1987, effective August 1, 1987; April 30, 1991, effective December 1, 1991; April 25, 2005, effective December 1, 2005; April 12, 2006, effective December 1, 2006; April 30, 2007, effective December 1, 2007; April 16, 2013, effective December 1, 2013.)

RULE 46. OBJECTING TO A RULING OR ORDER

A formal exception to a ruling or order is unnecessary. When the ruling or order is requested or made, a party need only state the action that it wants the court to take or objects to, along with the grounds for the request or objection. Failing to object does not prejudice a party who had no opportunity to do so when the ruling or order was made.

(Amended March 2, 1987, effective August 1, 1987; April 30, 2007, effective December 1, 2007.)

RULE 47. SELECTING JURORS

(a) Examining Jurors. The court may permit the parties or their attorneys to examine prospective jurors or may itself do so. If the court examines the jurors, it must permit the parties or their attorneys to make any further inquiry it considers proper, or must itself ask any of their additional questions it considers proper.

(b) Peremptory Challenges. The court must allow the number of peremptory challenges provided by 28 U.S.C. § 1870.

(c) Excusing a Juror. During trial or deliberation, the court may excuse a juror for good cause.

(Amended February 28, 1966, effective July 1, 1966; April 30, 1991, effective December 1, 1991; April 30, 2007, effective December 1, 2007.)

RULE 48. NUMBER OF JURORS; VERDICT; POLLING

(a) Number of Jurors. A jury must begin with at least 6 and no more than 12 members, and each juror must participate in the verdict unless excused under Rule 47(c).

(b) Verdict. Unless the parties stipulate otherwise, the verdict must be unanimous and must be returned by a jury of at least 6 members.

(c) Polling. After a verdict is returned but before the jury is discharged, the court must on a party's request, or may on its own, poll the jurors individually. If the poll reveals a lack of unanimity or lack of assent by the number of jurors that the parties stipulated to, the court may direct the jury to deliberate further or may order a new trial.

(Amended April 30, 1991, effective December 1, 1991; April 30, 2007, effective December 1, 2007; March 26, 2009, effective December 1, 2009.)

RULE 49. SPECIAL VERDICT; GENERAL VERDICT AND QUESTIONS

(a) Special Verdict.

(1) *In General.* The court may require a jury to return only a special verdict in the form of a special written finding on each issue of fact. The court may do so by:

(A) submitting written questions susceptible of a categorical or other brief answer;

(B) submitting written forms of the special findings that might properly be made under the pleadings and evidence; or

(C) using any other method that the court considers appropriate.

(2) *Instructions.* The court must give the instructions and explanations necessary to enable the jury to make its findings on each submitted issue.

(3) *Issues Not Submitted.* A party waives the right to a jury trial on any issue of fact raised by the pleadings or evidence but not submitted to the jury unless, before the jury retires, the party demands its submission to the jury. If the party does not demand submission, the court may make a finding on the issue. If the court makes no finding, it is considered to have made a finding consistent with its judgment on the special verdict.

(b) General Verdict with Answers to Written Questions.

(1) *In General.* The court may submit to the jury forms for a general verdict, together with written questions on one or more issues of fact that the jury must decide. The court must give the instructions and explanations necessary to enable the jury to render a general verdict and answer the questions in writing, and must direct the jury to do both.

(2) *Verdict and Answers Consistent.* When the general verdict and the answers are consistent, the court must approve, for entry under Rule 58, an appropriate judgment on the verdict and answers.

(3) *Answers Inconsistent with the Verdict.* When the answers are consistent with each other but one or more is inconsistent with the general verdict, the court may:

(A) approve, for entry under Rule 58, an appropriate judgment according to the answers, notwithstanding the general verdict;

(B) direct the jury to further consider its answers and verdict; or

(C) order a new trial.

(4) *Answers Inconsistent with Each Other and the Verdict.* When the answers are inconsistent with each other and one or more is also inconsistent with the general verdict, judgment must not be entered; instead, the court must direct the jury to further consider its answers and verdict, or must order a new trial.

(Amended January 21, 1963, effective July 1, 1963; March 2, 1987, effective August 1, 1987; April 30, 2007, effective December 1, 2007.)

RULE 50. JUDGMENT AS A MATTER OF LAW IN A JURY TRIAL; RELATED MOTION FOR A NEW TRIAL; CONDITIONAL RULING

(a) Judgment as a Matter of Law.

(1) *In General.* If a party has been fully heard on an issue during a jury trial and the court finds that a reasonable jury would not have a legally sufficient evidentiary basis to find for the party on that issue, the court may:

(A) resolve the issue against the party; and

(B) grant a motion for judgment as a matter of law against the party on a claim or defense that, under the controlling law, can be maintained or defeated only with a favorable finding on that issue.

(2) *Motion.* A motion for judgment as a matter of law may be made at any time before the case is submitted to the jury. The motion must specify the judgment sought and the law and facts that entitle the movant to the judgment.

(b) Renewing the Motion After Trial; Alternative Motion for a New Trial. If the court does not grant a motion for judgment as a matter of law made under Rule 50(a), the court is considered to have submitted the action to the jury subject to the court's later deciding the legal questions raised by the motion. No later than 28 days after the entry of judgment—or if the motion addresses a jury issue not decided by a verdict, no later than 28 days after the jury was discharged—the movant may file a renewed motion for judgment as a matter of law and may include an alternative or joint request for a new trial under Rule 59. In ruling on the renewed motion, the court may:

(1) allow judgment on the verdict, if the jury returned a verdict;

(2) order a new trial; or

(3) direct the entry of judgment as a matter of law.

(c) Granting the Renewed Motion; Conditional Ruling on a Motion for a New Trial.

(1) *In General.* If the court grants a renewed motion for judgment as a matter of law, it must also conditionally rule on any motion for a new trial by determining whether a new trial should be granted if the judgment is later vacated or reversed. The court must state the grounds for conditionally granting or denying the motion for a new trial.

(2) *Effect of a Conditional Ruling.* Conditionally granting the motion for a new trial does not affect the judgment's

finality; if the judgment is reversed, the new trial must proceed unless the appellate court orders otherwise. If the motion for a new trial is conditionally denied, the appellee may assert error in that denial; if the judgment is reversed, the case must proceed as the appellate court orders.

(d) Time for a Losing Party's New–Trial Motion. Any motion for a new trial under Rule 59 by a party against whom judgment as a matter of law is rendered must be filed no later than 28 days after the entry of the judgment.

(e) Denying the Motion for Judgment as a Matter of Law; Reversal on Appeal. If the court denies the motion for judgment as a matter of law, the prevailing party may, as appellee, assert grounds entitling it to a new trial should the appellate court conclude that the trial court erred in denying the motion. If the appellate court reverses the judgment, it may order a new trial, direct the trial court to determine whether a new trial should be granted, or direct the entry of judgment.

(Amended January 21, 1963, effective July 1, 1963; March 2, 1987, effective August 1, 1987; April 30, 1991, effective December 1, 1991; April 22, 1993, effective December 1, 1993; April 27, 1995, effective December 1, 1995; April 12, 2006, effective December 1, 2006; April 30, 2007, effective December 1, 2007; March 26, 2009, effective December 1, 2009.)

RULE 51. INSTRUCTIONS TO THE JURY; OBJECTIONS; PRESERVING A CLAIM OF ERROR

(a) Requests.

(1) *Before or at the Close of the Evidence.* At the close of the evidence or at any earlier reasonable time that the court orders, a party may file and furnish to every other party written requests for the jury instructions it wants the court to give.

(2) *After the Close of the Evidence.* After the close of the evidence, a party may:

(A) file requests for instructions on issues that could not reasonably have been anticipated by an earlier time that the court set for requests; and

(B) with the court's permission, file untimely requests for instructions on any issue.

(b) Instructions. The court:

(1) must inform the parties of its proposed instructions and proposed action on the requests before instructing the jury and before final jury arguments;

(2) must give the parties an opportunity to object on the record and out of the jury's hearing before the instructions and arguments are delivered; and

(3) may instruct the jury at any time before the jury is discharged.

(c) Objections.

(1) *How to Make.* A party who objects to an instruction or the failure to give an instruction must do so on the record, stating distinctly the matter objected to and the grounds for the objection.

(2) *When to Make.* An objection is timely if:

(A) a party objects at the opportunity provided under Rule 51(b)(2); or

(B) a party was not informed of an instruction or action on a request before that opportunity to object, and the party objects promptly after learning that the instruction or request will be, or has been, given or refused.

(d) Assigning Error; Plain Error.

(1) *Assigning Error.* A party may assign as error:

(A) an error in an instruction actually given, if that party properly objected; or

(B) a failure to give an instruction, if that party properly requested it and—unless the court rejected the request in a definitive ruling on the record—also properly objected.

(2) *Plain Error.* A court may consider a plain error in the instructions that has not been preserved as required by Rule 51(d)(1) if the error affects substantial rights.

(Amended March 2, 1987, effective August 1, 1987; March 27, 2003, effective December 1, 2003; April 30, 2007, effective December 1, 2007.)

RULE 52. FINDINGS AND CONCLUSIONS BY THE COURT; JUDGMENT ON PARTIAL FINDINGS

(a) Findings and Conclusions.

(1) *In General.* In an action tried on the facts without a jury or with an advisory jury, the court must find the facts specially and state its conclusions of law separately. The findings and conclusions may be stated on the record after the close of the evidence or may appear in an opinion or a memorandum of decision filed by the court. Judgment must be entered under Rule 58.

(2) *For an Interlocutory Injunction.* In granting or refusing an interlocutory injunction, the court must similarly state the findings and conclusions that support its action.

(3) *For a Motion.* The court is not required to state findings or conclusions when ruling on a motion under Rule 12 or 56 or, unless these rules provide otherwise, on any other motion.

(4) *Effect of a Master's Findings.* A master's findings, to the extent adopted by the court, must be considered the court's findings.

(5) *Questioning the Evidentiary Support.* A party may later question the sufficiency of the evidence supporting the findings, whether or not the party requested findings, objected to them, moved to amend them, or moved for partial findings.

(6) *Setting Aside the Findings.* Findings of fact, whether based on oral or other evidence, must not be set aside unless clearly erroneous, and the reviewing court must give due regard to the trial court's opportunity to judge the witnesses' credibility.

(b) Amended or Additional Findings. On a party's motion filed no later than 28 days after the entry of judgment, the court may amend its findings—or make additional findings—and may amend the judgment accordingly. The motion may accompany a motion for a new trial under Rule 59.

(c) Judgment on Partial Findings. If a party has been fully heard on an issue during a nonjury trial and the court finds against the party on that issue, the court may enter judgment against the party on a claim or defense that, under the controlling law, can be maintained or defeated only with a favorable finding on that issue. The court may, however, decline to render any judgment until the close of the evidence. A judgment on partial findings must be supported by findings of fact and conclusions of law as required by Rule 52(a).

(Amended December 27, 1946, effective March 19, 1948; January 21, 1963, effective July 1, 1963; April 28, 1983, effective August 1, 1983; April 29, 1985, effective August 1, 1985; April 30, 1991, effective December 1, 1991; April 22, 1993, effective December 1, 1993; April 27, 1995, effective December 1, 1995; April 30, 2007, effective December 1, 2007; March 26, 2009, effective December 1, 2009.)

RULE 53. MASTERS

(a) Appointment.

(1) *Scope.* Unless a statute provides otherwise, a court may appoint a master only to:

(A) perform duties consented to by the parties;

(B) hold trial proceedings and make or recommend findings of fact on issues to be decided without a jury if appointment is warranted by:

(i) some exceptional condition; or

(ii) the need to perform an accounting or resolve a difficult computation of damages; or

(C) address pretrial and posttrial matters that cannot be effectively and timely addressed by an available district judge or magistrate judge of the district.

(2) *Disqualification.* A master must not have a relationship to the parties, attorneys, action, or court that would require disqualification of a judge under 28 U.S.C. § 455, unless the parties, with the court's approval, consent to the appointment after the master discloses any potential grounds for disqualification.

(3) *Possible Expense or Delay.* In appointing a master, the court must consider the fairness of imposing the likely expenses on the parties and must protect against unreasonable expense or delay.

(b) Order Appointing a Master.

(1) *Notice.* Before appointing a master, the court must give the parties notice and an opportunity to be heard. Any party may suggest candidates for appointment.

(2) *Contents.* The appointing order must direct the master to proceed with all reasonable diligence and must state:

(A) the master's duties, including any investigation or enforcement duties, and any limits on the master's authority under Rule 53(c);

(B) the circumstances, if any, in which the master may communicate ex parte with the court or a party;

(C) the nature of the materials to be preserved and filed as the record of the master's activities;

(D) the time limits, method of filing the record, other procedures, and standards for reviewing the master's orders, findings, and recommendations; and

(E) the basis, terms, and procedure for fixing the master's compensation under Rule 53(g).

(3) *Issuing.* The court may issue the order only after:

(A) the master files an affidavit disclosing whether there is any ground for disqualification under 28 U.S.C. § 455; and

(B) if a ground is disclosed, the parties, with the court's approval, waive the disqualification.

(4) *Amending.* The order may be amended at any time after notice to the parties and an opportunity to be heard.

(c) Master's Authority.

(1) *In General.* Unless the appointing order directs otherwise, a master may:

(A) regulate all proceedings;

(B) take all appropriate measures to perform the assigned duties fairly and efficiently; and

(C) if conducting an evidentiary hearing, exercise the appointing court's power to compel, take, and record evidence.

(2) *Sanctions.* The master may by order impose on a party any noncontempt sanction provided by Rule 37 or 45, and may recommend a contempt sanction against a party and sanctions against a nonparty.

(d) Master's Orders. A master who issues an order must file it and promptly serve a copy on each party. The clerk must enter the order on the docket.

(e) Master's Reports. A master must report to the court as required by the appointing order. The master must file the report and promptly serve a copy on each party, unless the court orders otherwise.

(f) Action on the Master's Order, Report, or Recommendations.

(1) *Opportunity for a Hearing; Action in General.* In acting on a master's order, report, or recommendations, the court must give the parties notice and an opportunity to be heard; may receive evidence; and may adopt or affirm,

modify, wholly or partly reject or reverse, or resubmit to the master with instructions.

(2) *Time to Object or Move to Adopt or Modify.* A party may file objections to—or a motion to adopt or modify—the master's order, report, or recommendations no later than 21 days after a copy is served, unless the court sets a different time.

(3) *Reviewing Factual Findings.* The court must decide de novo all objections to findings of fact made or recommended by a master, unless the parties, with the court's approval, stipulate that:

(A) the findings will be reviewed for clear error; or

(B) the findings of a master appointed under Rule 53(a)(1)(A) or (C) will be final.

(4) *Reviewing Legal Conclusions.* The court must decide de novo all objections to conclusions of law made or recommended by a master.

(5) *Reviewing Procedural Matters.* Unless the appointing order establishes a different standard of review, the court may set aside a master's ruling on a procedural matter only for an abuse of discretion.

(g) Compensation.

(1) *Fixing Compensation.* Before or after judgment, the court must fix the master's compensation on the basis and terms stated in the appointing order, but the court may set a new basis and terms after giving notice and an opportunity to be heard.

(2) *Payment.* The compensation must be paid either:

(A) by a party or parties; or

(B) from a fund or subject matter of the action within the court's control.

(3) *Allocating Payment.* The court must allocate payment among the parties after considering the nature and amount of the controversy, the parties' means, and the extent to which any party is more responsible than other parties for the reference to a master. An interim allocation may be amended to reflect a decision on the merits.

(h) Appointing a Magistrate Judge. A magistrate judge is subject to this rule only when the order referring a matter to the magistrate judge states that the reference is made under this rule.

(Amended February 28, 1966, effective July 1, 1966; April 28, 1983, effective August 1, 1983; March 2, 1987, effective August 1, 1987; April 30, 1991, effective December 1, 1991; April 22, 1993, effective December 1, 1993; March 27, 2003, effective December 1, 2003; April 30, 2007, effective December 1, 2007; March 26, 2009, effective December 1, 2009.)

TITLE VII. JUDGMENT

RULE 54. JUDGMENT; COSTS

(a) Definition; Form. "Judgment" as used in these rules includes a decree and any order from which an appeal lies. A judgment should not include recitals of pleadings, a master's report, or a record of prior proceedings.

(b) Judgment on Multiple Claims or Involving Multiple Parties. When an action presents more than one claim for relief—whether as a claim, counterclaim, crossclaim, or third-party claim—or when multiple parties are involved, the court may direct entry of a final judgment as to one or more, but fewer than all, claims or parties only if the court expressly determines that there is no just reason for delay. Otherwise, any order or other decision, however designated, that adjudicates fewer than all the claims or the rights and liabilities of fewer than all the parties does not end the action as to any of the claims or parties and may be revised at any time before the entry of a judgment adjudicating all the claims and all the parties' rights and liabilities.

(c) Demand for Judgment; Relief to Be Granted. A default judgment must not differ in kind from, or exceed in amount, what is demanded in the pleadings. Every other final judgment should grant the relief to which each party is entitled, even if the party has not demanded that relief in its pleadings.

(d) Costs; Attorney's Fees.

(1) *Costs Other Than Attorney's Fees.* Unless a federal statute, these rules, or a court order provides otherwise, costs—other than attorney's fees—should be allowed to the prevailing party. But costs against the United States, its officers, and its agencies may be imposed only to the extent allowed by law. The clerk may tax costs on 14 days' notice. On motion served within the next 7 days, the court may review the clerk's action.

(2) *Attorney's Fees.*

(A) *Claim to Be by Motion.* A claim for attorney's fees and related nontaxable expenses must be made by motion unless the substantive law requires those fees to be proved at trial as an element of damages.

(B) *Timing and Contents of the Motion.* Unless a statute or a court order provides otherwise, the motion must:

(i) be filed no later than 14 days after the entry of judgment;

(ii) specify the judgment and the statute, rule, or other grounds entitling the movant to the award;

(iii) state the amount sought or provide a fair estimate of it; and

(iv) disclose, if the court so orders, the terms of any agreement about fees for the services for which the claim is made.

(C) *Proceedings.* Subject to Rule 23(h), the court must, on a party's request, give an opportunity for adversary submissions on the motion in accordance with Rule 43(c) or 78. The court may decide issues of liability for fees before receiving submissions on the value of services. The court must find the facts and state its conclusions of law as provided in Rule 52(a).

(D) *Special Procedures by Local Rule; Reference to a Master or a Magistrate Judge.* By local rule, the court may establish special procedures to resolve fee-related issues without extensive evidentiary hearings. Also, the court may refer issues concerning the value of services to a special master under Rule 53 without regard to the limitations of Rule 53(a)(1), and may refer a motion for attorney's fees to a magistrate judge under Rule 72(b) as if it were a dispositive pretrial matter.

(E) *Exceptions.* Subparagraphs (A)-(D) do not apply to claims for fees and expenses as sanctions for violating these rules or as sanctions under 28 U.S.C. § 1927.

(Amended December 27, 1946, effective March 19, 1948; April 17, 1961, effective July 19, 1961; March 2, 1987, effective August 1, 1987; April 22, 1993, effective December 1, 1993; April 29, 2002, effective December 1, 2002; March 27, 2003, effective December 1, 2003; April 30, 2007, effective December 1, 2007; March 26, 2009, effective December 1, 2009.)

RULE 55.   DEFAULT; DEFAULT JUDGMENT

(a) Entering a Default. When a party against whom a judgment for affirmative relief is sought has failed to plead or otherwise defend, and that failure is shown by affidavit or otherwise, the clerk must enter the party's default.

(b) Entering a Default Judgment.

(1) *By the Clerk.* If the plaintiff's claim is for a sum certain or a sum that can be made certain by computation, the clerk—on the plaintiff's request, with an affidavit showing the amount due—must enter judgment for that amount and costs against a defendant who has been defaulted for not appearing and who is neither a minor nor an incompetent person.

(2) *By the Court.* In all other cases, the party must apply to the court for a default judgment. A default judgment may be entered against a minor or incompetent person only if represented by a general guardian, conservator, or other like fiduciary who has appeared. If the party against whom a default judgment is sought has appeared personally or by a representative, that party or its representative must be served with written notice of the application at least 7 days before the hearing. The court may conduct hearings or make referrals—preserving any federal statutory right to a jury trial—when, to enter or effectuate judgment, it needs to:

(A) conduct an accounting;

(B) determine the amount of damages;

(C) establish the truth of any allegation by evidence; or

(D) investigate any other matter.

(c) Setting Aside a Default or a Default Judgment. The court may set aside an entry of default for good cause, and it may set aside a final default judgment under Rule 60(b).

(d) Judgment Against the United States. A default judgment may be entered against the United States, its officers, or its agencies only if the claimant establishes a claim or right to relief by evidence that satisfies the court.

(Amended March 2, 1987, effective August 1, 1987; April 30, 2007, effective December 1, 2007; March 26, 2009, effective December 1, 2009; April 29, 2015, effective December 1, 2015.)

RULE 56.   SUMMARY JUDGMENT

(a) Motion for Summary Judgment or Partial Summary Judgment. A party may move for summary judgment, identifying each claim or defense—or the part of each claim or defense—on which summary judgment is sought. The court shall grant summary judgment if the movant shows that there is no genuine dispute as to any material fact and the movant is entitled to judgment as a matter of law. The court should state on the record the reasons for granting or denying the motion.

(b) Time to File a Motion. Unless a different time is set by local rule or the court orders otherwise, a party may file a motion for summary judgment at any time until 30 days after the close of all discovery.

(c) Procedures.

(1) *Supporting Factual Positions.* A party asserting that a fact cannot be or is genuinely disputed must support the assertion by:

(A) citing to particular parts of materials in the record, including depositions, documents, electronically stored information, affidavits or declarations, stipulations (including those made for purposes of the motion only), admissions, interrogatory answers, or other materials; or

(B) showing that the materials cited do not establish the absence or presence of a genuine dispute, or that an adverse party cannot produce admissible evidence to support the fact.

(2) *Objection That a Fact Is Not Supported by Admissible Evidence.* A party may object that the material cited to support or dispute a fact cannot be presented in a form that would be admissible in evidence.

(3) *Materials Not Cited.* The court need consider only the cited materials, but it may consider other materials in the record.

(4) *Affidavits or Declarations.* An affidavit or declaration used to support or oppose a motion must be made on personal knowledge, set out facts that would be admissible in evidence, and show that the affiant or declarant is competent to testify on the matters stated.

(d) When Facts Are Unavailable to the Nonmovant. If a nonmovant shows by affidavit or declaration that, for specified reasons, it cannot present facts essential to justify its opposition, the court may:

(1) defer considering the motion or deny it;

(2) allow time to obtain affidavits or declarations or to take discovery; or

(3) issue any other appropriate order.

(e) Failing to Properly Support or Address a Fact. If a party fails to properly support an assertion of fact or fails to properly address another party's assertion of fact as required by Rule 56(c), the court may:

(1) give an opportunity to properly support or address the fact;

(2) consider the fact undisputed for purposes of the motion;

(3) grant summary judgment if the motion and supporting materials—including the facts considered undisputed—show that the movant is entitled to it; or

(4) issue any other appropriate order.

(f) Judgment Independent of the Motion. After giving notice and a reasonable time to respond, the court may:

(1) grant summary judgment for a nonmovant;

(2) grant the motion on grounds not raised by a party; or

(3) consider summary judgment on its own after identifying for the parties material facts that may not be genuinely in dispute.

(g) Failing to Grant All the Requested Relief. If the court does not grant all the relief requested by the motion, it may enter an order stating any material fact—including an item of damages or other relief—that is not genuinely in dispute and treating the fact as established in the case.

(h) Affidavit or Declaration Submitted in Bad Faith. If satisfied that an affidavit or declaration under this rule is submitted in bad faith or solely for delay, the court—after notice and a reasonable time to respond—may order the submitting party to pay the other party the reasonable expenses, including attorney's fees, it incurred as a result. An offending party or attorney may also be held in contempt or subjected to other appropriate sanctions.

(Amended December 27, 1946, effective March 19, 1948; January 21, 1963, effective July 1, 1963; March 2, 1987, effective August 1, 1987; April 30, 2007, effective December 1, 2007; March 26, 2009, effective December 1, 2009; April 28, 2010, effective December 1, 2010.)

RULE 57. DECLARATORY JUDGMENT

These rules govern the procedure for obtaining a declaratory judgment under 28 U.S.C. § 2201. Rules 38 and 39 govern a demand for a jury trial. The existence of another adequate remedy does not preclude a declaratory judgment that is otherwise appropriate. The court may order a speedy hearing of a declaratory-judgment action.

(Amended December 29, 1948, effective October 20, 1949; April 30, 2007, effective December 1, 2007.)

RULE 58. ENTERING JUDGMENT

(a) Separate Document. Every judgment and amended judgment must be set out in a separate document, but a separate document is not required for an order disposing of a motion:

(1) for judgment under Rule 50(b);

(2) to amend or make additional findings under Rule 52(b);

(3) for attorney's fees under Rule 54;

(4) for a new trial, or to alter or amend the judgment, under Rule 59; or

(5) for relief under Rule 60.

(b) Entering Judgment.

(1) *Without the Court's Direction.* Subject to Rule 54(b) and unless the court orders otherwise, the clerk must, without awaiting the court's direction, promptly prepare, sign, and enter the judgment when:

(A) the jury returns a general verdict;

(B) the court awards only costs or a sum certain; or

(C) the court denies all relief.

(2) Court's Approval Required. Subject to Rule 54(b), the court must promptly approve the form of the judgment, which the clerk must promptly enter, when:

(A) the jury returns a special verdict or a general verdict with answers to written questions; or

(B) the court grants other relief not described in this subdivision (b).

(c) Time of Entry. For purposes of these rules, judgment is entered at the following times:

(1) if a separate document is not required, when the judgment is entered in the civil docket under Rule 79(a); or

(2) if a separate document is required, when the judgment is entered in the civil docket under Rule 79(a) and the earlier of these events occurs:

(A) it is set out in a separate document; or

(B) 150 days have run from the entry in the civil docket.

(d) Request for Entry. A party may request that judgment be set out in a separate document as required by Rule 58(a).

(e) Cost or Fee Awards. Ordinarily, the entry of judgment may not be delayed, nor the time for appeal extended, in order to tax costs or award fees. But if a timely motion for attorney's fees is made under Rule 54(d)(2), the court may act before a notice of appeal has been filed and become effective to order that the motion have the same effect under Federal Rule of Appellate Procedure 4(a)(4) as a timely motion under Rule 59.

(Amended December 27, 1946, effective March 19, 1948; January 21, 1963, effective July 1, 1963; April 22, 1993, effective December 1, 1993; April 29, 2002, effective December 1, 2002; April 30, 2007, effective December 1, 2007.)

RULE 59. NEW TRIAL; ALTERING OR AMENDING A JUDGMENT

(a) In General.

(1) Grounds for New Trial. The court may, on motion, grant a new trial on all or some of the issues—and to any party—as follows:

(A) after a jury trial, for any reason for which a new trial has heretofore been granted in an action at law in federal court; or

(B) after a nonjury trial, for any reason for which a rehearing has heretofore been granted in a suit in equity in federal court.

(2) Further Action After a Nonjury Trial. After a nonjury trial, the court may, on motion for a new trial, open the judgment if one has been entered, take additional testimony, amend findings of fact and conclusions of law or make new ones, and direct the entry of a new judgment.

(b) Time to File a Motion for a New Trial. A motion for a new trial must be filed no later than 28 days after the entry of judgment.

(c) Time to Serve Affidavits. When a motion for a new trial is based on affidavits, they must be filed with the motion.

The opposing party has 14 days after being served to file opposing affidavits. The court may permit reply affidavits.

(d) New Trial on the Court's Initiative or for Reasons Not in the Motion. No later than 28 days after the entry of judgment, the court, on its own, may order a new trial for any reason that would justify granting one on a party's motion. After giving the parties notice and an opportunity to be heard, the court may grant a timely motion for a new trial for a reason not stated in the motion. In either event, the court must specify the reasons in its order.

(e) Motion to Alter or Amend a Judgment. A motion to alter or amend a judgment must be filed no later than 28 days after the entry of the judgment.

(Amended December 27, 1946, effective March 19, 1948; February 28, 1966, effective July 1, 1966; April 27, 1995, effective December 1, 1995; April 30, 2007, effective December 1, 2007; March 26, 2009, effective December 1, 2009.)

RULE 60. RELIEF FROM A JUDGMENT OR ORDER

(a) Corrections Based on Clerical Mistakes; Oversights and Omissions. The court may correct a clerical mistake or a mistake arising from oversight or omission whenever one is found in a judgment, order, or other part of the record. The court may do so on motion or on its own, with or without notice. But after an appeal has been docketed in the appellate court and while it is pending, such a mistake may be corrected only with the appellate court's leave.

(b) Grounds for Relief from a Final Judgment, Order, or Proceeding. On motion and just terms, the court may relieve a party or its legal representative from a final judgment, order, or proceeding for the following reasons:

(1) mistake, inadvertence, surprise, or excusable neglect;

(2) newly discovered evidence that, with reasonable diligence, could not have been discovered in time to move for a new trial under Rule 59(b);

(3) fraud (whether previously called intrinsic or extrinsic), misrepresentation, or misconduct by an opposing party;

(4) the judgment is void;

(5) the judgment has been satisfied, released or discharged; it is based on an earlier judgment that has been reversed or vacated; or applying it prospectively is no longer equitable; or

(6) any other reason that justifies relief.

(c) Timing and Effect of the Motion.

(1) Timing. A motion under Rule 60(b) must be made within a reasonable time—and for reasons (1), (2), and (3) no more than a year after the entry of the judgment or order or the date of the proceeding.

(2) Effect on Finality. The motion does not affect the judgment's finality or suspend its operation.

(d) Other Powers to Grant Relief. This rule does not limit a court's power to:

(1) entertain an independent action to relieve a party from a judgment, order, or proceeding;

(2) grant relief under 28 U.S.C. § 1655 to a defendant who was not personally notified of the action; or

(3) set aside a judgment for fraud on the court.

(e) Bills and Writs Abolished. The following are abolished: bills of review, bills in the nature of bills of review, and writs of coram nobis, coram vobis, and audita querela.

(Amended December 27, 1946, effective March 19, 1948; December 29, 1948, effective October 20, 1949; March 2, 1987, effective August 1, 1987; April 30, 2007, effective December 1, 2007.)

RULE 61. HARMLESS ERROR

Unless justice requires otherwise, no error in admitting or excluding evidence—or any other error by the court or a party—is ground for granting a new trial, for setting aside a verdict, or for vacating, modifying, or otherwise disturbing a judgment or order. At every stage of the proceeding, the court must disregard all errors and defects that do not affect any party's substantial rights.

(Amended April 30, 2007, effective December 1, 2007.)

RULE 62. STAY OF PROCEEDINGS TO ENFORCE A JUDGMENT

(a) Automatic Stay; Exceptions for Injunctions, Receiverships, and Patent Accountings. Except as stated in this rule, no execution may issue on a judgment, nor may proceedings be taken to enforce it, until 14 days have passed after its entry. But unless the court orders otherwise, the following are not stayed after being entered, even if an appeal is taken:

(1) an interlocutory or final judgment in an action for an injunction or a receivership; or

(2) a judgment or order that directs an accounting in an action for patent infringement.

(b) Stay Pending the Disposition of a Motion. On appropriate terms for the opposing party's security, the court may stay the execution of a judgment—or any proceedings to enforce it—pending disposition of any of the following motions:

(1) under Rule 50, for judgment as a matter of law;

(2) under Rule 52(b), to amend the findings or for additional findings;

(3) under Rule 59, for a new trial or to alter or amend a judgment; or

(4) under Rule 60, for relief from a judgment or order.

(c) Injunction Pending an Appeal. While an appeal is pending from an interlocutory order or final judgment that grants, dissolves, or denies an injunction, the court may suspend, modify, restore, or grant an injunction on terms for bond or other terms that secure the opposing party's rights. If the judgment appealed from is rendered by a statutory three-judge district court, the order must be made either:

(1) by that court sitting in open session; or

(2) by the assent of all its judges, as evidenced by their signatures.

(d) Stay with Bond on Appeal. If an appeal is taken, the appellant may obtain a stay by supersedeas bond, except in an action described in Rule 62(a)(1) or (2). The bond may be given upon or after filing the notice of appeal or after obtaining the order allowing the appeal. The stay takes effect when the court approves the bond.

(e) Stay Without Bond on an Appeal by the United States, Its Officers, or Its Agencies. The court must not require a bond, obligation, or other security from the appellant when granting a stay on an appeal by the United States, its officers, or its agencies or on an appeal directed by a department of the federal government.

(f) Stay in Favor of a Judgment Debtor Under State Law. If a judgment is a lien on the judgment debtor's property under the law of the state where the court is located, the judgment debtor is entitled to the same stay of execution the state court would give.

(g) Appellate Court's Power Not Limited. This rule does not limit the power of the appellate court or one of its judges or justices:

(1) to stay proceedings—or suspend, modify, restore, or grant an injunction—while an appeal is pending; or

(2) to issue an order to preserve the status quo or the effectiveness of the judgment to be entered.

(h) Stay with Multiple Claims or Parties. A court may stay the enforcement of a final judgment entered under Rule 54(b) until it enters a later judgment or judgments, and may prescribe terms necessary to secure the benefit of the stayed judgment for the party in whose favor it was entered.

(Amended December 27, 1946, effective March 19, 1948; December 29, 1948, effective October 20, 1949; April 17, 1961, effective July 19, 1961; March 2, 1987, effective August 1, 1987; April 30, 2007, effective December 1, 2007; March 26, 2009, effective December 1, 2009.)

RULE 62.1. INDICATIVE RULING ON A MOTION FOR RELIEF THAT IS BARRED BY A PENDING APPEAL

(a) Relief Pending Appeal. If a timely motion is made for relief that the court lacks authority to grant because of an appeal that has been docketed and is pending, the court may:

(1) defer considering the motion;

(2) deny the motion; or

(3) state either that it would grant the motion if the court of appeals remands for that purpose or that the motion raises a substantial issue.

(b) Notice to the Court of Appeals. The movant must promptly notify the circuit clerk under Federal Rule of Appellate Procedure 12.1 if the district court states that it would grant the motion or that the motion raises a substantial issue.

(c) Remand. The district court may decide the motion if the court of appeals remands for that purpose.

(Added March 26, 2009, effective December 1, 2009.)

RULE 63. JUDGE'S INABILITY TO PROCEED

If a judge conducting a hearing or trial is unable to proceed, any other judge may proceed upon certifying familiarity with the record and determining that the case may be completed without prejudice to the parties. In a hearing or a nonjury trial, the successor judge must, at a party's request, recall any witness whose testimony is material and disputed and who is available to testify again without undue burden. The successor judge may also recall any other witness.

(Amended March 2, 1987, effective August 1, 1987; April 30, 1991, effective December 1, 1991; April 30, 2007, effective December 1, 2007.)

TITLE VIII.   PROVISIONAL AND FINAL REMEDIES

RULE 64.   SEIZING A PERSON OR PROPERTY

(a) **Remedies Under State Law—In General.** At the commencement of and throughout an action, every remedy is available that, under the law of the state where the court is located, provides for seizing a person or property to secure satisfaction of the potential judgment. But a federal statute governs to the extent it applies.

(b) **Specific Kinds of Remedies.** The remedies available under this rule include the following—however designated and regardless of whether state procedure requires an independent action:

- arrest;
- attachment;
- garnishment;
- replevin;
- sequestration; and
- other corresponding or equivalent remedies.

(Amended April 30, 2007, effective December 1, 2007.)

RULE 65.   INJUNCTIONS AND RESTRAINING ORDERS

(a) **Preliminary Injunction.**

(1) *Notice.* The court may issue a preliminary injunction only on notice to the adverse party.

(2) *Consolidating the Hearing with the Trial on the Merits.* Before or after beginning the hearing on a motion for a preliminary injunction, the court may advance the trial on the merits and consolidate it with the hearing. Even when consolidation is not ordered, evidence that is received on the motion and that would be admissible at trial becomes part of the trial record and need not be repeated at trial. But the court must preserve any party's right to a jury trial.

(b) **Temporary Restraining Order.**

(1) *Issuing Without Notice.* The court may issue a temporary restraining order without written or oral notice to the adverse party or its attorney only if:

(A) specific facts in an affidavit or a verified complaint clearly show that immediate and irreparable injury, loss, or damage will result to the movant before the adverse party can be heard in opposition; and

(B) the movant's attorney certifies in writing any efforts made to give notice and the reasons why it should not be required.

(2) *Contents; Expiration.* Every temporary restraining order issued without notice must state the date and hour it was issued; describe the injury and state why it is irreparable; state why the order was issued without notice; and be promptly filed in the clerk's office and entered in the record. The order expires at the time after entry—not to exceed 14 days—that the court sets, unless before that time the court, for good cause, extends it for a like period or the adverse party consents to a longer extension. The reasons for an extension must be entered in the record.

(3) *Expediting the Preliminary–Injunction Hearing.* If the order is issued without notice, the motion for a preliminary injunction must be set for hearing at the earliest possible time, taking precedence over all other matters except hearings on older matters of the same character. At the hearing, the party who obtained the order must proceed with the motion; if the party does not, the court must dissolve the order.

(4) *Motion to Dissolve.* On 2 days' notice to the party who obtained the order without notice—or on shorter notice set by the court—the adverse party may appear and move to dissolve or modify the order. The court must then hear and decide the motion as promptly as justice requires.

(c) **Security.** The court may issue a preliminary injunction or a temporary restraining order only if the movant gives security in an amount that the court considers proper to pay the costs and damages sustained by any party found to have been wrongfully enjoined or restrained. The United States, its officers, and its agencies are not required to give security.

(d) **Contents and Scope of Every Injunction and Restraining Order.**

(1) *Contents.* Every order granting an injunction and every restraining order must:

(A) state the reasons why it issued;

(B) state its terms specifically; and

(C) describe in reasonable detail—and not by referring to the complaint or other document—the act or acts restrained or required.

(2) *Persons Bound.* The order binds only the following who receive actual notice of it by personal service or otherwise:

(A) the parties;

(B) the parties' officers, agents, servants, employees, and attorneys; and

(C) other persons who are in active concert or participation with anyone described in Rule 65(d)(2)(A) or (B).

(e) **Other Laws Not Modified.** These rules do not modify the following:

(1) any federal statute relating to temporary restraining orders or preliminary injunctions in actions affecting employer and employee;

(2) 28 U.S.C. § 2361, which relates to preliminary injunctions in actions of interpleader or in the nature of interpleader; or

(3) 28 U.S.C. § 2284, which relates to actions that must be heard and decided by a three-judge district court.

(f) Copyright Impoundment. This rule applies to copyright-impoundment proceedings.

(Amended December 27, 1946, effective March 19, 1948; December 29, 1948, effective October 20, 1949; February 28, 1966, effective July 1, 1966; March 2, 1987, effective August 1, 1987; April 23, 2001, effective December 1, 2001; April 30, 2007, effective December 1, 2007; March 26, 2009, effective December 1, 2009.)

RULE 65.1. PROCEEDINGS AGAINST A SURETY

Whenever these rules (including the Supplemental Rules for Admiralty or Maritime Claims and Asset Forfeiture Actions) require or allow a party to give security, and security is given through a bond or other undertaking with one or more sureties, each surety submits to the court's jurisdiction and irrevocably appoints the court clerk as its agent for receiving service of any papers that affect its liability on the bond or undertaking. The surety's liability may be enforced on motion without an independent action. The motion and any notice that the court orders may be served on the court clerk, who must promptly mail a copy of each to every surety whose address is known.

(Adopted February 28, 1966, effective July 1, 1966; amended March 2, 1987, effective August 1, 1987; April 12, 2006, effective December 1, 2006; April 30, 2007, effective December 1, 2007.)

RULE 66. RECEIVERS

These rules govern an action in which the appointment of a receiver is sought or a receiver sues or is sued. But the practice in administering an estate by a receiver or a similar court-appointed officer must accord with the historical practice in federal courts or with a local rule. An action in which a receiver has been appointed may be dismissed only by court order.

(Amended December 27, 1946, effective March 19, 1948; December 29, 1948, effective October 20, 1949; April 30, 2007, effective December 1, 2007.)

RULE 67. DEPOSIT INTO COURT

(a) Depositing Property. If any part of the relief sought is a money judgment or the disposition of a sum of money or some other deliverable thing, a party—on notice to every other party and by leave of court—may deposit with the court all or part of the money or thing, whether or not that party claims any of it. The depositing party must deliver to the clerk a copy of the order permitting deposit.

(b) Investing and Withdrawing Funds. Money paid into court under this rule must be deposited and withdrawn in accordance with 28 U.S.C. §§ 2041 and 2042 and any like statute. The money must be deposited in an interest-bearing account or invested in a court-approved, interest-bearing instrument.

(Amended December 29, 1948, effective October 20, 1949; April 28, 1983, effective August 1, 1983; April 30, 2007, effective December 1, 2007.)

RULE 68. OFFER OF JUDGMENT

(a) Making an Offer; Judgment on an Accepted Offer. At least 14 days before the date set for trial, a party defending against a claim may serve on an opposing party an offer to allow judgment on specified terms, with the costs then accrued. If, within 14 days after being served, the opposing party serves written notice accepting the offer, either party may then file the offer and notice of acceptance, plus proof of service. The clerk must then enter judgment.

(b) Unaccepted Offer. An unaccepted offer is considered withdrawn, but it does not preclude a later offer. Evidence of an unaccepted offer is not admissible except in a proceeding to determine costs.

(c) Offer After Liability is Determined. When one party's liability to another has been determined but the extent of liability remains to be determined by further proceedings, the party held liable may make an offer of judgment. It must be served within a reasonable time—but at least 14 days—before the date set for a hearing to determine the extent of liability.

(d) Paying Costs After an Unaccepted Offer. If the judgment that the offeree finally obtains is not more favorable than the unaccepted offer, the offeree must pay the costs incurred after the offer was made.

(Amended December 27, 1946, effective March 19, 1948; February 28, 1966, effective July 1, 1966; March 2, 1987, effective August 1, 1987; April 30, 2007, effective December 1, 2007; March 26, 2009, effective December 1, 2009.)

RULE 69. EXECUTION

(a) In General.

(1) *Money Judgment; Applicable Procedure.* A money judgment is enforced by a writ of execution, unless the court directs otherwise. The procedure on execution—and in proceedings supplementary to and in aid of judgment or execution—must accord with the procedure of the state where the court is located, but a federal statute governs to the extent it applies.

(2) *Obtaining Discovery.* In aid of the judgment or execution, the judgment creditor or a successor in interest whose interest appears of record may obtain discovery from any person—including the judgment debtor—as provided in these rules or by the procedure of the state where the court is located.

(b) Against Certain Public Officers. When a judgment has been entered against a revenue officer in the circumstances stated in 28 U.S.C. § 2006, or against an officer of Congress in the circumstances stated in 2 U.S.C. § 118, the judgment must be satisfied as those statutes provide.

(Amended December 29, 1948, effective October 20, 1949; March 30, 1970, effective July 1, 1970; March 2, 1987 effective August 1, 1987; April 30, 2007, effective December 1, 2007.)

RULE 70.   ENFORCING A JUDGMENT FOR A SPECIFIC ACT

(a) Party's Failure to Act; Ordering Another to Act. If a judgment requires a party to convey land, to deliver a deed or other document, or to perform any other specific act and the party fails to comply within the time specified, the court may order the act to be done—at the disobedient party's expense—by another person appointed by the court. When done, the act has the same effect as if done by the party.

(b) Vesting Title. If the real or personal property is within the district, the court—instead of ordering a conveyance—may enter a judgment divesting any party's title and vesting it in others. That judgment has the effect of a legally executed conveyance.

(c) Obtaining a Writ of Attachment or Sequestration. On application by a party entitled to performance of an act, the clerk must issue a writ of attachment or sequestration against the disobedient party's property to compel obedience.

(d) Obtaining a Writ of Execution or Assistance. On application by a party who obtains a judgment or order for possession, the clerk must issue a writ of execution or assistance.

(e) Holding in Contempt. The court may also hold the disobedient party in contempt.

(Amended April 30, 2007, effective December 1, 2007.)

RULE 71.   ENFORCING RELIEF FOR OR AGAINST A NONPARTY

When an order grants relief for a nonparty or may be enforced against a nonparty, the procedure for enforcing the order is the same as for a party.

(Amended March 2, 1987, effective August 1, 1987; April 30, 2007, effective December 1, 2007.)

TITLE IX.   SPECIAL PROCEEDINGS

RULE 71.1.   CONDEMNING REAL OR PERSONAL PROPERTY

(a) Applicability of Other Rules. These rules govern proceedings to condemn real and personal property by eminent domain, except as this rule provides otherwise.

(b) Joinder of Properties. The plaintiff may join separate pieces of property in a single action, no matter whether they are owned by the same persons or sought for the same use.

(c) Complaint.

(1) *Caption.* The complaint must contain a caption as provided in Rule 10(a). The plaintiff must, however, name as defendants both the property—designated generally by kind, quantity, and location—and at least one owner of some part of or interest in the property.

(2) *Contents.* The complaint must contain a short and plain statement of the following:

(A) the authority for the taking;

(B) the uses for which the property is to be taken;

(C) a description sufficient to identify the property;

(D) the interests to be acquired; and

(E) for each piece of property, a designation of each defendant who has been joined as an owner or owner of an interest in it.

(3) *Parties.* When the action commences, the plaintiff need join as defendants only those persons who have or claim an interest in the property and whose names are then known. But before any hearing on compensation, the plaintiff must add as defendants all those persons who have or claim an interest and whose names have become known or can be found by a reasonably diligent search of the records,

considering both the property's character and value and the interests to be acquired. All others may be made defendants under the designation "Unknown Owners."

(4) *Procedure.* Notice must be served on all defendants as provided in Rule 71.1(d), whether they were named as defendants when the action commenced or were added later. A defendant may answer as provided in Rule 71.1(e). The court, meanwhile, may order any distribution of a deposit that the facts warrant.

(5) *Filing; Additional Copies.* In addition to filing the complaint, the plaintiff must give the clerk at least one copy for the defendants' use and additional copies at the request of the clerk or a defendant.

(d) Process.

(1) *Delivering Notice to the Clerk.* On filing a complaint, the plaintiff must promptly deliver to the clerk joint or several notices directed to the named defendants. When adding defendants, the plaintiff must deliver to the clerk additional notices directed to the new defendants.

(2) *Contents of the Notice.*

(A) *Main Contents.* Each notice must name the court, the title of the action, and the defendant to whom it is directed. It must describe the property sufficiently to identify it, but need not describe any property other than that to be taken from the named defendant. The notice must also state:

(i) that the action is to condemn property;

(ii) the interest to be taken;

(iii) the authority for the taking;

(iv) the uses for which the property is to be taken;

(v) that the defendant may serve an answer on the plaintiff's attorney within 21 days after being served with the notice;

(vi) that the failure to so serve an answer constitutes consent to the taking and to the court's authority to proceed with the action and fix the compensation; and

(vii) that a defendant who does not serve an answer may file a notice of appearance.

(B) *Conclusion.* The notice must conclude with the name, telephone number, and e-mail address of the plaintiff's attorney and an address within the district in which the action is brought where the attorney may be served.

(3) *Serving the Notice.*

(A) *Personal Service.* When a defendant whose address is known resides within the United States or a territory subject to the administrative or judicial jurisdiction of the United States, personal service of the notice (without a copy of the complaint) must be made in accordance with Rule 4.

(B) *Service by Publication.*

(i) A defendant may be served by publication only when the plaintiff's attorney files a certificate stating that the attorney believes the defendant cannot be personally served, because after diligent inquiry within the state where the complaint is filed, the defendant's place of residence is still unknown or, if known, that it is beyond the territorial limits of personal service. Service is then made by publishing the notice—once a week for at least 3 successive weeks—in a newspaper published in the county where the property is located or, if there is no such newspaper, in a newspaper with general circulation where the property is located. Before the last publication, a copy of the notice must also be mailed to every defendant who cannot be personally served but whose place of residence is then known. Unknown owners may be served by publication in the same manner by a notice addressed to "Unknown Owners."

(ii) Service by publication is complete on the date of the last publication. The plaintiff's attorney must prove publication and mailing by a certificate, attach a printed copy of the published notice, and mark on the copy the newspaper's name and the dates of publication.

(4) *Effect of Delivery and Service.* Delivering the notice to the clerk and serving it have the same effect as serving a summons under Rule 4.

(5) *Amending the Notice; Proof of Service and Amending the Proof.* Rule 4(a)(2) governs amending the notice. Rule 4(*l*) governs proof of service and amending it.

(e) Appearance or Answer.

(1) *Notice of Appearance.* A defendant that has no objection or defense to the taking of its property may serve a notice of appearance designating the property in which it claims an interest. The defendant must then be given notice of all later proceedings affecting the defendant.

(2) *Answer.* A defendant that has an objection or defense to the taking must serve an answer within 21 days after being served with the notice. The answer must:

(A) identify the property in which the defendant claims an interest;

(B) state the nature and extent of the interest; and

(C) state all the defendant's objections and defenses to the taking.

(3) *Waiver of Other Objections and Defenses; Evidence on Compensation.* A defendant waives all objections and defenses not stated in its answer. No other pleading or motion asserting an additional objection or defense is allowed. But at the trial on compensation, a defendant—whether or not it has previously appeared or answered—may present evidence on the amount of compensation to be paid and may share in the award.

(f) Amending Pleadings. Without leave of court, the plaintiff may—as often as it wants—amend the complaint at any time before the trial on compensation. But no amendment may be made if it would result in a dismissal inconsistent with Rule 71.1(i)(1) or (2). The plaintiff need not serve a copy of an amendment, but must serve notice of the filing, as provided in Rule 5(b), on every affected party who has appeared and, as provided in Rule 71.1(d), on every affected party who has not appeared. In addition, the plaintiff must give the clerk at least one copy of each amendment for the defendants' use, and additional copies at the request of the clerk or a defendant. A defendant may appear or answer in the time and manner and with the same effect as provided in Rule 71.1(e).

(g) Substituting Parties. If a defendant dies, becomes incompetent, or transfers an interest after being joined, the court may, on motion and notice of hearing, order that the proper party be substituted. Service of the motion and notice on a nonparty must be made as provided in Rule 71.1(d)(3).

(h) Trial of the Issues.

(1) *Issues Other Than Compensation; Compensation.* In an action involving eminent domain under federal law, the court tries all issues, including compensation, except when compensation must be determined:

(A) by any tribunal specially constituted by a federal statute to determine compensation; or

(B) if there is no such tribunal, by a jury when a party demands one within the time to answer or within any additional time the court sets, unless the court appoints a commission.

(2) *Appointing a Commission; Commission's Powers and Report.*

(A) *Reasons for Appointing.* If a party has demanded a jury, the court may instead appoint a three-person commission to determine compensation because of the character, location, or quantity of the property to be condemned or for other just reasons.

(B) *Alternate Commissioners.* The court may appoint up to two additional persons to serve as alternate commissioners to hear the case and replace commissioners who, before a decision is filed, the court finds unable or disqualified to perform their duties. Once the commission renders its final decision, the court must discharge any alternate who has not replaced a commissioner.

(C) *Examining the Prospective Commissioners.* Before making its appointments, the court must advise the parties of the identity and qualifications of each prospective commissioner and alternate, and may permit the parties to examine them. The parties may not suggest appointees, but for good cause may object to a prospective commissioner or alternate.

(D) *Commission's Powers and Report.* A commission has the powers of a master under Rule 53(c). Its action and report are determined by a majority. Rule 53(d), (e), and (f) apply to its action and report.

(i) Dismissal of the Action or a Defendant.

(1) *Dismissing the Action.*

(A) *By the Plaintiff.* If no compensation hearing on a piece of property has begun, and if the plaintiff has not acquired title or a lesser interest or taken possession, the plaintiff may, without a court order, dismiss the action as to that property by filing a notice of dismissal briefly describing the property.

(B) *By Stipulation.* Before a judgment is entered vesting the plaintiff with title or a lesser interest in or possession of property, the plaintiff and affected defendants may, without a court order, dismiss the action in whole or in part by filing a stipulation of dismissal. And if the parties so stipulate, the court may vacate a judgment already entered.

(C) *By Court Order.* At any time before compensation has been determined and paid, the court may, after a motion and hearing, dismiss the action as to a piece of property. But if the plaintiff has already taken title, a lesser interest, or possession as to any part of it, the court must award compensation for the title, lesser interest, or possession taken.

(2) *Dismissing a Defendant.* The court may at any time dismiss a defendant who was unnecessarily or improperly joined.

(3) *Effect.* A dismissal is without prejudice unless otherwise stated in the notice, stipulation, or court order.

(j) Deposit and Its Distribution.

(1) *Deposit.* The plaintiff must deposit with the court any money required by law as a condition to the exercise of eminent domain and may make a deposit when allowed by statute.

(2) *Distribution; Adjusting Distribution.* After a deposit, the court and attorneys must expedite the proceedings so as to distribute the deposit and to determine and pay compensation. If the compensation finally awarded to a defendant exceeds the amount distributed to that defendant, the court must enter judgment against the plaintiff for the deficiency. If the compensation awarded to a defendant is less than the amount distributed to that defendant, the court must enter judgment against that defendant for the overpayment.

(k) Condemnation Under a State's Power of Eminent Domain. This rule governs an action involving eminent domain under state law. But if state law provides for trying an issue by jury—or for trying the issue of compensation by jury or commission or both—that law governs.

(*l*) Costs. Costs are not subject to Rule 54(d).

(Adopted April 30, 1951, effective August 1, 1951; amended January 21, 1963, effective July 1, 1963; April 29, 1985, effective August 1, 1985; March 2, 1987, effective August 1, 1987; April 25, 1988, effective August 1, 1988; amended by Pub.L. 100–690, Title VII, § 7050, November 18, 1988, 102 Stat. 4401 (although amendment by Pub.L. 100–690 could not be executed due to prior amendment by Court order which made the same change effective August 1, 1988); amended April 22, 1993, effective December 1, 1993; March 27, 2003, effective December 1, 2003; April 30, 2007, effective December 1, 2007; March 26, 2009, effective December 1, 2009.)

RULE 72. MAGISTRATE JUDGES: PRETRIAL ORDER

(a) Nondispositive Matters. When a pretrial matter not dispositive of a party's claim or defense is referred to a magistrate judge to hear and decide, the magistrate judge must promptly conduct the required proceedings and, when appropriate, issue a written order stating the decision. A party may serve and file objections to the order within 14 days after being served with a copy. A party may not assign as error a defect in the order not timely objected to. The district judge in the case must consider timely objections and modify or set aside any part of the order that is clearly erroneous or is contrary to law.

(b) Dispositive Motions and Prisoner Petitions.

(1) *Findings and Recommendations.* A magistrate judge must promptly conduct the required proceedings when assigned, without the parties' consent, to hear a pretrial matter dispositive of a claim or defense or a prisoner petition challenging the conditions of confinement. A record must be made of all evidentiary proceedings and may, at the magistrate judge's discretion, be made of any other proceedings. The magistrate judge must enter a recommended disposition, including, if appropriate, proposed findings of fact. The clerk must promptly mail a copy to each party.

(2) *Objections.* Within 14 days after being served with a copy of the recommended disposition, a party may serve and file specific written objections to the proposed findings and recommendations. A party may respond to another party's objections within 14 days after being served with a copy. Unless the district judge orders otherwise, the objecting party must promptly arrange for transcribing the record, or whatever portions of it the parties agree to or the magistrate judge considers sufficient.

(3) *Resolving Objections.* The district judge must determine de novo any part of the magistrate judge's disposition that has been properly objected to. The district judge may accept, reject, or modify the recommended disposition; receive further evidence; or return the matter to the magistrate judge with instructions.

(Former Rule 72 abrogated December 4, 1967, effective July 1, 1968; new Rule 72 adopted April 28, 1983, effective August 1, 1983; amended April 30, 1991, effective December 1, 1991; April 22, 1993, effective December 1, 1993; April 30, 2007, effective December 1, 2007; March 26, 2009, effective December 1, 2009.)

RULE 73. MAGISTRATE JUDGES: TRIAL BY CONSENT; APPEAL

(a) Trial by Consent. When authorized under 28 U.S.C. § 636(c), a magistrate judge may, if all parties consent, conduct a civil action or proceeding, including a jury or nonjury trial. A record must be made in accordance with 28 U.S.C. § 636(c)(5).

(b) Consent Procedure.

(1) *In General.* When a magistrate judge has been designated to conduct civil actions or proceedings, the clerk must give the parties written notice of their opportunity to consent under 28 U.S.C. § 636(c). To signify their consent, the parties must jointly or separately file a statement consenting to the referral. A district judge or magistrate judge may be informed of a party's response to the clerk's notice only if all parties have consented to the referral.

(2) *Reminding the Parties About Consenting.* A district judge, magistrate judge, or other court official may remind the parties of the magistrate judge's availability, but must also advise them that they are free to withhold consent without adverse substantive consequences.

(3) *Vacating a Referral.* On its own for good cause—or when a party shows extraordinary circumstances—the district judge may vacate a referral to a magistrate judge under this rule.

(c) Appealing a Judgment. In accordance with 28 U.S.C. § 636(c)(3), an appeal from a judgment entered at a magistrate judge's direction may be taken to the court of appeals as would any other appeal from a district-court judgment.

(Former Rule 73 abrogated December 4, 1967, effective July 1, 1968; new Rule 73 adopted April 28, 1983, effective August 1, 1983; amended March 2, 1987, effective August 1, 1987; April 22, 1993, effective December 1, 1993; April 11, 1997, effective December 1, 1997; April 30, 2007, effective December 1, 2007.)

RULE 74. METHOD OF APPEAL FROM MAGISTRATE JUDGE TO DISTRICT JUDGE UNDER TITLE 28, U.S.C. § 636(c)(4) AND RULE 73(d) [ABROGATED]

(Former Rule 74 abrogated December 4, 1967, effective July 1, 1968; new Rule 74 adopted April 28, 1983, effective August 1, 1983; amended April 22, 1993, effective December 1, 1993; abrogated April 11, 1997, effective December 1, 1997; April 30, 2007, effective December 1, 2007.)

RULE 75. PROCEEDINGS ON APPEAL FROM MAGISTRATE JUDGE TO DISTRICT JUDGE UNDER RULE 73(d) [ABROGATED]

(Former Rule 75 abrogated December 4, 1967, effective July 1, 1968; new Rule 75 adopted April 28, 1983, effective August 1, 1983; amended March 2, 1987, effective August 1, 1987; April 22, 1993, effective December 1, 1993; abrogated April 11, 1997, effective December 1, 1997; April 30, 2007, effective December 1, 2007.)

RULE 76. JUDGMENT OF THE DISTRICT JUDGE ON THE APPEAL UNDER RULE 73(d) AND COSTS [ABROGATED]

(Former Rule 76 abrogated December 4, 1967, effective July 1, 1968; new Rule 76 adopted April 28, 1983, effective August 1, 1983; amended April 22, 1993, effective December 1, 1993; abrogated April 11, 1997, effective December 1, 1997; April 30, 2007, effective December 1, 2007.)

TITLE X. DISTRICT COURTS AND CLERKS: CONDUCTING BUSINESS; ISSUING ORDERS

RULE 77. CONDUCTING BUSINESS; CLERK'S AUTHORITY; NOTICE OF AN ORDER OR JUDGMENT

(a) When Court Is Open. Every district court is considered always open for filing any paper, issuing and returning process, making a motion, or entering an order.

(b) Place for Trial and Other Proceedings. Every trial on the merits must be conducted in open court and, so far as convenient, in a regular courtroom. Any other act or proceeding may be done or conducted by a judge in chambers, without the attendance of the clerk or other court official, and anywhere inside or outside the district. But no hearing—other than one ex parte—may be conducted outside the district unless all the affected parties consent.

(c) Clerk's Office Hours; Clerk's Orders.

(1) *Hours.* The clerk's office—with a clerk or deputy on duty—must be open during business hours every day except Saturdays, Sundays, and legal holidays. But a court may, by local rule or order, require that the office be open for specified hours on Saturday or a particular legal holiday other than one listed in Rule 6(a)(6)(A).

(2) *Orders.* Subject to the court's power to suspend, alter, or rescind the clerk's action for good cause, the clerk may:

(A) issue process;

(B) enter a default;

(C) enter a default judgment under Rule 55(b)(1); and

(D) act on any other matter that does not require the court's action.

(d) Serving Notice of an Order or Judgment.

(1) *Service.* Immediately after entering an order or judgment, the clerk must serve notice of the entry, as provided in Rule 5(b), on each party who is not in default for failing to appear. The clerk must record the service on the docket. A party also may serve notice of the entry as provided in Rule 5(b).

(2) *Time to Appeal Not Affected by Lack of Notice.* Lack of notice of the entry does not affect the time for appeal or relieve—or authorize the court to relieve—a party for failing to appeal within the time allowed, except as allowed by Federal Rule of Appellate Procedure (4)(a).

(Amended December 27, 1946, effective March 19, 1948; January 21, 1963, effective July 1, 1963; December 4, 1967, effective July 1, 1968; March 1, 1971, effective July 1, 1971; March 2, 1987, effective August 1, 1987; April 30, 1991, effective December 1, 1991; April 23, 2001, effective December 1, 2001; April 30, 2007, effective December 1, 2007; April 25, 2014, effective December 1, 2014.)

RULE 78. HEARING MOTIONS; SUBMISSION ON BRIEFS

(a) Providing a Regular Schedule for Oral Hearings. A court may establish regular times and places for oral hearings on motions.

(b) Providing for Submission on Briefs. By rule or order, the court may provide for submitting and determining motions on briefs, without oral hearings.

(Amended March 2, 1987, effective August 1, 1987; April 30, 2007, effective December 1, 2007.)

RULE 79. RECORDS KEPT BY THE CLERK

(a) Civil Docket.

(1) *In General.* The clerk must keep a record known as the "civil docket" in the form and manner prescribed by the Director of the Administrative Office of the United States Courts with the approval of the Judicial Conference of the United States. The clerk must enter each civil action in the docket. Actions must be assigned consecutive file numbers, which must be noted in the docket where the first entry of the action is made.

(2) *Items to be Entered.* The following items must be marked with the file number and entered chronologically in the docket:

(A) papers filed with the clerk;

(B) process issued, and proofs of service or other returns showing execution; and

(C) appearances, orders, verdicts, and judgments.

(3) *Contents of Entries; Jury Trial Demanded.* Each entry must briefly show the nature of the paper filed or writ issued, the substance of each proof of service or other return, and the substance and date of entry of each order and judgment. When a jury trial has been properly demanded or ordered, the clerk must enter the word "jury" in the docket.

(b) Civil Judgments and Orders. The clerk must keep a copy of every final judgment and appealable order; of every order affecting title to or a lien on real or personal property; and of any other order that the court directs to be kept. The clerk must keep these in the form and manner prescribed by the Director of the Administrative Office of the United States Courts with the approval of the Judicial Conference of the United States.

(c) Indexes; Calendars. Under the court's direction, the clerk must:

(1) keep indexes of the docket and of the judgments and orders described in Rule 79(b); and

(2) prepare calendars of all actions ready for trial, distinguishing jury trials from nonjury trials.

(d) Other Records. The clerk must keep any other records required by the Director of the Administrative Office of the United States Courts with the approval of the Judicial Conference of the United States.

(Amended December 27, 1946, effective March 19, 1948; December 29, 1948, effective October 20, 1949; January 21, 1963, effective July 1, 1963; April 30, 2007, effective December 1, 2007.)

RULE 80. STENOGRAPHIC TRANSCRIPT AS EVIDENCE

If stenographically reported testimony at a hearing or trial is admissible in evidence at a later trial, the testimony may be proved by a transcript certified by the person who reported it.

(Amended December 27, 1946, effective March 19, 1948; April 30, 2007, effective December 1, 2007.)

TITLE XI. GENERAL PROVISIONS

RULE 81. APPLICABILITY OF THE RULES IN GENERAL; REMOVED ACTIONS

(a) Applicability to Particular Proceedings.

(1) *Prize Proceedings.* These rules do not apply to prize proceedings in admiralty governed by 10 U.S.C. §§ 7651–7681.

(2) *Bankruptcy.* These rules apply to bankruptcy proceedings to the extent provided by the Federal Rules of Bankruptcy Procedure.

(3) *Citizenship.* These rules apply to proceedings for admission to citizenship to the extent that the practice in those proceedings is not specified in federal statutes and has previously conformed to the practice in civil actions. The provisions of 8 U.S.C. § 1451 for service by publication and for answer apply in proceedings to cancel citizenship certificates.

(4) *Special Writs.* These rules apply to proceedings for habeas corpus and for quo warranto to the extent that the practice in those proceedings:

(A) is not specified in a federal statute, the Rules Governing Section 2254 Cases, or the Rules Governing Section 2255 Cases; and

(B) has previously conformed to the practice in civil actions.

(5) *Proceedings Involving a Subpoena.* These rules apply to proceedings to compel testimony or the production of documents through a subpoena issued by a United States officer or agency under a federal statute, except as otherwise provided by statute, by local rule, or by court order in the proceedings.

(6) *Other Proceedings.* These rules, to the extent applicable, govern proceedings under the following laws, except as these laws provide other procedures:

(A) 7 U.S.C. §§ 292, 499g(c), for reviewing an order of the Secretary of Agriculture;

(B) 9 U.S.C., relating to arbitration;

(C) 15 U.S.C. § 522, for reviewing an order of the Secretary of the Interior;

(D) 15 U.S.C. § 715d(c), for reviewing an order denying a certificate of clearance;

(E) 29 U.S.C. §§ 159, 160, for enforcing an order of the National Labor Relations Board;

(F) 33 U.S.C. §§ 918, 921, for enforcing or reviewing a compensation order under the Longshore and Harbor Workers' Compensation Act; and

(G) 45 U.S.C. § 159, for reviewing an arbitration award in a railway-labor dispute.

(b) Scire Facias and Mandamus. The writs of scire facias and mandamus are abolished. Relief previously available through them may be obtained by appropriate action or motion under these rules.

(c) Removed Actions.

(1) *Applicability.* These rules apply to a civil action after it is removed from a state court.

(2) *Further Pleading.* After removal, repleading is unnecessary unless the court orders it. A defendant who did not answer before removal must answer or present other defenses or objections under these rules within the longest of these periods:

(A) 21 days after receiving—through service or otherwise—a copy of the initial pleading stating the claim for relief;

(B) 21 days after being served with the summons for an initial pleading on file at the time of service; or

(C) 7 days after the notice of removal is filed.

(3) *Demand for a Jury Trial.*

(A) *As Affected by State Law.* A party who, before removal, expressly demanded a jury trial in accordance with state law need not renew the demand after removal. If the state law did not require an express demand for a jury trial, a party need not make one after removal unless the court orders the parties to do so within a specified time. The court must so order at a party's request and may so order on its own. A party who fails to make a demand when so ordered waives a jury trial.

(B) *Under Rule 38.* If all necessary pleadings have been served at the time of removal, a party entitled to a jury trial under Rule 38 must be given one if the party serves a demand within 14 days after:

(i) it files a notice of removal; or

(ii) it is served with a notice of removal filed by another party.

(d) Law Applicable.

(1) *"State Law" Defined.* When these rules refer to state law, the term "law" includes the state's statutes and the state's judicial decisions.

(2) *"State" Defined.* The term "state" includes, where appropriate, the District of Columbia and any United States commonwealth or territory.

(3) *"Federal Statute" Defined in the District of Columbia.* In the United States District Court for the District of Columbia, the term "federal statute" includes any Act of Congress that applies locally to the District.

(Amended December 28, 1939, effective April 3, 1941; December 27, 1946, effective March 19, 1948; December 29, 1948, effective October 20, 1949; April 30, 1951, effective August 1, 1951; January 21, 1963, effective July 1, 1963; February 28, 1966, effective July 1, 1966; December 4, 1967, effective July 1, 1968; March 1, 1971, effective July 1, 1971; March 2, 1987, effective August 1, 1987; April 23, 2001, effective December 1, 2001; April 29, 2002, effective December 1, 2002; April 30, 2007, effective December 1, 2007; March 26, 2009, effective December 1, 2009.)

RULE 82. JURISDICTION AND VENUE UNAFFECTED

These rules do not extend or limit the jurisdiction of the district courts or the venue of actions in those courts. An admiralty or maritime claim under Rule 9(h) is governed by 28 U.S.C. § 1390.

(Amended December 29, 1948, effective October 20, 1949; February 28, 1966, effective July 1, 1966; April 23, 2001, effective December 1, 2001; April 30, 2007, effective December 1, 2007; April 28, 2016, effective December 1, 2016.)

RULE 83. RULES BY DISTRICT COURTS; JUDGE'S DIRECTIVES

(a) Local Rules.

(1) *In General.* After giving public notice and an opportunity for comment, a district court, acting by a majority of its district judges, may adopt and amend rules governing its practice. A local rule must be consistent with—but not duplicate—federal statutes and rules adopted under 28 U.S.C. §§ 2072 and 2075, and must conform to any uniform numbering system prescribed by the Judicial Conference of the United States. A local rule takes effect on the date specified by the district court and remains in effect unless amended by the court or abrogated by the judicial council of the circuit. Copies of rules and amendments must, on their adoption, be furnished to the judicial council and the Administrative Office of the United States Courts and be made available to the public.

(2) *Requirement of Form.* A local rule imposing a requirement of form must not be enforced in a way that causes a party to lose any right because of a nonwillful failure to comply.

(b) Procedure When There Is No Controlling Law. A judge may regulate practice in any manner consistent with federal law, rules adopted under 28 U.S.C. §§ 2072 and 2075, and the district's local rules. No sanction or other disadvantage may be imposed for noncompliance with any requirement not in federal law, federal rules, or the local rules unless the alleged violator has been furnished in the particular case with actual notice of the requirement.

(Amended April 29, 1985, effective August 1, 1985; April 27, 1995, effective December 1, 1995; April 30, 2007, effective December 1, 2007.)

RULE 84. FORMS [ABROGATED]

(Amended December 27, 1946, effective March 19, 1948; April 30, 2007, effective December 1, 2007; abrogated April 29, 2015, effective December 1, 2015.)

RULE 85. TITLE

These rules may be cited as the Federal Rules of Civil Procedure.

(Amended April 30, 2007, effective December 1, 2007.)

RULE 86. EFFECTIVE DATES

(a) In General. These rules and any amendments take effect at the time specified by the Supreme Court, subject to 28 U.S.C. § 2074. They govern:

(1) proceedings in an action commenced after their effective date; and

(2) proceedings after that date in an action then pending unless:

(A) the Supreme Court specifies otherwise; or

(B) the court determines that applying them in a particular action would be infeasible or work an injustice.

(b) December 1, 2007 Amendments. If any provision in Rules 1–5.1, 6–73, or 77–86 conflicts with another law, priority in time for the purpose of 28 U.S.C. § 2072(b) is not affected by the amendments taking effect on December 1, 2007.

(Amended December 27, 1946, effective March 19, 1948; December 29, 1948, effective October 20, 1949; April 17, 1961, effective July 19, 1961; January 21, 1963, and March 18, 1963, effective July 1, 1963; April 30, 2007, effective December 1, 2007.)

APPENDIX OF FORMS [ABROGATED]

SUPPLEMENTAL RULES FOR ADMIRALTY OR MARITIME CLAIMS AND ASSET FORFEITURE ACTIONS

RULE A. SCOPE OF RULES

(1) These Supplemental Rules apply to:

(A) the procedure in admiralty and maritime claims within the meaning of Rule 9(h) with respect to the following remedies:

(i) maritime attachment and garnishment,

(ii) actions in rem,

(iii) possessory, petitory, and partition actions, and

(iv) actions for exoneration from or limitation of liability;

(B) forfeiture actions in rem arising from a federal statute; and

(C) the procedure in statutory condemnation proceedings analogous to maritime actions in rem, whether within the admiralty and maritime jurisdiction or not. Except as otherwise provided, references in these Supplemental Rules to actions in rem include such analogous statutory condemnation proceedings.

(2) The Federal Rules of Civil Procedure also apply to the foregoing proceedings except to the extent that they are inconsistent with these Supplemental Rules.

(Added Feb. 28, 1966, eff. July 1, 1966; amended Apr. 12, 2006, eff. Dec. 1, 2006.)

RULE B. IN PERSONAM ACTIONS: ATTACHMENT AND GARNISHMENT

(1) When Available; Complaint, Affidavit, Judicial Authorization, and Process. In an in personam action:

(a) If a defendant is not found within the district when a verified complaint praying for attachment and the affidavit required by Rule B(1)(b) are filed, a verified complaint may contain a prayer for process to attach the defendant's tangible or intangible personal property—up to the amount sued for—in the hands of garnishees named in the process.

(b) The plaintiff or the plaintiff's attorney must sign and file with the complaint an affidavit stating that, to the affiant's knowledge, or on information and belief, the defendant cannot be found within the district. The court must review the complaint and affidavit and, if the conditions of this Rule B appear to exist, enter an order so stating and authorizing process of attachment and garnishment. The clerk may issue supplemental process enforcing the court's order upon application without further court order.

(c) If the plaintiff or the plaintiff's attorney certifies that exigent circumstances make court review impracticable, the clerk must issue the summons and process of attachment and garnishment. The plaintiff has the burden in any post-attachment hearing under Rule E(4)(f) to show that exigent circumstances existed.

(d)(i) If the property is a vessel or tangible property on board a vessel, the summons, process, and any supplemental process must be delivered to the marshal for service.

(ii) If the property is other tangible or intangible property, the summons, process, and any supplemental process must be delivered to a person or organization authorized to serve it, who may be (A) a marshal; (B) someone under contract with the United States; (C) someone specially appointed by the court for that purpose; or, (D) in an action brought by the United States, any officer or employee of the United States.

(e) The plaintiff may invoke state-law remedies under Rule 64 for seizure of person or property for the purpose of securing satisfaction of the judgment.

(2) Notice to Defendant. No default judgment may be entered except upon proof—which may be by affidavit—that:

(a) the complaint, summons, and process of attachment or garnishment have been served on the defendant in a manner authorized by Rule 4;

(b) the plaintiff or the garnishee has mailed to the defendant the complaint, summons, and process of attachment or garnishment, using any form of mail requiring a return receipt; or

(c) the plaintiff or the garnishee has tried diligently to give notice of the action to the defendant but could not do so.

(3) Answer.

(a) By Garnishee. The garnishee shall serve an answer, together with answers to any interrogatories served with the complaint, within 21 days after service of process upon the garnishee. Interrogatories to the garnishee may be served with the complaint without leave of court. If the garnishee refuses or neglects to answer on oath as to the debts, credits, or effects of the defendant in the garnishee's hands, or any interrogatories concerning such debts, credits, and effects that may be propounded by the plaintiff, the court may award compulsory process against the garnishee. If the garnishee admits any debts, credits, or effects, they shall be held in the garnishee's hands or paid into the registry of the court, and shall be held in either case subject to the further order of the court.

(b) By Defendant. The defendant shall serve an answer within 30 days after process has been executed, whether by attachment of property or service on the garnishee.

(Added Feb. 28, 1966, eff. July 1, 1966; amended Apr. 29, 1985, eff. Aug. 1, 1985; Mar. 2, 1987, eff. Aug. 1, 1987; Apr. 17, 2000, eff. Dec. 1, 2000; Apr. 25, 2005, eff. Dec. 1, 2005; Mar. 26, 2009, eff. Dec. 1, 2009.)

RULE C. IN REM ACTIONS: SPECIAL PROVISIONS

(1) When Available. An action in rem may be brought:

(a) To enforce any maritime lien;

(b) Whenever a statute of the United States provides for a maritime action in rem or a proceeding analogous thereto.

Except as otherwise provided by law a party who may proceed in rem may also, or in the alternative, proceed in personam against any person who may be liable.

Statutory provisions exempting vessels or other property owned or possessed by or operated by or for the United States from arrest or seizure are not affected by this rule. When a statute so provides, an action against the United States or an instrumentality thereof may proceed on in rem principles.

(2) Complaint. In an action in rem the complaint must:

(a) be verified;

(b) describe with reasonable particularity the property that is the subject of the action; and

(c) state that the property is within the district or will be within the district while the action is pending.

(3) Judicial Authorization and Process.

(a) Arrest Warrant.

(i) The court must review the complaint and any supporting papers. If the conditions for an in rem action appear to exist, the court must issue an order directing the clerk to issue a warrant for the arrest of the vessel or other property that is the subject of the action.

(ii) If the plaintiff or the plaintiff's attorney certifies that exigent circumstances make court review impracticable, the clerk must promptly issue a summons and a warrant for the arrest of the vessel or other property that is the subject of the action. The plaintiff has the burden in any post-arrest hearing under Rule E(4)(f) to show that exigent circumstances existed.

(b) Service.

(i) If the property that is the subject of the action is a vessel or tangible property on board a vessel, the warrant and any supplemental process must be delivered to the marshal for service.

(ii) If the property that is the subject of the action is other property, tangible or intangible, the warrant and any supplemental process must be delivered to a person or organization authorized to enforce it, who may be: (A) a marshal; (B) someone under contract with the United States; (C) someone specially appointed by the court for that purpose; or, (D) in an action brought by the United States, any officer or employee of the United States.

(c) Deposit in Court. If the property that is the subject of the action consists in whole or in part of freight, the proceeds of property sold, or other intangible property, the clerk must issue—in addition to the warrant—a summons directing any person controlling the property to show cause why it should not be deposited in court to abide the judgment.

(d) Supplemental Process. The clerk may upon application issue supplemental process to enforce the court's order without further court order.

(4) Notice. No notice other than execution of process is required when the property that is the subject of the action

has been released under Rule E(5). If the property is not released within 14 days after execution, the plaintiff must promptly—or within the time that the court allows—give public notice of the action and arrest in a newspaper designated by court order and having general circulation in the district, but publication may be terminated if the property is released before publication is completed. The notice must specify the time under Rule C(6) to file a statement of interest in or right against the seized property and to answer. This rule does not affect the notice requirements in an action to foreclose a preferred ship mortgage under 46 U.S.C. §§ 31301 et seq., as amended.

(5) Ancillary Process. In any action in rem in which process has been served as provided by this rule, if any part of the property that is the subject of the action has not been brought within the control of the court because it has been removed or sold, or because it is intangible property in the hands of a person who has not been served with process, the court may, on motion, order any person having possession or control of such property or its proceeds to show cause why it should not be delivered into the custody of the marshal or other person or organization having a warrant for the arrest of the property, or paid into court to abide the judgment; and, after hearing, the court may enter such judgment as law and justice may require.

(6) Responsive Pleading; Interrogatories.

(a) Statement of Interest; Answer. In an action in rem:

(i) a person who asserts a right of possession or any ownership interest in the property that is the subject of the action must file a verified statement of right or interest:

(A) within 14 days after the execution of process, or

(B) within the time that the court allows;

(ii) the statement of right or interest must describe the interest in the property that supports the person's demand for its restitution or right to defend the action;

(iii) an agent, bailee, or attorney must state the authority to file a statement of right or interest on behalf of another; and

(iv) a person who asserts a right of possession or any ownership interest must serve an answer within 21 days after filing the statement of interest or right.

(b) Interrogatories. Interrogatories may be served with the complaint in an in rem action without leave of court. Answers to the interrogatories must be served with the answer to the complaint.

(Added Feb. 28, 1966, eff. July 1, 1966; amended Apr. 29, 1985, eff. Aug. 1, 1985; Mar. 2, 1987, eff. Aug. 1, 1987; Apr. 30, 1991, eff. Dec. 1, 1991; Apr. 17, 2000, eff. Dec. 1, 2000; Apr. 29, 2002, eff. Dec. 1, 2002; Apr. 25, 2005, eff. Dec. 1, 2005; Apr. 12, 2006, eff. Dec. 1, 2006; Apr. 23, 2008, eff. Dec. 1, 2008; Mar. 26, 2009, eff. Dec. 1, 2009.)

RULE D. POSSESSORY, PETITORY, AND PARTITION ACTIONS

In all actions for possession, partition, and to try title maintainable according to the course of the admiralty practice with respect to a vessel, in all actions so maintainable with respect to the possession of cargo or other maritime property, and in all actions by one or more part owners against the others to obtain security for the return of the vessel from any voyage undertaken without their consent, or by one or more part owners against the others to obtain possession of the vessel for any voyage on giving security for its safe return, the process shall be by a warrant of arrest of the vessel, cargo, or other property, and by notice in the manner provided by Rule B(2) to the adverse party or parties.

(Added Feb. 28, 1966, eff. July 1, 1966.)

RULE E. ACTIONS IN REM AND QUASI IN REM: GENERAL PROVISIONS

(1) Applicability. Except as otherwise provided, this rule applies to actions in personam with process of maritime attachment and garnishment, actions in rem, and petitory, possessory, and partition actions, supplementing Rules B, C, and D.

(2) Complaint; Security.

(a) Complaint. In actions to which this rule is applicable the complaint shall state the circumstances from which the claim arises with such particularity that the defendant or claimant will be able, without moving for a more definite statement, to commence an investigation of the facts and to frame a responsive pleading.

(b) Security for Costs. Subject to the provisions of Rule 54(d) and of relevant statutes, the court may, on the filing of the complaint or on the appearance of any defendant, claimant, or any other party, or at any later time, require the plaintiff, defendant, claimant, or other party to give security, or additional security, in such sum as the court shall direct to pay all costs and expenses that shall be awarded against the party by any interlocutory order or by the final judgment, or on appeal by any appellate court.

(3) Process.

(a) In admiralty and maritime proceedings process in rem or of maritime attachment and garnishment may be served only within the district.

(b) Issuance and Delivery. Issuance and delivery of process in rem, or of maritime attachment and garnishment, shall be held in abeyance if the plaintiff so requests.

(4) Execution of Process; Marshal's Return; Custody of Property; Procedures for Release.

(a) In General. Upon issuance and delivery of the process, or, in the case of summons with process of attachment and garnishment, when it appears that the defendant cannot be found within the district, the marshal or other person or organization having a warrant shall forthwith execute the process in accordance with this subdivision (4), making due and prompt return.

(b) Tangible Property. If tangible property is to be attached or arrested, the marshal or other person or organization having the warrant shall take it into the marshal's possession for safe custody. If the character or situation of the property is such that the taking of actual possession is impracticable, the marshal or other person executing the process shall affix a copy thereof to the property in a conspicuous place and leave a copy of the complaint and process with the person having possession or the person's agent. In furtherance of the marshal's custody of any vessel the marshal is authorized to make a written request to the collector of customs not to grant clearance to such vessel until notified by the marshal or deputy marshal or by the clerk that the vessel has been released in accordance with these rules.

(c) Intangible Property. If intangible property is to be attached or arrested the marshal or other person or organization having the warrant shall execute the process by leaving with the garnishee or other obligor a copy of the complaint and process requiring the garnishee or other obligor to answer as provided in Rules B(3)(a) and C(6); or the marshal may accept for payment into the registry of the court the amount owed to the extent of the amount claimed by the plaintiff with interest and costs, in which event the garnishee or other obligor shall not be required to answer unless alias process shall be served.

(d) Directions With Respect to Property in Custody. The marshal or other person or organization having the warrant may at any time apply to the court for directions with respect to property that has been attached or arrested, and shall give notice of such application to any or all of the parties as the court may direct.

(e) Expenses of Seizing and Keeping Property; Deposit. These rules do not alter the provisions of Title 28, U.S.C., § 1921, as amended, relative to the expenses of seizing and keeping property attached or arrested and to the requirement of deposits to cover such expenses.

(f) Procedure for Release From Arrest or Attachment. Whenever property is arrested or attached, any person claiming an interest in it shall be entitled to a prompt hearing at which the plaintiff shall be required to show why the arrest or attachment should not be vacated or other relief granted consistent with these rules. This subdivision shall have no application to suits for seamen's wages when process is issued upon a certification of sufficient cause filed pursuant to Title 46, U.S.C. §§ 603 and 604 or to actions by the United States for forfeitures for violation of any statute of the United States.

(5) Release of Property.

(a) Special Bond. Whenever process of maritime attachment and garnishment or process in rem is issued the execution of such process shall be stayed, or the property released, on the giving of security, to be approved by the court or clerk, or by stipulation of the parties, conditioned to answer the judgment of the court or of any appellate court. The parties may stipulate the amount and nature of such security. In the event of the inability or refusal of the parties so to stipulate the court shall fix the principal sum of the bond or stipulation at an amount sufficient to cover the amount of the plaintiff's claim fairly stated with accrued interest and costs; but the principal sum shall in no event exceed (i) twice the amount of the plaintiff's claim or (ii) the value of the property on due appraisement, whichever is smaller. The bond or stipulation shall be conditioned for the payment of the principal sum and interest thereon at 6 per cent per annum.

(b) General Bond. The owner of any vessel may file a general bond or stipulation, with sufficient surety, to be approved by the court, conditioned to answer the judgment of such court in all or any actions that may be brought thereafter in such court in which the vessel is attached or arrested. Thereupon the execution of all such process against such vessel shall be stayed so long as the amount secured by such bond or stipulation is at least double the aggregate amount claimed by plaintiffs in all actions begun and pending in which such vessel has been attached or arrested. Judgments and remedies may be had on such bond or stipulation as if a special bond or stipulation had been filed in each of such actions. The district court may make necessary orders to carry this rule into effect, particularly as to the giving of proper notice of any action against or attachment of a vessel for which a general bond has been filed. Such bond or stipulation shall be indorsed by the clerk with a minute of the actions wherein process is so stayed. Further security may be required by the court at any time.

If a special bond or stipulation is given in a particular case, the liability on the general bond or stipulation shall cease as to that case.

(c) Release by Consent or Stipulation; Order of Court or Clerk; Costs. Any vessel, cargo, or other property in the custody of the marshal or other person or organization having the warrant may be released forthwith upon the marshal's acceptance and approval of a stipulation, bond, or other security, signed by the party on whose behalf the property is detained or the party's attorney and expressly authorizing such release, if all costs and charges of the court and its officers shall have first been paid. Otherwise no property in the custody of the marshal, other person or organization having the warrant, or other officer of the court shall be released without an order of the court; but such order may be entered as of course by the clerk, upon the giving of approved security as provided by law and these rules, or upon the dismissal or discontinuance of the action; but the marshal or other person or organization having the warrant shall not deliver any property so released until the costs and charges of the officers of the court shall first have been paid.

(d) Possessory, Petitory, and Partition Actions. The foregoing provisions of this subdivision (5) do not apply to petitory, possessory, and partition actions. In such cases the property arrested shall be released only by order of the court, on such terms and conditions and on the giving of such security as the court may require.

(6) Reduction or Impairment of Security. Whenever security is taken the court may, on motion and hearing, for good cause shown, reduce the amount of security given; and if the surety shall be or become insufficient, new or additional sureties may be required on motion and hearing.

(7) Security on Counterclaim.

(a) When a person who has given security for damages in the original action asserts a counterclaim that arises from the transaction or occurrence that is the subject of the original action, a plaintiff for whose benefit the security has been given must give security for damages demanded in the counterclaim unless the court for cause shown, directs otherwise. Proceedings on the original claim must be stayed until this security is given unless the court directs otherwise.

(b) The plaintiff is required to give security under Rule E(7)(a) when the United States or its corporate instrumentality counterclaims and would have been required to give security to respond in damages if a private party but is relieved by law from giving security.

(8) Restricted Appearance. An appearance to defend against an admiralty and maritime claim with respect to which there has issued process in rem, or process of attachment and garnishment, may be expressly restricted to the defense of such claim, and in that event is not an appearance for the purposes of any other claim with respect to which such process is not available or has not been served.

(9) Disposition of Property; Sales.

(a) Interlocutory Sales; Delivery.

(i) On application of a party, the marshal, or other person having custody of the property, the court may order all or part of the property sold—with the sales proceeds, or as much of them as will satisfy the judgment, paid into court to await further orders of the court—if:

(A) the attached or arrested property is perishable, or liable to deterioration, decay, or injury by being detained in custody pending the action;

(B) the expense of keeping the property is excessive or disproportionate; or

(C) there is an unreasonable delay in securing release of the property.

(ii) In the circumstances described in Rule E(9)(a)(i), the court, on motion by a defendant or a person filing a statement of interest or right under Rule C(6), may order that the property, rather than being sold, be delivered to the movant upon giving security under these rules.

(b) Sales; Proceeds. All sales of property shall be made by the marshal or a deputy marshal, or by other person or organization having the warrant, or by any other person assigned by the court where the marshal or other person or organization having the warrant is a party in interest; and the proceeds of sale shall be forthwith paid into the registry of the court to be disposed of according to law.

(10) Preservation of Property. When the owner or another person remains in possession of property attached or arrested under the provisions of Rule E(4)(b) that permit execution of process without taking actual possession, the court, on a party's motion or on its own, may enter any order necessary to preserve the property and to prevent its removal.

(Added Feb. 28, 1966, eff. July 1, 1966; amended Apr. 29, 1985, eff. Aug. 1, 1985; Mar. 2, 1987, eff. Aug. 1, 1987; Apr. 30, 1991, eff. Dec. 1, 1991; Apr. 17, 2000, eff. Dec. 1, 2000; Apr. 12, 2006, eff. Dec. 1, 2006.)

RULE F. LIMITATION OF LIABILITY

(1) **Time for Filing Complaint; Security.** Not later than six months after receipt of a claim in writing, any vessel owner may file a complaint in the appropriate district court, as provided in subdivision (9) of this rule, for limitation of liability pursuant to statute. The owner (a) shall deposit with the court, for the benefit of claimants, a sum equal to the amount or value of the owner's interest in the vessel and pending freight, or approved security therefor, and in addition such sums, or approved security therefor, as the court may from time to time fix as necessary to carry out the provisions of the statutes as amended; or (b) at the owner's option shall transfer to a trustee to be appointed by the court, for the benefit of claimants, the owner's interest in the vessel and pending freight, together with such sums, or approved security therefor, as the court may from time to time fix as necessary to carry out the provisions of the statutes as amended. The plaintiff shall also give security for costs and, if the plaintiff elects to give security, for interest at the rate of 6 percent per annum from the date of the security.

(2) **Complaint.** The complaint shall set forth the facts on the basis of which the right to limit liability is asserted and all facts necessary to enable the court to determine the amount to which the owner's liability shall be limited. The complaint may demand exoneration from as well as limitation of liability. It shall state the voyage if any, on which the demands sought to be limited arose, with the date and place of its termination; the amount of all demands including all unsatisfied liens or claims of lien, in contract or in tort or otherwise, arising on that voyage, so far as known to the plaintiff, and what actions and proceedings, if any, are pending thereon; whether the vessel was damaged, lost, or abandoned, and, if so, when and where; the value of the vessel at the close of the voyage or, in case of wreck, the value of her wreckage, strippings, or proceeds, if any, and where and in whose possession they are; and the amount of any pending freight recovered or recoverable. If the plaintiff elects to transfer the plaintiff's interest in the vessel to a trustee, the complaint must further show any prior paramount liens thereon, and what voyages or trips, if any, she has made since the voyage or trip on which the claims sought to be limited arose, and any existing liens arising upon any such subsequent voyage or trip, with the amounts and causes thereof, and the names and addresses of the lienors, so far as known; and whether the vessel sustained any injury upon or by reason of such subsequent voyage or trip.

(3) **Claims Against Owner; Injunction.** Upon compliance by the owner with the requirements of subdivision (1) of this rule all claims and proceedings against the owner or the owner's property with respect to the matter in question shall cease. On application of the plaintiff the court shall enjoin the further prosecution of any action or proceeding against the plaintiff or the plaintiff's property with respect to any claim subject to limitation in the action.

(4) **Notice to Claimants.** Upon the owner's compliance with subdivision (1) of this rule the court shall issue a notice to all persons asserting claims with respect to which the complaint seeks limitation, admonishing them to file their respective claims with the clerk of the court and to serve on the attorneys for the plaintiff a copy thereof on or before a date to be named in the notice. The date so fixed shall be not less than 30 days after issuance of the notice. For cause shown, the court may enlarge the time within which claims may be filed. The notice shall be published in such newspaper or newspapers as the court may direct once a week for four successive weeks prior to the date fixed for the filing of claims. The plaintiff not later than the day of second publication shall also mail a copy of the notice to every person known to have made any claim against the vessel or the plaintiff arising out of the voyage or trip on which the claims sought to be limited arose. In cases involving death a copy of such notice shall be mailed to the decedent at the decedent's last known address, and also to any person who shall be known to have made any claim on account of such death.

(5) **Claims and Answer.** Claims shall be filed and served on or before the date specified in the notice provided for in subdivision (4) of this rule. Each claim shall specify the facts upon which the claimant relies in support of the claim, the items thereof, and the dates on which the same accrued. If a claimant desires to contest either the right to exoneration from or the right to limitation of liability the claimant shall file and serve an answer to the complaint unless the claim has included an answer.

(6) **Information to be Given Claimants.** Within 30 days after the date specified in the notice for filing claims, or within such time as the court thereafter may allow, the plaintiff shall mail to the attorney for each claimant (or if the claimant has no attorney to the claimant) a list setting forth (a) the name of each claimant, (b) the name and address of the claimant's attorney (if the claimant is known to have one), (c) the nature of the claim, i.e., whether property loss, property damage, death, personal injury etc., and (d) the amount thereof.

(7) **Insufficiency of Fund or Security.** Any claimant may by motion demand that the funds deposited in court or the security given by the plaintiff be increased on the ground that they are less than the value of the plaintiff's interest in the vessel and pending freight. Thereupon the court shall cause due appraisement to be made of the value of the plaintiff's interest in the vessel and pending freight; and if the court finds that the deposit or security is either insufficient or excessive it shall order its increase or reduction. In like manner any claimant may demand that the deposit or security be increased on the ground that it is insufficient to carry out the provisions of the statutes relating to claims in respect of loss of life or bodily injury; and, after notice and hearing, the court may similarly order that the deposit or security be increased or reduced.

(8) **Objections to Claims: Distribution of Fund.** Any interested party may question or controvert any claim without filing an objection thereto. Upon determination of liability the fund deposited or secured, or the proceeds of the vessel and pending freight, shall be divided pro rata, subject to all relevant provisions of law, among the several claimants in

proportion to the amounts of their respective claims, duly proved, saving, however, to all parties any priority to which they may be legally entitled.

(9) Venue; Transfer. The complaint shall be filed in any district in which the vessel has been attached or arrested to answer for any claim with respect to which the plaintiff seeks to limit liability; or, if the vessel has not been attached or arrested, then in any district in which the owner has been sued with respect to any such claim. When the vessel has not been attached or arrested to answer the matters aforesaid, and suit has not been commenced against the owner, the proceedings may be had in the district in which the vessel may be, but if the vessel is not within any district and no suit has been commenced in any district, then the complaint may be filed in any district. For the convenience of parties and witnesses, in the interest of justice, the court may transfer the action to any district; if venue is wrongly laid the court shall dismiss or, if it be in the interest of justice, transfer the action to any district in which it could have been brought. If the vessel shall have been sold, the proceeds shall represent the vessel for the purposes of these rules.

(Added Feb. 28, 1966, eff. July 1, 1966; amended Mar. 2, 1987, eff. Aug. 1, 1987.)

RULE G.   FORFEITURE ACTIONS IN REM

(1) Scope. This rule governs a forfeiture action in rem arising from a federal statute. To the extent that this rule does not address an issue, Supplemental Rules C and E and the Federal Rules of Civil Procedure also apply.

(2) Complaint. The complaint must:

(a) be verified;

(b) state the grounds for subject-matter jurisdiction, in rem jurisdiction over the defendant property, and venue;

(c) describe the property with reasonable particularity;

(d) if the property is tangible, state its location when any seizure occurred and—if different—its location when the action is filed;

(e) identify the statute under which the forfeiture action is brought; and

(f) state sufficiently detailed facts to support a reasonable belief that the government will be able to meet its burden of proof at trial.

(3) Judicial Authorization and Process.

(a) Real Property. If the defendant is real property, the government must proceed under 18 U.S.C. § 985.

(b) Other Property; Arrest Warrant. If the defendant is not real property:

(i) the clerk must issue a warrant to arrest the property if it is in the government's possession, custody, or control;

(ii) the court—on finding probable cause—must issue a warrant to arrest the property if it is not in the government's possession, custody, or control and is not subject to a judicial restraining order; and

(iii) a warrant is not necessary if the property is subject to a judicial restraining order.

(c) Execution of Process.

(i) The warrant and any supplemental process must be delivered to a person or organization authorized to execute it, who may be: (A) a marshal or any other United States officer or employee; (B) someone under contract with the United States; or (C) someone specially appointed by the court for that purpose.

(ii) The authorized person or organization must execute the warrant and any supplemental process on property in the United States as soon as practicable unless:

(A) the property is in the government's possession, custody, or control; or

(B) the court orders a different time when the complaint is under seal, the action is stayed before the warrant and supplemental process are executed, or the court finds other good cause.

(iii) The warrant and any supplemental process may be executed within the district or, when authorized by statute, outside the district.

(iv) If executing a warrant on property outside the United States is required, the warrant may be transmitted to an appropriate authority for serving process where the property is located.

(4) Notice.

(a) Notice by Publication.

(i) When Publication Is Required. A judgment of forfeiture may be entered only if the government has published notice of the action within a reasonable time after filing the complaint or at a time the court orders. But notice need not be published if:

(A) the defendant property is worth less than $1,000 and direct notice is sent under Rule G(4)(b) to every person the government can reasonably identify as a potential claimant; or

(B) the court finds that the cost of publication exceeds the property's value and that other means of notice would satisfy due process.

(ii) Content of the Notice. Unless the court orders otherwise, the notice must:

(A) describe the property with reasonable particularity;

(B) state the times under Rule G(5) to file a claim and to answer; and

(C) name the government attorney to be served with the claim and answer.

(iii) Frequency of Publication. Published notice must appear:

(A) once a week for three consecutive weeks; or

(B) only once if, before the action was filed, notice of nonjudicial forfeiture of the same property was published on an official internet government forfeiture site for at least 30 consecutive days, or in a newspaper of general circulation for three consecutive weeks in a district where publication is authorized under Rule G(4)(a)(iv).

(iv) Means of Publication. The government should select from the following options a means of publication reasonably calculated to notify potential claimants of the action:

(A) if the property is in the United States, publication in a newspaper generally circulated in the district where the action is filed, where the property was seized, or where property that was not seized is located;

(B) if the property is outside the United States, publication in a newspaper generally circulated in a district where the action is filed, in a newspaper generally circulated in the country where the property is located, or in legal notices published and generally circulated in the country where the property is located; or

(C) instead of (A) or (B), posting a notice on an official internet government forfeiture site for at least 30 consecutive days.

(b) Notice to Known Potential Claimants.

(i) Direct Notice Required. The government must send notice of the action and a copy of the complaint to any person who reasonably appears to be a potential claimant on the facts known to the government before the end of the time for filing a claim under Rule G(5)(a)(ii)(B).

(ii) Content of the Notice. The notice must state:

(A) the date when the notice is sent;

(B) a deadline for filing a claim, at least 35 days after the notice is sent;

(C) that an answer or a motion under Rule 12 must be filed no later than 21 days after filing the claim; and

(D) the name of the government attorney to be served with the claim and answer.

(iii) Sending Notice.

(A) The notice must be sent by means reasonably calculated to reach the potential claimant.

(B) Notice may be sent to the potential claimant or to the attorney representing the potential claimant with respect to the seizure of the property or in a related investigation, administrative forfeiture proceeding, or criminal case.

(C) Notice sent to a potential claimant who is incarcerated must be sent to the place of incarceration.

(D) Notice to a person arrested in connection with an offense giving rise to the forfeiture who is not incarcerated when notice is sent may be sent to the address that person last gave to the agency that arrested or released the person.

(E) Notice to a person from whom the property was seized who is not incarcerated when notice is sent may be sent to the last address that person gave to the agency that seized the property.

(iv) When Notice Is Sent. Notice by the following means is sent on the date when it is placed in the mail,

delivered to a commercial carrier, or sent by electronic mail.

(v) Actual Notice. A potential claimant who had actual notice of a forfeiture action may not oppose or seek relief from forfeiture because of the government's failure to send the required notice.

(5) Responsive Pleadings.

(a) Filing a Claim.

(i) A person who asserts an interest in the defendant property may contest the forfeiture by filing a claim in the court where the action is pending. The claim must:

(A) identify the specific property claimed;

(B) identify the claimant and state the claimant's interest in the property;

(C) be signed by the claimant under penalty of perjury; and

(D) be served on the government attorney designated under Rule G(4)(a)(ii)(C) or (b)(ii)(D).

(ii) Unless the court for good cause sets a different time, the claim must be filed:

(A) by the time stated in a direct notice sent under Rule G(4)(b);

(B) if notice was published but direct notice was not sent to the claimant or the claimant's attorney, no later than 30 days after final publication of newspaper notice or legal notice under Rule G(4)(a) or no later than 60 days after the first day of publication on an official internet government forfeiture site; or

(C) if notice was not published and direct notice was not sent to the claimant or the claimant's attorney:

(1) if the property was in the government's possession, custody, or control when the complaint was filed, no later than 60 days after the filing, not counting any time when the complaint was under seal or when the action was stayed before execution of a warrant issued under Rule G(3)(b); or

(2) if the property was not in the government's possession, custody, or control when the complaint was filed, no later than 60 days after the government complied with 18 U.S.C. § 985(c) as to real property, or 60 days after process was executed on the property under Rule G(3).

(iii) A claim filed by a person asserting an interest as a bailee must identify the bailor, and if filed on the bailor's behalf must state the authority to do so.

(b) Answer. A claimant must serve and file an answer to the complaint or a motion under Rule 12 within 21 days after filing the claim. A claimant waives an objection to in rem jurisdiction or to venue if the objection is not made by motion or stated in the answer.

(6) Special Interrogatories.

(a) Time and Scope. The government may serve special interrogatories limited to the claimant's identity and relationship to the defendant property without the court's leave at any time after the claim is filed and before discovery is closed. But if the claimant serves a motion to dismiss the action, the government must serve the interrogatories within 21 days after the motion is served.

(b) Answers or Objections. Answers or objections to these interrogatories must be served within 21 days after the interrogatories are served.

(c) Government's Response Deferred. The government need not respond to a claimant's motion to dismiss the action under Rule G(8)(b) until 21 days after the claimant has answered these interrogatories.

(7) Preserving, Preventing Criminal Use, and Disposing of Property; Sales.

(a) Preserving and Preventing Criminal Use of Property. When the government does not have actual possession of the defendant property the court, on motion or on its own, may enter any order necessary to preserve the property, to prevent its removal or encumbrance, or to prevent its use in a criminal offense.

(b) Interlocutory Sale or Delivery.

(i) Order to Sell. On motion by a party or a person having custody of the property, the court may order all or part of the property sold if:

(A) the property is perishable or at risk of deterioration, decay, or injury by being detained in custody pending the action;

(B) the expense of keeping the property is excessive or is disproportionate to its fair market value;

(C) the property is subject to a mortgage or to taxes on which the owner is in default; or

(D) the court finds other good cause.

(ii) Who Makes the Sale. A sale must be made by a United States agency that has authority to sell the property, by the agency's contractor, or by any person the court designates.

(iii) Sale Procedures. The sale is governed by 28 U.S.C. §§ 2001, 2002, and 2004, unless all parties, with the court's approval, agree to the sale, aspects of the sale, or different procedures.

(iv) Sale Proceeds. Sale proceeds are a substitute res subject to forfeiture in place of the property that was sold. The proceeds must be held in an interest-bearing account maintained by the United States pending the conclusion of the forfeiture action.

(v) Delivery on a Claimant's Motion. The court may order that the property be delivered to the claimant pending the conclusion of the action if the claimant shows circumstances that would permit sale under Rule G(7)(b)(i) and gives security under these rules.

(c) Disposing of Forfeited Property. Upon entry of a forfeiture judgment, the property or proceeds from selling the property must be disposed of as provided by law.

(8) Motions.

(a) Motion To Suppress Use of the Property as Evidence. If the defendant property was seized, a party with standing to contest the lawfulness of the seizure may move to suppress use of the property as evidence. Suppression does not affect forfeiture of the property based on independently derived evidence.

(b) Motion To Dismiss the Action.

(i) A claimant who establishes standing to contest forfeiture may move to dismiss the action under Rule 12(b).

(ii) In an action governed by 18 U.S.C. § 983(a)(3)(D) the complaint may not be dismissed on the ground that the government did not have adequate evidence at the time the complaint was filed to establish the forfeitability of the property. The sufficiency of the complaint is governed by Rule G(2).

(c) Motion To Strike a Claim or Answer.

(i) At any time before trial, the government may move to strike a claim or answer:

(A) for failing to comply with Rule G(5) or (6), or

(B) because the claimant lacks standing.

(ii) The motion:

(A) must be decided before any motion by the claimant to dismiss the action; and

(B) may be presented as a motion for judgment on the pleadings or as a motion to determine after a hearing or by summary judgment whether the claimant can carry the burden of establishing standing by a preponderance of the evidence.

(d) Petition To Release Property.

(i) If a United States agency or an agency's contractor holds property for judicial or nonjudicial forfeiture under a statute governed by 18 U.S.C. § 983(f), a person who has filed a claim to the property may petition for its release under § 983(f).

(ii) If a petition for release is filed before a judicial forfeiture action is filed against the property, the petition may be filed either in the district where the property was seized or in the district where a warrant to seize the property issued. If a judicial forfeiture action against the property is later filed in another district—or if the government shows that the action will be filed in another district—the petition may be transferred to that district under 28 U.S.C. § 1404.

(e) Excessive Fines. A claimant may seek to mitigate a forfeiture under the Excessive Fines Clause of the Eighth Amendment by motion for summary judgment or by motion made after entry of a forfeiture judgment if:

(i) the claimant has pleaded the defense under Rule 8; and

(ii) the parties have had the opportunity to conduct civil discovery on the defense.

(9) Trial. Trial is to the court unless any party demands trial by jury under Rule 38.

(Added Apr. 12, 2006, eff. Dec. 1, 2006; amended Mar. 26, 2009, eff. Dec. 1, 2009.)

INDEX TO
FEDERAL RULES OF CIVIL PROCEDURE

FEDERAL RULES OF EVIDENCE

Including Amendments Effective December 1, 2017

ARTICLE I. GENERAL PROVISIONS

RULE 101. SCOPE; DEFINITIONS

(a) **Scope.** These rules apply to proceedings in United States courts. The specific courts and proceedings to which the rules apply, along with exceptions, are set out in Rule 1101.

(b) **Definitions.** In these rules:

(1) "civil case" means a civil action or proceeding;

(2) "criminal case" includes a criminal proceeding;

(3) "public office" includes a public agency;

(4) "record" includes a memorandum, report, or data compilation;

(5) a "rule prescribed by the Supreme Court" means a rule adopted by the Supreme Court under statutory authority; and

(6) a reference to any kind of written material or any other medium includes electronically stored information.

(Pub.L. 93–595, § 1, Jan. 2, 1975, 88 Stat. 1929; Mar. 2, 1987, eff. Oct. 1, 1987; Apr. 25, 1988, eff. Nov. 1, 1988; Apr. 22, 1993, eff. Dec. 1, 1993; Apr. 26, 2011, eff. Dec. 1, 2011.)

RULE 102. PURPOSE

These rules should be construed so as to administer every proceeding fairly, eliminate unjustifiable expense and delay, and promote the development of evidence law, to the end of ascertaining the truth and securing a just determination.

(Pub.L. 93–595, § 1, Jan. 2, 1975, 88 Stat.1929; Apr. 26, 2011, eff. Dec. 1, 2011.)

RULE 103. RULINGS ON EVIDENCE

(a) **Preserving a Claim of Error.** A party may claim error in a ruling to admit or exclude evidence only if the error affects a substantial right of the party and:

(1) if the ruling admits evidence, a party, on the record:

(A) timely objects or moves to strike; and

(B) states the specific ground, unless it was apparent from the context; or

(2) if the ruling excludes evidence, a party informs the court of its substance by an offer of proof, unless the substance was apparent from the context.

(b) **Not Needing to Renew an Objection or Offer of Proof.** Once the court rules definitively on the record—either before or at trial—a party need not renew an objection or offer of proof to preserve a claim of error for appeal.

(c) **Court's Statement About the Ruling; Directing an Offer of Proof.** The court may make any statement about the character or form of the evidence, the objection made, and the ruling. The court may direct that an offer of proof be made in question-and-answer form.

(d) **Preventing the Jury from Hearing Inadmissible Evidence.** To the extent practicable, the court must conduct a jury trial so that inadmissible evidence is not suggested to the jury by any means.

(e) **Taking Notice of Plain Error.** A court may take notice of a plain error affecting a substantial right, even if the claim of error was not properly preserved.

(Pub.L. 93–595, § 1, Jan. 2, 1975, 88 Stat. 1929; Apr. 17, 2000, eff. Dec. 1, 2000; Apr. 26, 2011, eff. Dec. 1, 2011.)

RULE 104. PRELIMINARY QUESTIONS

(a) **In General.** The court must decide any preliminary question about whether a witness is qualified, a privilege exists, or evidence is admissible. In so deciding, the court is not bound by evidence rules, except those on privilege.

(b) **Relevance That Depends on a Fact.** When the relevance of evidence depends on whether a fact exists, proof must be introduced sufficient to support a finding that the fact does exist. The court may admit the proposed evidence on the condition that the proof be introduced later.

(c) **Conducting a Hearing So That the Jury Cannot Hear It.** The court must conduct any hearing on a preliminary question so that the jury cannot hear it if:

(1) the hearing involves the admissibility of a confession;

(2) a defendant in a criminal case is a witness and so requests; or

(3) justice so requires.

(d) **Cross–Examining a Defendant in a Criminal Case.** By testifying on a preliminary question, a defendant in a criminal case does not become subject to cross-examination on other issues in the case.

(e) **Evidence Relevant to Weight and Credibility.** This rule does not limit a party's right to introduce before the jury evidence that is relevant to the weight or credibility of other evidence.

(Pub.L. 93–595, § 1, Jan. 2, 1975, 88 Stat.1930; Mar. 2, 1987, eff. Oct. 1, 1987; Apr. 26, 2011, eff. Dec. 1, 2011.)

RULE 105. LIMITING EVIDENCE THAT IS NOT ADMISSIBLE AGAINST OTHER PARTIES OR FOR OTHER PURPOSES

If the court admits evidence that is admissible against a party or for a purpose—but not against another party or for another purpose—the court, on timely request, must restrict the evidence to its proper scope and instruct the jury accordingly.

(Pub.L. 93–595, § 1, Jan. 2, 1975, 88 Stat. 1930; Apr. 26, 2011, eff. Dec. 1, 2011.)

RULE 106.   REMAINDER OF OR RELATED WRITINGS OR RECORDED STATEMENTS

If a party introduces all or part of a writing or recorded statement, an adverse party may require the introduction, at that time, of any other part—or any other writing or recorded statement—that in fairness ought to be considered at the same time.

(Pub.L. 93–595, § 1, Jan. 2, 1975, 88 Stat. 1930; Mar. 2, 1987, eff. Oct. 1, 1987; Apr. 26, 2011, eff. Dec. 1, 2011.)

ARTICLE II.   JUDICIAL NOTICE

RULE 201.   JUDICIAL NOTICE OF ADJUDICATIVE FACTS

(a) **Scope.** This rule governs judicial notice of an adjudicative fact only, not a legislative fact.

(b) **Kinds of Facts That May Be Judicially Noticed.** The court may judicially notice a fact that is not subject to reasonable dispute because it:

(1) is generally known within the trial court's territorial jurisdiction; or

(2) can be accurately and readily determined from sources whose accuracy cannot reasonably be questioned.

(c) **Taking Notice.** The court:

(1) may take judicial notice on its own; or

(2) must take judicial notice if a party requests it and the court is supplied with the necessary information.

(d) **Timing.** The court may take judicial notice at any stage of the proceeding.

(e) **Opportunity to Be Heard.** On timely request, a party is entitled to be heard on the propriety of taking judicial notice and the nature of the fact to be noticed. If the court takes judicial notice before notifying a party, the party, on request, is still entitled to be heard.

(f) **Instructing the Jury.** In a civil case, the court must instruct the jury to accept the noticed fact as conclusive. In a criminal case, the court must instruct the jury that it may or may not accept the noticed fact as conclusive.

(Pub.L. 93–595, § 1, Jan. 2, 1975, 88 Stat. 1930; Apr. 26, 2011, eff. Dec. 1, 2011.)

ARTICLE III.   PRESUMPTIONS IN CIVIL CASES

RULE 301.   PRESUMPTIONS IN CIVIL CASES GENERALLY

In a civil case, unless a federal statute or these rules provide otherwise, the party against whom a presumption is directed has the burden of producing evidence to rebut the presumption. But this rule does not shift the burden of persuasion, which remains on the party who had it originally.

(Pub.L. 93–595, § 1, Jan. 2, 1975, 88 Stat. 1931; Apr. 26, 2011, eff. Dec. 1, 2011.)

RULE 302.   APPLYING STATE LAW TO PRESUMPTIONS IN CIVIL CASES

In a civil case, state law governs the effect of a presumption regarding a claim or defense for which state law supplies the rule of decision.

(Pub.L. 93–595, § 1, Jan. 2, 1975, 88 Stat. 1931; Apr. 26, 2011, eff. Dec. 1, 2011.)

ARTICLE IV.   RELEVANCE AND ITS LIMITS

RULE 401.   TEST FOR RELEVANT EVIDENCE

Evidence is relevant if:

(a) it has any tendency to make a fact more or less probable than it would be without the evidence; and

(b) the fact is of consequence in determining the action.

(Pub.L. 93–595, § 1, Jan. 2, 1975, 88 Stat.1931; Apr. 26, 2011, eff. Dec. 1, 2011.)

RULE 402.   GENERAL ADMISSIBILITY OF RELEVANT EVIDENCE

Relevant evidence is admissible unless any of the following provides otherwise:

● the United States Constitution;

● a federal statute;

● these rules; or

● other rules prescribed by the Supreme Court.

Irrelevant evidence is not admissible.

(Pub.L. 93–595, § 1, Jan. 2, 1975, 88 Stat. 1931; Apr. 26, 2011, eff. Dec. 1, 2011.)

RULE 403.   EXCLUDING RELEVANT EVIDENCE FOR PREJUDICE, CONFUSION, WASTE OF TIME, OR OTHER REASONS

The court may exclude relevant evidence if its probative value is substantially outweighed by a danger of one or more of the following: unfair prejudice, confusing the issues, misleading the jury, undue delay, wasting time, or needlessly presenting cumulative evidence.

(Pub.L. 93–595, § 1, Jan. 2, 1975, 88 Stat. 1932; Apr. 26, 2011, eff. Dec. 1, 2011.)

RULE 404. CHARACTER EVIDENCE; CRIMES OR OTHER ACTS

(a) Character Evidence.

(1) Prohibited Uses. Evidence of a person's character or character trait is not admissible to prove that on a particular occasion the person acted in accordance with the character or trait.

(2) Exceptions for a Defendant or Victim in a Criminal Case. The following exceptions apply in a criminal case:

(A) a defendant may offer evidence of the defendant's pertinent trait, and if the evidence is admitted, the prosecutor may offer evidence to rebut it;

(B) subject to the limitations in Rule 412, a defendant may offer evidence of an alleged victim's pertinent trait, and if the evidence is admitted, the prosecutor may:

(i) offer evidence to rebut it; and

(ii) offer evidence of the defendant's same trait; and

(C) in a homicide case, the prosecutor may offer evidence of the alleged victim's trait of peacefulness to rebut evidence that the victim was the first aggressor.

(3) Exceptions for a Witness. Evidence of a witness's character may be admitted under Rules 607, 608, and 609.

(b) Crimes, Wrongs, or Other Acts.

(1) Prohibited Uses. Evidence of a crime, wrong, or other act is not admissible to prove a person's character in order to show that on a particular occasion the person acted in accordance with the character.

(2) Permitted Uses; Notice in a Criminal Case. This evidence may be admissible for another purpose, such as proving motive, opportunity, intent, preparation, plan, knowledge, identity, absence of mistake, or lack of accident. On request by a defendant in a criminal case, the prosecutor must:

(A) provide reasonable notice of the general nature of any such evidence that the prosecutor intends to offer at trial; and

(B) do so before trial—or during trial if the court, for good cause, excuses lack of pretrial notice.

(Pub.L. 93–595, § 1, Jan. 2, 1975, 88 Stat.1932; Mar. 2, 1987, eff. Oct. 1, 1987; Apr. 30, 1991, eff. Dec. 1, 1991; Apr. 17, 2000, eff. Dec. 1, 2000; Apr. 12, 2006, eff. Dec. 1, 2006; Apr. 26, 2011, eff. Dec. 1, 2011.)

RULE 405. METHODS OF PROVING CHARACTER

(a) By Reputation or Opinion. When evidence of a person's character or character trait is admissible, it may be proved by testimony about the person's reputation or by testimony in the form of an opinion. On cross-examination of the character witness, the court may allow an inquiry into relevant specific instances of the person's conduct.

(b) By Specific Instances of Conduct. When a person's character or character trait is an essential element of a charge, claim, or defense, the character or trait may also be proved by relevant specific instances of the person's conduct.

(Pub.L. 93–595, § 1, Jan. 2, 1975, 88 Stat. 1932; Mar. 2, 1987, eff. Oct. 1, 1987; Apr. 26, 2011, eff. Dec. 1, 2011.)

RULE 406. HABIT; ROUTINE PRACTICE

Evidence of a person's habit or an organization's routine practice may be admitted to prove that on a particular occasion the person or organization acted in accordance with the habit or routine practice. The court may admit this evidence regardless of whether it is corroborated or whether there was an eyewitness.

(Pub.L. 93–595, § 1, Jan. 2, 1975, 88 Stat. 1932; Apr. 26, 2011, eff. Dec. 1, 2011.)

RULE 407. SUBSEQUENT REMEDIAL MEASURES

When measures are taken that would have made an earlier injury or harm less likely to occur, evidence of the subsequent measures is not admissible to prove:

- negligence;
- culpable conduct;
- a defect in a product or its design; or
- a need for a warning or instruction.

But the court may admit this evidence for another purpose, such as impeachment or—if disputed—proving ownership, control, or the feasibility of precautionary measures.

(Pub.L. 93–595, § 1, Jan. 2, 1975, 88 Stat. 1932; Apr. 11, 1997, eff. Dec. 1, 1997; Apr. 26, 2011, eff. Dec. 1, 2011.)

RULE 408. COMPROMISE OFFERS AND NEGOTIATIONS

(a) Prohibited Uses. Evidence of the following is not admissible—on behalf of any party—either to prove or disprove the validity or amount of a disputed claim or to impeach by a prior inconsistent statement or a contradiction:

(1) furnishing, promising, or offering—or accepting, promising to accept, or offering to accept—a valuable consideration in compromising or attempting to compromise the claim; and

(2) conduct or a statement made during compromise negotiations about the claim—except when offered in a criminal case and when the negotiations related to a claim by a public office in the exercise of its regulatory, investigative, or enforcement authority.

(b) Exceptions. The court may admit this evidence for another purpose, such as proving a witness's bias or prejudice, negating a contention of undue delay, or proving an effort to obstruct a criminal investigation or prosecution.

(Pub.L. 93–595, § 1, Jan. 2, 1975, 88 Stat. 1933; Apr. 12, 2006, eff. Dec. 1, 2006; Apr. 26, 2011, eff. Dec. 1, 2011.)

RULE 409. OFFERS TO PAY MEDICAL AND SIMILAR EXPENSES

Evidence of furnishing, promising to pay, or offering to pay medical, hospital, or similar expenses resulting from an injury is not admissible to prove liability for the injury.

(Pub.L. 93–595, § 1, Jan. 2, 1975, 88 Stat.1933; Apr. 26, 2011, eff. Dec. 1, 2011.)

RULE 410. PLEAS, PLEA DISCUSSIONS, AND RELATED STATEMENTS

(a) **Prohibited Uses.** In a civil or criminal case, evidence of the following is not admissible against the defendant who made the plea or participated in the plea discussions:

(1) a guilty plea that was later withdrawn;

(2) a nolo contendere plea;

(3) a statement made during a proceeding on either of those pleas under Federal Rule of Criminal Procedure 11 or a comparable state procedure; or

(4) a statement made during plea discussions with an attorney for the prosecuting authority if the discussions did not result in a guilty plea or they resulted in a later-withdrawn guilty plea.

(b) **Exceptions.** The court may admit a statement described in Rule 410(a)(3) or (4):

(1) in any proceeding in which another statement made during the same plea or plea discussions has been introduced, if in fairness the statements ought to be considered together; or

(2) in a criminal proceeding for perjury or false statement, if the defendant made the statement under oath, on the record, and with counsel present.

(Pub.L. 93–595, § 1, Jan. 2, 1975, 88 Stat. 1933; Pub.L. 94–149, § 1(9), Dec. 12, 1975, 89 Stat. 805; Apr. 30, 1979, eff. Dec. 1, 1980; Apr. 26, 2011, eff. Dec. 1, 2011.)

RULE 411. LIABILITY INSURANCE

Evidence that a person was or was not insured against liability is not admissible to prove whether the person acted negligently or otherwise wrongfully. But the court may admit this evidence for another purpose, such as proving a witness's bias or prejudice or proving agency, ownership, or control.

(Pub.L. 93–595, § 1, Jan. 2, 1975, 88 Stat.1933; Mar. 2, 1987, eff. Oct. 1, 1987; Apr. 26, 2011, eff. Dec. 1, 2011.)

RULE 412. SEX–OFFENSE CASES: THE VICTIM'S SEXUAL BEHAVIOR OR PREDISPOSITION

(a) **Prohibited Uses.** The following evidence is not admissible in a civil or criminal proceeding involving alleged sexual misconduct:

(1) evidence offered to prove that a victim engaged in other sexual behavior; or

(2) evidence offered to prove a victim's sexual predisposition.

(b) **Exceptions.**

(1) **Criminal Cases.** The court may admit the following evidence in a criminal case:

(A) evidence of specific instances of a victim's sexual behavior, if offered to prove that someone other than the defendant was the source of semen, injury, or other physical evidence;

(B) evidence of specific instances of a victim's sexual behavior with respect to the person accused of the sexual misconduct, if offered by the defendant to prove consent or if offered by the prosecutor; and

(C) evidence whose exclusion would violate the defendant's constitutional rights.

(2) **Civil Cases.** In a civil case, the court may admit evidence offered to prove a victim's sexual behavior or sexual predisposition if its probative value substantially outweighs the danger of harm to any victim and of unfair prejudice to any party. The court may admit evidence of a victim's reputation only if the victim has placed it in controversy.

(c) **Procedure to Determine Admissibility.**

(1) **Motion.** If a party intends to offer evidence under Rule 412(b), the party must:

(A) file a motion that specifically describes the evidence and states the purpose for which it is to be offered;

(B) do so at least 14 days before trial unless the court, for good cause, sets a different time;

(C) serve the motion on all parties; and

(D) notify the victim or, when appropriate, the victim's guardian or representative.

(2) **Hearing.** Before admitting evidence under this rule, the court must conduct an in camera hearing and give the victim and parties a right to attend and be heard. Unless the court orders otherwise, the motion, related materials, and the record of the hearing must be and remain sealed.

(d) **Definition of "Victim."** In this rule, "victim" includes an alleged victim.

(Added Pub.L. 95–540, § 2(a), Oct. 28, 1978, 92 Stat. 2046; amended Pub.L. 100–690, Title VII, § 7046(a), Nov. 18, 1988, 102 Stat. 4400; Apr. 29, 1994, eff. Dec. 1, 1994; Pub.L. 103–322, Title IV, § 40141(b), Sept. 13, 1994, 108 Stat. 1919; Apr. 26, 2011, eff. Dec. 1, 2011.)

RULE 413. SIMILAR CRIMES IN SEXUAL–ASSAULT CASES

(a) **Permitted Uses.** In a criminal case in which a defendant is accused of a sexual assault, the court may admit evidence that the defendant committed any other sexual assault. The evidence may be considered on any matter to which it is relevant.

(b) **Disclosure to the Defendant.** If the prosecutor intends to offer this evidence, the prosecutor must disclose it to the defendant, including witnesses' statements or a summary of the expected testimony. The prosecutor must do so at least 15 days before trial or at a later time that the court allows for good cause.

(c) Effect on Other Rules. This rule does not limit the admission or consideration of evidence under any other rule.

(d) Definition of "Sexual Assault." In this rule and Rule 415, "sexual assault" means a crime under federal law or under state law (as "state" is defined in 18 U.S.C. § 513) involving:

(1) any conduct prohibited by 18 U.S.C. chapter 109A;

(2) contact, without consent, between any part of the defendant's body—or an object—and another person's genitals or anus;

(3) contact, without consent, between the defendant's genitals or anus and any part of another person's body;

(4) deriving sexual pleasure or gratification from inflicting death, bodily injury, or physical pain on another person; or

(5) an attempt or conspiracy to engage in conduct described in subparagraphs (1)–(4).

(Added Pub.L. 103–322, Title XXXII, § 320935(a), Sept. 13, 1994, 108 Stat. 2136; Apr. 26, 2011, eff. Dec. 1, 2011.)

RULE 414. SIMILAR CRIMES IN CHILD–MOLESTATION CASES

(a) Permitted Uses. In a criminal case in which a defendant is accused of child molestation, the court may admit evidence that the defendant committed any other child molestation. The evidence may be considered on any matter to which it is relevant.

(b) Disclosure to the Defendant. If the prosecutor intends to offer this evidence, the prosecutor must disclose it to the defendant, including witnesses' statements or a summary of the expected testimony. The prosecutor must do so at least 15 days before trial or at a later time that the court allows for good cause.

(c) Effect on Other Rules. This rule does not limit the admission or consideration of evidence under any other rule.

(d) Definition of "Child" and "Child Molestation." In this rule and Rule 415:

(1) "child" means a person below the age of 14; and

(2) "child molestation" means a crime under federal law or under state law (as "state" is defined in 18 U.S.C. § 513) involving:

(A) any conduct prohibited by 18 U.S.C. chapter 109A and committed with a child;

(B) any conduct prohibited by 18 U.S.C. chapter 110;

(C) contact between any part of the defendant's body—or an object—and a child's genitals or anus;

(D) contact between the defendant's genitals or anus and any part of a child's body;

(E) deriving sexual pleasure or gratification from inflicting death, bodily injury, or physical pain on a child; or

(F) an attempt or conspiracy to engage in conduct described in subparagraphs (A)–(E).

(Added Pub.L. 103–322, Title XXXII, § 320935(a), Sept. 13, 1994, 108 Stat. 2135; Apr. 26, 2011, eff. Dec. 1, 2011.)

RULE 415. SIMILAR ACTS IN CIVIL CASES INVOLVING SEXUAL ASSAULT OR CHILD MOLESTATION

(a) Permitted Uses. In a civil case involving a claim for relief based on a party's alleged sexual assault or child molestation, the court may admit evidence that the party committed any other sexual assault or child molestation. The evidence may be considered as provided in Rules 413 and 414.

(b) Disclosure to the Opponent. If a party intends to offer this evidence, the party must disclose it to the party against whom it will be offered, including witnesses' statements or a summary of the expected testimony. The party must do so at least 15 days before trial or at a later time that the court allows for good cause.

(c) Effect on Other Rules. This rule does not limit the admission or consideration of evidence under any other rule.

(Added Pub.L. 103–322, Title XXXII, § 320935(a), Sept. 13, 1994, 108 Stat. 2137; Apr. 26, 2011, eff. Dec. 1, 2011.)

ARTICLE V. PRIVILEGES

RULE 501. PRIVILEGE IN GENERAL

The common law—as interpreted by United States courts in the light of reason and experience—governs a claim of privilege unless any of the following provides otherwise:

- the United States Constitution;
- a federal statute; or
- rules prescribed by the Supreme Court.

But in a civil case, state law governs privilege regarding a claim or defense for which state law supplies the rule of decision.

(Pub.L. 93–595, § 1, Jan. 2, 1975, 88 Stat. 1933; Apr. 26, 2011, eff. Dec. 1, 2011.)

RULE 502. ATTORNEY–CLIENT PRIVILEGE AND WORK PRODUCT; LIMITATIONS ON WAIVER

The following provisions apply, in the circumstances set out, to disclosure of a communication or information covered by the attorney-client privilege or work-product protection.

(a) Disclosure Made in a Federal Proceeding or to a Federal Office or Agency; Scope of a Waiver. When the disclosure is made in a federal proceeding or to a federal office or agency and waives the attorney-client privilege or work-product protection, the waiver extends to an undisclosed communication or information in a federal or state proceeding only if:

(1) the waiver is intentional;

(2) the disclosed and undisclosed communications or information concern the same subject matter; and

(3) they ought in fairness to be considered together.

(b) Inadvertent Disclosure. When made in a federal proceeding or to a federal office or agency, the disclosure does not operate as a waiver in a federal or state proceeding if:

(1) the disclosure is inadvertent;

(2) the holder of the privilege or protection took reasonable steps to prevent disclosure; and

(3) the holder promptly took reasonable steps to rectify the error, including (if applicable) following Federal Rule of Civil Procedure 26(b)(5)(B).

(c) Disclosure Made in a State Proceeding. When the disclosure is made in a state proceeding and is not the subject of a state-court order concerning waiver, the disclosure does not operate as a waiver in a federal proceeding if the disclosure:

(1) would not be a waiver under this rule if it had been made in a federal proceeding; or

(2) is not a waiver under the law of the state where the disclosure occurred.

(d) Controlling Effect of a Court Order. A federal court may order that the privilege or protection is not waived by disclosure connected with the litigation pending before the court—in which event the disclosure is also not a waiver in any other federal or state proceeding.

(e) Controlling Effect of a Party Agreement. An agreement on the effect of disclosure in a federal proceeding is binding only on the parties to the agreement, unless it is incorporated into a court order.

(f) Controlling Effect of This Rule. Notwithstanding Rules 101 and 1101, this rule applies to state proceedings and to federal court-annexed and federal court-mandated arbitration proceedings, in the circumstances set out in the rule. And notwithstanding Rule 501, this rule applies even if state law provides the rule of decision.

(g) Definitions. In this rule:

(1) "attorney-client privilege" means the protection that applicable law provides for confidential attorney-client communications; and

(2) "work-product protection" means the protection that applicable law provides for tangible material (or its intangible equivalent) prepared in anticipation of litigation or for trial.

(Pub.L. 110–322, § 1(a), Sept. 19, 2008, 122 Stat. 3537; Apr. 26, 2011, eff. Dec. 1, 2011.)

ARTICLE VI. WITNESSES

RULE 601. COMPETENCY TO TESTIFY IN GENERAL

Every person is competent to be a witness unless these rules provide otherwise. But in a civil case, state law governs the witness's competency regarding a claim or defense for which state law supplies the rule of decision.

(Pub.L. 93–595, § 1, Jan. 2, 1975, 88 Stat.1934; Apr. 26, 2011, eff. Dec. 1, 2011.)

RULE 602. NEED FOR PERSONAL KNOWLEDGE

A witness may testify to a matter only if evidence is introduced sufficient to support a finding that the witness has personal knowledge of the matter. Evidence to prove personal knowledge may consist of the witness's own testimony. This rule does not apply to a witness's expert testimony under Rule 703.

(Pub.L. 93–595, § 1, Jan. 2, 1975, 88 Stat. 1934; Mar. 2, 1987, eff. Oct. 1, 1987; Apr. 25, 1988, eff. Nov. 1, 1988; Apr. 26, 2011, eff. Dec. 1, 2011.)

RULE 603. OATH OR AFFIRMATION TO TESTIFY TRUTHFULLY

Before testifying, a witness must give an oath or affirmation to testify truthfully. It must be in a form designed to impress that duty on the witness's conscience.

(Pub.L. 93–595, § 1, Jan. 2, 1975, 88 Stat. 1934; Mar. 2, 1987, eff. Oct. 1, 1987; Apr. 26, 2011, eff. Dec. 1, 2011.)

RULE 604. INTERPRETER

An interpreter must be qualified and must give an oath or affirmation to make a true translation.

(Pub.L. 93–595, § 1, Jan. 2, 1975, 88 Stat. 1934; Mar. 2, 1987, eff. Oct. 1, 1987; Apr. 26, 2011, eff. Dec. 1, 2011.)

RULE 605. JUDGE'S COMPETENCY AS A WITNESS

The presiding judge may not testify as a witness at the trial. A party need not object to preserve the issue.

(Pub.L. 93–595, § 1, Jan. 2, 1975, 88 Stat. 1934; Apr. 26, 2011, eff. Dec. 1, 2011.)

RULE 606. JUROR'S COMPETENCY AS A WITNESS

(a) At the Trial. A juror may not testify as a witness before the other jurors at the trial. If a juror is called to testify, the court must give a party an opportunity to object outside the jury's presence.

(b) During an Inquiry Into the Validity of a Verdict or Indictment.

(1) Prohibited Testimony or Other Evidence. During an inquiry into the validity of a verdict or indictment, a juror may not testify about any statement made or incident that occurred during the jury's deliberations; the effect of anything on that juror's or another juror's vote; or any juror's mental processes concerning the verdict or indictment. The court may not receive a juror's affidavit or evidence of a juror's statement on these matters.

(2) Exceptions. A juror may testify about whether:

(A) extraneous prejudicial information was improperly brought to the jury's attention;

(B) an outside influence was improperly brought to bear on any juror; or

(C) a mistake was made in entering the verdict on the verdict form.

(Pub.L. 93–595, § 1, Jan. 2, 1975, 88 Stat. 1934; Pub.L. 94–149, § 1(10), Dec. 12, 1975, 89 Stat. 805; Mar. 2, 1987, eff. Oct. 1, 1987; Apr. 12, 2006, eff. Dec. 1, 2006; Apr. 26, 2011, eff. Dec. 1, 2011.)

RULE 607. WHO MAY IMPEACH A WITNESS

Any party, including the party that called the witness, may attack the witness's credibility.

(Pub.L. 93–595, § 1, Jan. 2, 1975, 88 Stat.1934; Mar. 2, 1987, eff. Oct. 1, 1987; Apr. 26, 2011, eff. Dec. 1, 2011.)

RULE 608. A WITNESS'S CHARACTER FOR TRUTHFULNESS OR UNTRUTHFULNESS

(a) Reputation or Opinion Evidence. A witness's credibility may be attacked or supported by testimony about the witness's reputation for having a character for truthfulness or untruthfulness, or by testimony in the form of an opinion about that character. But evidence of truthful character is admissible only after the witness's character for truthfulness has been attacked.

(b) Specific Instances of Conduct. Except for a criminal conviction under Rule 609, extrinsic evidence is not admissible to prove specific instances of a witness's conduct in order to attack or support the witness's character for truthfulness. But the court may, on cross-examination, allow them to be inquired into if they are probative of the character for truthfulness or untruthfulness of:

(1) the witness; or

(2) another witness whose character the witness being cross-examined has testified about.

By testifying on another matter, a witness does not waive any privilege against self-incrimination for testimony that relates only to the witness's character for truthfulness.

(Pub.L. 93–595, § 1, Jan. 2, 1975, 88 Stat.1935; Mar. 2, 1987, eff. Oct. 1, 1987; Apr. 25, 1988, eff. Nov. 1, 1988; Mar. 27, 2003, eff. Dec. 1, 2003; Apr. 26, 2011, eff. Dec. 1, 2011.)

RULE 609. IMPEACHMENT BY EVIDENCE OF A CRIMINAL CONVICTION

(a) In General. The following rules apply to attacking a witness's character for truthfulness by evidence of a criminal conviction:

(1) for a crime that, in the convicting jurisdiction, was punishable by death or by imprisonment for more than one year, the evidence:

(A) must be admitted, subject to Rule 403, in a civil case or in a criminal case in which the witness is not a defendant; and

(B) must be admitted in a criminal case in which the witness is a defendant, if the probative value of the evidence outweighs its prejudicial effect to that defendant; and

(2) for any crime regardless of the punishment, the evidence must be admitted if the court can readily determine that establishing the elements of the crime required proving—or the witness's admitting—a dishonest act or false statement.

(b) Limit on Using the Evidence After 10 Years. This subdivision (b) applies if more than 10 years have passed since the witness's conviction or release from confinement for it, whichever is later. Evidence of the conviction is admissible only if:

(1) its probative value, supported by specific facts and circumstances, substantially outweighs its prejudicial effect; and

(2) the proponent gives an adverse party reasonable written notice of the intent to use it so that the party has a fair opportunity to contest its use.

(c) Effect of a Pardon, Annulment, or Certificate of Rehabilitation. Evidence of a conviction is not admissible if:

(1) the conviction has been the subject of a pardon, annulment, certificate of rehabilitation, or other equivalent procedure based on a finding that the person has been rehabilitated, and the person has not been convicted of a later crime punishable by death or by imprisonment for more than one year; or

(2) the conviction has been the subject of a pardon, annulment, or other equivalent procedure based on a finding of innocence.

(d) Juvenile Adjudications. Evidence of a juvenile adjudication is admissible under this rule only if:

(1) it is offered in a criminal case;

(2) the adjudication was of a witness other than the defendant;

(3) an adult's conviction for that offense would be admissible to attack the adult's credibility; and

(4) admitting the evidence is necessary to fairly determine guilt or innocence.

(e) Pendency of an Appeal. A conviction that satisfies this rule is admissible even if an appeal is pending. Evidence of the pendency is also admissible.

(Pub.L. 93–595, § 1, Jan. 2, 1975, 88 Stat.1935; Mar. 2, 1987, eff. Oct. 1, 1987; Jan. 26, 1990, eff. Dec. 1, 1990; Apr. 12, 2006, eff. Dec. 1, 2006; Apr. 26, 2011, eff. Dec. 1, 2011.)

RULE 610. RELIGIOUS BELIEFS OR OPINIONS

Evidence of a witness's religious beliefs or opinions is not admissible to attack or support the witness's credibility.

(Pub.L. 93–595, § 1, Jan. 2, 1975, 88 Stat.1936; Mar. 2, 1987, eff. Oct. 1, 1987; Apr. 26, 2011, eff. Dec. 1, 2011.)

RULE 611. MODE AND ORDER OF EXAMINING WITNESSES AND PRESENTING EVIDENCE

(a) Control by the Court; Purposes. The court should exercise reasonable control over the mode and order of examining witnesses and presenting evidence so as to:

(1) make those procedures effective for determining the truth;

(2) avoid wasting time; and

(3) protect witnesses from harassment or undue embarrassment.

(b) Scope of Cross–Examination. Cross-examination should not go beyond the subject matter of the direct examination and matters affecting the witness's credibility. The court may allow inquiry into additional matters as if on direct examination.

(c) Leading Questions. Leading questions should not be used on direct examination except as necessary to develop the witness's testimony. Ordinarily, the court should allow leading questions:

(1) on cross-examination; and

(2) when a party calls a hostile witness, an adverse party, or a witness identified with an adverse party.

(Pub.L. 93–595, § 1, Jan. 2, 1975, 88 Stat. 1936; Mar. 2, 1987, eff. Oct. 1, 1987; Apr. 26, 2011, eff. Dec. 1, 2011.)

RULE 612. WRITING USED TO REFRESH A WITNESS'S MEMORY

(a) Scope. This rule gives an adverse party certain options when a witness uses a writing to refresh memory:

(1) while testifying; or

(2) before testifying, if the court decides that justice requires the party to have those options.

(b) Adverse Party's Options; Deleting Unrelated Matter. Unless 18 U.S.C. § 3500 provides otherwise in a criminal case, an adverse party is entitled to have the writing produced at the hearing, to inspect it, to cross-examine the witness about it, and to introduce in evidence any portion that relates to the witness's testimony. If the producing party claims that the writing includes unrelated matter, the court must examine the writing in camera, delete any unrelated portion, and order that the rest be delivered to the adverse party. Any portion deleted over objection must be preserved for the record.

(c) Failure to Produce or Deliver the Writing. If a writing is not produced or is not delivered as ordered, the court may issue any appropriate order. But if the prosecution does not comply in a criminal case, the court must strike the witness's testimony or—if justice so requires—declare a mistrial.

(Pub.L. 93–595, § 1, Jan. 2, 1975, 88 Stat. 1936; Mar. 2, 1987, eff. Oct. 1, 1987; Apr. 26, 2011, eff. Dec. 1, 2011.)

RULE 613. WITNESS'S PRIOR STATEMENT

(a) Showing or Disclosing the Statement During Examination. When examining a witness about the witness's prior statement, a party need not show it or disclose its contents to the witness. But the party must, on request, show it or disclose its contents to an adverse party's attorney.

(b) Extrinsic Evidence of a Prior Inconsistent Statement. Extrinsic evidence of a witness's prior inconsistent statement is admissible only if the witness is given an opportunity to explain or deny the statement and an adverse party is given an opportunity to examine the witness about it, or if justice so requires. This subdivision (b) does not apply to an opposing party's statement under Rule 801(d)(2).

(Pub.L. 93–595, § 1, Jan. 2, 1975, 88 Stat.1936; Mar. 2, 1987, eff. Oct. 1, 1987; Apr. 25, 1988, eff. Nov. 1, 1988; Apr. 26, 2011, eff. Dec. 1, 2011.)

RULE 614. COURT'S CALLING OR EXAMINING A WITNESS

(a) Calling. The court may call a witness on its own or at a party's request. Each party is entitled to cross-examine the witness.

(b) Examining. The court may examine a witness regardless of who calls the witness.

(c) Objections. A party may object to the court's calling or examining a witness either at that time or at the next opportunity when the jury is not present.

(Pub.L. 93–595, § 1, Jan. 2, 1975, 88 Stat.1937; Apr. 26, 2011, eff. Dec. 1, 2011.)

RULE 615. EXCLUDING WITNESSES

At a party's request, the court must order witnesses excluded so that they cannot hear other witnesses' testimony. Or the court may do so on its own. But this rule does not authorize excluding:

(a) a party who is a natural person;

(b) an officer or employee of a party that is not a natural person, after being designated as the party's representative by its attorney;

(c) a person whose presence a party shows to be essential to presenting the party's claim or defense; or

(d) a person authorized by statute to be present.

(Pub.L. 93–595, § 1, Jan. 2, 1975, 88 Stat.1937; Mar. 2, 1987, eff. Oct. 1, 1987; Apr. 25, 1988, eff. Nov. 1, 1988; Pub.L. 100–690, Nov. 18, 1988, Title VII, § 7075(a), 102 Stat. 4405; Apr. 24, 1998, eff. Dec. 1, 1998; Apr. 26, 2011, eff. Dec. 1, 2011.)

ARTICLE VII. OPINIONS AND EXPERT TESTIMONY

RULE 701. OPINION TESTIMONY BY LAY WITNESSES

If a witness is not testifying as an expert, testimony in the form of an opinion is limited to one that is:

(a) rationally based on the witness's perception;

(b) helpful to clearly understanding the witness's testimony or to determining a fact in issue; and

(c) not based on scientific, technical, or other specialized knowledge within the scope of Rule 702.

(Pub.L. 93–595, § 1, Jan. 2, 1975, 88 Stat.1937; Mar. 2, 1987, eff. Oct. 1, 1987; Apr. 17, 2000, eff. Dec. 1, 2000; Apr. 26, 2011, eff. Dec. 1, 2011.)

RULE 702. TESTIMONY BY EXPERT WITNESSES

A witness who is qualified as an expert by knowledge, skill, experience, training, or education may testify in the form of an opinion or otherwise if:

(a) the expert's scientific, technical, or other specialized knowledge will help the trier of fact to understand the evidence or to determine a fact in issue;

(b) the testimony is based on sufficient facts or data;

(c) the testimony is the product of reliable principles and methods; and

(d) the expert has reliably applied the principles and methods to the facts of the case.

(Pub.L. 93–595, § 1, Jan. 2, 1975, 88 Stat. 1937; Apr. 17, 2000, eff. Dec. 1, 2000; Apr. 26, 2011, eff. Dec. 1, 2011.)

RULE 703. BASES OF AN EXPERT'S OPINION TESTIMONY

An expert may base an opinion on facts or data in the case that the expert has been made aware of or personally observed. If experts in the particular field would reasonably rely on those kinds of facts or data in forming an opinion on the subject, they need not be admissible for the opinion to be admitted. But if the facts or data would otherwise be inadmissible, the proponent of the opinion may disclose them to the jury only if their probative value in helping the jury evaluate the opinion substantially outweighs their prejudicial effect.

(Pub.L. 93–595, § 1, Jan. 2, 1975, 88 Stat.1937; Mar. 2, 1987, eff. Oct. 1, 1987; Apr. 17, 2000, eff. Dec. 1, 2000; Apr. 26, 2011, eff. Dec. 1, 2011.)

RULE 704. OPINION ON AN ULTIMATE ISSUE

(a) In General—Not Automatically Objectionable. An opinion is not objectionable just because it embraces an ultimate issue.

(b) Exception. In a criminal case, an expert witness must not state an opinion about whether the defendant did or did not have a mental state or condition that constitutes an element of the crime charged or of a defense. Those matters are for the trier of fact alone.

(Pub.L. 93–595, § 1, Jan. 2, 1975, 88 Stat. 1937; Pub.L. 98–473, Title IV, § 406, Oct. 12, 1984, 98 Stat. 2067; Apr. 26, 2011, eff. Dec. 1, 2011.)

RULE 705. DISCLOSING THE FACTS OR DATA UNDERLYING AN EXPERT'S OPINION

Unless the court orders otherwise, an expert may state an opinion—and give the reasons for it—without first testifying to the underlying facts or data. But the expert may be required to disclose those facts or data on cross-examination.

(Pub.L. 93–595, § 1, Jan. 2, 1975, 88 Stat. 1938; Mar. 2, 1987, eff. Oct. 1, 1987; Apr. 22, 1993, eff. Dec. 1, 1993; Apr. 26, 2011, eff. Dec. 1, 2011.)

RULE 706. COURT–APPOINTED EXPERT WITNESSES

(a) Appointment Process. On a party's motion or on its own, the court may order the parties to show cause why expert witnesses should not be appointed and may ask the parties to submit nominations. The court may appoint any expert that the parties agree on and any of its own choosing. But the court may only appoint someone who consents to act.

(b) Expert's Role. The court must inform the expert of the expert's duties. The court may do so in writing and have a copy filed with the clerk or may do so orally at a conference in which the parties have an opportunity to participate. The expert:

(1) must advise the parties of any findings the expert makes;

(2) may be deposed by any party;

(3) may be called to testify by the court or any party; and

(4) may be cross-examined by any party, including the party that called the expert.

(c) Compensation. The expert is entitled to a reasonable compensation, as set by the court. The compensation is payable as follows:

(1) in a criminal case or in a civil case involving just compensation under the Fifth Amendment, from any funds that are provided by law; and

(2) in any other civil case, by the parties in the proportion and at the time that the court directs—and the compensation is then charged like other costs.

(d) Disclosing the Appointment to the Jury. The court may authorize disclosure to the jury that the court appointed the expert.

(e) Parties' Choice of Their Own Experts. This rule does not limit a party in calling its own experts.

(Pub.L. 93–595, § 1, Jan. 2, 1975, 88 Stat.1938; Mar. 2, 1987, eff. Oct. 1, 1987; Apr. 26, 2011, eff. Dec. 1, 2011.)

ARTICLE VIII. HEARSAY

RULE 801. DEFINITIONS THAT APPLY TO THIS ARTICLE; EXCLUSIONS FROM HEARSAY

(a) Statement. "Statement" means a person's oral assertion, written assertion, or nonverbal conduct, if the person intended it as an assertion.

(b) Declarant. "Declarant" means the person who made the statement.

(c) Hearsay. "Hearsay" means a statement that:

(1) the declarant does not make while testifying at the current trial or hearing; and

(2) a party offers in evidence to prove the truth of the matter asserted in the statement.

(d) Statements That Are Not Hearsay. A statement that meets the following conditions is not hearsay:

(1) A Declarant–Witness's Prior Statement. The declarant testifies and is subject to cross-examination about a prior statement, and the statement:

(A) is inconsistent with the declarant's testimony and was given under penalty of perjury at a trial, hearing, or other proceeding or in a deposition;

(B) is consistent with the declarant's testimony and is offered:

(i) to rebut an express or implied charge that the declarant recently fabricated it or acted from a recent improper influence or motive in so testifying; or

(ii) to rehabilitate the declarant's credibility as a witness when attacked on another ground; or

(C) identifies a person as someone the declarant perceived earlier.

(2) An Opposing Party's Statement. The statement is offered against an opposing party and:

(A) was made by the party in an individual or representative capacity;

(B) is one the party manifested that it adopted or believed to be true;

(C) was made by a person whom the party authorized to make a statement on the subject;

(D) was made by the party's agent or employee on a matter within the scope of that relationship and while it existed; or

(E) was made by the party's coconspirator during and in furtherance of the conspiracy.

The statement must be considered but does not by itself establish the declarant's authority under (C); the existence or scope of the relationship under (D); or the existence of the conspiracy or participation in it under (E).

(Pub.L. 93–595, § 1, Jan. 2, 1975, 88 Stat.1938; Pub.L. 94–113, § 1, Oct. 16, 1975, 89 Stat. 576; Mar. 2, 1987, eff. Oct. 1, 1987; Apr. 11, 1997, eff. Dec. 1, 1997; Apr. 26, 2011, eff. Dec. 1, 2011; Apr. 25, 2014, eff. Dec. 1, 2014.)

RULE 802. THE RULE AGAINST HEARSAY

Hearsay is not admissible unless any of the following provides otherwise:

- a federal statute;
- these rules; or
- other rules prescribed by the Supreme Court.

(Pub.L. 93–595, § 1, Jan. 2, 1975, 88 Stat. 1939; Apr. 26, 2011, eff. Dec. 1, 2011.)

RULE 803. EXCEPTIONS TO THE RULE AGAINST HEARSAY—REGARDLESS OF WHETHER THE DECLARANT IS AVAILABLE AS A WITNESS

The following are not excluded by the rule against hearsay, regardless of whether the declarant is available as a witness:

(1) Present Sense Impression. A statement describing or explaining an event or condition, made while or immediately after the declarant perceived it.

(2) Excited Utterance. A statement relating to a startling event or condition, made while the declarant was under the stress of excitement that it caused.

(3) Then–Existing Mental, Emotional, or Physical Condition. A statement of the declarant's then-existing state of mind (such as motive, intent, or plan) or emotional, sensory, or physical condition (such as mental feeling, pain, or bodily health), but not including a statement of memory or belief to prove the fact remembered or believed unless it relates to the validity or terms of the declarant's will.

(4) Statement Made for Medical Diagnosis or Treatment. A statement that:

(A) is made for—and is reasonably pertinent to—medical diagnosis or treatment; and

(B) describes medical history; past or present symptoms or sensations; their inception; or their general cause.

(5) Recorded Recollection. A record that:

(A) is on a matter the witness once knew about but now cannot recall well enough to testify fully and accurately;

(B) was made or adopted by the witness when the matter was fresh in the witness's memory; and

(C) accurately reflects the witness's knowledge.

If admitted, the record may be read into evidence but may be received as an exhibit only if offered by an adverse party.

(6) Records of a Regularly Conducted Activity. A record of an act, event, condition, opinion, or diagnosis if:

    (A) the record was made at or near the time by—or from information transmitted by—someone with knowledge;

    (B) the record was kept in the course of a regularly conducted activity of a business, organization, occupation, or calling, whether or not for profit;

    (C) making the record was a regular practice of that activity;

    (D) all these conditions are shown by the testimony of the custodian or another qualified witness, or by a certification that complies with Rule 902(11) or (12) or with a statute permitting certification; and

    (E) the opponent does not show that the source of information or the method or circumstances of preparation indicate a lack of trustworthiness.

(7) Absence of a Record of a Regularly Conducted Activity. Evidence that a matter is not included in a record described in paragraph (6) if:

    (A) the evidence is admitted to prove that the matter did not occur or exist;

    (B) a record was regularly kept for a matter of that kind; and

    (C) the opponent does not show that the possible source of the information or other circumstances indicate a lack of trustworthiness.

(8) Public Records. A record or statement of a public office if:

    (A) it sets out:

      (i) the office's activities;

      (ii) a matter observed while under a legal duty to report, but not including, in a criminal case, a matter observed by law-enforcement personnel; or

      (iii) in a civil case or against the government in a criminal case, factual findings from a legally authorized investigation; and

    (B) the opponent does not show that the source of information or other circumstances indicate a lack of trustworthiness.

(9) Public Records of Vital Statistics. A record of a birth, death, or marriage, if reported to a public office in accordance with a legal duty.

(10) Absence of a Public Record. Testimony—or a certification under Rule 902—that a diligent search failed to disclose a public record or statement if:

    (A) the testimony or certification is admitted to prove that

      (i) the record or statement does not exist; or

      (ii) a matter did not occur or exist, if a public office regularly kept a record or statement for a matter of that kind; and

    (B) in a criminal case, a prosecutor who intends to offer a certification provides written notice of that intent at least 14 days before trial, and the defendant does not object in writing within 7 days of receiving the notice—unless the court sets a different time for the notice or the objection.

(11) Records of Religious Organizations Concerning Personal or Family History. A statement of birth, legitimacy, ancestry, marriage, divorce, death, relationship by blood or marriage, or similar facts of personal or family history, contained in a regularly kept record of a religious organization.

(12) Certificates of Marriage, Baptism, and Similar Ceremonies. A statement of fact contained in a certificate:

    (A) made by a person who is authorized by a religious organization or by law to perform the act certified;

    (B) attesting that the person performed a marriage or similar ceremony or administered a sacrament; and

    (C) purporting to have been issued at the time of the act or within a reasonable time after it.

(13) Family Records. A statement of fact about personal or family history contained in a family record, such as a Bible, genealogy, chart, engraving on a ring, inscription on a portrait, or engraving on an urn or burial marker.

(14) Records of Documents That Affect an Interest in Property. The record of a document that purports to establish or affect an interest in property if:

    (A) the record is admitted to prove the content of the original recorded document, along with its signing and its delivery by each person who purports to have signed it;

    (B) the record is kept in a public office; and

    (C) a statute authorizes recording documents of that kind in that office.

(15) Statements in Documents That Affect an Interest in Property. A statement contained in a document that purports to establish or affect an interest in property if the matter stated was relevant to the document's purpose—unless later dealings with the property are inconsistent with the truth of the statement or the purport of the document.

(16) Statements in Ancient Documents. A statement in a document that was prepared before January 1, 1998, and whose authenticity is established.

(17) Market Reports and Similar Commercial Publications. Market quotations, lists, directories, or other compilations that are generally relied on by the public or by persons in particular occupations.

(18) Statements in Learned Treatises, Periodicals, or Pamphlets. A statement contained in a treatise, periodical, or pamphlet if:

    (A) the statement is called to the attention of an expert witness on cross-examination or relied on by the expert on direct examination; and

(B) the publication is established as a reliable authority by the expert's admission or testimony, by another expert's testimony, or by judicial notice.

If admitted, the statement may be read into evidence but not received as an exhibit.

(19) Reputation Concerning Personal or Family History. A reputation among a person's family by blood, adoption, or marriage—or among a person's associates or in the community—concerning the person's birth, adoption, legitimacy, ancestry, marriage, divorce, death, relationship by blood, adoption, or marriage, or similar facts of personal or family history.

(20) Reputation Concerning Boundaries or General History. A reputation in a community—arising before the controversy—concerning boundaries of land in the community or customs that affect the land, or concerning general historical events important to that community, state, or nation.

(21) Reputation Concerning Character. A reputation among a person's associates or in the community concerning the person's character.

(22) Judgment of a Previous Conviction. Evidence of a final judgment of conviction if:

(A) the judgment was entered after a trial or guilty plea, but not a nolo contendere plea;

(B) the conviction was for a crime punishable by death or by imprisonment for more than a year;

(C) the evidence is admitted to prove any fact essential to the judgment; and

(D) when offered by the prosecutor in a criminal case for a purpose other than impeachment, the judgment was against the defendant.

The pendency of an appeal may be shown but does not affect admissibility.

(23) Judgments Involving Personal, Family, or General History, or a Boundary. A judgment that is admitted to prove a matter of personal, family, or general history, or boundaries, if the matter:

(A) was essential to the judgment; and

(B) could be proved by evidence of reputation.

(24) [Other Exceptions.] [Transferred to Rule 807.]

(Pub.L. 93–595, § 1, Jan. 2, 1975, 88 Stat. 1939; Pub.L. 94–149, § 1(11), Dec. 12, 1975, 89 Stat. 805; Mar. 2, 1987, eff. Oct. 1, 1987; Apr. 11, 1997, eff. Dec. 1, 1997; Apr. 17, 2000, eff. Dec. 1, 2000; Apr. 26, 2011, eff. Dec. 1, 2011; Apr. 13, 2013, eff. Dec. 1, 2013; Apr. 25, 2014, eff. Dec. 1, 2014; Apr. 27, 2017, eff. Dec. 1, 2017.)

RULE 804. EXCEPTIONS TO THE RULE AGAINST HEARSAY—WHEN THE DECLARANT IS UNAVAILABLE AS A WITNESS

(a) Criteria for Being Unavailable. A declarant is considered to be unavailable as a witness if the declarant:

(1) is exempted from testifying about the subject matter of the declarant's statement because the court rules that a privilege applies;

(2) refuses to testify about the subject matter despite a court order to do so;

(3) testifies to not remembering the subject matter;

(4) cannot be present or testify at the trial or hearing because of death or a then-existing infirmity, physical illness, or mental illness; or

(5) is absent from the trial or hearing and the statement's proponent has not been able, by process or other reasonable means, to procure:

(A) the declarant's attendance, in the case of a hearsay exception under Rule 804(b)(1) or (6); or

(B) the declarant's attendance or testimony, in the case of a hearsay exception under Rule 804(b)(2), (3), or (4).

But this subdivision (a) does not apply if the statement's proponent procured or wrongfully caused the declarant's unavailability as a witness in order to prevent the declarant from attending or testifying.

(b) The Exceptions. The following are not excluded by the rule against hearsay if the declarant is unavailable as a witness:

(1) Former Testimony. Testimony that:

(A) was given as a witness at a trial, hearing, or lawful deposition, whether given during the current proceeding or a different one; and

(B) is now offered against a party who had—or, in a civil case, whose predecessor in interest had—an opportunity and similar motive to develop it by direct, cross-, or redirect examination.

(2) Statement Under the Belief of Imminent Death. In a prosecution for homicide or in a civil case, a statement that the declarant, while believing the declarant's death to be imminent, made about its cause or circumstances.

(3) Statement Against Interest. A statement that:

(A) a reasonable person in the declarant's position would have made only if the person believed it to be true because, when made, it was so contrary to the declarant's proprietary or pecuniary interest or had so great a tendency to invalidate the declarant's claim against someone else or to expose the declarant to civil or criminal liability; and

(B) is supported by corroborating circumstances that clearly indicate its trustworthiness, if it is offered in a criminal case as one that tends to expose the declarant to criminal liability.

(4) Statement of Personal or Family History. A statement about:

(A) the declarant's own birth, adoption, legitimacy, ancestry, marriage, divorce, relationship by blood, adoption, or marriage, or similar facts of personal or family history, even though the declarant had no way of acquiring personal knowledge about that fact; or

(B) another person concerning any of these facts, as well as death, if the declarant was related to the person by blood, adoption, or marriage or was so intimately associated with the person's family that the declarant's information is likely to be accurate.

(5) **[Other Exceptions.]** [Transferred to Rule 807.]

(6) **Statement Offered Against a Party That Wrongfully Caused the Declarant's Unavailability.** A statement offered against a party that wrongfully caused—or acquiesced in wrongfully causing—the declarant's unavailability as a witness, and did so intending that result.

(Pub.L. 93–595, § 1, Jan. 2, 1975, 88 Stat. 1942; Pub.L. 94–149, § 1(12), (13), Dec. 12, 1975, 89 Stat. 806; Mar. 2, 1987, eff. Oct. 1, 1987; Pub.L. 100–690, Title VII, § 7075(b), Nov. 18, 1988, 102 Stat. 4405; Apr. 11, 1997, eff. Dec. 1, 1997; Apr. 28, 2010, eff. Dec. 1, 2010; Apr. 26, 2011, eff. Dec. 1, 2011.)

RULE 805. HEARSAY WITHIN HEARSAY

Hearsay within hearsay is not excluded by the rule against hearsay if each part of the combined statements conforms with an exception to the rule.

(Pub.L. 93–595, § 1, Jan. 2, 1975, 88 Stat. 1943; Apr. 26, 2011, eff. Dec. 1, 2011.)

RULE 806. ATTACKING AND SUPPORTING THE DECLARANT'S CREDIBILITY

When a hearsay statement—or a statement described in Rule 801(d)(2)(C), (D), or (E)—has been admitted in evidence, the declarant's credibility may be attacked, and then supported, by any evidence that would be admissible for those purposes if the declarant had testified as a witness. The court

may admit evidence of the declarant's inconsistent statement or conduct, regardless of when it occurred or whether the declarant had an opportunity to explain or deny it. If the party against whom the statement was admitted calls the declarant as a witness, the party may examine the declarant on the statement as if on cross-examination.

(Pub.L. 93–595, § 1, Jan. 2, 1975, 88 Stat. 1943; Mar. 2, 1987, eff. Oct. 1, 1987; Apr. 11, 1997, eff. Dec. 1, 1997; Apr. 26, 2011, eff. Dec. 1, 2011.)

RULE 807. RESIDUAL EXCEPTION

(a) **In General.** Under the following circumstances, a hearsay statement is not excluded by the rule against hearsay even if the statement is not specifically covered by a hearsay exception in Rule 803 or 804:

(1) the statement has equivalent circumstantial guarantees of trustworthiness;

(2) it is offered as evidence of a material fact;

(3) it is more probative on the point for which it is offered than any other evidence that the proponent can obtain through reasonable efforts; and

(4) admitting it will best serve the purposes of these rules and the interests of justice.

(b) **Notice.** The statement is admissible only if, before the trial or hearing, the proponent gives an adverse party reasonable notice of the intent to offer the statement and its particulars, including the declarant's name and address, so that the party has a fair opportunity to meet it.

(Added Apr. 11, 1997, eff. Dec. 1, 1997; Apr. 26, 2011, eff. Dec. 1, 2011.)

ARTICLE IX. AUTHENTICATION AND IDENTIFICATION

RULE 901. AUTHENTICATING OR IDENTIFYING EVIDENCE

(a) **In General.** To satisfy the requirement of authenticating or identifying an item of evidence, the proponent must produce evidence sufficient to support a finding that the item is what the proponent claims it is.

(b) **Examples.** The following are examples only—not a complete list—of evidence that satisfies the requirement:

(1) **Testimony of a Witness with Knowledge.** Testimony that an item is what it is claimed to be.

(2) **Nonexpert Opinion About Handwriting.** A nonexpert's opinion that handwriting is genuine, based on a familiarity with it that was not acquired for the current litigation.

(3) **Comparison by an Expert Witness or the Trier of Fact.** A comparison with an authenticated specimen by an expert witness or the trier of fact.

(4) **Distinctive Characteristics and the Like.** The appearance, contents, substance, internal patterns, or other distinctive characteristics of the item, taken together with all the circumstances.

(5) **Opinion About a Voice.** An opinion identifying a person's voice—whether heard firsthand or through mechanical or electronic transmission or recording—based on hearing the voice at any time under circumstances that connect it with the alleged speaker.

(6) **Evidence About a Telephone Conversation.** For a telephone conversation, evidence that a call was made to the number assigned at the time to:

(A) a particular person, if circumstances, including self-identification, show that the person answering was the one called; or

(B) a particular business, if the call was made to a business and the call related to business reasonably transacted over the telephone.

(7) **Evidence About Public Records.** Evidence that:

(A) a document was recorded or filed in a public office as authorized by law; or

(B) a purported public record or statement is from the office where items of this kind are kept.

(8) Evidence About Ancient Documents or Data Compilations. For a document or data compilation, evidence that it:

(A) is in a condition that creates no suspicion about its authenticity;

(B) was in a place where, if authentic, it would likely be; and

(C) is at least 20 years old when offered.

(9) Evidence About a Process or System. Evidence describing a process or system and showing that it produces an accurate result.

(10) Methods Provided by a Statute or Rule. Any method of authentication or identification allowed by a federal statute or a rule prescribed by the Supreme Court.

(Pub.L. 93–595, § 1, Jan. 2, 1975, 88 Stat.1943; Apr. 26, 2011, eff. Dec. 1, 2011.)

RULE 902. EVIDENCE THAT IS SELF–AUTHENTICATING

The following items of evidence are self-authenticating; they require no extrinsic evidence of authenticity in order to be admitted:

(1) Domestic Public Documents That Are Sealed and Signed. A document that bears:

(A) a seal purporting to be that of the United States; any state, district, commonwealth, territory, or insular possession of the United States; the former Panama Canal Zone; the Trust Territory of the Pacific Islands; a political subdivision of any of these entities; or a department, agency, or officer of any entity named above; and

(B) a signature purporting to be an execution or attestation.

(2) Domestic Public Documents That Are Not Sealed but Are Signed and Certified. A document that bears no seal if:

(A) it bears the signature of an officer or employee of an entity named in Rule 902(1)(A); and

(B) another public officer who has a seal and official duties within that same entity certifies under seal—or its equivalent—that the signer has the official capacity and that the signature is genuine.

(3) Foreign Public Documents. A document that purports to be signed or attested by a person who is authorized by a foreign country's law to do so. The document must be accompanied by a final certification that certifies the genuineness of the signature and official position of the signer or attester—or of any foreign official whose certificate of genuineness relates to the signature or attestation or is in a chain of certificates of genuineness relating to the signature or attestation. The certification may be made by a secretary of a United States embassy or legation; by a consul general, vice consul, or consular agent of the United States; or by a diplomatic or consular official of the foreign country assigned or accredited to the United States. If all parties have been given a reasonable opportunity to investigate the document's authenticity and accuracy, the court may, for good cause, either:

(A) order that it be treated as presumptively authentic without final certification; or

(B) allow it to be evidenced by an attested summary with or without final certification.

(4) Certified Copies of Public Records. A copy of an official record—or a copy of a document that was recorded or filed in a public office as authorized by law—if the copy is certified as correct by:

(A) the custodian or another person authorized to make the certification; or

(B) a certificate that complies with Rule 902(1), (2), or (3), a federal statute, or a rule prescribed by the Supreme Court.

(5) Official Publications. A book, pamphlet, or other publication purporting to be issued by a public authority.

(6) Newspapers and Periodicals. Printed material purporting to be a newspaper or periodical.

(7) Trade Inscriptions and the Like. An inscription, sign, tag, or label purporting to have been affixed in the course of business and indicating origin, ownership, or control.

(8) Acknowledged Documents. A document accompanied by a certificate of acknowledgment that is lawfully executed by a notary public or another officer who is authorized to take acknowledgments.

(9) Commercial Paper and Related Documents. Commercial paper, a signature on it, and related documents, to the extent allowed by general commercial law.

(10) Presumptions Under a Federal Statute. A signature, document, or anything else that a federal statute declares to be presumptively or prima facie genuine or authentic.

(11) Certified Domestic Records of a Regularly Conducted Activity. The original or a copy of a domestic record that meets the requirements of Rule 803(6)(A)–(C), as shown by a certification of the custodian or another qualified person that complies with a federal statute or a rule prescribed by the Supreme Court. Before the trial or hearing, the proponent must give an adverse party reasonable written notice of the intent to offer the record—and must make the record and certification available for inspection—so that the party has a fair opportunity to challenge them.

(12) Certified Foreign Records of a Regularly Conducted Activity. In a civil case, the original or a copy of a foreign record that meets the requirements of Rule 902(11), modified as follows: the certification, rather than complying with a federal statute or Supreme Court rule, must be signed in a manner that, if falsely made, would subject the maker to a criminal penalty in the country where the certification is signed. The proponent must also meet the notice requirements of Rule 902(11).

(13) Certified Records Generated by an Electronic Process or System. A record generated by an electronic process or system that produces an accurate result, as shown by a certification of a qualified person that complies with the certification requirements of Rule 902(11) or (12).

The proponent must also meet the notice requirements of Rule 902(11).

(14) Certified Data Copied from an Electronic Device, Storage Medium, or File. Data copied from an electronic device, storage medium, or file, if authenticated by a process of digital identification, as shown by a certification of a qualified person that complies with the certification requirements of Rule 902(11) or (12). The proponent also must meet the notice requirements of Rule 902(11).

(Pub.L. 93–595, § 1, Jan. 2, 1975, 88 Stat. 1944; Mar. 2, 1987, eff. Oct. 1, 1987; Apr. 25, 1988, eff. Nov. 1, 1988; Apr. 17, 2000, eff. Dec. 1, 2000; Apr. 26, 2011, eff. Dec. 1, 2011; Apr. 27, 2017, eff. Dec. 1, 2017.)

RULE 903. SUBSCRIBING WITNESS'S TESTIMONY

A subscribing witness's testimony is necessary to authenticate a writing only if required by the law of the jurisdiction that governs its validity.

(Pub.L. 93–595, § 1, Jan. 2, 1975, 88 Stat. 1945; Apr. 26, 2011, eff. Dec. 1, 2011.)

ARTICLE X. CONTENTS OF WRITINGS, RECORDINGS, AND PHOTOGRAPHS

RULE 1001. DEFINITIONS THAT APPLY TO THIS ARTICLE

In this article:

(a) A "writing" consists of letters, words, numbers, or their equivalent set down in any form.

(b) A "recording" consists of letters, words, numbers, or their equivalent recorded in any manner.

(c) A "photograph" means a photographic image or its equivalent stored in any form.

(d) An "original" of a writing or recording means the writing or recording itself or any counterpart intended to have the same effect by the person who executed or issued it. For electronically stored information, "original" means any printout—or other output readable by sight—if it accurately reflects the information. An "original" of a photograph includes the negative or a print from it.

(e) A "duplicate" means a counterpart produced by a mechanical, photographic, chemical, electronic, or other equivalent process or technique that accurately reproduces the original.

(Pub.L. 93–595, § 1, Jan. 2, 1975, 88 Stat. 1945; Apr. 26, 2011, eff. Dec. 1, 2011.)

RULE 1002. REQUIREMENT OF THE ORIGINAL

An original writing, recording, or photograph is required in order to prove its content unless these rules or a federal statute provides otherwise.

(Pub.L. 93–595, § 1, Jan. 2, 1975, 88 Stat. 1946; Apr. 26, 2011, eff. Dec. 1, 2011.)

RULE 1003. ADMISSIBILITY OF DUPLICATES

A duplicate is admissible to the same extent as the original unless a genuine question is raised about the original's authenticity or the circumstances make it unfair to admit the duplicate.

(Pub.L. 93–595, § 1, Jan. 2, 1975, 88 Stat. 1946; Apr. 26, 2011, eff. Dec. 1, 2011.)

RULE 1004. ADMISSIBILITY OF OTHER EVIDENCE OF CONTENT

An original is not required and other evidence of the content of a writing, recording, or photograph is admissible if:

(a) all the originals are lost or destroyed, and not by the proponent acting in bad faith;

(b) an original cannot be obtained by any available judicial process;

(c) the party against whom the original would be offered had control of the original; was at that time put on notice, by pleadings or otherwise, that the original would be a subject of proof at the trial or hearing; and fails to produce it at the trial or hearing; or

(d) the writing, recording, or photograph is not closely related to a controlling issue.

(Pub.L. 93–595, § 1, Jan. 2, 1975, 88 Stat. 1946; Mar. 2, 1987, eff. Oct. 1, 1987; Apr. 26, 2011, eff. Dec. 1, 2011.)

RULE 1005. COPIES OF PUBLIC RECORDS TO PROVE CONTENT

The proponent may use a copy to prove the content of an official record—or of a document that was recorded or filed in a public office as authorized by law—if these conditions are met: the record or document is otherwise admissible; and the copy is certified as correct in accordance with Rule 902(4) or is testified to be correct by a witness who has compared it with the original. If no such copy can be obtained by reasonable diligence, then the proponent may use other evidence to prove the content.

(Pub.L. 93–595, § 1, Jan. 2, 1975, 88 Stat. 1946; Apr. 26, 2011, eff. Dec. 1, 2011.)

RULE 1006. SUMMARIES TO PROVE CONTENT

The proponent may use a summary, chart, or calculation to prove the content of voluminous writings, recordings, or photographs that cannot be conveniently examined in court. The proponent must make the originals or duplicates available for examination or copying, or both, by other parties at a reasonable time and place. And the court may order the proponent to produce them in court.

(Pub.L. 93–595, § 1, Jan. 2, 1975, 88 Stat. 1946; Apr. 26, 2011, eff. Dec. 1, 2011.)

RULE 1007. TESTIMONY OR STATEMENT OF A PARTY TO PROVE CONTENT

The proponent may prove the content of a writing, recording, or photograph by the testimony, deposition, or written statement of the party against whom the evidence is offered. The proponent need not account for the original.

(Pub.L. 93–595, § 1, Jan. 2, 1975, 88 Stat. 1947; Mar. 2, 1987, eff. Oct. 1, 1987; Apr. 26, 2011, eff. Dec. 1, 2011.)

RULE 1008. FUNCTIONS OF THE COURT AND JURY

Ordinarily, the court determines whether the proponent has fulfilled the factual conditions for admitting other evidence of the content of a writing, recording, or photograph under Rule 1004 or 1005. But in a jury trial, the jury determines—in accordance with Rule 104(b)—any issue about whether:

(a) an asserted writing, recording, or photograph ever existed;

(b) another one produced at the trial or hearing is the original; or

(c) other evidence of content accurately reflects the content.

(Pub.L. 93–595, § 1, Jan. 2, 1975, 88 Stat. 1947; Apr. 26, 2011, eff. Dec. 1, 2011.)

ARTICLE XI. MISCELLANEOUS RULES

RULE 1101. APPLICABILITY OF THE RULES

(a) **To Courts and Judges.** These rules apply to proceedings before:

- United States district courts;
- United States bankruptcy and magistrate judges;
- United States courts of appeals;
- the United States Court of Federal Claims; and
- the district courts of Guam, the Virgin Islands, and the Northern Mariana Islands.

(b) **To Cases and Proceedings.** These rules apply in:

- civil cases and proceedings, including bankruptcy, admiralty, and maritime cases;
- criminal cases and proceedings; and
- contempt proceedings, except those in which the court may act summarily.

(c) **Rules on Privilege.** The rules on privilege apply to all stages of a case or proceeding.

(d) **Exceptions.** These rules—except for those on privilege—do not apply to the following:

(1) the court's determination, under Rule 104(a), on a preliminary question of fact governing admissibility;

(2) grand-jury proceedings; and

(3) miscellaneous proceedings such as:

- extradition or rendition;
- issuing an arrest warrant, criminal summons, or search warrant;
- a preliminary examination in a criminal case;
- sentencing;
- granting or revoking probation or supervised release; and
- considering whether to release on bail or otherwise.

(e) **Other Statutes and Rules.** A federal statute or a rule prescribed by the Supreme Court may provide for admitting or excluding evidence independently from these rules.

(Pub.L. 93–595, § 1, Jan. 2, 1975, 88 Stat. 1947; Pub.L. 94–149, § 1(14), Dec. 12, 1975, 89 Stat. 806; Pub.L. 95–598, Title II, § 251, Nov. 6, 1978, 92 Stat. 2673; Pub.L. 97–164, Title I, § 142, Apr. 2, 1982, 96 Stat. 45; Mar. 2, 1987, eff. Oct. 1, 1987; Apr. 25, 1988, eff. Nov. 1, 1988; Pub.L. 100–690, Title VII, § 7075(c), Nov. 18, 1988, 102 Stat. 4405; Apr. 22, 1993, eff. Dec. 1, 1993; Apr. 26, 2011, eff. Dec. 1, 2011.)

RULE 1102. AMENDMENTS

These rules may be amended as provided in 28 U.S.C. § 2072.

(Pub.L. 93–595, § 1, Jan. 2, 1975, 88 Stat.1948; Apr. 30, 1991, eff. Dec. 1, 1991; Apr. 26, 2011, eff. Dec. 1, 2011.)

RULE 1103. TITLE

These rules may be cited as the Federal Rules of Evidence.

(Pub.L. 93–595, § 1, Jan. 2, 1975, 88 Stat.1948; Apr. 26, 2011, eff. Dec. 1, 2011.)

INDEX TO
FEDERAL RULES OF EVIDENCE

FEDERAL RULES OF APPELLATE PROCEDURE

Including Amendments Effective December 1, 2017

TITLE I. APPLICABILITY OF RULES

RULE 1. SCOPE OF RULES; DEFINITION; TITLE

(a) Scope of Rules.

(1) These rules govern procedure in the United States courts of appeals.

(2) When these rules provide for filing a motion or other document in the district court, the procedure must comply with the practice of the district court.

(b) Definition. In these rules, "state" includes the District of Columbia and any United States commonwealth or territory.

(c) Title. These rules are to be known as the Federal Rules of Appellate Procedure.

(As amended Apr. 30, 1979, eff. Aug. 1, 1979; Apr. 25, 1989, eff. Dec. 1, 1989; Apr. 29, 1994, eff. Dec. 1, 1994; Apr. 24, 1998, eff. Dec. 1, 1998; Apr. 29, 2002, eff. Dec. 1, 2002; Apr. 28, 2010, eff. Dec. 1, 2010.)

RULE 2. SUSPENSION OF RULES

On its own or a party's motion, a court of appeals may—to expedite its decision or for other good cause—suspend any provision of these rules in a particular case and order proceedings as it directs, except as otherwise provided in Rule 26(b).

(As amended Apr. 24, 1998, eff. Dec. 1, 1998.)

TITLE II. APPEAL FROM A JUDGMENT OR ORDER OF A DISTRICT COURT

RULE 3. APPEAL AS OF RIGHT—HOW TAKEN

(a) Filing the Notice of Appeal.

(1) An appeal permitted by law as of right from a district court to a court of appeals may be taken only by filing a notice of appeal with the district clerk within the time allowed by Rule 4. At the time of filing, the appellant must furnish the clerk with enough copies of the notice to enable the clerk to comply with Rule 3(d).

(2) An appellant's failure to take any step other than the timely filing of a notice of appeal does not affect the validity of the appeal, but is ground only for the court of appeals to act as it considers appropriate, including dismissing the appeal.

(3) An appeal from a judgment by a magistrate judge in a civil case is taken in the same way as an appeal from any other district court judgment.

(4) An appeal by permission under 28 U.S.C. § 1292(b) or an appeal in a bankruptcy case may be taken only in the manner prescribed by Rules 5 and 6, respectively.

(b) Joint or Consolidated Appeals.

(1) When two or more parties are entitled to appeal from a district-court judgment or order, and their interests make joinder practicable, they may file a joint notice of appeal. They may then proceed on appeal as a single appellant.

(2) When the parties have filed separate timely notices of appeal, the appeals may be joined or consolidated by the court of appeals.

(c) Contents of the Notice of Appeal.

(1) The notice of appeal must:

(A) specify the party or parties taking the appeal by naming each one in the caption or body of the notice, but an attorney representing more than one party may describe those parties with such terms as "all plaintiffs," "the defendants," "the plaintiffs A, B, et al.," or "all defendants except X";

(B) designate the judgment, order, or part thereof being appealed; and

(C) name the court to which the appeal is taken.

(2) A pro se notice of appeal is considered filed on behalf of the signer and the signer's spouse and minor children (if they are parties), unless the notice clearly indicates otherwise.

(3) In a class action, whether or not the class has been certified, the notice of appeal is sufficient if it names one person qualified to bring the appeal as representative of the class.

(4) An appeal must not be dismissed for informality of form or title of the notice of appeal, or for failure to name a party whose intent to appeal is otherwise clear from the notice.

(5) Form 1 in the Appendix of Forms is a suggested form of a notice of appeal.

(d) Serving the Notice of Appeal.

(1) The district clerk must serve notice of the filing of a notice of appeal by mailing a copy to each party's counsel of record—excluding the appellant's—or, if a party is proceeding pro se, to the party's last known address. When a defendant in a criminal case appeals, the clerk must also serve a copy of the notice of appeal on the defendant, either by personal service or by mail addressed to the defendant. The clerk must promptly send a copy of the notice of appeal and of the docket entries—and any later docket entries—to the clerk of the court of appeals named in the notice. The district clerk must note, on each copy, the date when the notice of appeal was filed.

(2) If an inmate confined in an institution files a notice of appeal in the manner provided by Rule 4(c), the district clerk must also note the date when the clerk docketed the notice.

(3) The district clerk's failure to serve notice does not affect the validity of the appeal. The clerk must note on the docket the names of the parties to whom the clerk mails

copies, with the date of mailing. Service is sufficient despite the death of a party or the party's counsel.

(e) Payment of Fees. Upon filing a notice of appeal, the appellant must pay the district clerk all required fees. The district clerk receives the appellate docket fee on behalf of the court of appeals.

(As amended Apr. 30, 1979, eff. Aug. 1, 1979; Mar. 10, 1986, eff. July 1, 1986; Apr. 25, 1989, eff. Dec. 1, 1989; Apr. 22, 1993, eff. Dec. 1, 1993; Apr. 29, 1994, eff. Dec. 1, 1994; Apr. 24, 1998, eff. Dec. 1, 1998.)

[RULE 3.1 APPEAL FROM A JUDGMENT OF A MAGISTRATE JUDGE IN A CIVIL CASE (ABROGATED APR. 24, 1998, EFF. DEC. 1, 1998)]

RULE 4. APPEAL AS OF RIGHT— WHEN TAKEN

(a) Appeal in a Civil Case.

(1) Time for Filing a Notice of Appeal.

(A) In a civil case, except as provided in Rules 4(a)(1)(B), 4(a)(4), and 4(c), the notice of appeal required by Rule 3 must be filed with the district clerk within 30 days after entry of the judgment or order appealed from.

(B) The notice of appeal may be filed by any party within 60 days after entry of the judgment or order appealed from if one of the parties is:

(i) the United States;

(ii) a United States agency;

(iii) a United States officer or employee sued in an official capacity; or

(iv) a current or former United States officer or employee sued in an individual capacity for an act or omission occurring in connection with duties performed on the United States' behalf—including all instances in which the United States represents that person when the judgment or order is entered or files the appeal for that person.

(C) An appeal from an order granting or denying an application for a writ of error coram nobis is an appeal in a civil case for purposes of Rule 4(a).

(2) Filing Before Entry of Judgment. A notice of appeal filed after the court announces a decision or order—but before the entry of the judgment or order—is treated as filed on the date of and after the entry.

(3) Multiple Appeals. If one party timely files a notice of appeal, any other party may file a notice of appeal within 14 days after the date when the first notice was filed, or within the time otherwise prescribed by this Rule 4(a), whichever period ends later.

(4) Effect of a Motion on a Notice of Appeal.

(A) If a party files in the district court any of the following motions under the Federal Rules of Civil Procedure—and does so within the time allowed by those rules—the time to file an appeal runs for all parties from the entry of the order disposing of the last such remaining motion:

(i) for judgment under Rule 50(b);

(ii) to amend or make additional factual findings under Rule 52(b), whether or not granting the motion would alter the judgment;

(iii) for attorney's fees under Rule 54 if the district court extends the time to appeal under Rule 58;

(iv) to alter or amend the judgment under Rule 59;

(v) for a new trial under Rule 59; or

(vi) for relief under Rule 60 if the motion is filed no later than 28 days after the judgment is entered.

(B)(i) If a party files a notice of appeal after the court announces or enters a judgment—but before it disposes of any motion listed in Rule 4(a)(4)(A)—the notice becomes effective to appeal a judgment or order, in whole or in part, when the order disposing of the last such remaining motion is entered.

(ii) A party intending to challenge an order disposing of any motion listed in Rule 4(a)(4)(A), or a judgment's alteration or amendment upon such a motion, must file a notice of appeal, or an amended notice of appeal—in compliance with Rule 3(c)—within the time prescribed by this Rule measured from the entry of the order disposing of the last such remaining motion.

(iii) No additional fee is required to file an amended notice.

(5) Motion for Extension of Time.

(A) The district court may extend the time to file a notice of appeal if:

(i) a party so moves no later than 30 days after the time prescribed by this Rule 4(a) expires; and

(ii) regardless of whether its motion is filed before or during the 30 days after the time prescribed by this Rule 4(a) expires, that party shows excusable neglect or good cause.

(B) A motion filed before the expiration of the time prescribed in Rule 4(a)(1) or (3) may be ex parte unless the court requires otherwise. If the motion is filed after the expiration of the prescribed time, notice must be given to the other parties in accordance with local rules.

(C) No extension under this Rule 4(a)(5) may exceed 30 days after the prescribed time or 14 days after the date when the order granting the motion is entered, whichever is later.

(6) Reopening the Time to File an Appeal. The district court may reopen the time to file an appeal for a period of 14 days after the date when its order to reopen is entered, but only if all the following conditions are satisfied:

(A) the court finds that the moving party did not receive notice under Federal Rule of Civil Procedure 77(d) of the entry of the judgment or order sought to be appealed within 21 days after entry;

(B) the motion is filed within 180 days after the judgment or order is entered or within 14 days after the moving party receives notice under Federal Rule of Civil Procedure 77(d) of the entry, whichever is earlier; and

(C) the court finds that no party would be prejudiced.

(7) Entry Defined.

(A) A judgment or order is entered for purposes of this Rule 4(a):

(i) if Federal Rule of Civil Procedure 58(a) does not require a separate document, when the judgment or order is entered in the civil docket under Federal Rule of Civil Procedure 79(a); or

(ii) if Federal Rule of Civil Procedure 58(a) requires a separate document, when the judgment or order is entered in the civil docket under Federal Rule of Civil Procedure 79(a) and when the earlier of these events occurs:

• the judgment or order is set forth on a separate document, or

• 150 days have run from entry of the judgment or order in the civil docket under Federal Rule of Civil Procedure 79(a).

(B) A failure to set forth a judgment or order on a separate document when required by Federal Rule of Civil Procedure 58(a) does not affect the validity of an appeal from that judgment or order.

(b) Appeal in a Criminal Case.

(1) Time for Filing a Notice of Appeal.

(A) In a criminal case, a defendant's notice of appeal must be filed in the district court within 14 days after the later of:

(i) the entry of either the judgment or the order being appealed; or

(ii) the filing of the government's notice of appeal.

(B) When the government is entitled to appeal, its notice of appeal must be filed in the district court within 30 days after the later of:

(i) the entry of the judgment or order being appealed; or

(ii) the filing of a notice of appeal by any defendant.

(2) Filing Before Entry of Judgment. A notice of appeal filed after the court announces a decision, sentence, or order—but before the entry of the judgment or order—is treated as filed on the date of and after the entry.

(3) Effect of a Motion on a Notice of Appeal.

(A) If a defendant timely makes any of the following motions under the Federal Rules of Criminal Procedure, the notice of appeal from a judgment of conviction must be filed within 14 days after the entry of the order disposing of the last such remaining motion, or within 14 days after the entry of the judgment of conviction, whichever period ends later. This provision applies to a timely motion:

(i) for judgment of acquittal under Rule 29;

(ii) for a new trial under Rule 33, but if based on newly discovered evidence, only if the motion is made no later than 14 days after the entry of the judgment; or

(iii) for arrest of judgment under Rule 34.

(B) A notice of appeal filed after the court announces a decision, sentence, or order—but before it disposes of any of the motions referred to in Rule 4(b)(3)(A)—becomes effective upon the later of the following:

(i) the entry of the order disposing of the last such remaining motion; or

(ii) the entry of the judgment of conviction.

(C) A valid notice of appeal is effective—without amendment—to appeal from an order disposing of any of the motions referred to in Rule 4(b)(3)(A).

(4) Motion for Extension of Time. Upon a finding of excusable neglect or good cause, the district court may—before or after the time has expired, with or without motion and notice—extend the time to file a notice of appeal for a period not to exceed 30 days from the expiration of the time otherwise prescribed by this Rule 4(b).

(5) Jurisdiction. The filing of a notice of appeal under this Rule 4(b) does not divest a district court of jurisdiction to correct a sentence under Federal Rule of Criminal Procedure 35(a), nor does the filing of a motion under 35(a) affect the validity of a notice of appeal filed before entry of the order disposing of the motion. The filing of a motion under Federal Rule of Criminal Procedure 35(a) does not suspend the time for filing a notice of appeal from a judgment of conviction.

(6) Entry Defined. A judgment or order is entered for purposes of this Rule 4(b) when it is entered on the criminal docket.

(c) Appeal by an Inmate Confined in an Institution.

(1) If an institution has a system designed for legal mail, an inmate confined there must use that system to receive the benefit of this Rule 4(c)(1). If an inmate files a notice of appeal in either a civil or a criminal case, the notice is timely if it is deposited in the institution's internal mail system on or before the last day for filing and:

(A) it is accompanied by:

(i) a declaration in compliance with 28 U.S.C. § 1746—or a notarized statement—setting out the date of deposit and stating that first-class postage is being prepaid; or

(ii) evidence (such as a postmark or date stamp) showing that the notice was so deposited and that postage was prepaid; or

(B) the court of appeals exercises its discretion to permit the later filing of a declaration or notarized statement that satisfies Rule 4(c)(1)(A)(i).

(2) If an inmate files the first notice of appeal in a civil case under this Rule 4(c), the 14–day period provided in Rule 4(a)(3) for another party to file a notice of appeal runs from the date when the district court dockets the first notice.

(3) When a defendant in a criminal case files a notice of appeal under this Rule 4(c), the 30–day period for the government to file its notice of appeal runs from the entry of the judgment or order appealed from or from the district court's docketing of the defendant's notice of appeal, whichever is later.

(d) Mistaken Filing in the Court of Appeals. If a notice of appeal in either a civil or a criminal case is mistakenly filed in the court of appeals, the clerk of that court must note on the notice the date when it was received and send it to the district clerk. The notice is then considered filed in the district court on the date so noted.

(As amended Apr. 30, 1979, eff. Aug. 1, 1979; Nov. 18, 1988, Pub.L. 100–690, Title VII, § 7111, 102 Stat. 4419; Apr. 30, 1991, eff. Dec. 1, 1991; Apr. 22, 1993, eff. Dec. 1, 1993; Apr. 27, 1995, eff. Dec. 1, 1995; Apr. 24, 1998, eff. Dec. 1, 1998; Apr. 29, 2002, eff. Dec. 1, 2002; Apr. 25, 2005, eff. Dec. 1, 2005; Mar. 26, 2009, eff. Dec. 1, 2009; Apr. 28, 2010, eff. Dec. 1, 2010; Apr. 26, 2011, eff. Dec. 1, 2011; Apr. 28, 2016, eff. Dec. 1, 2016; Apr. 27, 2017, eff. Dec. 1, 2017.)

RULE 5. APPEAL BY PERMISSION

(a) Petition for Permission to Appeal.

(1) To request permission to appeal when an appeal is within the court of appeals' discretion, a party must file a petition for permission to appeal. The petition must be filed with the circuit clerk with proof of service on all other parties to the district-court action.

(2) The petition must be filed within the time specified by the statute or rule authorizing the appeal or, if no such time is specified, within the time provided by Rule 4(a) for filing a notice of appeal.

(3) If a party cannot petition for appeal unless the district court first enters an order granting permission to do so or stating that the necessary conditions are met, the district court may amend its order, either on its own or in response to a party's motion, to include the required permission or statement. In that event, the time to petition runs from entry of the amended order.

(b) Contents of the Petition; Answer or Cross–Petition; Oral Argument.

(1) The petition must include the following:

(A) the facts necessary to understand the question presented;

(B) the question itself;

(C) the relief sought;

(D) the reasons why the appeal should be allowed and is authorized by a statute or rule; and

(E) an attached copy of:

(i) the order, decree, or judgment complained of and any related opinion or memorandum, and

(ii) any order stating the district court's permission to appeal or finding that the necessary conditions are met.

(2) A party may file an answer in opposition or a cross-petition within 10 days after the petition is served.

(3) The petition and answer will be submitted without oral argument unless the court of appeals orders otherwise.

(c) Form of Papers; Number of Copies; Length Limits. All papers must conform to Rule 32(c)(2). An original and 3 copies must be filed unless the court requires a different number by local rule or by order in a particular case. Except by the court's permission, and excluding the accompanying documents required by Rule 5(b)(1)(E):

(1) a paper produced using a computer must not exceed 5,200 words; and

(2) a handwritten or typewritten paper must not exceed 20 pages.

(d) Grant of Permission; Fees; Cost Bond; Filing the Record.

(1) Within 14 days after the entry of the order granting permission to appeal, the appellant must:

(A) pay the district clerk all required fees; and

(B) file a cost bond if required under Rule 7.

(2) A notice of appeal need not be filed. The date when the order granting permission to appeal is entered serves as the date of the notice of appeal for calculating time under these rules.

(3) The district clerk must notify the circuit clerk once the petitioner has paid the fees. Upon receiving this notice, the circuit clerk must enter the appeal on the docket. The record must be forwarded and filed in accordance with Rules 11 and 12(c).

(As amended Apr. 30, 1979, eff. Aug. 1, 1979; Apr. 29, 1994, eff. Dec. 1, 1994; Apr. 24, 1998, eff. Dec. 1, 1998; Apr. 29, 2002, eff. Dec. 1, 2002; Mar. 26, 2009, eff. Dec. 1, 2009; Apr. 28, 2016, eff. Dec. 1, 2016.)

[RULE 5.1 APPEAL BY LEAVE UNDER 28 U.S.C. § 636 (c)(5) (ABROGATED APR. 24, 1998, EFF. DEC. 1, 1998)]

RULE 6. APPEAL IN A BANKRUPTCY CASE

(a) Appeal From a Judgment, Order, or Decree of a District Court Exercising Original Jurisdiction in a Bankruptcy Case. An appeal to a court of appeals from a final judgment, order, or decree of a district court exercising jurisdiction under 28 U.S.C. § 1334 is taken as any other civil appeal under these rules.

(b) Appeal From a Judgment, Order, or Decree of a District Court or Bankruptcy Appellate Panel Exercising Appellate Jurisdiction in a Bankruptcy Case.

(1) Applicability of Other Rules. These rules apply to an appeal to a court of appeals under 28 U.S.C. § 158(d)(1) from a final judgment, order, or decree of a district court or bankruptcy appellate panel exercising appellate jurisdiction under 28 U.S.C. § 158(a) or (b), but with these qualifications:

(A) Rules 4(a)(4), 4(b), 9, 10, 11, 12(c), 13–20, 22–23, and 24(b) do not apply;

(B) the reference in Rule 3(c) to "Form 1 in the Appendix of Forms" must be read as a reference to Form 5;

(C) when the appeal is from a bankruptcy appellate panel, "district court," as used in any applicable rule, means "appellate panel"; and

(D) in Rule 12.1, "district court" includes a bankruptcy court or bankruptcy appellate panel.

(2) Additional Rules. In addition to the rules made applicable by Rule 6(b)(1), the following rules apply:

(A) Motion for Rehearing.

(i) If a timely motion for rehearing under Bankruptcy Rule 8022 is filed, the time to appeal for all parties runs from the entry of the order disposing of the motion. A notice of appeal filed after the district court or bankruptcy appellate panel announces or enters a judgment, order, or decree—but before disposition of the motion for rehearing—becomes effective when the order disposing of the motion for rehearing is entered.

(ii) If a party intends to challenge the order disposing of the motion—or the alteration or amendment of a judgment, order, or decree upon the motion—then the party, in compliance with Rules 3(c) and 6(b)(1)(B), must file a notice of appeal or amended notice of appeal. The notice or amended notice must be filed within the time prescribed by Rule 4—excluding Rules 4(a)(4) and 4(b)—measured from the entry of the order disposing of the motion.

(iii) No additional fee is required to file an amended notice.

(B) The Record on Appeal.

(i) Within 14 days after filing the notice of appeal, the appellant must file with the clerk possessing the record assembled in accordance with Bankruptcy Rule 8009—and serve on the appellee—a statement of the issues to be presented on appeal and a designation of the record to be certified and made available to the circuit clerk.

(ii) An appellee who believes that other parts of the record are necessary must, within 14 days after being served with the appellant's designation, file with the clerk and serve on the appellant a designation of additional parts to be included.

(iii) The record on appeal consists of:

- the redesignated record as provided above;
- the proceedings in the district court or bankruptcy appellate panel; and
- a certified copy of the docket entries prepared by the clerk under Rule 3(d).

(C) Making the Record Available.

(i) When the record is complete, the district clerk or bankruptcy-appellate-panel clerk must number the documents constituting the record and promptly make it available to the circuit clerk. If the clerk makes the record available in paper form, the clerk will not send documents of unusual bulk or weight, physical exhibits other than

documents, or other parts of the record designated for omission by local rule of the court of appeals, unless directed to do so by a party or the circuit clerk. If unusually bulky or heavy exhibits are to be made available in paper form, a party must arrange with the clerks in advance for their transportation and receipt.

(ii) All parties must do whatever else is necessary to enable the clerk to assemble the record and make it available. When the record is made available in paper form, the court of appeals may provide by rule or order that a certified copy of the docket entries be made available in place of the redesignated record. But any party may request at any time during the pendency of the appeal that the redesignated record be made available.

(D) Filing the Record. When the district clerk or bankruptcy-appellate-panel clerk has made the record available, the circuit clerk must note that fact on the docket. The date noted on the docket serves as the filing date of the record. The circuit clerk must immediately notify all parties of the filing date.

(c) Direct Review by Permission Under 28 U.S.C. § 158(d)(2).

(1) Applicability of Other Rules. These rules apply to a direct appeal by permission under 28 U.S.C. § 158(d)(2), but with these qualifications:

(A) Rules 3–4, 5(a)(3), 6(a), 6(b), 8(a), 8(c), 9–12, 13–20, 22–23, and 24(b) do not apply;

(B) as used in any applicable rule, "district court" or "district clerk" includes—to the extent appropriate—a bankruptcy court or bankruptcy appellate panel or its clerk; and

(C) the reference to "Rules 11 and 12(c)" in Rule 5(d)(3) must be read as a reference to Rules 6(c)(2)(B) and (C).

(2) Additional Rules. In addition, the following rules apply:

(A) The Record on Appeal. Bankruptcy Rule 8009 governs the record on appeal.

(B) Making the Record Available. Bankruptcy Rule 8010 governs completing the record and making it available.

(C) Stays Pending Appeal. Bankruptcy Rule 8007 applies to stays pending appeal.

(D) Duties of the Circuit Clerk. When the bankruptcy clerk has made the record available, the circuit clerk must note that fact on the docket. The date noted on the docket serves as the filing date of the record. The circuit clerk must immediately notify all parties of the filing date.

(E) Filing a Representation Statement. Unless the court of appeals designates another time, within 14 days after entry of the order granting permission to appeal, the attorney who sought permission must file a statement with the circuit clerk naming the parties that the attorney represents on appeal.

(Added Apr. 25, 1989, eff. Dec. 1, 1989; amended Apr. 30, 1991, eff. Dec. 1, 1991; Apr. 22, 1993, eff. Dec. 1, 1993; Apr. 24, 1998, eff. Dec. 1, 1998; Mar. 26, 2009, eff. Dec. 1, 2009; Apr. 25, 2014, eff. Dec. 1, 2014.)

RULE 7. BOND FOR COSTS ON APPEAL IN A CIVIL CASE

In a civil case, the district court may require an appellant to file a bond or provide other security in any form and amount necessary to ensure payment of costs on appeal. Rule 8(b) applies to a surety on a bond given under this rule.

(As amended Apr. 30, 1979, eff. Aug. 1, 1979; Apr. 24, 1998, eff. Dec. 1, 1998.)

RULE 8. STAY OR INJUNCTION PENDING APPEAL

(a) Motion for Stay.

(1) Initial Motion in the District Court. A party must ordinarily move first in the district court for the following relief:

(A) a stay of the judgment or order of a district court pending appeal;

(B) approval of a supersedeas bond; or

(C) an order suspending, modifying, restoring, or granting an injunction while an appeal is pending.

(2) Motion in the Court of Appeals; Conditions on Relief. A motion for the relief mentioned in Rule 8(a)(1) may be made to the court of appeals or to one of its judges.

(A) The motion must:

(i) show that moving first in the district court would be impracticable; or

(ii) state that, a motion having been made, the district court denied the motion or failed to afford the relief requested and state any reasons given by the district court for its action.

(B) The motion must also include:

(i) the reasons for granting the relief requested and the facts relied on;

(ii) originals or copies of affidavits or other sworn statements supporting facts subject to dispute; and

(iii) relevant parts of the record.

(C) The moving party must give reasonable notice of the motion to all parties.

(D) A motion under this Rule 8(a)(2) must be filed with the circuit clerk and normally will be considered by a panel of the court. But in an exceptional case in which time requirements make that procedure impracticable, the motion may be made to and considered by a single judge.

(E) The court may condition relief on a party's filing a bond or other appropriate security in the district court.

(b) Proceeding Against a Surety. If a party gives security in the form of a bond or stipulation or other undertaking with one or more sureties, each surety submits to the jurisdiction of the district court and irrevocably appoints the district clerk as the surety's agent on whom any papers affecting the surety's liability on the bond or undertaking may be served. On motion, a surety's liability may be enforced in the district court without the necessity of an independent action. The motion and any notice that the district court prescribes may be served on the district clerk, who must promptly mail a copy to each surety whose address is known.

(c) Stay in a Criminal Case. Rule 38 of the Federal Rules of Criminal Procedure governs a stay in a criminal case.

(As amended Mar. 10, 1986, eff. July 1, 1986; Apr. 27, 1995, eff. Dec. 1, 1995; Apr. 24, 1998, eff. Dec. 1, 1998.)

RULE 9. RELEASE IN A CRIMINAL CASE

(a) Release Before Judgment of Conviction.

(1) The district court must state in writing, or orally on the record, the reasons for an order regarding the release or detention of a defendant in a criminal case. A party appealing from the order must file with the court of appeals a copy of the district court's order and the court's statement of reasons as soon as practicable after filing the notice of appeal. An appellant who questions the factual basis for the district court's order must file a transcript of the release proceedings or an explanation of why a transcript was not obtained.

(2) After reasonable notice to the appellee, the court of appeals must promptly determine the appeal on the basis of the papers, affidavits, and parts of the record that the parties present or the court requires. Unless the court so orders, briefs need not be filed.

(3) The court of appeals or one of its judges may order the defendant's release pending the disposition of the appeal.

(b) Release After Judgment of Conviction. A party entitled to do so may obtain review of a district-court order regarding release after a judgment of conviction by filing a notice of appeal from that order in the district court, or by filing a motion in the court of appeals if the party has already filed a notice of appeal from the judgment of conviction. Both the order and the review are subject to Rule 9(a). The papers filed by the party seeking review must include a copy of the judgment of conviction.

(c) Criteria for Release. The court must make its decision regarding release in accordance with the applicable provisions of 18 U.S.C. §§ 3142, 3143, and 3145(c).

(As amended Apr. 24, 1972, eff. Oct. 1, 1972; Oct. 12, 1984, Pub.L. 98–473, Title II, § 210, 98 Stat. 1987; Apr. 29, 1994, eff. Dec. 1, 1994; Apr. 24, 1998, eff. Dec. 1, 1998.)

RULE 10. THE RECORD ON APPEAL

(a) Composition of the Record on Appeal. The following items constitute the record on appeal:

(1) the original papers and exhibits filed in the district court;

(2) the transcript of proceedings, if any; and

(3) a certified copy of the docket entries prepared by the district clerk.

(b) The Transcript of Proceedings.

(1) Appellant's Duty to Order. Within 14 days after filing the notice of appeal or entry of an order disposing of the last timely remaining motion of a type specified in Rule 4(a)(4)(A), whichever is later, the appellant must do either of the following:

(A) order from the reporter a transcript of such parts of the proceedings not already on file as the appellant considers necessary, subject to a local rule of the court of appeals and with the following qualifications:

(i) the order must be in writing;

(ii) if the cost of the transcript is to be paid by the United States under the Criminal Justice Act, the order must so state; and

(iii) the appellant must, within the same period, file a copy of the order with the district clerk; or

(B) file a certificate stating that no transcript will be ordered.

(2) Unsupported Finding or Conclusion. If the appellant intends to urge on appeal that a finding or conclusion is unsupported by the evidence or is contrary to the evidence, the appellant must include in the record a transcript of all evidence relevant to that finding or conclusion.

(3) Partial Transcript. Unless the entire transcript is ordered:

(A) the appellant must—within the 14 days provided in Rule 10(b)(1)—file a statement of the issues that the appellant intends to present on the appeal and must serve on the appellee a copy of both the order or certificate and the statement;

(B) if the appellee considers it necessary to have a transcript of other parts of the proceedings, the appellee must, within 14 days after the service of the order or certificate and the statement of the issues, file and serve on the appellant a designation of additional parts to be ordered; and

(C) unless within 14 days after service of that designation the appellant has ordered all such parts, and has so notified the appellee, the appellee may within the following 14 days either order the parts or move in the district court for an order requiring the appellant to do so.

(4) Payment. At the time of ordering, a party must make satisfactory arrangements with the reporter for paying the cost of the transcript.

(c) Statement of the Evidence When the Proceedings Were Not Recorded or When a Transcript Is Unavailable. If the transcript of a hearing or trial is unavailable, the appellant may prepare a statement of the evidence or proceedings from the best available means, including the appellant's recollection. The statement must be served on the appellee, who may serve objections or proposed amendments within 14 days after being served. The statement and any objections or proposed amendments must then be submitted to the district court for settlement and approval. As settled and approved, the statement must be included by the district clerk in the record on appeal.

(d) Agreed Statement as the Record on Appeal. In place of the record on appeal as defined in Rule 10(a), the parties may prepare, sign, and submit to the district court a statement of the case showing how the issues presented by the appeal arose and were decided in the district court. The statement must set forth only those facts averred and proved or sought to be proved that are essential to the court's resolution of the issues. If the statement is truthful, it—together with any additions that the district court may consider necessary to a full presentation of the issues on appeal—must be approved by the district court and must then be certified to the court of appeals as the record on appeal. The district clerk must then send it to the circuit clerk within the time provided by Rule 11. A copy of the agreed statement may be filed in place of the appendix required by Rule 30.

(e) Correction or Modification of the Record.

(1) If any difference arises about whether the record truly discloses what occurred in the district court, the difference must be submitted to and settled by that court and the record conformed accordingly.

(2) If anything material to either party is omitted from or misstated in the record by error or accident, the omission or misstatement may be corrected and a supplemental record may be certified and forwarded:

(A) on stipulation of the parties;

(B) by the district court before or after the record has been forwarded; or

(C) by the court of appeals.

(3) All other questions as to the form and content of the record must be presented to the court of appeals.

(As amended Apr. 30, 1979, eff. Aug. 1, 1979; Mar. 10, 1986, eff. July 1, 1986; Apr. 30, 1991, eff. Dec. 1, 1991; Apr. 22, 1993, eff. Dec. 1, 1993; Apr. 27, 1995, eff. Dec. 1, 1995; Apr. 24, 1998, eff. Dec. 1, 1998; Mar. 26, 2009, eff. Dec. 1, 2009.)

RULE 11. FORWARDING THE RECORD

(a) Appellant's Duty. An appellant filing a notice of appeal must comply with Rule 10(b) and must do whatever else is necessary to enable the clerk to assemble and forward the record. If there are multiple appeals from a judgment or order, the clerk must forward a single record.

(b) Duties of Reporter and District Clerk.

(1) Reporter's Duty to Prepare and File a Transcript. The reporter must prepare and file a transcript as follows:

(A) Upon receiving an order for a transcript, the reporter must enter at the foot of the order the date of its receipt and the expected completion date and send a copy, so endorsed, to the circuit clerk.

(B) If the transcript cannot be completed within 30 days of the reporter's receipt of the order, the reporter may request the circuit clerk to grant additional time to complete it. The clerk must note on the docket the action taken and notify the parties.

(C) When a transcript is complete, the reporter must file it with the district clerk and notify the circuit clerk of the filing.

(D) If the reporter fails to file the transcript on time, the circuit clerk must notify the district judge and do whatever else the court of appeals directs.

(2) District Clerk's Duty to Forward. When the record is complete, the district clerk must number the documents constituting the record and send them promptly to the circuit clerk together with a list of the documents correspondingly numbered and reasonably identified. Unless directed to do so by a party or the circuit clerk, the district clerk will not send to the court of appeals documents of unusual bulk or weight, physical exhibits other than documents, or other parts of the record designated for omission by local rule of the court of appeals. If the exhibits are unusually bulky or heavy, a party must arrange with the clerks in advance for their transportation and receipt.

(c) Retaining the Record Temporarily in the District Court for Use in Preparing the Appeal. The parties may stipulate, or the district court on motion may order, that the district clerk retain the record temporarily for the parties to use in preparing the papers on appeal. In that event the district clerk must certify to the circuit clerk that the record on appeal is complete. Upon receipt of the appellee's brief, or earlier if the court orders or the parties agree, the appellant must request the district clerk to forward the record.

(d) [Abrogated.]

(e) Retaining the Record by Court Order.

(1) The court of appeals may, by order or local rule, provide that a certified copy of the docket entries be forwarded instead of the entire record. But a party may at any time during the appeal request that designated parts of the record be forwarded.

(2) The district court may order the record or some part of it retained if the court needs it while the appeal is pending, subject, however, to call by the court of appeals.

(3) If part or all of the record is ordered retained, the district clerk must send to the court of appeals a copy of the order and the docket entries together with the parts of the original record allowed by the district court and copies of any parts of the record designated by the parties.

(f) Retaining Parts of the Record in the District Court by Stipulation of the Parties. The parties may agree by written stipulation filed in the district court that designated parts of the record be retained in the district court subject to call by the court of appeals or request by a party. The parts of the record so designated remain a part of the record on appeal.

(g) Record for a Preliminary Motion in the Court of Appeals. If, before the record is forwarded, a party makes any of the following motions in the court of appeals:

- for dismissal;
- for release;
- for a stay pending appeal;
- for additional security on the bond on appeal or on a supersedeas bond; or
- for any other intermediate order—

the district clerk must send the court of appeals any parts of the record designated by any party.

(As amended Apr. 30, 1979, eff. Aug. 1, 1979; Mar. 10, 1986, eff. July 1, 1986; Apr. 24, 1998, eff. Dec. 1, 1998.)

RULE 12. DOCKETING THE APPEAL; FILING A REPRESENTATION STATEMENT; FILING THE RECORD

(a) Docketing the Appeal. Upon receiving the copy of the notice of appeal and the docket entries from the district clerk under Rule 3(d), the circuit clerk must docket the appeal under the title of the district-court action and must identify the appellant, adding the appellant's name if necessary.

(b) Filing a Representation Statement. Unless the court of appeals designates another time, the attorney who filed the notice of appeal must, within 14 days after filing the notice, file a statement with the circuit clerk naming the parties that the attorney represents on appeal.

(c) Filing the Record, Partial Record, or Certificate. Upon receiving the record, partial record, or district clerk's certificate as provided in Rule 11, the circuit clerk must file it and immediately notify all parties of the filing date.

(As amended Apr. 30, 1979, eff. Aug. 1, 1979; Mar. 10, 1986, eff. July 1, 1986; Apr. 22, 1993, eff. Dec. 1, 1993; Apr. 24, 1998, eff. Dec. 1, 1998; Mar. 26, 2009, eff. Dec. 1, 2009.)

RULE 12.1 REMAND AFTER AN INDICATIVE RULING BY THE DISTRICT COURT ON A MOTION FOR RELIEF THAT IS BARRED BY A PENDING APPEAL

(a) Notice to the Court of Appeals. If a timely motion is made in the district court for relief that it lacks authority to grant because of an appeal that has been docketed and is pending, the movant must promptly notify the circuit clerk if the district court states either that it would grant the motion or that the motion raises a substantial issue.

(b) Remand After an Indicative Ruling. If the district court states that it would grant the motion or that the motion raises a substantial issue, the court of appeals may remand for further proceedings but retains jurisdiction unless it expressly dismisses the appeal. If the court of appeals remands but retains jurisdiction, the parties must promptly notify the circuit clerk when the district court has decided the motion on remand.

(Added Mar. 26, 2009, eff. Dec. 1, 2009.)

TITLE III. APPEALS FROM THE UNITED STATES TAX COURT

RULE 13. APPEALS FROM THE TAX COURT
(a) Appeal as of Right.

(1) How Obtained; Time for Filing a Notice of Appeal.

(A) An appeal as of right from the United States Tax Court is commenced by filing a notice of appeal with the Tax Court clerk within 90 days after the entry of the Tax Court's decision. At the time of filing, the appellant must furnish the clerk with enough copies of the notice to enable the clerk to comply with Rule 3(d). If one party files a timely notice of appeal, any other party may file a notice of appeal within 120 days after the Tax Court's decision is entered.

(B) If, under Tax Court rules, a party makes a timely motion to vacate or revise the Tax Court's decision, the time to file a notice of appeal runs from the entry of the order disposing of the motion or from the entry of a new decision, whichever is later.

(2) Notice of Appeal; How Filed. The notice of appeal may be filed either at the Tax Court clerk's office in the District of Columbia or by mail addressed to the clerk. If sent by mail the notice is considered filed on the postmark date, subject to § 7502 of the Internal Revenue Code, as amended, and the applicable regulations.

(3) Contents of the Notice of Appeal; Service; Effect of Filing and Service. Rule 3 prescribes the contents of a notice of appeal, the manner of service, and the effect of its filing and service. Form 2 in the Appendix of Forms is a suggested form of a notice of appeal.

(4) The Record on Appeal; Forwarding; Filing.

(A) Except as otherwise provided under Tax Court rules for the transcript of proceedings, the appeal is governed by the parts of Rules 10, 11, and 12 regarding the record on appeal from a district court, the time and manner of forwarding and filing, and the docketing in the court of appeals.

(B) If an appeal is taken to more than one court of appeals, the original record must be sent to the court named in the first notice of appeal filed. In an appeal to any other court of appeals, the appellant must apply to that other court to make provision for the record.

(b) Appeal by Permission. An appeal by permission is governed by Rule 5.

(As amended Apr. 30, 1979, eff. Aug. 1, 1979; Apr. 29, 1994, eff. Dec. 1, 1994; Apr. 24, 1998, eff. Dec. 1, 1998; Apr. 16, 2013, eff. Dec. 1, 2013.)

RULE 14. APPLICABILITY OF OTHER RULES TO APPEALS FROM THE TAX COURT

All provisions of these rules, except Rules 4, 6–9, 15–20, and 22–23, apply to appeals from the Tax Court. References in any applicable rule (other than Rule 24(a)) to the district court and district clerk are to be read as referring to the Tax Court and its clerk.

(As amended Apr. 24, 1998, eff. Dec. 1, 1998; Apr. 16, 2013, eff. Dec. 1, 2013.)

TITLE IV. REVIEW OR ENFORCEMENT OF AN ORDER OF AN ADMINISTRATIVE AGENCY, BOARD, COMMISSION, OR OFFICER

RULE 15. REVIEW OR ENFORCEMENT OF AN AGENCY ORDER—HOW OBTAINED; INTERVENTION
(a) Petition for Review; Joint Petition.

(1) Review of an agency order is commenced by filing, within the time prescribed by law, a petition for review with the clerk of a court of appeals authorized to review the agency order. If their interests make joinder practicable, two or more persons may join in a petition to the same court to review the same order.

(2) The petition must:

(A) name each party seeking review either in the caption or the body of the petition—using such terms as "et al.," "petitioners," or "respondents" does not effectively name the parties;

(B) name the agency as a respondent (even though not named in the petition, the United States is a respondent if required by statute); and

(C) specify the order or part thereof to be reviewed.

(3) Form 3 in the Appendix of Forms is a suggested form of a petition for review.

(4) In this rule "agency" includes an agency, board, commission, or officer; "petition for review" includes a petition to enjoin, suspend, modify, or otherwise review, or a notice of appeal, whichever form is indicated by the applicable statute.

(b) Application or Cross–Application to Enforce an Order; Answer; Default.

(1) An application to enforce an agency order must be filed with the clerk of a court of appeals authorized to enforce the order. If a petition is filed to review an agency order that the court may enforce, a party opposing the petition may file a cross-application for enforcement.

(2) Within 21 days after the application for enforcement is filed, the respondent must serve on the applicant an answer to the application and file it with the clerk. If the respondent fails to answer in time, the court will enter judgment for the relief requested.

(3) The application must contain a concise statement of the proceedings in which the order was entered, the facts upon which venue is based, and the relief requested.

(c) Service of the Petition or Application. The circuit clerk must serve a copy of the petition for review, or an application or cross-application to enforce an agency order, on each respondent as prescribed by Rule 3(d), unless a different manner of service is prescribed by statute. At the time of filing, the petitioner must:

(1) serve, or have served, a copy on each party admitted to participate in the agency proceedings, except for the respondents;

(2) file with the clerk a list of those so served; and

(3) give the clerk enough copies of the petition or application to serve each respondent.

(d) Intervention. Unless a statute provides another method, a person who wants to intervene in a proceeding under this rule must file a motion for leave to intervene with the circuit clerk and serve a copy on all parties. The motion—or other notice of intervention authorized by statute—must be filed within 30 days after the petition for review is filed and must contain a concise statement of the interest of the moving party and the grounds for intervention.

(e) Payment of Fees. When filing any separate or joint petition for review in a court of appeals, the petitioner must pay the circuit clerk all required fees.

(As amended Apr. 22, 1993, eff. Dec. 1, 1993; Apr. 24, 1998, eff. Dec. 1, 1998; Mar. 26, 2009, eff. Dec. 1, 2009.)

RULE 15.1   BRIEFS AND ORAL ARGUMENT IN A NATIONAL LABOR RELATIONS BOARD PROCEEDING

In either an enforcement or a review proceeding, a party adverse to the National Labor Relations Board proceeds first on briefing and at oral argument, unless the court orders otherwise.

(Added Mar. 10, 1986, eff. July 1, 1986; amended Apr. 24, 1998, eff. Dec. 1, 1998.)

RULE 16.   THE RECORD ON REVIEW OR ENFORCEMENT

(a) Composition of the Record. The record on review or enforcement of an agency order consists of:

(1) the order involved;

(2) any findings or report on which it is based; and

(3) the pleadings, evidence, and other parts of the proceedings before the agency.

(b) Omissions From or Misstatements in the Record. The parties may at any time, by stipulation, supply any omission from the record or correct a misstatement, or the court may so direct. If necessary, the court may direct that a supplemental record be prepared and filed.

(As amended Apr. 24, 1998, eff. Dec. 1, 1998.)

RULE 17.   FILING THE RECORD

(a) Agency to File; Time for Filing; Notice of Filing. The agency must file the record with the circuit clerk within 40 days after being served with a petition for review, unless the statute authorizing review provides otherwise, or within 40 days after it files an application for enforcement unless the respondent fails to answer or the court orders otherwise. The court may shorten or extend the time to file the record. The clerk must notify all parties of the date when the record is filed.

(b) Filing—What Constitutes.

(1) The agency must file:

(A) the original or a certified copy of the entire record or parts designated by the parties; or

(B) a certified list adequately describing all documents, transcripts of testimony, exhibits, and other material constituting the record, or describing those parts designated by the parties.

(2) The parties may stipulate in writing that no record or certified list be filed. The date when the stipulation is filed with the circuit clerk is treated as the date when the record is filed.

(3) The agency must retain any portion of the record not filed with the clerk. All parts of the record retained by the agency are a part of the record on review for all purposes and, if the court or a party so requests, must be sent to the court regardless of any prior stipulation.

(As amended Apr. 24, 1998, eff. Dec. 1, 1998.)

RULE 18.   STAY PENDING REVIEW

(a) Motion for a Stay.

(1) Initial Motion Before the Agency. A petitioner must ordinarily move first before the agency for a stay pending review of its decision or order.

(2) Motion in the Court of Appeals. A motion for a stay may be made to the court of appeals or one of its judges.

(A) The motion must:

(i) show that moving first before the agency would be impracticable; or

(ii) state that, a motion having been made, the agency denied the motion or failed to afford the relief requested and state any reasons given by the agency for its action.

(B) The motion must also include:

(i) the reasons for granting the relief requested and the facts relied on;

(ii) originals or copies of affidavits or other sworn statements supporting facts subject to dispute; and

(iii) relevant parts of the record.

(C) The moving party must give reasonable notice of the motion to all parties.

(D) The motion must be filed with the circuit clerk and normally will be considered by a panel of the court. But in an exceptional case in which time requirements make that procedure impracticable, the motion may be made to and considered by a single judge.

(b) Bond. The court may condition relief on the filing of a bond or other appropriate security.

(As amended Apr. 24, 1998, eff. Dec. 1, 1998.)

RULE 19. SETTLEMENT OF A JUDGMENT ENFORCING AN AGENCY ORDER IN PART

When the court files an opinion directing entry of judgment enforcing the agency's order in part, the agency must within 14 days file with the clerk and serve on each other party a proposed judgment conforming to the opinion. A party who disagrees with the agency's proposed judgment must within 10 days file with the clerk and serve the agency with a proposed judgment that the party believes conforms to the opinion. The court will settle the judgment and direct entry without further hearing or argument.

(As amended Mar. 10, 1986, eff. July 1, 1986; Apr. 24, 1998, eff. Dec. 1, 1998; Mar. 26, 2009, eff. Dec. 1, 2009.)

RULE 20. APPLICABILITY OF RULES TO THE REVIEW OR ENFORCEMENT OF AN AGENCY ORDER

All provisions of these rules, except Rules 3–14 and 22–23, apply to the review or enforcement of an agency order. In these rules, "appellant" includes a petitioner or applicant, and "appellee" includes a respondent.

(As amended Apr. 24, 1998, eff. Dec. 1, 1998.)

TITLE V. EXTRAORDINARY WRITS

RULE 21. WRITS OF MANDAMUS AND PROHIBITION, AND OTHER EXTRAORDINARY WRITS

(a) Mandamus or Prohibition to a Court: Petition, Filing, Service, and Docketing.

(1) A party petitioning for a writ of mandamus or prohibition directed to a court must file a petition with the circuit clerk with proof of service on all parties to the proceeding in the trial court. The party must also provide a copy to the trial-court judge. All parties to the proceeding in the trial court other than the petitioner are respondents for all purposes.

(2)(A) The petition must be titled "In re [name of petitioner]."

(B) The petition must state:

(i) the relief sought;

(ii) the issues presented;

(iii) the facts necessary to understand the issue presented by the petition; and

(iv) the reasons why the writ should issue.

(C) The petition must include a copy of any order or opinion or parts of the record that may be essential to understand the matters set forth in the petition.

(3) Upon receiving the prescribed docket fee, the clerk must docket the petition and submit it to the court.

(b) Denial; Order Directing Answer; Briefs; Precedence.

(1) The court may deny the petition without an answer. Otherwise, it must order the respondent, if any, to answer within a fixed time.

(2) The clerk must serve the order to respond on all persons directed to respond.

(3) Two or more respondents may answer jointly.

(4) The court of appeals may invite or order the trial-court judge to address the petition or may invite an amicus curiae to do so. The trial-court judge may request permission to address the petition but may not do so unless invited or ordered to do so by the court of appeals.

(5) If briefing or oral argument is required, the clerk must advise the parties, and when appropriate, the trial-court judge or amicus curiae.

(6) The proceeding must be given preference over ordinary civil cases.

(7) The circuit clerk must send a copy of the final disposition to the trial-court judge.

(c) Other Extraordinary Writs. An application for an extraordinary writ other than one provided for in Rule 21(a) must be made by filing a petition with the circuit clerk with proof of service on the respondents. Proceedings on the application must conform, so far as is practicable, to the procedures prescribed in Rule 21(a) and (b).

(d) Form of Papers; Number of Copies; Length Limits. All papers must conform to Rule 32(c)(2). An original and 3 copies must be filed unless the court requires the filing of a different number by local rule or by order in a particular case. Except by the court's permission, and excluding the accompanying documents required by Rule 21(a)(2)(C):

(1) a paper produced using a computer must not exceed 7,800 words; and

(2) a handwritten or typewritten paper must not exceed 30 pages.

(As amended Apr. 29, 1994, eff. Dec. 1, 1994; Apr. 23, 1996, eff. Dec. 1, 1996; Apr. 24, 1998, eff. Dec. 1, 1998; Apr. 29, 2002, eff. Dec. 1, 2002; Apr. 28, 2016, eff. Dec. 1, 2016.)

TITLE VI.   HABEAS CORPUS; PROCEEDINGS
IN FORMA PAUPERIS

RULE 22.   HABEAS CORPUS AND
SECTION 2255 PROCEEDINGS

(a) Application for the Original Writ. An application for a writ of habeas corpus must be made to the appropriate district court. If made to a circuit judge, the application must be transferred to the appropriate district court. If a district court denies an application made or transferred to it, renewal of the application before a circuit judge is not permitted. The applicant may, under 28 U.S.C. § 2253, appeal to the court of appeals from the district court's order denying the application.

(b) Certificate of Appealability.

(1) In a habeas corpus proceeding in which the detention complained of arises from process issued by a state court, or in a 28 U.S.C. § 2255 proceeding, the applicant cannot take an appeal unless a circuit justice or a circuit or district judge issues a certificate of appealability under 28 U.S.C. § 2253(c). If an applicant files a notice of appeal, the district clerk must send to the court of appeals the certificate (if any) and the statement described in Rule 11(a) of the Rules Governing Proceedings Under 28 U.S.C. § 2254 or § 2255 (if any), along with the notice of appeal and the file of the district-court proceedings. If the district judge has denied the certificate, the applicant may request a circuit judge to issue it.

(2) A request addressed to the court of appeals may be considered by a circuit judge or judges, as the court prescribes. If no express request for a certificate is filed, the notice of appeal constitutes a request addressed to the judges of the court of appeals.

(3) A certificate of appealability is not required when a state or its representative or the United States or its representative appeals.

(As amended Pub.L. 104–132, Title I, § 103, Apr. 24, 1996, 110 Stat. 1218; Apr. 24, 1998, eff. Dec. 1, 1998; Mar. 26, 2009, eff. Dec. 1, 2009.)

RULE 23.   CUSTODY OR RELEASE
OF A PRISONER IN A HABEAS
CORPUS PROCEEDING

(a) Transfer of Custody Pending Review. Pending review of a decision in a habeas corpus proceeding commenced before a court, justice, or judge of the United States for the release of a prisoner, the person having custody of the prisoner must not transfer custody to another unless a transfer is directed in accordance with this rule. When, upon application, a custodian shows the need for a transfer, the court, justice, or judge rendering the decision under review may authorize the transfer and substitute the successor custodian as a party.

(b) Detention or Release Pending Review of Decision Not to Release. While a decision not to release a prisoner is under review, the court or judge rendering the decision, or the court of appeals, or the Supreme Court, or a judge or justice of either court, may order that the prisoner be:

(1) detained in the custody from which release is sought;

(2) detained in other appropriate custody; or

(3) released on personal recognizance, with or without surety.

(c) Release Pending Review of Decision Ordering Release. While a decision ordering the release of a prisoner is under review, the prisoner must—unless the court or judge rendering the decision, or the court of appeals, or the Supreme Court, or a judge or justice of either court orders otherwise—be released on personal recognizance, with or without surety.

(d) Modification of the Initial Order on Custody. An initial order governing the prisoner's custody or release, including any recognizance or surety, continues in effect pending review unless for special reasons shown to the court of appeals or the Supreme Court, or to a judge or justice of either court, the order is modified or an independent order regarding custody, release, or surety is issued.

(As amended Mar. 10, 1986, eff. July 1, 1986; Apr. 24, 1998, eff. Dec. 1, 1998.)

RULE 24.   PROCEEDING IN FORMA PAUPERIS

(a) Leave to Proceed In Forma Pauperis.

(1) **Motion in the District Court.** Except as stated in Rule 24(a)(3), a party to a district-court action who desires to appeal in forma pauperis must file a motion in the district court. The party must attach an affidavit that:

(A) shows in the detail prescribed by Form 4 of the Appendix of Forms the party's inability to pay or to give security for fees and costs;

(B) claims an entitlement to redress; and

(C) states the issues that the party intends to present on appeal.

(2) **Action on the Motion.** If the district court grants the motion, the party may proceed on appeal without prepaying or giving security for fees and costs, unless a statute provides otherwise. If the district court denies the motion, it must state its reasons in writing.

(3) **Prior Approval.** A party who was permitted to proceed in forma pauperis in the district-court action, or who was determined to be financially unable to obtain an adequate defense in a criminal case, may proceed on appeal in forma pauperis without further authorization, unless:

(A) the district court—before or after the notice of appeal is filed—certifies that the appeal is not taken in good faith or finds that the party is not otherwise entitled to proceed in forma pauperis and states in writing its reasons for the certification or finding; or

(B) a statute provides otherwise.

(4) **Notice of District Court's Denial.** The district clerk must immediately notify the parties and the court of appeals when the district court does any of the following:

    (A) denies a motion to proceed on appeal in forma pauperis;

    (B) certifies that the appeal is not taken in good faith; or

    (C) finds that the party is not otherwise entitled to proceed in forma pauperis.

  (5) Motion in the Court of Appeals. A party may file a motion to proceed on appeal in forma pauperis in the court of appeals within 30 days after service of the notice prescribed in Rule 24(a)(4). The motion must include a copy of the affidavit filed in the district court and the district court's statement of reasons for its action. If no affidavit was filed in the district court, the party must include the affidavit prescribed by Rule 24(a)(1).

(b) Leave to Proceed In Forma Pauperis on Appeal from the United States Tax Court or on Appeal or Review of an Administrative–Agency Proceeding. A party may file in the court of appeals a motion for leave to proceed on appeal in forma pauperis with an affidavit prescribed by Rule 24(a)(1):

  (1) in an appeal from the United States Tax Court; and

  (2) when an appeal or review of a proceeding before an administrative agency, board, commission, or officer proceeds directly in the court of appeals.

(c) Leave to Use Original Record. A party allowed to proceed on appeal in forma pauperis may request that the appeal be heard on the original record without reproducing any part.

(As amended Apr. 30, 1979, eff. Aug. 1, 1979; Mar. 10, 1986, eff. July 1, 1986; Apr. 24, 1998, eff. Dec. 1, 1998; Apr. 29, 2002, eff. Dec. 1, 2002; Apr. 16, 2013, eff. Dec. 1, 2013.)

TITLE VII. GENERAL PROVISIONS

RULE 25. FILING AND SERVICE

(a) Filing.

  (1) Filing with the Clerk. A paper required or permitted to be filed in a court of appeals must be filed with the clerk.

  (2) Filing: Method and Timeliness.

    (A) In general. Filing may be accomplished by mail addressed to the clerk, but filing is not timely unless the clerk receives the papers within the time fixed for filing.

    (B) A brief or appendix. A brief or appendix is timely filed, however, if on or before the last day for filing, it is:

      (i) mailed to the clerk by First–Class Mail, or other class of mail that is at least as expeditious, postage prepaid; or

      (ii) dispatched to a third-party commercial carrier for delivery to the clerk within 3 days.

    (C) Inmate Filing. If an institution has a system designed for legal mail, an inmate confined there must use that system to receive the benefit of this Rule 25(a)(2)(C). A paper filed by an inmate is timely if it is deposited in the institution's internal mail system on or before the last day for filing and:

      (i) it is accompanied by:

        • a declaration in compliance with 28 U.S.C. § 1746—or a notarized statement—setting out the date of deposit and stating that first-class postage is being prepaid; or

        • evidence (such as a postmark or date stamp) showing that the paper was so deposited and that postage was prepaid; or

      (ii) the court of appeals exercises its discretion to permit the later filing of a declaration or notarized statement that satisfies Rule 25(a)(2)(C)(i).

    (D) Electronic filing. A court of appeals may by local rule permit or require papers to be filed, signed, or verified by electronic means that are consistent with technical standards, if any, that the Judicial Conference of the United States establishes. A local rule may require filing by electronic means only if reasonable exceptions are allowed. A paper filed by electronic means in compliance with a local rule constitutes a written paper for the purpose of applying these rules.

  (3) Filing a Motion with a Judge. If a motion requests relief that may be granted by a single judge, the judge may permit the motion to be filed with the judge; the judge must note the filing date on the motion and give it to the clerk.

  (4) Clerk's Refusal of Documents. The clerk must not refuse to accept for filing any paper presented for that purpose solely because it is not presented in proper form as required by these rules or by any local rule or practice.

  (5) Privacy Protection. An appeal in a case whose privacy protection was governed by Federal Rule of Bankruptcy Procedure 9037, Federal Rule of Civil Procedure 5.2, or Federal Rule of Criminal Procedure 49.1 is governed by the same rule on appeal. In all other proceedings, privacy protection is governed by Federal Rule of Civil Procedure 5.2, except that Federal Rule of Criminal Procedure 49.1 governs when an extraordinary writ is sought in a criminal case.

(b) Service of All Papers Required. Unless a rule requires service by the clerk, a party must, at or before the time of filing a paper, serve a copy on the other parties to the appeal or review. Service on a party represented by counsel must be made on the party's counsel.

(c) Manner of Service.

  (1) Service may be any of the following:

    (A) personal, including delivery to a responsible person at the office of counsel;

    (B) by mail;

    (C) by third-party commercial carrier for delivery within 3 days; or

    (D) by electronic means, if the party being served consents in writing.

(2) If authorized by local rule, a party may use the court's transmission equipment to make electronic service under Rule 25(c)(1)(D).

(3) When reasonable considering such factors as the immediacy of the relief sought, distance, and cost, service on a party must be by a manner at least as expeditious as the manner used to file the paper with the court.

(4) Service by mail or by commercial carrier is complete on mailing or delivery to the carrier. Service by electronic means is complete on transmission, unless the party making service is notified that the paper was not received by the party served.

(d) Proof of Service.

(1) A paper presented for filing must contain either of the following:

    (A) an acknowledgment of service by the person served; or

    (B) proof of service consisting of a statement by the person who made service certifying:

        (i) the date and manner of service;

        (ii) the names of the persons served; and

        (iii) their mail or electronic addresses, facsimile numbers, or the addresses of the places of delivery, as appropriate for the manner of service.

(2) When a brief or appendix is filed by mailing or dispatch in accordance with Rule 25(a)(2)(B), the proof of service must also state the date and manner by which the document was mailed or dispatched to the clerk.

(3) Proof of service may appear on or be affixed to the papers filed.

(e) Number of Copies. When these rules require the filing or furnishing of a number of copies, a court may require a different number by local rule or by order in a particular case.

(As amended Mar. 10, 1986, eff. July 1, 1986; Apr. 30, 1991, eff. Dec. 1, 1991; Apr. 22, 1993, eff. Dec. 1, 1993; Apr. 29, 1994, eff. Dec. 1, 1994; Apr. 23, 1996, eff. Dec. 1, 1996; Apr. 24, 1998, eff. Dec. 1, 1998; Apr. 29, 2002, eff. Dec. 1, 2002; Apr. 12, 2006, eff. Dec. 1, 2006; Apr. 30, 2007, eff. Dec. 1, 2007; Mar. 26, 2009, eff. Dec. 1, 2009; Apr. 28, 2016, eff. Dec. 1, 2016.)

RULE 26. COMPUTING AND EXTENDING TIME

(a) Computing Time. The following rules apply in computing any time period specified in these rules, in any local rule or court order, or in any statute that does not specify a method of computing time.

(1) Period Stated in Days or a Longer Unit. When the period is stated in days or a longer unit of time:

    (A) exclude the day of the event that triggers the period;

    (B) count every day, including intermediate Saturdays, Sundays, and legal holidays; and

    (C) include the last day of the period, but if the last day is a Saturday, Sunday, or legal holiday, the period

continues to run until the end of the next day that is not a Saturday, Sunday, or legal holiday.

(2) Period Stated in Hours. When the period is stated in hours:

    (A) begin counting immediately on the occurrence of the event that triggers the period;

    (B) count every hour, including hours during intermediate Saturdays, Sundays, and legal holidays; and

    (C) if the period would end on a Saturday, Sunday, or legal holiday, the period continues to run until the same time on the next day that is not a Saturday, Sunday, or legal holiday.

(3) Inaccessibility of the Clerk's Office. Unless the court orders otherwise, if the clerk's office is inaccessible:

    (A) on the last day for filing under Rule 26(a)(1), then the time for filing is extended to the first accessible day that is not a Saturday, Sunday, or legal holiday; or

    (B) during the last hour for filing under Rule 26(a)(2), then the time for filing is extended to the same time on the first accessible day that is not a Saturday, Sunday, or legal holiday.

(4) "Last Day" Defined. Unless a different time is set by a statute, local rule, or court order, the last day ends:

    (A) for electronic filing in the district court, at midnight in the court's time zone;

    (B) for electronic filing in the court of appeals, at midnight in the time zone of the circuit clerk's principal office;

    (C) for filing under Rules 4(c)(1), 25(a)(2)(B), and 25(a)(2)(C)—and filing by mail under Rule 13(a)(2)—at the latest time for the method chosen for delivery to the post office, third-party commercial carrier, or prison mailing system; and

    (D) for filing by other means, when the clerk's office is scheduled to close.

(5) "Next Day" Defined. The "next day" is determined by continuing to count forward when the period is measured after an event and backward when measured before an event.

(6) "Legal Holiday" Defined. "Legal holiday" means:

    (A) the day set aside by statute for observing New Year's Day, Martin Luther King Jr.'s Birthday, Washington's Birthday, Memorial Day, Independence Day, Labor Day, Columbus Day, Veterans' Day, Thanksgiving Day, or Christmas Day;

    (B) any day declared a holiday by the President or Congress; and

    (C) for periods that are measured after an event, any other day declared a holiday by the state where either of the following is located: the district court that rendered the challenged judgment or order, or the circuit clerk's principal office.

(b) Extending Time. For good cause, the court may extend the time prescribed by these rules or by its order to perform any act, or may permit an act to be done after that time expires. But the court may not extend the time to file:

(1) a notice of appeal (except as authorized in Rule 4) or a petition for permission to appeal; or

(2) a notice of appeal from or a petition to enjoin, set aside, suspend, modify, enforce, or otherwise review an order of an administrative agency, board, commission, or officer of the United States, unless specifically authorized by law.

(c) Additional Time after Certain Kinds of Service. When a party may or must act within a specified time after being served, 3 days are added after the period would otherwise expire under Rule 26(a), unless the paper is delivered on the date of service stated in the proof of service. For purposes of this Rule 26(c), a paper that is served electronically is treated as delivered on the date of service stated in the proof of service.

(As amended Mar. 1, 1971, eff. July 1, 1971; Mar. 10, 1986, eff. July 1, 1986; Apr. 25, 1989, eff. Dec. 1, 1989; Apr. 30, 1991, eff. Dec. 1, 1991; Apr. 23, 1996, eff. Dec. 1, 1996; Apr. 24, 1998, eff. Dec. 1, 1998; Apr. 29, 2002, eff. Dec. 1, 2002; Apr. 25, 2005, eff. Dec. 1, 2005; Mar. 26, 2009, eff. Dec. 1, 2009; Apr. 28, 2016, eff. Dec. 1, 2016.)

RULE 26.1   CORPORATE DISCLOSURE STATEMENT

(a) Who Must File. Any nongovernmental corporate party to a proceeding in a court of appeals must file a statement that identifies any parent corporation and any publicly held corporation that owns 10% or more of its stock or states that there is no such corporation.

(b) Time for Filing; Supplemental Filing. A party must file the Rule 26.1(a) statement with the principal brief or upon filing a motion, response, petition, or answer in the court of appeals, whichever occurs first, unless a local rule requires earlier filing. Even if the statement has already been filed, the party's principal brief must include the statement before the table of contents. A party must supplement its statement whenever the information that must be disclosed under Rule 26.1(a) changes.

(c) Number of Copies. If the Rule 26.1(a) statement is filed before the principal brief, or if a supplemental statement is filed, the party must file an original and 3 copies unless the court requires a different number by local rule or by order in a particular case.

(Added Apr. 25, 1989, eff. Dec. 1, 1989; amended Apr. 30, 1991, eff. Dec. 1, 1991; Apr. 29, 1994, eff. Dec. 1, 1994; Apr. 24, 1998, eff. Dec. 1, 1998; Apr. 29, 2002, eff. Dec. 1, 2002.)

RULE 27.   MOTIONS

(a) In General.

(1) Application for Relief. An application for an order or other relief is made by motion unless these rules prescribe another form. A motion must be in writing unless the court permits otherwise.

(2) Contents of a Motion.

(A) Grounds and relief sought. A motion must state with particularity the grounds for the motion, the relief sought, and the legal argument necessary to support it.

(B) Accompanying documents.

(i) Any affidavit or other paper necessary to support a motion must be served and filed with the motion.

(ii) An affidavit must contain only factual information, not legal argument.

(iii) A motion seeking substantive relief must include a copy of the trial court's opinion or agency's decision as a separate exhibit.

(C) Documents barred or not required.

(i) A separate brief supporting or responding to a motion must not be filed.

(ii) A notice of motion is not required.

(iii) A proposed order is not required.

(3) Response.

(A) Time to file. Any party may file a response to a motion; Rule 27(a)(2) governs its contents. The response must be filed within 10 days after service of the motion unless the court shortens or extends the time. A motion authorized by Rules 8, 9, 18, or 41 may be granted before the 10–day period runs only if the court gives reasonable notice to the parties that it intends to act sooner.

(B) Request for affirmative relief. A response may include a motion for affirmative relief. The time to respond to the new motion, and to reply to that response, are governed by Rule 27(a)(3)(A) and (a)(4). The title of the response must alert the court to the request for relief.

(4) Reply to Response. Any reply to a response must be filed within 7 days after service of the response. A reply must not present matters that do not relate to the response.

(b) Disposition of a Motion for a Procedural Order. The court may act on a motion for a procedural order—including a motion under Rule 26(b)—at any time without awaiting a response, and may, by rule or by order in a particular case, authorize its clerk to act on specified types of procedural motions. A party adversely affected by the court's, or the clerk's, action may file a motion to reconsider, vacate, or modify that action. Timely opposition filed after the motion is granted in whole or in part does not constitute a request to reconsider, vacate, or modify the disposition; a motion requesting that relief must be filed.

(c) Power of a Single Judge to Entertain a Motion. A circuit judge may act alone on any motion, but may not dismiss or otherwise determine an appeal or other proceeding. A court of appeals may provide by rule or by order in a particular case that only the court may act on any motion or class of motions. The court may review the action of a single judge.

(d) Form of Papers; Length Limits; Number of Copies.

(1) Format.

(A) Reproduction. A motion, response, or reply may be reproduced by any process that yields a clear black image on light paper. The paper must be opaque and unglazed. Only one side of the paper may be used.

(B) Cover. A cover is not required, but there must be a caption that includes the case number, the name of the court, the title of the case, and a brief descriptive title indicating the purpose of the motion and identifying the party or parties for whom it is filed. If a cover is used, it must be white.

(C) Binding. The document must be bound in any manner that is secure, does not obscure the text, and permits the document to lie reasonably flat when open.

(D) Paper size, line spacing, and margins. The document must be on 8½ by 11 inch paper. The text must be double-spaced, but quotations more than two lines long may be indented and single-spaced. Headings and footnotes may be single-spaced. Margins must be at least one inch on all four sides. Page numbers may be placed in the margins, but no text may appear there.

(E) Typeface and type styles. The document must comply with the typeface requirements of Rule 32(a)(5) and the type-style requirements of Rule 32(a)(6).

(2) Length Limits. Except by the court's permission, and excluding the accompanying documents authorized by Rule 27(a)(2)(B):

(A) a motion or response to a motion produced using a computer must not exceed 5,200 words;

(B) a handwritten or typewritten motion or response to a motion must not exceed 20 pages;

(C) a reply produced using a computer must not exceed 2,600 words; and

(D) a handwritten or typewritten reply to a response must not exceed 10 pages.

(3) Number of Copies. An original and 3 copies must be filed unless the court requires a different number by local rule or by order in a particular case.

(e) Oral Argument. A motion will be decided without oral argument unless the court orders otherwise.

(As amended Apr. 30, 1979, eff. Aug. 1, 1979; Apr. 25, 1989, eff. Dec. 1, 1989; Apr. 29, 1994, eff. Dec. 1, 1994; Apr. 24, 1998, eff. Dec. 1, 1998; Apr. 29, 2002, eff. Dec. 1, 2002; Apr. 25, 2005, eff. Dec. 1, 2005; Mar. 26, 2009, eff. Dec. 1, 2009; Apr. 28, 2016, eff. Dec. 1, 2016.)

RULE 28. BRIEFS

(a) Appellant's Brief. The appellant's brief must contain, under appropriate headings and in the order indicated:

(1) a corporate disclosure statement if required by Rule 26.1;

(2) a table of contents, with page references;

(3) a table of authorities—cases (alphabetically arranged), statutes, and other authorities—with references to the pages of the brief where they are cited;

(4) a jurisdictional statement, including:

(A) the basis for the district court's or agency's subject-matter jurisdiction, with citations to applicable statu-

tory provisions and stating relevant facts establishing jurisdiction;

(B) the basis for the court of appeals' jurisdiction, with citations to applicable statutory provisions and stating relevant facts establishing jurisdiction;

(C) the filing dates establishing the timeliness of the appeal or petition for review; and

(D) an assertion that the appeal is from a final order or judgment that disposes of all parties' claims, or information establishing the court of appeals' jurisdiction on some other basis;

(5) a statement of the issues presented for review;

(6) a concise statement of the case setting out the facts relevant to the issues submitted for review, describing the relevant procedural history, and identifying the rulings presented for review, with appropriate references to the record (see Rule 28(e));

(7) a summary of the argument, which must contain a succinct, clear, and accurate statement of the arguments made in the body of the brief, and which must not merely repeat the argument headings;

(8) the argument, which must contain:

(A) appellant's contentions and the reasons for them, with citations to the authorities and parts of the record on which the appellant relies; and

(B) for each issue, a concise statement of the applicable standard of review (which may appear in the discussion of the issue or under a separate heading placed before the discussion of the issues);

(9) a short conclusion stating the precise relief sought; and

(10) the certificate of compliance, if required by Rule 32(g)(1).

(b) Appellee's Brief. The appellee's brief must conform to the requirements of Rule 28(a)(1)–(8) and (10), except that none of the following need appear unless the appellee is dissatisfied with the appellant's statement:

(1) the jurisdictional statement;

(2) the statement of the issues;

(3) the statement of the case; and

(4) the statement of the standard of review.

(c) Reply Brief. The appellant may file a brief in reply to the appellee's brief. Unless the court permits, no further briefs may be filed. A reply brief must contain a table of contents, with page references, and a table of authorities—cases (alphabetically arranged), statutes, and other authorities—with references to the pages of the reply brief where they are cited.

(d) References to Parties. In briefs and at oral argument, counsel should minimize use of the terms "appellant" and "appellee." To make briefs clear, counsel should use the parties' actual names or the designations used in the lower court or agency proceeding, or such descriptive terms as "the employee," "the injured person," "the taxpayer," "the ship," "the stevedore."

(e) References to the Record. References to the parts of the record contained in the appendix filed with the appellant's brief must be to the pages of the appendix. If the appendix is prepared after the briefs are filed, a party referring to the record must follow one of the methods detailed in Rule 30(c). If the original record is used under Rule 30(f) and is not consecutively paginated, or if the brief refers to an unreproduced part of the record, any reference must be to the page of the original document. For example:

- Answer p. 7;
- Motion for Judgment p. 2;
- Transcript p. 231.

Only clear abbreviations may be used. A party referring to evidence whose admissibility is in controversy must cite the pages of the appendix or of the transcript at which the evidence was identified, offered, and received or rejected.

(f) Reproduction of Statutes, Rules, Regulations, etc. If the court's determination of the issues presented requires the study of statutes, rules, regulations, etc., the relevant parts must be set out in the brief or in an addendum at the end, or may be supplied to the court in pamphlet form.

(g) [Reserved]

(h) [Deleted]

(i) Briefs in a Case Involving Multiple Appellants or Appellees. In a case involving more than one appellant or appellee, including consolidated cases, any number of appellants or appellees may join in a brief, and any party may adopt by reference a part of another's brief. Parties may also join in reply briefs.

(j) Citation of Supplemental Authorities. If pertinent and significant authorities come to a party's attention after the party's brief has been filed—or after oral argument but before decision—a party may promptly advise the circuit clerk by letter, with a copy to all other parties, setting forth the citations. The letter must state the reasons for the supplemental citations, referring either to the page of the brief or to a point argued orally. The body of the letter must not exceed 350 words. Any response must be made promptly and must be similarly limited.

(As amended Apr. 30, 1979, eff. Aug. 1, 1979; Mar. 10, 1986, eff. July 1, 1986; Apr. 25, 1989, eff. Dec. 1, 1989; Apr. 30, 1991, eff. Dec. 1, 1991; Apr. 22, 1993, eff. Dec. 1, 1993; Apr. 29, 1994, eff. Dec. 1, 1994; Apr. 24, 1998, eff. Dec. 1, 1998; Apr. 29, 2002, eff. Dec. 1, 2002; Apr. 25, 2005, eff. Dec. 1, 2005; Apr. 16, 2013, eff. Dec. 1, 2013; Apr. 28, 2016, eff. Dec. 1, 2016.)

RULE 28.1 CROSS–APPEALS

(a) Applicability. This rule applies to a case in which a cross-appeal is filed. Rules 28(a)-(c), 31(a)(1), 32(a)(2), and 32(a)(7)(A)-(B) do not apply to such a case, except as otherwise provided in this rule.

(b) Designation of Appellant. The party who files a notice of appeal first is the appellant for the purposes of this rule and Rules 30 and 34. If notices are filed on the same day, the plaintiff in the proceeding below is the appellant. These desig-

nations may be modified by the parties' agreement or by court order.

(c) Briefs. In a case involving a cross-appeal:

(1) Appellant's Principal Brief. The appellant must file a principal brief in the appeal. That brief must comply with Rule 28(a).

(2) Appellee's Principal and Response Brief. The appellee must file a principal brief in the cross-appeal and must, in the same brief, respond to the principal brief in the appeal. That appellee's brief must comply with Rule 28(a), except that the brief need not include a statement of the case unless the appellee is dissatisfied with the appellant's statement.

(3) Appellant's Response and Reply Brief. The appellant must file a brief that responds to the principal brief in the cross-appeal and may, in the same brief, reply to the response in the appeal. That brief must comply with Rule 28(a)(2)–(8) and (10), except that none of the following need appear unless the appellant is dissatisfied with the appellee's statement in the cross-appeal:

(A) the jurisdictional statement;

(B) the statement of the issues;

(C) the statement of the case; and

(D) the statement of the standard of review.

(4) Appellee's Reply Brief. The appellee may file a brief in reply to the response in the cross-appeal. That brief must comply with Rule 28(a)(2)–(3) and (10) and must be limited to the issues presented by the cross-appeal.

(5) No Further Briefs. Unless the court permits, no further briefs may be filed in a case involving a cross-appeal.

(d) Cover. Except for filings by unrepresented parties, the cover of the appellant's principal brief must be blue; the appellee's principal and response brief, red; the appellant's response and reply brief, yellow; the appellee's reply brief, gray; an intervenor's or amicus curiae's brief, green; and any supplemental brief, tan. The front cover of a brief must contain the information required by Rule 32(a)(2).

(e) Length.

(1) Page Limitation. Unless it complies with Rule 28.1(e)(2), the appellant's principal brief must not exceed 30 pages; the appellee's principal and response brief, 35 pages; the appellant's response and reply brief, 30 pages; and the appellee's reply brief, 15 pages.

(2) Type-Volume Limitation.

(A) The appellant's principal brief or the appellant's response and reply brief is acceptable if it:

(i) contains no more than 13,000 words; or

(ii) uses a monospaced face and contains no more than 1,300 lines of text.

(B) The appellee's principal and response brief is acceptable if it:

(i) contains no more than 15,300 words; or

(ii) uses a monospaced face and contains no more than 1,500 lines of text.

(C) The appellee's reply brief is acceptable if it contains no more than half of the type volume specified in Rule 28.1(e)(2)(A).

(f) Time to Serve and File a Brief. Briefs must be served and filed as follows:

(1) the appellant's principal brief, within 40 days after the record is filed;

(2) the appellee's principal and response brief, within 30 days after the appellant's principal brief is served;

(3) the appellant's response and reply brief, within 30 days after the appellee's principal and response brief is served; and

(4) the appellee's reply brief, within 14 days after the appellant's response and reply brief is served, but at least 7 days before argument unless the court, for good cause, allows a later filing.

(As added April 25, 2005, eff. Dec. 1, 2005; amended Mar. 26, 2009, eff. Dec. 1, 2009; Apr. 16, 2013, eff. Dec. 1, 2013; Apr. 28, 2016, eff. Dec. 1, 2016.)

RULE 29. BRIEF OF AN AMICUS CURIAE

(a) During Initial Consideration of a Case on the Merits.

(1) Applicability. This Rule 29(a) governs amicus filings during a court's initial consideration of a case on the merits.

(2) When Permitted. The United States or its officer or agency or a state may file an amicus-curiae brief without the consent of the parties or leave of court. Any other amicus curiae may file a brief only by leave of court or if the brief states that all parties have consented to its filing.

(3) Motion for Leave to File. The motion must be accompanied by the proposed brief and state:

(A) the movant's interest; and

(B) the reason why an amicus brief is desirable and why the matters asserted are relevant to the disposition of the case.

(4) Contents and Form. An amicus brief must comply with Rule 32. In addition to the requirements of Rule 32, the cover must identify the party or parties supported and indicate whether the brief supports affirmance or reversal. An amicus brief need not comply with Rule 28, but must include the following:

(A) if the amicus curiae is a corporation, a disclosure statement like that required of parties by Rule 26.1;

(B) a table of contents, with page references;

(C) a table of authorities—cases (alphabetically arranged), statutes, and other authorities— with references to the pages of the brief where they are cited;

(D) a concise statement of the identity of the amicus curiae, its interest in the case, and the source of its authority to file;

(E) unless the amicus curiae is one listed in the first sentence of Rule 29(a)(2), a statement that indicates whether:

(i) a party's counsel authored the brief in whole or in part;

(ii) a party or a party's counsel contributed money that was intended to fund preparing or submitting the brief; and

(iii) a person—other than the amicus curiae, its members, or its counsel—contributed money that was intended to fund preparing or submitting the brief and, if so, identifies each such person;

(F) an argument, which may be preceded by a summary and which need not include a statement of the applicable standard of review; and

(G) a certificate of compliance under Rule 32(g)(1), if length is computed using a word or line limit.

(5) Length. Except by the court's permission, an amicus brief may be no more than one-half the maximum length authorized by these rules for a party's principal brief. If the court grants a party permission to file a longer brief, that extension does not affect the length of an amicus brief.

(6) Time for Filing. An amicus curiae must file its brief, accompanied by a motion for filing when necessary, no later than 7 days after the principal brief of the party being supported is filed. An amicus curiae that does not support either party must file its brief no later than 7 days after the appellant's or petitioner's principal brief is filed. A court may grant leave for later filing, specifying the time within which an opposing party may answer.

(7) Reply Brief. Except by the court's permission, an amicus curiae may not file a reply brief.

(8) Oral Argument. An amicus curiae may participate in oral argument only with the court's permission.

(b) During Consideration of Whether to Grant Rehearing.

(1) Applicability. This Rule 29(b) governs amicus filings during a court's consideration of whether to grant panel rehearing or rehearing en banc, unless a local rule or order in a case provides otherwise.

(2) When Permitted. The United States or its officer or agency or a state may file an amicus-curiae brief without the consent of the parties or leave of court. Any other amicus curiae may file a brief only by leave of court.

(3) Motion for Leave to File. Rule 29(a)(3) applies to a motion for leave.

(4) Contents, Form, and Length. Rule 29(a)(4) applies to the amicus brief. The brief must not exceed 2,600 words.

(5) Time for Filing. An amicus curiae supporting the petition for rehearing or supporting neither party must file its brief, accompanied by a motion for filing when necessary, no later than 7 days after the petition is filed. An amicus curiae opposing the petition must file its brief, accompanied by a motion for filing when necessary, no later than the date set by the court for the response.

(As amended Apr. 24, 1998, eff. Dec. 1, 1998; Apr. 28, 2010, eff. Dec. 1, 2010; Apr. 28, 2016, eff. Dec. 1, 2016.)

RULE 30. APPENDIX TO THE BRIEFS

(a) Appellant's Responsibility.

(1) Contents of the Appendix. The appellant must prepare and file an appendix to the briefs containing:

(A) the relevant docket entries in the proceeding below;

(B) the relevant portions of the pleadings, charge, findings, or opinion;

(C) the judgment, order, or decision in question; and

(D) other parts of the record to which the parties wish to direct the court's attention.

(2) Excluded Material. Memoranda of law in the district court should not be included in the appendix unless they have independent relevance. Parts of the record may be relied on by the court or the parties even though not included in the appendix.

(3) Time to File; Number of Copies. Unless filing is deferred under Rule 30(c), the appellant must file 10 copies of the appendix with the brief and must serve one copy on counsel for each party separately represented. An unrepresented party proceeding in forma pauperis must file 4 legible copies with the clerk, and one copy must be served on counsel for each separately represented party. The court may by local rule or by order in a particular case require the filing or service of a different number.

(b) All Parties' Responsibilities.

(1) Determining the Contents of the Appendix. The parties are encouraged to agree on the contents of the appendix. In the absence of an agreement, the appellant must, within 14 days after the record is filed, serve on the appellee a designation of the parts of the record the appellant intends to include in the appendix and a statement of the issues the appellant intends to present for review. The appellee may, within 14 days after receiving the designation, serve on the appellant a designation of additional parts to which it wishes to direct the court's attention. The appellant must include the designated parts in the appendix. The parties must not engage in unnecessary designation of parts of the record, because the entire record is available to the court. This paragraph applies also to a cross-appellant and a cross-appellee.

(2) Costs of Appendix. Unless the parties agree otherwise, the appellant must pay the cost of the appendix. If the appellant considers parts of the record designated by the appellee to be unnecessary, the appellant may advise the appellee, who must then advance the cost of including those parts. The cost of the appendix is a taxable cost. But if any party causes unnecessary parts of the record to be included in the appendix, the court may impose the cost of those parts on that party. Each circuit must, by local rule, provide for sanctions against attorneys who unreasonably and vexatiously increase litigation costs by including unnecessary material in the appendix.

(c) Deferred Appendix.

(1) Deferral Until After Briefs Are Filed. The court may provide by rule for classes of cases or by order in a particular case that preparation of the appendix may be deferred until after the briefs have been filed and that the appendix may be filed 21 days after the appellee's brief is served. Even though the filing of the appendix may be deferred, Rule 30(b) applies; except that a party must designate the parts of the record it wants included in the appendix when it serves its brief, and need not include a statement of the issues presented.

(2) References to the Record.

(A) If the deferred appendix is used, the parties may cite in their briefs the pertinent pages of the record. When the appendix is prepared, the record pages cited in the briefs must be indicated by inserting record page numbers, in brackets, at places in the appendix where those pages of the record appear.

(B) A party who wants to refer directly to pages of the appendix may serve and file copies of the brief within the time required by Rule 31(a), containing appropriate references to pertinent pages of the record. In that event, within 14 days after the appendix is filed, the party must serve and file copies of the brief, containing references to the pages of the appendix in place of or in addition to the references to the pertinent pages of the record. Except for the correction of typographical errors, no other changes may be made to the brief.

(d) Format of the Appendix. The appendix must begin with a table of contents identifying the page at which each part begins. The relevant docket entries must follow the table of contents. Other parts of the record must follow chronologically. When pages from the transcript of proceedings are placed in the appendix, the transcript page numbers must be shown in brackets immediately before the included pages. Omissions in the text of papers or of the transcript must be indicated by asterisks. Immaterial formal matters (captions, subscriptions, acknowledgments, etc.) should be omitted.

(e) Reproduction of Exhibits. Exhibits designated for inclusion in the appendix may be reproduced in a separate volume, or volumes, suitably indexed. Four copies must be filed with the appendix, and one copy must be served on counsel for each separately represented party. If a transcript of a proceeding before an administrative agency, board, commission, or officer was used in a district-court action and has been designated for inclusion in the appendix, the transcript must be placed in the appendix as an exhibit.

(f) Appeal on the Original Record Without an Appendix. The court may, either by rule for all cases or classes of cases or by order in a particular case, dispense with the appendix and permit an appeal to proceed on the original record with any copies of the record, or relevant parts, that the court may order the parties to file.

(As amended Mar. 30, 1970, eff. July 1, 1970; Mar. 10, 1986, eff. July 1, 1986; Apr. 30, 1991, eff. Dec. 1, 1991; Apr. 29, 1994, eff. Dec. 1, 1994; Apr. 24, 1998, eff. Dec. 1, 1998; Mar. 26, 2009, eff. Dec. 1, 2009.)

RULE 31. SERVING AND FILING BRIEFS

(a) Time to Serve and File a Brief.

(1) The appellant must serve and file a brief within 40 days after the record is filed. The appellee must serve and file a brief within 30 days after the appellant's brief is served. The appellant may serve and file a reply brief within 14 days after service of the appellee's brief but a reply brief must be filed at least 7 days before argument, unless the court, for good cause, allows a later filing.

(2) A court of appeals that routinely considers cases on the merits promptly after the briefs are filed may shorten the time to serve and file briefs, either by local rule or by order in a particular case.

(b) Number of Copies.
Twenty-five copies of each brief must be filed with the clerk and 2 copies must be served on each unrepresented party and on counsel for each separately represented party. An unrepresented party proceeding in forma pauperis must file 4 legible copies with the clerk, and one copy must be served on each unrepresented party and on counsel for each separately represented party. The court may by local rule or by order in a particular case require the filing or service of a different number.

(c) Consequence of Failure to File.
If an appellant fails to file a brief within the time provided by this rule, or within an extended time, an appellee may move to dismiss the appeal. An appellee who fails to file a brief will not be heard at oral argument unless the court grants permission.

(As amended Mar. 30, 1970, eff. July 1, 1970; Mar. 10, 1986, eff. July 1, 1986; Apr. 29, 1994, eff. Dec. 1, 1994; Apr. 24, 1998, eff. Dec. 1, 1998; Apr. 29, 2002, eff. Dec. 1, 2002; Mar. 26, 2009, eff. Dec. 1, 2009.)

RULE 32. FORM OF BRIEFS, APPENDICES, AND OTHER PAPERS

(a) Form of a Brief.

(1) Reproduction.

(A) A brief may be reproduced by any process that yields a clear black image on light paper. The paper must be opaque and unglazed. Only one side of the paper may be used.

(B) Text must be reproduced with a clarity that equals or exceeds the output of a laser printer.

(C) Photographs, illustrations, and tables may be reproduced by any method that results in a good copy of the original; a glossy finish is acceptable if the original is glossy.

(2) Cover.
Except for filings by unrepresented parties, the cover of the appellant's brief must be blue; the appellee's, red; an intervenor's or amicus curiae's, green; any reply brief, gray; and any supplemental brief, tan. The front cover of a brief must contain:

(A) the number of the case centered at the top;

(B) the name of the court;

(C) the title of the case (see Rule 12(a));

(D) the nature of the proceeding (e.g., Appeal, Petition for Review) and the name of the court, agency, or board below;

(E) the title of the brief, identifying the party or parties for whom the brief is filed; and

(F) the name, office address, and telephone number of counsel representing the party for whom the brief is filed.

(3) Binding.
The brief must be bound in any manner that is secure, does not obscure the text, and permits the brief to lie reasonably flat when open.

(4) Paper Size, Line Spacing, and Margins.
The brief must be on 8½ by 11 inch paper. The text must be double-spaced, but quotations more than two lines long may be indented and single-spaced. Headings and footnotes may be single-spaced. Margins must be at least one inch on all four sides. Page numbers may be placed in the margins, but no text may appear there.

(5) Typeface.
Either a proportionally spaced or a mono-spaced face may be used.

(A) A proportionally spaced face must include serifs, but sans-serif type may be used in headings and captions. A proportionally spaced face must be 14–point or larger.

(B) A monospaced face may not contain more than 10½ characters per inch.

(6) Type Styles.
A brief must be set in a plain, roman style, although italics or boldface may be used for emphasis. Case names must be italicized or underlined.

(7) Length.

(A) **Page Limitation.** A principal brief may not exceed 30 pages, or a reply brief 15 pages, unless it complies with Rule 32(a)(7)(B).

(B) **Type-Volume Limitation.**

(i) A principal brief is acceptable if it:

● contains no more than 13,000 words; or

● uses a monospaced face and contains no more than 1,300 lines of text.

(ii) A reply brief is acceptable if it contains no more than half of the type volume specified in Rule 32(a)(7)(B)(i).

(b) Form of an Appendix.
An appendix must comply with Rule 32(a)(1), (2), (3), and (4), with the following exceptions:

(1) The cover of a separately bound appendix must be white.

(2) An appendix may include a legible photocopy of any document found in the record or of a printed judicial or agency decision.

(3) When necessary to facilitate inclusion of odd-sized documents such as technical drawings, an appendix may be a size other than 8½ by 11 inches, and need not lie reasonably flat when opened.

(c) Form of Other Papers.

(1) **Motion.** The form of a motion is governed by Rule 27(d).

(2) Other Papers. Any other paper, including a petition for panel rehearing and a petition for hearing or rehearing en banc, and any response to such a petition, must be reproduced in the manner prescribed by Rule 32(a), with the following exceptions:

    (A) A cover is not necessary if the caption and signature page of the paper together contain the information required by Rule 32(a)(2). If a cover is used, it must be white.

    (B) Rule 32(a)(7) does not apply.

(d) Signature. Every brief, motion, or other paper filed with the court must be signed by the party filing the paper or, if the party is represented, by one of the party's attorneys.

(e) Local Variation. Every court of appeals must accept documents that comply with the form requirements of this rule and the length limits set by these rules. By local rule or order in a particular case, a court of appeals may accept documents that do not meet all the form requirements of this rule or the length limits set by these rules.

(f) Items Excluded from Length. In computing any length limit, headings, footnotes, and quotations count toward the limit but the following items do not:

- the cover page;
- a corporate disclosure statement;
- a table of contents;
- a table of citations;
- a statement regarding oral argument;
- an addendum containing statutes, rules, or regulations;
- certificates of counsel;
- the signature block;
- the proof of service; and
- any item specifically excluded by these rules or by local rule.

(g) Certificate of Compliance.

(1) Briefs and Papers That Require a Certificate. A brief submitted under Rules 28.1(e)(2), 29(b)(4), or 32(a)(7)(B)—and a paper submitted under Rules 5(c)(1), 21(d)(1), 27(d)(2)(A), 27(d)(2)(C), 35(b)(2)(A), or 40(b)(1)—must include a certificate by the attorney, or an unrepresented party, that the document complies with the type-volume limitation. The person preparing the certificate may rely on the word or line count of the word-processing system used to prepare the document. The certificate must state the number of words—or the number of lines of monospaced type—in the document.

(2) Acceptable Form. Form 6 in the Appendix of Forms meets the requirements for a certificate of compliance.

(As amended Apr. 24, 1998, eff. Dec. 1, 1998; Apr. 29, 2002, eff. Dec. 1, 2002; Apr. 25, 2005, eff. Dec. 1, 2005; Apr. 28, 2016, eff. Dec. 1, 2016.)

RULE 32.1   CITING JUDICIAL DISPOSITIONS

(a) Citation Permitted. A court may not prohibit or restrict the citation of federal judicial opinions, orders, judgments, or other written dispositions that have been:

    (i) designated as "unpublished," "not for publication," "non-precedential," "not precedent," or the like; and

    (ii) issued on or after January 1, 2007.

(b) Copies Required. If a party cites a federal judicial opinion, order, judgment, or other written disposition that is not available in a publicly accessible electronic database, the party must file and serve a copy of that opinion, order, judgment, or disposition with the brief or other paper in which it is cited.

(Added Apr. 12, 2006, eff. Dec. 1, 2006.)

RULE 33.   APPEAL CONFERENCES

The court may direct the attorneys—and, when appropriate, the parties—to participate in one or more conferences to address any matter that may aid in disposing of the proceedings, including simplifying the issues and discussing settlement. A judge or other person designated by the court may preside over the conference, which may be conducted in person or by telephone. Before a settlement conference, the attorneys must consult with their clients and obtain as much authority as feasible to settle the case. The court may, as a result of the conference, enter an order controlling the course of the proceedings or implementing any settlement agreement.

(As amended Apr. 29, 1994, eff. Dec. 1, 1994; Apr. 24, 1998, eff. Dec. 1, 1998.)

RULE 34.   ORAL ARGUMENT

(a) In General.

(1) Party's Statement. Any party may file, or a court may require by local rule, a statement explaining why oral argument should, or need not, be permitted.

(2) Standards. Oral argument must be allowed in every case unless a panel of three judges who have examined the briefs and record unanimously agrees that oral argument is unnecessary for any of the following reasons:

    (A) the appeal is frivolous;

    (B) the dispositive issue or issues have been authoritatively decided; or

    (C) the facts and legal arguments are adequately presented in the briefs and record, and the decisional process would not be significantly aided by oral argument.

(b) Notice of Argument; Postponement. The clerk must advise all parties whether oral argument will be scheduled, and, if so, the date, time, and place for it, and the time allowed for each side. A motion to postpone the argument or to allow longer argument must be filed reasonably in advance of the hearing date.

(c) Order and Contents of Argument. The appellant opens and concludes the argument. Counsel must not read at length from briefs, records, or authorities.

(d) Cross-Appeals and Separate Appeals. If there is a cross-appeal, Rule 28.1(b) determines which party is the appellant and which is the appellee for purposes of oral argument. Unless the court directs otherwise, a cross-appeal or separate appeal must be argued when the initial appeal is argued. Separate parties should avoid duplicative argument.

(e) Nonappearance of a Party. If the appellee fails to appear for argument, the court must hear appellant's argument. If the appellant fails to appear for argument, the court may hear the appellee's argument. If neither party appears, the case will be decided on the briefs, unless the court orders otherwise.

(f) Submission on Briefs. The parties may agree to submit a case for decision on the briefs, but the court may direct that the case be argued.

(g) Use of Physical Exhibits at Argument; Removal. Counsel intending to use physical exhibits other than documents at the argument must arrange to place them in the courtroom on the day of the argument before the court convenes. After the argument, counsel must remove the exhibits from the courtroom, unless the court directs otherwise. The clerk may destroy or dispose of the exhibits if counsel does not reclaim them within a reasonable time after the clerk gives notice to remove them.

(As amended Apr. 30, 1979, eff. Aug. 1, 1979; Mar. 10, 1986, eff. July 1, 1986; Apr. 30, 1991, eff. Dec. 1, 1991; Apr. 22, 1993, eff. Dec. 1, 1993; Apr. 24, 1998, eff. Dec. 1, 1998; Apr. 25, 2005, eff. Dec. 1, 2005.)

RULE 35.   EN BANC DETERMINATION

(a) When Hearing or Rehearing En Banc May Be Ordered. A majority of the circuit judges who are in regular active service and who are not disqualified may order that an appeal or other proceeding be heard or reheard by the court of appeals en banc. An en banc hearing or rehearing is not favored and ordinarily will not be ordered unless:

(1) en banc consideration is necessary to secure or maintain uniformity of the court's decisions; or

(2) the proceeding involves a question of exceptional importance.

(b) Petition for Hearing or Rehearing En Banc. A party may petition for a hearing or rehearing en banc.

(1) The petition must begin with a statement that either:

(A) the panel decision conflicts with a decision of the United States Supreme Court or of the court to which the petition is addressed (with citation to the conflicting case or cases) and consideration by the full court is therefore necessary to secure and maintain uniformity of the court's decisions; or

(B) the proceeding involves one or more questions of exceptional importance, each of which must be concisely stated; for example, a petition may assert that a proceeding presents a question of exceptional importance if it involves an issue on which the panel decision conflicts with the authoritative decisions of other United States Courts of Appeals that have addressed the issue.

(2) Except by the court's permission:

(A) a petition for an en banc hearing or rehearing produced using a computer must not exceed 3,900 words; and

(B) a handwritten or typewritten petition for an en banc hearing or rehearing must not exceed 15 pages.

(3) For purposes of the limits in Rule 35(b)(2), if a party files both a petition for panel rehearing and a petition for rehearing en banc, they are considered a single document even if they are filed separately, unless separate filing is required by local rule.

(c) Time for Petition for Hearing or Rehearing En Banc. A petition that an appeal be heard initially en banc must be filed by the date when the appellee's brief is due. A petition for a rehearing en banc must be filed within the time prescribed by Rule 40 for filing a petition for rehearing.

(d) Number of Copies. The number of copies to be filed must be prescribed by local rule and may be altered by order in a particular case.

(e) Response. No response may be filed to a petition for an en banc consideration unless the court orders a response.

(f) Call for a Vote. A vote need not be taken to determine whether the case will be heard or reheard en banc unless a judge calls for a vote.

(As amended Apr. 30, 1979, eff. Aug. 1, 1979; Apr. 29, 1994, eff. Dec. 1, 1994; Apr. 24, 1998, eff. Dec. 1, 1998; Apr. 25, 2005, eff. Dec. 1, 2005; Apr. 28, 2016, eff. Dec. 1, 2016.)

RULE 36.   ENTRY OF JUDGMENT; NOTICE

(a) Entry. A judgment is entered when it is noted on the docket. The clerk must prepare, sign, and enter the judgment:

(1) after receiving the court's opinion—but if settlement of the judgment's form is required, after final settlement; or

(2) if a judgment is rendered without an opinion, as the court instructs.

(b) Notice. On the date when judgment is entered, the clerk must serve on all parties a copy of the opinion—or the judgment, if no opinion was written—and a notice of the date when the judgment was entered.

(As amended Apr. 24, 1998, eff. Dec. 1, 1998; Apr. 29, 2002, eff. Dec. 1, 2002.)

RULE 37.   INTEREST ON JUDGMENT

(a) When the Court Affirms. Unless the law provides otherwise, if a money judgment in a civil case is affirmed, whatever interest is allowed by law is payable from the date when the district court's judgment was entered.

(b) When the Court Reverses. If the court modifies or reverses a judgment with a direction that a money judgment be entered in the district court, the mandate must contain instructions about the allowance of interest.

(As amended Apr. 24, 1998, eff. Dec. 1, 1998.)

RULE 38.   FRIVOLOUS APPEAL— DAMAGES AND COSTS

If a court of appeals determines that an appeal is frivolous, it may, after a separately filed motion or notice from the court and reasonable opportunity to respond, award just damages and single or double costs to the appellee.

(As amended Apr. 29, 1994, eff. Dec. 1, 1994; Apr. 24, 1998, eff. Dec. 1, 1998.)

RULE 39. COSTS

(a) **Against Whom Assessed.** The following rules apply unless the law provides or the court orders otherwise:

(1) if an appeal is dismissed, costs are taxed against the appellant, unless the parties agree otherwise;

(2) if a judgment is affirmed, costs are taxed against the appellant;

(3) if a judgment is reversed, costs are taxed against the appellee;

(4) if a judgment is affirmed in part, reversed in part, modified, or vacated, costs are taxed only as the court orders.

(b) **Costs For and Against the United States.** Costs for or against the United States, its agency, or officer will be assessed under Rule 39(a) only if authorized by law.

(c) **Costs of Copies.** Each court of appeals must, by local rule, fix the maximum rate for taxing the cost of producing necessary copies of a brief or appendix, or copies of records authorized by Rule 30(f). The rate must not exceed that generally charged for such work in the area where the clerk's office is located and should encourage economical methods of copying.

(d) **Bill of Costs: Objections; Insertion in Mandate.**

(1) A party who wants costs taxed must—within 14 days after entry of judgment—file with the circuit clerk, with proof of service, an itemized and verified bill of costs.

(2) Objections must be filed within 14 days after service of the bill of costs, unless the court extends the time.

(3) The clerk must prepare and certify an itemized statement of costs for insertion in the mandate, but issuance of the mandate must not be delayed for taxing costs. If the mandate issues before costs are finally determined, the district clerk must—upon the circuit clerk's request—add the statement of costs, or any amendment of it, to the mandate.

(e) **Costs on Appeal Taxable in the District Court.** The following costs on appeal are taxable in the district court for the benefit of the party entitled to costs under this rule:

(1) the preparation and transmission of the record;

(2) the reporter's transcript, if needed to determine the appeal;

(3) premiums paid for a supersedeas bond or other bond to preserve rights pending appeal; and

(4) the fee for filing the notice of appeal.

(As amended Apr. 30, 1979, eff. Aug. 1, 1979; Mar. 10, 1986, eff. July 1, 1986; Apr. 24, 1998, eff. Dec. 1, 1998; Mar. 26, 2009, eff. Dec. 1, 2009.)

RULE 40. PETITION FOR PANEL REHEARING

(a) **Time to File; Contents; Answer; Action by the Court if Granted.**

(1) **Time.** Unless the time is shortened or extended by order or local rule, a petition for panel rehearing may be filed within 14 days after entry of judgment. But in a civil case, unless an order shortens or extends the time, the petition may be filed by any party within 45 days after entry of judgment if one of the parties is:

(A) the United States;

(B) a United States agency;

(C) a United States officer or employee sued in an official capacity; or

(D) a current or former United States officer or employee sued in an individual capacity for an act or omission occurring in connection with duties performed on the United States' behalf—including all instances in which the United States represents that person when the court of appeals' judgment is entered or files the petition for that person.

(2) **Contents.** The petition must state with particularity each point of law or fact that the petitioner believes the court has overlooked or misapprehended and must argue in support of the petition. Oral argument is not permitted.

(3) **Answer.** Unless the court requests, no answer to a petition for panel rehearing is permitted. But ordinarily rehearing will not be granted in the absence of such a request.

(4) **Action by the Court.** If a petition for panel rehearing is granted, the court may do any of the following:

(A) make a final disposition of the case without reargument;

(B) restore the case to the calendar for reargument or resubmission; or

(C) issue any other appropriate order.

(b) **Form of Petition; Length.** The petition must comply in form with Rule 32. Copies must be served and filed as Rule 31 prescribes. Except by the court's permission:

(1) a petition for panel rehearing produced using a computer must not exceed 3,900 words; and

(2) a handwritten or typewritten petition for panel rehearing must not exceed 15 pages.

(As amended Apr. 30, 1979, eff. Aug. 1, 1979; Apr. 29, 1994, eff. Dec. 1, 1994; Apr. 24, 1998, eff. Dec. 1, 1998; Apr. 26, 2011, eff. Dec. 1, 2011; Apr. 28, 2016, eff. Dec. 1, 2016.)

RULE 41. MANDATE: CONTENTS; ISSUANCE AND EFFECTIVE DATE; STAY

(a) **Contents.** Unless the court directs that a formal mandate issue, the mandate consists of a certified copy of the judgment, a copy of the court's opinion, if any, and any direction about costs.

(b) When Issued. The court's mandate must issue 7 days after the time to file a petition for rehearing expires, or 7 days after entry of an order denying a timely petition for panel rehearing, petition for rehearing en banc, or motion for stay of mandate, whichever is later. The court may shorten or extend the time.

(c) Effective Date. The mandate is effective when issued.

(d) Staying the Mandate.

(1) On Petition for Rehearing or Motion. The timely filing of a petition for panel rehearing, petition for rehearing en banc, or motion for stay of mandate, stays the mandate until disposition of the petition or motion, unless the court orders otherwise.

(2) Pending Petition for Certiorari.

(A) A party may move to stay the mandate pending the filing of a petition for a writ of certiorari in the Supreme Court. The motion must be served on all parties and must show that the certiorari petition would present a substantial question and that there is good cause for a stay.

(B) The stay must not exceed 90 days, unless the period is extended for good cause or unless the party who obtained the stay files a petition for the writ and so notifies the circuit clerk in writing within the period of the stay. In that case, the stay continues until the Supreme Court's final disposition.

(C) The court may require a bond or other security as a condition to granting or continuing a stay of the mandate.

(D) The court of appeals must issue the mandate immediately when a copy of a Supreme Court order denying the petition for writ of certiorari is filed.

(As amended Apr. 29, 1994, eff. Dec. 1, 1994; Apr. 24, 1998, eff. Dec. 1, 1998; Apr. 29, 2002, eff. Dec. 1, 2002; Mar. 26, 2009, eff. Dec. 1, 2009.)

RULE 42. VOLUNTARY DISMISSAL

(a) Dismissal in the District Court. Before an appeal has been docketed by the circuit clerk, the district court may dismiss the appeal on the filing of a stipulation signed by all parties or on the appellant's motion with notice to all parties.

(b) Dismissal in the Court of Appeals. The circuit clerk may dismiss a docketed appeal if the parties file a signed dismissal agreement specifying how costs are to be paid and pay any fees that are due. But no mandate or other process may issue without a court order. An appeal may be dismissed on the appellant's motion on terms agreed to by the parties or fixed by the court.

(As amended Apr. 24, 1998, eff. Dec. 1, 1998.)

RULE 43. SUBSTITUTION OF PARTIES

(a) Death of a Party.

(1) After Notice of Appeal Is Filed. If a party dies after a notice of appeal has been filed or while a proceeding is pending in the court of appeals, the decedent's personal representative may be substituted as a party on motion filed with the circuit clerk by the representative or by any party. A party's motion must be served on the representative in accordance with Rule 25. If the decedent has no representative, any party may suggest the death on the record, and the court of appeals may then direct appropriate proceedings.

(2) Before Notice of Appeal Is Filed—Potential Appellant. If a party entitled to appeal dies before filing a notice of appeal, the decedent's personal representative—or, if there is no personal representative, the decedent's attorney of record—may file a notice of appeal within the time prescribed by these rules. After the notice of appeal is filed, substitution must be in accordance with Rule 43(a)(1).

(3) Before Notice of Appeal Is Filed—Potential Appellee. If a party against whom an appeal may be taken dies after entry of a judgment or order in the district court, but before a notice of appeal is filed, an appellant may proceed as if the death had not occurred. After the notice of appeal is filed, substitution must be in accordance with Rule 43(a)(1).

(b) Substitution for a Reason Other Than Death. If a party needs to be substituted for any reason other than death, the procedure prescribed in Rule 43(a) applies.

(c) Public Officer: Identification; Substitution.

(1) Identification of Party. A public officer who is a party to an appeal or other proceeding in an official capacity may be described as a party by the public officer's official title rather than by name. But the court may require the public officer's name to be added.

(2) Automatic Substitution of Officeholder. When a public officer who is a party to an appeal or other proceeding in an official capacity dies, resigns, or otherwise ceases to hold office, the action does not abate. The public officer's successor is automatically substituted as a party. Proceedings following the substitution are to be in the name of the substituted party, but any misnomer that does not affect the substantial rights of the parties may be disregarded. An order of substitution may be entered at any time, but failure to enter an order does not affect the substitution.

(As amended Mar. 10, 1986, eff. July 1, 1986; Apr. 24, 1998, eff. Dec. 1, 1998.)

RULE 44. CASE INVOLVING A CONSTITUTIONAL QUESTION WHEN THE UNITED STATES OR THE RELEVANT STATE IS NOT A PARTY

(a) Constitutional Challenge to Federal Statute. If a party questions the constitutionality of an Act of Congress in a proceeding in which the United States or its agency, officer, or employee is not a party in an official capacity, the questioning party must give written notice to the circuit clerk immediately upon the filing of the record or as soon as the question is raised in the court of appeals. The clerk must then certify that fact to the Attorney General.

(b) Constitutional Challenge to State Statute. If a party questions the constitutionality of a statute of a State in a proceeding in which that State or its agency, officer, or employee is not a party in an official capacity, the questioning party must give written notice to the circuit clerk immediately upon the filing of the record or as soon as the question is raised in the court of appeals. The clerk must then certify that fact to the attorney general of the State.

(As amended Apr. 24, 1998, eff. Dec. 1, 1998; Apr. 29, 2002, eff. Dec. 1, 2002.)

RULE 45. CLERK'S DUTIES

(a) General Provisions.

(1) Qualifications. The circuit clerk must take the oath and post any bond required by law. Neither the clerk nor any deputy clerk may practice as an attorney or counselor in any court while in office.

(2) When Court Is Open. The court of appeals is always open for filing any paper, issuing and returning process, making a motion, and entering an order. The clerk's office with the clerk or a deputy in attendance must be open during business hours on all days except Saturdays, Sundays, and legal holidays. A court may provide by local rule or by order that the clerk's office be open for specified hours on Saturdays or on legal holidays other than New Year's Day, Martin Luther King, Jr.'s Birthday, Washington's Birthday, Memorial Day, Independence Day, Labor Day, Columbus Day, Veterans' Day, Thanksgiving Day, and Christmas Day.

(b) Records.

(1) The Docket. The circuit clerk must maintain a docket and an index of all docketed cases in the manner prescribed by the Director of the Administrative Office of the United States Courts. The clerk must record all papers filed with the clerk and all process, orders, and judgments.

(2) Calendar. Under the court's direction, the clerk must prepare a calendar of cases awaiting argument. In placing cases on the calendar for argument, the clerk must give preference to appeals in criminal cases and to other proceedings and appeals entitled to preference by law.

(3) Other Records. The clerk must keep other books and records required by the Director of the Administrative Office of the United States Courts, with the approval of the Judicial Conference of the United States, or by the court.

(c) Notice of an Order or Judgment. Upon the entry of an order or judgment, the circuit clerk must immediately serve a notice of entry on each party, with a copy of any opinion, and must note the date of service on the docket. Service on a party represented by counsel must be made on counsel.

(d) Custody of Records and Papers. The circuit clerk has custody of the court's records and papers. Unless the court orders or instructs otherwise, the clerk must not permit an original record or paper to be taken from the clerk's office. Upon disposition of the case, original papers constituting the record on appeal or review must be returned to the court or agency from which they were received. The clerk must preserve a copy of any brief, appendix, or other paper that has been filed.

(As amended Mar. 1, 1971, eff. July 1, 1971; Mar. 10, 1986, eff. July 1, 1986; Apr. 24, 1998, eff. Dec. 1, 1998; Apr. 29, 2002, eff. Dec. 1, 2002; Apr. 25, 2005, eff. Dec. 1, 2005.)

RULE 46. ATTORNEYS

(a) Admission to the Bar.

(1) Eligibility. An attorney is eligible for admission to the bar of a court of appeals if that attorney is of good moral and professional character and is admitted to practice before the Supreme Court of the United States, the highest court of a state, another United States court of appeals, or a United States district court (including the district courts for Guam, the Northern Mariana Islands, and the Virgin Islands).

(2) Application. An applicant must file an application for admission, on a form approved by the court that contains the applicant's personal statement showing eligibility for membership. The applicant must subscribe to the following oath or affirmation:

"I, _____, do solemnly swear [or affirm] that I will conduct myself as an attorney and counselor of this court, uprightly and according to law; and that I will support the Constitution of the United States."

(3) Admission Procedures. On written or oral motion of a member of the court's bar, the court will act on the application. An applicant may be admitted by oral motion in open court. But, unless the court orders otherwise, an applicant need not appear before the court to be admitted. Upon admission, an applicant must pay the clerk the fee prescribed by local rule or court order.

(b) Suspension or Disbarment.

(1) Standard. A member of the court's bar is subject to suspension or disbarment by the court if the member:

(A) has been suspended or disbarred from practice in any other court; or

(B) is guilty of conduct unbecoming a member of the court's bar.

(2) Procedure. The member must be given an opportunity to show good cause, within the time prescribed by the court, why the member should not be suspended or disbarred.

(3) Order. The court must enter an appropriate order after the member responds and a hearing is held, if requested, or after the time prescribed for a response expires, if no response is made.

(c) Discipline. A court of appeals may discipline an attorney who practices before it for conduct unbecoming a member of the bar or for failure to comply with any court rule. First, however, the court must afford the attorney reasonable notice, an opportunity to show cause to the contrary, and, if requested, a hearing.

(As amended Mar. 10, 1986, eff. July 1, 1986; Apr. 24, 1998, eff. Dec. 1, 1998.)

RULE 47. LOCAL RULES BY COURTS OF APPEALS

(a) Local Rules.

(1) Each court of appeals acting by a majority of its judges in regular active service may, after giving appropriate public notice and opportunity for comment, make and amend rules governing its practice. A generally applicable direction to parties or lawyers regarding practice before a court must be in a local rule rather than an internal operating procedure or standing order. A local rule must be consistent with—but not duplicative of—Acts of Congress and rules adopted under 28 U.S.C. § 2072 and must conform to any uniform numbering system prescribed by the Judicial Conference of the United States. Each circuit clerk must send the Administrative Office of the United States Courts a copy of each local rule and internal operating procedure when it is promulgated or amended.

(2) A local rule imposing a requirement of form must not be enforced in a manner that causes a party to lose rights because of a nonwillful failure to comply with the requirement.

(b) Procedure When There Is No Controlling Law. A court of appeals may regulate practice in a particular case in any manner consistent with federal law, these rules, and local rules of the circuit. No sanction or other disadvantage may be imposed for noncompliance with any requirement not in federal law, federal rules, or the local circuit rules unless the alleged violator has been furnished in the particular case with actual notice of the requirement.

(As amended Apr. 27, 1995, eff. Dec. 1, 1995; Apr. 24, 1998, eff. Dec. 1, 1998.)

RULE 48. MASTERS

(a) Appointment; Powers. A court of appeals may appoint a special master to hold hearings, if necessary, and to recommend factual findings and disposition in matters ancillary to proceedings in the court. Unless the order referring a matter to a master specifies or limits the master's powers, those powers include, but are not limited to, the following:

(1) regulating all aspects of a hearing;

(2) taking all appropriate action for the efficient performance of the master's duties under the order;

(3) requiring the production of evidence on all matters embraced in the reference; and

(4) administering oaths and examining witnesses and parties.

(b) Compensation. If the master is not a judge or court employee, the court must determine the master's compensation and whether the cost is to be charged to any party.

(As amended Apr. 29, 1994, eff. Dec. 1, 1994; Apr. 24, 1998, eff. Dec. 1, 1998.)

APPENDIX OF FORMS

FORM 1. NOTICE OF APPEAL TO A COURT OF APPEALS FROM A JUDGMENT OR ORDER OF A DISTRICT COURT

United States District Court for the _____
District of _____
File Number _____

A.B., *Plaintiff*	)	
	)	
v.	)	*Notice of Appeal*
	)	
C.D., *Defendant*	)	

Notice is hereby given that [___ (here name all parties taking the appeal) ___ , (plaintiffs) (defendants) in the above named case,*] hereby appeal to the United States Court of Appeals for the _____ Circuit (from the final judgment) (from an order (describing it)) entered in this action on the _____ day of _____, 20___.

(s) _____
Attorney for [_____]
[Address:_____]

[Note to inmate filers: If you are an inmate confined in an institution and you seek the timing benefit of Fed. R. App. P. 4(c)(1), complete Form 7 (Declaration of Inmate Filing) and file that declaration along with this Notice of Appeal.]

* See Rule 3(c) for permissible ways of identifying appellants.

(As amended Apr. 22, 1993, eff. Dec. 1, 1993; Mar. 27, 2003, eff. Dec. 1, 2003; Apr. 28, 2016, eff. Dec. 1, 2016.)

FORM 2. NOTICE OF APPEAL TO A COURT OF APPEALS FROM A DECISION OF THE UNITED STATES TAX COURT

UNITED STATES TAX COURT

Washington, D.C.

A.B., Petitioner	)
	)
v.	) Docket No. _____
	)
Commissioner of Internal	)
Revenue, Respondent	)

Notice of Appeal

Notice is hereby given that [_____here name all parties taking the appeal [1]_____], hereby appeals to the United States Court of Appeals for the _____ Circuit from (that part of) the decision of this court entered in the above captioned proceeding on the _____ day of _____, 20___ (relating to _____).

                                           (s) _____
                                               Counsel for [_____]
                                               [Address:_____]

(As amended Apr. 22, 1993, eff. Dec. 1, 1993; Mar. 27, 2003, eff. Dec. 1, 2003.)

[1] See Rule 3(c) for permissible ways of identifying appellants.

FORM 3. PETITION FOR REVIEW OF ORDER OF AN AGENCY, BOARD, COMMISSION OR OFFICER

United States Court of Appeals for the _____ Circuit

A.B., Petitioner	)	
	)	
v.	)	Petition for Review
XYZ Commission, Respondent	)	

[____(here name all parties bringing the petition[1])____] hereby petitions the court for review of the Order of the XYZ Commission (describe the order) entered on _____, 20___.

[(s)] _____

Attorney for Petitioners

Address:_____

(As amended Apr. 22, 1993, eff. Dec. 1, 1993; Mar. 27, 2003, eff. Dec. 1, 2003.)

[1] See Rule 15.

FORM 4. AFFIDAVIT ACCOMPANYING MOTION FOR PERMISSION TO APPEAL IN FORMA PAUPERIS

UNITED STATES DISTRICT COURT
for the
<_____> DISTRICT OF <_____>

\<Name(s) of plaintiff(s)\>,	)
	)
Plaintiff(s)	)
	)
v.	)
	) Case No. \<Number\>
\<Name(s) of defendant(s)\>,	)
	)
Defendant(s)	)
	)

Affidavit in Support of Motion

I swear or affirm under penalty of perjury that, because of my poverty, I cannot prepay the docket fees of my appeal or post a bond for them. I believe I am entitled to redress. I swear or affirm under penalty of perjury under United States laws that my answers on this form are true and correct. (28 U.S.C. § 1746; 18 U.S.C. § 1621.)

Signed: _____

Instructions

Complete all questions in this application and then sign it. Do not leave any blanks: if the answer to a question is "0," "none," or "not applicable (N/A)," write in that response. If you need more space to answer a question or to explain your answer, attach a separate sheet of paper identified with your name, your case's docket number, and the question number.

Date: _____

My issues on appeal are:

1. *For both you and your spouse estimate the average amount of money received from each of the following sources during the past 12 months. Adjust any amount that was received weekly, biweekly, quarterly, semiannually, or annually to show the monthly rate. Use gross amounts, that is, amounts before any deductions for taxes or otherwise.*

Income source	Average monthly amount during the past 12 months		Amount expected next month	
	You	Spouse	You	Spouse
Employment	$____	$____	$____	$____
Self-employment	$____	$____	$____	$____
Income from real property (such as rental income)	$____	$____	$____	$____
Interest and dividends	$____	$____	$____	$____
Gifts	$____	$____	$____	$____
Alimony	$____	$____	$____	$____
Child support	$____	$____	$____	$____
Retirement (such as social security, pensions, annuities, insurance)	$____	$____	$____	$____
Disability (such as social security, insurance payments)	$____	$____	$____	$____
Unemployment payments	$____	$____	$____	$____
Public-assistance (such as welfare)	$____	$____	$____	$____

Other (specify): _____ $_____ $_____ $_____ $_____
                  Total monthly
                          income: $_____ $_____ $_____ $_____

2. List your employment history for the past two years, most recent employer first. (Gross monthly pay is before taxes or other deductions.)

Employer	Address	Dates of employment	Gross monthly pay
_____	_____	_____	_____
_____	_____	_____	_____

3. List your spouse's employment history for the past two years, most recent employer first. (Gross monthly pay is before taxes or other deductions.)

Employer	Address	Dates of employment	Gross monthly pay
_____	_____	_____	_____
_____	_____	_____	_____

4. How much cash do you and your spouse have? $_____
Below, state any money you or your spouse have in bank accounts or in any other financial institution.

Financial institution	Type of account	Amount you have	Amount your spouse has
_____	_____	$_____	$_____
_____	_____	$_____	$_____
_____	_____	$_____	$_____

If you are a prisoner seeking to appeal a judgment in a civil action or proceeding, you must attach a statement certified by the appropriate institutional officer showing all receipts, expenditures, and balances during the last six months in your institutional accounts. If you have multiple accounts, perhaps because you have been in multiple institutions, attach one certified statement of each account.

5. List the assets, and their values, which you own or your spouse owns. Do not list clothing and ordinary household furnishings.

Home	(Value)	Other real estate	(Value)	Motor vehicle #1	(Value)
_____		_____		Make & year: _____	
_____		_____		Model: _____	
				Registration #: _____	

Motor vehicle #2	(Value)	Other assets	(Value)	Other assets	(Value)
Make & year: _____		_____		_____	
Model: _____		_____		_____	
Registration #: _____					

6. State every person, business, or organization owing you or your spouse money, and the amount owed.

Person owing you or your spouse money	Amount owed to you	Amount owed to your spouse
_____	_____	_____
_____	_____	_____
_____	_____	_____

7. *State the persons who rely on you or your spouse for support.*

Name **[or, if under 18, initials only]**	**Relationship**	**Age**
_____	_____	_____
_____	_____	_____
_____	_____	_____

8. *Estimate the average monthly expenses of you and your family. Show separately the amounts paid by your spouse. Adjust any payments that are made weekly, biweekly, quarterly, semiannually, or annually to show the monthly rate.*

	You	**Your Spouse**
Rent or home-mortgage payment (include lot rented for mobile home)	$_____	$_____
Are real-estate taxes included? ☐ Yes ☐ No		
Is property insurance included? ☐ Yes ☐ No		
Utilities (electricity, heating fuel, water, sewer, and Telephone)	$_____	$_____
Home maintenance (repairs and upkeep)	$_____	$_____
Food	$_____	$_____
Clothing	$_____	$_____
Laundry and dry-cleaning	$_____	$_____
Medical and dental expenses	$_____	$_____
Transportation (not including motor vehicle payments)	$_____	$_____
Recreation, entertainment, newspapers, magazines, etc.	$_____	$_____
Insurance (not deducted from wages or included in mortgage payments)		
Homeowner's or renter's:	$_____	$_____
Life:	$_____	$_____
Health:	$_____	$_____
Motor Vehicle:	$_____	$_____
Other: _____	$_____	$_____
Taxes (not deducted from wages or included in mortgage payments) (specify): __	$_____	$_____
Installment payments		
Motor Vehicle:	$_____	$_____
Credit card (name): _____	$_____	$_____
Department store (name): _____	$_____	$_____
Other: _____	$_____	$_____
Alimony, maintenance, and support paid to others	$_____	$_____
Regular expenses for operation of business, profession, or farm (attach detailed statement)	$_____	$_____
Other (specify): _____	$_____	$_____
Total monthly expenses:	$_____	$_____

9. *Do you expect any major changes to your monthly income or expenses or in your assets or liabilities during the next 12 months?*

☐ Yes ☐ No   If yes, describe on an attached sheet.

10. *Have you spent—or will you be spending—any money for expenses or attorney fees in connection with this lawsuit?* ☐ Yes ☐ No

If yes, how much? $_____

11. *Provide any other information that will help explain why you cannot pay the docket fees for your appeal.*

12. *State the city and state of your legal residence.*

Your daytime phone number: (___) _____
Your age: _____ *Your years of schooling:* _____
Last four digits of your social-security number: _____

(As amended Apr. 24, 1998, eff. Dec. 1, 1998; Apr. 28, 2010, eff. Dec. 1, 2010; Apr. 16, 2013, eff. Dec. 1, 2013.)

FORM 5. NOTICE OF APPEAL TO A COURT OF APPEALS FROM A JUDGMENT OR ORDER OF A DISTRICT COURT OR A BANKRUPTCY APPELLATE PANEL

United States District Court for the ....

District of ....

In re   )

.................................,)

         Debtor   )

)   File No.. . . . .

.................................,)

         Plaintiff   )

         v.   )

.................................,)

         Defendant   )

Notice of Appeal to
United States Court of Appeals

for the .... Circuit

......................., the plaintiff [or defendant or other party] appeals to the United States Court of Appeals for the .... Circuit from the final judgment [or order or decree] of the district court for the district of .... [or bankruptcy appellate panel of the .... circuit], entered in this case on ...., 20.... [here describe the judgment, order, or decree] ....

The parties to the judgment [or order or decree] appealed from and the names and addresses of their respective attorneys are as follows:

Dated ....

Signed ....

Attorney for Appellant

Address: ....

....

*[**Note to inmate filers:** If you are an inmate confined in an institution and you seek the timing benefit of Fed. R. App. P. 4(c)(1), complete Form 7 (Declaration of Inmate Filing) and file that declaration along with this Notice of Appeal.]*

(Added Apr. 25, 1989, eff. Dec. 1, 1989; amended Mar. 27, 2003, eff. Dec. 1, 2003; Apr. 28, 2016, eff. Dec. 1, 2016.)

FORM 6.   CERTIFICATE OF COMPLIANCE WITH TYPE–VOLUME LIMIT

Certificate of Compliance With Type-Volume Limit, Typeface
Requirements, and Type-Style Requirements

1.   This document complies with [the type-volume limit of Fed. R. App. P. [*insert Rule citation; e.g., 32(a)(7)(B)*]] [the word limit of Fed. R. App. P. [*insert Rule citation; e.g., 5(c)(1)*]] because, excluding the parts of the document exempted by Fed. R. App. P. 32(f) [and [*insert applicable Rule citation, if any*]]:

☐ this document contains [*state the number of*] words, **or**

☐ this brief uses a monospaced typeface and contains [*state the number of*] lines of text.

2.   This document complies with the typeface requirements of Fed. R. App. P. 32(a)(5) and the type-style requirements of Fed. R. App. P. 32(a)(6) because:

☐ this document has been prepared in a proportionally spaced typeface using [*state name and version of word-processing program*] in [*state font size and name of type style*], **or**

☐ this document has been prepared in a monospaced typeface using [*state name and version of word-processing program*] with [*state number of characters per inch and name of type style*].

(s)_____

Attorney for _____

Dated: _____

(Added Apr. 29, 2002, eff. Dec. 1, 2002; amended Apr. 28, 2016, eff. Dec. 1, 2016.)

FORM 7.   DECLARATION OF INMATE FILING

[insert name of court; for example,
United States District Court for the District of Minnesota]

A.B., Plaintiff   )
)
      v.   ) *Case No.*
)
C.D., Defendant   )

I am an inmate confined in an institution. Today, _____ *[insert date]*, I am depositing the _____ *[insert title of document; for example, "notice of appeal"]* in this case in the institution's internal mail system. First-class postage is being prepaid either by me or by the institution on my behalf.

I declare under penalty of perjury that the foregoing is true and correct (see 28 U.S.C. § 1746; 18 U.S.C. § 1621).

Sign your name here _____

Signed on _____ *[insert date]*

[Note to inmate filers: If your institution has a system designed for legal mail, you must use that system in order to receive the timing benefit of Fed. R. App. P. 4(c)(1) or Fed. R. App. P. 25(a)(2)(C).]

(Added Apr. 28, 2016, eff. Dec. 1, 2016.)

APPENDIX

This chart summarizes the length limits stated in the Federal Rules of Appellate Procedure. Please refer to the rules for precise requirements, and bear in mind the following:

- In computing these limits, you can exclude the items listed in Rule 32(f).
- If you use a word limit or a line limit (other than the word limit in Rule 28(j)), you must file the certificate required by Rule 32(g).
- For the limits in Rules 5, 21, 27, 35, and 40:
  - You must use the word limit if you produce your document on a computer; and
  - You must use the page limit if you handwrite your document or type it on a typewriter.
- For the limits in Rules 28.1, 29(a)(5), and 32:
  - You may use the word limit or page limit, regardless of how you produce the document; or
  - You may use the line limit if you type or print your document with a monospaced typeface. A typeface is monospaced when each character occupies the same amount of horizontal space.

	Rule	Document type	Word limit	Page limit	Line limit
Permission to appeal	5(c)	• Petition for permission to appeal • Answer in opposition • Cross–petition	5,200	20	Not applicable
Extraordinary writs	21(d)	• Petition for writ of mandamus or prohibition or other extraordinary writ • Answer	7,800	30	Not applicable
Motions	27(d)(2)	• Motion • Response to a motion	5,200	20	Not applicable
	27(d)(2)	• Reply to a response to a motion	2,600	10	Not applicable
Parties' briefs (where no cross–appeal)	32(a)(7)	• Principal brief	13,000	30	1,300
	32(a)(7)	• Reply brief	6,500	15	650
Parties' briefs (where cross–appeal)	28.1(e)	• Appellant's principal brief • Appellant's response and reply brief	13,000	30	1,300
	28.1(e)	• Appellee's principal and response brief	15,300	35	1,500
	28.1(e)	• Appellee's reply brief	6,500	15	650
Party's supplemental letter	28(j)	• Letter citing supplemental authorities	350	Not applicable	Not applicable

	Rule	Document type	Word limit	Page limit	Line limit
Amicus briefs	29(a)(5)	• Amicus brief during initial consideration of case on merits	One–half the length set by the Appellate Rules for a party's principal brief	One–half the length set by the Appellate Rules for a party's principal brief	One–half the length set by the Appellate Rules for a party's principal brief
	29(b)(4)	• Amicus brief during consideration of whether to grant rehearing	2,600	Not applicable	Not applicable
Rehearing and en banc filings	35(b)(2) & 40(b)	• Petition for hearing en banc • Petition for panel rehearing; petition for rehearing en banc	3,900	15	Not applicable

(Added Apr. 28, 2016, eff. Dec. 1, 2016.)

INDEX TO
FEDERAL RULES OF APPELLATE PROCEDURE

UNITED STATES COURT OF APPEALS
FOR THE
SIXTH CIRCUIT

Including Amendments Received Through
January 1, 2018

TITLE I.   APPLICABILITY OF RULES

FRAP 1.   SCOPE OF RULES; DEFINITION; TITLE

[For text of rule, see the Federal Rules of Appellate Procedure]

RULE 1.   SCOPE OF RULES AND TITLE

Cite these rules as "6 Cir. R. ____."

[Effective December 1, 1998.   Amended effective August 16, 2012.]

IOP 1. SCOPE AND TITLE

(a) Purpose. The purpose of these internal operating procedures is to provide useful information about the court's procedures and facilities, as distinguished from requirements of practice and procedure. Although they include practices and procedures that the court and practitioners generally follow, the internal operating procedures are not rules and do not impose requirements of practice and procedure.

(b) General Content. These internal operating procedures describe the responsibilities, functions, organization, and procedures in the day-to-day administration of the court's operation. They also set out the work of the judges, bench assignments, calendaring, processing of opinions, and other operating procedures. The court may test and adopt new procedures that may not immediately be included in the internal operating procedures.

Cite these operating procedures as "6 Cir. I.O.P. ___."

[Effective December 1, 1998. Amended effective August 16, 2012.]

FRAP 2. SUSPENSION OF RULES

[For text of rule, see the Federal Rules of Appellate Procedure]

RULE 2. SUSPENSION OF RULES

The court may suspend any provision of these rules to expedite its decision or for other good cause.

[Effective December 1, 1998. Amended effective August 16, 2012.]

IOP 2. [RESERVED]

TITLE II. APPEAL FROM A JUDGMENT OR ORDER OF A DISTRICT COURT

FRAP 3. APPEAL AS OF RIGHT—HOW TAKEN

[For text of rule, see the Federal Rules of Appellate Procedure]

RULE 3. DISMISSAL FOR NONPAYMENT OF FEES

The court may dismiss an appeal if required fees are not paid.

[Amended effective August 16, 2012.]

IOP 3. FEES

(a) Generally. A fee schedule is available on the court's web site and from the clerk's office.

(b) Indigents. Fed. R. App. P. 24 governs proceedings in forma pauperis.

[Effective December 1, 1998. Amended effective August 16, 2012.]

FRAP 4. APPEAL AS OF RIGHT— WHEN TAKEN

[For text of rule, see the Federal Rules of Appellate Procedure]

RULE 4. [RESERVED]

IOP 4. [RESERVED]

FRAP 5. APPEAL BY PERMISSION

[For text of rule, see the Federal Rules of Appellate Procedure]

RULE 5. FILING OF PETITION AND SUBSEQUENT DOCUMENTS; FEE

A petition for permission to appeal and all subsequent documents shall be filed electronically as provided in 6 Cir. R. 25 and this court's Guide to Electronic Filing, unless otherwise ordered by the court. A fee is not required unless the court grants the petition.

[Effective June 1, 2008. Amended effective August 16, 2012.]

IOP 5. [RESERVED]

FRAP 5.1 APPEAL BY LEAVE UNDER 28 U.S.C. § 636(c)(5) [ABROGATED]

FRAP 6. APPEAL IN A BANKRUPTCY CASE

[For text of rule, see the Federal Rules of Appellate Procedure]

RULE 6. APPEAL IN BANKRUPTCY CASE FROM A FINAL JUDGMENT, ORDER, OR DECREE OF A DISTRICT COURT OR OF THE BANKRUPTCY APPELLATE PANEL—FEES

6 Cir. R. 10(b) applies to exhibits in bankruptcy appeals, except that when the appeal is from a bankruptcy appellate panel, the terms "district court" and "district clerk" mean "appellate panel" and "appellate panel clerk."

[Amended effective August 16, 2012.]

IOP 6. [RESERVED]

FRAP 7. BOND FOR COSTS ON APPEAL IN A CIVIL CASE

[For text of rule, see the Federal Rules of Appellate Procedure]

RULE 7. [RESERVED]

IOP 7. [RESERVED]

FRAP 8. STAY OR INJUNCTION PENDING APPEAL

[For text of rule, see the Federal Rules of Appellate Procedure]

RULE 8. STAY PENDING APPEAL IN DEATH PENALTY CASES

(a) Direct Federal Appeals.

(1) *Time for Filing Motion.* An appellant moving for a stay must do so as soon as possible after filing the notice of appeal.

(2) *Review of Merits on Motion for Stay.* The court may conclude it can appropriately address the merits of the case on a motion for a stay. If so, the court will order the parties to address the merits in expedited briefs. The court may grant a temporary stay pending consideration of the merits to prevent mooting the case. Any oral argument of the merits will be as soon as practicable after briefs are filed.

(b) State Cases. 6 Cir. R. 22(c)(3) governs stays in state death penalty cases.

[Amended effective August 16, 2012.]

IOP 8. [RESERVED]

FRAP 9. RELEASE IN A CRIMINAL CASE

[For text of rule, see the Federal Rules of Appellate Procedure]

RULE 9. RELEASE IN A CRIMINAL CASE

(a) Appellant.

(1) *What to File.*

(A) An appellant seeking review of an order regarding release or detention must file:

- the district court's order;
- relevant opinions;
- the judgment of conviction if the appeal is after conviction;
- a transcript of the relevant district court proceedings, if available; and
- a supporting brief complying with Fed. R. App. P. 27(d)(1), not exceeding 20 pages.

(B) The appellant may file other documents relevant to the appeal.

(2) *When to File.* The appellant must file the items required by 6 Cir. R. 9(a) as follows:

(A) When seeking relief by notice of appeal, not more than 7 days after the circuit clerk dockets the appeal.

(B) When seeking relief by motion, with the motion.

(b) Appellee.

(1) *What to File.* The appellee may file a response that includes:

- a brief complying with Fed. R. App. P. 27(d)(1), not exceeding 20 pages; and
- other documents relevant to the appeal.

(2) *When to File.* If filing a response, the appellee must file it not more than 7 days after the appellant's filing. The court may take action without a response.

(c) Appellant's Reply Brief. The appellant may file a reply brief not exceeding 5 pages and not more than 3 days after appellee's filing.

(d) Court May Change Requirements. On motion of a party or on its own, the court may order different filings and a different schedule.

[Effective December 1, 1998. Amended effective August 16, 2012.]

IOP 9. RELEASE IN A CRIMINAL CASE

Review of district court orders on pretrial release or detention is by appeal, not motion.

[Amended effective August 16, 2012.]

FRAP 10. THE RECORD ON APPEAL

[For text of rule, see the Federal Rules of Appellate Procedure]

RULE 10. THE RECORD ON APPEAL

(a) Transcripts.

(1) *Transcript Order.* A party ordering a transcript or certifying that a transcript is unnecessary must:

(A) Use Form 6CA–30, which is available on the court's web site and from the clerk's office;

(B) File the form in the district court;

(C) File the form in this court;

(D) Serve the form on the other parties; and

(E) Send four copies to each reporter from whom a transcript is ordered.

(2) *Failure to Comply With Transcript Requirements.* The court may dismiss an appeal for failure to timely order a transcript, to make satisfactory arrangements with the reporter for paying the cost of the transcript, or to certify that no transcript will be ordered.

(b) Exhibits. Exhibits should ordinarily be made part of the district court's electronic record. This subrule (b) applies to non-electronic exhibits that are necessary for the court to understand the issues and decide the appeal. If a party is uncertain as to how certain exhibits should be handled, the party should contact the case manager.

(1) *Appendix of Certain Paper Exhibits.* For paper exhibits that are not part of the district court's electronic record and that are necessary for the court to understand the issues and decide the appeal, a party may file an appendix with:

- manageable paper exhibits; and

- excerpts from documents of unusual bulk or weight that the district court would normally not transmit to this court.

(2) *Documents of Unusual Bulk or Weight; Physical Exhibits.* This subrule (b)(2) applies to documents of unusual bulk or weight and physical exhibits that the district clerk would not normally forward to this court. When a party deems it necessary for the court to have such items to understand the issues and decide the appeal, a party must:

(A) designate the items to be forwarded;

(B) obtain the circuit clerk's written permission to forward them; and

(C) request the district clerk to forward them.

[Effective December 1, 1998. Amended effective June 1, 2008; January 12, 2009; August 16, 2012.]

IOP 10.   THE RECORD ON APPEAL—EXHIBITS

(a) **Non–Electronic Exhibits.** Exhibits filed in the district court are part of the record on appeal. Fed. R. App. P. 10(a)(1). Generally, the district court does not send non-electronic exhibits to this court unless and until the circuit clerk requests them. 6 Cir. R. 10(b) gives guidance on handling non-electronic exhibits.

(b) **Bulky Exhibits.** 6 Cir. R. 10(b) distinguishes between "manageable paper exhibits" and "documents of unusual bulk or weight." The intent is (1) to allow parties to include in an appendix exhibits or exhibit excerpts without burdening the court with extremely voluminous exhibits and (2) to provide for forwarding of physical exhibits and documents of unusual bulk or weight when immediate availability to the court is important to the appeal.

(c) **Sealed Exhibits.** 6 Cir. R. 25(h) governs sealed documents, including sealed exhibits.

(d) **Video Exhibits.** A party may file with the clerk of the court of appeals four copies of a video exhibit which has been filed with the district court.

[Effective January 12, 2009. Amended effective August 16, 2012.]

FRAP 11.   FORWARDING THE RECORD

*[For text of rule, see the Federal Rules
of Appellate Procedure]*

RULE 11.   FORWARDING THE RECORD

(a) **District Clerk's Duty to Forward.**

(1) *Electronic Record.* The district clerk does not forward the electronic record. This court directly accesses the district court's electronic record.

(2) *Non–Electronic Record.* The district court will forward non-electronic parts of the record only when the circuit clerk requests it.

(b) **Transcripts; Reporter's Duties.** This subrule applies to transcripts that a party orders or that the court directs to be transcribed for appeal.

(1) *Criminal Appeals.* The reporter must give priority to preparing transcripts in criminal appeals except for in-courtroom obligations. Where necessary to ensure timely resolution of a criminal appeal, this court may direct preparation of the transcript out of the order otherwise prescribed by rule.

(2) *Extension of Time.* A request for additional time to complete the transcript under Fed. R. App. P. 11(b)(1)(B) must include:

- the date of the notice of appeal;
- the reasons for the extension;
- when the transcript was ordered;
- when the party ordering the transcript made satisfactory financial arrangements with the reporter;
- the estimated number of pages;
- the number of pages completed;
- the estimated completion date; and
- in a criminal case, the dates of conviction and sentencing.

(3) *Reduction of Fees.*

(A) If the transcript is not completed within 45 days from the reporter's receipt of the order, the reporter must reduce the usual fee by 10%.

(B) If the transcript is not completed within 60 days from the reporter's receipt of the order, the reporter must:

- reduce the usual fee by a total of 20%; and
- discontinue courtroom duties until the transcript is completed and filed in the district court.

(C) The circuit clerk may waive the fee reductions for good cause.

(4) *Request to Suspend Preparation.* The reporter must not honor a party's request to suspend transcript preparation unless the court directs otherwise.

(c) **Sealed Documents.**

(1) *Documents Remain Sealed.* If the district court forwards a sealed document, this court will give the document the same confidential treatment.

(2) *Unsealing.* A sealed document will be unsealed and made part of the public record only on this court's or the district court's order. A person seeking to unseal a document sealed by the district court must move to unseal first in the district court.

[Effective December 1, 1998. Amended effective August 16, 2012.]

IOP 11.   FORWARDING THE RECORD

(a) **Reporter's Duties; Extension of Time.** The circuit clerk monitors outstanding transcripts and delays in transcript preparation. Fed. R. App. P. 11(b)(1)(B) and 6 Cir. R. 11(b)(2) govern a reporter's request for an extension of time.

(b) **Presentence Reports.** The circuit clerk will obtain the presentence report and objections to it. The court will keep them confidential.

[Effective December 1, 1998. Amended effective January 12, 2009; August 16, 2012.]

FRAP 12. DOCKETING THE APPEAL; FILING A REPRESENTATION STATEMENT; FILING THE RECORD

[For text of rule, see the Federal Rules of Appellate Procedure]

RULE 12. FILING A REPRESENTATION STATEMENT—APPEARANCE OF COUNSEL; COUNSEL'S REPRESENTATION IN CRIMINAL CASES

(a) Required Appearance. An attorney must file a Form for Appearance of Counsel, 6CA–68, to file documents or argue. A party represented by more than one attorney or firm must designate a single attorney as lead counsel. Counsel must update his or her PACER account to reflect changes in address telephone number, fax number, and e-mail address, and must advise the clerk as well. The court will provide notices only to counsel who has filed an appearance. Failure to file an appearance may result in dismissal of the case.

(b) Exigent Circumstances. 6 Cir. R. 46(a)(1)(A) requires most counsel to be admitted to this court's bar to appear. In exigent circumstances that require filing or argument before admission, counsel should contact the clerk for directions.

(c) Counsel's Representation in Criminal Cases.

(1) *Continued Representation on Appeal.* Trial counsel in criminal cases must continue representation of the defendant on appeal unless relieved by the court.

(2) *Appointment of Trial Counsel as Appellate Counsel.* If the district court appointed trial counsel, this court will appoint trial counsel as appellate counsel when the notice of appeal is filed. Appellant need not provide further proof of indigence.

(3) *Appointment of Appellant's Counsel Under CJA.* When the court directs appointment of counsel for an appellant under the Criminal Justice Act, the clerk will select counsel as provided in the Sixth Circuit Criminal Justice Act Plan.

(4) *Withdrawal of Appellate Counsel.* A motion to withdraw as counsel on appeal in a criminal case must state reasons and be accompanied by one of the following:

(A) Proof that new counsel has been retained to represent the defendant, including a signed appearance by new counsel. If the defendant is indigent and seeks the appointment of counsel pursuant to the Criminal Justice Act application must first be made to the district court for leave for the defendant to proceed in forma pauperis.

(B) An affidavit or signed statement from the defendant stating:

- the defendant has been advised of the defendant's appellate rights; and
- the defendant withdraws the appeal.

(C) A brief following the procedure in *Anders v. California*, 386 U.S. 738 (1967), and—in addition to service otherwise required—proof that counsel served the following on the defendant:

- a copy of the brief;
- a copy of the motion; and
- notice that the defendant has 21 days from the date of service to file a brief in support of reversal of the conviction.

(D) A detailed statement of reasons why it would be unethical, unfair, or unreasonable to require counsel to continue to represent defendant, and—in addition to service otherwise required—proof that counsel served the following on the defendant:

- a copy of the motion, including this statement; and
- notice that the defendant has 14 days from service of the motion to file a response.

(5) *Petition for Writ of Certiorari.* Appointed counsel must file a petition for a writ of certiorari in the Supreme Court if the client requests it and, in counsel's considered judgment, there are grounds for seeking Supreme Court review.

[Effective December 1, 1998. Amended effective June 1, 2008; August 16, 2012.]

IOP 12. APPEARANCE

The appearance must be filed electronically. 6 Cir. R. 25(a)(1).

[Effective December 1, 1998. Amended effective August 16, 2012.]

FRAP 12.1 REMAND AFTER AN INDICATIVE RULING BY THE DISTRICT COURT ON A MOTION FOR RELIEF THAT IS BARRED BY A PENDING APPEAL

[For text of rule, see the Federal Rules of Appellate Procedure]

TITLE III. APPEALS FROM THE UNITED STATES TAX COURT

FRAP 13. APPEALS FROM THE TAX COURT

[For text of rule, see the Federal Rules of Appellate Procedure]

RULE 13. REVIEW OF A DECISION OF THE TAX COURT

The provisions in these rules for appeal from a judgment or order of a district court apply to appeals from the United States Tax Court, except as provided for appendices in 6 Cir. R. 30.

[Effective June 1, 2008.]

Comment

This rule is added to make clear that Tax Court appeals will generally be handled the same as district court appeals. However, the Tax Court's electronic records are not easily transferable to the court of appeals. Therefore, as set out in 6 Cir. R. 30, in Tax Court appeals there will be appendices instead of an electronic record on appeal.

IOP 13. [RESERVED]

FRAP 14. APPLICABILITY OF OTHER RULES TO APPEALS FROM THE TAX COURT

[For text of rule, see the Federal Rules of Appellate Procedure]

RULE 14. REVIEW OF A DECISION OF THE TAX COURT

The rules for appeals from a district court apply to appeals from the United States Tax Court, except that 6 Cir. R. 30(b)(3) governs the appendix.

[Amended effective August 16, 2012.]

IOP 14. REVIEW OF A DECISION OF THE TAX COURT

The Tax Court's electronic records are not easily transferable to this court. Therefore, a Tax Court appeal has an appendix instead of an electronic record on appeal. The appendix and all other filings generally must be filed electronically.

[Amended effective August 16, 2012.]

TITLE IV. REVIEW OR ENFORCEMENT OF AN ORDER OF AN ADMINISTRATIVE AGENCY, BOARD, COMMISSION, OR OFFICER

FRAP 15. REVIEW OR ENFORCEMENT OF AN AGENCY ORDER—HOW OBTAINED; INTERVENTION

[For text of rule, see the Federal Rules of Appellate Procedure]

RULE 15. ELECTRONIC FILING

A petition for review of an agency order and all subsequent documents shall be filed electronically, in accordance with 6 Cir. R. 25 and this court's Guide to Electronic Filing, unless otherwise ordered by the court.

[Effective June 1, 2008. Amended effective August 16, 2012.]

IOP 15. REVIEW OR ENFORCEMENT OF AN AGENCY ORDER—PAPER AND ELECTRONIC FILING

(a) Petition, Application. A party seeking review or enforcement of an agency order must file the petition for review or application for enforcement electronically as provided in 6 Cir. R. 25(b)(1).

(b) Motion for Stay. A party filing a motion for a stay at the same time as the petition for review must file the motion in paper format with an electronic copy as provided in 6 Cir. R. 25(b)(1).

(c) Other Documents. All other documents must be filed electronically unless the court orders otherwise. 6 Cir. R. 25(a).

[Amended effective August 16, 2012.]

FRAP 15.1 BRIEFS AND ORAL ARGUMENT IN A NATIONAL LABOR RELATIONS BOARD PROCEEDING

[For text of rule, see the Federal Rules of Appellate Procedure]

RULE 15.1 [RESERVED]

IOP 15.1 [RESERVED]

FRAP 16. THE RECORD ON REVIEW OR ENFORCEMENT

[For text of rule, see the Federal Rules of Appellate Procedure]

RULE 16. [RESERVED]

IOP 16. [RESERVED]

FRAP 17. FILING THE RECORD

[For text of rule, see the Federal Rules of Appellate Procedure]

RULE 17. FILING THE RECORD FOR AN IMMIGRATION REVIEW PETITION

See 6 Cir. R. 30(f)(2) for the requirements for filing the record in immigration cases.

[Amended effective August 16, 2012.]

IOP 17.   [RESERVED]

FRAP 18.   STAY PENDING REVIEW

[For text of rule, see the Federal Rules of Appellate Procedure]

RULE 18.   MOTION FOR STAY PENDING REVIEW

A motion for stay must be filed electronically as provided in 6 Cir. R. 25(b)(1).

[Effective June 1, 2008. Amended effective August 16, 2012.]

FRAP 19.   SETTLEMENT OF A JUDGMENT ENFORCING AN AGENCY ORDER IN PART

[For text of rule, see the Federal Rules of Appellate Procedure]

RULE 19.   [RESERVED]

IOP 19.   AMENDMENT, CORRECTION OR SETTLEMENT OF A JUDGMENT

The clerk refers the following matters to the panel that decided the case:

- a motion to amend or correct the judgment; and
- settlement of a judgment under Fed. R. App. P. 19.

[Effective December 1, 1998. Amended effective August 16, 2012.]

FRAP 20.   APPLICABILITY OF RULES TO THE REVIEW OR ENFORCEMENT OF AN AGENCY ORDER

[For text of rule, see the Federal Rules of Appellate Procedure]

RULE 20.   APPLICABILITY OF RULES TO THE REVIEW OR ENFORCEMENT OF AN AGENCY ORDER

The provisions of these rules, except 6 Cir. R. 3–14 and 22, apply to review or enforcement of an agency order. In these rules, "appellant" includes a petitioner or applicant, and "appellee" includes a respondent.

[Amended effective August 16, 2012.]

IOP 20.   [RESERVED]

TITLE V.   EXTRAORDINARY WRITS

FRAP 21.   WRITS OF MANDAMUS AND PROHIBITION, AND OTHER EXTRAORDINARY WRITS

[For text of rule, see the Federal Rules of Appellate Procedure]

RULE 21.   WRITS OF MANDAMUS AND PROHIBITION, AND OTHER EXTRAORDINARY WRITS—FILING FEE

A fee schedule is available on the court's web site and from the clerk's office. The clerk will not docket the petition if the fee is not paid, or if the petitioner has not been granted leave to proceed in forma pauperis.

[Effective December 1, 1998. Amended effective June 1, 2008; August 16, 2012.]

IOP 21.   WRIT OF MANDAMUS AND PROHIBITION, AND OTHER EXTRAORDINARY WRITS

(a) A party seeking an extraordinary writ may file the petition in paper format with an electronic copy as provided in 6 Cir. R. 25(b)(1) and (3).

(b) Status Report From Respondent. When a petition seeks to expedite a district court or tax court case, this court will request a status report from the respondent judge and send a copy of the request to petitioner.

(c) Petition Raising Substantive Issues. When a petition raises substantive legal issues, this court will invite a preliminary response from respondent and send a copy of the request to petitioner.

[Effective December 1, 1998. Amended effective August 16, 2012.]

TITLE VI.   HABEAS CORPUS; PROCEEDINGS IN FORMA PAUPERIS

FRAP 22.   HABEAS CORPUS AND SECTION 2255 PROCEEDINGS

[For text of rule, see the Federal Rules of Appellate Procedure]

RULE 22.   HABEAS CORPUS AND SECTION 2255 PROCEEDINGS—SECOND OR SUCCESSIVE APPLICATIONS—DEATH PENALTY CASES

(a) Certificate of Appealability. A party seeking a certificate of appealability from this court must do so as soon as possible after the filing of the notice of appeal.

(b) Motion to File a Second or Successive Application Under 28 U.S.C. § 2254 or § 2255.

(1) *Scope.* This subrule (b) applies to motions in this court for authorization to file a second or successive application in the district court under 28 U.S.C. § 2254 or § 2255.

(2) *Motion.*

(A) Information Sheet. The clerk will provide an information sheet and motion form for an applicant who advises that he or she will move for authorization. The information sheet and motion form is also available on the court's web site.

(B) What to File.

(i) Form. The applicant must use the court's form. The form is available on the court's web site.

(ii) Additional Documents. The applicant must file with the motion the following documents from prior § 2254 or § 2255 proceedings if they are reasonably available. The court may request respondent to provide these documents:

- the magistrate judge's report and recommendation; and

- the district judge's opinion.

(C) No Filing Fee. A filing fee is not required.

(3) *Response.* The respondent may file a response within 14 days after the later of service of the motion or respondent's service of supporting documentation.

(4) *Court Action.*

(A) Considering Response. The court may consider an untimely response. The court need not await a response in a death penalty case where execution is imminent.

(B) Forwarding Order. The clerk will forward the court's order to the district clerk.

(c) Death Penalty Cases.

(1) *Scope.* This subrule (c) applies to applications under 28 U.S.C. § 2254 or § 2255 by a person under a sentence of death.

(2) *Contacting the Clerk.* Counsel must contact the clerk's office by telephone at the earliest possible time—before filing a notice of appeal if possible—to inform the clerk of the status of the case and determine the procedures that apply.

(3) *Stay of Execution.*

(A) Time for Filing Motion. An applicant moving for a stay must do so as soon as possible after filing the notice of appeal.

(B) Review of Merits on Motion for Stay. The court may conclude it appropriately can address the merits of the case on a motion for a stay. If so, the court will order the parties to address the merits in expedited briefs. The court may grant a temporary stay pending consideration of the merits to prevent mooting the case. Any oral argument of the merits will be held as soon as practicable after briefs are filed.

(4) *Emergency Motions.* Counsel with an emergency motion or application must file it with the clerk rather than with an individual judge. The court encourages telephone communication with the clerk as soon as it becomes evident that an applicant will seek emergency relief.

(5) *Required Documents for Certificate of Appealability or Stay of Execution.* This subrule (c)(5) applies to an application for a certificate of appealability and a motion for stay of execution. The application or motion must include the following documents if they are not part of the district court's electronic record:

- available transcripts of the district court proceedings; and

- all state and federal opinions or judgments involving any issue presented to this court or, if the ruling was not made in a written opinion or judgment, the relevant portions of the transcript.

[Effective December 1, 1998. Amended effective December 1, 2009; August 16, 2012.]

IOP 22. HABEAS CORPUS AND SECTION 2255 PROCEEDINGS

(a) Motion to File a Second or Successive Application Under 28 U.S.C. § 2254 or § 2255. An applicant not represented by counsel seeking authorization to file a second or successive application in the district court under 28 U.S.C. § 2254 or § 2255 must file the motion in paper format. If an applicant is represented by counsel, the request for authorization to file the application should be filed electronically as provided in 6 Cir. R. 25 with an electronic copy as provided in 6 Cir. R. 25(b)(1).

(b) Death Penalty Cases.

(1) *Panel Assignment.* The court maintains a roster of active judges and those senior judges who so elect for making panel assignments in all death penalty cases, including direct appeals in federal death penalty cases. The clerk assigns the panel as soon as the case is docketed. The panel handles all matters in the case, including second or successive petitions, incidental and collateral matters, and separate proceedings questioning the conviction or sentence. An active judge assigned to a panel continues as a member after taking senior status.

(2) *Scheduling and Briefing.* Special scheduling and briefing requirements apply to death penalty cases. See 6 Cir. R. 31(c)(3) and 32(b)(2).

(c) Appointment of Counsel. When a pro se applicant is the appellee in a 28 U.S.C. §§ 2241, 2254, or 2255 case, the clerk will appoint counsel if the applicant is indigent.

(d) Single Judge Stay. The panel decision is the court's decision unless the en banc court changes it. However, it is the court's policy that an active judge—whether or not a member of the assigned panel—or a senior judge who is a member of the panel, may issue a stay for no longer than necessary to allow the court to rule on a petition for en banc review or a judge's request for en banc review. This policy is consistent with the authority granted a single judge by Rule 8 of the Federal Rules of Appellate Procedure to rule on motions in exceptional circumstances.

[Effective December 1, 1998. Amended effective August 27, 2002; August 16, 2012.]

FRAP 23. CUSTODY OR RELEASE OF A PRISONER IN A HABEAS CORPUS PROCEEDING

[For text of rule, see the Federal Rules of Appellate Procedure]

RULE 23. [RESERVED]

IOP 23. [RESERVED]

FRAP 24. PROCEEDING IN FORMA PAUPERIS

[For text of rule, see the Federal Rules of Appellate Procedure]

RULE 24. PROCEEDINGS IN FORMA PAUPER-IS—APPLICATION FOR PAUPER STATUS ON APPEAL—CRIMINAL

If a convicted defendant did not qualify to proceed in forma pauperis in the district court but appears to qualify on appeal, trial counsel must see that the defendant completes CJA Form 23 (for an incarcerated defendant) or Fed. R. App. P. Form 4 (for a defendant not incarcerated) and files it in the district court. The forms are available from the district court clerk and this court's web site.

[Effective December 1, 1998. Amended effective August 16, 2012.]

Committee Note

Former 6th Cir. R. 12(c). See also 6 Cir. R. 101.

IOP 24. [RESERVED]

TITLE VII. GENERAL PROVISIONS

FRAP 25. FILING AND SERVICE

[For text of rule, see the Federal Rules of Appellate Procedure]

RULE 25. FILING AND SERVICE; ELECTRONIC CASE FILING

(a) Electronic Filing Required.

(1) *Requirement.* All documents must be filed electronically using the Electronic Case Filing (ECF) system unless these rules or a court order provide otherwise. These rules and the Guide to Electronic Filing govern electronic filing.

(2) *Form of Electronic Filing.* Electronically filed documents must be in PDF format and must conform to technical requirements established by the Judicial Conference or the court. When possible, documents must be in Native PDF format and not created by scanning.

(3) *Paper Filings Not Accepted.* When these rules require electronic filing, the clerk will not accept a paper filing.

(b) Exceptions to Electronic Filing.

(1) *Case Initiating Documents—Exceptions to Electronic Filing.*

(A) Definition. The following are "case initiating documents" governed by this subrule (b)(1):

(i) A petition for permission to appeal under Fed. R. App. P. 5;

(ii) A petition for review or application for enforcement of an agency order under Fed. R. App. P. 15;

(iii) A motion for a stay filed with a petition for review of an agency order;

(iv) A petition for a writ of mandamus or prohibition or other extraordinary writ under Fed. R. App. P. 21;

(v) A motion to authorize filing in the district court of a second or successive application for a writ of habeas corpus under 6 Cir. R. 22(b); and

(vi) Any other document initiating an original action in this court.

(B) Manner of Filing. A party represented by counsel must file a case initiating document electronically, as either a PDF file attached to an e-mail directed to the clerk's office or in CD format, as provided in the Guide to Electronic Filing.

(2) *Other Exceptions.* The following must be filed in paper format:

(A) In Pro Per Filings. A document filed by a party not represented by counsel.

(B) Attorney Misconduct Proceedings. Documents involving complaints of attorney misconduct.

(C) CJA Representation. Documents involving compensation or expense reimbursement for representation under the Criminal Justice Act.

(D) Large Documents. A document that exceeds the limit for the size of electronic filing, as specified in the electronic case filing section of the court's web site.

(3) *Filing in Paper Format.* Unless these rules require otherwise, a party filing in paper format must file only a signed original.

(4) *Proof of Filing in Paper Format.* When the court allows or requires filing in paper format, the filer may obtain a file-stamped copy at the time of filing in person or by providing the clerk with a preaddressed stamped envelope and an extra copy of the document.

(c) ECF Registration and Use.

(1) *Requirements for ECF Registration.* To use the ECF system, an attorney must register. To register, an attorney must:

(A) be permitted to practice in this court and be in good standing;

(B) have a valid Public Access to Court Electronic Records (PACER) account or be a member of an office that has a valid PACER account;

(C) register for appellate court electronic filing at the PACER Service Center; and

(D) have a valid e-mail address.

(2) *Registration Is Consent to Electronic Service.* An attorney's registration is written consent:

(A) to electronic service of documents as provided by the Federal Rules of Appellate Procedure and these rules, and

(B) to receive electronic correspondence, orders, and opinions from the court.

(3) *Login Name and Password.* The clerk will issue a login name and password to an attorney who registers. The attorney may change the password after receiving it. Use of an attorney's login name and password by another, with the attorney's authorization, is deemed the attorney's use. If a login name or password is compromised, the attorney must notify the court as provided in the Guide to Electronic Filing.

(4) *Changes in Information.*

(A) Requirement to Give Notice. An attorney whose email address, mailing address, telephone number, or fax number has changed must change the information in his or her PACER account accordingly, and must file a notice of the change with the clerk and serve the notice on the parties in cases in which the attorney entered an appearance.

(B) Service on Obsolete Address. Service on an obsolete email address is valid service if the attorney failed to give notice of a change.

(d) Signatures.

(1) *Attorney Signature.* An attorney's use of the attorney's login name and password to submit a document electronically serves as that attorney's signature on the document. The attorney must use a signature block in substantially the following form, without a graphic or electronic signature:

/s/ Attorney Name
Attorney Name
ABC Law Firm
1234 First Street
Cincinnati, Ohio 45202
Telephone: (513) 987–6543
E-mail: AttorneyName@abclawfirm.com
Attorney for ___

(2) *Multiple Attorney Signatures.* The filer of a document with multiple signatures (such as a stipulation) must file in one of the following forms:

(A) Use an "/s/ Attorney Name" signature block for each attorney. By submitting the document, the filer certifies that the other attorneys expressly agreed to the form and substance of the document and authorized the filer to submit it electronically.

(B) Submit a scanned document with the signatures.

(3) *Clerk and Deputy Clerks; Court–Issued Documents.* The clerk's or a deputy clerk's filing of a document using that individual's login and password is the filing of a signed original. An order, opinion, judgment, or other court-issued document filed electronically without the signature of the judge, clerk, or deputy clerk has the same effect as if it were signed.

(e) Filing; Entry; Official Record.

(1) *Filing and Entry—ECF—Filed Documents.*

(A) Filing by Party.

(i) Filing and Entry. Electronic transmission of a document and transmission of the Notice of Docket Activity (NDA) from the court constitute filing the document under the Federal Rules of Appellate Procedure and entry of that document in the docket under Fed. R. App. P. 45(b)(1).

(ii) Time of Filing. An electronically-filed document is filed at the time shown on the NDA. Electronic filing does not alter a filing deadline. Where the deadline is a specific time of day, the electronic filing must be completed by that time.

(B) Filing by Court. Electronic filing of an order, decree, notice, opinion, or judgment constitutes entry in the docket under Fed. R. App. P. 36 and 45(b)(1) and (c).

(2) *Official Record.* The electronic version of filed documents—including those originally filed in paper format—is the official record. Modification of a filed document or docket entry is not permitted unless the court authorizes it.

(3) *Disposal of Paper Filings.* The clerk will discard paper documents once they have been made a part of the electronic record, unless the electronic copy is incomplete or of questionable quality or unless the court orders otherwise.

(f) Service of Documents Filed Electronically.

(1) *Method of Service.*

(A) NDA Constitutes Service. The ECF system sends a Notice of Docket Activity (NDA) to registered attorneys in the case. This constitutes service on them and no other service is necessary.

(B) Service on Unregistered Parties and Attorneys. The filer must serve parties not represented by counsel and attorneys not registered for electronic filing by other means under Fed. R. App. P. 25(c).

(2) *Certificate of Service.* A document presented for filing must contain a proof of service. Fed. R. App. P. 25(d). The NDA does not replace the proof of service.

(g) ECF Technical Failures.

(1) *Extension of Time.* There is a technical failure in the ECF system if the clerk finds that the system is unable to accept filings continuously or intermittently for more than one hour after 12:00 noon Eastern time. In that case, filings due that day that were not filed because of that technical failure are due the next business day. A delayed filing must include a declaration or affidavit attesting to the filer's failed attempts to file electronically at least two times after 12:00 noon separated by at least one hour on each day of delay because of the technical failure.

(2) *Help Desk.* A filer experiencing difficulty with electronic filing should contact the ECF help desk, as provided on the court's website and in the Guide to Electronic Filing.

(h) Sealed Documents.

(1) *Sealing or Limiting Access to Orders and Opinions.* An order or opinion is generally part of the public record. A party that seeks to seal or restrict access to an order or opinion must do so by motion.

(2) *Motion.* A motion to file sealed documents may be filed electronically unless prohibited by law, local rule, or court order. At the same time as filing the motion, the movant must provide the court and other parties a copy of the documents at issue. The movant must consult with the clerk before submitting the documents. The movant may provide the court's copy by sending a CD or an email to the clerk's office with a PDF file as provided in the Guide to Electronic Filing.

(3) *Order.* If the court grants the motion, the order authorizing filing of sealed documents may be filed electronically unless prohibited by law.

(4) *Filing.* Upon this court's entry of an order granting a motion to seal documents, those documents are to be filed via the court's electronic filing system (ECF).

(5) *Sealed Documents From Lower Court or Agency.* Documents sealed in the lower court or agency must continue to be filed under seal in this court. The filing must comply with the requirements of the court or agency that originally ordered or authorized the documents to be sealed.

[Effective December 1, 1998. Amended effective June 1, 2008; August 16, 2012.]

IOP 25.   [RESERVED]

FRAP 26.   COMPUTING AND EXTENDING TIME

[For text of rule, see the Federal Rules of Appellate Procedure]

RULE 26.   EXTENDING TIME; FAILURE TO FILE OR UNTIMELY FILING

(a) Extending Time.

(1) *How Sought.* A party seeking an extension of time must do so by written motion. The fact that the opposing party does not oppose the extension or previously received an extension is not dispositive of the motion. The court disfavors applications for extensions of time for the filing of briefs.

(2) *Extension of Time to File Brief in Criminal Appeal.* A motion to extend a briefing deadline in a criminal appeal must state whether the defendant is in custody or on bail.

(3) *Late Documents.* If a party files a document after the filing deadline, the party must also file a motion to extend the time for filing explaining the circumstances. If a party files without the required motion, the court will notify the party of the need to file the motion and await receipt of the motion before acting on the late-filed document.

(b) Failure to File or Untimely Filing. If the appellant does not timely process the appeal—including not timely filing a brief or required appendix or not meeting other deadlines—the court may dismiss the appeal for want of prosecution, impose sanctions, or both.

[Effective December 1, 1998. Amended effective August 16, 2012.]

IOP 26.   EXTENDING TIME

(a) Briefing Extensions Not Favored. The court does not favor motions to extend briefing deadlines.

(b) No Extension Until Granted. A party seeking a filing deadline extension should assume that there is no extension unless the clerk advises otherwise.

[Effective December 1, 1998. Amended effective August 16, 2012.]

FRAP 26.1   CORPORATE DISCLOSURE STATEMENT

[For text of rule, see the Federal Rules of Appellate Procedure]

RULE 26.1   CORPORATE DISCLOSURE STATEMENT

(a) Parties Required to Make Disclosure. With the exception of the United States government or agencies thereof or a state government or agencies or political subdivisions thereof, all parties and amici curiae to a civil or bankruptcy case, agency review proceeding, or original proceedings, and all corporate defendants in a criminal case shall file a corporate affiliate/financial interest disclosure statement. A negative report is required except in the case of individual criminal defendants.

(b) Financial Interest to Be Disclosed.

(1) Whenever a corporation that is a party to an appeal, or which appears as amicus curiae, is a subsidiary or affiliate of any publicly owned corporation not named in the appeal, counsel for the corporation that is a party or amicus shall advise the clerk in the manner provided by subdivision (c) of this rule of the identity of the parent corporation or affiliate and the relationship between it and the corporation that is a party or amicus to the appeal. A corporation shall be considered an affiliate of a publicly owned corporation for purposes of this rule if it controls, is controlled by, or is under common control with a publicly owned corporation.

(2) Whenever, by reason of insurance, a franchise agreement, or indemnity agreement, a publicly owned corporation or its affiliate, not a party to the appeal, nor an amicus, has a substantial financial interest in the outcome of litigation, counsel for the party or amicus whose interest is aligned with that of the publicly owned corporation or its affiliate shall advise the clerk in the manner provided by subdivision (c) of this rule of the identity of the publicly owned corporation and the nature of its or its affiliate's substantial financial interest in the outcome of the litigation.

(c) Form and Time of Disclosure. The disclosure statement shall be made on a form provided by the clerk and filed with the brief of a party or amicus or upon filing a motion, response, petition, or answer in this court, whichever first occurs.

[Effective December 1, 1998.]

Committee Note

Former 6th Cir. R. 25.

IOP 26.1   [RESERVED]

FRAP 27.   MOTIONS

[For text of rule, see the Federal Rules of Appellate Procedure]

RULE 27.   MOTIONS

(a) Where to File. All motions—including emergency motions and single judge motions—must be filed with the clerk. In an emergency when time does not permit this, counsel must contact the clerk's office by telephone to explain the situation and seek guidance.

(b) Service of Paper Motions. When a paper motion is allowed, the filer must serve one copy on each other party.

(c) Emergency Motions.

(1) *Notifying the Clerk.* When a party knows in advance that an emergency motion may be needed, the party must make every reasonable effort to notify the clerk at the earliest possible time that an emergency motion may be filed, the nature of the motion, and the relief to be sought.

(2) *Required Attachments.* Emergency motions must have the following copies attached:

- the notice of appeal;
- the order appealed from; and
- any other parts of the record necessary to decide the motion.

(d) Motion to Dismiss. A party may file a motion to dismiss for lack of jurisdiction. Ordinarily, the court will not grant other motions to dismiss.

(e) Motion to Affirm. The court will not consider a motion to affirm the judgment appealed from.

(f) Motion to Expedite. A party may move to expedite the appeal. The motion must show good cause to expedite.

(g) Motion for Reconsideration. A party may seek rehearing of a judgment of this court pursuant to Fed. R. App. P. 40. A party may file a motion for reconsideration of any other action of a panel, of a single judge or of the clerk. See 6 Cir. R. 45(b). A panel may reconsider its own action or may review the action of a single judge or of the clerk, but the panel reviewing a single judge's action shall not include that judge.

[Effective December 1, 1998. Amended effective June 1, 2008; January 12, 2009; December 1, 2009; August 16, 2012.]

IOP 27.   MOTIONS

(a) Motion Assignment.

(1) *Before Assignment to the Merits Panel. Composition of Motion Panels.* In cases not yet assigned to a merits panel, substantive motions are assigned to randomly assembled panels drawn from among active and senior circuit judges and visiting judges designated to sit with the court. Motions panels sit together for a calendar quarter and are assigned motions throughout that period. One member of the panel is designated the lead judge of each motions panel, to coordinate the actions of the panel.

(2) *After Assignment to the Oral Argument Calendar.* In cases assigned to the oral argument calendar, the court assigns motions to the merits panel rather than to a motions panel. The senior active judge on the panel initiates the panel's action.

(3) *Review of Single Judge Decision.* A panel reviewing a single judge's decision will not include that judge.

(b) Emergency Motions. Hearings on emergency motions, as with other motions, are extremely unusual. Parties should not expect that there will be a hearing and need not move for one. The clerk will inform the parties of the hearing time if the court decides to hold one.

[Effective December 1, 1998. Amended effective August 16, 2012.]

FRAP 28.   BRIEFS

[For text of rule, see the Federal Rules of Appellate Procedure]

RULE 28.   BRIEFS

(a) References to the Record. A brief must direct the court to the parts of the record it refers to.

(1) *District Court Appeals.* In an appeal from the district court, a brief must cite the "Page ID #" shown on the header or footer of the page(s) of the original record being referenced, along with a brief title and the record entry number of the document referenced. It is the responsibility of counsel to ensure that all documents referred to in the addendum have either been filed initially in digital format in the district court by way of ECF or, if not, have been scanned into digital format and then filed in the record in that format so that they bear the "Page ID #" designation referred to above. Counsel's failure to do so may result in rejection of the brief.

The description of relevant district court documents in the addendum shall include (i) a brief description of the document, (ii) the docket entry number of the document, and (iii) the "Page ID #" range for the relevant pages.

(2) *Other Appeals—References to the Record.* If there is an appendix or consecutively-numbered administrative record, the brief must also refer to the page number of the appendix or administrative record. For example, the brief should refer to "Record [or Appendix], pp. 69–70." Suitable abbreviations in these record references are acceptable.

(b) Additional Contents. The requirements of this subrule (b) are in addition to those in Fed. R. App. P. 28(a) and (b).

(1) *Principal Briefs.*

(A) Required Contents. Each principal brief must include:

(i) Designation of Relevant Lower Court Documents. A designation of relevant documents from the lower court record shall be included in an addendum to the brief; 6 Cir. R. 30(g)(1).

(ii) Designation of Record Items in Immigration Review Petitions. In cases where the government files the administrative record under 6 Cir. R. 30(f)(2), a designation of relevant record items under 6 Cir. R. 30(g)(2).

(B) Permitted Contents. A principal brief may include—before the jurisdictional statement—a statement of reasons why the court should hear oral argument under 6 Cir. R. 34(a).

(2) *Unpublished Dispositions.* When Fed. R. App. P. 32.1(b) or 6 Cir. R. 32.1(a) requires copies of unpublished opinions, the party must include the copies as an addendum to the brief.

(c) **Attachments.** A party may not attach documents to an electronically filed brief that are in an electronic record on appeal or are in a permitted appendix.

(d) **Briefs as Public Record.** Briefs filed with the court are public records. A brief that refers to sealed information is not automatically sealed. A party seeking to have a brief sealed in whole or in part must file a motion seeking such relief.

[Effective December 1, 1998. Amended effective January 24, 2007; June 1, 2008; January 12, 2009; August 16, 2012.]

IOP 28. BRIEFS

(a) **Length.** Briefs in excess of the lengths provided by the rules are seldom permitted.

(b) **Sample Briefs.** The clerk's office will not distribute sample briefs. However, copies are available for inspection in the clerk's office.

(c) **Expedited Cases.** In the following cases, this court directs the parties to file briefs on an expedited basis and then schedules an oral hearing or submission on briefs as soon as possible: recalcitrant witnesses under 28 U.S.C. § 1826 and grand jury contempt appeals. Issuance of a routine briefing schedule and expedited argument or submission on briefs is directed in the following cases: appeals from orders denying or granting preliminary or temporary injunctions; interlocutory appeals under 28 U.S.C. § 1292(b); direct criminal appeals; and appeals in cases filed pursuant to 28 U.S.C. §§ 2241, 2254 and 2255. See also Fed. R. App. P. 45(b).

Any other case may be expedited upon this court's granting of a motion under 6 Cir. R. 27(e). If an appeal is ordered expedited, the clerk will fix a briefing schedule which will permit the appeal to be set for oral argument at an early date, unless an earlier hearing date is directed by a judge. The clerk will usually have some idea of the approximate date of the hearing and will so advise counsel when the order is issued.

[Effective December 1, 1998. Amended effective June 1, 2008; August 16, 2012.]

FRAP 28.1 CROSS–APPEALS

[For text of rule, see the Federal Rules of Appellate Procedure]

RULE 28.1 [RESERVED]

IOP 28.1 [RESERVED]

FRAP 29. BRIEF OF AN AMICUS CURIAE

[For text of rule, see the Federal Rules of Appellate Procedure]

RULE 29. MOTION TO PARTICIPATE IN ORAL ARGUMENT

An amicus curiae may request to participate in oral argument by motion stating the reason oral argument will aid the court.

[Effective December 1, 1998. Amended effective August 16, 2012.]

IOP 29. [RESERVED]

FRAP 30. APPENDIX TO THE BRIEFS

[For text of rule, see the Federal Rules of Appellate Procedure]

RULE 30. APPENDIX TO THE BRIEFS; DESIGNATION OF RELEVANT DOCUMENTS; RECORD IN LIEU OF APPENDIX

(a) **When an Appendix Is Required.** An appendix is required only in the following cases, unless the court directs otherwise. In other cases, an appendix is unnecessary and must not be filed. The court will have the district court electronic record available.

(1) *District Court Appeal.* An appeal from a district court where 6 Cir. R. 30(b)(2) requires certain documents that are not part of the district court's electronic record to be included in an appendix—except social security cases (where the administrative record is filed instead of an appendix).

(2) *Tax Court Appeal.* An appeal from the United States Tax Court.

(3) *Agency Appeal.* A petition to review or application to enforce the decision of a federal administrative agency—except immigration review petitions described in 6 Cir. R. 30(f)(2) (where the administrative record is filed instead of an appendix).

(b) **Appendix Contents.**

(1) *General Requirement.* The parties and the court may rely on parts of the record not included in the appendix, except as provided in 6 Cir. R. 30(b)(5)(A). When required, the appendix is limited to parts of the record necessary for the court to understand the issues and decide the appeal. Inclusion of unnecessary parts or omission of necessary parts may result in sanctions under 6 Cir. R. 30(h).

(2) *District Court Appeals.* In an appeal from the district court, the appendix, when required, must include the current district court docket sheet and those items listed below that are not part of the district court's electronic record:

(A) in appeals in cases under 28 U.S.C. § 2254:

(i) all unpublished state court opinions in previous proceedings related to the issues raised in the petition;

(ii) the trial transcript;

(iii) the transcription of the state court record if required by 6 Cir. R. 30(b)(5); and

(iv) a transcript of any post-conviction state court hearing, if previously transcribed and available.

(B) other parts of the record—including all or part of exhibits or transcript pages—necessary for the court to understand the issues and decide the appeal, in chronological order; and

(C) certification that the documents in the appendix are properly part of the record.

(3) *Tax Court Appeals.* In an appeal from the Tax Court, the appendix must include:

(A) the current Tax Court docket sheet;

(B) the complaint;

(C) other pleadings or motions relevant to the arguments on appeal;

(D) the judgment from which the appeal is taken;

(E) relevant memorandum opinions, opinions from the bench, and findings of fact and conclusions of law;

(F) the notice of appeal;

(G) other parts of the record—including all or part of exhibits or transcript pages—necessary for the court to understand the issues and decide the appeal, in chronological order; and

(H) certification that the documents in the appendix are properly part of the record.

(4) *Agency Appeals.* In an agency appeal, the appendix must include:

(A) the order sought to be reviewed or enforced;

(B) supporting opinions, findings of fact, and conclusions of law;

(C) the petition for review or application for enforcement;

(D) other parts of the record—including all or part of exhibits or transcript pages—necessary for the court to understand the issues and decide the appeal, in chronological order; and

(E) certification that the documents in the appendix are properly part of the record.

(5) *State Habeas Corpus Appeals; Transcript Where There Is No Written State Court Record.*

(A) Transcript Required. Where the state court record is not in writing, the appendix must also include a written transcript of the parts of the state court record that each party deems necessary for the court to understand the issues and decide the appeal. The transcript may be prepared by any method that provides an adequate written record. A party may not rely on a part of the state court record not reduced to written form.

(B) Appellant's Duty to Provide Transcript. The appellant must provide the transcript to the appellee within 30 days of filing the notice of appeal. The circuit clerk may grant an additional 30 days. Where, because of the length of the record, more than 60 days are required, the appellant must request additional time by motion within the 60–day period.

(C) Appellee May Provide Additional Transcript. An appellee who believes that a transcript of other parts of the state court record is necessary must provide the transcript to the appellant within 30 days of the appellant's filing the transcript. The time may be extended as under subrule (b)(5)(B).

(D) Dispute About Accuracy of the Transcript. The parties must resolve disputes about accuracy of the transcript under Fed. R. App. P. 10(e).

(c) Who Must File the Appendix and When.

(1) *Generally.* This subrule (c)(1) applies in all cases where an appendix is required except those in subrules (c)(2)–(3).

(A) Appellant. The appellant must file and serve the appendix with its principal brief.

(B) Appellee. If the appellee determines that the appellant did not include a necessary part of the record, the appellee may file and serve the omissions as a separate appendix with its brief. The pagination must be consecutive, beginning with the next page number after the last page of the appellant's appendix.

(2) *State Habeas Corpus Appeals.* In a state habeas corpus appeal where the plaintiff is pro se and in forma pauperis, the defendant respondent must file the appendix with defendant's brief.

(3) *Black Lung Appeals.* In an appeal from an administrative decision on a claim for black lung benefits, where the appellant is pro se and in forma pauperis, the director must file the appendix with the director's brief.

(d) Manner of Filing.

(1) *Electronic Filing Required.* The appendix must be filed electronically, except as provided in subrule (d)(2).

(2) *Exceptions to Electronic Filing.* Five copies of the appendix must be filed in paper format in the following instances:

(A) In Pro Per Filings. An appendix filed by a party not represented by counsel.

(B) Large Documents. An appendix that exceeds the limit for the size of electronic filing, as specified in the electronic case filing section of the court's web site.

(C) State Death Penalty Cases. A case involving a state prisoner under a death sentence where the district court record includes parts of the state court record.

(e) Form.

(1) *Pagination and Transcript Identification.* The appendix must be paginated. The original pagination of a transcript must be placed in brackets.

(2) *Order of Items.* The appendix must contain the following items in the following order:

(A) Table of Contents. A table of contents at the beginning. For each document, the table must:

- describe the document;
- include the record entry number from the court or agency below, where available; and
- identify the appendix page where the document appears.

(B) Index. If the appendix contains a transcript of testimony, an alphabetical list of witnesses, with the date, the proceeding (such as trial, hearing, or deposition), and the appendix page where the testimony begins.

(C) Other Items. The items in the order set out in 6 Cir. R. 30(b).

(D) Proof of Service. The proof of service required by Fed. R. App. P. 25(d). The appendix will not be considered filed unless it includes the proof of service.

(3) *Multi–Volume Appendix.* Transcripts and exhibits may appear at the end of the appendix or in a separate volume or volumes. If the appendix has more than one volume, each volume must be consecutively paginated and must contain the full table of contents and index required by 6 Cir. R. 30(e)(2)(A) and (B). The table of contents and index in each volume must include the contents of all appendix volumes.

(f) Administrative Record Filed Instead of Appendix. The administrative record must be filed and no appendix is required in the following cases.

(1) *Social Security Cases.* In appeals from a district court on review of a decision of the Commissioner of Social Security, counsel for the Commissioner must file with the Commissioner's brief four paginated copies of the administrative record.

(2) *Immigration Review Petitions.* This subrule (f)(2) applies to a petition for review of a final order of exclusion, deportation, or removal under 8 U.S.C. § 1252. The government must file and serve the administrative record as provided below. The court will not accept a paper copy of the record unless it orders otherwise. The court will issue a scheduling notice specifying the time to file and serve the record and briefs.

(A) BIA Orders. In a case where the Board of Immigration Appeals issued the final order of exclusion, deportation, or removal, the Executive Office of Immigration Review must file four text-searchable, paginated copies of the certified administrative record on CD–ROM.*

(B) ICE Orders. In a case where U.S. Immigration and Customs Enforcement issued the final order of exclusion, deportation, or removal—where the Department of Homeland Security maintains the administrative record—the Attorney General must file the certified administrative record in one of the following ways:

(i) file one text-searchable, paginated copy on CD–ROM; or

(ii) file it using the electronic case filing system.

(C) Service. Service of the record is as follows, unless the court orders otherwise:

(i) Represented Petitioner. When petitioner is represented, service is by mailing a copy of the CD–ROM filed with the court or, when the record is filed using the electronic case filing system, by service as provided in 6 Cir. R. 25(f)(1).

(ii) Unrepresented Petitioner. Service on an unrepresented petitioner is by mailing one paper copy of the record.

(g) Designation of Relevant Documents in Certain Cases.

(1) *District Court Appeals.* A party may not include documents from the district court's electronic record in an appendix. To facilitate the court's reference to the electronic record, each party must include in its principal brief a designation of documents.

(A) Documents to Be Designated. The designation must include the following:

(i) the complaint or indictment;

(ii) other pleadings or motions relevant to the arguments on appeal;

(iii) the judgment from which the appeal is taken;

(iv) relevant memorandum opinions or opinions from the bench, findings of fact and conclusions of law, and reports and recommendations of a magistrate judge and objections to the reports and recommendations;

(v) the notice of appeal; and

(vi) other parts of the record—including all or part of exhibits or transcript pages—necessary for the court to understand the issues and decide the appeal, in chronological order.

(B) Form of Designation. The designation must be at the end of the brief as an addendum and include for each document:

- the district court's record entry number;
- a description of the document; and
- the page number of the consecutively-paginated electronic record.

(C) Counsel shall ensure that all documents included in the designation have been included in the electronic district court record and bear the "Page ID #" of the consecutively paginated record referred to above.

(2) *Immigration Review Petitions.* In cases where the government files the administrative record under 6 Cir. R. 30(f)(2), each party must include in its principal brief a designation of the documents in 6 Cir. R. 30(b)(4). The designation must be at the end of the brief as an addendum and include for each document:

- a description of the document; and
- the page number of the administrative record where the document is located.

(h) Sanctions. The court may dismiss the appeal or impose other sanctions for failing to file an appendix when required, filing an appendix substantially out of compliance with this rule, or otherwise violating this rule.

[Effective December 1, 1998. Amended effective June 1, 2008; January 12, 2009; December 1, 2009; August 16, 2012.]

* [Publisher's Note: On April 23, 2013, the Court entered Administrative Order 13–01, providing as follows: "The court hereby suspends that portion of 6 Cir. R. 30(f)(2)(A) which requires the Executive Office of Immigration Review to file the certified administrative record on CD–ROM. The record shall be filed in such electronic format as the clerk of this court shall permit."]

IOP 30.   [RESERVED]

FRAP 31.   SERVING AND FILING BRIEFS

*[For text of rule, see the Federal Rules
of Appellate Procedure]*

RULE 31.   SERVING AND FILING BRIEFS

(a) Electronic Briefs. When a party is required to file a brief electronically, the clerk will not accept a paper copy. Fed. R. App. P. 25(c) and 6 Cir. R. 25(f) govern service of a brief filed electronically.

(b) Paper Briefs. A party filing a paper brief must file a signed original and serve two copies on each other party.

(c) Time to File.

(1) *Generally.* The court will set a briefing schedule specifying the due dates for briefs. Except as specified in subrules (c)(2)–(3), the time limits in Fed. R. App. P. 31(a)(1) apply except that the time limit for the filing of the brief of the appellant is as indicated by the clerk, since the electronic record is no longer "filed" as that term was formerly construed.

(2) *Expedited Briefing.*

(A) Generally. The court schedules expedited briefing in the following cases:

- appeals from orders denying or granting preliminary injunctions,
- recalcitrant witness appeals under 28 U.S.C. § 1826,
- direct criminal appeals in which the sentence is 15 months or less, and
- grand jury contempt appeals.

(B) On Motion. A party may move to expedite other cases. See 6 Cir. R. 27(f).

(3) *Death Penalty Cases.* In an application under 28 U.S.C. § 2254 or § 2255 by a person under a death sentence and in an appeal from a federal sentence of death:

(A) Appellant. The appellant must serve and file a brief by the deadline set by the clerk.

(B) Appellee. The appellee must serve and file a brief within 60 days after the appellant's brief is served.

(C) Reply Brief. The appellant may serve and file a reply brief within 14 days after the appellee's brief is served,

but at least 7 days before argument. The court may, for good cause, allow a later filing.

[Effective December 1, 1998. Amended effective August 12, 2005; June 1, 2008; August 16, 2012.]

IOP 31.   [RESERVED]

FRAP 32.   FORM OF BRIEFS, APPENDICES, AND OTHER PAPERS

*[For text of rule, see the Federal Rules
of Appellate Procedure]*

RULE 32.   FORM OF BRIEFS

(a) Certificate of Compliance With Type–Volume Limitation. The certificate of compliance under Fed. R. App. P. 32(a)(7)(C) must immediately follow the signature at the end of the brief.

(b) Length.

(1) *Exclusions From Length Limits.* The following items do not count toward the length limitations in Fed. R. App. P. 32(a)(7)(A) and (B):

- the corporate disclosure statement required under Fed. R. App. P. 26.1;
- the designation of relevant district court documents required under 6 Cir. R. 28(b)(1)(A)(i) and 30(g)(1);
- the designation of relevant administrative record items required under 6 Cir. R. 28(b)(1)(A)(ii) and 30(g)(2);
- the statement of reasons for oral argument permitted under 6 Cir. R. 28(b)(1)(B); and
- copies of unpublished opinions required under Fed. R. App. P. 32.1(b) or 6 Cir. R. 32.1(a).

(2) *Death Penalty Cases.* In an application under 28 U.S.C. § 2254 or § 2255 by a person under a death sentence and in an appeal from a federal sentence of death, the briefs may not exceed one-and-a-half times the length allowed by Fed. R. App. P. 32(a)(7)(A) and (B).

[Effective December 1, 1998. Amended effective June 1, 2008; August 16, 2012.]

IOP 32.   [RESERVED]

FRAP 32.1   CITING JUDICIAL DISPOSITIONS

*[For text of rule, see the Federal Rules
of Appellate Procedure]*

RULE 32.1   CITING JUDICIAL DISPOSITIONS; EFFECT OF PUBLISHED DECISIONS

(a) Citing Unpublished Dispositions. The court permits citation of any unpublished opinion, order, judgment, or other written disposition. The limitations of Fed. R. App. P. 32.1(a) do not apply. If a party cites such an item that is not available in a publicly accessible electronic database, the party must file and serve a copy as an addendum to the brief or other paper in which it is cited.

(b) Binding Effect of Published Decisions. Published panel opinions are binding on later panels. A published opinion is overruled only by the court en banc.

[Amended effective August 16, 2012.]

IOP 32.1 PREPARATION AND RELEASE OF OPINIONS; PUBLICATION OF DECISIONS

(a) Preparation and Release of Opinions.

(1) *Case Conferences; Writing Assignments; Conference Reports.* At the conclusion of each day's arguments, the panel usually holds a conference concerning the cases submitted that day. The panel discusses a tentative decision. The presiding judge assigns opinion-writing responsibility.

(2) *Circulating Opinions to Panel Members.* After the proposed opinion is prepared, the opinion-writing judge circulates it to the other two panel judges to obtain their concurrence, dissent, or special concurrence. The panel gives high priority to review of a judge's proposed opinion.

(3) *Circulating Opinions to Non–Panel Members.* All judges receive copies of proposed published opinions.

(4) *Filing and Release of Decisions.* The clerk's office files and releases all decisions. The clerk sends copies to counsel and makes them available to the public on the date of filing. The clerk's office does not receive advance notice of when a decision will be rendered.

(b) Publication of Decisions.

(1) *Criteria for Publication.* When determining whether a decision will be published in the Federal Reporter, panels consider whether the decision:

(A) Establishes a new rule of law, modifies an existing rule of law, or applies an established rule to a novel factual situation.

(B) Creates or resolves a conflict of authority within this circuit or between this circuit and another.

(C) Discusses a legal or factual issue of continuing public interest.

(D) Is accompanied by a concurring or dissenting opinion.

(E) Reverses the decision below, unless:

(i) the reversal was because of an intervening change in law or fact; or

(ii) the reversal is a remand to the lower court or agency—without further comment—of a case reversed or remanded by the United States Supreme Court;

(F) Addresses a published lower court or agency decision; or

(G) Has been reviewed by the United States Supreme Court.

(2) *Designation for Publication.* Any panel member may request that a decision be published. The court may also publish on motion.

(3) *Unpublished Decisions.* Decisions not designated for publication are listed in table form in the Federal Reporter.

[Effective August 16, 2012.]

FRAP 33. APPEAL CONFERENCES

[For text of rule, see the Federal Rules of Appellate Procedure]

RULE 33. APPEAL CONFERENCES— MEDIATION

(a) Civil Appeal Statement of Parties and Issues. The appellant, petitioner, or applicant in a civil case must file with the court and serve on all parties a Civil Appeal Statement of Parties and Issues.

(1) *When to File.* The Civil Appeal Statement must be filed as directed by the court.

(2) *What to File.*

(A) In an appeal from the district court or Tax Court, the Civil Appeal Statement must be filed on Form 6CA–53.

(B) In an appeal from or application for enforcement of an administrative agency order, the Civil Appeal Statement must be filed on Form 6CA–54.*

(C) The forms are available on the court's website.

(3) *Exception.* A pro se appellant, petitioner, or applicant is not required to file a Civil Appeal Statement.

(4) *Response.* No response to the Civil Appeal Statement is permitted.

(b) Mediation Procedures.

(1) *Selection of Cases for Mediation.* The Office of the Circuit Mediators reviews civil appellate cases to determine whether mediation would be appropriate. If so, a mediation conference is scheduled. In addition, counsel may contact the mediation administrator and request a mediation conference. Requests will remain confidential unless counsel instructs otherwise.

(2) *Notice of Mediation Conference.* When a case is selected for mediation, counsel will receive a mediation conference notice stating the date and time of the conference and other relevant information about the process.

(3) *Submission of Confidential Mediation Background Information Form.* Counsel must submit the Confidential Mediation Background Information Form as directed in the mediation conference notice. The form is submitted directly to the mediation office and shall not be filed or otherwise disclosed to the court or other parties.

(4) *Mediation Conferences.*

(A) General. A Circuit Mediator conducts the conference. The clerk, at the direction of the mediator, may enter orders controlling the course of the proceedings.

(B) Purposes. The primary purpose of the conference is to explore, in depth, possibilities for settlement, including the parties' interests, objectives, and possible bases for resolution of the appeal. Procedural issues may also be addressed.

(C) Attendance/Participation. Lead counsel and any other attorney with primary authority on behalf of each party must participate in the conference. Co-counsel or other attorneys whose participation would be beneficial are welcome to participate as well. The mediator may conduct more than one conference. Clients' attendance in the initial conference is not mandatory but is welcome. The decision regarding client participation in the initial conference is left to counsel. The mediator may direct that clients participate in subsequent conferences.

(D) Confidentiality. Communications in mediation conferences or in connection with the mediation process are confidential. They may not be disclosed or otherwise used by any mediation participant, except as agreed in advance by all participants.

(c) Non–Compliance; Sanctions.

(1) *Failure to File Civil Appeal Statement.* The clerk may assess sanctions if the appellant, petitioner, or applicant fails to properly file the Civil Appeal Statement.

(2) *Failure to Submit the Confidential Mediation Background Information Form.* The clerk may assess sanctions if a party fails to properly submit the Confidential Mediation Background Information form.

(3) *Other Sanctions.* If an attorney or party fails to comply with a provision of this rule or a mediation order, the court may take any or all of the following actions:

(A) Remove the case from mediation;

(B) Assess reasonable expenses caused by the failure, including attorney's fees;

(C) Assess all or a portion of the appellate costs;

(D) Dismiss the appeal; and

(E) Impose further sanctions as the court deems appropriate.

[Effective December 1, 1998. Amended effective August 16, 2012.]

* [**Publisher's Note:** So in original. Form 6CA–54 has been discontinued.]

IOP 33.   [RESERVED]

FRAP 34.   ORAL ARGUMENT

[For text of rule, see the Federal Rules of Appellate Procedure]

RULE 34.   ORAL ARGUMENT

(a) Requesting Oral Argument. A party desiring oral argument must include a statement in the brief explaining why the court should hear oral argument. The statement must not exceed one page.

(b) Waiver of Oral Argument. The court may deem oral argument to have been waived:

(1) if a party fails to request it in the brief; or

(2) if the parties stipulate to waive it.

(c) Expedited Argument.

(1) *Generally.* The court may expedite oral argument, even if the time to file briefs has not expired by the date of the expedited hearing. The court may do so on its own or on motion of a party.

(2) *Expedited Cases.* Where the court determines that a case of one of the types listed below is to be orally argued, argument will generally be expedited.

- recalcitrant witness appeals under 28 U.S.C. § 1826;
- grand jury contempt appeals;
- appeals from orders denying or granting preliminary or temporary injunctions;
- interlocutory appeals under 28 U.S.C. § 1292(b);
- direct criminal appeals; and
- appeals in cases under 28 U.S.C. §§ 2241, 2254, and 2255.

(3) *Procedure.* When the court grants a motion to expedite, the clerk will schedule oral argument at an early date. A judge may direct an earlier hearing.

(d) Postponement of Hearing. After a case is set for hearing, the court will not postpone the hearing without good cause. A motion for postponement must be made immediately after notice of the hearing date. It must include notice to all counsel and state where possible the consent or objection of other counsel.

(e) Argument by Intervening Party. An intervening party may request oral argument. The request must

- be in writing;
- state whether the named parties have consented; and
- state the reason separate argument is needed.

(f) Time for Oral Argument.

(1) *Generally.* Each side has 15 minutes for oral argument unless the notice of oral argument provides otherwise.

(2) *Additional Time.* A party may move for additional time. The motion must be filed within 14 days of submission of the last brief, but not later than 7 days before the hearing.

(3) *En Banc.* In cases argued before the en banc court, each side will generally have 20 minutes for oral argument, unless the court directs otherwise.

(g) Presentation of Argument.

(1) *Purpose.* The purpose of oral argument is to emphasize and clarify the argument in the briefs.

(2) *Divided Argument.* The court may—in exceptional circumstances—permit divided arguments.

(3) *Teleconference.* The court may conduct oral argument by teleconference.

(4) *Cross–Appeals.* An appeal and cross-appeal will be argued together as one case in the time allotted for one case.

[Effective December 1, 1998. Amended effective June 1, 2008; December 1, 2009; August 16, 2012.]

IOP 34. ORAL ARGUMENT—CALENDARING; PANEL SELECTION AND IDENTITY; NOTICE OF HEARING, POSTPONEMENT, AND PRESENTATION OF ORAL ARGUMENT; SCREENING AND SUMMARY DECISIONS

(a) Calendaring.

(1) *Annual Schedule.* The court sits over two-week periods scheduled so as to afford all judges at least five weeks between sittings. All active judges are scheduled to sit four consecutive days during one of the two sitting weeks. At least six active judges are assigned to one of the two sitting weeks at random; the balance of the court's active judges are assigned to the other sitting week. Judges are later assigned to panels during the sitting weeks using an automated routine which searches the court's database to determine which active judges have the longest intervals between sitting pairing. The goal is to give every judge the opportunity to sit with as many different colleagues as possible.

(2) *Argument Calendars.* The clerk prepares the calendar for a session before the composition of panels is determined.

(3) *Case Typing.* The clerk balances the calendars by dividing the cases as evenly as possible among the panels according to case type and the district of origin.

(4) *Oral Argument.* Panels determine which of the cases assigned to them will receive oral argument and which do not require oral argument. Although there will generally be four panels hearing argument Tuesday through Friday of a sitting week, this will vary according to individual panels' preferences.

(b) Panel Selection and Identity.

(1) *Schedule of Panels.* The Sixth Circuit's automated panel assignment protocol attempts to maximize active circuit judges' opportunities to sit with every other judge on the court. This is accomplished by giving precedence in panel assembly to grouping judges with the longest time intervals between pairings. The panel assignment system gathers information from the case management system with respect to judges' past sittings, and then checks that information against judges available for assignment during a one-week period for purposes of grouping judges based on the longest intervals between sittings. The automated program first pairs active judges based on intervals between pairings and then adds senior circuit judges and visiting judges to pairings, again determined by the longest interval between pairings with either judge in the assembled pairs.

(2) *Subsequent Appeals Returned to Original Panel.* In appeals after this court returns a case to the lower court or agency for further proceedings, or after the Supreme Court of the United States remands a case to this court, the original panel will determine whether to hear the appeal or whether it should be assigned to a panel at random.

(3) *Replacement Judge.* Where it is necessary to bring in a new judge to complete a panel, the clerk will draw a name from among the active judges not already on the panel. That judge will sit on the panel regardless whether the judge is scheduled to sit during the same weeks as the other panel members.

(4) *Remands With Jurisdiction Retained.* Where the court remands and retains jurisdiction, the case will be assigned to the panel that ordered the retention of jurisdiction. The chief judge may order the case assigned to another panel.

(5) *Identity of Panels.* The names of the judges who will hear the case are posted on the court's web site and are available from the clerk's office on the first business day of the week two weeks before oral argument.

(c) Notice of Hearing, Postponement, and Presentation of Oral Argument.

(1) *Notice of Hearing.* The court seeks to give at least six weeks' advance notice of oral argument. The notice of hearing will remind counsel that 6 Cir. R. 36 allows the court to announce disposition of a case in open court following oral argument.

(2) *Request for Postponement.* Counsel's engagement in other courts is not necessarily good cause for postponement.

(3) *Checking in With Clerk's Office on Date of Hearing.* Counsel should check in with the clerk's office at least 15 minutes before court convenes. The clerk's office is open at 8:00 a.m. for check in.

(4) *Presenting Oral Argument.* Counsel should prepare for oral argument with the knowledge that the judges have already studied the briefs. Reading from briefs, decisions, or the record is disfavored and permitted only in unusual circumstances. Counsel should be prepared to answer questions from the court.

(5) *Additional Time.* The court rarely permits additional time for oral argument.

(d) Absence of Quorum; Adjournment. If less than a quorum is present, a judge in attendance may adjourn the court. If no judge is present, the clerk may adjourn the court.

[Effective December 1, 1998. Amended effective August 27, 2002; February 26, 2003; January 24, 2007; December 1, 2009; August 16, 2012.]

FRAP 35.   EN BANC DETERMINATION

[For text of rule, see the Federal Rules of Appellate Procedure]

RULE 35.   PETITION FOR REHEARING EN BANC

(a) Petition Content. A petition for rehearing containing a petition for rehearing en banc must so state plainly on the cover and in the title of the document. A copy of the opinion or final order sought to be reviewed must accompany the petition.

(b) Effect of Granting the Petition. A decision to grant rehearing en banc vacates the previous opinion and judgment of the court, stays the mandate, and restores the case on the docket as a pending appeal.

(c) Counsel Not Obligated to File. Counsel fully discharges his or her duty in a case without filing a petition for rehearing en banc unless the case meets the rigid standards of Fed. R. App. P. 35(a).

[Effective December 1, 1998. Amended effective June 1, 2008; August 16, 2012.]

IOP 35. EN BANC DETERMINATION

(a) Extraordinary Nature of Petition for Rehearing En Banc. A petition for rehearing en banc is an extraordinary procedure intended to bring to the attention of the entire court a precedent-setting error of exceptional public importance or an opinion that directly conflicts with Supreme Court or Sixth Circuit precedent. Alleged errors in the determination of state law or in the facts of the case (including sufficient evidence), or errors in the application of correct precedent to the facts of the case, are matters for panel rehearing but not for rehearing en banc.

(b) Voting to Sit En Banc. Only Sixth Circuit judges in regular active service who have not recused themselves from the case may vote in a poll on an en banc petition. See 28 U.S.C. § 46(c).

(c) Composition of En Banc Court. The en banc court is composed of all judges in regular active service at the time of a hearing or rehearing, any senior judge of the court who sat on the original panel, and, if no oral argument en banc is held, any judge in regular active service at the time that the en banc court agreed to decide the case without oral argument.

(d) General Procedure—Petition for Rehearing En Banc.

(1) The court will treat a petition for rehearing en banc as a petition for rehearing before the original panel.

(2) The clerk will circulate the petition to the original panel. The panel has 14 days to comment on the petition to the en banc coordinator in the clerk's office.

(A) If the panel changes the substance of its decision, it will provide its modified decision to the en banc coordinator. The modified decision will be filed and counsel notified. Counsel will then have 14 days to withdraw, modify, or maintain the pending petition for rehearing en banc or to file a new petition.

(B) If the panel does not substantially modify its decision, the coordinator will then circulate the petition and the panel's comments to the en banc court.

(3) Any active judge or any member of the panel whose decision is the subject of the rehearing may request a poll within 14 days from the date of circulation of the petition and the panel's comments. If a poll is requested, 14 days are allowed for voting.

(e) When a Poll Can Be Requested. Any active judge or any member of the original hearing panel whose decision is under review may request a poll. Usually a poll is requested after a party files a petition for rehearing en banc. However, any member of the en banc court may sua sponte request a poll for hearing or rehearing en banc before a party files an en banc petition. If the request for a poll is not based on a party's petition, the clerk will immediately circulate voting forms to the en banc court.

(f) Response to Petition. When a poll is requested, or if a judge requests a response, the clerk will ask for a response to the petition if none has been previously requested.

(g) Petitions Circulated to the Court. Petitions seeking rehearing en banc from an order that disposes of the case on the merits or on jurisdictional grounds are circulated to the whole court. The court will also circulate to all active judges, for a determination of whether or not the matter should be reheard by the en banc court, petitions for en banc review of:

(1) An order in a death penalty case in which a scheduled execution is imminent;

(2) An order allowing or disallowing appellate review under Fed. R. Civ. P. 23(f) of interlocutory grants or denials of class certification;

(3) An order denying in full or in part an application for a certificate of appealability under 28 U.S.C. § 2253(c); and

(4) An order allowing or disallowing appellate review of an interlocutory order certified as appealable under 28 U.S.C. § 1292(b).

(h) Rehearing of Motions Panel Decisions. Petitions seeking rehearing en banc from other orders will be treated in the same manner as a petition for panel rehearing: They will be circulated only to the panel judges.

[Effective December 1, 1998. Amended effective August 27, 2002; June 10, 2003; August 16, 2012.]

FRAP 36. ENTRY OF JUDGMENT; NOTICE

[For text of rule, see the Federal Rules of Appellate Procedure]

RULE 36. ENTRY OF JUDGMENT— DISPOSITIONS IN OPEN COURT

The court may announce its decision in open court when the decision is unanimous and each judge of the panel believes that a written opinion would serve no jurisprudential purpose. The clerk will enter a signed written judgment in accordance with the panel's decision from the bench. A person may pay a fee to obtain a recording of the decision announced from the bench.

[Amended effective August 16, 2012.]

IOP 36. [RESERVED]

FRAP 37. INTEREST ON JUDGMENT

[For text of rule, see the Federal Rules of Appellate Procedure]

RULE 37. [RESERVED]

IOP 37. [RESERVED]

FRAP 38. FRIVOLOUS APPEALS— DAMAGES AND COSTS

[For text of rule, see the Federal Rules of Appellate Procedure]

RULE 38. [RESERVED]

Committee Note

No corresponding 6 Cir. R. For rules regarding attorney discipline generally, see FRAP 46 and 6 Cir. R. 46.

IOP 38. [RESERVED]

FRAP 39. COSTS

[For text of rule, see the Federal Rules of Appellate Procedure]

RULE 39. COSTS RECOVERABLE FOR FILING PAPER BRIEFS

(a) Reproduction Costs. Costs are not available for electronic filings. For paper filings, costs are taxed at the lesser of the actual cost or 25 cents per page, including covers, index, and table of authorities, regardless of the reproduction process used.

(b) Number of Briefs. When the court allows or requires paper briefs or appendices to be filed, costs may be taxed for two copies for each party required to be served.

(c) Number of Appendices. When the court allows or requires a paper appendix, costs may be taxed for one copy for each party required to be served.

[Effective December 1, 1998. Amended effective June 1, 2008; August 16, 2012.]

IOP 39. BILL OF COSTS—ALLOWABLE COSTS AND MOTION TO EXTEND TIME

(a) Bills of Costs. Costs may include the court of appeals docket fee (where applicable) and production of the briefs and appendix, as limited by 6 Cir. R. 39. The court does not favor commercial printing or other expensive methods of producing the briefs and appendix. Therefore, 6 Cir. R. 39 limits the recoverable costs for production or reproduction of those documents. Generally, the court does not consider attorney fees costs of appeal.

(b) Motion to Extend Time to File Bill of Costs. The clerk decides uncontested motions to extend time to file a bill of costs. A single judge decides contested motions.

[Effective December 1, 1998. Amended effective August 16, 2012.]

FRAP 40. PETITION FOR PANEL REHEARING

[For text of rule, see the Federal Rules of Appellate Procedure]

RULE 40. PETITION FOR REHEARING— EXTENSION OF TIME

(a) Grounds. The court will grant a motion to extend time to file a petition for rehearing only for the most compelling reasons.

(b) Failure to File a Motion. If an untimely petition for rehearing is not accompanied by a motion to extend the filing time, the court will return the petition, unfiled, to the sending party.

[Effective December 1, 1998. Amended effective August 16, 2012.]

IOP 40. PETITIONS FOR REHEARING

(a) When Necessary.

(1) *Purpose.* The purpose of a rehearing is to bring a claimed error of fact or law in the opinion to the panel's attention. It is not to be used for re-argument of issues previously presented.

(2) *Not a Prerequisite to Supreme Court Filing.* A party is not required to petition for rehearing—with or without a petition for rehearing en banc—as a prerequisite to a petition for writ of certiorari in the Supreme Court of the United States.

(b) Review. Only the original panel members will review petitions for rehearing that are unaccompanied by a petition for rehearing en banc.

(c) Briefing, Reargument, and Disposition. If rehearing is granted, the court will usually make a final disposition without additional briefing or reargument. It may instead:

- allow additional briefing;
- restore the case to the calendar for reargument or resubmission; or
- enter other appropriate orders.

(d) Extension of Time or Leave to File Out-of-Time. The court will refer a motion for additional time to file a petition for rehearing or for permission to file out of time, as a single-judge matter, to the judge who authored the opinion. Counsel should not presume that the motion will be granted.

[Effective December 1, 1998. Amended effective August 16, 2012.]

FRAP 41. MANDATE: CONTENTS; ISSUANCE AND EFFECTIVE DATE; STAY

[For text of rule, see the Federal Rules of Appellate Procedure]

RULE 41. ISSUANCE OF MANDATE; STAY OF MANDATE

(a) Stay of Mandate. In the interest of minimizing unnecessary delay in the administration of justice, the issuance of the mandate will not be stayed simply upon request beyond the time necessary for disposition of a motion seeking a stay. The mandate ordinarily will issue pursuant to Fed. R. App. P. 41(b) unless there is a showing, or an independent determination by this court, that a petition for writ of certiorari would present a substantial question and that there is good cause for a stay.

(b) Time for Filing Motion to Stay. A motion to stay the mandate must be received in the clerk's office within 7 days after the time to file a petition for rehearing expires or seven days from entry of an order on petition for rehearing.

(c) Duration of Stay Pending Application for Certiorari. A stay of the mandate pending application to the Supreme

Court for a writ of certiorari shall not be effective later than the date on which the movant's application for a writ of certiorari must be filed pursuant to 28 U.S.C. § 2101 or Rule 13 of the Supreme Court Rules, as applicable. If during the period of the stay there is filed with the clerk a notice from the clerk of the Supreme Court that the party who has obtained the stay has filed a petition for the writ in that Court, the stay shall continue until final disposition by the Supreme Court. Upon the filing of a copy of an order of the Supreme Court denying the petition for writ of certiorari, the mandate shall issue immediately.

[Effective December 1, 1998. Amended effective August 16, 2012.]

Committee Note
Former 6th Cir. R. 15.

IOP 41. ISSUANCE OF MANDATE; STAY OF MANDATE—RIGHT TO CERTIORARI NOT AFFECTED

(a) Issuing a Mandate.

(1) *Purpose.* A mandate is the document by which this court relinquishes jurisdiction and authorizes the originating court or agency to enforce this court's judgment.

(2) *Distribution.* This court will distribute copies of the mandate to all parties and to the lower court or agency clerk. This court will then return the record to the lower court.

(b) Presiding Judge. The clerk will refer a motion for stay or recall of the mandate, as a single-judge matter, to the judge who wrote the opinion.

(c) Staying a Mandate. The court will not stay a mandate beyond the date on which the movant's application is due under 28 U.S.C. § 2101 or Rule 13 of the Supreme Court Rules.

(d) Right to Seek Certiorari. The issuance of a mandate does not affect a party's right to seek a writ of certiorari.

[Effective December 1, 1998. Amended effective August 16, 2012.]

FRAP 42. VOLUNTARY DISMISSAL

[For text of rule, see the Federal Rules of Appellate Procedure]

RULE 42. [RESERVED]

IOP 42. [RESERVED]

FRAP 43. SUBSTITUTION OF PARTIES

[For text of rule, see the Federal Rules of Appellate Procedure]

RULE 43. [RESERVED]

IOP 43. [RESERVED]

FRAP 44. CASES INVOLVING A CONSTITUTIONAL QUESTION WHEN THE UNITED STATES OR THE RELEVANT STATE IS NOT A PARTY

[For text of rule, see the Federal Rules of Appellate Procedure]

RULE 44. [RESERVED]

IOP 44. [RESERVED]

FRAP 45. CLERK'S DUTIES

[For text of rule, see the Federal Rules of Appellate Procedure]

RULE 45. DUTIES OF CLERKS— PROCEDURAL ORDERS

(a) Orders That the Clerk May Enter. The clerk may prepare, sign, and enter orders or otherwise dispose of the following matters without submission to the court or a judge, unless otherwise directed:

(1) Procedural motions;

(2) Motions involving production or filing of the appendix or briefs on appeal;

(3) Orders for voluntary dismissal of appeals or petitions, or for consent judgments in National Labor Relations Board cases;

(4) Orders for dismissal for want of prosecution;

(5) Orders appointing counsel under the Criminal Justice Act of 1984, as amended, in criminal cases in which the appellant is entitled to the appointment of counsel under the Sixth Circuit Plan for the Implementation of the Criminal Justice Act and in any other case in which an order directing the clerk to appoint counsel has been entered;

(6) Bills of costs under Fed. R. App. P. 39(d);

(7) Orders granting remands and limited remands where the motion includes a notice under Fed. R. App. P. 12.1(a); and

(8) Orders dismissing a second appeal as duplicative, where the court has docketed a jurisdictionally sound appeal from the same judgment or final order.

(b) Notice. A clerk's order must show that it was authorized under 6 Cir. R. 45(a).

(c) Reconsideration. A party adversely affected by a clerk's order may move for reconsideration by a judge or judges. The motion must be filed within 14 days of service of notice of entry of the order.

(d) Remand From the Supreme Court. The clerk refers remands from the Supreme Court of the United States to the panel that decided the case. Counsel need not file a motion concerning the remand—it is referred when the clerk receives a certified copy of the judgment. The clerk's office will advise counsel of further proceedings.

[Effective December 1, 1998. Amended effective January 24, 2007; December 1, 2009; August 16, 2012.]

IOP 45. DUTIES OF CLERKS— CLERK'S OFFICE

(a) Location and Hours. The clerk's office is the public business office for the court. It is at 100 E. Fifth Street,

Cincinnati, Ohio, 45202. The clerk's business office (Room 540 of the Potter Stewart U.S. Courthouse) is open Monday through Friday, 8:30 a.m. to 5:00 p.m. On days when the court is sitting to hear oral argument, the clerk's office will open at 8:00 a.m. to allow counsel to check in.

(b) Function. All filings of documents and entry of decisions or other rulings of the court are made at the clerk's office. Questions regarding practice in the court or case status information can be directed to the clerk's office by telephone, (513) 564–7000, or letter.

(c) Telephone Inquiries. The clerk's office welcomes telephone inquiries from counsel regarding rules and procedures. The clerk and the chief deputy are available to confer with counsel on special problems and matters of rule interpretation. They can be reached at (513) 564–7000.

(d) Web Site. The court maintains an Internet web site for access to docket information, Sixth Circuit Rules, Internal Operating Procedures, recently issued opinions, and other items of interest including the Sixth Circuit Guide to Electronic Filing and other related information. The address is http://www.ca6.uscourts.gov. The court charges a fee for access to docket information.

[Effective December 1, 1998. Amended effective February 26, 2003; June 1, 2008; August 16, 2012.]

FRAP 46. ATTORNEYS

[For text of rule, see the Federal Rules of Appellate Procedure]

RULE 46. ATTORNEYS—ADMISSION OF ATTORNEYS, ATTORNEY DISCIPLINE, LAW STUDENT PRACTICE

(a) Admission of Attorneys.

(1) *Prerequisite to Practice.*

(A) Generally. Except as provided in 6 Cir. R. 46(a)(1)(B), (C), and (D), an attorney must be admitted to the bar of this court and must file appearance Form 6CA–68 to file documents or participate in oral argument.

(B) Government Attorneys. An attorney representing the United States or its officer or agency may participate in the case without being admitted to the bar of this court.

(C) Attorneys employed by the Federal Public Defenders Office may participate in the case without being admitted to the bar of this court.

(D) Attorneys for Amici Curiae. An attorney for an amicus curiae may participate in the case without being admitted to the bar of this court.

(2) *Admission Fee.* Applicants for admission to the bar of this court must pay a fee. The amount is listed on the court's web site. No admission fee is required from:

- attorneys appointed by this court to represent a party in forma pauperis;
- attorneys employed by a federal public defender organization created under 18 U.S.C. § 3006A(g)(2)(A); and

- attorneys presently employed by a United States court.

(3) *Application Procedures.* Admissions are made on the motion of a member of the bar of this court. Application for admission is made by filing the form prescribed by the clerk. The form is available on the court's web site.

(4) *Failure to Secure Admission or File Notice of Appearance.* If counsel for the appellant fails to secure admission and file a notice of appearance within the time the clerk specifies, the court may dismiss the appeal.

(b) Code of Conduct. An attorney admitted to practice in this court is subject to the rules of professional conduct or other equivalent rules of the state where the attorney's principal office is located.

(c) Attorney Discipline.

(1) *Conduct Subject to Discipline.* This court may impose discipline on a member who:

(A) engages in conduct violating the Canons of Ethics or the Model Rules of Professional Conduct, whichever applies;

(B) fails to comply with the rules or orders of this court; or

(C) has been disciplined by a state or other court.

(2) *Records Sealed.* All records pertaining to disciplinary proceedings before the court must be filed under seal, unless the chief judge orders otherwise.

(3) *Scope of Discipline.* Discipline may include disbarment, suspension, reprimand, or other appropriate action. This rule does not limit the court's inherent contempt power or its authority under 28 U.S.C. § 1912 or 28 U.S.C. § 1927.

(4) *Initiation of Disciplinary Proceedings.* Formal disciplinary proceedings are initiated by an order to show cause, signed by the chief judge or by the circuit clerk, acting at the direction of the chief judge.

(A) Order to Show Cause. The court may issue an order to show cause on its own initiative or in response to a complaint filed by a member of the bar of this court or a party before the court.

(B) Contents of Complaint. A complaint of attorney misconduct must include:

(i) The name, address, and telephone number of the complainant;

(ii) The specific facts that require discipline, including the date, place, and nature of the alleged misconduct, and the names of all persons involved;

(iii) Copies of all documents or other evidence that support the factual allegations contained in subsection (ii), including a copy of any rule or order of this court that is alleged to have been violated; and

(iv) A statement under the penalty of perjury—at the end of the complaint—that the complainant has read the complaint and that the facts contained there are correct to the best of the complainant's knowledge.

(C) Action by Chief Judge. The clerk will send a complaint to the chief judge for initial review.

(i) If the chief judge determines that the complaint—on its face or after investigation—is without merit or does not warrant court action, the chief judge will dismiss the complaint.

(ii) If the chief judge determines that reasonable grounds exist for further investigation, the chief judge may order investigation. The chief judge may issue an order to show cause if the complaint appears meritorious, either before or after investigation.

(iii) If the chief judge issues an order to show cause, the clerk will mail the following to the respondent:

- the order to show cause;

- the complaint and supporting documents;

- a copy of Fed. R. App. P. 46;

- a copy of this rule; and

- a written statement that the respondent has 21 days from entry of the order to show cause to respond.

(iv) Alternatively, the chief judge may refer the matter to a state disciplinary authority for action.

(4)* *Response.* A respondent has 21 days from entry of the order to show cause to file a response. The response must include:

(A) The name, address, and telephone number of the respondent;

(B) An admission or denial of each factual allegation in the complaint and order to show cause;

(C) A specific statement of facts on which respondent relies, including all other relevant dates, places, persons, and conduct;

(D) All relevant documents or other supporting evidence not previously filed with the complaint or order;

(E) A statement requesting or declining a hearing; and

(F) A statement under the penalty of perjury that the respondent has read the response and that the facts contained there are correct to the best of respondent's knowledge.

(5) *Summary Dismissal.* The chief judge may dismiss the complaint if the response shows that it is without merit.

(6) *Conformity With Other Discipline.* When a court or other disciplinary authority has disbarred or suspended the respondent and the respondent admits the action complained of or does not respond to the order to show cause, the chief judge may enter a final order imposing similar discipline.

(7) *Judicial Officer.* After a response is filed, the chief judge may appoint a circuit judge, district judge, or other judicial officer from the circuit to investigate the allegations. The judicial officer must review the documents, conduct hearings if necessary, and issue a written recommendation.

(8) *Hearing.* A disciplinary hearing will be held if the respondent timely requested one and the judicial officer determines that a hearing is necessary for proper disposition of the charges.

(A) Notice. When a hearing is necessary, the judicial officer will provide the respondent with at least 21 days written notice of the hearing. The notice must contain the date and location of the hearing and a statement that the respondent is entitled to be represented by counsel, to present witnesses and other evidence, and to confront and cross-examine adverse witnesses.

(B) Procedure. The judicial officer will conduct the hearing. The judicial officer has authority to resolve procedural and evidentiary disputes. Witnesses must testify under penalty of perjury. Hearings are confidential and will be recorded.

(C) Rights of the Complainant and the Respondent. During the hearing, the respondent is entitled to be represented by counsel, to present witnesses and other evidence, and to confront and cross-examine adverse witnesses. The judicial officer may permit the complainant to participate through counsel.

(D) Burden of Proof. The respondent's violation of the applicable standards of conduct or rules or orders of this court must be proven by clear and convincing evidence. A certified copy of a final order of disbarment or judgment of conviction for a felony offense, entered in any state or federal court, constitutes clear and convincing evidence.

(E) Failure to Appear. The respondent's failure to appear at the hearing is grounds for discipline.

(9) *Recommendation.* The judicial officer must recommend—in writing—a proposed disposition of the charges.

(A) Filing of the Recommendation. The judicial officer must file the recommendation and send copies to the respondent.

(B) Response to the Recommendation. The respondent may file a written response to the recommendation within 14 days of service of the recommendation. The response must state concisely any inaccuracies, errors, or omissions that warrant a disposition other than the recommended disposition. The response must not exceed 25 pages.

(10) *Final Action on the Recommendation.* The court will enter a final order of disposition within 30 days of the filing of a response to the recommendation. It will send notice of the final order to the respondent and the complainant.

(11) *Reinstatement.* A suspended or disbarred attorney may petition the court for reinstatement. The petition must include a concise statement of the circumstances of the disciplinary proceedings, the discipline imposed, and the grounds that justify reinstatement.

(A) Automatic Reinstatement. The court will automatically reinstate an attorney suspended for a definite term at the end of the suspension period on receipt of:

- a petition for reinstatement; and

- an affidavit showing compliance with the suspension order.

(B) Petition for Reinstatement. The court will reinstate a disbarred or indefinitely suspended attorney on petition for reinstatement only for good cause shown. The chief judge will review the petition for clear and convincing evidence that the member has the moral qualifications, competency, and learning in the law required for readmission. After review, the chief judge will make a recommendation to the court.

(C) *Successive Petitions for Reinstatement.* A suspended or disbarred attorney may not petition for reinstatement within one year following an adverse determination on a prior petition.

(12) *Chief Judge's Designees.* The chief judge may designate a circuit judge or judges to perform the duties of the chief judge under this rule. References to "chief judge" in this rule include his or her designees.

(d) Law Student Practice.

(1) *Eligibility.* To make an appearance under this rule, a law student must:

(A) Be enrolled in a law school approved by the American Bar Association;

(B) Have completed legal studies for at least four semesters, or the equivalent if the school is on some basis other than a semester basis;

(C) Be certified—with certification filed—by the student's law school dean or authorized representative as being of good character and competent legal ability; and

(D) Certify in writing that he or she has read and is familiar with the Code of Professional Responsibility or Rules of Professional Conduct in force in the state where the student's law school is located.

(2) *Cases in Which a Law Student May Appear.* An eligible law student may appear in this court in the following circumstances:

(A) On behalf of an indigent, with the written consent of the indigent and the attorney of record.

(B) On behalf of the United States, with the written consent of the United States Attorney or authorized representative.

(C) On behalf of a state, with the written consent of the state attorney general or authorized representative.

In each case, the written consent must be filed with the clerk.

(3) *Preparation of Documents and Oral Argument.* An eligible law student may assist in the preparation of briefs and other documents to be filed in this court, but those briefs or other documents must also be signed by the attorney of record. The student may also participate in oral argument with leave of the court, but only in the presence of the attorney of record. The student must be introduced to the court by an attorney admitted to practice before it.

(4) *Responsibility of the Attorney of Record.* The attorney of record must assume personal professional responsibility for the law student's work and for supervising the quality of that work. The attorney must be familiar with the case and prepared to supplement any written or oral statement by the student.

(5) *Revocation.* The dean of the student's law school may withdraw certification at any time by mailing notice to the clerk. This court may terminate a student's privileges under this rule at any time. Neither the law school nor this court are required to provide notice, hearing, or any showing of cause.

(6) *Compensation.* A law student appearing under this rule may not ask for or receive compensation or remuneration from the individual or party on whose behalf the student renders services. But an attorney, legal aid bureau, law school, public defender agency, state, or the United States may compensate the eligible law student. This rule does not prevent an entity from charging a client or other recipient for its services.

[Effective December 1, 1998. Amended effective August 27, 2002; December 1, 2009; August 16, 2012.]

* [**Publisher's Note:** So in original.]

IOP 46. [RESERVED]

FRAP 47. LOCAL RULES BY COURT OF APPEALS

[For text of rule, see the Federal Rules of Appellate Procedure]

RULE 47. RULE AMENDMENTS

(a) Notice of Proposed Amendments. Generally, the clerk must provide notice and a 90–day comment period for proposed amendments to the rules. The clerk gives notice to the state bar association in each state in the circuit and to the distribution list that the clerk maintains. The clerk will include an interested publisher, bar association, or other law-related association in this list on request.

(b) Comments. Comments should be filed in writing with the clerk.

(c) Adoption After the Comment Period. The court may adopt a proposed amendment any time after the comment period closes.

(d) Adoption Without Prior Notice. If the court determines that an immediate need exists, it may amend the rules without prior notice and comment. If the court does not provide prior notice, it will promptly provide notice and an opportunity for comment after the amendment.

[Effective December 1, 1998. Amended effective August 16, 2012.]

IOP 47. ADVISORY COMMITTEE ON RULES

(a) Membership. The advisory committee on rules has 12 members, appointed by the chief judge. The committee includes:

(1) Three members from each state in the circuit;

(2) At least one member from each district in the circuit; and

(3) Broad representation of all aspects of litigation practiced before the court.

(b) Terms of Office. Each member is appointed for three years, in staggered terms. A member may not serve more than two successive three-year terms. An interim appointment of less than 2 years is not a term.

(c) Meetings. The committee meets annually. In even-numbered years, it meets during the judicial conference. In other years, the chair must call the annual meeting. When possible, the meeting is coordinated with the Sixth Circuit Rules Committee meeting. The chair or the chief judge may call additional committee meetings.

(d) Recommendations.

(1) *Recommendations From the Advisory Committee.* The advisory committee proposes amendments by resolution sent to the chief judge, with a copy to the chair of the Sixth Circuit Rules Committee.

(2) *Proposals From the Rules Committee.* The rules committee will send proposed amendments to the advisory committee for comment unless time or other circumstances make this impracticable.

[Amended effective August 16, 2012.]

FRAP 48. MASTERS

[For text of rule, see the Federal Rules of Appellate Procedure]

RULE 48. [RESERVED]

IOP 48. [RESERVED]

SUPPLEMENTAL PROCEDURAL RULES—RULE 100

RULE 101.   [RESERVED]

IOP 101.   [RESERVED]

RULE 102.   [RESERVED]

IOP 102.   [RESERVED]

RULE 103.   [RESERVED]

IOP 103.   [RESERVED]

RULE 104.   [RESERVED]

IOP 104.   [RESERVED]

RULE 105.   [RESERVED]

IOP 105.   COMPLAINTS OF JUDICIAL MISCONDUCT

A complaint of judicial misconduct filed with the circuit clerk will be referred to the circuit executive. See 28 U.S.C. § 351.

[Effective December 1, 1998. Amended effective August 16, 2012.]

ADMINISTRATIVE RULES—RULE 200

RULE 201. [RESERVED]

IOP 201. [RESERVED]

RULE 202. SESSIONS OF COURT

(a) Time and Place. Sessions of this court are held when the court deems advisable. All sessions are at the Potter Stewart U.S. Courthouse in Cincinnati, Ohio, unless otherwise ordered.

(b) Order of Business. Before the call of the calendar, the court will entertain motions to admit attorneys to the bar of the court. The court will then call the calendar for the day. The court will hear cases in the order in which they appear on the calendar, unless it directs otherwise.

[Effective December 1, 1998. Amended effective August 16, 2012.]

IOP 202. SESSIONS—COURT FACILITIES AND PERSONNEL

(a) Courtroom Deputies. The clerk's office provides courtroom deputies.

(b) Physical Facilities. The court is located in the Potter Stewart U.S. Courthouse at Fifth and Walnut Streets in Cincinnati, Ohio, 45202. The building contains three court-rooms for the Sixth Circuit and chambers for each active and senior circuit judge. The building also contains the circuit executive's office, the clerk's office, the staff attorneys' office, and the library.

(c) Judges and Other Supporting Personnel.

(1) *Judges.* The Sixth Circuit is authorized to have sixteen active judges. Each active judge is authorized to have three law clerks and two judicial assistants or, instead, four law clerks and one judicial assistant. The chief judge is authorized one additional law clerk and judicial assistant. The court is also served by senior circuit and visiting judges who sit with panels of the court.

(2) *Circuit Executive.* The circuit executive and staff are an arm of the Judicial Council of the circuit and provide administrative support to the court. The circuit executive's services are designed to assist judges to free them for their primary duty of adjudication and, particularly, to assist the chief judge with administrative duties.

(3) *Staff Attorneys.* The court appoints a senior staff attorney and supervisory staff attorneys to supervise the staff attorney's office. The office provides legal support to the court as a whole, rather than to individual judges by making dispositional recommendations in those cases that the court has decided do not require oral argument under Fed. R. App. P. 34(a)(2).

[Effective December 1, 1998. Amended effective June 1, 2008; August 16, 2012.]

RULE 203. ASSIGNMENT OF JUDGES; QUORUM

(a) Assignment of Judges; Quorum. As provided in 28 U.S.C. § 46, the judges of this court shall be assigned to sit upon the court and its panels in such order, at such sessions, and for the hearing of such cases, as the court directs. Cases and controversies shall be heard and determined by a panel of three judges, unless a hearing or rehearing before the court en banc is ordered as provided by FRAP 35. A majority of the number of judges authorized to constitute the court or a panel thereof shall constitute a quorum.

(b) Absence of Quorum; Adjournment. If on any day less than a quorum is present, any judge in attendance may adjourn the court until a later time or, if no judge is present, the clerk may adjourn the court from day to day.

[Effective December 1, 1998.]

Committee Note

Former 6th Cir. R. 3.

IOP 203. [RESERVED]

RULE 204. COURT LIBRARY AND MATERIALS

The court's libraries are available to federal court personnel. When library staff is present, other federal personnel and attorneys admitted to federal practice may use the libraries during regular hours. The court librarian may admit other users. The court librarian may permit court personnel or counsel acting on a judge's request to remove materials from a library, but library materials may not be removed from local courthouses or federal buildings.

[Effective December 1, 1998. Amended effective August 16, 2012.]

IOP 204. LIBRARY HOURS OF OPERATION

The Cincinnati library is open from 8:00 a.m. to 5:00 p.m., Monday through Friday. The satellite libraries in Chattanooga, Cleveland, Columbus, Detroit, Grand Rapids, Louisville, Memphis, and Nashville have varying hours of operation.

[Effective December 1, 1998. Amended effective August 16, 2012.]

RULE 205. JUDICIAL CONFERENCE OF THE SIXTH CIRCUIT

(a) Annual Conference. Unless the court determines otherwise, it will hold an annual conference of the court's circuit, district, bankruptcy, and magistrate judges at a time and place the chief judge designates.

(1) *Open Conferences.* Open conferences are held in even-numbered years.

(2) *Judges–Only Conferences.* Judges-only conferences are held in odd-numbered years.

(b) Purpose. The purpose of the conference is to consider the state of the courts and to consider ways to improve the administration of justice in the circuit.

(c) Attendees. The circuit, district, bankruptcy, and magistrate judges of the circuit may attend all conferences. Members of the bar who meet the following qualifications may attend open conferences:

(1) Attorneys admitted to practice in one or more federal courts in this circuit; and

(2) Delegates appointed under subrule (d).

(d) Delegates.

(1) *Eligibility.* An attorney who has demonstrated a willingness to work to improve the judicial system is eligible to serve as a delegate. The attorney must have practiced actively for at least five years in one or more federal courts of the circuit, in a manner that reflects integrity, honesty, capability, and civility. The appointing judge should know the attorney.

(2) *Selection.* The judges in the circuit appoint delegates to the open conferences. Appointment as a delegate for one conference does not imply appointment to succeeding conferences. In appointing delegates, judges should consider the composition of their court's bar with respect to areas of practice, race, sex, national origin, and level of experience. Delegates consist of:

(A) two or more lawyers appointed by the chief judge of the circuit;

(B) two lawyers appointed by each other circuit judge; and

(C) one lawyer appointed by each district judge.

(e) Life Members.

(1) *Membership.* Membership by Attendance. An attorney who has attended three conferences in one or more of the capacities below is a life member of the conference. For purposes of determining eligibility, an attorney may aggregate years of attendance as:

(A) A delegate;

(B) The president or president-elect of the state bar association of a state in the circuit;

(C) The vice presidents for the Sixth Circuit of the Federal Bar Association or a member of the Executive Committee of the Federal Bar Association who resides in the circuit;

(D) The dean or designated member of the faculty of an accredited law school in the circuit;

(E) A member of the Advisory Committee on Rules of the United States Court of Appeals for the Sixth Circuit;

(F) The United States Attorney for a judicial district in the Sixth Circuit;

(G) The Federal Public Defender or Executive Director of the Community Defender Organization for the judicial districts in the circuit that have established defender organizations; and

(H) The CJA attorney representative for each district in the circuit.

(2) *Retired or Former Judges.*

(A) A circuit or district judge who has retired from judicial office under honorable circumstances under 28 U.S.C. § 371(a) or who has resigned from judicial office under honorable circumstances after having served at least three years is a life member;

(B) A bankruptcy or magistrate judge who has retired from judicial office under honorable circumstances under 28 U.S.C. § 377(a) or who has resigned from judicial office under honorable circumstances after having served for a least ten years, is a life member if the majority of the district judges of the bankruptcy or magistrate judge's district recommend membership.

(3) *Petitioning for Membership.* An attorney who has attended three conferences since 2000 may petition the chief judge to become a life member. The chief judge will grant the petition if the attendee satisfies the requirements in subrule (e)(1)(C). The chief judge's decision is final unless a majority of active circuit judges determines that the chief judge clearly erred. The petition must include:

(A) a statement that the attorney meets the eligibility requirements of a delegate under subrule (d)(1);

(B) evidence that the attorney attended at least three open conferences after actively practicing in one or more federal courts of this circuit for five years; and

(C) the favorable recommendation of a circuit or district judge of this circuit.

(4) *Eligibility to Attend Conferences; Responsibility.* A life member may attend all open conferences. The life members, acting through the Life Member Committee, organize life member programs and collegial activities of open conferences.

(5) *Maintaining Life Member Status.* To maintain active life member status, a life member must attend three open conferences each decade and pay annual dues. If these requirements are not met, the life member will be assigned to inactive status, subject to qualification as a senior life member. Inactive life members will not receive a letter of invitation or registration information for open conferences, nor are they required to pay dues.

(A) Reinstating Active Life Member Status. An inactive life member may return to active status by showing reasonable cause. The chief judge decides the request after considering the Life Member Committee's recommendation.

(B) Senior Life Members Status. At age 70, a life member may elect senior status. A senior life member will continue to receive a letter of invitation and conference registration materials but is not required to attend. A senior life member may—but is not required to—pay annual dues.

(6) *Dues.* Active life members must pay $100 annually. The Life Member Committee may change this amount. Dues will be turned over to the circuit executive for deposit and expenditure as directed by the chair of the Life Member Committee.

(f) Committees. The chief judge may appoint the following committees to help plan and carry out conferences:

(1) *Standing Committee on Judicial Conference Planning.* The Standing Committee on Judicial Conference Planning consists of a representative number of circuit, district, bankruptcy, and magistrate judges of this circuit and members of the bar. Members serve five-year terms unless the chief judge extends the term. Terms rotate, so approximately one-fifth of the members' terms end each year. The committee plans and organizes the annual conferences. The chief judge appoints the chair of the Standing Committee on Judicial Conference Planning. The chair may appoint ad hoc committees to arrange particular aspects of an annual conference.

(2) *Life Member Committee.* The Life Member Committee consists of three life members from each of the four states in the circuit, with at least one member from each district. Members serve three-year terms. The chief judge may reappoint a committee member for one additional term. Alternatively, the chief judge may fix the length of terms so that approximately one-third of the terms expire each year. The chief judge appoints the chair of the Life Member Committee. The Life Member Committee organizes and oversees the life members' activities, including—in consultation with the chief judge and the chair of the Standing Committee on Judicial Conference Planning—the life members' participation in open conferences and dues collection.

(3) *Senior Counselors.* The members of the Life Member Committee and the life members serving on the Standing Committee on Judicial Conference Planning act as senior counselors to the circuit. Senior counselors provide advice, at the court's request, on issues, policies, and other matters of significant concern.

[Effective December 1, 1998. Amended effective February 26, 2003; August 16, 2012.]

IOP 205. [RESERVED]

RULE 206. [RESERVED]

IOP 206. [RESERVED]

APPENDIX OF FORMS

FRAP FORM 1.   NOTICE OF APPEAL TO A COURT OF APPEALS FROM A JUDGMENT OR ORDER OF A DISTRICT COURT

[For text of form, see the Federal Rules of Appellate Procedure]

FRAP FORM 2.   NOTICE OF APPEAL TO A COURT OF APPEALS FROM A DECISION OF THE UNITED STATES TAX COURT

[For text of form, see the Federal Rules of Appellate Procedure]

FRAP FORM 3.   PETITION FOR REVIEW OF ORDER OF AN AGENCY, BOARD, COMMISSION OR OFFICER

[For text of form, see the Federal Rules of Appellate Procedure]

FRAP FORM 4.   AFFIDAVIT ACCOMPANYING MOTION FOR PERMISSION TO APPEAL IN FORMA PAUPERIS

[For text of form, see the Federal Rules of Appellate Procedure]

FRAP FORM 5.   NOTICE OF APPEAL TO A COURT OF APPEALS FROM A JUDGMENT OR ORDER OF A DISTRICT COURT OR A BANKRUPTCY APPELLATE PANEL

[For text of form, see the Federal Rules of Appellate Procedure]

FRAP FORM 6.   CERTIFICATE OF COMPLIANCE WITH TYPE–VOLUME LIMIT

[For text of form, see the Federal Rules of Appellate Procedure]

FRAP FORM 7.   DECLARATION OF INMATE FILING

[For text of form, see the Federal Rules of Appellate Procedure]

APPENDIX: LENGTH LIMITS STATED IN THE FEDERAL RULES OF APPELLATE PROCEDURE

[For text of appendix, see the Federal Rules of Appellate Procedure]

SIXTH CIRCUIT GUIDE TO ELECTRONIC FILING

Introduction

The United States Court of Appeals for the Sixth Circuit requires attorneys to file documents electronically, subject to exceptions set forth in the Sixth Circuit Rules and this Guide, using the Electronic Case File (ECF) system.

1. Definitions.

1.1. *ECF (Electronic Case Filing)* means the system maintained by the court for receiving and storing documents in electronic format.

1.2. *PACER (Public Access to Court Electronic Records)* is an electronic system that allows the user to view, print, and download electronically maintained docket information and court documents from the federal courts over the Internet.

1.3. *PDF (Portable Document Format)* means a non-modifiable electronic file containing the ".pdf" file extension. **Native PDF** form means a text-searchable PDF file generated from an original word-processing file.

1.4. *Registered Attorney* means an attorney who has registered under section 2 below and is therefore authorized to file documents electronically and to receive service on the ECF system.

1.5. *Initiating Filing* means the motion, petition, or other document initiating an original proceeding in this court, including those filed under Rules 5, 15 or 21 of the Federal Rules of Appellate Procedure.

1.6. *Document* means any order, opinion, judgment, petition, application, notice, transcript, motion, brief or other document filed in the court of appeals.

1.7. *Traditionally filed document* means a document submitted to the clerk in paper form for filing.

1.8. *NDA (Notice of Docket Activity)* is a notice generated automatically by the ECF system at the time a document is filed and a docket entry results. This notice sets forth the time of filing, the text of the docket entry, and the name of the attorney(s) required to receive notice of the filing. If a PDF document is attached to the docket entry, the NDA will also identify the person filing the document, the type of document, and a hyperlink to the filed document. Any document filed by the court will similarly list those to whom electronic notice of the filing is being sent.

2. Registration; Passwords.

2.1. To participate in the ECF system, an attorney must register to file and serve documents electronically. Registration constitutes consent to receive electronic service of all documents as provided by the Federal Rules of Appellate Procedure and the Rules of the Sixth Circuit, as well as to receive electronic notice of correspondence, orders, and opinions issued by the court.

2.2. To be eligible to register as a user of the ECF system, an attorney must be admitted to practice in this court, be a member in good standing, and have submitted to the PACER Service Center a completed ECF Attorney Registration form. Registration forms may be obtained from:

PACER Service Center
P.O. Box 780549
San Antonio, TX 78278
Tel. (800)676–6856 or (210)301–6440
http://pacer.psc.uscourts.gov

In addition, the attorney or the attorney's firm must have a PACER account and an e-mail address.

2.3. Upon receipt of the attorney's registration information from the PACER Service Center, the clerk will issue a login name and user password to the attorney, who may thereafter change the password as he or she wishes. All registered attorneys have an affirmative duty to inform the clerk immediately of any change in their e-mail address. Service on an obsolete e-mail address will still constitute valid service on a registered attorney if the attorney has failed to notify the clerk of a new address. Authorized use of an attorney's login name and password by another is deemed to be the act of the attorney. If a login name and/or password should become compromised, the attorney is responsible for notifying the ECF Help Desk immediately at (513) 564–7000 or ca06-ecf-help@ca6.uscourts.gov.

2.4.   An attorney whose e-mail address, mailing address, telephone number, or fax number has changed from that disclosed on the attorney's original Attorney Registration Form shall file a notice of such change and serve the notice of such change on all parties in all cases in which the attorney has entered an appearance.

3.   Mandatory Electronic Filing; Exceptions.

3.1.   Except as otherwise required by the Sixth Circuit Rules or by order of the court, all documents submitted by attorneys in cases filed with the Sixth Circuit must be filed electronically, using the Electronic Case Filing (ECF) system.   The Sixth Circuit Rules and this Guide govern electronic filings.   If the Sixth Circuit Rules and this Guide are inconsistent, the Sixth Circuit Rules control.

3.2.   All electronically filed documents must be in PDF form and must conform to all technical requirements established by the Judicial Conference or the court.   Whenever possible, documents must be in Native PDF form and not created by scanning.   The following documents are exempted from the electronic filing requirement and are to be filed in paper format:

(1) Any document filed by a party that is unrepresented by counsel;

(2) Documents relating to complaints of attorney misconduct;

(3) Vouchers or other documents relating to claims for compensation and reimbursement of expenses incurred with regard to representation afforded under the Criminal Justice Act; and

(4) Documents that exceed any limit that the court may set for the size of electronic filings.

3.3.   No unrepresented party may file electronically; unrepresented parties must submit documents in paper format.   The clerk will scan such documents into the ECF system, and the electronic version scanned in by the clerk will constitute the appeal record of the court as reflected on its docket.

4.   [Reserved].

5.   Record on Appeal and Appendices.

5.1.   In an appeal in which the entire record of the lower court or administrative agency is available to this court in electronic form, no paper record on appeal will be transmitted to the clerk. If part of the record below is maintained in paper form, only that part must be transmitted to the circuit clerk when the court of appeals requests that the record be transmitted.

5.2.   Except as provided in 6 Cir. R. 30(a), appendices to briefs are no longer required.   The clerk will not accept an appendix for filing in cases where it is not required.

5.3.   In appeals from the district court where there is an electronic record in the district court, documents in the electronic record must not be included in an appendix.   To facilitate the court's reference to the electronic record in such cases, each party must include in its principal brief a designation of relevant district court documents; see 6 Cir. R. 30(g)(1).   The designation must include for each document the record entry number from the district court docket and a description of the document.

5.4.   In some instances the court's electronic filing system may not be able to accept large scanned documents that may be necessary for an appendix.   A filer encountering such a problem should contact the ECF Help Desk, available by phone at (513) 564–7000 during the hours 8:00 A.M. to 5:00 P.M.   Eastern time, Monday through Friday, or by e-mail at ca06-ecf-help@ca6.uscourts.gov.   The court will work with the filer to resolve technical problems with filing large documents.   If necessary, the court will extend the deadline for filing an appendix when such problems are encountered.

6.   Briefs on Appeal—Proof Briefs Eliminated.

6.1.   Proof briefs are no longer required to be filed.   The clerk will not accept a proof brief for filing.

6.2.   Only one version of each brief is to be filed.   Each brief will cite with specificity those parts of the record to which reference is made.   Citation shall be to the record item being referred to and to the page of the appendix, if there is an appendix.   See 6 Cir. R. 28(a).

7. Documents Filed Under Seal.

7.1. A motion to file documents under seal may be filed electronically unless prohibited by law, local rule, or court order. If the court grants the motion, the order authorizing the filing of documents under seal may be filed electronically unless prohibited by law.

7.2. Documents filed under seal in the court from which an appeal is taken shall continue to be filed under seal on appeal to this court. Documents filed under seal shall comply with all filing requirements of the court that originally ordered or otherwise authorized the documents to be filed under seal.

8. Signatures.

8.1. Attorneys—A registered attorney's use of the assigned login name and password to submit a document electronically serves as that attorney's signature on that document for all purposes. The identity of the registered attorney submitting the electronically filed document must be reflected at the end of the document by means of an "s/[attorney's name]" block showing the attorney's name, followed by the attorney's business address, telephone number, and e-mail address. Graphic and other electronic signatures are discouraged.

8.2. Multiple attorney signatures—The filer of any electronically filed document requiring multiple signatures (e.g., stipulations) must list thereon all the names of other attorney signatories by means of an "s/ [attorney's name]" block for each. By submitting such a document, the filer certifies that each of the other attorneys has expressly agreed to the form and substance of the document, and that the filer has their authority to submit the document electronically. In the alternative, the filer *may* submit a scanned document containing all necessary signatures.

8.3. Clerk of Court or Deputy Clerks—The electronic filing of any document by the clerk or a deputy clerk of this court by use of that individual's login and password shall be deemed the filing of a signed original document for all purposes.

9. Entry Onto the Docket; Official Court Record.

9.1. The electronic transmission of a document, together with transmission of the NDA from the court, in accordance with the policies, procedures, and rules adopted by the court, constitutes the filing of the document under the Federal Rules of Appellate Procedure and constitutes the entry of that document onto the official docket of the court maintained by the clerk pursuant to Fed. R. App. P. 45(b)(1). All orders, decrees, notices, opinions and judgments of the court will be filed and maintained by the ECF system and constitute entry on the docket kept by the clerk for purposes of Rules 36 and 45(b)(1) and (c) of the Federal Rules of Appellate Procedure.

9.2. The electronic version of filed documents, whether filed electronically in the first instance or received by the clerk in paper format and subsequently scanned into electronic format, constitutes the official record in the case. Later modification of a filed document or docket entry is not permitted except as authorized by the court. A document submitted electronically is deemed to have been filed on the date and at the time indicated in the system-generated NDA.

9.3. The clerk's office will discard all paper documents once they have been scanned and made a part of the official record, unless the electronic file thereby produced is incomplete or of questionable quality.

10. Service of Documents.

10.1. A certificate of service is required for all documents, and registered attorneys must comply with Fed. R. App. P. 25 when filing electronically. The ECF system will automatically generate and send by e-mail an NDA to all registered attorneys participating in any case. This notice constitutes service on those registered attorneys. Registration for electronic filing by the ECF system constitutes consent to service through the NDA. Independent service, either by paper or otherwise, need not be made on any registered attorney. *Pro se* litigants and attorneys who are not registered for electronic filing must be served by the filing party through the conventional means of service set forth in Fed. R. App. P. 25. The Notice of Docket Activity generated by the ECF system does not replace the certificate of service required by Fed. R. App. P. 25.

10.2. Except as may be otherwise provided by local rule or order of the court, all orders, opinions, judgments and other court-issued documents in cases maintained in the ECF system will be filed electronically, which filing will constitute entry on the docket maintained by the clerk under Fed. R. App. P. 36 and 45(b).

Any order, opinion, judgment, or other court-issued document filed electronically without the signature of the judge, clerk, or authorized deputy clerk has the same effect as if the judge or clerk had signed a paper copy of the filing.

11. Access to Documents.

11.1. Access to all documents maintained electronically, except those filed under seal, is available to any person through the PACER system. PACER accounts can be established through the PACER Service Center at: http://pacer.psc.uscourts.gov, or by contacting the PACER Service Center, P.O. Box 780549, San Antonio, Texas 78278, or by telephone at (800) 676–6856 or (210) 301–6440.

11.2. Under the PACER system, parties and counsel of record are entitled to one free copy of each document filed in their cases, within fifteen days of filing. Parties are encouraged to download a copy of the document and save it to their hard drives during this period, as subsequent access to those documents is subject to billing fees as set forth on the PACER website.

12. Privacy Protection and Redactions.

In accordance with Fed. R. App. P. 25(a)(5), registered attorneys must redact all documents, including briefs, consistent with the privacy policy of the Judicial Conference of the United States. Required redactions include social security numbers and taxpayer identification numbers (the filer shall include only the last four digits of a social security or tax identification number), birth dates (use year of birth only), minors' names (initials may be used), and financial account numbers (except those identifying property allegedly subject to forfeiture in a forfeiture proceeding). It is the responsibility of the filer to redact pleadings appropriately. Pursuant to the privacy policy of the Judicial Conference and applicable statutory provisions, remote electronic access to immigration and social security dockets is limited to the attorneys in the case who are registered in ECF. In this regard, the clerk will restrict electronic public access in these cases to judges, court staff, and the parties and attorneys in the appeal or agency proceeding. The court will not restrict access to orders and opinions in these cases. Parties seeking to restrict access to orders and opinions must file a motion explaining why that relief is required in a given case.

13. Filing Deadlines; Technical Failures.

13.1. Filing documents electronically does not in any way alter any filing deadlines. Where a specific time of day deadline is set by court order or stipulation, the electronic filing must be completed by that time. An electronically filed document is deemed filed upon completion of the transmission and issuance by the court's system of an NDA.

13.2. The clerk shall deem the court's website to be subject to a technical failure on a given day if the site is unable to accept filings continuously or intermittently over the course of any period of time greater than one hour after 12:00 noon (Eastern time) that day, in which case, filings due that day which were not filed due solely to such technical failures shall become due the next business day. Such delayed filings must be accompanied by a declaration or affidavit attesting to the filer's failed attempts to file electronically at least two times after 12:00 noon separated by at least one hour on each day of delay because of such technical failure. The initial point of contact for any practitioner experiencing difficulty filing a document electronically shall be the ECF Help Desk, available by phone at (513) 564–7000 during the hours 8:00 A.M. to 5:00 P.M. Eastern time, Monday though Friday, or by e-mail at ca06-ecf-help@ca6.uscourts.gov.

14. Training.

14.1. The clerk shall post and maintain on the court's website instructions for counsel on how to use the ECF system, and shall update the website as necessary when changes are made to the procedures for using ECF. These instructions, in such form as the clerk determines most effective, shall be clear and concise, giving the prospective user the information necessary to successfully file documents.

14.2. The court shall also staff and maintain an ECF Help Desk to which users can turn to for direction in accessing the ECF system successfully. In addition, the clerk shall offer whatever other assistance is practicable to ensure that attorneys become proficient in the use of the ECF system.

[Effective June 1, 2008. Amended effective January 12, 2009; August 16, 2012; November 18, 2015.]

RULES FOR JUDICIAL–CONDUCT AND JUDICIAL–DISABILITY PROCEEDINGS

PREFACE

These Rules were promulgated by the Judicial Conference of the United States, after public comment, pursuant to 28 U.S.C.

§§ 331 and 358, to establish standards and procedures for addressing complaints filed by complainants or identified by chief judges under the Judicial Conduct and Disability Act, 28 U.S.C. §§ 351–364.

ARTICLE I.   GENERAL PROVISIONS

RULE 1.   SCOPE

These Rules govern proceedings under the Judicial Conduct and Disability Act (the Act), 28 U.S.C. §§ 351–364, to determine whether a covered judge has engaged in conduct prejudicial to the effective and expeditious administration of the business of the courts or is unable to discharge the duties of office because of mental or physical disability.

[Adopted March 11, 2008, effective April 10, 2008. Amended effective September 17, 2015.]

Commentary on Rule 1

In September 2006, the Judicial Conduct and Disability Act Study Committee ("Breyer Committee"), appointed in 2004 by Chief Justice Rehnquist, presented a report ("Breyer Committee Report"), 239 F.R.D. 116 (Sept. 2006), to Chief Justice Roberts that evaluated implementation of the Judicial Conduct and Disability Act of 1980, 28 U.S.C. §§ 351–364. The Breyer Committee had been formed in response to criticism from the public and Congress regarding the effectiveness of the Act's implementation. The Executive Committee of the Judicial Conference directed its Committee on Judicial Conduct and Disability to consider the Breyer Committee's recommendations and to report on their implementation to the Conference.

The Breyer Committee found that it could not evaluate implementation of the Act without establishing interpretive standards, Breyer Committee Report, 239 F.R.D. at 132, and that a major problem faced by chief judges in implementing the Act was the lack of authoritative interpretive standards. *Id.* at 212–15. The Breyer Committee then established standards to guide its evaluation, some of which were new formulations and some of which were taken from the "Illustrative Rules Governing Complaints of Judicial Misconduct and Disability," discussed below. The principal standards used by the Breyer Committee are in Appendix E of its Report. *Id.* at 238.

Based on the Breyer Committee's findings, the Committee on Judicial Conduct and Disability concluded that there was a need for the Judicial Conference to exercise its power under Section 358 of the Act to fashion standards guiding the various officers and bodies that must exercise responsibility under the Act. To that end, the Committee on Judicial Conduct and Disability proposed rules that were based largely on Appendix E of the Breyer Committee Report and the Illustrative Rules.

The Illustrative Rules were originally prepared in 1986 by the Special Committee of the Conference of Chief Judges of the United States Courts of Appeals, and were subsequently revised and amended, most recently in 2000, by the predecessor to the Committee on Judicial Conduct and Disability. The Illustrative Rules were adopted, with minor variations, by circuit judicial councils, to govern complaints under the Judicial Conduct and Disability Act.

After being submitted for public comment pursuant to 28 U.S.C. § 358(c), the Judicial Conference promulgated the present Rules on March 11, 2008. They were amended on September 17, 2015.

RULE 2.   EFFECT AND CONSTRUCTION

(a) Generally. These Rules are mandatory; they supersede any conflicting judicial-council rules. Judicial councils may promulgate additional rules to implement the Act as long as those rules do not conflict with these Rules.

(b) Exception. A Rule will not apply if, when performing duties authorized by the Act, a chief judge, a special committee, a judicial council, the Committee on Judicial Conduct and Disability, or the Judicial Conference expressly finds that exceptional circumstances render application of that Rule in a particular proceeding manifestly unjust or contrary to the purposes of the Act or these Rules.

[Adopted March 11, 2008, effective April 10, 2008. Amended effective September 17, 2015.]

Commentary on Rule 2

Unlike the Illustrative Rules, these Rules provide mandatory and nationally uniform provisions governing the substantive and procedural aspects of misconduct and disability proceedings under the Act. The mandatory nature of these Rules is authorized by 28 U.S.C. §§ 358(a) and (c). Judicial councils retain the power to promulgate rules consistent with these Rules. For example, a local rule may authorize the electronic distribution of materials pursuant to Rule 8(b).

Rule 2(b) recognizes that unforeseen and exceptional circumstances may call for a different approach in particular cases.

RULE 3.   DEFINITIONS

(a) Chief Judge. "Chief judge" means the chief judge of a United States court of appeals, of the United States Court of International Trade, or of the United States Court of Federal Claims.

(b) Circuit Clerk. "Circuit clerk" means a clerk of a United States court of appeals, the clerk of the United States Court of International Trade, the clerk of the United States Court of Federal Claims, or the circuit executive of the United States Court of Appeals for the Federal Circuit.

(c) Complaint. A complaint is:

(1) a document that, in accordance with Rule 6, is filed by any person in his or her individual capacity or on behalf of a professional organization; or

(2) information from any source, other than a document described in (c)(1), that gives a chief judge probable cause to believe that a covered judge, as defined in Rule 4, has engaged in misconduct or may have a disability, whether or not the

information is framed as or is intended to be an allegation of misconduct or disability.

(d) Court of Appeals, District Court, and District Judge. "Court of appeals," "district court," and "district judge," where appropriate, include the United States Court of Federal Claims, the United States Court of International Trade, and the judges thereof.

(e) Disability. "Disability" is a temporary or permanent impairment, physical or mental, rendering a judge unable to discharge the duties of the particular judicial office. Examples of disability include substance abuse, the inability to stay awake during court proceedings, or impairment of cognitive abilities that renders the judge unable to function effectively.

(f) Judicial Council and Circuit. "Judicial council" and "circuit," where appropriate, include any courts designated in 28 U.S.C. § 363.

(g) Magistrate Judge. "Magistrate judge," where appropriate, includes a special master appointed by the Court of Federal Claims under 42 U.S.C. § 300aa–12(c).

(h) Misconduct. Cognizable misconduct:

(1) is conduct prejudicial to the effective and expeditious administration of the business of the courts. Misconduct includes, but is not limited to:

(A) using the judge's office to obtain special treatment for friends or relatives;

(B) accepting bribes, gifts, or other personal favors related to the judicial office;

(C) having improper discussions with parties or counsel for one side in a case;

(D) treating litigants, attorneys, or others in a demonstrably egregious and hostile manner;

(E) engaging in partisan political activity or making inappropriately partisan statements;

(F) soliciting funds for organizations;

(G) retaliating against complainants, witnesses, or others for their participation in this complaint process;

(H) refusing, without good cause shown, to cooperate in the investigation of a complaint under these Rules; or

(I) violating other specific, mandatory standards of judicial conduct, such as those pertaining to restrictions on outside income and requirements for financial disclosure.

(2) is conduct occurring outside the performance of official duties if the conduct might have a prejudicial effect on the administration of the business of the courts, including a substantial and widespread lowering of public confidence in the courts among reasonable people.

(3) does not include:

(A) an allegation that is directly related to the merits of a decision or procedural ruling. An allegation that calls into question the correctness of a judge's ruling, including a failure to recuse, without more, is merits-related. If the decision or ruling is alleged to be the result of an improper motive, *e.g.,* a bribe, ex parte contact, racial or ethnic bias, or improper conduct in rendering a decision or ruling, such

as personally derogatory remarks irrelevant to the issues, the complaint is not cognizable to the extent that it attacks the merits.

(B) an allegation about delay in rendering a decision or ruling, unless the allegation concerns an improper motive in delaying a particular decision or habitual delay in a significant number of unrelated cases.

(i) Subject Judge. "Subject judge" means any judge described in Rule 4 who is the subject of a complaint.

[Adopted March 11, 2008, effective April 10, 2008. Amended effective September 17, 2015.]

Commentary on Rule 3

Rule 3 is derived and adapted from the Breyer Committee Report and the Illustrative Rules.

Unless otherwise specified or the context otherwise indicates, the term "complaint" is used in these Rules to refer both to complaints identified by a chief judge under Rule 5 and to complaints filed by a complainant under Rule 6.

Under the Act, a "complaint" may be filed by "any person" or "identified" by a chief judge. *See* 28 U.S.C. §§ 351(a), (b). Under Rule 3(c)(1), complaints may be submitted by a person, in his or her individual capacity, or by a professional organization. Generally, the word "complaint" brings to mind the commencement of an adversary proceeding in which the contending parties are left to present the evidence and legal arguments, and judges play the role of an essentially passive arbiter. The Act, however, establishes an administrative, inquisitorial process. For example, even absent a complaint under Rule 6, chief judges are expected in some circumstances to trigger the process—"identify a complaint," *see* 28 U.S.C. § 351(b) and Rule 5—and conduct an investigation without becoming a party. *See* 28 U.S.C. § 352(a); Breyer Committee Report, 239 F.R.D. at 214; Illustrative Rule 2(j). Even when a complaint is filed by someone other than the chief judge, the complainant lacks many rights that a litigant would have, and the chief judge, instead of being limited to the "four corners of the complaint," must, under Rule 11, proceed as though misconduct or disability has been alleged where the complainant reveals information of misconduct or disability but does not claim it as such. *See* Breyer Committee Report, 239 F.R.D. at 183–84.

An allegation of misconduct or disability filed under Rule 6 is a "complaint," and the Rule so provides in subsection (c)(1). However, both the nature of the process and the use of the term "identify" suggest that the word "complaint" covers more than a document formally triggering the process. The process relies on chief judges considering known information and triggering the process when appropriate. "Identifying" a "complaint," therefore, is best understood as the chief judge's concluding that information known to the judge constitutes probable cause to believe that misconduct occurred or a disability exists, whether or not the information is framed as, or intended to be, an accusation. This definition is codified in subsection (c)(2).

Rule 3(e) relates to disability and provides only the most general definition, recognizing that a fact-specific approach is the only one available. A mental disability could involve cognitive impairment or any psychiatric or psychological condition that renders the judge unable to discharge the duties of office. Such duties may include those that are administrative. If, for example, the judge is a chief judge, the judicial council, fulfilling its obligation under 28 U.S.C. § 332(d)(1) to make "necessary and appropriate orders for the effective and expeditious administration of justice," may find, under 28 U.S.C. § 45(d) or § 136(e), that the judge is "temporarily unable to perform" his or her chief-judge duties. In that event, an appropriate remedy could involve, under Rule 20(b)(1)(D)(vii), temporary reassignment of chief-judge duties to the next judge statutorily eligible to perform them.

The phrase "prejudicial to the effective and expeditious administration of the business of the courts" is not subject to precise definition, and subsection (h)(1) therefore provides some specific examples. Although the Code of Conduct for United States Judges may be informative, its main precepts are highly general; the Code is in many potential applications aspirational rather than a set of disciplinary rules. Ultimately, the responsibility for determining what constitutes misconduct under the statute is the province of the judicial council of the circuit, subject to such review and limitations as are ordained by the statute and by these Rules.

Even where specific, mandatory rules exist—for example, governing the receipt of gifts by judges, outside earned income, and financial disclosure obligations—the distinction between the misconduct statute and these specific, mandatory rules must be borne in mind. For example, an inadvertent, minor violation of any one of these rules, promptly remedied when called to the attention of the judge, might still be a violation but might not rise to the level of misconduct under the statute. By contrast, a pattern of such violations of the Code might well rise to the level of misconduct.

Under Rule 3(h)(1)(G), a judge's efforts to retaliate against any person for his or her involvement in the complaint process may constitute cognizable misconduct. The Rule makes this explicit in the interest of public confidence in the complaint process.

Rule 3(h)(1)(H) provides that a judge's refusal, without good cause shown, to cooperate in the investigation of a complaint under these Rules may constitute cognizable misconduct. While the exercise of rights under the Fifth Amendment to the Constitution would constitute good cause under Rule 3(h)(1)(H), given the fact-specific nature of the inquiry, it is not possible to otherwise anticipate all circumstances that might also constitute good cause. The Commentary on Rule 13 provides additional discussion regarding Rule 3(h)(1)(H). The Rules contemplate that judicial councils will not consider commencing proceedings under Rule 3(h)(1)(H) except as necessary after other means to acquire the information have been tried or have proven futile.

Rule 3(h)(2) reflects that an allegation can meet the statutory standard even though the judge's alleged conduct did not occur in the course of the performance of official duties. And some conduct in the categories listed under subsection (h)(1), or in categories not listed, might, depending on the circumstances, amount to "misconduct" under subsection (h)(2), or under both subsection (h)(1) and subsection (h)(2). Also, the Code of Conduct for United States Judges expressly covers a wide range of extra-official activities, and some of these activities may constitute misconduct. For example, allegations that a judge solicited funds for a charity or participated in a partisan political event are cognizable under the Act.

On the other hand, judges are entitled to some leeway in extra-official activities. For example, misconduct may not include a judge being repeatedly and publicly discourteous to a spouse (not including physical abuse) even though this might cause some reasonable people to have diminished confidence in the courts. Rule 3(h)(2) states that conduct of this sort is covered, for example, when it might lead to a "substantial and widespread" lowering of such confidence.

Rule 3(h)(3)(A) tracks the Act, 28 U.S.C. § 352(b)(1)(A)(ii), in excluding from the definition of misconduct allegations "[d]irectly related to the merits of a decision or procedural ruling." This exclusion preserves the independence of judges in the exercise of judicial power by ensuring that the complaint procedure is not used to collaterally attack the substance of a judge's ruling. Any allegation that calls into question the correctness of an official action of a judge—without more—is merits-related. The phrase "decision or procedural ruling" is not limited to rulings issued in deciding Article III cases or controversies. Thus, a complaint challenging the correctness of a chief judge's determination to dismiss a prior misconduct complaint

would be properly dismissed as merits-related—in other words, a challenging the substance of the judge's administrative determination to dismiss the complaint—even though it does not concern the judge's rulings in Article III litigation. Similarly, an allegation that a judge had incorrectly declined to approve a Criminal Justice Act voucher is merits-related under this standard.

Conversely, an allegation—however unsupported—that a judge conspired with a prosecutor to make a particular ruling is not merits-related, even though it "relates" to a ruling in a colloquial sense. Such an allegation attacks the propriety of conspiring with the prosecutor and goes beyond a challenge to the correctness—"the merits"—of the ruling itself. An allegation that a judge ruled against the complainant because the complainant is a member of a particular racial or ethnic group, or because the judge dislikes the complainant personally, is also not merits-related. Such an allegation attacks the propriety of arriving at rulings with an illicit or improper motive. Similarly, an allegation that a judge used an inappropriate term to refer to a class of people is not merits-related even if the judge used it on the bench or in an opinion; the correctness of the judge's rulings is not at stake. An allegation that a judge treated litigants, attorneys, or others in a demonstrably egregious and hostile manner while on the bench is also not merits-related.

The existence of an appellate remedy is usually irrelevant to whether an allegation is merits-related. The merits-related ground for dismissal exists to protect judges' independence in making rulings, not to protect or promote the appellate process. A complaint alleging an incorrect ruling is merits-related even though the complainant has no recourse from that ruling. By the same token, an allegation that is otherwise cognizable under the Act should not be dismissed merely because an appellate remedy appears to exist (for example, vacating a ruling that resulted from an improper *ex parte* communication). However, there may be occasions when appellate and misconduct proceedings overlap, and consideration and disposition of a complaint under these Rules may be properly deferred by the chief judge until the appellate proceedings are concluded in order to avoid inconsistent decisions, among other things.

Because of the special need to protect judges' independence in deciding what to say in an opinion or ruling, a somewhat different standard applies to determine the merits-relatedness of a non-frivolous allegation that a judge's language in a ruling reflected an improper motive. If the judge's language was relevant to the case at hand—for example, a statement that a claim is legally or factually "frivolous"—then the judge's choice of language is presumptively merits-related and excluded, absent evidence apart from the ruling itself suggesting an improper motive. If, on the other hand, the challenged language does not seem relevant on its face, then an additional inquiry under Rule 11 is necessary.

With regard to Rule 3(h)(3)(B), a complaint of delay in a single case is excluded as merits-related. Such an allegation may be said to challenge the correctness of an official action of the judge—in other words, assigning a low priority to deciding the particular case. But, by the same token, an allegation of a habitual pattern of delay in a significant number of unrelated cases, or an allegation of deliberate delay in a single case arising out of an illicit motive, is not merits-related.

The remaining subsections of Rule 3 provide technical definitions clarifying the application of the Rules to the various kinds of courts covered.

RULE 4. COVERED JUDGES

A complaint under these Rules may concern the actions or capacity only of judges of United States courts of appeals, judges of United States district courts, judges of United States bankruptcy courts, United States magistrate judges, and judges of the courts specified in 28 U.S.C. § 363.

[Adopted March 11, 2008, effective April 10, 2008.]

ARTICLE II. INITIATION OF COMPLAINT

RULE 5. IDENTIFICATION OF COMPLAINT

(a) **Identification.** When a chief judge has information constituting reasonable grounds for inquiry into whether a covered judge has engaged in misconduct or has a disability, the chief judge may conduct an inquiry, as he or she deems appropriate, into the accuracy of the information even if no related complaint has been filed. A chief judge who finds probable cause to believe that misconduct has occurred or that a disability exists may seek an informal resolution that he or she finds satisfactory. If no informal resolution is achieved or is feasible, the chief judge may identify a complaint and, by written order stating the reasons, begin the review provided in Rule 11. If the evidence of misconduct is clear and convincing and no informal resolution is achieved or is feasible, the chief judge must identify a complaint. A chief judge must not decline to identify a complaint merely because the person making the allegation has not filed a complaint under Rule 6. This Rule is subject to Rule 7.

(b) **Submission Not Fully Complying with Rule 6.** A legible submission in substantial but not full compliance with Rule 6 must be considered as possible grounds for the identification of a complaint under Rule 5(a).

[Adopted March 11, 2008, effective April 10, 2008. Amended effective September 17, 2015.]

Commentary on Rule 5

This Rule is adapted from the Breyer Committee Report, 239 F.R.D. at 245–46.

The Act authorizes a chief judge, by written order stating reasons, to identify a complaint and thereby dispense with the filing of a written complaint. *See* 28 U.S.C. § 351(b). Under Rule 5, when a chief judge becomes aware of information constituting reasonable grounds to inquire into possible misconduct or disability on the part of a covered judge, and no formal complaint has been filed, the chief judge has the power in his or her discretion to begin an appropriate inquiry. A chief judge's decision whether to informally seek a resolution and/or to identify a complaint is guided by the results of that inquiry. If the chief judge concludes that there is probable cause to believe that misconduct has occurred or a disability exists, the chief judge may seek an informal resolution, if feasible, and if failing in that, may identify a complaint. Discretion is accorded largely for the reasons police officers and prosecutors have discretion in making arrests or bringing charges. The matter may be trivial and isolated, based on marginal evidence, or otherwise highly unlikely to lead to a misconduct or disability finding. On the other hand, if the inquiry leads the chief judge to conclude that there is clear and convincing evidence of misconduct or a disability, and no satisfactory informal resolution has been achieved or is feasible, the chief judge is required to identify a complaint.

An informal resolution is one agreed to by the subject judge and found satisfactory by the chief judge. Because an informal resolution under Rule 5 reached before a complaint is filed under Rule 6 will generally cause a subsequent Rule 6 complaint alleging the identical

Commentary on Rule 4

This Rule tracks the Act. Rule 8(c) and (d) contain provisions as to the handling of complaints against persons not covered by the Act, such as other court personnel, or against both covered judges and noncovered persons.

matter to be concluded, *see* Rule 11(d), the chief judge must be sure that the resolution is fully appropriate before endorsing it. In doing so, the chief judge must balance the seriousness of the matter against the particular judge's alacrity in addressing the issue. The availability of this procedure should encourage attempts at swift remedial action before a formal complaint is filed.

When a chief judge identifies a complaint, a written order stating the reasons for the identification must be provided; this begins the process articulated in Rule 11. Rule 11 provides that once a chief judge has identified a complaint, the chief judge, subject to the disqualification provisions of Rule 25, will perform, with respect to that complaint, all functions assigned to the chief judge for the determination of complaints filed by a complainant.

In high-visibility situations, it may be desirable for a chief judge to identify a complaint without first seeking an informal resolution (and then, if the circumstances warrant, dismiss or conclude the identified complaint without appointment of a special committee) in order to assure the public that the allegations have not been ignored.

A chief judge's decision not to identify a complaint under Rule 5 is not appealable and is subject to Rule 3(h)(3)(A), which excludes merits-related complaints from the definition of misconduct.

A chief judge may not decline to identify a complaint solely on the basis that the unfiled allegations could be raised by one or more persons in a filed complaint, but none of these persons has opted to do so.

Subsection (a) concludes by stating that this Rule is "subject to Rule 7." This is intended to establish that only (i) the chief judge of the home circuit of a potential subject judge, or (ii) the chief judge of a circuit in which misconduct is alleged to have occurred in the course of official business while the potential subject judge was sitting by designation, shall have the power or a duty under this Rule to identify a complaint.

Subsection (b) provides that submissions that do not comply with the requirements of Rule 6(d) must be considered under Rule 5(a). For instance, if a complaint has been filed but the form submitted is unsigned, or the truth of the statements therein are not verified in writing under penalty of perjury, then a chief judge must nevertheless consider the allegations as known information and as a possible basis for the identification of a complaint under the process described in Rule 5(a).

RULE 6. FILING OF COMPLAINT

(a) **Form.** A complainant may use the form reproduced in the appendix to these Rules or a form designated by the rules of the judicial council in the circuit in which the complaint is filed. A complaint form is also available on each court of appeals' website or may be obtained from the circuit clerk or any district court or bankruptcy court within the circuit. A form is not necessary to file a complaint, but the complaint must be written and must include the information described in (b).

(b) **Brief Statement of Facts.** A complaint must contain a concise statement that details the specific facts on which the claim of misconduct or disability is based. The statement of facts should include a description of:

(1) what happened;

(2) when and where the relevant events happened;

(3) any information that would help an investigator check the facts; and

(4) for an allegation of disability, any additional facts that form the basis of that allegation.

(c) Legibility. A complaint should be typewritten if possible. If not typewritten, it must be legible. An illegible complaint will be returned to the complainant with a request to resubmit it in legible form. If a resubmitted complaint is still illegible, it will not be accepted for filing.

(d) Complainant's Address and Signature; Verification. The complainant must provide a contact address and sign the complaint. The truth of the statements made in the complaint must be verified in writing under penalty of perjury. If any of these requirements are not met, the submission will be accepted, but it will be reviewed under only Rule 5(b).

(e) Number of Copies; Envelope Marking. The complainant shall provide the number of copies of the complaint required by local rule. Each copy should be in an envelope marked "Complaint of Misconduct" or "Complaint of Disability." The envelope must not show the name of any subject judge.

[Adopted March 11, 2008, effective April 10, 2008. Amended effective September 17, 2015.]

Commentary on Rule 6

The Rule is adapted from the Illustrative Rules and is self-explanatory.

RULE 7.   WHERE TO INITIATE COMPLAINT

(a) Where to File. Except as provided in (b),

(1) a complaint against a judge of a United States court of appeals, a United States district court, a United States bankruptcy court, or a United States magistrate judge must be filed with the circuit clerk in the jurisdiction in which the subject judge holds office.

(2) a complaint against a judge of the United States Court of International Trade or the United States Court of Federal Claims must be filed with the respective clerk of that court.

(3) a complaint against a judge of the United States Court of Appeals for the Federal Circuit must be filed with the circuit executive of that court.

(b) Misconduct in Another Circuit; Transfer. If a complaint alleges misconduct in the course of official business while the subject judge was sitting on a court by designation under 28 U.S.C. §§ 291–293 and 294(d), the complaint may be filed or identified with the circuit clerk of that circuit or of the subject judge's home circuit. The proceeding will continue in the circuit of the first-filed or first-identified complaint. The judicial council of the circuit where the complaint was first filed or first identified may transfer the complaint to the subject judge's home circuit or to the circuit where the alleged misconduct occurred, as the case may be.

[Adopted March 11, 2008, effective April 10, 2008. Amended effective September 17, 2015.]

Commentary on Rule 7

Title 28 U.S.C. § 351 states that complaints are to be filed with "the clerk of the court of appeals for the circuit." However, in many circuits, this role is filled by circuit executives. Accordingly, the term "circuit clerk," as defined in Rule 3(b) and used throughout these Rules, applies to circuit executives.

Section 351 uses the term "the circuit" in a way that suggests that either the home circuit of the subject judge or the circuit in which misconduct is alleged to have occurred is the proper venue for complaints. With an exception for judges sitting by designation, the Rule requires the filing or identification of a misconduct or disability complaint in the circuit in which the judge holds office, largely based on the administrative perspective of the Act. Given the Act's emphasis on the future conduct of the business of the courts, the circuit in which the judge holds office is the appropriate forum because that circuit is likely best able to influence a judge's future behavior in constructive ways.

However, when judges sit by designation, the non-home circuit has a strong interest in redressing misconduct in the course of official business, and where allegations also involve a member of the bar—*ex parte* contact between an attorney and a judge, for example—it may often be desirable to have the judicial and bar misconduct proceedings take place in the same venue. Rule 7(b), therefore, allows transfer to, or filing or identification of a complaint in, the non-home circuit. The proceeding may be transferred by the judicial council of the filing or identified circuit to the other circuit.

RULE 8.   ACTION BY CIRCUIT CLERK

(a) Receipt of Complaint. Upon receiving a complaint against a judge filed under Rule 6 or identified under Rule 5, the circuit clerk must open a file, assign a docket number according to a uniform numbering scheme promulgated by the Committee on Judicial Conduct and Disability, and acknowledge the complaint's receipt.

(b) Distribution of Copies. The circuit clerk must promptly send copies of a complaint filed under Rule 6 to the chief judge or the judge authorized to act as chief judge under Rule 25(f), and copies of complaints filed under Rule 6 or identified under Rule 5 to each subject judge. The circuit clerk must retain the original complaint. Any further distribution should be as provided by local rule.

(c) Complaint Against Noncovered Person. If the circuit clerk receives a complaint about a person not holding an office described in Rule 4, the clerk must not accept the complaint under these Rules.

(d) Complaint Against Judge and Another Noncovered Person. If the circuit clerk receives a complaint about a judge described in Rule 4 and a person not holding an office described in Rule 4, the clerk must accept the complaint under these Rules only with regard to the judge and must so inform the complainant.

[Adopted March 11, 2008, effective April 10, 2008. Amended effective September 17, 2015.]

Commentary on Rule 8

This Rule is adapted from the Illustrative Rules and is largely self-explanatory.

The uniform docketing scheme described in subsection (a) should take into account potential problems associated with a complaint that names multiple judges. One solution may be to provide separate docket numbers for each subject judge. Separate docket numbers would help avoid difficulties in tracking cases, particularly if a complaint is dismissed with respect to some, but not all of the named judges.

Complaints against noncovered persons are not to be accepted for processing under these Rules but may, of course, be accepted under other circuit rules or procedures for grievances.

RULE 9.   TIME FOR FILING OR IDENTIFYING COMPLAINT

A complaint may be filed or identified at any time. If the passage of time has made an accurate and fair investigation of a complaint impracticable, the complaint must be dismissed under Rule 11(c)(1)(E).

[Adopted March 11, 2008, effective April 10, 2008. Amended effective September 17, 2015.]

Commentary on Rule 9

This Rule is adapted from the Act, 28 U.S.C. §§ 351, 352(b)(1)(A)(iii), and the Illustrative Rules.

RULE 10.   ABUSE OF COMPLAINT PROCEDURE

(a) Abusive Complaints. A complainant who has filed repetitive, harassing, or frivolous complaints, or has otherwise abused the complaint procedure, may be restricted from filing further complaints. After giving the complainant an opportunity to show cause in writing why his or her right to file further complaints should not be limited, the judicial council may prohibit, restrict, or impose conditions on the complainant's use of the complaint procedure. Upon written request of the complainant, the judicial council may revise or withdraw any prohibition, restriction, or condition previously imposed.

(b) Orchestrated Complaints. When many essentially identical complaints from different complainants are received and appear to be part of an orchestrated campaign, the chief judge may recommend that the judicial council issue a written order instructing the circuit clerk to accept only a certain number of such complaints for filing and to refuse to accept additional complaints. The circuit clerk must send a copy of any such order to anyone whose complaint was not accepted.

[Adopted March 11, 2008, effective April 10, 2008. Amended effective September 17, 2015.]

Commentary on Rule 10

This Rule is adapted from the Illustrative Rules.

Rule 10(a) provides a mechanism for a judicial council to restrict the filing of further complaints by a single complainant who has abused the complaint procedure. In some instances, however, the complaint procedure may be abused in a manner for which the remedy provided in Rule 10(a) may not be appropriate. For example, some circuits have been inundated with submissions of dozens or hundreds of essentially identical complaints against the same judge or judges, all submitted by different complainants. In many of these instances, persons with grievances against a particular judge or judges used the Internet or other technology to orchestrate mass complaint-filing campaigns against them. If each complaint submitted as part of such a campaign were accepted for filing and processed according to these Rules, there would be a serious drain on court resources without any benefit to the adjudication of the underlying merits.

A judicial council may, therefore, respond to such mass filings under Rule 10(b) by declining to accept repetitive complaints for filing, regardless of the fact that the complaints are nominally submitted by different complainants. When the first complaint or complaints have been dismissed on the merits, and when further, essentially identical submissions follow, the judicial council may issue a second order noting that these are identical or repetitive complaints, directing the circuit clerk not to accept these complaints or any further such complaints for filing, and directing the clerk to send each putative complainant copies of both orders.

ARTICLE III.   REVIEW OF COMPLAINT BY CHIEF JUDGE

RULE 11.   CHIEF JUDGE'S REVIEW

(a) Purpose of Chief Judge's Review. When a complaint is identified by the chief judge or is filed, the chief judge must review it unless the chief judge is disqualified under Rule 25. If a complaint contains information constituting evidence of misconduct or disability, but the complainant does not claim it as such, the chief judge must treat the complaint as if it did allege misconduct or disability and give notice to the subject judge. After reviewing a complaint, the chief judge must determine whether it should be:

(1) dismissed;

(2) concluded on the ground that voluntary corrective action has been taken;

(3) concluded because intervening events have made action on the complaint no longer necessary; or

(4) referred to a special committee.

(b) Chief Judge's Inquiry. In determining what action to take under Rule 11(a), the chief judge may conduct a limited inquiry. The chief judge, or a designee, may communicate orally or in writing with the complainant, the subject judge, and any others who may have knowledge of the matter, and may obtain and review transcripts and other relevant documents. In conducting the inquiry, the chief judge must not determine any reasonably disputed issue. Any such determination must be left to a special committee appointed under Rule 11(f) and to the judicial council that considers the special committee's report.

(c) Dismissal.

(1) *Permissible Grounds.* A complaint must be dismissed in whole or in part to the extent that the chief judge concludes that the complaint:

(A) alleges conduct that, even if true, is not prejudicial to the effective and expeditious administration of the business of the courts and does not indicate a mental or physical disability resulting in the inability to discharge the duties of judicial office;

(B) is directly related to the merits of a decision or procedural ruling;

(C) is frivolous;

(D) is based on allegations lacking sufficient evidence to raise an inference that misconduct has occurred or that a disability exists;

(E) is based on allegations that are incapable of being established through investigation;

(F) has been filed in the wrong circuit under Rule 7; or

(G) is otherwise not appropriate for consideration under the Act.

(2) *Impermissible Grounds.* A complaint must not be dismissed solely because it repeats allegations of a previously dismissed complaint if it also contains material information not previously considered and does not constitute harassment of the subject judge.

(d) Corrective Action. The chief judge may conclude a complaint proceeding in whole or in part if:

(1) an informal resolution under Rule 5 satisfactory to the chief judge was reached before the complaint was filed under Rule 6; or

(2) the chief judge determines that the subject judge has taken appropriate voluntary corrective action that acknowledges and remedies the problems raised by the complaint.

(e) Intervening Events. The chief judge may conclude a complaint proceeding in whole or in part upon determining that intervening events render some or all of the allegations moot or make remedial action impossible.

(f) Appointment of Special Committee. If some or all of a complaint is not dismissed or concluded, the chief judge must promptly appoint a special committee to investigate the complaint or any relevant portion of it and to make recommendations to the judicial council. Before appointing a special committee, the chief judge must invite the subject judge to respond to the complaint either orally or in writing if the judge was not given an opportunity during the limited inquiry. In the chief judge's discretion, separate complaints may be joined and assigned to a single special committee. Similarly, a single complaint about more than one judge may be severed and more than one special committee appointed.

(g) Notice of Chief Judge's Action; Petition for Review.

(1) *When Chief Judge Appoints Special Committee.* If the chief judge appoints a special committee, the chief judge must notify the complainant and the subject judge that the matter has been referred to a committee, notify the complainant of a complainant's rights under Rule 16, and identify the members of the committee. A copy of the order appointing the special committee must be sent to the Committee on Judicial Conduct and Disability.

(2) *When Chief Judge Disposes of Complaint Without Appointing Special Committee.* If the chief judge disposes of a complaint under Rule 11(c), (d), or (e), the chief judge must prepare a supporting memorandum that sets forth the reasons for the disposition. If the complaint was initiated by identification under Rule 5, the memorandum must so indicate. Except as authorized by 28 U.S.C. § 360, the memorandum must not include the name of the complainant or of the subject judge. The order and memoranda incorporated by reference in the order must be promptly sent to the complainant, the subject judge, and the Committee on Judicial Conduct and Disability.

(3) *Right to Petition for Review.* If the chief judge disposes of a complaint under Rule 11(c), (d), or (e), the complainant and the subject judge must be notified of the right to petition the judicial council for review of the disposition, as provided in Rule 18. If the chief judge so disposes of a complaint that was identified under Rule 5 or filed by its subject judge, the chief judge must transmit the order and memoranda incorporated by reference in the order to the judicial council for review in accordance with Rule 19. In the event of such a transmission, the subject judge may make a written submission to the judicial council but will have no further right of review except as allowed under Rule 21(b)(1)(B). When a disposition is to be reviewed by the judicial council, the chief judge must promptly transmit all materials obtained in connection with the inquiry under Rule 11(b) to the circuit clerk for transmittal to the council.

(h) Public Availability of Chief Judge's Decision. The chief judge's decision must be made public to the extent, at the time, and in the manner provided in Rule 24.

[Adopted March 11, 2008, effective April 10, 2008. Amended effective September 17, 2015.]

Commentary on Rule 11

This Rule describes complaint-review actions available either to a chief judge or, where that judge is the subject judge or is otherwise disqualified under Rule 25, to the judge designated under Rule 25(f) to perform the chief judge's duties under these Rules. Subsection (a) of this Rule provides that where a complaint has been filed under Rule 6, the ordinary doctrines of waiver do not apply. The chief judge must identify as a complaint any misconduct or disability issues raised by the factual allegations of the complaint even if the complainant makes no such claim with regard to those issues. For example, an allegation limited to misconduct in fact-finding that mentions periods during a trial when the judge was asleep must be treated as a complaint regarding disability. Some formal order giving notice of the expanded scope of the proceeding must be given to the subject judge.

Subsection (b) describes the nature of the chief judge's inquiry. It is based largely on the Breyer Committee Report, 239 F.R.D. at 243–45. The Act states that dismissal is appropriate "when a limited inquiry . . . demonstrates that the allegations in the complaint lack any factual foundation or are conclusively refuted by objective evidence." 28 U.S.C. § 352(b)(1)(B). At the same time, however, Section 352(a) states that "[t]he chief judge shall not undertake to make findings of fact about any matter that is reasonably in dispute." These two statutory standards should be read together, so that a matter is not "reasonably" in dispute if a limited inquiry shows that the allegations do not constitute misconduct or disability, that they lack any reliable factual foundation, or that they are conclusively refuted by objective evidence.

In conducting a limited inquiry under subsection (b), the chief judge must avoid determinations of reasonably disputed issues, including reasonably disputed issues as to whether the facts alleged constitute misconduct or disability, which are ordinarily left to the judicial council and its special committee. An allegation of fact is ordinarily not "refuted" simply because the subject judge denies it. The limited inquiry must reveal something more in the way of refutation before it is appropriate to dismiss a complaint that is otherwise cognizable. If it is the complainant's word against the subject judge's—in other words, there is simply no other significant evidence of what happened or of the complainant's unreliability—then there must be a special-committee investigation. Such a credibility issue is a matter "reasonably in dispute" within the meaning of the Act.

However, dismissal following a limited inquiry may occur when a complaint refers to transcripts or to witnesses and the chief judge determines that the transcripts and witnesses all support the subject judge. Breyer Committee Report, 239 F.R.D. at 243. For example, consider a complaint alleging that the subject judge said X, and the complaint mentions, or it is independently clear, that five people may have heard what the judge said. *Id.* The chief judge is told by the subject judge and one witness that the judge did not say X, and the chief judge dismisses the complaint without questioning the other four possible witnesses. *Id.* In this example, the matter remains reasonably in dispute. If all five witnesses say the subject judge did not say X, dismissal is appropriate, but if potential witnesses who are reasonably accessible have not been questioned, then the matter remains reasonably in dispute. *Id.*

Similarly, under subsection (c)(1)(A), if it is clear that the conduct or disability alleged, even if true, is not cognizable under these Rules, the complaint should be dismissed. If that issue is reasonably in dispute, however, dismissal under subsection (c)(1)(A) is inappropriate.

Essentially, the standard articulated in subsection (b) is that used to decide motions for summary judgment pursuant to Fed. R. Civ. P. 56. Genuine issues of material fact are not resolved at the summary judgment stage. A material fact is one that "might affect the outcome of the suit under the governing law," and a dispute is "genuine" if "the evidence is such that a reasonable jury could return a verdict for the nonmoving party." *Anderson v. Liberty Lobby*, 477 U.S. 242, 248 (1986). Similarly, the chief judge may not resolve a genuine issue concerning a material fact or the existence of misconduct or a disability when conducting a limited inquiry pursuant to subsection (b).

Subsection (c) describes the grounds on which a complaint may be dismissed. These are adapted from the Act, 28 U.S.C. § 352(b), and the Breyer Committee Report, 239 F.R.D. at 239–45. Subsection (c)(1)(A) permits dismissal of an allegation that, even if true, does not constitute misconduct or disability under the statutory standard. The proper standards are set out in Rule 3 and discussed in the Commentary on that Rule. Subsection (c)(1)(B) permits dismissal of complaints related to the merits of a decision by a subject judge; this standard is also governed by Rule 3 and its accompanying Commentary.

Subsections (c)(1)(C)–(E) implement the statute by allowing dismissal of complaints that are "frivolous, lacking sufficient evidence to raise an inference that misconduct has occurred, or containing allegations which are incapable of being established through investigation." 28 U.S.C. § 352(b)(1)(A)(iii).

Dismissal of a complaint as "frivolous" under Rule 11(c)(1)(C) will generally occur without any inquiry beyond the face of the complaint. For instance, when the allegations are facially incredible or so lacking in indicia of reliability that no further inquiry is warranted, dismissal under this subsection is appropriate.

A complaint warranting dismissal under Rule 11(c)(1)(D) is illustrated by the following example. Consider a complainant who alleges an impropriety and asserts that he knows of it because it was observed and reported to him by a person who is identified. The subject judge denies that the event occurred. When contacted, the source also denies it. In such a case, the chief judge's proper course of action may turn on whether the source had any role in the allegedly improper conduct. If the complaint was based on a lawyer's statement that he or she had an improper *ex parte* contact with a judge,

the lawyer's denial of the impropriety might not be taken as wholly persuasive, and it would be appropriate to conclude that a real factual issue is raised. On the other hand, if the complaint quoted a disinterested third party and that disinterested party denied that the statement had been made, there would be no value in opening a formal investigation. In such a case, it would be appropriate to dismiss the complaint under Rule 11(c)(1)(D).

Rule 11(c)(1)(E) is intended, among other things, to cover situations when no evidence is offered or identified, or when the only identified source is unavailable. Breyer Committee Report, 239 F.R.D. at 243. For example, a complaint alleges that an unnamed attorney told the complainant that the subject judge did X. *Id.* The subject judge denies it. The chief judge requests that the complainant (who does not purport to have observed the subject judge do X) identify the unnamed witness, or that the unnamed witness come forward so that the chief judge can learn the unnamed witness's account. *Id.* The complainant responds that he has spoken with the unnamed witness, that the unnamed witness is an attorney who practices in federal court, and that the unnamed witness is unwilling to be identified or to come forward. *Id.* at 243–44. The allegation is then properly dismissed as containing allegations that are incapable of being established through investigation. *Id.*

If, however, the situation involves a reasonable dispute over credibility, the matter should proceed. For example, the complainant alleges an impropriety and alleges that he or she observed it and that there were no other witnesses; the subject judge denies that the event occurred. Unless the complainant's allegations are facially incredible or so lacking indicia of reliability as to warrant dismissal under Rule 11(c)(1)(C), a special committee must be appointed because there is a material factual question that is reasonably in dispute.

Dismissal is also appropriate when a complaint is filed so long after an alleged event that memory loss, death, or changes to unknown residences prevent a proper investigation.

Subsection (c)(2) indicates that the investigative nature of the process prevents the application of claim preclusion principles where new and material evidence becomes available. However, it also recognizes that at some point a renewed investigation may constitute harassment of the subject judge and should not be undertaken, depending of course on the seriousness of the issues and the weight of the new evidence.

Rule 11(d) implements the Act's provision for dismissal if voluntary appropriate corrective action has been taken. It is largely adapted from the Breyer Committee Report, 239 F.R.D. at 244–45. The Act authorizes the chief judge to conclude the complaint proceedings if "appropriate corrective action has been taken." 28 U.S.C. § 352(b)(2). Under the Rule, action taken after a complaint is filed is "appropriate" when it acknowledges and remedies the problem raised by the complaint. Breyer Committee Report, 239 F.R.D. at 244. Because the Act deals with the conduct of judges, the emphasis is on correction of the judicial conduct that was the subject of the complaint. *Id.* Terminating a complaint based on corrective action is premised on the implicit understanding that voluntary self-correction or redress of misconduct or a disability is preferable to sanctions. *Id.* The chief judge may facilitate this process by giving the subject judge an objective view of the appearance of the judicial conduct in question and by suggesting appropriate corrective measures. *Id.* Moreover, when corrective action is taken under Rule 5 satisfactory to the chief judge before a complaint is filed, that informal resolution will be sufficient to conclude a subsequent complaint based on identical conduct.

"Corrective action" must be voluntary action taken by the subject judge. Breyer Committee Report, 239 F.R.D. at 244. A remedial action directed by the chief judge or by an appellate court without the participation of the subject judge in formulating the directive or without the subject judge's subsequent agreement to such action does not constitute the requisite voluntary corrective action. *Id.* Neither the chief judge nor an appellate court has authority under the Act to impose a formal remedy or sanction; only the judicial council can impose a formal remedy or sanction under 28 U.S.C. § 354(a)(2). *Id.* Compliance with a previous judicial-council order may serve as corrective action allowing conclusion of a later complaint about the same behavior. *Id.*

Where a subject judge's conduct has resulted in identifiable, particularized harm to the complainant or another individual, appropriate corrective action should include steps taken by that judge to acknowledge and redress the harm, if possible, such as by an apology, recusal from a case, or a pledge to refrain from similar conduct in the future. *Id.* While the Act is generally forward-looking, any corrective action should, to the extent possible, serve to correct a specific harm to an individual, if such harm can reasonably be remedied. *Id.* In some cases, corrective action may not be "appropriate" to justify conclusion of a complaint unless the complainant or other individual harmed is meaningfully apprised of the nature of the corrective action in the chief judge's order, in a direct communication from the subject judge, or otherwise. *Id.*

Voluntary corrective action should be proportionate to any plausible allegations of misconduct in a complaint. The form of corrective action should also be proportionate to any sanctions that the judicial council might impose under Rule 20(b), such as a private or public reprimand or a change in case assignments. Breyer Committee Report, 239 F.R.D at 244–45. In other words, minor corrective action will not suffice to dispose of a serious matter. *Id.*

Rule 11(e) implements Section 352(b)(2) of the Act, which permits the chief judge to "conclude the proceeding" if "action on the complaint is no longer necessary because of intervening events," such as a resignation from judicial office. Ordinarily, however, stepping down from an administrative post such as chief judge, judicial-council member, or court-committee chair does not constitute an event rendering unnecessary any further action on a complaint alleging judicial misconduct. Breyer Committee Report, 239 F.R.D. at 245. As long as the

subject of a complaint performs judicial duties, a complaint alleging judicial misconduct must be addressed. *Id.*

If a complaint is not disposed of pursuant to Rule 11(c), (d), or (e), a special committee must be appointed. Rule 11(f) states that a subject judge must be invited to respond to the complaint before a special committee is appointed, if no earlier response was invited.

Subject judges, of course, receive copies of complaints at the same time that they are referred to the chief judge, and they are free to volunteer responses to them. Under Rule 11(b), the chief judge may request a response if it is thought necessary. However, many complaints are clear candidates for dismissal even if their allegations are accepted as true, and there is no need for the subject judge to devote time to a defense.

The Act requires that the order dismissing a complaint or concluding a proceeding contain a statement of reasons and that a copy of the order be sent to the complainant. 28 U.S.C. § 352(b). Rule 24, dealing with availability of information to the public, contemplates that the order will be made public, usually without disclosing the names of the complainant or the subject judge. If desired for administrative purposes, more identifying information can be included in a non-public version of the order.

When a complaint is disposed of by the chief judge, the statutory purposes are best served by providing the complainant with a full, particularized, but concise explanation, giving reasons for the conclusions reached. *See also* Commentary on Rule 24 (dealing with public availability).

Rule 11(g) provides that the complainant and the subject judge must be notified, in the case of a disposition by the chief judge, of the right to petition the judicial council for review. Because an identified complaint has no "complainant" to petition for review, the chief judge's dispositive order on such a complaint will be transmitted to the judicial council for review. The same will apply where a complaint was filed by its subject judge. A copy of the chief judge's order, and memoranda incorporated by reference in the order, disposing of a complaint must be sent by the circuit clerk to the Committee on Judicial Conduct and Disability.

ARTICLE IV. INVESTIGATION AND REPORT BY SPECIAL COMMITTEE

RULE 12. SPECIAL COMMITTEE'S COMPOSITION

(a) Membership. Except as provided in (e), a special committee appointed under Rule 11(f) must consist of the chief judge and equal numbers of circuit and district judges. These judges may include senior judges. If the complaint is about a district judge, bankruptcy judge, or magistrate judge, then, when possible, the district-judge members of the special committee must be from districts other than the district of the subject judge. For the courts named in 28 U.S.C. § 363, the special committee must be selected from the judges serving on the subject judge's court.

(b) Presiding Officer. When appointing the special committee, the chief judge may serve as the presiding officer or else must designate a committee member as the presiding officer.

(c) Bankruptcy Judge or Magistrate Judge as Adviser. If the subject judge is a bankruptcy judge or magistrate judge, he or she may, within 14 days after being notified of the special committee's appointment, ask the chief judge to designate as a committee adviser another bankruptcy judge or

magistrate judge, as the case may be. The chief judge must grant such a request but may otherwise use discretion in naming the adviser. Unless the adviser is a Court of Federal Claims special master appointed under 42 U.S.C. § 300aa–12(c), the adviser must be from a district other than the district of the subject bankruptcy judge or subject magistrate judge. The adviser cannot vote but has the other privileges of a special-committee member.

(d) Provision of Documents. The chief judge must certify to each other member of the special committee and to any adviser copies of the complaint and statement of facts, in whole or relevant part, and any other relevant documents on file.

(e) Continuing Qualification of Special–Committee Member. A member of a special committee may continue to serve on the committee even though the member relinquishes the position of chief judge, active circuit judge, or active district judge, as the case may be, but only if the member continues to hold office under Article III, Section 1, of the Constitution of the United States, or under 28 U.S.C. § 171.

(f) Inability of Special–Committee Member to Complete Service. If a member of a special committee can no longer serve because of death, disability, disqualification, resignation, retirement from office, or other reason, the chief judge must decide whether to appoint a replacement member, either a circuit or district judge as needed under (a). No special committee appointed under these Rules may function with only a single member, and the votes of a two-member committee must be unanimous.

(g) Voting. All actions by a special committee must be by vote of a majority of all members of the committee.

[Adopted March 11, 2008, effective April 10, 2008. Amended effective September 17, 2015.]

Commentary on Rule 12

This Rule is adapted from the Act and the Illustrative Rules.

Rule 12 leaves the size of a special committee flexible, to be determined on a case-by-case basis. The question of the size of a special committee is one that should be weighed with care in view of the potential for consuming the members' time; a large committee should be appointed only if there is a special reason to do so. Rule 12(a) acknowledges the common practice of including senior judges in the membership of a special committee.

Although the Act requires that the chief judge be a member of each special committee, 28 U.S.C. § 353(a)(1), it does not require that the chief judge preside. Accordingly, Rule 12(b) provides that if the chief judge does not preside, he or she must designate another member of the special committee as the presiding officer.

Rule 12(c) provides that the chief judge must appoint a bankruptcy judge or magistrate judge as an adviser to a special committee at the request of a bankruptcy or magistrate subject judge. Subsection (c) also provides that the adviser will have all the privileges of a member of the special committee except a vote. The adviser, therefore, may participate in all deliberations of the special committee, question witnesses at hearings, and write a separate statement to accompany the committee's report to the judicial council.

Rule 12(e) provides that a member of a special committee who remains an Article III judge may continue to serve on the committee even though the member's status otherwise changes. Thus, a special committee that originally consisted of the chief judge and an equal number of circuit and district judges, as required by the law, may continue to function even though changes of status alter that composition. This provision reflects the belief that stability of membership will contribute to the quality of the work of such committees.

Stability of membership is also the principal concern animating Rule 12(f), which deals with the case in which a special committee loses a member before its work is complete. The Rule permits the chief judge to determine whether a replacement member should be appointed. Generally, appointment of a replacement member is desirable in these situations unless the special committee has conducted evidentiary hearings before the vacancy occurs. However, cases may arise in which a special committee is in the late stages of its work, and in which it would be difficult for a new member to play a meaningful role. The Rule also preserves the collegial character of the special-committee process by prohibiting a single surviving member from serving as a committee and by providing that a committee of two surviving members will, in essence, operate under a unanimity rule.

Rule 12(g) provides that actions of a special committee must be by vote of a majority of all the members. All the members of a special committee should participate in committee decisions. In that circumstance, it seems reasonable to require that special-committee decisions be made by a majority of the membership, rather than a majority of some smaller quorum.

RULE 13. CONDUCT OF SPECIAL–COMMITTEE INVESTIGATION

(a) Extent and Methods of Special–Committee Investigation. A special committee should determine the appropriate extent and methods of its investigation in light of the allegations of the complaint and its preliminary inquiry. The investigation may include use of appropriate experts or other professionals. If, in the course of the investigation, the special committee has cause to believe that the subject judge may have engaged in misconduct or has a disability that is beyond the scope of the complaint, the committee must refer the new matter to the chief judge for a determination of whether action under Rule 5 or Rule 11 is necessary before the committee's investigation is expanded to include the new matter.

(b) Criminal Conduct. If the special committee's investigation concerns conduct that may be a crime, the committee must consult with the appropriate prosecutorial authorities to the extent permitted by the Act to avoid compromising any criminal investigation. The special committee has final authority over the timing and extent of its investigation and the formulation of its recommendations.

(c) Staff. The special committee may arrange for staff assistance to conduct the investigation. It may use existing staff of the Judiciary or may hire special staff through the Director of the Administrative Office of the United States Courts.

(d) Delegation of Subpoena Power; Contempt. The chief judge may delegate the authority to exercise the subpoena powers of the special committee. The judicial council or special committee may institute a contempt proceeding under 28 U.S.C. § 332(d) against anyone who fails to comply with a subpoena.

[Adopted March 11, 2008, effective April 10, 2008. Amended effective September 17, 2015.]

Commentary on Rule 13

This Rule is adapted from the Illustrative Rules.

Rule 13, as well as Rules 14, 15, and 16, are concerned with the way in which the special committee carries out its mission. They reflect the view that the special committee has two roles that are separated in ordinary litigation. First, the special committee has an investigative role of the kind that is characteristically left to executive branch agencies or discovery by civil litigants. 28 U.S.C. § 353(c). Second, it has a formalized fact-finding and recommendation-of-disposition role that is characteristically left to juries, judges, or arbitrators. *Id.* Rule 13 generally governs the investigative stage. Even though the same body has responsibility for both roles under the Act, it is important to distinguish between them in order to ensure that appropriate rights are afforded at appropriate times to the subject judge.

Rule 13(a) includes a provision making clear that a special committee may choose to consult appropriate experts or other professionals if it determines that such a consultation is warranted. If, for example, the special committee has cause to believe that the subject judge may be unable to discharge all of the duties of office by reason of mental or physical disability, the committee could ask the subject judge to respond to inquiries and, if necessary, request the judge to undergo a medical or psychological examination. In advance of any such examination, the special committee may enter into an agreement with the subject judge as to the scope and use that may be made of the examination results. In addition or in the alternative, the special committee may ask to review existing records, including medical records.

The extent of the subject judge's cooperation in the investigation may be taken into account in the consideration of the underlying complaint. If, for example, the subject judge impedes reasonable efforts to confirm or disconfirm the presence of a disability, the special committee may still consider whether the conduct alleged in the complaint and confirmed in the investigation constitutes disability. The same would be true of a complaint alleging misconduct.

The special committee may also consider whether such a judge might be in violation of his or her duty to cooperate in an investigation under these Rules, a duty rooted not only in the Act's definition of misconduct but also in the Code of Conduct for United States Judges, which emphasizes the need to maintain public confidence in the Judiciary, see Canon 2(A) and Canon 1 cmt., and requires judges to "facilitate the performance of the administrative responsibilities of other judges and court personnel," Canon 3(B)(1). If the special committee finds a breach of the duty to cooperate and believes that the breach may amount to misconduct under Rule 3(h)(1)(H), it should determine, under the final sentence of Rule 13(a), whether that possibility should be referred to the chief judge for consideration of action under Rule 5 or Rule 11. *See also* Commentary on Rule 3.

One of the difficult questions that can arise is the relationship between proceedings under the Act and criminal investigations. Rule 13(b) assigns responsibility for coordination to the special committee in cases in which criminal conduct is suspected, but gives the committee the authority to determine the appropriate pace of its activity in light of any criminal investigation.

Title 28 U.S.C. § 356(a) provides that a special committee will have full subpoena powers as provided in 28 U.S.C. § 332(d). Section 332(d)(1) provides that subpoenas will be issued on behalf of a judicial council by the circuit clerk "at the direction of the chief judge of the circuit or his designee." Rule 13(d) contemplates that, where the chief judge designates someone else as presiding officer of the special committee, the presiding officer also be delegated the authority to direct the circuit clerk to issue subpoenas related to committee proceedings. That is not intended to imply, however, that the decision to use the subpoena power is exercisable by the presiding officer alone. *See* Rule 12(g).

RULE 14. CONDUCT OF SPECIAL– COMMITTEE HEARINGS

(a) Purpose of Hearings. The special committee may hold hearings to take testimony and receive other evidence, to hear argument, or both. If the special committee is investigating allegations against more than one judge, it may hold joint or separate hearings.

(b) Special–Committee Evidence. Subject to Rule 15, the special committee must obtain material, nonredundant evidence in the form it considers appropriate. In the special committee's discretion, evidence may be obtained by committee members, staff, or both. Witnesses offering testimonial evidence may include the complainant and the subject judge.

(c) Counsel for Witnesses. The subject judge has the right to counsel. The special committee has discretion to decide whether other witnesses may have counsel present when they testify.

(d) Witness Fees. Witness fees must be paid as provided in 28 U.S.C. § 1821.

(e) Oath. All testimony taken at a hearing must be given under oath or affirmation.

(f) Rules of Evidence. The Federal Rules of Evidence do not apply to special-committee hearings.

(g) Record and Transcript. A record and transcript must be made of all hearings.

[Adopted March 11, 2008, effective April 10, 2008. Amended effective September 17, 2015.]

Commentary on Rule 14

This Rule is adapted from the Act, 28 U.S.C. § 353, and the Illustrative Rules.

Rule 14 is concerned with the conduct of fact-finding hearings. Special-committee hearings will normally be held only after the investigative work has been completed and the committee has concluded that there is sufficient evidence to warrant a formal fact-finding proceeding. Special-committee proceedings are primarily inquisitorial rather than adversarial. Accordingly, the Federal Rules of Evidence do not apply to such hearings. Inevitably, a hearing will have something of an adversary character. Nevertheless, that tendency should be moderated to the extent possible. Even though a proceeding will commonly have investigative and hearing stages, special-committee members should not regard themselves as prosecutors one day and judges the next. Their duty—and that of their staff—is at all times to be impartial seekers of the truth.

Rule 14(b) contemplates that material evidence will be obtained by the special committee and presented in the form of affidavits, live testimony, etc. Staff or others who are organizing the hearings should regard it as their role to present evidence representing the entire picture. With respect to testimonial evidence, the subject judge should normally be called as a special-committee witness. Cases may arise in which the subject judge will not testify voluntarily. In such cases, subpoena powers are available, subject to the normal testimonial privileges. Although Rule 15(c) recognizes the subject judge's statutory right to call witnesses on his or her own behalf, exercise of this right should not usually be necessary.

RULE 15. SUBJECT JUDGE'S RIGHTS

(a) Notice.

(1) *Generally.* The subject judge must receive written notice of:

(A) the appointment of a special committee under Rule 11(f);

(B) the expansion of the scope of an investigation under Rule 13(a);

(C) any hearing under Rule 14, including its purposes, the names of any witnesses the special committee intends to call, and the text of any statements that have been taken from those witnesses.

(2) *Suggestion of Additional Witnesses.* The subject judge may suggest additional witnesses to the special committee.

(b) Special–Committee Report. The subject judge must be sent a copy of the special committee's report when it is filed with the judicial council.

(c) Presentation of Evidence. At any hearing held under Rule 14, the subject judge has the right to present evidence, to compel the attendance of witnesses, and to compel the production of documents. At the request of the subject judge, the chief judge or the judge's designee must direct the circuit clerk to issue a subpoena to a witness under 28 U.S.C. § 332(d)(1). The subject judge must be given the opportunity to cross-examine special-committee witnesses, in person or by counsel.

(d) Presentation of Argument. The subject judge may submit written argument to the special committee and must be given a reasonable opportunity to present oral argument at an appropriate stage of the investigation.

(e) Attendance at Hearings. The subject judge has the right to attend any hearing held under Rule 14 and to receive copies of the transcript, of any documents introduced, and of any written arguments submitted by the complainant to the special committee.

(f) Representation by Counsel. The subject judge may choose to be represented by counsel in the exercise of any right enumerated in this Rule. As provided in Rule 20(e), the United States may bear the costs of the representation.

[Adopted March 11, 2008, effective April 10, 2008. Amended effective September 17, 2015.]

Commentary on Rule 15

This Rule is adapted from the Act and the Illustrative Rules.

The Act states that these Rules must contain provisions requiring that "the judge whose conduct is the subject of a complaint ... be afforded an opportunity to appear (in person or by counsel) at proceedings conducted by the investigating panel, to present oral and documentary evidence, to compel the attendance of witnesses or the production of documents, to cross-examine witnesses, and to present argument orally or in writing." 28 U.S.C. § 358(b)(2). To implement this provision, Rule 15(e) gives the subject judge the right to attend any hearing held for the purpose of receiving evidence of record or hearing argument under Rule 14.

The Act does not require that the subject judge be permitted to attend all proceedings of the special committee. Accordingly, the Rules do not give a right to attend other proceedings—for example, meetings at which the special committee is engaged in investigative activity, such as interviewing persons to learn whether they ought to be called as witnesses or examining for relevance purposes documents delivered pursuant to a subpoena duces tecum, or meetings in which the committee is deliberating on the evidence or its recommendations.

RULE 16. COMPLAINANT'S RIGHTS IN INVESTIGATION

(a) Notice. The complainant must receive written notice of the investigation as provided in Rule 11(g)(1). When the special committee's report to the judicial council is filed, the complainant must be notified of the filing. The judicial council may, in its discretion, provide a copy of the report of a special committee to the complainant.

(b) Opportunity to Provide Evidence. If the complainant knows of relevant evidence not already before the special committee, the complainant may briefly explain in writing the basis of that knowledge and the nature of that evidence. If the special committee determines that the complainant has information not already known to the committee that would assist in the committee's investigation, a representative of the committee must interview the complainant.

(c) Presentation of Argument. The complainant may submit written argument to the special committee. In its discretion, the special committee may permit the complainant to offer oral argument.

(d) Representation by Counsel. A complainant may submit written argument through counsel and, if permitted to offer oral argument, may do so through counsel.

(e) Cooperation. In exercising its discretion under this Rule, the special committee may take into account the degree of the complainant's cooperation in preserving the confidentiality of the proceedings, including the identity of the subject judge.

[Adopted March 11, 2008, effective April 10, 2008. Amended effective September 17, 2015.]

Commentary on Rule 16

This Rule is adapted from the Act and the Illustrative Rules.

In accordance with the view of the process as fundamentally administrative and inquisitorial, these Rules do not give the complainant the rights of a party to litigation and leave the complainant's role largely to the discretion of the special committee. However, Rule 16(b) gives the complainant the prerogative to make a brief written submission showing that he or she is aware of relevant evidence not already known to the special committee. (Such a submission may precede any written or oral argument the complainant provides under Rule 16(c), or it may accompany that argument.) If the special committee determines, independently or from the complainant's submission, that the complainant has information that would assist the committee in its investigation, the complainant must be interviewed by a representative of the committee. Such an interview may be in person or by telephone, and the representative of the special committee may be either a member or staff.

Rule 16 does not contemplate that the complainant will ordinarily be permitted to attend proceedings of the special committee except when testifying or presenting oral argument. A special committee may exercise its discretion to permit the complainant to be present at its proceedings, or to permit the complainant, individually or through counsel, to participate in the examination or cross-examination of witnesses.

The Act authorizes an exception to the normal confidentiality provisions where the judicial council in its discretion provides a copy of the report of the special committee to the complainant and to the subject judge. 28 U.S.C. § 360(a)(1). However, the Rules do not entitle the complainant to a copy of the special committee's report.

In exercising their discretion regarding the role of the complainant, the special committee and the judicial council should protect the confidentiality of the complaint process. As a consequence, subsection (e) provides that the special committee may consider the degree to which a complainant has cooperated in preserving the confidentiality of the proceedings in determining what role beyond the minimum required by these Rules should be given to that complainant.

RULE 17. SPECIAL–COMMITTEE REPORT

The special committee must file with the judicial council a comprehensive report of its investigation, including findings and recommendations for council action. The report must be accompanied by a statement of the vote by which it was adopted, any separate or dissenting statements of special-committee members, and the record of any hearings held under Rule 14. In addition to being sent to the subject judge under Rule 15(b), a copy of the report and any accompanying statements and documents must be sent to the Committee on Judicial Conduct and Disability.

[Adopted March 11, 2008, effective April 10, 2008. Amended effective September 17, 2015.]

Commentary on Rule 17

This Rule is adapted from the Illustrative Rules and is self-explanatory. The provision for sending a copy of the special-committee report and accompanying statements and documents to the Committee on Judicial Conduct and Disability is new.

ARTICLE V.   REVIEW BY JUDICIAL COUNCIL

RULE 18.   PETITION FOR REVIEW OF CHIEF-JUDGE DISPOSITION UNDER RULE 11(c), (d), OR (e)

(a) Petition for Review. After the chief judge issues an order under Rule 11(c), (d), or (e), the complainant or the subject judge may petition the judicial council of the circuit to review the order. By rules promulgated under 28 U.S.C. § 358, the judicial council may refer a petition for review filed under this Rule to a panel of no fewer than five members of the council, at least two of whom must be district judges.

(b) When to File; Form; Where to File. A petition for review must be filed in the office of the circuit clerk within 42 days after the date of the chief judge's order. The petition for review should be in letter form, addressed to the circuit clerk, and in an envelope marked "Misconduct Petition" or "Disability Petition." The name of the subject judge must not be shown on the envelope. The petition for review should be typewritten or otherwise legible. It should begin with "I hereby petition the judicial council for review of . . ." and state the reasons why the petition should be granted. It must be signed.

(c) Receipt and Distribution of Petition. A circuit clerk who receives a petition for review filed in accordance with this Rule must:

(1) acknowledge its receipt and send a copy to the complainant or subject judge, as the case may be;

(2) promptly distribute to each member of the judicial council, or its relevant panel, except for any member disqualified under Rule 25, or make available in the manner provided by local rule, the following materials:

(A) copies of the complaint;

(B) all materials obtained by the chief judge in connection with the inquiry;

(C) the chief judge's order disposing of the complaint;

(D) any memorandum in support of the chief judge's order;

(E) the petition for review; and

(F) an appropriate ballot; and

(3) send the petition for review to the Committee on Judicial Conduct and Disability. Unless the Committee on Judicial Conduct and Disability requests them, the circuit clerk will not send copies of the materials obtained by the chief judge.

(d) Untimely Petition. The circuit clerk must refuse to accept a petition that is received after the time allowed in (b).

(e) Timely Petition Not in Proper Form. When the circuit clerk receives a petition for review filed within the time allowed but in a form that is improper to a degree that would substantially impair its consideration by the judicial council— such as a document that is ambiguous about whether it is intended to be a petition for review—the circuit clerk must acknowledge its receipt, call the filer's attention to the deficiencies, and give the filer the opportunity to correct the deficiencies within the original time allowed for filing the petition or within 21 days after the date on which a notice of the deficiencies was sent to the complainant, whichever is later. If the deficiencies are corrected within the time allowed, the circuit clerk will proceed according to paragraphs (a) and (c) of this Rule. If the deficiencies are not corrected, the circuit clerk must reject the petition.

[Adopted March 11, 2008, effective April 10, 2008. Amended effective September 17, 2015.]

Commentary on Rule 18

Rule 18 is adapted largely from the Illustrative Rules.

Subsection (a) permits the subject judge, as well as the complainant, to petition for review of the chief judge's order dismissing a complaint under Rule 11(c), or concluding that appropriate corrective action or intervening events have remedied or mooted the problems raised by the complaint pursuant to Rule 11(d) or (e). Although the subject judge may ostensibly be vindicated by the dismissal or conclusion of a complaint, the chief judge's order may include language disagreeable to the subject judge. For example, an order may dismiss a complaint, but state that the subject judge did in fact engage in misconduct. Accordingly, a subject judge may wish to object to the content of the order and is given the opportunity to petition the judicial council of the circuit for review.

Subsection (b) contains a time limit of 42 days to file a petition for review. It is important to establish a time limit on petitions for review of chief judges' dispositions in order to provide finality to the process. If the complaint requires an investigation, the investigation should proceed; if it does not, the subject judge should know that the matter is closed.

The standards for timely filing under the Federal Rules of Appellate Procedure should be applied to petitions for review. *See* Fed. R. App. P. 25(a)(2)(A), (C).

Rule 18(e) provides for an automatic extension of the time limit imposed under subsection (b) if a person files a petition that is rejected for failure to comply with formal requirements.

RULE 19.   JUDICIAL-COUNCIL DISPOSITION OF PETITION FOR REVIEW

(a) Rights of Subject Judge. At any time after a complainant files a petition for review, the subject judge may file a written response with the circuit clerk. The circuit clerk must promptly distribute copies of the response to each member of the judicial council or of the relevant panel, unless that member is disqualified under Rule 25. Copies must also be distributed to the chief judge, to the complainant, and to the Committee on Judicial Conduct and Disability. The subject judge must not otherwise communicate with individual judicial-council members about the matter. The subject judge must be given copies of any communications to the judicial council from the complainant.

(b) Judicial–Council Action. After considering a petition for review and the materials before it, the judicial council may:

(1) affirm the chief judge's disposition by denying the petition;

(2) return the matter to the chief judge with directions to conduct a further inquiry under Rule 11(b) or to identify a complaint under Rule 5;

(3) return the matter to the chief judge with directions to appoint a special committee under Rule 11(f); or

(4) in exceptional circumstances, take other appropriate action.

(c) Notice of Judicial–Council Decision. Copies of the judicial council's order, together with memoranda incorporated by reference in the order and separate concurring or dissenting statements, must be given to the complainant, the subject judge, and the Committee on Judicial Conduct and Disability.

(d) Memorandum of Judicial–Council Decision. If the judicial council's order affirms the chief judge's disposition, a supporting memorandum must be prepared only if the council concludes that there is a need to supplement the chief judge's explanation. A memorandum supporting a judicial-council order must not include the name of the complainant or the subject judge.

(e) Review of Judicial–Council Decision. If the judicial council's decision is adverse to the petitioner, and if no member of the council dissented, the complainant must be notified that he or she has no right to seek review of the decision. If there was a dissent, the petitioner must be informed that he or she can file a petition for review under Rule 21(b).

(f) Public Availability of Judicial–Council Decision. Materials related to the judicial council's decision must be made public to the extent, at the time, and in the manner set forth in Rule 24.

[Adopted March 11, 2008, effective April 10, 2008. Amended effective September 17, 2015.]

Commentary on Rule 19

This Rule is adapted largely from the Act and is self-explanatory.

The judicial council should ordinarily review the decision of the chief judge on the merits, treating the petition for review for all practical purposes as an appeal. The judicial council may respond to a petition for review by affirming the chief judge's order, remanding the matter, or, in exceptional cases, taking other appropriate action. A petition for review of a judicial council's decision may be filed under Rule 21(b) in any matter in which one or more members of the council dissented from the order.

RULE 20. JUDICIAL–COUNCIL ACTION FOLLOWING APPOINTMENT OF SPECIAL COMMITTEE

(a) Subject Judge's Rights. Within 21 days after the filing of the report of a special committee, the subject judge may send a written response to the members of the judicial council. The subject judge must also be given an opportunity to present argument, personally or through counsel, written or oral, as determined by the judicial council. The subject judge must not otherwise communicate with judicial-council members about the matter.

(b) Judicial–Council Action.

(1) *Discretionary Actions.* Subject to the subject judge's rights set forth in subsection (a), the judicial council may:

(A) dismiss the complaint because:

(i) even if the claim is true, the claimed conduct is not conduct prejudicial to the effective and expeditious administration of the business of the courts and does not indicate a mental or physical disability resulting in inability to discharge the duties of office;

(ii) the complaint is directly related to the merits of a decision or procedural ruling;

(iii) the facts on which the complaint is based have not been established; or

(iv) the complaint is otherwise not appropriate for consideration under 28 U.S.C. §§ 351–364.

(B) conclude the proceeding because appropriate corrective action has been taken or intervening events have made the proceeding unnecessary.

(C) refer the complaint to the Judicial Conference with the judicial council's recommendations for action.

(D) take remedial action to ensure the effective and expeditious administration of the business of the courts, including:

(i) censuring or reprimanding the subject judge, either by private communication or by public announcement;

(ii) ordering that no new cases be assigned to the subject judge for a limited, fixed period;

(iii) in the case of a magistrate judge, ordering the chief judge of the district court to take action specified by the council, including the initiation of removal proceedings under 28 U.S.C. § 631(i) or 42 U.S.C. § 300aa–12(c)(2);

(iv) in the case of a bankruptcy judge, removing the judge from office under 28 U.S.C. § 152(e);

(v) in the case of a circuit or district judge, requesting the judge to retire voluntarily with the provision (if necessary) that ordinary length-of-service requirements be waived;

(vi) in the case of a circuit or district judge who is eligible to retire but does not do so, certifying the disability of the judge under 28 U.S.C. § 372(b) so that an additional judge may be appointed; and

(vii) in the case of a circuit chief judge or district chief judge, finding that the judge is temporarily unable to perform chief-judge duties, with the result that those duties devolve to the next eligible judge in accordance with 28 U.S.C. § 45(d) or § 136(e).

(E) take any combination of actions described in (b)(1)(A)–(D) of this Rule that is within its power.

(2) *Mandatory Actions.* A judicial council must refer a complaint to the Judicial Conference if the council determines that a circuit judge or district judge may have engaged in conduct that:

(A) might constitute ground for impeachment; or

(B) in the interest of justice, is not amenable to resolution by the judicial council.

(c) Inadequate Basis for Decision. If the judicial council finds that a special committee's report, recommendations, and record provide an inadequate basis for decision, it may return the matter to the committee for further investigation and a new report, or it may conduct further investigation. If the judicial council decides to conduct further investigation, the subject judge must be given adequate prior notice in writing of that decision and of the general scope and purpose of the additional investigation. The judicial council's conduct of the additional investigation must generally accord with the procedures and powers set forth in Rules 13 through 16 for the conduct of an investigation by a special committee.

(d) Judicial–Council Vote. Judicial-council action must be taken by a majority of those members of the council who are not disqualified. A decision to remove a bankruptcy judge from office requires a majority vote of all the members of the judicial council.

(e) Recommendation for Fee Reimbursement. If the complaint has been finally dismissed or concluded under (b)(1)(A) or (B) of this Rule, and if the subject judge so requests, the judicial council may recommend that the Director of the Administrative Office use funds appropriated to the Judiciary to reimburse the judge for reasonable expenses incurred during the investigation, when those expenses would not have been incurred but for the requirements of the Act and these Rules. Reasonable expenses include attorneys' fees and expenses related to a successful defense or prosecution of a proceeding under Rule 21(a) or (b).

(f) Judicial–Council Order. Judicial-council action must be by written order. Unless the judicial council finds that extraordinary reasons would make it contrary to the interests of justice, the order must be accompanied by a memorandum setting forth the factual determinations on which it is based and the reasons for the council action. Such a memorandum may incorporate all or part of any underlying special-committee report. If the complaint was initiated by identification under Rule 5, the memorandum must so indicate. The order and memoranda incorporated by reference in the order must be provided to the complainant, the subject judge, and the Committee on Judicial Conduct and Disability. The complainant and the subject judge must be notified of any right to review of the judicial council's decision as provided in Rule 21(b). If the complaint was identified under Rule 5 or filed by its subject judge, the judicial council must transmit the order and memoranda incorporated by reference in the order to the Committee on Judicial Conduct and Disability for review in accordance with Rule 21. In the event of such a transmission, the subject judge may make a written submission to the

Committee on Judicial Conduct and Disability but will have no further right of review.

[Adopted March 11, 2008, effective April 10, 2008. Amended effective September 17, 2015.]

Commentary on Rule 20

This Rule is largely adapted from the Illustrative Rules.

Rule 20(a) provides that within 21 days after the filing of the report of a special committee, the subject judge may address a written response to all of the members of the judicial council. The subject judge must also be given an opportunity to present argument to the judicial council, personally or through counsel, or both, at the direction of the council. Whether that argument is written or oral would be for the judicial council to determine. The subject judge may not otherwise communicate with judicial-council members about the matter.

Rule 20(b)(1)(D) recites the remedial actions enumerated in 28 U.S.C. § 354(a)(2) while making clear that this list is not exhaustive. A judicial council may consider lesser remedies. Some remedies may be unique to senior judges, whose caseloads can be modified by agreement or through statutory designation and certification processes.

Under 28 U.S.C. §§ 45(d) and 136(e), which provide for succession where "a chief judge is temporarily unable to perform his duties as such," the determination whether such an inability exists is not expressly reserved to the chief judge. Nor, indeed, is it assigned to any particular judge or court-governance body. Clearly, however, a chief judge's inability to function as chief could implicate "the effective and expeditious administration of justice," which the judicial council of the circuit must, under 28 U.S.C. § 332(d)(1), "make all necessary and appropriate orders" to secure. For this reason, such reassignment is among a judicial council's remedial options, as subsection (b)(1)(D)(vii) makes clear. Consistent with 28 U.S.C. §§ 45(d) and 136(e), however, any reassignment of chief-judge duties must not outlast the subject judge's inability to perform them. Nor can such reassignment result in any extension of the subject judge's term as chief judge.

Rule 20(c) provides that if the judicial council decides to conduct an additional investigation, the subject judge must be given adequate prior notice in writing of that decision and of the general scope and purpose of the additional investigation. The conduct of the investigation will be generally in accordance with the procedures set forth in Rules 13 through 16 for the conduct of an investigation by a special committee. However, if hearings are held, the judicial council may limit testimony or the presentation of evidence to avoid unnecessary repetition of testimony and evidence before the special committee.

Rule 20(d) provides that judicial-council action must be taken by a majority of those members of the council who are not disqualified, except that a decision to remove a bankruptcy judge from office requires a majority of all the members of the council as required by 28 U.S.C. § 152(e). However, it is inappropriate to apply a similar rule to the less severe actions that a judicial council may take under the Act. If some members of the judicial council are disqualified in the matter, their disqualification should not be given the effect of a vote against council action.

With regard to Rule 20(e), the judicial council, on the request of the subject judge, may recommend to the Director of the Administrative Office that the subject judge be reimbursed for reasonable expenses incurred, including attorneys' fees. The judicial council has the authority to recommend such reimbursement where, after investigation by a special committee, the complaint has been finally dismissed or concluded under subsection (b)(1)(A) or (B) of this Rule. It is contemplated that such reimbursement may be provided for the successful prosecution or defense of a proceeding under Rule 21(a) or (b), in other words, one that results in a Rule 20(b)(1)(A) or (B) dismissal or conclusion.

Rule 20(f) requires that judicial-council action be by order and, normally, that it be supported with a memorandum of factual determinations and reasons. Notice of the action must be given to the complainant and the subject judge, and must include notice of any right to petition for review of the judicial council's decision under Rule 21(b). Because an identified complaint has no "complainant" to peti-

tion for review, a judicial council's dispositive order on an identified complaint on which a special committee has been appointed must be transmitted to the Committee on Judicial Conduct and Disability for review. The same will apply where a complaint was filed by its subject judge.

ARTICLE VI. REVIEW BY COMMITTEE ON JUDICIAL CONDUCT AND DISABILITY

RULE 21. COMMITTEE ON JUDICIAL CONDUCT AND DISABILITY

(a) **Committee Review.** The Committee on Judicial Conduct and Disability, consisting of seven members, considers and disposes of all petitions for review under (b) of this Rule, in conformity with the Committee's jurisdictional statement. Its review of judicial-council orders is for errors of law, clear errors of fact, or abuse of discretion. Its disposition of petitions for review is ordinarily final. The Judicial Conference may, in its sole discretion, review any such Committee decision, but a complainant or subject judge does not have a right to this review.

(b) **Reviewable Matters.**

(1) *Upon Petition.* A complainant or subject judge may petition the Committee for review of a judicial-council order entered in accordance with:

(A) Rule 20(b)(1)(A), (B), (D), or (E); or

(B) Rule 19(b)(1) or (4) if one or more members of the judicial council dissented from the order.

(2) *Upon Committee's Initiative.* At its initiative and in its sole discretion, the Committee may review any judicial-council order entered under Rule 19(b)(1) or (4), but only to determine whether a special committee should be appointed. Before undertaking the review, the Committee must invite that judicial council to explain why it believes the appointment of a special committee is unnecessary, unless the reasons are clearly stated in the council's order denying the petition for review. If the Committee believes that it would benefit from a submission by the subject judge, it may issue an appropriate request. If the Committee determines that a special committee should be appointed, the Committee must issue a written decision giving its reasons.

(c) **Committee Vote.** Any member of the Committee from the same circuit as the subject judge is disqualified from considering or voting on a petition for review related to that subject judge. Committee decisions under (b) of this Rule must be by majority vote of the qualified Committee members. Those members hearing the petition for review should serve in that capacity until final disposition of the petition, whether or not their term of Committee membership has ended. If only six members are qualified to consider a petition for review, the Chief Justice shall select an additional judge to join the qualified members to consider the petition. If four or fewer members are qualified to consider a petition for review, the Chief Justice shall select a panel of five judges, including the qualified Committee members, to consider it.

(d) **Additional Investigation.** Except in extraordinary circumstances, the Committee will not conduct an additional investigation. The Committee may return the matter to the judicial council with directions to undertake an additional investigation. If the Committee conducts an additional investigation, it will exercise the powers of the Judicial Conference under 28 U.S.C. § 331.

(e) **Oral Argument; Personal Appearance.** There is ordinarily no oral argument or personal appearance before the Committee. In its discretion, the Committee may permit written submissions.

(f) **Committee Decision.** A Committee decision under this Rule must be transmitted promptly to the Judicial Conference. Other distribution will be by the Administrative Office at the direction of the Committee chair.

(g) **Finality.** All orders of the Judicial Conference or of the Committee (when the Conference does not exercise its power of review) are final.

[Adopted March 11, 2008, effective April 10, 2008. Amended effective September 17, 2015.]

Commentary on Rule 21

This Rule is largely self-explanatory.

Rule 21(a) is intended to clarify that the delegation of power to the Committee on Judicial Conduct and Disability to dispose of petitions for review does not preclude review of such dispositions by the Judicial Conference. However, there is no right to such review in any party.

Rules 21(b)(1)(B) and (b)(2) are intended to fill a jurisdictional gap as to review of a dismissal or a conclusion of a complaint under Rule 19(b)(1) or (4). Where one or more members of a judicial council reviewing a petition have dissented, the complainant or the subject judge has the right to petition for review by the Committee. Under Rule 21(b)(2), the Committee may review such a dismissal or conclusion in its sole discretion, whether or not a dissent occurred, and only as to the appointment of a special committee. Any review under Rule 21(b)(2) will be conducted as soon as practicable after the dismissal or conclusion at issue. No party has a right to such review, and such review will be rare.

Rule 21(c) provides for review only by Committee members from circuits other than that of the subject judge. The Rule provides that every petition for review must be considered and voted on by at least five, and if possible by seven, qualified Committee members to avoid the possibility of tie votes. If six, or four or fewer, members are qualified, the Chief Justice shall appoint other judges to join the qualified members to consider the petition for review. To the extent possible, the judges whom the Chief Justice selects to join the qualified members should be drawn from among former members of the Committee.

Under this Rule, all Committee decisions are final in that they are unreviewable unless the Judicial Conference, in its discretion, decides to review a decision. Committee decisions, however, do not necessarily constitute final action on a complaint for purposes of Rule 24.

RULE 22. PROCEDURES FOR REVIEW

(a) **Filing Petition for Review.** A petition for review of a judicial-council decision on a complaint referred to a special committee may be filed by sending a brief written statement to the Committee on Judicial Conduct and Disability at JCD_PetitionforReview@ao.uscourts.gov or to:

> Judicial Conference Committee on Judicial Conduct and Disability
> Attn: Office of General Counsel
> Administrative Office of the United States Courts
> One Columbus Circle, NE
> Washington, D.C. 20544

The Administrative Office will send a copy of the petition for review to the complainant or subject judge, as the case may be.

(b) **Form and Contents of Petition.** No particular form is required. The petition for review must contain a short statement of the basic facts underlying the complaint, the history of its consideration before the appropriate judicial council, a copy of the council's decision, and the grounds on which the petitioner seeks review. The petition for review must specify the date and docket number of the judicial council order for which review is sought. The petitioner may attach any documents or correspondence arising in the course of the proceeding before the judicial council or its special committee. A petition for review should not normally exceed 20 pages plus necessary attachments. A petition for review must be signed by the petitioner or his or her attorney.

(c) **Time.** A petition for review must be submitted within 42 days after the date of the order for which review is sought.

(d) **Action on Receipt of Petition.** When a petition for review of a judicial-council decision on a complaint referred to a special committee is submitted in accordance with this Rule, the Administrative Office shall acknowledge its receipt, notify the chair of the Committee on Judicial Conduct and Disability, and distribute the petition to the members of the Committee for their deliberation.

[Adopted March 11, 2008, effective April 10, 2008. Amended effective September 17, 2015.]

Commentary on Rule 22

Rule 22 is self-explanatory.

ARTICLE VII. MISCELLANEOUS RULES

RULE 23. CONFIDENTIALITY

(a) **General Rule.** The consideration of a complaint by a chief judge, a special committee, a judicial council, or the Committee on Judicial Conduct and Disability is confidential. Information about this consideration must not be disclosed by any judge or employee of the Judiciary or by any person who records or transcribes testimony except as allowed by these Rules. A chief judge may disclose the existence of a proceeding under these Rules when necessary or appropriate to maintain public confidence in the Judiciary's ability to redress misconduct or disability.

(b) **Files.** All files related to a complaint must be separately maintained with appropriate security precautions to ensure confidentiality.

(c) **Disclosure in Decisions.** Except as otherwise provided in Rule 24, written decisions of a chief judge, a judicial council, or the Committee on Judicial Conduct and Disability, and dissenting opinions or separate statements of members of a council or the Committee may contain information and exhibits that the authors consider appropriate for inclusion, and the information and exhibits may be made public.

(d) **Availability to Judicial Conference.** On request of the Judicial Conference or its Committee on Judicial Conduct and Disability, the circuit clerk must furnish any requested records related to a complaint. For auditing purposes, the circuit clerk must provide access to the Committee on Judicial Conduct and Disability to records of proceedings under the Act at the site where the records are kept.

(e) **Availability to District Court.** If the judicial council directs the initiation of proceedings for removal of a magistrate judge under Rule 20(b)(1)(D)(iii), the circuit clerk must provide to the chief judge of the district court copies of the report of the special committee and any other documents and records that were before the council at the time of its decision. On request of the chief judge of the district court, the judicial council may authorize release to that chief judge of any other records relating to the investigation.

(f) **Impeachment Proceedings.** If the Judicial Conference determines that consideration of impeachment may be warranted, it must transmit the record of all relevant proceedings to the Speaker of the House of Representatives.

(g) **Subject Judge's Consent.** If both the subject judge and the chief judge consent in writing, any materials from the files may be disclosed to any person. In any such disclosure, the chief judge may require that the identity of the complainant, or of witnesses in an investigation conducted under these Rules, not be revealed.

(h) **Disclosure in Special Circumstances.** The Judicial Conference, its Committee on Judicial Conduct and Disability, or a judicial council may authorize disclosure of information about the consideration of a complaint, including the papers, documents, and transcripts relating to the investigation, to the extent that disclosure is justified by special circumstances and is not prohibited by the Act. Disclosure may be made to judicial researchers engaged in the study or evaluation of experience under the Act and related modes of judicial discipline, but only where the study or evaluation has been specifically approved by the Judicial Conference or by the Committee on Judicial Conduct and Disability. Appropriate steps must be taken to protect the identities of the subject judge, the complainant, and witnesses from public disclosure. Other appropriate safeguards to protect against the dissemination of confidential information may be imposed.

(i) Disclosure of Identity by Subject Judge. Nothing in this Rule precludes the subject judge from acknowledging that he or she is the judge referred to in documents made public under Rule 24.

(j) Assistance and Consultation. Nothing in this Rule prohibits a chief judge, a special committee, a judicial council, or the Judicial Conference or its Committee on Judicial Conduct and Disability, in the performance of any function authorized under the Act or these Rules, from seeking the help of qualified staff or experts or from consulting other judges who may be helpful regarding the performance of that function.

[Adopted March 11, 2008, effective April 10, 2008. Amended effective September 17, 2015.]

Commentary on Rule 23

Rule 23 was adapted from the Illustrative Rules.

The Act applies a rule of confidentiality to "papers, documents, and records of proceedings related to investigations conducted under this chapter" and states that they may not be disclosed "by any person in any proceeding," with enumerated exceptions. 28 U.S.C. § 360(a). Three questions arise: Who is bound by the confidentiality rule, what proceedings are subject to the rule, and who is within the circle of people who may have access to information without breaching the rule?

With regard to the first question, Rule 23(a) provides that judges, employees of the Judiciary, and those persons involved in recording proceedings and preparing transcripts are obliged to respect the confidentiality requirement. This of course includes subject judges who do not consent to identification under Rule 23(i).

With regard to the second question, Rule 23(a) applies the rule of confidentiality broadly to consideration of a complaint at any stage.

With regard to the third question, there is no barrier of confidentiality among a chief judge, a judicial council, the Judicial Conference, and the Committee on Judicial Conduct and Disability. Each may have access to any of the confidential records for use in their consideration of a referred matter, a petition for review, or monitoring the administration of the Act. A district court may have similar access if the judicial council orders the district court to initiate proceedings to remove a magistrate judge from office, and Rule 23(e) so provides.

In extraordinary circumstances, a chief judge may disclose the existence of a proceeding under these Rules. The disclosure of such information in high-visibility or controversial cases is to reassure the public that the Judiciary is capable of redressing judicial misconduct or disability. Moreover, the confidentiality requirement does not prevent the chief judge from "communicat[ing] orally or in writing with . . . [persons] who may have knowledge of the matter" as part of a limited inquiry conducted by the chief judge under Rule 11(b).

Rule 23 recognizes that there must be some exceptions to the Act's confidentiality requirement. For example, the Act requires that certain orders and the reasons for them must be made public. 28 U.S.C. § 360(b). Rule 23(c) makes it explicit that written decisions, as well as dissenting opinions and separate statements, may contain references to information that would otherwise be confidential and that such information may be made public. However, subsection (c) is subject to Rule 24(a), which provides the general rule regarding the public availability of decisions. For example, the name of a subject judge cannot be made public in a decision if disclosure of the name is prohibited by that Rule.

The Act makes clear that there is a barrier of confidentiality between the judicial branch and the legislative branch. It provides that material may be disclosed to Congress only if it is believed necessary to an impeachment investigation or trial of a judge. 28 U.S.C. § 360(a)(2). Accordingly, Section 355(b) of the Act requires the Judicial Conference to transmit the record of a proceeding to the House of Representatives if the Conference believes that impeachment of a subject judge may be appropriate. Rule 23(f) implements this requirement.

The Act provides that confidential materials may be disclosed if authorized in writing by the subject judge and by the chief judge. 28 U.S.C. § 360(a)(3). Rule 23(g) implements this requirement. Once the subject judge has consented to the disclosure of confidential materials related to a complaint, the chief judge ordinarily will refuse consent only to the extent necessary to protect the confidentiality interests of the complainant or of witnesses who have testified in investigatory proceedings or who have provided information in response to a limited inquiry undertaken pursuant to Rule 11. It will generally be necessary, therefore, for the chief judge to require that the identities of the complainant or of such witnesses, as well as any identifying information, be shielded in any materials disclosed, except insofar as the chief judge has secured the consent of the complainant or of a particular witness to disclosure, or there is a demonstrated need for disclosure of the information that, in the judgment of the chief judge, outweighs the confidentiality interest of the complainant or of a particular witness (as may be the case where the complainant is delusional or where the complainant or a particular witness has already demonstrated a lack of concern about maintaining the confidentiality of the proceedings).

Rule 23(h) permits disclosure of additional information in circumstances not enumerated. For example, disclosure may be appropriate to permit a prosecution for perjury based on testimony given before a special committee. Another example might involve evidence of criminal conduct by a judge discovered by a special committee.

Subsection (h) also permits the authorization of disclosure of information about the consideration of a complaint, including the papers, documents, and transcripts relating to the investigation, to judicial researchers engaged in the study or evaluation of experience under the Act and related modes of judicial discipline. The Rule envisions disclosure of information from the official record of a complaint proceeding to a limited category of persons for appropriately authorized research purposes only, and with appropriate safeguards to protect individual identities in any published research results. In authorizing disclosure, a judicial council may refuse to release particular materials when such release would be contrary to the interests of justice, or when those materials constitute purely internal communications. The Rule does not envision disclosure of purely internal communications between judges and their colleagues and staff.

Under Rule 23(j), any of the specified judges or entities performing a function authorized under these Rules may seek expert or staff assistance or may consult with other judges who may be helpful regarding performance of that function; the confidentiality requirement does not preclude this. A chief judge, for example, may properly seek the advice and assistance of another judge who the chief judge deems to be in the best position to communicate with the subject judge in an attempt to bring about corrective action. As another example, a new chief judge may wish to confer with a predecessor to learn how similar complaints have been handled. In consulting with other judges, of course, a chief judge should disclose information regarding the complaint only to the extent the chief judge deems necessary under the circumstances.

RULE 24. PUBLIC AVAILABILITY OF DECISIONS

(a) General Rule; Specific Cases. When final action has been taken on a complaint and it is no longer subject to review, all orders entered by the chief judge and judicial council, including memoranda incorporated by reference in those orders and any dissenting opinions or separate statements by members of the judicial council, but excluding any orders under Rule 5 or 11(f), must be made public, with the following exceptions:

(1) if the complaint is finally dismissed under Rule 11(c) without the appointment of a special committee, or if it is concluded under Rule 11(d) because of voluntary corrective action, the publicly available materials must not disclose the name of the subject judge without his or her consent.

(2) if the complaint is concluded because of intervening events, or dismissed at any time after a special committee is appointed, the judicial council must determine whether the name of the subject judge should be disclosed.

(3) if the complaint is finally disposed of by a privately communicated censure or reprimand, the publicly available materials must not disclose either the name of the subject judge or the text of the reprimand.

(4) if the complaint is finally disposed of under Rule 20(b)(1)(D) by any action other than private censure or reprimand, the text of the dispositive order must be included in the materials made public, and the name of the subject judge must be disclosed.

(5) the name of the complainant must not be disclosed in materials made public under this Rule unless the chief judge orders disclosure.

(b) Manner of Making Public. The orders described in (a) must be made public by placing them in a publicly accessible file in the office of the circuit clerk and by placing the orders on the court's public website. If the orders appear to have precedential value, the chief judge may cause them to be published. In addition, the Committee on Judicial Conduct and Disability will make available on the Judiciary's website, www.uscourts.gov, selected illustrative orders described in paragraph (a), appropriately redacted, to provide additional information to the public on how complaints are addressed under the Act.

(c) Orders of Committee on Judicial Conduct and Disability. Orders of the Committee on Judicial Conduct and Disability constituting final action in a complaint proceeding arising from a particular circuit will be made available to the public in the office of the circuit clerk of the relevant court of appeals. The Committee on Judicial Conduct and Disability will also make such orders available on the Judiciary's website, www.uscourts.gov. When authorized by the Committee on Judicial Conduct and Disability, other orders related to complaint proceedings will similarly be made available.

(d) Complaint Referred to Judicial Conference. If a complaint is referred to the Judicial Conference under Rule 20(b)(1)(C) or 20(b)(2), materials relating to the complaint will be made public only if ordered by the Judicial Conference.

[Adopted March 11, 2008, effective April 10, 2008. Amended effective September 17, 2015.]

Commentary on Rule 24

Rule 24 is adapted from the Illustrative Rules and the recommendations of the Breyer Committee.

The Act requires the circuits to make available only written orders of a judicial council or the Judicial Conference imposing some form of sanction. 28 U.S.C. § 360(b). The Judicial Conference, however, has long recognized the desirability of public availability of a broader range of orders and other materials. In 1994, the Judicial Conference "urge[d] all circuits and courts covered by the Act to submit to the West Publishing Company, for publication in Federal Reporter 3d, and to Lexis all orders issued pursuant to [the Act] that are deemed by the issuing circuit or court to have significant precedential value to other circuits and courts covered by the Act." Report of the Proceedings of the Judicial Conference of the United States, Mar. 1994, at 28. Following this recommendation, the 2000 revision of the Illustrative Rules contained a public availability provision very similar to Rule 24. In 2002, the Judicial Conference again voted to encourage the circuits "to submit non-routine public orders disposing of complaints of judicial misconduct or disability for publication by on-line and print services." Report of the Proceedings of the Judicial Conference of the United States, Sept. 2002, at 58. The Breyer Committee Report further emphasized that "[p]osting such orders on the judicial branch's public website would not only benefit judges directly, it would also encourage scholarly commentary and analysis of the orders." Breyer Committee Report, 239 F.R.D. at 216. With these considerations in mind, Rule 24 provides for public availability of a wide range of materials.

Rule 24 provides for public availability of orders of a chief judge, a judicial council, and the Committee on Judicial Conduct and Disability, as well as the texts of memoranda incorporated by reference in those orders, together with any dissenting opinions or separate statements by members of the judicial council. No memoranda other than those incorporated by reference in those orders shall be disclosed. However, these orders and memoranda are to be made public only when final action on the complaint has been taken and any right of review has been exhausted. The provision that decisions will be made public only after final action has been taken is designed in part to avoid public disclosure of the existence of pending proceedings. Whether the name of the subject judge is disclosed will then depend on the nature of the final action. If the final action is an order predicated on a finding of misconduct or disability (other than a privately communicated censure or reprimand) the name of the subject judge must be made public. If the final action is dismissal of the complaint, the name of the subject judge must not be disclosed. Rule 24(a)(1) provides that where a proceeding is concluded under Rule 11(d) by the chief judge on the basis of voluntary corrective action, the name of the subject judge must not be disclosed. Shielding the name of the subject judge in this circumstance should encourage informal disposition.

If a complaint is dismissed as moot, or because intervening events have made action on the complaint unnecessary, after appointment of a special committee, Rule 24(a)(2) allows the judicial council to determine whether the subject judge will be identified. In such a case, no final decision has been rendered on the merits, but it may be in the public interest—particularly if a judicial officer resigns in the course of an investigation—to make the identity of the subject judge known.

Once a special committee has been appointed, and a proceeding is concluded by the full judicial council on the basis of a remedial order of the council, Rule 24(a)(4) provides for disclosure of the name of the subject judge.

Rule 24(a)(5) provides that the identity of the complainant will be disclosed only if the chief judge so orders. Identifying the complainant when the subject judge is not identified would increase the likelihood that the identity of the subject judge would become publicly known, thus circumventing the policy of nondisclosure. It may not always be practicable to shield the complainant's identity while making public disclosure of the judicial council's order and supporting memoranda; in some circumstances, moreover, the complainant may consent to public identification.

Rule 24(b) makes clear that circuits must post on their external websites all orders required to be made public under Rule 24(a).

Matters involving orders issued following a special-committee investigation often involve highly sensitive situations, and it is important that judicial councils have every opportunity to reach a correct and just outcome. This would include the ability to reach informal resolution before a subject judge's identity must be released. But there must also come a point of procedural finality. The date of finality—and thus the time at which other safeguards and rules such as the publication requirement are triggered—is the date on which the judicial council issues a Final Order. *See In re Complaint of Judicial Misconduct*, 751 F.3d 611, 617 (2014) (requiring publication of a judicial-council order "[e]ven though the period for review had not yet elapsed" and concluding that "the order was a final decision because the Council had adjudicated the matter on the merits after having received a report from a special investigating committee"). As determined in the cited case, modifications of this kind to a final order are subject to review by the Committee on Judicial Conduct and Disability.

RULE 25. DISQUALIFICATION

(a) **General Rule.** Any judge is disqualified from participating in any proceeding under these Rules if the judge, in his or her discretion, concludes that circumstances warrant disqualification. If a complaint is filed by a judge, that judge is disqualified from participating in any consideration of the complaint except to the extent that these Rules provide for a complainant's participation. A chief judge who has identified a complaint under Rule 5 is not automatically disqualified from considering the complaint.

(b) **Subject Judge.** A subject judge is disqualified from considering a complaint except to the extent that these Rules provide for participation by a subject judge.

(c) **Chief Judge Disqualified From Considering Petition for Review of Chief Judge's Order.** If a petition for review of the chief judge's order entered under Rule 11(c), (d), or (e) is filed with the judicial council in accordance with Rule 18, the chief judge is disqualified from participating in the council's consideration of the petition.

(d) **Member of Special Committee Not Disqualified.** A member of the judicial council who serves on a special committee, including the chief judge, is not disqualified from participating in council consideration of the committee's report.

(e) **Subject Judge's Disqualification After Appointment of Special Committee.** Upon appointment of a special committee, the subject judge is disqualified from participating in the identification or consideration of any complaint, related or unrelated to the pending matter, under the Act or these Rules. The disqualification continues until all proceedings on the complaint against the subject judge are finally terminated with no further right of review.

(f) **Substitute for Disqualified Chief Judge.** If the chief judge is disqualified from performing duties that the Act and these Rules assign to a chief judge, those duties must be assigned to the most-senior active circuit judge not disqualified. If all circuit judges in regular active service are disqualified, the judicial council may determine whether to request a transfer under Rule 26, or, in the interest of sound judicial administration, to permit the chief judge to dispose of the complaint on the merits. Members of the judicial council who are named in the complaint may participate in this determination if necessary to obtain a quorum of the council.

(g) **Judicial–Council Action When Multiple Judges Disqualified.** Notwithstanding any other provision in these Rules to the contrary,

(1) a member of the judicial council who is a subject judge may participate in its disposition if:

(A) participation by one or more subject judges is necessary to obtain a quorum of the judicial council;

(B) the judicial council finds that the lack of a quorum is due to the naming of one or more judges in the complaint for the purpose of disqualifying that judge or those judges, or to the naming of one or more judges based on their participation in a decision excluded from the definition of misconduct under Rule 3(h)(3); and

(C) the judicial council votes that it is necessary, appropriate, and in the interest of sound judicial administration that one or more subject judges be eligible to act.

(2) otherwise disqualified members may participate in votes taken under (g)(1)(B) and (g)(1)(C).

(h) **Disqualification of Members of Committee on Judicial Conduct and Disability.** No member of the Committee on Judicial Conduct and Disability is disqualified from participating in any proceeding under the Act or these Rules because of consultations with a chief judge, a member of a special committee, or a member of a judicial council about the interpretation or application of the Act or these Rules, unless the member believes that the consultation would prevent fair-minded participation.

[Adopted March 11, 2008, effective April 10, 2008. Amended effective September 17, 2015.]

Commentary on Rule 25

Rule 25 is adapted from the Illustrative Rules.

Subsection (a) provides the general rule for disqualification. Of course, a judge is not disqualified simply because the subject judge is on the same court. However, this subsection recognizes that there may be cases in which an appearance of bias or prejudice is created by circumstances other than an association with the subject judge as a colleague. For example, a judge may have a familial relationship with a complainant or subject judge. When such circumstances exist, a judge may, in his or her discretion, conclude that disqualification is warranted.

Subsection (e) makes it clear that the disqualification of the subject judge relates only to the subject judge's participation in any proceeding arising under the Act or these Rules. For example, the subject judge cannot initiate complaints by identification, conduct limited inquiries, or choose between dismissal and special-committee investigation as the threshold disposition of a complaint. Likewise, the subject judge cannot participate in any proceeding arising under the Act or these Rules as a member of any special committee, the judicial council of the circuit, the Judicial Conference, or the Committee on Judicial Conduct and Disability. The Illustrative Rule, based on Section 359(a) of the Act, is ambiguous and could be read to disqualify a subject judge from service of any kind on each of the bodies mentioned. This is undoubtedly not the intent of the Act; such a disqualification would be anomalous in light of the Act's allowing a subject judge to continue to decide cases and to continue to exercise the powers of chief circuit or district judge. It would also create a substantial deterrence to the appointment of special committees, particularly where a special committee is needed solely because the chief judge may not decide matters of credibility in his or her review under Rule 11.

While a subject judge is barred by Rule 25(b) from participating in the disposition of the complaint in which he or she is named, Rule 25(e) recognizes that participation in proceedings arising under the Act or these Rules by a judge who is the subject of a special committee investigation may lead to an appearance of self-interest in creating substantive and procedural precedents governing such proceedings. Rule 25(e) bars such participation.

Under the Act, a complaint against the chief judge is to be handled by "that circuit judge in regular active service next senior in date of commission." 28 U.S.C. § 351(c). The Rules do not purport to prescribe who is to preside over meetings of the judicial council. Consequently, where the presiding member of the judicial council is disqualified from participating under these Rules, the order of precedence prescribed by Rule 25(f) for performing "the duties and responsibilities of the chief circuit judge under these Rules" does not apply to determine the acting presiding member of the council. That is a matter left to the internal rules or operating practices of each judicial council. In most cases the most senior active circuit judge who is a member of the judicial council and who is not disqualified will preside.

Sometimes a single complaint is filed against a large group of judges. If the normal disqualification rules are observed in such a case, no court of appeals judge can serve as acting chief judge of the circuit, and the judicial council will be without appellate members. Where the complaint is against all circuit and district judges, under normal rules no member of the judicial council can perform the duties assigned to the council under the statute.

A similar problem is created by successive complaints arising out of the same underlying grievance. For example, a complainant files a complaint against a district judge based on alleged misconduct, and the complaint is dismissed by the chief judge under the statute. The complainant may then file a complaint against the chief judge for dismissing the first complaint, and when that complaint is dismissed by the next senior judge, still a third complaint may be filed. The threat is that the complainant will bump down the seniority ladder until, once again, there is no member of the court of appeals who can serve as acting chief judge for the purpose of the next complaint. Similarly, complaints involving the merits of litigation may involve a series of decisions in which many judges participated or in which a rehearing en banc was denied by the court of appeals, and the complaint may name a majority of the judicial council as subject judges.

In recognition that these multiple-judge complaints are virtually always meritless, the judicial council is given discretion to determine: (1) whether it is necessary, appropriate, and in the interest of sound judicial administration to permit the chief judge to dispose of a complaint where it would otherwise be impossible for any active circuit judge in the circuit to act, and (2) whether it is necessary, appropriate, and in the interest of sound judicial administration, after appropriate findings as to need and justification are made, to permit subject judges of the judicial council to participate in the disposition of a petition for review where it would otherwise be impossible to obtain a quorum.

Applying a rule of necessity in these situations is consistent with the appearance of justice. See, e.g., In re Complaint of Doe, 2 F.3d 308 (8th Cir. Jud. Council 1993) (invoking the rule of necessity); In re Complaint of Judicial Misconduct, No. 91–80464 (9th Cir. Jud. Council 1992) (same). There is no unfairness in permitting the chief judge to dispose of a patently insubstantial complaint that names all active circuit judges in the circuit.

Similarly, there is no unfairness in permitting subject judges, in these circumstances, to participate in the review of the chief judge's dismissal of an insubstantial complaint. The remaining option is to assign the matter to another body. Among other alternatives, the judicial council may request a transfer of the petition under Rule 26. Given the administrative inconvenience and delay involved in these

alternatives, it is desirable to request a transfer only if the judicial council determines that the petition for review is substantial enough to warrant such action.

In the unlikely event that a quorum of the judicial council cannot be obtained to consider the report of a special committee, it would normally be necessary to request a transfer under Rule 26.

Rule 25(h) recognizes that the jurisdictional statement of the Committee on Judicial Conduct and Disability contemplates consultation between members of the Committee and judicial participants in proceedings under the Act and these Rules. Such consultation should not automatically preclude participation by a member in that proceeding.

RULE 26. TRANSFER TO ANOTHER JUDICIAL COUNCIL

In exceptional circumstances, the chief judge or the judicial council may ask the Chief Justice to transfer a proceeding based on a complaint identified under Rule 5 or filed under Rule 6 to the judicial council of another circuit. The request for a transfer may be made at any stage of the proceeding before a reference to the Judicial Conference under Rule 20(b)(1)(C) or 20(b)(2) or a petition for review is filed under Rule 22. Upon receiving such a request, the Chief Justice may refuse the request or select the transferee judicial council, which may then exercise the powers of a judicial council under these Rules.

[Adopted March 11, 2008, effective April 10, 2008. Amended effective September 17, 2015.]

Commentary on Rule 26

Rule 26 is new; it implements the Breyer Committee's recommended use of transfers. Breyer Committee Report, 239 F.R.D. at 214–15.

Rule 26 authorizes the transfer of a complaint proceeding to another judicial council selected by the Chief Justice. Such transfers may be appropriate, for example, in the case of a serious complaint where there are multiple disqualifications among the original judicial council, where the issues are highly visible and a local disposition may weaken public confidence in the process, where internal tensions arising in the council as a result of the complaint render disposition by a less involved council appropriate, or where a complaint calls into question policies or governance of the home court of appeals. The power to effect a transfer is lodged in the Chief Justice to avoid disputes in a judicial council over where to transfer a sensitive matter and to ensure that the transferee council accepts the matter.

Upon receipt of a transferred proceeding, the transferee judicial council shall determine the proper stage at which to begin consideration of the complaint—for example, reference to the transferee chief judge, appointment of a special committee, etc.

RULE 27. WITHDRAWAL OF COMPLAINT OR PETITION FOR REVIEW

(a) Complaint Pending Before Chief Judge. With the chief judge's consent, the complainant may withdraw a complaint that is before the chief judge for a decision under Rule 11. The withdrawal of a complaint will not prevent the chief judge from identifying or having to identify a complaint under Rule 5 based on the withdrawn complaint.

(b) Complaint Pending Before Special Committee or Judicial Council. After a complaint has been referred to the special committee for investigation and before the committee files its report, the complainant may withdraw the complaint only with the consent of both the subject judge and either the special committee or the judicial council.

(c) Petition for Review. A petition for review addressed to the judicial council under Rule 18, or the Committee on Judicial Conduct and Disability under Rule 22, may be withdrawn if no action on the petition has been taken.

[Adopted March 11, 2008, effective April 10, 2008. Amended effective September 17, 2015.]

Commentary on Rule 27

Rule 27 is adapted from the Illustrative Rules and treats the complaint proceeding, once begun, as a matter of public business rather than as the property of the complainant. Accordingly, the chief judge or the judicial council remains responsible for addressing any complaint under the Act, even a complaint that has been formally withdrawn by the complainant.

Under subsection (a), a complaint pending before the chief judge may be withdrawn if the chief judge consents. Where the complaint clearly lacked merit, the chief judge may accordingly be saved the burden of preparing a formal order and supporting memorandum. However, the chief judge may, or be obligated under Rule 5, to identify a complaint based on allegations in a withdrawn complaint.

If the chief judge appoints a special committee, Rule 27(b) provides that the complaint may be withdrawn only with the consent of both the body before which it is pending (the special committee or the judicial council) and the subject judge. Once a complaint has reached the stage of appointment of a special committee, a resolution of the issues may be necessary to preserve public confidence. Moreover, the subject judge is given the right to insist that the matter be resolved on the merits, thereby eliminating any ambiguity that might remain if the proceeding were terminated by withdrawal of the complaint.

With regard to all petitions for review, Rule 27(c) grants the petitioner unrestricted authority to withdraw the petition. It is thought that the public's interest in the proceeding is adequately protected, because there will necessarily have been a decision by the chief judge and often by the judicial council as well in such a case.

RULE 28. AVAILABILITY OF RULES AND FORMS

These Rules and copies of the complaint form as provided in Rule 6(a) must be available without charge in the office of the circuit clerk of each court of appeals, district court, bankruptcy court, or other federal court whose judges are subject to the Act. Each court must also make these Rules, the complaint form, and complaint-filing instructions available on the court's website, or provide an Internet link to these items on the appropriate court of appeals website or on www.uscourts.gov.

[Adopted March 11, 2008, effective April 10, 2008. Amended effective September 17, 2015.]

RULE 29. EFFECTIVE DATE

These Rules will become effective 30 days after promulgation by the Judicial Conference of the United States.

[Adopted March 11, 2008, effective April 10, 2008.]

APPENDIX

COMPLAINT FORM

Judicial Council of the _____ Circuit

COMPLAINT OF JUDICIAL MISCONDUCT OR DISABILITY

To begin the complaint process, complete this form and prepare the brief statement of facts described in item 4 (below). The Rules for Judicial–Conduct and Judicial–Disability Proceedings, adopted by the Judicial Conference of the United States, contain information on what to include in a complaint (Rule 6), where to file a complaint (Rule 7), and other important matters. The Rules are available in federal court clerks' offices, on individual federal courts' websites, and on www.uscourts. gov.

Your complaint (this form and the statement of facts) should be typewritten and must be legible. For the number of copies to file, consult the local rules or clerk's office of the court in which your complaint is required to be filed. Enclose each copy of the complaint in an envelope marked "COMPLAINT OF MISCONDUCT" or "COMPLAINT OF DISABILITY" and submit it to the appropriate clerk of court. **Do not put the name of any judge on the envelope.**

1. Name of Complainant: _____
   Contact Address: _____
   _____

   Daytime telephone: (_____) _____

2. Name(s) of Judge(s): _____
   Court: _____

3. Does this complaint concern the behavior of the judge(s) in a particular lawsuit or lawsuits?
   　　　　[ ] Yes　　　　[ ] No
   If "yes," give the following information about each lawsuit:
   Court: _____
   Case Number: _____
   Docket number of any appeal to the _____ Circuit: _____
   Are (were) you a party or lawyer in the lawsuit?
   [ ] Party　　　　　　[ ] Lawyer　　　　　　[ ] Neither
   If you are (were) a party and have (had) a lawyer, give the lawyer's name, address, and telephone number:
   _____
   _____
   _____

4. **Brief Statement of Facts.** Attach a brief statement of the specific facts on which the claim of judicial misconduct or disability is based. Include what happened, when and where it happened, and any information that would help an investigator check the facts. If the complaint alleges judicial disability, also include any additional facts that form the basis of that allegation.

5. **Declaration and signature:**
   I declare under penalty of perjury that the statements made in this complaint are true and correct to the best of my knowledge.

   (Signature) _____ Date _____

[Adopted March 11, 2008, effective April 10, 2008. Amended effective September 17, 2015.]

CRIMINAL JUSTICE ACT PLAN

PREAMBLE

Pursuant to the Criminal Justice Act (hereinafter referred to as either "Act" or "CJA"), 18 U.S.C. § 3006A, and the Guidelines for the Administration of the Criminal Justice Act, Vol. VII, *Guide to Judiciary Policies and Procedures*, this Court adopts the following Plan for furnishing appellate representation to all persons who are financially eligible for representation under the CJA and related statutes. This Plan formally amends the Criminal Justice Act Plan adopted by the Sixth Circuit Judicial Council on February 11, 1971.

I. Appointment of Counsel

Counsel appointed by the district court must continue to represent the client until relieved by the United States Court of Appeals for the Sixth Circuit. 6th Cir. R. 101(a). While the Sixth Circuit recognizes that there may be benefits to maintaining continuity of counsel, it also recognizes that the skills necessary to proceed as appellate counsel may differ from those required for trial counsel. In adjudicating trial counsel's request to withdraw as appellate counsel, the Sixth Circuit will give considerable deference to trial counsel as to whether his or her continuing to act as appellate counsel is (1) in the best interests of the client; and (2) consistent with counsel's professional skills and obligations. Consequently, substitution of counsel shall not reflect negatively in anyway on the conduct of the lawyer involved. The Court will require, however, that trial counsel perfect the appeal prior to seeking to withdraw.

Once the notice of appeal has been filed and trial counsel seeks to withdraw as counsel of record, only the United States Court of Appeals for the Sixth Circuit may assign or relieve appellate counsel. Furthermore, absent a change in financial conditions, any determination that a person is eligible for representation by appointed counsel made in the district court shall continue on appeal. Even if trial counsel seeks to withdraw as counsel of record, in its discretion, the Court may continue the appointment of trial counsel or may appoint any Federal Public or Community Defender office located in the Circuit or any lawyer from the Court's Criminal Justice Act Panel (CJA Panel) to represent the indigent on appeal.

Should one or both attorneys who represented a capital defendant in the district court not continue as appellate counsel, the Court may consult with the state public defender's office in the state where the case originated or a Federal Public Defender or Community Defender Capital Habeas Unit located in the district in which the case was litigated in order to locate death penalty qualified counsel to appoint on appeal. After this consultation, the Court may: (1) appoint and compensate under the Act, an attorney or attorneys from a state public defender's office located in the state where the case originated; (2) appoint an attorney or attorneys from a Federal Public Defender or Community Defender Capital Habeas Unit located in the district in which the case was litigated; or (3) appoint counsel from the CJA Panel, giving consideration to the extent of counsel's experience litigating capital appellate issues in the Circuit.

The selection of counsel shall be the exclusive responsibility of the Court and no indigent defendant will be permitted to select his or her own attorney from the CJA Panel.

II. Composition of Panel of Private Attorneys

A. *CJA Panel.*

The Court will establish and maintain a panel of private attorneys (the CJA Panel) who are both eligible and willing to accept appointments in cases where representation is required under 18 U.S.C. § 3006A. These attorneys, along with attorneys from any Federal Public or Community Defender office located in the Circuit, shall constitute the core group from which appointments shall be made. The Court shall approve private attorneys for membership on the CJA Panel after receiving recommendations from the Standing Criminal Justice Act Committee (Standing Committee), established pursuant to Section III of this Plan.

B. *Size.*

The CJA Panel shall be large enough to provide a sufficient number of experienced attorneys who can handle the CJA caseload, yet small enough so that CJA Panel members will receive an adequate number of appointments to ensure that their proficiency in litigating federal criminal appeals is maintained. The CJA Panel will include adequate attorney representation from each of the districts in the Circuit. The Standing Committee will view applications for membership on the CJA Panel with the express goal of identifying qualified appellate counsel from each district in the Circuit.

C. *Eligibility.*

To be eligible for service on the CJA Panel, lawyers must be members in good standing of the Sixth Circuit's bar and maintain an office within the Circuit. Members of the CJA Panel must have a working knowledge of the Federal Rules of Appellate Procedure, Federal Rules of Evidence, Federal Rules of Criminal Procedure, United States Sentencing Guidelines, and the habeas corpus provisions found in Title 28 of the United States Code. CJA Panel members must also be willing to accept at least one appellate appointment each year.

D. *Term of Service.*

There are no fixed terms for panel membership. Continued membership shall be in the discretion of the Clerk of Court, in consultation with the Standing Committee.

E. *Application for Membership.*

Applications to become a CJA Panel member will be available in the office of the Clerk of Court and on the Circuit's website at www.ca6.uscourts.gov. Completed applications must be submitted to the Clerk of Court for transmittal to the Standing Committee.

F. *Maintenance of the List.*

The Clerk of Court shall maintain a public list of the members of the CJA Panel, including current street and email addresses and telephone numbers.

G. *Appointment Process.*

Appointments from the list of the members of the CJA Panel will be made on a rotational basis, with due regard given to the nature and complexity of the case, an attorney's experience, and geographic considerations. The primary consideration shall be to ensure quality representation for all persons who are financially eligible for representation under the CJA and related statutes.

H. *Removal From the Panel.*

The Court is very appreciative of the time and commitment required to accept appellate appointments. Membership on the CJA Panel is not a property right, however, and the refusal to accept appointments on a consistent basis will lead the Court to assume that the attorney has resigned from the panel. The attorney will be notified in writing of any change in status resulting from the failure to accept appointments.

Counsel may also be removed from the panel for any other reason. Such removal shall be in the discretion of the Clerk of Court, in consultation with the Standing Committee. For every case in which a CJA attorney represents an indigent on appeal, whether the case is argued orally or not, the Clerk is requested to provide the presiding judge with a rating sheet, the primary purpose of which is to determine whether the attorney's representation met prevailing professional standards. These evaluations shall be reviewed on an ongoing basis by a designee of the Clerk of Court. A rating at a less-than-professional level, or repeated marginal ratings, shall be referred to the Standing Committee, along with other ratings received by that attorney, for a recommendation as to whether the attorney should continue as a CJA Panel member.

Any attorney whose resignation is assumed because he or she has not accepted cases may file a request to return to active status. This request must include an explanation regarding counsel's refusal to accept appointments. The Standing Committee will make a recommendation to the Court on these requests for reinstatement.

Attorneys removed for any other reason may file a renewed application to be placed back on the CJA Panel no earlier than one year from the date of removal. In the renewed application, counsel must note the earlier removal and explain why they believe that they should be permitted to return to the panel. The Standing Committee will also make a recommendation to the Court on these requests for reinstatement.

III. Standing Criminal Justice Act Committee

A. *Membership and Structure.*

The Chief Judge of the Circuit or his designee, shall appoint the Standing Committee which shall be composed of one criminal defense lawyer from each of the districts comprising the Circuit and one member of the Court's Judicial Council. Non–Judicial Council members of the Standing Committee may be private attorneys or lawyers from the various Federal Public and Community Defender offices located in the Circuit and they should have experience litigating criminal appeals. The Standing Committee members shall serve staggered three year terms, and may serve two consecutive terms. The Chief Judge or his designee may also appoint a liaison to the Standing Committee from the Court's legal staff. This liaison will not be a Standing Committee member, but will be available to both the Court and members of the Committee for support and consultation. Finally, the Chief Judge or his designee shall appoint a chairperson for the Standing Committee.

B. *Duties.*

The Standing Committee shall review the qualifications of applicants for membership on the CJA Panel, conduct further inquiries as may be necessary, and shall make recommendations to the Court for placement of attorneys on as well as removal of attorneys from the CJA Panel. The Standing Committee shall also review the operation of the appellate panel on a periodic basis and shall make recommendations to the Court regarding any necessary changes. At the Court's discretion, the Standing Committee may also investigate complaints concerning deficient performance by CJA Panel members and report its findings to the Court. The Standing Committee's recommendations to the Court on any issue shall remain confidential.

IV. Change in Financial Conditions

If a party becomes financially unable to employ counsel on appeal and this determination is made before the notice of appeal is filed, a motion seeking a finding that the party is eligible for the appointment of counsel must be made in district court. 18 U.S.C. § 3006A. Because the district court must make factual findings regarding the defendant's financial eligibility, appropriate forms, such as a CJA 23 affidavit, should be filed in that court to assist in making this determination.

In cases where a request for the appointment of counsel under the Act is made for the first time after the notice of appeal is filed, the Chief Judge of the Circuit or his designee, before making the appointment, shall inquire into and make a finding as to whether the party applying for representation by the CJA Panel is financially able to employ counsel. Appropriate forms such as a CJA 23 affidavit shall be utilized in making this determination.

The Court may, at any time, examine or re-examine the financial status of the defendant. It is also incumbent on counsel appointed pursuant to the Act to apprise the Court of his or her client's change of financial circumstances that would impact their entitlement to representation pursuant to the Act as long as the source of counsel's information is not a privileged communication with his or her client. If at any time the Court finds that the defendant is financially able to retain counsel or make partial payments for representation, the Court may deny or terminate an appointment pursuant to 18 U.S.C. § 3006A(c) or require the defendant to make partial payment for services rendered, pursuant to 18 U.S.C. § 3006A(f).

V. Petition for Writ of *Certiorari*

If the judgment of this Court is adverse to the client, the attorney must inform the client of the right to petition the Supreme Court of the United States for a writ of *certiorari*. The attorney must file a petition for a writ of *certiorari* if the client requests the attorney to seek this discretionary review, and, in the attorney's considered judgment, there are grounds for seeking Supreme Court review that are not frivolous and are consistent with the standards for filing a petition embodied by the Rules of the Supreme Court and applicable case law. 6th Cir. R. 101(g). If, on the other hand, the client requests that the attorney file a petition for a writ of *certiorari* and, in the attorney's considered judgment, there are no such grounds for seeking Supreme Court review that are not frivolous, the attorney should promptly so advise the client and submit to this Court a written motion for leave to withdraw from the representation after the entry of judgment. If this Court grants the attorney's motion and terminates the attorney's appointment, the attorney must so advise the client in writing as soon as possible. The attorney must also advise the client of his or her right to file a pro se petition for a writ of *certiorari*.

VI. Quality of Representation

Attorneys appointed pursuant to any provision of the Act must conform to the highest standards of professional conduct, including, but not limited to, the provisions of the American Bar Association's Code of Professional Responsibility.

VII. Compensation

A. *Claims.*

At the conclusion of the attorney's representation, all claims for compensation and expenses must be submitted to the Clerk of Court on the CJA 20 voucher enclosed with the appointment. All claims must be supported by appropriate documentation and must be prepared consistent with the directives found in the "CJA 20 Voucher Submission Instructions" that are posted on this Court's website.

In each case, the Court will fix the compensation to be paid the attorney as provided in the Act. Although the Act provides for limited compensation, the Court recognizes that the compensation afforded often does not reflect the true value of the services rendered. Consequently, it is the Court's policy not to cut or reduce claims which are reasonable and necessary.

In evaluating a CJA 20 voucher for approval, the Court may take into account, among other considerations: (1) the extent to which the time claimed for brief preparation corresponds to the number and complexity of issues in the brief(s), the length of the brief(s), and the length of the record; (2) whether appellate counsel was also trial counsel; (3) whether there were "associates" involved in the preparation of the brief(s) or whether there was only one lawyer who worked the case up for the appeal; (4) the overall quality of the brief(s) and argument; and (5) the overall reasonableness of the time requested. After considering these factors and others, if the Court determines that a claim must be reduced, it will provide the attorney notice of its intent to reduce the attorney's claim and an opportunity to address this issue before final payment is made. Once the attorney is provided with notice of the Court's intention to reduce the submitted claim, the attorney must submit his or her written response to support the claim within ten days.

The Court will process all claims for compensation and expenses that are submitted by CJA Panel attorneys as expeditiously as possible.

B. *Other Payments.*

Except as authorized or directed by the Court, no person or organization authorized by the Court to furnish representation under the Act may request or accept any payment or promise of payment for representation from a source other than the Administrative Office of the United States Courts.

VIII. Amendments

Amendments to this Plan may be made from time to time by the Court, subject to the Sixth Circuit Judicial Council's approval.

CERTIFICATE OF APPROVAL

This is to certify that, in accordance with the Criminal Justice Act of 1964 as amended, 18 U.S.C. § 3006A, *et seq.*, the foregoing Amended Criminal Justice Act Plan for the United States Court of Appeals for the Sixth Circuit has been duly received and approved as complying with the law by the Judicial Council of the Sixth Circuit of the United States. The said Amended Plan shall become effective upon the date of this approval.

[Effective May 7, 2008.]

SELECTED FORMS AND INSTRUCTIONS

FORM 6CA–1. DISCLOSURE OF CORPORATE AFFILIATIONS AND FINANCIAL INTEREST

UNITED STATES COURT OF APPEALS
FOR THE SIXTH CIRCUIT

Disclosure of Corporate Affiliations and Financial Interest

Sixth Circuit
Case Number: _____   Case Name: _____

Name of counsel: _____

Pursuant to 6th Cir. R. 26.1, _____
                                          Name of Party
makes the following disclosure:

1.   Is said party a subsidiary or affiliate of a publicly owned corporation? If Yes, list below the
     identity of the parent corporation or affiliate and the relationship between it and the named
     party:

```
┌──────────────────────────────────────────────────────────────┐
│                                                                │
│                                                                │
│                                                                │
│                                                                │
│                                                                │
└──────────────────────────────────────────────────────────────┘
```

2.   Is there a publicly owned corporation, not a party to the appeal, that has a financial interest
     in the outcome? If yes, list the identity of such corporation and the nature of the financial
     interest:

```
┌──────────────────────────────────────────────────────────────┐
│                                                                │
│                                                                │
│                                                                │
│                                                                │
└──────────────────────────────────────────────────────────────┘
```

```
┌──────────────────────────────────────────────────────────────┐
│                    CERTIFICATE OF SERVICE                      │
│ I certify that on _____ the foregoing document was served on all │
│ parties or their counsel of record through the CM/ECF system if they are registered users or, if they are not, │
│ by placing a true and correct copy in the United States mail, postage prepaid, to their address of record. │
│                                                                │
│              s/_____                       │
│              _____                         │
│              _____                         │
└──────────────────────────────────────────────────────────────┘
```

This statement is filed twice: when the appeal is initially opened and later, in the principal briefs,
immediately preceding the table of contents. See 6th Cir. R. 26.1 on page 2 of this form.

6CA-1
8/08

6th Cir. R. 26.1
DISCLOSURE OF CORPORATE AFFILIATIONS
AND FINANCIAL INTEREST

(a) **Parties Required to Make Disclosure.** With the exception of the United States government or agencies thereof or a state government or agencies or political subdivisions thereof, all parties and amici curiae to a civil or bankruptcy case, agency review proceeding, or original proceedings, and all corporate defendants in a criminal case shall file a corporate affiliate/financial interest disclosure statement. A negative report is required except in the case of individual criminal defendants.

(b) **Financial Interest to Be Disclosed.**

(1) Whenever a corporation that is a party to an appeal, or which appears as amicus curiae, is a subsidiary or affiliate of any publicly owned corporation not named in the appeal, counsel for the corporation that is a party or amicus shall advise the clerk in the manner provided by subdivision (c) of this rule of the identity of the parent corporation or affiliate and the relationship between it and the corporation that is a party or amicus to the appeal. A corporation shall be considered an affiliate of a publicly owned corporation for purposes of this rule if it controls, is controlled by, or is under common control with a publicly owned corporation.

(2) Whenever, by reason of insurance, a franchise agreement, or indemnity agreement, a publicly owned corporation or its affiliate, not a party to the appeal, nor an amicus, has a substantial financial interest in the outcome of litigation, counsel for the party or amicus whose interest is aligned with that of the publicly owned corporation or its affiliate shall advise the clerk in the manner provided by subdivision (c) of this rule of the identity of the publicly owned corporation and the nature of its or its affiliate's substantial financial interest in the outcome of the litigation.

(c) **Form and Time of Disclosure.** The disclosure statement shall be made on a form provided by the clerk and filed with the brief of a party or amicus or upon filing a motion, response, petition, or answer in this Court, whichever first occurs.

6CA-1
8/08

218

FORM 6CA–3. NOTICE OF APPEAL

United States District Court for the _____

District of _____

Plaintiff,

vs.   Case No. _____

Defendant.

NOTICE OF APPEAL

Notice is hereby given that _____.
Name all parties taking the appeal

hereby appeal to the United States Court of Appeals for the Sixth Circuit from

_____
The final judgment, from an order describing it

entered in this action on the _____ day of _____, _____

(s)_____

Address:_____

_____

_____

Attorney for _____

Note to inmate filers: If you are an inmate confined in an institution and you seek the timing benefit of Fed. R. App. P. 4(c)(1), complete Form 7 (Declaration of Inmate Filing) and file that declaration along with this Notice of Appeal.

cc: Opposing Counsel ☐
     Court of Appeals ☐

6CA-3
11/16

[Revised November, 2016.]

FORM 6CA–14.   APPLICATION FOR ADMISSION TO THE BAR

United States Court of Appeals for the Sixth Circuit
APPLICATION FOR ADMISSION TO THE BAR

APPLICATION: I, _____, do
hereby make application for admission to the bar of the United States Court of Appeals for the Sixth Circuit. My Personal statement showing my eligibility for membership is as follows: I am admitted to practice in the following court(s)

_____

OATH: I, _____, do
solemnly swear (or affirm) that I will demean myself as an attorney and counselor of this Court, uprightly and according to law; and that I will support the Constitution of the United States of America.

Subscribed and sworn to before me this   _____
                                                          Signature of Applicant

_____ day of _____, 20_____

_____
Signature of Notary (or Court of Appeals Deputy Clerk)

FOR NOTARY: My commission expires on _____, 20_____

MOTION: I, _____, a
member of the bar of this court, do hereby move the admission of the above attorney.

_____
Signature of Movant

▬ ▬ ▬ ▬ ▬ ▬ ▬ ▬ ▬ ▬ ▬ ▬ ▬ ▬

APPLICATION INFORMATION: (Please print)

Mr.   Ms. Name: _____
                        (Last)   (First)   (Middle)

E-mail Address: _____

Firm: _____

Address: _____

City: _____ State: _____ Zip: _____

Last 4 digits
of SSN: _____ Phone: _____ Fax: _____

ADMISSION FEE: Fee for admission to the bar of this court is $231.00 (this includes a local fee of $50.00). Payment may be made by cash, check, money order, credit or debit card. Check and money order should be made payable to "Clerk, U.S. Court of Appeals, Sixth Circuit". Go to http://www.ca6.uscourts.gov/fees to pay with a credit or debit card.

FOR CLERK'S OFFICE USE: Fee Paid: ☐Yes ☐No   Date Paid: _____

Comments: _____

Admitted this _____ day of _____, 20_____

Deborah Hunt, Clerk
United States Court of Appeals for the Sixth Circuit

By: _____

6CA-14
11/16

[Revised April 6, 2016; November, 2016.]

FORM 6CA–27. ADMISSION TO THE BAR OF THE UNITED STATES COURT OF APPEALS FOR THE SIXTH CIRCUIT

Admission To The Bar
of
The United States Court Of Appeals
For The Sixth Circuit

Requirements and Eligibility. Attorneys must be admitted to the bar of the Sixth Circuit before they will be permitted to file pleadings or briefs on behalf of a party or participate in oral argument. An attorney who has been admitted to practice before the Supreme Court of the United States, the highest court of a state, another United States Court of Appeals, or a United States District Court and who is of good moral and professional character is eligible for admission to the Bar of the United States Court of Appeals for the Sixth Circuit. Any attorney representing the United States or any officer or agency thereof in an appeal will be permitted to participate in that case without the necessity of being admitted to the Bar of the Sixth Circuit. However, any such attorney desiring admittance to the bar of the court will be required to pay the fee.

Fee. Attorneys appointed by the court to represent clients *in forma pauperis* and who qualify under the standards of Fed. R. App. P. 46 and attorneys employed by a Federal Defender organization created pursuant to 18 U.S.C. § 3006A shall be admitted to practice in this court without payment of a fee. All other qualified counsel shall be **admitted upon payment of a $226.00 fee**. Payment may be made electronically, by credit/debit card (go to http://www.ca6.uscourts.gov/internet/electronic_payment/electronicpay.htm), or by cash, check or money order made payable to the "Clerk of the United States Court of Appeals."

Application Procedures. Admissions are made upon the motion of a member of the Bar of the Sixth Circuit. Application for admission is made by filing form 6CA- 14 via CM/ECF, in person, or by mail, with the Office of the Clerk of the United States Court of Appeals for the Sixth Circuit. (Form 6CA- 14 may be obtained from the Clerk's Office or on the Sixth Circuit's website.)

The completed form 6CA-14 must include the following:

- name and mailing address of the applicant;
- a statement of eligibility;
- an oath signed and notarized, with seal or stamp of the notary affixed; and
- the motion for admission signed by a fellow attorney previously admitted to the Bar of the Sixth Circuit. If there is no one who can move your admission, you may submit a certificate of good standing from the court (state or federal) wherein you are admitted to practice to. Upon admission, a certificate of admission will be forwarded to the applicant.

See Fed. R. App. P. 46 and 6th Cir. R. 46.

For Further Information, Contact:

Office of the Clerk
United States Court of Appeals For the Sixth Circuit
(513) 564-7000

6CA-27
07/14

[Revised April 6, 2016.]

FORM 6CA–53.   CIVIL APPEAL STATEMENT OF PARTIES AND ISSUES

**UNITED STATES COURT OF APPEALS
FOR THE SIXTH CIRCUIT
CIVIL APPEAL STATEMENT OF PARTIES AND ISSUES**

Case No: ___$226.00._____

Case Name: _____

Is this case a cross appeal?   ☐ Yes   ☐ No

Has this case or a related one been before this court previously?   ☐ Yes   ☐ No

If yes, state:

    Case Name: _____ Citation: _____

    Was that case mediated through the court's program?   ☐ Yes   ☐ No

Please Identify the Parties Against Whom this Appeal is Being Taken and the Specific Issues You Propose to Raise:

This is to certify that a copy of this statement was served on opposing counsel of record this ____ day of

_____, _____.

                                      _____

                                      Name of Counsel for Appellant

6CA-53
Rev. 6/08

FORM 6CA–68. APPEARANCE OF COUNSEL

UNITED STATES COURT OF APPEALS
FOR THE SIXTH CIRCUIT

Appearance of Counsel

Appeal No.: _____

Case Title: _____ vs. _____

List all clients you represent in this appeal:

```
┌─────────────────────────────────────────────────────┐
│                                                     │
│                                                     │
│                                                     │
│                                                     │
└─────────────────────────────────────────────────────┘
```

☐ Appellant   ☐ Petitioner   ☐ Amicus Curiae   ☐ Criminal Justice Act
☐ Appellee   ☐ Respondent   ☐ Intervenor   (Appointed)

☐ Check if a party is represented by more than one attorney.
☐ Check if you are lead counsel.

If you are substituting for another counsel, include that attorney's name here:

_____

By filing this form, I certify my admission and/or eligibility to file in this court.

Attorney Name: _____ Signature: s/_____

Firm Name: _____

Business Address: _____

City/State/Zip: _____

Telephone Number (Area Code): _____

Email Address: _____

Please ensure your contact information above matches your PACER contact information. If necessary, update your PACER account.

```
┌─────────────────────────────────────────────────────┐
│                  CERTIFICATE OF SERVICE             │
│  The electronic signature above certifies that all  │
│  parties or their counsel of record have been       │
│  electronically served with this document as of the │
│  date of filing.                                    │
└─────────────────────────────────────────────────────┘
```

6ca-68
8/17

[Revised October 29, 2014; June 28, 2017; August 4, 2017.]

FORM 6CA–70. PRO SE BRIEFS

UNITED STATES COURT OF APPEALS
FOR THE SIXTH CIRCUIT

Case Number: _____

Case Name: _____

Name:_____

Address:_____

City:_____ State:_____ Zip Code:_____

PRO SE APPELLANT'S BRIEF

Directions: Answer the following questions about the appeal to the best of your ability. Use additional sheets of paper, if necessary, not to exceed 30 pages. Please print or write legibly, or type your answers double-spaced. You need not limit your brief solely to this form, but you should be certain that the document you file contains answers to the questions below. The Court prefers short and direct statements.

Within the date specified in the briefing letter, you should return one signed original brief to:

United States Court of Appeals For The Sixth Circuit
540 Potter Stewart U.S. Courthouse
100 East Fifth Street
Cincinnati, Ohio   45202-3988

1. Did the District Court incorrectly decide the facts?   ☐ Yes   ☐ No

   If so, what facts?

   ┌──┐
   │ $226.00.   │
   │   │
   │   │
   └──┘

2. Do you think the District Court applied the wrong law?   ☐ Yes   ☐ No

   If so, what law do you want applied?

   ┌──┐
   │   │
   │   │
   │   │
   │   │
   │   │
   └──┘

6CA-70
03/10

3. Do you feel that there are any others reasons why the District Court's judgment was wrong?
    ☐ Yes   ☐ No
    If so, what are they?

4. What specific issues do you wish to raise on appeal?

5. What action do you want the Court of Appeals to take in this case?

I certify that a copy of this brief was sent to opposing counsel via U.S. Mail on the ____ day of
_____, 20____.

Signature (Notary not required)

_____

6CA-70
03/10

INDEX TO UNITED STATES COURT OF APPEALS
FOR THE SIXTH CIRCUIT

UNITED STATES BANKRUPTCY APPELLATE PANEL FOR THE SIXTH CIRCUIT

Including Amendments Received Through
January 1, 2018

RULE 8001–1. DEFINITIONS

(a) **Panel Clerk.** The words "panel clerk" as used in these rules mean the Clerk of the Bankruptcy Appellate Panel of the Sixth Circuit.

(b) **Judge.** The word "judge" as used in these rules, unless otherwise designated, means a judge of the Bankruptcy Appellate Panel of the Sixth Circuit.

(c) **Panel.** The word "panel" as used in these rules means a panel of three judges of the Bankruptcy Appellate Panel of the Sixth Circuit.

(d) **BAP.** The acronym "BAP" or the words "Bankruptcy Appellate Panel of the Sixth Circuit" as used in these rules mean the Bankruptcy Appellate Panel Service established by the Judicial Council of the Sixth Circuit pursuant to 28 U.S.C. § 158(b)(1).

[Adopted effective December 15, 2014.]

RULE 8001–2. CLERK OF THE BANKRUPTCY APPELLATE PANEL

(a) **Designation of Clerk.** The Clerk of the United States Court of Appeals for the Sixth Circuit shall serve as Clerk of the Bankruptcy Appellate Panel of the Sixth Circuit.

(b) **Communications to the BAP.** All communications to the BAP shall be addressed to the Clerk of the Bankruptcy Appellate Panel of the Sixth Circuit, 540 Potter Stewart U.S. Courthouse, 100 East Fifth Street, Cincinnati, Ohio 45202–3988.

[Adopted effective December 15, 2014.]

RULE 8003–1. DISMISSAL OF APPEAL FOR NON–PROSECUTION

(a) **After Notice by Panel Clerk.** If an appellant or cross-appellant fails to comply with the Federal Rules of Bankruptcy Procedure or with these rules, the panel clerk shall notify the appellant or cross-appellant that the appeal or cross-appeal will be dismissed for non-prosecution unless the default is remedied within fourteen days. If the appellant or cross-appellant fails to remedy the default within the fourteen-day period, the panel clerk shall enter an order dismissing the appeal or cross appeal for non-prosecution.

(b) **By a Panel.** A panel on its own initiative or on the motion of a party may dismiss an appeal or take other appropriate action, including an award of damages and attorney's fees, for the failure of any party to comply with the Federal Rules of Bankruptcy Procedure or with these rules. Dismissal by a panel is independent of the notice of default provided in subsection (a) of this rule.

[Adopted effective December 15, 2014.]

RULE 8005–1. ELECTION FOR DISTRICT COURT DETERMINATION OF APPEAL INSTEAD OF THE BAP

(a) **Statement of Election Required.** In districts that have authorized appeals to the BAP, every appeal filed in the bankruptcy court shall be heard by the Bankruptcy Appellate Panel of the Sixth Circuit unless a party makes an election to the district court in the manner required by Federal Rule of Bankruptcy Procedure 8005 and in the time required by 28 U.S.C. § 158(c)(1). The filing by any other party to the appeal of any paper (other than a notice of appearance) with the BAP waives the right of that party to elect to have the appeal heard by the district court.

(b) **Upon Motion for Leave to Appeal.** In districts that have authorized appeals to the BAP, every appeal upon motion for leave to appeal under Rule 8003 shall be heard by the Bankruptcy Appellate Panel of the Sixth Circuit unless a party makes an election to the district court in the manner required by Federal Rule of Bankruptcy Procedure 8005 and in the

231

time required by 28 U.S.C. § 158(c)(1). The filing by any other party to the appeal of any paper (other than a notice of appearance) with the BAP waives the right of that party to elect to have the appeal heard by the district court.

[Adopted effective December 15, 2014.]

RULE 8011–1. FILING PAPERS

The BAP requires attorneys to file documents electronically. The "Sixth Circuit Guide to Electronic Filing" is adopted to govern the filing of documents in cases filed with the BAP. Any amendments to the Guide adopted by the court of appeals shall apply to cases filed in the BAP. The current version of the Guide is available on the court of appeals' website, www.ca 6.uscourts.gov.

[Adopted effective December 15, 2014.]

RULE 8013–1. DETERMINATION OF PROCEDURAL MOTION

(a) By Panel Clerk. The panel clerk may act on the following motions without submission to a panel or judge:

(1) Motions that are procedural or relate to the preparation or filing of the record or briefs;

(2) Motions for voluntary dismissal of appeals;

(3) Motions to dismiss for want of prosecution;

(4) Motions for extensions of time;

(5) Motions to withdraw or for substitution of counsel; and

(6) Such other motions as the BAP may designate the panel clerk to act upon that are subject to disposition by a single judge under Rule 8013(e).

(b) Order by Panel Clerk. An order by the panel clerk disposing of a motion shall show that it was entered by the panel clerk pursuant to this rule. Any party adversely affected by an order entered by the panel clerk shall be entitled to reconsideration by a judge or panel if, within the deadline provided in Fed. R. Bankr. P. 8013(b), the party files a motion for reconsideration.

[Adopted effective December 15, 2014.]

RULE 8013–2. EMERGENCY MOTION

An emergency motion pursuant to Rule 8013(d) shall be electronically filed. The movant shall attach all documents relevant to the motion.

[Adopted effective December 15, 2014.]

RULE 8014–1. BRIEFS

(a) Briefs. The filing of the briefs is governed by the "Sixth Circuit Guide to Electronic Filing."

(b) Statement Regarding Oral Argument. The brief of the appellant and the brief of the appellee shall include a statement, not exceeding one page, explaining why oral argument should, or need not, be permitted. This statement shall follow the table of authorities and shall not be considered in determining the maximum number of pages in the brief.

(c) Citation of "Unpublished" Decisions. Citation in briefs and oral arguments of decisions designated "not for publication" by the Sixth Circuit, or given any similar limited precedential effect by the court rendering the decision, is disfavored, except for the purpose of establishing res judicata, estoppel, or the law of the case. Such decisions may be cited only if a copy thereof is served on all other parties and on the panel. Service may be accomplished by including a copy of the decision in an addendum to the brief.

(d) Format and Spacing of Type. Briefs shall be double-spaced in a font not less than 12 points in size with margins of not less than one inch.

(e) Extensions of Time. Extensions of time for the filing of briefs must be sought by motion and for good cause shown.

(f) Briefs as Public Record. Briefs filed with the BAP are public records. To have a brief sealed, a timely motion must be filed.

[Adopted effective December 15, 2014.]

RULE 8018–1. FORM OF RECORD ON APPEAL

The filing of the record on appeal is governed by the "Sixth Circuit Guide to Electronic Filing."

[Adopted effective December 15, 2014.]

RULE 8019–1. ORAL ARGUMENT

(a) Advancement of Hearing. A panel may, on its own motion or for good cause shown on motion of a party, advance any case to be heard, though the time permitted under the rules for filing briefs may not have expired as of the hearing date.

(b) Postponement of Hearing. After a case has been set for hearing, postponement must be sought by motion for good cause shown.

(c) Oral Argument.

(1) Oral argument will not be heard on behalf of any party for whom a brief has not been filed unless otherwise directed by the panel.

(2) An amicus curiae may, with the consent of a party, argue orally on the side of such party, provided that the time permitted for oral argument on behalf of that party will not thereby be exceeded. In the absence of such consent, argument for an amicus curiae may be made only upon motion to the panel in advance of the hearing date.

(d) Waiver of Oral Argument. Oral argument may be waived upon written stipulation of the parties, unless the panel orders otherwise.

[Adopted effective December 15, 2014.]

RULE 8024–1. DISPOSITION OF APPEAL

(a) In Open Court. In those cases in which the decision is unanimous and each judge of the panel believes that no jurisprudential purpose would be served by a written opinion, disposition of the case may be made in open court following oral argument. A written judgment shall be signed and entered by the clerk in accordance with the decision of the panel from the bench.

(b) Decisions as Precedent. A panel may limit the precedential effect of a decision to the case and parties before it by so stating in its decision. Absent such a statement, decisions of a panel shall not be limited as precedent for purposes of 6th Cir. BAP LBR 8014–1(c).

[Adopted effective December 15, 2014.]

RULE 8026–1. LOCAL RULES

The Rules of the Bankruptcy Appellate Panel of the Sixth Circuit shall be cited as: "**6th Cir. BAP LBR ___–___.**" For example, subsection (a) of Rule 8014–1 of these rules shall be cited as "6th Cir. BAP LBR 8014–1(a)."

[Adopted effective December 15, 2014.]

RULE 8027–1. PRE–ARGUMENT CONFERENCE AND MEDIATION

(a) Pre–Argument Conference. All bankruptcy appeals shall be reviewed by staff attorneys to determine if a pre-argument conference would be of assistance to the BAP or the parties. Such a conference may be conducted by a judge or a staff attorney. Any party may request a pre-argument conference by motion.

(b) Attendance. Any party may be required to attend a pre-argument conference, in person or by telephone. The possibility of settlement, simplification of issues, the use of mediation and any other matters which the judge or conference attorney determines may aid in disposition of the appeal may be considered at the pre-argument conference.

(c) Participating Judge Disqualified. Any judge who participates in a pre-argument conference or becomes involved in mediation or settlement discussions pursuant to this rule will not sit on a panel that considers any aspect of the case.

(d) Confidentiality. Statements made and information exchanged during a pre-argument conference or mediation are confidential, except to the extent disclosed by the pre-argument conference order, and shall not be disclosed by the conference judge or conference attorney nor by parties in briefs or argument.

(e) Pre–Argument Conference Order. To effectuate the purposes and results of this rule, a judge or the panel clerk at the request of the conference attorney shall enter a pre-argument conference order.

[Adopted effective December 15, 2014.]

RULE 8090–1. ATTORNEYS—ADMISSION TO PRACTICE

(a) Admission. Any attorney admitted to practice before a United States district court within the Sixth Circuit or before the United States Court of Appeals for the Sixth Circuit and who is in good standing before such court shall be deemed admitted to practice before the BAP. An attorney not so admitted may apply to the panel for permission to appear in a particular appeal.

(b) Notice of Appearance. Any attorney who wishes to file documents or argue on behalf of any party shall file a notice of appearance on a form available from the panel clerk.

[Adopted effective December 15, 2014.]

SELECTED FORMS
FORM 6BAP-1. APPELLATE PANEL APPEARANCE OF COUNSEL

**SIXTH CIRCUIT BANKRUPTCY APPELLATE
PANEL APPEARANCE OF COUNSEL**

IMPORTANT NOTICE:

Lead counsel must be designated if a party is represented by more than one attorney or law firm. While the Clerk's office will accept documents from any attorney who has entered an appearance and has been admitted to the Bar, only lead counsel will be on the BAP's service list. It is the responsibility of lead counsel to advise co-counsel of deadlines, orders, notice of argument, decisions and any other case-related activity. If counsel fails to designate lead counsel or designates more than one attorney as lead counsel, the Clerk's office will designate without notice.

BAP CASE NO. _____

Client's Name: _____

Appellant ☐   Appellee ☐   Other ☐

I AM LEAD COUNSEL ☐   OR   CO-COUNSEL ☐

Name: _____

Admitted (See 6th Cir. BAP R. 8090-1): _____

Signature: _____

Firm Name: _____

Business Address: _____

Suite: _____ City/State/Zip: _____

Telephone Number: (Area Code) _____ Fax: _____

Email Address: _____

CERTIFICATE OF SERVICE

I certify that on _____ the foregoing document was served on all parties or their counsel of record through the CM/ECF system if they are registered users or, if they are not, by placing a true and correct copy in the United States mail, postage prepaid, to their address of record.

s/ _____

6BAP-1
4/10

[Revised April, 2010.]

B.A.P. PRO SE APPELLANT'S BRIEF
UNITED STATES COURT OF APPEALS
FOR THE SIXTH CIRCUIT

Case Number: _____

Case Name: _____

B.A.P. PRO SE APPELLANT'S BRIEF

Directions: Answer the following questions about the appeal to the best of your ability. Use additional sheets of paper, if necessary, not to exceed 30 pages. Please type your answers double-spaced. You need not limit your brief solely to this form, but you should be certain that the document you file contains answers to the questions below. The Court prefers short and direct statements.

Within the date specified in the briefing letter, you should return your completed brief to:

United States Court of Appeals For The Sixth Circuit
532 Potter Stewart U.S. Courthouse
100 East Fifth Street
Cincinnati, Ohio 45202-3988

1. Did the Bankruptcy Court incorrectly decide the facts? If so, what facts?

2. Do you think the Bankruptcy Court applied the wrong law? If so, what law do you want applied?

1/16

United States Court of Appeals for the Sixth Circuit
B.A.P. Pro Se Appellant's Brief

3. Do you feel that there are any others reasons why the Bankruptcy Court's judgment was wrong? If so, what are they?

4. What action do you want the Court to take in this case?

5. What specific issues do you wish to raise on appeal?

I certify that a copy of this brief was sent to opposing counsel via U.S. Mail on the _____ day of _____, 20__.

_____
Signature (Notary not required)

[Revised February 8, 2016.]

UNITED STATES DISTRICT COURT FOR THE EASTERN DISTRICT OF MICHIGAN

Including Amendments Received Through
January 1, 2018

REVISED PLAN FOR IMPLEMENTING THE CRIMINAL JUSTICE ACT OF 1964, AS AMENDED, 18 U.S.C. § 3006A

JUROR SELECTION PLAN

SPEEDY TRIAL ACT PLAN

CIVILITY PRINCIPLES

SELECTED ADMINISTRATIVE ORDERS

LOCAL RULES FOR CIVIL CASES

LR 1.1   SCOPE OF RULES

(a) Title and Citation. These rules are to be known as the Local Rules of the United States District Court for the Eastern District of Michigan. They may be cited as "E.D.Mich. LR ___" and "E.D.Mich. LCrR ___".

(b) Effective Date. The Civil Rules became effective on January 1, 1992; the Criminal Rules on July 1, 1992. An amendment to these rules takes effect on the first day of the month following adoption unless otherwise ordered by the court. The effective date of the most recent amendment to a rule appears in the lower left hand corner of the page.

(c) Scope of Rules. These rules apply in civil and criminal actions. Special rules governing proceedings before magistrate judges may be found at LR 72.1, bankruptcy cases at LR 83.50, admiralty cases at LR B.1 through E.1, and criminal cases at LCrR 1.1 to 58.1. The Local Rules of the Bankruptcy Court for the Eastern District of Michigan govern practice in the bankruptcy court. In the absence of a specific provision in one of these special rules, the general provisions apply.

(d) Relationship to Prior Rules; Actions Pending on Effective Date. These Rules supersede all previous Rules promulgated by this Court or any Judge of this Court. They shall govern all applicable proceedings brought in this Court after they take effect. They also shall apply to all proceedings pending at the time they take effect, except to the extent that in the opinion of the Court the application thereof would not be feasible or would work injustice, in which event the former Rules shall govern.

[Effective January 1, 1992. Amended effective March 2, 1998; January 4, 1999, effective February 1, 1999.]

LR 1.2   EMERGENCY SUSPENSION OF THE LOCAL RULES

For good cause shown, for a particular matter, any Judge of this Court may temporarily suspend the operation of the Rules.

[Former LR 1.3 effective January 1, 1992. Renumbered as LR 1.2 effective March 3, 1997.]

LR 1.3   AVAILABILITY OF THE LOCAL RULES

Copies of these Rules as amended are available online at www.mied.uscourts.gov.

[Former LR 1.4 effective January 1, 1992. Amended effective October 5, 1992. Renumbered as LR 1.3 effective March 3, 1997. Amended effective January 1, 2016.]

LR 3.1   CIVIL CASE COVER SHEET

(a) A person filing a complaint or other document initiating a civil action must—

(1) when filing electronically, provide the information normally entered on the civil case cover sheet, or

(2) when not filing electronically, complete and file a civil case cover sheet.

(b) The clerk will accept for filing an initiating document without a civil case cover sheet and may enlist the cooperation of counsel or a pro se party in completing the civil case cover sheet.

[Effective January 1, 1992. Amended effective July 1, 2010.]

Comment

The civil case cover sheet is available at the clerk's office and the court's web site.

LR 3.2   METHOD OF PAYMENT

The United States District Court for the Eastern District of Michigan does not accept cash for payment of court fees, services, fines payments, bond payments or restitution. The Court accepts credit cards, checks and money orders as forms of payment. Checks should be made payable to Clerk, U.S. District Court. Court staff will not make change; exact amount whether in check or money order must be presented.

[Effective May 1, 2016.]

LR 4.1   ISSUANCE AND SERVICE OF PROCESS

(a) Issuance of process. A party requesting the issuance of any process or who initiates a proceeding in which the issuance of process is required by statute, rule, or order must prepare all required forms. Where necessary, the party must present the process to the Clerk for signature and sealing.

(b) Service of Process. Subject to subsection (c) of this rule, unless the plaintiff requests otherwise, the Clerk must arrange for service of the summons and complaint by the United States Marshal for a plaintiff authorized to proceed in forma pauperis under 28 U.S.C. § 1915 or as a seaman under 28 U.S.C. § 1916. A request for that assistance is not necessary.

(c) Represented parties. If an attorney represents a plaintiff authorized to proceed in forma pauperis under 28 U.S.C. § 1915, or as a seaman under 28 U.S.C. § 1916, that attorney is deemed specially appointed by the Court and must arrange for service of the summons and complaint.

[Effective November 1, 2017.]

Comment

This rule implements Federal Rule of Civil Procedure 4(c)(3). When a plaintiff who qualifies for pauper status is represented by an attorney, the attorney must arrange for service of process, but may seek assistance for service from the United States Marshal at government expense.

LR 5.1 FILING OF PAPERS

(a) Papers Presented for Filing. Under LR 5.1.1, unless specified otherwise in the ECF Policies and Procedures (Appendix ECF to these rules) or by court order, all papers must be filed electronically.

(1) *Required Information.* All papers presented for filing must include:

(A) the name of the court,

(B) the title and number of the case,

(C) the name or nature of the paper in sufficient detail for identification,

(D) the name of the district judge and magistrate judge to whom the case is assigned, and

(E) the following contact information:

(i) For an attorney: Name, office address, e-mail address, telephone number, and state bar identification number.

(ii) For a party without counsel: Name, address, e-mail address, and telephone number.

(2) *Format.* All papers must be on 8½ × 11 inch white paper of good quality, plainly typewritten, printed, or prepared by a clearly legible duplication process, and double-spaced, except for quoted material and footnotes. Margins must be at least one inch on the top, sides, and bottom. Each page must be numbered consecutively. This subsection does not apply to exhibits submitted for filing and documents filed in removed actions before removal from the state courts.

(3) *Type Size.* Except for standard preprinted forms that are in general use, type size of all text and footnotes must be no smaller than 10–1/2 characters per inch (non-proportional) or 14 point (proportional).

(b) Number of Copies Required.

(1) *Papers Filed Electronically.* Attorneys and parties without counsel should refer to the court's ECF Policies and Procedures and the court's website to determine those papers that each judge requests be provided as a judge's copy.

(2) *Papers Not Filed Electronically.* All papers not filed electronically with the clerk must include an original and one copy. The copy should be clearly marked "JUDGE'S COPY."

(c) Number of Copies Required for a Three–Judge Court. In any action or proceeding in which a three-judge court is requested, parties not filing electronically must file an original and three copies of papers until it is determined either that a three-judge court will not be convened or that the three-judge court has been convened and dissolved and the case remanded to a single judge. The court may allow fewer copies.

(d) Exhibits.

(1) *Filed Electronically.* Exhibits filed electronically must comply with the court's ECF Policies and Procedures.

(2) *Not Filed Electronically.* Bulky exhibits must be securely bound or fastened and clearly marked with the case number and the name of the judge to whom the case is assigned.

[Effective January 1, 1992. Amended effective September 12, 1994; March 2, 1998; March 1, 2010; July 1, 2013.]

Comment

LR 26.2 applies to filing discovery material.

LR 83.50 applies to filing papers in bankruptcy cases and proceedings.

Counsel and parties not filing electronically are advised that the handling and storage of documents are facilitated if they are received flat and without folds.

Under LR 5.1.1, the court may excuse a party from electronic filing on motion for good cause shown.

Attempts to circumvent the LR in any way may be considered an abusive practice which may result in papers being stricken as well as sanctions being imposed under LR 11.1.

[Comment amended March 1, 2010.]

LR 5.1.1 FILING AND SERVICE BY ELECTRONIC MEANS

(a) Governing Rules and Procedures. The local rules, the court's ECF Policies and Procedures (Appendix ECF to these rules), and court orders govern papers filed by electronic means. Except as specified otherwise in the ECF Policies and Procedures or by court order, all papers (not simply cases) filed after November 30, 2005 must be filed electronically. The court may excuse a party from electronic filing on motion for good cause shown. Except as specified otherwise in this rule, papers must also comply with LR 5.1.

(b) Service. Papers may be served through the court's electronic transmission facilities as authorized by the court's ECF Policies and Procedures. Transmission of the Notice of Electronic Filing is service on each party in the case registered as a filing user. Service of papers on other parties must be according to the local rules, the Federal Rules of Civil Procedure and the Federal Rules of Criminal Procedure.

(c) Judge's Copies.

(1) *Requirement.* The court's web site specifies those papers that each judge requests be provided directly to the judge as a judge's copy. Judge's copies otherwise need not be provided unless the judge specifically requests them.

(2) *Form.* The judge's copy must have the Notice of Electronic Filing attached to the front.

(3) *Submission to Judge.* The judge's copy must be submitted directly to the judge's chambers, not to the clerk's office. Furnishing a judge's copy is not filing.

(d) Facsimile Transmission. Filing by electronic means does not include filing by facsimile transmission.

[Effective October 1, 2003. Amended effective October 1, 2005.]

Comment

The Court will maintain electronic case files for all civil cases.

Administrative Order No. 04–AO–08, filed on February 4, 2004, suspended the original effective date of LR 5.1.1 from March 1, 2004, to June 1, 2004.

A judge may impose time or other limitations on the "good cause shown" referred to in (a).

LR 5.2   SERVICE OF NON–DISPOSITIVE AND DISPOSITIVE ORDERS; STIPULATIONS AND ORDERS

(a) Electronic Filing. The ECF Policies and Procedures (Appendix ECF to these rules) govern the filing and service of orders and proposed orders electronically.

(b) Service of Non–Dispositive Orders. Unless the court directs otherwise, the clerk will send the movant seeking a non-dispositive order a copy of the signed order. Within 14 days of the date of the order, unless the judge directs otherwise, the movant must serve, in accordance with Fed. R. Civ. P. 5, copies of the order on all other parties and other persons entitled to service of the order and promptly file a proof of service.

(c) Stipulations and Orders; Service of Orders. The person initiating a stipulation and proposing an order must submit a self-addressed stamped envelope and serve copies of the order on all other parties and other persons entitled to service of the order within 14 days of the date of the order, unless the judge directs otherwise. No proof of service is required.

(d) Service of Dispositive Orders. The preparer of a dispositive order, other than a stipulated order, must submit the proposed order to the court with an original, a copy for the court, and sufficient copies and addressed, stamped envelopes for all parties and other persons entitled to service of the order. The clerk will mail the order and provide a proof of service for the record.

(e) Definition of Dispositive Order. For purposes of this Rule, "dispositive order" means an order disposing of a motion for injunctive relief, for judgment on the pleadings, for summary judgment, to dismiss or quash an indictment or information made by a defendant, to suppress evidence in a criminal case, to certify or decertify a class, to dismiss for failure to state a claim upon which relief can be granted, and to involuntarily dismiss an action, whether the order grants or denies the motion in whole or in part.

[Former LR 5.4 adopted October 2, 1995. Renumbered as LR effective March 3, 1997. Amended effective December 1, 2009; March 1, 2010.]

Comment

In (b), the movant is responsible for service even if the movant does not prevail, in whole or in part.

In (c), the initiating person carries the same burden as the movant in (b). No proof of service is necessary because the order follows a stipulation.

In (d), the preparer includes the court. If the court prepares the dispositive order, then the court provides all documents, envelopes and postage for service. If the court directs a person to prepare the final order, then that person provides copies of the order, envelopes and postage for the court to complete service after the judicial officer signs the order.

LR 5.3   CIVIL MATERIAL FILED UNDER SEAL

(a) Sealing Items Authorized by Statute or Rule. When a statute or rule authorizes filing a document or other item under seal in a civil case, the item may be filed without a court order.

(1) A separate notice of filing under seal must be filed before filing an item under seal.

(2) The notice must include:

(A) a citation to the statute or rule authorizing the seal;

(B) an identification and description of each item submitted under seal; and

(C) a statement establishing that the items are within the statute or rule authorizing the seal.

(b) Sealing Items Not Authorized by Statute or Rule.

(1) Except as provided by statute or rule, documents (including settlement agreements) or other items may be sealed in a civil case only by court order. A party or other person may not file or tender to the clerk an item proposed for sealing under this subrule unless the court enters an order permitting sealing.

(2) A party or other person seeking to file an item under seal in a civil case under LR 5.3(b) must either file and serve a motion or submit a proposed stipulated order to authorize sealing.

(A) A motion or stipulated order to authorize sealing must:

(i) state the authority for sealing;

(ii) include an identification and description of each item proposed for sealing;

(iii) state the reason that sealing each item is necessary;

(iv) state the reason that a means other than sealing is not available or unsatisfactory to preserve the interest advanced by the movant in support of the seal; and

(v) have a supporting brief.

(B) When a motion to seal is filed, the movant must submit a proposed order with the motion. The proposed order submitted with the motion or a proposed stipulated order must state the reason the seal is required.

(c) Format of Documents to Be Sealed.

(1) All documents must comply with LR 5.1(a).

(2) Only the germane portion of a filing may be sealed. For example, if the sealed item is an exhibit to a motion, response, or reply, only the exhibit may be sealed.

(d) Unsealing Documents. When the court orders an item unsealed, the clerk will make it publicly available as any other public document.

(e) Disposition. Unless the court directs otherwise, the court will transfer sealed material to the Federal Records Center for maintenance under the judiciary's Records Disposition Schedule six months after expiration of the last applicable appeal period.

[Effective March 2, 1998. Amended effective June 1, 2002; March 3, 2008, effective April 1, 2008.]

Comment

Attorneys are cautioned that attempts to circumvent (a) may result in the imposition of sanctions.

Sealed settlement agreements are covered by LR 5.3(b)(1). Generally, except in extraordinary circumstances, the sealing of settlement agreements is disfavored.

Protective orders are covered under LR 26.4.

The delivery of papers filed under seal to federal court facilities must be in accordance with LR 83.31(a)(3)(B).

Other material provided by statute, e.g., Qui Tam cases, are not covered by this rule.

Documents filed electronically must comply with the Court's ECF Policies and Procedures (Appendix ECF to these rules).

[Comment amended effective June 1, 1998; June 1, 2002. Amended March 3, 2008, effective April 1, 2008. Amended effective July 1, 2008.]

LR 7.1 MOTION PRACTICE

(a) Seeking Concurrence in Motions and Requests.

(1) The movant must ascertain whether the contemplated motion, or request under Federal Rule of Civil Procedure 6(b)(1)(A), will be opposed. If the movant obtains concurrence, the parties or other persons involved may make the subject matter of the contemplated motion or request a matter of record by stipulated order.

(2) If concurrence is not obtained, the motion or request must state:

(A) there was a conference between attorneys or unrepresented parties and other persons entitled to be heard on the motion in which the movant explained the nature of the motion or request and its legal basis and requested but did not obtain concurrence in the relief sought;

(B) despite reasonable efforts specified in the motion or request, the movant was unable to conduct a conference; or

(C) concurrence in this motion has not been sought because the movant or nonmovant is an incarcerated prisoner proceeding pro se.

(3) The court may tax costs for unreasonable withholding of consent.

(b) Motions.

(1) Motions must comply with LR 5.1.

(2) A party must obtain leave of court to file more than one motion for summary judgment. For example, a challenge to several counts of a complaint generally must be in a single motion.

(c) Responses.

(1) A respondent opposing a motion must file a response, including a brief and supporting documents then available.

(2) Responses must comply with LR 5.1.

(3) A party must obtain leave of court to file more than one response to a motion for summary judgment. For example, a challenge to several arguments raised in a motion for summary judgment generally must be in a single response.

(d) Briefs.

(1) *Briefs Required and Permitted.*

(A) Unless the court permits otherwise, each motion and response to a motion must be accompanied by a single brief. The brief may be separate from or may be contained within the motion or response. If contained within the motion or response, the brief must begin on a new page and must be clearly identified as the brief. A movant may also file a reply brief.

(B) Briefs must comply with LR 5.1.

(2) *Form of Required Briefs.* A brief supporting a motion or response must, at the beginning, contain a concise statement of the issues presented and, on the following page, the controlling or most appropriate authority for the relief sought. The brief may contain a table of contents, an index of authorities, and an index of exhibits attached to the brief.

(3) *Length of Briefs.*

(A) The text of a brief supporting a motion or response, including footnotes and signatures, may not exceed 25 pages. A person seeking to file a longer brief may apply *ex parte* in writing setting forth the reasons.

(B) The text of a reply brief, including footnotes and signatures, may not exceed 7 pages.

(e) Briefing Schedule.

(1) *Dispositive Motions.*

(A) Dispositive motions are motions:

- for injunctive relief,
- for judgment on the pleadings,
- for summary judgment,
- to dismiss or quash an indictment or information made by a defendant,
- to suppress evidence in a criminal case,

- to certify or decertify a class,

- to dismiss for failure to state a claim upon which relief can be granted, and

- to involuntarily dismiss an action.

(B) A response to a dispositive motion must be filed within 21 days after service of the motion.

(C) If filed, a reply brief supporting a dispositive motion must be filed within 14 days after service of the response, but not less than 3 days before oral argument.

(2) *Nondispositive Motions.*

(A) Nondispositive motions are motions not listed in LR 7.1(e)(1)(A).

(B) A response to a nondispositive motion must be filed within 14 days after service of the motion.

(C) If filed, a reply brief supporting a nondispositive motion must be filed within 7 days after service of the response, but not less than 3 days before oral argument.

(f) Hearing on Motions.

(1) The court will not hold a hearing on a motion for rehearing or reconsideration, a motion for reduction of sentence, or a motion in a civil case where a person is in custody unless the judge orders a hearing.

(2) The court will hold a hearing on all other motions unless the judge orders submission and determination without hearing.

(3) The motion must be filed with the clerk, who will forward it to the assigned judge. The judge will set or cause to be set a date for hearing with notice to the parties and other persons entitled to be heard on the motion. Inquiries regarding time of hearing may be directed to the judge's chambers.

(g) Additional Time to File Supporting Documents and Brief.

(1) When a motion, response or written request states that the filing of additional affidavits or other documents in support or opposition is necessary, the assigned judge may specify the time within which the additional documents and brief must be filed by:

(A) entering an *ex parte* order prepared by the person making the request, or

(B) approving a written stipulation.

(2) A person obtaining such an order must immediately:

(A) serve it on opposing parties and other persons entitled to be heard on the motion, and

(B) notify them personally or by telephone, electronic mail, or facsimile of the signing of the order.

(3) A person against whom an *ex parte* enlargement of time has been granted may immediately move for a dissolution of the order granting enlargement.

(h) Motions for Rehearing or Reconsideration.

(1) *Time.* A motion for rehearing or reconsideration must be filed within 14 days after entry of the judgment or order.

(2) *No Response and No Hearing Allowed.* No response to the motion and no oral argument are permitted unless the court orders otherwise.

(3) *Grounds.* Generally, and without restricting the court's discretion, the court will not grant motions for rehearing or reconsideration that merely present the same issues ruled upon by the court, either expressly or by reasonable implication. The movant must not only demonstrate a palpable defect by which the court and the parties and other persons entitled to be heard on the motion have been misled but also show that correcting the defect will result in a different disposition of the case.

[Effective January 1, 1992. Amended effective November 7, 1994; September 8, 1998; December 1, 2005; June 2, 2008; December 1, 2009; March 1, 2010; July 1, 2013; October 1, 2015.]

Comment

Federal Rule of Civil Procedure 6(b)(1)(A) permits a person to seek an enlargement of time "with or without motion or notice ... if a request is made before the original time or its extension expires ...." Although the court generally prefers that such relief be sought by stipulation or motion, if a person chooses to seek relief by means of a "request," LR 7.1(a) requires contact with other parties and other persons entitled to be heard on the motion to seek concurrence in the relief requested. The court retains the inherent authority to alter the briefing schedule.

Attempts to circumvent the LR in any way may be considered an abusive practice which may result in the motion or response being stricken as well as sanctions being imposed under LR 11.1.

The following LR's also apply to specific types of motions:

1) LR 15.1, Form of a Motion to Amend and Its Supporting Documentation

2) LR 37.1, Motion to Compel Discovery

3) LR 37.2, Form of Discovery Motions

4) LR 54.2, Social Security Fee Motions

5) LR 59.1, Motion to Alter or Amend a Judgment

6) LR 65.1, Motions for Temporary Restraining Orders and for Preliminary Injunctions

7) LR 83.50, Bankruptcy Cases and Proceedings Stylistic amendments to the Federal Rules of Civil Procedure took effect on December 1, 2007. Pursuant to those amendments, the reference to Fed. R.Civ.P. 6(b)(1) in LR 7.1(a)(1) was changed to Fed.R.Civ.P. 6(b)(1)(A).

The movant must not include a "notice of hearing" unless the judge so directs.

LR 9.1 SPECIAL RULES OF PLEADING

(a) Notation of "Jury Demand" in the Pleading. If a party demands a jury trial by including it in a pleading, as permitted by Fed. R. Civ. P. 38(b)(1), the party must place a notation on the front page of the pleading, to the right of the caption, stating "Demand For Jury Trial" or the equivalent.

(b) Procedure for Notification of Any Claim of Unconstitutionality. In any action, suit or proceeding in which the United States or any agency, officer, or employee thereof is not a party and in which the constitutionality of an Act of Congress affecting the public interest is drawn in question, or in any action, suit or proceeding in which a State or any agency, officer, or employee thereof is not a party, and in which the constitutionality under the Constitution of the United States of any statute of that State affecting the public interest is drawn in question, the party raising the constitutional issue shall notify the Court of the existence of the question by stating on the paper that alleges the unconstitutionality, to the right of the caption, "Claim of Unconstitutionality" or the equivalent.

(c) Request for Three–Judge Court. In any action or proceeding which a party believes is required to be heard by a three-Judge court, the words "Three–Judge Court Requested" or the equivalent shall be included to the right of the caption of the first pleading in which the cause of action requiring a three-Judge court is pleaded. The words "Three–Judge Court Requested" or the equivalent on a pleading is a sufficient request under 28 U.S.C. § 2284. Together with the pleading requesting a three-Judge court, there shall be submitted a separate document entitled "Application for Three–Judge Court," together with a memorandum of points and authorities in support of the application.

(d) Designation of "Class Action" in the Caption. In any case sought to be maintained as a class action, the complaint, or other pleading asserting a class action, shall include to the right of the caption, the words "Class Action."

(e) Failure to Comply. The failure to comply with the requirements of this Rule shall not be grounds for denial of or construed as a waiver of rights otherwise provided by law.

[Former LR 5.3 effective January 1, 1992. Renumbered as LR 9.1 effective March 3, 1997. Amended effective November 1, 2004; July 1, 2010.]

LR 11.1 SANCTIONS FOR NON–COMPLIANCE WITH LOCAL RULES

If, after notice and a reasonable opportunity to respond, the Court determines that a provision of these Local Rules has been knowingly violated, the Court may impose an appropriate sanction upon the attorneys, law firms, or parties that have violated the Local Rule or are responsible for the violation. The procedures for imposing sanctions and the nature of sanctions shall be as set out in Fed.R.Civ.P. 11(c). For purposes of this rule, references in Fed.R.Civ.P. 11(c) to violations of "Rule 11(b)" are deemed to be references to violations of the Local Rules, and Fed.R.Civ.P. 11(c)(5)(A) does not apply.

[Effective January 1, 1992. Amended effective September 12, 1994; June 2, 2008.]

Comment

Stylistic amendments to the Federal Rules of Civil Procedure took effect on December 1, 2007. Pursuant to those amendments, the reference to "subdivision (b)" was changed to "Rule 11(b)" and the reference to Fed.R.Civ.P. 11(c)(2)(A) was changed to Fed.R.Civ.P. 11(c)(5)(A).

[Comment amended effective June 2, 2008.]

LR 11.2 FAILURE TO PROVIDE NOTIFICATION OF CHANGE OF ADDRESS

Every attorney and every party not represented by an attorney must include his or her contact information consisting of his or her address, e-mail address, and telephone number on the first paper that person files in a case. If there is a change in the contact information, that person promptly must file and serve a notice with the new contact information. The failure to file promptly current contact information may subject that person or party to appropriate sanctions, which may include dismissal, default judgment, and costs.

[Effective July 1, 2009.]

Comment

Notice should be filed with the Clerk and served on all parties.

LR 15.1 FORM OF A MOTION TO AMEND AND ITS SUPPORTING DOCUMENTATION

A party who moves to amend a pleading shall attach the proposed amended pleading to the motion. Any amendment to a pleading, whether filed as a matter of course or upon a motion to amend, must, except by leave of court, reproduce the entire pleading as amended, and may not incorporate any prior pleading by reference. Failure to comply with this Rule is not grounds for denial of the motion.

[Effective January 1, 1992.]

LR 16.1 PRETRIAL CONFERENCES

(a) All pretrial conferences shall be held as ordered by the Judges having jurisdiction of each case, with reasonable notice of the time thereof given to counsel or any party without counsel.

(b) Counsel or a party without counsel in any case may petition the Court to hold a pretrial conference at a time prior to the setting of a conference by order of the Court.

(c) Each represented party must be represented in the pretrial conference by at least one attorney who will participate actively in the trial of the action, and who has information and authority adequate for responsible and effective participation for all purposes, including settlement. At settlement conferences, all parties must be present, including, in the case of a party represented by an insurer, a claim representative with authority adequate for responsible and effective participation in the conference.

(d) If counsel for a party or a party without counsel fails to appear at a pretrial conference, the Judge may impose sanctions as appear proper, including costs and dismissal of the action or entry of default judgment.

(e) The following categories of action shall be exempted from the requirements of Fed.R.Civ.P. 16(b), unless otherwise ordered by the Judge to whom the action or proceeding is assigned:

(1) all actions in which one of the parties appears pro se and is incarcerated;

(2) all actions for judicial review of administrative decisions of government agencies or instrumentalities where the review is conducted on the basis of the administrative record (this includes social security actions);

(3) prize proceedings, actions for forfeitures and seizures, for condemnation, or for foreclosure of mortgages or sales to satisfy liens of the United States;

(4) proceedings in bankruptcy, for admission to citizenship or to cancel or revoke citizenship;

(5) proceedings for habeas corpus or in the nature thereof, whether addressed to federal or state custody;

(6) proceedings to compel arbitration or to confirm or set aside arbitration awards;

(7) proceedings to compel the giving of testimony or productions of documents under a subpoena or summons issued by an officer, agency or instrumentality of the United States not provided with authority to compel compliance;

(8) proceedings to compel the giving of testimony or production of documents in this District in connection with discovery, or testimony de bene esse, or for perpetuation of testimony, for use in a matter pending or contemplated in a U.S. District Court of another District;

(9) proceedings for the temporary enforcement of orders of the National Labor Relations Board;

(10) actions for recovery of erroneously paid educational assistance;

(11) proceedings involving efforts by the Internal Revenue Service to enforce the tax laws.

(f) If a timely-filed dispositive motion remains pending on the seventh day before the date for submitting the final pretrial order, that date will be postponed and rescheduled to a date no earlier than 7 days after the date of decision on the motion, unless the court orders otherwise. The court will also reschedule the final pretrial conference and the trial date accordingly. For purposes of this rule, "dispositive motion" means a motion for judgment on the pleadings, for summary judgment, to certify or decertify a class, to dismiss for failure to state a claim upon which relief can be granted, or to involuntarily dismiss an action, including such a motion directed to fewer than all claims, issues, or parties.

[Effective January 1, 1992. Amended effective December 2, 1996; July 1, 2010.]

Comment

The requirement that all parties be present at a pretrial conference held within 90 days of trial is eliminated. All parties are required to attend settlement conferences whenever they may be held.

LR 16.2   JOINT FINAL PRETRIAL ORDER

(a) Joint Final Pretrial Order. The parties shall furnish a joint final pretrial order in every civil case at, or if the judge requires, before the final pretrial conference. This joint final pretrial order shall fulfill the parties' disclosure obligations under Fed.R.Civ.P. 26(a)(3), unless the Judge orders otherwise. All objections specified in Rule 26(a)(3)(B) shall be made in this order. Counsel for plaintiff(s) or a plaintiff without counsel shall convene a conference for all parties to confer and collaborate in formulating a concise joint final pretrial order. Counsel for plaintiff(s) or a plaintiff without counsel shall compile the order. Counsel for all parties and any party without counsel shall approve and sign the order. Counsel for plaintiff(s) or a plaintiff without counsel shall submit an original and one copy of the order to the assigned Judge for approval and adoption. The order shall provide for

the signature of the Court and, when signed and filed in the Clerk's Office, becomes an order of the Court, superseding the pleadings and governing the course of trial unless modified by further order. The pretrial order shall not be a vehicle for adding claims or defenses. The order will not be filed in the Clerk's Office until the Judge has signed it.

(b) Contents of Order. The joint final pretrial order shall contain, under numbered and captioned headings, the following:

(1) *Jurisdiction.* The parties shall state the basis for Federal Court jurisdiction and whether jurisdiction is contested by any party.

(2) *Plaintiffs' Claims.* The statement of the claim or claims of plaintiffs shall include legal theories.

(3) *Defendants' Claims.* The statement of the defenses or claims of defendants, or third parties, shall include legal theories.

(4) *Stipulation of Facts.* The parties shall state, in separately numbered paragraphs, all uncontested facts.

(5) *Issues of Fact to Be Litigated.*

(6) *Issues of Law to Be Litigated.*

(7) *Evidence Problems Likely to Arise at Trial.* Include objections to exhibits and to the use of deposition testimony, including the objections required under Fed.R.Civ.P. 26(a)(3)(B). The order shall list all motions in limine of which counsel or a party without counsel should reasonably be aware.

(8) *Witnesses.* Each party shall list all witnesses whom that party will call and all witnesses whom that party may call. This listing shall include, but is not limited to, the disclosures required under Fed.R.Civ.P. 26(a)(3)(A)(i) and (ii). A party may, without further notice, call a witness listed by another party as a "will call" witness. Except as permitted by the Court for good cause a party may not list a witness unless the witness was included on a witness list submitted under a prior order or has been deposed. The list shall state whether the witness is an expert and whether testimony will be offered by deposition. Only listed witnesses will be permitted to testify at trial, except for rebuttal witnesses whose testimony could not be reasonably anticipated before trial, or except for good cause shown. The provisions of Fed.R.Civ.P. 37(c)(1) shall apply to a failure to list a witness.

(9) *Exhibits.* The parties must number and list, with appropriate identification, each exhibit, including summaries, as provided in Fed.R.Civ.P. 26(a)(3)(A)(iii). Objections to listed exhibits must be stated in the joint pretrial order. Only listed exhibits will be considered for admission at trial, except for rebuttal exhibits which could not be reasonably anticipated before trial, or except for good cause shown. The provisions of Fed.R.Civ.P. 37(c)(1) will apply to a failure to list an exhibit.

(10) *Damages.* The parties shall itemize all claimed damages and shall specify damages that can be calculated from objective data. The parties shall stipulate to those damages not in dispute.

(11) *Trial.*

(A) Jury or non-jury.

(B) Estimated length of trial.

(12) *Settlement.* Counsel or a party without counsel shall state that they have conferred and considered the possibility of settlement, giving the most recent place and date, and state the current status of negotiations and any plans for further discussions. They may state that they wish the Court to schedule a settlement conference.

(c) Failure to Cooperate. For failure to cooperate in preparing or submitting the joint final pretrial order or failure to comply strictly with the terms of the joint final pretrial order, the Court may dismiss claims, enter default judgment, refuse to permit witnesses to testify or to admit exhibits, assess costs and expenses, including attorney fees, or impose other appropriate sanctions.

(d) Filing of Trial Briefs, Findings and Instructions. The joint final pretrial order must further provide that trial briefs and requests for jury instructions must be filed on the first day of trial and proposed findings of fact and conclusions of law in nonjury cases must be filed before the last day of trial unless the court orders otherwise.

(e) Additional Requirements. A Judge, in an appropriate case, may add additional requirements to the joint final pretrial order, or may suspend application of this Rule, in whole or in part.

(f) Juror Costs Attributable to Parties. Each party shall also acknowledge that the Court may assess juror expenses under LR 38.2.

[Effective January 1, 1992. Amended May 6, 1996; March 2, 1998; November 2, 1998; June 2, 2008.]

Comment

Under LR 16.2(b)(9), any objection based on foundation or authenticity will be deemed waived if not raised before trial.

Stylistic amendments to the Federal Rules of Civil Procedure took effect on December 1, 2007. Pursuant to those amendments:

1) The reference to Fed.R.Civ.P. 26(a)(3) in the third sentence of LR 16.2(a) was changed to Fed.R.Civ.P. 26(a)(3)(B).

2) The reference to Fed.R.Civ.P. 26(a)(3) in LR 16.2(b)(7) was changed to Fed.R.Civ.P. 26(a)(3)(B).

3) The reference to Fed.R.Civ.P. 26(a)(3)(A) and (B) in LR 16.2(b)(8) was changed to Fed.R.Civ.P. 26(a)(3)(A)(i) and (ii).

4) The reference to Fed.R.Civ.P. 26(a)(3)(C) in LR 16.2(b)(9) was changed to Fed.R.Civ.P. 26(a)(3)(A)(iii).

[Comment amended effective June 2, 2008.]

LR 16.3 ALTERNATIVE DISPUTE RESOLUTION: GENERAL PROVISIONS

(a) ADR Favored. Alternative dispute resolution (ADR) refers to a set of procedures that seek to provide litigants a more informal, less expensive, and less adversarial method for resolving their disputes than is afforded by traditional litigation procedures. The judges of this district favor ADR methods in cases where the court determines, after consultation with the parties, that ADR may help resolve the case. The ADR methods approved by these rules include facilitative mediation (LR 16.4); case evaluation (LR 16.5); settlement conferences (LR 16.6); and other procedures (LR 16.7). The court will also consider other ADR methods that the parties propose.

(b) Court Administration of the ADR Program. ADR is authorized in all civil actions in this district under 28 U.S.C. § 651(b). Each ADR program is governed by these rules.

(c) Consideration of ADR. In appropriate cases, as part of the conference held under Rule 26(f) of the Federal Rules of Civil Procedure, or at some other conference ordered by the court, all litigants and counsel must consider and discuss the use of an appropriate ADR process at a suitable stage of the litigation.

(d) Confidentiality. Communications in ADR proceedings are confidential. They are not subject to discovery, are not admissible in a proceeding, and may not be disclosed to anyone other than the ADR participants unless the court permits disclosure. No party may compel a mediator to produce documents that relate to, or testify to matters discussed during, ADR proceedings except on order of the court.

(e) Judicial Officers. District judges and magistrate judges performing alternative dispute resolution functions, such as serving as mediators or settlement conference judges, act in their capacity as federal judicial officers.

(f) Neutrality of Evaluators, Mediators and Arbitrators.

(1) *Standards for Disqualification.* The standards for disqualification of a judicial officer under 28 U.S.C. § 455 apply to an evaluator and mediator. If the parties agree to the rules of an arbitration tribunal (such as the American Arbitration Association), the standards for disqualification of an arbitrator in those rules apply. If the rules of an arbitration tribunal do not apply, the standards for disqualification of a judicial officer under 28 U.S.C. § 455 apply to an arbitrator.

(2) *Procedure for Disqualification.* If an evaluator, mediator, or arbitrator becomes aware of facts that may require disqualification, or a party raises an issue about disqualification, the evaluator, mediator or arbitrator must disclose the relevant facts to the parties. If a party requests that the person withdraw, the person may withdraw and notify the court that another person should be appointed. If the person determines that withdrawal is not warranted, the person may elect to continue. The objecting party may then ask the court to remove the person by filing a motion. This procedure does not apply if the parties have agreed to another procedure.

(g) Status of Discovery, Motions and Trial During the ADR Process. Cases referred to ADR continue to be subject to the case management schedule established by the judge assigned to the case. Unless otherwise ordered, parties are not precluded from filing pretrial motions or pursuing discovery. Referral of a case to ADR is not grounds to avoid or postpone any deadline or obligation imposed by the case management order unless ordered by the court.

(h) Attorney's Responsibility for Payment of Fees. The attorney or law firm representing a party participating in ADR is directly responsible for fees payable to the court, mediators, or arbitrators. Parties not represented by an attorney are personally responsible for fees. To the extent consistent with ethical rules, the attorney or law firm may seek reimbursement from the client. If any attorney or unrepresented party is delinquent in paying any fee required to be paid to a mediator or arbitrator under these rules, the mediator or arbitrator may petition the court for an order directing payment, and any judge or magistrate judge assigned to the case may order payment, upon pain of contempt.

[Effective February 1, 2015.]

Comment

Responsibility for payment of fees to mediators can be adjusted by the Court, considering the fairness in allocating likely expenses among the parties. In cases in which a party is represented by a *pro bono* attorney under the Court's *pro bono* counsel program, volunteer mediators are available at no cost to the parties. See also LR 16.4(d).

LR 16.4   FACILITATIVE MEDIATION

(a) Definition.

(1) *Mediators.* Mediators are neutral persons who meet with the litigants and facilitate settlement negotiations.

(2) *Mediation.* Facilitative Mediation (mediation) is a flexible, nonbinding dispute resolution process in which an impartial third party—the mediator—facilitates negotiations among the parties to help them reach settlement. Mediation seeks to expand traditional settlement discussions and broaden resolution options, often by going beyond the issues in controversy. The mediator, who may meet jointly and separately with the parties, serves as a facilitator only and does not decide issues or make findings of fact. Cases will be assigned to mediation if the district or magistrate judge, after consultation with counsel or the parties, is satisfied that the selection of mediation will assist in the resolution of the case.

(b) Qualification of Mediators. Mediators must be qualified by training or experience. Completion of a mediator training course approved by the Michigan Supreme Court Administrative Office is sufficient to establish qualifications. A judge may maintain a list of qualified mediators to assist the parties in selecting a mediator.

(c) Mediator Selection. The parties may select a mediator. The court may disapprove the selection. If the parties cannot agree on a mediator, the judge may -

- appoint a mediator from the parties' nominations

- appoint a mediator from the judge's qualified mediator list, or

- appoint another federal judicial officer, including a magistrate judge.

Once a mediator is selected, the court will enter an order appointing the mediator and referring the case to mediation.

COMMENT

The parties' choice of mediator will generally be honored and disapproval is expected to be exceedingly rare.

(d) Mediator Compensation. The mediator must be paid his or her standard hourly rate, assessed in as many equal parts as there are separately represented parties, unless the parties agree in writing or the court orders otherwise. The mediator is responsible for billing counsel and unrepresented parties.

COMMENT

Responsibility for payment of fees to mediators can be adjusted by the Court, considering the fairness in allocating likely expenses among the parties. In cases in which a party is represented by a pro bono attorney under the Court's pro bono counsel program, volunteer mediators are available at no cost to the parties. See also LR 16.3(h).

(e) The Mediation Process.

(1) *Agreement.* The mediator may require the parties to sign an agreement consistent with this rule regarding confidentiality of the proceedings, discovery for the proceedings, and other procedural matters.

(2) *Notice.* The mediator must send a notice of the time and place of the mediation session(s) to participating parties.

(3) *Parties' Memoranda.* Unless the mediator directs otherwise, no later than seven calendar days before the mediation session, each party must provide the mediator with a concise memorandum stating the party's position, including issues of both liability and damages. Mediators may establish formal requirements for the memoranda. The mediator may circulate the parties' memoranda if the mediator gives the parties notice before they submit them.

(4) *Process.* The mediator will preside over the mediation session(s). The mediator may determine the length and timing of the session(s) and the order in which issues are presented. The mediator may meet jointly with the parties and separately with each party or group of parties. The mediator is expected to encourage and assist the parties in reaching a settlement but not to compel or coerce the parties to settle.

(5) *Party Responsibilities.* All parties or individuals with settlement authority must attend the mediation session(s), unless the court orders otherwise. Corporate parties must be represented by an agent with authority to negotiate a binding settlement. In cases involving insurance carriers, an insurer representative with settlement authority must attend in person. Each party must be accompanied by the lawyer expected to be primarily responsible for handling trial of the matter. The court will excuse a party or lawyer from attending in person only on a showing of extraordinary circumstances.

(6) *Completion of Mediation.* The mediator must advise the court of completion of mediation within seven days of completion, stating only the date of completion, who participated, whether settlement was reached, and whether further ADR proceedings are contemplated.

(7) *Settlement.* If the case is settled, the parties must notify the court without delay and submit appropriate documents to conclude the case within 21 days of settlement.

[Effective February 1, 2015.]

LR 16.5   CASE EVALUATION

(a) Case Evaluation Under Mich. Ct. R. 2.403. The court may refer a case to case evaluation under Michigan Court Rule 2.403, as amended from time to time, with or without the parties' consent, and subject to the provisions of this rule. The court may not enforce the sanctions provisions of that rule unless the parties consent to be bound by those provisions before the referral is made. The court may approve other procedures different from those in Mich. Ct. R. 2.403.

(b) Excepted Cases. Cases in which the United States is a party are not subject to case evaluation.

(c) Case Evaluation Panel; Stipulation of the Parties. The Wayne County Mediation Tribunal Association or another Michigan state trial court case evaluation system will evaluate cases, unless the court orders otherwise. For cases evaluated by the Wayne County Mediation Tribunal Association, the tribunal clerk is the case evaluation clerk. With the court's approval, the parties may stipulate to different procedures that apply.

(d) Actual Costs and Attorney's Fees. Actual costs, including attorney fees, may be awarded under this rule. However, if a statute or Federal Rule of Civil Procedure also authorizes the payment of attorney's fees, duplicate costs and attorney's fees may not be awarded.

[Effective February 1, 2015. Amended effective November 1, 2017.]

Comment

For example, if attorney's fees are awarded pursuant to Fed. R. Civ. P. 68—Offers of Judgment, or 42 U.S.C. 1988—Civil Rights Cases, the same fees may not be awarded pursuant to this Local Rule.

LR 16.6 SETTLEMENT CONFERENCES

The judge assigned to the case may order a settlement conference to be held before that judge, another district judge, or a magistrate judge. The court may require parties to be present. For parties that are not natural persons, the court may require a natural person representing that party who possesses ultimate settlement authority to attend in person. In cases where an insured party does not have full settlement authority, the court may require an official of the insurer with ultimate settlement authority to attend.

[Effective February 1, 2015.]

Comment

The court may consider assigning a settlement conference to another judicial officer rather than ordering a case to facilitative mediation when the amount in controversy is low or a party appears pro se.

LR 16.7 OTHER ADR PROCEDURES

A judge may use other methods of alternative dispute resolution, including summary jury trials, summary bench trials, and (with the parties' consent) arbitration, or recommend or facilitate the use of any extrajudicial procedures for dispute resolution not otherwise provided for by these rules.

[Effective February 1, 2015.]

LR 16.8 PRETRIAL FILINGS AND EXCHANGES

(a) Applicability. These requirements apply unless the court orders otherwise.

(b) Trial Briefs. Parties in civil cases must file and serve trial briefs on the first day of trial.

(c) Exhibits. Parties in civil cases must mark, number, and exchange all trial exhibits before trial. For good cause, the court may admit exhibits that are not marked, numbered, and exchanged before trial. During trial, each party must have its exhibits available as needed. After trial, each party must retain its exhibits.

(d) Jury Instructions.

(1) Parties in jury trials must file and serve on opposing counsel requested instructions on the first day of trial. In civil cases, they must include an instruction stating concisely the party's claim and theory of the issues. At any time before closing argument, a party may file and serve additional requested instructions that could not have reasonably been anticipated before trial.

(2) A party may file and serve with the requests a legal memorandum in support of the requested instructions. Parties may file and serve legal memoranda opposing requested instructions at any time before settlement of the instructions.

(3) Each requested instruction must:

    (A) start on a separate page;

    (B) be consecutively numbered;

    (C) bear the case number;

    (D) identify the requesting party; and

    (E) cite supporting authority.

[Former LR 16.4 effective March 2, 1998. Renumbered effective February 1, 2015.]

Comment

In criminal cases, the court's Standing Order for Discovery and Inspection and Fixing Motion Cut–Off Date in Criminal Cases governs certain pretrial obligations.

LR 26.1 FORM OF CERTAIN DISCOVERY DOCUMENTS

The party serving interrogatories, pursuant to Fed.R.Civ.P. 33, serving requests for production of documents or things, pursuant to Fed.R.Civ.P. 34, or serving requests for admission, pursuant to Fed.R.Civ.P. 36, shall provide a space after each such interrogatory, request, or admission, for the answer, response, or objection thereto. The party answering, responding, or objecting to written interrogatories, requests for production of documents or things, or requests for admission shall either set forth the answer, response, or objection in the space provided or shall quote each such interrogatory or request in full immediately preceding the statement of any answer, response, or objection thereto. Each party shall also number its interrogatories, requests, answers, responses, or objections sequentially, regardless of the number of sets of interrogatories or requests. In cases involving multiple parties, the sequential numbering required by this rule operates for each plaintiff and defendant. A separate numerical sequence shall be maintained for each discovery device and for each party from whom discovery is sought.

[Effective January 1, 1992.]

Comment

Fed. R. Civ. P. 33(a)(1) limits interrogatories to 25 without leave of court. [Stylistic amendments to the Federal Rules of Civil Procedure took effect on December 1, 2007. Pursuant to those amendments, the above reference to Fed.R.Civ.P. 33(a) was changed to Fed.R.Civ.P. 33(a)(1).]

[Comment amended effective April 3, 1995; June 2, 2008.]

LR 26.2 FILING DISCOVERY MATERIAL

(a) A party or other person may not file discovery material specified in Fed.R.Civ.P. 5(d)(1) and certificates of service for such discovery material except:

(1) when it provides factual support for a motion, response or reply. The party or other person relying on the material must file only the germane portion of it as an exhibit or attachment to the motion, response, or reply.

(2) when it is read or otherwise used during a trial or other proceeding. The party or other person relying on the material must file it at the conclusion of the trial or other proceeding in which it was used or at a later time that the court permits.

(3) on order of the court.

(4) if discovery material not previously filed is needed for an appeal, the party or other person with custody of the discovery material must file it either by stipulation or court order.

(b) Deposition material must be filed in written form. A written transcript of an audio taped or videotaped deposition will be accepted.

(c) The originating party or other person must maintain discovery material for six months after expiration of the last applicable appeal period, or until the court directs otherwise.

(d) If the court orders filing, the party or other person with custody of the discovery material must file it within 14 days of service of the order.

[Effective January 1, 1992. Amended effective May 2, 1994; November 7, 1994; May 5, 1997; July 1, 2001; March 3, 2008, effective April 1, 2008; October 8, 2008, nunc pro tunc April 1, 2008.]

Comment

Documents filed electronically must comply with the Court's ECF Policies and Procedures (Appendix ECF to these rules).

[Comment amended effective November 7, 1994. Amended May 5, 1997; July 1, 2001. Amended March 3, 2008, effective April 1, 2008.]

LR 26.3 DISCLOSURES REQUIRED BY FED. R. CIV. P. 26(a)(3)

The parties must make the disclosures and objections required by Fed. R. Civ. P. 26(a)(3) in the joint final pretrial order as specified in LR 16.2 unless the Court orders otherwise.

[Former LR 16.3 adopted effective September 12, 1994. Renumbered and amended as LR 26.3 effective December 5, 1994. Amended effective May 6, 1996; paragraph (a) repealed by 00–AO–079, effective December 1, 2000; July 1, 2001.]

Comment

Effective December 1, 2000, courts are no longer allowed to opt-out of the provisions of Fed.R.Civ.P. 26(a).

[Comment added July 1, 2001.]

LR 26.4 PROTECTIVE ORDERS ON GROUND OF PRIVILEGE OR OTHER PROTECTION

(a) Motions for Protective Orders.

(1) This rule governs motions for protective orders based on a claim that information is privileged or subject to protection. It does not apply to a motion for a protective order on other grounds. The motion must:

(A) state the claim that information, otherwise discoverable, is either privileged or subject to protection, and

(B) without revealing privileged or protected information, describe the nature of the documents, communications, or things not produced or disclosed, to enable the court to assess application of the privilege or protection.

(2) A party or other person may not file or tender to the clerk an item proposed for sealing under a protective order unless the court enters a protective order authorizing sealing.

(b) Proposed Orders. The movant must submit as an exhibit to the motion a proposed order that states that the information is either privileged or subject to protection and describes the type of information to be protected.

(c) Filing Protected Material. If a motion for protective order is granted, protected material shall not be filed with the Clerk except:

(1) when it provides factual support for a motion, response or reply. The party or other person relying on the material must file only the germane portion of it as an exhibit or attachment to the motion, response or reply.

(2) if it is read or otherwise used during a trial or other proceeding. The party or other person relying on the material must file it at the conclusion of the trial or other proceeding in which it was used or at a later time that the court permits.

(3) on order of the court.

(4) if privileged or protected material not previously filed is needed for an appeal, the party or other person with custody of the material must file it either by stipulation or court order.

(d) Sealing, Unsealing, and Disposition of Material. LR 5.3(d)–(e) govern the method of filing sealed items, unsealing, and disposition of sealed material.

[Adopted March 8, 2008, effective April 1, 2008.]

Comment

Sealed settlement agreements are covered under LR 5.3(b)(1).

Filing of depositions under seal is covered under LR 26.2(b).

Stipulated protective orders must be submitted as directed in the ECF Policies and Procedures (Appendix ECF to these rules).

The retention of protected material is addressed in Appendix ECF.

LR 37.1   MOTION TO COMPEL DISCOVERY

With respect to all motions to compel discovery, counsel for each of the parties or a party without counsel shall confer in advance of the hearing in a good faith effort to narrow the areas of disagreement. The conference shall be held a sufficient time in advance of the hearing so as to enable the parties to narrow the areas of disagreement to the greatest possible extent. It shall be the responsibility of counsel for the movant or a party without counsel to arrange for the conference.

[Effective January 1, 1992.]

Comment

Motions to compel discovery are also subject to LR 7.1.

LR 37.2   FORM OF DISCOVERY MOTIONS

Any discovery motion filed pursuant to Fed.R.Civ.P. 26 through 37, shall include, in the motion itself or in an attached memorandum, a verbatim recitation of each interrogatory, request, answer, response, and objection which is the subject of the motion or a copy of the actual discovery document which is the subject of the motion.

[Effective January 1, 1992.]

LR 38.1   JURY SELECTION

(a) The random selection of grand and petit jurors for service in this Court is provided for in a plan adopted by the Court in compliance with the requirements and provisions of the Jury Selection and Service Act of 1968, 28 U.S.C. § 1861, et seq. The plan is available for inspection at the offices of the Clerk.

(b) Jurors are summoned from the following counties for each place of holding court:

(1) Ann Arbor—Jackson, Lenawee, Monroe, Oakland, Washtenaw and Wayne.

(2) Bay City—Alcona, Alpena, Arenac, Bay, Cheboygan, Clare, Crawford, Gladwin, Gratiot, Huron, Iosco, Isabella, Midland, Montmorency, Ogemaw, Oscoda, Otsego, Presque Isle, Roscommon, Saginaw and Tuscola.

(3) Detroit—Jackson, Lenawee, Macomb, Monroe, Oakland, St. Clair, Sanilac, Washtenaw and Wayne.

(4) Flint—Genesee, Lapeer, Livingston and Shiawassee.

(5) Port Huron—Macomb, Oakland, St. Clair, Sanilac and Wayne.

[Effective January 1, 1992.]

LR 38.2   ASSESSMENT OF JUROR EXPENSES

The expense to the United States of bringing jurors to the courthouse for a trial may be assessed to one or more of the parties or counsel if the jury trial is not begun as scheduled or the jurors are not used for that trial for any reason attributable to the parties or counsel.

[Former LR 38.3 effective January 1, 1992. Renumbered as LR 38.2 effective March 3, 1997.]

Comment

It is the policy of the Judicial Conference of the United States that last minute settlements and continuances which result in unnecessary juror fees and expenses be penalized by the assessment of costs against the responsible attorney or party. See also LR 40.2.

LR 40.1   ASSIGNMENT OF CASES FOR TRIAL

Pursuant to Fed.R.Civ.P. 40, cases shall be set for trial in the manner and at the time designated by the Judge before whom the case is pending.

[Effective January 1, 1992. Amended effective March 2, 1998.]

Comment

For reassignment of civil cases, see LR 83.11(b).

LR 40.2   CONTINUANCES

Counsel or any party without counsel shall be prepared and present themselves as ready in all cases set for trial or for pretrial on the date set unless, on timely application and good cause shown, the cases are continued. Where application is made for the continuance of the trial of a case, such application shall be made to the Court as soon as the need arises.

[Former LR 39.1 effective January 1, 1992. Renumbered as LR 40.2 effective March 3, 1997.]

Comment

It is the policy of the Judicial Conference of the United States that last-minute settlements and continuances which result in unnecessary juror fees and expenses be penalized by the assessment of costs against the responsible attorney or party. See also LR 38.2.

LR 41.1   SETTLEMENTS

Whenever an action pending in this Court is to be settled by the parties thereto, otherwise disposed of out of Court, or obviously will not be tried, to the knowledge of counsel or a party without counsel, it shall be the duty of counsel for all parties or any party without counsel to see that immediate notice of such fact is given to the courtroom deputy clerk of the Judge handling the case.

[Effective January 1, 1992.]

Comment

Failure to provide the notice required by this Rule may, in an appropriate case, lead to the assessment of juror expenses under LR 38.2.

LR 41.2   DISMISSAL FOR LACK OF SUBJECT MATTER JURISDICTION OR FAILURE TO PROSECUTE

Subject to Fed.R.Civ.P. 23(e) and LR 81.1, when it appears that the court lacks subject matter jurisdiction or that the parties have taken no action for a reasonable time, the court may, on its own motion after reasonable notice or on application of a party, enter an order dismissing or remanding the case unless good cause is shown. An application for a continuance or pending discovery may not preclude a dismissal for failure to prosecute.

[Effective January 1, 1992. Amended effective March 2, 1998.]

LR 42.1   MOTIONS TO CONSOLIDATE

(a) A party seeking to consolidate cases under Federal Rule of Civil Procedure 42(a) must:

(1) file a motion in the case with the earliest case number; and

(2) file a notice of the motion in each related case.

(b) The district judge presiding in the earliest numbered case will decide the motion. However, the motion may not be granted unless the judges presiding in the related cases consent.

(c) If the motion is granted, the consolidated cases will be reassigned to the judge presiding in the earliest numbered case.

[Effective November 1, 2013.]

LR 43.1   EXAMINATION OF WITNESSES

Not more than one counsel on the same side shall be allowed to examine the same witness unless leave of Court is obtained.

[Effective January 1, 1992.]

LR 47.1   JUROR COMMUNICATION

(a) During the course of a trial, parties and attorneys must refrain from having contact with jurors before a verdict is returned.

(b) Once summoned to a courtroom for selection and until discharged, jurors must refrain from any outside contact or communication that relates to the case, which includes the use of cell phones, BlackBerries, iPhones, and other smartphone devices, the Internet, e-mail, text messaging, instant messaging, chat rooms, blogs, or the use of social networking websites such as Facebook, MySpace, LinkedIn, YouTube, or Twitter.

(c) Parties, attorneys, and jurors learning of a violation of this rule must immediately notify the judicial officer presiding over the trial.

(d) Any person wilfully violating this rule is subject to sanctions.

[Effective February 1, 2011.]

Comment

The court is encouraged to instruct the jury at the beginning of trial and before deliberations about these restrictions. See, for example, the suggested jury instruction prepared by the Judicial Conference Committee on Court Administration and Case Management, December 2009.

LR 52.1   PROPOSED FINDINGS AND CONCLUSIONS

Parties in civil non-jury trials must file and serve proposed findings of fact and conclusions of law before the last day of trial unless the court orders otherwise.

[Former LR 39.4 effective January 1, 1992. Renumbered as LR 52.1 effective March 3, 1997. Amended effective March 2, 1998.]

LR 54.1   TAXATION OF COSTS

A party seeking costs must file a bill of costs no later than 28 days after the entry of judgment. The clerk will tax costs under Fed. R. Civ. P. 54(d)(1) as provided in the Bill of Costs Handbook available from the clerk's office and the court's web site.

[Effective January 1, 1992. Amended effective June 1, 2007.]

Comment

A post-judgment motion that extends the time to appeal also extends the time to file a bill of costs under this rule until 28 days after the court rules on the post-judgment motion. *Miltimore Sales, Inc. v. International Rectifier, Inc.*, 412 F.3d 685 (6th Cir. 2005).

LR 54.1.2   ATTORNEYS' FEES

(a) A motion for attorneys' fees and related non-taxable expenses pursuant to Fed.R.Civ.P. 54(d)(2) must be filed no later than 28 days after entry of judgment.

(b) A motion for an award of attorneys' fees shall be supported by a memorandum brief as to the authority of the court to make such an award, and as to why the movant should be considered the "prevailing party," if such is required for the award. The motion shall also be supported by an affidavit of counsel setting out in detail the number of hours spent on each aspect of the case, the rate customarily charged by counsel for such work, the prevailing rate charged in the community for similar services, and any other factors which the court should consider in making the award. Within 14 days after filing of the motion, the party or parties against whom the award is requested shall respond with any objections thereto and accompanying memorandum setting forth why the award is excessive, unwarranted, or unjust.

[Effective June 1, 2007.]

Comment

Where a request for reconsideration under Fed.R.Civ.P. 59(e) has been filed, the time limit shall begin to run upon the denial of the motion. See *Miltimore Sales, Inc. v. International Rectifier*, 412 F.3d 685 (6th Cir. 2005).

LR 54.2   SOCIAL SECURITY FEE MOTIONS

(a) Attorneys representing clients in social security disability claims under Title II of the Social Security Act who seek District Court approval under 42 U.S.C. § 406 must file and serve a social security fee motion no later than 14 days after entry of judgment or receipt of the social security certificate award (notice of award), whichever is later. Attorneys representing clients in social security disability claims who seek District Court approval under 28 U.S.C. § 2412(d), the Equal Access to Justice Act, shall file a motion within 30 days of final judgment in the action.

(b) The social security fee motion must include the following information and any other information that the applicable statute requires:

(1) the past due benefits due the claimant,

(2) the past due benefits due any dependents,

(3) the dollar amount under (1) and (2) withheld by the Secretary for attorney's fees,

(4) the fees sought under 42 U.S.C. § 406 and court costs, fees and/or expenses sought under 28 U.S.C. § 2412,

(5) separate totals of hours counsel spent preparing and presenting the case in the District Court and before the Social Security Administration, and a certification by counsel that these hours are accurate and they are derived from contemporaneous time records, and

(6) a statement of whether counsel has represented the client in any other matter that involved the impairments in the disability claim. If so, indicate:

(A) whether the attorney has or may obtain an attorney fee from that matter and the amount or means of calculation;

(B) which medical evidence or reports prepared for or used in that matter were also used in the social security proceedings.

(c) The social security fee motion shall be accompanied by the following documents:

(1) a legible copy of the notice of award showing the amount of past due benefits and the amount withheld by the Secretary under 42 U.S.C. § 406,

(2) an itemized statement of services rendered showing chronological time entries for services at the administrative agency and District Court levels. These chronological time entries shall indicate the specific task(s) performed by the attorney.

(3) a copy of any fee agreement entered into between the plaintiff and the attorney.

(4) a certificate of service that the attorney's fee motion and attachments have been served on the U.S. Attorney and on the plaintiff. The certificate of service on the plaintiff shall include a statement that the plaintiff has received the following notice on a cover page of his or her copy of the motion and attachments:

NOTICE

Under the Social Security Act, the District Court must review and approve a reasonable attorney fee for legal services rendered in your case. This fee will be paid from a portion of your past due benefits that the Social Security Administration has withheld. This fee cannot be more than 25% of your past due benefits. It can, however, be an amount less than 25% of your past due benefits even if you have signed an agreement with your attorney for the full 25%. The attorney is not legally permitted to accept more from you or Social Security than the Federal Court allows. Enclosed is a copy of the attorney's fee application and attachments. If you have any objections to the fee or consider it to be unreasonable, or if you believe that any of the statements in the fee application are incorrect, you should send a brief statement of your concerns to the Judge whose name is on the motion, c/o U.S. District Court, 231 W. Lafayette, Detroit, MI 48226. Your statement will be given to the Judge, and the Court will send a copy of it to your attorney and will consider your statement in arriving at a reasonable fee for your attorney.

[Former LR 54.2 deleted and former LR 54.3 renumbered as LR 54.2 effective June 6, 1994. Amended effective March 2, 1998.]

LR 55.1 CLERK'S ENTRY OF DEFAULT

Requests for, with affidavits in support of, a Clerk's Entry of Default shall contain the following information:

(a) A statement identifying the specific defendant who is in default.

(b) A statement attesting to the date the summons and complaint were served upon the defendant who is in default.

(c) A statement indicating the manner of service and the location where the defendant was served.

[Effective January 1, 1992.]

Comment

The Clerk's Office provides a form for the Clerk's Entry of Default.

LR 55.2 CLERK'S ENTRY OF JUDGMENT BY DEFAULT

Requests for a Clerk's Entry of Judgment by Default must be accompanied by an affidavit which sets forth:

(a) The sum certain or the information necessary to allow the computation of a sum certain.

(b) The name of the defendant who is subject to default.

(c) A statement that the defendant is not:

(1) an infant or an incompetent person, or

(2) in the military service.

(d) A statement that a default has been entered because the defendant failed to plead or otherwise defend in accordance with Fed.R.Civ.P. 55(a).

[Effective January 1, 1992.]

Comment

The Clerk's Office has forms for requests for a Clerk's Entry of Judgment by Default and Affidavit of Sum Certain to assist parties and attorneys in complying with LR 55.2.

LR 58.1 PROCEDURE FOR ENTRY OF JUDGMENTS AND ORDERS

The court may enter a judgment or order by one of the following methods:

(a) The court may sign the judgment or order at or after the time it grants the relief in the judgment or order.

(b) The court will sign the judgment or order when the parties and any other person entitled to be heard on entry of the judgment or order approve its form.

(c) Within seven days after granting the judgment or order, or later if the court allows, a person seeking entry of a judgment or order may serve a copy of the proposed judgment or order on the other parties and any other person entitled to be heard on entry of the judgment or order, with notice that it will be submitted to the court for signing if no written objections are filed within seven days after service of the notice. The person seeking entry of the judgment or order must file the original and proof of service with the court.

(1) If no written objections are filed within seven days, the court will then sign the judgment or order if, in the court's determination, it comports with the court's decision. If the proposed judgment or order does not comport with the decision, the court will notify the parties and any other person entitled to be heard on entry of the judgment or order to appear before the court on a specified date for settlement of the matter; or, in the court's discretion, the court may enter its own order consistent with the court's decision.

(2) A person filing the objections must serve them on all parties and other persons entitled to be heard on entry of the judgment or order.

(3) If objections are filed, within seven days after receiving notice of the objections, the person who proposed the judgment or order must notice it for settlement before the court.

(d) A person seeking entry of a judgment or order may prepare a proposed judgment or order and notice it for settlement before the court.

[Effective January 1, 1992. Amended effective March 2, 1998; March 1, 2010.]

Comment

Pursuant to the recent amendments to Fed. R. Civ. P. 6(a)(1)(B), effective December 1, 2009, the counting of seven days under this rule includes Saturdays, Sundays, and legal holidays.

[Comment amended March 1, 2010.]

LR 59.1   MOTION TO ALTER OR AMEND A JUDGMENT

No response to a motion to alter or amend a judgment and no oral argument are permitted unless the court directs otherwise.

[Effective March 2, 1998.]

LR 65.1   MOTIONS FOR TEMPORARY RESTRAINING ORDERS AND FOR PRELIMINARY INJUNCTIONS

Requests for temporary restraining orders and for preliminary injunctions must be made by a separate motion and not by order to show cause. Motions for temporary restraining orders and preliminary injunctions and responses must comply with the briefing requirements of LR 7.1(b)–(d). A request under LR 7.1(a) to the opposing party for concurrence in the relief sought is not necessary for a temporary restraining order if Fed.R.Civ.P. 65(b)(1) permits an ex parte order. The court may set a different time schedule for motions and briefing and may grant an ex parte temporary restraining order under Fed.R.Civ.P. 65(b)(1).

[Effective January 1, 1992. Amended effective March 2, 1998; June 2, 2008.]

Comment

Stylistic amendments to the Federal Rules of Civil Procedure took effect on December 1, 2007. Pursuant to those amendments, the references to Fed.R.Civ.P. 65(b) were changed to Fed.R.Civ.P. 65(b)(1).

[Comment amended effective June 2, 2008.]

LR 65.1.1   ATTORNEY OR OFFICER AS SURETY

The court will not accept a member of the bar in active practice, or officer or employee of the court or the United States Marshals Service as a surety, except that a district judge may approve a member of the bar as a surety for a family member if the attorney is not counsel of record in the case.

[Effective March 2, 1998.]

LR 67.1   DEPOSIT AND WITHDRAWAL OF FUNDS IN INTEREST–BEARING ACCOUNTS

(a) **Deposit Order.** The Clerk of Court shall accept only certified check, cashier's check or money order for deposit in an interest bearing account. A proposed order directing the Clerk to deposit funds in an interest-bearing account shall include the following information:

(1) the amount to be invested; and

(2) language which directs the Clerk to deduct from the account any fee authorized by the Judicial Conference of the United States.

The proposed order shall be reviewed by the Clerk or his designee for approval as to form before it is submitted to the Judge. After signature, the movant shall personally serve a copy of the order on the Clerk or his designee who shall deposit the funds as soon as the business of the Clerk's Office allows.

(b) **Withdrawal Order.** An order for the withdrawal of funds held in an interest-bearing account shall state:

(1) the name and address of each recipient of the funds and, except for any governmental entity, the corresponding social security or employer identification number of each recipient, and

(2) the exact amount of principal and the percentage of interest to be paid to each recipient.

The proposed withdrawal order shall be reviewed by the Clerk or his designee for approval as to form before it is submitted to the Judge. After signature, the movant shall personally serve a copy of the order on the Clerk or his designee who shall execute the order as soon as the business of the Clerk's Office allows.

[Effective January 1, 1992. Amended effective November 1, 2014.]

LR 69.1   GARNISHMENTS

Except in cases in which the United States is the judgment creditor and unless the Court orders otherwise, a garnishment writ shall direct the garnishee to make all payments by check directly to the plaintiff by first-class mail to the plaintiff's attorney.

[Former LR 41.1 adopted effective November 7, 1994. Renumbered as LR 69.1 effective March 3, 1997.]

Comment

The Federal Debt Collection Procedures Act of 1990 and revised MCR 3.101 authorize this simplified procedure.

LR 72.1 UNITED STATES MAGISTRATE JUDGES

(a) Authority of Magistrate Judges.

(1) *General.* Pursuant to 28 U.S.C. § 636(b)(4), each United States magistrate judge appointed by this court is authorized to exercise all powers and perform all duties conferred upon magistrate judges by 28 U.S.C. § 636, as amended.

(2) *Specific Duties.* A magistrate judge may:

(A) conduct extradition proceedings, in accordance with 18 U.S.C. § 3184;

(B) direct the probation department to conduct a presentence investigation in a case in which the magistrate judge has exercised trial jurisdiction under 18 U.S.C. § 3401;

(C) hear and determine any nondispositive pretrial motions in civil and criminal cases, and hear and recommend the determination of any dispositive motions in such cases;

(D) exercise general supervision of civil and criminal calendars, conduct calendar and status calls, determine motions to expedite or postpone the trial of cases for the district judges;

(E) conduct pretrial conferences, settlement conferences, and related pretrial proceedings in civil and criminal cases;

(F) conduct arraignments in criminal cases not triable by the magistrate judge and take not guilty pleas in such cases;

(G) receive grand jury returns in accordance with Fed. R. Crim. P. 6(f);

(H) accept waivers of indictment, pursuant to Fed. R. Crim. P. 7(b);

(I) conduct voir dire and select petit juries for the court, with the consent of the parties;

(J) accept petit jury verdicts in civil cases in the absence of a district judge;

(K) conduct necessary proceedings leading to the potential revocation of probation;

(L) issue subpoenas, writs of habeas corpus ad testificandum or habeas corpus ad prosequendum, or other orders necessary to obtain the presence of parties, witnesses or evidence needed for court proceedings;

(M) order the exoneration or forfeiture of bonds;

(N) conduct proceedings for the collection of civil penalties of not more than $200 assessed under the Federal Boat Safety Act of 1971, 46 U.S.C. § 4311(d);

(O) conduct examinations of judgment debtors in accordance with Fed. R. Civ. P. 69;

(P) conduct proceedings for initial commitment of narcotics addicts under the Narcotic Addict Rehabilitation Act, 42 U.S.C. § 3412;

(Q) supervise proceedings conducted pursuant to letters rogatory in accordance with 28 U.S.C. § 1782;

(R) consider and, when appropriate, grant applications of the United States to enter premises for the purpose of seizing property or the rights to property subject to levy, pursuant to 26 U.S.C. § 6331;

(S) submit to a district judge of the court a report containing proposed findings of fact and recommendations for disposition by the district judge on motions for review of default judgments;

(T) perform any additional duties not inconsistent with the Constitution and laws of the United States.

(3) *Consent Jurisdiction.* Upon the consent of the judge to whom the case is assigned, and with the consent of the parties, magistrate judges are authorized to conduct civil proceedings (LR 73.1).

(4) *Other Duties.* A magistrate judge may perform any other duty authorized by 28 U.S.C. § 636.

(b) Assignment of Duties to Magistrate Judges.

(1) *General.* A magistrate judge may perform any of the duties authorized above upon specific reference by a judge of the court or pursuant to a general order of the court assigning duties. In performing such duties the magistrate judge will conform to the general procedural rules of this court, the instructions of the district judge to whom the case is assigned, and the Plan for the Administration of the Magistrate Judge System.

(2) *Prisoner Cases Under 28 U.S.C. §§ 2254, 2255 and 42 U.S.C. § 1983.* In addition to the authority granted in 28 U.S.C. § 636(b)(1)(B), Rule 10 of the Rules Governing Section 2254 Cases in the United States District Courts and Rule 8(b) of the Rules Governing Section 2255 Proceedings in the United States District Courts, a magistrate judge may issue any preliminary orders and conduct any necessary evidentiary or other appropriate hearings in prisoner cases under 28 U.S.C. §§ 2254, 2255 and 42 U.S.C. § 1983.

(3) *Social Security Benefits Cases.* All cases seeking review of a denial of social security benefits will be assigned both to a district judge and a magistrate judge by the clerk of the court at the time of filing. The clerk will provide for the random selection of a magistrate judge so that each magistrate judge in this district receives an equal share of all such cases from each division of the court. The magistrate judge will determine all non-dispositive motions in such cases pursuant to 28 U.S.C. § 636(b)(1)(A) and will file a report and recommendation in each such case pursuant to 28 U.S.C. § 636(b)(1)(B) and (C).

(c) Registry Funds.

A magistrate judge is authorized to enter an order of the court under 28 U.S.C. § 2042 to withdraw registry funds in any matter in which the magistrate judge is authorized by law to enter judgment, including but not limited to:

(1) misdemeanor and petty offense cases disposed of by a magistrate judge pursuant to 18 U.S.C. § 3401; 28 U.S.C. § 636(a)(3);

(2) bail release proceedings in which a magistrate judge has ordered bail money to be deposited into court pursuant to 18 U.S.C. § 3141 et seq.; 28 U.S.C. § 636(a)(2); and

(3) pretrial matters referred to the magistrate judge for determination pursuant to 28 U.S.C. § 636(b)(1)(A).

(d) Review and Appeal.

(1) Objections under Fed. R. Civ. P. 72 must:

  (A) specify the part of the order, proposed findings, recommendations, or report to which a person objects; and

  (B) state the basis for the objection.

(2) A person serving objections permitted by Fed. R. Civ. P. 72 must serve them on the magistrate judge and all parties and other persons entitled to be heard on the matter.

(3) A person may respond to objections within 14 days of service.

(4) A person may file a reply brief within 7 days of service of a response.

(5) LR 7.1 governs the form of objections, responses, and replies.

[Effective January 1, 1992. Amended effective November 2, 1993; December 6, 1993; September 8, 1998; December 1, 2009; March 1, 2010.]

Comment

28 U.S.C. § 636(b)(4) requires that "Each district court shall establish rules pursuant to which the magistrate judges shall discharge their duties."

LR 72.1(d) conforms procedures for the filing of objection to a Magistrate judge's order or report and recommendation to the provisions of Fed. R. Civ. P. 72 and provides that the form and time limits for the filing of responses to objections are to be governed by LR 7.1.

Review of matters referred under LR 72.1 is by the district judge. Review of matters referred under LR 73.1 is in the court of appeals.

Effective December 1, 2009, the time to file objections under Fed. R. Civ. P. 72 will change from 10 days to 14 days.

[Comment amended September 8, 1998; March 1, 2010.]

LR 72.2 EFFECT OF MAGISTRATE JUDGE RULING PENDING APPEAL TO A DISTRICT JUDGE

When an objection is filed to a magistrate judge's ruling on a non-dispositive motion, the ruling remains in full force and effect unless and until it is stayed by the magistrate judge or a district judge.

[Effective February 1, 2011.]

LR 73.1 SPECIAL DESIGNATION TO EXERCISE CIVIL CONSENT AUTHORITY

(a) Authority of a Magistrate Judge. Upon consent of all of the parties, and upon approval of the district judge to whom the case is assigned through entry of an order of reference, a magistrate judge may conduct all proceedings in a civil case and order entry of judgment in the case.

(b) Notice of Consent Option. Upon the filing of a complaint or notice of removal in a civil case, the clerk will give the plaintiff or plaintiff's counsel or the removing defendant or removing defendant's counsel a notice/consent form (form) informing the parties that they may consent to have a magistrate judge conduct all proceedings in the case and order the entry of final judgment. The parties or their attorneys must sign the form if they consent to the exercise of dispositive authority by the magistrate judge. Plaintiff or plaintiff's counsel must attach a copy of the form to each copy of the complaint and summons served. A removing defendant or removing defendant's counsel must include the form with the notice of removal required under 28 U.S.C. § 1446(a). Additional copies of the form may be furnished to the parties at later stages of the proceedings. The parties are free to withhold consent without adverse consequences, and any notice or other communication from the court under authority of this LR will so advise them. This section will not apply if the district judge so instructs the clerk.

(c) Execution of Consent. If all of the parties in a civil case consent to have the magistrate judge exercise the authority described in (a), the plaintiff or plaintiff's counsel must file with the clerk the form described in (b), signed by all parties or their attorneys. The clerk will not accept the form without all such signatures, and neither the form nor its contents may be made known or available to a district judge or magistrate judge if it lacks any signatures required under this LR. A party's decision regarding consent will not be communicated to a district judge or magistrate judge before a fully-executed form is filed. Consent in a civil case under (a) may be entered until 28 days before scheduled trial of the case unless otherwise ordered by the district judge.

(d) Reference of Civil Consent Case. Upon filing of an executed form as described in (c), the clerk will send it to the district judge. The district judge may then refer the case to the magistrate judge for all further proceedings. A magistrate judge may exercise consent jurisdiction only if the district judge enters an order specifically referring the case.

(e) Party Added After Consent Occurs. A party added to a civil case after reference of the case to a magistrate judge on consent will be given an opportunity to consent to the continued exercise of case-dispositive authority by the magistrate judge. The clerk will give the party a copy of the form described in (b). A party choosing to consent must, within 28 days of appearance, file with the clerk the form signed by the party or attorney. The case will be returned to the district judge for all further proceedings unless a form is properly signed and filed.

[Effective September 8, 1998. Amended effective December 1, 2009; March 1, 2010.]

Comment

Review of matters referred under LR 73.1 is in the court of appeals. Review of matters referred under LR 72.1 is by the district judge.

LR 77.1 SESSIONS OF THE COURT

This court shall be in continuous session for transacting judicial business on all business days throughout the year.

[Effective January 1, 1992. Amended effective March 2, 1998.]

Comment

28 U.S.C. § 141 reads:

"Special sessions; places; notices. Special sessions of the district court may be held at such places in the district as the nature of the business may require, and upon such notice as the court orders. Any business may be transacted at a special session which might be transacted at a regular session."

LR 77.2 PRESIDING JUDGE

(a) Presiding Judge Calendar (Detroit). The presiding judge calendar is compiled by the Chief Judge and is based on the availability of each district judge (including senior judges who consent) in Detroit. The presiding judge normally acts for designated one-week periods. The identity of the presiding judge may not be disclosed before Monday at 8:30 a.m.

(b) Role of Presiding Judge. The presiding judge may act in the absence or unavailability of the assigned judge. Since judges often make specific arrangements with other judges to act if they are absent or unavailable, counsel or a person without counsel should always contact the chambers of the assigned judge. If it appears that no such arrangements have been made, counsel or a person without counsel may contact the presiding judge. The first presiding judge to act for the assigned judge concerning any case or matter will hear all other issues arising in the case or matter in the absence or unavailability of the assigned judge. Unless other arrangements have been made, the presiding judge normally presides over naturalization ceremonies.

(c) Judge Absent or Unavailable. The presiding judge will be present in the courthouse during business hours through the week assigned as presiding judge. If the presiding judge is absent or unavailable, counsel or a person without counsel should contact the clerk's office to determine if arrangements have been made for another judge to act as presiding judge. If it appears that no such arrangements have been made, the clerk's office will contact judges, beginning with the most senior district judge in Detroit (including senior judges who consent), until an available judge is found to act as presiding judge.

(d) Ann Arbor and Port Huron. The presiding judge in Detroit acts as presiding judge for the Ann Arbor and Port Huron court locations.

(e) Bay City. In Bay City, the presiding judge is the resident district judge at that court location. If that judge is not available, the matter will be referred by the Clerk's Office to the presiding judge in Detroit.

(f) Flint. In Flint, the more senior resident judge will establish the presiding judge calendar, which will designate one of the resident district judges at that court location as the presiding judge for the period. The presiding judge normally acts for designated one-week periods. If that judge is not available, the matter will be referred by the Clerk's Office to the presiding judge in Detroit.

[Effective January 1, 1992. Amended effective January 1, 2001; March 1, 2010; June 1, 2014.]

Comment

The role of presiding judge when an appeal of a magistrate judge's decision in a preliminary criminal proceeding which has not been assigned to a district judge is defined in LCrR 57.2.

The role of presiding judge in determining whether exigent circumstances exist in proceedings commenced by attachment and garnishment and actions in rem is defined in LR B.1.

The designated period referred to in LR 77.2(a) begins at 8:30 a.m. on Monday and ends at 8:29 a.m. on the following Monday unless that Monday is a Federal holiday, in which case the designated period would extend until 8:29 a.m. on Tuesday.

[Comment amended March 1, 2010; July 1, 2014.]

LR 80.1 ORDERS FOR TRANSCRIPT FROM OFFICIAL COURT REPORTERS

(a) All requests for transcripts from any proceeding held in the United States District Court for the Eastern District of Michigan shall be in writing and addressed to the court reporter for the District Judge before whom the matter was heard.

(b) A copy of a transcript must not be represented as an official transcript of a court proceeding unless a court reporter of the court or electronic transcriber performing services for the court certifies the transcript.

(c) The Clerk shall post and make available upon request the schedule of fees approved by the Judicial Conference of the United States and this Court.

[Effective January 1, 1992. Amended effective March 2, 1998; November 1, 2014.]

LR 81.1 REMOVAL OF DIVERSITY ACTIONS

(a) This rule applies to actions removed on the basis of diversity of citizenship in which the complaint does not plead a specific amount in controversy in excess of the jurisdictional amount required under 28 U.S.C. § 1332.

(b) The removing defendant must:

(1) allege in the notice of removal that the amount in controversy exceeds the required jurisdictional amount, and

(2) set forth the facts or other reasons that the removing defendant possesses that support that allegation or state that the removing defendant has no such facts at that time.

(c) If the notice of removal does not establish that the case meets the jurisdictional requirement, the court may issue an order to the defendant to show cause, either orally or in writing, why the case should not be remanded to state court.

(d) If a plaintiff moves to remand, contending that the amount in controversy does not exceed the required jurisdictional amount, the plaintiff must include with the motion a signed statement of damages claimed, itemizing all damages by category and amount, or, for those categories for which the plaintiff is unable to specify a precise amount, an estimate of the maximum amount and a detailed description of the factual basis for the estimate.

(e) The court will not enter an order to remand on the ground that the amount in controversy does not exceed the required jurisdictional amount without an opportunity to be heard.

[Adopted effective January 6, 1992. Amended effective December 6, 1993; March 2, 1998.]

Comment

Nothing in LR 81.1 is intended to alter the otherwise applicable burden of proof. A form of Notice of Removal may be obtained from the Clerk's Office in Ann Arbor, Bay City, Detroit and Flint.

At both a show cause hearing or hearing on a motion to remand, both parties may file statements of facts supporting their jurisdictional allegations. These statements may be supported by affidavits or documentary evidence. The statements and supporting materials are "papers" within the meaning of Fed.R.Civ.P. 11.

LR 83.1 AMENDMENTS TO LOCAL RULES; EFFECTIVE DATE

(a) When the court proposes an amendment to or amends these rules, it must provide public notice of the proposal or amendment on its website and via other sources that will reach a wide audience.

(b) An amendment to these rules takes effect on the first day of the month following adoption unless otherwise ordered by the court.

[Effective January 1, 1992. Amended effective March 2, 1998; January 4, 1999, effective February 1, 1999; December 1, 2008.]

Comment

These Rules may be amended in compliance with Fed. R. Civ. P. 83 and Fed. R. Crim. P. 57.

In addition to the Court's website, sources as used in LR 83.1(a) will include legal newspapers throughout the Eastern District, and the roster of persons registered to file papers electronically (filing users).

A notice will appear in each issue of the Michigan Bar Journal advising persons that proposed and final amendments to the Court's local rules will be posted on its website.

LR 83.20(a) requires that "a person practicing in this court must know these rules, including the provisions for sanctions for violating the rules." For the most up-to-date information, persons practicing in this court are encouraged to visit the Court's website frequently.

[Comment amended effective December 1, 2008.]

LR 83.2 REPORTERS AND ADVISORY COMMITTEE

The Chief Judge of this Court shall appoint one or more reporters who shall be empowered to recommend amendments to these Rules. The reporters shall collect material relevant to proposed changes. The Chief Judge of this Court shall also appoint an advisory committee composed of members of the Bar who will assist the reporters in these functions. This provision does not limit the authority of the Judges of this Court to adopt amendments independent of the reportorial process.

[Effective January 1, 1992.]

LR 83.3 ADMINISTRATIVE ORDERS

When authorized by the Court, the Chief Judge may issue administrative orders of general scope which apply to all cases pending in the district and administrative orders of a more limited nature which apply to smaller groups of cases. Administrative orders shall be transmitted to the Clerk who shall maintain a public file of all administrative orders currently in force. The Clerk shall transmit administrative orders to the State Bar United States Courts Committee, the Federal Bar Association Eastern District of Michigan Chapter, and the Local Rules Advisory Committee. When directed by the Chief Judge, the Clerk shall arrange for publication of an administrative order.

[Former LR 1.2 effective January 1, 1992. Amended and redesignated as LR 83.3 October 2, 1995.]

LR 83.4 DISCLOSURE OF CORPORATE AFFILIATIONS AND FINANCIAL INTEREST

(a) Parties Required to Make Disclosure. With the exception of the United States Government or agencies thereof, or a state government or agencies or political subdivisions thereof, all corporate parties to a civil case and all corporate defendants in a criminal case must file a Statement of Disclosure of Corporate Affiliations and Financial Interest. A negative report is also required.

(b) Financial Interest to Be Disclosed.

(1) Whenever a corporation which is a party to a case is a subsidiary or affiliate of any publicly owned corporation not named in the case, counsel for the corporation which is a party must file the statement of disclosure provided in (c) identifying the parent corporation or affiliate and the relationship between it and the corporation which is a party to the case. A corporation is considered an affiliate of a publicly owned corporation for purposes of this Rule if it controls, is controlled by, or is under common control with a publicly owned corporation.

(2) Whenever, by reason of insurance, a franchise agreement, lease, profit sharing agreement, or indemnity agreement, a publicly owned corporation or its affiliate, not a party to the case, has a substantial financial interest in the outcome of the litigation, counsel for the party whose interest is aligned with that of the publicly owned corporation or its affiliate must file the statement of disclosure provided in (c) identifying the publicly owned corporation and the nature of its or its affiliate's substantial financial interest in the outcome of the litigation.

(3) The duty of disclosure by the corporate parties described in this Rule is continuing.

(c) Statement of Disclosure. The statement of disclosure must be made on a form provided by the Clerk and filed, as part of the first pleading or paper filed by the party in this Court, or as soon as the party becomes aware of the corporate affiliation or financial interest, or as otherwise ordered by the judge to whom the case is assigned.

[Effective May 1, 1999.]

Comment

LR 83.4 is based on 6th Cir. R. 26.1. It is the responsibility of the courtroom deputy clerk for the judge to whom the case is assigned to monitor compliance with this Rule, including but not limited to sending out copies of the statement of disclosure to new defendants, third-party defendants, and others affected under (b).

LR 83.10 ASSIGNMENT OF CIVIL CASES TO PLACES OF HOLDING COURT

(a) Counties and Places of Holding Court. Except as provided in LR 83.11, civil cases arising in or related to one or more of the following counties shall be assigned as provided in (b):

(1) Genesee, Jackson, Lapeer, Lenawee, Livingston, Macomb, Monroe, Oakland, St. Clair, Sanilac, Shiawassee, Washtenaw and Wayne counties for which the places of holding court are Detroit, Ann Arbor, Flint and Port Huron.

(2) Alcona, Alpena, Arenac, Bay, Cheboygan, Clare, Crawford, Gladwin, Gratiot, Huron, Iosco, Isabella, Midland, Montmorency, Ogemaw, Oscoda, Otsego, Presque Isle, Roscommon, Saginaw and Tuscola counties for which the place of holding court is Bay City.

(b) Assignment of Cases. Civil cases shall be assigned by the Clerk to a place of holding court by reference to the counties in (a) in the following order of priority:

(1) If an action is removed from State Court, the county in which the case was pending in State Court (28 U.S.C. § 1441(a)).

(2) If an action is local in nature, the county in which the real estate is located.

(3) The county in which a plaintiff resides.

(4) The county in which the claim arose.

(5) In a case in which a defendant is an officer or employee of the United States or any agency thereof acting in his or her official capacity, or under color of legal authority, or an agency of the United States, the county in which an office of a defendant is located.

(6) A county in which a defendant resides or has a place of business.

(7) The place of holding court in which the case is filed.

(c) Improper Assignments. A case improperly assigned to a place of holding court shall be transferred to the proper location by order of the Court.

[Former LR 100.1 effective January 1, 1992. Amended effective April 3, 1995. Renumbered as LR 83.10 effective March 3, 1997. Amended effective October 1, 2003.]

LR 83.11 ASSIGNMENT AND REASSIGNMENT OF CIVIL CASES TO JUDGES

(a) Random Method for Assignment of Cases to Judges.

(1) In Ann Arbor, Detroit, Flint and Port Huron, the Clerk shall employ a random method for the assignment of civil cases (excluding social security cases and special civil cases) to Judges. Special civil cases are defined as those cases arising under 28 U.S.C. §§ 2241 and 2254 and 42 U.S.C. §§ 1983 and 1985 in which the plaintiff is an inmate or resident of any facility of the Michigan Department of Corrections, the United States Bureau of Prisons, or of any county or local jail.

(2) In Bay City, the Clerk shall assign civil cases to the Judge regularly holding court in Bay City.

(3) In Ann Arbor, Bay City, Detroit, Flint and Port Huron, the Clerk shall employ a random method for the assignment of social security cases and special civil cases to Judges.

(4) A case in which a three-Judge court is requested under 28 U.S.C. § 2284 shall be assigned by random method regardless of the place of holding court in which the case is filed.

(5) Assignment of cases to the Chief Judge, to Senior Judges, and, in cases of emergency, to Judges in active service, shall be as provided by administrative order of the Court.

(6) Miscellaneous matters shall be assigned to a judge at the place of holding court where the miscellaneous matter is filed.

(b) Reassignment of Civil Cases.

(1) Cases shall be reassigned only by order of the Court.

(2) To promote docket efficiency, or to conform to the requirement of any case management plan adopted by the Court, or upon consent of the parties, or after notice and hearing, or in the interests of justice, the Chief Judge may order a civil case to be reassigned, but only with the consent of the Judge to whom the case was originally assigned and with the consent of the Judge to whom it is to be reassigned.

(3) To promote judicial efficiency in cases not requiring reassignment under these Rules, the Judges, after notice to the parties and opportunity to respond, may jointly order consolidation of some or all aspects of related cases.

(4) Reassignment of cases because of a change in judicial personnel shall be in accordance with an administrative order authorized by the Court.

(5) Successive habeas corpus petitions challenging the same conviction or sentence regardless of grounds asserted shall be assigned to the Judge to whom the original petition was assigned or to the Judge who is appointed to fill the vacancy of that Judge. If no judge has been appointed to fill that vacancy, the matter will be reassigned by random method under (a).

(6) Motions for relief filed under 28 U.S.C. § 2255 shall be assigned to the Judge who imposed sentence on the defendant or to the Judge who is appointed to fill the vacancy of the sentencing Judge. If no judge has been appointed to fill that vacancy, the matter will be reassigned by random method under (a).

(7) Companion Cases.

(A) Companion cases are cases in which it appears that:

(i) substantially similar evidence will be offered at trial, or

(ii) the same or related parties are present and the cases arise out of the same transaction or occurrence, or

(iii) they are Social Security cases filed by the same claimant.

(B) Cases may be companion cases even though one of them has been terminated.

(C) Counsel or a party without counsel must bring companion cases to the court's attention by responding to the questions on the civil case cover sheet or in the electronic filing system.

(D) When it becomes apparent to the Judge to whom a case is assigned and to a Judge having an earlier case number that two cases are companion cases, upon consent of the Judge having the earlier case number, the Judge shall sign an order reassigning the case to the Judge having the earlier case number.

(8) Matters arising from a civil, special civil (as defined in (a)(1)), or miscellaneous case assigned to (1) a judge who has retired from the court, or (2) a senior judge no longer receiving special civil or miscellaneous cases, will be assigned to the judge who is appointed to fill the vacancy of that judge. If no judge has been appointed to fill that vacancy, the matter will be reassigned by random method under (a).

(c) Refiled, Dismissed, and Remanded Civil Cases.

(1) If an action is filed or removed to this court and assigned to a judge and then is discontinued, dismissed, or remanded to a state court and later refiled, it shall be assigned to the same judge who received the initial case assignment without regard for the place of holding court where the case was refiled. Counsel or a party without counsel must bring such cases to the court's attention by responding to the questions on the civil case cover sheet or in the electronic filing system.

(2) When it becomes apparent to the Judge to whom a case is assigned that the case has been previously filed in this Court and assigned to another Judge and has later been discontinued, dismissed without prejudice or remanded to a State Court, the two Judges shall sign an order reassigning the case to the Judge who had been assigned the earlier case.

(d) Disqualification of Judge. When a Judge to whom a case is assigned is disqualified from hearing it, the Clerk shall reassign the case in accordance with (a)(1) or (a)(3).

[Former LR effective January 1, 1992. Amended effective March 2, 1992; April 3, 1995. Renumbered as LR 83.11 effective March 3, 1997. Amended effective May 1, 1999; October 1, 2003; July 1, 2010; June 1, 2014.]

Comment

The "earlier case number" referred to in (b)(7)(D) will mean the earlier case filed as determined by date and time. Miscellaneous matters referred to in LR 83.11(a)(6) include, but are not limited to, the following:

1) matters sealed in the early stages of criminal proceedings;

2) registrations of judgment from other districts;

3) actions to enforce administrative subpoenas and summons;

4) proceedings ancillary to an action pending in another district, e.g., deposition subpoenas;

5) supplementary proceedings brought in aid of execution;

6) applications for writs of habeas corpus ad testificandum or ad prosequendum;

7) appointments of counsel under the Criminal Justice Act;

8) disciplinary proceedings for attorneys;

9) incoming letters rogatory.

NOTE: Any of these may be changed into a civil case if contested before a district judge.

The civil case cover sheet referred to in (b)(7)(C) and (c)(1) is available at the clerk's office and the court's web site.

[Comment amended December 4, 2000. Amended July 1, 2010.]

LR 83.20   ATTORNEY ADMISSION

(a) Definitions.

(1) As used in this rule, except as provided in LR 83.20(i)(1)(D), "practice in this court" means, in connection with an action or proceeding pending in this court, to appear in, commence, conduct, prosecute, or defend the action or proceeding; appear in open court; sign a paper; participate in a pretrial conference; represent a client at a deposition; or otherwise practice in this court or before an officer of this court. A person practicing in this court must know these rules, including the provisions for sanctions for violating the rules. A person is not permitted to circumvent this rule by directing the conduct of litigation if that person would not be eligible to practice in this court.

(2) As used in this rule, "chief judge" includes his or her designee.

(b) Roll of Attorneys. The bar of this court consists of those currently admitted to practice in this court. The clerk will maintain the roll of admitted attorneys.

(c) Eligibility for Admission.

(1) A person who is admitted to practice in a court of record in a state, territory, commonwealth, or possession of the United States, the District of Columbia, or a United States District Court and who is in good standing is eligible for admission to the bar of this court, except as provided in (c)(2). Pro hac vice admission is not permitted.

(2) If the applicant has been held in contempt, subject to public or private discipline administered by a court or the Michigan Attorney Discipline Board or other similar disciplinary authority of another state, is not in compliance with an order of a court directed to the applicant as a party, or convicted of a crime, the chief judge will make an independent determination as to whether the applicant is fit to be entrusted with professional matters and to aid in the administration of justice as an attorney and officer of the court.

(d) Procedure for Admission.

(1) An applicant for admission to the bar of this court must pay the fee established by the court and complete the application provided by the clerk. The following information must be included in the application:

(A) applicant's name, firm/agency name (if applicable), office address, e-mail address, office telephone and fax numbers;

(B) the date of admission for each jurisdiction where the applicant has been admitted to practice and appropriate I.D. number;

(C) whether the applicant has ever been held in contempt, or the subject of an order of discipline as defined in LR 83.22(a)(1). If so, the applicant must state the facts and the final disposition of each such instance;

(D) whether the applicant is not in compliance with an order of a court directed to the applicant as a party, or been convicted of a crime. If so, the applicant must state the facts and the final disposition of each instance; and

(E) any other name under which the applicant has received legal education or has practiced or been licensed and the periods during which the names were used.

(2) An applicant for admission to the bar of this court must submit an original certificate of good standing issued within the last 30 days from a court of record identified in (c)(1).

(3) A sponsor is not required for an applicant under (c)(1), unless directed by the chief judge. A sponsor is required for an applicant under (c)(2) and for an applicant taking the oath of office by telephone or video conference in (d)(4). A sponsor is a member of the bar of this court who must sign a declaration supporting the application for admission. The sponsor must declare that the applicant is of good character and reputation and is qualified to practice as a member of the bar of this court. A sponsor who knowingly and willfully provides a false or fraudulent declaration will be subject to sanctions under 18 U.S.C. § 1001.

(4) If the court grants the application, the applicant must take the oath of office. An applicant with an office in the district must personally appear to take the oath before a judicial officer. A judicial officer may designate the clerk or a deputy clerk to administer the oath. An applicant without an office in the district may take the oath by telephone or video conference before a judicial officer. The clerk then will issue a certificate of admission.

(e) Maintaining Eligibility for Admission. An attorney immediately must report to the chief judge a change of the status of his or her permission to practice law in any other jurisdiction if:

(1) the attorney's license to practice law becomes inactive in any jurisdiction for any reason other than under an order of discipline as defined in LR 83.22(a)(1);

(2) the change to inactive status leaves the attorney unlicensed to practice law in all other states and the District of Columbia; and

(3) the attorney has a case pending in this court or seeks to appear in a case.

The chief judge then will make an independent determination whether the attorney may continue to practice in this court. The chief judge may issue a show cause order to assist in making the determination. The failure to make a timely report may itself be grounds for discipline. The obligation to report orders of discipline from other jurisdictions is governed by LR 83.22(g)(3).

(f) Local Counsel.

(1) *General Requirement.* A member of the bar of this court who appears as attorney of record in the district court and is not an active member of the State Bar of Michigan must specify as local counsel a member of the bar of this court with an office in the district. Local counsel must enter an appearance and have the authority and responsibility to conduct the case if non-local counsel does not do so. On application, the court may relieve an attorney who is not an active member of the State Bar of Michigan of the obligation to specify local counsel.

(2) *Appearances of Local Counsel.* Local counsel must attend each scheduled appearance on the case unless the court, on its own motion or on motion or request of a party, dispenses with the requirement.

(g) Government Attorneys. An attorney representing the United States or an agency of the United States may practice in this court in an official capacity without applying for admission. If the attorney does not have an office in the district, he or she must designate the United States attorney or an assistant United States attorney for this district to receive service of all notices and papers. Service of notice on the United States attorney or designated assistant will constitute service on the nonresident government attorney.

(h) Law Student Practice. Law students may practice in this court only as permitted by LR 83.21, Law Student Practice.

(i) Unauthorized Practice.

(1) A person must be a member in good standing of the bar of this court to practice in this court or to hold himself or herself out as being authorized to practice in this court, except that—

(A) a party may proceed in pro per.

(B) government attorneys may practice under LR 83.20(g).

(C) law students may practice under LR 83.21.

(D) an actively-licensed attorney who is not under suspension or disbarment in this or another federal or state court may—

(i) cosign papers or participate in pretrial conferences in conjunction with a member of the bar of this court.

(ii) represent a client in a deposition, provided that an attorney who is not a member of the bar of this court who conducts a deposition will be subject to the disciplinary rules of this court.

(iii) counsel a client in an action or proceeding pending in this court.

(E) an attorney may issue a subpoena under Fed.R.Civ.P. 45(a)(3)(B).

(2) A person knowingly violating this provision may, on notice and after hearing, be found guilty of criminal contempt.

(j) Consent to Standards of Conduct and Disciplinary Authority. An attorney admitted to the bar of this court or who practices in this court as permitted by this rule is subject to the Rules of Professional Conduct adopted by the Michigan Supreme Court, as amended from time to time, and consents to the jurisdiction of this court and the Michigan Attorney Grievance Commission and Michigan Attorney Discipline Board for purposes of disciplinary proceedings.

[Former LR 110.1 effective January 1, 1992. Renumbered as LR 83.20 effective March 3, 1997. Amended effective September 8, 1997; July 1, 2008; March 1, 2010; July 1, 2012.]

Comment

Admission to practice pro hac vice has not been permitted in the Eastern District since 1981. The provision of LR 83.20(c)(1) is subordinate to any provision of federal law or rules to the contrary, e.g., Rule 6 of the Rules of Procedure of the Judicial Panel on Multidistrict Litigation promulgated pursuant to 28 U.S.C. § 1407(f).

The application referred to in LR 83.20(d)(1) requires attorneys to swear (or affirm) that they have read and will abide by the Civility Principles approved by the Court (APPENDIX CIVILITY to these rules).

Under (d)(4), an applicant taking the oath of office in person will be referred to the presiding judge, a volunteer judge, or a judge with whom the applicant has made a previous arrangement.

Local counsel appearances under (f) do not apply to bankruptcy cases, which are governed by the bankruptcy court's orders, rules, and policies, or to criminal cases, which are governed by LCrR 57.1.

LR 83.21 LAW STUDENT PRACTICE

(a) Purpose. Effective legal service for each person in the Eastern District of Michigan, regardless of that person's ability to pay, is important to the directly affected person, to our system of justice and to the whole citizenry. Law students and recent law graduates, under supervision by a member of the Bar of this Court, may assist the United States Attorney's Office, the Federal Defender's Office and the Pro Bono Civil Assignment Panel of this Court or an accredited law school or a legal aid clinic funded pursuant to the Legal Services Corporation Act. Law students and recent law graduates may participate in legal training programs organized in the offices of the United States Attorney, the Federal Defender and the Pro Bono Civil Assignment Panel.

(b) Eligible Persons. A student in a law school approved by the American Bar Association who has received a passing grade in law school courses and has completed the first year is eligible to participate in a legal aid clinic or United States Attorney's Office or Federal Defender's Office or Pro Bono Civil Assignment Panel, if the student meets the academic and moral standards established by the dean of the school. For the purpose of this rule, a "recent law graduate" is a person who has graduated from law school within the last year.

(c) Scope; Procedure.

(1) A member of the legal aid clinic, in representing an indigent person, is authorized to advise the person and to negotiate and appear on the person's behalf before this Court.

(2) Representation must be conducted under the supervision of a member of the Bar of this Court. Supervision by a member of the Bar of this Court includes the duty to examine and sign all pleadings filed. It does not require the member of the Bar of this Court to be present:

(A) while a law student or graduate is advising an indigent person or negotiating on the person's behalf, or

(B) during a courtroom appearance of a law student or graduate, except in a criminal case exposing the client to a penalty of more than six months.

(3) A law student or graduate may not appear in a case before any judicial officer of this Court without the approval of the judicial officer. If the judicial officer grants approval, the judicial officer may suspend the proceedings at any stage if he or she determines that the representation by the law student or graduate:

(A) is professionally inadequate, and

(B) substantial justice requires suspension.

(4) A law student or graduate serving in a United States Attorney's Office, Federal Defender's Office or Pro Bono Civil Assignment Panel may be authorized to perform comparable functions and duties assigned by the United States Attorney or Federal Defender, except that

(A) the law student or graduate is subject to the conditions and restrictions of this Rule; and

(B) the law student or graduate may not be appointed as an Assistant United States Attorney or Assistant Federal Defender.

[Former LR 114.1 effective January 1, 1992. Renumbered as LR 83.21 effective March 3, 1997.]

Comment

LR 83.21 is based on MCR 8.120 which governs law student practice before the Michigan Courts.

LR 83.22 ATTORNEY DISCIPLINE

(a) Definitions. The following definitions apply in this rule.

(1) "Order of discipline" means an order entered against an attorney by the Michigan Attorney Discipline Board, a similar disciplinary authority of another state, or a court

(A) revoking or suspending an attorney's license or admission before a court to practice law,

(B) placing an attorney on probation or inactive status,

(C) reprimanding an attorney for misconduct,

(D) requiring an attorney to make restitution, or

(E) transferring an attorney to inactive status in lieu of discipline.

(2) "State" means a state, territory, commonwealth, or possession of the United States, and the District of Columbia.

(3) "Serious crime" means:

(A) a felony.

(B) a crime, a necessary element of which, as determined by the statutory or common law definition of the crime in the jurisdiction of the conviction, involves interference with the administration of justice, false swearing, misrepresentation, fraud, willful failure to file income tax returns, willful failure to pay income tax, deceit, bribery, extortion, misappropriation, theft, or an attempt, conspiracy, or solicitation of another to commit a serious crime.

(C) a crime that reflects adversely on the attorney's honesty, trustworthiness, or fitness as an attorney.

(4) "Chief judge" includes his or her designee.

(b) Standards of Professional Conduct. The Rules of Professional Conduct adopted by the Michigan Supreme Court, as amended from time to time, apply to members of the bar of this court and attorneys who practice in this court as permitted by LR 83.20. A violation of those rules is ground for discipline.

(c) Disciplinary Proceedings. When misconduct or allegations of misconduct that, if substantiated, would warrant discipline of an attorney who is a member of the bar of this court or has practiced in this court as permitted by LR 83.20 come to the attention of a judicial officer, including a bankruptcy judge or a magistrate judge, whether by complaint or otherwise, the judicial officer may refer the matter to:

(1) the Michigan Attorney Grievance Commission for investigation and prosecution,

(2) another disciplinary authority that has jurisdiction over the attorney, or

(3) the chief district judge for institution of disciplinary proceedings by this court under LR 83.22(e).

(d) Discipline Other Than Suspension or Disbarment. In addition to the discipline authorized by (c), a judicial officer may impose discipline, except suspension or disbarment from this court, on any attorney who engages in conduct violating the Rules of Professional Conduct, these rules, the Federal Rules of Civil or Bankruptcy Procedure, or orders of the court; or engages in other conduct unbecoming of a member of the bar of this court. Prior to the imposition of discipline, the attorney shall be afforded an opportunity to show good cause, within such time as the court shall prescribe, why the discipline should not be imposed. Upon the attorney's response, and after a hearing, if requested and allowed by the judicial officer, or upon expiration of the time prescribed for a response if no response is made, the court shall enter an appropriate order. The provisions of this rule do not preclude contempt proceedings including those pursuant to 18 U.S.C. §§ 401 and 402 and Fed.R.Crim.P. 42 or proceedings under 28 U.S.C. § 1927 and Fed.R.Civ.P. 11.

(e) Discipline by Court After Hearing.

(1) *Hearing Panel.* On receipt of a request by a judicial officer under LR 83.22(c), the chief judge will assign a three judge panel to hear and determine the matter. The three judicial officers shall be randomly selected, except that the judicial officer who made the request for discipline or before whom the conduct giving rise to the request took place may not be appointed. At least one member of the panel must be a district judge. If the alleged misconduct occurred in relation to a bankruptcy proceeding, the panel must include one bankruptcy judge. If the alleged misconduct occurred in relation to a magistrate judge's proceeding, the panel must include one magistrate judge. Otherwise the panel must consist of three district judges. The most senior district judge will preside and has the authority to resolve issues of procedure and evidence.

(2) *Order to Show Cause.* The panel will determine whether to issue an order to show cause. The order to show cause will include the specific facts that give rise to the proposed discipline, including the date, place and nature of the alleged misconduct, and the names of all persons involved. The clerk must mail to the attorney who is the subject of investigation a copy of the order and any supporting documents.

(3) *Response.* The respondent must respond to the order to show cause within 21 days from entry of the order. The response must—

(A) specifically admit or deny each factual allegation in the order and,

(B) state specific facts on which the respondent relies, including all other material dates, places, persons and conduct, and all documents or other supporting evidence not previously filed with the order that are relevant to the charges of misconduct.

(4) *Notice of the Hearing.* The court must give the respondent 21 days written notice of the date and location of the hearing and notice of the respondent's rights under LR 83.22(e)(6)(B).

(5) *Discovery.* The panel may order prehearing discovery for good cause shown.

(6) *Hearing and Decision.*

(A) Prosecuting Counsel. The chief judge must appoint an attorney to present the evidence supporting the allegations giving rise to the request for discipline when a hearing is necessary to resolve disputed facts. An attorney appointed under this rule will be paid at a rate not to exceed the Criminal Justice Act rate in effect at the time.

(B) Respondent's Rights. The respondent may be represented by counsel, to present witnesses and other evidence, and to confront and cross examine adverse witnesses.

(C) Subpoenas. The presiding judge may authorize a party to subpoena witnesses or documents for the hearing for good cause shown.

(D) Witnesses. Witnesses must testify under oath. The judicial officer who initiated the referral may be called as a witness at the hearing at the panel's discretion.

(E) Burden of Proof. The conduct giving rise to the request for discipline must be proven by a preponderance of the evidence.

(F) Failure to Appear. The respondent's failure to appear at the hearing is grounds for discipline.

(G) Confidentiality; Recording. The hearing will be confidential and recorded.

(H) Decision. Decision is by a majority of the panel. The panel may order suspension, disbarment, or any other remedy or sanction it deems appropriate, including costs and attorney's fees. The panel will prepare a written order including the panel's findings and disposition of the disciplinary charges. The order will be a public record. The court will send the order to the respondent and the complainant.

(7) *Appeal.* The decision of the panel will be the final decision of the district court.

(8) *Required Notice on Suspension or Disbarment.* Within 14 days after service of an order suspending or disbarring an attorney under LR 83.22(e)(6)(H), the respondent must:

(A) Send a copy of the order to:

(i) the Michigan Attorney Grievance Commission,

(ii) the licensing authority of any other state in which the respondent is licensed to practice law, and

(iii) the clerk of every other federal court in which the respondent is admitted to practice.

(B) Notify each client of the respondent in matters that the disciplinary action may affect of the following:

(i) the nature and duration of the discipline;

(ii) the effective date of the discipline;

(iii) the attorney's inability to act as an attorney in this court after the effective date of the discipline;

(iv) the location and identity of the custodian of the client's files and records, which will be made available to the client or to substitute counsel;

(v) that the client may wish to seek legal advice and counsel elsewhere, but, if the attorney was a member of a law firm, the firm may continue to represent the client with the client's express written consent; and

(vi) the address to which all correspondence to the attorney may be addressed.

(C) In every matter in which the respondent is representing a client in litigation affected by the disciplinary action, send a copy of the order of discipline to all parties and other persons entitled to notice of matters in the litigation.

(9) *Affidavit of Compliance.* Within 14 days after service of an order suspending or disbarring an attorney under LR 83.22(e)(6)(H), the respondent must file an affidavit with the clerk certifying compliance with LR 83.22(e)(8). The affidavit must include as an appendix copies of the disclosure notices required under LR 83.22(e)(8).

(f) Attorneys Convicted of Crimes.

(1) *Serious Crimes.*

(A) When an attorney admitted to practice before this court is convicted of a serious crime, the attorney is automatically suspended from practice in this court without further action of the court, regardless of the pendency of an appeal. A conviction occurs upon the return of a verdict of guilty or upon the acceptance of a plea of guilty or nolo contendere. On receipt of written notice of conviction of a serious crime of an attorney admitted to practice before this court, the chief judge will enter an order suspending the attorney. The suspension will continue until after final disposition of an appeal of the conviction, proceedings on remand after an appeal, and any disciplinary investigation and proceeding based on the conduct that resulted in the conviction. The court shall serve a copy of the order on the attorney by certified mail.

(B) On application, the chief judge may reinstate the attorney on a showing that—

(i) there is a jurisdictional deficiency that establishes that the suspension may not properly be ordered, such as that the crime did not constitute a serious crime or that the attorney is not the individual convicted; or

(ii) the conviction has been reversed and there is no likelihood of further criminal prosecution or disciplinary action related to the conduct that resulted in the conviction. A reinstatement will not terminate any disciplinary investigation or proceeding based on the conduct that resulted in the conviction.

(2) *Other Crimes.* LR 83.22(c) applies if the court receives written notice of conviction of an attorney admitted to practice before this court of a crime not constituting a serious crime.

(3) *Obligation to Report Conviction.* An attorney admitted to practice before this court must, on being convicted of a serious crime, immediately inform the clerk. If the conviction was in this court, the attorney must notify all other jurisdictions in which the attorney is admitted to practice. An attorney knowingly violating this provision may, on notice and after hearing, be found guilty of criminal contempt.

(g) Discipline by Other Jurisdictions.

(1) *Order of Discipline.*

(A) On receipt of written notice that another jurisdiction imposed discipline against an attorney admitted to practice in this court, the chief judge will enter an order imposing the same discipline, effective as of the date that the discipline was effective in the other jurisdiction. If the discipline imposed in the other jurisdiction has been stayed there, the court may defer discipline until the stay expires. If the order of discipline includes a period of suspension or disbarment, an attorney may be reinstated to this court only by application pursuant to LR 83.22(i)(1).

(B) When this court enters an order of discipline against an attorney, the attorney must provide to the clerk a list of all other jurisdictions in which the attorney is admitted to practice.

(2) *Application to Modify Order of Discipline.*

(A) Within 28 days after the effective date of the order of discipline in this court, the attorney may apply to the chief judge for modification or vacation of the discipline.

(B) The court shall modify or vacate the discipline if, on the record supporting the order of discipline in the other jurisdiction, the attorney demonstrates or the court finds that it clearly appears that—

(i) the procedure in the other jurisdiction constituted a deprivation of due process; or

(ii) there was such an infirmity of proof establishing the misconduct as to give rise to the clear conviction that this court could not accept as final the conclusion on that subject; or

(iii) imposing the same discipline in this court would result in grave injustice; or

(iv) the misconduct warrants substantially different discipline.

If the court determines that any of these grounds exist, it shall order other appropriate discipline or no discipline.

(3) *Obligation to Report Discipline.*

(A) An attorney admitted to practice before this court appearing or participating in a pending matter must, on being subjected to an order of discipline, immediately inform the clerk of the order of discipline.

(B) An attorney admitted to practice before this court must, before appearing or participating in a matter in the court after being subjected to an order of discipline that has not previously been reported to the court, immediately inform the clerk of the order of discipline.

(C) An attorney knowingly violating this provision may, on notice and after hearing, be found guilty of criminal contempt.

(4) *Administrative Suspension and Reinstatement.* An attorney who is suspended for nonpayment of dues to the State Bar of Michigan or any other bar association on which the attorney's admission to practice in this court may be based will be automatically suspended in this court without any action by the court other than written notice to the attorney. On receipt of notice that the attorney has been reinstated for payment of dues and penalties and payment of the court's attorney renewal fee, the attorney will be automatically reinstated in this court.

(h) Resignation in Other Jurisdictions.

(1) If an attorney resigns from the bar of another court of the United States or the bar of a state while an investigation into allegations of misconduct is pending,

(A) the attorney will immediately and automatically be disbarred from this court, and

(B) the attorney must promptly inform the clerk of the resignation. An attorney knowingly violating this notification provision may, on notice and after hearing, be found guilty of criminal contempt.

(2) On receipt of written notice that an attorney has resigned from the bar of another court of the United States or the bar of a state while an investigation into allegations of misconduct was pending, the chief judge will enter an order disbarring the attorney, effective as of the date of resignation in the other jurisdiction.

(3) An attorney disbarred under (h)(1)(A) may be reinstated if the attorney is readmitted in the jurisdiction from which the attorney resigned and there has been a final disposition of the investigation into allegations of misconduct without an order of discipline.

(i) Reinstatement.

(1) When this court has suspended or disbarred an attorney under LR 83.22(g) or (h), the attorney may apply for reinstatement by filing in this court an affidavit that the jurisdiction that entered the order of discipline on which this court based its discipline has reinstated the attorney. When this court has suspended or disbarred an attorney under LR 83.22(e), the attorney may apply for reinstatement by filing an application for reinstatement. The affidavit or application must be accompanied by payment of the court's attorney renewal fee. The clerk will assign the affidavit or application to a panel of three judges chosen randomly from among the active and senior judges.

(2) The attorney seeking reinstatement must prove by clear and convincing evidence that—

(A) the attorney has complied with the orders of discipline of this court and all other disciplinary authorities.

(B) the attorney has not practiced in this court during the period of disbarment or suspension and has not practiced law contrary to any other order of discipline.

(C) the attorney has not engaged in any other professional misconduct since disbarment or suspension.

(D) the attorney has the moral qualifications, competency and learning in the law required for admission to practice before this court, and that his or her resumption of the practice of law will not be detrimental to the integrity and standing of the bar or to the administration of justice, or subversive of the public interest.

(3) The court may invite any judge of the court, the Michigan Attorney Grievance Commission or other disciplinary counsel to present grounds why the attorney should not be reinstated and may conduct an evidentiary hearing if factual issues are contested.

(4) If the attorney seeking reinstatement has met the burden of proof in subsections (2)(A)–(D), and unless the court finds such irregularities in the proceedings conducted in the other jurisdiction so as to undermine confidence in the result, or finds that there are other compelling reasons for not reinstating the attorney, the application will be granted.

(5) In addition to payment of the attorney renewal fee, the court may condition reinstatement on—

(A) payment of all or part of the costs of the disciplinary and reinstatement proceedings in this court and may impose any of the conditions of reinstatement imposed in the other jurisdiction, or such other conditions as are warranted.

(B) partial or complete restitution to the persons harmed by the misconduct that led to disbarment or suspension.

(C) if the disbarment or suspension has been for five years or more, certification by the bar examiners of a state or other jurisdiction of the attorney's successful completion of an examination for admission to practice after the date of disbarment or suspension.

(6) An attorney may not file an application for reinstatement under this rule within one year following denial of such an application.

(j) Service of Papers.
Service of papers on an attorney under this rule may be by mail to the address of the attorney shown on the court's roll of attorneys or the address in the most recent paper the attorney filed in a proceeding in this court.

(k) Duties of the Clerk.

(1) On being informed that an attorney admitted to practice before this court has been convicted of a serious crime, the clerk will determine whether the court in which the conviction occurred sent a certificate of the conviction to this court. If not, the clerk will promptly obtain a certificate and file it with the court.

(2) On being informed that another court or a state has entered an order of discipline against an attorney admitted to practice before this court, the clerk will determine whether a certified copy of the order has been filed with this court. If

not, the clerk will promptly obtain a certified copy of the order and file it with the court.

(3) When this court convicts an attorney of a serious crime or enters an order of discipline against an attorney, the clerk will promptly notify the National Discipline Data Bank operated by the American Bar Association.

(*l*) **Other Authority.** Nothing in this rule abridges the court's power to control proceedings before it, including the power to initiate proceedings for contempt under Title 18, United States Code or Fed. R. Crim. P. 42.

[Former LR 111.1 effective January 1, 1992. Renumbered as LR 83.22 effective March 3, 1997. Amended effective September 26, 1997; October 1, 2005; December 1, 2009; March 1, 2010; July 1, 2013.]

Comment

The United States Supreme Court has held that "conduct unbecoming" [referred to in (d)], is conduct "contrary to professional standards that show an unfitness to discharge continuing obligations to clients or courts, or conduct inimical to the administration of justice." In re Snyder, 472 U.S. 634, 645 (1985).

Under LR 83.22(e)(1), a hearing panel assigned as a result of alleged misconduct in relation to a bankruptcy proceeding will consist of two district judges and one bankruptcy judge. Likewise, a hearing panel assigned as a result of alleged misconduct in relation to a magistrate judge's proceeding will consist of two district judges and one magistrate judge.

28 U.S.C. § 1291 applies to LR 83.22(e)(7).

In 1997, the Judicial Conference of the United States authorized courts to charge, at their option, a fee for renewal of an attorney's admission to practice. The Eastern District of Michigan established the attorney renewal fee effective January 1, 2000 (Administrative Order 99-AO-059).

LR 83.25   ATTORNEY'S APPEARANCE

(a) **Appearance.** An attorney must appear before representing a person or a party, except for practice permitted under LR 83.20(i)(1)(D) or (E). An attorney appears and becomes an attorney of record by filing a pleading or other paper or a notice of appearance. The attorney's office address, e-mail address, and telephone number must be included in the appearance.

(b) **Duration of Appearance.**

(1) An attorney's appearance continues until entry of—

(A) a final order or judgment disposing of all claims by or against the party the attorney represents, or

(B) a withdrawal or substitution order.

(2) An attorney may withdraw or be substituted for only on order of the court.

[Effective July 1, 2012.]

LR 83.30   COURTROOM DECORUM

(a) **Attorney as a Witness.** No attorney shall, without leave of the Court secured in advance of trial when feasible, conduct the trial of an action in which he or she is to be a witness.

(b) **Presence During In–Court Proceedings.** Unless other arrangements have been made with the Court, it is the duty of attorneys to be present in Court at all times the Court may be in session in their case. In civil cases, any attorney who absents himself or herself during such times or during the deliberation of the jury waives his or her right to be present and consents to such proceedings as may occur in the courtroom during his or her absence.

[Former LR 112.1 effective January 1, 1992. Renumbered as LR 83.30 effective March 3, 1997. Amended effective March 2, 1998; July 1, 2012.]

LR 83.31   CONDUCT IN FEDERAL COURT FACILITIES

(a) **Security.**

(1) As used in this rule, "federal court facility" includes any facility occupied by the United States District Court or the United States Bankruptcy Court for the Eastern District of Michigan, or any temporary facility occupied by a judicial officer of the Eastern District of Michigan.

(2) All persons entering a federal court facility are required to pass through a magnetometer and have all belongings and packages subject to physical and/or x-ray examination by the United States Marshals Service.

(3) All mail and packages addressed to any office within a federal court facility are subject to physical and/or x-ray examination by the United States Marshals Service.

(A) Except as provided in (B), sealed envelopes brought by courier may not be delivered to any office within a federal court facility. They must be given to a court security officer for processing in that facility's mail room.

(B) Sealed filings authorized by statute, rule, or court order in accordance with LR 5.3 must have the court order or notice of filing under seal affixed to the top of the sealed envelope. Such filings may be delivered to the clerk's office.

(b) **Soliciting, Loitering and Disruptive Behavior.**

(1) The solicitation of business relating to bail bonds or to employment as counsel is prohibited.

(2) Loitering in or about federal court facilities is prohibited.

(3) Any behavior which impedes or disrupts the orderly conduct of the business of the court is prohibited. Cards, signs, placards, or banners may not be brought into any courtroom or its environs.

(c) **Cameras and Recording Devices.**

(1) The taking of photographs in connection with any judicial proceeding and the recording or broadcasting of judicial proceedings by radio, television or other means is prohibited.

(A) As used in this rule, "judicial proceeding" includes proceedings before district, bankruptcy or magistrate judges, and sessions of the grand jury.

(B) As used in this rule, "in connection with any judicial proceeding" includes all participants in a judicial proceeding while they are in a courtroom or its environs.

(2) A judicial officer may authorize, by written notice to the United States Marshal the use of electronic or photographic

means for the presentation of evidence or for the perpetuation of the record.

(3) A district judge may authorize, by written notice to the United States Marshal:

(A) the broadcasting, televising, recording, or photographing of investitive, ceremonial, or naturalization proceedings; and

(B) the radio or television broadcasting, audio or video recording or photographing of court proceedings pursuant to a resolution of the Judicial Conference of the United States.

(d) Firearms and Weapons.

(1) Firearms, knives, explosives, and other weapons are prohibited from federal court facilities and subject to confiscation.

(2) Exceptions to this rule may include:

(A) the United States Marshal, deputy marshals, court security officers, and employees of the Federal Protective Service in accordance with 18 U.S.C. § 930(d);

(B) federal law enforcement agencies having offices in a federal court facility are exempt from the provisions regarding the carrying of weapons while entering the building and while going to and from the floor where their offices are located; or

(C) state, county, and local law enforcement officers who are:

(i) escorting prisoners to and from court under the direction of the United States Marshals Service, or

(ii) assisting the Marshals Service by supporting or providing additional security, as directed, in and around federal court facilities.

(3) All other federal, state or local law enforcement officers are required to identify themselves and store their weapons at the office of the United States Marshal.

(4) The handling of firearms as exhibits in trials is governed by an administrative order authorized by the court.

(5) An exception to this Rule regarding weapons or firearms may only be made by the Chief Judge or the Judge in whose courtroom the proceedings are occurring.

(e) Laptop Computers. Laptop computers are permitted in federal court facilities, but may not be used in any courtroom without the written permission of the appropriate judicial officer.

(f) Cellular Telephones and Other Communication Devices.

(1) *Policy Governing Non–Attorneys.* Except as provided in (2) and other court orders, cellular telephones and any other device with wireless communication capabilities, hereinafter "phones," are not permitted in federal court facilities.

(2) *Policy Governing Attorneys.* An attorney appearing in connection with any judicial proceeding or presenting evidence of bar membership may bring a phone into a federal court facility. The United States Marshal, his deputies, and court security officers may demand from any individual in possession of a phone identification in aid of enforcement of this rule, and if the identification does not satisfy the officer that the person in possession of a phone is authorized in accordance with the terms of this rule to bring the phone or use it in a court space, the officer may refuse admittance to any person in possession of a phone. The following conditions shall apply:

(A) the phone may not be used and must be turned off except in designated areas of the court facility; and

(B) the phone cannot be initiated, "answered," examined or otherwise manipulated while in a courtroom; and

(C) the phone may be used for communication only in posted designated areas; and

(D) any camera-like function or audio recording capability of a phone is subject to the provisions of (c) of this Rule (i.e., strictly prohibited except with the specific permission of the court).

(3) *District Judge Authority.* A district judge may institute another policy in his or her courtroom, including requiring that attorneys store their cellular telephones in chambers during court proceedings. A district judge located in a court facility at a duty station away from the Theodore Levin Courthouse in Detroit, Michigan may make appropriate orders regulating the possession and use of phones in the buildings in which he or she presides.

(4) *Co–Located Court Facilities.* Court facilities in the Eastern District of Michigan that are co-located with other government agencies shall be governed by this rule concerning the possession and use of phones in all court spaces, and the rules prescribed herein shall take precedence over other rules applicable elsewhere in the building.

(5) *Violations.*

(A) Attorney Discipline. An attorney violating this rule may be subject to discipline, including debarment, in accordance with Local Rule 83.22.

(B) Confiscation. A violation of this rule, including without limitation unauthorized possession of a phone, use of a phone in an unauthorized space, possession of a phone in an audible mode, and failing to turn off a phone when required, **SHALL** result in immediate confiscation of the phone. Any judicial officer may order confiscation of a phone. Any United States Marshal or Deputy Marshal or court security officer may also confiscate a phone.

(C) Contempt of Court. A violation of this rule may be punished as criminal contempt of court. A violation that disrupts a judicial proceeding may be punished by summary proceedings.

(6) *Relief From Confiscation of a Phone.* An attorney whose phone has been confiscated may apply in writing within twenty-eight (28) days after confiscation for return of the phone. The application shall be made to the judicial officer whose proceedings were disturbed by the violation, or, if there is no such judicial officer, to the chief judge. The judicial officer may grant or refuse the request. If the judicial officer determines that no violation of this rule occurred, he or she shall order the phone returned. If a violation has occurred and the request for return is granted, the judicial officer shall assess an appropriate monetary payment as a condition of

returning the phone. Confiscated phones that are not returned, either because no request has been made within the
time provided or the request for return has been denied, shall
be disposed of in a manner directed by the chief judge.

(7) *Consent to Provisions.* Any attorney bringing in a phone
shall be determined to have consented to the provisions of this
rule.

(g) Communication Devices. Communication devices (tape
and audio recorders and devices and dictating devices) are
prohibited from federal court facilities unless otherwise ordered by a judge in a particular case.

(h) Pagers; Beepers. Pagers and beepers are permitted in
federal court facilities, but must be programmed to an inaudi-
ble mode.

**(i) Access to Federal Court Facilities Outside of Regular
Court Hours.**

(1) A judicial officer is responsible for all aspects of conducting a judicial proceeding outside of regular court hours. This
rule supplements and does not limit the authority of the
judicial officer.

(2) If any person in attendance at an initial appearance
conducted in a federal court facility outside of regular court
hours is aware of the presence of persons outside the facility
who wish to attend the proceeding, such person should advise
the judicial officer promptly and prior to commencement of the
proceeding.

(3) If the judicial officer is aware that there are persons
outside the facility who wish to attend the proceeding, the
judicial officer should then confer with the United States
Marshal (or designee) to determine whether court security
officers and/or deputy marshals must be summoned to ensure
the security of the facility and the safety of those already
present if the persons outside are allowed to enter. This
determination will take into account the requirement of this
rule that all persons entering the facility must pass through
the magnetometer as well as the need to ensure that the
persons who enter do not have unrestricted access to areas of
the facility other than the courtroom in which the judicial
proceeding is to take place.

(4) The United States Marshal (or designee) may confer
with any law enforcement officers who are present to determine whether there are a sufficient number of such officers
already in the facility for security purposes. The United States
Marshal (or designee) may exercise, in his or her discretion,
one of the following options:

(A) utilize federal law enforcement officers already present in the facility to assume the additional duties involved in
providing adequate security; or

(B) summon court security officers or deputy marshals to
the facility for the purpose of providing adequate security.

(5) If adequate security arrangements are not possible that
will allow for a court proceeding to take place without unnecessary delay, the judicial officer may proceed to conduct the
initial appearance of the defendant or material witness without
ordering that any persons outside the facility be allowed to
enter and attend. If any persons are excluded, the judicial
officer at the outset of the initial appearance will place on the

record the actions taken and the reasons for these actions. The
parties who are present shall be permitted to place any
objections on the record.

(j) Compliance.

(1) The United States Marshals Service, or any judicial
officer sua sponte, and the custodians of federal court facilities
may enforce this rule, or

(2) the United States Attorney may require any person who
violates this rule to appear before a judge of this court to
answer to a charge of contempt.

[Former LR 113.1 effective January 1, 1992. Renumbered as LR
83.31 effective March 3, 1997. Amended effective July 1, 1999;
October 1, 2005; July 1, 2008.]

LR 83.40   CERTIFICATION OF ISSUES
TO STATE COURTS

(a) Upon motion or after a hearing ordered by the Judge
sua sponte, the Judge may certify an issue for decision to the
highest Court of the State whose law governs its disposition.
An order of certification shall be accompanied by written
findings that:

(1) the issue certified is an unsettled issue of State law, and

(2) the issue certified will likely control the outcome of the
federal suit, and

(3) certification of the issue will not cause undue delay or
prejudice.

Such order shall also include citation to precedent, statutory
or court rule authority authorizing the State Court involved to
resolve certified questions.

(b) In all such cases, the order of certification shall stay
federal proceedings for a fixed time which shall be subsequently enlarged only upon a showing that such additional time is
required to obtain a State Court decision and is not the result
of dilatory actions on the part of the litigants.

(c) In cases certified to the Michigan Supreme Court, in
addition to the findings required by this Rule, the United
States District Court shall approve an agreed statement of
facts which shall be subsequently transmitted to the Michigan
Supreme Court by the parties as an appendix to briefs filed
therein.

[Former LR 118.1 effective January 1, 1992. Renumbered as LR
83.40 effective March 3, 1997.]

LR 83.50   BANKRUPTCY CASES
AND PROCEEDINGS

(a) Matters Referred to the Bankruptcy Judges.

(1) Unless withdrawn by a district judge, all cases under
Title 11 of the United States Code and any or all proceedings
arising under Title 11 or arising in or related to a case under
Title 11 are referred to bankruptcy judges. The court intends
to give bankruptcy judges the broadest possible authority to
administer cases and proceedings properly within their jurisdiction.

(2) Under 28 U.S.C. § 157(b)(1), bankruptcy judges will hear and determine all cases under Title 11 and all core proceedings (including those listed in 28 U.S.C. § 157(b)(2)) arising under Title 11, or arising in or related to a case under Title 11, and will enter appropriate orders and judgments, subject to review under 28 U.S.C. § 158.

(3) Bankruptcy judges will hear all the non-core proceedings related to a case under Title 11.

(A) By Consent. With the parties' express consent, bankruptcy judges may conduct hearings and enter appropriate orders or judgments in the proceeding, subject only to review under 28 U.S.C. § 158.

(B) Absent Consent. Absent consent of the parties, bankruptcy judges will conduct hearings and file proposed findings of fact and conclusions of law and a proposed order or judgment with the bankruptcy clerk. Bankruptcy judges may also file recommendations for expedited review. The bankruptcy clerk will immediately serve copies on all parties by mail and enter the date of mailing on the docket. Objections to a bankruptcy judge's proposed findings of fact and conclusions of law must be filed as required by Fed. R.Bankr.P. 9033(b) and (c).

(b) Motions to Withdraw. District judges will hear motions to withdraw cases or proceedings. The district clerk will serve a copy of the order on the bankruptcy clerk and the bankruptcy judge.

(c) Matters to Be Heard and Determined or Tried by District Judges. District judges will hear and determine cases or proceedings withdrawn under 28 U.S.C. § 157(d). District judges will also try personal injury tort and wrongful death claims under 28 U.S.C. § 157(b)(5). If necessary, parties may move under (b) to withdraw a personal injury tort or wrongful death claim from a bankruptcy judge.

(d) Filing Papers.

(1) While cases or proceedings are pending before a bankruptcy judge, or before entry of an appeal on the district court docket under Fed.R.Bankr.P. 8007(b), all papers—including removal notices under 28 U.S.C. § 1452(a) and motions to withdraw the reference—will be filed with the bankruptcy clerk. If a notice of removal is mistakenly filed with the district clerk, the district clerk will note on the notice the date on which it was received and transmit it to the bankruptcy clerk. It will be deemed filed with the bankruptcy clerk on the date noted.

(2) After a contested matter or proceeding is assigned to a district judge, all papers in the matter or proceeding must bear a civil case number in addition to the bankruptcy case number(s) and must be filed with the district clerk.

(3) With the exception of papers required under Fed. R.Bankr.P. 8006, after the district clerk gives notice of the date on which the appeal was docketed, all papers must bear a civil case number in addition to the bankruptcy case number(s) and must be filed with the district clerk.

(e) Submitting Papers, Records or Files to the District Court; Assigning District Judges.

(1) The bankruptcy clerk will submit the necessary papers to the district clerk when:

(A) the time for filing objections under Fed.R.Bankr.P. 9033(b) expires;

(B) a district judge enters an order under 28 U.S.C. § 157(d);

(C) a party files a motion to withdraw a case or proceeding;

(D) a bankruptcy judge determines that a case or proceeding is one in which a personal injury tort or wrongful death claim is to be tried in a district court under 28 U.S.C. § 157(b)(5); or

(E) the record is complete for purposes of appeal under Fed.R.Bankr.P. 8007(b).

(2) In connection with matters other than appeals, the bankruptcy clerk will send a notice to the parties identifying the papers submitted to the district clerk.

(3) Subject to (4), below, the district clerk will assign a civil case number to each matter submitted. The district clerk will assign all cases and proceedings arising out of a bankrupt estate to the district judge to whom the case was first assigned. If there is no prior assignment, the district clerk will assign the matter under LR 83.11.

(4) If the assigned judge believes that a bankruptcy case is one of unusual complexity, then, with the consent of the assigned judge, the chief judge may reassign to other judges of this court by random draw subsequent cases, motions to withdraw the reference under 28 U.S.C. § 157(d), proceedings withdrawn under 28 U.S.C. § 157(d), and appeals under 28 U.S.C. § 158, arising from that bankruptcy case for the purpose of docket efficiency and to expedite the resolution of such matters. In such a case, the following case management guidelines apply:

(A) In motions and appeals, expedited briefing schedules should be ordered.

(B) Oral argument should be allowed, unless the court finds explicitly that oral argument will delay or inhibit the decision.

(C) The order or opinion deciding motions and appeals should be filed within 28 days of oral argument.

[Former LR 150.1 effective January 1, 1992. Renumbered as LR 83.50 effective March 3, 1997. Amended effective November 2, 1998; July 1 2010.]

Comment

If multiple matters are reassigned under (e)(4), the chief judge will consider whether each subsequent matter should be treated as a companion case and reassigned under the companion case rule in LR 83.11(b)(7).

LR B.1 EXIGENT CIRCUMSTANCES IN PROCEEDINGS COMMENCED BY ATTACHMENT AND GARNISHMENT AND ACTIONS IN REM

Exigent circumstances shall exist when the assigned judge, presiding judge and Chief Judge of the district are unavailable to make a determination as to whether the conditions for the issuance of a warrant for arrest or writ for attachment or garnishment of maritime property exist and the property to be subject to the arrest or attachment may in the immediate future leave the District. For purposes of this Local Rule, a Judge shall be deemed unavailable, unless the Judge indicates that he or she will immediately consider the proposed order.

[Former LR 140.1(c) effective January 1, 1992. Renumbered as LR B.1 effective March 3, 1997.]

LR E.1   ACTIONS IN REM AND QUASI IN REM

(a) **Advance Deposit for Cost.** The United States Marshal shall collect in advance of the arrest, attachment or garnishment only that amount sufficient to cover the cost of service or process, United States Marshal's insurance and 10 days' keeper and maintenance fees. If the plaintiff is represented by an attorney duly authorized to practice in this District, then the advance deposit for cost may be satisfied by tendering to the United States Marshal a check from the attorney or attorney's firm in the amount of the required deposit. The United States Marshal shall not deliver any property so released until costs and charges of the Court have been paid.

(b) **Custody and Operation of Seized Vessels.** On seizure of a vessel by arrest or attachment, the marshal must appoint as custodian of the vessel the master or other officer in control of the vessel if the master or other officer accepts the responsibilities and liabilities of the appointment. Absent such acceptance, the marshal must make other satisfactory arrangements for the safekeeping of the vessel. The marshal in either event may require the party at whose instance the vessel was seized to pay the fees and costs as incurred. On motion of the plaintiff or another person claiming an interest in the vessel, the court may appoint a different custodian. In that event the person at whose instance the appointment was made must pay the fees and costs as incurred. Unless restriction of the vessel is necessary for its safekeeping, the loading or discharging of cargo or other normal working of the vessel shall not be impeded. The marshal may permit the vessel to be moved from berth to berth within a marine terminal or to a local anchorage within the district without further court order.

(c) **Release of Maritime Property.** The United States Marshal shall release property under arrest, attachment or garnishment upon receipt of any of the following:

(1) An order of the Court expressly authorizing the release; or

(2) A stipulation signed by the party on whose behalf the property is detained, or his or her attorney, expressly authorizing the release; or

(3) A voluntary dismissal under Fed.R.Civ.P. 41(a) signed by the party on whose behalf the property is detained, or his or her attorney, which expressly authorizes the release.

(4) Under (2) and (3), it is not necessary that the defendant or his or her attorney sign the pleading.

[Former LR 140.1(a) and (b) and former LR 140.2 effective January 1, 1992. Renumbered as LR E.1 effective March 3, 1997. Amended effective March 1, 2010.]

LR–APPENDIX ECF
ELECTRONIC FILING POLICIES AND PROCEDURES
PREFACE

In December 2002, the Administrative Office of the United States Courts advised the Eastern District of Michigan that it had been identified to begin implementation of Case Management / Electronic Case Files (CM/ECF) in January 2003.

On December 18, 2002, Chief Judge Lawrence P. Zatkoff approved a recommendation from the Court's Automation and Technology Committee and appointed an *Ad Hoc* Committee on Electronic Filing. The Committee's charge was to discuss and recommend to the Court a position on various policy issues underlying the creation of a new Local Rule governing electronic filing.

At its regular meeting on September 8, 2003, the Court approved Local Rules establishing the authority for electronic filing in civil and criminal cases in the Eastern District of Michigan. The Court also agreed that papers filed by electronic means must comply with the technical standards in the Electronic Case Filing (ECF) Policies and Procedures (this document), which is also included as an appendix to the Local Rules. This document was approved by the Court at its regular meeting on December 1, 2003.

At its regular meeting on February 2, 2004, the Court approved a delay in the implementation date of ECF from March 1, 2004, to June 1, 2004. At its meeting on September 6, 2005, the Court approved amendments to LR 5.1.1, which mandated that all papers—not simply cases—filed after November 30, 2005, be filed electronically.

In anticipation of mandatory e-filing, the Court also approved mandatory training for all ECF filing users effective September 19, 2005.

The Court expresses its appreciation to the original members of the *Ad Hoc* Committee on Electronic Filing who worked diligently on this document:

Chief Judge Lawrence P. Zatkoff (Ex Officio)

Judge Robert H. Cleland, Chair

Judge Arthur J. Tarnow

Judge Victoria A. Roberts

Judge David M. Lawson

Magistrate Judge Charles E. Binder

Attorney Daniel J. LaCombe (Barris, Sott, Denn & Driker, PLLC)

Attorney Patrick G. Seyferth (Bush, Seyferth & Kethledge)

Assistant United States Attorney Sheldon N. Light

Deputy Federal Defender Andrew N. Wise

Court Administrator David J. Weaver

Deputy Court Administrator Mary E. Miers (ECF Project Manager)

Operations Manager Kevin B. Williams

Management Analyst Jerri Torolski

Secretary to Court Administrator Stephanie Miszkowski (Reporter)

INTRODUCTION

As of June 1, 2004, the official record of filed cases shall be maintained electronically. These policies and procedures set forth the scope and requirements for filing users.

R1. DEFINITIONS

The following terms appear in these Electronic Filing Policies and Procedures:

(a) "E–Government Act of 2002" establishes a broad framework for the use of technology to enhance public access to government information and services. Pub. L. No. 107–347, 116 Stat. 2899. See 44 U.S.C. §§ 3601, et seq.

(b) "Electronic Filing" means filing a paper over the Internet by a registered attorney or a non-incarcerated *pro se* party.

(c) "Electronic Filing System" (hereinafter ECF) refers to the Court's automated system that receives and stores papers filed in electronic form. The program is part of the CM/ECF (Case Management/Electronic Case Files) software, which was developed for the Federal Judiciary by the Administrative Office of the United States Courts.

(d) "Filing User" is a registered attorney or a *pro se* party who has a district court-issued login and password to file papers electronically over the Internet in the Eastern District of Michigan. *Pro se* party refers to a non-incarcerated person only.

(e) "Hyperlink" is a selectable connection from a word, picture, or information object to another, providing a mechanism for navigating to information between or within electronic documents or to Internet material. Hyperlinks are activated when the user clicks on an "active" region on the document. The active region is usually indicated by the highlighting or underlining of text.

(f) "Initiating Papers" are comprised of the following: civil complaints, statements of disclosure of corporate affiliations and financial interest, notices of removal, criminal complaints, indictments or informations, and any other document filed with the Court that creates a new case and new case number on the Court's docket.

(g) "Notice of Electronic Filing" (hereinafter NEF) is a notice automatically generated by ECF at the time a paper is filed, setting forth the time of filing, the name of the filing user, the type of paper, the text of the docket entry, the name of the filing user receiving the notice, and an electronic link (hyperlink) to the filed paper, which allows recipients to retrieve the paper automatically.

(h) "Paper" is defined as a pleading, motion, exhibit, declaration, affidavit, memorandum, order, notice, and any other filing by or to the Court.

(i) "Portable Document Format" (hereinafter PDF) refers to a non-modifiable, electronic file that is converted to a format that will look the same on a computer screen and in print, regardless of the printer used to print it, and regardless of the software package originally used to create it (see R5(c)).

(j) "Proposed Order" is a draft paper submitted for a judge's editing, if necessary, and signature, in a format compatible with Word or WordPerfect and not in PDF (see R11(a)).

(k) "Public Access to Court Electronic Records" (hereinafter PACER) is an electronic public access service that allows users to obtain case and docket information online from federal appellate, district, and bankruptcy courts.

(*l*) "Technical Failure" is defined as a malfunction of Court-owned/leased equipment (e.g., hardware, software or telecommunication facility) that occurs continuously or intermittently for more than one hour after 12:00 noon (Eastern Time) that day, and which results in the inability of a filing user to file papers electronically. Technical failure does not include malfunctioning of a filing user's equipment.

(m) "Text–Only Order" is a docket entry that itself constitutes the order; no PDF or paper order is issued. These text-only orders, which are generally only used for routine matters, are official and binding.

(n) "Traditional Manner" means filing a paper (hard copy) or a physical object at a Clerk's Office (see R18(c)).

(o) "Web–Based Resource" is material made available on the World Wide Web, accessed by means of a universal record locater (URL).

R2. SCOPE OF ELECTRONIC FILING

All papers (not simply cases) filed June 1, 2004 and thereafter will be maintained as electronic case files no matter when a case was originally filed.

R3. ELIGIBILITY, REGISTRATION, PASSWORDS

(a) A filing user must be an attorney admitted and in good standing to practice in the Eastern District of Michigan, an attorney authorized to represent the United States Government, or a non-incarcerated *pro se* party granted permission to file on a case-by-case basis.

(1) Attorneys already admitted to practice who have a case pending before the Court must immediately comply with (b).

(2) Newly-admitted attorneys who have a case pending before the Court at the time of admission have up to two weeks to comply with (b). Newly-admitted attorneys do not need to comply with (b) until such time as the attorney has a case pending before the Court.

(b) Each filing user must complete the ECF Registration Requirements outlined on the Court's website to receive a login and password to ECF. Filing users must complete mandatory ECF Training.

(c) A filing user must have a PACER account.

(d) Each filing user is responsible for maintaining valid and current contact information in his or her ECF Registration account profile. When a user's contact information changes, the user must promptly update his or her ECF Registration account profile. If the filing user has a pending case before the Court, the user must also promptly notify all parties in all cases. Electronic service upon an obsolete e-mail address will constitute valid service if the user has not updated the account profile with the new e-mail address.

R4. NON–COMPLIANCE

(a) The Court may excuse a party from electronic filing on motion for good cause shown (LR 5.1.1(a)).

(b) The Court may issue an order to show cause for repeated filing errors or other instances of non-compliance with these Policies and Procedures. The Court may also subject a filing user to sanctions in accordance with LR 11.1. See Procedure to Address Non–Compliance with ECF Policies and Procedures (EXHIBIT A).

R5. FILING—IN GENERAL

(a) Filing users are required to file papers electronically.

(b) Filing users must present one "courtesy" or "chambers copy" of all dispositive motion papers, as defined in LR 7.1(e)(1)(A), (including responses and replies) and all accompanying exhibits must be submitted directly to the judge's chambers on paper. Any exhibits must be properly tabbed and all papers firmly bound, usually along the left margin ("book-style"). Good practice requires that in appropriate cases, relevant portions of lengthy documents be highlighted. A printed copy of the Notice of Electronic Filing must be attached to the front of the paper.

The chambers copy must be sent via first class mail the same day the document is e-filed, unless it relates to a court proceeding scheduled within the next five days or otherwise requires the immediate attention of the Court, in which case the chambers copy must be hand-delivered to chambers not later than the morning of the next business day after the document is e-filed.

(c) A file created with a word processor, or a paper that has been scanned, must be converted to PDF to be filed electronically with the Court. Converted files contain the extension ".pdf". All fonts embedded in PDF records (except in papers that have been scanned) must have been publicly identified as a font that may be legally embedded (i.e., the font license permits embedding) in a file for unlimited, universal viewing and printing. Common font styles include but are not limited to the following: Courier, Arial, Times New Roman, Calibri, Century Schoolbook, Symbol and ZapfDingbats (see R1(i)).

(d) A hyperlink (as defined in R1(e)) contained in an electronic filing is merely a convenient mechanism created by the author for accessing Web-based resources (see R1(*o*)). A hyperlink is not a part of the Court's record. Accordingly, the Court does not endorse nor exercise any responsibility over the content at the destination. Any hyperlink to a case or other authority included in an electronic filing must be expressed in the full traditional citation method for the cited authority.

(e) A cited Web-based resource that refers to information that has not already been made part of the record, must be captured, preserved in PDF, and attached to the paper. The attachment should include a notation of the date it was viewed and the case to which it relates.

(f) A complaint must not be combined with a motion for preliminary relief and a response or reply to a motion must not be combined with a counter-motion. Papers filed in violation of this rule will be stricken.

(g) Papers containing advertisements, which may be generated as a result of the use of free or trial-run PDF conversion software, will be stricken.

R6. FILING—CIVIL INITIATING PAPERS

(a) Filing users must file civil initiating papers and request for issuance of a summons electronically. A case is not considered filed until an initiating paper has been uploaded and a judicial officer has been assigned to the case.

(b) Payment of initial filing fees may be accomplished electronically at the time the initiating papers are filed and is the Court's preferred method. If payment is not made at that time, the filing user has seven calendar days to remit payment to the Clerk's Office or file an application to proceed *in forma pauperis*, or the case may be dismissed by the assigned judicial officer.

(c) Corporate plaintiffs must file the Statement of Disclosure of Corporate Affiliations and Financial Interest in accordance with LR 83.4, along with initiating papers. Corporate defendants in either civil or criminal cases should e-file the Statement as one of the first pleadings or papers filed with the Court, or as soon as the party becomes aware of the corporate affiliation or financial interest, or as otherwise ordered by the judge to whom the case is assigned.

(d) A *pro se* party does not have permission to file civil initiating papers electronically in ECF.

R7. FILING—CRIMINAL INITIATING PAPERS

Criminal initiating papers may be filed in the traditional manner or may be filed electronically by the United States Government.

R8. SERVICE

(a) Fed. R. Civ. P. 5(b) and Fed. R. Crim. P. 49(b) do not permit electronic service of process for purposes of obtaining personal jurisdiction, i.e., Rule 4 service. Therefore, service of process must be effected in the traditional manner.

(b) Whenever a paper is filed electronically in accordance with these procedures, ECF will generate a NEF to all filing users associated with that case and to the judge to whom the case is assigned.

(c) If the recipient is a filing user, the NEF shall constitute service of the paper by electronic means under Federal Rule of Civil Procedure 5(b)(2)(E).

(d) A certificate of service on all parties entitled to service or notice is still required when a party files a paper electronically. The certificate must state the manner in which service or notice was accomplished on each party so served. This should be included as part of the paper rather than a separate filing. See Sample Certificate of Service (EXHIBIT B).

(e) A party who is *pro se* and not a filing user, or a party excused from electronic filing, is entitled to a hard copy of any paper filed electronically. Service of such copy must be made according to the federal rules of procedure (civil and criminal) and local rules. Unless otherwise ordered by the Court, an attorney who is not a filing user is not entitled to this traditional service.

R9. SIGNATURES

(a) The user login and password serve as the filing user's signature on all papers filed electronically with the Court. They serve as a signature for purposes of Fed.R.Civ.P. 11, all other federal rules (civil and criminal), the local rules, and for any other purpose for which a signature is required in connection with proceedings before the Court.

(b) A paper filed electronically must include a signature block containing the name of the filing user represented by "s/", "/s/" or a scanned signature, firm name (if applicable), street address, telephone number, primary e-mail address, and bar ID number (where applicable). The format of the signature block should substantially conform to the following sample:

> SAMPLE: s/John Doe
> Doe Law Firm
> 123 Main Street
> Detroit, MI 48200
> (313) 555–1234
> jdoe@doelaw.com
> P12345

(c) A paper containing the signature of a defendant in a criminal case shall be scanned and filed by filing users or Court personnel.

(d) An affidavit, declaration or paper containing the signature of a non-attorney shall be scanned and filed electronically.

(e) A paper requiring the signature of more than one party shall be filed electronically by:

(1) representing the consent of the other parties on the paper by including the name of the consenting party in a separate signature block as shown in the following sample:

> SAMPLE: s/ with consent of Jane Roe
> Law Office of Roe & Roe
> 456 Mockingbird Lane
> Ann Arbor, MI 49888
> (734) 555–6789
> jroe@roeroe.com
> P23456

or

(2) submitting a scanned paper containing all necessary signatures, or

(3) in any other manner approved by the Court.

(f) No filing user may submit a paper with an electronic signature unless the filing user has permission of the signatory.

R10. ENTRY OF COURT–ISSUED PAPERS

(a) All signed orders will be filed by Court personnel. Any order signed electronically (with s/judge's name) shall have the same force and effect as if the judge had affixed his or her signature to a hard copy of the order and it had been entered on the docket in the traditional manner.

(b) The judge to whom a case is assigned may issue routine text-only notices and orders for which ECF will generate a NEF. The text-only order entry shall constitute the Court's only order on the matter. In civil cases, such notices and orders may include but are not limited to notices setting or modifying a schedule, orders extending time, and orders granting leave to file papers. In criminal cases, such orders could include orders of dismissal filed under Fed. R. Crim. P. 48(a) and orders unsealing documents.

R11. PROPOSED ORDERS

(a) Proposed orders (see R1(j)) must be submitted to the judge to whom the case is assigned or to the magistrate judge to whom the matter is referred via the link located under the Utilities section of ECF. This link may not be used for any other purpose. Proposed orders must not include the judge's electronic signature.

(1) If the movant (filing user) obtains concurrence pursuant to E.D. Mich. LR 7.1(a)(1), the proposed stipulated order must be submitted via the link referred to in (a).

(2) If concurrence is obtained and the movant (filing user) prepares a separate stipulation and separate proposed order, the stipulation must be submitted with the proposed order via the link referred to in (a), unless:

(i) the stipulation requires the signature of a *pro se* party who is not a filing user or a non-attorney, in which case the stipulation is to be electronically filed and the proposed order submitted via the link referred to in (a); or

(ii) the stipulation is regarding trial exhibits for appeal purposes and does not require an order signed by a district or magistrate judge.

(3) Proposed orders shall not be combined with *ex-parte* motions. The *ex-parte* motion must be filed electronically first and the proposed order must be submitted via the link referred to in (a).

(4) An exception to the submission of proposed orders via the link referred to in (a) is found in E.D. Mich. LR 58.1(c).

(b) The movant (filing user) must provide all other parties a copy of the proposed order either by e-mail or other form. ECF does not automatically generate an NEF or a copy of the proposed order for them.

(c) Alternatively, a motion or stipulation may request that routine relief be granted by text-only order. Such orders are official and binding.

R12. DOCKET/OFFICIAL COURT RECORD

A paper filed electronically in accordance with these policies and procedures shall constitute entry of that paper on the docket kept by the Clerk under Fed. R. Civ. P. 58 and 79, and Fed. R. Crim. P. 55.

R13. TECHNICAL FAILURE OF COURT EQUIPMENT; MALFUNCTION OF FILING USER'S EQUIPMENT

(a) If a filing user encounters technical failure of Court equipment (as defined in R1(l)), the paper may be submitted to the Court as indicated below, provided that it is accompanied by an affidavit of the filing user's failed attempts to file electronically at least two times after 12:00 noon, each attempt separated by at least one hour. The following methods of filing are acceptable in the case of a technical failure:

(1) Via e-mail sent that day with PDF attachment to the e-mail address for technical failures (technicalfailures@mied.uscourts.gov); or

(2) Via electronic filing the next business day that ECF is operational.

(b) The Court will attempt to send email updates to primary and secondary email addresses when technical failures occur and when they are resolved, however some technical failures may preclude the possibility of a Court email update.

(c) A filing user who suffers prejudice as a result of a malfunction of the filing user's own equipment may seek appropriate relief from the Court.

R14. CORRECTING DOCKET ENTRIES INCLUDING PAPERS FILED IN ERROR

Once a paper is filed electronically and becomes part of the docket, corrections to the docket may be made only by the Clerk's Office. If a paper is filed in error, the filing user must seek appropriate relief from the Court.

R15. DEADLINES

(a) A paper filed electronically is deemed filed on the date and time stated on the NEF.

(b) Filing electronically does not alter the filing deadline for a paper. Filing users are encouraged to file electronically during ordinary business hours; however, filing electronically must be completed before 12:00 midnight (Eastern Time) in order to be considered timely filed that day, unless a technical failure (see R13(a)) or malfunction of filing user's equipment occurs (see R13(b)). In accordance with Fed.R.Civ.P. 6(d) and Fed.R.Crim.P. 45(c), service by electronic means is governed by Federal Rule of Civil Procedure 5(b)(2)(E). [See R8(c).]

R16. TRANSCRIPTS AND AUDIO FILES OF FEDERAL COURT PROCEEDINGS

(a) Transcripts of federal court proceedings will be filed electronically in ECF by the court reporter, transcriber, or Court personnel.

(b) Access to transcripts of federal court proceedings will be governed by the Court's Procedures Governing the Electronic Availability and Redaction of Transcripts (EXHIBIT C).

(c) An audio file uploaded in ECF by the Court is a copy of the original audio recording and provided as a convenience to filing and PACER users. A transcript must still be produced in accordance with 28 U.S.C. § 753(b).

R17. RETENTION REQUIREMENTS

The official Court record shall be the electronic file maintained on the Court's servers and any papers allowed to be filed in the traditional manner. The Clerk's Office will discard all papers brought to the Clerk's Office for entry on the docket after those papers are scanned and uploaded to ECF. Therefore, the Court encourages filing users to retain the originals of papers with intrinsic value.

R18. EXHIBITS

(a) **In General.** An exhibit available in original electronic format must be converted to PDF and filed electronically, subject to size limitations contained herein. A filing user must scan a paper exhibit that is less than 50 megabytes (filing users are directed to file only portions of exhibits that are germane and not include any paper that is already part of the record) and submit the exhibit as a

PDF file. Because PDF files containing scanned papers take up considerably more space on ECF than PDF files containing electronically-generated papers, filing users may submit PDF files containing scanned papers of more than 50 megabytes only if they are filed in separate 50 megabyte segments.

The offering party shall retain hard copies, or accurate electronic copies, of exhibits until entry of final orders by the District Court and, if applicable, appellate courts.

(b) Filing Exhibits to Papers Electronically. Exhibits must be filed electronically according to the following procedure:

(1) If there is only one exhibit, an index of exhibits is not necessary.

(2) The filing user must prepare an index of exhibits and file the index as the first attachment to the paper. Each exhibit must be described on the index both by an exhibit identifier and by a brief narrative description. See Sample Index of Exhibits (EXHIBIT D).

(3) Each exhibit must then be filed and identified as a separate attachment to the paper, and must be labeled in the electronic record with an exhibit identifier and brief narrative description.

SAMPLE DOCKET ENTRY: Motion for Summary Judgment filed by ABC Company (Attachments: #1 Index of Exhibits #2 Exhibit A—Affidavit of John Smith #3 Exhibit B—Excerpts from Jane Doe's Deposition #4 Exhibit C1—Contract Between XYZ Company and ABC Company, pages 1–35 #5 Exhibit C2—Contract Between XYZ Company and ABC Company, pages 36–69 #6 Exhibit D—XYZ Company General Ledgers)

(c) Video Tapes, DVDs and Physical Objects. A filing user must obtain leave of court to file in the traditional manner exhibits that are physical objects that cannot authentically be converted to PDF as required in R18(a). Examples include but are not limited to media files such as .mp3 and .wav. CDs and DVDs that contain files such as briefs, motions, and exhibits that can be authentically converted to PDF shall not be submitted. See Ex Parte Motion for Leave to File Exhibits in the Traditional Manner (EXHIBIT E). If the Court grants a filing user leave of court to file exhibits in the traditional manner, the Notice of Filing Exhibits in the Traditional Manner (EXHIBIT F) must be completed and accompany the original and judge's courtesy copy. The exhibits then must be filed according to the following procedures:

(1) The filing user must prepare an index of exhibits. This index must be filed as an attachment to the main paper and must state that the exhibits are being filed in the traditional manner rather than electronically.

(2) The filing user shall file the exhibits in the traditional manner accompanied by a cover sheet identifying the paper to which the exhibits relate (e.g., "Exhibits in Support of Defendant XYZ Company's Memorandum in Support of Motion for Summary Judgment"). Objects must have a label physically attached that include case number and description. The Clerk's Office will note on the docket its receipt of the exhibits.

(3) A filing user must serve materials filed in the traditional manner on other parties in accordance with the federal and local rules, and file a notice electronically (see R8(d)).

R19. ACCESS TO PAPERS IN ECF

(a) A person may retrieve information from ECF at the Court's Internet site by obtaining a PACER login and password. A person who has PACER access may retrieve the docket and papers in civil cases, except immigration and social security benefits cases. In immigration and social security benefits cases, only counsel of record or parties in the case may retrieve papers. Judicial Conference of the United States policy prohibits routine public access via the Internet of immigration and social security benefits cases.

(b) A person who has PACER access may retrieve the docket and papers filed after November 1, 2004 in a criminal case. However, only counsel of record in a case, or a *pro se* defendant with PACER access, may retrieve papers filed before November 1, 2004.

R20. E–GOVERNMENT ACT OF 2002

Privacy protection for filings made with the Court is governed by Fed.R.Civ.P. 5.2 and Fed.R.Crim.P. 49.1. To supplement the federal rules, the Court has entered an administrative order (EXHIBIT G) which makes it clear that counsel and the parties are responsible for redacting filings with the Court. The Clerk's Office will not review papers for compliance with the federal rules.

EXHIBIT A

UNITED STATES DISTRICT COURT
EASTERN DISTRICT OF MICHIGAN

**PROCEDURE TO ADDRESS NON–COMPLIANCE
WITH ECF POLICIES AND PROCEDURES**

(Revised September 2009)

I. Authority. At the May 2007 Judges' Meeting, the Court approved a Procedure to Address Non–Compliance with the ECF Policies and Procedures (Appendix ECF to the Local Rules).

II. Overview. With each e-filing error or instance of non-compliance a Notice of E–Filing Error or Notice of Non–Compliance will be generated and served on the filing user, opposing counsel, and the judge's chambers. Action will be taken after there have been a combined threshold of three occurrences of e-filing errors, or non-compliance, or a combination of the two within a six-month period. The threshold will be met whether three violations occur in a single case or a single violation occurs in three different cases.

With each violation, the offending filing user will receive a Notice of E–filing Error or Notice of Non–Compliance that will identify the problem and the course of action that should be taken. The Notice will caution the offending filing user that sanctions may result from repeated errors and/or instances of non-compliance.

III. Definitions.

(A) *E–Filing Error.* Electronically filing a document which violates the local and/or federal rules.

(B) *Non–Compliance.*

(1) Registered filing users filing a document in paper without leave of Court.

(2) Failure to update the Court with current contact information resulting in an e-mail being returned to the Court's electronic mailbox as undeliverable.

(3) An attorney who is admitted to practice before this Court, and has an active case or cases, but has not registered for electronic filing.

(4) Any other violation of local and/or federal rules.

(C) *Chief Judge's Designee.* For purposes of this procedure, the Chief Judge has designated Judge Robert H. Cleland to act for the Court.

IV. Clerk's Office Contact. After the third violation within a six-month period, the offending filing user will be contacted in writing by CM/ECF Help Desk personnel. The offending filing user will be instructed to follow a prescribed course of action appropriate for the violations that have occurred. Appropriate action may include, but not be limited to, completion of online training, a violation warning or direction to review specific online content related to electronic filing. The user will be warned that further violations will be referred to the Chief Judge's designee for further action.

V. Further Violations. Upon the fourth violation within a six-month period, the Chief Judge's designee may issue an Order to Show Cause directing the offending filing user to explain the offending conduct. The Chief Judge's designee may take any remedial action deemed appropriate.

Any additional violations within a six-month period may be considered contempt of court. If held in contempt, an appropriate monetary fine will be imposed.

VI. Newly–Admitted attorneys. Newly admitted attorneys, who have a pending case at the time of admission, have up to two weeks from their admission date to register and otherwise comply with the ECF Policies and Procedures. Attorneys who do not have any active cases pending at the time of admission are not required to register until such time as the attorney has appeared in an active case.

Approved: May 7, 2007

Revised: September 2009

EXHIBIT B

MIED (Rev. 6/05) Sample Certificate of Service Form

CERTIFICATE OF SERVICE

I hereby certify that on _____ [Date], I electronically filed the foregoing paper with the Clerk of the Court using the ECF system which will send notification of such filing to the following: _____

_____,

and I hereby certify that I have mailed by United States Postal Service the paper to the following non-ECF participants: _____

_____.

                                             s/Name of Filing User
                                             Firm Name (if applicable)
                                             Street Address
                                             City, State, Zip Code
                                             Telephone Number
                                             Primary Email Address
                                             Attorney Bar No. (if applicable)

EXHIBIT C

UNITED STATES DISTRICT COURT
EASTERN DISTRICT OF MICHIGAN

**PROCEDURES GOVERNING THE ELECTRONIC AVAILABILITY
AND
REDACTION OF TRANSCRIPTS**

(Revised September 2009)

A. Authority. At its September 2007 session, the Judicial Conference of the United States approved a new policy regarding the availability of transcripts of courtroom proceedings. The language from that session states:

(1) A transcript provided to a court by a court reporter or transcriber will be available at the office of the clerk of court for inspection only, for a period of 90 days after it is delivered to the clerk.

(2) During the 90–day period, a copy of the transcript may be obtained from the court reporter or transcriber at the rate established by the Judicial Conference, the transcript will be available within the court for internal use, and an attorney or party who obtains the transcript from the court reporter or transcriber may obtain remote electronic access to the transcript through the court's CM/ECF system for the purposes of creating hyperlinks to the transcript in court filings or for other purposes.

(3) After the 90–day period has ended, the filed transcript will be available for inspection and copying in the clerk's office and for downloading from the court's CM/ECF system through the judiciary's PACER system.

In addition, amendments to the Federal Civil and Criminal Rules of Procedure that took effect on December 1, 2007, require that personal identification information be redacted from documents filed with the court—individuals' Social Security numbers, names of minor children, financial account numbers, dates of birth, and, in criminal cases, home addresses.

B. Procedures. These procedures apply to all transcripts of federal court proceedings, or parts of federal court proceedings, filed by official court reporters, contract court reporters, and transcribers.

The responsibility to review the transcripts and request redactions, if necessary, rests solely with the attorneys and parties to the case.

Nothing in these procedures creates a private right of action against the court, the official court reporter, the contract court reporter, or transcriber.

1. Transcripts of federal court proceedings, or parts of federal court proceedings, will be filed electronically in CM/ECF by the court reporter or transcriber. Transcripts will not be made electronically available for 90 calendar days from the date of filing, however they may be viewed at the clerk's office using the public terminal. CM/ECF will calculate the release of transcript restriction deadlines.

2. Upon receipt of payment from the ordering party, the court reporter or transcriber will grant the attorney or party electronic access to the transcript in CM/ECF. If the transcript is ordered by a Federal Government agency, the agency will be granted access to the transcript in CM/ECF upon its completion.

3. Any attorney or party needing to review the transcript for redaction purposes may purchase a copy from the court reporter or transcriber, or view the transcript at the clerk's office using the public terminal.

4. Once a prepared transcript is filed with the clerk's office, the attorneys or parties in the case are responsible for reviewing it for the personal data identifiers required by the federal rules to be redacted, and providing the court reporter or transcriber with a statement of the redactions to be made to comply with the rules. Attorneys and parties must request the redaction of the following personal data identifiers:

• Social Security numbers (or taxpayer identification numbers) to the last four digits;

- financial account numbers to the last four digits;

- dates of birth to the year;

- names of minor children to the initials; and

- in criminal cases, any home addresses stated in court to the city and state.

5.   Unless otherwise ordered by the court, attorneys and parties must review the following portions of the transcript:

- opening and closing statements made on the party's behalf;

- statements of the party;

- the testimony of any witnesses called by the party;

- sentencing proceedings; and

- any other portion of the transcript as ordered by the court.

6.   An attorney serving as "standby" counsel appointed to assist a *pro se* defendant in his or her defense in a criminal case must review the same portions of the transcript as if the *pro se* defendant were his or her client.   The attorney conducting the review is entitled to compensation under the Criminal Justice Act for functions reasonably performed to fulfill the redaction obligation and for reimbursement for related reasonable expenses.

7.   Within 21 days from the filing of the transcript, or longer if the court so orders, an attorney or party must submit to the court reporter or transcriber a statement (Redaction Request) indicating where the personal data identifiers appear in the transcript, by page and line number, and how they are to be redacted.   A copy must also be filed with the clerk's office.   [NOTE: The Court's standard Redaction Request is attached.   It is also available on the Court's website.]

8.   If an attorney or party wishes to redact additional information, he or she may make a motion to the court within the 21–day period, with a copy served on the court reporter or transcriber.   The transcript will not be electronically available until the court has ruled on any such motion, even though the 90–day restriction period may have ended.

9.   If redaction is requested, the court reporter or transcriber must, within 31 days from the filing of the original transcript, or longer if the court so orders, perform the requested redactions and file a redacted version of the transcript with the clerk of court.   A copy of the redaction request must be retained by the court reporter or transcriber in order to have a record to support the redactions made.

10.   The redacted transcript will be available for remote access after 90 calendar days from the date the original transcript was filed.   The unredacted, original transcript will be retained by the clerk of court as a restricted document, and will continue to be available at the clerk's office public terminal for viewing only.

11.   If, at the end of the 90–day restriction period, there are no redaction documents or motions linked to the transcript, CM/ECF will automatically remove the access restrictions.

12.   Transcripts that include voir dire or other juror information will only be available to parties in the case if they are specifically requested.   The voir dire transcript will be sealed to ensure a juror's right to privacy.   Parties to the case will be required to seek permission of the Court to use the transcript in any other proceeding except an appeal of the same case.   Members of the public must receive permission from the judge that ordered the voir dire transcript sealed prior to obtaining a copy of the transcript, and the transcript may be subject to redaction before it is given to any member of the public.

C.   **Purchase of Transcripts by the Public.**   Members of the public, including the news media, who purchase a transcript from the court reporter or transcriber within the 90–day restriction period, will not be granted remote electronic access during the restriction period.   At the end of the restriction period, the public will be provided remote electronic access to the redacted transcript, or if no redaction was done, to the transcript originally submitted, unless it is under seal.

If both redacted and unredacted versions exist at the time a transcript is ordered by a member of the public, including the news media, the redacted transcript is the version that should be sold.

D.   **Redaction Procedures.**   Court reporters and transcribers may perform the requested redactions manually or with the assistance of various software programs.   To manually redact, an "x" should be placed in the space of each redacted character. Regardless of the method used, the page and line numbers of the original transcript must be preserved.

E. Certification of Redacted Transcripts. The title page of the transcript will include a notation of "REDACTED TRANSCRIPT" on a blank line immediately below the case caption and before the volume number and the name and title of the Judge.

At the end of the transcript, and without affecting the page number, the redacted transcript should be certified by the court reporter or transcriber by stating:

"I (we) certify that the foregoing is a true and correct copy of the transcript originally filed with the clerk of court on mm/dd/yy, and incorporating redactions of personal identifiers requested by the following attorneys of record or parties: _____ in accordance with Judicial Conference policy. Redacted characters appear as an "x" (or black box) in the transcript."

F. Remote Access and PACER Charges. Charges for access through PACER will accrue during and after the 90–day restriction period. Charges will accrue for the entire transcript rather than being capped at 30 pages. The user will incur PACER charges each time the transcript is accessed even though he or she may have purchased it from the court reporter or transcriber and obtained remote access through CM/ECF. There will not be a remote free copy of the transcript. In addition, the transcript policy approved by the Judicial Conference does not provide for a free copy of the transcripts for the Department of Justice at the clerk's office.

G. Effective Date. These procedures apply to transcripts of court proceedings, or parts of proceedings, filed on or after June 16, 2008.

Attachment

MIED (Rev. 6/08) Redaction Request—Transcript

UNITED STATES DISTRICT COURT
EASTERN DISTRICT OF MICHIGAN

Plaintiff(s),   Case No.

v.

Defendant(s).

_____/

REDACTION REQUEST—TRANSCRIPT

Pursuant to Judicial Conference policy, _____ requests redaction of transcript(s) on file in this case:

(Please list the document number, page, and line number and a redacted identifier for each redaction necessary; *e.g.*, Doc. No. 15, Page 12, Line 9, Social Security No. to read xxx–xx–6130.)

Document Number	Page Number	Line Number(s)	Redacted Identifier

_____

_____

_____

_____

_____

The undersigned understands that redaction of information other than personal identifiers listed below requires an order of the court.

Social Security or taxpayer-identification numbers to the last four digits

Dates of birth to the year

Names of minor children to the initials

Financial account numbers to the last four digits

Home addresses to the city and state (in a criminal case)

The requesting party is responsible for providing a copy of this request to the Court Reporter.

Date: _____   _____
                                     Signature

                                     _____
                                     Bar No.

                                     _____
                                     Street Address

                                     _____
                                     City, State, Zip Code

                                     _____
                                     Telephone Number

                                     _____
                                     Primary Email Address

EXHIBIT D

**UNITED STATES DISTRICT COURT
EASTERN DISTRICT OF MICHIGAN**

SAMPLE INDEX OF EXHIBITS

Exhibit	Description
A	Affidavit of John Smith
B	Excerpts from Jane Doe's Deposition
C–1	Contract Between XYZ Company and ABC Company (Part 1, Pages 1–35)
C–2	Contract Between XYZ Company and ABC Company (Part 2, Pages 36–69)
D	XYZ Company General Ledgers

EXHIBIT E

MIED (Rev. 6/05) Sample Ex Parte Motion for Leave to File Exhibits in the Traditional Manner

UNITED STATES DISTRICT COURT
EASTERN DISTRICT OF MICHIGAN

Plaintiff(s),   Case No.

    v.   Judge

                         Magistrate Judge

Defendant(s).

_____/

**EX PARTE MOTION FOR LEAVE TO FILE
EXHIBITS IN THE TRADITIONAL MANNER**

NOW COMES the undersigned _____, and pursuant to the Electronic Filing Policies and Procedures, seeks leave of this Court to file exhibits in the traditional manner.

The exhibits to _____ cannot be authentically converted to electronic form for the following reason(s): _____

_____

_____

_____.

For the foregoing reasons, the undersigned respectfully requests that this Court grant the leave sought in this motion.

Date: _____   s/Name of Filing User
                                 Firm Name (if applicable)
                                 Street Address
                                 City, State, Zip Code
                                 Telephone Number
                                 Primary Email Address
                                 Attorney Bar No. (if applicable)

EXHIBIT F

MIED (Rev. 6/05) Sample Notice of Filing Exhibits in the Traditional Manner

UNITED STATES DISTRICT COURT
EASTERN DISTRICT OF MICHIGAN

Plaintiff(s),   Case No.

v.   Judge

                                 Magistrate Judge

Defendant(s).

_____/

NOTICE OF FILING EXHIBITS IN THE TRADITIONAL MANNER

Please take notice that the undersigned has filed exhibits to the following paper in the traditional manner.

Leave of Court was previously granted on _____ [Date] by the above judicial officer.

Title of Paper: _____

_____

_____

_____

The exhibits have been served in hard copy on all parties pursuant to federal and local rules.

Date: _____   s/Name of Filing User _____
                             Firm Name (if applicable)
                             Street Address
                             City, State, Zip Code
                             Telephone Number
                             Primary Email Address
                             Attorney Bar No. (if applicable)

EXHIBIT G

UNITED STATES DISTRICT COURT
EASTERN DISTRICT OF MICHIGAN

Administrative Order No. 07–AO–030.   In re: Federal Rules Governing Privacy
Protection for Filings Made with the Court—Responsibility for Redaction

ADMINISTRATIVE ORDER

It appearing that privacy protection for filings made with this Court have been governed by Administrative Orders 05–AO–025 (civil) and 05–AO–026 (criminal); and

It further appearing that new federal rules, Fed.R.Civ.P.5.2 and Fed.R.Crim.P.49.1, governing privacy protection for filings made with the Court will take effect on December 1, 2007, absent contrary Congressional action;

NOW THEREFORE IT IS ORDERED that counsel and the parties are responsible for redacting filings with the Court. The Clerk's Office will not review papers filed with the Court for compliance with the federal rules.

This administrative order supersedes Administrative Orders 05–AO–025 and 05–AO–026 in their entirety, and remains in effect until amendments to the appropriate local rule have been approved by the Court.

IT IS ORDERED.

FOR THE COURT:

Bernard A. Friedman
Chief Judge

[Effective November 30, 2007. Amended effective August, 2008; November, 2008; March, 2010; May 1, 2016; December 1, 2016.]

LOCAL RULES FOR CRIMINAL CASES

LCrR 1.1   SCOPE OF RULES

In addition to these local criminal rules, the general local rules apply to criminal actions as provided in LR 1.1(c).

[Amended effective March 2, 1998.]

LCrR 5.1   INITIAL APPEARANCES BY DEFENDANT

(a) All initial appearances shall comply with Fed.R.Crim.P. 5.

(b) If a defendant is appearing voluntarily, the defendant shall report to the Pretrial Services Agency for the purpose of a bond recommendation and to the United States Marshals Service before the defendant's initial appearance in court.

(c) The United States Attorney shall provide the Magistrate Judge a copy of the complaint, removal petition, other papers and information relating to the defendant's initial appearance.

[Former LR 205.1 adopted effective July 1, 1992. Renumbered as LCrR 5.1 effective March 3, 1997.]

LCrR 6.1   GRAND JURIES

(a) All grand juries are under the direct supervision of the Court. The Chief Judge shall act for the Court. The Chief Judge, by Administrative Order, may designate District Judges to act for the Court.

(b) A motion or application filed in connection with a grand jury subpoena or other matter occurring before a grand jury, all other papers filed in support of or in opposition to such a motion or application, and all orders entered by the Court in connection therewith, shall be filed under seal.

(c) The moving party shall prepare a motion and order to seal and shall bring such papers to the District Judge to whom the matter has been assigned rather than file them in the Clerk's Office.

(d) The moving party shall contact the Assistant United States Attorney assigned to the investigation to determine whether a prior miscellaneous matter in the same grand jury investigation has resulted in the assignment of a District Judge.

(e) All miscellaneous matters regarding grand juries sitting in Detroit shall be assigned by random method to District Judges in active service in Detroit, except the Chief Judge. All miscellaneous matters regarding grand juries sitting in Bay City or Flint shall be assigned to the District Judge designated by the Chief Judge to act for the Court in supervising the grand jury in that place of holding court.

[Former LR 206.1 adopted effective July 1, 1992. Renumbered as LCrR 6.1 effective March 3, 1997.]

Comment

LCrR 6.1(e) makes clear that miscellaneous matters relating to grand juries, e.g., motions to quash grand jury subpoenas, are as-

signed by random method to District Judges in Detroit and are not directed to the Chief Judge under LCrR 6.1(a).

LCrR 10.1   ARRAIGNMENTS

(a) If a defendant is arrested on a warrant or is otherwise in custody, the United States Attorney shall schedule the case for arraignment. In the case of a voluntary appearance, the United States Attorney shall schedule the arraignment and inform defendant or defendant's attorney, if defendant is represented by counsel, of the time and date of the arraignment.

(b) On the scheduled arraignment date, the defendant's attorney shall inform the defendant to report to the Pretrial Services Agency for a bond recommendation prior to the arraignment. If the defendant is not represented by counsel, the United States Attorney shall so inform the defendant.

(c) The defendant's attorney shall inform the defendant to report to the United States Marshals Service for processing after completion of the Pretrial Services Agency interview.

(d) All arraignments shall be conducted pursuant to Fed. R.Crim.P. 10.

[Former LR 210.1 adopted effective July 1, 1992. Renumbered as LCrR 10.1 effective March 3, 1997.]

LCrR 12.1   MOTION PRACTICE

(a) Motions in criminal cases shall be filed in accordance with the procedures set forth in LR 7.1.

(b) Pretrial motions shall be filed within the time specified in the standing order of discovery and inspection and fixing motion cut-off date in criminal cases unless modified by order of the District Judge.

[Former LR 247.1 adopted effective July 1, 1992. Renumbered as LCrR 12.1 effective March 3, 1997.]

Comment

LCrR 12.1 should be read with Fed.R.Crim.P. 47.

LCrR 12.2   EX PARTE MOTION UNDER THE CRIMINAL JUSTICE ACT

Ex parte motions permitted pursuant to the Criminal Justice Act, 18 U.S.C. § 3006A(e)(1), shall be filed with the District Judge or Magistrate Judge assigned to the case rather than in the Clerk's Office and shall be filed under seal.

[Former LR 244.2 adopted effective July 1, 1992. Renumbered as LCrR 12.2 effective March 3, 1997.]

Comment

While ex parte motions are not routinely permitted, the Criminal Justice Act authorizes ex parte motions under limited circumstances.

LCrR 17.1   SUBPOENAS

(a) Defendant Unable to Pay.

(1) *Subpoenas Served Within 100 Miles.* For subpoenas to ⸀e served within 100 miles from the place of holding court, ⸀efense counsel appointed under the Criminal Justice Act and ⸀ederal defenders may obtain witness subpoenas from the ⸀lerk's office. The clerk must issue those subpoenas signed, ⸀ealed, and designated *in forma pauperis*, but otherwise in ⸀lank. By completing such a subpoena, defense counsel certi⸗es that in counsel's opinion the witness's presence is neces⸗ary to an adequate defense.

(2) *Subpoenas Served More Than 100 Miles Away.* For ⸀ubpoenas to be served more than 100 miles from the place of ⸀olding court, an application for issuance of a subpoena *in ⸀orma pauperis* must be made to the Court. The application ⸀nay be made *ex parte*.

(b) A party seeking a subpoena for books, papers, documents, data, or other objects under Fed. R. Crim. P. 17(c) in advance of trial must seek prior approval from the court. An application for approval may be made *ex parte*. The subpoena must state that the requested items must be returned to the chambers of the assigned judge.

[Former LR 217.1 adopted effective July 1, 1992. Renumbered as LCrR 17.1 effective March 3, 1997. Amended effective March 2, 1998; July 1, 2017.]

Comment

LCrR 17.1 should be read with Fed. R. Crim. P. 17 (which is substantially similar to Fed R. Civ. P. 45). Paragraph (b) provides guidance for the issuance and return of subpoenas under Fed. R. Crim. P.17(c). That rule was "not intended to provide a means of discovery for criminal cases," but it was designed "to expedite the trial by providing a time and place before trial for the inspection of subpoenaed materials." United States v. Nixon, 418 U.S. 683, 698–99 (1974). To facilitate court supervision of subpoenas directed to third parties, subpoenas issued under that rule must specify that the items sought be returned to the court, and not elsewhere, such as a lawyer's office.

LCrR 18.1 ASSIGNMENT OF CRIMINAL CASES TO PLACES OF HOLDING COURT

(a) **Counties and Places of Holding Court.** Criminal cases shall be assigned to the place of holding court which serves the county in which the offense is alleged to have been committed:

(1) Jackson, Lenawee, Macomb, Monroe, Oakland, St. Clair, Sanilac, Washtenaw and Wayne counties for which the places of holding court are Ann Arbor, Detroit and Port Huron.

(2) Genesee, Lapeer, Livingston and Shiawassee counties for which the place of holding court is Flint.

(3) Alcona, Alpena, Arenac, Bay, Cheboygan, Clare, Crawford, Gladwin, Gratiot, Huron, Iosco, Isabella, Midland, Montmorency, Ogemaw, Oscoda, Otsego, Presque Isle, Roscommon, Saginaw and Tuscola counties for which the place of holding court is Bay City.

(b) **Improper Assignments.** A case improperly assigned to a place of holding court shall be transferred to the proper location by order of the Court.

[Former LR 200.1 adopted effective July 1, 1992. Amended effective April 3, 1995. Renumbered as LCrR 18.1 effective March 3, 1997.]

LCrR 32.1 GUIDELINE SENTENCING

(a) Not less than 35 days before the sentencing date, the probation officer must disclose the presentence investigation report, excluding the probation officer's recommendation, to the *pro se* defendant or to defense counsel and government counsel. The presentence report is disclosed under 18 U.S.C. § 3552(d):

(1) when it is physically or electronically delivered, or

(2) three days after it is mailed.

(b) Within 14 days after disclosure, the *pro se* defendant or counsel for the defendant and counsel for the Government shall communicate to the probation officer and to each other any objections to any material information, sentencing classifications, sentencing guideline ranges, and policy statements which are contained in, or omitted from, the report. Such communication shall be in writing and shall be signed by the defendant or counsel for the defendant or counsel for the Government, or in another manner as the Court directs. Any response to an objection shall be in writing and submitted directly to the probation officer, with copies furnished to all parties.

(c) After receiving a timely objection or response, the probation officer shall immediately conduct a further investigation and make such revisions to the presentence report as are warranted. The probation officer may require each counsel or pro se defendant to meet with the officer to discuss any unresolved factual and legal issues.

(d) Prior to the date set for sentencing, the probation officer shall submit the presentence report to the sentencing judge. The report shall be accompanied by

(1) an addendum which shall set forth any unresolved objections that counsel or the pro se defendant may have and any response thereto, and

(2) the comments of the probation officer. The probation officer shall certify that the contents of the report, including any revisions and the addendum, have been disclosed to the defendant and counsel for the defendant and counsel for the Government, and that the addendum to the presentence report, if any, fairly states all of the remaining objections.

(e) After reviewing the presentence report and addendum, the Court, upon a showing of good cause, may allow a new objection to be raised at any time prior to the imposition of sentence.

(f) When the Court resolves disputed sentencing factors, it shall notify the parties of its tentative findings and provide a reasonable opportunity for the submission of oral or written objections to the Court before the imposition of sentence. If the Court determines that a hearing is necessary to resolve disputed sentencing factors, a hearing shall be held for that purpose upon reasonable notice to all interested parties. See Fed.R.Crim.P. 32.

(g) A party who submits a document to the Court shall serve a copy of the document on the probation officer.

(h) The times set forth in this LCrR may be modified by the Court upon a showing of good cause.

(i) The presentence report, any objections thereto, and any correspondence between counsel and a probation officer concerning any such objections shall be maintained in confidence and shall not be disclosed to any person other than the defendant, counsel for the defendant, counsel for the Government, other persons assisting counsel in the discharge of their professional responsibility representing the client, the probation officer, the Court, and the United States Sentencing Commission without a prior order of the Court authorizing such disclosure.

[Former LR 232.1 adopted effective July 1, 1992. Amended effective November 7, 1994. Renumbered as LCrR 32.1 effective March 3, 1997. Amended effective March 2, 1998; November 1, 2017.]

Comment

LCrR 32.1(g) requires service on the probation officer of a copy of any document submitted to the Court under LCrR 32.1.

LCrR 32.1(a) provides that disclosure is "under 18 U.S.C. § 3552(d)." The statute requires disclosure "at least ten days prior to the date set for sentencing, unless this minimum period is waived by the defendant." The 35–day requirement of Fed R Crim P 32(e)(2) supersedes the statutory ten-day requirement.

LCrR 46.1   RELEASE FROM CUSTODY

(a) Eligibility for release prior to trial shall be in accordance with the Bail Reform Act, 18 U.S.C. §§ 3141–3142.

(b) An individual posting bond with the Clerk's Office shall present a copy of the order setting conditions of the bond signed by the District Judge or Magistrate Judge.

(1) Only money order or cashier's check made payable to "Clerk, United States District Court", or credit card is acceptable for a cash bond.

(2) Unless approved in writing by a District Judge, property shall not be accepted as collateral for a bond.

(3) Court personnel shall not recommend specific bail bonding agencies.

(c) To recover money posted as bond, a District Judge's or Magistrate Judge's order releasing the bond must be on file in the Clerk's Office and the individual must present the original receipt and personal identification. The Clerk's Office will issue a check in the name of the owner of the cash identified in the affidavit accompanying the original bond.

(d) The court will not accept a member of the bar in active practice, or officer or employee of the court or the United States Marshals Service as a surety, except that a district judge may approve a member of the bar as a surety for a family member if the attorney is not counsel of record in the case.

[Former LR 246.1 adopted effective July 1, 1992. Amended effective September 12, 1994. Renumbered as LCrR 46.1 effective March 3, 1997. Amended effective March 2, 1998; July 1, 2008; November 1, 2014.]

Comment

The Court accepts the following credit cards for a cash bond: VISA, MasterCard, American Express, Discover, and Diners Club.

[Comment effective July 1, 2008.]

LCrR 49.1   FILING AND SERVICE BY ELECTRONIC MEANS

LR 5.1.1 governs filing and service by electronic means.

[Effective October 1, 2003.]

Comment

The Court will maintain electronic case files for all criminal cases.

LCrR 50.1   PROMPT DISPOSITION OF CRIMINAL CASES

The Judges of the United States District Court for the Eastern District of Michigan have adopted a Speedy Trial Act Plan which has been approved by the Chief Judge of the United States Court of Appeals for the Sixth Circuit, to minimize undue delay and further the prompt disposition of criminal cases. A copy of the Plan is available in the Clerk's Office for use by counsel and the public.

[Former LR 250.1 adopted effective July 1, 1992. Renumbered as LCrR 50.1 effective March 3, 1997.]

LCrR 57.1   APPEARANCES BY ATTORNEYS IN CRIMINAL CASES

(a) An attorney, whether retained or appointed, who enters a post-indictment appearance shall continue to represent the defendant until the case is dismissed, the defendant is acquitted, or the direct appeal is completed unless the attorney is granted leave to withdraw by the District Court or the Court of Appeals if notice of appeal has been filed.

(b) An attorney who has appeared in a criminal case may thereafter withdraw only by written motion served upon the defendant personally or at the defendant's last-known address and upon all other parties. The Court may deny a motion to withdraw if the attorney's withdrawal would unduly delay trial of the case, or be unfairly prejudicial to any party, or otherwise not be in the interest of justice.

(c) The United States Attorney shall advise the Clerk and the District Judge to whom the case is assigned regarding any change in the attorney for the United States responsible for the prosecution.

[Former LR 244.1 adopted effective July 1, 1992. Renumbered as LCrR 57.1 effective March 3, 1997.]

Comment

LCrR 57.1 should be read with Fed.R.Crim.P. 44.

LCrR 57.2   REVIEW OF ORDER OF MAGISTRATE JUDGE

A motion for review of a release or detention order as provided in 18 U.S.C. § 3145 (a) and (b) entered by a magistrate judge in a preliminary criminal proceeding which has not been assigned to a district judge shall be heard and decided by the district judge who was the presiding judge on the date the magistrate judge's order was entered. If that judge is not available, the motion will be heard and decided by a district judge selected by random method. If the judge selected is not available, the motion will be heard and decided by the district judge who was the presiding judge on the date the motion was filed.

Former LR 205.2 adopted effective July 1, 1992. Amended effective May 6, 1996. Renumbered as LCrR 57.2 effective March 3, 1997. Amended effective July 1, 2001.]

Comment

As an example of a matter covered by LCrR 57.2, an appeal of a magistrate judge's bond order is properly before the judge who was presiding judge on the date the bond order was entered if the case has not been assigned to a district judge.

Pursuant to LR 77.2(c), if the district judge who was the presiding judge on the date the motion was filed is not available, and no arrangements have been made for another judge to act as presiding judge, the Clerk's Office will contact judges, beginning with the most senior district judge in active service in Detroit until an available judge is found to act as presiding judge.

[Comment amended effective July 1, 2001.]

LCrR 57.3　RECORDING OF PROCEEDINGS

All initial appearances and arraignments shall be recorded. Attorneys may order copies of these proceedings from the Court Reporting Supervisor.

[Former LR 255.1 adopted effective July 1, 1992. Renumbered as LCrR 57.3 effective March 3, 1997.]

LCrR 57.10　ASSIGNMENT AND REASSIGNMENT OF CRIMINAL CASES TO JUDGES

(a) Assignment of Criminal Cases to Judges.

(1) In Ann Arbor, Detroit and Port Huron, the Clerk shall employ a random method for the assignment of criminal cases to Judges.

(2) In Flint, the Clerk shall assign criminal cases to the Judge regularly holding court in Flint.

(3) In Bay City, the Clerk shall assign criminal cases to the Judge regularly holding court in Bay City.

(4) Assignment of criminal cases to the Chief Judge, to senior Judges, and, in cases of emergency to Judges in active service, shall be as provided by administrative order authorized by the Court.

(b) Reassignment of Criminal Cases.

(1) Cases shall be reassigned only by order of the Court.

(2) To promote docket efficiency, or to conform to the requirement of any case management plan adopted by the Court, or upon consent of the parties, or after notice and hearing, or in the interests of justice, the Chief Judge may order a criminal case to be reassigned, but only with the consent of the Judge to whom the case was originally assigned and with the consent of the Judge to whom it is to be reassigned.

(3) Reassignment of cases because of a change in judicial personnel shall be in accordance with an administrative order authorized by the Court.

(4) Companion Cases.

(A) Companion cases are those cases in which it appears that:

(i) substantially similar evidence will be offered at trial, or

(ii) the same or related parties are present, and the cases arise out of the same transaction or occurrence. Cases may be companion cases even though one of them may have already been terminated.

(B) Counsel, including the United States Attorney, or a party without counsel shall be responsible for bringing such cases to the attention of the Court by responding to the questions included on the criminal case cover sheet.

(C) When it becomes apparent to the Judge to whom a case is assigned and to a Judge having an earlier case number that two cases are companion cases, upon consent of the Judge having the earlier case number, the Judge shall sign an order reassigning the case to the Judge having the earlier case number.

(5) Matters arising from a criminal case assigned to (1) a judge who has retired from the court, or (2) a senior judge no longer receiving criminal cases, will be assigned to the judge who is appointed to fill the vacancy of that judge. If no judge has been appointed to fill that vacancy, the matter will be reassigned by random method under (a).

(c) Disqualification of Judge.

(1) In Ann Arbor, Detroit and Port Huron, when a Judge to whom a criminal case is assigned is disqualified from hearing it, the Clerk shall reassign the case by random method.

(2) In Flint, when a Judge to whom a criminal case is assigned is disqualified from hearing it, the Clerk shall reassign the case in accordance with an administrative order authorized by the Court.

(3) In Bay City, when a Judge to whom a case is assigned is disqualified from hearing it, the Clerk shall reassign the case in accordance with an administrative order authorized by the Court.

(d) Superseding Indictments or Informations.

(1) A superseding indictment or information shall be assigned to the Judge to whom the superseded matter was assigned when:

(A) it merely corrects errors in names, dates and places, etc., or

(B) it is a follow-up to an indictment or information terminated on motion of the government, or

(C) it is a follow-up information involving different charges or added counts for purpose of a plea only, or

(D) it is a follow-up to an indictment or information embracing the same subject matter terminated by motion of the defendant or on the Court's motion, or

(E) it is a follow-up to an indictment or information embracing the same subject matter but containing additional defendants or charges.

(2) The United States Attorney shall attach a cover sheet in a form prescribed by the Clerk's Office to permit assignments according to this Rule.

(3) Superseding indictments and informations shall not be filed in closed cases or cases where the last defendant has pleaded guilty and is awaiting sentencing.

[Former LR 200.2 adopted effective April 3, 1995. Renumbered as LCrR 57.10 effective March 3, 1997. Amended effective May 1, 1999; June 1, 2014.]

Comment

The "earlier case number" referred to in (b)(4)(C) will mean the earlier case filed as determined by date and time.

[Comment added December 4, 2000.]

LCrR 58.1 FORFEITURE OF COLLATERAL IN LIEU OF APPEARANCE IN ACCORDANCE WITH FED. R. CRIM. P. 58(d)(1)

(a) A person who is charged with a violation of a federal wildlife act, parking regulations governing federal buildings, national forest offenses, conduct on Postal Service property, motor vehicle violations on Postal Service property, violations of law on military property, or any other petty offense as defined in 18 U.S.C. § 19, may, in lieu of appearance, post collateral in the amount indicated for the offense, waive appearance before a Magistrate Judge, and consent to the forfeiture of collateral. The offenses for which collateral may be posted and forfeited are set forth in an administrative order from the Court which may be obtained from the Clerk's Office. Those offenses marked with an asterisk and for which no amount of collateral is shown require a mandatory appearance before a Magistrate Judge.

(b) If a person charged with an offense under (a) fails to post and forfeit collateral, any punishment, including fine, imprisonment or probation, may be imposed within the limits established by law upon conviction or after trial.

(c) If, within the discretion of the law enforcement officer, the offense is of an aggravated nature, the law enforcement officer may require appearance, and any punishment, including fine, imprisonment or probation, may be imposed within the limits established by law upon conviction or after trial.

(d) Nothing in this LCrR shall prohibit a law enforcement officer from arresting a person for the commission of any offense, including those for which collateral may be posted and forfeited, and requiring the person charged to appear before a Magistrate Judge or, upon arrest, taking the person immediately before a Magistrate Judge.

[Former LR 258.1 adopted effective July 1, 1992. Renumbered as LCrR 58.1 effective March 3, 1997.]

REVISED PLAN FOR IMPLEMENTING THE CRIMINAL JUSTICE ACT OF 1964, AS AMENDED, 18 U.S.C. § 3006A

PREAMBLE

Pursuant to the provisions of the Criminal Justice Act of 1964, as amended, 18 U.S.C. § 3006A, [hereinafter referred to as "The Act"], the Judges of the United States District Court for the Eastern District of Michigan adopt the following amended plan for the representation of any person otherwise financially unable to obtain adequate representation.

(1) Representation shall be provided for any financially eligible person who:

(i) is charged with a felony or with a misdemeanor other than a petty offense as defined in section 1 of title 18, United States Code (but see paragraph (2)(i), infra);

(ii) is a juvenile alleged to have committed an act of juvenile delinquency as defined in section 5031 of title 18, U.S.C. (see section 5034 of title 18, U.S.C., with regard to appointment of counsel);

(iii) is charged with a violation of probation;

(iv) is under arrest, when such representation is required by law;

(v) is entitled to appointment of counsel in parole proceedings pursuant to chapter 311 of title 18, U.S.C.;

(vi) is charged with a violation of supervised release or faces modification, reduction, or enlargement of a condition, or extension or revocation of a term of supervised release;

(vii) is subject to a mental condition hearing under chapter 313 of title 18, U.S.C.;

(viii) is in custody as a material witness; and

(ix) is entitled to appointment of counsel under the sixth amendment to the Constitution; or

(x) faces loss of liberty in a case and federal law requires the appointment of counsel.

(2) Whenever the United States magistrate judge or district judge determines that the interests of justice so require, representation may be provided for any financially eligible person who:

(i) is charged with a petty offense for which a sentence to confinement is authorized; or

(ii) is seeking relief under section 2241, 2254, or 2255 of title 28;

(iii) is charged with civil or criminal contempt and faces loss of liberty;

(iv) could be subject to a criminal prosecution, a civil or criminal contempt proceeding, or face loss of liberty as a result of an appearance before a grand jury or court;

(v) is proposed by the U.S. Attorney for processing under a "pretrial diversion" program;

(vi) is held for international extradition under chapter 209, title 18, United States Code;

(vii) is involved in "ancillary matters appropriate to the proceedings" pursuant to subsection (c) of the Act.

In determining whether a matter is ancillary to the proceedings, the court should consider whether the matter, or the issues of law or fact in the matter, arose from, or are the same as or closely related to, the facts and circumstances surrounding the principal criminal charge.

In determining whether representation in an ancillary matter is appropriate to the proceedings, the court should consider whether such representation is reasonably necessary to accomplish, inter alia, one of the following objectives:

(a) to protect a Constitutional right;

(b) to contribute in some significant way to the defense of the principal criminal charge;

(c) to aid in preparation for the trial or disposition of the principal criminal charge;

(d) to enforce the terms of a plea agreement in the principal criminal charge;

(e) to preserve the claim of the CJA client to an interest in real or personal property subject to a civil forfeiture proceeding pursuant to 21 U.S.C. § 881, 19 U.S.C. § 1602 or similar statutes, which property, if recovered by the CJA client, may be considered for reimbursement under subsection (f) of the Act; or

(f) to effectuate the return of real or personal property belonging to the CJA client which may be subject to a motion for return of property pursuant to Fed. R. Crim. P. 41(e), which property, if recovered by the CJA client, may be considered for reimbursement under subsection (f) of the Act.

Representation shall include counsel and investigative, expert, and other services necessary for an adequate defense.

I. PROVISION FOR FURNISHING COUNSEL

A. This plan provides for the furnishing of legal services by a Community Defender Organization, serving the United States District Court for the Eastern District of Michigan, and for the appointment and compensation of private counsel in a substantial proportion of cases. The term "private counsel" includes counsel furnished by a bar association, a legal aid agency, and a state or local defender association, and a claim by such an entity for compensation will be approved on the same basis as in the case of the appointment of private counsel.

B. The determination of whether a party entitled to representation will be represented by the Community Defender Organization or by private counsel is within the discretion of the appointing district judge or magistrate judge. Insofar as practical, private attorney appointments will be made in at least 25 percent of the cases.

II. COMMUNITY DEFENDER ORGANIZATION

A. Metropolitan Justice Center of Southeast Michigan, a non-profit defense counsel service, is authorized by this Plan to provide representation as a Community Defender Organization, and shall be eligible to furnish attorneys and receive payments pursuant to subsection (g)(2)(B) of the Act. The by-laws of MJCSEM are incorporated as part of the Plan, and a copy of said by-laws shall be maintained by the Clerk of the Court and attached to the original of this Plan.

B. The Community Defender Organization shall operate pursuant to the provisions of subsection (g)(2)(B) of the Act, the terms and conditions of the sustaining grant, and the Guidelines for the Administration of the Criminal Justice Act, Guide to Judiciary Policies and Procedures), promulgated by the United States Judicial Conference pursuant to subsection (h) of the Act.

C. The Community Defender Organization shall submit to the Judicial Conference of the United States an annual report setting forth its activities and financial position and the anticipated caseload and expenses for the next fiscal year.

D. The Community Defender shall furnish to this court the roster of staff attorneys and shall report any changes thereto to the court.

E. In order to ensure the effective supervision and management of the Community Defender Organization, its Chief Attorney (hereinafter the Community Defender) will be responsible for the assignment of cases among the staff attorneys in that office. Accordingly, the court will assign cases in the name of the Community Defender Organization rather than in the name of individual staff attorneys.

III. PANEL OF PRIVATE ATTORNEYS

A. Composition of Panel of Private Attorneys.

1. *Approval.* The court shall establish a panel of private attorneys (hereinafter referred to as the "CJA Panel") who are eligible and willing to be appointed to provide representation under the Criminal Justice Act. The court shall approve attorneys for membership on the panel after receiving recommendations from the "Panel Selection Committee," established pursuant to Part B of this title. Members of the CJA Panel shall serve at the pleasure of the court.

2. *Size.* The court shall fix, periodically, the size of the CJA Panel. The panel shall be large enough to provide a sufficient number of experienced attorneys to handle the CJA caseload, yet small enough so that panel members will receive an adequate number of appointments to maintain their proficiency in federal criminal defense work, and thereby provide a high quality of representation.

3. *Eligibility.* Attorneys who serve on the CJA Panel must be members in good standing of the federal bar of this district, and have sufficient experience to demonstrate competence in, and knowledge of, the Federal Rules of Criminal Procedure and the Federal Rules of Evidence.

4. *Pro Hac Vice Admission.* Subsection (b) of the Act provides, in part, that:

> Counsel furnishing representation under the plan shall be selected from a panel of attorneys designated or approved by the court, or from a bar association, legal aid agency, or defender organization furnishing representation pursuant to the plan.

However, when the district judge presiding over the case, or the chief judge if a district judge has not yet been assigned to the case, determines that the appointment of an attorney, who is not a member of the CJA panel, is in the interest of justice, judicial economy or continuity of representation, or there is some other compelling circumstance warranting his or her appointment, the attorney may be admitted to the CJA panel pro hac vice and appointed to represent the CJA defendant. Consideration for preserving the integrity of the panel selection process suggests that such appointments should be made only in exceptional circumstances. Further, the attorney, who may or may not maintain an office in this district, should possess such qualities as would qualify him or her for admission to this district's CJA panel in the ordinary course of panel selection. Notice of such appointment shall be sent to the Clerk of Court at the time of the appointment.

5. *Application.* Application forms for membership on the CJA Panel shall be made available, upon request, by the Federal Defender Office. Completed applications shall be transmitted to the Federal Defender Office.

B. Panel Selection Committee.

1. *Membership.* A Panel Selection Committee shall be established by the Court. One experienced federal criminal law practitioner from each of the following bar associations shall be invited to sit on the committee:

SOUTHERN DIVISION, DETROIT:
Detroit
Jackson County
Metropolitan Justice Center of Southeast Michigan
Lenawee County
Macomb County
Monroe County
Oakland County
St. Clair County
Sanilac County
Washtenaw County
Wolverine

SOUTHERN DIVISION, FLINT:
Genesee County
Lapeer County
Livingston County
Shiawassee County

NORTHERN DIVISION, BAY CITY:
Bay County
Cheboygan County
Gratiot County
Huron County
Midland County
Saginaw County
Tuscola County
21st Judicial Circuit (Isabella)
23rd Judicial Circuit (Iosco, Oscoda)
26th Judicial Circuit (Alcona, Alpena,
Montmorency, Presque Isle)
34th Judicial Circuit (Arenac, Ogemaw,
Roscommon)
46th Judicial Circuit (Crawford, Otsego)
55th Judicial Circuit (Clare, Gladwin)

2. *Duties.* The Committee shall review the qualifications of applicants and recommend, for approval by the court, those applicants best qualified to fill the vacancies.

C. Disqualification From Membership on CJA Panel.

1. *Removal From List (Automatic); Reinstatement by Request.* Any attorney whose license is revoked or suspended by the Attorney Discipline Board for more than 119 days shall be removed automatically from the CJA Panel list. In the event of such an attorney's reinstatement to membership in good standing in the State Bar of Michigan and the Bar of this Court, an attorney who desires to be reinstated to the CJA Panel shall proceed as on original application. If such attorney receives a recommendation by the Panel Selection Committee for appointment to the CJA Panel, the Court shall be advised of the recommendation and shall discuss and decide the appointment.

2. *Suspension From List (Automatic); Reinstatement by Request.* Any attorney whose license is suspended by the Attorney Discipline Board for 119 days or less or for any other reason is no longer a member in good standing of the State Bar of Michigan shall be suspended automatically form active status on the list of CJA Panel attorneys. Upon reinstatement to membership in good standing in the State Bar of Michigan and the Bar of this Court, a suspended CJA panel attorney shall be responsible for initiating any request for return to active status on the Panel list. Such request shall be made to the Panel Selection Committee, which shall in turn recommend appropriate action to the Chief Judge. The Chief Judge shall either notify the Court of his or her intended action on the recommendation, or refer the recommendation to the Court for discussion and decision.

3. *Suspension From List (Provisional); Reinstatement by Request.* The Chief Judge may provisionally suspend an attorney from membership on the CJA Panel for reasons other than bar membership status, including but not limited to formal accusation of a crime, conviction of crime not resulting in action by the Attorney Discipline Board, indications of lack of professional competence or lack of adherence to ethical standards, and indications of mental or emotional instability affecting professional responsibilities. A district judge in possession of any such information concerning a panel attorney should immediately make the Chief Judge aware of that information and any recommendation the district judge may have concerning the panel attorney's continued status. Upon such a provisional suspension, the attorney shall be given written notice and shall have the opportunity to seek relief from suspension. Any such application shall be to the Chief Judge, who shall either refer the matter to the Panel Selection Committee for study and recommendation, or shall notify the Court of his or her intended decision on the matter or shall refer the matter to the Court for discussion and decision.

4. None of the foregoing reinstatement procedures shall be construed to alter the principle stated in section III.A.1., i.e. that all Panel attorneys serve at the pleasure of the Court.

IV. SELECTION FOR APPOINTMENT

A. Maintenance of List and Distribution of Appointments. The Community Defender shall maintain a current list of all attorneys included on the CJA Panel, with current office addresses and telephone numbers as well as a statement of qualifications and experience. The Community Defender shall furnish a copy of this list to each district judge and magistrate judge. The Community Defender shall also maintain a public record of assignments to private counsel, and, when appropriate, statistical data reflecting the proration of appointments between attorneys from the Community Defender Organization and private attorneys, according to the formula described in title I(B) of this plan.

B. Method of Selection. Appointments from the list of private attorneys should be made on a rotational basis, subject to discretion to make exceptions due to the nature and complexity of the case, an attorney's experience, and geographical considerations. This procedure should result in a balanced distribution of appointments and compensation among the members of the CJA Panel, and quality representation for each CJA defendant.

Upon the determination of a need for the appointment of counsel, the district judge or magistrate judge shall notify the Community Defender of the need for counsel and the nature of the case.

V. DETERMINATION OF NEED FOR COUNSEL

A. Advice of Right, Financial Inquiry, Appointment, Procedure. Counsel should be provided to persons financially eligible for representation as soon as feasible after they are taken into custody, when they appear before a federal judge or magistrate judge, when formally charged, or when otherwise entitled to counsel under the Act, whichever occurs earliest. The determination of eligibility for representation under the Criminal Justice Act is a judicial function to be performed by a federal judge or magistrate judge after making appropriate inquiries regarding the person's financial condition.

To effectuate this objective, federal law enforcement and prosecutorial agencies in this district, and those acting on their behalf, shall promptly ask any person who is in custody, or who might otherwise be entitled to counsel under the Act, whether the person desires court appointed counsel, and shall, in such cases in which the person indicates that he or she does seek representation, promptly arrange to have the person presented before a magistrate judge or district judge of this court for determination of financial eligibility and assignment of counsel.

Unless it will result in undue delay, factfinding concerning the person's eligibility for appointment of counsel should be completed prior to the person's first appearance in court. Pretrial Services officers are designated by the court to obtain or verify the facts upon which such determination is to be made. Relevant information bearing on the person's financial eligibility should be reflected on a financial eligibility affidavit (CJA Form 23) and the form shall be completed and executed before a judicial officer or employee. Employees of law enforcement agencies or United States attorney offices should not participate in the completion of the CJA Form 23 or seek to obtain information from a person requesting the appointment of counsel concerning his or her eligibility.

Upon the appearance of a person before a magistrate judge or district judge as provided above, or at any proceeding in which a person who is entitled to representation under this plan appears without counsel, the court shall advise the person of the right to be represented by counsel and that counsel will be appointed if the person is financially unable to afford adequate representation. Unless the person waives representation by counsel, the court, if satisfied after appropriate inquiry that the person is financially unable to obtain counsel, shall appoint counsel to represent the person. If the need for the assistance of counsel is immediate and apparent, and the person states under oath that he or she is financially unable to obtain counsel, the inquiry may follow the appointment of counsel as soon thereafter as is practical. All statements made by a person in requesting counsel or during the inquiry into eligibility shall be either (a) by affidavit sworn to before the court, a court clerk or deputy, or a notary public, or (b) under oath in open court.

Appointment of counsel may be made retroactive to include representation furnished pursuant to this plan prior to appointment.

The court shall appoint separate counsel for persons having interests that cannot be represented by the same counsel or when other good cause is shown.

B. Continuity and Duration of Appointment. A person for whom counsel is appointed shall be represented at every stage of the proceedings from initial appearance before the United States magistrate judge or the district court judge through appeal, including ancillary matters appropriate to the proceedings. In determining whether a matter is ancillary to the proceedings the court should consider whether the matter, or the issues of law or fact in the matter, arose from, or are the same as or closely related to, the facts and circumstances surrounding the principal charge. If a United States magistrate judge appoints counsel to represent a person and the person is later before a district court judge in connection with the same charge, the same counsel shall appear before the judge to represent the person until the judge has had the opportunity to make an independent determination as to whether appointment of counsel in the proceeding is appropriate and, if so, who should be appointed.

C. Appeal. In the event that a defendant enters a plea of guilty or is convicted following trial, counsel appointed hereunder shall advise the defendant of the right of appeal and of the right to counsel on appeal. If requested to do so by the defendant in a criminal case, counsel shall file a timely Notice of Appeal. The attorney shall continue to represent the defendant on appeal unless or until relieved by the district court or the court of appeals. Representation continues with regard to consideration of and, if proper, the filing of a Rule 35 motion to reduce sentence.

D. Partial Payment or Reimbursement. If at any time after appointment of counsel the court finds that the person is financially able to obtain counsel or to make partial payment for the representation, or that funds are available for payment from or on behalf of a person furnished representation, the court may terminate the appointment of counsel or authorize payment as provided in subsection (f) of the Act, as the interests of justice may dictate.

If at any time after appointment counsel obtains information that a client is financially able to make payment, in whole or in part, for legal or other services in connection with the representation and the source of the attorney's information is not protected as a privileged communication, counsel shall advise the court. The court will then take appropriate action, which may include permitting assigned counsel to continue to represent the party with part or all of the cost of representation defrayed by such party. In such event, the amount so paid or payable by the party shall be considered by the court in determining the total compensation to be allowed to such attorney. No appointed counsel may require, request, or accept any payment or promise of payment for representing a party, unless such payment is approved by order of the court.

If at any stage of the proceedings, including an appeal, the court finds that the party is financially unable to pay counsel whom he or she had retained, the court may appoint counsel as provided in the Act, and authorize such payment as therein provided, as the interests of justice may dictate.

The court, in the interests of justice, may substitute one appointed counsel for another at any stage of the proceedings.

VI. INVESTIGATIVE, EXPERT, AND OTHER SERVICES

A. With Prior Authorization (Ex Parte Motions). Counsel (whether or not appointed under the Act) for a party who is financially unable to obtain investigative, expert, or other services necessary for adequate representation may request such services in an ex parte motion filed under seal in the Court's operating system, currently CM/ECF, before a district judge or before a United States magistrate judge, if the services are required in connection with a matter over which the magistrate judge has jurisdiction or if a district judge otherwise refers such application to a magistrate judge for findings and report. Upon finding, after appropriate inquiry in such ex parte proceedings, that the services are necessary, and that the person is financially unable to obtain them, the district judge or the magistrate judge, as the case may be, shall authorize counsel to obtain the services by issuing an order under seal granting the ex parte motion. Ex parte motions for services other than counsel shall be heard in camera, if necessary, and shall not be revealed without the consent of the person represented. The motion shall remain under seal until the final disposition of the case in the trial court, subject to further order of the district judge or magistrate judge. The maximum which may be paid to a person or organization for services so authorized shall not exceed the CJA maximum exclusive of reimbursement for expenses reasonably incurred, unless payment in excess of that limit is certified by the district judge, or by the magistrate judge if the services were rendered in connection with a case disposed of entirely before the magistrate judge, as necessary to provide fair compensation for services of an unusual character or duration, and the amount of the excess payment is approved by the chief judge of the Court of Appeals for the Sixth Circuit, (or an active circuit judge to whom excess compensation approval authority has been delegated). If it can be anticipated that the compensation will exceed the statutory maximum, advance approval should be obtained from the court and the chief judge of the circuit (or the active circuit judge to whom excess compensation approval authority has been delegated).

B. Without Prior Authorization. Counsel appointed under the Act may obtain, subject to later review, investigative, expert, or other services without prior authorization, if necessary for adequate representation. However, the total cost for services obtained without prior authorization may not exceed the CJA maximum and expenses reasonably incurred, for each person or organization providing the services. This limit may be waived, however, if the presiding district judge or magistrate judge (if the services were rendered in a case disposed of entirely before the magistrate judge) in the interest of justice finds that timely procurement of necessary services could not wait prior authorization. (Refer to CJA Guidelines)

C. Transcripts. Counsel (whether or not appointed under the Act) for a party who is financially unable to obtain a transcript of a proceeding for adequate representation may request authorization to obtain such transcript using the appropriate CJA form in the electronic payment system. (Instructions are available on the Court's website)

D. Claims. Claims for compensation of persons providing investigative, expert, and other services under the Act shall be submitted on the appropriate CJA form, using the electronic payment system. Claims will be reviewed for mathematical and technical accuracy and for conformity with the Guidelines for the Administration of the Criminal Justice Act, Guide to Judiciary Policies and Procedures), and if correct, shall be approved for payment by the appropriate district judge or magistrate judge.

If prior authorization was obtained, a copy of the order must be uploaded into the electronic payment system and submitted with the claim.

E. Community Defender Organization. The Community Defender Organization may obtain investigative, expert, or other services without regard to the requirements and limitations of this title, provided that total expenditures of the organization for investigative, expert, and other services do not exceed its grant authorization for these specific categories.

VII. PAYMENT FOR REPRESENTATION BY PRIVATE COUNSEL

A. Hourly Rates. Any private attorney appointed under this plan shall, at the conclusion of the representation, or any segment thereof, be compensated at a rate not exceeding the applicable CJA hourly rate for time expended in and out of court. Such attorney shall be reimbursed for expenses reasonably incurred, including the costs of transcripts authorized by the court.

B. Case Budgeting. Counsel must use case-budgeting techniques in representations that appear likely to become or have become extraordinary in terms of potential costs (generally, a representation in which attorneys hours are expected to exceed 300 hours or total expenditures are expected to exceed 300 times the prevailing CJA panel attorney non-capital hourly rate, rounded up to the nearest thousand, for appointed counsel and services other than counsel for an individual CJA defendant.)

Counsel must submit an ex parte motion seeking court approval of a proposed initial litigation budget, subject to modification in light of facts and developments that emerge as the case proceeds. The motion must be filed under seal in the Court's operating system, currently CM/ECF. All claims for payment must be submitted using the electronic payment system.

C. Interim Payments.

(1) *Non–Death Penalty Cases.* Counsel who has been appointed to represent a defendant under CJA may file a motion seeking interim payments to alleviate financial hardships in extended and complex cases.

Motions for interim payments must be filed under seal in the Court's operating system, currently CM/ECF. Orders for interim payments approved by the district judge must be sent to the chief judge of the circuit or his/her designee for approval. The order will be filed under seal in the Court's operating system, currently CM/ECF.

Circuit approval is required before an interim claim may be submitted and processed for payment. All interim claims for payment must be submitted using the electronic payment system.

(2) *Death Penalty Cases.* The Anti–Drug Abuse Act of 1988 effectively repealed the case compensation maximum with respect to death penalty cases. However, counsel who has been appointed to represent a defendant under CJA may file a motion seeking interim payments to alleviate financial hardships.

Motions for interim payments must be filed under seal in the Court's operating system, currently CM/ECF. Orders for interim payments approved by the district judge must be sent to the chief judge of the circuit or his/her designee for approval. The order will be filed under seal in the Court's operating system, currently CM/ECF.

Circuit approval is required before an interim claim may be submitted and processed for payment. All interim claims for payment must be submitted using the electronic payment system.

D. Maximum Amounts. For representation of a person before the district judge or the United States magistrate judge, or both, the compensation to be paid to a private attorney appointed under this plan shall not exceed the CJA maximum compensation rate for each attorney in a case in which one or more felonies are charged, and for each attorney in a case in which only misdemeanors (including petty offenses as set forth in subsection (a)(2)(A) of the Act) are charged. For any other representation required or authorized by the Act compensation is limited to the applicable CJA maximum compensation rate for each attorney in each proceeding. This includes, but is not limited to, representation of persons charged with a violation of probation, a person charged with a violation of supervised release or a person who faces modification, reduction, or enlargement of a condition, or extension or revocation of a term of supervised release, or persons entitled to appointment of counsel in parole proceedings under chapter 311 of title 18, U.S.C., material witnesses in custody, and persons seeking relief under section 2241, 2254 or 2255 of title 28, U.S.C.

E. Waiving Maximum Amounts. Payment in excess of any maximum amount provided in the previous paragraph may be made for extended or complex representation whenever the presiding district judge, or the United States magistrate judge, if the representation was furnished exclusively before the magistrate judge, certifies that the amount of the excess payment is necessary to provide fair compensation and the payment is approved by the chief judge of the Court of Appeals for the Sixth Circuit (or by an active circuit judge to whom excess compensation approval authority has been delegated).

F. Filing Claims. Claims for compensation shall be submitted, on the appropriate CJA form, using the electronic payment system. Claims will be reviewed for mathematical and technical accuracy, and for conformity with the Guidelines for the Administration of the Criminal Justice Act, Guide to Judiciary Policies and Procedures) and, if correct, the claim form will be forwarded for consideration and action of the presiding district judge, or to the United States magistrate judge if the representation was furnished exclusively before the magistrate judge. In cases where representation is furnished other than before the district judge, magistrate judge, or an appellate court, the district judge shall fix the compensation and reimbursement to be paid.

In cases where the amount of compensation and reimbursement approved by the reviewing judicial officer is less than was requested by appointed counsel, the judicial officer should notify appointed counsel that the claim has been reduced, and provide an explanation for the reasons for the reduction.

VIII. MISCELLANEOUS

A. Forms. Standard forms for payment that have been approved by the Judicial Conference of the United States or an appropriate committee thereof, shall be used by the court, the clerk, the Community Defender Organization, and other appointed counsel and are available in the electronic payment system.

B. Guidelines for the Administration of the Criminal Justice Act. The court, clerk of the court, Community Defender Organization, and private attorneys appointed under the Act and this plan, shall comply with the provisions of the Judicial Conference's Guidelines for the Administration of the Criminal Justice Act, Guide to Judiciary Policies and Procedures.

IX. EFFECTIVE DATE

This plan as amended shall take effect immediately upon its approval by the Judicial Council of the Sixth Circuit.

CERTIFICATE OF APPROVAL

This is to certify that, in accordance with the Criminal Justice Act of 1964 as amended, 18 U.S.C. § 3006A, *et seq.*, the foregoing Revised Plan for Implementing the Criminal Justice Act of 1964, As Amended for the United States District Court for the Eastern District of Michigan, has been duly received and approved via mail ballot dated June 3, 2016 as complying with the law by the Judicial Council of the Sixth Circuit of the United States. The said Revised Plan shall become effective upon the date of this approval.

[Amended effective November 7, 1987; February 7, 1994; June 16, 2016.]

JUROR SELECTION PLAN

(a) Declaration of Policy. All litigants in this court entitled to trial by jury have the right to grand and petit juries selected at random from a fair cross section of the community. All citizens resident within the district have the opportunity to be considered for service on grand and petit juries and have an obligation to serve as jurors when summoned for that purpose.

This court utilizes the one-step summoning and qualification procedure, as authorized by 28 U.S.C. § 1878. Accordingly, jurors will be summoned and qualified in a single procedure.

(b) Definitions. The definitions contained in 28 U.S.C. § 1869, as amended, will apply in this Juror Selection Plan (plan) except:

(1) "division" means a set of counties deemed a unit for the purpose of defining the geographic area of the master jury wheels; and

(2) "chief judge" includes his or her designee.

(c) Discrimination Prohibited. No citizen will be excluded from service as a grand or petit juror in this court on account of race, color, religion, sex, national origin, or economic status.

(d) Designation of Divisions. The Eastern District of Michigan is divided into the following divisions for juror selection purposes:

(1) Grand and petit jurors serving in the Detroit division will be selected from citizens residing in the following counties:

Jackson	Monroe	Sanilac
Lenawee	Oakland	Washtenaw
Macomb	St. Clair	Wayne

(2) Grand and petit jurors serving in the Flint division will be selected from citizens residing in the following counties:

Genesee	Livingston
Lapeer	Shiawassee

(3) Grand and petit jurors serving in the Bay City division will be selected from citizens residing in the following counties:

Alcona	Gladwin	Ogemaw
Alpena	Gratiot	Oscoda
Arenac	Huron	Otsego
Bay	Iosco	Presque Isle
Cheboygan	Isabella	Roscommon
Clare	Midland	Saginaw
Crawford	Montmorency	Tuscola

(4) Petit jurors serving in the Port Huron division will be selected from citizens residing in the following counties:

Macomb	St. Clair
Oakland	Sanilac
	Wayne

(5) Petit jurors serving in the Ann Arbor division will be selected from citizens residing in the following counties:

Jackson	Oakland
Lenawee	Washtenaw
Monroe	Wayne

(e) Management of the Juror Selection Process.

(1) The clerk will manage the juror selection process under the supervision of the chief judge.

(2) Orders of the court relating to the general operation of the jury system and public notices concerning the drawing of names for assignment to grand and petit jury panels will be available in the clerk's office and on the court's website, and distributed to the judicial officers of the court.

(f) Data Sources.

(1) Grand and petit jurors will be selected randomly from the following data sources:

(A) registered voters in the Qualified Voter File (QVF) compiled by the Michigan Secretary of State;

(B) persons licensed by the Michigan Secretary of State to drive motor vehicles;

(C) persons who have been issued a personal identification card by the Michigan Secretary of State; and

(D) persons who have filed Michigan state income tax, if available.

(2) The clerk will obtain data sources in the electronic form most compatible with the computer hardware and software used by the court for the random selection of names.

(g) Random Selection.

(1) The clerk may use electronic data processing systems for any tasks associated with the administration of the jury system including, but not limited to:

(A) the random selection of names from the data sources for master jury wheels;

(B) the random selection of names of qualified jurors for grand and petit jury panels;

(C) the random assignment of prospective jurors to pools;

(D) the summoning of jurors;

(E) the payment of jurors;

(F) the preparation of documents; and

(G) statistical reports necessary for the efficient and effective administration of the jury system.

(2) For all purposes for which random selection is required by this plan, the clerk will use a purely randomized process through a properly programmed electronic data processing system.

(3) If a contractor is used for any tasks associated with the administration of the jury system, the contractor will submit to the court a certification that work has been completed pursuant to the detailed instructions from the clerk.

(h) Master Jury Wheels.

(1) The clerk will maintain master jury wheels for each division.

(2) The clerk will ensure that each county within a division is proportionally represented in the master jury wheel for that division. For the purpose of determining proportional representation in master jury wheels, the number of registered voters in each county in each division will be used.

(3) To increase the probability that the names and addresses on the data sources are as current as possible, the clerk will empty and refill the master jury wheels as frequently as is practicable, but at least once every four years, between March 1 and November 1 in the year following general elections.

(4) The clerk will determine the total number of names to be selected at random from the data sources and placed in master jury wheels.

(5) The minimum number of names to be placed in the respective master jury wheels is as follows:

Ann Arbor division	10,000
Bay City division	10,000
Detroit division	300,000
Flint division	10,000
Port Huron division	10,000

(6) The clerk will use the most current data sources referenced in (f) for the creation of each master jury wheel.

(7) After determining the total number of names needed for any master jury wheel and the percentage of names to be drawn from each county, the clerk will direct the random selection of names from the data sources.

(i) Drawing of Names From the Master Jury Wheels.

(1) The clerk will direct the random drawing of the names of as many persons from the master jury wheels as may be needed to maintain an adequate number of names of qualified jurors.

(2) The clerk will maintain records of the names drawn from the master jury wheels.

(j) Juror Summons and Qualification Forms. The clerk will mail a juror summons and qualification form to every person drawn with instructions for the recipient to complete, sign, and return the form within 10 days. 28 U.S.C. § 1864(a). The clerk will send a subsequent form to any person not responding to an earlier mailing.

(k) Supplemental Draw.

(1) For each juror summons and qualification form returned as undeliverable by the United States Postal Service to the court, the clerk will randomly draw the name of another person residing in the same zip code and mail a new juror summons and qualification form to that person.

(2) The clerk will implement the supplemental draw process for a period of two years following the date of approval by the reviewing panel of the Judicial Council for the Sixth Circuit.

(l) Determination of Juror Qualifications. Under the supervision of the chief judge, the clerk will determine whether a person is (1) unqualified for, (2) exempt from, or (3) to be excused from, jury service. These determinations will be based solely on information provided in the juror qualification form and other competent evidence. The clerk will produce reports on qualification information upon request of the court.

(m) Qualifications for Jury Service. Under 28 U.S.C. § 1865(b), a person will be deemed qualified to serve on grand and petit juries unless he or she:

(1) is not a citizen of the United States 18 years old who has resided for a period of one year within the judicial district;

(2) is unable to read, write, and understand the English language with a degree of proficiency sufficient to complete satisfactorily the juror qualification form;

(3) is unable to speak the English language;

(4) is incapable, by reason of mental or physical infirmity, to render satisfactory jury service, or

(5) has a charge pending against him/her for the commission of, or has been convicted in a state or federal court of record of, a crime punishable by imprisonment for more than one year and his/her civil rights have not been restored. Application of this provision is governed by state law. Since there is no provision in Michigan law for the restoration of an individual's civil rights, the clerk must deem any individual convicted of a felony in Michigan as not qualified to serve as a juror in this court.

(n) Exemption From Jury Service. Under 28 U.S.C. § 1863(b)(6), the following are exempt from jury service:

(1) members in active service in the Armed Forces of the United States;

(2) members of fire or police departments; and

(3) public officers in the executive, legislative or judicial branches of the government of the United States, or of any state or subdivision of any state, who are actively engaged in the performance of official duties.

(o) Excuses on Individual Request.

(1) The court finds that jury service by the following persons would entail undue hardship or extreme inconvenience and to excuse them from jury service on individual request is not inconsistent with 28 U.S.C. §§ 1861 and 1862:

(A) persons over the age of 73;

(B) persons who have served on a grand or petit jury in a federal court within the last two years; and

(C) persons who are members of a volunteer fire department, rescue squad or ambulance crew for a public agency.

(2) Additionally, under supervision of the chief judge, the clerk may excuse persons summoned for jury service upon a showing of undue hardship, extreme inconvenience, or other ground of excusal as set forth in 28 U.S.C. §§ 1866(c) and 1869(j), for such period of time as the court may deem

necessary and proper. The court finds that jury service by members of the following groups of persons may entail undue hardship and extreme inconvenience to the members thereof:

(A) persons who have active care and custody of a child under the age of six whose health and/or safety would be jeopardized by their absence;

(B) persons who are essential to the care of aged or infirm persons;

(C) persons having no access to a private vehicle and residing in a remote location where public transportation is unavailable or is not feasible; and

(D) persons whose services are so essential to the operation of a business, commercial, or agricultural enterprise that it may close or cease to function if they were required to perform jury duty.

The clerk may only defer or excuse jurors under the categories defined in this plan. All other categories will be referred to the chief judge for disposition.

(p) Postponement of Jury Service.

(1) If a person requests a postponement of his or her jury service for a specific reason, such as a pre-planned vacation, business commitment, health problem or similar episodic event, the clerk may reassign the juror to a different pool within the same jury wheel. All requests for postponement must be in writing.

(2) The clerk will record any postponements granted and will report on the status of any individual juror or group of jurors upon request of the court.

(q) Qualified Jurors.

(1) At all times, the clerk will maintain an adequate number of qualified jurors not exempt or excused under this plan.

(2) Qualified jurors will be randomly assigned to grand and petit jury panels.

(3) The clerk will maintain records of persons summoned and assigned to grand and petit jury panels.

(r) Petit Jury Panels. Petit jurors in the Detroit division will serve for a period of one week. Petit jurors in other divisions will serve for a period of two weeks. An additional period of two weeks may be authorized by the chief judge.

(s) Failure to Report for Jury Service. A person who does not report for jury service on the date and at the time stated on his or her summons may be subject to prosecution. 28 U.S.C. § 1866(g).

(t) Maintenance of Records.

(1) During the life of a master jury wheel, the contents of records or papers used by the clerk in connection with the juror selection process will not be disclosed, except as necessary in the preparation or presentation of a jury challenge under 28 U.S.C. § 1867(f) or as indicated in this plan. If the challenge is based on race, ethnicity, or sex, the order will be limited to the disclosure of a person's juror number, race, ethnicity, or sex. If the challenge seeks additional information, the matter will be referred to the chief judge for disposition, who may order disclosure upon a showing of good cause.

(2) Names and personal information of grand and petit jurors will not be disclosed to attorneys, parties, the public, or the media, subject to the following exceptions:

(A) upon order of the court, names and counties of residence of prospective petit jurors may be disclosed to the attorneys or parties in a case set for trial after those jurors have appeared for service. Unless otherwise directed by the court, the clerk will provide attorneys or parties a written list of the jurors' names and counties of residence, which may not be copied or shared except as necessary for selecting a jury. The list and any copies must be returned to the clerk immediately following jury selection.

(B) upon order of the court, names and counties of residence of petit jurors selected in a case set for trial may be disclosed after the conclusion of the jury selection. Unless otherwise directed by the court, the clerk will provide the attorneys, parties, the public, or the media with a written list of the jurors' names and counties of residence.

(3) Any district judge may order juror names to be kept confidential in any case when the interests of justice so require.

(4) After a master jury wheel is emptied and refilled, and after all persons selected have completed their jury service, the clerk will maintain and preserve all records and papers pertaining to all master jury wheels for four years or for such longer period as may be ordered by the court. These records and papers will be available for public inspection for the purpose of determining the validity of the selection of any jury.

(5) The clerk will retain and, when requested, provide the public access to the following:

(A) Juror Selection Plan for the Eastern District of Michigan;

(B) a description of the procedure used by the electronic data processing system to randomly select and assign names during the implementation of this plan; and

(C) the clerk's directives to any contractor that implements any portion of this plan, including the execution of any pure random selection procedures, and that contractor's certifications required under (g)(3) of this plan.

(u) General Provisions.

(1) The clerk will collect information to monitor the court's compliance with statutes, this plan, and the quality of the data sources provided by the Michigan Secretary of State and will distribute it periodically to the judges of the court.

(2) Incorporated in this plan by reference are the provisions of 28 U.S.C. §§ 1861–1971, any amendments to these sections as may be made from time to time, and all statutes enacted after this plan is approved pertaining to grand and petit jurors and trials by jury in federal courts.

CERTIFICATE OF APPROVAL

This is to certify that, in accordance with 28 U.S.C. § 1863(a), the foregoing Juror Selection Plan of the United States District Court for the Eastern District of Michigan has been duly received and approved as complying with the law by a reviewing panel consisting of the members of the Judicial Council for the Sixth Circuit of the United States and the Chief Judge of the District to which the plan is applicable.

This 6th day of March, 2013.

CERTIFICATE OF FILING

This is to certify that, in accordance with 28 U.S.C. § 1863(a), a true copy of the foregoing Juror Selection Plan for the United States District Court for the Eastern District of Michigan was filed with the Administrative Office of the United States Courts, Washington, D.C., and the Attorney General of the United States.

[Filed March 18, 2013. Approved by the Sixth Circuit Judicial Council March 6, 2013.]

SPEEDY TRIAL ACT PLAN

1. Authority. Pursuant to the Speedy Trial Act of 1974, as amended, 18 U.S.C. §§ 3161–3174, and Rule 50 of the Federal Rules of Criminal Procedure, the Judges of the United States District Court for the Eastern District of Michigan have adopted this Speedy Trial Act Plan which sets forth time limits and procedures to minimize undue delay and to further the prompt disposition of criminal cases.

This Plan shall take effect upon approval by the Sixth Circuit Judicial Council and supersedes the Speedy Trial Act Revised Final Plan dated July 1, 1980.

2. Applicability.

(a) *Offenses.* The time limits set forth herein apply to all criminal offenses triable in this court, including cases triable by United States Magistrate Judges, except for Class B misdemeanors, Class C misdemeanors, and infractions. [18 U.S.C. § 3172(2).]

(b) *District.* The term "district" refers to the Eastern District of Michigan.

(c) *Judicial Officer.* The term "judicial officer" refers to any United States District Judge or United States Magistrate Judge. [18 U.S.C. § 3172(1).]

(d) *Court.* The term "court" refers either to the United States District Court for the Eastern District of Michigan or to the judicial officer to whom a specific case is assigned.

(e) *Clerk.* The term "clerk" refers to Clerk of Court and includes his or her designee.

(f) *United States Attorney.* As used in this Plan, the term "United States Attorney" also includes Assistant United States Attorneys.

3. Priorities in Scheduling Criminal Cases. Preference shall be given to criminal proceedings as far as practicable, as required by Rule 50 of the Federal Rules of Criminal Procedure. The trial of defendants in custody solely because they are awaiting trial should be given preference over other criminal cases. [18 U.S.C. § 3164(a).]

4. Time Within Which an Indictment or Information Must Be Filed.

(a) *Time Limits.* If an individual is arrested or served with a summons and the complaint charges an offense to be prosecuted in this district, any indictment or information charging that offense shall be filed within 30 days of arrest or service. [18 U.S.C. § 3161(b).]

(b) *Measurement of Time Periods.* If a person has not been arrested or served with a summons on a federal complaint, an arrest will be deemed to have been made at such time as the person (1) is held in custody solely for the purpose of responding to the complaint; (2) is delivered to the custody of a federal official in connection with the complaint, or (3) appears before a judicial officer in connection with the complaint.

(c) *Related Procedures.*

(1) At the time of the earliest appearance before a judicial officer of a person who has been arrested for an offense charged in a complaint, the judicial officer shall establish for the record the date on which the arrest took place. The United States Attorney appearing at the earliest appearance shall have the arrest information available to provide to the judicial officer.

(2) In absence of a showing to the contrary, a summons shall be considered to have been served on the date of service shown on the return thereof.

5. Time Within Which Trial Must Commence.

(a) *Time Limits.* The trial of a defendant shall commence not later than 70 days after the last to occur of the following dates:

(1) The date on which an indictment or information is filed in this district;

(2) The date on which a sealed indictment or information is unsealed; or

(3) The date of the defendant's first appearance before a judicial officer of this district. [18 U.S.C. § 3161(c)(1).]

(b) *Retrial: Trial After Reinstatement of an Indictment or Information.* The retrial of a defendant shall commence within 70 days from the date the order occasioning the retrial becomes final, as shall the trial of a defendant upon an indictment or information dismissed by the court and reinstated following an appeal. If the retrial or trial follows an appeal or collateral attack, the court may extend the period if unavailability of witnesses or other factors resulting from passage of time make trial within 70 days impractical. The extended period shall not exceed 180 days. [18 U.S.C. § 3161(d)(2) and (e).]

(c) *Withdrawal of Plea.* If a defendant enters a plea of guilty or nolo contendere to any or all charges in an indictment or information and is subsequently permitted to withdraw it, the time limit shall be determined for all counts as if the indictment or information were filed on the day the order permitting withdrawal of the plea became final. [18 U.S.C. § 3161(i).]

(d) *Superseding Charges.* If, after an indictment or information has been filed, a complaint, indictment, or information is filed which charges the defendant with the same offense or with an offense required to be joined with that offense, the time limit applicable to the subsequent charge will be determined as follows:

(1) If the original indictment or information was dismissed on motion of the defendant before the filing of the subsequent charge, the time limit shall be determined without regard to the existence of the original charge. [18 U.S.C. § 3161(d).]

(2) If the original indictment or information is pending at the time the subsequent charge is filed, the trial shall commence within the time limit for commencement of trial on the original indictment or information, unless the court finds that the new charge is not for the same offense charged in the original indictment or information or an offense required to be joined by them.

(3) If the original indictment or information was dismissed on motion of the United States Attorney before the filing of the subsequent charge, the trial shall commence within the time limit for commencement of trial on the original indictment or information, but the period during which the defendant was not under charges shall be excluded from the computations. Such period is the period between the dismissal of the original indictment or information and the date the time would have commenced to run on the subsequent charge had there been no previous charge. [18 U.S.C. § 3161(h)(5).]

(4) If the subsequent charge is contained in a complaint, the formal time limit within which an indictment or information must be obtained on the charge shall be determined without regard to the existence of the original indictment or information but earlier action may in fact be required if the time limit for commencement of trial is to be satisfied.

(e) *Measurement of Time Periods.* For the purposes of this section:

(1) If a defendant signs a written consent to be tried before a magistrate judge on a complaint, the time limit shall run from the date of such consent.

(2) In the event of a transfer to this district under Rule 20 of the Federal Rules of Criminal Procedure, the indictment or information shall be deemed filed in this district when the papers in the proceeding or certified copies thereof are received by the clerk.

(3) A trial in a jury case shall be deemed to commence at the beginning of voir dire.

(4) A trial in a non-jury case shall be deemed to commence on the day the case is called, provided that some step in the trial procedure immediately follows.

(f) *Related Procedures.*

(1) At the time of the defendant's earliest appearance before a judicial officer of this district, the judicial officer will take appropriate steps to assure that the defendant is represented by counsel and shall appoint counsel where appropriate under the Criminal Justice Act, 18 U.S.C. § 3006A, or Rule 44 of the Federal Rules of Criminal Procedure.

(2) The court shall have sole responsibility for setting cases for trial after consultation with counsel. At the time of arraignment or as soon thereafter as is practicable, each case will be set for trial on a day certain or listed for trial on a weekly or other short-term calendar. [18 U.S.C. § 3161(a).]

(3) Individual calendars shall be managed so that it will be reasonably anticipated that every criminal case set for trial will be reached during the week of original setting. A conflict in schedules of the United States Attorney or defense counsel will be grounds for a continuance or delayed setting only if approved by the court and called to the court's attention at the earliest practicable time. The court will not force substitution of defense counsel in an attempt to comply with the Speedy Trial Act. This includes a request to transfer an assigned case from one attorney to another attorney within the Federal Defender Office.

(4) In the event a complaint, indictment, or information is filed against a defendant charged in a pending indictment or information or in an indictment or information dismissed on motion of the United States Attorney, the trial on the new charge shall commence within the time limit for commencement of trial on the original indictment or information unless the court finds that the new charge is not for the same offense charged in the original indictment or information or an offense required to be joined by them.

(5) At the time of filing of a complaint, indictment or information described in paragraph (4), the United States Attorney shall give written notice to the court of that circumstance and of his position with respect to the computation of the time limits.

(6) All pretrial hearings shall be conducted as soon after the arraignment as possible, consistent with the priorities of other matters on the court's criminal docket.

6. Defendants in Custody.[1]

(a) *Time Limits.* Notwithstanding any longer time periods that may be permitted under sections 4 and 5, the trial of a defendant held in custody solely for the purpose of trial on a federal charge shall commence within 90 days following the beginning of continuous custody. [18 U.S.C. § 3164(b).]

(b) *Measurement of Time Periods.* For the purposes of this section:

(1) A defendant is deemed to be in detention awaiting trial when he is arrested on a federal charge or otherwise held for the purpose of responding to a federal charge. Detention is deemed to be solely because the defendant is awaiting trial unless the person exercising custodian authority has an independent basis (not including a detainer) for continuing to hold the defendant.

(2) If a case is transferred pursuant to Rule 20 of the Federal Rules of Criminal Procedure and the defendant subsequently rejects disposition under Rule 20, or the court declines to accept the plea, a new period of continuous detention awaiting trial will begin at that time.

(3) A trial shall be deemed to commence as provided in section 5(e)(3) and (4).

(c) *Related Procedures.* If a defendant is being held in custody solely for the purpose of awaiting trial, the United States Attorney shall advise the court at the earliest practicable time of the date of the beginning of such custody.

7. Exclusion of Time From Computations.

(a) *Applicability.* In computing any time limit under sections 4, 5, or 6, the periods of delay set forth in 18 U.S.C. § 3161(h) and in section 14 infra, dealing with pretrial diversion, shall be excluded. Such periods of delay shall not be excluded in computing the minimum period for commencement of trial under section 8.

(b) *Records of Excludable Time.* The clerk shall enter on the docket, in the form prescribed by the Administrative Office of the United States Courts, information with respect to the excludable periods of time for each criminal defendant. With respect to proceedings prior to the filing of an indictment or information, excludable time shall be reported to the clerk by the United States Attorney.

(c) *Pre–Indictment Procedures.*

(1) In the event that the United States Attorney anticipates that an indictment or information will not be filed within the time limit set forth in section 4, he may file a written motion with the court for a determination of excludable time. In the event that the United States Attorney seeks a continuance under 18 U.S.C. § 3161(h)(7), he shall file a written motion with the court requesting such a continuance.

(2) The motion of the United States Attorney shall state (i) the period of time proposed for exclusion, and (ii) the basis of the proposed exclusion. If the motion is for continuance under 18 U.S.C. § 3161(h)(7), it shall also state whether or not the defendant is being held in custody on the basis of the complaint. In appropriate circumstances, the motion may include a request that some or all of the supporting material be considered ex parte and *in camera.*

(3) The court may grant a continuance under 18 U.S.C. § 3161(h)(7) for either a specific period of time or a period to be determined by reference to an event (such as recovery from illness) not within the control of the government. If the continuance is to a date not certain, the court shall require one or both parties to inform the court promptly when and if the circumstances that justify the continuance no longer exist. In addition, the court shall require one or both parties to file

periodic reports bearing on the continued existence of such circumstance. The court shall determine the frequency of such reports in the light of the facts of the particular case.

(d) *Post–Indictment Procedures.*

(1) The United States Attorney may file a written motion with the court for a determination of excludable time.

(2) In the event that the United States Attorney or the defendant seeks a continuance under 18 U.S.C. § 3161(h)(7), he shall file a written motion with the court requesting such a continuance. The United States Attorney and the defendant may also stipulate that there are grounds for such a continuance.

(3) If it is determined that a continuance is justified, the court shall set forth its findings in the record, either orally or in writing. If the continuance is granted under 18 U.S.C. § 3161(h)(7), the court shall also set forth its reasons for finding that the ends of justice served by granting the continuance outweigh the best interests of the public and the defendant in a speedy trial. If the continuance is to a date not certain, the court shall require one or both parties to inform the court promptly when and if the circumstances that justify the continuance no longer exist. In addition, the court shall require one or both parties to file periodic reports bearing on the continued existence of such circumstances. The court shall determine the frequency of such reports in the light of the facts of the particular case.

(4) Because of the importance of scheduling trial dates, each counsel has a duty to notify the court at an early stage of the proceedings of any motion for continuance on the grounds that the case is unusual or complex.

8. Minimum Period for Defense Preparation. Unless the defendant consents in writing to the contrary, the trial shall not commence earlier than 30 days from the date on which the indictment or information is filed or, if later, from the date on which counsel first enters an appearance or on which the defendant expressly waives counsel and elects to proceed pro se. In circumstances in which the 70–day time limit for commencing trial on a charge in an indictment or information is determined by reference to an earlier indictment or information pursuant to section 5(d), the 30–day minimum period shall also be determined by reference to the earlier indictment or information. When prosecution is resumed on an original indictment or information following a mistrial, appeal, or withdrawal of a guilty plea, a new 30–day minimum period will not begin to run. The court will in all cases schedule trials so as to permit defense counsel adequate preparation time in the light of all the circumstances. [18 U.S.C. § 3161(c)(2).]

9. Time Within Which Defendant Should Be Sentenced.

(a) *Time Limit.* A defendant shall ordinarily be scheduled for sentence not less than 90 days after the date of conviction by verdict, plea of guilty or nolo contendere.

(b) *Related Procedures.* If the defendant and counsel consent thereto, a presentence investigation may be commenced prior to a plea of guilty or nolo contendere or a conviction.

10. Sanctions.

(a) *Dismissal or Release from Custody.* Failure to comply with the requirements of Title I of the Speedy Trial Act may entitle the defendant to dismissal of the charges or to release from pretrial custody. Nothing in this Plan shall be construed to require that a case be dismissed or a defendant released from custody in circumstances in which such action would not be required by 18 U.S.C. §§ 3162 and 3164.

(b) *Discipline of Attorneys.* In a case in which counsel (1) knowingly allows the case to be set for trial without disclosing the fact that a necessary witness would be unavailable for trial, (2) files a motion solely for the purpose of delay which counsel knows is frivolous and without merit, (3) makes a statement for the purpose of obtaining a continuance which counsel knows to be false and which is material to the granting of the continuance, or (4) otherwise willfully fails to proceed to trial without justification consistent with 18 U.S.C. § 3161, the court may punish such counsel as provided in 18 U.S.C. § 3162(b) and (c).

11. Persons Serving Terms of Imprisonment. If the United States Attorney knows that a person charged with an offense is serving a term of imprisonment in any penal institution, the United States Attorney shall promptly seek to obtain the presence of the prisoner for trial, or cause a detainer to be filed, in accordance with the provisions of 18 U.S.C. § 3161(j).

12. **Discovery Materials.** Discovery is governed by the Court's Standing Order for Discovery and Inspection and Fixing Motion Cut–Off Date in Criminal Cases.

13. **Reassignment of Cases Between Judges.** The reassignment of criminal cases between judges is governed by local rule.

14. **Pretrial Diversion.** Because a pretrial diversion determination is not part of the typical criminal proceeding and because of the time delay necessary to make that determination, the actual number of days from the date consent for investigation is signed until the investigation report is completed, or 30 days, whichever is less, is excludable, and the actual number of days from the date the investigation report is received by the United States Attorney until the date the United States Attorney makes a decision on the diversion recommendation, or 30 days, whichever is less, is excludable.

15. **Computation of Time.** The time limits set forth herein shall be calculated in accordance with Rule 45(a) of the Federal Rules of Criminal Procedure.

16. **Statement of Procedures and Innovations That Have Been or Will Be Adopted by the District Court to Expedite the Disposition of Criminal Cases in Accordance With the Speedy Trial Act (18 U.S.C. § 3167(b)).**

(a) *Clerk of the Court.* The Administrative Office has developed the following categories of intervals or "clocks" to use in calculating the three time limits, established by the Speedy Trial Act of 1974 and subsequent amendments; Procedural, Location and Excludable Intervals are used to track compliance with the Act.

Procedural Intervals are used to track the progress of the case and to monitor the case's compliance with the 30 and 70 day clocks. Location Intervals are used to keep track of the defendant's location (custody or not) and to monitor the case's compliance with 90–day continuous custody clock. Excludable Intervals are used to keep track of the time excluded by various statutory delays.

The Clerk's Office maintains the case management system that produces various criminal reports to assist in monitoring Speedy Trial compliance. Case managers are responsible for regularly reviewing the Non–Fugitive Pending Trial report for their assigned judicial officer to ensure compliance with the Act.

Magistrate Judges' case managers are responsible for serving copies of all orders of dismissal on the attorneys listed on the docket and on the Pretrial Services Agency.

(b) *Probation Department.* The Court shall whenever possible schedule plea hearings in the morning to allow for the immediate presentence interview of the defendant by the Probation Department. When an immediate interview cannot be completed, the interview shall be completed within 7 days following the date of referral to the Probation Department.

Upon conviction by verdict, plea of guilty or nolo contendere, the defense attorney shall immediately escort the defendant or take the referral form (for defendants in custody), to the Probation Department for processing and commencement of the presentence investigation.

The above procedures for immediate interviews will save time, reduce travel expenses, and allow for the effective use of interpreter services when necessary. It will further assure that presentence reports are submitted in a timely manner.

17. **Statistical Information.** The statistical information referenced in 18 U.S.C. § 3166(c) can be obtained at www.uscourts.gov.

Certificate of Approval

The foregoing Amended Speedy Trial Act Plan was approved pursuant to 18 U.S.C. § 3165(c) by a reviewing panel consisting of the members of the Judicial Council of the Sixth Circuit and the Chief Judge of the United States District Court for the Eastern District of Michigan this 1st day of December 2009.

[Effective November 6, 2007. Amended effective December 1, 2009.]

1 If a defendant's presence has been obtained through the filing of a detainer with state authorities, the Interstate Agreement on Detainers, 18 U.S.C., Appendix 2, may require that trial commence before the deadline established by the Speedy Trial Act. See United States v. Mauro, 436 U.S. 340, 356–57 n.24 (1978).

CIVILITY PRINCIPLES

PREAMBLE

An attorney's conduct should be characterized at all times by personal courtesy and professional integrity in the fullest sense of those terms.   In fulfilling our duty to represent a client vigorously as attorneys, we will be mindful of our obligations to the administration of justice, which is a truth-seeking process designed to resolve human and societal problems in a rational, peaceful and efficient manner.

A judge's conduct should be characterized at all times by courtesy and patience toward all participants.   As judges we owe all participants in a legal proceeding respect, diligence, punctuality and protection against unjust and improper criticism or attack.

Conduct that may be characterized as uncivil, abrasive, abusive, hostile or obstructive impedes the fundamental goal of resolving disputes rationally, peacefully and efficiently.   Such conduct tends to delay, and often deny, justice.

The following standards are designed to encourage us, judges and attorneys, to meet our obligations to each other, to litigants and to the system of justice, and thereby achieve the twin goals of civility and professionalism, both of which are hallmarks of a learned profession dedicated to public service.

We expect judges and attorneys will make a mutual and firm commitment to these standards. Voluntary adherence is expected as part of a commitment by all participants to improve the administration of justice throughout the Eastern District.

These standards shall not be used alone as a basis for litigation, sanctions or penalties.   However, nothing in these standards supersedes or detracts from existing disciplinary codes or alters existing standards of conduct against which attorney negligence or misconduct may be determined.

These standards should be reviewed and followed by all judges and attorneys participating in any proceeding in the Eastern District.   Copies may be made available to clients to reinforce our obligation to maintain and foster these standards.

ATTORNEYS' RESPONSIBILITIES TO OTHER COUNSEL

(1) We will practice our profession with a continuing awareness that our role is to advance the legitimate interest of our clients.   In our dealings with others, we will not reflect the ill feelings of our clients.   We will treat all other counsel, parties and witnesses in a civil and courteous manner, not only in court, but also in all other written and oral communications.

(2) We will not, even when called upon by a client to do so, abuse or indulge in offensive conduct directed to other counsel, parties or witnesses.   We will abstain from disparaging personal remarks or acrimony toward other counsel, parties, or witnesses.   We will treat adverse witnesses and parties with fair consideration.

(3) We will not encourage or knowingly authorize any person under our control to engage in conduct that would be improper if we were to engage in such conduct.

(4) We will not, absent good cause, attribute bad motives or improper conduct to other counsel or bring the profession into disrepute by unfounded accusations of impropriety.

(5) We will not seek court sanctions without first conducting a reasonable investigation and unless fully justified by the circumstances and necessary to protect our client's lawful interests.

(6) We will adhere to all express promises and agreements with other counsel, whether oral or in writing, and will adhere in good faith to all agreements implied by the circumstances or local customs.

(7) When we reach an oral understanding on a proposed agreement or stipulation and decide to commit it to writing, the drafter will endeavor in good faith to state the oral understanding accurately and completely.   The drafter will provide other counsel the opportunity to review the writing.   As drafts are exchanged between or among counsel, changes from prior drafts will be identified in the draft or otherwise explicitly brought to the attention of other counsel.   We will not include in a draft

matters to which there has been no agreement without explicitly advising other counsel in writing of the addition.

(8) We will endeavor to confer early with other counsel to assess settlement possibilities. We will not falsely hold out the possibility of settlement as a means to adjourn discovery or to delay trial.

(9) In civil actions, we will stipulate to relevant matters if they are undisputed and if no good-faith advocacy basis exists for not stipulating.

(10) We will not use any form of discovery or discovery scheduling as a means of harassment.

(11) We will make good faith efforts to resolve by agreement our objections to matters contained in pleadings, discovery requests and objections.

(12) We will not time the filing or service of motions or pleadings in any way that unfairly limits another party's opportunity to respond.

(13) We will not request an extension of time solely for the purpose of unjustified delay or to obtain tactical advantage.

(14) We will consult other counsel regarding scheduling matters in a good-faith effort to avoid scheduling conflicts.

(15) We will endeavor to accommodate previously scheduled dates for hearings, depositions, meetings, conferences, vacations, seminars or other functions that produce good-faith calendar conflicts on the part of other counsel. If we have been given an accommodation because of a calendar conflict, we will notify those who have accommodated us as soon as the conflict has been removed.

(16) We will notify other counsel and, if appropriate, the Court or other persons, at the earliest possible time when hearings, depositions, meetings or conferences are to be canceled or postponed. Early notice avoids unnecessary travel and expense of counsel and may enable the Court to use the previously-reserved time for other matters.

(17) We will agree to reasonable requests for extensions of time and for waiver of procedural formalities, recognizing that it is the attorney, and not the client, who has the sole discretion to determine the accommodations to be granted opposing counsel in all matters not materially or adversely affecting the client's legitimate rights. We will affirm that in such matters no client has a right to demand that his or her counsel shall be illiberal or that we do anything therein repugnant to our own sense of honor and propriety.

(18) We will not cause any default or dismissal to be entered without first notifying opposing counsel, when we know his or her identity.

(19) We will take depositions only when actually needed to ascertain facts or information or to perpetuate testimony. We will not take depositions for the purposes of harassment or to increase litigation expenses.

(20) We will not engage in any conduct during a deposition that would not be appropriate in the presence of a judge.

(21) We will not obstruct questioning during a deposition or object to deposition questions unless appropriate under the applicable rules.

(22) During depositions, we will ask only those questions we reasonably believe are necessary for the prosecution or defense of an action.

(23) We will carefully craft document production requests and/or interrogatories so they are limited to those documents we reasonably believe are necessary for the prosecution or defense of an action. We will not design production requests to place an undue burden or expense on a party.

(24) We will respond to document requests and interrogatories reasonably and not strain to interpret the requests or interrogatories in an artificially restrictive manner to avoid disclosure of relevant and non-privileged documents and information fairly within the scope of the requests or interrogatories. We will not produce documents or answer interrogatories in a manner designed to hide or obscure the existence of particular documents or information.

(25) We will base our discovery objections on a good-faith belief in their merit and will not object solely for the purpose of withholding or delaying the disclosure of relevant information.

(26) When a draft order is to be prepared by counsel to reflect a court ruling, we will draft an order that accurately and completely reflects the Court's ruling. We will promptly prepare and

submit a proposed order to other counsel and attempt to reconcile any differences before the draft order is presented to the Court.

(27) We will not ascribe a position to another counsel that counsel has not taken or otherwise seek to create an unjustified inference based on counsel's statements or conduct.

(28) Unless specifically permitted or invited by the Court, or unless otherwise necessary, we will not send copies of correspondence between counsel to the Court.

ATTORNEYS' RESPONSIBILITIES TO THE COURT

(1) We will speak and write civilly and respectfully in all communications with the Court.

(2) We will be punctual and prepared for all Court appearances so that all hearings, conferences and trials may commence on time; if delayed, we will notify the Court and counsel, if possible.

(3) We will be considerate of the time constraints and pressures on the Court and Court staff inherent in their efforts to administer justice.

(4) We will not engage in conduct that brings disorder or disruption to the courtroom. We will advise our clients and witnesses appearing in Court of the proper conduct expected and required there and, to the best of our ability, prevent our clients and witnesses from creating disorder or disruption.

(5) We will not knowingly misrepresent, mischaracterize, misquote, or miscite facts or authorities in any oral or written communication.

(6) We will not send letters to the Court (whether addressed to the Court or copies of letters to opposing counsel) that contain argument or criticize counsel in connection with a pending action, unless invited or permitted by the Court or as appropriate exhibits to Court filings, in which event a copy shall be provided to opposing counsel in such a manner as to insure delivery to opposing counsel on that same day that it is delivered to the Court.

(7) Before dates for hearings or trials are set, or if that is not feasible, immediately after such date has been set, we will attempt to verify the availability of necessary participants and witnesses so we can promptly notify the Court of any likely problems.

(8) We will act and speak civilly to marshals, clerks, court reporters, secretaries and law clerks with an awareness that they, too, are an integral part of the judicial system.

COURT'S RESPONSIBILITIES TO ATTORNEYS

(1) We will endeavor to be courteous, respectful and civil to attorneys, parties and witnesses. We will maintain control of the proceedings, recognizing that judges have both the obligation and the authority to insure that all litigation proceedings are conducted in a civil manner.

(2) We will not employ hostile, demeaning or humiliating words in opinions or in written or oral communications with attorneys, parties or witnesses.

(3) We will be punctual in convening hearings, meetings and conferences; if delayed, we will notify counsel, if possible.

(4) The Court, recognizing the existence of family and business obligations of parties, witnesses and attorneys, will attempt, in scheduling all hearings, meetings and conferences, to be considerate of time schedules of attorneys, parties and witnesses.

(5) We will make reasonable efforts to decide promptly matters presented to us for decision.

(6) While endeavoring to resolve disputes efficiently, we will be considerate of the time constraints and pressures imposed on attorneys.

(7) We recognize that an attorney has a right and a duty to present a cause fully and properly, and that a litigant has a right to fair and impartial consideration.

(8) We will not impugn the integrity or professionalism of any attorney on the basis of the clients whom, or the causes which, an attorney represents.

(9) We will do our best to insure that Court personnel act civilly toward attorneys, parties and witnesses.

(10) We will not adopt procedures that needlessly increase litigation expense.

(11) We will bring to an attorney's attention uncivil conduct which we observe.

JUDGES' RESPONSIBILITIES TO EACH OTHER

(1) We will be courteous, respectful and civil in opinions, ever mindful that a position articulated by another judge is the result of that judge's earnest effort to interpret the law and the facts correctly.

(2) In all written and oral communications, we will abstain from disparaging personal remarks or criticisms, or sarcastic or demeaning comments about another judge.

(3) We will endeavor to work with other judges in an effort to foster a spirit of cooperation in our mutual goal of enhancing the administration of justice.

LAWYER'S COMMITMENT OF PROFESSIONAL CIVILITY

A lawyer shall conduct him/herself in accordance with the standards of professional integrity and personal courtesy set forth in the Civility Principles of the United States District Court for the Eastern District of Michigan.

A lawyer shall honor and respect the Constitution of the United States, the judicial system, the legal profession and will strive to uphold the dignity of each.

A lawyer shall be guided by a fundamental sense of integrity, candor and fair play.

A lawyer shall abstain from disrespectful, disruptive and/or abusive behavior, and will at all times act with dignity, decency and courtesy.

A lawyer shall seek to resolve and not prolong legal disputes, without lessening your obligations to client interests.

A lawyer shall respect the time and commitments of others and will be diligent and punctual in communicating with others and fulfilling in your own responsibilities.

A lawyer shall exercise independent judgment and will not be guided by ill will, deceit or avarice.

As a lawyer you shall further your profession's dedication to public service.

A lawyer shall strive to do honor to the search for truth and justice.

As a lawyer your word is your bond.

[Approved February 5, 1996. Amended effective December 3, 2007.]

SELECTED ADMINISTRATIVE ORDERS

ADMINISTRATIVE ORDER NO. 08–AO–046   IN RE: FILING A NEW CIVIL CASE OR CIVIL INITIATING PAPERS UNDER SEAL

Rule 6(a) of the Electronic Filing Policies and Procedures requires that civil initiating papers be filed electronically.

CM/ECF does not currently allow a new civil case or civil initiating papers to be immediately sealed when filed electronically.

In addition, sealing a new civil case or civil initiating papers cannot be done until the assigned judge has decided the motion requesting the sealing;

NOW THEREFORE IT IS ORDERED THAT filing users wishing to electronically file a new civil case or civil initiating papers under seal must contact the CM/ECF Help Desk at 313–234–5042 before filing the case or the papers.

IT IS FURTHER ORDERED THAT when a party files a motion to seal a new civil case or civil initiating papers the Clerk is directed to "shield" the new civil case or civil initiating papers from public view until the assigned judge has decided the motion requesting the sealing.

[Dated: October 4, 2008.]

ADMINISTRATIVE ORDER NO. 11–AO–025.   IN RE: TRANSCRIPT FEE RATES

At their regular meeting on May 2, 2011, the Judges of the United States District Court for the Eastern District of Michigan approved the attached Maximum Transcript Fee Rates, effective immediately.

These rates are consistent with, and do not exceed, the maximum transcript fee rates approved by the Judicial Conference of the United States at its March 2011 session.

Transcripts ordered prior to May 2, 2011 should be billed at the rates in effect at the time the transcript order was placed with the official court reporter or transcriber.

This administrative order supersedes Administrative Order No. 07–AO–026.

MAXIMUM TRANSCRIPT FEE RATES—ALL PARTIES PER PAGE

(Effective May 2, 2011)

	Original	First Copy to Each Party	Each Add'l Copy to the Same Party
Ordinary Transcript (30 day) A transcript to be delivered within thirty (30) calendar days after receipt of an order.	$3.65	$0.90	$0.60
14–Day Transcript A transcript to be delivered within fourteen (14) calendar days after receipt of an order.	$4.25	$0.90	$0.60
Expedited Transcript (7 day) A transcript to be delivered within seven (7) calendar days after receipt of an order.	$4.85	$0.90	$0.60
Daily Transcript A transcript to be delivered following adjournment and prior to the normal opening hour of the court	$6.05	$1.20	$0.90

	Original	First Copy to Each Party	Each Add'l Copy to the Same Party
on the following morning whether or not it actually is a court day.			
Hourly Transcript A transcript of proceedings ordered under unusual circumstances to be delivered within two (2) hours.	$7.25	$1.20	$0.90
Realtime Transcript A draft unedited transcript produced by a certified realtime reporter as a byproduct of realtime to be delivered electronically during proceedings or immediately following adjournment.	One feed, $3.05 per page; two-to-four feeds, $2.10 per page; five or more feeds, $1.50 per page.		

[Dated: May 2, 2011.]

UNITED STATES BANKRUPTCY COURT FOR THE
EASTERN DISTRICT OF MICHIGAN

Including Amendments Received Through
January 1, 2018

SELECTED GUIDELINES

CHAPTER 13 MODEL PLAN

ADMINISTRATIVE ORDERS AND NOTICES

ADMINISTRATIVE PROCEDURES FOR ELECTRONIC CASE FILING

RULE 1002–1. BANKRUPTCY PETITION AND COVER SHEET

(a) Number of Copies. When a Paper Filing has been authorized under the ECF Procedures, only the original must be filed, except that the debtor must file an original and one copy of a chapter 9 petition or a chapter 11 petition.

(b) Cover Sheet. A petition must be accompanied by a completed form "Bankruptcy Petition Cover Sheet," available on the court's website.

[Effective May 5, 2008. Amended effective February 1, 2016.]

RULE 1007–1. SCHEDULES AND OTHER INITIAL PAPERS

(a) Failure to Timely File Initially Required Documents. If the debtor fails to timely file the schedules, statement of financial affairs or other required documents and fails to timely move for an extension of time under Local Rule 9006–1(a) before the deadline for filing those documents, the debtor's voluntary petition may be dismissed without a hearing unless, within 21 days after the petition is filed, a party files a request for a hearing. If a party files a timely request for a hearing, the court will schedule a hearing with notice to any party who requested it, the debtor, the trustee and the United States trustee.

(b) Pro Se Declarations. In a case in which the debtor is not represented by an attorney, the debtor must file a completed form "Declaration Under Penalty of Perjury for Debtor(s) Without An Attorney," available on the court's website. The deadline to file the declaration form is 14 days after the petition is filed.

(c)* Payment Order in a Chapter 13 Case.

(1) Within 14 days after filing a chapter 13 petition or converting a case to chapter 13, the debtor must submit for entry one or more proposed initial payment orders, as necessary to make plan payments, using the following forms available on the court's website:

(A) "Third Party Payment Order" or

(B) "Electronic Transfer of Funds Payment Order," but only if a Third Party Payment Order cannot be effectuated.

(2) The initial Third Party Payment Order must be submitted on an *ex parte* basis and need not be submitted to the trustee for concurrence. An Electronic Transfer of Funds Payment Order may only be submitted for entry upon a filed stipulation with the trustee. Upon entry, the trustee must serve a copy of the payment order(s) as appropriate.

(3) By the deadline under subpart (c)(1), the debtor may instead file a motion under Local Rule 9014–1, supported by an affidavit, or a stipulation with the trustee, for an order excusing the requirement of a payment order, for good cause.

(4) A payment order may be amended only by:

(A) an order entered upon a motion under Local Rule 9014–1;

(B) an order entered upon a stipulation with the trustee; or

(C) a provision in an order confirming the plan.

(5) This rule does not affect a debtor's duty to commence or continue plan payments.

(d) Service of the Plan in a Chapter 13 Case. The debtor must promptly serve a copy of the plan on all creditors and other parties in interest and file a certificate of service. The debtor need not serve a copy of the plan on the trustee.

(e) Application to Pay the Filing Fee in Installments. The deadline to file an application and a proposed order authorizing payment of the filing fee in installments is 14 days after the petition is filed.

(f) Section 521(a)(1)(B)(iv) Material. The debtor need not file the material identified in § 521(a)(1)(B)(iv)—"copies of all payment advices or other evidence of payment received within 60 days before the date of the filing of the petition, by the debtor from any employer of the debtor." Instead, if the debtor is represented by an attorney, the debtor's attorney must transmit this material to the trustee in PDF format by email at least seven days prior to the first date set for the meeting of creditors, but not later than 45 days after the date of the filing of the petition. If the debtor is not represented by counsel, the debtor must mail or deliver this material to the trustee at least seven days before the first date set for the meeting of creditors, but not later than 45 days after the petition was filed.

(g) Schedule C in a Joint Case. Each debtor in a joint case must file a separate schedule C.

[Effective October 1, 1998. Amended effective November 30, 1999 by General Order No. 99–03; December 1, 2003; January 3, 2005; October 17, 2005; May 5, 2008; August 21, 2008; December 1, 2009; February 1, 2016.]

* **[Publisher's Note:** *See also* Administrative Order No. 08–10, *post.*]

RULE 1007–2. THE LIST OF CREDITORS AND THE MATRIX

(a) When a Matrix of Creditors and Matrix of Equity Security Holders Are Required; Contents. The requirements of this subpart (a) apply when a voluntary bankruptcy petition is filed by a Paper Filing as authorized under ECF Procedures. The petition must be accompanied by (1) a matrix listing the names, addresses and zip codes in alphabetical order, of all creditors; and (2) in a chapter 11 case, a separately labeled matrix listing the names, addresses and zip codes of equity security holders. These matrices must comply with the "Guidelines for a Paper Filing Matrix," available on the court's website. A debtor with more than 100 creditors must, instead of filing a printed matrix, provide the matrix to the clerk by electronic media prepared using the guidelines available on the court's website.

(b) ECF Filed Petition. When a petition is filed by ECF, the matrices described in subpart (a) must be uploaded.

(c) Requirements for Listing Government Agencies. This subpart (c) applies to the list of creditors uploaded in ECF when a petition is filed and to the creditor matrix when a petition is filed by a Paper Filing. When any department or agency of the United States is listed in the matrix, the list of creditors must also include the United States Attorney for the

Eastern District of Michigan (Attention: Civil Division). The address for the office of the United States Attorney must correspond to the court location where the petition is assigned and all subsequent service on the United States Attorney must be at that address. When an agency or department of the United States is listed, the proper address must be obtained from the United States Attorney's Office and must be included. The United States trustee's office need not be included.

[Effective October 1, 1998. Amended effective October 29, 2003; May 5, 2008; February 1, 2016.]

RULE 1007–3. CREDIT COUNSELING COMPLIANCE

(a) Certification Procedures. A debtor who files a certification under § 109(h)(3)(A) must also file a motion for approval of the certification. The debtor must file the certification and the motion with the petition, serve it on all parties and file a certificate of service. The deadline to file a response is 14 days after service. If no timely response is filed, the certification will be deemed satisfactory under § 109(h)(3)(A)(iii) without a hearing or further order. The motion must be accompanied by a notice that the deadline to file a response is 14 days after service and that if no response is filed, the court will deem the certification satisfactory under § 109(h)(3)(A)(iii) without a hearing.

(b) Additional Extension of Time. A motion for an extension of time under § 109(h)(3)(B) must be served on all parties and may be accompanied by an *ex parte* motion for an expedited hearing. If the court grants an expedited hearing, the debtor must promptly serve a notice of the hearing on all parties and file a certificate of service.

(c) Motion to Excuse Credit Counseling. A motion seeking relief under § 109(h)(4) must be filed under Local Rule 9014–1.

[Former interim rule effective October 17, 2005. Renumbered as Rule 1007–6 and amended effective May 5, 2008. Amended effective December 1, 2009. Renumbered and amended effective February 1, 2016.]

RULE 1007–4. LISTS, SCHEDULES, STATEMENTS AND OTHER DOCUMENTS; TIME LIMITS

(a) Schedules, Statements and Other Documents Required. Unless either (A) § 707(b)(2)(D)(i) applies, or (B) § 707(b)(2)(D)(ii) applies and the exclusion from means testing granted therein extends beyond the period specified by F.R.Bankr.P. 1017(e), an individual debtor in a chapter 7 case must file a statement of current monthly income prepared as prescribed by the appropriate Official Form, and, if the current monthly income exceeds the median family income for the applicable state and household size, the information, including calculations, required by § 707(b), prepared as prescribed by the appropriate Official Form.

(b) Time Limits. In a voluntary case, the schedules, statements and other documents required by F.R.Bankr.P. 1007(b)(1), (4), (5) and (6) must be filed with the petition or within 14 days thereafter, except as otherwise provided in F.R.Bankr.P. 1007(d), (e), (f) and (h) or in subpart (c) of this rule. In an involuntary case, the list in F.R.Bankr.P. 1007(a)(2), and the schedules, statements and other documents required by F.R.Bankr.P. 1007(b)(1) must be filed by the debtor within 14 days of the entry of the order for relief. In a voluntary case, the documents required by subparts (A), (C) and (D) of F.R.Bankr.P. 1007(b)(3) must be filed with the petition. Unless the court orders otherwise, a debtor who has filed a statement under F.R.Bankr.P. 1007(b)(3)(B), must file the documents required by F.R.Bankr.P. 1007(b)(3)(A) within 14 days of the order for relief. In a chapter 7 case, the debtor must file the statement required by F.R.Bankr.P. 1007(b)(7) within 45 days after the first date set for the meeting of creditors under § 341 of the Code, and in a chapter 11 or 13 case no later than the date when the last payment was made by the debtor as required by the plan or the filing of a motion for a discharge under § 1141(d)(5)(B) or § 1328(b) of the Code. The court may, at any time and in its discretion, enlarge the time to file the statement required by F.R.Bankr.P. 1007(b)(7). The debtor must file the statement required by F.R.Bankr.P. 1007(b)(8) no earlier than the date of the last payment made under the plan or the date of the filing of a motion for a discharge under §§ 1141(d)(5)(B), 1228(b), or 1328(b) of the Code. Lists, schedules, statements and other documents filed prior to the conversion of a case to another chapter will be deemed filed in the converted case unless the court directs otherwise. Except as provided in § 1116(3), any extension of time to file schedules, statements and other documents required under this rule may be granted only on motion for cause shown and on notice to the United States trustee, any committee elected under § 705 or appointed under § 1102 of the Code, trustee, examiner or other party as the court may direct. Notice of an extension must be given to the United States trustee and to any committee, trustee or other party as the court may direct.

(c) Time Limits For, and Notice To, Debtors Temporarily Excluded from Means Testing.

(1) An individual debtor who is temporarily excluded from means testing pursuant to § 707(b)(2)(D)(ii) of the Code must file any statement and calculations required by F.R.Bankr.P. 1007(b)(4) no later than 14 days after the expiration of the temporary exclusion if the expiration occurs within the time specified by F.R.Bankr.P. 1017(e) for filing a motion pursuant to § 707(b)(2).

(2) If the temporary exclusion from means testing under § 707(b)(2)(D)(ii) terminates due to the circumstances specified in subpart (c)(1) of this rule, and if the debtor has not previously filed a statement and calculations required by F.R.Bankr.P. 1007(b)(4), the clerk must promptly notify the debtor that the required statement and calculations must be filed within the time specified in subpart (c)(1) of this rule.

[Former Rule 1007–7 effective December 1, 2009. Renumbered and amended effective February 1, 2016.]

RULE 1007–5. IDENTIFICATION REQUEST

The clerk of the court must require any individual presenting a bankruptcy petition for filing at intake to produce a government-issued photo identification and must refuse such filing if such identification is not produced upon request. The court may grant relief from this requirement upon request in a specific case.

[Effective February 1, 2016.]

RULE 1009–1. AMENDMENT OF INITIAL PAPERS

(a) Procedure. An amended petition, schedule, statement of financial affairs or matrix must be accompanied by a completed form "Cover Sheet for Amendments," available on the court's website. The amended paper must be signed by the amending party. If several papers are contemporaneously amended, the amending party may file one signed affirmation relating to all of the amended papers in the same form as required on the original documents. The amended paper must completely disclose all information required by the form. A "supplemental" paper that merely provides additional information may not be filed.

(b) Service of Amendment. The debtor must serve a copy of the amendment and the "Cover Sheet for Amendments" on all entities affected by the amendment and file a certificate of service.

(c) Adding an Omitted Creditor More Than 14 Days Prior to the Meeting of Creditors. A debtor who, more than 14 days prior to the commencement of the meeting of creditors, amends a schedule to add a creditor not previously listed, must comply with subparts (a) and (b).

(d) Adding an Omitted Creditor After 14 Days Prior to the Meeting of Creditors. If an amendment adding a creditor is filed after 14 days prior to the commencement of the meeting of creditors:

(1) the deadlines under F.R.Bankr.P. 4007 and F.R.Bankr.P. 4004 for the filing of complaints under § 523 or § 727, respectively, and the deadline under F.R.Bankr.P. 4003(b) to object to the debtor's claim of exemptions are extended to allow the added creditor the same number of days in which to file such a complaint or objection as the creditor would have had if the creditor had been properly scheduled when the order for relief was entered;

(2) the creditor added by the amendment is entitled to examine the debtor under oath with any reasonable expense to be borne by the debtor; and

(3) the debtor must serve the amended document, a notice containing a copy of subpart (d) of this rule and a copy of the notice of commencement on the added creditor and file a certificate of service.

[Effective October 1, 1998. Amended effective October 1, 2003; May 5, 2008; December 1, 2009; February 1, 2016.]

RULE 1015–1. JOINT ADMINISTRATION OF CASES OF AFFILIATED DEBTORS

(a) The Motion. A motion for joint administration of affiliated debtors filed under F.R.Bankr.P. 1015(b) and (c) must contain detailed information concerning:

(1) the disclosure required by F.R.Bankr.P. 1007(a)(3);

(2) any inter-debtor claims and whether they are disputed or undisputed;

(3) any guaranties or co-obligations among the debtors and non-debtor equity holders;

(4) whether any of the debtors is a publicly traded entity; and

(5) inter-company transfers within one year before the order for relief.

(b) The Proposed Order. The proposed order attached to the motion must include a paragraph identifying the proposed caption to be used for the jointly administered cases. The caption must use the name of a publicly traded entity, if any, with the other debtors indicated by the phrase, "et al." If there is no publicly traded entity, the name of the debtor to be used must be the name of the debtor with the first filed case. The case number to be used for the jointly administered cases must be the lowest number of the cases. There must also be a footnote to the caption stating that the case is jointly administered with the cases of other debtors, identifying the names and case numbers of the cases of the other debtors.

(c) Service of the Motion. A motion requesting joint administration must be served on the United States trustee, the members and counsel of any official committees (or, if no official committee is yet formed, the list of creditors filed by the debtors under F.R.Bankr.P. 1007(d)), secured creditors, taxing authorities and any other persons as directed by the court.

(d) Service of the Order. The debtors must serve the joint administration order on all of the creditors in each of the jointly administered cases and file a certificate of service.

(e) Subsequent Filings. Except as provided in subpart (f), if the motion for joint administration is granted, then thereafter all papers must be filed only in the lead case and must include the footnote described in subpart (b).

(f)* Proof of Claim. Unless the court orders otherwise, a proof of claim in a jointly administered case must be filed in the case of the specific debtor against whom the claim is asserted. Unless the court orders otherwise, all objections to any proof of claim filed in a jointly administered case must be filed only in the lead case.

(g) Joint Cases. Unless the court orders otherwise, the estates in a joint case filed by a husband and wife under § 302(a) will be jointly administered, but in such circumstances there is no lead case for purposes of this rule.

[Effective January 3, 2005. Amended effective May 5, 2008; February 1, 2016.]

* **[Publisher's Note:** *See also* Administrative Order No. 08–11.]

RULE 1017–1. CONVERSION FROM CHAPTER 13 TO A DIFFERENT CHAPTER

(a) Requirements for the Debtor After Conversion to Chapter 7. When a debtor whose debts are primarily consumer debts converts a chapter 13 case to a chapter 7 case, the debtor must file Official Form 122A–1 within 14 days after filing the notice of conversion or the entry of an order converting the case. If the case is dismissed because the debtor failed to timely file the statement in the converted case, this dismissal is without prejudice to the debtor's right to move to reinstate the case under Local Rule 9024–1(c) within 14 days after entry of the dismissal order.

(b) Chapter 13 Trustee's Final Report. In a case converted from chapter 13 to a different chapter, the chapter 13 trustee must file a final report within 45 days of all checks clearing in the debtor's chapter 13 case.

(c) Service on the Chapter 13 Trustee After Conversion. After conversion of a chapter 13 case to a different chapter, the chapter 13 trustee must be served by first class mail with any paper that relates to the chapter 13 case or which may require action by the chapter 13 trustee.

[Effective May 5, 2008. Amended effective December 1, 2009; February 1, 2016.]

RULE 1017–2. DISMISSAL FOR FAILURE TO FURNISH TAX RETURNS UNDER § 521(E)(2)(B) OR (C)

Immediately after filing a motion under § 521(e)(2)(B) or (C), the movant must contact the judge's courtroom deputy clerk to obtain a hearing date. The clerk will cause a notice of the hearing to be served on all parties in interest. Any party in interest may be heard at the hearing. Written objections are permitted but not required. If the movant seeks a hearing on the motion before the meeting of creditors, the movant must file the motion no later than three days after the expiration of the deadline in § 521(e)(2)(A)(i).

[Effective May 5, 2008. Amended effective February 1, 2016.]

RULE 1020–1. PROCEDURES FOR A SMALL BUSINESS CHAPTER 11 CASE

(a) Objection to Designation. An objection to the debtor's designation as a small business debtor under F.R.Bankr.P. 1020(b) must be made by motion under Local Rule 9014–1 served on all parties in interest.

(b) Request for F.R.Bankr.P. 1020(c) Determination. A request for a determination under F.R.Bankr.P. 1020(c) must be made by motion under Local Rule 9014–1 served on all parties in interest.

[Effective October 17, 2005. Amended effective May 5, 2008; February 1, 2016.]

RULE 1071–1. COURT DIVISIONS AND THE TRANSFER OF A CASE OR PROCEEDING

(a) Court Locations. The work of the court is divided by county among court locations as follows:

Detroit: Jackson, Lenawee, Macomb, Monroe, Oakland, St. Clair, Sanilac, Washtenaw and Wayne Counties;

Flint: Genesee, Lapeer, Livingston and Shiawassee Counties;

Bay City: Alcona, Alpena, Arenac, Bay, Cheboygan, Clare, Crawford, Gladwin, Gratiot, Huron, Iosco, Isabella, Midland,

Montmorency, Ogemaw, Oscoda, Otsego, Presque Isle, Roscommon, Saginaw and Tuscola Counties.

(b) Identifying the Appropriate County. A petition initiating a bankruptcy case must identify the county in which the domicile, residence, principal place of business or principal assets of the person or entity that is the subject of such case has been located for the 180 days immediately preceding such commencement, or for a longer portion of such 180–day period than the domicile, residence, principal place of business, or principal assets of such person were located in any other court location.

(c) Transfer of Case or Proceeding.

(1) Upon notice and hearing, a judge may, in the interest of justice or for the convenience of the parties, transfer a case or proceeding filed in a proper location to any other court location within the district.

(2) If a case is filed in an improper court location, a judge may transfer it to a proper court location on stipulation of the debtor and the United States trustee or upon motion of the United States trustee or any party in interest.

[Effective October 1, 1998. Amended effective November 30, 1999 by General Order No. 99–03; May 5, 2008; February 1, 2016.]

RULE 1073–1. ASSIGNMENTS OF CASES

(a) Assignments to Judges.

(1) A petition from a county assigned or transferred to the Detroit location under Local Rule 1071–1 will be assigned to a judge by a blind draw system adopted by the court except that a companion case will be assigned to the judge to whom the first companion case was assigned or to the judge who is appointed to fill the vacancy of that judge.

(2) A petition from a county assigned or transferred to the Bay City or Flint locations under Local Rule 1071–1 will be assigned to the judge responsible for those court locations.

(3) All adversary proceedings arising in a case will be assigned to the judge to whom the case is assigned. If the case in which the adversary proceeding arose is pending in another district, the adversary proceeding will be assigned in accordance with the assignment practices of the court location where the adversary proceeding is filed.

(4) When a judge enters an order for recusal with respect to a case, a particular matter arising therein or an adversary proceeding, reassignment will be by blind draw to a judge at Detroit.

(5) If any matter requires urgent or immediate attention and the judge to whom the matter has been assigned is not or will not be available, then the clerk will assign the matter to another judge available at Detroit by blind draw.

(b) Companion Cases. Companion cases are cases involving:

(1) identical individuals or entities;

(2) a corporation and any majority shareholder thereof;

(3) affiliated corporations;

(4) a partnership and any of its general partners;

(5) an individual and his or her general partner;

(6) an individual and his or her spouse; or

(7) any substantial identity of financial interest or assets.

(c) Reassignment of a Case or a Proceeding.

(1) Consolidated cases or jointly administered cases under F.R.Bankr.P. 1015 will normally be reassigned to the judge to whom the case with the lowest filing number is assigned.

(2) To facilitate the administration of the court's docket and for good cause shown, a case or proceeding may be reassigned by the chief judge from one judge to another judge with the consent of the judges involved.

[Effective May 5, 2008. Amended effective February 1, 2016.]

RULE 1074–1. FILING AUTHORIZATION FOR A CORPORATION, A PARTNERSHIP OR AN ENTITY OTHER THAN AN INDIVIDUAL

In a case commenced by a voluntary petition, filed by a corporation, partnership or any other entity other than an individual, the debtor must file a copy of the duly attested resolution or other appropriate document authorizing the bankruptcy filing. The deadline to file this paper is 14 days after the filing of the petition.

[Effective October 1, 1998. Amended effective December 1, 2009; February 1, 2016.]

RULE 2002–1. AUTHORIZATION FOR A SPECIAL SERVICE LIST

(a) Order for Special Service List. In a Large Bankruptcy Case, counsel for the debtor may submit a proposed order for a Special Service List, as described in subpart (b). In any other case, such an order may be entered upon the filing of a motion for cause shown, served on all parties designated in subpart (b) and the 20 largest unsecured creditors. Upon entry of the order, counsel for the movant must serve the order on all parties on the matrix and file a certificate of service.

(b) The List. For matters requiring notice under F.R.Bankr.P. 2002(a)(2)–(6), the Special Service List must include, at a minimum:

(1) the United States trustee;

(2) the debtor;

(3) the debtor's general and local bankruptcy counsel;

(4) general and local counsel for each committee;

(5) any secured creditors and their counsel;

(6) all taxing authorities; and

(7) parties added to the Special Service List under subpart (c).

(c) Additions and Deletions. Parties may seek to be added to or deleted from the Special Service List by filing a written request and serving it on the parties designated in subpart (b).

(d) Maintaining the List. At least every 14 days during the first 56 days of the case and thereafter at least every 28 days, the debtor's counsel (or counsel for the trustee, if one is appointed) must maintain and update the Special Service List by:

(1) making any requested additions and deletions;

(2) filing the updated Special Service List;

(3) serving the updated Special Service List on the parties listed thereon who are not ECF participants; and

(4) filing a certificate of service.

(e) Claims and Noticing Agents. Unless otherwise ordered by the court, in any case where an individual or entity is appointed as a claims and/or noticing agent under 28 U.S.C. § 156(c), the order approving appointment of the claims and/or noticing agent must contain the following language:

"Upon completion of administration of the bankruptcy case, the claims and/or noticing agent must:

(1) deliver to the clerk of the court electronic images of the claims register maintained by the claims agent and electronic images of all claims and supporting documentation for such claims received by the claims agent;

(2) file in the bankruptcy case in which the claims agent was appointed, an affidavit:

(A) attesting that the electronic images delivered to the clerk of the court are true and correct copies of the claims register, claims and supporting documentation; and

(B) stating the location and the contact information of the individual or entity in possession of the claims register, claims and supporting documentation; and

(3) retain the claims register, claims and supporting documentation, and must not deliver them to the clerk or destroy them, unless and until specifically authorized to do so by the court in the case in which the claims agent was appointed."

[Effective January 3, 2005. Amended effective May 5, 2008; December 1, 2009; February 1, 2016.]

RULE 2002–2. SERVICE IN A CHAPTER 7 CASE AFTER THE CLAIMS FILING DEADLINE

Under F.R.Bankr.P. 2002(h), after the claims filing deadline in a chapter 7 case, a notice required by F.R.Bankr.P. 2002(a) needs to be served on only the debtor, the trustee, all indenture trustees, creditors that hold claims for which proofs of claim have been filed and creditors that may still file timely claims. If the trustee determines that additional assets will be available for distribution after distributions under § 726(a)(1)–(5) are made, the trustee must give notice to that effect to all parties on the matrix, so that additional late filed claims may be filed and distributions made under § 726(a)(3) prior to making distributions under § 726(a)(6).

[Former Rule 2002–4 effective May 5, 2008. Renumbered and amended effective February 1, 2016.]

RULE 2002–3. REQUEST TO BE ADDED TO THE ELECTRONIC NOTICE LIST

To receive notice in a case, an ECF Filer must file an appearance.

[Former Rule 2002–5 effective May 5, 2008. Renumbered and amended effective February 1, 2016.]

RULE 2002–4. NOTICE TO EQUITY SECURITY HOLDERS

The debtor must serve all notices under F.R.Bankr.P. 2002(d) and file a certificate of service.

[Former Rule 2002–6 effective May 5, 2008. Renumbered and amended effective February 1, 2016.]

RULE 2003–1. DEBTOR'S FAILURE TO APPEAR AT THE MEETING OF CREDITORS IN A CHAPTER 7, CHAPTER 12 OR CHAPTER 13 CASE

(a) When the Debtor Fails to Appear. If a debtor in a voluntary Chapter 7, Chapter 12 or Chapter 13 case fails to appear at a meeting of creditors, the trustee may give notice to creditors of the trustee's intent to file a motion to dismiss the case by an announcement at the meeting of creditors. The announcement must advise that:

(1) the trustee intends to file a motion to dismiss the case for the debtor's failure to attend the meeting;

(2) the deadline for a creditor to file an objection to dismissal is 14 days after the motion is filed; and

(3) if an objection is not timely filed, the court may enter an order dismissing the case without a hearing.

The trustee must promptly file a proof of such oral notice with the motion to dismiss.

(b) Response to Motion to Dismiss. The deadline to file a response to the motion is 14 days after the motion is filed. The debtor's response must include affidavits or declarations of persons with actual knowledge of any facts explaining or justifying the debtor's failure to appear at the meeting of creditors together with any documentary corroborating evidence.

(c) Upon a Failure to Respond. If no party files a timely response, the trustee may file a certification of non-response. The court may thereafter enter an order dismissing the case without a hearing.

(d) Upon a Timely Response. If a timely response is filed, the court will schedule a hearing with notice to the trustee, the debtor and any creditor that filed a timely objection.

(e) A New Date for a Meeting of Creditors. When a debtor fails to appear at a meeting of creditors and subsequently a new date for a meeting of creditors is established, then:

(1) the new date must be stated in an order entered upon either a motion or a stipulation between the trustee and the debtor, with the proposed order attached;

(2) the deadlines under F.R.Bankr.P. 4007 and F.R.Bankr.P. 4004 for filing a complaint under § 523 or § 727, respectively, are extended as if the new date for the meeting of creditors is the first date scheduled;

(3) in a chapter 13 case that is dismissed and then reinstated, the clerk will issue a notice of the new date for the meeting of creditors, the new deadlines under subpart (e)(2) and, if established, the new date for the hearing on confirmation of the chapter 13 plan; and

(4) in all other cases, the debtor must serve notice of the new date for the meeting of creditors and the new deadlines under subpart (e)(2), except that the clerk will serve the notice if the debtor is pro se.

[Effective October 1, 1998. Amended effective May 5, 2008; December 1, 2009; February 1, 2016.]

RULE 2003–2. DEBTOR'S DOCUMENTS AT THE MEETING OF CREDITORS

(a) In a case under chapter 7, 12 or 13, or in an individual case under chapter 11, to the extent they are in the debtor's possession or are readily available, the debtor must have available at the meeting of creditors, neatly arranged, all of the following:

(1) documents for one year pre-petition to support all entries on schedule I, other than previously provided payment advices and tax returns;

(2) documents for one year pre-petition to support all entries on schedule J, including canceled checks, paid bills or other proof of expenses;

(3) copies of life insurance policies either owned by the debtor or insuring the debtor's life;

(4) keys to non-exempt buildings and vehicles;

(5) divorce judgments and property settlement agreements;

(6) documents establishing the scheduled amounts of joint debts, if the debtor claims an entireties exemption;

(7) the name, address and telephone number of each holder of a domestic support obligation; and

(8) any other specific document requested by the trustee relating to the schedules or statement of financial affairs, if requested in writing at least seven days before the first meeting of creditors.

(b) In a case under chapter 7, 12 or in an individual case under chapter 11, to the extent they are in the debtor's possession or are readily available, the debtor must provide to the trustee or, in a chapter 11 case to the United States trustee, no later than seven days prior to the meeting of creditors, neatly arranged, all of the following:

(1) certificate of title (originals if available, otherwise copies) for currently owned titled assets, including vehicles, boats and mobile homes (regardless of when acquired);

(2) a current statement from each secured creditor stating the amount owed;

(3) originals of bank books, check registers, other financial accounts, bonds, stock certificates and bank, brokerage and credit card statements for one year pre-petition;

(4) copies of leases, recorded mortgages, recorded and unrecorded deeds and recorded land contracts for the time period six years pre-petition;

(5) current property tax statements;

(6) asset appraisals;

(7) casualty insurance policies; and

(8) if the debtor owns a business, business financial statements and business tax returns for the past three years, and business bank statements for the past six months.

(c) In a case under chapter 13, to the extent they are in the debtor's possession or are readily available, the debtor must provide to the trustee no later than 14 days prior to the meeting of creditors, neatly arranged, all of the following:

(1) tax returns for the last two years pre-petition;

(2) payment advices or other proof of current income for the 60 days pre-petition;

(3) proof of all income for one year pre-petition stated on schedule I, including year to date profit and loss statements if the debtor is self employed or engaged in business;

(4) if the debtor owns a business, business financial statements and business tax returns for the past three years, and business bank statements for the past six months; and

(5) any other specific document requested in writing by the trustee relating to the schedules or statement of financial affairs.

[Effective October 1, 1998. Amended effective May 5, 2008; February 1, 2016.]

RULE 2003–3. INFORMATION FOR THE APPOINTMENT OF A COMMITTEE

In all chapter 11 cases, the debtor must immediately provide to the United States trustee the email address and contact person for each entity listed on the debtor's filing under F.R.Bankr.P. 1007(d). If an email address is not available, the debtor must immediately provide to the United States trustee the name of the contact person, address and telephone number of each entity listed on the debtor's filing under F.R.Bankr.P. 1007(d).

[Effective January 3, 2005. Renumbered and amended effective May 5, 2008. Amended effective February 1, 2016.]

RULE 2003–4. DUTIES OF A COMMITTEE REGARDING CREDITOR ACCESS TO INFORMATION

Any committee appointed under § 1102 must serve a notice of the appointment of the committee on all creditors holding claims of the kind represented by that committee and file a certificate of service. The deadline to serve this notice is 45 days after appointment of the committee. This notice must also provide for a procedure for creditors and their attorneys to be placed on a service list, maintained by the committee, of those who elect to receive information under § 1102(b)(3). This notice must also provide for a procedure for creditors to provide comments to the committee.

[Effective May 5, 2008. Amended effective February 1, 2016.]

RULE 2004–1. MOTION TO EXAMINE UNDER F.R.BANKR.P. 2004

(a) Motion to Examine the Debtor. Any person who seeks to examine the debtor under F.R.Bankr.P. 2004 must contact the debtor's attorney to arrange a mutually convenient date, time and place before filing a motion. If agreed, a stipulation for an order must be filed, stating the date, time and place for the examination, and the documents to be produced. If the debtor's attorney does not agree, after the requesting party has made all reasonable efforts, a motion for examination of the debtor may be filed under Local Rule 9014–1, stating specifically the efforts that were made, the proposed date, time and place of the examination, and the documents sought.

(b) Motion to Examine Any Other Person. Any other motion under F.R.Bankr.P. 2004 must be filed under Local Rule 9014–1. The moving party must serve the motion on the party proposed to be examined.

[Effective October 1, 1998. Amended effective May 5, 2008; February 1, 2016.]

RULE 2014–1. APPLICATION FOR COURT APPROVAL OF THE EMPLOYMENT OF A PROFESSIONAL

(a) Disclosing Connections. An application for the approval of the employment of a professional must include or be accompanied by a statement of the professional that the employment complies with § 327(a). This statement must also disclose all of the connections of the professional and associates of the professional with the debtor, creditors or any other party in interest, and their respective attorneys and accountants as required by F.R.Bankr.P. 2014. The term "connection" as used herein is defined also to include any family relationship as defined in § 101(45).

(b) United States Trustee Concurrence. If the United States trustee concurs in an application for the approval of the employment of a professional, the concurrence must be indicated by the signature of the United States trustee on a statement of concurrence to the proposed order appointing the professional, which must be filed. If a statement of concurrence is filed, the proposed order approving the employment may be submitted for entry. If the United States trustee does not concur within seven days, the applicant may contact the judge's courtroom deputy clerk and obtain a hearing date on the application. The order will be deemed effective as of the date of the filing of the application, unless the court orders otherwise.

(c) Appointing Chapter 7 Trustee As Attorney. Unless the trustee is also a creditor in the case, whenever a chapter 7 panel trustee seeks to be appointed as trustee's attorney, an order appointing that person as attorney will be deemed to have been entered without the formal entry of an order, effective upon the filing of the verified statement required by the last sentence in F.R.Bankr.P. 2014(a).

(d) Other Appointments. An application for the appointment of an auctioneer, appraiser or real estate sales agent must also contain a statement of the fee or commission proposed to be paid. With respect to the appointment of an auctioneer or an appraiser, the application must further contain a statement as to the amount of expenses and the number of hours of labor anticipated.

(e) Using Local Rule 9014–1. Nothing herein precludes a party from utilizing Local Rule 9014–1 to seek an order approving the employment of a professional.

[Effective October 1, 1998. Amended effective May 5, 2008; December 1, 2009; February 1, 2016.]

RULE 2014–2. PROHIBITED CONDUCT IN CONNECTION WITH THE APPOINTMENT OF AN ATTORNEY, ACCOUNTANT OR AGENT FOR AN OFFICIAL COMMITTEE

Neither the debtor, nor an attorney or accountant for, or insider of, the debtor may attempt directly or indirectly to influence the selection of attorneys, accountants or other agents by any official committee. It is the affirmative duty of any member of the bar of the court to inform the United States trustee in writing of any conduct in violation of this rule.

[Effective October 1, 1998. Amended effective February 1, 2016.]

RULE 2015–1. TRUSTEE'S REPORT OF UNDISCLOSED ASSETS

If a trustee discovers an asset that the debtor failed to disclose and the trustee's discovery of the asset occurs after the debtor has testified at the meeting of creditors that the schedules are accurate, then the trustee must, as promptly as practicable after the discovery, file a completed form "Trustee's Report of Undisclosed Asset," available on the court's website.

[Effective May 5, 2008. Amended effective February 1, 2016.]

RULE 2015–2. QUARTERLY INCOME AND EXPENSE STATEMENT IN A BUSINESS CHAPTER 13 CASE

Within 28 days of the close of each calendar quarter, a chapter 13 debtor engaged in business must file a statement of income and expenses for that quarter.

[Effective October 1, 1998. Amended effective May 5, 2008; December 1, 2009; February 1, 2016.]

RULE 2015–3. TRUSTEE'S PROCEDURES UPON CHAPTER 13 PLAN COMPLETION

(a) Procedure Leading to Entry of the Debtor's Discharge. Within 30 days after the completion of plan payments by the debtor to the trustee, the trustee must file and serve on the debtor and all holders of allowed claims a notice stating that:

(1) the debtor's payments to the trustee under the plan have been completed;

(2) the order of discharge will include findings that:

(A) all allowed claims have been paid in accordance with the plan; and

(B) with respect to any secured claim that continues beyond the term of the plan, any pre-petition or post-petition defaults have been cured;

(3) the order of discharge will direct that:

(A) any creditor who held a secured claim that was fully paid must execute and deliver to the debtor a release, termination statement, discharge of mortgage or other appropriate certificate suitable for recording; and

(B) any creditor who holds a secured claim that continues beyond the term of the plan must take no action inconsistent with the above findings;

(4) in addition to the requirements for holders of claims governed by F.R.Bankr.P. 3002.1, any party may file with the court an objection to the trustee's notice under subpart (a)(1); to assert that the debtor is not current in the payments that the debtor was authorized to make directly to a creditor; to the proposed findings as stated in subpart (a)(2); or to the proposed terms of the order of discharge as stated in subpart (a)(3). (The provisions of this subpart (a)(4) do not apply to a creditor with respect to whom the automatic stay has been terminated.);

(5) the deadline to file an objection is 21 days after service of the notice. If no objection is timely filed with the court under this rule, and no statement disagreeing with the notice of final cure payment is timely filed under F.R.Bankr.P. 3002.1(g), the court may enter an order of discharge containing the provisions of subparts (a)(2) and (a)(3) without a hearing. If either a timely objection is filed with the court under this rule, or a timely statement disagreeing with the notice of final cure payment is filed under F.R.Bankr.P. 3002.1(g), the court will delay entry of the order of discharge until it resolves such objection or statement, after a hearing that will be scheduled by the court upon the filing of such objection or statement with notice to the party filing such objection or statement, the debtor and the trustee;

(6) to avoid defaulting on any continuing secured debt obligation, the debtor must immediately begin making the required payments on that obligation; and

(7) the chapter 13 discharge does not discharge the debtor from any obligation on any continuing secured debt payments that are due after the last contractually due payment to which the trustee's last disbursement is applied. The trustee must file a certificate of service of this notice.

(b) Additional Notice. The notice under subpart (a) must also state that unless a party timely objects under subpart (a)(4), the court may find without a hearing that there is no reasonable cause to believe that:

(1) § 522(q)(1) may be applicable to the debtor; and

(2) there is pending any proceeding in which the debtor may be found guilty of a felony of the kind specified in § 522(q)(1)(A) or liable for a debt of the kind described in § 522(q)(1)(B).

(c) Application. Subparts (a)(2)(B) and (a)(3)(B) will not apply to the extent that the court has entered an order providing otherwise.

(d) Trustee's Final Report and Account. Within 120 days after the trustee files the notice required under subpart (a), the trustee must file the final report and account and serve it or a summary thereof on all holders of allowed claims and file a certificate of service.

(1) The final report must state the allowed amount of each claim and the amount paid thereon.

(2) The report and any summary thereof that is served must also state that the deadline to file an objection to the trustee's final report and account is 30 days after service of the final report; that if no objection is timely filed, the trustee may be discharged and the case may be closed without a hearing; and that if a timely objection is filed, a hearing will be scheduled with notice to the objecting party, the debtor and the trustee.

[Former Rule 2015–5 effective October 1, 1998. Amended effective October 17, 2005; May 5, 2008; December 1, 2009; November 23, 2011; October 26, 2012. Renumbered and amended effective February 1, 2016.]

RULE 2016–1. APPROVAL OF FEES

(a) An Application by an Attorney or Accountant. An application by an attorney or an accountant for compensation and reimbursement under § 330 or § 331 must contain the disclosures required by F.R.Bankr.P. 2016(a), must comply with the following subparts (1)–(10), numbered as such, and must include the exhibits described in subparts (11)–(17).

(1) *State separately.*

(A) the total amount of compensation sought to be approved;

(B) the amount of expenses sought to be approved; and

(C) the balance of any retainer on deposit with the applicant that remains after the payment of prior fee awards.

This statement must be incorporated into the notice of the fee application served on all parties in interest.

(2) Identify the time period during which the services for which the award is sought were rendered.

(3) Provide a narrative summary explaining the services performed and how the services benefitted the estate. In addition, in a chapter 13 case, a pre-confirmation or post-confirmation fee application that requests approval of fees and expenses totaling more than $3,500.00 in that application must specifically identify the circumstances of the case that make the amount requested reasonable.

(4) Unless unduly burdensome, with respect to each adversary proceeding, state or other federal litigation or administrative proceeding in which the applicant is or was involved, describe:

(A) the nature of the action instituted;

(B) the relief requested;

(C) the dollar amount directly or indirectly involved;

(D) the issues, both factual and legal, in sufficient detail to permit the court to evaluate the problems confronting the attorney; and

(E) the results obtained since the prior fee application, if any.

(5) Describe the current status of the bankruptcy case. In addition:

(A) in a chapter 7 case, provide a summary of the administration of the case, including all money received and disbursed in the case, the total amount of funds in the estate, the date the case is expected to close, and whether it is appropriate to make an interim disbursement to creditors without prejudicing the rights of any creditors;

(B) in a chapter 11 case, state whether all monthly operating reports have been timely filed and whether a plan has been or will be timely filed; and

(C) in a chapter 13 case, state the impact on the plan resulting from approval of the fee application.

(6) Describe the nature of any professional services to be provided in the future.

(7) State the amount and nature of accrued unpaid administrative expenses.

(8) Identify each specific instance in which an award is sought for the services of more than one professional and paraprofessional and the justification for each such specific instance.

(9) State the amount of compensation sought in prior applications in the case by the applicant and the court's disposition of each application.

(10) State that:

(A) the party on whose behalf the applicant is employed was given the opportunity to review the application at least seven days before filing and state the substance of the party's response; or

(B) the applicant has obtained the written approval of the application from the party on whose behalf the applicant is employed prior to filing the application.

(11) Exhibit 1 must be the proposed order granting the application.

(12) Exhibit 2 must be a copy of the order approving the employment of the applicant.

(13) Exhibit 3 must be a copy of the applicant's statement under F.R.Bankr.P. 2016(b) or if none was filed, a copy of the applicant's retention agreement.

(14) Exhibit 4 must be a summary statement of the number of hours of service rendered by each professional and paraprofessional, the hourly rate of each and the blended hourly rate of the professionals not including the paraprofessionals.

(15) Exhibit 5 must be in the format required by either subpart (A) or subpart (B).

(A) This subpart (A) applies if the cumulative amount of the fee application and the applicant's prior interim fee applications is equal to or less than the following:

$15,000 for an attorney or an accountant for a chapter 7 trustee;

$20,000 for an attorney or an accountant for a chapter 11 debtor in possession or a chapter 11 trustee; or

$5,000 for an attorney for a chapter 13 debtor.

These amounts may be amended from time to time by administrative order. Exhibit 5 must be an itemized time record in chronological order, of each specific service for which an award of compensation is sought. This itemized time record must:

(i) state the date each service was rendered;

(ii) identify the attorney or paralegal who performed the service;

(iii) describe with particularity the services rendered; and

(iv) state the time spent performing the service in increments of a tenth of an hour.

(B) This subpart (B) applies if the cumulative amount of the fee application and the applicant's prior interim applications is greater than the applicable amount in subpart (A). Unless otherwise ordered by the court, exhibit 5 must comply with the United States Trustee Guidelines for Reviewing Applications for Compensation and Reimbursement of Expenses, 28 C.F.R. Part 58 Appendix A. The United States Trustee Fee Guidelines are available on the court's website. In a chapter 13 case, the project categories in the "List of Chapter 13 Project Categories for Fee Applications," available on the court's website, must be used.

(16) Exhibit 6 must be a brief biographical statement of the professional experience of each professional for whom an award of compensation is sought. This statement must include a list of all continuing professional education programs taught or attended by each professional in the two years before the application, specifying for each program the dates, the number of hours attended, the organizer and the subject or title of the program. The applicant is also encouraged to disclose for each professional any published articles and books, and any professional memberships, positions, activities, honors and board certifications.

(17) Exhibit 7 must be an itemized statement of expenses for which reimbursement is sought. For each expense, this statement must disclose its date and a description of the nature and purpose of the expense. For example, a request for mileage must include the date, the destination, the number of miles, the mileage rate and the reason for the trip.

(b) An Application Filed by a Chapter 7 Trustee or by Any Other Professional. This subpart applies to an application for compensation and reimbursement filed by a chapter 7 trustee or by a professional other than one addressed in subpart (a), including an appraiser, auctioneer, real or personal property sales broker, investment advisor or consultant. In addition to the requirements of F.R.Bankr.P. 2016(a), the application must state the manner by which the requested compensation was computed and sufficient facts for the court to determine reasonable compensation under § 330. A request for reimbursement of expenses must be supported by a statement disclosing for each expense its date and a description of the nature and purpose of the expense. Vouchers and invoices must be made available for review by the United States trustee.

(c) Compensation for a Chapter 13 Debtor's Attorney Without a Fee Application. Notwithstanding subpart (a), an order confirming plan in a chapter 13 case may award the debtor's attorney fees and expenses up to $3,500.00 in total for pre-confirmation services.

(d) Compensation for a Chapter 13 Debtor's Attorney Under a Fixed Amount. Notwithstanding subpart (a), the debtor's attorney in a chapter 13 case may file an *ex parte* application that seeks allowance of fees and expenses that does not exceed the amount identified in F.R.Bankr.P. 2002(a)(6) if it has the endorsed approval of the debtor and the chapter 13 trustee. If the application lacks the endorsements, the applicant must utilize Local Rule 9014–1 but notice needs to be sent only to the trustee and the debtor. The debtor's endorsement must state as follows:

"I, the debtor, understand that:

I do not have to sign this document unless I agree with it;

I signed this document on the date stated below;

When I signed this document, all the blanks were filled in;

I agree that the fees and expenses requested should be allowed.

Date signed: _____ Debtor signature: _____"

[Effective October 1, 1998. Amended effective May 5, 2008; October 29, 2008; February 1, 2016.]

RULE 2016–2. INTERIM PAYMENT OF FEES

(a) Motion for Interim Fee Payments. In a chapter 11 case, for cause shown, any professional appointed under § 327 or any official committee may move for an order authorizing interim payments of fees and expenses pending a formal fee application. A motion seeking interim payment of fees or expenses pending a formal fee application must address the following factors and any other relevant factors:

(1) whether a large amount of fees will accrue each month;

(2) whether a failure to allow interim payments would cause an undue hardship; and

(3) whether the professional or committee will be able to disgorge the interim payments if required.

In determining whether to permit an interim fee procedure, the court will consider all the facts and circumstances.

(b) Interim Fee Procedure. When the court enters an order granting a motion for interim fee payments to a professional or committee:

(1) that professional or committee may file an itemized monthly fee and expense statement in compliance with the provisions of these Local Rules and, when applicable, the United States Trustee Fee Guidelines, setting forth in detail

he fees and expenses for which payment is sought for the preceding month, and must serve a copy of the statement on he debtor and such additional parties as the court may designate and file a certificate of service;

(2) each statement must include, as an exhibit, records that itemize services and expenses in conformity with the Federal Rules of Bankruptcy Procedure, these Local Rules and the United States Trustee Fee Guidelines;

(3) the deadline to file an objection to the interim fee statement is 14 days from the date of service of the interim statement. If no objection is timely filed, the debtor is authorized to pay in the ordinary course of business: (A) 80% of the professional fees; (B) 100% of the expenses incurred by the professional; and (C) 100% of the expenses incurred by committee members. The 20% professional fee hold back will be paid only in accordance with the Federal Rules of Bankruptcy Procedure, Local Rule 2016–1 and the Bankruptcy Code sections governing the award of fees;

(4) any objection to any interim statement must be filed and served on the affected professional or committee. The objection must specify in detail the nature and basis of the objection and the amount not disputed. Pending resolution of the objection, the debtor is authorized to pay the professional or committee the amount requested in the particular monthly statement less the greater of: (A) the amount in dispute, or (B) the professional fee hold back provided in subpart (3) above. The parties must endeavor to resolve any objection within 5 days. If a resolution is not achieved, the professional or committee may request a hearing; and

(5) the failure of any party to object to an interim fee statement within the objection period does not constitute a waiver of the right to object to any interim or final fee application filed by any professional or committee or preclude any disgorgement of fees or expenses paid.

(c) Interim Fee Applications Required. If the court permits interim fee payments under this rule, the professional must file interim fee applications every 120 days under § 331 and committee members must file requests for allowance of administrative expenses every 120 days under § 503(b)(3)(F).

[Former Rule 2016–3 effective January 3, 2005. Amended effective May 5, 2008; December 1, 2009. Renumbered and amended effective February 1, 2016.]

RULE 2018–1. INTERVENTION

When the court has entered an order allowing a party to intervene in a case, the intervening party must file an appearance to request that the clerk add its name to the case.

[Effective October 1, 1998. Amended effective May 5, 2008; February 1, 2016.]

RULE 2019–1. DISCLOSURES

Any group, committee or entity required to file a disclosure under F.R.Bankr.P. 2019 must file such disclosure at the same time as the group, committee or entity's first paper is filed.

[Effective February 1, 2016.]

RULE 3001–1. TRANSFER OF CLAIM

Any assignments or other evidence of a transfer of claim filed after the proof of claim has been filed must include the claim number of the claim to be transferred.

[Effective February 1, 2016.]

RULE 3001–2. ADJUSTMENT IN A PERIODIC PAYMENT ON A SECURED CLAIM IN CHAPTER 13

(a) Creditor's Notice. A creditor with a claim under § 1322(b)(5) or (b)(7) that is not governed by F.R.Bankr.P. 3002.1 must file and serve on the debtor, debtor's counsel and the trustee, a notice of any proposed increase or decrease of periodic payments and file a certificate of service. The deadline to file this notice is 21 days before the effective date of the adjustment of the payment amount. The notice must fully disclose the calculations on which the adjustment is based.

(b) Objection. The deadline to file an objection to a creditor's notice under subpart (a) or to a notice of mortgage payment change filed under F.R.Bankr.P. 3002.1(b) is 21 days after service of the notice. If an objection is filed, the court will schedule a hearing with notice to the debtor, the creditor and the trustee.

(c) Effective Date of Proposed Change. A proposed payment change under subpart (a) or under F.R.Bankr.P. 3002.1(b) will be effective 21 days after service of the notice, unless the court orders otherwise.

(d) Notice of Inability to Comply with Timing Requirements. This subpart (d) applies to a creditor whose claim is secured by a mortgage for which the amount of the debtor's payment obligations is subject to change more frequently than once every 60 days. Such a creditor may file a "Notice of Inability To Comply With Local Rule 3001–2(a) Deadline" as an attachment to any statement of proposed payment change filed under subpart (a) of this Local Rule. Upon the filing of a notice under this subpart (d), unless there is an objection filed within 14 days or the court orders otherwise, the trustee must effectuate the payment change stated in the notice of payment change.

[Effective October 1, 1998. Amended effective May 5, 2008; March 24, 2009; December 1, 2009; June 11, 2010; November 23, 2011; October 26, 2012; February 1, 2016.]

RULE 3003–1. DEADLINE TO FILE A PROOF OF CLAIM, A PROOF OF INTEREST OR A § 503(B)(9) MOTION IN A CHAPTER 11 CASE

In a chapter 11 case, unless the court orders otherwise, the deadline for filing a required proof of claim or equity interest or a motion for the allowance of a claim under § 503(b)(9) is 90 days after the first date set for the meeting of creditors.

[Effective October 1, 1998. Amended effective May 5, 2008; February 1, 2016.]

RULE 3007–1. OBJECTION TO A CLAIM

(a) Procedure. An objection to claim must be filed with a completed form "Notice of Hearing on Objection to Claim," available on the court's website, and a certificate of service. The date and time for the hearing stated on the notice of hearing must be obtained from the schedule of available hearing dates for claims objections on the court's website. The date of the hearing must be at least 30 days after the date of service of the hearing notice. The notice of hearing must state that if the creditor does not file a response by seven days before the date set for the hearing on the objection, the court may cancel the hearing and enter an order sustaining the objection.

(b) Deadline for Response. The deadline for a creditor whose proof of claim is subject to an objection to file a response to the objection is seven days before the date set for the hearing on the objection.

(c) No Response. If a response is not timely filed, the objecting party may file a certificate to that effect and submit a proposed order sustaining the objection. If the court decides to proceed with the scheduled hearing, the court will notify the objecting party.

(d) Initial Hearing. Unless the court orders otherwise, the initial hearing on an objection to claim will not be an evidentiary hearing. If the court determines that an evidentiary hearing is necessary, the court will schedule a separate evidentiary hearing.

[Effective October 1, 1998. Amended effective May 5, 2008; December 1, 2009; February 1, 2016.]

RULE 3013–1. CLASSIFICATION OF CLAIMS IN A CHAPTER 11 PLAN

Unless unduly burdensome due to the large number involved, the disclosure statement must identify by name the entities who hold a claim or equity interest within each class and the amount of each entity's claim or equity interest within each class. However, specific identification is not required for convenience classes or for a class of unsecured nonpriority claims when there is only one such class.

[Effective October 1, 1998. Amended effective February 1, 2016.]

RULE 3014–1. ELECTION UNDER § 1111(B)

When the court has entered an order requiring a combined plan and disclosure statement, the deadline to file an election under § 1111(b) is seven days before the first scheduled date of the confirmation hearing.

[Effective May 5, 2008. Amended effective February 1, 2016.]

RULE 3015–1. THE CHAPTER 13 PLAN

(a) Plan Contents. In addition to the requirements of § 1322(a), a plan must contain:

(1) a statement of the value of each item of encumbered property;

(2) the time within which the debtor proposes to cure any default on any secured claim;

(3) a direction to the trustee to either assume or reject any executory contracts or unexpired leases; and if the plan proposes an assumption of a contract or lease that is in default, then a statement as to the method and time to cure the default and an explanation of how to satisfy each of the other § 365(b) requirements for assumption of a defaulted contract or lease;

(4) a method by which the trustee can determine the point at which the plan is completed;

(5) a statement of the order in which claims are to be paid;

(6) a statement of the rate of interest to be paid with respect to each secured claim, articulated as a number and not in formula fashion;

(7) a statement of whether all tax returns due have been filed and if not, which returns were not filed;

(8) a statement of whether the debtor, if self-employed, incurs trade credit;

(9) if the plan provides for the payment of a claim governed by § 1322(b)(5) or (b)(7), a provision that payments by the debtor to the trustee and by the trustee to the creditor on such claim will be adjusted as provided in Local Rule 3001–2;

(10) if the plan provides for a surrender of real property to a secured creditor, a statement that the requirements of Local Rule 3001–2 are terminated as to that creditor upon confirmation of the plan; and

(11) if the plan provides for a surrender of property to a secured creditor, a statement that the automatic stay, and any applicable co-debtor automatic stay, are terminated as to that creditor upon confirmation of the plan.

(b) Plan Attachments. The debtor must attach to the plan:

(1) an analysis of what creditors would receive if the case were a chapter 7 case; and

(2) a completed form "Chapter 13 Worksheet," available on the court's website, estimating the total amount of non-priority unsecured claims and the anticipated dividend to non-priority unsecured creditors if the debtor successfully performs the plan.

[Effective October 1, 1998. Amended effective May 5, 2008; February 1, 2016.]

RULE 3015–2. MODIFICATION OF PLAN IN A CHAPTER 13 CASE

(a) Pre–Confirmation Modification of Plan.

(1) In a chapter 13 case, a pre-confirmation modification of a proposed plan that does not materially and adversely affect any party in interest may be incorporated in the proposed order confirming the plan.

(2) A pre-confirmation modification to a proposed plan that materially and adversely affects any party in interest:

(A) may be incorporated in the proposed order confirming the plan that is executed by the adversely affected party; or in the alternative,

(B) must be incorporated into a completely restated plan that must be dated and identified as "First Modified Plan," "Second Modified Plan," etc., as the case may be. The debtor must serve a copy of the modified plan on all creditors and parties in interest that are adversely affected by the modification and file a certificate of service. The debtor must attach to the plan the papers required under Local Rule 3015–1(b).

(3) All amended schedules that are necessary for confirmation of a modified plan must be filed prior to or contemporaneously with the modified plan.

(b) Post–Confirmation Plan Modification.

(1) The proponent of a post-confirmation plan modification must:

(A) serve the modification as required by F.R.Bankr.P. 3015(g) and file a certificate of service;

(B) comply with Local Rule 3015–1(b);

(C) state with specificity the impact of the proposed plan modification on each class of creditors;

(D) file the form "Notice of Deadline to Object to Chapter 13 Plan Modification," available on the court's website; and

(E) file the post-confirmation plan modification using the ECF event, "Chapter 13 Post–Confirmation Plan Modification."

(2) If a timely objection is filed, the court will schedule a hearing with notice of such hearing given to the debtor, the proponent of the plan modification, the trustee and any objecting parties.

(3) A post-confirmation plan modification may not be proposed by motion. If a post-confirmation plan modification is proposed by motion, the court will enter an order denying it without prejudice to the proponent's right to properly file a proposed post-confirmation plan modification.

(4) If the post-confirmation plan modification is proposed by the debtor, the debtor must file, either prior to or contemporaneously with the modified plan, all amended schedules that are necessary for the approval of the plan modification, and a proposed order modifying the plan.

(5) If no timely responses are filed to a proposed post-confirmation plan modification, the proponent may file a certificate of no response and request entry of an order approving the plan modification.

(6) A post-confirmation plan modification will only become effective when the court enters an order approving the plan modification, either upon the filing of a certificate of no response or after ruling on all objections to the plan modification.

(7) If the post-confirmation plan modification provides for a surrender of real property to a secured creditor, the requirements of Local Rule 3001–2 are terminated as to that creditor upon entry of an order approving the plan modification.

(8) If the post-confirmation plan modification provides for a surrender of property to a secured creditor, the automatic stay, and any applicable co-debtor automatic stay, are terminated as to that creditor upon entry of an order approving the plan modification.

(c) Payment of a § 1305(a) Post–Petition Claim.

(1) The debtor must serve a notice of the filing of a § 1305(a) post-petition claim on all creditors whose claims are allowed and file a certificate of service. The notice must state: the name of the post-petition creditor; the amount of the claim; the nature of the debt; the impact that allowance of the claim would have upon disbursements to other creditors; and the following procedural information:

"If no objection to paying the post-petition claim as provided for in the plan is filed within 14 days, the trustee may pay the claim in the manner provided in the plan. If you have any objection to the claim itself or to the effect that payment of the claim will have on your dividend, then you must file a written objection within 14 days or the objection will be deemed waived."

The debtor must file a certificate of service of such notice.

(2) If no party files an objection, the chapter 13 trustee may disburse payments to a creditor that has filed a post-petition proof of claim commencing 18 days after the notice is served. If a party timely files an objection, the court will schedule a hearing with notice to the debtor, the creditor and the trustee.

[Effective October 1, 1998. Amended effective May 5, 2008; December 1, 2009; February 1, 2016.]

RULE 3015–3. CONFIRMATION OF A CHAPTER 13 PLAN

(a) Objection to Confirmation of a Plan.

(1) In a chapter 13 case, an objection to confirmation of the plan must be filed by the deadline established in the notice of the commencement of the case.

(2) A party who fails to file an objection to confirmation may be deemed to have consented to confirmation of the plan and if the party is a secured creditor, the party may be deemed to have accepted the plan for purposes of § 1325(a)(5)(A).

(3) A secured creditor who disputes the value ascribed to collateral that the debtor proposes to retain under the terms of the plan must file an objection to confirmation of the plan. The debtor must forthwith make the collateral available to the creditor for examination and appraisal. The resulting hearing under F.R.Bankr.P. 3012 must be conducted as part of the plan confirmation hearing.

(4) The deadline to file an objection to the confirmation of a modified plan is 28 days after service of the modified plan.

(5) An objection to confirmation of a plan need not be refiled with respect to a subsequently filed pre-confirmation modified plan that does not cure such objection.

(6) Unless announced on the record at the confirmation hearing, a withdrawal of an objection to confirmation of a plan must be evidenced by a filed withdrawal of the objection or by

the signature of the objecting party or its counsel on the proposed order confirming the plan.

(b) Hearing on Confirmation of Plan.

(1) Neither the debtor nor debtor's counsel need appear at the confirmation hearing if:

(A) either no timely objection to confirmation has been filed or all timely objections have been withdrawn or resolved; and

(B) the chapter 13 trustee has approved the proposed order confirming the plan.

(2) If the court declines to confirm the plan or if a party appears at the confirmation hearing and is permitted for cause to argue an untimely objection, the court will reschedule the hearing with notice to the debtor, debtor's counsel, the trustee and the objecting creditor.

[Effective October 1, 1998. Amended effective May 5, 2008; December 1, 2009; February 1, 2016.]

RULE 3016–1. A PREPACKAGED CHAPTER 11 PLAN

(a) Definition. A prepackaged chapter 11 plan is a plan for which the debtor has solicited acceptances before filing the petition.

(b) Procedure. Immediately upon filing a prepackaged chapter 11 plan, the debtor must file a motion to set a deadline to object to confirmation of the plan and to schedule a confirmation hearing not more than 90 days following the petition date. The motion must be accompanied by a copy of the plan and the disclosure statement or other solicitation document.

[Effective January 3, 2005. Amended effective May 5, 2008; February 1, 2016.]

RULE 3017–1. OBTAINING APPROVAL OF A DISCLOSURE STATEMENT

(a) When Applicable. Subparts (b)–(d) of this Local Rule apply only when the court has not entered an order requiring a combined plan and disclosure statement.

(b) Requirements Upon Filing. The filing of a disclosure statement will be deemed to include a motion for its approval, to which Local Rule 9014–1 applies.

(c) Service of Notice. When a disclosure statement is filed, the movant must obtain a form of notice from the court's website and promptly serve the notice on all parties entitled to notice under F.R.Bankr.P. 2002(b). In addition, the proponent must serve a copy of the disclosure statement and the notice on the United States trustee and the chairperson and counsel for each official committee. The proponent must file a certificate of service.

(d) Approval on No Objection. Upon a certification by the movant that no timely objection to the approval of the disclosure statement was filed, the court may enter an order approving the disclosure statement without a hearing.

[Effective October 1, 1998. Amended effective May 5, 2008; February 1, 2016.]

RULE 3018–1. THE DUTIES OF A PLAN PROPONENT AFTER DISCLOSURE STATEMENT APPROVAL

Within seven days after the entry of the order approving the disclosure statement, the plan proponent must cause that order, the plan, the disclosure statement, any statement approved by the court under F.R.Bankr.P. 3017(d) and a ballot to be served. The court may approve the service of these papers in electronic format with such conditions as the court deems appropriate. The plan proponent must file a certificate of service. Unless the court orders otherwise, ballots must be returned to the attorney for the plan proponent. At least two Business Days before the confirmation hearing, the plan proponent must file a verified summary of the ballot count under § 1126(c) and (d) with a copy of all original ballots attached. The proponent must have the originals of the ballots available at the confirmation hearing and the originals must be retained by the plan proponent under the ECF Procedures.

[Effective October 1, 1998. Amended effective February 3, 2003; May 5, 2008; December 1, 2009; February 1, 2016.]

RULE 3020–1. PROOFS AT AN UNCONTESTED CONFIRMATION HEARING IN A CHAPTER 11 CASE

At the hearing on the confirmation of a chapter 11 plan, if no objection to confirmation has been filed or if all filed objections have been resolved, and if no class of claims or equity interests has rejected the plan, upon consent of all parties present, the court may dispense with an evidentiary hearing and based on the lack of objection and the consents, may find that each of the elements necessary for confirmation under § 1129(a) has been established.

[Effective October 1, 1998. Amended effective May 5, 2008.]

RULE 3021–1. POST–CONFIRMATION PROCEDURES IN A LARGE BANKRUPTCY CASE

(a) Unless the court orders otherwise, within 14 days after the entry of an order confirming a chapter 11 plan in a Large Bankruptcy Case, the plan proponent or other responsible person under the plan must file with the court a statement that contains a timetable with the steps proposed for achieving substantial consummation of the plan and entry of a final decree, including resolution of claims and resolution of avoidance and other bankruptcy court litigation outstanding or contemplated. Any law firm or individual responsible for safeguarding and accounting for the proceeds of all recoveries on behalf of the estate must be identified.

(b) Unless the court orders otherwise, the plan proponent or other responsible person under the plan must file with the court a report whenever necessary, but no less frequently than every six months after the entry of the order issued in accordance with subpart (a) of this Local Rule, identifying the actions taken under the order, location of and steps taken to rotect any funds or other property recovered on behalf of the state, and any necessary revisions to the timetable.

[Effective February 1, 2016.]

RULE 3070–1. CLAIMS TO BE PAID BY THE CHAPTER 13 TRUSTEE

In a chapter 13 case, all claims must be paid by and through the chapter 13 trustee unless the debtor's plan establishes cause for remitting payments on a claim directly to the creditor. Any timely objection to such a plan provision will be heard at the confirmation hearing.

[Effective October 1, 1998. Amended effective February 1, 2016.]

RULE 4001–1. MOTION FOR RELIEF FROM THE STAY OR STIPULATION TO APPROVE AGREEMENT FOR RELIEF FROM THE STAY

(a) Parties to be Served. A party seeking relief from the stay must file a motion under Local Rule 9014–1, or a stipulation providing for entry of an order approving an agreement regarding relief from the stay. A motion seeking relief from the stay must be served upon the parties required to be served under F.R.Bankr.P. 4001, the debtor, any trustee, any other parties asserting an interest in the property that is the subject of the motion, and on any other party who has requested notice, and file a certificate of service. A stipulation providing for entry of an order approving an agreement regarding relief from the stay must be signed by the debtor, any trustee, and any other parties asserting an interest in the property that is the subject of the agreement.

(b) Contents of the Motion. If applicable, the motion under subpart (a) must identify the property, state the names and purported interests of all parties that are known or discoverable upon a reasonable investigation to claim an interest in the property, state the amount of the outstanding indebtedness, and state the fair market value of the property. The motion must have attached a legible and complete copy of any relevant agreements and documents establishing perfection, including notes, assignments of instruments, mortgages and UCC–1 financing statements. All exhibits must be redacted as necessary to comply with F.R.Bankr.P. 9037. A motion for relief from the stay must be so entitled.

(c) The Preliminary Hearing. Unless the court notifies the parties in or contemporaneously with the notice of the preliminary hearing, the preliminary hearing will not be an evidentiary hearing and the court will determine whether to schedule a final hearing based on the parties' papers and arguments. At the preliminary hearing, the court may decide issues of law or define the factual or legal issues to be determined at the final hearing and may issue appropriate scheduling orders. The parties may request or the court may order that the preliminary hearing be treated as the final hearing.

[Effective October 1, 1998. Amended effective May 5, 2008; February 1, 2016.]

RULE 4001–2. MOTION FOR USE OF CASH COLLATERAL OR TO OBTAIN FINANCING

(a) Contents of the Motion. In addition to the requirements of F.R.Bankr.P. 4001(b)(1)(B) and F.R.Bankr.P. 4001(c)(1)(B), a motion for use of cash collateral under § 363(c)(2) or to obtain credit under § 364(c) or (d) must explicitly state the moving party's position as to the value of each of the secured interests to be protected. Pertinent appraisals and projections must be summarized in the motion.

(b) Cover Sheet.

(1) The motion must be filed with a completed form "Cover Sheet for Motion to Use Cash Collateral or to Obtain Financing," available on the court's website. When a cover sheet is not filed, the court may enter an order striking or denying the motion without prejudice to the movant's right to re-file the motion in compliance with this rule.

(2) If any proposed order granting interim or final relief would alter any information given in the initial cover sheet, then the movant must file an amended cover sheet concurrently with the submission of the proposed order indicating where appropriate all changes from the original proposed order.

(c) Motion to Approve Agreement. A motion for the entry of an order approving an agreement for the use of cash collateral or to obtain credit on an expedited basis may be granted without a hearing if the motion complies with F.R.Bankr.P. 4001(d)(1)(B) and if:

(1) the proposed order is approved by all creditors who may have an interest in the cash collateral to be used or the credit to be extended, by the chairperson or attorney for each official committee and by the United States trustee;

(2) the proposed order provides for the debtor to use cash collateral or to obtain credit in a maximum specified dollar amount necessary to avoid immediate and irreparable harm only until the earlier of the date of the final hearing or the date that the order would become a final order;

(3) the proposed order provides for a final hearing, the date and time for which will be filled in by the court when the proposed order is entered;

(4) the proposed order provides that the debtor must, within 24 hours of its entry, serve a copy of the motion with its attachments and the entered order on all parties who are required to be served under F.R.Bankr.P. 4001(d);

(5) the proposed order provides that:

(A) the deadline to file an objection to the proposed order is 14 days from the entry of the order, except that an official committee may file objections within 14 days after it is served with the entered order;

(B) if an objection is timely filed, the final hearing will be held; and

(C) if no objection is timely filed, the interim or preliminary order may become a final order; and

(6) the motion is accompanied by an affidavit or declaration of the debtor or a principal of the debtor stating the facts upon which the debtor relies in seeking the entry of the proposed

order on an expedited basis and the amount of money needed to avoid immediate and irreparable harm.

(d) Interim Order on Expedited Basis. If a debtor files a motion for authority to use cash collateral or to obtain post-petition financing but the debtor's pre-petition secured creditors have not consented to the relief sought in the motion, the court may enter an interim order granting the relief requested on an expedited basis if:

(1) the debtor has served a copy of the motion, a proposed order and a notice of the hearing on the motion on the non-consenting secured creditors in the manner set forth in Local Rule 9013–1;

(2) the court has held a hearing on the motion at which the non-consenting secured creditors were given an opportunity to be heard;

(3) the proposed order complies with each of the requirements of subparts (c)(2)–(c)(6) of this rule; and

(4) the court makes a specific finding of fact that the protection offered to the non-consenting secured creditors is adequate and such adequate protection is incorporated into the proposed order.

(e) Effect of Interim Order. If the court enters an interim order under subpart (d) of this rule over the objection of a secured creditor or if a secured creditor does not appear at the hearing or object to the motion, such secured creditor retains the right to object to the interim order as provided in subpart (c)(5)(A) of this rule.

(f) Reducing or Enlarging Time for Objections. On timely motion, the court may enlarge or reduce the time within which an objection must be filed, except that the court may not reduce the time within which a non-consenting secured creditor must file an objection under subpart (c)(5)(A) of this rule. In its discretion, the court may schedule a hearing on the debtor's motion at any time, with such notice as it deems appropriate, provided such notice and hearing are consistent with subpart (d) of this rule.

[Effective October 1, 1998. Amended effective January 3, 2005; May 5, 2008; December 1, 2009; February 1, 2016.]

RULE 4001–3. MOTION FOR PAYMENT OF PRE–PETITION CLAIMS OF CRITICAL VENDORS

(a) Contents of Motion. A motion requesting the authority to pay the pre-petition claims of creditors that a debtor deems critical to its operations or to the preservation of the estate (a "Critical Vendor") must, at a minimum, include the following information:

(1) the aggregate amount to be paid to all Critical Vendors;

(2) the names of, and the amount proposed to be paid to, each Critical Vendor;

(3) the reasons why each of the subject creditors is a Critical Vendor;

(4) the potential loss of economic advantage to the estate or to the debtor's going concern value by the nonpayment of the pre-petition claim of each of the Critical Vendors;

(5) the steps taken or to be taken by which the debtor might deal with the Critical Vendors, other than by payment of the pre-petition claim, and whether it is necessary to pay 100% of the pre-petition claim of the Critical Vendors to obtain the required post-petition goods or services;

(6) the extent to which the claims of the Critical Vendors may be entitled to payment as administrative priority or secured claim;

(7) the terms by which the debtor will seek to do business with the Critical Vendors post-petition, including the terms of any post-petition credit; and

(8) the impact of granting the requested relief on the creditors deemed not to be Critical Vendors.

(b) Not First Day Motion. Consistent with F.R.Bankr.P. 6003(b), a Critical Vendor motion will not be considered a First Day Motion.

(c) Service of Motion. The motion must be served on all creditors.

[Former Rule 4001–4 effective October 1, 1998. Amended effective May 5, 2008. Renumbered and amended effective February 1, 2016.]

RULE 4001–4. ADDITIONAL PROCEDURES TO EXTEND STAY AND TO ORDER STAY TO TAKE EFFECT

(a) Motion to Extend the Stay. The deadline to file and serve a motion to extend the stay under § 362(c)(3)(B) and to file a certificate of service is seven days after the petition is filed. When such a motion is filed, the court will schedule a hearing with a notice to all parties in interest. If the movant has not received a notice of hearing within seven days after filing the motion, the movant may contact the judge's courtroom deputy clerk to obtain a hearing date within the time limit established by law. Any party in interest may be heard at the hearing. Written objections are permitted but not required.

(b) Motion to Order the Stay to Take Effect. A motion to order the stay to take effect under § 362(c)(4)(B) may be accompanied by an *ex parte* motion for an expedited hearing. Otherwise, the court will schedule a hearing in due course. In either event, the court will cause a notice of the hearing to be served on all parties in interest. If the movant has not filed a motion for an expedited hearing and has not received a notice of hearing within seven days after filing the motion, the movant may contact the judge's courtroom clerk to obtain a hearing date. Any party in interest may be heard at the hearing. Written objections are permitted but not required.

(c) Objection Under § 362(l)(3)(A). When an objection under § 362(l)(3)(A) is filed, the court will schedule a hearing with notice to all parties in interest. If the objecting party has not received a notice of hearing within three Business Days after filing the objection, the objecting party must contact the judge's courtroom deputy clerk to obtain a hearing date; otherwise, the requirement to hold a hearing within 10 days under § 362(l)(3)(A) is waived.

(d) Objection Under § 362(m)(2)(B). When an objection under § 362(m)(2)(B) is filed, the court will schedule a hearing with notice to all parties in interest. If the debtor has not received a notice of hearing within three Business Days after filing the objection, the debtor must contact the judge's courtroom deputy clerk to obtain a hearing date; otherwise, the debtor's objection is deemed waived and the 15 day period of § 362(m)(1) will continue to run.

(e) Order Regarding the Existence of the Stay. A party seeking relief under either § 362(c)(4)(A)(ii), § 362(j) or § 521(a)(6) must file a motion under Local Rule 9014–1. The motion must be titled, "Motion for an Order Confirming That No Stay Is in Effect," or "Motion for an Order Confirming That the Stay Has Been Terminated." The moving party must serve the debtor and the trustee and file a certificate of service. The motion may be accompanied by an *ex parte* motion for an expedited hearing.

[Former Rule 4001–5 effective January 3, 2005. Amended effective May 5, 2008; December 1, 2009. Renumbered and amended effective February 1, 2016.]

RULE 4001–5. PRE–CONFIRMATION PAYMENTS IN A CHAPTER 13 CASE

(a) Payment by the Trustee.

(1) *Conditions of Disbursements.* Without a court order, the trustee must disburse pre-confirmation payments under § 1326(a)(1) to a creditor holding a purchase money security interest in personal property and to a lessor of personal property if:

(A) funds are available;

(B) the creditor or lessor has, by the 14th day of the month prior to the trustee's next regularly scheduled disbursement, filed a proof of claim with adequate proof of a security interest attached setting forth the amount of the debtor's contractual monthly payment obligation;

(C) either the plan proposes that the claim will be paid by the trustee or the debtor was not current in the debtor's contractual monthly payment obligation when the petition was filed;

(D) the plan proposes that the debtor will retain possession of the secured or leased property; and

(E) a stay is in effect as to the secured or leased property.

If any objection to the proof of claim is filed, the trustee must escrow the amount of distributions on such proof of claim until further order of the court.

(2) *Timing of Disbursement.* The trustee's disbursements must be made monthly until an order of confirmation is entered.

(3) *Amount of Disbursement.* Unless the court orders otherwise for good cause shown under § 1326(a)(3), the disbursements must be 30% of the debtor's contractual monthly payment obligation to each secured creditor and 100% of the debtor's contractual monthly payment obligation to each personal property lessor. If the trustee does not have sufficient funds on hand to make all of the required disbursements, the disbursements must be made pro rata based on the monthly payments required.

(4) *Dismissal.* Upon dismissal of the case, the trustee must make the required pre-confirmation disbursements before disbursing any funds to the debtor.

(5) *Trustee's Statutory Fee.* For all pre-confirmation disbursements, the trustee will be awarded and paid a fee equal to the applicable percentage fee established by the United States trustee.

(b) Direct Payment by the Debtor.

(1) *Conditions of Payment.* Without a court order, the debtor must make pre-confirmation payments under § 1326(a)(1) to a creditor holding purchase money security interests in personal property and to a lessor of personal property if:

(A) the creditor or lessor has filed a proof of claim with adequate proof of a security interest attached setting forth the amount of the debtor's contractual monthly payment obligation;

(B) the debtor was current in the contractual monthly payment obligation when the petition was filed;

(C) the plan proposes that the claim will be paid directly by the debtor;

(D) the plan proposes that the debtor will retain possession of the secured or leased property; and

(E) a stay is in effect as to the secured or leased property.

(2) *Timing and Amount of Payment by the Debtor.* The debtor's payments must be made as required by the debtor's contract.

(c) Amended Proof of Claim. Within 28 days after confirmation, a creditor receiving any pre-confirmation payments must file an amended proof of claim clearly showing the application of the pre-confirmation payments.

[Former Rule 4001–6 effective October 17, 2005, as amended by Administrative Order 05–8. Amended effective May 5, 2008; December 1, 2009. Renumbered and amended effective February 1, 2016.]

RULE 4002–1. CONTINUED PRE–PETITION CASH MANAGEMENT

A motion in a chapter 11 case to continue using pre-petition bank accounts or pre-petition cash management systems for good cause must contain the following information:

(a) identification of the accounts by name of bank, description or title of the accounts and purpose of the accounts;

(b) a thorough explanation of the cash management system, including, if applicable, the relationship between parent and subsidiaries and other entities that participate in the cash management system;

(c) the reason for continuing to use the pre-petition accounts or system, including the costs and inconvenience of compliance with the guidelines requiring closure of pre-petition accounts;

(d) the mechanism and steps to be taken to ensure that unauthorized pre-petition checks will not clear the bank accounts post-petition;

(e) the steps that will be taken to have the face of each check and bank statement identify the payer as a debtor in possession; and

(f) the steps that will be taken to ensure compliance with § 345.

[Effective January 3, 2005. Amended effective May 5, 2008; February 1, 2016.]

RULE 4003–1. ENTIRETIES EXEMPTION

A married debtor not filing a joint petition who claims property as exempt under tenants by the entireties law must state whether each debt listed on schedules D and E/F is a joint debt with the non-filing spouse or is the sole debt of the debtor. For purposes of determining whether the debtor's claim of exemption under state entireties law should be allowed, there will be a rebuttable presumption that any debt listed on schedule D or E/F that is not clearly disclosed as the sole debt of the filing spouse is the joint debt of both spouses.

[Effective May 5, 2008. Amended effective February 1, 2016.]

RULE 4004–1. DOMESTIC SUPPORT CERTIFICATION IN A CHAPTER 13 CASE

In a chapter 13 case, within 28 days after the trustee files a notice of the completion of all payments under the plan under Local Rule 2015–3(a), the debtor must file a completed form "Certification Regarding Domestic Support Obligations," available on the court's website. This certification must state whether the debtor has been the subject of any domestic support obligation and if so, whether the debtor is current in that obligation as required by § 1328(a) to obtain a discharge. The debtor must serve the certification on any domestic support obligation creditor and file a certificate of service. If the debtor fails to file this certification, the case may be closed without a discharge, without prejudice to the debtor's right to file a motion to reopen under Local Rule 5010–1 to file the certification in order to obtain a discharge.

[Effective October 17, 2005. Amended effective May 5, 2008; December 1, 2009; February 1, 2016.]

RULE 4008–1. REAFFIRMATION AGREEMENTS AND THE PRESUMPTION OF UNDUE HARDSHIP

(a) Reaffirmation With Attorney Certification. If the debtor's attorney certifies that a reaffirmation agreement does not impose an undue hardship on the debtor, neither a motion nor court action is required. This subpart (a) applies even if it appears that a presumption of undue hardship may apply. The court may in its discretion schedule a hearing regarding any reaffirmation agreement, even if the debtor's attorney certifies that the reaffirmation agreement does not impose an undue hardship on the debtor.

(b) Reaffirmation Without Attorney Certification. If a presumption of undue hardship under § 524(m) applies and the debtor's attorney has not certified that the agreement does not impose an undue hardship, either the debtor or the creditor must file a separate motion for approval of the reaffirmation agreement. The motion must be accompanied by the papers specified in § 524(k)(1) and F.R.Bankr.P. 4008. The motion must be titled and filed in the ECF event, "Motion for Approval of Reaffirmation—Presumption of Undue Hardship Applies." The court will schedule a hearing with notice to the debtor and the creditor.

(c) Reaffirmation by a Debtor Not Represented by an Attorney in the Case. If a reaffirmation agreement is filed and the debtor is not represented by an attorney in the bankruptcy case, the debtor must sign a motion for approval of the reaffirmation agreement under § 524(k)(7), attached as Part E. The reaffirmation agreement, including Parts A—E, must be filed in ECF with the event "Reaffirmation Agreement by Debtor Not Represented by An Attorney." The court will schedule a hearing with notice to the debtor and the creditor. The creditor may file the motion even though the motion is signed by the debtor.

(d) Reaffirmation by a Debtor Represented by an Attorney Who Did Not Negotiate the Agreement. The requirements and procedures of subpart (c) of this rule apply to a reaffirmation agreement by a debtor represented by an attorney who did not negotiate the agreement.

[Effective October 17, 2005. Amended effective May 5, 2008; February 1, 2016.]

RULE 5005–1. ELECTRONIC FILING

All papers must be filed using the ECF Procedures. Paper Filings may be authorized only as provided in those procedures.

[Former Rule 5005–4 effective May 5, 2008. Renumbered and amended effective February 1, 2016.]

RULE 5010–1. MOTION TO REOPEN A BANKRUPTCY CASE

(a) A motion to reopen a closed bankruptcy case may be filed *ex parte*.

(b) After a case is closed, a debtor seeking to file either a Certification About Financial Management Course or a Certification Regarding Domestic Support Obligations must first file a motion to reopen the case. When a case is reopened to permit a debtor to file a missing paper, the debtor must file the missing paper within 14 days after entry of the order reopening the case. If the missing paper is not timely filed, the case will be closed again.

[Effective May 5, 2008. Amended effective February 1, 2016.]

RULE 5011–1. MOTION TO WITHDRAW THE REFERENCE

When filing a motion to withdraw the reference, the filing party must also file contemporaneously the form "Bankruptcy

Matter Civil Case Cover Sheet," available on the court's website.

[Effective February 1, 2016.]

RULE 5071-1. ADJOURNMENT OF A PRETRIAL CONFERENCE, HEARING OR TRIAL

Each judge's adjournment procedures are available on the court's website and must be followed as posted. If a judge has not posted adjournment procedures, the following procedures apply:

(a) Pretrial Conferences and Oral Arguments on Motions. The court will normally grant one adjournment of a pretrial conference or oral arguments on a motion upon a written stipulation of all interested parties. Where the interested parties stipulate, the court will consider further adjournments only upon a showing of good cause. Where the interested parties do not stipulate, a party requesting an adjournment must file a motion establishing good cause.

(b) Evidentiary Hearings or Trials. The court will consider an adjournment of an evidentiary hearing or a trial only on a motion or a stipulation of all interested parties, establishing good cause, submitted at least three Business Days before the hearing or trial. A motion must state whether opposing counsel objects to the requested adjournment.

(c) Submission of an Order. A proposed order adjourning the conference, the hearing or the trial must be submitted and must provide a blank space for the new date and time.

(d) Procedure Upon Adjournment. After entry, the movant must immediately serve the order on all interested parties whose counsel are not ECF Filers and file a certificate of service. If there is insufficient time for mailing notice of the order of adjournment, the moving party must personally or telephonically provide any required notice of the adjournment order.

[Effective May 5, 2008. Amended effective December 1, 2009; February 1, 2016.]

RULE 5072-1. CONDUCT IN COURT

Except as otherwise provided in these Local Rules, E.D. Mich. LR 83.31, entitled "Conduct in Federal Court Facilities," applies in the bankruptcy court facilities in this district.

[Effective May 5, 2008. Amended effective February 1, 2016.]

RULE 5073-1. ELECTRONIC DEVICES

Subject to security screening, the following may be carried into the bankruptcy court facilities: laptop or notebook computers, cellular telephones or tablets, personal digital assistants, pagers, calculators and portable dictating devices. These devices must be turned off in all courtrooms and chambers, except that: (1) computers may be used with the volume muted; (2) calculators may be used; and (3) personal digital assistants, cellular telephones, tablets and paging devices may be used only in the vibration or silent mode. Telephone communication in a courtroom is prohibited. In the Theodore Levin United States Courthouse in Detroit, the rules

of the United States District Court for the Eastern District of Michigan relating to electronic devices will apply.

[Effective October 1, 1998. Amended effective May 5, 2008; February 1, 2016.]

RULE 5077-1. REQUEST FOR A COURT TRANSCRIPT

A request for the preparation of a court transcript must be filed on a completed form "Transcript Order Form," available on the court's website.

[Effective May 5, 2008. Amended effective February 1, 2016.]

RULE 5081-1. TRANSACTIONS REQUIRING THE PAYMENT OF MONEY

ECF Filers must pay fees to the clerk by using the internet payment service authorized by the court. Payment of fees to the clerk by others must be in one of the following forms:

(a) cash (exact change only);

(b) cashier's check;

(c) money order;

(d) from attorneys and non-debtor businesses only-business checks; or

(e) credit card in accordance with the clerk's guidelines. Personal checks will not be accepted. Checks must be made payable to "Clerk, U.S. Bankruptcy Court."

[Effective October 1, 1998. Amended effective May 5, 2008; February 1, 2016.]

RULE 6004-1. USE, SALE OR LEASE OF ESTATE PROPERTY OTHER THAN CASH COLLATERAL

(a) Use, Sale or Lease By Notice. Except for the use of cash collateral, use, sale or lease of property of the estate must be effected in accordance with § 363, F.R.Bankr.P. 2002 and F.R.Bankr.P. 6004. The notice of use, sale or lease must be served by the trustee or debtor in possession as the case may be. The notice must include a statement that the deadline for filing an objection is 14 days from the date the notice is served. Neither a court proceeding nor an order is necessary to authorize the transactions set forth in the notice unless an objection is timely filed and is not formally withdrawn. The 14 day period in this subpart begins to run contemporaneously with the 21 day notice in F.R.Bankr. P. 2002(a)(2).

(b) Sale By Motion. A motion for authority to sell property free and clear of liens and other interests under F.R.Bankr.P. 6004(c), with liens and interests transferred to the proceeds of the sale, must be filed under Local Rule 9014-1 with service to all parties required under F.R.Bankr.P. 2002 and to all parties who have an interest in the property that is proposed to be sold. The movant must file a certificate of service.

(c) Approval of Sale Procedures. A motion for approval of procedures for the sale of assets must be filed with a completed form "Cover Sheet for Motion to Approve Sale

Procedures," available on the court's website. If a cover sheet is not filed as required, the court may enter an order striking or denying the motion without prejudice to the movant's right to refile the motion in compliance with this rule.

[Effective October 1, 1998. Amended effective May 5, 2008; December 1, 2009; February 1, 2016.]

RULE 6004–2. REQUEST FOR INCENTIVE COMPENSATION

If the debtor files a motion for entry of an order allowing incentive compensation for executives, employees or groups of employees, the motion must detail for each employee:

(a) the name of employee;

(b) the present position and responsibilities;

(c) whether the employee is an equity holder, creditor, debtor or guarantor of the debtor;

(d) the employee's work experience, with emphasis on how this experience qualifies or impacts the employee in the present position;

(e) the length of service with the debtor;

(f) the present compensation, including contractual bonuses and benefits, monetary and otherwise (any written employment agreement must be attached to the motion);

(g) the requested compensation (including benefits, monetary and otherwise);

(h) how the requested increase in compensation (or the amount requested) will benefit and impact the debtor;

(i) the consequences to the debtor of denying the request;

(j) the timing of the payment of the compensation and any conditions precedent;

(k) the terms of any job offer that the employee has received;

(*l*) if the requested payment is a severance payment to an insider, facts establishing that the requirements of § 503(c)(2) are met; and

(m) any other information relevant under § 503(c).

[Effective October 1, 1998. Amended effective May 5, 2008; February 1, 2016.]

RULE 6007–1. DISPOSITION OF THE BOOKS AND RECORDS OF A CHAPTER 7 DEBTOR

Unless otherwise ordered by the court or required by the Executive Office for United States Trustees, a chapter 7 trustee may dispose of the debtor's books and records in the trustee's possession 60 days after the entry of the order closing the estate. Notice of the proposed disposition of the debtor's books and records must be provided in the trustee's final report.

[Effective October 1, 1998. Amended effective May 5, 2008; February 1, 2016.]

RULE 6007–2. FEDERAL TAX REFUND IN A CHAPTER 7 CASE

Unless directed otherwise in writing by the trustee, the Internal Revenue Service may in the ordinary course of business make an income tax refund to a debtor in a chapter 7 case 60 days after the first date set for the meeting of creditors.

[Renumbered effective May 5, 2008.]

RULE 7004–1. SERVICE ON AN INSURED DEPOSITORY INSTITUTION

Unless one of the exceptions set forth in F.R.Bankr.P. 7004(h)(1)–(3) is applicable, service on an insured depository institution will be presumed proper if the summons and complaint in an adversary proceeding or a motion governed by F.R.Bankr.P. 9014 is made by serving a copy of the paper by certified mail addressed to either (a) an officer of the institution in care of the resident agent of the institution, or (b) the chief executive officer of the institution at the institution's principal place of business.

[Effective October 1, 1998. Amended effective May 5, 2008; February 1, 2016.]

RULE 7007–1.1 CORPORATE OWNERSHIP STATEMENT IN AN ADVERSARY PROCEEDING

A corporate ownership statement required by F.R.Bankr.P. 7007.1 must be filed as a separate paper, not as an attachment to another paper.

[Effective February 1, 2016.]

RULE 7016–1. THE JOINT FINAL PRETRIAL ORDER AND THE PREPARATION OF EXHIBITS

(a) Duty to Prepare Proposed Joint Final Pretrial Order. If the court orders the parties to prepare a proposed joint final pretrial order, it must be prepared in accordance with this rule. In a contested matter, the movant will be considered the plaintiff for purposes of this rule and the court will designate the other parties responsible to participate. Counsel for plaintiff must:

(1) convene a conference for all parties to confer and collaborate in formulating a concise proposed joint final pretrial order;

(2) compile and submit the proposed order; and

(3) file a stipulation to the entry of the proposed order signed by all parties.

If the plaintiff is without counsel, the defendant's counsel must perform these obligations. Unless the court orders otherwise, the deadline to file the stipulation and to submit the proposed order is seven days before the final pretrial conference or, if no final pretrial conference is scheduled, seven days before the hearing or trial. When entered, the order supersedes the pleadings and governs the course of trial unless modified by further order. The pretrial order must not be a vehicle for adding claims or defenses.

(b) Contents of Order. The proposed joint final pretrial order must contain, under the following numbered and captioned headings, the following:

(1) *Jurisdiction.* The parties must state the basis for bankruptcy court jurisdiction, whether the matter is core and whether jurisdiction is contested by any party.

(2) *Plaintiff's Claims.* The statement of the claim or claims of plaintiff must include legal theories.

(3) *Defendant's Claims.* The statement of the claim or claims of defendants or third parties must include legal theories.

(4) *Stipulation of Facts and Law.* The parties must state, in separately numbered paragraphs, all uncontested facts and all undisputed points of law.

(5) *Issues of Fact to Be Litigated.*

(6) *Issues of Law to Be Litigated.*

(7) *Evidence Problems Likely to Arise at Trial.* Each party must state its objections to exhibits and to the use of deposition testimony, including the objections required under F.R.Civ.P. 26(a)(3)(B).

(8) *Witnesses.* Each party must separately list all witnesses whom that party will call and all witnesses whom that party may call. A party may, without further notice, call a witness listed by another party as a "will call" witness. The list must state whether the witness is an expert and whether testimony will be offered by deposition. Only listed witnesses will be permitted to testify at trial, except for rebuttal witnesses whose testimony could not be reasonably anticipated before trial, or except for good cause shown.

(9) *Exhibits.* Each party must number and list each exhibit with appropriate identification according to subpart (e), below. Only listed exhibits will be considered for admission, except for rebuttal exhibits that could not be reasonably anticipated before trial, or except for good cause shown. The parties are encouraged to agree upon a joint list of exhibits, without duplicates, to be admitted.

(10) *Objections to Exhibits.* Each party must state its objections to the other party's listed exhibits. Objections not stated in the proposed order may be deemed waived and exhibits not objected to may be admitted into evidence.

(11) *Damages.* The parties must itemize all claimed damages and must specify damages that can be calculated from objective data. The parties must stipulate to those damages not in dispute.

(12) *Trial.*

(A) Jury or non-jury.

(B) Estimated length of trial.

(13) *Settlement or Mediation.* Counsel or a party without counsel must state that they have conferred and considered the possibility of settlement, giving the most recent place and date, and state the current status of negotiations and any plans for further discussions. They may request the court to schedule a settlement conference or mediation.

(14) *Filing of Trial Briefs, Proposed Findings of Fact and Requests for Jury Instructions.* Unless the court otherwise orders, at least three Business Days before trial, the parties must file trial briefs, proposed findings of fact and conclusions of law in a non-jury case or requests for instructions in a jury case.

(15) *Additional Requirements.* A judge, in an appropriate case, may add requirements to the proposed joint final pretrial order or may suspend application of this rule in whole or in part.

(16) *Juror Costs Attributable to Parties.* The court may assess juror expenses under E. D. Mich. LR 38.2.

(c) Failure to Cooperate. For failure to comply with the requirements of this rule or with the terms of the joint final pretrial order, the court may dismiss claims, enter a default judgment, refuse to permit witnesses to testify or to admit exhibits, assess costs and expenses including attorney fees or impose other appropriate sanctions.

(d) Pre–marking and Exchange of Documentary Exhibits. If there has been no final pretrial conference and at least one week's notice of the trial or the evidentiary hearing has been provided to counsel, then at least one Business Day prior to the trial or evidentiary hearing, counsel must arrange with the judge's chambers staff to have all documentary exhibits marked and must provide copies of all exhibits to opposing counsel. In any event, all proposed exhibits and an exhibit list must be provided to the court at the start of the trial or hearing and an extra copy of each exhibit must be available for witnesses' use during testimony. Unless the court orders otherwise, each party will be responsible for the care and custody of the party's own exhibits.

(e) Exhibit Identification. Exhibits must be marked using numbers for the plaintiff or movant and letters for the defendant or respondent. If the defendant has more than 26 exhibits, the defendant may use exhibit numbers starting, for example, with 101 or 1001. Each separate document must be separately marked. Grouping exhibits is strongly discouraged.

[Effective October 1, 1998. Amended effective May 5, 2008; December 1, 2009; February 1, 2016.]

RULE 7016–2. MEDIATION

(a) The Mediation Process. Upon its own initiative, the stipulation of the parties or a motion filed under Local Rule 9014–1, the court may order the parties to engage in mediation. If the court orders mediation on its own initiative, a party may within seven days file a motion under Local Rule 9014–1 objecting to mediation.

(1) If mediation is stipulated or ordered, the parties must choose one mediator from the court's panel of mediators. If that mediator is not available or has a conflict that the parties do not waive, the parties must choose another mediator. The parties may request the court's assistance in selecting a mediator if they cannot agree.

(2) When a mediator is chosen, the parties must submit a proposed mediation order for entry, unless the court has already entered a mediation order. If a mediation order has

not been entered by the time of the mediation, the mediator must submit a proposed mediation order. A form "Mediation Order" is available on the court's website.

(3) Mediation may be ordered at any time during the case. Mediation must be completed within 14 days after the entry of the mediation order or within such other time as the court has fixed in the mediation order.

(4) Unless otherwise ordered by the court, each of the parties to the mediation process must pay $200.00 to the mediator before or at the commencement of the mediation session. The mediator, with the consent of the parties, may retain professionals to assist the mediator. The expenses of such professionals must be equally paid by all parties to the mediation and may not exceed $2,000.00, unless otherwise ordered by the court.

(5) All proceedings and writings incident to the mediation will be privileged and confidential, and must not be reported or placed in evidence. No party will be bound by mediation unless a settlement is reached. If a settlement is reached, the agreement must be reduced to writing. If necessary, the parties must file a motion for approval of the settlement under F.R.Bankr.P. 9019 within 14 days after the agreement is fully executed.

(6) The mediator will have the duty and authority to establish the mediation process, including the submission of documents, the attendance of parties with authority to settle, the procedure governing the mediation and a schedule for the parties to act upon the mediator's recommendation. The mediator will have no obligation to make any written recommendation, but may provide the attorneys for the parties or unrepresented parties with a written settlement memorandum. Such memorandum will be governed by the first sentence of subpart (a)(5) and must not be filed or made available to the court. The mediator must not be called as a witness.

(7) Within seven days after the conclusion of the mediation, the mediator must file a certification (A) demonstrating that there has been compliance with the mediation requirements of this rule, and (B) stating whether a settlement was achieved, without referring to any substantive matters involved in the mediation.

(b) The Mediation Panel.

(1) The court will appoint mediators to the mediation panel as necessary from time to time. The court may select one or more chairpersons to assist the court with the administration of the mediation panel.

(2) Before serving as a mediator, a professional must have participated in a court-approved training seminar in alternative dispute resolution and must provide to the court a certificate of such training. The clerk will maintain a list of such seminars.

(3) A list of the mediators on the panel is maintained by the clerk and is available on the court's website.

(4) Individuals who wish to serve on the mediation panel must inform the clerk in writing and must provide the clerk with information that the applicant or the court deems pertinent.

(5) The court may meet periodically with the panel of mediators or its chairpersons as necessary to discuss improving the mediation process.

[Effective October 1, 1998. Amended effective November 21, 2002; May 5, 2008; December 1, 2009; February 1, 2016.]

RULE 7026–1. FILING DISCOVERY

(a) Discovery to be Filed. The following must be filed: deposition notices; interrogatories; requests for the production of documents, and the responses thereto; and requests for admissions and the responses thereto.

(b) Discovery Not to be Filed. Except to the extent necessary in support or defense of a contested matter or an adversary proceeding, the following must not be filed: deposition transcripts; answers to interrogatories; and documents produced in response to a request for the production of documents.

[Effective October 1, 1998. Amended effective December 1, 2000 by Administrative Order No. 00–04; May 5, 2008; February 1, 2016.]

RULE 7026–2. FURNISHING AN ELECTRONIC FORMATTED DISCOVERY REQUEST

Upon the request of a party responding to interrogatories, a request for documents or a request for admissions, the party serving the discovery request must, if feasible, furnish the discovery request in Word or WordPerfect format (not PDF format), as designated by the responding party, so that the responding party need not re-type these discovery requests to prepare a response.

[Effective May 5, 2008. Amended effective February 1, 2016.]

RULE 7026–3. DISCOVERY IN A CONTESTED MATTER

Discovery in a contested matter is permitted only upon a court order for cause shown.

[Effective May 5, 2008.]

RULE 7026–4. DISCOVERY OF ELECTRONICALLY STORED INFORMATION

Unless the court orders otherwise, in any adversary proceeding or contested matter where discovery involves the exchange of electronically stored information, the Model Order Relating To The Discovery Of Electronically Stored Information approved by the United States District Court for the Eastern District of Michigan on September 20, 2013, subject to any amendments or revisions made to such Model Order by the United States District Court for the Eastern District of Michigan, will apply.

[Effective February 1, 2016.]

RULE 7041–1. DISMISSAL OF A COMPLAINT OBJECTING TO THE DISCHARGE OF THE DEBTOR

When the parties to an action under § 727 propose to dismiss the action, they must file a joint statement of the consideration received or to be received by the plaintiff. The plaintiff must then serve the joint statement on all creditors and the trustee, with a notice stating that the deadline to file objections is 14 days after service, and file a certificate of service. If no timely objection is filed, the plaintiff must promptly file a certificate of no response and submit the agreed proposed dismissal order. If a timely response is filed, the court will set the matter for hearing. An original signature from a pro se party is not necessary to authorize the filing of a joint statement under this rule; a fax, email or written signature or consent is sufficient.

[Effective October 1, 1998. Amended effective May 5, 2008; December 1, 2009; February 1, 2016.]

RULE 7054–1. PROCEDURE TO OBTAIN FEES AND COSTS UNDER F.R.BANKR.P. 7054

(a) Unless the court orders otherwise, a party who has been awarded attorney fees and related nontaxable costs under F.R.Bankr.P. 7054(b) must, within 14 days after the award, file an application for allowance of the fees and costs with the following information stated separately:

(1) the total amount of fees sought to be awarded;

(2) the amount of expenses to be awarded;

(3) the time period during which the services for which the award is sought were rendered;

(4) a summary statement of the number of hours of service rendered by each professional and paraprofessional and the hourly rates of each;

(5) an itemized time record in chronological order of each specific service for which an award is sought. This itemized time record must:

(i) state the date each service was rendered;

(ii) identify the professional or paraprofessional who performed the service; and

(iii) describe with particularity the services rendered; and

(6) an itemized statement of expenses for which reimbursement is sought.

In addition, the application must include a proposed order awarding and ordering payment of the fees and costs, and a certificate of service.

(b) Any party opposing the allowance or payment of the fees and costs will have 14 days from service of the application to object.

(c) If no objection is timely filed, the court may grant the application without a hearing.

(d) Any objection must specify in detail the nature and basis of the objection and the amount, if any, that is not disputed. Pending resolution of the objection, the court may enter an order awarding and ordering the payment of any undisputed fees and costs.

(e) The initial hearing on the application will not be an evidentiary hearing. If the court determines that an evidentiary hearing is needed, the court will schedule a separate evidentiary hearing.

[Effective February 1, 2016.]

RULE 7055–1. DEFAULT JUDGMENT

The deadline to file an application for the entry of a default judgment and submit a proposed default judgment is 14 days after the clerk has entered the opposing party's default. The application for the default judgment need not be served on the party in default unless the court orders otherwise or unless service is required by F.R.Civ.P. 55(b).

[Effective October 1, 1998. Amended effective May 5, 2008; December 1, 2009.]

RULE 7067–1. DEPOSIT, WITHDRAWAL AND INVESTMENT OF FUNDS IN THE COURT REGISTRY INVESTMENT SYSTEM

(a) Deposit Order. A proposed order for deposit of funds into the Court Registry Investment System ("CRIS") must state:

(1) the amount to be deposited;

(2) that the deposit is being made pursuant to 28 U.S.C. § 2041;

(3) that funds on deposit in CRIS are administered by the Administrative Office of the United States Court ("AOUSC") pursuant to 28 U.S.C. § 2045;

(4) that an account for the case, including case name and number, will be established in the CRIS titled in the name of the case giving rise to the investment in the fund;

(5) that the director of AOUSC, as custodian for CRIS, is authorized and directed to deduct the investment service fee for the management of investments in CRIS and the registry fee for maintaining accounts deposited with the court.

(b) Order for Withdrawal of Funds. A proposed order for withdrawal of funds held in CRIS must state:

(1) the names, addresses and last four digits of the social security or full employer identification numbers of the recipients of the funds;

(2) the amount of any fee payable to the United States in accordance with the CRIS fee schedule; and

(3) the amount of principal and interest to be paid to each recipient.

The proposed order must be submitted to the clerk or to the clerk's designee for approval as to form before it is submitted to the judge. After entry, the moving party must deliver the order to the clerk.

(c) Receipt of Funds.

(1) Money must not be sent to the court or its officers for deposit in the court's registry without an order signed by the presiding judge in the case.

(2) The party making the deposit or transferring the funds to the court's registry must serve the order permitting the deposit or transfer on the clerk of the court.

(d) Investment of Registry Funds. Where, by order of the court, funds on deposit with the court are to be placed in some form of interest-bearing account, the CRIS, administered by the AOUSC under 28 U.S.C. § 2045 will be the only investment mechanism authorized.

(e) Transition From Former Investment Procedures. Parties not wishing to transfer certain existing registry deposits into the CRIS may seek leave to transfer them to the litigants or their designees on motion for approval of the judge assigned to the specific case.

[Effective October 1, 1998. Amended effective December 1, 2003; May 5, 2008; February 1, 2016; December 6, 2016; December 1, 2017.]

RULE 8001–1. TRANSMITTING A BANKRUPTCY MATTER TO THE DISTRICT COURT

When filing a notice of appeal or a motion for leave to appeal, the filing party must also file with the bankruptcy court the form "District Court Bankruptcy Matter Civil Case Cover Sheet," available on the court's website.

[Effective October 1, 1998. Amended effective May 5, 2008; February 1, 2016.]

RULE 9001–1. DEFINITIONS

(a) Large Bankruptcy Cases. Upon a motion or the court's own initiative, the court may enter an order without a hearing designating a chapter 11 case as a "Large Bankruptcy Case."

(b) First Day Motion. A "First Day Motion" is a motion filed within the first 14 days after an order for relief in a chapter 11 case and designated as such under Local Rule 9013–1. It is a motion that the debtor believes is so important to the initial stages of the case that the best interests of the bankruptcy estate warrant granting a hearing on the motion upon shortened or limited notice.

(c) ECF Terms. The terms defined in the court's ECF Procedures have the same meanings herein.

(d) Business Day. A Business Day is a day when the court is open for business. A Business Day does not include a Saturday, a Sunday, a legal holiday such as New Year's Day, Birthday of Martin Luther King, Jr., Washington's Birthday, Memorial Day, Independence Day, Labor Day, Columbus Day, Veterans Day, Thanksgiving Day, Christmas Day, any other day appointed as a holiday by the President or the Congress of the United States, or by the State of Michigan, or a day on which weather or other conditions have made the Clerk's Office inaccessible.

[Effective January 3, 2005. Amended effective October 17, 2005; May 5, 2008; December 1, 2009.]

RULE 9004–1. THE CAPTION AND FILING OF PAPERS

(a) Caption. The caption on a paper must substantially conform to the applicable official form (if any) and must also state:

(1) the chapter number under which the petition is pending;

(2) the judge to whom the case is assigned;

(3) a concise statement of the nature of the document and:

(A) for a motion, identification of the movant and specific relief sought; and

(B) for a response, identification of the respondent and the title of the motion to which the response is directed, including the name of the movant and the specific relief sought.

(b) Paper Filings. When a Paper Filing is filed with the clerk of the court, such filing may only be made in accordance with the ECF Procedures. The paper, other than a proof of claim, may use only one side of a page and under the signature line must state any attorney's name, mailing address and telephone number and the name of the client. The pages, excluding exhibits, must be numbered.

(c) Use of Forms. The use of a form pleading that contains extraneous factual allegations or legal arguments not applicable to the matter before the court may subject the individual who submits it to sanctions under F.R.Bankr.P. 9011. Factual allegations in pleadings must be made with the proper respect for the applicable rules regarding relevance, specificity and accuracy.

[Former Rule 9004–2 effective October 1, 1998. Amended effective May 5, 2008. Renumbered and amended effective February 1, 2016.]

RULE 9006–1. REDUCTION OR ENLARGEMENT OF TIME

(a) Motion for Extension of Time Under F.R.Bankr.P. 1007(c) or F.R.Bankr.P. 3015(b).

(1) Before filing a motion for extension of time to file papers under F.R.Bankr.P. 1007(c) or to file a chapter 13 plan under F.R.Bankr.P. 3015(b), the movant must request the concurrence of the trustee, if any, or if no trustee has been appointed, the United States trustee.

(2) The motion must state:

(A) the date set for the meeting of creditors;

(B) the date on which the movant intends to file the papers;

(C) the grounds establishing good cause for the relief sought;

(D) that an objection to the relief requested in the motion must be filed within three Business Days of filing of the motion; and

(E) the efforts made by the moving party to obtain concurrence.

(3) The deadline to file an objection is three Business Days after the motion is filed. Upon the filing of an objection, the

court will schedule an expedited hearing with notice to the movant and the objecting party.

(4) The movant may submit a proposed order granting the relief requested after the movant files a certification that no response was timely filed.

(5) If the movant obtains concurrence under subpart (1), the movant may file a stipulation for the entry of a proposed order and submit a proposed order for entry by the court.

(b) Any Other Reduction or Enlargement of Time. Unless prohibited by F.R.Bankr.P. 9006 and to the extent otherwise permitted by the Code and the Federal Rules of Bankruptcy Procedure, a party may file a motion for an *ex parte* order reducing or enlarging the time for a party to take any action or file any paper. Prior to making the motion, if the motion is made in an adversary proceeding or a contested matter, the movant must attempt to obtain the acquiescence of opposing counsel, unless unduly burdensome. The movant must also immediately notify opposing counsel personally or by telephone of the entry of the order and must serve the order on any opposing counsel who does not receive service by ECF and file a certificate of service. A party aggrieved by such an order may move for a dissolution of the order.

[Effective October 1, 1998. Amended effective May 5, 2008; June 25, 2008; December 1, 2009; February 1, 2016.]

RULE 9010–1. APPEARANCE BEFORE THE COURT AND AT A MEETING OF CREDITORS

(a) Appearance by Attorney.

(1) Except as otherwise provided by law, appearance before the court on behalf of a person or entity may be made only by an attorney admitted to the bar of, or permitted to practice before, the United States District Court for the Eastern District of Michigan, under E. D. Mich. LR 83.20. A corporation, partnership or other entity other than an individual may not file a petition or other paper, nor appear as a debtor, plaintiff, defendant or other party in an adversary proceeding, unless it is represented by an attorney duly admitted to, and in good standing with, the bar of the United States District Court for this district. The following do not constitute the practice of law for purposes of these rules:

(A) the signing or filing of a request for notice;

(B) the signing or filing of a proof of claim or a ballot;

(C) the attendance and participation at a meeting of creditors or of an official committee;

(D) the signing or filing of a pleading or paper resolving an objection to a proof of claim;

(E) the signing or filing of a stipulation adjourning a hearing or extending a deadline; or

(F) the filing of an appearance under Local Rule 2002–3.

(2) An attorney appearing before the court is expected to have read and to be familiar with the Federal Rules of Bankruptcy Procedure, these rules, the ECF Procedures, the rules of the United States District Court for the Eastern District of Michigan and the Civility Principles. Unless otherwise instructed by the court, counsel must:

(A) at the onset of the hearing, place the attorney's name on the record and state the name of the party that the attorney represents;

(B) stand when speaking or when addressed by the judge;

(C) speak in the vicinity of a microphone;

(D) refrain from confrontation or colloquy with opposing counsel;

(E) address all persons by their surnames;

(F) state all objections concisely and with specificity; and

(G) be fully prepared and knowledgeable of the issues and matters to be addressed.

(b) Required Appearance by Debtor's Attorney or Firm of Record. The debtor's attorney or firm of record must, except as provided in subpart (c) below, attend and represent the debtor at the meeting of creditors, any hearing on any reaffirmation agreement and all hearings within the scope of representation. The appearing attorney must have sufficient familiarity and knowledge of the case and its prior proceedings as to permit informed discussion and argument.

(c) Attorney Appearing on Behalf of Attorney of Record. An attorney whose appearance in a particular hearing or a meeting of creditors is made at the request of the debtor's attorney of record must file prior to such appearance a written notice of special appearance and a completed form "Statement of Attorney for Debtor(s) Under F.R.Bankr.P. 2016(b)," available on the court's website. At the time of appearance, the attorney must furnish, on request, a copy of the notice of appearance that evidences the fact of filing. An attorney making a special appearance will be accountable for adequately representing the interests of the person or entity on whose behalf the appearance is made.

(d) Disclosure of Scope of Representation of Debtor's Attorney. The attorney for a debtor must file a completed form "Statement of Attorney for Debtor(s) Under F.R.Bankr.P. 2016(b)," available on the court's website, in which the scope of the attorney's appearance and representation must be accurately stated. The "Statement of Attorney for Debtor(s) Under F.R.Bankr.P. 2016(b)" must be countersigned by the debtor.

(e) Scope of Appearance of Debtor's Attorney in a Chapter 9, 11, 12 or 13 Case. The attorney for a debtor under chapter 9, 11, 12 or 13, is presumed to appear for the case and all proceedings in the case, unless otherwise ordered by the court, and has a continuing duty to represent the debtor in all proceedings in the bankruptcy court, including relief from automatic stay motions, hearings on claims or adversary proceedings, until the occurrence of the earliest of:

(1) dismissal of the case;

(2) closing of the case; or

(3) the entry of an order allowing the attorney to withdraw from further representation of the debtor.

(f) Scope of Appearance of Debtor's Attorney in a Chapter 7 Case. In a case filed under or converted to chapter 7, the scope of appearance of the debtor's attorney will be as disclosed in the F.R.Bankr.P. 2016(b) statement, as may be amended from time to time.

(g) Withdrawal of Attorney.

(1) An attorney who has appeared on behalf of a party may not withdraw without permission of the court. A request for permission to withdraw may be made by stipulation between the attorney and the party or upon motion filed under Local Rule 9014–1. Immediately upon the entry of an order permitting the attorney's withdrawal, the attorney must serve it on parties in interest, file a certificate of service, and to the extent available, provide the parties' contact information and telephone number to opposing counsel upon withdrawal in an adversary proceeding, and to the trustee upon withdrawal in a bankruptcy case.

(2) Except as required under subpart (g)(1), no order is required for a consensual substitution of attorney that is signed by the represented party, the withdrawing attorney and the substituting attorney. A notice of substitution of attorney must be filed and served on the trustee and any interested parties involved in pending litigation.

(h) Required Approval for Employment. If an order approving the employment of the withdrawing attorney under § 327 or § 1103 was required, any new attorney must also comply with F.R.Bankr.P. 2014; the employment will not be deemed approved merely by filing a notice of substitution of attorney.

(i) Appearance for Settlement Purposes Only. Local counsel need not appear solely to sign and file a paper resolving a contested matter or an adversary proceeding.

[Effective October 1, 1998. Amended effective January 3, 2005; May 5, 2008; February 1, 2016.]

RULE 9010–2. RESTRICTION ON THE LAW PRACTICE OF A FORMER LAW CLERK

(a) A Former Law Clerk for a Specific Bankruptcy Judge. A former law clerk for a judge in this district may not appear before that judge for two years after such service or participate in any capacity in any case that was pending before that judge during the clerkship.

(b) A Former Law Clerk for the Court. A former law clerk for the court, such as a shared law clerk, may not appear before any judge in the district for six months after such service or participate in any capacity in any case that was pending during the clerkship.

(c) A Former Law Clerk's Firm. The prohibitions of subparts (a) and (b) do not extend to an individual or entity that employs a former law clerk, nor to its partners, members or associates.

[Former Rule 9010–3 effective May 5, 2008. Renumbered and amended effective February 1, 2016.]

RULE 9011–1. SANCTIONS

For failure to comply with any applicable rules, sanctions may be imposed upon: (1) any counsel appearing before the court; (2) any person appearing without counsel; (3) any person acting in a fiduciary capacity in a case or proceeding; and (4) other professional persons whose employment was approved by the court. Sanctions in the form of an admonition, the assessment of costs or any other sanction deemed appropriate may be imposed upon notice and opportunity for hearing when it is determined that such non-compliance has obstructed the effective conduct of the business of the court. These sanctions are in addition to the sanctions that the court may impose upon counsel under E. D. Mich. LR 11.1, the Federal Rules of Bankruptcy Procedure or the Federal Rules of Civil Procedure.

[Former Rule 9011–3 effective October 1, 1998. Renumbered effective February 1, 2016.]

RULE 9013–1. FIRST DAY MOTIONS

(a) Filing Requirements. The title of each First Day Motion and of each proposed order granting a First Day Motion must contain the words "First Day." When filing the motion through ECF, the debtor's counsel must select the prefix "First Day." The debtor's counsel must promptly notify the judge's courtroom deputy clerk that First Day Motions have been filed. The term "First Day Motion" must also be included on all exhibits, budgets, proposed orders, affidavits and all other papers that the debtor files in support of a First Day Motion.

(b) Service of Motion. A First Day Motion and all related papers must be served on the United States trustee, all secured creditors, the creditors included on the list filed under F.R.Bankr.P. 1007(d) and any adverse party relative to the relief requested in the First Day Motion. This service must be completed within 24 hours after the First Day Motion is filed even if the hearing on the First Day Motion has not yet been scheduled by the court. First Day Motions must also be served by:

(1) transmission to a Registered Filer or User consistent with F.R.Bankr.P. 9036 and ECF Procedure 4(e);

(2) hand delivery;

(3) delivery by overnight delivery service;

(4) facsimile transmission to the extent that facsimile number(s) are available; or

(5) email to the extent that email addresses are available.

The movant must promptly file a certificate of service.

(c) Scheduling a Hearing. The movant is not required to file a separate motion for an expedited hearing on a First Day Motion. The movant must submit a proposed order scheduling the First Day Motions for hearing, leaving blank the hearing date and time. As expeditiously as possible, the court will determine whether each motion qualifies as a First Day Motion and will enter an order scheduling a prompt hearing on those that do. The order may specify the means and deadline for service of the notice of hearing. The movant must serve the order scheduling the hearing on the parties and by the means identified in subpart (b) and file a certificate of service.

[Effective January 3, 2005. Amended effective May 5, 2008; February 1, 2016.]

RULE 9013–2. FIXED HEARING DATES IN A LARGE BANKRUPTCY CASE

(a) Motion to Establish Fixed Hearing Dates. Upon motion of the debtor, the court may enter an order establishing fixed dates and times as the scheduled hearing date and time for consideration of all motions and contested matters in a Large Bankruptcy Case.

(b) Procedure for Fixed Hearing Dates. If the court establishes fixed dates, the following procedures will apply unless the court orders otherwise:

(1) any notice of an opportunity to object must conspicuously contain above the title of the notice the date and time that the hearing will be held in the event that an objection is filed in accordance with applicable rules;

(2) any motion or contested matter filed and properly served in accordance with applicable rules and as to which the applicable response time will elapse at least three Business Days before a fixed hearing date, may be set for hearing on such a fixed date;

(3) if the requisite time period set forth in Local Rule 9014–1(b)(1) has passed, the movant may file a certificate of no response and then must submit a proposed order and promptly notify the court that a hearing on the motion is unnecessary;

(4) debtor's counsel must file and serve on all affected parties at least seven days before the hearing a list of all matters scheduled to be considered by the court and file a certificate of service. The list must set forth all motions and responses and whether the matter is resolved, disputed or adjourned;

(5) if a party intends to present a proposed order at the hearing different from the proposed order attached to the motion, debtor's counsel must state on the list filed in accordance with subpart (b)(4) above that a different proposed order will be presented for entry;

(6) debtor's counsel together with any affected party or parties may, without leave of the court, unless the court orders otherwise, adjourn any matter to a subsequent fixed hearing date. If a matter is adjourned, debtor's counsel must immediately update the list filed in accordance with subpart (b)(4) above; and

(7) upon request, the court may allow counsel to participate in any hearing by telephone.

(c) Other Hearing Dates. The establishment of fixed dates for hearings does not preclude any party in interest from requesting and obtaining a different date for a hearing on a particular matter.

[Former Rule 9013–4 effective January 3, 2005. Amended effective May 5, 2008; December 1, 2009. Renumbered and amended effective February 1, 2016.]

RULE 9013–3. CORPORATE OWNERSHIP STATEMENT IN A CONTESTED MATTER

A corporation that is a party to a contested matter must file, contemporaneous with the filing of its first paper in such contested matter, a statement of corporate ownership that contains the information required by F.R.Bankr.P. 7007.1 for a corporation that is a party to an adversary proceeding. The corporate ownership statement must be filed as a separate paper, not as an attachment to another paper. A party subject to this rule must file a supplemental statement promptly upon any change in circumstances that this rule requires the party to identify or disclose.

[Former Rule 9013–5 effective January 3, 2005. Amended effective May 5, 2008. Amended effective February 1, 2016.]

RULE 9014–1. MOTION PROCEDURE GENERALLY

(a) Motion Required. Unless permitted otherwise by applicable rule, a party seeking relief must file a motion. This rule also applies to a fee application under Local Rule 2016–1(a) or (b). For purposes of this rule, an objection to a claim of exemption will be deemed to be a motion.

(b) Deadline for Response. Except as otherwise ordered by the court or applicable rule, the deadline to respond to any motion is 14 days after service (21 days after service for matters covered by F.R.Bankr.P. 2002(a)).

(c) Attachments. The moving party must attach the following to the motion:

(1) a copy of the proposed order, labeled as Exhibit 1;

(2) a completed form "Notice of Motion and Opportunity to Object," available on the court's website, labeled as Exhibit 2, stating that: the deadline to file an objection to the motion is within 14 days (21 days for matters covered by F.R.Bankr.P. 2002(a)) after service; objections must comply with F.R.Civ.P. 8(b), (c) and (e); and if an objection is not timely filed, the court may grant the motion without a hearing;

(3) a brief, when required under subpart (f), labeled as Exhibit 3;

(4) a certificate of service showing service on those parties entitled to service under ECF Procedure 12(b), labeled as Exhibit 4;

(5) affidavits, labeled as Exhibit 5; and

(6) documentary exhibits, labeled as Exhibit 6.

(d) No Timely Response. If a response is not timely filed, the movant may file a certification of no response so stating, attaching thereto a copy of the original certificate of service, and may submit the proposed order. The movant may file a certification of no response only after the deadline for response has passed, including the addition of days to the deadline in order to comply with F.R.Bankr.P. 9006(a) and (f). The court may enter the submitted proposed order without a hearing. If the court decides not to enter the proposed order, the court will schedule a hearing with notice to the movant and the other parties that are entitled to notice, unless the court determines that a hearing is unnecessary to resolve the motion.

(e) Timely Response. If a response is timely filed, the court will schedule a hearing with notice to the movant and all respondents, unless the court determines that a hearing is unnecessary to resolve the motion.

(f) Briefing Requirements. A brief, not more than 25 pages in length, including footnotes and signatures, must be filed in support of and in opposition to the following:

(1) a motion in an adversary proceeding;

(2) a motion for relief from stay or abandonment in a chapter 11 case;

(3) a motion for the appointment of a trustee or examiner in a chapter 11 case;

(4) an objection to a claim of exemptions; or

(5) a motion for payment of pre-petition claims.

Unless otherwise ordered by the court, there is no requirement to file a brief in support of or in opposition to other types of motions. A reply brief of not more than seven pages in length, including footnotes and signatures, may be filed and served not less than three Business Days before the hearing on the motion. A party seeking to file a brief in excess of the page length in this rule, must file an *ex parte* motion requesting permission to do so, setting forth the reasons to do so and specifying the page length for such brief.

(g) Rule Not Applicable. This rule does not apply to:

(1) an objection to claim under Local Rule 3007–1;

(2) a motion for reconsideration under Local Rule 9024–1(a);

(3) a motion to amend an order or judgment under Local Rule 9024–1(b);

(4) a motion to reinstate a dismissed case under Local Rule 9024–1(c);

(5) a motion to reduce or enlarge time under Local Rule 9006–1, including a motion for extension of time to file papers under Local Rule 9006–1(a);

(6) a motion to withdraw the reference under F.R.Bankr.P. 5011(a);

(7) a motion for leave to appeal under F.R.Bankr.P. 8004;

(8) a motion to dismiss under Local Rule 2003–1;

(9) a motion to dismiss under Local Rule 1017–2;

(10) a matter covered by Local Rule 1007–3(a) and (b), relating to credit counseling compliance;

(11) a motion seeking approval of a reaffirmation agreement under Local Rule 4008–1;

(12) an application to waive the filing fee;

(13) an application to pay the filing fee in installments;

(14) a motion to extend the stay under Local Rule 4001–4(a);

(15) a motion to order the stay to take effect under Local Rule 4001–4(b);

(16) a motion to reopen a case to file missing papers under Local Rule 5010–1;

(17) a motion for a default judgment under Local Rule 7055–1;

(18) a motion to file by Paper Filing under ECF Procedure 3(b); or

(19) a motion for an order restricting public access to a paper that contains unredacted information in violation of F.R.Bankr.P. 9037(a).

(h) Statement of Concurrence Sought. In an adversary proceeding, or in a bankruptcy case unless it is unduly burdensome, the motion must affirmatively state that concurrence of opposing counsel in the relief sought has been requested on a specified date and that the concurrence was denied.

(i) Discovery Motions. With respect to a matter relating to discovery to which F.R.Bankr.P. 7026 through 7037 apply, counsel for each of the parties must meet and confer in advance of the hearing in a good faith effort to narrow the areas of disagreement. The conference must be held a sufficient time in advance of the hearing so as to enable the parties to narrow the areas of disagreement to the greatest extent possible. It is the responsibility of counsel for the movant to arrange for the conference and, in the absence of an agreement to the contrary, the conference must be held in the office of the attorney nearest to the court in which the motion is pending.

(j) Withdrawal of a Motion. After a response has been filed, a motion may be withdrawn only upon stipulation of the moving and responding parties or a court order.

(k) Evidentiary hearings. Unless the court orders otherwise, the initial hearing on a contested matter will not be an evidentiary hearing. The court may determine at the initial hearing whether an evidentiary hearing is necessary and, if so, will schedule it at that initial hearing. No further notice of the evidentiary hearing need be served.

[Effective October 1, 1998. Amended effective October 17, 2005; December 13, 2005; October 21, 2006; May 5, 2008; December 1, 2009; February 1, 2016; September 28, 2017; December 1, 2017.]

RULE 9015–1. JURY TRIAL DEMAND AND CONSENT

(a) In a Contested Matter or Adversary Proceeding Initiated in Bankruptcy Court. A party who demands a jury trial in a contested matter or adversary proceeding initiated in the bankruptcy court must indicate in its jury trial demand whether it consents to the bankruptcy judge conducting the jury trial. Any other party has until 14 days after the later of (a) the service of a jury demand, or (b) the deadline to file an answer or other responsive pleading, to file a statement indicating whether it consents to the bankruptcy judge conducting the jury trial. Any party that does not timely file a statement indicating that it does not consent to the bankruptcy judge conducting the jury trial, will be deemed to have consented to the bankruptcy judge conducting the jury trial.

(b) In an Adversary Proceeding Removed From State Court in Which a Jury Trial Demand Was Timely Filed. In an adversary proceeding removed from state court in which a jury trial demand was timely filed, the jury demand need not be re-filed in this court to be effective. A party will be deemed to have consented to the bankruptcy judge conducting the jury trial unless, within 28 days after the removal, the party files a statement indicating that it does not consent to the bankruptcy judge conducting the jury trial.

(c) In an Adversary Proceeding Removed from State Court in Which a Jury Trial Demand Was Not Filed and the Time to File Has Not Yet Expired. In an adversary proceeding removed from state court in which a jury trial demand was not filed and the time to file a jury demand under applicable state law has not expired, the deadline to file a jury demand is 28 days after the removal. If a jury trial demand is filed, the parties' consents to the bankruptcy judge conducting the jury trial will be determined under the provisions of subpart (a).

(d) Motion to Withdraw the Reference or Motion to Strike Jury Demand. With respect to subparts (a), (b) and (c) of this rule, if all parties do not consent to the bankruptcy judge conducting a jury trial, at the initial hearing on a contested matter, or at the initial status conference held in an adversary proceeding, the court may consider setting a deadline for the filing of a motion to withdraw the reference or a motion to strike the jury demand.

[Effective October 1, 1998. Amended effective May 5, 2008; December 1, 2009; February 1, 2016.]

RULE 9019–1. SETTLEMENT

Counsel must notify the court immediately upon the settlement of an adversary proceeding or contested matter. If, by the date set for the trial or hearing, the attorneys have not submitted a proposed order disposing of the matter, then the attorneys must appear and state the settlement on the record, and must submit a proposed order within 14 days. Failure to submit a proposed order within 14 days is cause for dismissal.

[Effective October 1, 1998. Amended effective May 5, 2008; December 1, 2009; February 1, 2016.]

RULE 9021–1. ENTRY OF AN ORDER OR JUDGMENT IN A CONTESTED MATTER OR ADVERSARY PROCEEDING

(a) Procedure for the Entry of an Order or Judgment. An order or judgment may be entered by one of the following methods:

(1) upon notice to the parties, the court may prepare and enter an order or a Text Order;

(2) the court may at the hearing excuse presentment of a proposed order or judgment for approval;

(3) the court may enter a proposed order or judgment when a stipulation to its form is filed and if, in the court's determination, it conforms with the court's decision; or

(4) unless the court has excused presentment for approval, the prevailing party must file a proposed order or judgment with a notice that it will be submitted for entry if written objections are not filed within seven days.

(A) If a written objection is not timely filed and served, the prevailing party must file a certification that no objections have been filed and must submit the proposed judgment or order. If the proposed judgment or order conforms with the decision, the court may then enter it. If the proposed judgment or order does not conform with the

decision, the court may schedule a hearing with notice to the parties.

(B) If an objection is filed, a proposed order must be attached. The court will schedule a hearing with notice to the parties, unless the court determines that a hearing is unnecessary to resolve the matter.

(C) If all filed objections to a proposed order are withdrawn, then the court may enter the proposed order or judgment under subpart (a)(4)(A).

(5) If the prevailing party fails to act within a reasonable time, any other party may prepare the proposed order or judgment and follow the appropriate steps for entry.

(b) Costs. The court may impose costs upon any party or attorney who:

(1) unreasonably withholds approval as to form;

(2) files a frivolous objection under this rule; or

(3) submits a proposed order that does not reasonably conform with the court's decision.

(c) Order Granting Different Relief. When the court enters an order granting relief different from that requested, the court may require the prevailing party to serve a copy of the order on all parties who are not served through ECF and who might be materially and adversely affected by the difference. In such case, the party serving the order must include, with the copy of the order, a notice that a request for a rehearing must be filed and served within a time period that will be fixed by the court. Unless the court orders otherwise, until such period is concluded, the order will be stayed insofar as it affects parties not present at the hearing of the underlying motion.

[Effective October 1, 1998. Amended effective May 5, 2008; February 1, 2016.]

RULE 9024–1. POST–JUDGMENT MOTIONS

(a) A Motion for Reconsideration.

(1) *Deadline.* The deadline to file a motion for reconsideration of an order or judgment on the grounds that it was erroneous in fact or law is 14 days after the entry of the order or judgment.

(2) *No Response and No Hearing Allowed.* No response to the motion and no oral argument thereon will be allowed unless the court otherwise orders.

(3) *Grounds.* Generally, and without restricting the discretion of the court, a motion for reconsideration that merely presents the same issues ruled upon by the court, either expressly or by reasonable implication, will not be granted. The movant must not only demonstrate a palpable defect by which the court and the parties have been misled but also show that a different disposition of the case must result from a correction thereof.

(4) *Brief.* The movant must file a brief in support of the motion not exceeding 25 pages in length.

(5) *Application.* Subparts (a)(1)–(4) do not apply to a motion to reconsider an order disallowing a claim under F.R.Bankr.P. 3008.

(b) A Motion to Amend an Order or Judgment. If a motion is filed to amend an order or a judgment under F.R.Civ.P. 59(e), no response may be filed and no oral argument will be scheduled unless the court so orders.

(c) A Motion to Reinstate a Dismissed Case. If a motion is filed to reinstate a dismissed case on the grounds that the default that caused the dismissal has been or can be cured, no response may be filed and no oral argument will be scheduled unless the court so orders. A motion to reopen a closed case to file missing papers is covered by Local Rule 5010–1.

(d) Other Post–Judgment Motions. The following post-judgment motions must be filed under Local Rule 9014–1:

(1) a motion for relief from an order due to mistake, inadvertence, excusable neglect, newly discovered evidence, fraud, etc., under F.R.Civ.P. 60(b);

(2) a motion for a new or reopened evidentiary hearing or trial under F.R.Civ.P. 59(a)–(c);

(3) a motion to reopen a closed bankruptcy case under § 350, except as provided in Local Rule 5010–1; and

(4) a motion to reconsider an order disallowing a claim under F.R.Bankr.P. 3008.

[Effective October 1, 1998. Amended effective May 5, 2008; December 1, 2009; February 1, 2016.]

RULE 9029–1.   RULES OF PROCEDURE

(a) Rules of General Applicability. The rules of procedure in cases and proceedings in this court will be as prescribed by the laws of the United States, the rules promulgated by the Supreme Court of the United States, any applicable rules of the United States Court of Appeals for the Sixth Circuit, any applicable Local Rules of the United States District Court for the Eastern District of Michigan, these rules and the court's ECF Procedures.

(b) Title and Authority. These rules are promulgated under F.R.Bankr.P. 9029 and are referred to as the Local Rules of the Bankruptcy Court for the Eastern District of Michigan, cited as E. D. Mich. LBR _____-__.

(c) References in These Rules. In these rules the United States Bankruptcy Code, 11 U.S.C. §101 et seq., is referred to as the "Code." References in these rules to any specific section of the Code are "§_____." References in these rules to the Local Rules for the United States District Court for the Eastern District of Michigan are "E. D. Mich. LR _____." References in these rules to the Federal Rules of Bankruptcy Procedure are "F.R.Bankr.P. _____." References in these rules to the Federal Rules of Civil Procedure are "F.R.Civ.P. _____." Within these rules, these rules are referred to as "Local Rule _____." In these rules, the court's Administrative Procedures for Electronic Case Filing are referred to as the "ECF Procedures." References in these rules to any particular section of the ECF Procedures are "ECF Procedure _____." Undefined capitalized terms in these rules that are defined in the ECF Procedures have the meanings set forth in the ECF Procedures.

(d) Procedural Orders in a Specific Case or Proceeding. A judge may issue orders governing matters of procedure not addressed by these rules.

(e) Suspension of the Local Rules. Upon notice and for cause in a particular case or proceeding, a judge may temporarily suspend the applicability of any of these rules.

(f) Prior Rules Superseded. These rules supersede all prior local rules and all prior administrative orders on the matters covered in these rules.

(g) References to Other Rules or Statutes. When these rules refer to F.R.Bankr.P., the rules of the United States District Court for the Eastern District of Michigan or sections of the Code, they refer to such as they existed on the effective date of the last amendments to these rules. If the statute or rule referred to is re-codified, the reference in these rules will be deemed to be amended to track the re-codification. If these rules refer to an interim rule promulgated by the Judicial Conference of the United States and adopted by this court and that interim rule is subsequently adopted as part of the Federal Rules of Bankruptcy Procedure, the reference will then be deemed to that rule in the Federal Rules of Bankruptcy Procedure.

(h) Format and Type Size. All papers filed with the court must be on 8–½ inch × 11 inch white paper of good quality, plainly typewritten, printed or prepared by a clearly legible duplication process, and double-spaced, except for quoted material and footnotes. Margins must be at least 1 inch on the top, sides and bottom. Each page must be numbered consecutively. Except for standard preprinted forms that are in general use, type size of all text and footnotes must be no smaller than 10–½ characters per inch (non-proportional) or 14 point (proportional). This subpart applies to attached exhibits consisting of materials that are created for filing with the court but does not apply to attached exhibits consisting of previously printed materials that are only copied as attachments to a paper filed with the court.

[Effective October 1, 1998. Amended effective May 5, 2008; February 1, 2016.]

RULE 9029–2.   ADMINISTRATIVE ORDERS OF GENERAL SCOPE

When authorized by the court, the chief judge may issue administrative orders of general scope. The orders will be transmitted to the clerk, who will arrange for their appropriate publication and will maintain a public file containing copies of all such orders currently in effect.

[Effective May 5, 2008.]

RULE 9029–3.   CIVILITY PRINCIPLES

The Civility Principles as adopted and amended by the United States District Court for the Eastern District of Michigan are adopted and are available on the court's website.

[Effective May 5, 2008. Amended effective February 1, 2016.]

RULE 9029–4.   APPLICABILITY OF AMENDMENTS

Amendments to these rules will apply to pending cases and proceedings, except to the extent that in the opinion of the court their application in a particular case or proceeding would not be feasible or would result in an injustice.

[Effective October 1, 1998. Amended effective February 1, 2016.]

RULE 9037–1. PROCEDURE FOR RESTRICTING ACCESS TO DOCUMENTS CONTAINING PROTECTED PRIVATE INFORMATION

If a document contains unredacted information in violation of F.R.Bankr.P. 9037(a), a party seeking to restrict access to such document may file an *ex parte* motion or a stipulation signed by the party that filed such document, requesting the entry of an order restricting public access to such document. If an order is entered upon such motion or stipulation, a redacted copy of the document must be filed within seven days from the date of the order.

[Effective February 1, 2016.]

SELECTED GUIDELINES
GUIDELINE 1. NOTIFYING THE UNITED STATES TRUSTEE AND THE CLERK OF FIRST DAY MOTIONS

Before filing a chapter 11 case that is accompanied by First Day Motions, counsel for the debtor is encouraged to communicate with the United States trustee's office and the clerk's office. With respect to contact with the clerk's office, counsel should contact the clerk of the court. If the clerk is not available, contact may be made with the chief deputy clerk or the operations manager of the clerk's office. Counsel for the debtor may discuss any relevant issues in the case with the United States trustee and the clerk of the court.

The court strongly encourages the parties to discuss the following with the United States trustee's office:

(1) The nature of the first day relief to be requested.

(2) The debt structure of the business, including the public and trade debt.

(3) Description of the debtor's cash management system and issues under § 345.

(4) Issues that may be resolved by consent (*e.g.*, extensions of time to file schedules, adequate assurances of utility payments, wage and benefit payments up to statutory limitation(s), joint administration, necessity doctrine payments, professional employment issues, including conflicts and indemnification requests).

(5) Corporate governance issues.

(6) Collateral issues including Federal Trade Commission issues, taxing authority issues, Security and Exchange Commission issues, pension and other Department of Labor issues, Environmental Protection Agency and Michigan Department of Environmental Quality issues and insurance issues.

(7) The status of any attempted out-of-court workout, including perceived impediments to a successful reorganization and whether there was an unofficial prepetition committee.

(8) The number of creditors and any special needs due to the size of the case.

(9) The need for a noticing vendor for the notice of the meeting of creditors and any other notice requirement.

The court strongly encourages the parties to discuss the following with the clerk:

(1) The number of creditors and any special needs due to the size of the case.

(2) The need for a noticing vendor for the notice of the meeting of creditors and any other notice requirement.

(3) The need for the availability of the clerk or staff outside of ordinary business hours.

[Effective January 3, 2005. Amended effective May 5, 2008.]

GUIDELINE 2. EXPEDITED FORMATION OF COMMITTEE IN A LARGE BANKRUPTCY CASE

In Large Bankruptcy Cases, the United States trustee's office is encouraged to appoint a committee of creditors within 3 Business Days after receiving the information from the debtor required by Local Rule 2003–3, provided that creditors are willing to serve in accordance with § 1102.

[Effective January 3, 2005. Amended effective May 5, 2008; December 1, 2009.]

GUIDELINE 3. MISSING PAPERS

The clerk will not issue a discharge in a chapter 13 case if the debtor has not filed a Debtor's Certification Regarding Domestic Support Obligations, as required by Local Rule 4004–1.

[Effective October 17, 2005. Amended effective May 5, 2008; February 12, 2016.]

GUIDELINE 4.   WAIVER OF FILING FEE

An application to waive the filing fee must be filed on the official form. The court will review all such applications in chambers. The court may deny an application without a hearing. If the court schedules a hearing, the court will give notice to the debtor and the trustee.

[Effective October 17, 2005. Amended effective May 5, 2008.]

GUIDELINE 5.   TAX RETURN COMPLIANCE

A motion under §§ 521(j), 1307(e) or 1308 must be filed under Local Rule 9014–1.

[Effective October 17, 2005. Amended effective May 5, 2008; February 12, 2016.]

GUIDELINE 6.   CHAPTER 13 POST–CONFIRMATION MOTIONS TO EXCUSE PLAN PAYMENTS OR TAX REFUNDS IN CHAPTER 13 CASES AND PLAN MODIFICATIONS

Because post-confirmation motions to excuse plan payments or tax refunds in chapter 13 cases are actually plan modifications, for which the national and local rules establish a procedure, the Court will no longer consider such motions. Upon the filing of such a post-confirmation motion, the Court will enter an order denying it without prejudice to the debtor's right to file a proposed plan modification.

Any such proposed plan modification must comply with LBR 3015–2(b); and be filed in ECF using the event, "Chapter 13 Post–Confirmation Plan Modification."

[Effective May 1, 2008. Amended effective February 12, 2016.]

GUIDELINE 7.   ENTRY OF A DISCHARGE IN AN INDIVIDUAL CHAPTER 11 CASE

11 U.S.C. § 1141(d)(5) provides that in an individual chapter 11 case, a discharge is entered after the completion of all payments under the confirmed plan and after the court makes the findings required by § 1141(d)(5)(C). Rather than await those events to close the case, which may take several years, the Court will close such a case upon plan confirmation and resolution of all post-confirmation litigation. To request the entry of a discharge upon the completion of plan payments, the debtor must file a motion to reopen for that purpose. The Court will waive any applicable reopening fee for such a motion. The motion should request the findings required by § 1141(d)(5)(C) and should be filed under LBR 9014–1 with notice to all parties in interest.

[Former Guideline 11 effective September 10, 2008. Renumbered effective February 12, 2016.]

GUIDELINE 8.   PROCEDURE FOR LIEN STRIP OF A JUNIOR MORTGAGE IN CHAPTER 13 [ABROGATED EFFECTIVE DECEMBER 1, 2017]

GUIDELINE 9.   RESPONSIBILITIES OF DEBTOR'S COUNSEL RELATING TO A REAFFIRMATION AGREEMENT

As a matter of fulfilling the obligations of counsel for a debtor in a Chapter 7 case, counsel may not exclude from representation services relating to a reaffirmation agreement.

[Former Guideline 13 effective December 16, 2009. Renumbered and amended effective February 12, 2016.]

GUIDELINE 10.   NEW CHAPTER 13 MODEL PLAN [ABROGATED EFFECTIVE DECEMBER 1, 2017]

CHAPTER 13 MODEL PLAN

CHAPTER 13 Plan

UNITED STATES BANKRUPTCY COURT
EASTERN DISTRICT OF MICHIGAN

IN RE:

S.S.# XXX-XX-_____
            Debtor

and

S.S.# XXX-XX-_____
        Joint-Debtor
                Debtor(s)   /

CASE NO.
CHAPTER 13
JUDGE

PLAN SUMMARY

For informational purposes only.

ACP: _____ Months
Minimum Plan Length: ____ Months
Plan payment: $_____ per Month
Minimum dividend to Class 9 Creditors $_____
Percentage of Tax Refunds committed   _____%

CHAPTER 13 PLAN

[ ] Original   **OR**   [ ] Pre-Confirmation Modification # _____

I. NOTICES

TO CREDITORS: YOUR RIGHTS MAY BE AFFECTED BY THIS PLAN. THIS PLAN MAY BE CONFIRMED AND BECOME BINDING WITHOUT FURTHER NOTICE OR HEARING UNLESS A TIMELY WRITTEN OBJECTION IS FILED. READ THIS DOCUMENT CAREFULLY AND CONSIDER SEEKING THE ADVICE OF AN ATTORNEY.

Debtor must check one box on each line to state whether or not the Plan includes each of the following items:		
A. Nonstandard Provisions set out in Section IV. Under Federal Rule of Bankruptcy Procedure 3015(c), a "nonstandard provision" means a provision that is not otherwise included in the approved form for a Chapter 13 Plan in the Eastern District of Michigan.	☐ Included	☐ Not included
B. A limit on the amount of a secured claim based on a valuation of the collateral for the claim.	☐ Included	☐ Not included
C. Avoidance of a security interest or lien.	☐ Included	☐ Not included
• IF AN ITEM IS CHECKED AS "NOT INCLUDED" OR IF BOTH BOXES ARE CHECKED, THE PROVISION IS VOID EVEN IF OTHERWISE INCLUDED IN THE PLAN.		
• ANY "NONSTANDARD PROVISION" THAT IS NOT SPECIFICALLY IDENTIFIED IN SECTION IV IS VOID.		

- IF THIS SECTION I INDICATES THAT THIS PLAN DOES NOT INCLUDE ANY "NONSTANDARD PROVISIONS", ANY "NONSTANDARD PROVISIONS" IN THIS PLAN (INCLUDING ANY OTHERWISE SPECIFICALLY LISTED IN SECTION IV) ARE VOID.

THIS PLAN IS SUBJECT TO AND INCORPORATES BY REFERENCE THE ADDITIONAL STANDARD PROVISIONS WHICH MAY BE FOUND AT WWW.13EDM.COM OR WWW.MIEB.USCOURTS.GOV OR FROM DEBTOR'S COUNSEL UPON WRITTEN REQUEST.

II. **APPLICABLE COMMITMENT PERIOD; PLAN PAYMENTS; PLAN LENGTH; EFFECTIVE DATE AND ELIGIBILITY FOR DISCHARGE:**

A. □ Debtor's Current Monthly Income exceeds the applicable State median income. Debtor's Applicable Commitment Period is 60 months. Debtor's Plan Length shall be 60 months from the date of entry of the Order Confirming Plan.

□ Debtor's Current Monthly Income is less than or equal to the applicable State median income. Debtor's Applicable Commitment Period is 36 months. Debtor's Plan Length shall be _____ months from the date of entry of the Order Confirming Plan. **This is a minimum Plan length.** If the Plan has not been completed in the minimum Plan length, the Plan length shall be extended as necessary for completion of the requirements of the Plan; provided that in no event will the Plan term continue beyond 60 months from the date of entry of the Order Confirming Plan. *See Paragraph J of the Additional Terms, Conditions and Provisions for additional information regarding Completion of Plan.*

If neither or both of the above boxes is checked, then the Applicable Commitment Period and the Plan Length shall be 60 months from the date of entry of the Order Confirming Plan.

B. Debtor's Plan payment amount is $_____ per month.

C. Future Tax Refunds. *See Paragraph A of the Additional Terms, Conditions and Provisions for additional information regarding Tax Refunds and Tax Returns.*

FOR CASES ASSIGNED TO BAY CITY DIVISION: *Check only one box. If none are checked or more than one box is checked, paragraph 2 shall apply:*

1. □ Debtor's Plan proposes a 100% dividend to unsecured creditors. Therefore, debtor is not required to remit any future Tax Refunds.

2. □ Debtor's Plan proposes less than a 100% dividend to unsecured creditors and debtor's Schedule I *does not* include a pro-ration for anticipated Tax Refunds. Debtor will remit 50% of all Federal and State Tax Refunds that debtor receives or is entitled to receive after commencement of the case.

3. □ Debtor's Plan proposes less than a 100% dividend to unsecured creditors and debtor's Schedule I *includes* a pro-ration for anticipated Federal Tax Refunds. Debtor will remit 100% of all Federal and State Tax Refunds that debtor receives or is entitled to receive after commencement of the case to the extent the Refund exceeds the sum of twelve times the amount of the Federal and State Tax Refund pro-ration shown in Schedule I.

> **FOR CASES ASSIGNED TO DETROIT DIVISION:** *Check only one box. If none are checked or more than one box is checked, paragraph 2 shall apply:*
>
> 1. ☐ Debtor's Plan proposes a 100% dividend to unsecured creditors. Therefore, debtor is not required to remit any future Tax Refunds.
>
> 2. ☐ Debtor's Plan proposes less than a 100% dividend to unsecured creditors and debtor's Schedule I *does not* include a pro-ration for anticipated Tax Refunds. Debtor will remit 100% of all Federal Tax Refunds that debtor receives or is entitled to receive after commencement of the case.
>
> 3. ☐ Debtor's Plan proposes less than a 100% dividend to unsecured creditors and debtor's Schedule I *includes* a pro-ration for anticipated Federal Tax Refunds. Debtor will remit 100% of all Federal Tax Refunds that debtor receives or is entitled to receive after commencement of the case to the extent the Refund exceeds the sum of twelve times the amount of the Federal Tax Refund pro-ration shown in Schedule I.

> **FOR CASES ASSIGNED TO FLINT DIVISION:** *Check only one box. If none are checked or more than one box is checked, paragraph 2 shall apply:*
>
> 1. ☐ Debtor's Plan proposes a 100% dividend to unsecured creditors. Therefore, debtor is not required to remit any future Tax Refunds.
>
> 2. ☐ Debtor's Plan proposes less than a 100% dividend to unsecured creditors and debtor's Schedule I *does not* include a pro-ration for anticipated Tax Refunds. Debtor will remit 100% of all Federal Tax Refunds that debtor receives or is entitled to receive after commencement of the case.
>
> 3. ☐ Debtor's Plan proposes less than a 100% dividend to unsecured creditors and debtor's Schedule I *includes* a pro-ration for anticipated Federal Tax Refunds. Debtor is not required to remit Federal Tax Refunds in excess of the amount of the proration shown on Schedule I.

D. ☐ If the box to the immediate left is "checked", the debtor acknowledges that debtor **is not** eligible for a discharge pursuant to 11 USC §1328.

☐ If the box to the immediate left is "checked", the joint debtor acknowledges that joint debtor **is not** eligible for a discharge pursuant to 11 USC §1328.

E. ☐ If the box to the immediate left is "checked", the debtor or joint debtor is self-employed **AND** incurs trade credit in the production of income from such employment. Debtor shall comply with the requirements of Title 11, United States Code, and all applicable Local Bankruptcy Rules regarding operation of the business and duties imposed upon the debtor.

III. <u>**DESIGNATION AND TREATMENT OF CLASSES OF CLAIMS:**</u> *See Paragraph F of the Additional Terms, Conditions and Provisions for additional information regarding the order in which claims are to be paid.*

A. Cʟᴀss Oɴᴇ – **TRUSTEE FEES** as determined by statute.

B. Cʟᴀss Two – **ADMINISTRATIVE CLAIMS, INCLUDING ATTORNEYS FEES AND COSTS:**

    1. **PRE-CONFIRMATION ATTORNEY FEES:** At confirmation of the Plan, Counsel shall elect to either:
       a. In lieu of filing a separate fee application pursuant to 11 USC §327 and §330, accept the sum of $_____ for services rendered plus $_____ for costs advanced by Counsel, for total Attorney Fees and Costs of $_____ through the Effective Date of the Plan. The total Attorney Fees and Costs less the sum paid to Counsel prior to the commencement of this case as reflected in the Rule 2016(b) Statement leaving a net balance due of $_____, will be paid as an Administrative Expense Claim; **or**

      b.   Request an award of compensation for services rendered and recovery of costs advanced by filing a separate Application for Compensation for services rendered up through the date of entry of the Order Confirming Plan pursuant to 11 USC §327 and §330. If Counsel elects to file a fee application pursuant to this sub-paragraph, the Trustee shall escrow $_____ for this purpose. *See Paragraph B of the Additional Terms, Conditions and Provisions for additional information.*

  2. **POST-CONFIRMATION ATTORNEY FEES:** *See Paragraph D of the Additional Terms, Conditions and Provisions for additional information.*

  3. **RETENTION OF OTHER PROFESSIONALS FOR POST-PETITION SERVICES:** Debtor □ has retained or □ intends to retain the services of _____(name of person to be retained) as _____ (capacity or purpose for retention) to perform professional services post-petition with fees and expenses of the professional to be paid as an Administrative Expense. *See Paragraph C of the Additional Terms, Conditions and Provisions for additional information.*

  4. **OTHER ADMINISTRATIVE EXPENSE CLAIMS:** Any administrative expense claims approved by Order of Court pursuant to 11 USC §503 shall be paid as a Class Two administrative claim. *See Paragraph E of the Additional Terms, Conditions and Provisions for additional information.*

C. **CLASS THREE – SECURED CLAIMS TO BE STRIPPED OR AVOIDED FROM THE COLLATERAL AND TREATED AS UNSECURED CLAIMS TO BE PAID BY TRUSTEE.** *See Paragraph G and Paragraph N of the Additional Terms, Conditions and Provisions for additional information.*

  Class 3.1 Liens to be Stripped. 11 USC §506(a).

Creditor	Collateral

  Class 3.2 Judicial Liens and Non-Possessory, Non-Purchase Money Liens to be Avoided. 11 USC §522(f).

Creditor	Collateral

D. **CLASS FOUR - SECURED CLAIMS ON WHICH THE LAST CONTRACTUAL PAYMENT IS DUE BEYOND THE LENGTH OF THE PLAN. 11 USC §1322(b)(5).**

  Class 4.1 Continuing Payments on a claim secured by the debtor's principal residence that come due on and after the date of the Order for Relief. (*See Paragraph P, Paragraph L and Paragraph EE of the Additional Terms, Conditions and Provisions for additional information*).

Creditor	Collateral	Monthly Payment	Direct or Via Trustee

Class 4.2 Pre-Petition Arrearages on a claim secured by the debtor's principal residence to be paid by Trustee: Those amounts which were due as of the filing of the Order for Relief:

Creditor	Collateral	Arrears Amount	Estimated Average Monthly Payment	Months to Cure From Confirmation Date

Class 4.3 Continuing Payments other than on a claim secured by the debtor's principal residence that come due on and after the date of the Order for Relief. (*See Paragraph P, Paragraph L and Paragraph EE of the Additional Terms, Conditions and Provisions for additional information*).

Creditor	Collateral	Monthly Payment	Direct or Via Trustee

Class 4.4 Pre-Petition Arrearages other than on a claim secured by the debtor's principal residence to be paid by Trustee: Those amounts which were due as of the filing of the Order for Relief:

Creditor	Collateral	Arrears Amount	Estimated Average Monthly Payment	Months to Cure From Confirmation Date

E. **CLASS FIVE - SECURED CLAIMS ON WHICH THE LAST PAYMENT WILL BECOME DUE WITHIN THE PLAN DURATION**. (*See Paragraph H, Paragraph L, Paragraph O and Paragraph S of the Additional Terms, Conditions and Provisions for additional information*).

Class 5.1 Secured Claims not excluded from 11 USC §506 to be paid Equal Monthly Payments. 11 USC §1325(a)(5)(B):

Creditor/Collateral	Indicate if "crammed" *** or modified	Interest rate (Present Value Rate)	Total to be paid Including Interest	Monthly Payment	Direct or Via Trustee

*** See debtor's Schedule A/B for more information about values.

Class 5.2   Secured Claims not excluded from 11 USC §506 *not* to be paid Equal Monthly Payments. 11 USC §1325(a)(5)(B):

Creditor/Collateral	Indicate if "crammed" *** or modified	Interest rate (Present Value Rate)	Total to be paid including interest	Estimated Average Monthly Payment	Direct or Via Trustee

*** See debtor's Schedule A/B for more information about values.

Class 5.3   Secured claims excluded from 11 USC §506 by the "hanging paragraph" at the end of 11 USC §1325 (a)(9) to be paid "Equal Monthly Payments". 11 USC §1325(a)(5)(B).

Creditor/Collateral	Indicate if modified	Interest rate (Present Value Rate)	Total to be paid Including Interest	Monthly Payment	Direct or Via Trustee

Class 5.4   Secured claims excluded from 11 USC §506 by the "hanging paragraph" at the end of 11 USC §1325 (a)(9) *not* to be paid Equal Monthly Payments. 11 USC §1325(a)(5)(B).

Creditor/Collateral	Indicate if "modified	Interest rate (Present Value Rate)	Total to be paid including interest	Estimated Average Monthly Payment	Direct or Via Trustee

CLASS 5.5   **Surrender of collateral.** (*See Paragraph P of the Additional Terms, Conditions and Provisions for additional information*).

The debtor surrenders debtor's interest in the following collateral. Any allowed unsecured claim remaining after disposition of the collateral will be treated as a Class 9 General Unsecured Creditor.

Creditor Name	Description of Collateral

F. CLASS SIX – EXECUTORY CONTRACTS AND/OR UNEXPIRED LEASES. 11 USC §§365, 1322(b)(7): Debtor assumes the executory contracts and unexpired leases listed in subparagraph 1. *(See Paragraph K of the Additional Terms, Conditions and Provisions for additional information).*

Class 6.1   Continuing Lease/Contract Payments:

Creditor	Property	Monthly Payment	Lease/Contract expiration date	Direct or Via Trustee

Class 6.2   Pre-petition Arrearages on Assumed Executory Contracts and Leases *(to be paid by Trustee):*

Creditor	Property	Arrears Amount	Estimated Average Monthly Payment	Months to Cure From Confirmation Date

Class 6.3   Debtor rejects the executory contracts and unexpired leases listed in this subparagraph 3. Any unexpired lease or executory contract that is neither expressly assumed in Class 6.1 above or expressly rejected below shall be deemed rejected as of the date of confirmation of debtor's chapter 13 Plan to the same extent as if that unexpired lease or executory contract was listed below. *(See Paragraph K of the Additional Terms, Conditions and Provisions for additional information):*

Creditor	Property

G. CLASS SEVEN – PRIORITY UNSECURED CLAIMS. 11 USC §§507, 1322(a)(2).

Class 7.1   Domestic Support Obligations: Continuing Payments that come due on and after the date of the Order for Relief:

Creditor	Monthly Payment	Direct or Via Trustee

Class 7.2   Domestic Support Obligations: Pre-Petition Arrearages due as of the filing of the Order for Relief:

Creditor	Arrears Amount	Estimated Average Monthly Payment	Direct or Via Trustee

Class 7.3   All Other Priority Unsecured Claims [11 USC §1322(a)(2)]

Creditor	Amount	Direct or via Trustee

H.   **CLASS EIGHT – SEPARATELY CLASSIFIED UNSECURED CLAIMS.** 11 USC §1322(b)(1):   *(To be paid by Trustee)*:
(*See Paragraph M of the Additional Terms, Conditions and Provisions for additional information*):

Creditor	Amount	Interest Rate	Reason for Special Treatment

I.   **CLASS NINE - GENERAL UNSECURED CLAIMS** *(to be paid by Trustee)*: – *See Paragraph N of the Additional Terms, Conditions and Provisions for additional information.*

☐   This Plan shall provide a total sum for distribution to creditors holding Class 9 General Unsecured claims in an amount that is not less than the Amount Available in Chapter 7 shown on Attachment 1, Liquidation Analysis and Statement of Value of Encumbered Property (the "Unsecured Base Amount").   This Plan shall provide either (i) the Unsecured Base Amount; or (ii) will continue for the full Plan Length as indicated in Paragraph II.A of this Plan, whichever yields the greater payment to Class 9 Unsecured Creditors.   *See Attachment 2, Chapter 13 Model Worksheet, Line 8, for additional information concerning funds estimated to be available for payment to Class 9 Unsecured Creditors.*

☐   This Plan shall provide a dividend to holders of Class 9 General Unsecured Claims equal to 100% of allowed claims.

If neither box is checked or if both boxes are checked, then the Plan shall pay the Unsecured Base Amount.

☐ If the box to the immediate left is "checked", creditors holding claims in Class Seven, Eight and Nine shall receive interest on their allowed claims at the rate of ____% per annum as required by 11 USC §1325(a)(4).

IV.   **Nonstandard Plan Provisions**:

> • ANY "NONSTANDARD PROVISION" THAT IS NOT BOTH INCLUDED IN SECTION 1.A AND SPECIFICALLY STATED IN THIS SECTION IS VOID.

A.   _____
B.   _____
C.   _____
D.   _____
E.   _____

I, _____, **Attorney for debtor (or debtor if not represented by an attorney),**
certify that this Plan contains no "Nonstandard Provisions" other than those set out in Section IV above.

Attorney for Debtor   Debtor

Street Address

City, State and Zip Code   Joint Debtor

E-Mail Address

Phone Number   Date

<u>ATTACHMENT 1</u>

<u>LIQUIDATION ANALYSIS AND STATEMENT OF VALUE OF ENCUMBERED PROPERTY</u>:

TYPE OF PROPERTY	FAIR MARKET VALUE	LIENS	DEBTOR'S SHARE OF EQUITY	EXEMPT AMOUNT	NON-EXEMPT AMOUNT
PERSONAL RESIDENCE					
REAL ESTATE OTHER THAN PERSONAL RESIDENCE					
HHG/PERSONAL EFFECTS					
JEWELRY					
CASH/BANK ACCOUNTS					
VEHICLES					
OTHER *(itemize)*					
OTHER *(itemize)*					
OTHER *(itemize)*					

Amount available upon liquidation .... $ _____

Less administrative expenses and costs .... $ _____

Less priority claims .... $ _____

Amount Available in Chapter 7 .... $ _____

ATTACHMENT 2

CHAPTER 13 MODEL WORKSHEET
LOCAL BANKRUPTCY RULE 3015-1(B)(2) E.D.M.

1.   Proposed length of Plan: _____ months

2.   Initial Plan payment:
        $_____ per month x _____ months = $_____   (subtotal)

        Step payment #1
        $_____ per month x _____ months = $_____   (subtotal)

        Step payment #2
        $_____ per month x _____ months = $_____   (subtotal)

3.   Additional payments: $_____ per _____ = $_____   (subtotal)

4.   Lump sum payments   = $_____   (subtotal)

5.   Total to be paid into Plan (total of lines 2 through 4) $_____

6.   Estimated disbursements other than to Class 9 General Unsecured Creditors

        a.   Estimated Trustee Fees $_____

        b.   Estimated Attorney Fees and costs
             through confirmation of Plan $_____

        c.   Estimated Attorney Fees and costs
             post-confirmation through duration of Plan $_____

        d.   Estimated fees of other Professionals $_____

        e.   Total mortgage and other
             continuing secured debt payments $_____

        f.   Total non-continuing secured
             debt payments (including interest) $_____

        g.   Total priority claims $_____

        h.   Total arrearage claims $_____

7.   Total disbursements other than to Class 9 General Unsecured Creditors
        (Total of lines 6.a through 6.h) $_____

8.   Funds *estimated* to be available for Class 9 General Unsecured Creditors
        (Line 5 minus Line 7) $_____

9.   Estimated dividend to Class 9 General Unsecured Creditors
        in Chapter 7 proceeding (see Liquidation Analysis) $_____

Comments:

359

V. ADDITIONAL STANDARD PROVISIONS

THE FOLLOWING STANDARD PROVISIONS ARE APPLICABLE TO ALL PLANS AND PRE-CONFIRMATION MODIFIED PLANS FILED ON OR AFTER DECEMBER 1, 2017, IN THE UNITED STATES BANKRUPTCY COURT FOR THE EASTERN DISTRICT OF MICHIGAN

A. **DEBTOR'S OBLIGATION TO REMIT TAX REFUNDS:** Debtor shall not alter any withholding deductions/exemptions without Court approval. If the Internal Revenue Service or any State taxing authority remits to the Trustee any sum which the debtor is not required to remit pursuant to this Plan, then upon written request of the debtor and concurrence of the Trustee, the Trustee shall be authorized to refund those sums to the debtor from funds first available without further motion, notice or Order of Court. The Trustee shall not be required to recoup or recover funds disbursed to creditors prior to receipt of the debtor's written request.

If debtor is married and debtor's spouse is not a joint-debtor in this case, debtor's Tax Refund(s) for any calendar year shall be 50% of the aggregate net Tax Refunds received by debtor and debtor's non-filing spouse, regardless of whether debtor and spouse file a joint tax return or file separate tax returns.

B. **ALLOWANCE AND PAYMENT OF PRE-CONFIRMATION ATTORNEY FEES:** If Class 2.1 of the Plan indicates that Counsel intends to file a Separate Application for compensation for services rendered up through the date of entry of the Order Confirming Plan pursuant to 11 USC §327 and §330, the Trustee shall withhold the amount designated in Class 2.1 from funds remaining after payment of claims required to be paid prior to attorney fees pending further Order of Court.

C. **RETENTION AND COMPENSATION OF OTHER PROFESSIONALS FOR POST-PETITION PRE-CONFIRMATION SERVICES:** If Class 2.3 indicates that debtor has retained or intends to retain the services of any Professional (as that term is defined in 11 USC §327) to perform professional services after the commencement of this case, debtor will file a timely Application to Employ Professional Person stating the identity of the person to be retained and the capacity or purpose for retention, accompanied by a Certification of Disinterestedness signed by the Professional and obtain Court permission to retain the Professional. The Professional may seek compensation in an amount not to exceed $400.00 by filing a Proof of Claim designated as an Administrative Expense without further notice, hearing or Order of Court. If the Professional seeks compensation in excess of $400.00, the Professional shall file an Application for Compensation for services rendered pursuant to 11 USC §327.

D. **POST-CONFIRMATION ATTORNEY FEES & COSTS BY SEPARATE APPLICATION:** Counsel reserves the right to file Applications for compensation for services rendered subsequent to the Confirmation of this Plan. Upon entry of an Order Awarding Post Confirmation Attorney Fees, if debtor's Plan will not complete within 60 months of the date of the Order Confirming Plan, all unpaid Attorney Fees and costs shall be paid by the Trustee only after a Plan modification that allows debtor's Plan to complete within 60 months from the date of the Order Confirming Plan is approved with notice as is appropriate to the parties interested.

E. **PAYMENT OF ADMINISTRATIVE EXPENSE CLAIMS:** Administrative Expense Claims as defined in 11 USC §503, other than those claims provided for in Paragraphs B, C and D of these Additional Terms, Conditions and Provisions, will be deemed allowed and will be paid only upon entry of a specific Order of this Court determining the allowance and amount of that claim.

F. **ORDER OF PAYMENT OF CLAIMS:** All claims for which this Plan proposes payment through the Trustee shall be paid in the following order to the extent that funds are available:

Level 1:	Class 1
Level 2:	Class 5.1, 5.3 and 6.1
Level 3:	Class 2.1 and 2.3
Level 4:	Class 2.2 and 2.4
Level 5:	Classes 4.1 and 4.3
Level 6:	Classes 4.2, 4.4, 5.2, 5.4 and 6.2
Level 7:	Class 7
Level 8:	Classes 3.1, 3.2, 5.5, 6.3, 8 and 9

Each level shall be paid as provided in this Plan before any disbursements are made to any subordinate class. If there are not sufficient funds to pay all claims within a level, then the claims in that level shall be paid *pro rata*.

G. **SECURED CLAIMS TO BE STRIPPED OR AVOIDED FROM THE COLLATERAL AND TREATED AS UNSECURED:** Claims for which the creditor holds a lien that is listed as "Stripped" in Class 3.1 or "Avoided" in Class 3.2 are avoided and will be paid as a General Unsecured Creditor as provided in Class 9 of the Plan. Upon completion of the Plan, the creditor will record a Satisfaction of the Lien in the applicable Public Records to discharge and release the lien. If the creditor fails to do so, the debtor may file a motion for an order declaring that the lien has been satisfied by completion of the confirmed Plan, which the debtor may then have certified and recorded in the applicable Public Records.

H. **CLASS 5.1, CLASS 5.3 AND CLASS 6.1 CREDITORS SPECIFIED TO RECEIVE EQUAL MONTHLY PAYMENTS:** Creditors identified in Class 5.1, Class 5.3, and Class 6.1 will receive Equal Monthly Payments to the extent funds are available at the date of each disbursement. If more than one creditor is scheduled in Class 5.1, Class 5.3, and Class 6.1 and the funds available in any disbursement are insufficient to pay the full Equal Monthly Payments to all of the listed creditors, payments shall be made on a *pro rata* basis determined by the ratio of the Equal Monthly Payment specified to each creditor to the total amount of Equal Monthly Payments to all creditors scheduled in Class 5.1, Class 5.3, and Class 6.1. The amount of the Equal Monthly Payment to any creditor shall be the amount stated in Class 5.1, Class 5.3, and Class 6.1 as may be applicable and the amount of the Equal Monthly Payment specified in the Plan will supersede any monthly payment amount specified in a Proof of Claim at variance with the Equal Monthly Payment amount set forth in the Plan unless otherwise Ordered by the Court.

The monthly post-confirmation disbursement to any creditor designated in Class 5.1, Class 5.3, and Class 6.1 will not exceed the Equal Monthly Payment amount for that creditor for the month in which disbursement is being made plus any previously unpaid Equal Monthly Payments accruing before the date of disbursement.

I. **APPLICATION OF DISBURSEMENTS BY CREDITORS:** Creditors shall apply all disbursements under the Plan only in the manner consistent with the terms of the Plan and to the account(s) or obligation(s) as designated on the voucher or check provided to the Creditor with each disbursement.

J. **COMPLETION OF PLAN:** For purposes of 11 USC §1328, the debtor shall be deemed to have completed all payments under the Plan:

1. Upon the expiration of the Plan Length as defined in Paragraph II.A of the Plan commencing on the date of entry of the Order Confirming Plan; *and*

2. Debtor has remitted all Plan payments (as defined in Paragraph II.A and II.B of the Plan) coming due after the date of entry of the Order Confirming Plan; *and*

3. Debtor has remitted all Federal Income Tax Refunds as required by Paragraph II.C of the Plan and Paragraph A of these Additional Terms, Conditions and Provisions; *and*

4. Debtor has remitted a sum sufficient to pay all allowed claims as amended and/or supplemented as provided in the Plan.

K. **EXECUTORY CONTRACTS AND/OR UNEXPIRED LEASES:**

1. Any executory contract or unexpired lease not expressly assumed in Class 6.1 or in the Order Confirming Plan shall be deemed rejected effective as of the Effective Date of this Plan.

2. Upon rejection of any Executory Contract or Unexpired Lease, the property and debtor's interest in the rejected executory contract or unexpired lease will no longer be property of the estate and the stay under 11 USC §362(a) and the co-debtor stay under 11 USC §1301 shall automatically terminate as to such property. Any claims arising from the rejection of an executory contract or unexpired lease shall be treated as a general unsecured claim in Class Nine, subject to further Order of Court.

3. For all assumed executory contracts and unexpired leases, confirmation of this Plan shall constitute a finding that this Plan complies with all requirements for assumption of the executory contracts and unexpired leases being assumed, including all requirements set forth in 11 USC §365(b).

4. Upon the termination of the Lease (whether as a result of the expiration of the contractual lease term, repossession of the property which is the subject of the Lease, or otherwise), the Lessor shall have the right to file a Supplemental Claim for any damages or charges permitted under or pursuant to the Lease.

5. If Class 6.1 provides for the Continuing Lease/Contract Payments to be made by the Trustee, the Supplemental Claim as filed and allowed shall be paid by the Trustee over the remaining term of the Plan.

6. If Class 6.1 provides for the Continuing Lease Payments to be made directly by the debtor to the Lessor, the Supplemental Claim as filed and allowed shall be paid directly by the debtor to the creditor over the remaining term of the Plan. If there is a balance outstanding on the supplemental claim as of the completion of debtor's confirmed Chapter 13 Plan, this balance shall not prevent or preclude the entry of a discharge in this case; instead, this balance shall be deemed non-dischargeable and debtor shall be responsible for payment of the remaining balance of the Supplemental Claim following the entry of a Discharge.

L. **SECURED CLAIMS – POST-PETITION FEES, COSTS AND CHARGES**:

1. Any Supplement to Claim that is filed with the Court as to which there is no objection filed or as to which any objection has been overruled, shall be deemed allowed.

2. If Class 4.1, 4.3, 5.1, 5.2, 5.3 or 5.4 provides for the Creditor's Secured Claim to be paid by the Trustee, the Supplement to Claim as filed and allowed shall be paid by the Trustee over the remaining term of the Plan.

3. If Class 4.1, 4.3, 5.1, 5.2, 5.3 or 5.4 provides for the Creditor's Secured Claim to be paid directly by the debtor to the creditor, the Supplement to Claim as filed and allowed shall be paid directly by the debtor to the creditor before completion of the Plan. If there is a balance outstanding on the Supplement to Claim as of the completion of debtor's confirmed Chapter 13 Plan, this balance shall not prevent or preclude the entry of a discharge in this case; instead, any unpaid balance shall be non-dischargeable.

M. **SEPARATELY CLASSIFIED UNSECURED CLAIMS:** Claims classified as "Separately Classified Unsecured Claims" are unsecured claims that qualify for discriminatory and preferred treatment pursuant to 11 USC §1322(b)(1). The basis for separate classification is specified in Paragraph III.H of the Plan. Each Separately Classified Unsecured Claims shall receive payments that total 100% of the allowed amount of the claim plus interest if specified in Class Eight of the Plan. *See also Paragraph F of the Additional Terms, Conditions and Provisions for additional information concerning the timing of payments to be made on these claims.*

N. **GENERAL UNSECURED CREDITORS**: Unless Class 9 of the Plan provides a dividend to holders of General Unsecured Claims equal to 100% of allowed claims, the Plan shall produce a total sum for distribution to General Unsecured Creditors (the "Unsecured Base Amount"). The Unsecured Base Amount shall be not less than the aggregate amount which creditors in this class would have received had the estate of the debtor been liquidated under Chapter 7 of Title 11, United States Code. *See* 11 USC §1325(a)(4). Each holder of a duly filed and allowed General Unsecured Claim shall receive the holder's *pro rata* share of the Unsecured Base Amount, based on the creditor's claim as a fraction of the total General Unsecured Claims duly filed and allowed. The *pro rata* dividend for each holder of an allowed unsecured claim will be calculated by the Trustee upon review of allowed claims.

This Plan shall provide either the total Unsecured Base Amount or shall continue for the Plan Length as stated in Paragraph II.A of the Plan, whichever will offer the greater dividend to general unsecured creditors.

O. **VESTING, POSSESSION OF ESTATE PROPERTY AND LIEN RETENTION**: Upon the Effective Date of the Plan, all property of the estate shall vest in the debtor and shall cease to be property of the estate. The debtor shall remain in possession of all property during the pendency of this case unless specifically provided herein, and shall not seek to sell, transfer or otherwise dispose of such property (except in the ordinary course of debtor's business) without prior Court approval.

P. **SURRENDER OF COLLATERAL**: Those claims that are treated pursuant to 11 USC §1325(a)(5)(C) (surrender of collateral) are so designated in Class 5.5 of the Plan. Upon confirmation, the Automatic Stay and co-debtor Stay is lifted as to the collateral and any creditor holding a lien on the collateral and the collateral shall no longer constitute property of the estate. No disbursements shall be made by the Trustee to any creditor whose claim is secured by the collateral being surrendered unless the holder of such claim files a Proof of Claim (or Amended Proof of Claim) after the Effective Date of the Plan setting forth the amount of any deficiency remaining after disposition of the collateral. Any allowed deficiency claim shall be paid as a general unsecured claim in Class 9 of the Plan. *See Federal Rule of Bankruptcy Procedure 3002.1.*

Q. **PROHIBITION AGAINST INCURRING POST-PETITION DEBT**: While this case is pending, the debtor shall not incur a debt in excess of $2,000.00 without first obtaining approval of either this Court or of the Chapter 13 Trustee. If the Chapter 13 Trustee stipulates to entry of an Order allowing debtor to incur post-petition debt, debtor shall be permitted to file the Stipulation signed by the Trustee and to submit an Order to the Court on an *ex parte* basis without notice to creditors or other parties in interest.

R. **UNSCHEDULED CLAIMS**: If an unscheduled proof of claim is filed, the Trustee is authorized to exercise sole discretion to classify the claim into one of the existing classes under this Plan and to schedule the claim for payment within that class, without prejudice to debtor's right to object to the allowance of the claim and/or to modify the Plan to provide a different treatment.

S. **PROOFS OF CLAIM FILED AT VARIANCE WITH THE PLAN**: In the event that a Proof of Claim is filed and allowed that is at variance with the provisions of this Plan, the following method is to be employed to resolve the conflict:

    1.   Regarding claims for which the Plan does not propose a "cramdown" or modification, the Proof of Claim shall supersede the Plan as to the claim amount, percentage rate of interest, monthly payments, valuation of collateral and classification of the claim.

    2.   As to claims for which the Plan proposes a "cramdown" or modification, the Proof of Claim governs only as to the claim amount. The Plan governs valuation, interest rate and any other contractual term.

    3.   If a Proof of Claim is filed that is at variance with this Plan or related schedules, the Trustee shall automatically treat that claim as the holder indicated, unless provided otherwise in the confirmed Plan; these Additional Terms, Conditions and Provisions; or by Order of Court.

    4.   As to claims specified in Class 3.1 or Class 3.2 (Secured Claims to be Stripped or Avoided), the Proof of Claim shall control only as to the allowed amount of the claim. *See also Paragraph G of the Additional Terms, Conditions and Provisions for additional information concerning payments to be made on these claims.*

T. **TAX RETURNS AND TAX SET-OFFS**: All Tax Returns which have become due prior to the filing of the Plan have been filed. The Internal Revenue Service and the United States Department of Treasury are prohibited from setting off against post-petition Tax Refunds for payment of pre-petition tax obligations.

U. **DEBTOR DUTY TO MAINTAIN INSURANCE – REMEDY FOR FAILURE TO MAINTAIN INSURANCE**: Debtor shall maintain all insurance required by law and contract upon property of the estate and the debtor's property. After confirmation of this Plan, if the debtor fails to maintain insurance as required by law or contract, any party in interest may submit a notice of default, served on debtor, debtor's counsel and the Chapter 13 Trustee, permitting 10 days from service of the notice in which to cure the default. If the default is not cured within the time permitted, the party in interest may submit an Order Granting Relief from the Automatic Stay as to the collateral to the Court along with an affidavit attesting to the debtor's failure to cure, and the Stay may thereafter be lifted without further motion, notice or hearing.

V. **SECURED CREDITORS, LESSORS AND PARTIES TO EXECUTORY CONTRACTS UPON ENTRY OF ORDER LIFTING AUTOMATIC STAY**: Any secured creditor and any party to an assumed executory contract or unexpired lease as to whom the Automatic Stay is lifted shall not receive any further disbursements until a Proof of Claim for the balance remaining after liquidation of the collateral is filed.

W. **PROVIDING FUTURE TAX RETURNS TO TRUSTEE:** Debtor shall timely file each Federal Income Tax Return required to be filed under applicable law during the pendency of this case, and shall provide to the Trustee a copy of each Return at the same time the Return is filed with the taxing authority.

X. **DEADLINES IN EVENT OF CONVERSION:** In the event of conversion of this case to a case under Chapter 7 of the United States Bankruptcy Code, the rights of the Chapter 7 Trustee and all creditors (including but not limited to the right to object to exemptions and the right to object to discharge pursuant to 11 USC §727 and/or dischargeability pursuant to 11 USC §523) will be determined as if the Petition was filed on the date of conversion. The date of the Order converting this case to one under Chapter 7 will be treated as the date of the Order For Relief and all applicable deadlines shall be determined as if the post-conversion Meeting of Creditors pursuant to 11 USC §341 was the initial Meeting of Creditors.

Y. **OBJECTIONS TO PROOFS OF CLAIM:** Any party in interest shall have the right to object to Proofs of Claim. Confirmation of this Plan shall not constitute a waiver of any objection and shall not constitute or have any *res judicata* or collateral estoppel effect on or against any objection to Proof of Claim. If any objection to Proof of Claim is filed and sustained, in whole or in part, after the Trustee has begun making disbursements under this Plan as confirmed, Trustee shall have no obligation or duty to recoup any payments or disbursements made to the creditor whose Proof of Claim was the subject of the objection.

Z. **CREDITOR'S AUTHORIZATION TO CONTACT DEBTOR:** Notwithstanding the provisions of the Automatic Stay and co-debtor Stay, creditors holding claims in Classes 4 and 5 for which the debtor proposes to retain the collateral and parties to any assumed unexpired lease or executory contract in Class 6 may contact debtor for purposes of sending periodic statements and annual or periodic summaries of accounts including but not limited to account reconciliations pursuant to the Real Estate Settlement Procedures Act.

AA.   **IDENTITY OF DISBURSING AGENT**: All claims in all classes of creditors shall be paid by the Trustee as Disbursing Agent except those claims which are specified to be paid directly by either the debtor or a third party, in which event the debtor or third party making those payments shall be the Disbursing Agent for those claims.

BB.   **SPECIAL PROVISIONS APPLICABLE TO GOVERNMENTAL UNITS RESPONSIBLE FOR ENFORCING DOMESTIC SUPPORT OBLIGATIONS:** Notwithstanding the provisions of 11 USC §362 and §1327, the Automatic Stay is modified to permit any governmental unit or agency responsible for enforcing a domestic support obligation to send notices, to take other actions to the extent not inconsistent with the terms of the Plan, and to collect domestic support obligations from property that is not property of the estate.

CC.   **PRE- AND POST-PETITION LITIGATION AND CAUSES OF ACTION:** Debtor and the Chapter 13 Trustee shall have concurrent standing to prosecute all Pre- and Post-Petition causes of action, including but not limited to actions arising under Title 11, United States Code. Any compromise or settlement of any litigation or cause of action shall be subject to the provisions of Federal Rule of Bankruptcy Procedure 9019. Any proceeds or damages recovered by or on behalf of the debtor shall be retained pending Order of the Bankruptcy Court.

DD.   **SUBSTANTIVE CONSOLIDATION OF JOINTLY FILED CASES:** If this case has been filed jointly by a husband and wife pursuant to 11 USC §302, entry of an Order Confirming Plan shall also constitute an Order for Substantive Consolidation of the debtors.

EE.   **NON-APPLICABILITY OF FEDERAL RULE OF BANKRUPTCY PROCEDURE 3002.1:** The requirements and provisions of Federal Rule of Bankruptcy Procedure 3002.1 shall not apply to any property that the Plan as confirmed surrenders to the Creditor as provided in 11 USC §1325(a)(5)(C); or to any property as to which the Automatic Stay is lifted for purposes of allowing the secured creditor to exercise rights and remedies pursuant to applicable State Law, regardless of whether the Order Lifting Automatic Stay is entered before or after entry of an Order Confirming the Plan.

FF.   **TIME TO CURE PARAMOUNT:** For any class of claims where the Months to Cure From Confirmation Date may be specified, if the Plan does not specify the number of months to cure, the Months to Cure From Confirmation Date shall be the Plan Length specified in Paragraph II.A of the Plan. For any class of claims or creditors for which the Plan specifies an Estimated Average Monthly Payment that is inconsistent with or contradicts the Months to Cure From Confirmation Date, the Months to Cure From Confirmation Date controls. The Chapter 13 Trustee is authorized to make any changes to the amount of disbursements to the creditor to implement this provision.

GG.   **SECURED CLAIMS EXCLUDED FROM 11 USC § 506 BY THE "HANGING PARAGRAPH" AT THE END OF 11 USC §1325 (a)(9):** Claims treated in Class 5.3 or Class 5.4 are claims that were either (1) incurred within 910 days before the petition date and secured by a purchase money security interest in a motor vehicle acquired for the personal use of the debtor, or (2) incurred within 1 year of the petition date and secured by a purchase money security interest in any other thing of value.

[Dated: December 1, 2017.]

ADMINISTRATIVE ORDERS AND NOTICES

ADMINISTRATIVE ORDER NO. 04–05. ADMINISTRATIVE ORDER REGARDING CERTAIN CHAPTER 13 PROCEDURES

The Court concludes that the following procedures should be required in chapter 13 cases filed in this district:

1.   Within 5 business days after an order is entered confirming the plan, the debtor's counsel shall serve a copy of the order upon all parties in interest by mail and file a proof of service. If the debtor is unrepresented, the clerk will serve the order.

2.   Within 5 days after either (a) the filing of a certificate of no objection to a post-confirmation plan modification under Local Bankruptcy Rule 3015–2(b) (E.D.M.), (b) the entry of an order overruling objections to a post-confirmation plan modification, or (c) the entry of an order confirming a post-confirmation modified plan, the proponent of the plan modification shall serve a copy of the certificate or order upon all parties in interest by mail and file a proof of service. If the debtor is unrepresented, the clerk will provide for service.

3.   When a debtor seeks the entry of an order modifying or vacating a payment order previously entered as required by Local Bankruptcy Rule 1007(g)(1)(B) (E.D.M.), the debtor shall first seek the stipulation of the chapter 13 trustee. If that stipulation is obtained, the debtor may submit a stipulated order to the court. If that stipulation is not obtained, the debtor shall file a motion to amend the payment order, supported by an affidavit establishing good cause, utilizing the procedures of Local Bankruptcy Rule 9014–1 (E.D.M.) with service upon the chapter 13 trustee. Ex parte orders amending payment orders previously entered shall not be submitted to the court for entry.

This order is effective for pending and new cases as of November 1, 2004.

[Dated: September 28, 2004.]

ADMINISTRATIVE ORDER NO. 05–22. IN RE: ADMINISTRATIVE ORDER REGARDING MANDATORY ELECTRONIC FILING OF MONTHLY FINANCIAL REPORTS AND DOCUMENTS BY A NOTICING AND CLAIMS AGENTS

The monthly financial reports of a debtor in possession in a chapter 11 case would normally be filed in paper because the debtor in possession is not an entity that may register as an ECF Filer pursuant to the Court's Administrative Procedures for Electronic Case Filing.

For the same reason, documents filed by a noticing agent or a claims agent in a chapter 11 case would normally be filed in paper.

These documents may be voluminous and therefore burdensome for the Clerk's Office staff to scan in the Court's electronic records system.

Accordingly, it is ordered that the monthly financial reports of a debtor in possession and all documents to be filed by a noticing agent or a claims agent shall be filed electronically by the attorney for the debtor, based on the attorney's mandatory ECF date pursuant to Administrative Order 05–04.

[Dated: November 15, 2005.]

ADMINISTRATIVE ORDER NO. 06–08. IN RE: REGARDING THE FILING OF STATEMENT OF CURRENT MONTHLY INCOME AND MEANS TEST CALCULATION FORM IN CONVERTED CASES

The Statement of Current Monthly Income and Calculation of Commitment Period and Disposable Income (Form B22C) is required to be filed by in each chapter 13 case. The Statement of Current Monthly Income and Means Test Calculation (Form B22A) is required to be filed by an individual chapter 7 debtor whose debts are primarily consumer debts.

The Court has determined that it is appropriate to clarify that when a debtor whose debts are primarily consumer debts converts a chapter 13 case to a chapter 7 case, the debtor is required to file

Form B22A. This requirement only affects cases filed on or after October 17, 2005, that later convert to a chapter 7.

Accordingly, an individual debtor whose debts are primarily consumer debts shall file the Statement of Current Monthly Income and Means Test Calculation (Form B22A) within 15 days from the notice of conversion or from an order converting the case from a chapter 13 case to a chapter 7 case. If the debtor fails to timely file the statement in the converted case, the case shall be dismissed pursuant to L.B.R. 1007–1(d) (E.D.M.).

[Dated: February 14, 2006.]

REVISED NOTICE REGARDING REAFFIRMATION AGREEMENTS

11 U.S.C. § 524(c) and (k) clearly prescribe the language required in a reaffirmation agreement. A reaffirmation agreement that does not comply with the requirements of these subsections will be considered deficient and may be stricken.

The Court has made a determination regarding the actions that should be taken for the various types of reaffirmation agreements:

Reaffirmation With Attorney Certification

- If the debtor's attorney certifies that the agreement does not impose an undue hardship on the debtor, *neither a motion nor court action is required. The Court will not act on a motion to approve the reaffirmation agreement in these circumstances.*

- If the debtor's attorney certifies that a presumption of undue hardship has been established with respect to an agreement, *a motion for approval of the reaffirmation agreement is required pursuant to L.B.R. 4008–1. The motion shall be filed in the ECF event "Motion for Approval of Reaffirmation Agreement—Presumption of Undue Hardship Applies."* **Otherwise, a notice of deficiency be will issued.** Such a motion will be set for hearing.

Reaffirmation by a Debtor Not Represented by an Attorney in the Case

- If a reaffirmation agreement is filed and the debtor is not represented by an attorney in the bankruptcy case, *the debtor must sign a motion for approval of the reaffirmation agreement pursuant to 11 U.S.C. § 524(k)(7), attached as Part E. The reaffirmation agreement, including Parts A–E shall be filed in ECF with the event "Reaffirmation Agreement by Debtor Not Represented by An Attorney."* **Otherwise, a notice of deficiency will be issued.** Such a motion will be set for hearing. The creditor may file the motion even though the motion is signed by the debtor.

Reaffirmation by a Debtor Represented by an Attorney Who Did Not Negotiate the Agreement

- This circumstance will be addressed in the same way as a reaffirmation by a debtor not represented by an attorney in the bankruptcy case.

In addition, if a reaffirmation agreement is signed by the debtor's attorney but the attorney has failed to certify whether or not the agreement will pose an undue hardship, *a notice of deficiency will be issued and the pleading may be stricken if not corrected.*

[Dated: June 26, 2007.]

NOTICE TO BANKRUPTCY PRACTITIONERS REGARDING REQUESTS FOR COMPENSATION FOR TIME EXPENDED BY ATTORNEYS FILING PAPERS IN THE COURT'S ELECTRONIC FILING SYSTEM (ECF)

It has recently come to the Court's attention that there may exist some confusion over whether an attorney may be compensated for the time expended by that attorney electronically filing a paper in the Court's ECF systems. This notice is intended to address that issue.

ECF Procedure 2(f) defines a "Filer" as an individual with an approved login and password, registered to use the ECF system in this Court under ECF Procedure 4(a). ECF Procedure 4(a)(1) provides that attorneys admitted to practice in the United States District Court for the Eastern District of Michigan shall register as Filers in the Court's ECF system. That same ECF Procedure also provides that members of a Filer's staff are encouraged to participate in ECF training but will not themselves receive a separate login and password. ECF Procedure 4(d) provides that each Filer is required to protect the security of the assigned password. ECF Procedure 11(a) provides that an electronic filing of a paper is the equivalent of signing a paper for all purposes. ECF Procedure 11(c) provides that a Filer "shall not knowingly permit or cause to permit the Filer's ... password to be used by anyone other than an agent specifically authorized by the Filer ..."

The Court's ECF Procedures make clear that only an attorney may be a Filer. The attorney is responsible for the login and password. That does not mean, however, that only the attorney may perform the task of electronic filing. ECF Procedure 11(c) specifically provides authority for a Filer to authorize a secretary, clerical person or other agent of the Filer to use the Filer's password. The Court considers the performance of the electronic filing task itself to be a clerical task that can be delegated to personnel performing clerical services for such attorney and, as such, non-compensable. The Court does not consider the task of electronic filing to be a service required to be performed by an attorney. Accordingly, requests for compensation for an attorney's time in performing an ECF filing, pulling documents off of the ECF system via the internet, reviewing notices of electronic filing that merely confirm that a particular pleading has actually been filed, and pulling off of the internet ECF notifications of documents filed by such attorney, shall be denied.

[Dated: June 28, 2006.]

ADMINISTRATIVE ORDER NO. 08-10. IN RE: ADMINISTRATIVE ORDER REGARDING LBR 1007-1(c)

LBR 1007-1(c) requires the debtor in a chapter 13 case to submit a payment order for entry within 15* days after filing or conversion to chapter 13. This local rule permits the debtor to file either a Third Party Payment Order or an Electronic Transfer of Funds Payment Order. However, the local rule states that the debtor can submit an Electronic Transfer of Funds Payment Order only if a Third Party Payment Order cannot be effectuated.

To compel compliance with this local rule, the debtor shall, before submitting an Electronic Transfer of Funds Payment Order, file an affidavit stating in detail why a Third Party Payment Order cannot be effectuated.

It is so ordered. This order is effective upon entry.

[Dated: June 10, 2008.]

  * So in original. But see LBR 1007-1(c)(1).

ADMINISTRATIVE ORDER NO. 08-11. IN RE: ADMINISTRATIVE ORDER REGARDING LBR 1015-1(f)

LBR 1015-1(f) provides, "A proof of claim in jointly administered cases shall be filed in the case of the debtor against whom the claim is asserted rather than in the lead case." The rule does not address in which case an objection to a proof of claim should be filed. To minimize confusion, the Court concludes that any objection to a proof of claim should also be filed in the case in which was filed the proof of claim that is the subject of the objection, rather than in the lead case.

It is so ordered. This order is effective upon entry.

[Dated: June 10, 2008.]

ADMINISTRATIVE ORDER NO. 08-12. IN RE: ADMINISTRATIVE ORDER ADOPTING REVISED CERTIFICATION REGARDING DOMESTIC SUPPORT OBLIGATIONS

It is hereby ordered that the attached revised "Certification Regarding Domestic Support Obligations" is adopted for use under LBR 4004-1, and to enable the Chapter 13 trustee to comply with 11 U.S.C. § 1302(d)(1)(C).

UNITED STATES BANKRUPTCY COURT
EASTERN DISTRICT OF MICHIGAN

In re:

                                    Chapter 13

         Debtor(s)   Case No.
_____ Judge:

CERTIFICATION REGARDING DOMESTIC SUPPORT OBLIGATIONS

(To be filed *separately* by each debtor after completion of all payments
under the plan in cases filed on or after October 17, 2005)

The Chapter 13 debtor, being first duly sworn, states the following:

SECTION I—TO BE COMPLETED BY EACH DEBTOR

Disclosure of Domestic Support Obligations

During the chapter 13 case, was the debtor required by a judicial or administrative order, or by statute, to pay a domestic support obligation as defined in 11 U.S.C. § 101(14A)?

Check one: Yes _____   No _____

If yes: Complete Sections II and III below

If no: Complete Section III below

SECTION II—TO BE COMPLETED BY A DEBTOR WHO WAS REQUIRED TO PAY A DOMESTIC SUPPORT OBLIGATION DURING THE CHAPTER 13 CASE

1. Has the debtor paid all amounts due under the domestic support obligation, including amounts due before the petition was filed to the extent provided for in the plan?

Check one: Yes _____   No _____

2. List the name and address of each spouse, former spouse or child to or for whom alimony, maintenance or support is paid or required to be paid (if more space is needed, please attach a separate sheet):

Name _____

Address _____

City, State and Zip _____

Account Number _____

3. Has any debt been determined to be non-dischargeable or is any action currently pending to determine a debt to be non-dischargeable pursuant to:? *(check one)*:

Section	Yes	No
11 U.S.C. Section 523(a)(2)		
11 U.S.C. Section 523(a)(4)		

If you answered "yes" to any of the above, please identify the creditor and the legal basis for the action

Name of Creditor: _____ ☐ 11 USC § 523(a)(2)
Address of Creditor: _____ ☐ 11 USC § 523(a)(4)
City, State and ZIP: _____

If more space is needed, please attach a separate sheet.

4. Has any debt been reaffirmed pursuant to 11 U.S.C. Section 524(c)?

Check one: Yes _____   No _____

If yes, please state:

Name of Creditor: _____

Address of Creditor: _____

City, State and ZIP: _____

If more space is needed, please attach a separate sheet.

5. Debtor's Current Address: _____

_____

_____

Name of Debtor's Current Employer: _____

Debtor's Current Employer's Address: _____

_____

_____

SECTION III—TO BE COMPLETED BY EACH DEBTOR

CERTIFICATION

I declare under penalty of perjury that the foregoing statements are true and correct to the best of my knowledge, information, and belief.

_____   _____
Debtor's Signature   Date

[Dated: June 25, 2008.]

ADMINISTRATIVE ORDER NO. 08–20. IN RE: ORDER REGARDING THE POLICY AND PROCEDURES FOR REDACTED INFORMATION IN TRANSCRIPTS

In December 2002, the E–Government Act of 2002, Pub. L. No. 107–347, was adopted to protect the privacy and security of publicly available electronic filings. Section 205(c)(3) specified that if federal rules relating to the electronic filing of documents provided for the redaction of certain personal data identifiers, they also had to allow a party wishing to file a document containing such information to file an unredacted copy of the document under seal, which the court must retain as part of the record.

At its September 2007 session, the Judicial Conference adopted a policy regarding electronic availability of transcripts of court proceedings. Under 28 U.S.C. § 753(b), the court reporter or transcriber must deliver promptly a certified copy of any transcript made to the clerk of court for the records of the court.

Rule 9037(a) of the Federal Rules of Bankruptcy Procedure, which was effective December 1, 2007, states:

Unless the court orders otherwise, in an electronic or paper filing made with the court that contains an individual's social security number and taxpayer identification number, or birth date, the name of an individual, other than the debtor, known to be and identified as a minor, or a financial account number, a party or nonparty making the filing may include only:

(1) the last four digits of the social security number and taxpayer identification number;

(2) the year of the individual's birth;

(3) the minor's initials; and

(4) the last four digits of the financial account number.

369

This policy applies to transcripts made available remotely via CM/ECF and PACER. The redaction procedures for transcripts, as well as the 91–day restriction policy, apply only to transcripts of federal courtroom proceedings. **This policy and procedures are effective as of October 6, 2008.**

Procedures

1. A party will electronically file a request for a transcript of a court proceeding. Chambers staff will forward the transcript request to a court reporter/transcriber to complete. A revised transcript request form can be found on the court's web site.

2. The transcriber files an electronic transcript of the court proceedings with the clerk's office through CM/ECF. An email notification is automatically sent to chambers staff of the transcript filing.

The CM/ECF docket event for the transcript automatically restricts access to the electronic transcript to court staff only for 91 days.

The Notice of Electronic Filing (NEF) of the transcript event informs parties and attorneys of record that:

    (a) A transcript has been filed;

    (b) A 91–day restriction period is in effect;

    (c) Specific deadlines are associated with redaction; and

    (d) Procedures must be followed for obtaining the transcript during the restriction period.

3. If any party participated in the proceeding and does not receive electronic notice, chambers staff will file and mail to the party a Notice of Filing of Official Transcript and of Deadlines Related to Restriction and Redaction.

4. The attorneys or pro se parties who attended the court proceeding are responsible for reviewing the transcript for the personal data identifiers required by the federal rules to be redacted. Unless otherwise ordered by the court, the parties must review the following portions of the transcript:

    (a) opening and closing statements made on the party's behalf;

    (b) statements of the party;

    (c) the testimony of any witnesses called by the party; and

    (d) any other portion of the transcript as ordered by the court.

Any party needing to review the transcript for redaction purposes may purchase a copy from the transcriber. If an attorney purchases the transcript from the transcriber, the clerk's office will provide the attorney remote access to the transcript as well as to any redacted transcript via CM/ECF and PACER. Pro se parties may view the transcript at the clerk's office.

5. If redaction is not necessary, no further action needs to be taken. Public access to the electronic transcript will be **91 days** from the date of filing of the transcript if no motions to extend time or for a protective order are filed.

6. If redaction of information is necessary, parties have **21 days** from the date of filing of the electronic transcript to file with the court a **Transcript Redaction Request** pursuant to Fed. R. Bankr. P. 9037(a). **The redaction request shall list the information to be redacted by page and line number**.

Parties shall also serve the transcriber with the Transcript Redaction Request. The transcriber will also automatically receive email notification that this request has been filed with the court.

If a party fails to file the Transcript Redaction Request by the deadline set by the Court, it will be deemed the party has waived his/her right to request redaction and the Court will enter an order denying any untimely request.

7. The transcriber has **28 days** from the date of filing of the electronic transcript to file with the court an electronic **Redacted Transcript**. The transcriber is not authorized to sell a copy of an unredacted transcript to the public if a redacted version is filed with the Court.

8. If a redacted transcript is filed, the **redacted version** will be available to the public for viewing and printing at the public terminal in the clerk's office and available for download from CM/ECF through PACER for a fee, 91 days from the date of filing of the original electronic transcript. The

unredacted version of the transcript will NOT be available to the public and will be retained by the clerk of the court as a restricted document.

    9. **Remote Access and PACER Charges.** Charges for access through PACER apply during and after the 91–day restriction period. <u>Charges are not capped at 30 pages.</u> The user will incur PACER charges each time the transcript is accessed even though the party may have purchased it from the transcriber and obtained remote access through CM/ECF. **A free copy of the electronic transcript is not available via remote access.** If an attorney only purchases a redacted version of the transcript, the attorney will not be given remote electronic access to the unredacted transcript in CM/ECF.

    10. **Extension of Deadlines.** If a party wishes to request an extension of a deadline, the party may file a motion to extend time pursuant to Fed. R. Bankr. P. 9037(d). The transcript will not be electronically available until the court has ruled on any such motion, even though the 91–day restriction period may have ended. These motions will be handled by the court expeditiously given the 91–day restriction period as well as the need for access to the transcript by the attorneys and parties.

    11. **Redaction of Additional Information.** If an attorney wishes to redact additional information other than the specific personal data identifiers listed in the rules, the attorney may file a motion for a protective order pursuant to Fed. R. Bankr. P. 9037(d). The transcript will not be electronically available until the court has ruled on any such motion, even though the 91–day restriction period may have ended. These motions will be handled by the court expeditiously given the 91–day restriction period as well as the need for access to the transcript by the attorneys and parties.

[Dated: October 1, 2008.]

ADMINISTRATIVE ORDER NO. 08–23. IN RE: ADMINISTRATIVE ORDER GRANTING THE CLERK AUTHORITY TO REQUEST PHOTO IDENTIFICATION IN INTAKE

    Pursuant to this Court's authority and responsibility under 11 U.S.C. § 105(a) to prevent abuse of process, it is hereby ordered that the clerk of the court is granted the authority to require any individual presenting a bankruptcy petition for filing at intake to produce a government-issued photo identification and to refuse such filing if such identification is not produced upon request. Upon request in a specific case, the chief judge may grant relief from this order. This order is effective immediately.

[Dated: October 29, 2008.]

ADMINISTRATIVE ORDER NO. 08–24. IN RE: REGARDING THE ASSIGNMENT OF CERTAIN CASES

    This order is entered to secure the just, speedy and efficient administration of cases filed in this Court and to provide a means of facilitating that purpose by making available all of the Court's available judicial resources in appropriate cases. It is entered under the authority of E.D. Mich. LBR 1073–1(c)(2).

    This order is applicable upon the filing of a bankruptcy case that the chief bankruptcy judge determines is a very large, complex case of national significance.

    It is hereby ordered that upon the filing of such a case, the case shall not be assigned by the Court's blind draw system under E.D. Mich. LBR 1073–1(a)(1). Instead, after consulting with the other bankruptcy judges, the chief bankruptcy judge shall assign the case to a bankruptcy judge.

    It is further ordered that the bankruptcy judge to whom the case is assigned shall have the authority to assign adversary proceedings and contested matters to other bankruptcy judges as necessary and appropriate to carry out the purposes of this order.

[Dated: December 10, 2008.]

AMENDED NOTICE REGARDING NEW PROCEDURES FOR
STRIKING PLEADINGS FILED IN CLOSED CASES

On February 17, 2009, the Court issued a Notice Regarding New Procedures for Striking Pleadings in Closed Cases. That notice explained that the Court will strike, without prejudice, any pleadings filed in a closed case unless a motion to reopen such case is first filed under 11 U.S.C. § 350. The notice contained a list of exceptions for certain pleadings that may be filed after a case is closed without first filing a motion to reopen the case. The purpose of this amended notice is to add three pleadings to that list of exceptions.

Effective immediately, only the following pleadings may be filed in a closed case without first filing a motion to reopen the case. Pleadings listed in bold print have been added to the original list.

> Motion to Reopen
>
> Requests and Writs of Garnishment
>
> Garnishee Disclosure
>
> Certificate of Service
>
> Applications to Pay Unclaimed Funds
>
> Affidavit of Claimant for Unclaimed Funds
>
> Request to Be Removed From Receiving Electronic Filings
>
> Affidavit of Non–Compliance
>
> **Motion to Restrict Public Access to Pleading or Claim Containing Personal Identification Information Not Permitted Under Bankruptcy Rule 9037(a)**
>
> **Notice of Recision**
>
> **Chapter 7 Trustee Reports**

This amended notice makes it clear that a motion may be filed in a closed case to restrict public access to a pleading or claim containing personal identification information not permitted under Bankruptcy Rule 9037(a), and that the Court may grant such motion by order entered in the closed case. This does not mean that the moving party may then also file another pleading, claim or amended claim in the closed case without first filing a motion to reopen the case.

[Dated: May 26, 2009.]

ADMINISTRATIVE ORDER NO. 09–07. IN RE: ADMINISTRATIVE ORDER
PERTAINING TO MANDATORY ELECTRONIC FILING OF CLAIMS

ECF Administrative Procedure 3(b)(3) specifies that proofs of claim may be filed by a traditional filing of a paper claim. Upon review the court has determined that any party filing 10 or more claims per year will be required to file all claims using the electronic filing system.

IT IS ORDERED that ECF Administrative Procedure 3(b)(3) is amended to require the electronic filing of claims by any party who files 10 or more claims per calendar year.

[Dated: April 29, 2009.]

NOTICE REGARDING DISMISSAL OF CASE FOR FAILURE
TO FILE PETITION PURSUANT TO 11 U.S.C. § 301(a)

Effective immediately, the Court will dismiss any electronically filed case in which the petition is not filed as the lead event. Pursuant to 11 U.S.C. § 301(a), a voluntary case is commenced by the filing of a petition. If the voluntary petition is not associated with the initial entry, no case exists, therefore, the filing will be dismissed.

[Dated: September 29, 2009.]

NOTICE REGARDING PROCESSING OF APPLICATIONS
FOR WAIVER OF CHAPTER 7 FILING FEE

Federal Rule of Bankruptcy Procedure 1006(c) provides that a voluntary Chapter 7 petition filed by an individual shall be accepted for filing if accompanied by the debtor's application requesting a waiver of the filing fee under 28 U.S.C. § 1930(f) prepared on the prescribed Official Form.

PLEASE TAKE NOTICE that effective immediately, no application to waive the Chapter 7 filing fee will be granted until seven (7) days after the conclusion of the § 341 meeting of creditors. After such date, the Court will either grant the application, deny the application, or set the application for hearing. In the event that the Court schedules a hearing on the application, the debtor shall attend the hearing. If the debtor fails to attend the hearing, the Court will deny the application. The Chapter 7 trustee is not required to attend the hearing, but may attend the hearing or participate in the hearing by telephone, provided that advance arrangements are made with the chambers for the bankruptcy judge assigned to the case. Although this procedure provides that no application for waiver of the Chapter 7 filing fee will be granted until seven (7) days after the conclusion of the § 341 meeting of creditors, an application for waiver of the Chapter 7 filing fee may be denied prior to that date if the Court determines that the debtor is not eligible for a waiver pursuant to 28 U.S.C. § 1930(f).

[Dated: July 13, 2012.]

ADMINISTRATIVE ORDER NO. 13–02. IN RE: DEPOSIT
AND INVESTMENT OF REGISTRY FUNDS*

The Court, having determined that it is necessary to adopt local procedures to ensure uniformity in the deposit and investment of funds in the Court's Registry,

IT IS ORDERED that the following shall govern the receipt, deposit and investment of registry funds:

I. Receipt of Funds

A. No money shall be sent to the Court or its officers for deposit in the Court's registry without a court order signed by the presiding judge in the case or proceeding.

B. The party making the deposit or transferring funds to the Court's registry shall serve the order permitting the deposit or transfer on the Clerk of Court.

C. Unless provided for elsewhere in this Order, all monies ordered to be paid to the Court or received by its officers in any case pending or adjudicated shall be deposited with the Treasurer of the United States in the name and to the credit of this Court pursuant to 28 U.S.C. § 2041 through depositories designated by the Treasury to accept such deposit on its behalf.

II. Investment of Registry Funds

A. Where, by order of the Court, funds on deposit with the Court are to be placed in some form of interest-bearing account, the Court Registry Investment System ("CRIS"), administered by the Administrative Office of the United States Courts under 28 U.S.C. § 2045, shall be the only investment mechanism authorized.

B. The Director of Administrative Office of the United States Courts is designated as custodian for CRIS. The Director or the Director's designee shall perform the duties of custodian. Funds held in the CRIS remain subject to the control and jurisdiction of the Court.

C. Money from each case deposited in the CRIS shall be "pooled" together with those on deposit with Treasury to the credit of other courts in the CRIS and used to purchase Government Account Series securities through the Bureau of Public Debt, which will be held at Treasury, in an account in the name and to the credit of the Director of Administrative Office of the United States Courts. The pooled funds will be invested in accordance with the principals of the CRIS Investment Policy as approved by the Registry Monitoring Group.

D.   An account for each case will be established in the CRIS titled in the name of the case giving rise to the investment in the fund. Income generated from fund investments will be distributed to each case based on the ratio each account's principal and earnings has to the aggregate principal and income total in the fund. Reports showing the interest earned and the principal amounts contributed in each case will be prepared and distributed to each court participating in the CRIS and made available to litigants and/or their counsel.

III.   Deductions of Fees

A.   The custodian is authorized and directed by this Order to deduct the investment services fee for the management of investments in the CRIS and the registry fee for maintaining accounts deposited with the Court.

B.   The investment services fee is assessed from interest earnings to the pool according to the Court's Miscellaneous Fee Schedule and is to be assessed before a pro rata distribution of earnings to court cases.

C.   The registry fee is assessed by the custodian from each case's pro rata distribution of the earnings and is to be determined on the basis of the rates published by the Director of the Administrative Office of the United States Courts as approved by the Judicial Conference of the United States.

IV.   Transition From Former Investment Procedure

A.   The Clerk of Court is further directed to develop a systematic method of redemption of all existing investments and their transfer to the CRIS.

B.   Parties not wishing to transfer certain existing registry deposits into the CRIS may seek leave to transfer them to the litigants or their designees on proper motion and approval of the judge assigned to the specific case.

C.   This Order supersedes and abrogates all prior orders of this Court regarding the deposit and investment of registry funds.

[Dated: February 7, 2013.]

  * [**Publisher's Note:** *See also* Administrative Order 13–05, *post.*]

ADMINISTRATIVE ORDER NO. 13–05.   ADMINISTRATIVE ORDER AMENDING ORDER REGARDING DEPOSIT AND INVESTMENT REGISTRY FUNDS

Local Bankruptcy Rule 7067–1 governs the deposit and withdrawal of funds in an interest bearing account in the registry of the Court. Under 28 U.S.C. § 2045, the Administrative Office of the United States Courts administers the Court Registry Investment System ("CRIS") for the purpose of providing a safe, efficient market rate of return for registry funds. On February 7, 2013, this Court entered Administrative Order No. 13–02, which requires any funds on deposit with this Court to be deposited and administered in CRIS. The Court is entering this order to clarify that L.B.R. 7067–1 remains in full force and effect, except to the extent that it is expressly modified by Administrative Order No. 13–02.

[Dated: April 4, 2013.]

ADMINISTRATIVE ORDER NO. 13–09.   ORDER REQUIRING CHAPTER 11 DEBTORS TO PROVIDE EMAIL ADDRESS FOR THE 20 LARGEST UNSECURED CREDITORS

Chapter 11 debtors are required by Federal Rule of Bankruptcy Procedure 1007(d) to file with their petition Official Form B4, which contains a list of the debtor's 20 largest unsecured claims. This form requires the debtor to provide certain contact information for each of the 20 largest unsecured creditors, including telephone number, mailing address and other information, but it does not require the debtor to provide an email address for each creditor. In a Chapter 11 case designated under Local Bankruptcy Rule 9001–1(a) as a "Large Bankruptcy Case," the debtor is required by Local Bankruptcy Rule 2003–3 to "immediately email, fax or hand deliver" to the United States Trustee an email address for each creditor shown on Official Form B4. Because of the increasingly widespread use of email by debtors and creditors, the Court concludes that it is now appropriate to require all Chapter 11 debtors to provide the United States Trustee with an email address for each of the 20 largest unsecured creditors, if the debtor already has email addresses for such creditors at the time that the Chapter 11 petition is filed. Accordingly,

It Is Hereby Ordered that in all Chapter 11 cases filed after the date of this order, the debtor must immediately email, fax or hand deliver to the United States Trustee an email address for each of the 20 largest unsecured creditors, if and to the extent that the debtor already has email addresses for such creditors in its possession at the time that the Chapter 11 petition is filed.

[Dated: June 24, 2013.]

ADMINISTRATIVE ORDER NO. 14–02. IN RE: ADMINISTRATIVE ORDER ADOPTING RECOMMENDATION OF THE LOSS MITIGATION AND MORTGAGE MODIFICATION COMMITTEE IN CHAPTER 13 CASES

In 2011, approximately twenty individuals, consisting of Chapter 13 trustees, attorneys for debtors in Chapter 13 cases, and attorneys for creditors in Chapter 13 cases, volunteered to form and serve on an ad hoc committee ("Committee") in the Eastern District of Michigan for the purpose of reviewing various voluntary programs adopted by bankruptcy courts throughout the country to help facilitate resolution of loss mitigation and mortgage modifications in Chapter 13 cases. The Honorable Walter Shapero served as the chairperson for the Committee.

After completing its work, the Committee submitted a written Report and Recommendation to the Bankruptcy Court for the Eastern District of Michigan on February 4, 2014. A copy of the Report and Recommendation can be found on the Court's website under "Notices & Announcements". The Committee's Report and Recommendation recognized that mortgage loan modifications in Chapter 13 cases are voluntary and cannot be forced upon the parties. It further recognized that there have been many improvements made in the mortgage loan modification process over time. Notwithstanding these facts, the Committee reported its belief that bankruptcy court involvement can still be useful in moving the mortgage loan modification process forward in a timely and efficient fashion without adding unnecessary and unaffordable costs to the parties involved. Accordingly, the Committee recommended that the Bankruptcy Court approve and adopt the use of specific forms and a uniform procedure for debtors in Chapter 13 cases in the Eastern District of Michigan to request a mortgage modification review, for creditors to respond to such request, and for the Court to adjudicate such request.

The Bankruptcy Court has considered the Committee's Report and Recommendation and has determined to adopt it and approve the use of the forms that it has recommended, with minor changes. Accordingly,

It Is Hereby Ordered that the Court approves and adopts the Committee's Report and Recommendation.

It Is Further Ordered that in Chapter 13 cases in the Eastern District of Michigan, the exclusive way in which debtors may request the Bankruptcy Court to order a mortgage loan modification review is by means of the Debtor's Motion Requesting Mortgage Modification Review in the form attached as exhibit A to this order. A specific event code shall be created by the Court for use in Chapter 13 cases for such motion.

It Is Further Ordered that the Debtor's Motion Requesting Mortgage Modification Review shall be filed and served in accordance with Local Bankruptcy Rule 9014–1.

It Is Further Ordered that if the Court grants a debtor's motion filed on the prescribed form, the Court will do so by entering an Order Granting Debtor's Motion Requesting Mortgage Modification Review in the form attached as exhibit B to this order, subject to such revisions as the assigned bankruptcy judge may determine in his or her discretion.

IT IS FURTHER ORDERED that forms approved by this order shall be used as the exclusive means for addressing a debtor's request for a mortgage modification review in a Chapter 13 case effective April 1, 2014.

[Dated: March 12, 2014.]

APPENDIX A. ORDER GRANTING DEBTOR'S MORTGAGE
REQUESTING MORTGAGE MODIFICATION REVIEW

UNITED STATES BANKRUPTCY COURT
EASTERN DISTRICT OF MICHIGAN
SOUTHERN DIVISION

In re: Chapter 13

*,   Case No. *

    Debtor.   Hon. *

_____ /

DEBTOR'S MOTION REQUESTING
MORTGAGE MODIFICATION REVIEW

Debtor, by and through counsel, *, requests entry of an order setting deadlines and other parameters for Creditor, *, to respond to Debtor's request for mortgage modification, and in support states as follows:

1. The Debtor filed this Chapter 13 case in an attempt to retain his/her primary residence.

2. The Debtor would like to modify the terms of the mortgage encumbering his/her primary residence. The Debtor's household income will now allow him/her to contribute to a modified mortgage debt.

3. An order setting forth certain deadlines and other parameters will assist the parties in negotiation of a modification of the relevant mortgage.

Wherefore, Debtor requests the entry of an order setting deadlines and other parameters for a mortgage modification, and such other relief as this Court deems just and proper.

Dated: _____   _____
                                                    (P   )
                                            Attorney for Debtor

APPENDIX B. ORDER GRANTING DEBTOR'S MOTION REQUESTING MORTGAGE MODIFICATION REVIEW

UNITED STATES BANKRUPTCY COURT
EASTERN DISTRICT OF MICHIGAN
SOUTHERN DIVISION

In re:	Chapter 13
*,	Case No. *
Debtor.	Hon. *

_____ /

ORDER GRANTING DEBTOR'S MOTION
REQUESTING MORTGAGE MODIFICATION REVIEW

This matter having come before the Court on Debtor's Motion Requesting Mortgage Modification Review and to encourage the parties to engage in the modification process in good faith;

NOW, THEREFORE,

IT IS HEREBY ORDERED that:

1. <u>Notice of Applicable Programs</u>. Within 21 days after service of this order upon Creditor, Creditor shall supply and notify Debtor and Debtor's counsel of the Creditor's required loan modification package.

2. <u>Debtor's Financial Documents</u>. Within 35 days after service of this order, Debtor shall submit to Creditor a fully complete Loan Modification Package with all timely supporting documentation. Such exchange of information shall be through the mechanism as specified by Creditor or as otherwise agreed upon.

3. <u>Creditor Request for Additional or Updated Documents</u>. Creditor and/or its counsel shall review the Loan Modification Package submitted by Debtor and notify the Debtor and his/her counsel of any additional or updated financial records that must be supplied to Creditor. Debtor shall provide Creditor all required additional financial records within 10 days.

4. <u>Point of Contact</u>. Creditor shall designate a point of contact for loss mitigation purposes including phone number and/or email address. The point of contact may be Creditor's counsel.

5. <u>Status of Review</u>. Any document(s) or exchanges of information, not otherwise protected by any privilege, exchanged between the Debtor, Creditor and/or Creditor's representative counsel (as applicable) may be presented to the Court for purposes of providing a status of the loan modification review by either party. Where the parties agree, dates and times may be established for filing a mutually prepared status report or the Court may, on ex parte request of any party or sua sponte, set status conferences at reasonable intervals to allow the parties to provide the Court with updates as to the process.

6. <u>Lack of Prosecution</u>. In the event that this case is converted under any other chapter of the Bankruptcy Code, the Debtor fails to pursue the modification with appropriate submission of the package within the above stated time frames, or if the Debtor declines an offered trial payment plan or permanent modification, this order shall become null and void unless otherwise extended by the Court.

7. <u>Court Approval of Mortgage Modification</u>. The parties shall seek any necessary Court approval to formalize any fully executed and completed modification.

8. <u>Creditor Fee</u>. If applicable, any fees and costs incurred by Creditor for all work involved in connection with the mortgage modification shall be recoverable from the borrower as permitted by law.

9. <u>Debtor's counsel's fee</u>. Counsel for the Debtor is entitled to receive reasonable compensation for all work involved in connection with the mortgage modification and shall file an application for allowance of attorney fees and costs for allowance by the Court to be paid as an administrative expense.

10. <u>Confidential Communications</u>. All statements made by parties, attorneys, and other participants associated with the mortgage modification request are confidential and subject to Federal Rule of Evidence 408 and may not be construed for any purposes as an admission.

11. <u>Stay Modified to Allow Loan Modification</u>. The automatic stay is modified, to the extent necessary, to facilitate the terms pursuant to this Order.

12. <u>Service</u>. Debtor shall serve a copy of this order on the Creditor and file a proof of service.

[Dated: April 1, 2014.]

ADMINISTRATIVE ORDER NO. 14–09. IN RE: ORDERS BARRING DEBTORS FROM REFILING BANKRUPTCY CASES

From time to time, the bankruptcy court enters an order in a bankruptcy case barring the debtor from later filing another bankruptcy case for a specified time or based upon other terms or conditions set forth in the order. This administrative order is entered to make it clear that when a debtor who is subject to a bar order later attempts to file a bankruptcy petition in violation of the bar order, the Clerk of the Court is directed not to accept the bankruptcy petition for filing. In such circumstances, the Clerk of the Court is authorized to provide a copy of this administrative order to the debtor attempting to file the bankruptcy petition in violation of the bar order. This administrative order applies to all debtors who are presently subject to a bar order, and to any debtors who hereafter become subject to a bar order.

[Dated: June 27, 2014.]

ADMINISTRATIVE ORDER NO. 14–10. IN RE: ADMINISTRATIVE ORDER ADDRESSING EXCEPTION TO LOCAL BANKRUPTCY RULE 9010–1(a)(1)

Local Bankruptcy Rule 9010–1(a)(1) provides that a corporation, partnership or other entity other than an individual may not appear in a case or adversary proceeding unless it is represented by an attorney duly admitted to and in good standing with the bar of the United States District Court for the Eastern District of Michigan. The rule sets forth the following six exceptions:

(A) The signing or filing of a request for notice;

(B) The signing or filing of a proof of claim or a ballot;

(C) The attendance and participation at a meeting of creditors or of an official committee;

(D) The signing or filing of a pleading or paper resolving an objection to a proof of claim;

(E) The signing or filing of a stipulation adjourning a hearing or extending a deadline; or

(F) The filing of an appearance under Local Rule 2002–5.

The Court is entering this administrative order to create another exception for a recurring circumstance in Chapter 13 cases that is not specifically addressed by this rule. The Court has observed in some Chapter 13 cases and adversary proceedings to strip liens from a debtor's real property that the entity that holds the mortgage that is being stripped expressly consents to the lien strip by having an employee, officer or individual, other than an attorney admitted to practice in the District Court for the Eastern District of Michigan, sign a stipulation on behalf of the entity, indicating a representative capacity. The stipulation is then filed either in the Chapter 13 case or in the adversary proceeding. The issue is whether a stipulation signed in this manner must also be signed by an attorney admitted to practice in the District Court for the Eastern District of Michigan. The Court finds that the signing and filing of a stipulation consenting to a lien strip either in a Chapter 13 case or in an adversary proceeding does not constitute the practice of law, and is therefore excepted from the requirement of L.B.R. 9010–1(a)(1).

[Dated: September 16, 2014.]

ADMINISTRATIVE PROCEDURES FOR ELECTRONIC CASE FILING

ECF Procedure 1—Title

The Administrative Procedures for Electronic Case Filing in this Court may be abbreviated as the "Procedures" or, individually, as "ECF Procedure _____." These Procedures are available in their current version on the Court's Website at www.mieb.uscourts.gov.

ECF Procedure 2—Definitions

The following terms appear in these Procedures for Electronic Case Filing:

(a) The "Court's Website" address is www.mieb.uscourts.gov.

(b) The "E–Government Act of 2002" establishes a broad framework for the use of technology to enhance public access to government information and services. Pub. L. No. 107–347, 116 Stat. 2899. *See* 44 U.S.C. §§ 3601, *et seq.*

(c) "Electronic Filing" means the filing of a Paper over the internet by a Filer or a User.

(d) "Electronic Case Filing" or "Electronic Filing System" ("ECF") refers to the Court's automated system that receives and stores Papers filed in electronic format. The program is part of the CM/ECF (Case Management/Electronic Case Files) software, developed for the Federal Judiciary by the Administrative Office of the United States Courts.

(e) "Electronically Generated Text" is electronic text generated by converting or printing from an original word processing file to the Portable Document Format ("PDF"), so that the text of the Paper may be electronically searched and copied.

(f) A "Filer" is an individual with an approved login and password, registered to use the ECF system in this Court under ECF Procedure 4(a).

(g) A "Hyperlink" is a selectable connection from a word, picture, or information object to another, providing a mechanism for navigating to information between or within Papers filed electronically. Hyperlinks are activated when a reader clicks on an "active" region on the Paper. The active region is usually indicated by the highlighting or underlining of text. In the context of ECF, an example of a useful Hyperlink would be a case citation that leads the reader to the text of the cited case, maintained on the internet, outside of the ECF system.

(h) A "Notice of Electronic Filing" ("NEF") is a notice automatically generated by ECF when a Paper is filed, stating the time of filing, the name of the Filer or User filing the Paper, the type of Paper, the text of the docket entry, the names of those receiving the notice, and a Hyperlink to the filed Paper, which allows recipients to retrieve the Paper automatically.

(i) A "Paper" includes a petition, schedules, a statement of financial affairs, a pleading, a motion, an exhibit, a declaration, an affidavit, a brief, a judgment, an order, a notice, a proof of claim, an application to withdraw unclaimed funds, an appearance, an assignment of a claim, a reaffirmation agreement, and any other document filed by or with the Court.

(j) "Paper Filing" means filing a hard copy of a Paper with the clerk.

(k) "Portable Document Format" or "PDF" refers to a non-modifiable, electronic file in a format that will look the same on a computer screen and in print, regardless of the printer used to print it and regardless of the software package originally used to create it. A PDF file is created either by converting a word processing file or by scanning or imaging a Paper Filing.

(*l*) A "Proposed Order" is a draft of an order submitted for a judge's editing and signature in Word or WordPerfect format, and not in PDF. The process for submitting a Proposed Order to the judge is established by the Court on its website.

(m) "Public Access to Court Electronic Records" or "PACER" is an automated system that allows any individual to view, print and download docket information over the internet.

(n) "Scanned Material" is an electronic image of text or other material in PDF format produced by a scanning or imaging process.

(o) A "Text–Only Order" is a docket entry that constitutes an order. A Text–Only Order is official and binding. See ECF Procedure 7(f).

(p) A "User" is an individual with an approved login and limited password, registered for restricted use of the ECF system in this Court under ECF Procedure 4(b).

ECF Procedure 3—Scope of Electronic Filing

(a) **Electronic Filing Required.** The Court will only accept Papers filed electronically in compliance with these Procedures, unless upon motion showing good cause, the Court enters a specific order authorizing a Paper Filing of a particular Paper.

(b) **Paper Filing Authorized.** The following Papers must be filed by a Paper Filing:

(1) Papers under seal in compliance with ECF Procedure 9;

(2) Papers filed by *pro se* parties;

(3) Proofs of claim filed by entities who are neither Filers nor Users, except that any entity that files ten or more proofs of claims in a calendar year must file such proofs of claims by Electronic Filing;

(4) A Paper commencing or related to a miscellaneous matter; and

(5) Other Papers on a limited basis, if permitted by the assigned judge upon motion showing good cause.

ECF Procedure 4—Registration, Waiver of Notice and Service by Mail, Consent to Electronic Notice and Service, and Withdrawal from Electronic Filing System

(a) **Required Registration Procedure for Filers.** The following must register as Filers in the Court's ECF system:

(1) Attorneys admitted to practice in the United States District Court for the Eastern District of Michigan;

(2) Case trustees and examiners;

(3) Assistant United States Trustees;

(4) Assistant United States Attorneys; and

(5) Others as the Court determines appropriate.

To register as a Filer, a Filer registration must be completed through the on-line registration process available on the Court's Website. To be assigned a Filer login and password, a Filer must either receive ECF training from the Court or training from another U.S. Bankruptcy Court and complete the registration for a login and password in the Bankruptcy Court for the Eastern District of Michigan through the Court's website. (A Filer who has a login name issued only by a district court is still required to receive training from a bankruptcy court.) Members of a Filer's staff are encouraged to participate in ECF training, but will not receive a separate login and password.

(b) **Required Registration for Users.** The following entities must register as ECF Users:

(1) Entities authorized to appear on behalf of a child support creditor;

(2) Entities authorized to file applications to withdraw unclaimed funds;

(3) Entities authorized to submit reaffirmation agreements;

(4) Entities authorized to submit notices of transferred claims; and

(5) Entities authorized to file a certificate of completion of postpetition instructional course concerning personal financial management.

Any entity, including those who file proofs of claim, may register as a User.

To register as a User, a User Registration must be completed through the on-line registration process available on the Court's Website. For instructional material on how to file proofs of claim, reaffirmation agreements, etc., Users must consult the Court's "ECF Creditor Manual" available on the Court's Website. As a general rule, a User will receive one login and password, but upon a written request and a sufficient explanation of business necessity, members of a User's staff may receive separate logins and passwords, although the principal User remains responsible for usage of a staff member's login and password.

(c) **Login and Password.** After the Filer or User's on-line registration is processed and training, if required, is completed, the Court will send an email message notifying the Filer or User of the login and password assigned. The email message ensures that the Filer or User has a properly functioning email address which will be used by the Court's ECF system.

(d) **Password Security.** Each Filer or User is required to protect the security of the assigned password. If there is any reason to believe the security of the assigned password may have been compromised, the Filer or User must immediately notify the Information Technology Department both by email addressed to cmecfhelpdesk@mieb.uscourts.gov *and* by telephone to the clerk at (313) 234–0065. This email message must originate from the primary email address of the registered Filer or User making the report; if that email address is no longer available, the Filer or User may submit the notice by a signed letter on the Filer or User's printed letterhead. A Filer or User may be subject to civil liability, sanctions or other consequences for failure to take required action in connection with the security of the assigned password.

(e) **Electronic Notice And Service Request, Waiver and Consent.** Registration as a Filer or User constitutes waiver of the right to personal service and first class mail service. Registration as a Filer or User also constitutes a written request for, and consent to, electronic service by receipt of a NEF from ECF of all filed Papers to which the Filer or User is entitled, except when service of a hard paper copy is required. (See ECF Procedure 12—"Service on Filers, Users and Others.")

(f) **Withdrawal as Filer or User.** To withdraw from ECF, a Filer or a User must file a written request with the clerk who will then forward the request to the Court for entry of an order authorizing the withdrawal. Upon the entry of such an order, the User's or Filer's password will be deactivated.

(g) **Suspension or Revocation of Use.** Upon notice and opportunity for hearing, the Court may for cause enter an order suspending or revoking participation in ECF by any Filer or User. Upon receiving information indicating a potential risk or harm to ECF, the Court may temporarily suspend participation in ECF by any Filer or User without prior notice, and will provide prompt notification of such action to the Filer or User.

(h) **Payment of Required Fees.** All required fees must be promptly paid; the ECF system permits one credit card payment for a series of filings performed during one log-on session. Failure to complete prompt payment will result in suspension from the ECF system. Upon suspension, an email will be sent for the payments due and the *Internet Payments* option will become the only ECF payment option available. Upon completion of the payments due, the suspension will be automatically terminated and the ECF system will become available.

(i) **Notification of Changes in Information for a Filer or User.** Each Filer and User has a continuing responsibility to notify the Court of any change in any information provided through on-line registration, by promptly completing a Notice of Change of Information Form available on the Court's Website. The Filer or User must also promptly serve a notice of such changes on all other parties in that Filer's or User's open cases. Service upon an obsolete email address will constitute valid service if the Filer or User has not notified the Court of a new email address.

(j) **Accounts Required.** Filers and Users must have both a PACER account and an ECF account in this Court.

ECF Procedure 5—Consequences of Electronic Filing

(a) **Filing and Entry on the Docket.** Once electronic transmission of a Paper to ECF, consistent with these rules, has been received by the Court, the Paper has been filed for all purposes required by the Bankruptcy Code, Federal Rules of Bankruptcy Procedure and the Local Rules of this Court, and is entered upon the docket kept by the clerk under Rule 5003.

(b) **Official Record.** When a Paper has been filed through ECF, the official record is the electronic recording of the Paper as stored by the Court and the filing party is bound by the Paper as if filed by a Paper Filing.

(c) **Filing Date and Time.** A Paper filed through ECF is deemed filed at the date and time stated on the NEF from the Court. Filing a Paper electronically does not alter the filing deadline for the filing of that Paper. Unless otherwise ordered, a filing must be completed before midnight local time where the Court is located in order to be considered timely filed that day.

(d) **Appropriate Title of ECF Filed Papers.** A Filer or User electronically filing a Paper is responsible for designating the appropriate title for that Paper when making a selection from the ECF event menu. Assistance in selecting the appropriate title is available on the Court's website under "Quick Links, Dictionary Events." If a Paper is filed under the wrong event code, the Court will enter an order striking the Paper.

ECF Procedure 6—Filing a Motion Under LBR 9014–1

(a) **Filing a Motion Under LBR 9014–1.** A party filing a motion under LBR 9014–1 must file the following as part of the same PDF file as the motion, with each exhibit separately bookmarked by an identifying tab in the PDF file:

Exhibit 1—The Proposed Order

Exhibit 2—The Notice of Opportunity to Respond

Exhibit 3—The Brief in Support

Exhibit 4—The Proof of Service

Exhibit 5—Affidavits

Exhibit 6—Documentary Exhibits, beginning with a list of the exhibits (See Exhibit A of these Administrative Procedures) and with each exhibit separately bookmarked by an identifying tab in the PDF file.

At the Filer's option, each of these exhibits may be filed as separate attachments to the motion.

The requirement to file a blank notice of hearing is abrogated. The clerk will serve a notice of hearing.

(b) Filing a Certificate of No Response Under LBR 9014–1(c). See ECF Procedure 7(a)(3) and (b).

ECF Procedure 7—Orders

(a) Step One in Obtaining the Entry of an Order. The following must be electronically filed, separately and before a Proposed Order may be submitted, and, except as provided below, <u>may not</u> be combined into one Paper with the Proposed Order:

(1) Approvals as to the form of a Proposed Order under LBR 9021–1(a)(3);

(2) A certificate of no response under LBR 9021–1(a)(4)(A);

(3) A certificate of no response under LBR 9014–1(c), except the requirement to file a copy of the proof of service with this certificate is abrogated;

(4) A stipulation for the entry of an attached Proposed Order;

(5) A statement of consent to the entry of an attached Proposed Order;

(6) A joint motion for the entry of an attached Proposed Order; and,

(7) An *ex parte* motion. (In addition, unless the Court orders otherwise, before submitting a Proposed Order, the *ex parte* motion must be served on all interested parties, either by email or other means.)

If the Court excuses presentment of a Proposed Order under LBR 9021–1(a)(2), the Proposed Order may be submitted as set forth in subpart (b).

The following Papers may have the electronic signatures of consenting parties as otherwise required: a Proposed Order confirming a chapter 13 plan; a stipulation and a Proposed Order adjourning a chapter 13 confirmation hearing. The submission of such a Proposed Order is governed by subpart (b), below.

(b) Step Two in Obtaining the Entry of an Order. The Proposed Order must be submitted in Word or WordPerfect format and <u>not</u> in PDF using the procedure available on the Court's website. The Proposed Order must <u>not</u> contain a signature block for the judge's signature, and must be left blank after the text of the Proposed Order. No other special formatting is required for a Proposed Order submitted by this procedure.

(c) Consideration of a Proposed Order. If the judge declines to enter a Proposed Order, the judge may prepare and enter an order, or the judge may direct that counsel submit a revised Proposed Order.

(d) Effect of a Judge's Electronic Signature. The electronic signature of a bankruptcy judge on any order, judgment or other Paper filed in ECF will have the same force and effect as if the judge had manually signed a hard paper copy.

(e) Text–Only Orders. Upon request or upon its own initiative, the Court may cause the entry of a Text–Only Order. A motion or stipulation may suggest language for a proposed Text–Only Order. A Text–Only Order will have the same force and effect as if the judge had manually signed a hard paper copy. Upon the entry of a Text–Only Order, ECF will generate a NEF. When a Text–Only Order is entered, the judge will not generally issue an order in PDF.

(f) Entry on the Docket. The entry of an order or a judgment on the docket required to be kept by the clerk under Bankruptcy Rules 5003 and 9021 results when the Court either (1) files an order or a judgment in ECF, or (2) enters a Text–Only Order.

(g) Notice of an Order or a Judgment. Immediately upon the entry of an order or a judgment, the clerk will:

(1) Electronically transmit a NEF to all Filers and Users who are or who represent contesting parties, and to other Filers and Users that the Court directs, which constitutes the notice required by Bankruptcy Rule 9022; and

(2) Give notice to contesting parties who are neither Filers nor Users, and to others as the Court directs, in accordance with the Federal Rules of Bankruptcy Procedure.

(h) Format of Orders. Proposed orders should be in a basic text format. The following must **not** be a part of a Proposed Order: party or attorney signatures; textboxes; saved as "read-only"; linked fields; attached templates; add–ons; lines at the end of the final paragraph; and signature block for judge. Six single spaced lines must be left at the end for the Court to insert the judge's signature block and date stamp. If necessary, the last page should be broken up so that the signature block and date stamp does not become appended to an additional page. (NOTE: The best method to determine where the signature block and date stamp will be inserted is to hold down the **ctrl** key and press the **end** key. This will place the cursor at the insertion point.)

(i) Orders Resolving Multi–Part Motions. A Proposed Order resolving a motion requesting more than one type of relief must specify a disposition for each such request. Any request for relief not addressed in the Proposed Order will be deemed denied without prejudice.

ECF Procedure 8—Filing Format Requirements

(a) PDF Requirements. All Papers transmitted to ECF must be Electronically Generated Text in PDF format so that the text of the Paper may be searched and copied, except as provided in subpart (c) below. The file name of a converted file must contain the extension ".pdf". All fonts embedded in PDF records (except in Papers that have been scanned) must have been publicly identified as legally embeddable (i.e., the font license permits embedding) in a file for unlimited, universal viewing and printing. The most commonly used font styles are: Courier (Regular, Bold, Italic, and Bold Italic); Arial MT (Regular, Bold, Oblique, and Bold Oblique); Times New Roman PS MT (Roman, Bold, Italic, and Bold Italic); Symbol; and ZapfDingbats.

(b) Hyperlinks. A Hyperlink contained in an Electronic Filing is merely a convenient mechanism created by the author for accessing material cited in a Paper. A Hyperlink is not a part of the Court's record. Accordingly, the Court does not endorse nor exercise any responsibility over the content at the Hyperlink destination. Any Hyperlink to a case or other authority included in a Paper must be expressed in the full traditional citation method for the cited authority.

(c) Attachments and Exhibits. All attachments and exhibits available in original electronic format must be converted to PDF and filed electronically, subject to the size limitations and formatting requirements contained herein. All attachments and exhibits not available as Electronically Generated Text (i.e., those that must be scanned) must be transmitted to ECF as Scanned Material in PDF format. The filing party must retain a paper copy, or an accurate electronic copy, of all attachments and exhibits until entry of a final order by the Court and, if applicable, appellate courts.

(d) Size Limitations Per Transmission. Each transmission to ECF must not exceed five (5) megabytes total file size. Files which exceed five (5) megabytes must be broken into smaller files and transmitted to ECF in multiple transmissions. The ECF system may refuse to accept a Paper in excess of this limitation.

(e) Use of Bookmarks Required for Grouped Papers. In some circumstances, the ECF event menu permits a group of Papers to be filed together as a single PDF file (e.g., the petition and accompanying Papers); when such a group of Papers is filed, each such separate Paper (including each separate schedule, the statement of financial affairs, etc.) must be separately bookmarked by an identifying tab in the PDF file.

(f) Requirement to File Separate Document. Official Form 122A–1, Chapter 7 Statement of Your Current Monthly Income (along with Official Form 122A–1 Supp.; Statement of Exemption from Presumption of Abuse Under § 707(b)(2), if applicable), which is required to be filed by every individual chapter 7 debtor whose debts are primarily consumer debts, must be filed *as a separate Paper* and must not be filed within a group of Papers described in ECF Procedure 8(e).

ECF Procedure 9—Filing a Paper Under Seal

Unless otherwise ordered by the Court, a motion to file a Paper under seal must be filed electronically. The motion must not contain confidential or privileged information. The proposed order authorizing the filing of a Paper under seal must be submitted under ECF Procedure 7(b). The Paper ordered to be filed under seal must be filed with the clerk both in hard paper copy, placed in a sealed envelope, with a statement on the envelope indicating the title of the Paper to be sealed, the case number and case name, and in PDF on diskette, compact disc (CD), or digital video disc (DVD), accompanied by a copy of the order to seal the Paper. The Court may sua sponte order a Paper to be sealed.

ECF Procedure 10—Retention Requirements

(a) Retention of a Paper with an Original Signature. Each Paper that must contain an original signature by a person other than the Filer or User, or that is required to be verified under Rule 1008 or as provided in 28 U.S.C. § 1746 by a person other than the Filer or User, must be filed electronically by a Filer or a User. The Filer or User who files the Paper must retain for five years after the closing of the case or adversary proceeding either (1) the Paper containing the original signature or (2) an electronically scanned copy of the Paper containing the original signature. This retention does not affect or replace any other retention period required by other applicable laws or rules.

(b) Sanctions; Production of Original Papers. Failure to comply with subpart (a) will subject the Filer or User to sanctions, including disgorgement of fees. On request of the Court or any party in interest, the Filer or User must provide the Paper containing the original signature or an electronically scanned copy of the Paper containing the original signature for review.

ECF Procedure 11—Signatures

(a) Electronic Filing Constitutes Signature. The filing by a Filer or User of any Paper constitutes any required signature of that Filer or User on such Paper. The Filer or User need not manually sign a transmitted Paper. The filing is the equivalent of signing a Paper for all purposes, including, without limitation, the Federal Rules of Bankruptcy Procedure, including Rule 9011, the Bankruptcy Code, and the Local Bankruptcy Rules of this Court.

(b) Electronic Filing Constitutes Certification. The filing by a Filer or User of any Paper constitutes certification of the Filer or User that all persons other than the Filer or User indicated to have signed the Paper have actually executed an original prior to filing with the Court.

(c) Use of Password. A Filer or User must not knowingly permit or cause to permit the Filer's or User's password to be used by anyone other than an agent specifically authorized by the Filer or User.

(d) Form of Electronic Signatures.

(1) *Required Information for Filers and Users.* A Paper filed by ECF must be signed in the following form and must include the following information:

/s/ Name of Filer or User
Address
City, State, Zip Code
Phone: (xxx) xxx-xxxx
Email: xxx@xxx.xxx
[attorney bar number, if applicable]

(2) *Filing a Paper with Multiple Signatures.* A Paper with more than one signature must contain the signature form and information required by subpart (d)(1) for each signature. The filing of such a Paper constitutes certification that all persons indicated to have signed the Paper have actually signed an original prior to filing or have consented to their signature on the Paper.

ECF Procedure 12—Service on Filers, Users and Others

(a) Service Upon Filers and Users. Pursuant to the consent of a Filer or User through ECF registration:

(1) The transmission from the Court to the Filer or User of the NEF of a Paper constitutes notice and service of the filed Paper upon that Filer or User.

(2) If two or more attorneys appear on behalf of a party, service on one of the attorneys will be sufficient, unless otherwise required by law.

(3) Service of a Paper filed through ECF is complete upon transmission of the NEF by ECF.

(b) When Service of a Hard Paper Copy is Required. A hard paper copy of the following must be served in accordance with the rules applicable to them:

(1) In a bankruptcy case, a motion under Rule 9014, except that service by mail is not required to any respondent's attorney who is on the Electronic Email Notice List of the case, which is available through the ECF Utilities screen by clicking on –> Mailings... –> Mailing Info for a Case –> [Enter Case Number –> Submit];

(2) In an adversary proceeding,

(i) a summons and complaint under Rule 7004; and,

(ii) a motion filed with a complaint, such as a motion for a temporary restraining order or a motion for a preliminary injunction.

In an adversary proceeding, any other motion may be filed and served electronically.

(c) Issuance of a Summons in an Adversary Proceeding. The issuance of a summons in an adversary proceeding must be completed electronically as follows:

(1) After the complaint is filed by ECF, the Filer must download the issued summons in PDF format by clicking on the appropriate Hyperlink in the NEF.

(2) The Filer must then print and serve as required a hard copy of the summons. The Filer must not bring the summons to the clerk's office for issuance.

(3) The summons is deemed issued when the complaint is filed.

(d) Issuance of a Summons in an Involuntary Bankruptcy Case. The issuance of a summons in an involuntary bankruptcy case must be completed electronically as follows:

(1) After filing the involuntary petition, the Filer must download the issued summons in PDF format by clicking on the appropriate Hyperlink in the NEF.

(2) The Filer must then print and serve as required a hard paper copy of the completed and filed summons.

(3) The summons is deemed issued when the involuntary petition is filed.

(e) Issuance of a Subpoena. A PDF form of subpoena is available through the Court's website. This form can be downloaded, completed, printed and then served as appropriate. No filing is necessary, except that a proof of service may be filed.

(f) [Deleted]

(g) Service Upon Others. Service upon anyone who has not registered as a Filer or User must be made according to the Federal Rules of Bankruptcy Procedure and any applicable Local Bankruptcy Rules.

(h) Certificate of Service Required. A party serving a Paper must file a certificate of service. The certificate must state the Paper served, the manner in which service was accomplished, and the parties served. This certificate of service may not be included as part of the Paper that was served; it must be a separate filing. Appendix B is a sample certificate of service.

ECF Procedure 13—Technical Failure

In the event of a technical failure in the ECF system, the Court will determine whether to extend deadlines under Rule 9006(a).

ECF Procedure 14—Public Access

(a) Public Access at the Court. The public may view all Papers in the ECF System at no charge at the clerk's offices in Bay City, Detroit and Flint during regular business hours.

(b) Internet Access. Internet access to the ECF system is limited to subscribers to PACER. In accordance with the Bankruptcy Court Fee Schedule established by the Judicial Conference of the United States pursuant to 28 U.S.C. § 1930, fees are charged for accessing certain detailed case information. Information regarding subscribing to PACER is available on the Court's Website and at the clerk's offices in Bay City, Detroit and Flint.

(c) Copies and Certified Copies. Copies and certified copies of electronically filed Papers may be purchased at the clerk's office. The fee for copying and certification is in accordance with 28 U.S.C. § 1930.

ECF Procedure 15—Privacy

In compliance with the policy of the Judicial Conference of the United States, and the E-Government Act of 2002, and in order to promote electronic access to case files while also protecting personal privacy and other legitimate interests, parties must refrain from including, or must partially redact where inclusion is necessary, the following personal data identifiers from all Papers filed with the Court, including exhibits thereto, whether filed electronically or by a Paper Filing, unless otherwise ordered by the Court or required by statute, the Federal Rules of Bankruptcy Procedure, or the Official Bankruptcy Forms.

(a) Social Security Numbers. If an individual's social security number must be included in a Paper, only the last four digits of that number should be used.

(b) Names of Minor Children. If the involvement of a minor child must be mentioned, only the initials of that child should be used. On Schedule J of Official Bankruptcy Form 106, list the relationship and age of the debtor's dependents (e.g., Son, Age 6).

(c) Dates of Birth. If an individual's date of birth must be included in a Paper, only the year should be used. On Schedule J of Official Bankruptcy Form 106, list the age of each of the debtor's dependents.

(d) Financial Account Numbers. If financial account numbers are relevant, only the last four digits of these numbers should be used. On Schedules D and E/F of Official Bankruptcy Form 106, debtors, if they so choose, may include their full account numbers to assist the trustee and creditors.

In compliance with the E-Government Act of 2002, a party wishing to file a Paper containing the personal data identifiers listed above may file a motion to file an unredacted Paper under seal as set forth under ECF Procedure 9. This Paper will be retained by the Court as part of the record. The Court may still require the party to file a redacted copy for the public file.

The responsibility for redacting these personal identifiers rests solely with counsel and the parties. The clerk will not review each Paper for compliance with this rule.

Appendix A—Sample Exhibit List

UNITED STATES BANKRUPTCY COURT
EASTERN DISTRICT OF MICHIGAN

[CASE CAPTION]

Exhibit List

Exhibit	Description
A	Affidavit of John Smith
B	Excerpts from Jane Doe's Deposition
C–1	Contract between XYZ Company and ABC Company (Part 1, Pages 1–35)
C–2	Contract between XYZ Company and ABC Company (Part 1, Pages 36–69)
D	XYZ Company General Ledgers

Appendix B—Sample Certificate of Service

UNITED STATES BANKRUPTCY COURT
EASTERN DISTRICT OF MICHIGAN

[CASE CAPTION]

Certificate of Service

I hereby certify that on ___(date)___, I served the following Paper:

_____

_____

_____,

on the following parties at these addresses:

_____

_____

_____

By the following means:

_____

/s/ Name of Filer or User

Address

City, State, Zip Code

Phone: (xxx) xxx-xxxx

Email: xxx@xxx.xxx

[attorney bar number, if applicable]

[Adopted effective May 16, 2005. Amended effective September 26, 2005; November 15, 2005; February 14, 2006; June 13, 2006; August 23, 2006; May 7, 2008; February 1, 2016; December 8, 2016.]

UNITED STATES DISTRICT COURT FOR THE WESTERN DISTRICT OF MICHIGAN

Including Amendments Received Through
January 1, 2018

LOCAL RULES OF CIVIL PRACTICE AND PROCEDURE

PREFACE TO THE 1998 EDITION

On March 12, 1996, the Judicial Conference approved the recommendation of the Committee on Rules of Practice and Procedure to "adopt a numbering system for local rules of court that corresponds with the relevant Federal Rules of Practice and Procedure." The action of the Judicial Conference implements the December 1, 1995 amendments to the Federal Rules of Appellate, Bankruptcy, Civil, and Criminal Procedure, which provide that all local rules of court "must conform to any uniform numbering system prescribed by the Judicial Conference." (See Appellate Rule 47, Bankruptcy Rules 8018 and 9029, Civil Rule 83, and Criminal Rule 57.)

In addition to the substantive changes to the local rules found in the 1998 Edition, the Rules have been renumbered to comply with this mandate. The result is that, rather than being consecutively numbered, the rules have been assigned numbers which best correspond to the numbering scheme of the Federal Rules of Civil and Criminal Procedure. The renumbered Local Civil Rules and the renumbered Local Criminal Rules have been compiled as separate sets of Rules. Many of the rules familiar to practitioners under the prior edition remain substantively intact, but have had their provisions redistributed to two or more new rules within the newly-mandated numbering system.

Local Civil Rules which do not correspond to any rule within the Federal Rules of Civil Procedure have been assigned to Rule 83, which, in the Federal Rules of Civil Procedure, governs the rulemaking authority of the courts of the various districts.

I.   SCOPE OF RULES

LOCAL CIVIL RULE 1.   AUTHORITY; SCOPE; CONSTRUCTION

1.1.   Authority. These rules are promulgated pursuant to 28 U.S.C. § 2071 and Rule 83 of the Federal Rules of Civil Procedure. Amendment of these rules is governed by LCivR 83.3(f).

1.2.   Short Title. These rules may be cited and referred to individually as "W.D. Mich. LCivR _____."

1.3.   Effective Date. The effective date of these rules is June 1, 1998, including amendments through September 18, 2017.

1.4.   Applicability. These rules apply to all civil proceedings in this Court.

1.5.   Scope. These rules govern the procedure in the United States District Court for the Western District of Michigan, govern the practice of attorneys before this Court, and supersede all previous rules promulgated by this Court or any judge thereof. Administrative orders and single-judge standing orders shall be maintained by the Clerk and made available upon request. All such orders shall be consistent with these rules and the Federal Rules of Civil Procedure.

1.6.   Construction. These rules shall be construed to achieve an orderly administration of the business of this Court and to secure the just, speedy and inexpensive determination of every action. References to statutes, regulations or rules shall be interpreted to include all revisions and amendments thereto. References to the Clerk shall be interpreted to mean the Clerk of this Court or any deputy clerk. Wherever used in these rules, the term "party," whether in the singular or plural, shall include all parties appearing in the action pro se and the attorney or attorneys of record for represented parties, where appropriate.

[Effective June 1, 1998. Amended effective September 3, 2003; April 5, 2004; April 19, 2010; May 27, 2011; February 8, 2012; May 9, 2012; December 2, 2013; March 19, 2014; September 28, 2015; July 14, 2016; September 18, 2017.]

II. COMMENCEMENT OF ACTION; SERVICE OF PROCESS, PLEADINGS, MOTIONS, AND ORDERS

LOCAL CIVIL RULE 3. COMMENCEMENT OF ACTION; ASSIGNMENT TO DIVISION AND JUDGE

3.1. Fee Payment. The fee provided by 28 U.S.C. § 1914 shall be paid to the Clerk. The Clerk may require that any payment be in cash or certified check.

3.2. Assignment of Cases to Divisions. This district is composed of a Northern Division and a Southern Division. The residence of corporations, partnerships, and unincorporated associations shall be the division where the principal place of business is maintained. The Southern Division comprises the counties of Allegan, Antrim, Barry, Benzie, Berrien, Branch, Calhoun, Cass, Charlevoix, Clinton, Eaton, Emmet, Grand Traverse, Hillsdale, Ingham, Ionia, Kalamazoo, Kalkaska, Kent, Lake, Leelanau, Manistee, Mason, Mecosta, Missaukee, Montcalm, Muskegon, Newaygo, Oceana, Osceola, Ottawa, Saint Joseph, Van Buren, and Wexford. The Northern Division comprises the counties of Alger, Baraga, Chippewa, Delta, Dickinson, Gogebic, Houghton, Iron, Keweenaw, Luce, Mackinac, Marquette, Menominee, Ontonagon, and Schoolcraft. 28 U.S.C. § 102(b). All cases shall be assigned to a division by application of the following order of priorities:

(a) if an action is removed from state court, the division embracing the county in which the case was pending in state court;

(b) in bankruptcy appeals, the division in which the bankruptcy matter is pending;

(c) if the action is local in nature, the division in which the real property is located;

(d) in prisoner civil rights cases, the division in which the claim arose;

(e) the division in which all plaintiffs reside;

(f) the division in which all defendants reside;

(g) the division in which the claim arose;

(h) in a case in which a defendant is an officer or employee of the United States or any agency thereof acting in an official capacity, or under color of legal authority, or an agency of the United States, the division in which an office of a defendant is located; or

(i) the division in which the case is filed.

3.3.1. Assignment of Cases to District Judges.

(a) *Method.* Each civil action (except social security cases) and each bankruptcy appeal, shall be assigned to a district judge, who shall continue in the case or matter until its final disposition, except as hereinafter provided. Each Social Security action shall be assigned at random to a magistrate judge at the time of filing. The parties will thereafter be given an opportunity to consent voluntarily to the dispositive jurisdiction of the assigned magistrate judge pursuant to 28 U.S.C. § 636(c). If all parties do not timely consent, the case will be assigned to a district judge at random and will be referred to

the originally assigned magistrate judge under 28 U.S.C. § 636(b)(1).

(b) *Sequence.* At the commencement of each civil case, the Clerk shall assign the case a sequential case number and assign the case to a judge in accordance with the next subsection. The numbering and assignment of each case shall be completed before processing of the next case is commenced.

(c) *Procedure.* The Clerk shall use automated or manual means to assign new cases to judges at random in accordance with administrative orders issued by the Court from time to time. The Clerk shall mark the name of the assigned judge on the first document of the case and preserve a record of such assignments.

(d) *Exceptions.*

(i) Refilings. If a case is dismissed or remanded to state court and later refiled, either in the same or similar form, upon refiling it shall be assigned or transferred to the judge to whom it was originally assigned.

(ii) Subsequent Proceedings. Subsequent proceedings in cases shall be assigned to the judge assigned to the original case, if that judge is still hearing cases.

(iii) Related Cases. Cases related to cases already assigned to a judge shall be assigned or transferred as set out below.

(A) Definition. Cases are deemed related when a filed case (1) relates to property involved in an earlier numbered pending suit, or (2) arises out of the same transaction or occurrence and involves one or more of the same parties as a pending suit, or (3) involves the validity or infringement of a patent already in suit in any pending earlier numbered case.

(B) Determination. When it appears to the Clerk that two or more cases may be related cases, they shall be referred to the magistrate judge assigned to the judge who has the earliest case to determine whether or not the cases are related. If related, the cases will be assigned to the same judge. If cases are found to be related cases after assignment to different judges, they may be reassigned by the Chief Judge to the judge having the related case earliest filed.

(e) *Miscellaneous Docket.* The miscellaneous docket of the Court shall be assigned at random to a magistrate judge at the time of filing. If a miscellaneous docket matter is contested and requires proceedings conducted before a district judge, the case will be randomly reassigned to a district judge and a new civil action number will be assigned.

(f) *Effect.* This rule is intended to provide for an orderly division of the business of the Court and not to grant any right to any litigant.

(g) *Duty of Parties.* All parties shall notify the Court in writing of all pending related cases and any dismissed or remanded prior cases.

3.3.2. Reassignment of Cases.

(a) *Reassignment of Cases on Grounds of Geographic Convenience.* Promptly after all parties have appeared in any civil action, the parties may file a stipulation and motion requesting transfer of the action to a judge located in a different city, on the basis of the convenience of counsel, the parties, or witnesses. Reassignment of the action shall be at the discretion of the Court and shall require the consent of all parties and of both the transferor and transferee judge.

(b) *Reassignment to Promote Judicial Economy.* The Court may reassign cases from one district judge to another (i) to equalize and balance workloads among judges; (ii) to assign cases to senior or visiting judges or remove cases from their dockets as necessary; or (iii) for other reasons of judicial economy. Any case may be reassigned under this rule from one judge to another judge with the consent of both judges. Cases may also be reassigned by administrative order of the Chief Judge if approved by a majority of active district judges.

(c) *Reassignment of Cognate Cases.*

(i) Definition. Cognate cases are pending civil actions involving the same or similar questions of fact or law such that their assignment to a single judge is likely to effect a substantial saving of judicial effort and to avoid wasteful and duplicative proceedings for the court and the parties.

(ii) Procedure for Reassignment. When any judge determines that reassignment of cognate cases would serve the interests of justice and judicial economy, the judge will contact all other judges to whom cognate cases have been assigned. If all those judges agree to reassignment, the Chief Judge will enter an administrative order reassigning such cognate cases to the judge with the earliest numbered case. The administrative order may also provide for automatic assignment of future cognate cases to that judge, and for an adjustment in future case assignments to that judge to compensate for the increased workload.

3.4. In Forma Pauperis Proceedings.

(a) *Motion and Supporting Documents.* All persons applying to proceed in forma pauperis in this Court or on appeal shall file with their complaint or notice of appeal a motion for leave to proceed in forma pauperis supported by the financial affidavit required under 28 U.S.C. § 1915(a)(1). In addition, any person incarcerated under a state or federal criminal conviction shall submit a certified copy of the prison trust fund account statement for the prisoner for the six-month period immediately preceding the filing of the complaint or notice of appeal, obtained from the appropriate official of each prison at which the prisoner is or was confined. The statement shall disclose

(i) the amount then in the trust fund account;

(ii) all deposits and withdrawals from the account during the six-month period immediately preceding the filing of the complaint or notice of appeal as required by 28 U.S.C. § 1915(a)(2).

(b) *Determination of Pauper Status.* A petition for leave to proceed in forma pauperis shall be presented by the Clerk to any available magistrate judge. If the financial affidavit discloses that the person is unable to pay the full filing fee or fees for service of process, the magistrate judge shall grant the petition for pauper status. The magistrate judge shall nevertheless order that a prisoner pay, within a specified period, an initial partial filing fee and make monthly payments thereafter in accordance with 28 U.S.C. § 1915(b). If the person fails to comply with the order for payment of all or any part of the filing fee, the complaint may be dismissed by a district judge or the appeal may be dismissed for want of prosecution by the Sixth Circuit Court of Appeals.

[Effective June 1, 1998. Amended effective June 20, 2005; February 15, 2007; May 27, 2011; February 21, 2017.]

LOCAL CIVIL RULE 4.1 FEE PAYMENT TO MARSHAL

4.1.1. A deposit in a sum deemed sufficient by the marshal to cover fees for the service to be performed shall be made in every instance in which the marshal is required to perform service. The marshal may require that any payment be in cash or certified check.

[Effective June 1, 1998.]

LOCAL CIVIL RULE 5. SERVICE AND FILING OF PLEADINGS AND OTHER PAPERS

5.1. Cover Sheet. A cover sheet obtained from the Clerk shall be filed with each new case and all required information shall be supplied.

5.2. Proof of Service. Proof of service of all pleadings and other papers required or permitted to be served shall be filed promptly after service and may be made by written acknowledgment of service, by affidavit of the person making service or by written certification of counsel. Proof of service shall state the date and manner of service. Proof of service is unnecessary for documents served electronically on a registered attorney.

5.3. Filing of Discovery Materials.

(a) Interrogatories, requests for production or inspection, requests for admissions, and responses or objections shall be served upon other parties, but shall not be filed with the Court. Only a proof of service shall be filed with the Court. The party responsible for service of these discovery materials shall retain the original and become the custodian.

(b) Transcripts of depositions shall not be filed with the Court.

(c) If discovery materials are to be used at trial, relevant portions of the materials to be used shall be filed with the Clerk at or before trial. If discovery materials are necessary to any motion, relevant portions of the materials shall be filed with the Clerk with the motion or response.

5.4. Place of Filing. Pleadings and other papers may be filed with the Clerk at any divisional office during walk-in business hours. If a hearing is scheduled, it is incumbent upon the party to insure that the judge or magistrate judge receives a copy of such relevant pleadings or other papers sufficiently in advance of the hearing.

5.5. Rejection of Filings. The Court may order the Clerk to reject any pleading or other paper that does not comply with these rules or the Federal Rules of Civil Procedure unless such noncompliance is expressly approved by the Court. The Clerk shall return any rejected filing to the party tendering it, along with a statement of the reasons for rejection.

5.6. Pleadings and Other Papers in Particular Cases.

(a) *Actions by Prisoners.* Habeas corpus petitions or complaints brought under the Civil Rights Acts by prisoners proceeding pro se shall be in the form specified by the Court. The Clerk shall make such forms available to prisoners desiring to file such actions.

(b) *In Pro Per Petitions.* Absent good cause, in all proceedings brought in propria persona or in forma pauperis, the petition or complaint shall not be accepted for filing unless it is accompanied by a copy or copies in number sufficient for service on the respondent(s) or the defendant(s).

5.7. Filing and Service by Electronic Means.

(a) *General Information; Definitions.* Pursuant to Rule 5(d) of the Federal Rules of Civil Procedure, the Clerk will accept pleadings and other papers filed and signed by electronic means in accordance with this rule. All papers filed by electronic means must comply with technical standards, if any, now or hereafter established by the Judicial Conference of the United States.

This rule shall apply to all civil actions maintained in the court's electronic case filing system. All documents, whether filed electronically or on paper, will be placed into the electronic case filing system, except as provided below. Attorneys must file and serve all documents electronically by use of the ECF system unless (1) the attorney has been specifically exempted by the Court for cause or (2) a particular document is not eligible for electronic filing under this rule.

As used in this rule, the term

- "ECF system" means the electronic case filing system maintained by this Court;
- "registered attorney" means an attorney who is authorized pursuant to Rule 5.7(b) to file documents electronically and to receive service on the ECF system;
- "initial pleading" means the complaint, petition or other document by which a civil action is initiated;
- "electronically filed document" means any order, opinion, judgment, pleading, notice, transcript, motion, brief or other paper submitted electronically to the ECF system;
- "traditionally filed document" means a pleading or other paper submitted to the Clerk in paper form for filing;
- "NEF" means the Notice of Electronic Filing generated by the ECF system;
- "nonelectronic means of service" means one of the methods of service authorized by Rule 5(b) of the Federal Rules of Civil Procedure, except electronic service under Rule 5(b)(2)(E).

(b) *Mandatory Registration; Attorney Training.*

(i) Every attorney practicing in this Court must register to file and serve documents electronically by the ECF system.

(ii) To be entitled to register as a user of the ECF system, an attorney must be admitted to practice in this District, be a member in good standing, and have filed with the Clerk a completed ECF Attorney Registration form. In addition, the attorney or the attorney's firm must have a Public Access to Court Electronic Records (PACER) account and an e-mail address.

Detailed registration information is available on the Court's Website (www.miwd.uscourts.gov). Upon receipt of the ECF Attorney Registration form, the Court will issue a login name and a user password to qualified attorneys. All registered attorneys have an affirmative duty to update their accounts with any change in their e-mail address. A registered attorney may not knowingly cause or allow another person to file a document using the attorney's login name and password, except for members of the attorney's staff. Authorized use of an attorney's login name and password by a staff member is deemed to be the act of the attorney. However, a registered attorney must not allow an unregistered attorney, even a member of the same firm, to use his or her login name and password. If a login name and/or password should become compromised, the attorney is responsible for notifying the ECF Help Desk immediately.

(iii) The Clerk's Office will provide periodic training sessions on use of the ECF system. The Court will also provide on its Website a User's Manual containing instructions on the use of the ECF system and an on-line tutorial. Law firms are encouraged to have individuals responsible for electronic filing (attorney, paralegal or automation specialist) attend a live training session or use the on-line tutorial.

(c) *Initial Pleading.* All attorneys must submit complaints and other initial pleadings in civil cases electronically, following the "Case Opening Protocol" posted by the Clerk on the Court's Website, unless the pleading is exempt from electronic filing under subrule (d)(ii) of this rule, or the attorney is granted an exception by the Chief Judge for good cause shown. Filing fees must be paid (or a motion for leave to proceed in forma pauperis must be filed) electronically at the time the initial pleading is electronically submitted. A civil case is not commenced until the initial pleading has been accepted by the ECF system and a Notice of Electronic Filing has issued. Unrepresented parties must file initial pleadings and pay the filing fee (or seek in forma pauperis status) by the traditional method.

(d) *Electronic Filing.*

(i) Mandatory Electronic Filing. All attorneys must file all pleadings and other papers permitted by the Federal Rules and the Local Rules of this Court electronically in all civil cases, subject to the exceptions set forth below. All electronically filed documents must be in PDF digital format and must be submitted in accordance with the instructions set forth in the User's Manual. *Pro se* parties who are not members of the bar of the Court may not file pleadings or other papers electronically, but must submit them in paper form.

(ii) Papers That May Not Be Filed Electronically. The following documents must not be filed electronically, but must be submitted in paper form:

(A) Documents submitted by a person who is not a registered attorney (for example, a *pro se* litigant);

(B) [Repealed]

(C) Documents that are required by statute to be filed *in camera*, such as complaints and certain other filings submitted under the Federal False Claims Act or analogous state statutes.

(D) Papers filed in cases that have been sealed in their entirety.

(E) Garnishee disclosures and other documents submitted by unrepresented third parties in response to writs or other court process;

(iii) Electronic Filing of Affidavits and Other Original Documents. The following documents must be filed electronically by submission of a scanned PDF version of the original document:

(A) Affidavits in support of or in opposition to a motion (this rule does not apply to affidavits of service);

(B) Declarations under penalty of perjury;

(C) Certified copies of judgments or orders of other Courts.

The electronically filed version of such documents must bear a scanned image of all original manuscript signatures. The filer must meet the requirements of Rule 5.7(e)(viii) regarding evidence of an original signature.

(iv) Deadlines. Filing documents electronically does not in any way alter any filing deadlines. An electronically filed document is deemed filed upon completion of the transmission and issuance by the Court's system of an NEF. In situations where Rule 5.7(d)(vii) requires that attachments to an electronically filed document be submitted in paper form, the electronic document is deemed filed upon issuance of the NEF, provided that the paper exhibits are filed and served within 72 hours thereof. All electronic transmissions of documents must be completed (i.e., received completely by the Clerk's Office) prior to midnight, Eastern Time, in order to be considered timely filed that day. Where a specific time of day deadline is set by Court order or stipulation, the electronic filing must be completed by that time.

(v) Technical Failures. The Clerk shall deem the Court's Website to be subject to a technical failure on a given day if the site is unable to accept filings continuously or intermittently over the course of any period of time greater than one hour after 12:00 noon (Eastern Time) that day, in which case, filings due that day which were not filed due solely to such technical failures shall become due the next business day. Such delayed filings must be accompanied by a declaration or affidavit attesting to the filer's failed attempts to file electronically at least two times after 12:00 noon separated by at least one hour on each day of delay because of such technical failure. The initial point of contact for any practitioner experiencing difficulty filing a document electronically shall be the ECF Help Desk, available via phone at (616) 456–2206 or (800) 290–2742, or via e-mail at ecfhelp@miwd.uscourts.gov.

(vi) Official Record; Discarding of Traditionally Filed Documents. For purposes of Rule 79 of the Federal Rules of Civil Procedure, the record of filings and entries created by the ECF system for each case constitutes the docket. The official record of all proceedings in civil cases filed on and after August 1, 2001, is the electronic file maintained on the Court's ECF system. The Clerk's Office will discard all traditionally filed documents after they have become part of the electronic record, unless the document produces a low-quality electronic file.

(vii) Exhibits and Attachments.

(A) Oversized Documents. No PDF document exceeding 10 MB in size may be filed in the CM/ECF system. Filers must divide such documents into component parts, each part not to exceed 10 MB in size, for purposes of electronic filing. The docket entry must clearly indicate that the document is filed in parts. An exhibit may be filed traditionally only if it is exempt from electronic filing under subrule (d)(ii) of this rule.

(B) Requirements. Filers must not attach as an exhibit any pleading or other paper already on file with the Court, but shall merely refer to that document. All exhibits and attachments, whether filed electronically or traditionally, must contain on their face a prominent exhibit number or letter. If one or more attachments or exhibits to an electronically filed document are being submitted traditionally under this rule, the electronically filed document must contain a notice of that fact in its text.

(e) *Signature.*

(i) Attorneys. A registered attorney's use of the assigned login name and password to submit an electronically filed document serves as the registered attorney's signature on that document for purposes of Fed. R. Civ. P. 11 and for all other purposes under the Federal Rules of Civil Procedure and the Local Rules of this Court. The identity of the registered attorney submitting the electronically filed document must be reflected at the end of the document by means of an " s/[attorney's name]" block showing the attorney's name, followed by the attorney's business address, telephone number, and e-mail address. Graphic and other electronic signatures are discouraged.

(ii) Multiple Attorney Signatures. The filer of any electronically filed document requiring multiple signatures (e.g., stipulations, joint status reports) must list thereon all the names of other attorney signatories by means of an " s/[attorney's name]" block for each. By submitting such a document, the filer certifies that each of the other attorneys has expressly agreed to the form and substance of the document, that the filer has their actual authority to submit the document electronically, and that the requirements of Rule 5.7(e)(viii) regarding evidence of original signature have been met. This paragraph does not apply to pro-se or unrepresented parties, whose manuscript signature, in original or scanned form, must appear on the face of the document.

(iii) Court Reporters. The electronic filing of a transcript by a court reporter by use of the court reporter's login name and password shall be deemed the filing of a signed and certified original document for all purposes.

(iv) Judges. The electronic filing of an opinion, order, judgment or other document by a judge (or authorized member of the judge's staff) by use of the judge's login and password shall be deemed the filing of a signed original document for all purposes.

(v) Clerk of Court or Deputy Clerks. The electronic filing of any document by the Clerk or a Deputy Clerk of this Court, of the Bankruptcy Court of this District, or of any Circuit Court of Appeals by use of that individual's login and password shall be deemed the filing of a signed original document for all purposes.

(vi) Office of the U.S. Marshal. The office of the U.S. Marshal for this District is authorized to file and serve documents electronically. The electronic filing of any document by the Office of the U.S. Marshal by use of the assigned login and password shall be deemed the filing of a signed original document for all purposes.

(vii) Officers of the Court. If the court has appointed a special master, monitor, or other court adjunct who is required to make regular filings, the Court may authorize the officer to file and serve documents electronically. The officer of the court shall complete a registration form, and upon assignment of a login and password to the system, has authority to file and serve documents electronically in the case in which the officer was appointed. The electronic filing of any document by a court officer by use of the assigned login and password shall be deemed the filing of a signed original document for all purposes.

(viii) Evidence of Original Signature. Filers of documents containing signatures authorized by Rule 5.7(e)(ii) (multiple attorney signatures) must maintain any records evidencing concurrence, and filers of documents containing signatures authorized by Rule 5.7(d)(iii) (electronically filed affidavits, etc.) must maintain the documents bearing the original manual signature for subsequent production to the Court or for inspection by a party until one year after the final resolution of the action (including appeal, if any). A non-filing signatory or party who disputes the authenticity of a signature on an electronically filed document must file an objection to the document within fourteen (14) days after service of that document.

(f) *Proposed Pleadings.* Except for proposed sealed filings, if the filing of an electronically submitted document requires leave of court, such as an amended complaint or brief in excess of page limits, the proposed document must be attached as an exhibit to the motion seeking leave to file. If the Court grants leave to file the document, the Clerk of Court will electronically file the document without further action by the attorney. Requests to file documents under seal are governed by Local Civil Rule 10.6.

(g) *Proposed Orders.* Proposed orders may be submitted electronically. All proposed orders must be in PDF format and must be: (1) attached as an exhibit to a motion or stipulation; or (2) contained within the body of a stipulation; or (3) submitted separately. If the Judge approves the proposed order, it will be refiled electronically under a separate document number.

(h) *Court Orders, Judgments, Writs and Other Process.* Judgments and orders may be filed electronically by the Court or authorized Court personnel. Any order or other Court-issued document filed electronically without the image of the manuscript signature of the judge or clerk has the same force and effect as a document bearing an original signature. The Clerk may electronically affix the Seal of the Court on writs, summons, and other process, which shall have the same legal force and effect as process bearing an imprinted seal.

(i) *Service of Electronically Filed Documents.*

(i) Summons and Initial Pleading. Summons, writs and other court process may be issued in electronic form with electronically affixed signatures and seal. Service of the summons and complaint or other initial pleading, however, must be made by one of the methods allowed by Rule 4 of the Federal Rules of Civil Procedure and may not be made electronically.

(ii) Service on Registered Attorneys. By registering under this rule, an attorney automatically consents to electronic service by both the Court and any opposing attorney of any electronically filed document in any civil action in which the registered attorney appears. Consequently, service of an electronically filed document upon a registered attorney is deemed complete upon the transmission of an NEF to that attorney under subsection (i)(iv) of this rule and no separate certificate of service should be filed. Traditionally filed documents and sealed documents must be served on registered attorneys by nonelectronic means of service. A proof of service must be filed.

(iii) Service on Unregistered Attorneys and *Pro Se* Parties. Counsel filing any pleading or other paper must serve attorneys not registered under this rule and *pro se* parties by nonelectronic means of service under Rule 5. A proof of service must be filed.

(iv) Method of Electronic Service. At the time a document is filed either electronically or by scanning paper submissions, the Court's system will generate an NEF, which will be transmitted by e-mail to the filer and all registered attorneys who have appeared on that case. The NEF will contain a hyperlink to the filed document. The attorney filing the document should retain a paper or digital copy of the NEF, which serves as the Court's date-stamp and proof of filing. Except in the case of sealed documents (see Local Civil Rule 10.6(d)) and *ex parte* filings (see Local Civil Rule 10.5(a)), transmission of the NEF to the registered e-mail address constitutes service of an electronically filed document upon any registered attorney. Only service of the NEF by the Court's system constitutes electronic service; transmission of a document by one party to another by regular e-mail does not constitute service.

(v) Effect on Time Computation. [Repealed]

(j) *Remote Access to Electronically Stored Documents.* The general public, as well as any party to the litigation, may access and download any electronically stored document, with the following exceptions: (1) remote access to documents filed in social security and immigration cases is restricted as required by Fed. R. Civ. P. 5.2(c); (2) access to certain documents may be restricted to the Court or to the parties of record, by order or local rule; and (3) the Court may restrict access to other classes of documents by future order in conformity with resolutions of the Judicial Conference of the United States.

(k) Facsimile Transmissions. The Clerk will not accept for filing any pleading or other paper submitted by facsimile transmission.

[Effective June 1, 1998. Amended effective October 1, 2001; January 2, 2002; September 3, 2003; January 1, 2005; February 15, 2007; December 1, 2007; December 15, 2008; December 1, 2009; April 19, 2010; January 2, 2011; February 8, 2012; April 1, 2012; May 9, 2012; March 19, 2014; December 1, 2016.]

III. PLEADINGS AND MOTIONS

LOCAL CIVIL RULE 7. MOTION PRACTICE

7.1. Motions in General.

(a) *Briefs.* All motions, except those made during a hearing or trial, shall be accompanied by a supporting brief. Any party opposing a written motion shall do so by filing and serving a brief conforming to these rules. All briefs filed in support of or in opposition to any motion shall contain a concise statement of the reasons in support of the party's position and shall cite all applicable federal rules of procedure, all applicable local rules, and the other authorities upon which the party relies. Briefs shall not be submitted in the form of a letter to the judge.

(b) *Supporting Documents.* When allegations of facts not appearing of record are relied upon in support of or in opposition to any motion, all affidavits or other documents relied upon to establish such facts shall accompany the motion. All discovery motions shall set forth verbatim, or have attached, the relevant discovery request and answer or objection.

(c) *Modification of Limits.* In its discretion, the Court may in a particular case shorten or enlarge any time limit or page limit established by these rules, with or without prior notice or motion.

(d) *Attempt to Obtain Concurrence.* With respect to all motions, the moving party shall ascertain whether the motion will be opposed. In addition, in the case of all non dispositive motions, counsel or pro se parties involved in the dispute shall confer in a good-faith effort to resolve the dispute. All non dispositive motions shall be accompanied by a separately filed certificate setting forth in detail the efforts of the moving party to comply with the obligation created by this rule.

(e) *Motion for Expedited Consideration.* Where the relief requested by a motion may be rendered moot before the motion is briefed in accordance with the schedules set forth herein, the party shall so indicate by inserting the phrase "EXPEDITED CONSIDERATION REQUESTED," in bold-face type, below the case caption, and shall identify in the motion the reason expedited consideration is necessary.

(f) *Unavailability of Judge.* If it appears that any matter requires immediate attention, and the judge to whom the case has been assigned, or in the usual course would be assigned, is not available, the matter shall be referred to the judge's assigned magistrate judge, who shall decide the matter if it is within the magistrate judge's jurisdiction. If the matter can only be decided by a judge, the magistrate judge shall determine whether the matter can be set for a hearing at a time when the assigned judge is available. If the matter is determined by a magistrate judge to require an immediate hearing before a judge, the case will be referred to the Chief Judge, or in the Chief Judge's absence, the next available judge by seniority for decision or reassignment to an available judicial officer. After disposition of this emergency matter, the case will be returned to the originally assigned judge.

7.2. Dispositive Motions.

(a) *Definition.* Dispositive motions are motions for injunctive relief, for judgment on the pleadings, for summary judgment, to dismiss or to permit maintenance of a class action, to dismiss for failure to state a claim upon which relief can be granted, to involuntarily dismiss an action, and other dispositive motions as defined by law. Motions for dismissal as a sanction pursuant to Federal Rules of Civil Procedure 16 or 37 shall be subject to the briefing schedule for nondispositive motions.

(b) *Length of Briefs.* Any brief filed in support of or in opposition to a dispositive motion shall not exceed twenty-five (25) pages in length, exclusive of cover sheet, tables, and indices.

(c) *Briefing Schedule.* Any party opposing a dispositive motion shall, within twenty-eight (28) days after service of the motion, file a responsive brief and any supporting materials. The moving party may, within fourteen (14) days after service of the response, file a reply brief not exceeding ten (10) pages. The Court may permit or require further briefing.

(d) *Oral Argument.* Any party desiring oral argument shall include a request for oral argument in the caption and the heading of the party's brief. In its discretion, the Court may schedule oral argument or may dispose of the motion without argument at the end of the briefing schedule. The time for oral argument on all motions shall be scheduled and noticed by the Court at the earliest convenient date.

7.3. Nondispositive Motions.

(a) *Definition.* Nondispositive motions are all motions not specifically listed in LCivR 7.2.

(b) *Length of Briefs.* Any brief filed in support of or in opposition to a nondispositive motion shall not exceed ten (10) pages in length, exclusive of cover sheet, tables, and indices.

(c) *Briefing Schedule.* Any party opposing a nondispositive motion shall, within fourteen (14) days of service of the motion, file a responsive brief and supporting materials. Reply briefs may not be filed without leave of court.

(d) *Oral Argument.* Any party desiring oral argument shall include a request for oral argument in the caption and the heading of the party's brief. In its discretion, the Court may schedule oral argument or may dispose of the motion without argument at the end of the briefing schedule. The time for oral argument on all motions shall be scheduled and noticed by the Court at the earliest convenient date.

7.4. Motions for Reconsideration.

(a) *Grounds.* Generally, and without restricting the discretion of the Court, motions for reconsideration which merely present the same issues ruled upon by the Court shall not be granted. The movant shall not only demonstrate a palpable defect by which the Court and the parties have been misled, but also show that a different disposition of the case must result from a correction thereof.

(b) *Response to Motions for Reconsideration.* No answer to a motion for reconsideration will be allowed unless requested by the Court, but a motion for reconsideration will ordinarily not be granted in the absence of such request. Any oral argument on a motion for reconsideration is reserved to the discretion of the Court.

[Effective June 1, 1998. Amended effective December 1, 2009; February 8, 2012; September 28, 2015.]

LOCAL CIVIL RULE 8. GENERAL RULES OF PLEADING

8.1. Complaints in Social Security Cases. Complaints filed pursuant to § 205(g) of the Social Security Act, 42 U.S.C. § 405(g), for benefits under Titles II, XVI and XVII of the Social Security Act shall contain, in addition to what is required under Rule 8(a) of the Federal Rules of Civil Procedure, the following information: (1) the type of benefit claimed, for example, disability, retirement, survivor, health insurance, supplemental security income; (2) in cases involving claims for retirement, survivors, disability, or health insurance, the last four digits of the social security number of the worker (who may or may not be the plaintiff) on whose wage record the application for benefits was filed; and (3) in cases involving claims for supplemental security income benefits, the social security number of the plaintiff.

8.2. Answers and Replies. Except in cases brought by a pro se plaintiff, a responsive pleading under Fed. R. Civ. P. 8(b) shall recite verbatim that paragraph of the pleading, or amended pleading, to which it is responsive, followed by the response. Upon request, an attorney must provide to opposing counsel a copy of the complaint or other pleading to which a response is due, in native word-processing format, so that opposing counsel may comply with this rule.

[Effective June 1, 1998. Amended effective July 1, 2008.]

LOCAL CIVIL RULE 10. FORM OF PLEADINGS AND OTHER PAPERS; FILING REQUIREMENTS

10.1. Paper Size and Format. All documents must be double spaced in 8½ x 11 inch format with writing on only the face of each sheet. Type must be no smaller than 12 point type and all margins must be at least one inch.

10.2. Binding. All pleadings and other papers that have numerous pages must be bound with a fastener. Originals should be stapled or bound on the top margin with a two-hole fastener. Copies may be bound in the same manner as originals or in a binder. Paper clips and other types of clips shall not be used; fasteners shall pass through the pages.

10.3. Date, Address and Telephone Number. All pleadings and other papers shall contain the date of signing and the address and telephone number of the signing attorney or pro se party.

10.4. Number of Copies. All traditionally filed documents must be filed in duplicate—the original and one copy. If service of any paper is to be made by the United States Marshal, sufficient additional copies shall be supplied for service upon each other party. If file stamped copies of documents are requested to be returned to the offering party, a suitable self-addressed, postage paid envelope shall be supplied.

10.5*

Ex Parte Submissions

(a) *Filing of Ex Parte Submissions.* If the law allows a party to submit a pleading or other paper ex parte, the party may file the document with the Clerk without serving a copy on any other party. The document shall be properly identified on its face as Ex Parte. A registered attorney must submit any ex parte filing electronically by use of the appropriate CM/ECF event. An NEF will be generated for the ex parte document and will be transmitted to all parties. Unless modified by the filer, the NEF and docket entry will identify the document only as "Ex Parte Document" or "Ex Parte Motion".

(b) *Access to Ex Parte Filings.* The docket entry and the NEF for any ex parte filing will be available for public viewing. Unless the Court specifically orders otherwise, access to ex parte documents will be available only to the party submitting the filing (or that party's registered attorneys) and to the personnel of this Court and the Court of Appeals, but not to the public or any other party.

(c) *Filings by the Court.* The court may issue restricted access orders in response to ex parte filings. Access to these orders will be restricted to the moving party, the personnel of this Court and the Court of Appeals. The docket entry and the NEF for any restricted access order will be identified as such and available for public viewing.

(d) *Sealed Cases.* If an entire case has been sealed, either by order or by operation of statute, then neither the ex parte submission nor any docket entry relating thereto will be available for public viewing, until such time as the Court orders otherwise.

10.6. Filing Documents Under Seal.

(a) *Policy.* To preserve the qualified, common-law presumption of public access to judicial files in civil cases, the filing of documents under seal should be the exception. Sealing is to be limited to information that is truly proprietary or confidential. The Court strongly resists the sealing of entire civil pleadings, motions or briefs, as it is rare that the entire document will merit confidential treatment. In lieu of seeking leave to file an entire document under seal, parties should incorporate the confidential material in a separate document and seek leave to file only that document under seal.

(b) *Requests to Seal.* The procedures set forth in this rule apply to cases that have not been sealed in their entirety. Documents may be submitted under seal only if authorized by statute or by the Court for good cause shown. A person seeking leave to file a document under seal must file a motion requesting such relief, unless the Court has entered a previous order authorizing the submission of the document under seal or submission under seal is authorized by statute. The motion seeking leave to file under seal should generally be a public filing, unless the submitting party believes in good faith that public access to the motion will compromise the confidential matter. A proposed sealed document submitted by a registered attorney must be submitted electronically under seal as a separate document, under a separate docket entry, by use of the appropriate CM/ECF event. The docket entry and the NEF for any sealed document will be available for public viewing; the description of the sealed document should therefore be general in nature (e.g., sealed affidavit, sealed exhibit). The proposed sealed document shall be appropriately identified on its face as sealed, but should not contain the word "proposed". Proposed sealed documents submitted by persons other than registered attorneys must be filed in a sealed envelope bearing the case caption and number, the identity of the party submitting the documents, and a general description of the contents; the proposed sealed document will be scanned and maintained electronically under seal. If the Court denies the motion to seal in whole or in part, the proposed sealed document will remain sealed, but the Court may order the submitting party to tender a modified document, either sealed or not under seal, as the Court directs. If the Court grants leave to file the document under seal, the Clerk of Court will modify the docket entry to remove reference to "proposed".

(c) *Access to Sealed Documents.* A document filed under seal may be accessed electronically only by authorized personnel of this Court and the Court of Appeals and not by the public or any attorney or party.

(d) *Service of Sealed Documents.* A party submitting a document under seal must serve it by non-electronic means of service on all other parties.

10.7. Privacy [Repealed] *

Exhibits. All exhibits or attachments to pleadings, motions, briefs, or other papers must contain on their face a prominent exhibit number or letter.

[Effective June 1, 1998. Amended effective April 16, 2003; September 3, 2003; January 1, 2005; February 15, 2007; December 1, 2007.]

  * **[Publisher's Note:** So in original.]

LOCAL CIVIL RULE 16. CIVIL PRETRIAL CONFERENCES; ALTERNATIVE DISPUTE RESOLUTION

16.1. Early Scheduling Conference. The Court may order that an early scheduling conference be held before a magistrate judge or Article III judge either in open court, in chambers, or at the discretion of the Court, by telephone. Following this conference, the Court will issue a case management order establishing a timetable for disposition of the case. The timetable may contain deadlines for joinder of parties and amendment of pleadings; discovery disclosures and exchange of witnesses; completion of discovery and dispositive motions; a methodology of ADR; a settlement conference date; a final pretrial conference date; and a trial date. Upon good cause shown or on the Court's own initiative, the Court may modify the case management order in the interest of justice. The following provisions shall apply to all conferences conducted by the Court pursuant to Rule 16 of the Federal Rules of Civil Procedure:

(a) *Recording.* At the request of any party or the direction of the Court, the conference may be recorded. For good cause, the Court may direct that portions of the conference be unrecorded or sealed.

(b) *Scope.* The conference shall cover the matters specified in Rules 16 and 26 of the Federal Rules of Civil Procedure and any other matters specified by the Court.

(c) *Attendance.* The attorney who is to have charge of the actual trial of the case shall attend the conference unless the judge directs otherwise. Pro se parties shall attend on their own behalf.

(d) *Authority.* The Court may in its discretion require the actual parties (i.e., a party who is a natural person or a representative—other than counsel—of a party which is not a natural person) to attend the conference and may require that counsel be authorized to discuss final settlement of the case.

(e) *Scheduling.* The Court shall set the date, time and place of the conference and shall notify all parties thereof in writing.

(f) *Pretrial Order.* A proposed order shall be prepared and filed by the parties in accordance with written instructions from the judge to whom the case has been assigned.

(g) *Exemptions From Scheduling and Planning Order.* The following categories of actions are exempt from the requirement in Rule 16(b) of the Federal Rules of Civil Procedure that a scheduling and planning order be entered:

(i) actions brought pursuant to the Freedom of Information Act;

(ii) petitions for writ of habeas corpus;

(iii) motions filed pursuant to 28 U.S.C. § 2255;

(iv) all other petitions brought by prisoners incarcerated in federal or state facilities;

(v) appeals from bankruptcy decisions;

(vi) all actions brought by the United States to collect student loans and all other debts owed to the United States government;

(vii) actions involving the review of Social Security benefit denials;

(viii) all applications for attorneys' fees and costs;

(ix) multidistrict litigation;

(x) condemnation proceedings;

(xi) forfeiture actions by the United States;

(xii) appeals from a decision by a United States magistrate judge;

(xiii) motions to quash or enforce administrative subpoenas; and

(xiv) petitions to enforce Internal Revenue Service summonses.

16.2. Alternative Dispute Resolution: General Provisions.

(a) *ADR Favored.* The judges of this District favor alternative dispute resolution (ADR) methods in those cases where the parties and the Court agree that ADR may help resolve the case. The ADR methods approved by these rules include Voluntary Facilitative Mediation (LCivR 16.3); Early Neutral Evaluation (LCivR 16.4); Case Evaluation (LCivR 16.5); Summary Jury Trials, Summary Bench Trials (LCivR 16.7); and Settlement Conferences (LCivR 16.8). In addition, the Court will consider other ADR methods proposed by the parties.

(b) *Court Administration of the ADR Program.*

(i) Program Description and Administration. Each ADR program is governed by these rules and the provisions of a Program Description, which is incorporated into these rules by reference. The Program Description for each ADR method is available on the Court's website and is published in a form suitable for reference by attorneys and their clients. The ADR program is administered by the Clerk's Office. Problems are initially handled by the ADR Administrator.

(ii) Evaluation of the Program. In an effort to gather information, the Court may develop questionnaires for participants, counsel and neutrals, to be completed and returned at the close of the ADR process. Responses will be kept confidential and not divulged to the Court, the attorneys or the parties. Only aggregate information about the program will be reported.

(c) *Consideration of ADR in Appropriate Cases.* In connection with the conference held pursuant to Rule 26(f) of the Federal Rules of Civil Procedure, all litigants and counsel must consider and discuss the use of an appropriate ADR process at a suitable stage of the litigation.

(d) *Confidentiality.* All ADR proceedings are considered to be compromise negotiations within the meaning of Fed. R. Evid. 408.

(e) *Status of Discovery, Motions and Trial During the ADR Process.* Any case referred to ADR continues to be subject to management by the Judge to whom it is assigned. Parties may file motions and engage in discovery. Selection of a case for ADR has no effect on the normal progress of the case toward trial. Referral of a case to ADR is not grounds to avoid or postpone any deadline or obligation imposed by the case management order unless so ordered by the Court.

(f) *Qualifications for Neutrals.* To be qualified to act as a neutral (i.e., facilitative mediator, early neutral evaluator, case evaluator, or arbitrator), an attorney must have at least ten (10) years of experience in the practice of law and must satisfy any special requirements applicable to a particular ADR program. No person may serve as a neutral in any action in which any of the circumstances specified in 28 U.S.C. § 455 exist or in good faith are believed to exist. An attorney shall accept the neutral's role only if he or she can be fair and impartial and can avoid a conflict of interest or the appearance of a conflict of interest. For example, see the Model Standards Of Conduct For Mediators, jointly adopted in 2005 by the American Bar Association, the American Arbitration Association and the Association For Conflict Resolution.

(g) *Attorneys' Responsibility for Payment of Fees.* The attorney or law firm representing a party participating in ADR is directly responsible for fees payable to the Court or to neutrals. Pro se parties are personally responsible for fees. To the extent consistent with ethical rules, the attorney or firm may seek reimbursement from the client. If any attorney or pro se party is delinquent in paying any fee required to be paid to a neutral under these rules, the neutral may petition the Court for an order directing payment, and any judge or magistrate judge assigned to the case may order payment, upon pain of contempt.

(h) *Pro Bono Service.* In cases in which one or more parties cannot afford the fees of a neutral, the Court may request that the neutral serve pro bono, by waiving or reducing the fee for the indigent party. All other parties are expected to pay the full fee.

16.3. Voluntary Facilitative Mediation.

(a) *Definition.* Voluntary Facilitative Mediation (VFM) is a flexible, nonbinding dispute resolution process in which an impartial third party—the mediator—facilitates negotiations among the parties to help them reach settlement. VFM seeks to expand traditional settlement discussions and broaden resolution options, often by going beyond the issues in controversy. The mediator, who may meet jointly and separately with the parties, serves as a facilitator only and does not decide issues or make findings of fact. Cases will be assigned to VFM only if the district or magistrate judge is satisfied that the selection of VFM is purely voluntary and with full approval of all parties.

(b) *Qualification, Certification and Removal of Mediators.* The Clerk's Office maintains a current list of certified mediators. Criteria for training, certification, retention and removal of mediators are governed by the VFM Program Description.

(c) *Mediation Assessment.* The Court shall assess a fee per referral in accordance with the VFM procedures adopted by the Court. The monies are deposited into the Voluntary Facilitative Mediation Training Fund. In a pro bono mediation, the assessment is waived for any indigent party.

(d) *Selection and Compensation of Mediator.*

(i) Selection of Mediator. Within fourteen (14) days of the issuance of the case management order, the parties jointly select one mediator from the list of court certified mediators. The plaintiff is responsible for notifying the ADR Administrator of the name of the selected mediator by electronically filing a Notice of Selection of Facilitative Mediator. If the parties are unable to agree on a mediator, the ADR Administrator selects the mediator for them. The proposed mediator will then check for conflicts of interest. Once the selection of a mediator is finalized, the ADR

Administrator electronically files a Notice of Appointment of Facilitative Mediator.

(ii) Compensation of Mediator. The mediator is paid his or her normal hourly rate, assessed in as many equal parts as there are separately represented parties, unless otherwise agreed in writing. The mediator is responsible for billing counsel and pro se parties.

(e) *The Mediation Process.*

(i) The details of the VFM process, including establishment and timing of VFM sessions and submissions by the parties to the mediator, are set forth in general in the VFM Program Description, and, with regard to each specific case, in the Notice of Appointment of Facilitative Mediator.

(ii) Party Responsibilities. Individual parties and representatives of corporate or government parties with settlement authority are required to attend the mediation session(s) in person. In cases involving insurance carriers, the insurer representative with settlement authority must attend in person. Each party must be accompanied at the VFM session by the lawyer expected to be primarily responsible for handling the trial of the matter. A party or lawyer will be excused from attending the mediation session in person only after approval by the Court upon showing extraordinary circumstances to excuse attendance.

(f) *Filing of Outcome.* Within fourteen (14) days of the completion of the mediation process, the mediator will electronically file a Facilitative Mediation Report with the Court. The report will indicate only who participated in the mediation session and whether settlement was reached. If settlement is reached, the mediator will help the parties draft a settlement agreement. The settlement agreement, absent unusual circumstances, must be completed and signed by the parties within fourteen (14) days. The parties shall file a stipulation and proposed order to dismiss with the Court within twenty-eight (28) days of reaching a settlement. If settlement is not reached, the parties have seven (7) days following the mediation session to inform the mediator whether they desire to continue with the mediation process.

16.4. Early Neutral Evaluation.

(a) *Definition.* Early Neutral Evaluation (ENE) is a flexible, nonbinding dispute resolution process in which an experienced neutral attorney meets with the parties early in the case to evaluate its strengths and weaknesses and the value that it may have, and also attempts to negotiate a settlement.

(b) *Selection and Compensation of Evaluator.*

(i) Selection of Evaluator. Counsel for the parties jointly select an evaluator who meets the criteria for neutrals under this rule. If the parties are unable to agree on an evaluator, the ADR Administrator selects the evaluator for them. No listing of evaluators is maintained by the Court or the Clerk. The proposed evaluator will check for conflicts of interest. Once the selection process is finalized, the judge issues an order of referral.

(ii) Compensation of Evaluator. The evaluator is paid his or her normal hourly rate, assessed in as many equal parts as there are separately represented parties, unless other-

wise agreed in writing. The evaluator is responsible for billing counsel and pro se parties.

(c) *The Early Neutral Evaluation Process.*

(i) Program Description. The details of the ENE process, including the duties of the evaluator, the establishment and timing of ENE sessions, and submissions of the parties to the evaluator, are set forth in the ENE Program Description. Parties participating in ENE must follow the requirements of the Program Description, including the special requirements applying to patent, copyright and trademark cases.

(ii) Party Responsibilities. Individual parties and representatives of corporate or government parties with ultimate settlement authority are required to attend the ENE session(s). In cases involving insurance carriers, the insurer representative with ultimate settlement authority must attend. Each party must be accompanied at the ENE session by the lawyer expected to be primarily responsible for handling the trial of the matter.

(d) *Filing of Outcome.* Within fourteen (14) days following the conclusion of ENE, if settlement is reached, the evaluator, if requested, helps the parties draft a settlement agreement along with a stipulation and proposed order to dismiss, which when executed is filed with the Court. If settlement is not reached, the parties have seven (7) days to inform the evaluator whether they desire to continue with the ENE process. Within fourteen (14) days of the completion of the ENE process, the evaluator files a brief report with the ADR Administrator, with copies to all parties. The report indicates only who participated in the ENE session and whether issues were narrowed or settlement was reached.

16.5. Case Evaluation.

(a) *Definition.* The case evaluation program affords litigants an ADR process patterned after that extensively used in the courts of the State of Michigan. See Mich. Comp. Laws §§ 600.4951–.4969; Mich. Ct. R. 2.403. Case evaluation principally involves establishment of the settlement value of a case by a three-member panel of attorneys. The court may order that any civil case in which damages are sought be submitted to case evaluation; certain tort cases in which the rule of decision is supplied by Michigan law must be submitted to case evaluation, unless the parties unanimously agree to submit the case to Voluntary Facilitation Mediation.

(b) *Standard Case Evaluation.*

(i) Adoption of Michigan State–Court Procedures; Exceptions. The procedures governing standard case evaluation are generally set forth in Rule 2.403 of the Michigan Rules of Court. Unless modified by these rules, the Program Description, or order of court in a particular case, the provisions of Mich. Ct. R. 2.403, as amended from time to time, will govern in cases referred to standard case evaluation, except as follows:

(A) Panel Selection. The ADR Administrator selects all three case evaluators.

(B) Fees. Each party must send each evaluator a check for $200.00, for a total fee of $600 per party. Promptly thereafter, a proof of payment must be filed with the ADR Administrator. Failure to submit a proof showing timely payment subjects the offending attorney to a $150.00 penalty, which may not be charged to the client. The rules set forth in Mich. Ct. R. 2.403 for allocation of fees among multiple parties or claims apply. Once paid, the fee is not subject to refund.

(C) Submission of Documents. The rules for submission of documents set forth in Mich. Ct. R. 2.403 apply, except that case evaluation summaries are limited to 20 pages and attachments must not exceed 20 pages. Documents must be submitted directly to the evaluators, with a proof of service filed with the ADR Administrator. Failure to file or serve such documents in a timely manner subjects the offending party to a $150.00 penalty, which may not be charged to the client.

(D) Time Limit at Hearing. Each side's presentation at the case evaluation hearing is limited to 30 minutes.

(E) Time in Which Award Must Be Rendered. The evaluators render a written evaluation at the close of the hearing and serve it personally on the parties at that time.

(F) Rejecting Party's Liability for Costs.

(1) In diversity tort cases where Michigan law provides the rule of decision, this Court has determined that the state statute and court rules requiring case evaluation form a part of state substantive law. Such tort cases will be referred to mandatory case evaluation, unless the parties unanimously agree to Voluntary Facilitative Mediation. In all tort cases ordered to mandatory case evaluation, the provisions of Rule 2.403 governing liability for costs, including taxation of a reasonable attorney fee for rejection of a case evaluation award, apply.

(2) In cases in which case evaluation is not mandatory, the provisions of Mich. Ct. R. 2.403 governing liability for costs apply, except that attorneys' fees will not be taxed for rejection of a case evaluation award.

(3) In any case referred to case evaluation, the parties may stipulate in writing to the assessment of attorneys' fees in accordance with Mich. Ct. R. 2.403.

(c) *Blue Ribbon Case Evaluation.* Blue Ribbon case evaluation allows the parties to choose their own evaluators and to request that the evaluators devote substantial time to the evaluation process. A case may be referred to Blue Ribbon case evaluation only with the unanimous and voluntary consent of the parties. All procedures applicable to standard case evaluation apply, except:

(i) Selection of Evaluators. The parties jointly select the evaluators, who need not be members of the Court's certified list.

(ii) Fees. Evaluators are compensated at their customary hourly rate, to be assessed in as many equal parts as there are separately represented parties, or as otherwise agreed by the parties at the time case evaluation is ordered. No late fees are imposed for untimely submissions.

(iii) Mediation Briefs and Hearings. No limits apply to length of Blue Ribbon case evaluation hearings or to the length of case evaluation briefs, unless agreed to in writing by the parties.

(iv) Time for Rendering Award. In an extraordinary case, where the award cannot reasonably be rendered at the conclusion of the hearing, the evaluators may render their written evaluation no later than seven days after the hearing.

16.6. Court–Annexed Arbitration. [Repealed]

16.7. Summary Jury Trials; Summary Bench Trials.

(a) *Summary Jury Trial.* The summary jury trial is an abbreviated proceeding during which the parties' attorneys summarize their case before a six-person jury. Unless the parties stipulate otherwise, the verdict is advisory only.

(b) *Summary Bench Trial.* A summary bench trial is an abbreviated proceeding during which the parties' attorneys summarize their case before a judge or magistrate judge. Unless the parties stipulate otherwise, the verdict is advisory only.

16.8. Settlement Conferences. The Court may order a settlement conference to be held before a district judge or a magistrate judge. All parties may be required to be present. For parties that are not natural persons, a natural person representing that party who possesses ultimate settlement authority may be required to attend the settlement conference. In cases where an insured party does not have full settlement authority, an official of the insurer with ultimate authority to negotiate a settlement may also be required to attend.

[Effective June 1, 1998. Amended effective June 1, 1998; March 4, 1999; May 21, 2002; December 16, 2002; April 5, 2004; January 1, 2005; June 20, 2005; December 1, 2009; December 13, 2010; May 9, 2012; July 14, 2016.]

VI. TRIALS

LOCAL CIVIL RULE 39. TRIAL PROCEDURES

39.1. Exhibits During Trial. Exhibits shall be premarked in accordance with the order issued by the Court.

39.2. Exhibits After Trial.

(a) Unless the Court orders otherwise, exhibits shall not be filed with the Clerk, but shall be retained in the custody of the respective attorneys who produced them in court.

(b) In case of an appeal, a party, upon written request of any party or by order of the Court, shall make available all the original exhibits in that party's possession, or true copies thereof, to enable such other party to prepare the record on appeal, at which time and place such other party shall also make available all the original exhibits in that party's possession. The parties are encouraged to designate which exhibits are necessary for the determination of the appeal. The parties are to submit to the Clerk of this Court a list of those exhibits so designated indicating in whose custody they remain. The attorney who has custody of the exhibits shall be charged with the responsibility for their safekeeping and transportation to the Court of Appeals. All exhibits which are not designated as necessary for the determination of the appeal shall remain in the custody of the respective attorneys who shall have the responsibility of promptly forwarding same to the Clerk of the Court of Appeals upon request.

(c) For good cause shown, the Court may order the Clerk to take custody of any or all exhibits on behalf of a party. If the Clerk does take custody of any exhibits, parties are to remove them within twenty-eight (28) days after the mandate of the final reviewing court is filed. Parties failing to comply with this rule shall be notified by the Clerk to remove their exhibits and upon their failure to do so within twenty-eight (28) days, the Clerk may dispose of them as the Clerk may see fit.

[Effective June 1, 1998. Amended effective December 1, 2009.]

LOCAL CIVIL RULE 40. TRIAL DATE

40.1. Scheduling. Cases shall be set for trial in the manner and at the time designated by the judge before whom the cause is pending. Any case may be assigned from one judge to another with the consent of both judges to promote the efficient administration of justice or to comply with the Speedy Trial Act in another case.

40.2. Continuances. A motion for a continuance of a trial or other proceeding shall be made only for good cause and as soon as the need arises.

40.3. Notice of Settlement. Whenever a case is settled or otherwise disposed out of Court, counsel for all parties shall assure that immediate notice is given to the Court. Should a failure to provide immediate notice result in having jurors unnecessarily report for service in connection with the case, the Court may, on its own motion, for good cause shown, assess costs incurred in having jurors report for service equally between the parties or against one or more of the parties responsible for failure to notify the Court.

[Effective June 1, 1998. Amended effective June 1, 1998.]

LOCAL CIVIL RULE 41. INVOLUNTARY DISMISSAL FOR WANT OF PROSECUTION OR FAILURE TO FOLLOW RULES

41.1. A judicial officer may issue an order to show cause why a case should not be dismissed for lack of prosecution or for failure to comply with these rules, the Federal Rules of Civil Procedure, or any court order. If good cause is not shown within the time set in the show cause order, a district judge may enter an order of dismissal with or without prejudice, with or without costs. Failure of a plaintiff to keep the

Court apprised of a current address shall be grounds for dismissal for want of prosecution.

[Effective June 1, 1998.]

LOCAL CIVIL RULE 43. ATTORNEY AS WITNESS

43.1. Leave of court to conduct the trial of an action in which the attorney is to be a witness shall be sought in advance of trial when feasible.

[Effective June 1, 1998.]

LOCAL CIVIL RULE 45. SERVICE OF SUBPOENAS

45.1. All subpoenas delivered to the United States Marshal's Office for service shall allow a minimum of seven (7) days if within the Western District of Michigan, or fourteen (14) days if outside the district, prior to the required appearance.

[Effective June 1, 1998. Amended effective December 1, 2009.]

LOCAL CIVIL RULE 47. CONFIDENTIALITY OF JUROR INFORMATION

47.1. Confidentiality of Juror Information.

(a) All information obtained from juror questionnaires is confidential and may be used only for jury selection and in accordance with this rule.

(b) All copies of juror questionnaires must be destroyed or returned to the Court upon completion of jury selection, or at any earlier time determined by the Court.

(c) For represented parties, counsel of record is responsible for maintaining the confidentiality and security of juror questionnaires, and must apply security practices no less stringent than those applicable to confidential client information. Unrepresented parties may use juror questionnaires only under supervision of the Court, and may not reproduce the juror questionnaires in any form, or distribute them to anyone.

(d) Juror questionnaires will be electronically filed under restricted access three (3) business days before trial. Electronic access will be available to the Court and counsel of record only. The Court will provide unrepresented parties with one paper copy of the juror questionnaires at the beginning of jury selection. Juror questionnaires will not be available via mail or facsimile transmission.

[Effective June 1, 1998. Amended effective July 15, 2004; September 11, 2015.]

VII. JUDGMENT

LOCAL CIVIL RULE 54. COSTS AND ATTORNEY'S FEES

54.1. Taxation of Costs. If the parties in a case can agree on costs, it is not necessary to file a cost bill with the Clerk. If the parties cannot agree, a bill of costs shall be filed with

the Clerk within twenty-eight (28) days from the entry of judgment. If a bill of costs is filed, any party objecting to the taxation of costs must file a motion to disallow all or part of the claimed costs within fourteen (14) days of service of the bill of costs on that party. The motion and response thereto shall be governed by LCivR 7.1 and 7.3.

54.2. Attorney's Fees in Certain Social Security Cases.

(a) *Scope of Rule.* The procedures set forth in this rule apply to motions for attorney's fees brought under 42 U.S.C. § 406(b)(1)(A) (Social Security Disability Claims) or 42 U.S.C. § 1383(d)(2)(A) (Supplemental Security Income Claims), which allow an attorney to obtain fees from the client's award of past-due benefits for work performed in the District Court. It is necessary to prescribe a special procedure for such cases, because the amount of past-due benefits is unknown at the time judgment for the claimant is entered in the District Court. This rule does not apply to motions for fees under the Equal Access to Justice Act (EAJA), which are governed by the procedures set forth in that Act. 28 U.S.C. § 2412(d).

(b) *Procedure.*

(i) Commencement of Time Period. The time in which an attorney must file a motion for approval of fees under 42 U.S.C. §§ 406(b)(1)(A) or 1383(d)(2)(A) commences on the date shown on the face of the Notice of Award issued by the Social Security Administration. This time period does not commence until the Administration has issued all of the Notices of Award necessary to calculate the total amount of retroactive benefits payable. In the case of multiple or amended notices, the time period commences on the date shown on the face of the last notice.

(ii) Deadline for Filing Motion. The time to file a motion for fees expires 35 days after the commencement date calculated under subparagraph (i) above. Any motion filed after this 35–day deadline will be considered only by a specific showing of excusable neglect by plaintiff's attorney.

(iii) Requirements for Motion. The motion must be accompanied by a supporting brief and all necessary documentation. The motion must state the following:

(A) The past due benefits due the claimant.

(B) The past due benefits due any dependents.

(C) The total dollar amount withheld by the Commissioner out of these past due benefits.

(D) The dollar amount (if any) of fees the attorney was awarded, has sought, or intends to seek pursuant to 42 U.S.C. § 406(a) for services performed at the administrative level of review.

(E) Whether the attorney has knowledge of any other representative(s) who were awarded, sought, or will seek authorization for fees under 42 U.S.C. § 406(a).

(F) The dollar amount of fees sought pursuant to 42 U.S.C. § 406(b).

(G) The dollar amount of court costs, fees, and/or expenses sought or already awarded under the Equal Access to Justice Act (28 U.S.C. § 2412).

(H) The dollar amount, if different from that provided in compliance with subsection (b)(iii)(C), that is currently being withheld by the Commissioner to cover a potential award of attorney's fees in this Court.

(I) An itemization of the services provided in judicial proceedings, specifying the hours worked, the work performed, and the attorney's hourly billing rate.

(J) An itemization of the services provided in administrative proceedings and, if the attorney maintains time records for administrative work, a specification of the hours worked and the billing rate. The itemization for administrative proceedings is an aid to the Court's assessment of the reasonableness of the fee yielded by the fee agreement.

(K) Whether counsel has represented the client in any other matter that involved the impairments in the disability claim. If so, indicate:

(1) whether the attorney has or may obtain an attorney fee from that matter and the amount or means of calculation;

(2) which medical evidence or reports prepared for or used in that matter were also used in the social security proceedings.

(L) An argument establishing that the fees sought are authorized under any applicable fee agreement, are reasonable, and do not exceed applicable statutory limits.

(M) In addition to complying with the requirements of W.D. Mich. LCivR 7.1, an affirmative statement that the attorney has discussed the matter of fees with the plaintiff and the plaintiff either has no objection to the amount of fees sought in the motion, or that the plaintiff and the attorney disagree as to the reasonableness of the fees sought.

(iv) The fee motion must be accompanied by:

(A) Legible copies of all of the Notices of Award showing the amount of past due benefits and the amount(s) withheld by the Commissioner under 42 U.S.C. §§ 406, 1383.

(B) A copy of any fee agreement entered into between the plaintiff and the attorney.

(C) A certificate of service that the attorney's fee motion and attachments have been served on the U.S. Attorney and on the plaintiff.

(v) Response. Any response by the client or defendant must be filed within twenty-one (21) days after the motion for attorney's fees is served.

(vi) Reply Brief. Because it is plaintiff's attorney's burden to establish entitlement to and the reasonableness of the attorney's fees requested, it should seldom be necessary to file a reply brief. Plaintiff's attorney may not file a reply brief absent leave of Court.

[Effective June 1, 1998. Amended effective December 1, 2009; December 2, 2013.]

VIII.   PROVISIONAL AND FINAL REMEDIES

LOCAL CIVIL RULE 65.   BONDS AND SURETIES

65.1. In all civil actions the Clerk shall accept as surety upon bonds and other undertakings a surety company approved by the United States Department of Treasury, cash or an individual personal surety residing within the district. The Clerk shall maintain a list of approved surety companies. Any personal surety must qualify as the owner of real estate within this district of the full net value of twice the face amount of the bond. Attorneys or other officers of this Court shall not serve as sureties. This rule shall apply to supersedeas bonds and any other bonds required by law.

[Effective June 1, 1998.]

LOCAL CIVIL RULE 67.   DEPOSIT IN COURT; PAYMENT OF JUDGMENT

67.1. Deposit of Funds. Any order requiring the Clerk to make investment of funds in an interest bearing account shall not be effective until such order is personally served on the Clerk.

67.2. Payment of Judgment. Except with respect to litigation in which the United States is a party, the Clerk will not, unless authorized by order of the Court, accept payment of judgments. Upon receipt of payment of a judgment, however, the party shall file with the Clerk an acknowledgment of payment.

[Effective June 1, 1998.]

IX.   SPECIAL PROCEEDINGS

LOCAL CIVIL RULE 71A.   CONDEMNATION CASES

71A.1. When the United States files separate land condemnation actions and concurrently files a single declaration of taking relating to those separate actions, the Clerk is authorized to establish a master file so designated, in which the declaration of taking shall be filed, and the filing of the declaration of taking therein shall constitute a filing of the same in each of the actions in which it relates.

[Effective June 1, 1998.]

LOCAL CIVIL RULE 72.   AUTHORITY OF UNITED STATES MAGISTRATE JUDGES

72.1. The United States magistrate judges of this district are hereby empowered to perform all duties authorized by 28 U.S.C. § 636 and any other duty not inconsistent with the Constitution and laws of the United States, as more fully set forth below.

(a) *Duties Under 28 U.S.C. § 636(a).* Each magistrate judge of this Court is empowered to perform all duties prescribed by 28 U.S.C. § 636(a).

(b) *Determination of Nondispositive Pretrial Matters—28 U.S.C. § 636(b)(1)(A).* A magistrate judge may hear and determine any procedural or discovery motion or other pretrial matter in a case, other than the motions which are specified in subsection (c) of this rule.

(c) *Recommendations Regarding Case–Dispositive Motions—28 U.S.C. § 636(b)(1)(B).*

(i) A magistrate judge may submit to a judge of the Court a report containing proposed findings of fact and recommendations for disposition by the judge of the following pretrial motions in civil cases:

(A) motion for injunctive relief, including temporary restraining orders and preliminary and permanent injunctions;

(B) motions for judgment on the pleadings;

(C) motions for summary judgment;

(D) motions to dismiss or permit the maintenance of a class action;

(E) motions to dismiss for failure to state a claim upon which relief may be granted;

(F) motions to involuntarily dismiss an action; or

(G) motions for review of default judgments.

(ii) A magistrate judge may determine any preliminary matters and conduct any necessary evidentiary hearing or other proceeding arising in the exercise of the authority conferred by this rule.

(d) *Prisoner Cases Under 28 U.S.C. §§ 2254 and 2255.* A magistrate judge may perform any or all of the duties imposed upon a judge by the rules governing proceedings in the United States District Courts under §§ 2254 and 2255 of Title 28, United States Code, and may review all other applications for relief made under 28 U.S.C. Chapter 153. In so doing, a magistrate judge may issue any preliminary orders and conduct any necessary evidentiary hearing or other appropriate proceeding and may submit to a judge a report containing proposed findings of fact and recommendations for disposition of the petition by the judge. Any order disposing of the petition may only be made by a judge.

(e) *Prisoner Cases Under 42 U.S.C. § 1983.* A magistrate judge may issue any preliminary orders and conduct any necessary evidentiary hearing or other appropriate proceeding and may submit to a judge a report containing proposed findings of fact and recommendations for the disposition of petitions filed by prisoners challenging the conditions of their confinement.

(f) *Other Duties.* A magistrate judge is also authorized to:

(i) exercise all authority conferred upon United States magistrate judges by the Federal Rules of Civil Procedure;

(ii) conduct pretrial conferences, settlement conferences, omnibus hearings, and related pretrial proceedings in cases;

(iii) conduct voir dire and select petit juries to the extent allowed by law;

(iv) accept petit jury verdicts in cases in the absence of a judge;

(v) issue subpoenas, writs of habeas corpus ad testificandum or habeas corpus ad prosequendum, or other orders necessary to obtain the presence of parties witnesses or evidence needed for investigations or for court proceedings;

(vi) order the exoneration or forfeiture of bonds;

(vii) conduct proceedings for the collection of civil penalties of not more than $200 assessed under the Federal Boat Safety Act of 1971, in accordance with 46 U.S.C. §§ 4311(d) and 12309(c);

(viii) conduct examinations of judgment debtors in accordance with Rule 69 of the Federal Rules of Civil Procedure;

(ix) conduct proceedings for initial commitment of narcotics addicts under Title III of the Narcotic Addict Rehabilitation Act;

(x) perform the functions specified in 18 U.S.C. §§ 4107, 4108, and 4109, regarding proceedings for verification of consent by offenders to transfer to or from the United States and the appointment of counsel therein;

(xi) conduct final hearings and decide routine motions for dismissal and continuance in naturalization cases in which petitioners are recommended by the Immigration and Naturalization Service without reservation;

(xii) issue summons, search warrants, orders or other process authorizing agents and officers of the Internal Revenue Service or other authorized persons to enter premises and to make such search as is necessary in order to levy and seize property pursuant to Section 6331 of the Internal Revenue Code or other applicable provision of law;

(xiii) conduct proceedings in accordance with 26 U.S.C. §§ 7402(b) and 7604(b) regarding enforcement of Internal Revenue Service summonses; and

(xiv) perform any additional duty not inconsistent with the Constitution and laws of the United States.

72.2. Assignment of Matters to Magistrate Judges. Unless otherwise ordered by the judge to whom a case is assigned, the magistrate judge assigned to any case may hear and determine any nondispositive pretrial matters in that case without any further order of reference.

(a) *General Cases.* The method for assignment and reassignment of duties to a magistrate judge and for the allocation of duties among the several magistrate judges of the Court shall be made in accordance with orders of the Court or by special designation of a judge.

(b) *Habeas Corpus and Prisoner Civil Rights Cases.* At the time of filing any habeas corpus or prisoner civil rights case, the Clerk shall assign the case to a judge and to a magistrate judge in accordance with procedures established by these rules and the implementing orders of the Court. The assigned magistrate judge may enter such orders and conduct such proceedings in that case as are authorized by statute or rule, without any further order of reference. An order disposing of the case may only be entered by a judge.

72.3. Review and Appeal of Magistrate Judges' Decisions.

(a) *Appeal of Nondispositive Matters—28 U.S.C. § 636(b)(1)(A).* Any party may appeal from a magistrate judge's order determining any motion or matter within fourteen (14) days after service of the magistrate judge's order, unless a longer time is prescribed by the magistrate judge or a judge. Such party shall file and serve a written statement of appeal which shall specifically designate the order, or part thereof, appealed from and the basis for any objection thereto. In any case in which the decision of the magistrate judge is reflected only in an oral opinion on the record, the appealing party shall provide the district judge with a transcript of the oral opinion, unless excused by the district judge. Any party may respond to another party's objections within fourteen (14) days of service. Objections and responses shall conform to the page limits for briefs set forth in LCivR 7.3(b). A judge of the Court shall consider the appeal and shall set aside any portion of the magistrate judge's order found to be clearly erroneous or contrary to law.

(b) *Review of Case–Dispositive Motions and Prisoner Litigation—28 U.S.C. § 636(b)(1)(B).* Any party may object to a magistrate judge's proposed findings, recommendations or report within fourteen (14) days after being served with a copy thereof unless a longer time is prescribed by the magistrate judge or a judge. Such party shall file and serve written objections which shall specifically identify the portions of the proposed findings, recommendations or report to which objections are made and the basis for such objections. Any party may respond to another party's objections within fourteen (14) days after being served with a copy thereof. Objections and responses shall conform to the page limits for briefs set forth in LCivR 7.2(b). A judge shall make a de novo determination of those portions of the report or specified proposed findings or recommendations to which objection is made and may accept, reject, or modify, in whole or in part, the findings or recommendations made by the magistrate judge. The judge, however, need conduct a new hearing only where required by law, and may consider the record developed before the magistrate judge, making a de novo determination on the basis of that record. The judge may also receive further evidence, recall witnesses or recommit the matter to the magistrate judge with instructions.

(c) *Special Master Reports—28 U.S.C. § 636(b)(2).* Any party may seek review of, or action on, a special master report filed by a magistrate judge in accordance with the provisions of Rule 53(f) of the Federal Rules of Civil Procedure.

(d) *Appeals From Other Orders of a Magistrate Judge.* Appeals from any other decisions and orders of a magistrate judge not provided for in this rule should be taken as provided by governing statute, rule, or decisional law.

[Effective June 1, 1998. Amended effective December 1, 2007; December 1, 2009; September 18, 2017.]

LOCAL CIVIL RULE 73. CONSENT JURISDICTION OF MAGISTRATE JUDGES

73.1. Conduct of Trials and Disposition of Cases Upon Consent of the Parties—28 U.S.C. § 636(c). Upon the consent of all parties, a magistrate judge may conduct any or all proceedings in any case, including the conduct of a jury or non-jury trial, and may order the entry of a final judgment, in accordance with 28 U.S.C. § 636(c). In the course of conducting such proceedings, a magistrate judge may hear and determine any and all pretrial and post-trial motions, including case-dispositive motions.

73.2. Notice. The Clerk shall notify the parties in cases of their option to consent to have a magistrate judge conduct any or all proceedings as provided by law.

73.3. Execution of Consent. The Clerk shall not accept a consent form unless it has been signed by all the parties in a case. No consent form will be made available, nor will its contents be made known, to any judge or magistrate judge, unless all parties have consented to the reference to a magis-

trate judge. No magistrate judge or other court official may attempt to persuade or induce any party to consent to the reference of any matter to a magistrate judge. This rule, however, shall not preclude a judge or magistrate judge from informing the parties that they have the option of referring a case to a magistrate judge.

73.4. Reference. After the consent form has been executed and filed, the Clerk shall transmit it to the judge to whom the case has been assigned for approval and referral of the case to a magistrate judge. Once the case has been assigned to a magistrate judge, the magistrate judge shall have the authority to conduct any and all proceedings to which the parties have consented and to direct the Clerk of Court to enter a final judgment in the same manner as if a judge had presided.

73.5. Suspension of Rule. This rule may be suspended in those instances when the Court determines that the other duties of the magistrate judges preclude their availability for this purpose.

[Effective June 1, 1998.]

X. DISTRICT COURTS AND CLERKS

LOCAL CIVIL RULE 77. DISTRICT COURTS AND CLERKS; ISSUANCE OF PROCESS

77.1. Time and Place of Holding Court. The Court shall be deemed to be in continuous session for transacting judicial business on all business days throughout the year. Proceedings may be held at such times and places within the district as the judge to whom the case is assigned shall designate.

77.2. Clerk's Office. The Court maintains Southern Division offices in Grand Rapids, Kalamazoo and Lansing, and a Northern Division office in Marquette.

77.3. Issuance of Process. Any party requesting the issuance of any process or who initiates any proceeding in which the issuance of process is required by statute, rule or order, shall prepare all required forms, including the following: (a) Summons; (b) Warrants of Seizure and Monition; (c) Subpoenas to Witnesses; (d) Certificates of Judgment; (e) Writs of Execution; (f) Orders of Sale; (g) All process in garnishment or other aid in execution; and (h) Civil cover sheet. The party where necessary shall present the process to the Clerk for signature and sealing. The Clerk shall, upon request, and subject to current availability, make reasonable supplies of all

blank official forms of process available to attorneys admitted to practice in this Court, or their agents or employees.

77.4. Notice of State Interests. [Repealed].

[Effective June 1, 1998. Amended effective February 15, 2007.]

LOCAL CIVIL RULE 79. BOOKS AND RECORDS KEPT BY THE CLERK

79.1. Custody of Files. Files in Southern Division cases shall be maintained in the divisional office where the judge or magistrate judge assigned to the case sits. All Northern Division files shall be maintained in Marquette.

79.2. Removal of Files, Exhibits and Papers. No files, pleadings, exhibits or papers shall be removed from the offices of the Clerk except upon order of the Court. Whenever files, pleadings, exhibits or papers are removed from an office of the Clerk, the person receiving them shall sign and deliver to the Clerk a receipt therefor.

79.3. Duplication of Papers. The Clerk shall make reasonable arrangements for the duplication of unrestricted papers in any court file.

[Effective June 1, 1998.]

XI. GENERAL PROVISIONS

LOCAL CIVIL RULE 83. ATTORNEYS; BANKRUPTCY; MISCELLANEOUS; CONDUCT IN FEDERAL COURT FACILITIES

83.1. Attorneys.

(a) *Definitions.* As used in Local Rules 83.1(a) through 83.1(q), these terms are defined below.

(i) "Discipline" means an order entered against an attorney by the Michigan Attorney Discipline Board, a similar disciplinary authority of another state, or a state or federal court, revoking or suspending an attorney's license or admission before a court to practice law, placing an attorney on probation or inactive status, requiring restitution, or a transfer to inactive status in lieu of discipline.

(ii) "Chief Judge" means the Chief Judge or another district judge designated to perform the Chief Judge's functions under these rules.

(iii) "Practice in this Court," means, in connection with an action or proceeding pending in this Court, to appear in, commence, conduct, prosecute, or defend the action or proceeding; appear in open court; sign a paper; participate in a pretrial conference; represent a client at a deposition; counsel a client in the action or proceeding for compensation; or otherwise practice in this Court or before an officer of this Court.

(iv) "State" means a state, territory, commonwealth, or possession of the United States, and the District of Columbia.

(v) "Serious crime" means:

(A) a felony; or

(B) a crime, a necessary element of which, as determined by the statutory or common law definition of the crime in the jurisdiction of the conviction, involves interference with the administration of justice, false swearing, misrepresentation, fraud, willful failure to file income tax returns, willful failure to pay income tax, deceit, bribery, extortion, misappropriation, theft, or an attempt, conspiracy, or solicitation of another to commit a serious crime.

(b) *Roll of Attorneys.* The bar of this Court consists of those currently admitted to practice in this Court. The Clerk shall maintain the roll of admitted attorneys.

(c) *Eligibility for Admission.*

(i) Eligibility. A person who is duly admitted to practice in a court of record of a state, and who is in active status and in good standing, may apply for admission to the bar of this Court, except as provided in (ii) below.

(ii) Effect of Prior Discipline. If the applicant has been held in contempt, disciplined, or convicted of a crime, the Chief Judge shall make an independent determination as to whether the applicant is qualified to be entrusted with professional matters and to aid in the administration of justice as an attorney and officer of the Court. An applicant dissatisfied with the decision of the Chief Judge may within twenty-eight (28) days file a petition for a hearing before a three judge panel as described in LCivR 83.1(m)(iii).

(iii) Pro Hac Vice Admissions. This Court disfavors pro hac vice admission and prefers that all lawyers appearing before it become full members of the bar of the Court. Pro hac vice admission may nevertheless be allowed on a temporary basis pending full admission, or in unusual circumstances.

(d) *Procedure for Admission.*

(i) An applicant for admission to the bar of this Court shall pay the fee established by the Court and complete the application provided by the Clerk. The following information must be included in the application:

(A) office address and telephone number;

(B) the date of admission and each jurisdiction where the applicant has been admitted to practice; and

(C) whether the applicant has ever been held in contempt, subjected to discipline as defined by these rules or convicted of a crime. If so, the applicant shall state the facts and the final disposition of each such instance.

(ii) A sponsor must sign a declaration supporting the application for admission. A sponsor may be a member of the bar of this Court or, for applicants residing in another state, a judge of a court of record of that state, or a federal judge. The Chief Judge may waive the sponsorship requirement for recent law school graduates.

(iii) If an applicant has been subject to discipline as defined by these rules, the application must be accompanied by a copy of the entire disciplinary record, including complaints, answers, hearing transcripts and orders entered in the disciplinary proceedings.

(iv) The Chief Judge may grant or deny the application for admission. Alternatively, the Chief Judge may refer the application to a three-judge panel constituted pursuant to subsection (m)(iii)(A) of this rule for decision. A panel may grant or deny the application or may grant it subject to conditions. A decision of a majority of the three–judge panel shall be final and binding. If the Court grants the application, the Clerk shall issue a certificate of admission.

(e) *Limited Pre–Admission Practice.* An attorney may appear on record and file papers in a case or proceeding before actual admission to practice in this Court if:

(i) the attorney pays the fee established by the Court;

(ii) the attorney files the application required by this rule with the Clerk; and

(iii) the attorney is admitted before a personal appearance in court.

(f) *Local Counsel.* The Court may, in its discretion, require any attorney whose office is a great distance from the courthouse to retain local counsel. Local counsel shall enter an appearance in the case and shall have both the authority and responsibility for the conduct of the case should lead counsel be unavailable for any appearance, hearing or trial.

(g) *Government Attorneys.* An attorney representing the United States, or an agency of the United States may practice in this Court in official capacity without applying for admission. If the attorney does not have an office in the district, he or she shall designate the United States Attorney or an Assistant United States Attorney for this district to receive service of all notices and papers. Service of notice on the United States Attorney or designated assistant shall constitute service on the nonresident government attorney.

(h) *Law Student Practice.*

(i) Admission. Upon a satisfactory showing of eligibility and taking of the prescribed oath, a law student in an approved program may appear before the Court under the supervision of an attorney who has been duly certified. The supervising attorney may be an attorney in the U.S. Attorney's Office, an attorney in private practice admitted to practice before this Court, or a faculty member of an ABA-approved law school teaching in an eligible law school clinical program as defined in (iii) below.

(ii) Eligibility of Law Student. To be eligible to practice, a law student must:

(A) be enrolled in, or have graduated from, a law school approved by the American Bar Association;

(B) have completed at least two-thirds of the credit hours necessary for graduation from that law school;

(C) be certified by the dean of the law school as being of good character and of sufficient legal ability and training to perform as a legal intern;

(D) have a working knowledge of the Federal Rules of Civil and Criminal Procedure, Evidence, and Code of Professional Responsibility;

(E) have been certified by the Court pursuant to this rule;

(G) if the student qualifies as a legal intern under a supervising law school faculty member, be registered for credit in a law school clinical program which has been certified by the Court; and

(H) have been appropriately introduced to the Court by a member of the bar of this Court or by the supervising faculty member.

(iii) Eligibility of Program.

(A) An eligible law school clinical program:

(1) must be offered for credit at a law school approved by the American Bar Association;

(2) must be supervised by a full-time or adjunct law school faculty member who is admitted to practice before this Court;

(3) must include academic and practical advocacy training within the program;

(4) must be certified by this Court;

(5) must provide malpractice insurance for its activities, supervisors and student participants in the legal representation of any clients;

(6) must designate an official within the Western District to whom all notices may be sent in connection with this rule or any legal representation provided pursuant to this rule; and

(7) may arrange for a supervisor to accept compensation other than from a client, such as compensation under the Criminal Justice Act.

(B) An eligible non-law school clinical program:

(1) must be supervised by a member of a bar who is admitted to practice before this Court;

(2) must be developed to provide practical advocacy training within the program;

(3) must provide direct supervision by the supervising attorney;

(4) must be for a period of no less than fourteen (14) weeks;

(5) must be certified by the Court;

(6) must provide malpractice insurance for its activities, supervisors and student participants in the legal representation of any client under this program;

(7) may be, but need not be, under the direction of a full-time or adjunct faculty member of a law school; and

(8) must identify the supervising attorney to whom all notices may be sent.

(iv) Requirements for Supervisor. A supervisor must:

(A) if a full-time or adjunct member of a law school faculty, be certified by the dean of the law school as being of good character, and as having sufficient legal ability and adequate litigation experience to fulfill the responsibilities as the supervisor. If the supervisor is not a member of a law school faculty, the certification may be provided by a practicing member of the bar;

(B) be admitted to practice in this Court;

(C) be present with the student in court and at other proceedings in which testimony is taken and as required under subsection (e) of this rule;

(D) cosign all pleadings or other documents filed with the Court;

(E) assume full personal and professional responsibility for a student's guidance in any work undertaken and for the quality of a student's work, and be available for consultation with represented clients;

(F) assist and counsel the student in activities pursuant to this rule and review all such activities with the student to the extent required for the proper practical training of the student and protection of the client; and

(G) be responsible for supplemental oral or written work for the student as is necessary to ensure proper representation of the client.

(v) Approved Activities. A certified student under the personal supervision of a supervisor may participate in activities as set out below.

(A) A student may represent any client, including federal, state or local government bodies, if the client on whose behalf the student is appearing has indicated in writing consent to that appearance and the supervising attorney has also indicated in writing approval of that appearance.

(B) A student may represent a client in any criminal, civil or administrative matter on behalf of any person or governmental body. However, any judge or magistrate judge of this Court retains the authority to limit a student's participation in any individual case before that judge or magistrate judge.

(C) Representation shall include holding of consultations, preparation of documents for filing or submission to the Court, participation in discovery proceedings and the participation in trials and other court proceedings.

(D) The supervising attorney must be present with the student for all court appearances or for the taking of oral depositions except that a legal intern under a law school clinical program may appear in court without the supervising attorney unless the Court directs the presence of the supervisor. The Court shall be advised in advance whenever a legal intern is scheduled to appear in court without a supervising attorney.

(E) A student may make no binding commitments on behalf of an absent client prior to client and supervisor approval. Documents or papers filed with the Court must be read, approved and cosigned by the supervising attorney. The Court retains the authority to establish exceptions to such activities.

(F) A judge of this Court may terminate the admission of the legal intern at any time without prior notice or hearing or showing of cause.

(vi) Compensation. An eligible law student may neither solicit nor accept compensation or remuneration of any kind for services performed pursuant to this rule from the person on whose behalf services are rendered; but this rule will not prevent an attorney, legal aid bureau, law school or state or federal agency from paying compensation to an eligible law student, or making such charges for services as may be proper.

(vii) Certification of Student. Certification of a student by the law school dean or designee, if such certification is approved by the Court, shall be filed with the Clerk and unless it is sooner withdrawn, shall remain in effect until the expiration of twelve (12) months. Certification will automatically terminate if the student does not take the first bar examination following graduation, or if the student fails to achieve a passing grade in the bar examination, or if the student is admitted to full practice before this Court. Certification of a student to appear in a particular case may be withdrawn by the Court at any time, in the discretion of the Court and without any showing of cause.

(viii) Certification of Program. Certification of a program by the Court shall be filed with the Clerk and shall remain in effect indefinitely unless withdrawn by the Court. Certification of a program may be withdrawn by the Court at any time, in the discretion of the Court and without any showing of cause.

(ix) Certification of Supervisor. Certification of a supervisor by the law school dean or member of the bar, if such certification is approved by the Court, shall be filed with the Clerk and shall remain in effect indefinitely unless withdrawn by the Court. Certification of a supervisor may be withdrawn by the Court at any time, in the discretion of the Court and without any showing of cause. Any judge or magistrate judge of this Court retains the authority to withdraw or limit a supervisor's participation in any individual case before that judge or magistrate judge. Certification of a supervisor may be withdrawn by the dean or attorney who originally certified the supervisor by mailing the notices of withdrawal to the Clerk.

(i) *Unauthorized Practice.*

(i) A person must be a member in good standing of the bar of this Court to practice in this Court or to hold himself or herself out as being authorized to practice in this Court, except that:

(A) a party may proceed in pro per;

(B) government attorneys may practice under LCivR 83.1(g); and

(C) law students may practice under LCivR 83.1(h).

(D) A licensed attorney who is not under suspension or disbarment in this or another federal or state court may:

(1) cosign papers or participate in pretrial conferences in conjunction with a member of the bar of this Court;

(2) represent a client in a deposition; and

(3) counsel a client in an action or proceeding pending in this Court.

(j) *Consent to Standards of Conduct and Disciplinary Authority.* An attorney admitted to the bar of this Court or who practices in this Court as permitted by this Rule is subject to the Rules of Professional Conduct adopted by the Michigan Supreme Court, except those rules a majority of the judges of this Court exclude by administrative order, and consents to the jurisdiction of this Court and the Michigan Attorney Grievance Commission and Michigan Attorney Discipline Board for purposes of disciplinary proceedings. Any person practicing or purporting to practice in this Court shall be presumed to know the Local Rules of this Court, including those provisions relating to sanctions for violations of these Rules.

(k) *Attorney Discipline.*

(i) Discipline Other Than Suspension or Disbarment. In accordance with the provisions of this Rule, a district judge or magistrate judge may impose discipline, except suspension or disbarment from this Court, on any attorney who engages in conduct violating the Rules of Professional Conduct; willfully violates these rules, the Federal Rules of Civil Procedure, or orders of the Court; or engages in other conduct unbecoming of a member of the bar of this Court. Prior to the imposition of discipline, the attorney shall be afforded an opportunity to show good cause, within such time as the Court shall prescribe, why the discipline should not be imposed. Upon the attorney's response to show cause, and after hearing, if requested and allowed by the district judge, or upon expiration of the time prescribed for a response if no response is made, the Court shall enter an appropriate order.

(ii) Suspension or Disbarment.

(A) Initiation of Proceedings. Formal disciplinary proceedings leading up to possible suspension or disbarment shall be initiated by the issuance of an order to show cause, signed by the Chief Judge. Such order may be issued by the Court, on its own initiative or in response to allegations brought to the attention of the Court in a written complaint, if the Court determines further investigation is warranted. The Chief Judge may dismiss a complaint and refuse to issue an order to show cause if the complaint is found to be frivolous. The order to show cause issued by the Court shall include the specific facts that give rise to the proposed discipline, including the date, place and nature of the alleged misconduct, and the names of all persons involved. A copy of the order and any supporting documents shall be mailed to the attorney who is the subject of investigation. The attorney shall have twenty-one (21) days from the entry of the order in which to respond. The response shall contain a specific admission or denial of each of the factual allegations contained in the order and, in addition, a specific statement of facts on which the respondent relies, including all other material dates, places, persons and conduct, and all documents or other supporting evidence not previously filed with the order that are relevant to the charges of misconduct alleged. The response shall contain a specific request for a hearing, if so desired by the respondent.

(B) Hearing. A disciplinary hearing shall be held only when the attorney under investigation has requested such a hearing in a timely response.

(1) Procedures. If it is determined that a hearing is necessary, the Chief Judge shall provide the attorney with written notice of the hearing a minimum of twenty-one (21) days before its scheduled date. The notice shall contain the date and location of the hearing and a statement that the attorney is entitled to be represented by counsel, to present witnesses and other evidence, and to confront and cross examine adverse witnesses.

(2) Conduct of the Hearing. The hearing shall be conducted by a panel of three judicial officers appointed by the Chief Judge, consisting of at least one active or senior district judge. The other members of the panel may include senior judges, bankruptcy judges, and magistrate judges. Any judge who initiated the request for discipline or before whom the allegation giving rise to the request took place shall not be appointed to the panel. The presiding judicial officer shall have the authority to resolve all disputes on matters of procedure and evidence which arise during the course of the proceeding. The presiding judicial officer may appoint an attorney to assist in the preparation and presentation of the evidence supporting the allegations giving rise to the request for discipline. All witnesses shall testify under penalty of perjury. Such hearings shall be confidential and be recorded. A decision of a majority of the three judge panel shall be final and binding. A written order shall be prepared which shall include the findings of the panel and disposition of the disciplinary charges. The order shall be a matter of public record and be sent to the respondent and complainant.

(3) Burden of Proof. The conduct giving rise to the request for discipline shall be proven by a preponderance of the evidence.

(4) Failure to Appear. The failure of the respondent to appear at the hearing shall itself be grounds for discipline.

(iii) Reinstatement After Expiration of Court–Imposed Discipline. After expiration of a period of suspension imposed by this Court, an attorney may apply for reinstatement by filing an affidavit under LCivR 83.1(m)(iii). The application for reinstatement will be decided in accordance with the process set forth in that rule. Unless and until reinstated, a suspended attorney must not practice before this Court.

(*l*) *Attorneys Convicted of Crimes.*

(i) Serious Crimes.

(A) When an attorney admitted to practice before this Court is convicted of a serious crime, the attorney is automatically suspended from practice in this Court without further action of the Court, whether the conviction resulted from a plea of guilty or nolo contendere or from a verdict after trial or otherwise, and regardless of the pendency of an appeal. On receipt of written notice of conviction of a serious crime of an attorney admitted to practice before this Court, the Chief Judge shall enter an order suspending the attorney. The suspension shall continue until after final disposition of an appeal of the conviction, proceedings on remand after an appeal, and any disciplinary investigation and proceeding based on the conduct that resulted in the conviction. The Court shall serve a copy of the order on the attorney by certified mail.

(B) On application, the Chief Judge shall reinstate the attorney on a showing that:

(1) there is a jurisdictional deficiency that establishes that the suspension may not properly be ordered; such as that the crime did not constitute a serious crime or that the attorney is not the individual convicted; or

(2) the conviction has been reversed and there is no likelihood of further criminal prosecution or disciplinary action related to the conduct that resulted in the conviction. A reinstatement will not terminate any disciplinary investigation or proceeding based on the conduct that resulted in the conviction.

(ii) Other Crimes. If the Court receives written notice of conviction of an attorney admitted to practice before this Court of a crime not constituting a serious crime, the matter shall be referred to the Chief Judge who may initiate proceedings under subsection (k)(i) or (ii) of this rule.

(iii) Obligations to Report Conviction. An attorney admitted to practice before this Court shall, on being convicted of any crime, immediately inform the Clerk. If the conviction was in this Court, the attorney shall also provide to the Clerk a list of all other jurisdictions in which the attorney is admitted to practice. An attorney knowingly violating this provision may, on notice and after hearing, be charged with criminal contempt.

(m) *Discipline by Other Jurisdictions.*

(i) Reciprocal Discipline.

(A) On receipt of written notice that another jurisdiction entered an order of discipline against an attorney admitted to practice in this Court, the Chief Judge shall enter an order imposing the same discipline, effective as of the date that the discipline was effective in the other jurisdiction. If the discipline imposed in the other jurisdiction has been stayed there, the Court shall defer reciprocal discipline until the stay expires.

(B) When this Court enters an order of discipline against an attorney, the attorney shall provide to the Clerk a list of all other jurisdictions in which the attorney is admitted to practice.

(ii) Application to Modify Reciprocal Discipline.

(A) Within twenty-eight (28) days after the effective date of the order of discipline in this Court, the attorney may apply to the Chief Judge for modification or vacation of the discipline.

(B) The Chief Judge shall modify or vacate the discipline if, on the record supporting the order of discipline in the other jurisdiction, the attorney demonstrates or the Chief Judge finds that it clearly appears that:

(1) the procedure in the other jurisdiction constituted a deprivation of due process;

(2) there was such an infirmity of proof establishing the misconduct as to give rise to the clear conviction that this Court could not accept as final the conclusion on that subject;

(3) imposing the same discipline in this Court would result in grave injustice; or

(4) the misconduct warrants substantially different discipline.

If the Chief Judge determines that any of these grounds exist, the Chief Judge shall order other appropriate discipline or no discipline.

(iii) Reinstatement After Expiration of Discipline.

(A) An attorney may apply for reinstatement by filing an affidavit of reinstatement stating that the jurisdiction that entered the underlying order of discipline has reinstated the attorney. The application for reinstatement must be accompanied by a copy of the entire disciplinary record, including complaints, answers, hearing transcripts, and orders entered in the disciplinary proceedings. The Chief Judge shall assign such applications to a panel of three judicial officers consisting of at least one active or senior district judge. The other members of the panel may include senior judges, bankruptcy judges and magistrate judges. Any judge who initiated the request for discipline or before whom the allegation giving rise to request for discipline took place shall not be appointed to the panel. A decision of the majority of the three judge panel shall be final and binding.

(B) The judicial officers assigned to the matter shall within twenty-eight (28) days after assignment schedule a hearing at which the attorney shall have the burden of demonstrating by clear and convincing evidence that:

(1) the attorney has complied with the orders of discipline of this Court and all other disciplinary authorities;

(2) the attorney has not practiced in this Court during the period of disbarment or suspension and has not practiced law contrary to any other order of discipline;

(3) the attorney has not engaged in any other professional misconduct since disbarment or suspension;

(4) the attorney has the moral qualifications, competency and learning in the law required for admission to practice law before this Court; and

(5) the attorney's resumption of the practice of law will not be detrimental to the integrity and standing of the bar or to the administration of justice, or subversive of the public interest.

The Court may condition reinstatement on payment of all or part of the costs of the proceedings in this Court and may impose any of the conditions of reinstatement imposed in the other jurisdiction, or such other conditions as are warranted.

(C) An attorney shall not file an application for reinstatement under this Rule within one year following denial of such an application.

(iv) Obligation to Report Discipline.

(A) An attorney admitted to practice before this Court appearing or participating in a pending matter shall, on being subjected to an order of discipline, immediately inform the Clerk of the order of discipline.

(B) An attorney admitted to practice before this Court shall, before appearing or participating in a matter in the Court after being subjected to an order of discipline that has not previously been reported to the Court, immediately inform the Clerk of the order of discipline.

(C) An attorney knowingly violating this provision may be charged with criminal contempt.

(n) *Resignation in Other Jurisdictions.*

(i) If an attorney resigns from the bar of another court of the United States while an investigation into allegations of misconduct is pending:

(A) the attorney shall immediately and automatically be disbarred from this Court; and

(B) the attorney shall promptly inform the Clerk of the resignation. An attorney knowingly violating this notification provision may be charged with criminal contempt.

(ii) On receipt of written notice that an attorney has resigned from the bar of another court of the United States or the bar of a state while an investigation into allegations of misconduct was pending, the Chief Judge shall enter an order disbarring the attorney, effective as of the date of resignation in the other jurisdiction.

(iii) An attorney disbarred under this subsection may apply to the Chief Judge for modification or vacation of the disbarment pursuant to LCivR 83.1(m)(ii).

(iv) An attorney disbarred under this subsection may be reinstated if the attorney is readmitted in the jurisdiction from which the attorney resigned and there has been a final disposition of the investigation into allegations of misconduct without an order of discipline.

(o) *Service of Papers.* Service of papers on an attorney under this Rule may be by mail to the address of the attorney shown on the Court's roll of attorneys or the address in the most recent paper the attorney filed in a proceeding in this Court.

(p) *Duties of the Clerk.*

(i) On being informed that an attorney admitted to practice before this Court has been convicted of a crime, the Clerk shall determine whether the Court in which the conviction occurred sent a certificate of the conviction to this

Court. If not, the Clerk shall promptly obtain a certificate and file it with the Court.

(ii) On being informed that another court or a state has entered an order of discipline against an attorney admitted to practice before this Court, the Clerk shall determine whether a certified copy of the order has been filed with this Court. If not, the Clerk shall promptly obtain a certified copy of the order and file it with the Court.

(iii) When this Court convicts an attorney of a crime or enters an order of discipline against an attorney, the Clerk shall promptly notify the National Discipline Data Bank operated by the American Bar Association and any other authority that licensed or authorized the attorney to practice.

(q) *Other Authority.* Nothing in this Rule abridges the Court's power to control proceedings before it, including the power to initiate proceedings for contempt under Fed. R. Crim. P. 42 or sanction or disqualify an attorney in a particular case.

83.2. Bankruptcy.

(a) *Referral of Cases Under Title 11 to Bankruptcy Judges.* Pursuant to the powers granted by 28 U.S.C. § 157(a) any or all cases under Title 11 and any or all proceedings arising under Title 11 or arising in or related to a case under Title 11 previously filed or hereafter filed shall be referred to the bankruptcy judges of this district.

(b) *Bankruptcy Court Jurisdiction in Core and Noncore Related Proceedings.* The bankruptcy judge shall determine whether proceedings are core, or noncore related, and shall enter appropriate orders and judgments subject to those appeal rights afforded by 28 U.S.C. § 158 and Fed. R. Bankr. P. 8001–8009. In those noncore related proceedings in which the parties timely object to the entry of a final judgment or order by the bankruptcy judge, the bankruptcy court shall file and serve proposed findings of fact and conclusions of law on all dispositive matters. Objections shall be filed in accordance with Fed. R. Bankr. P. 9033. Upon submission by the bankruptcy court clerk to the district court clerk of the proposed findings of fact and conclusions of law and all objections timely filed thereto, the matter will be randomly assigned to a district judge who will conduct all further proceedings and enter a dispositive order.

(c) *Jury Trials.* Pursuant to 28 U.S.C. §§ 157(e) and 1411(e), the bankruptcy judges in this district are specially designated to conduct jury trials with the express consent of all parties, if the right to jury trial applies in any proceeding that may be heard by a bankruptcy judge. All bankruptcy judges shall adhere to the Jury Selection and Service Act, 18 U.S.C. §§ 1861–1878, and this Court's jury selection plan. Upon request, the district court clerk shall supply a sufficient number of jurors for jury trials in the bankruptcy court. Procedure in jury cases, including time and form of jury demand, waiver, advisory juries and trial by consent shall be governed by local rule of the bankruptcy court.

(d) *Local Bankruptcy Rules.* Pursuant to Rule 83 of the Federal Rules of Civil Procedure and the rules governing bankruptcy practice, a majority of the bankruptcy judges of this district are authorized to make rules of practice and procedure consistent with the Bankruptcy Rules.

83.3. Miscellaneous.

(a) *Courthouse Conduct.* [Repealed]

(b) *Certification of Issues to State Courts.* Upon motion or after a hearing ordered by the judge sua sponte, the Court may certify an issue for decision to the highest court of the state whose law governs any issue, claim or defense in the case. An order of certification shall be accompanied by written findings that: (a) the issue certified is an unsettled issue of state law; (b) the issue certified will likely affect the outcome of the federal suit; and (c) certification of the issue will not cause undue delay or prejudice. The order shall also include citation to authority authorizing the state court involved to resolve certified questions. In all such cases, the order of certification shall stay federal proceedings for a fixed time, which shall be subsequently enlarged only upon a showing that such additional time is required to obtain a state court decision. In cases certified to the Michigan Supreme Court, in addition to the findings required by this rule, the Court must approve a statement of facts to be transmitted to the Michigan Supreme Court by the parties as an appendix to briefs filed therein.

(c) *Sealed Cases.* The court may enter an order sealing an entire civil case file only if (a) sealing is required by statute or court rule, or (b) sealing is justified by a showing of extraordinary circumstances and the absence of narrower feasible and effective alternatives (such as sealing discrete documents or redacting specific information), such that sealing an entire case file is a last resort. Any order sealing an entire case file under ground (b) of this rule must contain specific findings justifying sealing. The order may be vacated on motion of any party or on the court's own motion when the reason for sealing has ended. Government attorneys of record in miscellaneous cases involving Grand Jury matters will be afforded remote electronic access to the miscellaneous case.

(d) *Appearance.* An attorney appears by filing any pleading or other paper or by acknowledging in court that the attorney acts in the proceeding on behalf of a party. The appearance of an attorney is deemed to be the appearance of the law firm. Any attorney in the firm may be required by the Court to conduct a court-ordered conference or trial. Withdrawal of appearance may be accomplished only by leave of court.

(e) *Amendment.* These rules may be amended by a majority vote of the judges of this district in conformity with Rule 83 of the Federal Rules of Civil Procedure.

(f) *Payment to Court Reporters.* All parties ordering a transcript must pay in advance by cash or certified check unless the court reporter agrees to other arrangements.

83.4. Conduct in Federal Court Facilities.

(a) *Security.*

(i) As used in this rule, "federal court facility" includes any facility occupied by the United States District Court or any temporary facility occupied by a District Judge or Magistrate Judge serving in the Western District of Michigan.

(ii) All persons entering a federal court facility in the Western District of Michigan are required to present a valid government issued identification card with photo, pass through a magnetometer, and have all belongings and packages subject to physical and/or x-ray examination by the United States Marshals' Service. Any person who refuses to present a valid form of identification or pass through screening shall be denied entrance.

(b) *Soliciting, Loitering, and Disruptive Behavior.*

(i) The solicitation of business relating to bail bonds or to employment as counsel is prohibited.

(ii) Loitering in or about federal court facilities is prohibited.

(iii) Any behavior which impedes or disrupts the orderly conduct of the business of the court is prohibited. Signs, placards, or banners may not be brought into a federal court facility or its environs.

(c) *Recording of Court Proceedings.*

(i) Except as specifically provided herein, no camera or recording device shall be permitted in a federal court facility. This prohibition shall include any device or contrivance capable of preserving or transmitting a visual image and any device or contrivance capable of recording, transmitting, or preserving any audible communication (except cell phones with camera features).

(ii) The taking of photographs or video recordings in connection with any judicial proceeding and the recording or broadcasting of judicial proceedings by radio, television or other means is prohibited.

(A) As used in this rule, "judicial proceeding" includes proceedings before district, bankruptcy or magistrate judges, and sessions of the grand jury.

(B) As used in this rule, "in connection with any judicial proceeding" includes all participants in a judicial proceeding while they are in a courtroom or its environs.

(iii) A judicial officer may authorize, by written notice to the United States Marshal, the use of electronic or photographic means for the presentation of evidence or for the perpetuation of the record.

(iv) A district judge or magistrate judge may authorize, by written notice to the United States Marshal:

(A) The broadcasting, televising, recording, or photographing of investiture, ceremonial, or naturalization proceedings; and

(B) The radio or television broadcasting, audio or video recording or photographing of court proceedings pursuant to a resolution of the Judicial Conference of the United States.

(v) By written notice to the U.S. Marshals' Service, the General Service Administration Property Manager or his designee can authorize an individual or contract group to possess a camera or recording device for the purpose of maintaining or enhancing the facility, to include repair and alterations.

(d) *Firearms and Weapons.*

(i) It is illegal to possess a firearm or other dangerous weapon in a federal court facility with or without the intent to commit a crime (Title 18, USC 930). Firearms, knives, explosives, and other weapons are prohibited in federal court facilities and subject to confiscation.

(ii) Exceptions to this rule include:

(A) Judicial officers, the United States Marshal, deputy marshals, court security officers, and employees of the Federal Protective Service.

(B) Federal law enforcement agencies having offices in a federal court facility are exempt from the provisions regarding the carrying of weapons while entering the building and while going to and from the floor where their offices are located.

(C) Employees of the United States Probation Office who are authorized by law and agency regulations to carry firearms in the performance of their official duties may possess firearms in this facility to the extent necessary to transport such firearms by the most direct route available to and from the offices of the Probation Department. In accordance with regulations of the U.S. Probation Department, all firearms shall be secured while present within the offices of the Probation Department. The Chief U.S. Probation Officer will notify the United States Marshals' Service in writing of all officers authorized to carry firearms. Employees of the United States Probation Office are prohibited from carrying firearms into courtrooms.

(D) State, county, and local law enforcement officers who are:

(1) Escorting prisoners to and from court under the direction of the United States Marshals' Service, or

(2) Assisting the Marshals' Service by supporting or providing additional security, as directed, in and around federal court facilities.

(iii) All other federal, state or local law enforcement officers are required to identify themselves and store their weapons in weapons lock boxes maintained by the United States Marshals' Service. For security purposes, officers *may* be required to be screened after securing their weapons.

(iv) The handling of firearms as exhibits in trials is governed by an administrative order issued by the court.

(v) An exception to this Rule regarding weapons or firearms may only be made by the Chief Judge or the Judge in whose courtroom the proceedings are occurring.

(e) *Cellular Telephones and Laptop Computers.*

(i) General Policy. Except as provided in (ii) and other court orders, cellular telephones and laptop computers, are not permitted in federal court facilities.

(ii) Exempted Persons. The following persons are permitted to carry and use cellular telephones and laptop computers, within federal court facilities in the Western District of Michigan:

(A) Officers of the Court. Attorneys appearing in their official capacity as officers of the Court.

(B) Building Tenants. Employees and visiting employees of the federal court facility.

(C) Parties to Litigation. Parties, other than defendants in criminal cases, who enter a federal court facility accompanied by their attorney, if their counsel certifies to security staff that such devices are necessary to facilitate litigation pending before the court.

(D) U.S. Marshals' Service Personnel. Including Court Security Officers and contract guards.

(E) Other Federal, State, Local Law Enforcement. When appearing in their official capacity.

(F) GSA Approved Contractors. By written notice to the U.S. Marshals' Service, the General Service Administration Property Manager or his designee may authorize an individual or contract group to possess a cellular telephone, laptop computer, or other wireless communication device for the purpose of maintaining or enhancing the facility, to include repair and alterations.

(G) Jurors. Grand jury members, petit jury members, and persons appearing as directed pursuant to a jury summons.

(H) Judicial Authority. Upon request to the court, a judicial officer may issue an order granting permission to an individual or group, otherwise not authorized to possess a cell phone or laptop computer. The U.S. Marshal shall be notified of such order.

(I) Members of the Press. Bona fide members of the press who present official credentials satisfactory to the U.S. Marshal.

(iii) Conditions for Authorized Use of Cellular Telephones.* Unless express permission to the contrary is given by the presiding judicial officer, the following conditions and restrictions apply to those individuals authorized to carry a cellular telephone:

(A) While in a courtroom, cellular telephones shall be in the "off" position at all times, unless the presiding judicial officer give express permission for use of the device.

(B) The device may not be used and must be turned off except in designated areas of the court facility.

(C) The device cannot be initiated, "answered," or examined or manipulated (for text messaging or otherwise) while in a courtroom.

(D) The device may be used for communication by non-building tenants only in designated areas. Designated areas will be identified by each court facility by administrative order, to be posted prominently in each facility and on the court's Internet website.

(E) The cell phone or computer may not be used for purposes of taking pictures or making any audio or video recording in violation of subsection (c) of this rule.

(f) *Enforcement.* The United States Marshal, his deputies, and court security officers may demand from any individual in possession of a cellular telephone or wireless communication device, to produce identification in aid of enforcement of this rule, and if the identification does not satisfy the officer that the person in possession of the device is authorized in accordance with the terms of this rule, the officer may refuse admittance to this person and/or confiscate the device.

(g) *Violations.*

(i) Attorney Discipline. An attorney violating this rule may be subject to discipline, including disbarment, in accordance with Local Criminal Rule 57 and/or Local Civil Rule 83.

(ii) Confiscation. A violation of this rule, including without limitation, unauthorized possession, use in an unauthorized space, possession of a device in an audible mode, and failing to turn off a device when required, *SHALL* result in immediate confiscation of the device. Any judicial officer may order confiscation of a cellular telephone or wireless communications device. Any United States Marshal or Deputy Marshal or court security officer may also confiscate such a device. The U.S. Marshal's Service will develop a procedure for handling and storing confiscated devices.

(iii) Contempt of Court. A violation of this rule may be punished as criminal contempt of court. A violation that disrupts a judicial proceeding may be punished by summary proceedings.

(h) *Relief From Confiscation of a Device.* An individual whose device has been confiscated may apply in writing not less than seven (7) days after confiscation for its return. The application shall be made to the judicial officer whose proceedings were disturbed by the violation, or, if there is no such judicial officer, to the chief judge. The judicial officer may grant or refuse the request. Confiscated devices that are not returned, either because no request has been made within the time provided or the request for return has been denied, shall be disposed of in a manner directed by the chief judge. Nothing in this paragraph shall prohibit the judicial officer or his designee to return a device after the conclusion of a court matter if the violation was totally inadvertent.

(i) *Consent to Provisions.* Any person bringing in a cellular telephone, laptop computer, or other wireless communication device shall be determined to have consented to the provisions of this rule.

[Effective June 1, 1998. Amended effective January 2, 2002; January 1, 2005; June 21, 2006; February 15, 2007; November 3, 2008; December 1, 2009; May 27, 2011; October 13, 2011; February 8, 2012; July 2, 2012; May 6, 2013; February 21, 2017.]

* [**Publisher's Note:** *See also* Administrative Order No. 08–143, *post.*]

LOCAL RULES OF CRIMINAL PRACTICE AND PROCEDURE

PREFACE TO THE 1998 EDITION

On March 12, 1996, the Judicial Conference approved the recommendation of the Committee on Rules of Practice and Procedure to "adopt a numbering system for local rules of court that corresponds with the relevant Federal Rules of Practice and Procedure." The action of the Judicial Conference implements the December 1, 1995 amendments to the Federal Rules of Appellate, Bankruptcy, Civil, and Criminal Procedure, which provide that all local rules of court "must conform to any uniform numbering system prescribed by the Judicial Conference." (See Appellate Rule 47, Bankruptcy Rules 8018 and 9029, Civil Rule 83, and Criminal Rule 57).

In addition to the substantive changes to the local rules found in the 1998 Edition, the Rules have been renumbered to comply with this mandate. The result is that, rather than being consecutively numbered, the rules have been assigned numbers which best correspond to the numbering scheme of the Federal Rules of Civil and Criminal Procedure. The renumbered Local Civil Rules and the renumbered Local Criminal Rules have been compiled as separate sets of Rules. Many of the rules familiar to practitioners under the prior edition remain substantively intact, but have had their provisions redistributed to two or more new rules within the newly-mandated numbering system.

Local Criminal Rules which do not correspond to any rule within the Federal Rules of Criminal Procedure have been assigned to Rule 57, which, in the Federal Rules of Criminal Procedure, governs the rulemaking authority of the courts of the various districts.

I. SCOPE, PURPOSE AND CONSTRUCTION

LOCAL CRIMINAL RULE 1. AUTHORITY; SCOPE; CONSTRUCTION

1.1. Authority. These rules are promulgated pursuant to 28 U.S.C. § 2071 and Rule 57 of the Federal Rules of Criminal Procedure. Amendment of these rules is governed by LCrR 57.3(a).

1.2. Short Title. These rules may be cited and referred to individually as "W.D. Mich. LCrR ___."

1.3. Effective Date. The effective date of these rules is June 1, 1998, including amendments through February 21, 2017.

1.4. Applicability. These rules apply to all criminal proceedings in this Court.

1.5. Scope. These rules govern the procedure in the United States District Court for the Western District of Michigan, govern the practice of attorneys before this Court, and supersede all previous rules promulgated by this Court or any judge thereof. Administrative orders and single-judge standing orders shall be maintained by the Clerk and made available upon request. All such orders shall be consistent with these rules and the Federal Rules of Criminal Procedure.

1.6. Construction. These rules shall be construed to achieve an orderly administration of the business of this Court and to secure the just, speedy and inexpensive determination of every action. References to statutes, regulations or rules shall be interpreted to include all revisions and amendments thereto. References to the Clerk shall be interpreted to mean the Clerk of this Court or any deputy clerk. Wherever used in these rules, the term "party," whether in the singular or plural, shall include all parties appearing in the action pro se and the attorney or attorneys of record for represented parties, where appropriate.

[Effective June 1, 1998. Amended effective September 3, 2003; May 27, 2011; January 17, 2012; February 8, 2012; March 12, 2013; September 24, 2013; March 19, 2014; September 28, 2015; February 21, 2017.]

III. INDICTMENT AND INFORMATION

LOCAL CRIMINAL RULE 6. GRAND JURIES

6.1. All grand juries are under the direct supervision of the Court. They shall convene at such times and dates as ordered by the Chief Judge.

[Effective June 1, 1998.]

LOCAL CRIMINAL RULE 9. WARRANTS AND SUMMONSES [REPEALED EFFECTIVE FEBRUARY 8, 2012]

IV. ARRAIGNMENT AND PREPARATION FOR TRIAL

LOCAL CRIMINAL RULE 10. ARRAIGNMENT

10.1. Whenever the U.S. Attorney wishes to have a defendant appear for arraignment or change of plea, a date should be obtained from the office of the responsible judge or magistrate judge. When a defendant has previously appeared before a judicial officer in this district, the date of an arraignment should not be more than seven (7) days after the date of indictment. Thereafter, the U.S. Attorney's Office is responsible for notifying all necessary parties of the date and time for the proceeding. This includes the marshal, the person responsible for issuing a writ, if needed, the probation office, the defendant and/or defendant's attorney.

[Effective June 1, 1998. Amended effective December 1, 2009.]

LOCAL CRIMINAL RULE 11. GUILTY PLEAS

11.1. Guilty Pleas in Felony Prosecutions. With the consent of the district judge to whom the case is assigned, a magistrate judge may preside over the taking of guilty pleas in felony matters pursuant to Fed. R. Crim. P. 11 in the circumstances below.

(a) The magistrate judge shall carefully explain to the defendant that he or she has the right to have all proceedings, including the plea hearing, conducted by a district judge. The magistrate judge shall not proceed unless after such explanation, the defendant, defendant's attorney, and the attorney for the government all consent in writing and on the record to allow the magistrate judge to preside over the guilty-plea proceedings.

(b) If the magistrate judge finds on the record that defendant's consent is knowingly and voluntarily given, the magistrate judge shall conduct guilty-plea proceedings, following the procedures set forth in Rule 11 of the Federal Rules of Criminal Procedure. The magistrate judge shall set forth on the record findings concerning the knowing and voluntary nature of the guilty plea, the adequacy of the factual basis for the plea, and any other relevant matter. If satisfied that all requirements of law have been met, the magistrate judge shall accept the plea and order the preparation of a presentence investigation report. The magistrate judge shall inquire concerning the existence of a plea agreement but shall not accept or reject any such agreement, but shall specifically reserve acceptance of the plea agreement for the district judge at the time of sentencing.

(c) A magistrate judge shall not have authority to accept a conditional guilty plea or a plea of nolo contendere in a felony case.

(d) Upon application of a party or sua sponte, the district judge shall conduct a de novo review of the magistrate judge's findings. In conducting such review, the district judge may reconduct all or any part of the guilty-plea hearing and may affirm, set aside, or cure any finding or proceeding before the magistrate judge. Any application for review made by a party must be in writing, must specify the portions of the findings or proceedings objected to, and must be filed and served no later than fourteen (14) days after the plea hearing, unless the time is extended by the district judge.

[Effective June 1, 1998. Amended effective December 17, 2008; December 1, 2009.]

LOCAL CRIMINAL RULE 12. MOTION PRACTICE

12.1. Briefs. All motions, except those made during a hearing or trial, shall be accompanied by a supporting brief. Any party opposing a written motion shall do so by filing and serving a brief conforming to these rules. All briefs filed in support of or in opposition to any motion shall contain a concise statement of the reasons in support of the party' position and shall cite all applicable federal rules of procedure all applicable local rules, and the other authorities upon which the party relies. Briefs shall not be submitted in the form of letter to the judge.

12.2. Supporting Documents. When allegations of facts not appearing of record are relied upon in support of or in opposition to any motion, all affidavits or other documents relied upon to establish such facts shall accompany the motion. All discovery motions shall set forth verbatim, or have attached, the relevant discovery request and answer or objection.

12.3. Modification of Limits. In its discretion, the Court may in a particular case shorten or enlarge any time limit or page limit established by these rules, with or without prior notice or motion.

12.4. Attempt to Obtain Concurrence. With respect to all motions, the moving party shall ascertain whether the motion will be opposed. In addition, in the case of all non dispositive motions, counsel or pro se parties involved in the dispute shall confer in a good-faith effort to resolve the dispute. All non dispositive motions shall be accompanied by a separately filed certificate setting forth in detail the efforts of the moving party to comply with the obligation created by this rule.

12.5. Motion for Expedited Consideration. Where the relief requested by a motion may be rendered moot before the motion is briefed in accordance with the schedules set forth herein, the party shall so indicate by inserting the phrase "EXPEDITED CONSIDERATION REQUESTED," in boldface type, below the case caption, and shall identify in the motion the reason expedited consideration is necessary.

12.6. Unavailability of Judge. If it appears that any matter requires immediate attention, and the judge to whom the case has been assigned, or in the usual course would be assigned, is not available, the matter shall be referred to the judge's assigned magistrate judge, who shall decide the matter if it is within the magistrate judge's jurisdiction. If the matter can only be decided by a judge, the magistrate judge shall determine whether the matter can be set for a hearing at a time when the assigned judge is available. If the matter is determined by a magistrate judge to require an immediate hearing before a judge, the case will be referred to the Chief Judge, or in the Chief Judge's absence, the next available judge by seniority for decision or reassignment to an available judicial officer. After disposition of this emergency matter, the case will be returned to the originally assigned judge.

12.7. Privacy. [Repealed]

[Effective June 1, 1998. Amended effective April 16, 2003; January 1, 2005; December 1, 2007; September 28, 2015.]

LOCAL CRIMINAL RULE 17. SERVICE OF SUBPOENAS

17.1. All subpoenas delivered to the United States Marshal's Office for service shall allow a minimum of seven (7) days if within the Western District of Michigan, or fourteen (14) days if outside the district, prior to the required appearance. A leposit in a sum deemed sufficient by the marshal to cover 'ees for the service to be performed shall be made in every nstance in which the marshal is required to perform service.

The marshal may require that any payment be in cash or certified check.

[Effective June 1, 1998. Amended effective December 1, 2009.]

V. VENUE

LOCAL CRIMINAL RULE 18. ASSIGNMENT OF CASES

18.1. All cases shall be assigned to the division in which the offense is alleged to have been committed.

[Effective June 1, 1998.]

VI. TRIAL

LOCAL CRIMINAL RULE 23. TRIAL DATE

23.1. Scheduling. Cases shall be set for trial in the manner and at the time designated by the judge before whom the cause is pending. Any case may be assigned from one judge to another with the consent of both judges to promote the efficient administration of justice or to comply with the Speedy Trial Act in another case.

23.2. Continuances. A motion for a continuance of a criminal matter shall be made only for good cause and in conjunction with the Speedy Trial Act.

23.3. Notice of Settlement. Whenever a case is settled or otherwise disposed out of Court, counsel for all parties shall assure that immediate notice is given to the Court. Should a failure to provide immediate notice result in having jurors unnecessarily report for service in connection with the case, the Court may, on its own motion, for good cause shown, assess costs incurred in having jurors report for service equally between the parties or against one or more of the parties responsible for failure to notify the Court.

[Effective June 1, 1998. Amended effective June 1, 1998.]

LOCAL CRIMINAL RULE 24. CONFIDENTIALITY OF JUROR INFORMATION

24.1. Confidentiality of Juror Information.

(a) All information obtained from juror questionnaires is confidential and may be used only for jury selection and in accordance with this rule.

(b) All copies of juror questionnaires must be destroyed or returned to the Court upon completion of jury selection, or at any earlier time determined by the Court.

(c) For represented parties, counsel of record is responsible for maintaining the confidentiality and security of juror questionnaires, and must apply security practices no less stringent than those applicable to confidential client information. Unrepresented parties may use juror questionnaires only under supervision of the Court, and may not reproduce the juror questionnaires in any form, or distribute them to anyone.

(d) Juror questionnaires will be electronically filed under restricted access three (3) business days before trial. Electronic access will be available to the Court and counsel of record only. The Court will provide unrepresented parties with one paper copy of the juror questionnaires at the beginning of jury selection. Juror questionnaires will not be available via mail or facsimile transmission.

[Effective June 1, 1998. Amended effective July 15, 2004; September 11, 2015.]

LOCAL CRIMINAL RULE 26. ATTORNEY AS WITNESS

26.1. Leave of court to conduct the trial of an action in which the attorney is to be a witness shall be sought in advance of trial when feasible.

[Effective June 1, 1998.]

VII. JUDGMENT

LOCAL CRIMINAL RULE 32. SENTENCING

32.1. Notice. The office of the responsible judge or magistrate judge setting the sentence will notify all necessary parties of the date of sentencing. This includes the marshal, the person responsible for issuing a writ, if needed, the probation office, the U.S. Attorney, the defendant and/or defendant's attorney. This date may be set at the time of taking a plea or a verdict of guilty.

32.2. Presentence Report. Unless waived pursuant to Fed. R. Crim. P. 32(c), a presentence report must be prepared in every felony case and may be prepared in misdemeanor cases in the Court's discretion.

(a) *Initial Interview.* The initial interview with the defendant, defendant's counsel, and the probation officer must be conducted within seven (7) days of the date of the order setting sentencing date. Counsel for the government must make available the offense conduct information, including all relevant conduct, within seven (7) days of the date of such order.

(b) *Disclosure of Presentence Report.* At least thirty-five (35) days before the date scheduled for sentencing, the probation officer must provide a copy of the presentence report (except the sentencing rationale) to (1) counsel for the government, and (2) counsel for the defendant or, where the defendant is pro se, to the defendant. The sentencing judge may additionally direct the probation officer not to disclose the officer's recommendation on the sentence. Disclosure of the presentence investigation report (and any subsequent revisions and addenda thereto) to a defense attorney is deemed to be disclosure to the defendant. Defense counsel must provide a copy of the report to the defendant forthwith.

(c) *Time of Disclosure.*

(1) To Represented Parties: The presentence report is deemed disclosed to counsel for a represented defendant and to counsel for the government when it is filed electronically by the Probation Office on the CM/ECF system (access restricted to the Court, the probation office, attorneys of record for the government and for the relevant defendant).

(2) To an Unrepresented Party: The presentence report is deemed disclosed to a pro se defendant when a copy of the report is physically delivered or three (3) days after a copy of the report has been mailed. The presentence report must contain the date of mailing.

(d) *Objections to Presentence Report.* Within fourteen (14) days after disclosure of the presentence report, each counsel or pro se defendant must file a written response to the presentence report acknowledging disclosure and containing all objections, and supporting reasons, to any material information, sentencing classifications, sentencing guideline ranges, and policy statements contained in or omitted from the report. Alternatively, the response may affirmatively state that there is no objection to the report. Counsel for the government and for defendant must submit objections electronically by the CM/ECF system (access restricted to the Court, the probation office, attorneys of record for the government and for the relevant defendant); the government must also serve objections pertaining to an unrepresented defendant on that defendant alone by traditional means, with proof of service. Unrepresented defendants must file their objections in writing with the Clerk of the Court, with a proof of service on government counsel. The Clerk shall file the objections electronically by the CM/ECF system (access restricted to the Court, the probation office, and attorneys of record for the government).

(e) *Non–Judicial Resolution of Objections.* After receiving a timely objection, the probation officer must promptly conduct any further investigation and make any revisions to the presentence report that may be necessary. The probation officer may require each counsel and pro se defendant to meet with the officer to discuss unresolved factual and legal issues, and may request that such persons meet with each other for the same purpose.

(f) *Submission of Presentence Report to the Court.* Not less than nine (9) days before the date set for sentencing, the probation officer must submit the final presentence report

electronically by the CM/ECF system (access restricted to the Court, the probation office, attorneys of record for the government and for the relevant defendant). The report will be accompanied by an addendum setting forth any unresolved objections that counsel or the pro se defendant may have together with the officer's comments thereon. The probation officer must certify that the contents of the report, including any revisions and the addendum, have been disclosed to counsel and any pro se defendant, and that the addendum fairly states any remaining objections.

(g) *Motions for Departure or Variance; Sentencing Memoranda.* Not less than seven (7) days before the date set for sentencing, any party seeking an upward or downward departure under the Sentencing Guidelines or a variance based on the application of the factors set forth in 18 U.S.C. § 3553(a), or both, must submit a separate and clearly captioned motion seeking such relief. All sentencing memoranda, including memoranda in support of a motion for departure or variance, must be filed by the same date. Counsel must submit such motions and memoranda by the CM/ECF system and may move for leave to restrict access to the Court, the probation office, attorneys of record for the government and for the relevant defendant, if sensitive or confidential information is contained therein. Pro se parties must file and serve such documents in the traditional manner, with proof of service on the opposing party.

(h) *Judicial Resolution of Objections.* Upon receipt of the final report and attachments, the sentencing judge will determine the extent of any further proceedings necessary in light of the nature of any unresolved objections. The judge may hold all objections for resolution at the time of sentencing. In the alternative, the judge may resolve any objections prior to sentencing and may afford the parties a reasonable opportunity for the submission of further written objections before the imposition of sentence. Any objections must be made in the same manner as provided for in this rule. Where the Court determines that a hearing is necessary to resolve the disputed sentencing matters, a hearing may be held for that purpose, either on the date of sentencing or at an earlier time.

(i) *Late Objections.* Upon a showing of good cause, the Court may allow a new objection to be raised at any time prior to the imposition of sentence.

(j) *Modified or Expedited Procedures.* The time periods set forth in this rule may be modified by the Court for good cause shown, or upon its own motion, except that in no event shall sentence be imposed less than ten (10) days following disclosure of the presentence report without the consent of the defendant. The parties may agree in writing or on the record to an expedited sentencing procedure that shortens the times set forth in this rule or abbreviates the information otherwise required in the presentence report.

(k) *Limitations on Disclosure.* Nothing in this rule requires the disclosure of any portions of the presentence report that are not disclosable under the Federal Rules of Criminal Procedure.

(*l*) *Relationship to Fed. R. Crim. P. 32.* This rule shall not be construed to limit any sentencing procedure modifications permitted by Rule 32 of the Federal Rules of Criminal Procedure.

(m) *Release of Presentence Report to Other Officers.* The Chief Probation Officer may, in his or her discretion, disclose a presentence report to a federal or state probation or parole officer in connection with that officer's conduct of official duties regarding a person previously sentenced by this Court.

32.3. Judgments and Commitments. [Repealed]

[Effective June 1, 1998. Amended effective March 25, 1999; February 15, 2007; October 5, 2007; December 1, 2009; January 17, 2012; February 8, 2012.]

LOCAL CRIMINAL RULE 32.1. ACTIONS AGAINST PERSONS ON PROBATION OR SUPERVISED RELEASE

32.1.1. Whenever the probation office requests action against a probationer or person on supervised release, the probation office shall secure a date from the office of the judge or magistrate judge conducting the preliminary, revocation, or modification hearing and notify all necessary parties. This includes the marshal, the person responsible for issuing a writ, if needed, the U.S. Attorney, and the defendant and/or defendant's attorney.

[Effective June 1, 1998.]

X. GENERAL PROVISIONS

LOCAL CRIMINAL RULE 44. MOTION FOR APPOINTMENT

44.1. If trial counsel was appointed under the Criminal Justice Act and intends to prosecute the appeal, counsel should file a motion with the Clerk of the Court of Appeals for appointment on appeal. Whether on such a motion or otherwise, no further proof of the defendant's indigency need be submitted unless specifically required by the Court of Appeals.

[Effective June 1, 1998.]

LOCAL CRIMINAL RULE 47. MOTIONS

47.1. Dispositive Motions.

(a) *Definition.* Dispositive motions are motions to dismiss or quash an indictment or information made by the defendant, to suppress evidence in a case, to involuntarily dismiss an action, and other dispositive motions as defined by law.

(b) *Length of Briefs.* Any brief filed in support of or in opposition to a dispositive motion shall not exceed twenty-five (25) pages in length, exclusive of cover sheet, tables, and indices.

(c) *Briefing Schedule.* Any party opposing a dispositive motion shall, within twenty-eight (28) days after service of the motion, file a responsive brief and any supporting materials. The Court may permit or require further briefing.

(d) *Oral Argument.* Any party desiring oral argument shall include a request for oral argument in the caption and the heading of the party's brief. In its discretion, the Court may schedule oral argument or may dispose of the motion without argument at the end of the briefing schedule. The time for oral argument on all motions shall be scheduled and noticed by the Court at the earliest convenient date.

47.2. Nondispositive Motions.

(a) *Definition.* Nondispositive motions are all motions not specifically listed in LCrR 47.1.

(b) *Length of Briefs.* Any brief filed in support of or in opposition to a nondispositive motion shall not exceed ten (10) pages in length, exclusive of cover sheet, tables, and indices.

(c) *Briefing Schedule.* Any party opposing a nondispositive motion shall, within fourteen (14) days of service of the motion, file a responsive brief and supporting materials. The Court may permit or require further briefing. Reply briefs may not be filed without leave of court.

(d) *Oral Argument.* Any party desiring oral argument shall include a request for oral argument in the caption and the heading of the party's brief. In its discretion, the Court may schedule oral argument or may dispose of the motion without argument at the end of the briefing schedule. The time for oral argument on all motions shall be scheduled and noticed by the Court at the earliest convenient date.

47.3. Motions for Reconsideration.

(a) *Grounds.* Generally, and without restricting the discretion of the Court, motions for reconsideration which merely present the same issues ruled upon by the Court shall not be granted. The movant shall not only demonstrate a palpable defect by which the Court and the parties have been mislead, but also show that a different disposition of the case must result from a correction thereof.

(b) *Response to Motions for Reconsideration.* No answer to a motion for reconsideration will be allowed unless requested by the Court, but a motion for reconsideration will ordinarily not be granted in the absence of such request. Any oral argument on a motion for reconsideration is reserved to the discretion of the Court.

[Effective June 1, 1998. Amended effective February 8, 2012.]

LOCAL CRIMINAL RULE 49. FORM OF PLEADINGS AND OTHER PAPERS; FILING REQUIREMENTS

49.1. Place of Filing. Pleadings and other papers may be filed with the Clerk at any divisional office during walk-in business hours. If a hearing is scheduled, it is incumbent upon the party to insure that the judge or magistrate judge receives a copy of such relevant pleadings or other papers sufficiently in advance of the hearing.

49.2. Paper Size and Format. All documents must be double spaced in 8½ × 11 inch format with writing on only the face of each sheet. Type must be no smaller than 12 point type and all margins must be at least one inch.

49.3. Binding. All pleadings and other papers that have numerous pages must be bound with a fastener. Originals should be stapled or bound on the top margin with a two-hole fastener. Copies may be bound in the same manner as originals or in a binder. Paper clips and other types of clips shall not be used; fasteners shall pass through the pages.

49.4. Date, Address and Telephone Number. All pleadings and other papers shall contain the date of signing and the address and telephone number of the signing attorney or pro se party.

49.5. Number of Copies. All traditionally filed documents must be filed in duplicate — the original and one copy. If service of any paper is to be made by the United States Marshal, sufficient additional copies shall be supplied for service upon each other party. If file stamped copies of documents are requested to be returned to the offering party, a suitable self-addressed, postage paid envelope shall be supplied.

49.6. Proof of Service. Proof of service of all pleadings and other papers required or permitted to be served shall be filed promptly after service and may be made by written acknowledgment of service, by affidavit of the person making service or by written certification of counsel. Proof of service shall state the date and manner of service. Proof of service is unnecessary for documents served electronically on a registered attorney.

49.7. Tendering of Orders. [Repealed]

Ex parte submissions

(a) *Filing of Ex Parte Submissions.* If the law allows a party to submit a pleading or other paper *ex parte*, the party may file the document with the Clerk without serving a copy on any other party. The document shall be properly identified on its face as *Ex Parte*. A registered attorney must submit any *ex parte* filing electronically by use of the appropriate CM/ECF event. An NEF will be generated for the *ex parte* document and will be transmitted to all parties. Unless modified by the filer, the NEF and docket entry will identify the document only as "*Ex Parte* Document" or "*Ex Parte* Motion."

(b) *Access to Ex Parte Filings.* The docket entry and the NEF for any *ex parte* filing will be available for public viewing. Unless the Court specifically orders otherwise, access to *ex parte* documents will be available only to the party submitting the filing (or that party's registered attorneys) and to the personnel of this Court and the Court of Appeals, but not to the public or any other party.

(c) *Filings by the Court.* The court may issue restricted access orders in response to *ex parte* filings. Access to these orders will be restricted to the moving party, the personnel of this Court and the Court of Appeals. The docket entry and the NEF for any restricted access order will be identified as such and available for public viewing.

(d) *Sealed Cases.* If an entire case has been sealed, either by order or by operation of statute, then neither the *ex parte* submission nor any docket entry relating thereto will be available for public viewing, until such time as the Court orders otherwise.

49.8. Filing Documents Under Seal.

(a) *Requests to Seal.* The procedures set forth in this rule apply to cases that have not been sealed in their entirety. Documents may be submitted under seal only if authorized by the Court for good cause shown. A person seeking leave to file a document under seal must file a motion requesting such relief, unless the Court has entered a previous order authorizing the submission of the document under seal or submission under seal is authorized by statute. The motion seeking leave to file under seal should generally be a public filing, unless the submitting party believes in good faith that public access to the motion will compromise the confidential matter. A proposed sealed document submitted by a registered attorney must be submitted electronically under seal as a separate document, under a separate docket entry, by use of the appropriate CM/ECF event. The docket entry and the NEF for any sealed document will be available for public viewing; the description of the sealed document should therefore be general in nature (*e.g.*, sealed affidavit, sealed exhibit, sealed motion). The proposed sealed document shall be appropriately identified on its face as sealed, but should not contain the word "proposed." Proposed sealed documents submitted by persons other than registered attorneys must be filed in a sealed envelope bearing the case caption and number, the identity of the party submitting the documents, and a general description of the contents; the proposed sealed document will be scanned and maintained electronically under seal. If the Court denies the motion to seal in whole or in part, the proposed sealed document will remain sealed, but the Court may order the submitting party to tender a modified document, either sealed or not under seal, as the Court directs. If the Court grants leave to file the document under seal, the Clerk of Court will modify the docket entry to remove reference to "proposed."

(b) *Access to Sealed Documents.* A document filed under seal may be accessed electronically only by authorized personnel of this Court and the Court of Appeals and not by the public or any attorney or party.

(c) *Service of Sealed Documents.* A party submitting a document under seal must serve it by non-electronic means of service on all other parties.

(d) *Death Penalty and Other Complex Litigation.* The parties to a death-eligible case, a death-penalty case, or other complex litigation involving numerous sealed documents may be ordered to comply with a special protocol for submission of sealed and *ex parte* documents, which will supersede the procedures set forth in this rule.

49.9. Rejection of Filings. The Court may order the Clerk to reject any pleading or other paper that does not comply with these rules or the Federal Rules of Criminal Procedure unless such noncompliance is expressly approved by the Court. The Clerk shall return any rejected filing to the party tendering it, along with a statement of the reasons for rejection.

49.10. Filing and Service by Electronic Means.

(a) *General Information; Definitions.* Pursuant to Rule 49(d) of the Federal Rules of Criminal Procedure, the Clerk will accept pleadings and other papers filed and signed by electronic means in accordance with this rule. All papers filed by electronic means must comply with technical standards, if any, now or hereafter established by the Judicial Conference of the United States.

This rule shall apply to all criminal actions maintained in the court's electronic case filing system. All documents, whether filed electronically or on paper, will be placed into the electronic case filing system, except as provided below. Attorneys must file and serve all documents electronically by use of the ECF system unless (1) the attorney has been specifically exempted by the Court for cause or (2) a particular document is not eligible for electronic filing under this rule.

As used in this rule, the term

- "ECF system" means the electronic case filing system maintained by this Court;
- "registered attorney" means an attorney who is authorized pursuant to Rule 49.10(b) to file documents electronically and to receive service on the ECF system;
- "charging document" means the original complaint, indictment (or any superseding indictment), information or other document by which charges are brought in a criminal case;
- "electronically filed document" means any order, opinion, judgment, pleading, notice, transcript, motion, brief or other paper submitted electronically to the ECF system;
- "traditionally filed document" means a pleading or other paper submitted to the Clerk in paper form for filing;
- "NEF" means the Notice of Electronic Filing generated by the ECF system;
- "nonelectronic means of service" means one of the methods of service authorized by Rule 49(b) of the Federal Rules of Criminal Procedure and Rule 5(b) of the Federal Rules of Civil Procedure, except electronic service under FED. R. CIV. P. 5(b)(2)(E).

(b) *Mandatory Registration; Attorney Training.*

(i) Every attorney practicing in this Court must register to file and serve documents electronically by the ECF system.

(ii) To be entitled to register as a user of the ECF system, an attorney must be admitted to practice in this District, be a member in good standing, and have filed with the Clerk a completed ECF Attorney Registration form. In addition, the attorney or the attorney's firm must have a Public Access to Court Electronic Records (PACER) account and an e-mail address.

Detailed registration information is available on the Court's Website (www.miwd.uscourts.gov). Upon receipt of the ECF Attorney Registration form, the Court will issue a login name and a user password to qualified attorneys. All registered attorneys have an affirmative duty to update their accounts with any change in their e-mail address. A registered attorney may not knowingly cause or allow another person to file a document using the attorney's login name and password, except for members of the attorney's staff.

Authorized use of an attorney's login name and password by a staff member is deemed to be the act of the attorney. However, a registered attorney must not allow an unregistered attorney, even a member of the same firm, to use his or her login name and password. If a login name and/or password should become compromised, the attorney is responsible for notifying the ECF Help Desk immediately.

(iii) The Clerk's Office will provide periodic training sessions on use of the ECF system. The Court will also provide on its Website a User's Manual containing instructions on the use of the ECF system and an on-line tutorial. Law firms are encouraged to have individuals responsible for electronic filing (attorney, paralegal or automation specialist) attend a live training session or use the on-line tutorial.

(c) *Charging Documents.* Charging documents may be filed in the following ways:

(i) traditionally, bearing manuscript signatures; or

(ii) electronically, with facsimile signatures created by use of the electronic signature pad; or

(iii) in a scanned PDF document containing the image of original manuscript signatures.

The Court may issue a summons or warrant electronically, but such process may be served only in accordance with Rule 4(c) of the Federal Rules of Criminal Procedure.

(d) *Electronic Filing.*

(i) Mandatory Electronic Filing. All attorneys must file all pleadings and other papers permitted by the Federal Rules and the Local Rules of this Court (except charging documents) electronically in all criminal cases, subject to the exceptions set forth below. All electronically filed documents must be in PDF digital format and must be submitted in accordance with the instructions set forth in the User's Manual. *Pro se* parties who are not members of the bar of the Court may not file pleadings or other papers electronically, but must submit them in paper form.

(ii) Papers That May Not Be Filed Electronically. The following documents may not be filed electronically, but must be submitted in paper form:

(A) Documents submitted by a person who is not a registered attorney (for example, a *pro se* litigant);

(B) Papers filed in cases that have been sealed in their entirety;

(C) Documents that are required by statute to be filed *in camera*;

(D) Garnishee disclosures and other documents submitted by unrepresented third parties in response to writs or other court process;

(iii) Electronic Filing of Affidavits and Other Original Documents. The following documents must be filed electronically by submission of a scanned PDF version of the original document:

(A) Affidavits in support of or in opposition to a motion (This rule does not apply to affidavits of service);

(B) Declarations under penalty of perjury;

(C) Certified copies of judgments or orders of other Courts.

The electronically filed version of such documents must bear a scanned image of all original manuscript signatures. The filer must meet the requirements of Rule 49.10(e)(vii) regarding evidence of an original signature.

(iv) Deadlines. Filing documents electronically does not in any way alter any filing deadlines. An electronically filed document is deemed filed upon completion of the transmission and issuance by the Court's system of an NEF. In situations where attachments to an electronically filed document are submitted in paper form, the electronic document is deemed filed upon issuance of the NEF, provided that the paper exhibits are filed and served within 72 hours thereof. All electronic transmissions of documents must be completed (i.e., received completely by the Clerk's Office) prior to midnight, Eastern Time, in order to be considered timely filed that day. Where a specific time of day deadline is set by Court order or stipulation, the electronic filing must be completed by that time.

(v) Technical Failures. The Clerk shall deem the Court's Website to be subject to a technical failure on a given day if the site is unable to accept filings continuously or intermittently over the course of any period of time greater than one hour after 12:00 noon (Eastern Time) that day, in which case, filings due that day which were not filed due solely to such technical failures shall become due the next business day. Such delayed filings must be accompanied by a declaration or affidavit attesting to the filer's failed attempts to file electronically at least two times after 12:00 noon separated by at least one hour on each day of delay because of such technical failure. The initial point of contact for any practitioner experiencing difficulty filing a document electronically shall be the ECF Help Desk, available via phone at (616) 456–2206 or (800) 290–2742, or via e-mail at ecfhelp@miwd.uscourts.gov.

(vi) Official Record; Discarding of Traditionally Filed Documents. For purposes of Rule 55 of the Federal Rules of Criminal Procedure, the official record of all proceedings filed on and after November 3, 2003, is the electronic file maintained on the Court's ECF system. The Clerk's Office will discard all traditionally filed documents after they have become part of the electronic record, unless the document produces a low-quality electronic file.

(vii) Exhibits and Attachments.

(A) Oversized Documents. No PDF document exceeding 10 MB in size may be filed in the CM/ECF system. Filers must divide such documents into component parts, each part not to exceed 10 MB in size, for purposes of electronic filing. The docket entry must clearly indicate that the document is filed in parts. An exhibit may be filed traditionally only if it is exempt from electronic filing under subrule (d)(ii) of this rule.

(B) Requirements. Filers must not attach as an exhibit any pleading or other paper already on file with the Court, but shall merely refer to that document. All exhibits and attachments, whether filed electronically or traditionally, must contain on their face a prominent exhibit number or letter. If one or more attachments or exhibits to an electronically filed document are being submitted traditionally under this rule, the electronically filed document must contain a notice of that fact in its text.

(e) *Signature.*

(i) Attorneys. A registered attorney's use of the assigned login name and password to submit an electronically filed document serves as the registered attorney's signature on that document, for purposes of Fed. R. Civ. P. 11 and for all other purposes under the Federal Rules of Criminal and Civil Procedure and the Local Rules of this Court. The identity of the registered attorney submitting the electronically filed document must be reflected at the end of the document by means of an "s/ [attorney's name]" block showing the attorney's name, followed by the attorney's business address, telephone number, and e-mail address. Graphic and other electronic signatures are discouraged.

(ii) Multiple Attorney Signatures. The filer of any electronically filed document requiring multiple signatures (e.g., stipulations, joint motions) must list thereon all the names of other attorney signatories by means of an "s/[attorney's name]" block for each. By submitting such a document, the filer certifies that each of the other attorneys has expressly agreed to the form and substance of the document, that the filer has their actual authority to submit the document electronically, and that the requirements of Rule 49.10(e)(viii) regarding evidence of signature have been met. This paragraph does not apply to pro-se or unrepresented parties, whose manuscript signature, in original or scanned form, must appear on the face of the document.

(iii) Court Reporters. The electronic filing of a transcript by a court reporter by use of the court reporter's login name and password shall be deemed the filing of a signed and certified original document for all purposes.

(iv) Judges. The electronic filing of an opinion, order, warrant, judgment or other document by a judge (or authorized member of the judge's staff) by use of the judge's login and password shall be deemed the filing of a signed original document for all purposes.

(v) Clerk of Court or Deputy Clerks. The electronic filing of any document by the Clerk or a Deputy Clerk of this Court or of the Circuit Court of Appeals by use of that individual's login and password shall be deemed the filing of a signed original document for all purposes.

(vi) Probation Office and Office of the U.S. Marshal. The Probation Office and Office of the United States Marshal for this district are authorized to file and serve documents electronically. The electronic filing of any document by the Probation Office and Office of the United States Marshal by use of the assigned login and password shall be deemed the filing of a signed original document for all purposes.

(vii) Signature of Defendant. Documents containing the original signature of the defendant must be submitted in one of three ways: (1) by use of the in-court electronic signature pad; (2) in a scanned PDF document containing the image of defendant's manuscript signature; or, (3) if neither of the foregoing is feasible in traditional form.

(viii) *Evidence of Original Signature.* Filers of documents containing signatures authorized by Rule 49(e)(ii) (multiple attorney signatures) must maintain any records evidencing concurrence, and filers of documents containing signatures authorized by Rule 49(d)(iii) (electronically filed affidavits, etc.) and 49(e)(vii) (documents containing defendant's signature) must maintain the documents bearing the original manual signature for subsequent production to the Court or for inspection by a party until one year after the final resolution of the action (including appeal, if any). A non-filing signatory or party who disputes the authenticity of a signature on an electronically filed document must file an objection to the document within fourteen (14) days after service of that document.

(f) *Proposed Pleadings.* Except for proposed sealed filings, if the filing of an electronically submitted document requires leave of Court, such as a brief in excess of page limits, the proposed document must be attached as an exhibit to the motion seeking leave to file. If the Court grants leave to file the document, the Clerk of Court will electronically file the document without further action by the attorney. Requests to file documents under seal are governed by Local Criminal Rule 49.8.

(g) *Proposed Orders.* Proposed orders must be submitted electronically. All proposed orders must be in PDF format and must be: (1) attached as an exhibit to a motion or stipulation; or (2) contained within the body of a stipulation; or (3) submitted separately. If the Judge approves the proposed order, it will be refiled electronically under a separate document number.

(h) *Service of Electronically Filed Documents.*

(i) *Summons and Warrants.* Warrants and summons may be issued in electronic form with electronically affixed signatures and seal. Service of warrants and summons, however, must be made in accordance with FED. R. CRIM. P. 4(c) and may not be made electronically.

(ii) *Service on Registered Attorneys.* By registering under this rule, an attorney automatically consents to electronic service by both the Court and any opposing attorney of any electronically filed document in any case in which the registered attorney appears. Consequently, service of an electronically filed document upon a registered attorney is deemed complete upon the transmission of an NEF to that attorney and no separate certificate of service should be filed. Traditionally filed documents and sealed documents must be served on registered attorneys by nonelectronic means of service, and a proof of service filed.

(iii) *Service on United States Probation Office.* A registered attorney may serve the United States Probation Office electronically with a copy of sentencing memoranda, motions for departure, or any other document that the Federal Rules of Criminal Procedure or these rules require to be served on the Probation Office. If such documents are filed by a registered attorney electronically, service will be accomplished by the ECF system automatically. If such documents are filed traditionally, they must be served on the Probation Office by nonelectronic means of service.

(iv) *Service on Unregistered Attorneys and pro se Parties.* Counsel filing any pleading or other paper must serve attorneys not registered under this rule and *pro se* parties by nonelectronic means of service. A proof of service must be filed.

(v) *Method of Electronic Service.* At the time a document is filed either electronically or by scanning paper submissions, the Court's system will generate an NEF, which will be transmitted by e-mail to the filer and all registered attorneys who have appeared on that case. The NEF will contain a hyperlink to the filed document. The attorney filing the document should retain a paper or digital copy of the NEF, which serves as the Court's date-stamp and proof of filing. Except in the case of sealed documents (see Local Criminal Rule 49.8(c)) and *ex parte* filings (see Local Criminal Rule 49.7(b), (c)), transmission of the NEF to the registered e-mail address constitutes service of an electronically filed document upon any registered attorney. Only service of the NEF by the Court's system constitutes electronic service; transmission of a document by one party to another by regular e-mail does not constitute service.

(vi) Effect on Time Computation. [Repealed]

(i) *Court Orders, Judgments, Writs and Other Process.* Judgments and orders may be filed electronically by the Court or authorized Court personnel. Any order or other Court-issued document filed electronically without the image of the manuscript signature of the judge or clerk has the same force and effect as a document bearing an original signature. Upon entry of an order or judgment in a criminal proceeding, the clerk will transmit an NEF to all registered attorneys. Such transmission constitutes the notice to registered attorneys required by FED. R. CRIM. P. 49(c). The clerk will provide notice to attorneys not registered under this rule and *pro se* parties by nonelectronic means of service. The Clerk may electronically affix the Seal of the Court on writs, summons, and other process, which shall have the same legal force and effect as process bearing an imprinted seal.

(j) *Access to Electronically Stored Documents.* Any person may review at the Clerk's Office filings in a criminal case that have not been sealed by the Court or filed *ex parte*. Any person may retrieve a docket sheet in a criminal case through the PACER system and may access electronically the text of documents (except sealed documents, *ex parte* documents, and transcripts) stored on the ECF system and filed on or after November 1, 2004.

(k) *Facsimile Transmissions.* The Clerk will not accept for filing any pleading or other paper submitted by facsimile transmission.

[Effective June 1, 1998. Amended effective January 1, 2005; February 15, 2007; December 1, 2007; December 17, 2008; December 1, 2009; May 27, 2011; February 8, 2012; March 12, 2013; March 19, 2014; December 1, 2016.]

LOCAL CRIMINAL RULE 50. PROMPT DISPOSITION OF CRIMINAL CASES

50.1. Pursuant to statutory requirements, the judges of the United States District Court for the Western District of

Michigan have adopted a plan to minimize undue delay and further the prompt disposition of cases. Copies of the plan are available on the Court's website or in the Clerk's Office.

[Effective June 1, 1998. Amended effective February 15, 2007.]

LOCAL CRIMINAL RULE 56. DISTRICT COURTS AND CLERKS; ISSUANCE OF PROCESS

56.1. Time and Place of Holding Court. The Court shall be deemed to be in continuous session for transacting judicial business on all business days throughout the year. Proceedings may be held at such times and places within the district as the judge to whom the case is assigned shall designate.

56.2. Clerk's Office. The Court maintains Southern Division offices in Grand Rapids, Kalamazoo and Lansing and a Northern Division office in Marquette. The Southern Division comprises the counties of Allegan, Antrim, Barry, Benzie, Berrien, Branch, Calhoun, Cass, Charlevoix, Clinton, Eaton, Emmet, Grand Traverse, Hillsdale, Ingham, Ionia, Kalamazoo, Kalkaska, Kent, Lake, Leelanau, Manistee, Mason, Mecosta, Missaukee, Montcalm, Muskegon, Newaygo, Oceana, Osceola, Ottawa, Saint Joseph, Van Buren, and Wexford. The Northern Division comprises the counties of Alger, Baraga, Chippewa, Delta, Dickinson, Gogebic, Houghton, Iron, Keweenaw, Luce, Mackinac, Marquette, Menominee, Ontonagon, and Schoolcraft. 28 U.S.C. § 102(b).

56.3. Issuance of Process. Any party requesting the issuance of any process or who initiates any proceeding in which the issuance of process is required by statute, rule or order, shall prepare all required forms. The party shall present the process to the Clerk for signature and sealing when required. The Clerk shall, upon request, and subject to current availability, make reasonable supplies of all blank official forms of process available to attorneys admitted to practice in this Court, or their agents or employees.

56.4. Books and Records Kept by the Clerk.

(a) *Custody of Files.* Files in Southern Division cases shall be maintained in the divisional office where the judge or magistrate judge assigned to the case sits. All Northern Division files shall be maintained in Marquette.

(b) *Removal of Files, Exhibits and Papers.* No files, pleadings, exhibits or papers shall be removed from the offices of the Clerk except upon order of the Court. Whenever files, pleadings, exhibits or papers are removed from an office of the Clerk, the person receiving them shall sign and deliver to the Clerk a receipt therefor.

(c) *Duplication of Papers.* The Clerk shall make reasonable arrangements for the duplication of unrestricted papers in any court file.

56.5. Assignment of Cases to Judges.

(a) *New Criminal Cases.* Upon the filing of an initial indictment or information, the Clerk must assign the case the next sequential number. The case must be assigned to a district judge by automated means at random, in the proportions established from time to time by administrative order.

The Clerk will cause the case number and the name of the assigned judge to be reflected on the official record.

(b) [Repealed.]

(c) [Repealed.]

(d) *Exceptions.*

(i) Refilings. If a case is dismissed and later refiled either in the same or similar form, upon refiling it shall be assigned or transferred to the judge to whom it was originally assigned.

(ii) Subsequent Proceedings. Post–conviction proceedings in criminal cases (including motions under section 2255 and proceedings to modify or revoke probation or supervised release) shall be assigned to the judge who sentenced the defendant.

(iii) Related Cases.

(A) Definition. Cases are deemed related when (1) a superseding indictment or information has been filed; or (2) any other indictment or information is pending against the same defendant(s); (3) an indictment or information charges contempt of court or other crime arising from alleged violation of an order entered in a previous case; (4) an indictment is returned against a defendant who is then on probation or supervised release to a judge, provided the new case involves only the same defendant; or (5) two or more cases are based upon a substantial common nucleus of facts, events, or transactions.

(B) Determination. When it appears to the United States Attorney that two or more cases may be related cases, the United States Attorney shall file at the earliest practicable time a statement in all affected cases, describing the basis for concluding that the cases may be related. The duty magistrate judge shall promptly determine whether the cases are related. If related, the cases will be assigned to the same judge. If cases are found to be related cases after assignment to different judges, they may be reassigned by the Chief Judge to the judge having the related case earliest filed.

(e) *Miscellaneous Docket.* The miscellaneous docket of the Court shall be conducted and assigned at random to a magistrate judge at the time of filing, and it shall include all grand jury matters. If a miscellaneous docket matter is contested and requires proceedings conducted before a district judge, the case will be randomly reassigned to a district judge and a new civil action number will be assigned.

(f) *Effect.* This rule is intended to provide for an orderly division of the business of the Court and not to grant any right to any litigant.

(g) *Duty of Parties.* All parties shall notify the Court in writing of all pending related cases and any dismissed or remanded prior cases.

56.6. Reassignment of Cases.

(a) *Reassignment to Promote Judicial Economy.* The Court may reassign cases from one district judge to another (i) to equalize and balance workloads among judges; (ii) to assign cases to senior or visiting judges or remove cases from their dockets as necessary; (iii) to comply with the requirements of he Speedy Trial Act, or (iv) for other reasons of judicial economy. Any case may be reassigned under this rule from ne judge to another judge with the consent of both judges. Cases may also be reassigned by administrative order of the Chief Judge if approved by a majority of active district judges.

(b) *Reassignment of Cognate Cases.*

(i) Definition. Cognate cases are pending criminal actions that have substantial questions of fact or law in common such that their assignment to a single judge is likely to effect a substantial saving of judicial effort and to avoid wasteful and duplicative proceedings for the court and the parties.

(ii) Procedure for Reassignment. When a judge determines that reassignment of cognate cases would serve the interests of justice and judicial economy, the judge will contact all other judges to whom cognate cases have been assigned. If all those judges agree to reassignment, the Chief Judge will enter an administrative order reassigning such cognate cases to the judge with the earliest numbered case. The administrative order may also provide for automatic assignment of future cognate cases to that judge, and for an adjustment of future case assignments to that judge to compensate for the increased workload.

56.7. Criminal Matters in the Northern Division. With the permission of the district judge to whom a case is assigned, any available judge may take a guilty plea, preside over trial, or sentence a defendant in Northern Division cases.

[Effective June 1, 1998. Amended effective June 1, 1998; June 20, 2005; March 12, 2013; March 1, 2016; February 21, 2017.]

LOCAL CRIMINAL RULE 57. ATTORNEYS; MAGISTRATE JUDGES; MISCELLANEOUS; CONDUCT IN FEDERAL COURT FACILITIES

57.1. Attorneys.

(a) *Definitions.* As used in Local Rules 57.1(a) through 57.1(q), these terms are defined below.

(i) "Discipline" means an order entered against an attorney by the Michigan Attorney Discipline Board, a similar disciplinary authority of another state, or a state or federal court revoking or suspending an attorney's license or admission before a court to practice law, placing an attorney on probation or inactive status, requiring restitution, or a transfer to inactive status in lieu of discipline.

(ii) "Chief Judge" means the Chief Judge or another district judge designated to perform the Chief Judge's functions under these rules.

(iii) "Practice in this Court," means, in connection with an action or proceeding pending in this Court, to appear in, commence, conduct, prosecute, or defend the action or proceeding; appear in open court; sign a paper; participate in a pretrial conference; represent a client at a deposition; counsel a client in the action or proceeding for compensation; or otherwise practice in this Court or before an officer of this Court.

(iv) "State" means a state, territory, commonwealth, or possession of the United States, and the District of Columbia.

(v) "Serious crime" means:

(A) a felony; or

(B) a crime, a necessary element of which, as determined by the statutory or common law definition of the crime in the jurisdiction of the conviction, involves interference with the administration of justice, false swearing, misrepresentation, fraud, willful failure to file income tax returns, willful failure to pay income tax, deceit, bribery, extortion, misappropriation, theft, or an attempt, conspiracy, or solicitation of another to commit a serious crime.

(b) *Roll of Attorneys.* The bar of this Court consists of those currently admitted to practice in this Court. The Clerk shall maintain the roll of admitted attorneys.

(c) *Eligibility for Admission.*

(i) Eligibility. A person who is duly admitted to practice in a court of record of a state, and who is in active status and in good standing, may apply for admission to the bar of this Court, except as provided in (ii) below.

(ii) Effect of Prior Discipline. If the applicant has been held in contempt, disciplined, or convicted of a crime, the Chief Judge shall make an independent determination as to whether the applicant is qualified to be entrusted with professional matters and to aid in the administration of justice as an attorney and officer of the Court. An applicant dissatisfied with the decision of the Chief Judge may within twenty-eight (28) days file a petition for a hearing before a three judge panel as described in LCivR 57. 1(m)(iii).

(iii) Pro Hac Vice Admissions. This Court disfavors pro hac vice admission and prefers that all lawyers appearing before it become full members of the bar of the Court. Pro hac vice admission may nevertheless be allowed on a temporary basis pending full admission, or in unusual circumstances.

(d) *Procedure for Admission.*

(i) An applicant for admission to the bar of this Court shall pay the fee established by the Court and complete the application provided by the Clerk. The following information must be included in the application:

(A) office address and telephone number;

(B) the date of admission and each jurisdiction where the applicant has been admitted to practice; and

(C) whether the applicant has ever been held in contempt, subjected to discipline as defined by these rules or convicted of a crime. If so, the applicant shall state the facts and the final disposition of each such instance.

(ii) A sponsor must sign a declaration supporting the application for admission. A sponsor may be a member of the bar of this Court or, for applicants residing in another state, a judge of a court of record of that state, or a federal judge. The Chief Judge may waive the sponsorship requirement for recent law school graduates.

(iii) If an applicant has been subject to discipline as defined by these rules, the application must be accompanied by a copy of the entire disciplinary record, including complaints, answers, hearing transcripts and orders entered in the disciplinary proceedings.

(iv) The Chief Judge may grant or deny the application for admission. Alternatively, the Chief Judge may refer the application to a three-judge panel constituted pursuant to subsection (m)(iii)(A) of this rule for decision. A panel may grant or deny the application or may grant it subject to conditions. A decision of a majority of the three-judge panel shall be final and binding. If the Court grants the application, the Clerk shall issue a certificate of admission.

(e) *Limited Pre–Admission Practice.* An attorney may appear of record and file papers in a case or proceeding before actual admission to practice in this Court if:

(i) the attorney pays the fee established by the Court;

(ii) the attorney files the application required by this rule with the Clerk; and

(iii) the attorney is admitted before a personal appearance in court.

(f) *Local Counsel.* The Court may, in its discretion, require any attorney whose office is a great distance from the courthouse to retain local counsel. Local counsel shall enter an appearance in the case and shall have both the authority and responsibility for the conduct of the case should lead counsel be unavailable for any appearance, hearing or trial.

(g) *Government Attorneys.* An attorney representing the United States, or an agency of the United States may practice in this Court in official capacity without applying for admission. If the attorney does not have an office in the district, he or she shall designate the United States Attorney or an Assistant United States Attorney for this district to receive service of all notices and papers. Service of notice on the United States Attorney or designated assistant shall constitute service on the nonresident government attorney.

(h) *Law Student Practice.*

(i) Admission. Upon a satisfactory showing of eligibility and taking of the prescribed oath, a law student in an approved program may appear before the Court under the supervision of an attorney who has been duly certified. The supervising attorney may be an attorney in the U.S. Attorney's Office, an attorney in private practice admitted to practice before this Court, or a faculty member of an ABA-approved law school teaching in an eligible law school clinical program as defined in (iii) below.

(ii) Eligibility of Law Student. To be eligible to practice, a law student must:

(A) be enrolled in, or have graduated from, a law school approved by the American Bar Association;

(B) have completed at least two-thirds of the credit hours necessary for graduation from that law school;

(C) be certified by the dean of the law school as being of good character and of sufficient legal ability and training to perform as a legal intern;

(D) have a working knowledge of the Federal Rules of Civil and Criminal Procedure, Evidence, and Code of Professional Responsibility;

(E) have been certified by the Court pursuant to this rule;

(F) if the student qualifies as a legal intern under a supervising law school faculty member, be registered for credit in a law school clinical program which has been certified by the Court; and

(G) have been appropriately introduced to the Court by a member of the bar of this Court or by the supervising faculty member.

(iii) Eligibility of Program.

(A) An eligible law school clinical program:

(1) must be offered for credit at a law school approved by the American Bar Association;

(2) must be supervised by a full-time or adjunct law school faculty member who is admitted to practice before this Court;

(3) must include academic and practical advocacy training within the program;

(4) must be certified by this Court;

(5) must provide malpractice insurance for its activities, supervisors and student participants in the legal representation of any clients;

(6) must designate an official within the Western District to whom all notices may be sent in connection with this rule or any legal representation provided pursuant to this rule; and

(7) may arrange for a supervisor to accept compensation other than from a client, such as compensation under the Criminal Justice Act.

(B) An eligible non-law school clinical program:

(1) must be supervised by a member of a bar who is admitted to practice before this Court;

(2) must be developed to provide practical advocacy training within the program;

(3) must provide direct supervision by the supervising attorney;

(4) must be for a period of no less than fourteen (14) weeks;

(5) must be certified by the Court;

(6) must provide malpractice insurance for its activities, supervisors and student participants in the legal representation of any client under this program;

(7) may be, but need not be, under the direction of a full-time or adjunct faculty member of a law school; and

(8) must identify the supervising attorney to whom all notices may be sent.

(iv) Requirements for Supervisor. A supervisor must:

(A) if a full-time or adjunct member of a law school faculty, be certified by the dean of the law school as being of good character, and as having sufficient legal ability and adequate litigation experience to fulfill the responsibilities as the supervisor. If the supervisor is not a member of a law school faculty, the certification may be provided by a practicing member of the bar;

(B) be admitted to practice in this Court;

(C) be present with the student in court and at other proceedings in which testimony is taken and as required under subsection (v) of this rule;

(D) cosign all pleadings or other documents filed with the Court;

(E) assume full personal and professional responsibility for a student's guidance in any work undertaken and for the quality of a student's work, and be available for consultation with represented clients;

(F) assist and counsel the student in activities pursuant to this rule and review all such activities with the student to the extent required for the proper practical training of the student and protection of the client; and

(G) be responsible for supplemental oral or written work for the student as is necessary to ensure proper representation of the client.

(v) Approved Activities. A certified student under the personal supervision of a supervisor may participate in activities as set out below.

(A) A student may represent any client, including federal, state or local government bodies, if the client on whose behalf the student is appearing has indicated in writing consent to that appearance and the supervising attorney has also indicated in writing approval of that appearance.

(B) A student may represent a client in any criminal, civil or administrative matter on behalf of any person or governmental body. However, any judge or magistrate judge of this Court retains the authority to limit a student's participation in any individual case before that judge or magistrate judge.

(C) Representation shall include holding of consultations, preparation of documents for filing or submission to the Court, participation in discovery proceedings and the participation in trials and other court proceedings.

(D) The supervising attorney must be present with the student for all court appearances or for the taking of oral depositions except that a legal intern under a law school clinical program may appear in court without the supervising attorney unless the Court directs the presence of the supervisor. The Court shall be advised in advance whenever a legal intern is scheduled to appear in court without a supervising attorney.

(E) A student may make no binding commitments on behalf of an absent client prior to client and supervisor approval. Documents or papers filed with the Court must be read, approved and cosigned by the supervising attorney. The Court retains the authority to establish exceptions to such activities.

(F) A judge of this Court may terminate the admission of the legal intern at any time without prior notice or hearing or showing of cause.

(vi) Compensation. An eligible law student may neither solicit nor accept compensation or remuneration of any kind for services performed pursuant to this rule from the person on whose behalf services are rendered; but this rule will not prevent an attorney, legal aid bureau, law school or state or federal agency from paying compensation to an eligible law student, or making such charges for services as may be proper.

(vii) Certification of Student. Certification of a student by the law school dean or designee, if such certification is approved by the Court, shall be filed with the Clerk and unless it is sooner withdrawn, shall remain in effect until the expiration of twelve (12) months. Certification will automatically terminate if the student does not take the first bar examination following graduation, or if the student fails to achieve a passing grade in the bar examination, or if the student is admitted to full practice before this Court. Certification of a student to appear in a particular case may be withdrawn by the Court at any time, in the discretion of the Court and without any showing of cause.

(viii) Certification of Program. Certification of a program by the Court shall be filed with the Clerk and shall remain in effect indefinitely unless withdrawn by the Court. Certification of a program may be withdrawn by the Court at any time, in the discretion of the Court and without any showing of cause.

(ix) Certification of Supervisor. Certification of a supervisor by the law school dean or member of the bar, if such certification is approved by the Court, shall be filed with the Clerk and shall remain in effect indefinitely unless withdrawn by the Court. Certification of a supervisor may be withdrawn by the Court at any time, in the discretion of the Court and without any showing of cause. Any judge or magistrate judge of this Court retains the authority to withdraw or limit a supervisor's participation in any individual case before that judge or magistrate judge. Certification of a supervisor may be withdrawn by the dean or attorney who originally certified the supervisor by mailing the notices of withdrawal to the Clerk.

(i) *Unauthorized Practice.* A person must be a member in good standing of the bar of this Court to practice in this Court or to hold himself or herself out as being authorized to practice in this Court, except that:

(A) a party may proceed in pro per;

(B) government attorneys may practice under LCivR 57.1(g); and

(C) law students may practice under LCivR 57.1(h).

(D) A licensed attorney who is not under suspension or disbarment in this or another federal or state court may:

(1) cosign papers or participate in pretrial conferences in conjunction with a member of the bar of this Court;

(2) represent a client in a deposition; and

(3) counsel a client in an action or proceeding pending in this Court.

(j) *Consent to Standards of Conduct and Disciplinary Authority.* An attorney admitted to the bar of this Court or who practices in this Court as permitted by this Rule is subject to the Rules of Professional Conduct adopted by the Michigan Supreme Court, except those rules a majority of the judges of this Court exclude by administrative order, and consents to the jurisdiction of this Court and the Michigan Attorney Grievance Commission and Michigan Attorney Discipline Board for purposes of disciplinary proceedings. Any person practicing or purporting to practice in this Court shall be presumed to know the Local Rules of this Court, including those provisions relating to sanctions for violations of these Rules.

(k) *Attorney Discipline.*

(i) Discipline Other Than Suspension or Disbarment. In accordance with the provisions of this Rule, a district judge or magistrate judge may impose discipline, except suspension or disbarment from this Court, on any attorney who engages in conduct violating the Rules of Professional Conduct; willfully violates these rules, the Federal Rules of Criminal Procedure, or orders of the Court; or engages in other conduct unbecoming of a member of the bar of this Court. Prior to the imposition of discipline, the attorney shall be afforded an opportunity to show good cause, within such time as the Court shall prescribe, why the discipline should not be imposed. Upon the attorney's response to show cause, and after hearing, if requested and allowed by the district judge, or upon expiration of the time prescribed for a response if no response is made, the Court shall enter an appropriate order.

(ii) Suspension or Disbarment.

(A) Initiation of Proceedings. Formal disciplinary proceedings leading up to possible suspension or disbarment shall be initiated by the issuance of an order to show cause, signed by the Chief Judge. Such order may be issued by the Court, on its own initiative or in response to allegations brought to the attention of the Court in a written complaint, if the Court determines further investigation is warranted. The Chief Judge may dismiss a complaint and refuse to issue an order to show cause if the complaint is found to be frivolous. The order to show cause issued by the Court shall include the specific facts that give rise to the proposed discipline, including the date, place and nature of the alleged misconduct, and the names of all persons involved. A copy of the order and any supporting documents shall be mailed to the attorney who is the subject of investigation. The attorney shall have twenty-one (21) days from the entry of the order in which to respond. The response shall contain a specific admission or denial of each of the factual allegations contained in the order and, in addition, a specific statement of facts on which the respondent relies, including all other material dates, places, persons and conduct, and all documents or other supporting evidence not previously filed with the order that are relevant to the charges of misconduct alleged. The response shall contain a specific request for a hearing, if so desired by the respondent.

(B) Hearing. A disciplinary hearing shall be held only when the attorney under investigation has requested such a hearing in a timely response.

(1) Procedures. If it is determined that a hearing is necessary, the Chief Judge shall provide the attorney with written notice of the hearing a minimum of twenty-one (21) days before its scheduled date. The notice shall contain the date and location of the hearing and a statement that the attorney is entitled to be represented by counsel, to present witnesses and other evidence, and to confront and cross examine adverse witnesses.

(2) Conduct of the Hearing. The hearing shall be conducted by a panel of three judicial officers appointed by the Chief Judge, consisting of at least one active or senior district judge. The other members of the panel may include senior judges, bankruptcy judges, and magistrate judges. Any judge who initiated the request for discipline or before whom the allegation giving rise to the request took place shall not be appointed to the panel. The presiding judicial officer shall have the authority to resolve all disputes on matters of procedure and evidence which arise during the course of the proceeding. The presiding judicial officer may appoint an attorney to assist in the preparation and presentation of the evidence supporting the allegations giving rise to the request for discipline. All witnesses shall testify under penalty of perjury. Such hearings shall be confidential and be recorded. A decision of a majority of the three judge panel shall be final and binding. A written order shall be prepared which shall include the findings of the panel and disposition of the disciplinary charges. The order shall be a matter of public record and be sent to the respondent and complainant.

(3) Burden of Proof. The conduct giving rise to the request for discipline shall be proven by a preponderance of the evidence.

(4) Failure to Appear. The failure of the respondent to appear at the hearing shall itself be grounds for discipline.

(iii) Reinstatement After Expiration of Court–Imposed Discipline. After expiration of a period of suspension imposed by this Court, an attorney may apply for reinstatement by filing an affidavit under LCrR 57.1(m)(iii). The application for reinstatement will be decided in accordance with the process set forth in that rule. Unless and until reinstated, a suspended attorney must not practice before this Court.

(*l*) *Attorneys Convicted of Crimes.*

(i) Serious Crimes.

(A) When an attorney admitted to practice before this Court is convicted of a serious crime, the attorney is automatically suspended from practice in this Court without further action of the Court, whether the conviction resulted from a plea of guilty or nolo contendere or from a verdict after trial or otherwise, and regardless of the pendency of an appeal. On receipt of written notice of conviction of a serious crime of an attorney admitted to practice before this Court, the Chief Judge shall enter an order suspending the attorney. The suspension shall continue until after final disposition of an appeal of the conviction, proceedings on remand after an appeal, and any disciplinary investigation and proceeding based on the conduct that resulted in the conviction. The Court shall serve a copy of the order on the attorney by certified mail.

(B) On application, the Chief Judge shall reinstate the attorney on a showing that:

(1) there is a jurisdictional deficiency that establishes that the suspension may not properly be ordered; such as that the crime did not constitute a serious crime or that the attorney is not the individual convicted; or

(2) the conviction has been reversed and there is no likelihood of further criminal prosecution or disciplinary action related to the conduct that resulted in the conviction. A reinstatement will not terminate any disciplinary investigation or proceeding based on the conduct that resulted in the conviction.

(ii) Other Crimes. If the Court receives written notice of conviction of an attorney admitted to practice before this Court of a crime not constituting a serious crime, the matter shall be referred to the Chief Judge who may initiate proceedings under subsection (k)(i) or (ii) of this rule.

(iii) Obligations to Report Conviction. An attorney admitted to practice before this Court shall, on being convicted of any crime, immediately inform the Clerk. If the conviction was in this Court, the attorney shall also provide to the Clerk a list of all other jurisdictions in which the attorney is admitted to practice. An attorney knowingly violating this provision may, on notice and after hearing, be charged with criminal contempt.

(m) *Discipline by Other Jurisdictions.*

(i) Reciprocal Discipline.

(A) On receipt of written notice that another jurisdiction entered an order of discipline against an attorney admitted to practice in this Court, the Chief Judge shall enter an order imposing the same discipline, effective as of the date that the discipline was effective in the other jurisdiction. If the discipline imposed in the other jurisdiction has been stayed there, the Court shall defer reciprocal discipline until the stay expires.

(B) When this Court enters an order of discipline against an attorney, the attorney shall provide to the Clerk a list of all other jurisdictions in which the attorney is admitted to practice.

(ii) Application to Modify Reciprocal Discipline.

(A) Within twenty-eight (28) days after the effective date of the order of discipline in this Court, the attorney may apply to the Chief Judge for modification or vacation of the discipline.

(B) The Chief Judge shall modify or vacate the discipline if, on the record supporting the order of discipline in the other jurisdiction, the attorney demonstrates or the Chief Judge finds that it clearly appears that:

(1) the procedure in the other jurisdiction constituted a deprivation of due process;

(2) there was such an infirmity of proof establishing the misconduct as to give rise to the clear conviction that this Court could not accept as final the conclusion on that subject;

(3) imposing the same discipline in this Court would result in grave injustice; or

(4) the misconduct warrants substantially different discipline.

If the Chief Judge determines that any of these grounds exist, the Chief Judge shall order other appropriate discipline or no discipline.

(iii) Reinstatement After Expiration of Discipline.

(A) An attorney may apply for reinstatement by filing an affidavit of reinstatement stating that the jurisdiction that entered the underlying order of discipline has reinstated the attorney. The application for reinstatement must be accompanied by a copy of the entire disciplinary record, including complaints, answers, hearing transcripts, and orders entered in the disciplinary proceedings. The Chief Judge shall assign such applications to a panel of three judicial officers consisting of at least one active or senior district judge. The other members of the panel may include senior judges, bankruptcy judges, and magistrate judges. Any judge who initiated the request for discipline or before whom the allegation giving rise to request for discipline took place shall not be appointed to the panel. A decision of the majority of the three judge panel shall be final and binding.

(B) The judicial officers assigned to the matter shall within twenty-eight (28) days after assignment schedule a hearing at which the attorney shall have the burden of demonstrating by clear and convincing evidence that:

(1) the attorney has complied with the orders of discipline of this Court and all other disciplinary authorities;

(2) the attorney has not practiced in this Court during the period of disbarment or suspension and has not practiced law contrary to any other order of discipline;

(3) the attorney has not engaged in any other professional misconduct since disbarment or suspension;

(4) the attorney has the moral qualifications, competency and learning in the law required for admission to practice law before this Court; and

(5) the attorney's resumption of the practice of law will not be detrimental to the integrity and standing of the bar or to the administration of justice, or subversive of the public interest.

The Court may condition reinstatement on payment of all or part of the costs of the proceedings in this Court and may impose any of the conditions of reinstatement imposed in the other jurisdiction, or such other conditions as are warranted.

(C) An attorney shall not file an application for reinstatement under this Rule within one year following denial of such an application.

(iv) Obligation to Report Discipline.

(A) An attorney admitted to practice before this Court appearing or participating in a pending matter shall, on being subjected to an order of discipline, immediately inform the Clerk of the order of discipline.

(B) An attorney admitted to practice before this Court shall, before appearing or participating in a matter in the Court after being subjected to an order of discipline that has not previously been reported to the Court, immediately inform the Clerk of the order of discipline.

(C) An attorney knowingly violating this provision may be charged with criminal contempt.

(n) *Resignation in Other Jurisdictions.*

(i) If an attorney resigns from the bar of another court of the United States while an investigation into allegations of misconduct is pending:

(A) the attorney shall immediately and automatically be disbarred from this Court; and

(B) the attorney shall promptly inform the Clerk of the resignation. An attorney knowingly violating this notification provision may be charged with criminal contempt.

(ii) On receipt of written notice that an attorney has resigned from the bar of another court of the United States or the bar of a state while an investigation into allegations of misconduct was pending, the Chief Judge shall enter an order disbarring the attorney, effective as of the date of resignation in the other jurisdiction.

(iii) An attorney disbarred under this subsection may apply to the Chief Judge for modification or vacation of the disbarment pursuant to LCivR 83.1(m)(ii).

(iv) An attorney disbarred under this subsection may be reinstated if the attorney is readmitted in the jurisdiction from which the attorney resigned and there has been a final disposition of the investigation into allegations of misconduct without an order of discipline.

(o) *Service of Papers.* Service of papers on an attorney under this Rule may be by mail to the address of the attorney shown on the Court's roll of attorneys or the address in the most recent paper the attorney filed in a proceeding in this Court.

(p) *Duties of the Clerk.*

(i) On being informed that an attorney admitted to practice before this Court has been convicted of a crime, the Clerk shall determine whether the Court in which the conviction occurred sent a certificate of the conviction to this Court. If not, the Clerk shall promptly obtain a certificate and file it with the Court.

(ii) On being informed that another court or a state has entered an order of discipline against an attorney admitted to practice before this Court, the Clerk shall determine whether a certified copy of the order has been filed with this Court. If not, the Clerk shall promptly obtain a certified copy of the order and file it with the Court.

(iii) When this Court convicts an attorney of a crime or enters an order of discipline against an attorney, the Clerk shall promptly notify the National Discipline Data Bank operated by the American Bar Association and any other

authority that licensed or authorized the attorney to practice.

(q) *Other Authority.* Nothing in this Rule abridges the Court's power to control proceedings before it, including the power to initiate proceedings for contempt under Fed. R. Crim. P. 42 or sanction or disqualify an attorney in a particular case.

57.2. Magistrate Judges.

(a) *Determination of Nondispositive Pretrial Matters—28 U.S.C. § 636(b)(1)(A).* A magistrate judge may hear and determine any procedural or discovery motion or other pretrial matters, other than motions to dismiss or quash an indictment or information made by a defendant and motions to suppress evidence.

(b) *Recommendations Regarding Case–Dispositive Motions—28 U.S.C. § 636(b)(1)(B).* A magistrate judge may submit to a judge of the Court a report containing proposed findings of fact and recommendations for disposition by the judge of motions to dismiss or quash an indictment or information made against a defendant or motions to suppress evidence. A magistrate judge may determine any preliminary matters and conduct evidentiary hearing or other proceeding in connection with such recommendations.

(c) *Other Duties.* A magistrate judge is also authorized to:

(i) exercise all authority conferred upon United States magistrate judges by the Federal Rules of Criminal Procedure, including exercising case-dispositive jurisdiction in petty offense and other misdemeanor prosecutions under Fed. R. Crim. P. 58 and 18 U.S.C. § 3401;

(ii) conduct pretrial conferences, settlement conferences, omnibus hearings, and related pretrial proceedings in cases;

(iii) conduct all nondispositive proceedings in cases not triable to the magistrate judge, including initial appearances, bond hearings, detention hearings, hearings on motion to revoke bond, arraignments, the taking of not-guilty pleas and the entering of not-guilty pleas for defendants standing mute;

(iv) impanel grand juries, and receive grand jury returns in accordance with Rule 6(f) of the Federal Rules of Criminal Procedure;

(v) accept waivers of indictment and waivers of counsel;

(vi) conduct voir dire and select petit juries to the extent allowed by law;

(vii) accept petit jury verdicts in cases in the absence of a judge;

(viii) conduct necessary proceedings leading to the potential revocation of probation;

(ix) issue subpoenas, writs of habeas corpus ad testificandum or habeas corpus ad prosequendum, or other orders necessary to obtain the presence of parties witnesses or evidence needed for investigations or for court proceedings;

(x) order the exoneration or forfeiture of bonds;

(xi) perform the functions specified in 18 U.S.C. §§ 4107, 4108, and 4109, regarding proceedings for verification of consent by offenders to transfer to or from the United States and the appointment of counsel therein;

(xii) issue summons, search warrants, orders or other process authorizing agents and officers of the Internal Revenue Service or other authorized persons to enter premises and to make such search as is necessary in order to levy and seize property pursuant to Section 6331 of the Internal Revenue Code or other applicable provision of law;

(xiii) conduct proceedings in accordance with 26 U.S.C. §§ 7402(b) and 7604(b) regarding enforcement of Internal Revenue Service summonses;

(xiv) conduct extradition proceedings in accordance with 18 U.S.C. § 3184;

(xv) preside over the acceptance of guilty pleas in felony prosecutions in the circumstances allowed by LCrR 11; and

(xvi) perform any additional duty not inconsistent with the Constitution and laws of the United States.

(d) *Appeal From Judgments in Misdemeanor Cases—18 U.S.C. § 3402.* A defendant may appeal a judgment of conviction by a magistrate judge in a misdemeanor case by filing a notice of appeal within fourteen (14) days after entry of the judgment, and by serving a copy of the notice upon the United States Attorney. If the case was previously assigned to a district judge, that judge shall hear any appeal from the decision of the magistrate judge; otherwise, the appeal shall be assigned to a district judge at random. The scope of appeal shall be the same as on an appeal from a judgment of the District Court to the Court of Appeals.

(e) *Appeals From Other Orders of a Magistrate Judge.* Appeals from any other decisions and orders of a magistrate judge not provided for in this rule should be taken as provided by governing statute, rule, or decisional law. Such appeals shall be taken in accordance with the procedures set forth in LCivR 72.3.

(f) Any magistrate judge of this Court may exercise nondispositive jurisdiction and perform the duties authorized by this rule in any criminal case, without the necessity of an order of reference.

7.3. Miscellaneous.

(a) *Amendment.* These rules may be amended by a majority vote of the judges of this district in conformity with Rule 57 of the Federal Rules of Criminal Procedure.

(b) *Probation Office.* No employee of the U.S. Probation Office shall, except as required by law, disclose to any person or organization any information obtained or maintained pursuant to official duties. Any order, subpoena or other demand for the testimony of a probation officer or the official records of the Probation Office must be made in accordance with the procedures set forth in the applicable Regulations of the Judicial Conference of the United States. Whenever a probation officer of this Court is served with an order, subpoena or other demand for testimony or the production of confidential presentence or probation records, the probation officer must not provide testimony or access to official records without the prior written approval of the Chief Probation Officer. Except when the request is made by a federal or state probation or parole officer, the Chief Probation Officer must consult with the Chief Judge of this Court regarding the proper response to the order, subpoena, or other demand. This rule does not apply to officers' testimony before this Court.

(c) *Bonds and Sureties.* In all proceedings the Clerk shall accept as surety upon bonds and other undertakings a surety company approved by the United States Department of Treasury, cash or an individual personal surety residing within the district. The Clerk shall maintain a list of approved surety companies. Any personal surety must qualify as the owner of real estate within this district of the full net value of twice the face amount of the bond. Attorneys or other officers of this Court shall not serve as sureties. This rule shall apply to supersedeas bonds and any other bonds required by law.

(d) *Appearance.* An attorney appears by filing any pleading or other paper or by acknowledging in court that the attorney acts in the proceeding on behalf of a party. The appearance of an attorney is deemed to be the appearance of the law firm. Any attorney in the firm may be required by the Court to conduct a court-ordered conference or trial. Withdrawal of appearance may be accomplished only by leave of court.

(e) *Courthouse Conduct.* [Repealed]

(f) *Other Matters.* All other matters scheduled before a judge shall be scheduled by the judge's case manager, who shall notify all parties or counsel of scheduled dates and the purpose of all court appearances.

(g) *Writs of Habeas Corpus.*

(i) Requirements. All writs of habeas corpus ad prosequendum or testificandum for an individual shall, in addition to stating a specific date and time, include the following phrase: "and at such other times and dates as the Court may decree." Every effort shall be made to allow fourteen (14) days after service prior to the required appearance.

(ii) Requests to Seal. A request that the writ be issued under seal must state facts showing good cause supporting the request. The caption of both the application and the proposed order granting the writ must clearly identify the document as being filed under seal.

(h) *Suppression Orders.* For good cause shown, any party may obtain a protective order for the suppression of any action or of any pleading or other paper. Upon the entry of a suppression order, the Clerk shall prevent all persons, except those designated by the Court, from having access to the suppressed material.

(i) *Payment to Court Reporters.* All parties, except defendants represented by CJA counsel, ordering a transcript must pay in advance by cash or certified check unless the court reporter agrees to other arrangements.

57.4. Conduct in Federal Court Facilities.

(a) *Security.*

(i) As used in this rule, "federal court facility" includes any facility occupied by the United States District Court or any temporary facility occupied by a District Judge or Magistrate Judge serving in the Western District of Michigan.

(ii) All persons entering a federal court facility in the Western District of Michigan are required to present a valid government issued identification card with photo, pass through a magnetometer, and have all belongings and packages subject to physical and/or x-ray examination by the United States Marshals' Service. Any person who refuses to present a valid form of identification or pass through screening shall be denied entrance.

(b) *Soliciting, Loitering, and Disruptive Behavior.*

(i) The solicitation of business relating to bail bonds or to employment as counsel is prohibited.

(ii) Loitering in or about federal court facilities is prohibited.

(iii) Any behavior which impedes or disrupts the orderly conduct of the business of the court is prohibited. Signs, placards, or banners may not be brought into a federal court facility or its environs.

(c) *Recording of Court Proceedings.*

(i) Except as specifically provided herein, no camera or recording device shall be permitted in a federal court facility. This prohibition shall include any device or contrivance capable of preserving or transmitting a visual image and any device or contrivance capable of recording, transmitting, or preserving any audible communication (except cell phones with camera features).

(ii) The taking of photographs or video recordings in connection with any judicial proceeding and the recording or broadcasting of judicial proceedings by radio, television or other means is prohibited.

(A) As used in this rule, "judicial proceeding" includes proceedings before district, bankruptcy or magistrate judges, and sessions of the grand jury.

(B) As used in this rule, "in connection with any judicial proceeding" includes all participants in a judicial proceeding while they are in a courtroom or its environs.

(iii) A judicial officer may authorize, by written notice to the United States Marshal, the use of electronic or photographic means for the presentation of evidence or for the perpetuation of the record.

(iv) A district judge or magistrate judge may authorize, by written notice to the United States Marshal:

(A) The broadcasting, televising, recording, or photographing of investiture, ceremonial, or naturalization proceedings; and

(B) The radio or television broadcasting, audio or video recording or photographing of court proceedings pursuant to a resolution of the Judicial Conference of the United States.

(v) By written notice to the U.S. Marshals' Service, the General Service Administration Property Manager or his designee can authorize an individual or contract group to possess a camera or recording device for the purpose of maintaining or enhancing the facility, to include repair and alterations.

(d) *Firearms and Weapons.*

(i) It is illegal to possess a firearm or other dangerous weapon in a federal court facility with or without the intent to commit a crime (Title 18, USC 930). Firearms, knives, explosives, and other weapons are prohibited in federal court facilities and subject to confiscation.

(ii) Exceptions to this rule include:

(A) Judicial officers, the United States Marshal, deputy marshals, court security officers, and employees of the Federal Protective Service.

(B) Federal law enforcement agencies having offices in a federal court facility are exempt from the provisions regarding the carrying of weapons while entering the building and while going to and from the floor where their offices are located.

(C) Employees of the United States Probation Office who are authorized by law and agency regulations to carry firearms in the performance of their official duties may possess firearms in this facility to the extent necessary to transport such firearms by the most direct route available to and from the offices of the Probation Department. In accordance with regulations of the U.S. Probation Department, all firearms shall be secured while present within the offices of the Probation Department. The Chief U.S. Probation Officer will notify the United States Marshals' Service in writing of all officers authorized to carry firearms. Employees of the United States Probation Office are prohibited from carrying firearms into courtrooms.

(D) State, county, and local law enforcement officers who are:

(1) Escorting prisoners to and from court under the direction of the United States Marshals' Service, or

(2) Assisting the Marshals' Service by supporting or providing additional security, as directed, in and around federal court facilities.

(iii) All other federal, state or local law enforcement officers are required to identify themselves and store their weapons in weapons lock boxes maintained by the United States Marshals' Service. For security purposes, officers *may* be required to be screened after securing their weapons.

(iv) The handling of firearms as exhibits in trials is governed by an administrative order issued by the court.

(v) An exception to this Rule regarding weapons or firearms may only be made by the Chief Judge or the Judge in whose courtroom the proceedings are occurring.

(e) *Cellular Telephones and Laptop Computers.*

(i) General Policy. Except as provided in (ii) and other court orders, cellular telephones and laptop computers, are not permitted in federal court facilities.

(ii) Exempted Persons. The following persons are permitted to carry and use cellular telephones and laptop computers, within federal court facilities in the Western District of Michigan:

(A) Officers of the Court. Attorneys appearing in their official capacity as officers of the Court.

(B) Building Tenants. Employees and visiting employees of the federal court facility.

(C) Parties to Litigation. Parties, other than defendants in criminal cases, who enter a federal court facility accompanied by their attorney, if their counsel certifies to security staff that such devices are necessary to facilitate litigation pending before the court.

(D) U.S. Marshals' Service Personnel. Including Court Security Officers and contract guards.

(E) Other Federal, State, Local Law Enforcement. When appearing in their official capacity.

(F) GSA Approved Contractors. By written notice to the U.S. Marshals' Service, the General Service Administration Property Manager or his designee may authorize an individual or contract group to possess a cellular telephone, laptop computer, or other wireless communication device for the purpose of maintaining or enhancing the facility, to include repair and alterations.

(G) Jurors. Grand jury members, petit jury members, and persons appearing as directed pursuant to a jury summons.

(H) Judicial Authority. Upon request to the court, a judicial officer may issue an order granting permission to an individual or group, otherwise not authorized to possess a cell phone or laptop computer. The U.S. Marshal shall be notified of such order.

(I) Members of the Press. Bona fide members of the press who present official credentials satisfactory to the U.S. Marshal.

(iii) Conditions for Authorized Use of Cellular Telephones.* Unless express permission to the contrary is given by the presiding judicial officer, the following conditions and restrictions apply to those individuals authorized to carry a cellular telephone:

(A) While in a courtroom, cellular telephones shall be in the "off" position at all times, unless the presiding judicial officer give express permission for use of the device.

(B) The device may not be used and must be turned off except in designated areas of the court facility.

(C) The device cannot be initiated, "answered," or examined or manipulated (for text messaging or otherwise) while in a courtroom.

(D) The device may be used for communication by non-building tenants only in designated areas. Designated areas will be identified by each court facility by administrative order, to be posted prominently in each facility and on the court's Internet website.

(E) The cell phone or computer may not be used for purposes of taking pictures or making any audio or video recording in violation of subsection (c) of this rule.

(f) *Enforcement.* The United States Marshal, his deputies, and court security officers may demand from any individual in possession of a cellular telephone or wireless communication device, to produce identification in aid of enforcement of this rule, and if the identification does not satisfy the officer that the person in possession of the device is authorized in accordance with the terms of this rule, the officer may refuse admittance to this person and/or confiscate the device.

(g) *Violations.*

(i) Attorney Discipline. An attorney violating this rule may be subject to discipline, including disbarment, in accordance with Local Criminal Rule 57 and/or Local Civil Rule 83.

(ii) Confiscation. A violation of this rule, including without limitation, unauthorized possession, use in an unauthorized space, possession of a device in an audible mode, and failing to turn off a device when required, *SHALL* result in immediate confiscation of the device. Any judicial officer may order confiscation of a cellular telephone or wireless communications device. Any United States Marshal or Deputy Marshal or court security officer may also confiscate such a device. The U.S. Marshal's Service will develop a procedure for handling and storing confiscated devices.

(iii) Contempt of Court. A violation of this rule may be punished as criminal contempt of court. A violation that disrupts a judicial proceeding may be punished by summary proceedings.

(h) *Relief From Confiscation of a Device.* An individual whose device has been confiscated may apply in writing not less than seven (7) days after confiscation for its return. The application shall be made to the judicial officer whose proceedings were disturbed by the violation, or, if there is no such judicial officer, to the chief judge. The judicial officer may grant or refuse the request. Confiscated devices that are not returned, either because no request has been made within the time provided or the request for return has been denied, shall be disposed of in a manner directed by the chief judge. Nothing in this paragraph shall prohibit the judicial officer or his designee to return a device after the conclusion of a court matter if the violation was totally inadvertent.

(i) *Consent to Provisions.* Any person bringing in a cellular telephone, laptop computer, or other wireless communication device shall be determined to have consented to the provisions of this rule.

[Effective June 1, 1998. Amended effective January 2, 2002; June 20, 2005; June 21, 2006; February 15, 2007; November 3, 2008; December 1, 2009; May 27, 2011; July 2, 2012; March 12, 2013; May 6, 2013; September 24, 2013.]

* [**Publisher's Note:** *See also* Administrative Order No. 08–143, *post.*]

LOCAL CRIMINAL RULE 58. MISDEMEANORS; PETTY OFFENSES AND COLLATERAL FORFEITURES

58.1. Disposition of Misdemeanor Cases—18 U.S.C. § 3401. Each magistrate judge of this Court is empowered to exercise all jurisdiction conferred by 18 U.S.C. § 3401, including jurisdiction to:

(a) try persons accused of, and sentence persons convicted of, misdemeanors in this District, after receiving such consent as may be required by 18 U.S.C. § 3401;

(b) direct the probation service of the Court to conduct a presentence investigation in such misdemeanor case;

(c) conduct a jury trial in any misdemeanor case where the defendant so requests and is entitled to trial by jury under the Constitution and laws of the United States; and

(d) conduct all post judgment proceedings, including petitions to revoke or modify probation or supervised release, for any misdemeanor defendant who was originally sentenced by a magistrate judge.

58.2. Petty Offenses and Collateral Forfeitures.

(a) *Posting Collateral in Lieu of Appearance.* A person who is charged with a violation of a Federal Wildlife Act, parking regulations governing the Federal Building, National Forest Offenses, Conduct on Postal Service Property, Violation of Law on Military Property or any other petty offense as defined in 18 U.S.C. § 1(3), may, in lieu of appearance, post collateral in the amount indicated for the offense, waive appearance before a United States magistrate judge, and consent to the forfeiture of collateral to the United States. The posting of said collateral shall signify that the offender does not contest the charge or request a hearing before the designated United States magistrate judge. If the collateral is forfeited, such action shall be tantamount to a finding of guilty. Collateral will be permitted only for those offenses specifically authorized by the Court in separate orders. There shall be maintained in the office of the Clerk and with each United States magistrate judge a current list of the petty offenses and collateral applicable thereto which the Court has established as collateral forfeiture offenses.

(b) *Failure to Post and Forfeit Collateral.* If a person charged with an offense under this rule fails to post and forfeit collateral, any punishment, including fine, imprisonment or probation, may be imposed within the limits established by law upon conviction or after trial.

(c) *Aggravated Offenses.* If, within the discretion of the law enforcement officer, the offense is of an aggravated nature, the law enforcement officer may require appearance, and any punishment including fine, imprisonment or probation, may be imposed within the limits established by law upon conviction or after trial.

(d) *Appearance Required.* Nothing contained in this rule shall prohibit law enforcement officers from arresting a person for the commission of any offense, including those for which collateral may be posted and forfeited, and requiring the person charged to appear before a United States magistrate judge or, upon arrest, taking the person immediately before a United States magistrate judge.

[Effective June 1, 1998.]

VOLUNTARY FACILITATIVE MEDIATION PROGRAM DESCRIPTION

I. Voluntary Facilitative Mediation (VFM)

VFM is a "flexible, nonbinding dispute resolution process in which an impartial neutral third party—the mediator—facilitates negotiations among the parties to help them reach settlement. A hallmark of mediation is its capacity to expand traditional settlement discussion and broaden resolution options, often by going beyond the legal issues in controversy."[1] The mediator, who may meet jointly or separately with the parties, serves as a facilitator only and does not decide issues or make findings of fact.

II. VFM Advisory Committee

A. A standing VFM Advisory Committee ("the Committee") is appointed by the Court from the following constituencies: certified mediators, attorney users of the VFM process, judicial officers, and the Court's ADR Administrator.

B. Taking into account comments solicited from client-users of the VFM process, the Committee will periodically review the VFM program and its effectiveness and make recommendations to the Court on such issues as the qualification, certification and removal of mediators, the demographic and diversity balance of the panel, optimal size of the panel, mediator training, changes in policy or procedures, and requests for review by applicants or mediators.

III. Mediators

A. Qualifications.

1. To be considered for certification, a mediator-applicant must:

(a) be an attorney with a minimum of ten (10) years of federal practice experience, with preference given to those applicants whose principal practice is in the state and federal courts in the Western District of Michigan,

(b) be a member in good standing of this Court's bar,

(c) have appeared as counsel of record or served as a facilitative mediator in at least five (5) cases over the past (5) years in this Court or another federal court,

(d) have completed a minimum of 16 hours of training sponsored or approved by the Court,

(e) agree to pay the Court's $100 mediator certification fee, and

(f) agree to serve in a *pro bono* capacity once each year. Additional requests by the Court for pro bono service in a calendar year may be declined.

2. To maintain certification, a mediator must:

(a) continue to meet all certification criteria specified in section III. A., above,

(b) after three (3) successive years as a panelist, be selected twice in two (2) years by the parties,

(c) attend periodic refresher seminars or additional training sponsored by the Court,

(d) pay an annual $25.00 recertification fee.

3. As mediators serve at the pleasure of the Court, the Court may remove a mediator from the certified list at any time for any reason. In addition, the Court retains discretion to waive or modify the criteria for qualification, certification or removal of any mediator in order to maintain the panel's balance in geography, practice area, and demography.

4. No person shall serve as a mediator in any action in which any of the circumstances specified in 28 USC sec. 455 exist or in good faith are believed to exist. An attorney shall accept the neutral's role only if he or she can be fair and impartial and can avoid a conflict of interest or the appearance of a conflict of interest. For example, see the Model Standards Of Conduct For Mediators, jointly adopted in 2005 by the American Bar Association, the American Arbitration Association and the Association For Conflict Resolution.

5.   In lieu of one selection by the parties, new mediators may seek out a mentor mediator from the Court's Panel to observe a federal court mediation with the consent of the parties, their respective attorneys and the mentor mediator.   Participation in this opportunity will substitute as one of the required party selections as described in Section III (2)(b) of the VFM Program Description.   New mediators may participate as often as desired, but are limited to receiving one selection credit for taking advantage of the opportunity.   A new mediator is defined as one with four years or less of service on the VFM Panel, while the selected mentor must be a current Panel member with at least five years of service on the Panel.   Mentees are responsible for locating their own mentors from the Court certified list.   Upon conclusion, the new mediator shall present to the mentor a "Mentorship Completion Form" for signature, which will be forwarded to the ADR Administrator for review.

B.   Immunity.   Certified mediators are entitled to quasi-judicial immunity as officers of the Court.

IV.   Mediator Panel

A.   It is the objective of the Court to maintain a panel of mediators who offer diversity in geography, practice area, and demographics.

B.   The panel is limited to fifty (50) certified mediators, or such other number as the Court may determine is appropriate from time to time to serve the needs of the program and provide sufficient experience for each mediator to maintain an adequate level of expertise.

C.   Panel Maintenance.

1.   Not later than November 15 of each calendar year, the ADR Administrator shall deliver a letter and biography form to all mediators who continue to meet certification requirements inquiring about each individual's interest in continuing to serve as a panel member during the upcoming calendar year.   Mediators' with interest in continuing as a panel mediator must return the biography form and recertification fee to the ADR Administrator not later than December 15.   Persons serving as mediators at the end of a calendar year retain their certified status if interested in doing so and unless removed from the panel.

2.   Not later than November 15 of each calendar year, the ADR Administrator shall deliver a letter to all mediators who appear not to meet all qualifications criteria listed in section III above and may thus be subject to removal.   Mediators will be invited to offer information to the Court that may bear upon the mediator's continued qualification.   For example, a certified mediator who does not meet the retention criterion by reason of illness or other extraordinary cause outside the mediator's control may offer this information in support of a request to be retained as a panel mediator.   Mediators must return this information to the Court not later than December 15.   Mediators who appear to no longer meet the qualifications criteria will be removed from the panel as of December 15, subject to action by the Committee.

3.   The ADR Administrator will report to the Committee in January regarding panelists' ongoing interest and qualifications.   The Committee, by a majority of members present, will determine if a mediator who has not continued to meet all qualifications criteria will be removed from the panel.

4.   All decisions of the Committee are subject to review by the ADR Judge upon written application filed by a mediator with the ADR Judge no later than ten (10) days after receipt of the decision for which the mediator seeks review.

D.   Panel Vacancies.   When the VFM panel drops below fifty (50) members, or under other circumstances identified by the Committee, additional mediators may be solicited as directed by the Committee.

V.   Case Selection

A.   Eligible Cases.   All civil cases except prisoner civil rights complaints, habeas corpus and social security cases, and § 2255 motions are eligible for voluntary facilitative mediation.

B.   Referral Method and Notice to Parties.   In preparation for the initial Rule 16 scheduling conference, all parties are required to discuss the use of alternative dispute resolution and indicate their preference in the joint status report.   If the district or magistrate judge is satisfied that the selection of facilitative mediation is *purely voluntary* and has the full approval of all parties, the

Judge will incorporate that selection in the case management order with instructions to the parties to jointly select a mediator within fourteen (14) days.

VI. The Mediation Process

A. Selection of Mediator.

1. Within fourteen (14) days of the issuance of the case management order, the parties must jointly select one mediator from the list of court certified mediators. The plaintiff is responsible for notifying the ADR Administrator of the name of the selected mediator by electronically filing a Notice of Selection of Facilitative Mediator.

2. If the parties are unable to agree on a mediator, the ADR Administrator will select the mediator for the parties. The ADR Administrator will contact the selected mediator, and request that the mediator check for potential conflicts of interest. If a conflict is found to exist, the mediator will contact the ADR Administrator, who will either select an alternate mediator or request the parties make a new selection.

3. Once the selection of a mediator is finalized, the ADR Administrator will electronically file the Notice of Appointment of Facilitative Mediator.

B. Mediation Assessment. The Court assesses a fee of $50 per referral, of which $25 is to be paid by the plaintiff(s) and $25 is to be paid by the defendant(s). The monies are deposited into the Voluntary Facilitative Mediation Training Fund. In a pro bono mediation, the assessment is waived for any indigent party.

C. Compensation of Mediator. The mediator is paid his or her normal hourly rate, assessed in as many equal parts as there are separately represented parties, unless otherwise agreed in writing. The mediator is responsible for billing counsel and pro se parties. In the event of noncompliance, the mediator may petition the district or magistrate judge for an order directing payment of his or her fees.

D. Timing for the Mediation Session. Within 14 days of the issuance of the Notice of Appointment of Facilitation Mediator, the mediator will consult with the parties and set a time and place for the mediation session. This section is not intended to impose any time limitations on the mediation process, but to encourage its prompt initiation. If the parties and the mediator agree, mediation may continue throughout the life of the case. The mediator will electronically file a Notice of Hearing of Mediation Session as soon as practicable.

E. Timing and Nature of Submissions Required Before the Mediation Session. Not less than seven (7) days before the initial mediation session, each party will provide the mediator with a concise memorandum, no more than 10 double-spaced pages in length, setting forth the party's position concerning the issues to be resolved through mediation, including issues relative to both liability and damages. The mediator may circulate the parties' memoranda with the consent of all parties.

F. Duration of the Mediation Process. The format for the session is developed by the parties and the mediator. The developed format may involve one session or several sessions. The parties are free to continue with the process as long as they feel it is productive.

G. Attendance at the Mediation Session. The *parties themselves* must attend the mediation session in person. A party other than a natural person (e.g., a corporation or association) satisfies this attendance requirement if it is represented at the session by a person (other than outside counsel) with authority to bind the party to terms of a settlement. A party that is a unit of government need not have present at the session the persons who would be required to approve a settlement before it could become final (e.g., the members of a city council or the chief executive of a major agency), but must send to the session an executive officer, in addition to counsel, knowledge-able about the facts of the case and the governmental unit's position. In cases involving insurance carriers, representatives of the insurance companies, with authority, must attend the mediation session in person. Each party must be accompanied at the mediation session by the lawyer expected to be primarily responsible for handling the trial of the matter. A party or lawyer will be excused from attending the mediation session in person only after approval by the Court upon showing extraordinary circumstances to excuse attendance.

H. Status of Discovery and Motions During Mediation Process. Any case referred to mediation continues to be subject to management by the Judge to whom it is assigned. Unless otherwise ordered, parties are not precluded from filing pretrial motions or pursuing discovery.

I. Mediation Logistics and Location. The mediator will establish the time and place of the mediation session(s). Mediations may take place at the mediator's office or at any other location to which the parties consent. The mediator will determine the length and timing of the sessions and the order in which issues are presented, and will send a notice of the agreed upon time and place to all participating parties.

J. Filing of Mediation Outcome.

1. Within fourteen (14) days of the completion of the mediation process, the mediator will electronically file a Facilitative Mediation Report with the Court. The report will indicate only who participated in the mediation session and whether settlement was reached.

2. If settlement is reached, the mediator will help the parties draft a settlement agreement. The settlement agreement, absent unusual circumstances, must be completed and signed by the parties within fourteen (14) days. The parties shall file a stipulation and proposed order to dismiss with the Court within twenty-eight (28) days of reaching a settlement.

3. If settlement is not reached, the parties have seven (7) days following the mediation session to inform the mediator whether they desire to continue with the mediation process.

K. Confidentiality. All mediation proceedings are considered to be compromise negotiations within the meaning of Fed. R. of Evid. 408.

VII. Court Administration of the Mediation Program

A. Administrative Structure. The mediation program is administered by the Office of the Clerk of Court.

B. Evaluation of the Program. The ADR Administrator will gather data relevant to a careful, in-depth analysis of the efficacy of the program, and will report to the ADR Judge on a regular basis. In an effort to gather information, the Court may develop questionnaires for participants, counsel and mediators to be completed and returned at the close of the mediation process. Only aggregate information about the program will be reported; specific responses will be kept confidential and will not be divulged to the Court, the attorneys or the parties.

[Effective February, 2010. Amended effective December, 2010; February 27, 2015.]

1 Judge's Deskbook on Court ADR, National ADR Institute for Federal Judges, Harvard Law School, November 12–13, 1993, p. 3.

EARLY NEUTRAL EVALUATION PROGRAM DESCRIPTION

Definition

Early Neutral Evaluation (ENE) is a form of alternative dispute resolution conducted by an experienced, objective and neutral attorney, who generally meets with the parties early in their case to evaluate its strengths, weaknesses and value, and who also attempts to negotiate a settlement.

Authorization

W.D. Mich. LCivR 16.4.

THE EARLY NEUTRAL EVALUATORS

Evaluators

The Court does not maintain a list of early neutral evaluators. The parties may choose as an evaluator any attorney who is qualified as a neutral under W.D. Mich. LCivR 16.2.

Disqualification Rules

No person serves as an evaluator in any action in which any of the circumstances specified in 28 U.S.C. § 455 exist, or, in good faith, are believed to exist.

Immunity

Early neutral evaluators are entitled to quasi-judicial immunity as officers of the Court.

CASE SELECTION

Eligible Cases

All civil cases except habeas corpus and social security cases are eligible for early neutral evaluation.

Referral Method and Notice to Parties

In preparation for the initial Rule 16 scheduling conference, all parties are required to discuss the use of alternative dispute resolution and indicate their preference in the joint status report. If the district or magistrate judge is satisfied that the selection of early neutral evaluation has the full approval of all parties, the judge incorporates that selection in the case management order with instructions to the parties to jointly select an evaluator within fourteen (14) days.

THE EARLY NEUTRAL EVALUATION PROCESS

Selection of Early Neutral Evaluator

The parties jointly choose one early neutral evaluator within fourteen (14) days of the issuance of the case management order. Plaintiff is responsible for notifying the ADR Administrator of the name of the selected evaluator. If the parties are unable to reach agreement, they notify the ADR Administrator, who then selects an evaluator for them. The ADR Administrator notifies the selected evaluator, and requests a check for potential conflicts of interest. If a conflict is found to exist, the evaluator notifies the ADR Administrator, who either selects an alternate evaluator or requests the parties make a new selection. Once an evaluator's selection is finalized, the ADR Administrator notifies the judge, who issues an order of referral for early neutral evaluation.

Fees

Evaluators are paid their normal hourly rate, assessed in as many equal parts as there are separately represented parties. The evaluator is responsible for billing counsel. In the event of noncompliance, the evaluator may petition the district or magistrate judge for an order directing payment of his or her fees.

Timing for the Early Neutral Evaluation Session

Within fourteen days of the issuance of the order of referral, the evaluator consults with the parties and sets a time and place for the evaluation session. The session is held within the timeframe ordered by the Court. The evaluator sends a notice of hearing as soon as practicable to all parties and the ADR Administrator.

Timing and Nature of Submissions Required Before the Early Neutral Evaluation Session

A. Seven (7) days before the evaluation session, each party provides the evaluator with a written evaluation statement with copies to all counsel. The evaluation statement must not exceed fifteen (15) pages (not counting exhibits and attachments). The statements should: 1) identify in addition to counsel, which person(s) with decision-making authority will attend the session, 2) identify persons connected to a party opponent, including an insurance carrier, whose presence at the session would enhance the prospects for making the session productive, 3) describe briefly the substance of the action, 4) address whether there are legal or factual issues whose early resolution might appreciably reduce the scope of the dispute or contribute significantly to settlement negotiations, and 5) identify the discovery that promises to contribute most to equipping the parties for meaningful settlement negotiations.

B. The parties attach to their written evaluation statements copies of documents out of which the action arose (e.g., contracts) or the availability of which would materially advance the purposes of the evaluation session (e.g., medical reports or documents by which special damages might be determined).

C. The written evaluations are not filed with the Court and/or shown to the assigned judge.

Special Provisions for Patent, Copyright, and Trademark Cases

A Patent Cases: In a case where a party is basing claims on a patent, that party must attach to its written statement an element-by-element analysis of the relationship between the applicable claims in the patent and the allegedly infringing product. In addition, each party who asserts a patent claim must describe in its written statement its theory or theories of damages and must set forth as much information that supports each theory as is then available. Any party who asserts a defense against the patent based on "prior art" must attach an exhibit that identifies each known example of alleged prior art and that describes the relationship between each such example of prior art and the claims of the patent. In addition, if such party denies infringement, it must describe the basis for such denial.

B. Copyright Cases: A party who bases a claim on copyright must include as exhibits the copyright registration and exemplars of both the copyrighted work and the allegedly infringing work(s), and must make a systematic comparison showing points of similarity. Such party also must present whatever direct or indirect evidence it has of copying, and must indicate whether it intends to elect statutory or actual damages. Each party in a copyright case who is accused of infringing must set forth in its written statement the dollar volume of sales of and profits from the allegedly infringing works that it and any entities for which it is legally responsible have made.

C. Trademark Cases: A party who bases a claim on trademark or trade dress infringement, or on other unfair competition, must include as an exhibit its registration, if any, exemplars of both its use of its mark and use of the allegedly infringing mark, both including a description or representation of the goods or services on or in connection with which the marks are used, and any evidence it has of actual confusion. If "secondary meaning" is in issue, such a party also must describe the nature and extent of the advertising it has done with its mark and the volume of goods it has sold under its mark. Both parties must describe in their evaluation statements how the consuming public is exposed to their respective marks and goods or services, including, if available, photographic or other demonstrative evidence. Each party in a trademark or unfair competition case who is accused of infringement must set forth the dollar volume or sales of and profits from goods or services bearing the allegedly infringing mark.

Duration of the Evaluation Process

The process may involve a minimum of one session or several, at the discretion of the evaluator, counsel and the parties. Parties are free to continue the process as long as they feel it is productive.

Attendance at the Evaluation Session

The *parties themselves* must attend the evaluation session. A party other than a natural person (e.g., a corporation or association) satisfies this attendance requirement if it is represented at the session by a person (other than outside counsel) with ultimate authority to bind the party to terms of a settlement. A party that is a unit of government need not have present at the session the persons who would be required to approve a settlement before it could become final (e.g., the members of a city council or the chief executive of a major agency), but must send to the session an executive officer, in addition to counsel, knowledgeable about the facts of the case and the governmental unit's position. In cases involving insurance carriers, representatives of the insurance companies, with ultimate authority, must attend the evaluation session. A party or lawyer will be excused from attending the evaluation session only after a showing that attendance would impose an extraordinary or otherwise unjustifiable hardship.

Status of Discovery and Motions During Evaluation Process

Any case referred to early neutral evaluation continues to be subject to management by the judge to whom it is assigned. Unless otherwise ordered, parties are not precluded from filing pretrial motions or pursuing discovery.

Evaluation Logistics and Location

A. The evaluator has considerable discretion in structuring the evaluation session. The session proceeds informally. Rules of evidence do not apply. There is no formal examination or cross examination of witnesses.

B. The evaluator permits each party to make an oral presentation; helps identify areas of agreement; assesses the relative strengths and weaknesses of the parties' positions and evidence, giving reasons; estimates the likelihood of liability and the dollar range of damages.

C. The evaluator may assist parties to explore the possibility of settlement; to draft stipulations where agreement is reached; to devise a plan for sharing the important information and/or to conduct the key discovery or to posture the case for disposition by other means, and to determine if some form of follow-up to the session would contribute to the case development process or to settlement.

Filing of Evaluation Outcome

At the conclusion of evaluation, if settlement is reached, the evaluator helps the parties draft a settlement agreement, along with a stipulation and proposed order to dismiss, which is then filed with the Court. If settlement is not reached, the parties have seven (7) days to inform the evaluator whether they desire to continue with the early neutral evaluation process. Within seven (7) days of the completion of evaluation, the evaluator files a brief report with the ADR Administrator, with copies to all parties. The report indicates only who participated in the evaluation session, and whether settlement was reached, or in the event of no settlement, whether the process will be continuing. The ADR Administrator is responsible for keeping the Court informed of the status of the early neutral evaluation process.

Confidentiality

All evaluation proceedings are considered to be compromise negotiations within the meaning of Fed. R. Evid. 408.

COURT ADMINISTRATION OF THE EARLY NEUTRAL EVALUATION PROGRAM

Administrative Structure

The early neutral evaluation program is administered by the Clerk's Office. Problems are initially handled by the ADR Administrator.

Evaluation of the Program

The ADR Administrator gathers data relevant to a careful, in-depth analysis of the efficacy of the program, and reports to the Court on a regular basis. In an effort to gather information, the Court may develop questionnaires for participants, counsel and evaluators, to be completed and returned at the close of the evaluation process. Responses will be kept confidential and not divulged to the Court, the attorneys or the parties. Only aggregate information about the program will be reported.

[Amended effective January, 2010.]

CASE EVALUATION PROGRAM DESCRIPTION

Definition

Case evaluation affords litigants an ADR process patterned after that extensively used in the state courts of Michigan. *See* MICH. COMP. LAWS §§ 600.4951–.4969; MICH. CT. R. 2.403. Case evaluation principally involves establishment of the settlement value of a case by a panel of three attorneys.

Authorization

W.D. Mich. LCivR 16.5

THE CASE EVALUATORS

List of Case Evaluators

The ADR Administrator maintains current lists of case evaluators certified by practice area for the Northern and Southern Divisions and updates the lists from time to time in order to maintain the minimum number of evaluators established by the Court. The ADR Administrator appoints evaluators for standard track case evaluations from these lists.

Certification of Case Evaluators

Standard Track—A certified case evaluator:

    1) is a member in good standing of the Bar of this Court with ten (10) years practice experience;

    2) agrees to serve *pro bono* on at least one case per year, and

    3) has acted as a case evaluator three times, in either state or federal court, in a particular substantive area in the previous five (5) years to be certified in that area.

Blue Ribbon Track: Not certified by the Court.

Disqualification Rules

No person serves as a case evaluator in any action in which any of the circumstances specified in 28 U.S.C. § 455 exist, or, in good faith, is believed to exist.

Immunity

Case evaluators are entitled to quasi-judicial immunity as officers of the Court.

CASE SELECTION

Eligible Cases

All civil cases in which damages are sought, except social security cases, are eligible for case evaluation. Certain tort cases in which the rule of decision is supplied by Michigan law must be submitted to case evaluation, unless the parties have agreed to use voluntary facilitative mediation.

Referral Method and Notice to Parties

In preparation for the initial Rule 16 scheduling conference, all parties are required to discuss the use of alternative dispute resolution and indicate their preference in the joint status report. Qualified cases may be referred to case evaluation with or without the parties' consent.

Selection of Case Evaluators

Standard Track: Case evaluators are selected by the ADR Administrator.

Blue Ribbon: Case evaluators are selected by the parties.

Compensation of Evaluators

A. Standard Panel: Within seven (7) days after the mailing of the notice of case evaluation hearing, each plaintiff and each defendant pays each case evaluator the sum of two hundred dollars ($200.00) for a total of three hundred dollars ($600.00) per party. Proof of payment must be filed with the ADR Administrator upon payment.

    1) Multiple parties, derivative claims: Multiple parties with derivative claims (e.g., husband/wife or parent/child) are treated as one party. Multiple parties, non-derivative claims: Each party shall

pay the sum of six hundred dollars ($600.00) for each award. However, in those cases in which an attorney certifies at the time of paying the case evaluation fees that the attorney represents multiple parties without conflict of interest and that there presently exists a substantial unity of interest between the parties on all issues, the parties may pay one fee. The case evaluation may include one lump sum award or separate awards to these parties, or a combination thereof, in the panel's discretion.

2) Multiple claims by members of a single family: When the plaintiffs are members of a single family, they may elect to treat the case as involving one claim, with the payment of one fee and the rendering of one lump sum award to be accepted or rejected. If no such election is made, a separate fee must be paid by each plaintiff, and the case evaluation panel will then make separate awards for each claim.

3) A party failing to pay fees within the time designated must pay an additional fee of fifty dollars ($50.00) per evaluator. If any evaluator waives this fee, it is paid to the Court instead.

B.   Blue Ribbon Panel: Evaluators are paid their normal hourly rate, to be assessed in as many equal parts as there are separately represented parties, or as otherwise agreed by the parties at the time the case is submitted to evaluation. The evaluators bill counsel directly.

C.   Noncompliance: In the event of noncompliance, a case evaluator may petition the Court for an order directing payment of fees.

Chairperson

Each case evaluation panel has a chairperson. The ADR Administrator chooses the chairperson for standard track case evaluation; the attorneys agree on a chairperson for Blue Ribbon mediation. The duties of the chairperson are:

A.   presiding at the case evaluation session to ensure a fair and orderly presentation;

B.   filing with the ADR Administrator and serving upon all parties the evaluation award, with proof of service; and

C.   in Blue Ribbon evaluation only, coordinating the scheduling of hearings and deciding whether a request for an adjournment should be granted and, if so, coordinating the rescheduled evaluation session with the other evaluators and counsel, and filing and serving the notice thereof.

Timing for the Case Evaluation Hearing

Within a time frame fixed by the Court:

A.   Standard Track: Plaintiff's counsel coordinates a specific time, date and place for the case evaluation hearing. The hearing is held in a suitably neutral setting (e.g., at the office of an evaluator or in the courthouse). Plaintiff's counsel files with the ADR Administrator and serves upon all parties the notice of hearing. Thereafter, adjournments of the hearing are by unanimous stipulation only.

B.   Blue Ribbon Track: The chairperson in consultation with the parties and evaluators, arranges the date, time and place of the case evaluation hearing. The chairperson files with the ADR Administrator and serves upon all parties the notice of hearing. Thereafter, the chairperson may grant an adjournment of the case evaluation session for good cause, within the time limit set by the Court. The chairperson is responsible for coordinating the scheduling of the original or adjourned session and for filing with the ADR Administrator and serving a notice of the date and time thereof.

C.   Any notices of hearing or adjournment may be made by e-mail.

Timing and Nature of Submissions Required Before the Case Evaluation Session

A.   *Standard Track:* Not less than fourteen (14) days before the evaluation session, each party provides each evaluator with a written evaluation statement, with copies to all counsel and a proof of service to the ADR Administrator. The evaluation statement must not exceed twenty (20) pages, and any attachments to the brief must not exceed twenty (20) pages. Failure to submit such documents in a timely manner subjects the offending party or attorney to a one hundred fifty dollar ($150.00) penalty.

B.   *Blue Ribbon Track:* There are no limits for the filing of case evaluation briefs or their length, unless agreed to in writing by all parties.

Status of Discovery and Motions During Case Evaluation Process

Any case referred to case evaluation continues to be subject to management by the judge to whom it is assigned. Unless otherwise ordered, parties are not precluded from filing pretrial motions or pursuing discovery.

Procedure at the Case Evaluation Hearing

A. The parties may attend but do not actively participate. If scars, disfigurement, or other conditions exist, that may be demonstrated to the panel by a personal appearance. However, no testimony is taken or permitted of any party.

B. The rules of evidence do not apply before the case evaluation panel. Factual information having a bearing on damages or liability must be supported by documentary evidence, if possible.

C. Oral presentation:

1) Standard Track: Each attorney is limited to 30 minutes oral presentation.

2) Blue Ribbon Track: Oral presentations are not limited.

Panel's Decision

A. At the conclusion of the hearing, the panel will make a written evaluation and personally serve a copy upon each party. In an extraordinary case, where the award cannot reasonably be rendered at the conclusion of the hearing, the evaluators in a Blue Ribbon evaluation may render their written evaluation within seven days of the conclusion of the hearing. In such circumstances, the chairperson is responsible for serving a copy on each party, with proof of service. The original evaluation is forwarded to the ADR Administrator. This document may not be electronically filed.

B. The evaluation must include a separate award as to the plaintiff's claim against each defendant and as to each cross-claim, counterclaim, or third-party claim that has been filed in the action. All such claims filed by any one party against any other party are treated as a single claim.

C. The evaluation may not include a separate award on any claim for equitable relief, but the panel may consider such claims in determining the amount of an award.

D. In a tort case to which MICH. COMP. LAWS § 600.4915(2) or MICH. COMP. LAWS § 600.4963(2) applies, if the panel unanimously finds that a party's action or defense as to any other party is frivolous, the panel must so indicate on the evaluation. For these purposes, an action or defense is "frivolous" if, as to all of a plaintiff's claims or all of a defendant's defenses to liability, at least one of the following conditions is met:

1) The party's primary purpose in initiating the action or asserting the defense was to harass, embarrass, or injure the opposing party;

2) The party had no reasonable basis to believe that the facts underlying that party's legal position were in fact true; or

3) The party's legal position was devoid of arguable legal merit.

E. In an action alleging medical malpractice to which MICH. COMP. LAWS § 600.4915 applies, the evaluation must include a specific finding that:

1) there has been a breach of the applicable standard of care;

2) there has not been a breach of the applicable standard of care; or

3) reasonable minds could differ as to whether there has been a breach of the applicable standard of care.

Acceptance or Rejection of the Case Evaluation

F. Each party must file with the ADR Administrator a written acceptance or rejection of the panel's evaluation within 28 days after service of the panel's evaluation. If there are separate awards on multiple claims, each party must either accept or reject the evaluation in its entirety as to each opposing party. The failure to file a written acceptance or rejection within 28 days constitutes rejection.

G. There must be no disclosure of a party's acceptance or rejection of the panel's evaluation until the expiration of the 28–day period, at which time the ADR Administrator sends a notice indicating each party's acceptance or rejection of the panel's evaluation.

H. In case evaluations involving multiple parties the following rules apply:

1) Each party has the option of accepting all of the awards covering the claims by or against that party or of accepting some and rejecting others. However, as to any particular opposing party, the party must either accept or reject the evaluation in its entirety.

2) A party who accepts all of the awards may specifically indicate that he or she intends the acceptance to be effective only if all opposing parties accept, or only if the opposing parties accept as to specified coparties. If such a limitation is not included in the acceptance, an accepting party is deemed to have agreed to entry of judgment or dismissal as provided below [Effect of acceptance of evaluation, ¶A] as to that party and those of the opposing parties who accept, with the action to continue between the accepting party and those opposing parties who reject.

3) If a party makes a limited acceptance under the preceding provision [¶C. 2 *above*], and some of the opposing parties accept and others reject, for the purposes of the cost provisions [Rejecting party's liability for costs, *below*] the party who made the limited acceptance is deemed to have rejected as to those opposing parties who accept.

Effect of Acceptance of Evaluation

A. If all of the parties accept the panel's evaluation, judgment will be entered in accordance with the evaluation unless the amount of the award is paid within 28 days after notification of the acceptances, in which case the Court dismisses the action with prejudice. The judgment or dismissal is deemed to dispose of all claims in the action and includes all fees, costs, and interest to the date it is entered.

B. In a case involving multiple parties, judgment or dismissal is entered as to those opposing parties who have accepted the portions of the evaluation that apply to them.

Proceedings after Rejection

A. If all or part of the evaluation by the panel is rejected, the action proceeds to trial as to all remaining claims.

B. If the panel finds a party's claim or defense to be frivolous, that party may request that the Court review the panel's finding by filing a motion within 14 days after the ADR Administrator sends notice of the rejection.

1) The motion must be submitted to the Court on the case evaluation summaries and documents that were considered by the case evaluation panel. No other exhibits or testimony may be submitted. However, oral argument on the motion is permitted.

2) After reviewing the material submitted, the Court determines whether the action or defense is frivolous.

3) If the Court agrees with the panel's determination, the provisions below [C.] apply, except that the bond must be filed within 28 days after the entry of the Court's order determining the action or defense to be frivolous.

4) The judge who hears a motion under this provision may not preside at a nonjury trial of the action.

C. Unless the finding is overturned by the Court, if the panel finds unanimously a party's claim or defense to be frivolous in a tort case governed by Mich. Comp. Laws 600.4915(2) or Mich. Comp. Laws § 600.4963(2) [Panel's decision, ¶ D.], that party must post a cash or surety bond in the amount of $5,000 for each party against whom the action or defense was determined to be frivolous.

1) The bond must be posted within 56 days after the case evaluation hearing or at least 14 days before trial, whichever is earlier.

2) If a surety bond is filed, an insurance company that insures the defendant against a claim made in the action may not act as the surety.

3) If the bond is not posted as required, the Court dismisses a claim found to have been frivolous, or enters a default of a defendant whose defense was found to be frivolous. The action proceeds to trial as to the remaining claims and parties, and as to the amount of damages against a defendant in default.

4) If judgment is entered against the party who posted the bond, the bond shall be used to pay any costs awarded against that party by the Court under any applicable law or court rule.

D. The ADR Administrator places a copy of the case evaluation and the parties' acceptances and rejections in a sealed envelope for filing with the Clerk of the Court. In a nonjury action, the envelope may not be opened and the parties may not reveal the amount of the evaluation until the judge has rendered judgment.

Rejecting Party's Liability for Costs

A. If a party has rejected an evaluation and the action proceeds to verdict, that party must pay the opposing party's actual costs unless the verdict is more favorable to the rejecting party than the case evaluation. However, if the opposing party has also rejected the evaluation, that party is entitled to costs only if the verdict is more favorable to that party than the case evaluation.

B. For the purpose of this provision, "verdict" includes 1) a jury verdict, 2) a judgment by the Court after a nonjury trial, and 3) a judgment entered as a result of a ruling on a motion after rejection of the case evaluation.

C. For the purpose of this provision, a verdict must be adjusted by adding to it assessable costs and interest on the amount of the verdict from the filing of the complaint to the date of the case evaluation, and, if applicable, by making the adjustment of future damages as provided by MICH. COMP. LAWS § 600.6306. After this adjustment, the verdict is considered more favorable to a defendant if it is more than 10 percent below the evaluation, and it is considered more favorable to the plaintiff if it is more than 10 percent above the evaluation. If the evaluation was zero, a verdict finding that a defendant is not liable to the plaintiff is deemed more favorable to the defendant.

D. In cases involving multiple parties, the following rules apply:

1) Except as provided below [D.2], in determining whether the verdict is more favorable to a party than the case evaluation, the Court considers only the amount of the evaluation and adjusted verdict as to the particular pair of parties, rather than the aggregate evaluation or verdict as to all parties. However, costs may not be imposed on a plaintiff who obtains an aggregate adjusted verdict more favorable to the plaintiff than the aggregate evaluation.

2) If the verdict against more than one defendant is based on their joint and several liability, the plaintiff may not recover costs unless the verdict is more favorable to the plaintiff than the total case evaluation as to those defendants, and a defendant may not recover costs unless the verdict is more favorable to that defendant than the case evaluation as to that defendant.

3) Except as provided below [J], in a personal injury action, the verdict against a particular defendant is not adjusted by applying that defendant's proportion of fault as determined under MICH. COMP. LAWS § 600.6304(1)–(2).

E. If the verdict awards equitable relief, costs may be awarded if the Court determines that taking into account both monetary relief (adjusted as provided above [C]) and equitable relief, the verdict is not more favorable to the rejecting party than the evaluation, and that it is fair to award costs under all of the circumstances.

F. For the purpose of this provision, "actual costs" include only those costs taxable in any civil action. The party entitled to recover actual costs shall be considered the prevailing party for the purpose of determining taxable costs.

G. Costs shall not be awarded if the case evaluation award was not unanimous.

H. A request for costs under this provision must be filed and served within 14 days after the entry of the judgment or entry of an order denying a timely motion for a new trial or to set aside the judgment.

I. In an action governed by MICH. COMP. LAWS § 436.22, if the plaintiff rejects the award against the minor or alleged intoxicated person, or is deemed to have rejected such an award under "Acceptance or Rejection of the Case Evaluation" above, the Court does not award costs against the plaintiff in favor of the minor or alleged intoxicated person unless it finds that the rejection was not motivated by the need to comply with Mich. Comp. Laws § 436.22(6).

J. A verdict awarding damages for personal injury, property damage, or wrongful death shall be adjusted for relative fault as provided by MICH. COMP. LAWS § 600.6304.

K. If the verdict is the result of a motion as provided above [B.3], the Court may, in the interest of justice, refuse to award actual costs.

Taxation of Attorney's Fees as Costs

A. In diversity tort cases where Michigan law provides the rule of decision, this Court has determined that the state statute and court rules requiring case evaluation form a part of state substantive law. Such tort cases will be referred to mandatory case evaluation, unless the parties unanimously agree to Voluntary Facilitative Mediation. In all tort cases ordered to mandatory case evaluation, the provisions of Rule 2.403 governing liability for costs, including taxation of a reasonable attorney fee for rejection of a case evaluation award, apply.

B. In any case referred to case evaluation, the parties may stipulate in writing to the taxation of attorney fees as costs pursuant to Mich. Ct. Rule 2.403(O)(6). Such stipulation must be filed before the mediation award is rendered.

Confidentiality

All case evaluation proceedings are considered compromise negotiations within the meaning of Fed. R. Evid. 408.

COURT ADMINISTRATION OF THE CASE EVALUATION PROGRAM

Administrative Structure

The case evaluation program is administered by the Clerk's Office. Problems are initially handled by the ADR Administrator.

Evaluation of the Program

The ADR Administrator gathers data relevant to a careful, in-depth analysis of the efficacy of the program, and reports to the Court on a regular basis. In an effort to gather information, the Court may develop questionnaires for participants, counsel and evaluators, to be completed and returned at the close of the evaluation process. Responses will be kept confidential and not divulged to the Court, the attorneys or the parties. Only aggregate information about the program will be reported.

[Amended effective January, 2010; October 26, 2016.]

STANDARDS FOR CIVILITY IN PROFESSIONAL CONDUCT

PREAMBLE

An attorney's conduct should be characterized at all times by personal courtesy and professional integrity in the fullest sense of those terms. In fulfilling our duty to represent a client vigorously as attorneys, we will be mindful of our obligations to the administration of justice, which is a truth-seeking process designed to resolve human and societal problems in a rational, peaceful and efficient manner.

Uncivil, abrasive, abusive, hostile or obstructive conduct impedes the fundamental goal of resolving disputes rationally, peacefully and efficiently. Incivility tends to delay, and often deny, justice.

A judicial officer's conduct should be characterized at all times by courtesy and patience toward all participants. Judicial officers owe all participants in a legal proceeding respect, diligence and punctuality. Judicial officers should lead by example.

These standards are designed to encourage attorneys and judicial officers to meet our obligations to each other, to litigants and to the system of justice, and thereby achieve the twin goals of civility and professionalism, both of which are hallmarks of a learned profession dedicated to public service.

Civility and professionalism are hallmarks of a learned profession dedicated to public service. The lawyers and judicial officers of this district are firmly committed to meet their obligations of civility and professionalism to each other, to litigants, and to the system of justice.

These standards are voluntary and shall not be used as a basis for litigation or sanctions. However, it is expected that all lawyers and judicial officers will make a commitment to adhere to these standards in all aspects of their dealings with one another and with other participants in the legal process.

These standards should be incorporated as an integral component of the teaching of professionalism to law students and practicing lawyers alike. Copies may be made available to clients to reinforce our obligation to maintain and foster these standards.

ATTORNEYS' RESPONSIBILITIES TO OTHER COUNSEL

1. We will treat all other counsel, parties and witnesses in a civil and courteous manner, not only in court, but also in all other written and oral communications.

2. We will not, even when called upon by a client to do so, abuse, or indulge in offensive conduct directed to other counsel, parties or witnesses. We will abstain from disparaging personal remarks or acrimony toward other counsel, parties, or witnesses.

3. We will not encourage or knowingly authorize any person under our control to engage in conduct that would be uncivil if we were to engage in such conduct.

4. We will not, absent good cause, attribute bad motives or improper conduct to other counsel or bring the profession into disrepute by unfounded accusations of impropriety.

5. We will avoid ex parte communications with the court or tribunal, including the judge's staff, on pending matters, except when permitted by law.

6. Honesty and fair dealing are integral components of civility. Promises and agreements fairly reached, whether orally or in writing, will be adhered to in good faith. When reiterating oral promises or agreements in writing, counsel shall fairly, completely and in good faith restate all elements of the parties' oral agreement.

7. We will endeavor to confer early with other counsel to assess settlement possibilities. We will not falsely hold out the possibility of settlement as a means to adjourn discovery or to delay trial.

8. In civil actions, we will stipulate to relevant matters if they are undisputed and if no good-faith advocacy basis exists for not stipulating.

9. We will not use any form of discovery or discovery scheduling as a means of harassment, or for any other improper purpose.

10. We will make good faith efforts to resolve by agreement our objections to matters contained in pleadings, discovery requests and objections.

450

11. We will not time the filing or service of motions or pleadings in any way that unfairly limits another party's opportunity to respond.

12. We will not request an extension of time solely for the purpose of unjustified delay.

13. We will consult other counsel regarding scheduling matters in a good-faith effort to avoid scheduling conflicts.

14. We will endeavor to accommodate previously scheduled dates for hearings, depositions, meetings, conferences, vacations, seminars or other functions of other counsel.

15. We will notify other counsel and, if appropriate, the Court or other persons, at the earliest possible time when hearings, depositions, meetings or conferences are to be canceled or postponed.

16. We accept primary responsibility, after consultation with the client, for making decisions about procedural agreements. We will explain to our clients that cooperation between counsel in such matters is the professional norm and may be in the clients' interests. We will explain the nature of the matter at issue in any such proposed agreements and explain how such agreements do not compromise the clients' interests.

17. We will take depositions only when actually needed to ascertain facts or information or to perpetuate testimony. We will not take depositions for the purposes of harassment or to increase litigation expenses.

18. We will not engage in any conduct during a deposition that is inappropriate under court rule or rule of evidence, including:

(a) obstructive questioning;

(b) inappropriate objections;

(c) irrelevant questioning.

19. Document requests and interrogatories shall be drafted in accordance with court rule, without placing an undue burden or expense on any party.

20. Responses to document requests and interrogatories shall be submitted in accordance with the court rules, fairly meeting the request or question without strained interpretation. We will not produce documents or answer interrogatories in a manner designed to hide or obscure the existence of particular documents or information.

21. We will base discovery objections on the court rules or rules of evidence, without withholding disclosable information.

22. When a draft order is to be prepared by counsel to reflect a court ruling, we will draft an order that accurately and completely reflects the court's ruling. We will promptly prepare and submit a proposed order to other counsel and attempt to reconcile any differences before the draft order is presented to the court.

23. We will not ascribe a position to other counsel that counsel has not taken, or otherwise seek to create an unjustified inference based on counsel's statements or conduct.

ATTORNEYS' RESPONSIBILITIES TO THE COURT

1. We will speak and write civilly and respectfully in all communications with the Court.

2. We will be punctual and prepared for all Court appearances so that all hearings, conferences and trials may commence on time; if delayed, we will notify the Court and counsel, if possible.

3. We will be considerate of the time constraints and pressures on the Court and Court staff inherent in their efforts to administer justice.

4. We will not engage in conduct that brings disorder or disruption to the courtroom. We will advise our clients and witnesses appearing in Court of the proper conduct expected and, to the best of our ability, prevent our clients and witnesses from creating disorder or disruption.

5. We will not knowingly misrepresent, mischaracterize, misquote or miscite facts or authorities in any oral or written communication.

6. We will act and speak civilly to marshals, clerks, court reporters, secretaries and law clerks with an awareness that they, too, are an integral part of the judicial system.

COURT'S RESPONSIBILITIES TO ATTORNEYS AND LITIGANTS

1.   We will be courteous, respectful, and civil to lawyers, parties, agency personnel, and witnesses. We will maintain control of the proceedings, recognizing that judges have both the obligation and the authority to ensure that judicial proceedings are conducted with dignity, decorum and courtesy.

2.   We will not employ hostile, demeaning or humiliating words in opinions or in written or oral communications with attorneys, parties or witnesses.

3.   We will be punctual in convening hearings, meetings and conferences; if delayed, we will notify counsel, if possible.

4.   In scheduling hearings, meetings and conferences, we will be considerate of time schedules of lawyers, parties, and witnesses and of other courts and tribunals. We will inform counsel promptly of any rescheduling, postponement, or cancellation of hearings, meetings, or conferences.

5.   We will make reasonable efforts to decide promptly matters presented to us for decision.

6.   While endeavoring to resolve disputes efficiently, we will be considerate of the time constraints and pressures imposed on attorneys.

7.   We recognize that a lawyer has a right and duty to present a cause fully and properly, and that a litigant has a right to a fair and impartial hearing. Within the practical limits of time, we will allow lawyers to present proper arguments, to make a complete and accurate record, and to represent a case free from unreasonable or unnecessary judicial interruption. At an appropriate time and in an appropriate manner, we will bring to a lawyer's attention conduct which we observe that is inconsistent with these standards.

8.   We will not impugn the integrity or professionalism of any attorney on the basis of the clients whom, or the causes, which, an attorney represents.

9.   We will do our best to insure that court personnel act civilly toward attorneys, parties and witnesses.

JUDICIAL OFFICERS' RESPONSIBILITIES TO EACH OTHER

1.   We will be courteous, respectful and civil regarding opinions, written or oral, authored by another judicial officer.

2.   In all written and oral communications, we will abstain from disparaging personal remarks or criticisms about another judicial officer.

3.   We will endeavor to work with other judicial officers in an effort to foster a spirit of cooperation in our mutual goal of enhancing the administration of justice.

[Dated: May 29, 2003.]

PRIVACY POLICY FOR TRANSCRIPTS

Whereas, recent resolutions were imposed by the United States Judicial Conference at its September 2007 and March 2008 sessions, enforcing redaction requirements on electronically filed transcripts;

Whereas, the Judicial Conference has directed that its policies be implemented by May 15, 2008;

NOW THEREFORE, the attached Policy and Procedure Regarding Electronic Availability of Transcripts shall be effective immediately.

On December 1, 2007, amendments to the Federal Civil, Criminal and Appellate Rules of Procedure took effect, implementing privacy requirements of the E–Government Act of 2002. The amendments to Fed. R. Civ. P. 5.2, Fed. R. Crim. P. 49.1, and Fed. R. App. P. 25(a)(5) require that personal identification information be redacted from documents filed with the court. This includes Social Security numbers, taxpayer identification numbers, names of minor children, financial account numbers, dates of birth, and in criminal cases, home addresses. In September 2007 and March 2008, the Judicial Conference approved procedures for applying redaction requirements to transcripts of court proceedings. In early 2008, an upgrade to the CM/ECF software provided the ability to implement these procedures.

As used in this policy, the term

- "transcript" means the official record of federal courtroom proceedings. This policy does not apply to sealed transcripts and other transcripts, such as those of depositions or of proceedings of state courts or other jurisdictions. Other transcripts are subject to the rules and redaction requirements applicable to other filings by parties.

- "counsel of record" means an attorney who has appeared on behalf of a client, including an attorney serving as "standby" counsel appointed to assist a pro se defendant in the defense of a criminal case.

I. FILING AND INITIAL ACCESS TO TRANSCRIPT

A. Filing of Transcript. Under 28 U.S.C. § 753(b), the court reporter or transcriber must deliver promptly a certified copy of any transcript to the clerk of court for the records of the court. The court reporter, contract court reporter, or transcriber will electronically file the official transcript in CM/ECF. Notice of this filing will be sent electronically to all registered counsel of record. The Notice of Electronic Filing (NEF) informs parties and registered attorneys of the redaction requirements, the 90–day restriction, and how to obtain the transcript during the restriction period. This notice will be sent manually by the clerk to unregistered attorneys and pro se parties.

B. Initial Access to Transcript. For a period of 90 days[1] after filing, access to the transcript document will be restricted to:

- court staff
- public terminal users
- counsel of record or parties who have purchased the transcript from the court reporter/transcriber and who have requested remote electronic access to same; and
- other persons as directed by the court, e.g., appellate attorneys

During this 90–day period, court staff may not copy or print the transcript for a requester. All requests for the transcript during this time will be referred to the court reporter or transcriber.

II. REDACTION REQUIREMENT

A. Responsibility to Review Transcript.

1. The responsibility of reviewing transcripts and identifying items for redaction rests solely with counsel of record.[2] Unless otherwise ordered by the court, counsel of record must review the following portions[3] within 14 days of the filing of the transcript:

- opening and closing statements made on the party's behalf;
- statements of the party;
- testimony of any witnesses called by the party;
- all voir dire; and
- any other portion of the transcript as ordered by the court

2. Counsel of record must identify the following personal data identifiers eligible for mandatory redaction:

- Social Security numbers
- taxpayer identification numbers
- names of minor children
- financial account numbers
- dates of birth
- in criminal cases, home addresses

B. Notice of Intent. Parties will have fourteen (14) days from the date of filing of the transcript within which to file with the court a Notice of Intent to Request Redaction of the transcript. The notice of intent must not contain any redaction information, but shall only state a party's intent to redact. Any party needing to review the transcript for redaction purposes may purchase a copy from the court reporter/transcriber, or view the transcript at the courthouse using the public terminal located in the lobby of the Clerk's office.

A hard copy of the notice of intent must be served upon the court reporter or transcriber manually, and a proof of service must be filed electronically. If no notice of intent is filed within the allotted time, the court will assume redaction of personal data identifiers from the transcript is not necessary.

Filing a notice of intent does not in any way prevent a transcript from being made public at the expiration of the 90 days. If a notice of intent to redact is filed, and no subsequent request for redaction is filed, the transcript will be available to the public at the expiration of the 90–day deadline.

C. Request for Redaction.

1. *Party Responsibility.* Any party requesting redaction must file a request within 21 days[4] of the filing of the transcript. The request must specify all personal data identifiers to be redacted and identify where each one appears in the transcript, by page and line number. For example:

Redact the Social Security number 123–45–6789 appearing on page 10, line 11 to read xxx–xx–6789.

Access to the redaction request in CM/ECF will be restricted to the case participants. A hard copy of the redaction request must be served upon the court reporter or transcriber manually, and a proof of service must be filed electronically.

2. *Court Reporter/Transcriber Responsibility.* When a request for redaction is served upon the court reporter or transcriber, he or she must, within 31 days of the filing of the original transcript, perform the requested redactions and electronically file a redacted version of the transcript with the clerk of court. Unless otherwise ordered, the court reporter/transcriber shall redact eligible items identified by counsel of record in a request for redaction document as follows:

- Social Security numbers to the last four digits;
- financial account numbers to the last four digits;
- taxpayer identification numbers to the last four digits;
- dates of birth to the year;
- names of minor children to the initials; and
- home addresses to the city and state.

D. Extensions of Time. Extensions of time to comply with the deadlines set forth in this procedure will <u>not</u> be routinely granted, especially when an extension might delay Court of Appeals proceedings.

III.   AVAILABILITY OF TRANSCRIPT

A.   Transcripts Not Requiring Redaction. At the expiration of the 90–day restriction period, if there are no redaction requests or motions related to the transcript, the transcript will be made available for remote electronic access via PACER. PACER charges will apply as outlined in section (C)(2) below.

B.   Transcripts Requiring Redaction. After making all requested redactions, the court reporter/transcriber will electronically file a redacted transcript. The original transcript will remain restricted and only the redacted transcript will be available for remote access via PACER at the expiration of the 90–day restriction period.

If redaction is identified by the parties or counsel of record after the 90–day restriction period has already elapsed, redaction will only occur as ordered by the court.

C.   Remote Electronic Access.

1.   During the 90–day restriction period, remote electronic access will be limited as set forth in I(B). Case participants who purchase the transcript and desire remote electronic access to the document through CM/ECF must submit a written request to the court reporter or transcriber in order to be provided such access.

2.   PACER charges will apply for the entire transcript; there is no 30–page cap. The user will incur PACER charges each time a transcript is accessed, even though the user may have previously purchased it from the court reporter and obtained remote access through CM/ECF.

3.   Members of the public, including the news media, who purchase a transcript during the 90–day restriction period will <u>not</u> be granted remote electronic access during the restriction period. Remote electronic access will be available as set forth in III(A) and III(B) of this policy.

IV.   TRIAL TRANSCRIPTS

To avoid unnecessary effort and expense to the parties and the Court, counsel of record shall meet and confer regarding the anticipated use of personal identification information at trial. If personal identification information may be offered at trial, counsel shall, at the time of the final pretrial conference, electronically file a stipulated redaction request, identifying such personal identification information to be used at trial and authorizing the court reporter to automatically redact the references in the original transcript in the manner required by Fed. R. Civ. P. 5.2(a)(1) through (4) or Fed. R. Crim. P. 49.1(a)(1) through (5). At the commencement of trial, counsel of record shall manually serve a hard copy of the stipulation upon the court reporter, or if the proceeding is to be digitally recorded, upon the courtroom deputy. A proof of service must be filed electronically.

V.   REPRESENTATION UNDER CJA

An attorney representing a criminal defendant under the Criminal Justice Act (CJA), including an attorney serving as standby counsel, is entitled to compensation under the CJA for functions reasonably performed to fulfill the obligation to review and redact transcripts, and for reimbursement for related reasonable expenses, including the following:

- traveling to gain access to the transcript, if needed;
- reviewing a transcript to determine whether to file notice of intent to redact;
- filing a notice of intent to redact or a motion for an extension of time;
- reviewing a transcript to determine the location of information to be redacted;
- preparing and filing a redaction request or motion; and
- other actions (including creating pleadings, attending hearings or other follow–up).

The attorney is also entitled to reimbursement under the CJA for the costs of obtaining a transcript for purposes of review. In a closed case involving CJA representation in which the original attorney or standby counsel is no longer available, new counsel may be appointed under the CJA and compensated as outlined above. In the event that the original appointed counsel is still available, but has filed a final voucher for the underlying case, the attorney shall be permitted to file a supplemental voucher for compensation.

[Effective May 15, 2008. Amended effective January 3, 2011.]

1 The 90–day period may be extended by the court.

2 The redaction responsibilities apply to counsel of record even if the requestor of the transcript is a judge or a member of the public/media. The court reporter, transcriber, and clerk's office staff have no obligation or responsibility in identifying redaction items.

3 If only a portion of the transcript is ordered, counsel of record is only responsible for reviewing those portions ordered.

4 The 21–day deadline may be extended by the court.

JUROR SELECTION PLAN

1. Declaration of Policy. All litigants entitled to trial by jury shall have the right to grand and petit juries selected at random from a fair cross-section of the community in the division where the court convenes. All qualified citizens within the District shall have the opportunity to be considered for service on the grand and petit juries of this Court, and shall have an obligation to serve as jurors when summoned for that purpose.

This Court utilizes the one-step summoning and qualification procedure, as authorized by 28 U.S.C. § 1878. Accordingly, jurors will be summoned and qualified in a single procedure.

2. Definitions. The definitions contained in 28 U.S.C. § 1869, as amended, will apply in this Juror Selection Plan (Plan) except:

a. "Division" means a set of counties deemed a unit for the purpose of defining the geographic area of the master jury wheels; and

b. "Chief Judge" includes his or her designee.

3. Discrimination Prohibited. No citizen shall be excluded from service as a grand, petit or summary trial juror in this Court on account of race, color, religion, sex, national origin or economic status.

4. Designation of Divisions and Applicability of Plan. The Western District of Michigan is divided into the following divisions for juror selection purposes and this plan applies to each of the listed Divisions, unless otherwise specifically indicated:

a. Southern Division at Grand Rapids comprising the counties of:

Antrim	Kent	Oceana
Benzie	Lake	Osceola
Charlevoix	Leelanau	Ottawa
Clinton	Manistee	Wexford
Eaton	Mason	
Emmet	Mecosta	
Grand Traverse	Missaukee	
Ingham	Montcalm	
Ionia	Muskegon	
Kalkaska	Newaygo	

b. Southern Division at Kalamazoo comprising the counties of:

Allegan	Branch	Kalamazoo
Barry	Calhoun	St. Joseph
Berrien	Cass	Van Buren

c. Southern Division at Lansing* comprising the counties of:

Branch	Eaton	Ingham
Clinton	Hillsdale	

d. Northern Division at Marquette comprising the counties of:

Alger	Gogebic	Mackinac
Baraga	Houghton	Marquette
Chippewa	Iron	Menominee
Delta	Keweenaw	Ontonagon
Dickinson	Luce	Schoolcraft

5. Management and Supervision of the Juror Selection Process.

a. The Clerk will manage the jury selection process under the supervision of the Chief Judge.

b. Orders of the Court relating to the general operation of the jury system and public notices concerning the drawing of names for assignment to grand, petit and summary jury panels will be available in the Clerk's Office, on the Court's website, and distributed to the judicial officers of the court.

6. Juror Selection Sources.

a.   Grand and petit jurors will be selected randomly from the merged lists, of the following data sources, after elimination of known duplicates:

    i.   registered voters in the Qualified Voter File compiled by the Michigan Secretary of State;

    ii.   persons over the age of 18 licensed by the Michigan Secretary of State to drive motor vehicles; and

    iii.   persons over the age of 18 who have been issued a personal identification card by the Michigan Secretary of State.

b.   The Clerk will obtain data sources in the electronic form most compatible with the computer hardware and software used by the Court for the random selection of names.

7. Random Selection.

a.   The Clerk may use electronic data processing systems for any tasks associated with the administration of the jury system including, but not limited to:

    i.   the random selection of names from the data sources for master jury wheels;

    ii.   the random selection of names of qualified jurors for grand, petit, and summary jury panels;

    iii.   the random assignment of prospective jurors to pools;

    iv.   the preparation of documents; and

    v.   statistical reports necessary for the efficient and effective administration of the jury system.

b.   For all purposes for which random selection is required by this plan, the Clerk will use a purely randomized process through a properly programmed electronic data processing system.

c.   If a contractor is used for any tasks associated with the administration of the jury system, the contractor will submit to the Court a certification that work has been completed pursuant to the detailed instructions from the Clerk.

d.   The selection of names from the source lists and the master jury wheels must ensure that the mathematical odds of any single name being picked is substantially equal.

8. Master Jury Wheels.

a.   The Clerk will maintain master jury wheels for each division.

b.   The Clerk will ensure that each county within a division is proportionally represented in the master jury wheel for that division in accordance with 28 U.S.C. § 1863. In creating the master jury wheels, the number of names drawn from each county shall be substantially in the same proportion to the total number drawn from all counties within the division as the number of names on that county's source lists bears to the total number of names on the source lists for all counties within a division.

c.   To increase the probability that the names and addresses on the data sources are as current as possible, the Clerk will empty and refill the master jury wheels every two (2) years, as soon as possible after the most recent federal general election held in the fall of even-numbered years. Jury panels already drawn, or jurors selected and sworn in for a particular case, shall continue to serve until this has been accomplished.

d.   The Chief Judge, upon recommendation of the Clerk will determine the total number of names to be selected at random from the data sources and placed in the master jury wheels.

e.   The minimum number of names to be placed in the respective master jury wheels is one thousand (1,000).

f.   If it should appear at any time that the names in a given master jury wheel will be exhausted before the prescribed time for refilling, the Chief Judge may order it refilled in advance of that time from the most recent source lists available. Such a refilling shall be in lieu of, and not in addition to, the next prescribed refilling.

9. Drawing of Names From the Master Jury Wheel.

a.   The Clerk will direct the random drawing of names of as many persons from the master jury wheels as may be needed to qualify and summon a sufficient number of jurors for a term of service.

b.   The number of names drawn will be determined by the Clerk based upon anticipated juror demands of the court, plus a margin of extra names sufficient to compensate for the estimated number that may be unavailable or ineligible.

c.   The Clerk will maintain records of the names drawn from the master jury wheels.

10.   Juror Summons and Qualification Forms. The Clerk will mail to each person drawn, a juror summons and qualification questionnaire form, accompanied by instructions to execute and return the questionnaire duly signed and sworn within ten (10) days in accordance with 28 U.S.C. § 1864(a).

11.   Determination of Juror Qualifications. The Chief Judge, or Clerk under the supervision of the Chief Judge, will determine whether a person is (1) unqualified for, (2) exempt from, or (3) to be excused from, jury service. These determinations will be based solely on information provided in the juror qualification questionnaire and other competent evidence.

12.   Qualifications for Jury Service.

a.   Under 28 U.S.C. § 1865(b), a person will be deemed qualified to serve on grand and petit juries unless he or she:

i.   is not a citizen of the United States, is not 18 years old, and has not resided for a period of one year within the judicial district;

ii.   is unable to read, write, and understand the English language with a degree of proficiency sufficient to satisfactorily complete the juror qualification form;

iii.   is unable to speak the English language;

iv.   is incapable, by reason of mental or physical infirmity, to render satisfactory jury service; or

v.   has a charge pending against him/her for the commission of, or has been convicted in a state or federal court of record of, a crime punishable by imprisonment for more than one year and his/her civil rights have not been restored by pardon or amnesty.

13.   Exemption From Jury Service.

a.   Under 28 U.S.C. § 1863(b)(6), the following are exempt from jury service:

i.   members in active service in the Armed Forces of the United States;

ii.   members of fire or police departments; and

iii.   public officers in the executive, legislative or judicial branches of the government of the United States, or of any state, district, territory, possession, or subdivision thereof, who are actively engaged in the performance of official duties. "Public officer" shall mean a person who is either elected to public office or who has been directly appointed by a person elected to public office.

14.   Excuses on Individual Request.

a.   The Court finds that jury service by the following persons would entail undue hardship or extreme inconvenience and to excuse them from jury service on individual request is not inconsistent with 28 U.S.C. §§ 1861 and 1862:

i.   persons over the age of 70;

ii.   persons who have served on a grand or petit jury in a federal court within the last two years; and

iii.   persons who are members of a volunteer fire department, rescue squad or ambulance crew for a public agency.

b.   Additionally, the Chief Judge, or the Clerk under supervision of the Chief Judge, may excuse persons summoned for jury service upon a showing of undue hardship, extreme inconvenience, or other ground for excuse as set forth in 28 U.S.C. §§ 1866(c) and 1869(j), for such period as the Court may deem necessary and proper.

15.   Deferral of Jury Service.

a.   If a person requests deferral of his or her jury service for a specific reason, such as a pre-planned vacation, business commitment, health problem or similar episodic event, the Clerk may reassign the juror to a different pool within the same jury wheel. All requests for deferral must be in writing, which includes electronically submitted requests.

b.   The Clerk will record any deferral granted and will report on the status of any individual juror or group of jurors upon request of the Court.

16.   Qualified Jurors.

a.   At all times, the Clerk will maintain an adequate number of qualified jurors not exempt or excused under this Plan.

b.   Qualified jurors will be randomly assigned to grand, petit and summary trial panels.

c.   The Clerk will maintain records of persons summoned and assigned to grand, petit and summary trial panels.

17.   Petit Jury Panels.

a.   Petit jurors will serve for a period of four (4) weeks, or as needed dependent upon the needs of each division.

b.   Persons whose names are selected and then qualified from the master jury wheel shall be called to appear as prospective jurors for trials in their respective divisions unless otherwise directed by the Chief Judge or the judge assigned to try the case.   Pursuant to 28 U.S.C. § 1866(e), no person shall be required to serve or attend court for prospective service as a petit juror for a total of more that thirty (30) days, except when necessary to complete service in a particular case.

c.   If the current panel for an area contains more persons than reasonably needed for the selection of a jury in a specific case, the Clerk shall select at random the number of individuals to be called.

d.   If two or more jury trials are to commence on the same day in the same city in this district, a central jury pool may be used.   The names of prospective jurors directed to report to any specific courtroom shall be determined at random by the Clerk.   Persons excluded from service in a particular case upon peremptory challenge or upon challenge by a party for good cause shown, shall be returned to the central jury pool.

e.   The Clerk shall prepare a separate list of the names of persons assigned to each petit jury panel.   These lists shall upon request, be disclosed to the parties three (3) business days prior to the trial date, unless otherwise directed by the Chief Judge or the judge assigned to try the case.

f.   A request for disclosure of jury names to the media or the public may be made to the judge assigned to try the case.   The Clerk shall not release juror names to the media or the public unless specifically authorized, in writing, by the assigned judge.   The Chief Judge or judge assigned to try the case may order such lists to be kept confidential in any case where the interests of justice so require.

18.   Failure to Report for Jury Service.   A person who does not report for jury service on the date and time on his or her summons, or as otherwise notified by the court, may be subject to prosecution in accordance with 28 U.S.C. § 1866(g).

19.   Reporting the Names of Non–Citizens to State Election Officials.   The Clerk shall report to the Michigan Secretary of State the names of prospective jurors that identify themselves as non-citizens at any time during the jury qualification or jury selection process.

20.   Summary Trial Jurors.   Jurors to be used for the purpose of summary trials will be drawn from a pool of jurors summoned and unused at the end of their term.

21.   Selection of Grand Jurors.

a.   The grand jury for the Southern Division shall be drawn from the Grand Rapids, Kalamazoo and Lansing jury wheels.   The grand jury for the Northern Division shall be drawn from the Marquette jury wheel.

b.   When the Court orders impanelment of a grand jury, the Clerk shall draw at random, from the master jury wheels, the names of as many persons as may be required for grand jury service.

c.   The Clerk shall select a proportionate share of names from each of the master jury wheels for each division.   That proportionate share shall be based on the total number of persons in the source list for each divisional office compared to the total number of persons on the source list for the entire district.   The Clerk shall issue summons and qualification forms for each person selected.

d.   Each grand jury shall serve for a period not to exceed eighteen (18) months, unless extended by an order of the Court, and such service shall not be affected by the emptying and refilling of the master wheels from which it was drawn.

e.   Upon request for excuse, and if inspection of the juror questionnaire of the person selected reflects that the person should be excused from grand jury service but not from petit jury service, that person shall be returned to the master wheel.

f.   Information of grand jurors shall not be disclosed to anyone at any time, except as may be directed by written Court order.

22.   Maintenance of Records.

a.   The Clerk shall preserve all records and papers compiled and maintained for the jury process for four (4) years after the master wheel is emptied, or for such longer period as may be ordered by the Court. Such records may then be destroyed, providing the means used is such to ensure privacy of their contents.

b.   Such records shall be available for public inspection for the purpose of determining the validity of the selection of any jury, pursuant to 28 U.S.C. § 1868 et seq.

c.   The Clerk shall retain and provide public access to the following documents:

i.   the Court's "Juror Selection Plan";

ii.   a copy of the Court's authorization and instruction order to the person or computer service organization which carries out automated name selection tasks for the Court and the affidavit by the representative of the facility certifying compliance with the same; and

iii.   orders of the Court for selection of grand and petit jury panels.

23.   Maintenance of Records. Incorporated in this Plan by reference are the provisions of 28 U.S.C. §§ 1861–1871, any amendments to these sections as may be made from time to time, and all statutes enacted after this Plan is approved pertaining to grand and petit jurors and trials by jury in federal courts.

[Effective September 20, 2013, approved by the Judicial Council of the Sixth Circuit November 6, 2013.]

* Pursuant to Administrative Order 07–90 dated August 8, 2007 (copy attached). Temporary changes to the Lansing jury wheel were made pending a permanent judge in residence.

SPEEDY TRIAL PLAN

I. INTRODUCTORY MATERIAL

A. Adoption of Plan. This final plan is adopted by the court pursuant to the requirements of the Speedy Trial Act of 1974 (18 U.S.C. Chapter 208) and the Speedy Trial Act Amendments of 1979 (Pub. L. No. 96–43, 93 Stat. 327).

B. Planning Group. The members of the Speedy Trial Act Planning Group of the court are as follows:

Honorable Wendell A. Miles	Chief District Judge
Honorable Douglas W. Hillman	District Judge
Honorable Benjamin F. Gibson	District Judge
Honorable Richard A. Enslen	District Judge
Honorable Stephen W. Karr	United States Magistrate
Honorable Hugh W. Brenneman, Jr.	United States Magistrate
James S. Brady	United States Attorney
Gerald H. Liefer	Clerk of the Court
Arthur Langeveld	Chief Deputy Clerk
Ted O. Wisner	Chief Probation Officer
Bruce W. Neckers	Criminal Attorney
Robert W. Dilley	Civil Attorney

C. Availability of Plan. Copies of this plan and recommendations of the Planning Group are available for public inspection at the office of the Clerk of the Court during normal business hours, and copies may be obtained at that office.

II. STATEMENT OF TIME LIMITS AND PROCEDURES FOR ACHIEVING PROMPT DISPOSITION OF CRIMINAL CASES

Pursuant to the requirements of rule 50(b) of the Federal Rules of Criminal Procedure, the Speedy Trial Act of 1974 (18 U.S.C. chapter 208), the Speedy Trial Act Amendments Act of 1979 (Pub. L. No. 96–43, 93 Stat. 327), and the Federal Juvenile Delinquency Act (18 U.S.C. §§ 5036, 5037), the judges of the United States District Court for the Western District of Michigan have adopted the following time limits and procedures to minimize undue delay and to further the prompt disposition of criminal cases and certain juvenile proceedings:

1. Applicability.

(a) *Offenses.* The time limits set forth herein are applicable to all criminal offenses triable in this court, including cases triable by United States Magistrates, except for petty offenses as defined in 18 U.S.C. § 1(3). Except as specifically provided, they are not applicable to proceedings under the Federal Juvenile Delinquency Act. [§ 3172]

(b) *Persons.* The time limits are applicable to persons accused who have not been indicted or informed against as well as those who have, and the word "defendant" includes such persons unless the context indicates otherwise.

2. Priorities in Scheduling Criminal Cases. Preference shall be given to criminal proceedings as far as practicable as required by rule 50(a) of the Federal Rules of Criminal Procedure. The trial of defendants in custody solely because they are awaiting trial and of high-risk defendants as defined in section 5 should be given preference over other criminal cases. [§ 3164(a)]

3. Time Within Which an Indictment or Information Must Be Filed.

(a) *Time Limits.* If an individual is arrested or served with a summons and the complaint charges an offense to be prosecuted in this district, any indictment or information subsequently filed in connection with such charge shall be filed within 30 days of arrest or service. [§ 3161(b)]

(b) *Grand Jury Not in Session.* If the defendant is charged with a felony to be prosecuted in this district, and no grand jury in the district has been in session during the 30–day period prescribed in subsection (a), such period shall be extended an additional 30 days. [§ 3161(b)]

(c) *Measurement of Time Periods.* If a person has not been arrested or served with a summons on a Federal charge, an arrest will be deemed to have been made at such time as the person (i) is held in custody solely for the purpose of responding to a Federal charge; (ii) is delivered to the custody of a Federal official in connection with a Federal charge; or (iii) appears before a judicial officer in connection with a Federal charge.

(d) *Related Procedures.*

(1) At the time of the earliest appearance before a judicial officer of a person who has been arrested for an offense not charged in an indictment or information, the judicial officer shall establish for the record the date on which the arrest took place.

(2) In the absence of a showing to the contrary, a summons shall be considered to have been served on the date of service shown on the return thereof.

4.   Time Within Which Trial Must Commence.

(a) *Time Limits.* The trial of a defendant shall commence not later than 70 days after the last to occur of the following dates:

(1) The date on which an indictment or information is filed in this district;

(2) The date on which a sealed indictment or information is unsealed; or

(3) The date of the defendant's first appearance before a judicial officer of this district. [§ 3161(c)(1)]

(b) *Retrial; Trial After Reinstatement of an Indictment or Information.* The retrial of a defendant shall commence within 70 days from the date the order occasioning the retrial becomes final, as shall the trial of a defendant upon an indictment or information dismissed by a trial court and reinstated following an appeal. If the retrial or trial follows an appeal or collateral attack, the court may extend the period if unavailability of witnesses or other factors resulting from passage of time make trial within 70 days impractical. The extended period shall not exceed 180 days. [§§ 3161(d)(2), (e)]

(c) *Withdrawal of Plea.* If a defendant enters a plea of guilty or nolo contendere to any or all charges in an indictment or information and is subsequently permitted to withdraw it, the time limit shall be determined for all counts as if the indictment or information were filed on the day the order permitting withdrawal of the plea became final. [§ 3161(i)]

(d) *Superseding Charges.* If, after an indictment or information has been filed, a complaint, indictment, or information is filed which charges the defendant with the same offense or with an offense required to be joined with that offense, the time limit applicable to the subsequent charge will be determined as follows:

(1) If the original indictment or information was dismissed on motion of the defendant before the filing of the subsequent charge, the time limit shall be determined without regard to the existence of the original charge. [§ 3161(d)(1)]

(2) If the original indictment or information is pending at the time the subsequent charge is filed, the trial shall commence within the time limit for commencement of trial on the original indictment or information. [§ 3161(h)(6)]

(3) If the original indictment or information was dismissed on motion of the United States attorney before the filing of the subsequent charge, the trial shall commence within the time limit for commencement of trial on the original indictment or information, but the period during which the defendant was not under charges shall be excluded from the computations. Such period is the period between the dismissal of the original indictment or information and the date the time would have commenced to run on the subsequent charge had there been no previous charge. [§ 3161(h)(6)]

If the subsequent charge is contained in a complaint, the form time limit within which an indictment or information must be obtained on the charge shall be determined without regard to the existence of the original indictment or information, but earlier action may in fact be required if the time limit for commencement of trial is to be satisfied.

(e) *Measurement of Time Periods.* For the purposes of this section:

(1) If a defendant signs a written consent to be tried before a magistrate and no indictment or information charging the offense has been filed, the time limit shall run from the date of such consent.

(2) In the event of a transfer to this district under Rule 20 of the Federal Rules of Criminal Procedure, the indictment or information shall be deemed filed in this district when the papers in the proceeding or certified copies thereof are received by the clerk.

(3) A trial in a jury case shall be deemed to commence at the beginning of voir dire.

(4) A trial in a non-jury case shall be deemed to commence on the day the case is called, provided that some step in the trial procedure immediately follows:

(f) *Related Procedures.*

(1) At the time of the defendant's earliest appearance before a judicial officer of this district, the officer will take appropriate steps to assure that the defendant is represented by counsel and shall appoint counsel where appropriate under the Criminal Justice Act and Rule 44 of the Federal Rules of Criminal Procedure.

(2) The court shall have sole responsibility for setting cases for trial after consultation with counsel. At the time of arraignment or as soon thereafter as is practicable, each case will be set for trial on a day certain or listed for trial on a weekly or other short-term calendar [§ 3161(a)]

(3) Individual calendars shall be managed so that it will be reasonably anticipated that every criminal case set for trial will be reached during the week of original setting. A conflict in schedules of Assistant United States Attorneys or defense counsel will be ground for a continuance or delayed setting only if approved by the court and called to the court's attention at the earliest practicable time.

(4) In the event that a complaint, indictment, or information is filed against a defendant charged in a pending indictment or information or in an indictment or information dismissed on motion of the United States Attorney, the trial on the new charge shall commence within the time limit for commencement of trial on the original indictment or information unless the court finds that the new charge is not for the same offense charged in the original indictment or information or an offense required to be joined therewith.

(5) At the time of the filing of a complaint, indictment, or information described in paragraph (4), the United States Attorney shall give written notice to the court of that circumstance and of his position with respect to the computation of the time limits.

(6) All pretrial hearings shall be conducted as soon after the arraignment as possible, consistent with the priorities of other matters on the court's criminal docket.

5. Defendants in Custody and High–Risk Defendants.

(a) *Time Limits.* Notwithstanding any longer time periods that may be permitted under sections 3 and 4, the following time limits will also be applicable to defendants in custody and high-risk defendants as herein defined:

(1) The trial of a defendant held in custody solely for the purpose of trial on a Federal charge shall commence within 90 days following the beginning of continuous custody.

(2) The trial of a high-risk defendant shall commence within 90 days of the designation as a high-risk. [§ 3164(b)]

(b) *Definition of "High–Risk Defendant."* A high-risk defendant is one reasonably designated by the United States Attorney as posing a danger to himself or any other person or to the community.

(c) *Measurement of Time Periods.* For the purposes of this section:

(1) A defendant is deemed to be in detention awaiting trial when he is arrested on a Federal charge or otherwise held for the purpose of responding to a Federal charge. Detention is deemed to be solely because the defendant is awaiting trial unless the person exercising custodial authority has an independent basis (not including a detainer) for continuing to hold the defendant.

(2) If a case is transferred pursuant to Rule 20 of the Federal Rules of Criminal Procedure and the defendant subsequently rejects disposition under Rule 20 or the court declines to accept the plea, a new period of continuous detention awaiting trial will begin at that time.

(3) A trial shall be deemed to commence as provided in sections 4(e)(3) and 4(e)(4).

(d) *Related Procedures.*

(1) If a defendant is being held in custody solely for the purpose of awaiting trial, the United States Attorney shall advise the court at the earliest practicable time of the date of the beginning of such custody.

(2) The United States Attorney shall advise the court at the earliest practicable time (usually at the hearing with respect to bail) if the defendant is considered by him to be high risk.

(3) If the court finds that the filing of a "high-risk" designation as a public record may result in prejudice to the defendant, it may order the designation sealed for such period as is necessary to protect the defendant's right to a fair trial, but not beyond the time that the court's judgment in the case becomes final. During the time the designation is under seal, it shall be made known to the defendant and his counsel but shall not be made known to other persons without the permission of the court.

6. Exclusion of Time From Computations.

(a) *Applicability.* In computing any time limit under section 3, 4, or 5, the periods of delay set forth in 18 U.S.C. § 3161(h) shall be excluded. Such periods of delay shall not be excluded in computing the minimum period for commencement of trial under section 7.

(b) *Records of Excludable Time.* The clerk of the court shall enter on the docket, in the form prescribed by the Administrative Office of the United States Courts, information with respect to excludable periods of time for each criminal defendant. With respect to proceedings prior to the filing of an indictment or information, excludable time shall be reported to the clerk by the United States Attorney.

(c) *Stipulations.*

(1) The attorney for the government and the attorney for the defendant may at any time enter into stipulations with respect to the accuracy of the docket entries recording excludable time.

(2) To the extent that the amount of time stipulated by the parties does not exceed the amount recorded on the docket for any excludable period of delay, the stipulation shall be conclusive as between the parties unless it has no basis in fact or law. It shall similarly be conclusive as to a codefendant for the limited purpose of determining, under 18 U.S.C. § 3161(h)(7), whether time has run against the defendant entering into the stipulation.

(3) To the extent that the amount of time stipulated exceeds the amount recorded on the docket, the stipulation shall have no effect unless approved by the court.

(d) *Pre–Indictment Procedures.*

(1) In the event that the United States Attorney anticipates that an indictment or information will not be filed within the time limit set forth in section 3, he may file a written motion with the court for a determination of excludable time. In the event that the United States Attorney seeks a continuance under 18 U.S.C. § 3161(h)(8), he shall file a written motion with the court requesting such a continuance.

(2) The motion of the United States Attorney shall state (i) the period of time proposed for exclusion, and (ii) the basis of the proposed exclusion. If the motion is for a continuance under 18 U.S.C. § 3161(h)(8), it shall also state whether or not the defendant is being held in custody on the basis of the complaint. In appropriate circumstances, the motion may include a request that some or all of the supporting material be considered ex parte and in camera.

(3) The court may grant a continuance under 18 U.S.C. § 3161(h)(8) for either a specific period of time or a period to be determined by reference to an event (such as recovery from illness) not within the control of the government. If the continuance is to a date not certain, the court shall require one or both parties to inform the court promptly when and if the circumstances that justify the continuance no longer exist. In addition, the court shall require one or both parties to file periodic reports bearing on the continued existence of such circumstances. The court shall determine the frequency of such reports in the light of the facts of the particular case.

(e) *Post–Indictment Procedures.*

(1) At each appearance of counsel before the court, counsel shall examine the clerk's records of excludable time for completeness and accuracy and shall bring to the court's immediate attention any claim that the clerk's record is in any way incorrect.

(2) In the event that the court continues a trial beyond the time limit set forth in section 4 or 5, the court shall determine whether the limit may be recomputed by excluding time pursuant to 18 U.S.C. § 3161(h).

(3) If it is determined that a continuance is justified, the court shall set forth its findings in the record, either orally or in writing. If the continuance is granted under 18 U.S.C. § 3161(h)(8), the

court shall also set forth its reasons for finding that the ends of justice served by granting the continuance outweigh the best interests of the public and the defendant in a speedy trial. If the continuance is to a date not certain, the court shall require one or both parties to inform the court promptly when and if the circumstances that justify the continuance no longer exist. In addition, the court shall require one or both parties to file periodic reports bearing on the continued existence of such circumstances. The court shall determine the frequency of such reports in the light of the facts of the particular case.

7. Minimum Period for Defense Preparation. Unless the defendant consents in writing to the contrary, the trial shall not commence earlier than 30 days from the date on which the indictment or information is filed or, if later, from the date on which counsel first enters an appearance or on which the defendant expressly waives counsel and elects to proceed pro se. In circumstances in which the 70–day time limit for commencing trial on a charge in an indictment or information is determined by reference to an earlier indictment or information pursuant to section 4(d), the 30–day minimum period shall also be determined by reference to the earlier indictment or information. When prosecution is resumed on an original indictment or information following a mistrial, appeal, or withdrawal of a guilty plea, a new 30–day minimum period will not begin to run. The court will in all cases schedule trials so as to permit defense counsel adequate preparation time in the light of all the circumstances. [§ 3161(c)(2)]

8. Time Within Which Defendant Should Be Sentenced.

(a) *Time Limit.* A defendant shall ordinarily be sentenced within 45 days of the date of his conviction or plea of guilty or nolo contendere.

(b) *Related Procedures.* If the defendant and his counsel consent thereto, a presentence investigation may be commenced prior to a plea of guilty or nolo contendere or a conviction.

9. Juvenile Proceedings.

(a) *Time Within Which Trial Must Commence.* An alleged delinquent who is in detention pending trial shall be brought to trial within 30 days of the date on which such detention was begun, as provided in 18 U.S.C. § 5036.

(b) *Time of Dispositional Hearing.* If a juvenile is adjudicated delinquent, a separate dispositional hearing shall be held no later than 20 court days after trial, unless the court has ordered further study of the juvenile in accordance with 18 U.S.C. § 5037(c).

10. Sanctions.

(a) *Dismissal or Release From Custody.* Failure to comply with the requirements of Title I of the Speedy Trial Act may entitle the defendant to dismissal of the charges against him or to release from pretrial custody. Nothing in this plan shall be construed to require that a case be dismissed or a defendant released from custody in circumstances in which such action would not be required by 18 U.S.C. §§ 3162 and 3164.

(b) *High–Risk Defendants.* A high-risk defendant whose trial has not commenced within the time limit set forth in 18 U.S.C. § 3164(b) shall, if the failure to commence trial was through no fault of the attorney for the government, have his release conditions automatically reviewed. A high-risk defendant who is found by the court to have intentionally delayed the trial of his case shall be subject to an order of the court modifying his nonfinancial conditions of release under chapter 207 of title 18, U.S.C., to ensure that he shall appear at trial as required. [§ 3164(c)]

(c) *Discipline of Attorneys.* In a case in which counsel (1) knowingly allows the case to be set for trial without disclosing the fact that a necessary witness would be unavailable for trial, (2) files a motion solely for the purpose of delay which he knows is frivolous and without merit, (3) makes a statement for the purpose of obtaining a continuance which he knows to be false and which is material to the granting of the continuance, or (4) other-wise willfully fails to proceed to trial without justification consistent with 18 U.S.C. § 3161, the court may punish such counsel as provided in 18 U.S.C. §§ 3162(b) and (c).

(d) *Alleged Juvenile Delinquents.* An alleged delinquent in custody whose trial has not commenced within the time limit set forth in 18 U.S.C. § 5036 shall be entitled to dismissal of his case pursuant to that section unless the Attorney General shows that the delay was consented to or caused by the juvenile or his counsel, or would be in the interest of justice in the particular case.

11. Persons Serving Terms of Imprisonment. If the United States Attorney knows that a person charged with an offense is serving a term of imprisonment in any penal institution, he shall promptly seek to obtain the presence of the prisoner for trial, or cause a detainer to be filed, in accordance with the provisions of 18 U.S.C. § 3161(j).

12. Continuances for Unusual or Complex Cases. Because of the importance of scheduling trial dates, each counsel has a duty to notify the court at any early stage of the proceedings of any motion for continuance in an unusual or complex case.

13. Computation of Time. Notwithstanding any directions regarding the computation of time under the Speedy Trial Act in this plan, if the ending date of any time interval falls on a non-business day, that interval will be treated as ending on the next business day.

14. Effective Dates.

(a) The amendments to the Speedy Trial Act made by Public Law 96–43 became effective August 2, 1979. To the extent that this revision of the district's plan does more than merely reflect the amendments, the revised plan shall take effect upon approval of the reviewing panel designated in accordance with 18 U.S.C. § 3165(c). However, the dismissal sanction and the sanctions against attorneys authorized by 18 U.S.C. § 3162 and reflected in sections 10(a) and (c) of this plan shall apply only to defendants whose cases are commenced by arrest or summons on or after July 1, 1980, and to indictments and informations filed on or after that date.

(b) If a defendant was arrested or served with a summons before July 1, 1979, the time within which an information or indictment must be filed shall be determined under the plan that was in effect at the time of such arrest or service.

(c) If a defendant was arraigned before August 2, 197 9, the time within which the trial must commence shall be determined under the plan that was in effect at the time of such arraignment.

(d) If a defendant was in custody on August 2, 1979, solely because he was awaiting trial, the 90–day period under section 5 shall be computed from that date.

III. SUMMARY OF EXPERIENCE UNDER THE ACT WITHIN THE DISTRICT

A. Progress Toward Meeting the Permanent Time Limits. The data in Table 1, attached, indicates the progress the district has made in complying with the Speedy Trial Act. It will be noted that during the last six months of the reporting period, there were only three defendants in whose cases there was not full compliance with the time requirements of the Act.

B. Problems Encountered. Most of the problems heretofore encountered in complying with the requirements of the Speedy Trial Act were or will be solved by the liberalizing 1979 amendments to the Act, particularly the expansion and redefinitions of the excludable time periods set forth in section 3161(h).

C. Incidence of, and Reasons for, Requests or Allowances of Extensions of Time Beyond the District's Standards (28 U.S.C. § 3166(b)(1), (4)).

None.

D. Reasons Why the Exclusions Were Inadequate to Accommodate Reasonable Period of Delay (18 USC § 3167(b)). In those cases not in compliance with the time limits for indictment and commencement of trial under 18 U.S.C. § 3161(b) and (c), the primary reason for the inadequacy of the exclusions to accommodate reasonable period of delay was the narrow statutory definitions of excludable time. For example, the exclusion for motions was limited to "delay resulting from hearings on pretrial motions." This exclusion has now been expanded to cover "delay resulting from any pretrial motion, from the filing of the motion through the conclusion of the hearing on, or any prompt disposition of, such motion." The former narrowness of the exclusion definitions is indicated by the 1979 amendments of the Act, which widened the scope and added to the number of excludable time periods.

E. The Effect on Criminal Justice Administration of the Prevailing Time Limits (18 U.S.C. § 3166(b)(5)). Although the Act was well intended, activities directed towards compliance may have the effect of wasting time which could more profitably be spent in the preparation for trial, and the short interval time periods may have the effect of decreasing the amount of time available for the preparation for trial, thereby, perhaps, contributing to the ineffective assistance of counsel. Furthermore, if the procedures necessary for complying with the Act become too onerous for private counsel, diligent and dedicated defense attorneys may refuse to take criminal cases in the federal courts thereby decreasing the effectiveness of federal court practitioners.

F. Effect of Compliance With the Time Limits on the Civil Calendar (18 U.S.C. § 3166(b)(9)). As indicated by Table 6, attached, compliance with the time limits of the Speedy Trial Act has tended to increase the length of time civil cases have been pending.

G. Frequency of Use of Sanctions Under 18 U.S.C. § 3164 (18 U.S.C. § 3166(b)(3)). No sanctions have been applied.

IV. STATEMENT OF PROCEDURES AND INNOVATIONS THAT HAVE BEEN OR WILL BE ADOPTED BY THE DISTRICT COURT TO EXPEDITE THE DISPOSITION OF CRIMINAL CASES IN ACCORDANCE WITH THE SPEEDY TRIAL ACT (18 U.S.C. § 3167(b))

The Court, the United States Attorney's Office, and the Office of the Clerk have made changes in their practices and procedures in order to facilitate compliance with the Act. However, no local rule changes have been made.

Over the past few years the grand jury had been called on an irregular basis, sometimes not appearing for several months. Starting January, 1978, the grand jury has met monthly. The U.S. Magistrate now takes Grand Jury Returns as permitted by Rule 6(f) of the Federal Rules of Criminal Procedure as amended. In addition, Monday has been designated as arraignment day. The Magistrate has been available every Monday to arraign any defendant.

Whenever a defendant wishes to enter a plea of guilty or nolo contendere under Rule 11 of the Federal Rules of Criminal Procedure and the judge to whom the case is assigned is not available, the judges have agreed that another judge may accept the plea. The sentence, however, still will be imposed by the judge to whom the case was originally assigned.

The United States Attorney has adopted two new procedures to aid compliance with the Act. First, a report describing the present status of all pending criminal cases is kept and is constantly updated by using a mechanized typewriter. The "target date" for the expiration of the speedy trial intervals is listed. Furthermore, each month the United States Attorney meets with all the Assistant United States Attorneys in a group office meeting in which the status of each pending case is checked to determine whether the "target date" for the intervals will be met and to discuss remedial measures for cases which appear will exceed interval time limits.

A number of changes have been adopted by the Clerk's Office to monitor compliance with the speedy trial time limits. It has become the duty of a deputy clerk to monitor pending cases under the Act. A locally developed criminal-defendant status card is maintained on each defendant and is used as part of a warning system to provide notice if the case approaches the maximum time limits permitted under the Act. A list of all cases pending before each judge or magistrate is sent to the respective judicial officer. At least once a month a list of all cases pending before each judge is sent to the judge along with the date interval 2 will expire or has expired. In addition, defendants who are subject to the 90–day continuous-custody provisions are specially noted.

V. STATEMENT OF ADDITIONAL RESOURCES NEEDED TO ACHIEVE COMPLIANCE WITH THE ACT (18 U.S.C. § 3166(d))

None.

VI. RECOMMENDATIONS FOR CHANGES IN STATUTES, RULES OR ADMINISTRATIVE PROCEDURES (18 U.S.C. §§ 3166(b)(7), (d), (e))

A. Statutes.

1. *Speedy Trial Act.*

a. Suggestions, if any, as to kinds of cases which should have separate or different time limits as a matter of statutory classification.

It is believed that classification of cases by kind is too arbitrary a criteria for imposing separate or different time limits. Use of the safety-valve provisions of section 3168(h)(8) is better suited to obtaining exclusions of time beyond the statutory limits in unusual or complex cases, such as antitrust, mail fraud, conspiracy, and net worth tax cases.

b. *Other.* Serious consideration should be given to repeal of the Act's stringent time limitations and a return to the more flexible standards of Rule 50(b) administered in light of the constitutional guarantee of speedy trial.

2. *Other Statutes.* A judicial impact statement should be required for all subsequent legislation. Any legislative changes which would substantially increase civil filings or substantially broaden federal criminal jurisdiction, and thereby increase criminal filings, will necessitate additional judgeships for continued compliance with the Speedy Trial Act.

B. Rules.

1. *Federal Rules of Criminal Procedure.* None

2. *Other.* None

C. Forms, Reporting Procedures, and Reporting Requirements. None

D. Other. None

VII. INCIDENCE AND LENGTH OF, REASONS FOR, AND REMEDIES FOR DETENTION PRIOR TO TRIAL (18 U.S.C. § 3166(b)(6))

As indicated by Table III, attached, only one defendant was detained beyond the 90–day period referred to in section 3164 of the Act. However, the period of "151 plus" days which is shown in the table as the period of detention is wrong. The Clerk's office advises that it is the result of a clerical error, and that the correct detention figure was 119 days. The prolonged detention of this defendant, who was charged with threats against the President of the United States, was due to several psychiatric examinations and extensive plea bargaining. Hereafter, the expanded exclusions of the 1979 amendments of the Act should result in compliance with the detention provisions of the Act.

The amendments to the Speedy Trial Act made by Public Law 96–43 became effective August 2, 1979. To the extent that this revision of the district's plan does more than merely reflect the amendments, the revised plan shall take effect upon approval of the reviewing panel designated in accordance with 18 U.S.C. § 3165(c).

[Effective June 7, 2005.]

CJA PLAN

I. AUTHORITY

Pursuant to the Criminal Justice Act of 1964 (CJA), as amended, 18 U.S.C. § 3006A, and Guide to Judiciary Policy (Guide), Volume 7A, the judges of the United States District Court for the Western District of Michigan adopt this Plan, as approved by the circuit, for furnishing representation in federal court for any person financially unable to obtain adequate representation in accordance with the CJA.

II. STATEMENT OF POLICY

A. Objectives.

1. The objective of this Plan is to attain the ideal of equality before the law for all persons. Therefore, this Plan shall be administered so that those accused of a crime, or otherwise eligible for services pursuant to the CJA, will not be deprived, because they are financially unable to pay for adequate representation, of any element of representation necessary to an adequate defense.

2. The further objective of this Plan is to particularize the requirements of the CJA, the USA Patriot Improvement and Reauthorization Act of 2005 (recodified at 18 U.S.C. § 3599), and the Guide, Volume 7A, in a way that meets the needs of this district.

B. Compliance.

1. The Court, its Clerk, the Federal Public Defender, and private attorneys appointed under the CJA shall comply with the Guide, Volume 7A, approved by the Judicial Conference of the United States and/or its Committee on Defender Services and with this Plan.

2. The Court will ensure that a current copy of the CJA Plan is made available on the Court's website. Each private attorney shall be provided by the Federal Public Defender with a current copy of this Plan upon the attorney's first appointment under the CJA or designation as a member of the panel of private attorneys under the Criminal Justice Act (CJA Panel). The Federal Public Defender shall also maintain a current copy of the Guide, Volume 7A for the use of members of the CJA Panel, and shall make its availability known to such attorneys. Failure to familiarize him or herself with this Plan shall not excuse an attorney from complying with its provisions.

III. DEFINITIONS

A. "Representation" includes counsel and investigative, expert, and other services.

B. "Appointed attorney" includes private attorneys, the Federal Public Defender, and staff attorneys of the Federal Public Defender recognized under paragraph V of this Plan.

C. "CJA Panel Administrator" is a person designated by the Federal Public Defender to administer the CJA Panel.

IV. PROVISION OF REPRESENTATION

A. Circumstances.

1. *Mandatory:* Representation <u>shall</u> be provided for any financially eligible person who:

    a. is charged with a felony or with a Class A misdemeanor;

    b. is a juvenile alleged to have committed an act of juvenile delinquency as defined in 18 U.S.C. § 5031;

    c. is charged with a violation of probation, or faces a change of a term or condition of probation (unless the modification sought is favorable to the probationer and the government has not objected to the proposed change);

    d. is under arrest, when such representation is required by law;

    e. is entitled to appointment of counsel in parole proceedings;

f. is charged with a violation of supervised release or faces modification, reduction, or enlargement of a condition, or extension or revocation of a term of supervised release;

g. is subject to a mental condition hearing under 18 U.S.C. §§ 4241–4248;

h. is in custody as a material witness;

i. is seeking to set aside or vacate a death sentence under 28 U.S.C. §§ 2254 or 2255;

j. is entitled to appointment of counsel in verification of consent proceedings pursuant to a transfer of an offender to or from the United States for the execution of a penal sentence under 18 U.S.C. § 4109;

k. is entitled to appointment of counsel under the Sixth Amendment to the Constitution; or

l. faces loss of liberty in a case and federal law requires the appointment of counsel.

2. *Discretionary:* Whenever a District Judge or United States Magistrate Judge determines that the interests of justice so require, representation may be provided for any financially eligible person who:

a. is charged with a petty offense (Class B or C misdemeanor, or an infraction) for which a sentence of confinement is authorized;

b. is seeking relief, other than to set aside or vacate a death sentence, under 28 U.S.C. §§ 2241, 2254, or 2255;

c. is charged with civil or criminal contempt and faces loss of liberty;

d. has been called as a witness before a grand jury, a court, the Congress, or a federal agency or commission that has the power to compel testimony, and there is reason to believe, either prior to or during testimony, that the witness could be subject to a criminal prosecution, a civil or criminal contempt proceeding, or face loss of liberty;

e. is proposed by the United States Attorney for processing under a pretrial diversion program;

f. is held for international extradition under 18 U.S.C. §§ 3181–3196;

g. has received a letter indicating that he or she is a "target" of a federal criminal investigation, as that term is defined in the United States Attorneys' Manual;

h. is involved in "ancillary matters appropriate to the proceedings" pursuant to subsection (c) of the CJA. In determining whether representation in an ancillary matter is appropriate to the proceedings, the court should consider whether such representation is reasonably necessary to accomplish, *inter alia*, one of the following objectives:

(1) to protect a Constitutional right;

(2) to contribute in some significant way to the defense of the principal criminal charge;

(3) to aid in preparation for the trial or disposition of the principal criminal charge;

(4) to enforce the terms of a plea agreement in the principal criminal charge;

(5) to preserve the claim of the CJA client to an interest in real or personal property subject to a civil forfeiture proceeding pursuant to 18 U.S.C. § 983, 21 U.S.C. § 881, 19 U.S.C. § 1602, or similar statutes, which property, if recovered by the CJA client, may be considered for reimbursement under subsection (f) of the CJA; or

(6) to effectuate the return of real or personal property belonging to the CJA client which may be subject to a motion for return of property pursuant to Fed. R. Crim. P. 41(g), which property, if recovered by the CJA client, may be considered for reimbursement under subsection (f) of the CJA.

B. When Counsel Shall Be Provided. Counsel shall be provided to eligible persons as soon as feasible after they are taken into custody, when they appear before a District Judge or United States Magistrate Judge, when they are formally charged or notified of charges if formal charges are sealed, or when a District Judge or United States Magistrate Judge otherwise considers appointment of counsel appropriate under the CJA, whichever occurs earliest. Such appointment may be made retroactive to include any representation furnished pursuant to the Plan prior to appointment.

C.   **Number and Qualifications of Counsel.**

1.   *Number:* More than one attorney may be appointed in any case determined by the Court to be extremely difficult. In a capital case, two or more attorneys may be appointed as required by 18 U.S.C. §§ 3005 and 3599 and other applicable law.

2.   *Qualifications:* In capital cases, at least one of the attorneys appointed shall be learned in the law applicable to such cases pursuant to 18 U.S.C. § 3005. Learned counsel should have distinguished prior experience in the trial, appeal, or post-conviction review of federal death penalty cases, or distinguished prior experience in state death penalty trials, appeals, or post-conviction review that, in combination with co-counsel, will assure high quality representation.

Pursuant to 18 U.S.C. § 3005, in appointing counsel in federal capital prosecutions, the Court shall consider the recommendation of the Federal Public Defender.

D.   **Eligibility for Representation.**

1.   *Fact Finding:* The determination of eligibility for representation under the CJA is a judicial function to be performed by a District Judge or United States Magistrate Judge after making appropriate inquiries concerning the person's financial condition.

2.   *Disclosure of Change in Eligibility:* If, at any time after appointment, appointed counsel obtains information that a client is financially able to make payment in whole or in part, for legal or other services in connection with his or her representation, and the source of the attorney's information is not protected as a privileged communication, counsel shall advise the Court.

V.   FEDERAL PUBLIC DEFENDER ORGANIZATION

A.   **Establishment.**

1.   The Office of the Federal Public Defender for the Western District of Michigan, previously established in this District pursuant to the provisions of the CJA, is hereby recognized as the Federal Public Defender Organization for this District.

2.   The Federal Public Defender Organization shall be capable of providing legal services in the Southern and Northern Divisions of the District and shall maintain offices in Grand Rapids and Marquette, Michigan.

B.   **Supervision of Defender Organization:** The Federal Public Defender shall be responsible for the supervision and management of the Federal Public Defender Organization. Accordingly, the Federal Public Defender shall be appointed in all cases assigned to that organization, and these cases may be subsequently reassigned to staff attorneys or CJA Panel attorneys at the discretion of the Federal Public Defender. Not later than January 31 of each year, the Federal Public Defender Organization shall provide the Court with a list of all defendants assigned to that office during the preceding calendar year, along with such related information which will assist the Court in reviewing the distribution of case assignments between the Federal Public Defender Organization and the CJA Panel.

C.   **CJA Panel:** Acting under the supervision of the Federal Public Defender, the CJA Panel Administrator within the Federal Public Defender Organization shall be responsible for the systematic distribution of cases to, and for the management of, the CJA Panel.

VI.   CJA PANEL ATTORNEYS

A.   **Establishment:** The Court shall establish a Panel of private attorneys who are eligible and willing to be appointed to provide representation under the Criminal Justice Act. The Court shall approve attorneys for membership on the Panel after receiving recommendations from the Court's Criminal Law Committee and the Federal Public Defender. Members of the CJA Panel shall serve at the pleasure of the Court.

B.   **Size:** The Court shall fix, periodically, the size of the CJA Panel. The CJA Panel shall be large enough to provide a sufficient number of experienced attorneys to handle the CJA caseload, yet small enough so that Panel members will receive an adequate number of appointments to maintain their proficiency in federal criminal defense work, and thereby provide a high quality of representation.

C.   **Eligibility:** Attorneys who serve on the CJA Panel must be members in good standing of the federal bar of this District, have criminal trial experience, and have demonstrated experience in knowledge of federal criminal law, the Federal Rules of Criminal Procedure, the Federal Rules of Evidence, and the Federal Sentencing Guidelines.

In exceptional circumstances, if the Court determines that the appointment of an attorney, who is not a member of the CJA Panel or the Federal Public Defender Organization, is in the interest of justice, judicial economy, or continuity of representation, or there is some other compelling circumstance warranting his or her appointment, an attorney may be admitted to the CJA Panel *pro hac vice* and appointed to represent a CJA defendant. Consideration for preserving the integrity of the Panel selection process suggests that such appointments should be made only in exceptional circumstances. Further, the attorney should possess such qualities as would qualify him or her for admission to the District's CJA Panel in the ordinary course of panel selection.

D. Application: Application forms for membership on the CJA Panel shall be made available, upon request, by the Federal Public Defender Organization. Completed applications shall be submitted to the Federal Public Defender who will transmit the applications to the Court.

E. Terms: Lawyers selected for the CJA Panel after 2006 will serve a three-year term. Any member selected with no previous panel experience shall serve a one-year probationary period.

F. Equal Opportunity: All qualified attorneys shall be encouraged to apply for membership without regard to race, color, religion, sex, age, national origin, or disabling condition.

G. Facilities and Technology Requirements:

1. CJA panel attorneys must have facilities, resources, and technological capability to effectively and efficiently manage assigned cases.

2. CJA panel attorneys must comply with the requirements of electronic filing and eVoucher.

H. Maintenance of List and Distribution of Appointments: The Federal Public Defender shall maintain a current list of all attorneys included on the CJA Panel, with current office addresses and telephone numbers, as well as a statement of qualifications and experience. The Federal Public Defender shall furnish a copy of this list to each District Judge and United States Magistrate Judge. The Federal Public Defender shall also maintain a record of assignments to private counsel, and when appropriate, statistical data reflecting the proration of appointments between attorneys from the Federal Public Defender's Office and private attorneys, according to the formula described in this Plan.

I. Method of Appointment: Appointments from the CJA Panel should generally be made on a rotational basis, subject to the Court's discretion to make exceptions due to the nature and complexity of the case, an attorney's experience, and geographical considerations. This procedure should result in a balanced distribution of appointments and compensation among the members of the CJA Panel, and quality representation for each CJA defendant.

Upon determination of a need for the appointment of counsel, the District Judge or United States Magistrate Judge shall advise the Federal Public Defender as to the need for counsel and the nature of the case.

The Federal Public Defender, through the CJA Panel Administrator, shall then determine whether to continue the representation personally, reassign the case to a staff attorney, or assign the case to a CJA Panel attorney. Under exceptional circumstances, the Federal Public Defender may assign a case to a private attorney not on the CJA Panel list.

In the event of an emergency, i.e., weekends, holidays, or other non-working hours of the Federal Public Defender's office, the presiding judge or United States Magistrate Judge may appoint any attorney from the CJA Panel list. In all cases where members of the CJA Panel are appointed by the Court, the Court shall notify the Federal Public Defender as to the name of the attorney appointed and the date of appointment.

J. Ratio of Appointment: Where practical and cost effective, attorneys from the CJA Panel shall be appointed in a substantial portion of the cases in which the accused is determined to be financially eligible for representation under the CJA. "Substantial" shall usually be defined as approximately 25% of the appointments under the CJA annually throughout the District.

K. Investigative, Expert, and Other Necessary Services: Investigative, expert, or other services reasonably necessary to provide adequate representation, as authorized by the CJA, shall be available as provided by statute to persons who are eligible for representation under the CJA, including eligible persons who have elected to proceed *pro se* and persons who have retained counsel but who are found by the Court to be financially unable to obtain necessary services.

L. Removal of a Lawyer from the CJA Panel.

1. *Automatic Removal; Reinstatement:* Any attorney whose license is revoked or suspended by an Attorney Discipline Board of any state or for any other reason is no longer a member in good standing of the state bar and the Bar of this Court, shall be removed automatically from the CJA Panel. Upon reinstatement to membership in good standing of his or her state bar and the Bar of this Court, an attorney who desires to be reinstated to the CJA Panel shall proceed as on original application.

2. *Other Removal; Reinstatement:* In the event that a District Judge or United States Magistrate Judge considers that an attorney should be removed from the CJA Panel for reasons other than bar membership status including, but not limited to, formal accusation of a crime, conviction of a crime not resulting in action by the Attorney Discipline Board, indications of lack of professional competence or lack of adherence to ethical standards, indications of mental or emotional instability affecting professional responsibilities, and indications of a lack of desire to accept or handle case assignments, referral of the matter shall be made to the Court's Criminal Law Committee. Upon consideration of the Committee's report, the Court may remove the attorney from the CJA Panel, either permanently or for a period of time. Prior to making its determinations, the Court may, within its sole discretion, give the attorney written notice of its intended action and may also afford the attorney an opportunity to be heard before a hearing panel designated by the Chief Judge, which panel shall then submit a report to the Court. Any attorney removed under this provision who desires to be reinstated to the CJA Panel shall proceed as on original application.

In the event that a District Judge or United States Magistrate Judge identifies a problem with a CJA Panel attorney not serious enough to warrant removal, the Judge may refer the matter to the Federal Public Defender for appropriate action.

None of the foregoing removal provisions shall be construed to limit or alter the provision stated in Section VI that all CJA Panel attorneys serve at the pleasure of the Court.

VII. DUTIES OF APPOINTED COUNSEL

A. Standards: The services to be rendered a person represented by appointed counsel shall be commensurate with those rendered if counsel were privately employed by the person.

B. Professional Conduct: Attorneys appointed pursuant to the CJA shall conform to the highest standards of professional conduct including, but not limited to, the provisions of Local Criminal Rule 57.1.

C. No Receipt of Other Payment: Appointed counsel may not require, request, or accept any payment or promise of payment, or any other valuable consideration, for representation under the appointment, unless such payment is approved by order of the Court.

D. Continuing Representation: Once counsel is appointed under the CJA, counsel shall continue the representation until the matter, including appeals or review by certiorari (as governed by the circuit CJA Plan provisions concerning representation on appeal), is closed, until substitute counsel has filed a notice of appearance, until an order has been entered allowing or requiring the person represented to proceed *pro se*, or until the appointment is terminated by court order. The Circuit CJA Plan is currently available on the Sixth Circuit Court of Appeals website.

VIII. DUTIES OF LAW ENFORCEMENT AND RELATED AGENCIES

A. Presentation of Accused for Appointment of Counsel. The United States Probation and Pretrial Services Office shall promptly ask any person who is in custody, or who otherwise may be entitled to counsel under the CJA, whether he or she is financially able to secure representation, and, whenever such person indicates that he or she is not able, shall assist in the completion of a financial affidavit (CJA Form 23) and notify and provide the completed form to the Court. If the Court determines that the appointment of counsel is appropriate, the Court shall enter an order directing the Office of the Federal Public Defender to provide representation. The United States Attorney's Office has no obligation to discuss with persons accused of a crime their right to the appointment of counsel or their eligibility for such appointment. The United States Attorney's Office and federal law enforcement agencies recognize their obligation to continue to comply with, all applicable law, standards, and procedures related to appointment of counsel.

B. Notice of Indictment or Criminal Information: At or before the initial appearance of a person accused of a crime, upon the return or unsealing of an indictment, the filing of a criminal information, or the filing of a complaint or petition to modify or revoke probation or supervised release, the accused shall be provided a copy of the charging document by the United States Marshals Service prior to the initial appearance or, if not so received, by the Assistant United States Attorney at the initial appearance. When the accused is directed by summons to appear to answer to an indictment, information, or complaint, the United States Attorney's Office will provide a copy of the charging document along with the cover letter notifying him or her of the date to appear. When the accused is directed by summons to appear to answer to a petition to modify or revoke probation or supervised release, the United States Probation and Pretrial Services Office will provide a copy of the petition along with the cover letter notifying him or her of the date to appear.

IX. MISCELLANEOUS

A. Compensation: Claims for compensation shall be submitted no later than 90 days after final disposition of the case, unless good cause is shown. Claims for compensation shall be submitted on the appropriate CJA form, to the office of the Federal Public Defender through the Court's eVoucher system. The CJA Panel Administrator within the Federal Public Defender Office shall review the claim form for mathematical and technical accuracy and for conformity with the Guide, Volume 7A, and, if correct, shall forward the claim form for the consideration of the appropriate District Judge or United States Magistrate Judge. The Court will exert its best effort to avoid delays in reviewing payment vouchers and submitting them for further processing.

In non-capital representations of unusual complexity that are likely to become extraordinary in terms of cost, the Court may require development of a case budget consistent with the Guide, Volume 7A, Ch.2, §§ 230.26.10–20.

B. Supersession: This Plan supersedes all prior Criminal Justice Act Plans of this Court.

X. EFFECTIVE DATE

This plan shall become effective when approved by the Judicial Council of the Sixth Circuit.

[Amended June 14, 2017, approved by the Judicial Council of the Sixth Circuit October 18, 2017.]

SELECTED ADMINISTRATIVE ORDERS
NOTICE REGARDING PUBLIC ACCESS

The United States District Court for the Western District of Michigan requires attorneys to file and retrieve documents electronically using the Court's Case Management/Electronic Case Files (CM/ECF) docketing system.

CIVIL CASES

The Court has determined that all civil cases filed on or after August 1, 2001 will be maintained electronically in the CM/ECF system. The CM/ECF system is capable of accepting electronic filings over the Internet. In addition, all documents that are filed on paper will be scanned by the Clerk's office and placed into the CM/ECF system for electronic access. Electronic filing and service is governed by Local Civil Rule 5.7.

Information on civil cases pending in 1989 and thereafter is available through Public Access to Court Electronic Records (PACER) or via the Court's web site (www.miwd.uscourts.gov). Any subscriber to PACER will be able to read, download, store and print the full content of all documents filed in those matters, whether they are filed on paper or electronically. The Court will not make electronically available documents that have been sealed or otherwise restricted by Local Rule or Court order.

CRIMINAL CASES

The Court has determined that all criminal cases filed on or after November 1, 2003 will be maintained electronically in the Court's Case Management/Electronic Case Files (CM/ECF) system. The CM/ECF system is capable of accepting electronic filings over the Internet. In addition, all documents that are filed on paper will be scanned by the Clerk's office and placed into the CM/ECF system for electronic file maintenance. Electronic filing and service is governed by Local Criminal Rule 49.10.

Current docket information on criminal cases pending in 1992 and thereafter is available through Public Access to Court Electronic Records (PACER) or via the Court's web site (www.miwd.uscourts. gov). Electronic access to the documents in criminal files that were filed prior to November 1, 2004, is available only to the participating registered attorneys, the U.S. Probation Office, the U.S. Marshal and the Court. On and after November 1, 2004, however, access to documents in criminal files is electronically available to the public over the Internet, in accordance with policies established by the Judicial Conference of the United States.

Any subscriber to PACER will be able to read, download, store and print the full content of all documents filed, whether they are filed on paper or electronically. In no event, however, will the Court make electronically available documents that have been sealed or otherwise restricted by Local Rule or Court order.

PERSONAL DATA AND IDENTIFIERS

In light of the current public access to civil and criminal files over the Internet, you should not include sensitive information in any document filed with the Court unless such inclusion is necessary and relevant to the case. Any sensitive information not otherwise protected may be available over the Internet via PACER. If sensitive information must be included in the filing, the following personal data and identifiers must be redacted from the pleading, whether it is filed traditionally or electronically:

- Social Security and tax–payer–identification number (redacted identifier is last four digits)
- financial account numbers (redacted identifier is last four digits)
- names of minor children (redacted identifier is initials)
- dates of birth (redacted identifier is year)
- in criminal filings, home addresses (redacted identifier is city and state)

Redaction of personal identifiers is not required for certain documents (see Fed. R. Civ. P. 5.2 and Fed. R. Crim. P. 49.1).

In compliance with the E–Government Act of 2002, a party wishing to file a document containing the personal data identifiers specified above may a) file an unredacted document under seal, or b) file a reference list under seal. The reference list shall contain the complete personal data identifier(s) and the redacted identifier(s) used in its (their) place in the filing. All references in the case to the redacted identifiers included in the reference list will be construed to refer to the corresponding complete identifier. The reference list must be filed under seal, and may be amended as of right. The unredacted version of the document or the reference list will be retained by the court as part of the record. The party is nevertheless required to file a redacted copy for the public file.

In addition, exercise caution when filing documents that contain the following: (1) personal identifying numbers, such as driver's license numbers; (2) medical records, treatment and diagnosis; (3) employment history; (4) individual financial information; (5) proprietary or trade secret information; (6) information regarding an individual's cooperation with the government; (7) information regarding the victim of any criminal activity; (8) national security information; (9) sensitive security information as described in 49 U.S.C. § 114(s).

Counsel is strongly urged to share this notice with all clients so that an informed decision about the inclusion of certain materials may be made. It is the sole responsibility of counsel and the parties to be sure that all pleadings comply with the Federal Rules of Civil and Criminal Procedure requiring redaction of personal data identifiers.

SERVICE

Court Orders and Notices. The Court will issue its orders and notices electronically to all registered counsel. The Court will send its orders and notices through regular U.S. mail to all counsel who have not registered. Parties who are not represented by counsel will be sent Court orders and notices through regular U.S. mail.

Service of Documents

Documents Filed on Paper by Non–Registered Attorneys and Pro Se Parties. All documents filed with the Court on paper must be served on other parties on paper in the traditional manner pursuant to the applicable Federal and Local Rules.

Documents Filed on Paper by Registered Attorneys. When a registered attorney does not use the electronic filing capabilities of the system and instead files documents with the Court on paper, the attorney must serve those documents in the traditional manner pursuant to the applicable Federal and Local Rules. Scanning of your documents by the Court and the resulting electronic notice by the Court does not constitute service upon the other parties in the case.

Documents Filed Electronically. When a document is filed electronically, a Notice of Electronic Filing will be generated by the system and will indicate which counsel have been served electronically. If opposing counsel has registered, they will be served electronically and no further service upon them is necessary. If opposing counsel has not registered, or if you are filing paper documents, then the document must be served upon that counsel on paper in the traditional manner pursuant to the applicable Federal and Local Rules.

ELECTRONIC FILING INFORMATION

Help Desk. The Clerk's Office has established an Electronic Filing Help Desk to answer questions and to provide assistance should difficulties arise. The Help Desk can be reached by phone at (616) 456–2206, toll free at (800) 290–2742, or via e-mail at ecfhelp@miwd.uscourts.gov. The Help Desk is staffed weekdays from 8:00 a.m. until 5:00 p.m., excluding Federal Holidays.

Additional Information. Additional information and materials are available on the Court's website (www.miwd.uscourts.gov). On the website, you will find Local Civil Rule 5.7, Local Criminal Rule 49.10, an electronic filing registration form, an on-line tutorial, a User's Guide, FAQ's and more.

[Dated: March 26, 2009.]

ADMINISTRATIVE ORDER NO. 05–108. IN THE MATTER OF AUTOMATIC REASSIGNMENT OF CRIMINAL DEFENDANTS TO THE SENTENCING JUDGE

WHEREAS for purposes of judicial economy, the sentencing judge may differ from the judge originally assigned to the case;

WHEREAS to ensure proper statistical accounting for the sentencing, the sentencing judge must also be the judge assigned to the case;

THEREFORE, IT IS HEREBY ORDERED that when it becomes known that the sentencing judge differs from the judge assigned to the case, the clerk's office shall automatically reassign the criminal defendant's case to the sentencing judge.

[Dated: September 12, 2005.]

ADMINISTRATIVE ORDER NO. 06–085. STANDING ORDER
REGARDING DISCOVERY IN CRIMINAL CASES

Unless otherwise ordered in a particular case, the parties in all criminal proceedings in this Court must comply with the following requirements:

A. Upon request of the defendant, to be made within seven (7) days from the date of arraignment of the defendant, the government shall permit the defendant to inspect and copy the following items or copies thereof, or supply copies thereof, which are within the possession, custody, or control of the government, or the existence of which is known or by the exercise of due diligence may become known to the attorney for the government:

1. Any relevant written or recorded statements made by the defendant including, but not limited to, the rough notes of any interrogations of the defendant before or after arrest by any persons then known to be government agents.

2. The defendant's arrest and conviction record.

3. Results or reports of physical or mental examinations, and of scientific tests, including, without limitation, any handwriting analysis or experiments, which are material to the preparation of the defense or are intended for use by the government as evidence in chief at the trial.

4. The substance of any oral statement made by the defendant before or after his arrest in response to interrogation by a person then known to be a government agent which the government intends to offer in evidence at trial.

5. Recorded grand jury testimony of the defendant relating to the offenses charged.

6. Books, papers, documents, photographs, tangible objects, buildings or places which the government intends to use as evidence at trial to prove its case in chief, or were obtained from or belong to each defendant.

B. Upon receipt by a defendant of materials in A(3) or A(6) from the government, the defendant shall permit the government to inspect and copy the following items or copies thereof, or supply copies thereof, which are within the possession, custody or control of the defendant, the existence of which is known or by the exercise of due diligence may become known to the defendant:

1. Books, papers, documents, photographs or tangible objects which each defendant intends to introduce as evidence in chief at trial.

2. Any results or reports of physical or mental examinations and of scientific tests or experiments made in connection with this case which the defendant intends to introduce as evidence in chief at trial, or which were prepared by a defense witness who will testify concerning the contents thereof.

C. If a defendant intends to rely upon the defense of insanity at the time of the alleged crime, or intends to introduce expert testimony relating to a mental disease, defect or other condition bearing upon the issue of whether he had the mental state required for the offense charged, he shall give written notice thereof to the government. This notice shall be given within twenty (21) days from the date of arraignment of the defendant.

D. The government shall reveal to the defendant and permit inspection and copying all information and material known to the government which may be favorable to the defendant on the issues of guilt or punishment within the scope of Brady v. Maryland, 373 U.S. 83 (1963), and United States v. Agurs, 427 U.S. 97 (1976).

E. The government shall obtain and copy impeachment information relating to its witnesses that is within the ambit of the Jencks Act and within the ambit of Brady, including any prior criminal record of any alleged informant who will testify for the government at trial, so that the documents are available for effective use at the time of trial. This Court cannot compel the government to disclose Jencks Act statements prior to the trial. United States v. Presser, 844 F.2d 1275, 1283 (6th Cir. 1988). The Sixth Circuit Court of Appeals has noted, however, that "the better practice . . . is for the government to produce such material well in advance of trial so that defense counsel may have an adequate opportunity to examine that which is not in dispute and the court may examine the rest in camera, usually in chamber." United States v. Minsky, 963 F.2d 870, 876 (6th Cir. 1992). This Court urges the government to follow the recommendation of the Sixth Circuit and produce Jencks Act and other impeachment material in a timely fashion.

F.   The government shall state whether the defendant was identified in any lineup, showup, photo spread or similar identification proceeding, and produce any picture utilized or resulting therefrom.

G.   The government shall advise its agents and officers involved in this case to preserve all rough notes.

H.   The government shall advise the defendant of its intention to introduce during its case in chief proof of evidence, pursuant to Rule 404(b) of the Federal Rules of Evidence pursuant to Rule 12(b)(4) of the Federal Rules of Criminal Procedure.

I.   The government shall state whether the defendant was an aggrieved person, as defined in 18 U.S.C. Section 2510(11) of any electronic surveillance conducted in connection with the investigation of the charges pending herein, if so, shall set forth in detail the circumstances thereof.

J.   Upon request of the defendant, to be made within seven (7) days from the date of arraignment of the defendant, the government shall provide the defense, for independent expert examination, copies of all latent fingerprints or palm prints which have been identified by a government expert as those of the defendant.

K.   The parties shall make every possible effort in good faith to stipulate all facts or points of law, the truth and existence of which is not contested and the early resolution of which will expedite the trial.

L.   The parties shall collaborate in preparation of a written statement to be signed by counsel for each side, generally describing all discovery material exchanged, and setting forth all stipulations entered into at the conference. No stipulation made by defense counsel at the conference shall be used against the defendant unless the stipulation is reduced to writing, signed by the defendant and his counsel, and filed with the court.

M.   It shall be the continuing duty of counsel for both sides to immediately reveal to opposing counsel all newly discovered information or other material within the scope of this order.

N.   Upon a sufficient showing, the Court may at any time, upon motion properly filed, order that the discovery or inspection provided for by this order be denied, restricted or deferred, or make such other order as is appropriate. It is expected by the Court, however, that counsel for both sides shall make every good faith effort to comply with the letter and spirit of this order.

O.   In setting forth the discovery required by this order, the Court notes that "in most criminal prosecutions, the Brady rule [Brady v. Maryland, 373 U.S. 83 (1963)], Rule 16 [Fed. R. Crim. P. 161] and the Jencks Act [18 U.S.C. § 3500], exhaust the universe of discovery to which the defendant is entitled." United States v. Presser, 844 F.2d 1275, 1285, n. 12 (6th Cir. 1988). The Court accordingly directs the parties to engage in discovery consistent with Brady, Rule 16, and the Jencks Act, including the requirement pertaining to expert witnesses. If any party discovers additional information required to be disclosed under Rule 16, it is to advise opposing counsel, in writing, regarding that information. The parties must also be prepared to comply with the provisions of Rule 26.2 at trial.

This order is designed to exhaust the discovery to which a defendant is ordinarily entitled and to avoid the necessity of counsel for the defendant(s) filing routine motions for routine discovery. Accordingly, counsel for the defendant(s) shall make a request of the government for each item of discovery sought and be declined the same prior to the filing of any motion. Further, any motion filed on behalf of the defendant(s) shall include an accompanying certification by counsel for the defendant(s) that either:

   1.   The item of discovery sought in the motion is not included in or covered by this discovery order; that a formal request for the item has been made to the government, and the government has declined-the request, or

   2.   The item of discovery sought in the motion is included in or covered by this discovery order; that a formal request for the item has been made to the government, and the government has declined the request.

Unless otherwise indicated above, the parties must comply with this order within 21 days of the initial arraignment. Failure to abide by this order may result in the imposition of sanctions.

[Dated: August 28, 2006.]

ADMINISTRATIVE ORDER NO. 07–026.　RE: JUDGES' COURTESY COPY POLICY

The Court hereby implements a Judges' Courtesy Copy Policy which applies to all papers filed through its electronic filing system (ECF):

One "courtesy" or "chambers copy" of all dispositive motion papers, as defined in W.D. Mich. LCivR 7.2, (including responses and replies) and all accompanying exhibits must be submitted directly to the judge's chambers on paper. Any exhibits must be properly tabbed and all papers firmly bound, usually along the left margin ("book–style"). A printed copy of the Notice of Electronic Filing must be attached to the front of the paper.

The chambers copy must be hand-delivered or sent via first class mail the same day the document is e-filed, unless it relates to a court proceeding scheduled within the next five days or otherwise requires the immediate attention of the Court, in which case the chambers copy must be hand-delivered to chambers not later than the morning of the next business day after the document is e-filed.

Questions regarding the courtesy copy policy should be directed to the ECF Help Desk (616–456–2206 or 800–290–2742) or submitted electronically to ecfhelp@miwd.uscourts.gov.

This policy is necessary because of the voluminous attachments to dispositive motions. It takes effect immediately. Any counsel wishing to comment on the policy is invited to do so by submitting written comments to ecfhelp@miwd.uscourts.gov.

The Clerk shall send a copy of this policy by e-mail to all registered attorneys and post a copy on the Court's website.

[Dated: March 21, 2007.]

ADMINISTRATIVE ORDER NO. 08–019.　IN RE: MOTIONS FOR SENTENCE MODIFICATION UNDER 18 U.S.C. § 3582(c)(2)

At a special meeting conducted on February 21, 2008, the district judges of this Court adopted guidelines for the handling of motions for sentence modification under 18 U.S.C. § 3582(c)(2) arising from the retroactive application of Amendments 706 and 711 of the Federal Sentencing Guidelines. A copy of the procedure adopted by the Court is attached to this order, along with copies of form motions to be used in such cases. All attorneys and pro se parties filing such motions must adhere to the attached procedures, unless a judge of this Court orders an exception in a particular case.

The Clerk is directed to make these materials available to the public on the Court's website and at the Clerk's divisional offices.

UNITED STATES DISTRICT COURT
FOR THE WESTERN DISTRICT OF MICHIGAN

PROCEDURES FOR HANDLING MOTIONS FOR
SENTENCING MODIFICATIONS UNDER 18 U.S.C. § 3582(c)(2)

This memorandum sets forth the procedures adopted by the United States District Court for the Western District of Michigan for consideration of motions by defendants for sentence modifications arising from Amendments 706 and 711 of the United States Sentencing Guidelines. These amendments, effective March 3, 2008, retroactively modified the Drug Quantity Table with regard to cocaine base (crack cocaine). These procedures are intended to govern the expeditious handling of motions for sentence modification in the majority of cases; an individual judge, however, is free to alter these procedures to address the circumstances of any particular case.

As used in this memorandum, an *eligible defendant* means: (1) a person serving a term of imprisonment under a criminal judgment issued by this court; (2) whose sentencing guideline offense level was computed in whole or in part by reference to a quantity of crack cocaine; and (3) whose guideline range is lowered by application of Amendments 706 and 711 of the U.S. Sentencing Guidelines.

I. FORM AND FILING OF MOTIONS

A. Form of Motions. Motions must be filed on the court-approved form. No memorandum of law or attachments may accompany the motion. Non-conforming motions will be returned to the submitting party by order of court.

B. Filing of Motion

1. *By the Federal Defender—*

   a. E-filed, with a copy automatically sent by CM/ECF to the U.S. Attorney's Office;

   b. The motion will include a request for appointment of FPD and financial affidavit.

2. *By a panel attorney who represented defendant at sentencing or on appeal—*

   a. E-filed, with a copy automatically sent by CM/ECF to the U.S. Attorney's Office;

   b. The motion will include a request for appointment of the panel attorney and financial affidavit.

3. *By retained counsel*—E-filed, with a copy automatically sent by CM/ECF to the U.S. Attorney's Office.

4. *By a pro se defendant—*

   a. Filed on paper and scanned into the CM/ECF system, with a copy automatically sent by CM/ECF to the U.S. Attorney's Office;

   b. May request appointment of counsel in body of the form motion.

C. Appointment of Counsel. Appointment of counsel is discretionary with the court at any stage of the proceedings.

II. INITIAL CONSIDERATION

A. Initial Review.

1. Immediately upon filing, the judge's office will review the motion to determine whether the defendant has been previously identified by the Sentencing Commission or the Administrative Office as an inmate potentially affected by Amendments 706 and 711.

   a. If so, the court will move to Step B.

   b. If not, the case will be referred to Probation for a review of the file, to determine whether the movant is an *eligible defendant*. This report should be filed within 7 business days, unless the Probation Office file is in storage.

   c. The Probation Office will file a short report, which will be served on the parties, stating whether or not the movant appears to be an *eligible defendant* and the basis for that conclusion. Any party objecting to the conclusion of the Probation Office must file the objection within 14 days of service.

2. If the defendant is clearly ineligible, the court may dismiss the motion. If the court determines that the movant may be an *eligible defendant*, the court will move to Step B.

B. Triage of Motions.

1. Motions by potentially *eligible defendants* with release dates before January 1, 2012, will receive priority, and the court will immediately move to Step C.

2. Motions by potentially *eligible defendants* with release dates on and after January 1, 2012, will be held in abeyance. The court will reach those motions, moving to Step C, as more urgent cases are decided.

C. Issuance of Order for Sentence Modification Report.

1. The court will order the Probation Office to prepare a Sentence Modification Report, addressing the following issues:

   a. a brief procedural history of sentencing decisions, including whether the original sentence was imposed pursuant to *Booker*, reflected any departures or variances, or was reduced under U.S.S.G. § 5K1.1 or Rule 35(b);

b.   the original Guideline calculation and a recalculation of the Guideline range in accordance with U.S.S.G. § 1B1.10(b)(1);

c.   a statement whether the movant is an *eligible defendant* and the basis for that conclusion;

d.   any information readily available to Probation from the BOP concerning defendant's post-sentencing conduct or misconduct;

e.   any information available to Probation concerning the danger to any person or the community that may be posed by a reduction in defendant's sentence;

f.   a recommendation for disposition of the motion.

2.   The U.S. Probation Office will be directed to prepare Sentence Modification Reports in a sequence consistent with projected release dates of the moving defendants, assuring those defendants eligible for imminent release are addressed first by the Court. Once all requested reports for inmates with projected release dates before January 1, 2012, are submitted to the Court, the U.S. Probation Office will prepare reports for moving defendants with release dates on or after January 1, 2012, in a sequence reflecting their projected release dates.

3.   Upon request, the Probation Office will provide a copy of the original Presentence Investigation Report to either party.

D.   Submissions by the Parties.

1.   Defendant (or counsel) will have 21 days after service of the Sentence Modification Report to file a brief and supporting documents, addressing any legal or factual issue relevant to the motion for reduction of sentence.

2.   Within 21 days of service of defendant's brief, the Government may file its brief and supporting materials, addressed to the same subjects.

3.   Submissions in support of or in opposition to a motion must not exceed 20 pages, including attachments.

4.   At any time before a decision on the motion, the parties may file with the court a joint recommendation for disposition of the motion, understanding that the ultimate decision is in the court's discretion.

E.   Hearing. A hearing will be scheduled only if the court determines that a genuine issue of material fact must be resolved or that oral argument will be beneficial to the court. A defendant's presence for sentence modification is not required by the Federal Rules of Criminal Procedure. FED. R. CRIM. P. 43(b)(4). If either party seeks a hearing or defendant's personal presence, the party's brief must specifically request such relief and give reasons in support.

UNITED STATES DISTRICT COURT
WESTERN DISTRICT OF MICHIGAN

UNITED STATES OF AMERICA,

               Plaintiff,

     File No. _____

      v.

     Hon. _____

_____,

               Defendant.

Motion for Modification or Reduction of Sentence Pursuant to 18 U.S.C. § 3582(c)(2)

Defendant, through his counsel, hereby requests a modification or reduction of sentence pursuant to 18 U.S.C. § 3582(c)(2) and Amendments 706 and 711 to the United States Sentencing Guidelines, which made a reduction in the base offense level for crack-cocaine offenses retroactive as of March 3, 2008. In support of this motion, defendant states as follows:

1.   I am serving a term of imprisonment.

2.   My sentence was based, at least in part, on crack cocaine. _____ (Yes or No)

3. I was sentenced in the Western District of Michigan on _____ (date) to a term of _____ months in prison. My total offense level was _____ and my criminal history category was _____.

4. My projected release date is _____.

5. I hereby request a court-appointed attorney. _____ (Yes or No)

If yes, please complete the Financial Affidavit available on the Court's website at www.miwd. uscourts.gov. (Note: appointment of counsel is discretionary with the Court.)

PLEASE DO NOT ATTACH ANY OTHER MATERIALS AT THIS TIME OR YOUR MOTION WILL BE REJECTED AND RETURNED. IF APPLICABLE, SUBMIT THE FINANCIAL AFFIDAVIT TO THE COURT ON PAPER.

_____   Date: _____
Counsel for Petitioner

Name: _____
Address: _____
Telephone Number: _____   Email Address: _____

UNITED STATES DISTRICT COURT
WESTERN DISTRICT OF MICHIGAN

_____

UNITED STATES OF AMERICA,

Plaintiff,   File No. _____

                                   Hon. _____

v.

_____,

Defendant.

Motion for Modification or Reduction of Sentence Pursuant to 18 U.S.C. § 3582(c)(2)

I hereby request a modification or reduction of my sentence pursuant to 18 U.S.C. § 3582(c)(2) and Amendments 706 and 711 to the United States Sentencing Guidelines, which made a reduction in the base offense level for crack-cocaine offenses retroactive as of March 3, 2008, and in support of my motion state as follows:

1. I am serving a term of imprisonment.

2. My sentence was based, at least in part, on crack cocaine. _____ (Yes or No)

3. I was sentenced in the Western District of Michigan on _____ (date) to a term of _____ months in prison. My total offense level was _____ and my criminal history category was _____.

4. My projected release date is _____.

5. I hereby request a court-appointed attorney. _____ (Yes or No)

If yes, please complete the attached Financial Affidavit.

(Note: appointment of counsel is discretionary with the Court)

WITH THE EXCEPTION OF THE FINANCIAL AFFIDAVIT, PLEASE DO NOT SUBMIT OR ATTACH ANY OTHER MATERIALS AT THIS TIME OR YOUR MOTION WILL BE REJECTED AND RETURNED.

Signature of Petitioner: _____   Date: _____

Print or Type Name: _____   Register #: _____

Current Address: _____

[Dated: February 26, 2008.]

483

ADMINISTRATIVE ORDER NO. 08–143.   IN RE: CELL PHONE USE UNDER LOCAL CIVIL RULE 83.4 AND LOCAL CRIMINAL RULE 57.4

By order entered September 3, 2008, this Court adopted and promulgated amendments to Local Civil Rule 83.4 and Local Criminal Rule 57.4, governing conduct in federal court facilities. Those rules, which go into effect on November 3, 2008, provide that cell phones may be used in federal court facilities only in designated areas, as established by Administrative Order. The purpose of this Administrative Order is to designate areas for cell phone use by those persons authorized in this Court's local rules to carry and use cellular phones within federal court facilities in this district.

Cell phones may be used in the following areas, but only by those persons permitted to use and carry cell phones by this court's local rules:

The Chambers Suites of all Judges

Gerald R. Ford Federal Building & Courthouse—Grand Rapids:

Sub-basement:	Elevator Lobby and Snack Bar Area
Basement:	Elevator Lobby
First Floor:	Elevator Lobby
Second Floor:	No Restrictions
Third Floor:	Elevator lobby
Fourth Floor:	Not allowed
Fifth Floor:	Elevator lobby
Sixth Floor:	Not allowed
Seventh Floor:	Elevator lobby

U.S. Courthouse—Kalamazoo:

Basement:	No Restrictions
First Floor:	West Lobby adjacent to Security Station

U.S. Post Office & Courthouse—Marquette:

Basement:	No Restrictions
Post Office:	No Restrictions
Second Floor:	Outside Security Screening Area Only
Third Floor:	Outside Security Screening Area Only

Charles E. Chamberlain Courthouse—Lansing:

Basement:	No Restrictions
First Floor:	East Lobby, Adjacent to Stairwell
	Jury Assembly Area–Jurors Only
Second Floor:	No Restrictions

Logans Place West—Traverse City:
Outside Security Screening Area Only

This Administrative Order takes effect on November 3, 2008, and will remain in effect until superseded by future order or local rule. This order shall be posted in each federal court facility in this district and on the Court's website.

[Dated: October 15, 2008.]

ADMINISTRATIVE ORDER NO. 16–MS–017.   IN RE: REFERENCING THE COURT RECORD

A record wide sequential pagination of the electronic court record initiates with the first filing in a case. The purpose of this is to clearly, uniquely, and permanently identify each page of the court record. The sequential page identification, referred to as the PageID, eliminates the need to define the date, document type and document page number when citing to the record.

The document header displayed at the top of every page of every electronically filed document clearly identifies the unique page identification, and is available to all who have electronic access to the document.[1] Reference to a page of the record by PageID ensures that the same document page is referenced by all, and eliminates any opportunity for misunderstanding. In addition, the Sixth Circuit Court of Appeals requires reference to the PageID in briefs on appeal (6 Cir. R. 28).

NOW, THEREFORE, IT IS ORDERED that any reference by a registered attorney to a portion of the record in which it is to be electronically filed shall be made by reference to the PageID identified thereon, following the cite form identified below, for any documents filed on or after March 7, 2016. Pro se litigants are exempt from this requirement.

To reference	Cite form example
A single page	PageID.234
Multiple sequential pages	PageID.234–235
Multiple pages that are not in succession	PageID.234, 238, 245

IT IS FURTHER ORDERED that the cite form for any filing that references a portion of a different case record within the Western District of Michigan shall be preceded with the 13–digit case number for that other case (e.g., 1:15–cv–99999 PageID.234).

[Dated: February 9, 2016.]

[1] The Court recognizes that some documents are filed with access restrictions, including under seal. If a document is restricted in some way and electronic access to the document is not available based on that restriction, access to the PageID number(s) for that document are likewise not available.

UNITED STATES BANKRUPTCY COURT FOR THE WESTERN DISTRICT OF MICHIGAN

**Including Amendments Received Through
January 1, 2018**

MEDIATION RULES

ELECTRONIC CASE FILING

ADMINISTRATIVE PROCEDURES FOR THE ELECTRONIC FILING, SIGNING, VERIFICATION AND SERVICE OF DOCUMENTS

POLICY—TRANSCRIPTS OF COURT PROCEEDINGS

LBR 1001. SCOPE, CITATION, AND DEFINITIONS

(a) Scope. These Local Bankruptcy Rules are promulgated pursuant to Fed. R. Bankr. P. 9029 to supplement the Federal Rules of Bankruptcy Procedure.

(b) Citation. These Local Bankruptcy Rules may be cited by number using the format "LBR [#]."

(c) Definitions.

(1) "Clerk" means the Clerk of the United States Bankruptcy Court for the Western District of Michigan or a designated Deputy Clerk.

(2) "CM/ECF" means the Case Management/Electronic Case Filing System.

(3) "Court" means the United States Bankruptcy Court for the Western District of Michigan and includes any judicial officer before whom a case or proceeding is pending.

(4) "Code" means the United States Bankruptcy Code, Title 11 of the United States Code.

(5) "Domestic Support Obligation" has the same meaning as prescribed in the Code.

(6) "ECF Filer" means a person registered to file a document using CM/ECF.

(7) "Over the counter" or "conventional" with respect to the filing of any document with the Court means delivery of that document to the Court by any method other than electronic transmission using CM/ECF.

(8) "Paper" or "Papers" as applied to cases and proceedings assigned to CM/ECF includes documents in electronic format presented for filing unless the context clearly indicates otherwise.

(9) "Paper Filer" means a person authorized to file a document "over the counter" without using CM/ECF.

(10) "Payment Advices" has the same meaning as prescribed in the Code.

(11) "Practice in the Court" means, in connection with a case or proceeding pending in this Court, (A) to appear in, commence, conduct, prosecute, or defend a matter in that case or proceeding; (B) to appear in open court; (C) to sign a document; (D) to participate in a pretrial conference; (E) to represent a client at a deposition; (F) to counsel a client in the

action or proceeding for compensation; or (G) to otherwise practice in this Court or before an officer of this Court.

(12) "Scanned Image" includes any electronically-generated graphic depiction of any original or duplicate document stored in electronic format and compatible with CM/ECF, unless the context requires otherwise.

(d) **Application of Local Bankruptcy Rules.** These Rules apply to all cases and proceedings except to the extent that they are inconsistent with the Code, the Federal Rules of Bankruptcy Procedure, or any rule promulgated by the Judicial Conference of the United States.

(e) **Use of Forms.** Whenever the use of an Official Form is required under these Rules, Fed. R. Bankr. P. 9009 applies. Whenever the use of a Local Form is required under these Rules, LBR 9029(d) applies.

[Effective August 1, 2012.]

LBR 1002. DISCLOSURE OF NONFILING SPOUSE AND CONTRIBUTIONS TO HOUSEHOLD EXPENSES

In Schedule I, a married debtor must disclose the full legal name, address, and income of a nonfiling spouse unless the spouses are separated and the information is not available. An individual debtor is not required to disclose a nonspouse cohabitant's income on Schedule I, but must include the nonspouse cohabitant's contributions to household expenses as income to the debtor.

[Effective August 1, 2012.]

LBR 1004. PARTNERSHIP PETITION

When a voluntary petition is filed by a partnership, evidence of the consent of all general partners must be attached to the petition. If a written partnership agreement permits less than unanimous consent for the filing of a voluntary bankruptcy petition, a declaration to that effect must be attached to the petition.

[Effective August 1, 2012.]

LBR 1006. FILING FEE

The Clerk may approve an application by an individual to pay the filing fee in installments.

[Effective August 1, 2012.]

LBR 1007-1. PAPER FILERS

(a) **No Copies Required.** When filing an original document or amendment, a Paper Filer is not required to provide the Clerk with extra copies unless a time-stamped copy is desired.

(b) **Time–Stamped Copies.** The Clerk will time stamp any copy provided by a Paper Filer and, if the document is filed by mail, return the copy by mail as long as a self-addressed envelope with sufficient postage has also been provided.

[Effective August 1, 2012.]

LBR 1007–2. ADDITIONAL REQUIRED DOCUMENTS

(a) **Corporate Resolution.** When filing a bankruptcy petition, a corporate debtor must file a copy of the corporate resolution that authorizes such filing.

(b) **Schedule C in a Joint Case.** Each individual in a joint case must file a separate Schedule C.

(c) **Mailing Matrix.**

(1) *Paper Filers.* A debtor who is a Paper Filer must file a mailing matrix with the petition that conforms with the matrix guidelines published by the Clerk. (Instructions for the preparation of matrices are appended to these Rules as Exhibit 1.)

(2) *ECF Filers.* ECF Filers must upload a mailing matrix in accordance with established procedures for submission into CM/ECF.

(3) *Verification of Creditor Matrix.* The debtor must file a Verification of Creditor Matrix along with a copy of the matrix. (A Verification of Creditor Matrix form is appended to these Rules as Exhibit 2.)

(d) **Asset Protection Report.**

(1) *With Original Petition.* A Chapter 7 debtor must file an asset protection report with the original petition.

(2) *On Conversion.* Any debtor who converts a case from Chapter 11, 12, or 13 to Chapter 7 must file an asset protection report with the motion to convert. If the conversion is involuntary, the debtor must file the asset protection report within 7 days after entry of the order for conversion.

(3) *Failure to Comply.* Failure to comply with this Rule may result in the dismissal of the case or other appropriate relief as determined by the Court.

(4) *Form.* Copies of the approved Asset Protection Report form may be obtained from the Clerk or via the Court's website at www.miwb.uscourts.gov. (A copy of the Asset Protection Report form is also appended to these Rules as Exhibit 3.)

(e) **Notice of Alternatives.**

(1) *Form.* In accordance with 11 U.S.C. § 342(b), the Notice of Alternatives is available under the "Official Forms" link on the Court's website at www.miwb.uscourts.gov. The Notice of Alternatives indicates each chapter of Title 11 under which an individual may proceed.

(2) *Mandatory Filing; Exceptions.* Every petition filed by an individual debtor must be accompanied by a Notice of Alternatives signed by the debtor. However, no Notice of Alternatives is required if:

(A) the debtor's attorney has completed Exhibit B on the Voluntary Petition (Official Form 1); or

(B) the schedules are filed contemporaneously with the petition and the schedules clearly show that the debts are not primarily consumer debts.

(f) **Documentation Required by Trustees.** In every individual chapter 7 and 13 case, the debtor must submit the following documents to the trustee at least 7 days before the date first set for the meeting of creditors. The trustee may adjourn the meeting of creditors or file a motion to dismiss if the documents are not provided by the required deadline.

(1) Copies of all payment advices or other evidence of payment received by the debtor from any employer within 60 days of the date of filing. This documentation must be provided to the trustee instead of being filed with the Court as prescribed by 11 U.S.C. § 521(a)(1)(B)(iv);

(2) Copies of the federal and state income-tax returns, together with all W–2s, for the most recent tax year ending immediately before the commencement of the case, or a debtor's certification explaining why those tax returns are not available. This documentation must be provided to the trustee instead of being filed with the Court as prescribed by 11 U.S.C. § 521(e)(2);

(3) For each financial account held by the debtor, copies of account statements or transaction histories that reflect the account's activity for the 90 days immediately preceding the commencement of the case;

(4) Copies of all certificates of title issued with respect to personal property owned by the debtor as of the commencement of the case;

(5) Copies of all recorded deeds and mortgages (if any) and the current year's SEV for all real property in which the debtor holds an interest as of the commencement of the case;

(6) The declarations pages of all insurance policies that provide coverage for any real or personal property owned by the debtor as of the commencement of the case;

(7) An account statement showing the current value of all IRAs, 401(k)s, pensions, or similar retirement or investment accounts held by the debtor as of the commencement of the case;

(8) If the debtor has been divorced within the last 10 years, a complete copy of the judgment of divorce and all related agreements; and

(9) If the debtor is required to pay a Domestic Support Obligation, written documentation showing:

(A) the name, address, and telephone number of the Domestic Support Obligation recipient; and

(B) the name, address, and telephone number of any Friend of the Court or similar out-of-state agency; and the case or account number used by the agency in the Domestic Support Obligation matter.

The foregoing list is not exclusive and the trustee may require the debtor to provide additional documentation. Similarly, a debtor's compliance with this Rule does not excuse the debtor from his or her obligation to continue cooperating with the trustee as required by 11 U.S.C. § 521(a)(3).

(g) Creditor Request for Payment Advices.

(1) *Timely Request.* In addition to the requirements of (f)(1) above, the debtor must submit payment advices directly to any creditor who timely requests a copy. A creditor makes a timely request for payment advices if the request is filed with the Court and served on the debtor and any attorney for the debtor by U.S. mail or CM/ECF no later than 14 days before the date first set for the meeting of creditors.

(2) *Form of Request.* A creditor's request for payment advices must be made in a separate document captioned "Request for Debtor's Pay Advices" or a substantially similar designation and must contain:

(A) the name; address; and telephone number, facsimile number, or email address of the requesting creditor; and

(B) the name; address; and telephone number, facsimile number, or email address of any attorney representing the creditor.

(3) *Compliance With Creditor's Request.* Transmitting payment advices to the designated facsimile number or email address contained in the request or mailing payment advices via U.S. Mail to the mailing address of the creditor or its attorney constitutes compliance with the creditor's request. The debtor must contemporaneously file with the Court a proof of service indicating that the required payment advices were provided.

(h) Creditor's Request for Pre–Petition Tax Information.

(1) *Timely Request.* In addition to the requirements of (f)(2) above, the debtor must submit pre-petition tax information directly to any creditor who timely requests a copy pursuant to 11 U.S.C. § 521(e)(2). A creditor makes a timely request for pre-petition tax information if the request is filed with the Court and served on the debtor and any attorney for the debtor by U.S. mail or CM/ECF no later than 14 days before the date first set for the meeting of creditors.

(2) *Form of Request.* A creditor's request for tax information must be made in a separate document captioned "Request for Debtor's Tax Return Information" or a substantially similar designation and must contain:

(A) the name; address; and telephone number, facsimile number, or email address of the requesting creditor; and

(B) the name; address; and telephone number, facsimile number, or email address of any attorney representing the creditor.

(3) *Compliance With Creditor's Request.* Transmitting tax information to the designated facsimile number or email address contained in the request or mailing tax information via U.S. Mail to the mailing address of the creditor or its attorney constitutes compliance with the creditor's request. The debtor must also contemporaneously file with the Court a proof of service indicating that the required tax returns or transcripts were provided.

(i) Debtor's Post–Petition Tax Information.

(1) *Information Required.* On the timely request of the United States Trustee or a party in interest pursuant to 11 U.S.C. § 521(f), the debtor must furnish the following tax information at the same time it is filed with the taxing authority:

(A) tax transcripts or returns filed for each post-petition year the bankruptcy case remains open;

(B) tax transcripts or returns for any year ending within the 3–year period before the commencement of the case that are filed post-petition while the bankruptcy case remains open; and

(C) a copy of any amended tax transcript or return filed while the bankruptcy case remains open.

(2) *Form of Request.* If the United States Trustee or a party in interest desires to receive a copy of the debtor's post-petition tax information, it must file a "Motion for Order Requiring Debtor to Provide Tax Return Information" or a motion with a substantially similar designation. The motion must contain (A) a citation to the applicable Code section; (B) the name; address; and telephone number, facsimile number, or email address of the party filing the motion and of any attorney representing that party; and (C) a request for relief.

(3) *Court Order Requiring Production.* On receipt of a motion requesting the debtor's post-petition tax information, the Court may (A) set the matter for hearing with notice to the moving party, any attorney for the moving party, the debtor, and any attorney for the debtor; or (B) issue an appropriate order without a hearing. If the Court enters an order requiring the debtor to produce post-petition tax information, the debtor must furnish the information according to the terms and procedures specified in the order. The debtor must also contemporaneously file with the Court a proof of service indicating that the required tax returns or transcripts were provided.

(j) Further Discovery. Nothing in this Rule precludes the discovery of other information or documents pursuant to the Code or the Federal Rules of Bankruptcy Procedure.

[Effective August 1, 2012.]

LBR 1008. VERIFICATION OF ELECTRONICALLY FILED PETITIONS, LISTS, SCHEDULES, STATEMENTS, AMENDMENTS, AND OTHER DOCUMENTS SIGNED UNDER OATH; RETENTION OF ORIGINALLY SIGNED DOCUMENTS; AND ADMISSIBILITY OF SCANNED DOCUMENTS

(a) Approved Methods for Signing Documents. A signature on an affidavit, stipulation, or other document, including one signed under penalty of perjury or verifying a bankruptcy petition, list, schedule, statement, plan, or any amendment thereto, is indicated by:

(1) filing a scanned image of the originally signed document;

(2) filing a scanned image of the signature page of the electronic document; or

(3) affixing "/s/ NAME" to the document where the handwritten signature or mark would otherwise appear.

(b) Retention of Signed Documents. If a document is filed with an electronic signature indicated by "/s/", the ECF Filer must retain the original signed document or the written authorization for the electronic signature for a minimum of 5 years from the date of filing.

(c) Admissibility of Scanned Documents. Unless the Court orders otherwise, any scanned document that is filed with the Court may be admitted as evidence of the contents of

the document scanned as long as the requirements of Fed. R. Evid. 1004 have been met.

[Effective August 1, 2012.]

LBR 1009. AMENDMENTS TO PETITIONS, LISTS, SCHEDULES, AND STATEMENTS

(a) General Procedure. When filing an amendment to the petition or a list, schedule, or any statement, the debtor must file the entire amended document and highlight the amendment in some fashion. Unless otherwise ordered by the Court, the debtor must sign every amended document. However, the debtor may attach a single signed verification if several documents are contemporaneously amended.

(b) Adding Creditors. If the amendment adds a creditor or creditors, each new creditor's name and address must be uploaded into CM/ECF. The debtor must also promptly serve each newly added creditor with a copy of the Notice of Commencement of Case, Notice of Meeting of Creditors, and Fixing of Deadlines.

(c) Service of Amendments. The debtor must serve the amendment on the trustee and all other entities adversely affected by the amendment, and must promptly file a proof of service showing compliance with Fed. R. Bankr. P. 1009.

[Effective August 1, 2012.]

LBR 1014. DETERMINATION OF PLACE OF HOLDING COURT

(a) Clerk to Determine Location for Hearings. Unless otherwise ordered by the Court, the Clerk will set the location for all hearings, trials, and other matters based on the county of residence or principal place of business listed on the debtor's petition.

(1) For the following counties, the designated location for holding court is Grand Rapids:

Barry	Ionia	Kent	Mecosta	Montcalm
Muskegon	Newaygo	Oceana	Ottawa	

(2) For the following counties, the designated location for holding court is Kalamazoo:

Allegan	Berrien	Branch	St. Joseph	Van Buren
Hillsdale	Cass	Calhoun	Kalamazoo	

(3) For the following counties, the designated location for holding court is Lansing:

Clinton	Eaton	Ingham

(4) For the following counties, the designated location for holding court is Traverse City:

Antrim	Benzie	Charlevoix	Emmet	Lake
Kalkaska	Leelanau	Grand Traverse	Manistee	Mason
Missaukee	Osceola	Wexford		

(5) For the following counties, the designated location for holding court is Marquette:

All of the counties in the Upper Peninsula of Michigan.

(b) Change of Location. The Court may change the location for holding hearings in a bankruptcy case or adversary proceeding if the change is in the interests of justice or convenient to the parties. A debtor, creditor, or other party in interest may request a change in the location for holding hearings by filing a motion with notice to all interested parties pursuant to LBR 9013.

(c) Exception in Pro Bono Cases. Notwithstanding subparagraph (b) of this Rule, an attorney who is affiliated with a pro bono program and who has agreed as part of the program to represent an indigent client before this Court without charge to the client may file a motion and ex parte order transferring the case to the location for holding court which is located nearest the principal office of that attorney. In ruling on the motion, the Court may consider the indigent party's ability to retain representation if the transfer request is denied.

(1) The Court may issue an order transferring the location for holding court without prior hearing.

(2) The Clerk will serve the order on all interested parties with notice and an opportunity to object. If an objection is filed, a hearing will be scheduled at the designated location where the case would normally be assigned absent a request for redesignation.

[Effective August 1, 2012.]

LBR 2002. NOTICING

(a) General Rule. The Clerk will serve:

(1) § 341 meeting notices in Chapter 7, 9, 11 and 13 cases;

(2) notices of the provisions under 11 U.S.C. § 522(q)(1) in individual Chapter 7, 11, 12, and 13 cases;

(3) notices to file Official Form 23 in individual Chapter 7, 11, and 13 cases;

(4) notices of possible dividends and discharges;

(5) notices or orders that are required to be served on all creditors by the United States Trustee, including notices of final accounting and orders of distribution;

(6) notices of sale sent to the Buyers' List maintained by the Clerk; and

(7) notices, orders, or other documents when:

(A) the hearing is expedited and the judicial officer determines that the Clerk is able to serve the parties quicker than the otherwise designated party; or

(B) the party having the burden of service is indigent.

(b) Chapter 12 Notices. The Chapter 12 trustee must serve the § 341 meeting notice unless the trustee requests in writing that the Clerk serve the notice. In that case, the Clerk will serve the notice. The Chapter 12 trustee may charge as an administrative expense of the Chapter 12 estate a per notice fee in an amount determined by general order of the Court. The notice fee is not to be included in the calculation of the combined percentage fee permitted by 11 U.S.C. § 330.

(c) Other Documents. Unless the Court orders otherwise, any other document must be served by the party who pre-

pared it or, if prepared by the Court, by the party for whom the document was prepared.

[Effective August 1, 2012.]

LBR 2004. EXAMINATION OF A PARTY IN INTEREST

(a) Prerequisite to Filing Application. Any entity seeking to examine a party in interest pursuant to Fed. R. Bankr. P. 2004 must first contact the party's attorney (or the party directly if not represented by counsel) to arrange a mutually convenient date, time, and place before filing an application pursuant to that rule. If an agreement is reached, the application must include the agreed-upon date, time, and place of the examination.

(b) Filing of Application Without Agreement. If, after making all reasonable efforts, the applicant is unable to set a mutually acceptable date, time, and place for the examination, the application must include a specific description of the efforts made and the proposed date, time, and place for the examination.

[Effective August 1, 2012.]

LBR 2007. APPOINTMENT OF PATIENT CARE OMBUDSMAN IN A HEALTH CARE BUSINESS CASE

If the debtor in a case under Chapter 7, 9, or 11 is a health care business, the debtor must, at the same time as the petition, file a separate motion to determine whether appointment of a patient care ombudsman is necessary pursuant to 11 U.S.C. § 333(a).

[Effective August 1, 2012.]

LBR 2014. APPOINTMENT OF PROFESSIONAL PERSONS

(a) Scope. This Rule governs all applications for employment of professional persons made in connection with a case.

(b) Application and Order of Employment. A committee in a chapter 11 case, a standing trustee, an appointed trustee, or a debtor-in-possession may file an application for employment of professionals pursuant to Fed. R. Bankr. P. 2014. The application and proposed order must be filed with the Clerk and served electronically on the United States Trustee. A hearing will not be held on the application unless a timely objection is received from the United States Trustee or the Court indicates otherwise.

(1) *Objection Filed.* The United States Trustee may file an objection to the application within 28 days from the date of entry of the application. The objection must be served on the applicant and any party in interest. If a hearing is scheduled, the Clerk will serve notice of the hearing on the United States Trustee, the applicant, and any other person the Court may direct.

(2) *No Objection Filed.* If no objection or request for hearing is filed within 28 days after entry of the application, the applicant may file a certification stating that no timely

response or request for hearing has been filed. No such certification is required if the United States Trustee has previously filed a Statement of No Objection and served the Statement of No Objection on the applicant.

(c) Emergency Applications. If the applicant requires emergency approval of the application for employment, the United States Trustee may certify on the applicant's proposed order that it has no objection to the application. The Court may immediately enter the certified order unless the Court requires further notice or a hearing.

[Effective August 1, 2012.]

LBR 2016–1. DISCLOSURE OF COMPENSATION PAID OR PROMISED TO ATTORNEY OR BANKRUPTCY PETITION PREPARER

Within 14 days after the order for relief, every debtor's attorney or bankruptcy petition preparer must file a statement disclosing any fee paid or agreed to be paid during the 12 months preceding the filing, the source of any such fee paid or promised, and a description of the services included or excluded from that fee. If the debtor is represented by an attorney, the statement must also disclose the nature of any fee-sharing agreement. In Chapter 7 cases only, the statement must be filed as a separate docket entry from the petition and schedules. In all cases, a supplemental statement must be filed within 14 days of any payment or agreement not previously disclosed.

[Effective August 1, 2012.]

LBR 2016–2. FEE APPLICATIONS FILED PURSUANT TO FED. R. BANKR. P. 2016

(a) Scope. This Rule governs all applications for compensation or reimbursement filed pursuant to Fed. R. Bankr. P. 2016.

(b) Fee Applications for $1,000 or Less.

(1) *By Stipulation.* The Court may approve an application for compensation or reimbursement of $1,000 or less without notice and opportunity to object if a stipulation that complies with this subsection is filed with the Clerk. The stipulation must be accompanied by the application, supporting documents, and proposed order. It must also clearly state that no signatory to the agreement intends to pursue an objection. The stipulation must be signed by the applicant and the following parties:

(A) the trustee and United States Trustee in a Chapter 7 case;

(B) the debtor-in-possession; trustee, if any; United States Trustee; and counsel for the committees of record in a Chapter 11 case; and

(C) the debtor and the trustee in a Chapter 12 or 13 case.

Regardless of the amount requested, this procedure may not be used by a debtor's attorney to apply for fees beyond the "no look" fee in a Chapter 13 case.

(2) *By Motion.* An entity applying for compensation or reimbursement of $1,000 or less may proceed by motion with notice and opportunity to object as set forth in LBR 9013(c), except that the movant must use the Notice to Creditors and Other Parties in Interest form appended as Exhibit 4 to these Rules. The notice, motion, supporting documents, and proposed order must be filed with the Clerk and served on all parties who would otherwise be required to sign a stipulation.

(c) Fee Applications for More Than $1,000. An entity applying for compensation or reimbursement in excess of $1,000 must proceed by motion with notice and opportunity to object as set forth in LBR 9013(c), except that the movant must use the Notice to Creditors and Other Parties in Interest form appended as Exhibit 4 to these Rules. The notice, motion, supporting documents, and proposed order must be served on all interested parties, including the United States Trustee, the trustee, creditors, equity security holders' committees, and their attorneys.

(d) Exception for Final Fees in a Chapter 7 Case. No Notice to Creditors or proposed order is required with an application for fees and expenses if the fees and expenses are already included in the trustee's final report and account to creditors in a Chapter 7 case.

(e) Special Rules for Fee Applications in Chapter 12 and 13 Cases.

(1) *Fee Applications by Professionals.*

(A) Initial Fee Application. No less than 21 days after the filing of a Chapter 12 or 13 petition, a professional person entitled to compensation must file a copy of the executed fee agreement with the Clerk and serve the trustee as agent for the United States Trustee. The fee agreement must plainly indicate the basis for calculating the fee and the services included in the fee. The agreement must also specifically describe all matters that may require additional compensation and the method by which this additional compensation will be computed. No Chapter 12 or 13 plan containing a provision for payment of professional fees will be confirmed unless all relevant fee agreements have been timely filed. Any objection to the fee agreement will be heard at the confirmation hearing or at such other time as the Court may set.

(B) Applications for Additional Fees. An application for additional fees may be filed by motion with notice and opportunity to object pursuant to LBR 9013(c). If the confirmed plan does not provide for the payment of additional fees and approval of the fees would negatively impact the distribution to unsecured creditors, then the motion must be accompanied by a plan amendment explaining how the additional fees will (i) be paid through the plan; (ii) affect the distribution to creditors; (iii) affect the duration of the plan; and (iv) otherwise adversely affect the parties in interest. The fee application and plan amendment must be served on all interested parties.

(2) *Attorney Fees in Chapter 13 Cases.*

(A) "No Look" Attorney Fee. In a chapter 13 case, the Court may approve compensation of a debtor's attorney up to the "no look" fee without requiring the attorney to file a formal fee application or an itemized statement of services rendered. As a condition to receiving the "no look" fee, the attorney must provide the chapter 13 trustee with a copy of the fee agreement. The fee agreement must be executed by both the debtor and the debtor's attorney and must state the agreed-on fee for pre-confirmation services.

The current "no look" fee is designated by this Court's Memorandum, Regarding Allowance of Compensation and Reimbursement of Expenses for Court–Appointed Professionals, as amended from time to time. (A copy of the most recent Memorandum is appended to these Rules as Exhibit 5.) An attorney requesting the higher "no look" fees pursuant to item 16 of the Court's Memorandum must first file a certificate in the form appended to these Rules as Exhibit 6. The Clerk will retain these certificates for judicial review.

(B) Fee Applications Beyond the "No Look" Fee. The Court will not approve additional fees beyond the "no look" fee unless the attorney files a formal fee application and submits an itemized statement or other documentation which comports with the method for computing additional compensation as set forth in the attorney's fee agreement. The itemized statement must document all services provided from the beginning of the case, including services that were covered by the "no look" fee. Any application for fees beyond the "no look" fee must comply with the requirements of subpart (e)(1)(B) of this Rule, and may not be requested by stipulation.

[Effective August 1, 2012.]

LBR 2030. INTERIM EXPENSES TO PRESERVE THE ESTATE

(a) **Administrative Expenses Under $1,000.** In a Chapter 7 case, the trustee may pay the following § 503(b) administrative expenses without prior notice and a hearing if the expenses are incurred in the ordinary course of the estate's administration and the aggregate amount of all such expenses does not exceed $1,000:

(1) Expenses related to changing locks on premises included in the estate;

(2) Storage (or rent) expenses for estate property;

(3) Expenses associated with winterizing estate property;

(4) Insurance for estate property;

(5) Advertising proposed sales of estate property;

(6) Moving expenses related to transportation of estate property;

(7) Expenses related to determining the existence or perfection of liens (but excluding the compensation of any professional person conducting the investigation);

(8) Bank fees for obtaining copies of bank documents;

(9) Transcript or court-reporter fees; and

(10) Taxes incurred by the estate.

Any time after an expense has been allowed pursuant to this subparagraph, a creditor or other party in interest may request a hearing to reconsider the allowance of the expense.

(b) **Administrative Expenses Over $1,000.** The trustee must file a motion with notice and opportunity to object pursuant to LBR 9013(c) before paying any administrative expense that exceeds the $1,000 aggregate amount. The notice must be served pursuant to Fed. R. Bankr. P. 2002(a).

(c) **Notice Required Before Expenditures Made.**

(1) *Notice to Creditors Directly Affected.* Except as provided in subparagraph (a), the trustee must give advance notice of a proposed expenditure to any creditor directly affected by the expenditure.

(2) *Notice to Others.* Any creditor or the United States Trustee may demand advance notice of expenditures in any case. If a demand is made, the trustee must give notice of the expenditure as far in advance as is reasonably practicable. If in the trustee's judgment funds must be expended on an emergency basis to avoid damage to the estate's property, notice must be given to the requesting party promptly after payment.

(d) **Objection Filed.** If the United States Trustee or a party in interest objects to any expenditure, written notice of the objection must be filed with the Court and served on the trustee and all interested parties. If an objection is filed before the expense is paid, the trustee may not pay the expense without obtaining a court order.

(e) **Expenses Not Covered by This Rule.** This Rule does not authorize payment of wages or professional compensation or authorize the payment of estate funds to the trustee or anyone employed by the bankruptcy estate.

[Effective August 1, 2012.]

LBR 3002. CHAPTER 12 AND 13 CLAIMS

To file a Chapter 12 or 13 claim, a signed claim form that includes all necessary attachments in support of the claim as required by Fed. R. Bankr. P. 3001(c) and (d) must be filed with the Clerk. Claims are deemed filed on the date and time received by the Clerk unless the Court orders otherwise.

[Effective August 1, 2012.]

LBR 3013. CLASSIFICATION OF CLAIMS AND INTERESTS IN CHAPTER 11 PLAN

If a Chapter 11 plan classifies secured claims, priority unsecured claims, or equity interests, it must identify by name each entity holding a claim or interest in that class and the amount of that claim or interest.

[Effective August 1, 2012.]

LBR 3015. CHAPTER 12 AND 13 PLANS

(a) **Service of § 341 Meeting Notices and Plans.** Except as otherwise provided in this subsection, the Clerk will serve the § 341 meeting notice and a copy of the debtor's plan or plan summary on all creditors and parties in interest listed on the mailing matrix. If the debtor fails to file a mailing matrix with the petition or if the debtor adds creditors to the mailing matrix after the case is filed, then the debtor must serve the § 341 meeting notice and a copy of the debtor's plan or plan mmary on all creditors and other parties in interest or on e newly added creditors, as the case may be. The debtor ust also file a proof of service with the Court.

(b) Dismissal When Debtor Fails to File Schedules, tatements, or a Plan. If a debtor files a Chapter 13 petition ut does not also file the schedules and statements as required y Fed. R. Bankr. P. 1007(b) or a plan as required by Fed. R. Bankr. P. 3015(b), the Court may send the debtor and debtor's ttorney a notice stating that the case may be dismissed without further hearing unless:

(1) the debtor files the required documents within 14 days of the filing of the petition;

(2) the debtor moves for an extension of time to file the required documents within 14 days of filing the petition; or

(3) the case has been converted to Chapter 13 from another chapter of the Code.

(c) Payroll Orders in Chapter 13 Cases. A payroll order must be entered in every Chapter 13 case unless it would be impractical or the debtor files a motion showing good cause why a payroll order should not be entered. (The Payroll Order form is appended to these Rules as Exhibit 7.)

(d) Model Chapter 13 Plan.

(1) *Mandatory Use.* The Court will maintain on its website a Chapter 13 plan adopted by the Chapter 13 trustees that will serve as a model for drafting Chapter 13 plans in this district. Absent exceptional circumstances, a Chapter 13 debtor must use the model plan but may make modifications to the plan to meet his or her particular needs. If a modification is made, the modification must be conspicuously described in Section IV.P. of the model plan unless the modification has otherwise been excepted from disclosure by the Chapter 13 trustee assigned to the case. (The Model Chapter 13 Plan as of the effective date of these Rules is appended to these Rules as Exhibit 8.)

(2) *Future Amendments.* The Chapter 13 trustees will regularly consult with attorneys who represent debtors and creditors in Chapter 13 cases in this district to discuss any needed changes to the model plan. Unless otherwise ordered by the Court, amendments may not be made more than once a year, with the Chapter 13 trustees submitting proposed amendments, if any, to the Court for final approval in August of each year.

(e) Objections to Confirmation. A creditor who objects to confirmation of the debtor's plan as last amended must file a written objection with the Court at least 7 days before confirmation of that plan is heard.

(f) Pre–Confirmation Amendments to Plans. All preconfirmation amendments to a plan must be numbered chronologically and entitled "First Pre–Confirmation Plan Amendment ..., Second Pre–Confirmation Plan Amendment ...", etc. The amendment must (1) include only the provisions that differ from the original plan, and (2) explain how each new or amended provision changes the plan. The debtor must serve the amendment, together with a notice of the hearing date for confirmation, on the trustee and any creditors or parties in interest who may be adversely affected; and must file a proof of service with the Clerk. The debtor may not file a plan

amendment that adversely affects the rights of non-objecting creditors less than 21 days before the plan is finally confirmed.

(g) Post–Confirmation Amendments to Plans. All amendments to a confirmed plan must filed by the debtor on a "notice and opportunity" basis pursuant to LBR 9013(c). Post-confirmation amendments to a plan must be numbered chronologically and entitled "First Post–Confirmation Plan Amendment ..., Second Post–Confirmation Plan Amendment ..., etc. The amendment must (1) include only the provisions that differ from the plan as confirmed, and (2) explain how each new or amended provision changes the plan. The debtor must serve the trustee and any creditors or parties in interest who may be adversely affected by the amendment with a copy of the amendment and the LBR 9013(c) notice; and must file a proof of service with the Clerk.

(h) Refunds to Debtors. As long as the confirmed plan so provides, the Chapter 13 trustee may refund estate monies to the debtor, including income-tax refunds, without amending the plan or otherwise securing a court order. The Chapter 13 trustee may also refund estate monies to the debtor on an emergency basis, even if the confirmed plan does not so allow and without prior court order, if the debtor stipulates in writing to repay the refund to the estate before completion of the plan.

[Effective August 1, 2012.]

LBR 3016. PRE–CONFIRMATION LEASE AND ADEQUATE PROTECTION PAYMENTS

(a) Plan Requirements. Unless the Court orders otherwise, when a debtor files a Chapter 13 plan providing that a lease or adequate protection payment be paid by the trustee to a creditor listed in the plan, the plan must:

(1) list the name, address, account number, and payment amount for each lessor or secured creditor receiving a payment;

(2) provide that the trustee may not disburse any adequate protection payments to a secured creditor until a proof of claim is filed; and

(3) provide that the trustee may only pay that portion of an allowed, secured claim that comes due after the order for relief.

(b) Trustee's Duties. As long as the information required by subparagraph (a) has been provided, the trustee may begin making lease or adequate protection payments within 28 days after a proof of claim is properly filed, subject to the availability of funds and the trustee's monthly disbursement cycle. However, the trustee will make no lease or adequate protection payments until administrative expenses have been paid. The trustee will reduce the principal amount of any lessor's or secured creditor's claim by the amount of the lease or adequate protection payments remitted. If a secured creditor files a pre-confirmation motion for relief from the automatic stay, the trustee will suspend lease or adequate protection payments until a final decision on the motion has been made. If the motion is denied, the trustee will resume making lease and adequate protection payments, including the suspended payments, unless the Court orders otherwise.

(c) Trustee's Fee.* The trustee may charge such percentage fee as may periodically be fixed by the Attorney General pursuant to 28 U.S.C. § 586(e) and may collect such fee at the time of distribution to the creditor.

(d) Dismissal or Conversion to Another Chapter. If a Chapter 13 case is dismissed or converted to another chapter before confirmation of the plan, the trustee will make pre-confirmation lease and adequate protection payments that are owed through the date of dismissal or conversion to the extent that funds are available for that purpose and the requirements of subparagraph (a) have been met.

[Effective August 1, 2012.]

* [**Publisher's Note:** *See* Administrative Order No. 2014–5, *post.*]

LBR 3018. BALLOTS

Unless the Court orders otherwise, all original ballots accepting or rejecting a Chapter 11 plan must be filed with the Clerk. The Clerk will scan paper ballots into CM/ECF and may draft and file an electronic vote-tally report. The Clerk's vote-tally report is for informational purposes only and does not constitute the Court's findings of fact or conclusions of law regarding confirmation of that plan.

[Effective August 1, 2012.]

LBR 3022. FINAL DECREE AND CLOSING

On entry of the final decree and after all contested matters and adversary proceedings are completed, the Clerk will close the case. Unless the Court orders otherwise, a Chapter 11 debtor must file an application for entry of a final decree upon substantial consummation of the plan.

[Effective August 1, 2012.]

LBR 4001–1. MOTIONS FOR RELIEF FROM THE AUTOMATIC STAY

(a) Scope. This Rule governs all motions made pursuant to Fed. R. Bankr. P. 4001(a) for relief from the automatic stay as provided for in 11 U.S.C. § 362(a).

(b) Use of "Notice and Opportunity" Procedures. A creditor may request relief from the automatic stay by filing a motion with notice and opportunity to object pursuant to LBR 9013(c). However, nothing in this subparagraph prohibits a party from seeking relief from stay using other motion procedures permitted by LBR 9013. A secured party seeking relief from the automatic stay by motion with notice and opportunity to object must attach to its motion documentary proof that any lien it asserts has been perfected in accordance with applicable law.

(1) *Combined With Motion for Abandonment.* Notwithstanding LBR 9013(e), a creditor may combine a motion for abandonment of estate property with the motion for relief from the automatic stay as long as the words "abandon" or "abandonment" clearly appear in the title of the document. Notwithstanding the filing of a combined motion, the creditor still has the burden of proof under 11 U.S.C. § 554 to show that the proposed abandoned property is of inconsequential value to the estate. The combined motion must be served on the entire matrix, and combining the two motions does not

waive either of the filing fees associated with the respective motions.

(2) *Response Filed.* If a response is filed by a party, only the final hearing will be scheduled under LBR 9013(c)(3). The response must set forth with specificity the party's good-faith reasons for objecting to the motion and for believing that relief from the stay will be denied if a hearing is held. Notwithstanding the filing of a response, the Court may enter an order lifting the stay without conducting a final hearing if the response does not establish a good-faith basis for objecting to the motion.

(c) Use of Contested Motion Procedures. If a movant does not proceed under subparagraph (b) or if the Court determines that a relief from stay motion should proceed by preliminary and final hearing, the Clerk will schedule the preliminary hearing on the motion within 30 days from the filing of the motion and a final hearing within an additional 30 days. Should such scheduling exceed the time limits established by the Code, the Federal Rules of Bankruptcy Procedure, or these Rules, the Clerk will make such alternative arrangements as are required to comply with the time limitations of 11 U.S.C. § 362(e). The Clerk will transmit a copy of the notice of hearing to the movant, who must serve the notice and motion in compliance with Fed. R. Bankr. P. 4001. The movant must file a proof of service of the notice and motion before any relief may be granted on the motion.

(1) *Preliminary Hearing.* At the preliminary hearing, the Court will determine: (A) whether material, disputed issues of fact exist, and (B) whether there is a reasonable likelihood that the party opposing the relief will prevail. These issues will be decided solely on the arguments of counsel and will be limited to no more than one hour unless the Court, on its own or on prior request of counsel, permits otherwise. The parties may further request that a preliminary hearing be treated as a final hearing. If the Court finds the existence of material, disputed facts and a likelihood that the party opposing relief will prevail, the hearing may be adjourned to a final hearing. At the conclusion of the preliminary hearing, the Court may decide questions of law, may define factual or legal issues to be decided at the final hearing, and may issue an appropriate scheduling order. If the preliminary hearing is adjourned to a final hearing, the stay will remain in effect until the Court orders otherwise. The Court may also grant adequate protection to the movant in the interim.

(2) *Final Hearing.* The Court may hear testimony at the final hearing or schedule a different time and date for testimony.

(d) Settlements. Nothing in this Rule prohibits the parties from filing a stipulated settlement of the motion in accordance with LBR 4001–3.

[Effective August 1, 2012.]

LBR 4001–2. MOTIONS FOR USE OF CASH COLLATERAL OR TO OBTAIN CREDIT

(a) Adequate Protection and Valuation of Secured Interests. A motion for use of cash collateral under § 363(c) of the Code or a motion to obtain credit under § 364(c) or (d) of the

Code must explicitly state the adequate protection offered the creditor and aver the moving party's position as to the value of each of the secured interests to be protected. Appraisals and projections, to the extent pertinent and available, must be summarized in the motion.

(b) Expedited Motion. If a debtor files a motion for entry of an order approving an agreement to use cash collateral or to obtain credit on an expedited basis, the Court may enter the order without a hearing if:

(1) the order is approved by:

(A) all creditors who have an interest in the cash collateral to be used,

(B) any entity extending the requested credit,

(C) the chairperson or attorney for each official committee (if any), and

(D) the United States Trustee;

(2) the order provides for the debtor to use cash collateral or to obtain credit in a maximum specified dollar amount necessary to avoid immediate and irreparable harm only until the earlier of:

(A) a final hearing, or

(B) the date the order becomes a final order;

(3) the order provides for a final hearing, to be scheduled by the Court when the order is entered;

(4) the order provides that the debtor will serve a copy of the motion with its attachments and the order on all parties who are required to be served under Fed. R. Bankr. P. 4001(d);

(5) the order provides that:

(A) objections to the order shall be filed within 14 days from the service of the order, except that an unsecured creditors' committee may file an objection within 14 days of its formation;

(B) on the filing of an objection, a final hearing will be held; and

(C) if no objections are timely filed, an order may become final; and

(6) the motion is accompanied by an affidavit or a declaration of the debtor, or a principal of the debtor, stating the facts on which the debtor relies in seeking the entry of the order on an expedited basis and the amount of money needed to avoid immediate and irreparable harm.

(c) Enlargement or Reduction of Time for Objecting; Hearing. On timely motion, the Court may enlarge or reduce the time within which an objection must be filed. The Court may schedule a hearing on the debtor's motion at any time with such notice as it deems appropriate.

[Effective August 1, 2012.]

LBR 4001–3. MOTIONS FOR APPROVAL OF AGREED RELIEF

(a) Agreements Subject to This Rule. A party may use the notice and opportunity procedure of LBR 9013(c) to request Court approval of an agreement to: (1) provide adequate protection; (2) modify or terminate the stay under § 362 of the Code; (3) use cash collateral; or (4) create a lien senior or equal to an entity's lien or interest in property of the estate. Any motion under this subsection must be accompanied by a copy of the agreement.

(b) Service of Motion. The moving party must serve the notice, motion, agreement, and proposed order on the following parties:

(1) *In a Chapter 7 Case*—the parties to the agreement, the Chapter 7 trustee, the United States Trustee, and any entity that claims an interest in the subject property.

(2) *In a Chapter 11 Case*—the parties to the agreement; any creditors' or equity security holders' committee appointed under § 1102 of the Code and its authorized agent, or if no creditors' committee has been appointed, on the 20 largest creditors holding unsecured claims; the United States Trustee; and any other entity the Court directs.

(3) *In a Chapter 12 Case*—the parties to the agreement, the Chapter 12 trustee, the United States Trustee, and any entity that claims an interest in the subject property.

(4) *In a Chapter 13 Case*—the parties to the agreement, the Chapter 13 trustee, the United States Trustee, and any entity that claims an interest in the subject property.

[Effective August 1, 2012.]

LBR 4001–4. RENT DEPOSITS

(a) Debtor's Duties. A debtor complies with 11 U.S.C. § 362(l)(1) by:

(1) making the required certification and disclosing the lessor's name and address where indicated in the voluntary petition under the section entitled "Statement by a Debtor who Resides as a Tenant of Residential Property";

(2) serving a copy of the petition on the lessor; and

(3) delivering to the Clerk, together with the petition (or within 1 day of electronically filing the petition):

(A) cash, a money order, or a cashier's or certified check made payable to the lessor in the amount of any rent that would come due during the 30–day period after the filing of the petition; and

(B) a copy of the pre-petition judgment of possession.

(b) Forwarding of Rent Deposits. No sooner than 14 days and no later than 30 days after the debtor deposits the rent as provided in subparagraph (a)(3), the Clerk will mail the deposited amount to the lessor at the address specified in the petition or such other address as the lessor directs in writing. If the debtor tendered cash to the Clerk, the Clerk will deposit the cash into the Court's account and issue a check to the lessor in the amount tendered by the debtor.

(c) Clerk's Notice to Lessor. The Clerk will send a notice of the filing to the lessor (the "Clerk's Notice to Lessor") advising the lessor that the lessor may file an objection stating with particularity how the debtor has failed to comply with the requirements of 11 U.S.C. § 362(l) and this Rule if the debtor:

(1) complies with subparagraph (a); and

(2) within 30 days after filing the petition:

(A) files a further certification that, under applicable non-bankruptcy law, the debtor has cured the entire monetary default giving rise to the judgment of possession;

(B) serves the certification on the lessor; and

(C) files a proof of service.

(d) **Opportunity to Object.** Within 14 days after service of the Clerk's Notice to Lessor, the lessor may file an objection to the debtor's certifications, stating with particularity how the debtor has failed to comply with the requirements of 11 U.S.C. § 362(*l*) and this Rule. If the lessor fails to timely file an objection, the automatic stay remains in effect notwithstanding 11 U.S.C. § 362(b)(22), the lessor is deemed to have consented to receiving the check, and the Clerk will forthwith mail the check to the lessor at the address set forth in the debtor's certification.

(e) **Timely Objection Filed.** If the lessor files a timely objection and serves such objection on the trustee, the United States Trustee, and the debtor (and debtor's counsel, if applicable), the Court will schedule a hearing to take place within 14 days of service of the objection.

[Effective August 1, 2012.]

LBR 4001–5.   MOTIONS TO EXTEND STAY

Unless the Court orders otherwise, the debtor or a party in interest may request a § 362(c)(3) extension of the automatic stay by filing a motion with notice and opportunity to object pursuant to LBR 9013. However, any such motion must be filed within 7 days of the filing of the petition.

[Effective August 1, 2012.]

LBR 4004–1.   DELAYED DISCHARGE

(a) **Request for Delay of Discharge.** A debtor may request that the Court defer granting a discharge for 30 days after entry of the order approving the request or until a date certain. The request must be made by written motion using the official Court form. (A copy of the Debtor's Motion to Defer Entry of Discharge is appended to these Rules as Exhibit 9.)

(b) **Clerk's Authority to Grant or Deny.** The Clerk may grant or deny the motion on behalf of the Court by endorsing the motion where indicated on the form and serving a copy on the appropriate parties.

(c) **Objections to Delay of Discharge.** Any party in interest objecting to the Clerk's action in subparagraph (b) may move for judicial review within 21 days after entry of the Clerk's order on the docket.

[Effective August 1, 2012.]

LBR 4004–2.   CERTIFICATION REGARDING DOMESTIC SUPPORT OBLIGATIONS

In every Chapter 13 case, the debtor must file a written certification that the debtor is current on any domestic support obligation that came due after the case was filed and on any prepetition domestic support obligation to the extent

provided for by the plan. (A copy of the Debtor's Certification Regarding Domestic Support Obligations is appended to these Rules as Exhibit 10.) This certification is a prerequisite to receiving a discharge in the Chapter 13 case.

[Effective August 1, 2012.]

LBR 5001.   PLACE OF FILING

(a) **Parties Required to File Electronically (ECF Filers).** All attorneys who practice in this Court are required to be registered users of CM/ECF. Subject to the provisions of Fed. R. Bankr. P. 5001, 5005, and the ECF Guidelines, all documents must be filed electronically using CM/ECF at http://ecf.miwb.uscourts.gov.

(b) **Parties Not Required to File Electronically (Paper Filers).** Those parties not required to file electronically may file documents at the following locations in the Western District of Michigan:

(1) *Western District of Michigan—Lower Peninsula.* The petition and any subsequent documents for a bankruptcy case with venue in a county located in the Lower Peninsula must be filed with the Clerk of the Bankruptcy Court, One Division Avenue North, Grand Rapids, Michigan 49503.

(2) *Western District of Michigan—Upper Peninsula.* The petition and any subsequent documents for a bankruptcy case with venue in a county located in the Upper Peninsula must be filed with the Clerk of the Bankruptcy Court, U.S. Post Office, 202 West Washington Street, Marquette, Michigan 49855 (Postal Address: P.O. Box 909, Marquette, Michigan 49855–0909).

[Effective August 1, 2012.]

LBR 5003.   CLERK—GENERAL AUTHORITY

(a) **Clerk's Authority to Sign Orders and Notices.** The Clerk is authorized to sign and enter the following orders and notices without further direction by the Court:

(1) orders allowing installment payments of filing fees;

(2) notice and orders of abandonment;

(3) Chapter 13 payroll orders;

(4) orders reducing, disallowing, withdrawing, or transferring claims when requested by the claimant;

(5) writs of garnishment, executions, and orders to pay;

(6) orders dismissing bankruptcy proceedings and adversary complaints due to CM/ECF error;

(7) orders granting motions to delay entry of discharge;

(8) orders permitting pleadings or other documents to be filed conventionally (i.e., on paper); and

(9) orders correcting administrative errors (e.g., erroneously closed cases and mistakenly entered discharges).

(b) **Clerk's Actions Reviewable.** An order signed and entered by the Clerk under this Rule may be reviewed, suspended, altered, or rescinded by the Court if requested by a party affected by that order.

(c) Clerk's Authority to Redact. The Clerk's authority under this Rule includes the authority to redact filings that disclose personal identifiers in violation of Fed. R. Bankr. P. 9037(a). However, nothing in this Rule imposes a duty on the Clerk to make the redaction. If the Clerk does redact a document, the redacted document will replace the original that appears for public viewing in CM/ECF.

(d) Assignment of New Cases. The Clerk will assign new cases to a judge consistent with a formula approved by the sitting judges of the Court. If a debtor has filed a prior bankruptcy case that was assigned to a particular judge and the debtor subsequently files another bankruptcy case, the Clerk will immediately reassign the subsequent case to the bankruptcy judge who was assigned to preside over the prior bankruptcy case, except:

(1) when the prior judge was assigned to a particular location for holding court but is no longer responsible for that location; or

(2) when the current judge who is handling a subsequently filed case advises the Clerk that the current judge desires to continue to preside over the subsequent case.

[Effective August 1, 2012.]

LBR 5005–1. FILING OF DOCUMENTS

(a) Filing by Electronic Transmission. Unless otherwise provided in subparagraph (b) or by Court order, all documents filed in all cases and proceedings must be filed electronically according to the ECF Administrative Procedures. Other documents filed over the counter (via paper) may be rejected by the Court pursuant to LBR 5005–2 and ECF Administrative Procedures available on the Court's website at www.miwb. uscourts.gov.

(b) Filing Over the Counter. The following persons are excused from filing by electronic transmission and may file documents over the counter:

(1) Individuals who are not represented by counsel;

(2) Filers experiencing internet failure provided the documents are accompanied by a "Motion for Leave to File Over the Counter";

(3) Filers relying on Section III of the ECF Administrative Procedures; and

(4) Filers of documents accompanied by a "Motion for Leave to File Over the Counter" that includes a clear statement why electronic filing is not feasible.

(c) Facsimile Filing. Except for the bankruptcy petition, any document may be filed by facsimile with prior Court approval.

[Effective August 1, 2012.]

LBR 5005–2. DEFECTIVE PLEADINGS AND PAPERS

(a) Time Stamp on Filed Documents. The Clerk will time stamp every document presented for filing over the counter as soon as practicable.

(b) Rejection for Nonpayment of Fee or Case Closed. The Clerk may reject, without filing, a document:

(1) not accompanied by the fee required to be paid at the time of filing pursuant to 28 U.S.C. § 1930. A fee is not paid unless made in cash, by a certified check or money order, with an attorney's credit or debit card or, at the Clerk's discretion, with a check drawn on an attorney's account; or

(2) that is to be filed in a case that does not exist in this Court or which has been closed, unless the document relates to post-judgment remedies or a motion to reopen a closed case.

(c) Clerk's Authority to Strike Defective Documents; Notice. The Clerk may strike after filing any document that is not signed or verified as required by Fed. R. Bankr. P. 9011. The Clerk will send notice that the document has been stricken to the filing party as soon as practicable. A stricken document that is amended to correct the defect and filed within 14 days is considered filed as of the date the document was originally filed with the Court.

(d) Request for Judicial Review of Clerk's Action. Any entity affected by a notice of rejection or an order to strike a document may file a motion for judicial review of such action within 14 days of the date of service of the notice of rejection or order to strike. If the Court determines that the action of the Clerk was improper, the Court may order that the document be deemed properly filed and determine the effective time and date of filing. The moving party must serve the motion for judicial review on all affected parties and file a proof of service.

(e) Notice to Correct Defective Filing. If the Clerk determines that a document is defective but does not warrant rejection or striking, the Clerk may issue and serve a notice of defective filing that advises the Filer of the corrective action needed to be taken or already taken by the Clerk.

(f) Failure to Correct Defective Filing. If any document required by LBR 1007 to be filed with the petition is not filed at that time, the Clerk will notify the filing attorney (or debtor if pro se) of the deficiency. If the deficiency is not corrected within 14 days of service of the notice, the case may be dismissed by the Court without further hearing.

[Effective August 1, 2012.]

LBR 5005–3. SERVICE OF DOCUMENTS ON THE UNITED STATES TRUSTEE

(a) Mandatory Service. In addition to the requirements of the Federal Rules of Bankruptcy Procedure, copies of the following documents must be transmitted electronically by CM/ECF to the United States Trustee contemporaneously with their filing with the Clerk:

(1) all documents (including notice of appeals) filed in a Chapter 7 or 11 case;

(2) a notice of appeal filed in an adversary proceeding related to a Chapter 7 or 11 case;

(3) any complaint to except a debt from discharge pursuant to 11 U.S.C. § 523 or to deny or revoke a discharge pursuant to 11 U.S.C. § 727; and

(4) all settlement papers filed in an adversary proceeding or a contested matter in a case under Chapter 7 or 11.

(b) Service of Additional Documents. The United States Trustee may also file a motion requesting service of additional documents in a particular case.

[Effective August 1, 2012.]

LBR 5005–4. ELECTRONIC SERVICE OF DOCUMENTS ON PARTIES

(a) Electronic Service. When service of a document is required by the Federal Rules of Bankruptcy Procedure, these Rules, or the Court, service may be made through CM/ECF. No proof of service is required if all parties entitled to notice are Electronic Filers. When a proof of service is nonetheless required, the proof of service must identify the parties served by CM/ECF.

(b) Service Completed. If the intended recipient is an ECF Filer, service is deemed complete when the Notice of Electronic Filing is transmitted to the Filer.

(c) Proof of Service. When a proof of service is required by the Federal Rules of Bankruptcy Procedure, these Rules, or Court order, the proof of service must indicate the method of service (U.S. Mail, private courier, facsimile, electronically, etc.).

[Effective August 1, 2012.]

LBR 5011. WITHDRAWAL OF REFERENCE

(a) Form of Request. A request for withdrawal of the reference of all or part of a case or proceeding referred to the Bankruptcy Court must be made by filing a motion with the Clerk. The motion must clearly and conspicuously state that "RELIEF IS SOUGHT FROM A UNITED STATES DISTRICT JUDGE."

(b) Time for Filing. A motion to withdraw the reference of the entire bankruptcy case must be filed by the time first set for the meeting of creditors. A motion to withdraw the reference of all or part of an adversary proceeding must be filed by the date on which the answer, reply, or motion under Fed. R. Bankr. P. 7012 or 7015 is first due. A motion to withdraw the reference of a contested matter within a case must be filed not later than 14 days after service of the motion, application, or objection that initiates the contested matter. Notwithstanding the foregoing, a motion to withdraw the reference may still be filed within 14 days of the filing of any pleading or paper that for the first time raises the reason for seeking the withdrawal.

(c) Proceedings Unaffected. The filing of a motion to withdraw the reference does not stay proceedings in the Bankruptcy Court. The procedures relating to stay are set forth in Fed. R. Bankr. P. 5011.

(d) Designation of Record. The moving party must file with the Clerk of the Bankruptcy Court and serve on interested parties a designation of those portions of the record of the case or proceeding in the Bankruptcy Court that the moving party believes will reasonably be necessary or pertinent to the United States District Court's consideration of the motion.

Within 14 days after service of such designation of record, any other party may serve and file a designation of additional portions of the record. If the record designated by any party includes a transcript of any hearing or trial, that party must immediately after filing the designation, deliver to the Bankruptcy Court's electronic court recorder operator or contract court reporter a written request for the transcript and make satisfactory arrangements for payment of its cost. The parties must take all steps necessary to enable the Clerk to assemble and transmit the record.

(e) Response Filed; Reply. If a party opposes the requested withdrawal, it must file and serve its objection within 14 days of service of the motion to withdraw the reference. The moving party may then file and serve a reply within 14 days after service of the objection.

(f) Transmittal to and Proceedings in the United States District Court. When the record is complete except for transcripts, the Clerk of the Bankruptcy Court will promptly transmit to the Clerk of the United States District Court the motion and the designated portions of the record.

[Effective August 1, 2012.]

LBR 5090. COURTHOUSE CONDUCT

(a) Solicitation. Solicitation of business relating to bonds or to employment as counsel is prohibited in the courthouse.

(b) Loitering. Loitering in or about the rooms or corridors of the courthouse is prohibited.

(c) Disruptive Behavior. Any behavior that impedes or disrupts the orderly conduct of the Court's business is prohibited.

(d) Signs. Card, signs, placards, or banners may not be brought into any of the courtrooms or on any floor where a courtroom is located.

(e) Enforcement. The United States Marshal, deputy marshals, court security officers, and the authorized employees of the courthouse may enforce this Rule by ejecting violators from the courthouse or by having them appear before one of the judges of this Court.

[Effective August 1, 2012.]

LBR 5091. CELL PHONES, PHOTOGRAPHY, AND RECORDING

(a) Prohibited Uses. Use of cell phones inside any courtroom is prohibited. Video equipment inside any courtroom is prohibited unless the Court specifically orders otherwise. The taking of photographs in any courtroom or its environs in connection with a judicial proceeding; the broadcast of a judicial proceedings by radio, television, or other means; and the audio or video recording of a judicial proceeding are all strictly prohibited.

(b) Exceptions. The judicial officer in whose courtroom the proceedings occurs may authorize the use of appropriate devices to preserve or present evidence and to broadcast or memorialize investiture, ceremonial, or naturalization proceedings.

(c) Adoption of Supreme Court Rules. Rules or regulations promulgated by the United States Supreme Court relating to photographing, recording, or broadcasting judicial proceedings are also incorporated by reference into this Rule.

[Effective August 1, 2012.]

LBR 6004.   USE, SALE, OR LEASE OF PROPERTY

(a) Descriptions of Real Property. A motion, complaint, or proposed orders regarding the use, sale, or lease of real property or liens on such property must include:

(1) the complete legal description in recordable form; and

(2) the common street address.

(b) Report of Sale.

(1) *Sale by a Chapter 7 Trustee.* The trustee must file a report regarding the sale of all real or personal property, whether tangible or intangible, and serve a copy of the report on the debtor and the United States Trustee. The report must include:

(A) an itemized statement of the property sold;

(B) a list of bidders;

(C) the name of each purchaser;

(D) the price received for each item or lot, or for the property as a whole if sold in bulk;

(E) the date, time, and place of each sale;

(F) a calculation of compensation allowable under the order of appointment of any professional retained to effectuate each sale;

(G) copies of the sale advertisement; and

(H) a summary listing of all sale expenses including advertising expenses, sign expenses, labor, postage, and other mailing expenses.

(2) *Sale by a Chapter 13 Debtor.* A Chapter 13 debtor who sells real or personal property, whether tangible or intangible, must provide a copy of the closing statement for the sale to the Chapter 13 trustee within 14 days after close.

[Effective August 1, 2012.]

LBR 6005.   AUCTIONEERS

(a) Bond Required. An auctioneer employed pursuant to 11 U.S.C. § 327 must be bonded unless the Court specifically orders otherwise. The bond must be drawn in favor of the United States and cover the faithful performance of the auctioneer's duties to the estate. Unless otherwise directed by the Court, the bond must be in the amount of at least $100,000.

(b) Proceedings on Auctioneer's Bond. A proceeding on the auctioneer's bond may be brought in the name of the United States by any party in interest claiming injury because of the auctioneer's actions.

[Effective August 1, 2012.]

LBR 6007.   ABANDONMENTS INITIATED BY TRUSTEE

(a) Notice of Abandonment. A trustee's notice of abandonment pursuant to Fed. R. Bankr. P. 6007(a) must substantially conform to the form appended to these Rules as Exhibit 11.

(b) Service of Notice. If a Chapter 7 trustee intends to abandon estate property, service of the notice must be made by the filing party as follows:

(1) cases in which a report of no distribution has been filed: on the debtor; debtor's attorney, if any; the United States Trustee; and those parties who have filed a specific request pursuant to subparagraph (c);

(2) cases in which a report of no distribution has not been filed: on the debtor; debtor's attorney, if any; the United States Trustee; and all creditors.

(c) Language of Notice. The Clerk will insert the following provision in the § 341 meeting notice (Official Forms 9A and 9B):

Abandonments—Trustees may abandon property in no asset estates without notice to creditors or other interested parties. Anyone wishing to receive notice of such abandonment must file a request with the Court.

[Effective August 1, 2012.]

LBR 7008.   CONSENT TO FINAL JUDGMENT OR ORDER IN CORE PROCEEDINGS

In any adversary proceeding before the Court, the complaint, counterclaim, cross-claim, or third-party complaint must contain a statement that the proceeding is core or noncore and, without regard to whether the proceeding is alleged to be core or non-core, that the pleader does or does not consent to entry of a final order or judgment by the Court.

[Effective August 1, 2012.]

LBR 7026.   APPLICABILITY OF FED. R. CIV. P. 26 TO CONTESTED MATTERS

Unless the Court orders otherwise, Fed. R. Civ. P. 26(a)(1), (d), and (f) do not apply to contested matters.

[Effective August 1, 2012.]

LBR 7090.   SETTLEMENT OF ADVERSARY PROCEEDINGS

Counsel must notify the Court immediately upon reaching a settlement of an adversary proceeding. If, by the date set for trial, the attorneys have not submitted an order disposing of the proceeding, then counsel may be required to appear and state the settlement on the record. In any event, unless otherwise ordered by the Court, counsel must submit the appropriate order within 14 days after notifying the Court of a settlement. The failure to submit an appropriate order within 14 days or as otherwise ordered may be cause for dismissal.

[Effective August 1, 2012.]

LBR 8001. APPEALS FROM THE BANKRUPTCY COURT

All appeals from the Bankruptcy Court will be heard and determined by the Bankruptcy Appellate Panel of the Sixth Circuit Court of Appeals unless a party to the appeal files a timely election to "opt out" and have the appeal heard by the United States District Court for the Western District of Michigan. Any such election must be made in accordance with the applicable procedural rules of the Bankruptcy Appellate Panel.

[Effective August 1, 2012.]

LBR 8006–1. DESIGNATION OF RECORD AND ISSUES ON APPEAL

(a) **Specific Designation Required.** The designation of record and issues on appeal required by Fed. R. Bankr. P. 8006 must expressly identify the specific issues on appeal and each item to be included in the record, including the item's entry number if docketed by the Court. General designations such as "all bankruptcy files" or "the entire case and/or proceeding record" are not acceptable and will result in the record on appeal being considered incomplete. Only that part of the record necessary for the appeal should be designated. Non-specific statements of the issues on appeal are also not acceptable.

(b) **Exhibits and Undocketed Items.** Any party who wishes to designate for the record on appeal a trial exhibit or item not appearing in the docket record must provide to the Clerk and all parties to the appeal a copy of the exhibit or item.

(c) **Failure to Comply.** Failure of any party to comply with the foregoing may be grounds for the dismissal of the appeal or cross appeal by the reviewing court.

[Effective August 1, 2012.]

LBR 9004. GENERAL REQUIREMENTS OF FORM

(a) **Current Bankruptcy Chapter.** All documents filed after the commencement of the case must include the debtor's current bankruptcy chapter in the caption immediately below the case number.

(b) **Designation of Character of Document.** All documents filed after the commencement of the case must include a description of the document in the caption. The description must be centered and placed immediately before the body of the document. The description should be as specific as possible and must include the number of the document (i.e., first, second, third), if applicable, and the name of the moving party.

(c) **Dates of Filing, Conversion, and Dismissal.** Every motion, pleading, or other request for relief must state the date of filing of the debtor's petition as well as the dates of any subsequent conversion, dismissal, or reinstatement of the case. In complaints or amended complaints governed by Part VII of the Federal Rules of Bankruptcy Procedure, this statement must be made immediately after the jurisdictional paragraph required by Fed. R. Bank. P. 7008(a). In an application or motion governed by Fed. R. Bankr. P. 9014, this statement must be made in the first paragraph.

(d) **Attorney Information.** Every pleading, motion, or other request for relief filed with the Clerk and signed by an attorney must state the attorney's telephone number, office address, email address, and state bar identification number directly below the attorney's signature or in some other prominent place.

(e) **Orders.** Each order must include a brief, specific description of the order, the number of the order, if applicable, and the name of the moving party.

(f) **Proper Format.** Except for exhibits, official forms, and preprinted forms generated by bankruptcy software packages, all documents filed with the Clerk must be double-spaced and typewritten in at least 12–point type.

[Effective August 1, 2012.]

LBR 9006. COMPUTING TIME

When computing time as prescribed in these Rules, in the Federal Rules of Bankruptcy Procedure, or in orders, weekends and holidays are included. However, if the last day ends on a Saturday, Sunday or holiday, the period runs to the end of the next business day.

[Effective August 1, 2012.]

LBR 9010–1. ADMISSION, DISCIPLINE, SUSPENSION, AND DISBARMENT

(a) **Admission, Suspension, and Disbarment.** Except as provided in subparagraph (b) and § 304(g) of Pub. L. 103–394, Oct. 22, 1994, 108 Stat. 4106 (providing special rules for child-support creditors and their representatives), W.D. Mich. L. Civ. R. 83.1 governs the admission, suspension, discipline, and disbarment of an attorney or law student who seeks to practice in the Court or who is practicing in the Court. An attorney or law student who is admitted to practice in the United States District Court for the Western District of Michigan is admitted to practice in this Court. If complaint filed with the United States District Court for the Western District of Michigan as contemplated in W.D. Mich. L. Civ. R. 83.1(k)(ii) (Initiation of Proceedings) includes allegations related to proceedings before this Court, a copy of the complaint must also be filed with the Clerk.

(b) **Discipline Other Than Suspension or Disbarment.** Except for suspension or disbarment, a bankruptcy judge may discipline an attorney who (1) engages in conduct violating the Michigan Rules of Professional Conduct, (2) willfully violates these Rules, the Federal Rules of Bankruptcy Procedure, or a Court order, or (3) engages in other conduct unbecoming of a member of the bar of the Court. Prior to imposing discipline, the Court will notify the attorney that discipline may be imposed and give the attorney an opportunity to respond in writing why discipline should not be imposed. If requested, the Court may also schedule a hearing.

[Effective August 1, 2012.]

LBR 9010–2. REPRESENTATION AND APPEARANCES

(a) Representation of Individuals. Only individuals may represent themselves in matters or proceedings before this Court.

(b) Representation of Entities. An entity other than an individual may act on its own behalf for purposes of filing a proof of claim, participating in a § 341 meeting, or filing a reaffirmation agreement. For all other purposes, an entity must be represented by an attorney unless a statute or applicable rule provides otherwise.

Effective August 1, 2012.]

LBR 9010–3. PRO HAC VICE ADMISSION

(a) Attorneys Who May Not Apply for Pro Hac Vice Admission. Attorneys licensed to practice law in the State of Michigan or licensed to practice in another state who maintain a regular office within the State of Michigan may *not* apply for pro hac vice admission. Instead, they must apply for admission to practice before the United States District Court for the Western District of Michigan.

(b) Attorneys Who May Apply for Pro Hac Vice Admission. Licensed attorneys not subject to subparagraph (a) may apply for pro hac vice admission to appear in a specific case and all contested matters and adversary proceedings arising in that case. The application must be made by motion and must:

(1) State the attorney's full name, business address, telephone number, email address, professional number if applicable, and the state in which the attorney is licensed to practice law;

(2) Identify the other federal (bankruptcy, district, or circuit) courts in which the attorney is licensed to practice law; and

(3) Verify that the attorney is bound by all rules, practices, and ethics that are applicable to attorneys admitted to practice before the United States District Court for the Western District of Michigan.

The movant need not be sponsored by a member of the bar.

(c) Pro Hac Vice Admission Fee. Admission pro hac vice requires payment of a fee to the Clerk of the Bankruptcy Court within 14 days of entry of the order granting admission. The fee, which is set by the Court, must be by check or money order made payable to the United States District Court for the Western District of Michigan, and must include the designation "Pro hac vice admission," the name of the case, and the case number. The Clerk of the Bankruptcy Court will then promptly forward the admission fee to the Clerk of the District Court for deposit in its account.

(d) Failure to Pay Fee. Failure to pay the pro hac vice admission fee in compliance with subparagraph (c) will immediately revoke, without notice, the attorney's privilege to appear pro hac vice notwithstanding the previously entered order.

[Effective August 1, 2012.]

LBR 9011. SIGNATURES ON ELECTRONICALLY FILED DOCUMENTS, DECLARATIONS RE: ELECTRONIC FILING, AND STATEMENTS OF SOCIAL SECURITY NUMBER(S)

(a) Facsimile Signatures. A signature transmitted by facsimile is deemed to be an original signature for purposes of Fed. R. Bankr. P. 9011.

(b) Mandatory Electronic Filing. ECF Filers must file through CM/ECF all petitions, lists, schedules, statements, amendments, pleadings, affidavits, and other documents containing original signatures or requiring verification under Fed. R. Bankr. P. 1008 or an unsworn declaration as provided in 28 U.S.C. § 1746.

(1) *Electronic Filing as Signature.* Electronic filing of a petition, pleading, motion, proof of claim, or other document by an ECF Filer constitutes the signature of that individual for all purposes, including those under Fed. R. Bankr. P. 9011 and 28 U.S.C. § 1746, and has the same effect as if the individual had affixed that individual's signature on a paper copy of the document being filed.

(2) *Declaration Re: Electronic Filing.* When the petition is filed through CM/ECF, the Filer must also file a separate Declaration Re: Electronic Filing pursuant to ECF Administrative Procedures. (A copy of the Declaration Re: Electronic Filing is appended to these Rules as Exhibit 12.) The Clerk will make a text entry in the electronic docket to reflect that the declaration has been filed. However, the declaration itself will not be available for public viewing.

(c) Statement of Social Security Number(s). If the debtor has not filed a Declaration Re: Electronic Filing containing the debtor's social security number, then the debtor must conventionally file a completed Official Form B21 (Statement of Social–Security Number(s)) containing the full 9–digit social security number and original signature of each debtor. If the debtor does not have a social security number, the debtor must file Official Form B21 stating that the debtor does not have a social security number. Failure to submit this form within 14 days from the date of the Notice to File Statement of Social Security Number(s) will result in dismissal of the case without further hearing.

(d) Acceptable Methods for Signing Documents. A signature on a document filed with the Court may be indicated by:

(1) filing a scanned image of the originally signed document;

(2) filing a scanned image of the signature page of the electronic document; or

(3) affixing "/s/ NAME" to the document where the handwritten signature or mark would otherwise appear.

(e) Retention of Signed Documents. If a document is filed with an electronic signature indicated by "/s/" or "/s/ NAME", the ECF Filer must retain the original signed document or the written authorization for the electronic signature for a minimum of 5 years from the date of filing.

(f) Filing of Documents With Multiple Signatures. If a stipulation or other document to be filed electronically includes the signatures of two or more persons, the ECF Filer must:

(1) confirm that the content of the document is acceptable to all persons required to sign and must obtain the actual signature of all signing parties; and

(2) retain the original in accordance with subparagraph (e).

[Effective August 1, 2012.]

LBR 9013. MOTION PRACTICE

(a) Scope. This Rule applies to relief requested pursuant to Fed. R. Bankr. P. 9013 and 9014 regardless of how the request is made.

(b) Ex Parte Relief. If the requested ex parte relief may be granted without a hearing and without prior notice, the movant may file the motion and proposed order with a request that the order be signed.

(c) Notice With Opportunity to Object. A party seeking relief with notice and an opportunity to object must follow the procedures set forth in this subsection unless the Code, the Federal Rules of Bankruptcy Procedure, or these Rules provide otherwise, or the Court otherwise directs.

(1) *Documents Filed With Motion.* The following documents must be filed with any motion under subparagraph (c):

(A) A notice to the debtor and all other parties upon whom service is required that states that the party served has 14 days (21 days for matters under Fed. R. Bankr. P. 2002(a) and 2016; and 30 days for objections to claims) from the date of service to file and serve a response or request for a hearing or both. In either event, the response must include the specific reasons for objecting or for requesting a hearing;

(B) A copy of the proposed order; and

(C) Unless otherwise excepted by these Rules, a proof of service indicating the parties served and the date and manner of service.

(2) *No Response Filed.* The Court may grant relief without a hearing if no timely response or request for hearing is filed. The movant may file with the Court no earlier than 21 days from the date of service of the notice (28 days for matters under Fed. R. Bankr. P. 2002(a) and 2016, and 35 days for objections to claims) a certification stating that no timely response or request for hearing has been filed. On receipt of the certification, the Court may sign the proposed order, require the moving party to prepare a new proposed order, draft and enter its own order, or schedule a hearing.

(3) *Response Filed.* If a timely response or request for hearing is filed or if the Court has directed that a hearing be held, the Clerk will schedule a hearing on the motion and prepare a notice of hearing for the movant to serve on all required parties.

(4) *When "Notice and Opportunity" Procedures May Not Be Used.* Except as provided in subparagraph (d), the procedures set forth in this Rule may not be used for plan confirmation hearings, disclosure statement approval hearings, dismissal or conversion hearings, or hardship discharge hearings.

(d) Dismissal Motions by Chapter 13 Trustee. A Chapter 13 trustee's motion to dismiss the case must state with particularity the grounds for dismissal (e.g., a debtor's failure to make timely payments). The motion may be served pursuant to subparagraph (c). Any response or request for hearing filed by the debtor or debtor's attorney must be filed with the Court and served on the Chapter 13 trustee within 30 days of when the trustee served the motion to dismiss. The response filed by the debtor or debtor's attorney must state with particularity the good faith reasons for opposing the motion and for believing that dismissal will not occur if a hearing is held.

(1) *Remedy If Proper Response Not Filed.* If the debtor or debtor's attorney does not file a proper response or request for hearing within 30 days of the date the trustee served a the motion to dismiss, the trustee may file with the Court a certification stating that no timely response or request for hearing has been filed together with a proposed order to dismiss. The Court may then dismiss the case without further hearing.

(2) *Hearing Date If Timely Response Filed.* If a debtor or debtor's attorney files a timely response or request for hearing, the Court will either hear the motion as already noticed or schedule a hearing.

(e) Procedure for Contested Motions. For all motions not filed pursuant to subparagraph (c), the Clerk will schedule the matter for hearing. Absent good cause, a party filing a brief or response to a motion must file and serve its brief or response at least 7 days before the scheduled hearing.

(f) Combined Motions Prohibited. Except as otherwise provided in these Rules, every request for an order from the Court must be filed in a separate motion. However, requests for alternative relief may be contained in one motion.

(g) Request for Emergency Hearing. An "emergency" is a matter that requires a hearing in less than 7 days, and that involves an injury which outweighs procedural concerns. If a motion requires an emergency hearing, a separate motion for the emergency hearing must be filed. The motion for emergency hearing must contain the following:

(1) sufficient information for the Court to schedule an emergency hearing (e.g., why relief is needed immediately and why affected parties will not be prejudiced if a hearing is held with only limited notice);

(2) a certificate of service; and

(3) a proposed order scheduling the hearing, with blank spaces for the date, time, and location of the hearing and for the manner and deadline for giving notice of the hearing.

The moving party must telephone the presiding Judge's chambers to promptly advise the Court staff that a request for an emergency hearing has been filed. Nothing in this Rule precludes the Court from utilizing different procedures for scheduling emergency hearings.

(h) Request for Expedited Hearing. If a motion requires a hearing on shortened notice but is not an emergency, a motion to shorten notice or to schedule an expedited hearing must be filed in accordance with Fed. R. Bankr. P. 9006(c). The request for expedited hearing must be accompanied by a proposed order.

[Effective August 1, 2012.]

LBR 9013–1. ALLOWANCE OF COMPENSATION AND REIMBURSEMENT OF EXPENSES FOR PROFESSIONALS

(a) Court Approval Required. Professional persons employed by the bankruptcy estate or a committee must be approved by the Court pursuant to 11 U.S.C. §§ 327, 332, 333, and 1103; and Fed. R. Bankr. P. 2016.

(b) Fees Requested by Application; Burden of Proof. A professional must file an application for fees and expenses under LBR 2016–2 before receiving any payment from the estate or applying any retainer that is property of the estate. The applicant has the burden of proof.

(c) Contents of Application.

(1) *General Requirements.* Every fee application must state the case filing date, the current chapter, and all dates of conversion. The application must also state the amount of any retainer paid, the date of each previous application, the amount of compensation and expenses previously requested, the date of each approval, and the total amount received to date.

The Court will not allow compensation for services that do not benefit the estate (e.g., fees for reading another's work product simply as a matter of interest, for services that mainly benefit the debtor or the debtor's principals, or for general research of law well known to practitioners in the area of law involved). The Court will determine whether tasks have been performed within a reasonable number of hours and whether the requested hourly rate is reasonable based on the customary rate charged by experienced practitioners. The reasonableness of the work done and the fee charged may depend on the results attained. An attorney may be required to estimate the probability of success, the amount to be realized, and the overall benefit to creditors with respect to each prospective matter or proceeding.

(2) *Itemization of Services Performed.* An application for compensation must identify each activity by date and the professional who performed the work. It must also include a description of the work performed, its purpose, and the time expended.

(A) Detail Required. Except as protected by the attorney-client privilege: (i) time entries for telephone calls must list the person with whom the applicant spoke and give a brief description of the conversation; (ii) time entries for correspondence must state the addressee and give a brief explanation of the contents; (iii) time entries involving documents must specify the specific document; and (iv) time entries for legal research must describe the matter for which the research was conducted and the research conducted. If abbreviations are used in the application or if computer sheets are added to supplement the application, the application must also include an appendix that explains the abbreviations or any code keys.

(B) Time Increments; No Rounding or "Lumping" Allowed. Each type of service must be listed with a corresponding specific time allotted. The time listed must represent the actual time expended to perform the activity and should be stated in tenths (.10) of an hour. "Rounding up" of time is not permitted. Applicants may not circumvent minimum time requirements or any detail requirement by "lumping" or "bunching" more than one activity into a single entry.

(C) Multiple Professionals. The application must indicate the total hours charged and give a summary of the hours and hourly rate charged by each professional. If more than one professional has charged time for an activity such as intra-office conferences or joint court appearances, the applicant must explain the need for each professional's participation in the activity.

(D) Reasonableness of Rates Charged. Rates must be commensurate with the level of skill required for a particular task. Professional fees may not be charged for non-professional services such as copying or delivering documents, preparing or filing proofs of service, or for trustee duties generally performed without the assistance of an attorney or other professional. When paralegals are utilized to perform legal services for an estate, they may be compensated as paraprofessionals rather than treated as an overhead expense.

(E) Reimbursement for Application Fees. Fees for reasonable time spent by an attorney in preparing and reviewing an application for compensation may also be included.

(3) *Itemization of Expenses.* An application for reimbursement of expenses must include a description of each expense and its purpose together with the date it was paid. Requests for mileage must include the date, destination, miles, per-mile rate, and the reason for the trip. In allowing expenses, the Court will consider economy (e.g., coach airfare, moderately priced accommodations, commercial duplication of large copy orders) and necessity (e.g., unnecessary use of overnight mail).

(d) Deferral of Fees. On the motion of a party in interest, the Court may order that the payment of all or a portion of an allowed interim fee be withheld for a specified period of time. The Court may do so with or without a hearing. However, if the order is without a hearing, the applicant may move to have the order modified or rescinded.

(e) Fees in Chapter 13 Cases. For compensation in Chapter 13 cases, see LBR 2016–2(e)(1).

[Effective August 1, 2012.]

LBR 9015. JURY TRIALS

(a) Applicability of Certain Federal Rules of Civil Procedure. Fed. R. Civ. P. 38, 39, and 47–51 apply in this Court's cases, except that a demand made under Fed. R. Civ. P. 38(b) must be filed in accordance with Fed. R. Bankr. P. 5005. Fed. R. Civ. P. 81(c) also applies to jury trials before this Court.

(b) Consent. If the right to a jury trial applies and a timely demand has been filed under Fed. R. Civ. P. 38(b), the parties may consent to have a trial by jury conducted by a bankruptcy judge under 28 U.S.C. 157(e) by jointly or separately filing a statement of consent no later than the date set for the filing of a Joint Final Pretrial Order.

[Effective August 1, 2012.]

LBR 9016. USE OF COURTROOM ELECTRONIC EQUIPMENT

Any person who intends to use electronic equipment in the courtroom during a hearing or trial must become familiar with the Court's systems prior to the scheduled court appearance. If needed, the person may contact the Automation Department of the Clerk's office and request an appropriate time for training. Anyone who fails to comply with this Rule may be subject to sanctions, including paying the cost to repair any Court system damaged by the person's use.

[Effective August 1, 2012.]

LBR 9016–1. ALTERNATIVE DISPUTE RESOLUTION [RESCINDED EFFECTIVE JANUARY 5, 2016.]

LBR 9017. TELECONFERENCING AND VIDEOCONFERENCING

The Court may permit a party or witness to appear at any proceeding before the Court by teleconference or video conference. Unless the Court orders otherwise, application to appear by telephone or video conference may be made informally and without a written request if timely notice is given to the other parties. The Court may grant such a request without a written order.

[Effective August 1, 2012.]

LBR 9019–1. BANKRUPTCY ALTERNATIVE DISPUTE RESOLUTION PROGRAM

The following Local Rules govern the Bankruptcy Alternative Dispute Resolution Program (the "Program") in the United States Bankruptcy Court for the Western District of Michigan and supersede LBR 9016–1 which is hereby rescinded.

[Effective January 5, 2016.]

LBR 9019–2. ADR FAVORED

(a) Purpose. The Court recognizes that formal litigation of disputes in bankruptcy cases, contested matters and adversary proceedings frequently imposes significant economic burdens on parties and often delays resolution of those disputes. The procedures established by these Local Rules are intended primarily to provide litigants with the means to resolve their disputes more quickly, at less cost, and often without the stress and pressure of litigation.

A court-authorized dispute resolution program, in which litigants and counsel meet with one or more neutral third parties, offers an opportunity for parties to resolve disputes promptly and less expensively, to their mutual satisfaction. By these Local Rules, the Program is adopted for the United States Bankruptcy Court for the Western District of Michigan. It is the Court's intention for the Program to allow participants to take advantage of and utilize mediation, negotiation and case evaluation to resolve disputes. The specific method or methods employed will be those which the Court or the parties determine appropriate and applicable, and may vary from matter to matter.

(b) Scope—These Local Rules Apply to All Matters Referred to the Program. All other Local Rules apply, except to the extent inconsistent with these Local Rules.

[Effective January 5, 2016.]

LBR 9019–3. ADMINISTRATION OF THE PROGRAM

The Court will designate personnel to maintain and collect applications, maintain a Panel of Qualified Neutrals, track and compile results of the Program, and handle such other administrative duties as necessary (collectively, the "ADR Administrator").

[Effective January 5, 2016.]

LBR 9019–4. ELIGIBLE MATTERS

Unless otherwise ordered by the Judge handling the particular matter, all controversies arising in an adversary proceeding, contested matter, or other dispute in a bankruptcy case, will be eligible for referral to the Program EXCEPT contested matters or adversary proceedings:

(a) initiated by the Office of the United States Trustee (including objections filed by that Office); or

(b) for contempt or other types of sanctions, other than alleged stay and discharge violations.

[Effective January 5, 2016.]

LBR 9019–5. *PRO BONO* MEDIATIONS

(a) *Pro bono* mediations include those matters in which the mediator determines one or both parties are unable to pay their share of the mediator's posted fee.

(b) Any party who is unable to pay their share of the mediator's posted fee must complete a form requesting *pro bono* services available from the Clerk of the Court or the ADR Administrator. See Form #1.*

(c) If one or more parties are unable to pay their share of the mediator's fee, the other party or parties may still pay their share of the mediator's fee, but will not be required to pay any portion of the non-paying party's share of the fee.

(d) The mediator may agree to a reduced fee for one or more parties so long as it does not render him or her unable to serve due to lack of neutrality.

[Effective January 5, 2016.]

* **[Publisher's Note:** Please see court website for forms.]

LBR 9019–6. PANEL OF QUALIFIED NEUTRALS

(a) The Bankruptcy Court shall establish and maintain a Panel of Qualified Neutrals (the "Panel") who have offered to serve as mediators or case evaluators for the possible resolution of matters referred to the Program.

(b) Neutrals may serve as members of the Panel for five-year terms without the need to re-apply.

(c) Applications to serve as a member of the Panel shall be submitted to the ADR Administrator by the deadlines established by the Court, shall set forth the qualifications described below, and should conform to forms promulgated by the Court. See Form #2.*

(d) Applicants must agree to mediate at least one *pro bono* matter per year.

Effective January 5, 2016.]

* [**Publisher's Note:** Please see court website for forms.]

LBR 9019–7. QUALIFICATIONS AND CRITERIA FOR PANEL OF QUALIFIED NEUTRALS

(a) In order to qualify for service on the Court's Panel of Qualified Neutrals, each applicant shall certify to the Court that the applicant:

(1) Is willing to serve as a Neutral and to undertake to evaluate or mediate settlement of matters subject only to unavailability due to conflicts, personal or professional commitments, or other matters which would make such service inappropriate;

(2) Is, and has been, a member in good standing of the bar of the United States District Court for the Western District of Michigan, and has regularly practiced in Bankruptcy Court for at least 10 years;

(3) Has served as the principal attorney of record in active matters in at least 10 bankruptcy cases (without regard to the party represented) from case commencement to the earlier of the date of the application or conclusion of the case, or has served as the principal attorney of record for a party in interest in at least 10 adversary proceedings or contested matters from commencement through conclusion;

(4) Shall be governed by any standards of professional conduct and ethical rules adopted by the Michigan Supreme Court for state-court mediators, currently set forth at MCR 4.211(G), as those standards and rules may be amended.

(b) Before serving on any assigned matters, mediators on the Court's Panel shall have:

(1) Completed a 40–hour mediation training program approved by the Court;

(2) Observed at least two mediations to completion conducted by an approved mediator; and

(3) Conducted at least one mediation to conclusion under the supervision and observation of an approved mediator.

a. The Court will appoint members to the Panel of Qualified Neutrals from the applications submitted, giving due regard to alternative dispute resolution training and experience and such matters as professional experience and location so as to make the Panel appropriately representative of the public being served by the Program. Appointments will be limited to keep the Panel at an appropriate size and to ensure that the panel is comprised of individuals who have broad-based experience, superior skills and qualifications.

b. The Neutrals on the Panel will indicate to the ADR Administrator the city or cities within the District in which they are willing to act or serve.

[Effective January 5, 2016.]

LBR 9019–8. SERVICE OF NEUTRALS

(a) No Neutral may serve in any matter in violation of the standards set forth in 28 U.S.C. § 455.

(b) Although parties shall not be considered their clients, a Neutral shall promptly determine all conflicts or potential conflicts in the same manner as an attorney would under the Michigan Rules of Professional Conduct as if any party to the dispute were their client. If the Neutral is a member of a firm and the firm has represented one or more of the parties, the Neutral shall promptly disclose that circumstance to all parties in writing.

(c) A party who believes that the assigned Neutral has a conflict of interest shall promptly bring the matter to the attention of the Neutral. If the Neutral does not withdraw from the assignment, the matter shall be brought to the attention of the Court by the Neutral or any of the parties.

(d) Promptly after appointment, any Neutral unavailable to serve in the matter shall notify the parties and the ADR Administrator so the parties may select an alternate Neutral in accordance with these Rules.

[Effective January 5, 2016.]

LBR 9019–9. ASSIGNMENT OF DISPUTES TO THE PROGRAM

(a) A contested matter in a bankruptcy case, adversary proceeding, or other dispute may be referred to the Program by order of the Judge at any time. While participation in the Program is intended to be voluntary, any Judge, on the request of a party or *sua sponte*, may refer specific matters to mediation under the Program. If all parties consent, the Court will refer a matter to case evaluation.

(b) If a party objects to referral to the Program, the party may file an objection within 14 days of the order of referral. For good cause shown, the matter may be removed from the Program with or without a hearing. Such cause may include certification of a party's inability to pay for ADR, incarceration or other matter making ADR inappropriate.

(c) When a matter is assigned to the Program, the parties will be presented with the order assigning the matter to the Program and a current roster of the Panel or directed to the location of the roster in electronic format.

(d) Within 14 days after the issuance of a case management order or other order referring a matter to the Program, the parties shall mutually agree upon the selection of one Mediator (or, in the cases referred to Blue Ribbon Case Evaluation only, three Blue Ribbon case evaluators).

(e) The neutral(s) may be selected from the Court's list of approved Neutrals or, by mutual agreement, any person or entity, including a Michigan community dispute resolution program. The plaintiff in an adversary proceeding or movant in a contested matter shall file a *Notice of Selection of*

Neutral(s) with the Court and provide a copy to the selected neutral(s). See Form #3.*

(f) Whenever the parties cannot agree or fail to file a *Notice of Selection of Neutral(s)*, the ADR Administrator's staff assistant shall randomly select a mediator or three case evaluators from the Court's Panel of Qualified Neutrals and notify the parties and neutral(s) of their selection.

(g) An order assigning a matter to the Program shall be docketed and served on the assigned Neutral and by first class mail to any interested parties to the dispute who do not have ECF capabilities.

(h) Subject to availability and by prior arrangement with the Clerk of the Court, mediators and case evaluators may use court facilities to conduct mediations and case evaluations.

[Effective January 5, 2016.]

* [**Publisher's Note:** Please see court website for forms.]

LBR 9019–10.   EFFECT ON DISCOVERY

Unless otherwise ordered by the Court, the assignment to mediation or case evaluation shall act to stay discovery, but will not stay the mandatory disclosures required under Fed.

R.Civ.P. 26(a). Any party may file a motion seeking proceed with discovery or to stay Rule 26(a) disclosure [Effective January 5, 2016.]

LBR 9019–11.   CERTIFICATION OF ADR CONFERENCE

(a) Unless otherwise ordered, no later than 14 days befor the initial scheduling conference set in an Adversary Proceed ing and whenever ordered by the Court in other conteste matters, counsel (or unrepresented parties) shall confer an discuss ADR options. Counsel for parties should:

(1) Provide a copy of the information sheet entitled *Bank ruptcy Dispute Resolution Program Instructions for Partie* (See Form #4 *) to their client;

(2) Discuss the available dispute resolution options provide by the Court and private entities with other counsel or unrep resented parties;

(3) Consider whether the dispute could benefit from any o the available dispute resolution options; and

(4) Determine whether they choose to participate in the Program and, if so, advise the Court whether they have selected Mediation or Case Evaluation.

[Effective January 5, 2016.]

* [**Publisher's Note:** Please see court website for forms.]

MEDIATION RULES

The following "Mediation Rules" apply only to mediation.

LBR 9019–12.   CONFIDENTIALITY & PRIVILEGE

(a) Definitions. As used in this rule on confidentiality and privilege, "Mediation Communication" means an oral or written statement, or nonverbal conduct intended to make an assertion, by or to a Mediation Participant made during the course of the mediation, whether during a Mediation Conference or prior to a mediation if made in furtherance of a mediation; "Mediation Participant" means a Party or any person who attends a mediation whether in person or by telephone, videoconference, or other electronic means; "Party" means a person participating in a mediation directly or through a designated representative, who is a named party, a real party in interest, or who would be a named party or real party in interest if an action or third-party complaint relating to the subject matter of the mediation were filed in a court of law; and "Other Proceeding" means any adjudicative process, including related discovery proceedings.

(b) Confidential Mediation Communications. Except as provided in this section, all Mediation Communications are confidential and the mediator and the Mediation Participants shall not disclose any Mediation Communication outside of the mediation, and no person may introduce in any Other Proceeding evidence pertaining to any aspect of the mediation process. However, information contained in a Mediation Communication which is otherwise admissible or subject to discovery does not become inadmissible or protected from discovery merely because of its disclosure or use in mediation.

(c) Evidence Rules and Laws. Without limiting subsection (b) and subject to any exceptions in subsection (d), Rule 408 of the Federal Rules of Evidence and any applicable federal or Michigan statute, rule, common law, or judicial precedent relating to the privileged nature of settlement discussions or Mediation Communications apply.

(d) Exceptions to Confidentiality. Notwithstanding subsections (b) and (c), upon order of the Court, Mediation Communications may be revealed in the following situations:

1. *Settlement Agreements.* Terms of a signed, written agreement reached during or as a result of a mediation, unless the Parties agree that those terms are to be kept confidential, including Mediation Communications which are relevant and material to a determination of insurance coverage for amounts at issue in the mediated settlement agreement;

2. *Waiver.* Mediation Communications for which the confidentiality or privilege against disclosure has been waived by all Parties in writing or on the record in Other Proceedings or by an individual Mediation Participant who discloses a Mediation Communication, but only to the extent necessary for another Mediation Participant to respond to the disclosure;

3. *Malpractice Claims.* Mediation Communications relevant and material to a Party's claim of legal malpractice or other tort committed during the mediation concerning the actions of a Party's attorney or other agent involved in the mediation.

(e) Required Disclosures. A mediator may disclose information from a Mediation Communication to a law enforcement agency or similar authority if required by law or if the mediator has a reasonable belief such disclosure will prevent a Mediation Participant from committing a criminal or illegal act likely to result in death or serious bodily harm.

(f) Attorneys, Agents, etc. This rule shall not prevent a Party from revealing Mediation Communications to that Party's attorney, agent, employee or partner for an artificial entity, such as a corporation, partnership or limited liability company.

(g) Preservation of Privileges. The disclosure by a Mediation Participant of privileged information (e.g., attorney/client, doctor/patient, etc.) in a Mediation Communication to the mediator, or another Mediation Participant does not waive or otherwise adversely affect the privileged nature of the information.

(h) Mediation Participants Shall Not:

(1) call or subpoena the mediator as a witness or expert in any proceeding relating to the mediation, to testify as to the subject matter of the mediation or any thoughts or impressions which the mediator may have about the parties or merits of the dispute; or

(2) subpoena or otherwise seek discovery of any notes, documents or other material prepared by the mediator in the course of or in connection with the mediation; or

(3) offer into evidence (or reveal in any argument) any statements, views, or opinions of the mediator.

(i) Communications With Court Personnel. Nothing in this rule shall be construed to prevent Parties, counsel or mediators from responding in absolute confidentiality to inquiries or surveys by persons authorized by this Court to evaluate the Program.

[Effective January 5, 2016.]

LBR 9019–13. MEDIATION PROCEDURE

(a) Initial Telephone Conference. As soon as practicable after notification of appointment, the mediator shall conduct a telephone conference with counsel for the parties and any unrepresented parties to discuss the nature of the matter, the expectations of the parties concerning the scheduling and nature of the mediation process, and anything else which will facilitate the mediation process.

(b) Mediation Conference Scheduling. Within 14 days of the telephonic conference, the mediator shall give notice to the parties of the time and place for the mediation, which shall be held at a time and location convenient to the parties.

(c) Mediation Summaries. At the request of the mediator, no later than seven days before the date of the Mediation Conference, each party shall submit a written Mediation Statement directly to the mediator and serve copies on all other parties. Mediation Summaries shall not exceed 15 pages (excluding exhibits and attachments). While Mediation Summaries may include any useful information, it is helpful to:

(1) Identify the person(s), in addition to counsel, who will attend the session as representative of the party with decision-making authority;

(2) Describe briefly the substance of the dispute;

(3) Identify any legal or factual issues whose early resolution might appreciably reduce the scope of the dispute or contribute significantly to settlement;

(4) Identify any outstanding discovery which could contribute most to equipping the parties for meaningful settlement discussions;

(5) Set forth the history of past settlement discussions, including disclosure of prior and any presently outstanding offers and demands;

(6) Make an estimate of the cost and time to be expended for further discovery, pretrial motions, expert witnesses and trial (this information may be included in a separate, confidential communication between the party and the mediator only); and

(7) Indicate presently scheduled dates for further status conferences, pretrial conferences, trial or otherwise.

(d) Summaries Not To Be Filed With Court. The written Mediation Summaries shall not be filed with or disclosed to the Court and the Court shall not have access to them.

(e) Identification of Mediation Participants. Parties may identify in their Mediation Summaries persons connected to a party opponent (including a representative of a party opponent's insurance carrier) whose presence at the Mediation Conference could make it more productive; the fact a person has been so identified, shall not, by itself, result in an order compelling that person to attend the Mediation Conference.

(f) Documents. Parties shall attach to their written Mediation Summaries copies of any documents which would materially advance the purposes of the Mediation Conference.

(g) Confidential Communications With Mediator. In the mediator's discretion, the mediator may meet with any party or confer with them or their representatives privately and confidentially.

[Effective January 5, 2016.]

LBR 9019–14. ATTENDANCE AT MEDIATION CONFERENCE

(a) Counsel. Counsel for each party primarily responsible for resolving the matter (and unrepresented parties) shall personally attend the Mediation Conference and any adjourned sessions. All counsel and parties shall come prepared to discuss all liability issues, all damage issues, and the position of the party relative to settlement.

(b) Parties. All individual parties, and representatives with authority to negotiate and to settle the matter on behalf of parties other than individuals, shall personally attend the Mediation Conference unless excused by the mediator for cause. A bankruptcy trustee need not be physically present so long as the trustee is represented by counsel, their counsel personally attends the mediation and the trustee can be reached throughout the entirety of the Mediation Conference.

(c) Telephonic Attendance. A party or lawyer who is excused by the Court or the mediator from appearing in person at the Mediation Conference may be required to participate by telephone.

[Effective January 5, 2016.]

LBR 9019–15. CONDUCT OF THE MEDIATION CONFERENCE

The Mediation Conference shall proceed informally and rules of evidence shall not apply. There shall be no formal examination or cross-examination of witnesses. In the mediator's discretion, the mediator may:

(a) Meet privately and confidentially with each party to discuss settlement or the mediation process;

(b) Permit each party, through counsel or otherwise, to make an oral presentation of its position;

(c) Help the parties identify areas of agreement and, where feasible, formulate stipulations;

(d) Help the parties assess the relative strengths and weaknesses of the parties' contentions and evidence;

(e) Help the parties estimate the likelihood of liability and the dollar range of damages;

(f) Help the parties devise a plan for sharing the important information and/or conducting the key discovery which will equip them to participate as expeditiously as possible in meaningful settlement discussions or to posture the dispute for disposition by other means; and

(g) Determine whether some form of follow-up to the Mediation Conference would contribute to the process of case development or settlement and, if so, conduct additional Mediation Conferences after the initial Mediation Conference.

[Effective January 5, 2016.]

LBR 9019–16. SUGGESTIONS AND RECOMMENDATIONS OF MEDIATOR

The mediator shall have no obligation to make any written comments or recommendations, but may, at the request of all parties and in the mediator's discretion, provide the parties with a written settlement recommendation to resolve an impasse. No copy of any such recommendation may be filed with the Clerk or revealed, in whole or in part, directly or indirectly, to the Court or Court staff, or be provided to anyone other than the parties.

[Effective January 5, 2016.]

LBR 9019–17. CONCLUSION OF THE MEDIATION CONFERENCE

Upon the conclusion of the Mediation Conference, the following procedure shall be followed:

(a) If the parties have reached an agreement regarding the disposition of the matter, the parties shall determine who shall prepare the writing to dispose of the matter, and they may continue the Mediation Conference to a date convenient to all parties and the mediator if necessary.

(b) Within 14 days following the conclusion of any Mediation Conference, the mediator shall file a report (See Form #5 *) with the Court and serve a copy on the parties. The report shall only indicate:

(1) The date of the Mediation Conference; the names and roles of all attendees; and whether the dispute was resolved.

(2) If the matter was not completely resolved, the mediator will indicate whether further mediation or other ADR procedures are contemplated by the parties.

(3) If the matter was completely resolved, the mediator will report when appropriate pleadings will be filed with the Court and the party or parties responsible for such filing.

(c) Regardless of the outcome of the Mediation Conference, the mediator will not provide the Court with any details of the substance of the conference.

[Effective January 5, 2016.]

* [Publisher's Note: Please see court website for forms.]

LBR 9019–18. FAILURE TO ATTEND MEDIATION CONFERENCE

Failure to attend the Mediation Conference may result in the imposition of sanctions by the Court.

[Effective January 5, 2016.]

LBR 9019–19. COMPENSATION OF MEDIATORS

(a) The mediator shall be paid their customary hourly rate for mediation by counsel for represented parties (or directly by *pro se* parties).

(b) Unless otherwise agreed in writing, the mediator's fees and expenses shall be assessed in as many equal parts as there are separately represented or participating parties.

(c) The mediator is responsible for billing counsel and pro se parties who shall pay said bills in full within 30 days of billing or as otherwise agreed by the mediator.

(d) In their discretion, a mediator may waive or agree to a reduced fee for any party without affecting the obligations of any other party.

[Effective January 5, 2016.]

LBR 9019–20. EVALUATION OF MEDIATION PROGRAM

In order to assist the ADR Administrator in compiling useful data to evaluate the Program and to aid the Court in assessing the efforts of the members of the Panel, the mediator shall report to the ADR Administrator such statistical and evaluative information as may be required without violating confidentiality on a form provided by the Court.

[Effective January 5, 2016.]

CASE EVALUATION

The following rules apply only to Case Evaluation.

LBR 9019–21. DEFINITION OF CASE EVALUATION

Case evaluation affords litigants an ADR process patterned after one extensively used in Michigan state courts. (See Mich. Comp. Laws §§ 600.4951–.4969; Mich. Ct. R. 2.403.) Case Evaluation involves establishment of a settlement value for a dispute by a three-member panel of attorneys. There are two types of Case Evaluation available in this Court: Standard Case Evaluation and Blue Ribbon Case Evaluation.

The Court may order any dispute to Standard Case Evaluation unless the parties unanimously agree to submit the case to Blue Ribbon Case Evaluation.

[Effective January 5, 2016.]

LBR 9019–22. STANDARD CASE EVALUATION

(a) Adoption of Michigan State–Court Procedures. The procedures governing Standard Case Evaluation are generally set forth in Rule 2.403 of the Michigan Rules of Court. Unless modified by these rules, the Program Description, or court order in a particular case, the provisions of Mich. Ct. R. 2.403, as amended from time to time, will govern in cases referred to Standard Case Evaluation, except as follows:

1. *Panel Selection.* The ADR Administrator will select all three case evaluators from the Court's Panel of Qualified Neutrals.

2. *Fees.* Each party must pay each case evaluator $100.00 apiece, for a total case evaluation fee of $300 per party, within 14 days of the notice of the ADR Administrator's notice of selection of the case evaluators. Allocation of Fees—The rules set forth in Mich. Ct. R. 2.403 for allocation of fees among multiple parties or claims apply. Once paid, the fee is not subject to refund.

(b) Submission of Documents. The rules for submission of documents set forth in Mich. Ct. R. 2.403 apply, except that case evaluation summaries are limited to 20 pages. Documents must be submitted directly to the evaluators, with a proof of service filed with the ADR Administrator. Failure to file or serve such documents in a timely manner subjects the offending party to a $150.00 penalty, with $50 payable to each case evaluator, which may not be charged to the client.

(c) Hearing Time Limit. Each side's presentation at the case evaluation hearing is limited to 30 minutes.

(d) Time for Rendering Award. The case evaluators shall render a written evaluation at the close of the hearing and serve copies personally on the parties or their counsel at that time and provide the original to the ADR Administrator's office. See Form #6* (top portion of form).

(e) Time for Acceptance or Rejection of Award. Parties shall have 14 days to accept or reject a case evaluation award. If any party fails to file an acceptance or rejection with the ADR Clerk within 14 days of service of the award, that party shall be deemed to have rejected the award. See Form #6 (bottom portion of form).

(f) Rejecting Party's Liability for Costs.

1. In cases submitted to Standard Case Evaluation, the provisions of Mich. Ct. R. 2.403 governing liability for costs apply, except that attorneys' fees will not be taxed for rejection of a case evaluation award absent the agreement of all parties.

2. In cases submitted to Standard Case Evaluation, the parties may stipulate in writing to the assessment of attorneys' fees in accordance with Mich. Ct. R. 2.403.

[Effective January 5, 2016.]

* [**Publisher's Note:** Please see court website for forms.]

LBR 9019–23. BLUE RIBBON CASE EVALUATION

Blue Ribbon Case Evaluation allows parties to choose their own evaluators and to request that the evaluators devote substantial time to the evaluation process. A case may be referred to Blue Ribbon Case Evaluation only with the unanimous consent of the parties. All procedures applicable to Standard Case Evaluation apply, except:

(a) Selection of Evaluators. The parties jointly select the Blue Ribbon case evaluators, who need not be members of the Court's Panel of Qualified Neutrals.

(b) Fees. Case evaluators are compensated at their customary hourly rate, to be assessed in as many equal parts as there are separately represented parties, or as otherwise agreed by the parties at the time Blue Ribbon Case Evaluation is ordered.

(c) Case Evaluation Briefs and Hearings. No limits apply to the length of Blue Ribbon Case Evaluation hearings or to the length of case evaluation briefs, unless agreed to in writing by the parties. No late fees are imposed for untimely submissions of case evaluation briefs.

(d) Time for Rendering Award. In an extraordinary case, where the award cannot reasonably be rendered at the conclusion of the hearing, the evaluators may render their written evaluation no later than seven days after the hearing concludes.

(e) Time for Acceptance or Rejection of Award. Parties shall have 14 days to accept or reject a case evaluation award. If any party fails to timely file an acceptance or rejection with the ADR Clerk within 14 days of service of the award, that party shall be deemed to have rejected the award.

[Effective January 5, 2016.]

LBR 9021. ENTRY OF ORDERS AND JUDGMENTS

Unless otherwise directed by the Court, orders and judgments must be prepared in writing by the prevailing party.

The prevailing party must serve a copy of the order or judgment on the required parties promptly after entry by the Court.

[Effective August 1, 2012.]

LBR 9029. GENERAL PROVISIONS

(a) Prior Rules Superseded. These Rules provide standardized procedures for the convenience of the bench and bar. They supersede all previous Local Rules and Court Administrative Orders, except for Court Administrative Order No. 2010–3 and any other Court Administrative Order that does not conflict with these Rules.

(b) Administrative Orders. If any matter of practice or procedure requires the attention of the Court prior to further amendment of these Rules, the Court may enter an administrative order to serve as an interim rule. The Clerk will maintain a file that numbers each administrative order as it is entered. Administrative orders are available for public inspection in the office of the Clerk and on the Court's website at www.miwb.uscourts.gov.

(c) Technical Corrections. Technical corrections to these Rules may be made by the Court at any time. Notice of such corrections will be provided on the Court's website at www. miwb.uscourts.gov and posted in the Clerk's office.

(d) Use of Local Forms. The documents attached as exhibits to these Rules are for reference purposes only. Only the official documents posted under the "Local Forms" link on the Court's website may be used.

(e) Suspension or Modification. Any judge of this Court may suspend or modify a provision of these Rules in a particular case, adversary proceeding, or contested matter on the Court's own initiative or on motion of a party.

[Effective August 1, 2012.]

LBR 9037–1. REDACTING PERSONAL IDENTIFIERS

(a) Redaction Requirement. Unless the Court orders otherwise, a filer must redact "personal identifiers" from any document filed with the Court or submitted to the trustee pursuant to LBR 1007–2(f). "Personal identifiers" means Social Security numbers, taxpayer-identification numbers, dates of birth, names of minor children, and financial account numbers. A filing is properly redacted if it includes only:

(1) the last four digits of the Social Security number or the taxpayer-identification number;

(2) the year of the individual's birth;

(3) the minor's initials; and

(4) the last four digits of the financial-account number.

For cause shown, the Court may require the redaction of additional information or limit a nonparty's electronic access to a document filed with the Court.

(b) Trustee's Authority to Redact. The trustee in an individual chapter 7, 11, or 13 case has the authority to redact any document that is inadvertently submitted with personal

identifiers. However, nothing in this Rule imposes a duty o[f] the trustee to make the redaction.

[Effective August 1, 2012.]

LBR 9037–2. USE OF ELECTRONIC TRANSCRIPTS

(a) Access to Electronic Transcripts. The Court ma[y] direct that a transcript of all or part of a digitally recorde[d] proceeding be made available through CM/ECF. All ECF Filers who attended the proceeding will be notified once a[n] electronic transcript is available.

(1) *Limited Access.* No electronic transcript will be available for viewing or downloading for the first 90 days after the transcript is filed with the Court unless the transcript is purchased from the court reporter or transcriber by an attorney of record, in which case the transcript will be available for remote electronic viewing and use by that attorney. Otherwise, an electronic transcript will only be available during the first 90 days for viewing from a public terminal at the Clerk's office.

(2) *Unrestricted Access.* The original electronic transcript (or a redacted transcript, if applicable) will be available for unrestricted viewing and printing—either remotely or from the Clerk's public terminal—beginning on the 91st day after the transcript is filed with the Court. PACER charges apply for all remote viewing regardless of whether the viewer purchased access to the transcript, and charges are not limited to 30 pages.

(b) Redaction of Electronic Transcripts.

(1) *Redacting Personal Identifiers.* The responsibility for redacting personal identifiers rests solely with the parties and their counsel. Any person who wishes to redact personal identifiers from an electronic transcript must file a "Notice of Intent to Request Redaction" with the Clerk and serve a copy on the transcriber within 7 days after the transcript is filed. The requesting party must then submit a Request for Redaction within 21 days of the transcript's filing that lists (A) the personal identifiers to be redacted, and (B) where those personal identifiers appear in the transcript by page and line.

(2) *Redacting Information Other Than Personal Identifiers.* If a person wishes to redact information other than personal identifiers from an electronic transcript, the person must file a motion for a protective order pursuant to Fed. R. Bankr. P. 9037(d). The electronic transcript will not be available for unrestricted viewing, downloading, or printing until the Court rules on the motion for the protective order.

[Effective August 1, 2012.]

LBR 9037–3. DOCKETED AUDIO FILES

The Court may direct that all or part of a digitally recorded proceeding be posted as an audio file on the CM/ECF docket. No transcript of an audio file may be included in a document that is filed with the Court unless the transcript has been prepared by an authorized court reporter.

[Effective August 1, 2012.]

LBR 9037–4. FILING DOCUMENTS UNDER SEAL

(a) **Court Order Required.** Before filing any document under seal, a party must file a written motion consistent with 11 U.S.C. § 107 explaining why the relief is necessary. The explanation must be as comprehensive as possible without disclosing the substance of the information to be filed under seal. If the motion is granted, the movant must conventionally file the document in a sealed envelope with a copy of the order attached to the envelope. A sealed document may be filed unredacted. The Clerk will maintain the document under seal until further Court order.

(b) **Request for *In Camera* Review.** In a motion requesting permission to file a document under seal, the moving party may include a request that the Court review the document *in camera* before deciding the motion. Any such request must include an explanation as to how an *in camera* review will assist the Court in deciding whether the document should be filed under seal. If the Court grants a request for *in camera* review, the Court will establish procedures to ensure the confidentiality of the document and the fairness of the process.

[Effective August 1, 2012.]

EXHIBITS
EXHIBIT INDEX

[Effective February 1, 2002. Amended effective February 1, 2007; August 1, 2012.]

EXHIBIT 1. PREPARATION OF CREDITOR MATRIX

The following instructions will guide you to correctly format a creditor matrix and save it as a **.txt** file to upload in to the court's Case Management/Electronic Filing (CM/ECF) System or for filing over-the-counter.

A creditor matrix shall contain each creditor's name and mailing address. This information is used for noticing and also for claims information when applicable.

Uploading in to CM/ECF: The creditor matrix must be in an ASCII file format with an appropriate text extension such as **.txt** before it can be successfully uploaded into the CM/ECF system. (If you have access to Notepad, it will automatically save matrices in **.txt** format).

Filing Matrix Over-The-Counter: The matrix must list all creditors in a single column down the center of the page.

Creditor Matrix Specifications: (Do not include the name and address of the debtor(s) and/or attorney for the debtor on the matrix)

- ◆ When preparing a matrix, there **must** be at least one blank line separating each creditor.

- ◆ The name and address of each creditor cannot be more than 5 lines.

- ◆ Each line may contain no more than 40 characters including blanks.

- ◆ One or more spaces in the first position of the address will cause that particular creditor to not be placed on the matrix.

- ◆ Do not use special characters such as ~, ½ or ^.

- ◆ Account numbers or "attention" lines should be reflected on the second address line.

- ◆ City, State & Zip Code must appear on the last line.

- ◆ Nine-digit ZIP codes must contain a hyphen which separates the first five digits from the last four digits.

- ◆ All states must be two-letter, standard postal abbreviations.

- ◆ Do not include page numbers, headers, footers, etc.

- ◆ Only the following fonts are acceptable:

  Courier, Helvetica, Arial or Times New Roman

U.S. Bankruptcy Court-Western District of Michigan   **August, 2006**

[Effective February 1, 2002. Amended effective February 1, 2007.]

Exhibit 2   U.S. BANKRUPTCY COURT

EXHIBIT 2.   VERIFICATION OF CREDITOR MATRIX

UNITED STATES BANKRUPTCY COURT
FOR THE WESTERN DISTRICT OF MICHIGAN

IN RE: _____

Case No.: _____

_____ Debtor(s)

<u>Verification of Creditor Matrix</u>

I(we), hereby declare, under penalty of perjury, that the attached list of creditors is true and correct to the best of my(our) knowledge.

Date: _____

At: _____

_____
Attorney for the Debtor(s)

- OR -

_____
Debtor

_____
Joint Debtor (if any)

[Effective February 1, 2002. Amended effective February 1, 2007.]

EXHIBIT 3. ASSET PROTECTION REPORT

UNITED STATES BANKRUPTCY COURT
WESTERN DISTRICT OF MICHIGAN

In re:

Case No. _____

Chapter 7

Debtor(s).

_____/

ASSET PROTECTION REPORT

Pursuant to Local Bankruptcy Rule 1007-2(d), debtors filing a Chapter 7 petition and debtors in a case converting to Chapter 7 must file an Asset Protection Report. List below any property referenced on **Schedule D** (Creditors Holding Secured Claims); or **Schedule G** (Executory Contracts and Unexpired Leases); and **any insurable asset in which there is nonexempt equity.** For each asset listed, provide the following information regarding property damage or casualty insurance:

INSURABLE ASSET (from schedules)	IS ASSET INSURED? (Yes/No)	NAME & ADDRESS OF AGENT OR INSURANCE CO.	POLICY EXPIRATION DATE (MM/YYYY)	WILL DEBTOR RENEW INSURANCE ON EXPIRATION? (Yes/No)

If the debtor is self-employed, does the debtor have general liability insurance for business activities?
Yes ☐   No ☐

I declare, under penalty of perjury, that the above information is true and accurate to the best of my knowledge. I intend to provide insurance protection for any exemptible interests in real or personal property of the estate, and I request that the trustee not expend estate funds to procure insurance coverage for my exemptible assets.

Dated:_____   _____
                                                                                   Debtor

Dated:_____   _____
                                                                              Joint Debtor (if any)

Pursuant to LBR 1007-2(f), debtor is required to provide the trustee with a copy of the Declarations Page for any insurance policy covering an insurable asset at least 7 days before the date first set for the meeting of creditors.

[Effective February 1, 2002.   Amended effective February 1, 2007.]

Exhibit 4   U.S. BANKRUPTCY COURT

EXHIBIT 4. NOTICE TO CREDITORS AND OTHER PARTIES IN INTEREST OF APPLICATION FOR PROFESSIONAL FEES PURSUANT TO FED. R. BANKR. P. 2016 AND NOTICE OF THE RIGHT TO OBJECT

UNITED STATES BANKRUPTCY COURT
FOR THE WESTERN DISTRICT OF MICHIGAN

In re: Case No. _____

                                     Chapter _____

           Debtors.

_____/

**NOTICE TO CREDITORS AND OTHER PARTIES IN
INTEREST OF APPLICATION FOR PROFESSIONAL
FEES PURSUANT TO FED. R. BANKR. P. 2016
AND NOTICE OF THE RIGHT TO OBJECT**

       Notice is hereby given that the following professional persons have made application to the Bankruptcy Court for the allowance of fees and expenses as listed below:

Professional (Name & Address)	Fees Requested	Expenses Requested	Fees Previously Allowed by Court

PLEASE NOTE: The application is available for public review at the Clerk's Office, One Division North, Grand Rapids, Michigan, Monday through Friday, from 8 a.m. – 4 p.m. No hearing will be set before the Court unless a written objection to this application is timely filed with the Clerk of the Bankruptcy Court. If you have any objection, you have 21 days from the date of service of this notice in which to file such written objection. If an objection is filed, a subsequent notice will be sent to you of the date, time, and location of the hearing on the objection.

ANY OBJECTION MUST BE TIMELY FILED WITH:

United States Bankruptcy Court
One Division North
Grand Rapids, MI 49503
[Use Marquette address if applicable]

A COPY OF ANY OBJECTION MUST ALSO BE SENT TO:

[Name & Address of the Applicant or attorney for Applicant]

Date Notice Served: _____   _____

                                                Applicant or Attorney

[Effective February 1, 2002. Amended effective February 1, 2007. Formerly Exhibit 6 redesignated as Exhibit 4 effective August 1, 2012.]

EXHIBIT 5.   MEMORANDUM REGARDING ALLOWANCE OF COMPENSATION AND REIMBURSEMENT OF EXPENSES FOR COURT–APPOINTED PROFESSIONALS

UNITED STATES BANKRUPTCY COURT
FOR THE WESTERN DISTRICT OF MICHIGAN

_____

MEMORANDUM REGARDING ALLOWANCE OF COMPENSATION
AND REIMBURSEMENT OF EXPENSES
FOR COURT-APPOINTED PROFESSIONALS

AS AMENDED EFFECTIVE OCTOBER 1, 2013

The Federal Bar Association (Western Michigan) Bankruptcy Section has requested that the court adjust the no-look fees and hourly rates in chapter 13 cases. The court has determined that it is in the interests of all debtors, creditors, and other parties in interest, and their respective attorneys, and the United States Trustee, that the following general guidelines regarding fee applications and reimbursement of expenses be established and published.

1.   Professional persons are appointed by the United States Bankruptcy Court for the Western District of Michigan, pursuant to 11 U.S.C. §§ 328 and 330(a)(1) and FED. R. BANKR. P. 2016.   The burden of proof regarding all fee applications submitted by court-appointed professionals is upon the applicant.

2.   Every application must succinctly itemize each activity, the date of the activity, the professional who performed the work, a description of both the nature and substance of the work, and the time expended thereon (the "itemization").   An itemization which lacks explanation of activities performed will be deemed inadequate and shall be non-compensable.

3.   In order for time spent on activities such as court appearances, preparation for court appearances, conferences, telephone calls, drafting documents, and research to be compensable, the nature and purpose of the activity must be stated.   Time entries for telephone calls must list the person with whom the applicant spoke and give a brief description of the conversation.   Time entries for correspondence must state the addressee and give a brief explanation of the contents.   Time entries involving documents must specify the specific document. Time entries for legal research must describe the matter or proceeding researched, and the legal issue that was researched.

Exhibit 5   U.S. BANKRUPTCY COURT

4.   Applicants shall not attempt to circumvent minimum time requirements or any detail requirement by "lumping" or "bunching" a number of activities into a single itemization entry. Each type of service must be listed with a corresponding specific time which was spent on the activity.

5.   Time entries with unexplained abbreviations are non-compensable. (Where abbreviations are used, an appendix explaining the abbreviations shall be attached.) Where computer time sheets are submitted to substantiate entries, a code key must be supplied, or the application will not be considered. In more complex petitions, a glossary of persons involved may be helpful.

6.   All applications shall state the case filing date, the chapter, whether conversion has occurred, and the date of conversion. The application must state the amount of any retainer paid, as well as the date of each previous application, the amount of compensation and expenses requested, the amount of compensation and expenses approved, the date of approval, and the amount previously received. The application must also indicate the total hours charged and give a summary of the hours and hourly rate charged by each professional.

7.   If more than one professional has charged time for activities such as intra-office conference or joint court appearances, the applicant must explain the need for each professional's participation in the activity.

8.   All time listed must represent the actual time required to perform the activity and should be stated in tenths (0.10) of an hour. "Rounding up" of time or minimum time increments, e.g. 0.25 hours, is not permitted.

9.   The rate charged must be commensurate with the level of skill required for a particular task; for example, attorney rates or paralegal rates may not be charged for non-legal work, such as copying or delivering documents, preparing or filing proofs of service, or for trustee duties generally performed without the assistance of an attorney. When paralegals are utilized to perform legal services for an estate, they may be compensated as paraprofessionals rather than treated as an overhead expense.

10.   No fees shall be allowed for general research on law well known or that should be well known to practitioners in the area of law involved.

11.   Reasonable time spent by an attorney in preparing and reviewing an application for compensation may be compensable.

12. The court will consider whether tasks performed within a reasonable number of hours and whether the requested hourly rate is reasonable based upon the customary rate charged by experienced practitioners.

13. Except as otherwise allowed by statute, e.g., 11 U.S.C. § 330(a)(4)(B), the court will not allow compensation for services which do not benefit the debtor's estate; for example, fees for reading the work product of another attorney simply as a matter of interest or performing legal services mainly beneficial to the debtor, or the debtor's principals.

14. An application for reimbursement of expenses must explicitly list each expense, its date incurred/paid, and a general description of the nature and purpose of the expense. For example, requests for mileage must include the date, destination, miles, per mile rate, and the reason for the trip. Professionals should utilize the most economical method for necessary expenses; for example, coach air fare, moderately priced accommodations, and commercial firm duplication for large number of copies. Courier service, express mail service and fax transmissions should not be used routinely, but, if used, should be as a result of justifiable reasons including time constraints.

15. Although the State Bar of Michigan does not require attorneys to participate in continuing legal education ("CLE"), the judges of this court continue to encourage bankruptcy CLE. The Clerk may maintain a list of attorneys who have attended CLE for each calendar year. Those attorneys who fail to attend CLE in any given calendar year may be required to attend fees hearings.

16. In view of the court's continued interest in promoting and rewarding attorney CLE, the court shall utilize a sliding scale to award compensation to chapter 13 debtors' attorneys. Commencing October 1, 2013 and continuing until modified or rescinded, the court may approve a "no look" fee in an amount not to exceed $2,600.00 (a $175.00 per hour presumptive hourly rate) for services rendered through confirmation. Attorneys who have and continue to personally attend bankruptcy education seminars (with at least seven hours of legal education attended) during the calendar year immediately prior to the date the chapter 13 was filed and who certify in writing as to the seminar(s) attended, and thus have attained chapter 13 expertise, may be awarded a "no look" fee up to $3,200.00 (a $220.00 per hour presumptive hourly rate) for services rendered through confirmation. Attorneys who are or become certified by the American Board of Certification ("ABC") may be awarded a "no look" fee up to $3,650.00 (a $250.00

Exhibit 5   U.S. BANKRUPTCY COURT

per hour presumptive hourly rate). These fees are not "entitlements" as there still may be simple consumer cases in which the attorney should request and will be awarded less than the "no look" fee stated above. Attorneys shall file with the court a copy of the fee agreement executed between the debtor and the debtor's attorney. If services are performed with a reasonable value in excess of the "no look" fees and are documented by the filing of an itemized fee application, covering both the initial "no look" fee awarded and the additional fees requested, upon review, the court may award fees in excess of the "no look" fees stated above.

17. In complicated chapter 13 cases, the hourly rate will be determined on a case-by-case basis and the court may approve a higher presumptive hourly rate. If an attorney seeks an hourly rate higher than the presumptive chapter 13 hourly rate, upon request and submission of an application and itemized statement, a hearing will be scheduled to permit the attorney to prove the "reasonableness" of the higher requested hourly rate. The court will follow *In re Boddy*, 950 F.2d 334 (6th Cir. 1991); *cf. In re Williams,* 357 B.R. 434, 439 (B.A.P. 6th Cir. 2007).

18. The court may consider applications for fees and expenses on a notice and opportunity to object basis as permitted by the Local Bankruptcy Rules for the Bankruptcy Court for the Western District of Michigan. The court may, *sua sponte*, or upon the motion or objection of any party in interest or the United States Trustee after notice and hearing, order that payment of all, or some portion of, allowed interim fees be withheld for a specified period of time. Whenever payment of an applicant's fee has been deferred by the court, that applicant may file at any time a motion to rescind or modify the deferral. Motions to rescind or modify deferral shall be scheduled for hearing and heard by the court.

19. In most cases, the reasonableness of the work done and the fee charged will depend upon the results attained. A part of the service to be performed by an attorney is to estimate, as to each prospective matter or proceeding, the probability of success, the amount to be realized and the overall benefit to debtor or creditors. Attorneys who routinely claim a "no look" fee award for simple cases which do not warrant payment of the "no look" fee may discover that the court may require itemization in all future cases.

The court will consider applications for allowance of compensation and reimbursement of expenses which comport with the guidelines set forth in this memorandum.

_____   _____
Hon. Scott W. Dales   Hon. James D. Gregg
Chief U.S. Bankruptcy Judge   U.S. Bankruptcy Judge

[Amended effective October 1, 2013.]

Exhibit 6   U.S. BANKRUPTCY COURT

EXHIBIT 6. CERTIFICATE REGARDING APPLICATIONS FOR ATTORNEY FEES BEYOND THE "NO LOOK" FEE IN ACCORDANCE WITH LBR 2016–2(e)(2)(A)

UNITED STATES BANKRUPTCY COURT
FOR THE WESTERN DISTRICT OF MICHIGAN

**Certificate Regarding Applications For Attorney
Fees Beyond the "No Look" Fee
In Accordance with LBR 2016-2(e)(2)(A)**

I, _____ hereby certify that I have attended the below-referenced seminars or obtained certification by the American Board of Certification in accordance with LBR 2016-2(e)(2)(A) and this Court's fee memorandum effective January 1, 2010.

Bankruptcy Educational Seminar(s) Attended:

Date(s) of Attendance

Description of Seminar(s)
(i.e.: FBA, ABI, etc.)

_____   _____

_____   _____

_____   _____

_____   _____

American Board Certification:

Date of Certification: _____

Dated:_____   _____

Attorney Name
Address
Telephone Number
Bar ID:_____

[Effective February 1, 2002. Amended effective February 1, 2007. Formerly Exhibit 5 redesignated as Exhibit 6 effective August 1, 2012.]

EXHIBIT 7. ORDER TO EMPLOYER TO PAY THE TRUSTEE

**UNITED STATES BANKRUPTCY COURT
FOR THE WESTERN DISTRICT OF MICHIGAN**

In re: _____ SSN: xxx-xx-_____   Case No. _____

ORDER TO EMPLOYER TO PAY THE TRUSTEE

The Court finds that:

1. The above-named debtor has a proceeding pending in this Court for a wage-earner's plan under Chapter 13 of the Bankruptcy Code.
2. Pursuant to the Code requirements and the debtor's plan, the debtor has submitted all future earnings and wages to the exclusive jurisdiction of this Court for the purpose of consummating the plan.
3. Under the provisions of §§ 1306(a)(2) and 1322(a)(1) of the Bankruptcy Code, the debtor's employer may be required by court order to pay over that portion of the debtor's wages or earnings as may be needed to effectuate the plan.
4. Such an order is necessary and proper.

NOW, THEREFORE, IT IS ORDERED:

1. Until further order of this Court, the debtor's employer: _____ _____ shall deduct from the debtor's earnings $_____ per _____ **pay period**, beginning on the next pay day following receipt of this Order.
2. The debtor's employer shall continue to deduct a similar amount from each subsequent pay period – including any pay period in which the debtor receives a periodic or lump-sum payment of vacation, termination, or other benefits arising out of the debtor's present or past employment.
3. Debtor's employer shall immediately remit the sums so deducted to the Trustee appointed in this case, or to his or her successor in interest, as follows:

> [Name and address of Chapter 13 Trustee's
> Payment Account, and line for signature
> Approval of Chapter 13 Trustee.]   _____

4. All of the debtor's earnings and wages–except amounts required to be withheld by federal, state, or local law; by any insurance, pension, retirement, or union-dues agreement between the employer and the debtor; or by order of the court–must be paid to debtor in accordance with the employer's usual payroll procedure.
5. The employer shall notify the trustee if the debtor's employment is terminated and shall state the reason for the termination.
6. The employer may not make a deduction from the debtor's earnings for any garnishment, wage assignment, credit union, or other purpose not specifically authorized by the Court; except the employer may make deductions for the Friend of the Court, if applicable, and (Other Possible Deductions).
7. This order supersedes all previous orders, if any, that may have been directed to the above-referenced employer in this case.

Dated:_____   _____
                                     Clerk of the Court for Bankruptcy Judge

The undersigned certifies that a copy of the foregoing Payroll Order was served by regular, first-class mail addressed to the following:

Trustee: See above
Employer: See above
Debtor:
Attorney:

                                     _____

[Effective February 1, 2002. Amended effective February 1, 2007.]

Exhibit 8   U.S. BANKRUPTCY COURT

EXHIBIT 8.   ORIGINAL CHAPTER 13 PLAN
UNITED STATES BANKRUPTCY COURT
FOR THE WESTERN DISTRICT OF MICHIGAN

In re:

_____,

Case No. _____

Chapter 13

Hon. _____

Debtor(s)

Filed: _____

_____/

ORIGINAL CHAPTER 13 PLAN

A limit on the amount of a secured claim, set out in Paragraph III.C.2.c and III.C.1.f., which may result in a partial payment or no payment at all to the secured creditor	☐ Included	☐ Not included
Avoidance of a judicial lien or nonpossessory, nonpurchase-money security interest, set out in Paragraph IV.R.	☐ Included	☐ Not included
Nonstandard provisions, set out in Paragraph IV.R.	☐ Included	☐ Not included

I.   **PLAN PARAMETERS**

A.   **APPLICABLE COMMITMENT PERIOD (ACP) - 11 U.S.C. § 1325(b)(4).**

(   ) The ACP is 60 months.

(   ) The ACP is 36 months. However, the duration of payments may be extended to complete the Plan.

B.   **LIQUIDATION ANALYSIS.**

1.   The amount to be distributed to holders of allowed unsecured claims shall not be less than the value of the non-exempt equity of the Debtor(s) less the costs of sale. The liquidation value of the estate as required by 11 U.S.C. § 1325(a)(4) is $_____.

2.   The estimated base amount to be paid to the general unsecured creditors is $_____.

1- As updated on 11-23-16

II. FUNDING

A. PLAN PAYMENT. The Debtor(s) shall make payments in the amount of $_____ per ( ) week, ( ) bi-weekly, ( ) semi-monthly, ( ) monthly, and/or ( ) other (see Additional Plan Payment Provisions) for the minimum of the ACP.

( ) Additional Plan Payment Provisions:

III. DISBURSEMENTS

A. ADMINISTRATIVE CLAIMS. The Debtor(s) shall pay in full, in deferred cash payments, all allowed claims entitled to priority under 11 U.S.C. § 507, including:

1. Court filing fee.

2. Trustee fee.

3. Attorney fees exclusive of costs and expenses: An initial fee of $_____ less fees paid of $_____, leaving a fee balance in the amount of $_____ to be paid by the Trustee pursuant to the priorities set forth in paragraph IV.H of the Plan, unless otherwise marked below:

    a. ( ) Attorney fees shall be paid at the rate of $_____ per month until paid in full pursuant to paragraph IV.H of the Plan.

    b. ( ) Attorney fees shall be paid after all necessary equal monthly payments on secured continuing claims, secured claims, assumed executory contract/unexpired lease claims which is a modification of paragraph IV.H.

4. Expenses advanced to the Debtor(s) (paid by the attorney to the Clerk of the Court or the service provider) include:

    $_____ filing fee (enter amount or N/A);

    $_____ mandatory credit counseling or financial management class (enter amount or N/A); and

    $_____ other (explain and enter amount, or enter N/A).

B. PRIORITY CLAIMS.

1. **Domestic Support Obligation (DSO)**[i]: Prepetition DSO payment arrears as of the petition date shall be paid directly by the Debtor(s) unless marked below:

    ( ) by the Trustee.

Mandatory information:

Name of DSO Payee(s)	Monthly Amount	Estimated Arrears

2. a. **Prepetition Priority Tax Claims:** Prepetition priority tax claims are allowed claims entitled to priority under 11 U.S.C. § 507 and shall be paid in full by the Trustee.

Mandatory information:

Creditor Name	Estimated Amount[ii]	Nature of Debt

    b. **Post-Petition Priority Tax Claims:** Absent objection, post-petition priority tax claims shall be paid in full pursuant to 11 U.S.C. § 1305(a)(1) and (b). Any portion of a post-petition claim under 11 U.S.C. § 1305 that is not paid through the Plan for whatever reason, including dismissal or conversion to Chapter 7, will remain non-dischargeable, even if the Debtor(s) receive(s) a discharge.

---

[i] The Debtor(s) will comply with 11 U.S.C. § 1325(a)(8) and shall, prior to confirmation of the Plan, provide the Trustee with an affidavit or other evidence (*e.g.,* wage deduction, a statement from friend of the court, or a statement from the recipient) that all post-petition, pre-confirmation DSO payments are current.

[ii] The amount stated is an estimate only and the proof of claim controls as to the amount of the claim. This provision does not preclude any party in interest from filing an objection to the claim.

2- As updated on 11-23-16

Exhibit 8

U.S. BANKRUPTCY COURT

3. **Other Priority Claims and Plan Treatment:**

C. **SECURED CLAIMS.**

1. **Real Property:**

    a. **Mortgage Payments:** Unless otherwise stated, the Trustee shall commence paying the first post-petition mortgage payment on the first day of the month following the month of the petition date.

    b. **Principal Residence Post-Petition Mortgage Payments and Prepetition Arrears:** The following is the street address and the tax ID parcel no. for the principal residence of the Debtor(s):

Property No. 1_____ Property No. 2_____

Creditor Name	Estimated Monthly Payment Amount[iii]	Estimated Arrears[iv]	Taxes & Insurance Escrowed With Lender? Y/N
#1			
#2			

    c. **Non-Residential Post-Petition Mortgage Payments and Prepetition Arrears:** The following is the street address and the tax ID parcel no. for the non-residential real property of the Debtor(s):

Property No. 1_____ Property No. 2_____

Creditor Name	Estimated Monthly Payment Amount[iii]	Estimated Arrears[iv]	Taxes & Insurance Escrowed With Lender? Y/N
#1			
#2			

    d. **Prepetition Real Property Tax Claims:** Claims of taxing authorities on real property pursuant to State law will be paid pro-rata as set forth in paragraph IV.H unless a fixed monthly payment is set forth below after the post-petition on-going mortgage payment(s).[v]

Taxing Authority	Amount	Delinquent Tax Years	Optional Equal Monthly Payment

    e. **Real Property Tax Escrow:**

The Debtor(s) will not utilize a tax escrow with the Trustee unless marked below.

( ) The Debtor(s) will utilize a tax escrow through the Plan. The Debtor(s) must provide the tax bill to the Trustee and verify taxes are paid each year until completion of the Plan. Tax escrow accounts will fund after on-going monthly mortgage payments but prior to other secured creditors.

[iii] The monthly payment amount is an estimate and the Trustee shall pay the monthly payment amount based on the proof of claim as filed. The Plan authorizes the Trustee to make post-petition regular mortgage or land contract payments prior to the proof of claim being filed. This provision does not preclude any party in interest from filing an objection to the claim.

[iv] The amount of prepetition arrears is an estimate and the Trustee shall pay the prepetition arrears based on the proof of claim as filed. Any claim filed for prepetition arrears shall be paid through the Plan over a reasonable period of time and pro-rata with other secured creditors without interest.

[v] Any creditor in this class shall retain its lien on the real property pursuant to applicable State law and shall be entitled to receive its statutory interest and collection fees as set forth in its proof of claim.

Real Property Address	Parcel Number	Taxing Authority	Monthly Escrow Amount

f. **Wholly Unsecured Liens:** The following claims shall be treated as unsecured by this Plan because there is no equity in the property to secure the claim. Upon completion of the Plan, the lien shall be discharged and removed from the property. The Debtor(s) may move under Fed. R. Bankr. P. 7070, on notice to the holder of such a claim who refuses to release the lien, for an order declaring the lien released and for related relief. These claims are as follows:

Property Address	Creditor	Claim Amount[vi]	Property Value	Senior Lien Amount

2. **Personal Property:**

a. **Pre-Confirmation Adequate Protections Payments (APP):** If the Trustee is to pay pre-confirmation APP the secured creditor's name, address, the account number and the payment amount must be provided and it must be signified by entering the monthly payment amount in the box marked "Pre-Conf. APP" under b. or c. of this paragraph. The Trustee will not disburse an APP until a proof of claim is filed with documentation of a perfected lien satisfactory to the Trustee.

b. **Secured Claims Subject to Final Paragraph of 11 U.S.C. § 1325(a):** Each secured creditor in this class has a lien that is not subject to 11 U.S.C. § 506.[vii] Claims in this class shall be paid as follows plus an additional pro-rata amount that may be available from funds on hand at an interest rate specified below or the contract rate specified in the proof of claim, whichever is lower.

Creditor, Address & Account No.	Collateral	Balance Owing	Interest Rate	Pre-Conf. APP	Equal Monthly Payment

c. **Secured Claims Subject to 11 U.S.C. § 506[viii]:** Claims in this class shall be paid as follows plus an additional pro-rata amount that may be available from funds on hand at an interest rate specified below or the contract rate specified in the proof of claim whichever is lower. Creditor will be paid the fair market value (FMV) as a secured claim and any balance due as a general unsecured claim.

Creditor, Address & Account No.[ix]	Collateral	FMV	Interest Rate	Pre-Conf. APP	Equal Monthly Payment

---

[vi] This is the estimate of the Debtor(s) as to the amount owing to the creditor. The proof of claim shall control as to amount of the claim. This provision does not preclude any party in interest from filing an objection to the claim.

[vii] Such a claim is not subject to "cramdown" and will be paid the full balance owing. If the collateral is a motor vehicle and is destroyed, the Debtor(s), with consent from the secured creditor and Trustee, or by order of the Court, may use the collateral insurance proceeds to purchase replacement collateral, to which the creditor's lien shall attach.

[viii] If the collateral is a motor vehicle and is destroyed, the Debtor(s), with consent from the secured creditor and Trustee or by order of the Court, may use the collateral insurance proceeds to purchase replacement collateral, to which the creditor's lien shall attach.

[ix] If the creditor files a proof of claim with a balance owing which is different from the amount listed above, the proof of claim shall control as to the amount of the debt, unless a party in interest objects to the proof of claim.

4- As updated on 11-23-16

Exhibit 8

U.S. BANKRUPTCY COURT

3. <u>Secured Claims of Taxing Authorities</u>: Secured claims of taxing authorities shall be paid as follows:

Creditor & Address	Collateral Real/Personal Property	Secured Claim Amount[x]	Interest Rate[xi]	Equal Monthly Payment

4. <u>Collateral to Be Surrendered/Executory Contracts to Be Rejected</u>: The property listed below is surrendered to the creditor, and the executory contracts/unexpired leases are rejected:

Creditor	Property/Contract Description

The automatic stay shall be terminated upon entry of the confirmation order and any deficiency claim or claim arising from rejection shall be treated as a general unsecured claim, subject to paragraph IV.G.

5. <u>Junior Lien Holders on Surrendered Property</u>: If a creditor holding a junior lien has filed a secured proof of claim, such claim shall be treated as a general unsecured claim if the value of the property, set forth below in the column entitled "Property Value," is equal to or less than the amount of the senior secured claim, absent an objection. These creditors are as follows:

Creditor, Address & Account No.	Property Address	Claim Amount[x]	Property Value	Senior Lien Amount

D. <u>ASSUMED EXECUTORY CONTRACTS AND UNEXPIRED LEASES.</u> The following executory contracts and/or unexpired leases, including land contract(s), are assumed:

Creditor, Address & Account No.	Property Description	Monthly Payment Amount	No. of Months Remaining	Cure Amount

E. <u>DIRECT PAYMENT BY THE DEBTOR(S) OF THE FOLLOWING DEBTS.</u> All claims shall be paid by the Trustee unless listed herein:

Creditor, Address & Account No.	Collateral/Obligation	Balance Owing	Interest Rate

F. <u>UNSECURED CREDITORS.</u>

<u>General Unsecured Creditors</u>: Claims in this class are paid from funds available after payment to all other classes. The allowed claims of general unsecured creditors will be satisfied by:

( ) Payment of a dividend of 100%, plus present value of _____% interest, if necessary to satisfy 11 U.S.C. § 1325(a)(4), **OR**

( ) Payment of a pro-rata share of a fixed amount of $_____ or payment from all disposable income to be received by the Debtor(s) in the ACP, whichever pays more. This fixed amount shall be reduced by additional administrative

---

[x] The amount stated is an estimate only and the proof of claim controls as to the amount of the claim. This provision does not preclude any party in interest from filing an objection to the claim.

[xi] The interest rate on tax claims that is in effect during the calendar month in which the plan is confirmed shall control. 11 U.S.C. § 511(b). The Trustee has the authority to make adjustments to its records to comply with the Bankruptcy Code.

5- As updated on 11-23-16

expenses including attorney fees approved under 11 U.S.C. § 330(a). However, this fixed amount shall not be reduced below the liquidation value specified in paragraph I.B.

G. **SPECIAL UNSECURED CREDITORS.** The special unsecured claims listed below are an exception pursuant to 11 U.S.C. § 1322(b)(1) and may include, but are not limited to, non-sufficient funds (NSF) checks, continuing professional services and non-dischargeable debts (*e.g.*, student loans, criminal fines).[xii] These special unsecured claims shall be paid as follows:

In a 36 month ACP case with the base to general unsecured creditors paid **within** 36 months, the special unsecured creditors will be paid pro rata with other general unsecured claims during the first 36 months and then that portion of the special unsecured creditor's claim that can be paid during the remainder of the 60 months from the date the first Plan payment is due will be paid exclusive of all other general unsecured claims during the remaining 60 months.

In a 36 month ACP case with the base to general unsecured creditors paid **beyond** 36 months, the special class unsecured creditors will be paid pro rata with other general unsecured claims during the first 36 months and until the specific fixed base amount to the general unsecured creditors is satisfied and then that portion of the special unsecured creditor's claim that can be paid during the remainder of the 60 months from the date the first Plan payment is due will be paid exclusive of all other general unsecured claims during the remaining 60 months.

In a 60 month ACP case, special unsecured creditors will be paid pro rata with the general unsecured creditors during the 60 months.

Special Unsecured Creditor Name	Reason For Special Treatment	Interest Rate

IV. **GENERAL PROVISIONS**

A. **DISPOSABLE INCOME, TAX RETURNS & TAX REFUNDS.** Debtor(s) submit(s) all or such portion of future earnings or other future income of Debtor(s) to the supervision and control of the Trustee as is necessary for the execution of the Plan. Unless this Plan provides for a dividend of 100% to all allowed general unsecured claims, the Debtor(s) shall pay all disposable income as defined in 11 U.S.C. § 1325(b) during the ACP. Unless otherwise provided in this Plan, Debtor(s) shall remit to the Trustee tax returns and tax refunds and other disposable income for the ACP for administration pursuant to the Plan or as otherwise ordered by the Court. Income tax refunds and other disposable income paid to the Trustee in a Plan with a 36 month ACP will operate to decrease the term of the Plan to the ACP but not below the 36 month ACP, rather than increase the dividend paid to general unsecured creditors. The Debtor(s) shall continue the same level of tax deductions as when the case was filed except as affected by changes in dependents and/or marital status.

Based on the disposable income available, the Trustee shall have the discretion without further notice to creditors to:

1. Increase the percentage to the unsecured creditors as a result of additional payments made under this provision subject to the limitation set forth in this paragraph;

2. Reduce the term of the Plan but not below the ACP; and

3. Determine if available funds are not disposable income when the Debtor(s) provide(s) the Trustee with supporting documentation.

B. **VESTING OF ESTATE PROPERTY.** Upon confirmation of the Plan, all property of the estate shall remain property of the estate until discharge unless marked below:

( ) Pursuant to 11 U.S.C. § 1327(b) upon confirmation of the Plan, all property of the estate shall vest in the Debtor(s), except (i) future earnings of the Debtor(s); (ii) additional disposable income, and (iii) other real and personal property necessary to fund the Plan which is identified as follows:

Regardless of whether any real or personal property is vested in the Debtor(s) or the estate, insurance proceeds derived from such real or personal property shall be deemed property of the estate. Subject to footnotes vii and viii of paragraph III.C.2, such insurance proceeds may be used by the Debtor(s), upon prior Court approval, to purchase replacement collateral.

In any case, all property of which Debtor(s) retain(s) possession and control shall be insured by the Debtor(s). The Trustee is not required to insure property and has no liability for damage or loss to any property in the possession and control of the Debtor(s).

[xii] If the table below is blank, or this case has a 60 month ACP, then there will be no special treatment for special unsecured creditors.

C.   <u>POST-PETITION ACTION BY DEBTOR(S)</u>.

    1.   <u>Post-Petition Sale of Property of Estate</u>: In the event that the Debtor(s) seek(s) to sell, before entry of the discharge, property of the estate constituting personal property with a value in excess of $2,500, or any real property regardless of value, the Debtor(s) shall request prior Court approval pursuant to 11 U.S.C. § 363 and any applicable rules.

    2.   <u>Post-Petition Sale of Property of Debtor(s)</u>: In the event that the Debtor(s) seek(s) to sell, before entry of the discharge, personal property of the Debtor(s) with a value in excess of $2,500, or any real property regardless of value, the Debtor(s) shall seek prior Court approval with notice to any parties in interest as the Court may direct.

    3.   <u>Post-Petition Incurrence of Debt by Debtor(s) and Related Relief</u>: Upon the prior written approval of the Trustee, the Debtor(s) may incur post-petition debt for a motor vehicle, whether through financing or lease transaction. The Debtor(s) may trade in an existing motor vehicle provided that the Debtor(s) satisfy in full any obligations related to such motor vehicle. The Debtor(s) may incur other, similar post-petition debt as allowed by the Court.

D.   <u>UNSCHEDULED CREDITORS FILING CLAIMS</u>. If a creditor's claim is not listed in the schedules, but the creditor files a proof of claim, the Trustee is authorized to classify the claim into one of the classes under this Plan and to pay the claim within the class, unless the claim is disallowed.

E.   <u>LATE FILED CLAIMS</u>. If a claim is not timely filed, the Trustee may in his/her discretion provide notice of intent to pay the claim.

F.   <u>LIMITATION ON NOTICES</u>.

    1.   <u>General</u>: If the Debtor(s) file(s) a plan modification pursuant to 11 U.S.C. § 1329 or a motion requesting relief, the plan modification or motion, and appropriate notice thereof, shall be served on (a) the Trustee, (b) the United States Trustee, and (c) any party or entity adversely affected by the plan modification or request for relief. If service under (c) requires service on the creditor matrix, subsequent to the claims bar date pursuant to Fed. R. Bankr. P. 3002, service may be made on creditors that hold claims for which proofs of claim have been filed, and any governmental unit that is a creditor in the case.

    2.   <u>Fee Applications</u>: Subsequent to the claims bar date pursuant to Fed. R. Bankr. P. 3002, if an attorney for the Debtor(s) files an application for compensation pursuant to 11 U.S.C. § 330, the application, including appropriate notice and an opportunity to object, shall be served on (a) the Trustee, (b) the Debtor(s), and (c) the United States Trustee. Appropriate notice of the application, including an opportunity to object in the same form as attached to the Local Bankruptcy Rules, shall be served on (a) creditors that hold claims for which proofs of claim have been filed, and (b) any governmental unit that is a creditor in the case.

    If service is made pursuant to this paragraph, the Debtor(s) shall file a certificate of service specifying parties and entities served.

G.   <u>CLAIMS AND AMENDED CLAIMS</u>. If a proof of claim is filed and Trustee has previously made a distribution to general unsecured creditors, the claim shall be entitled to the same pro rata distribution as that previously paid to general unsecured claims, to the extent possible, even if the base to general unsecured claims exceeds the amount stated in the confirmed Plan. The Trustee shall not be required to recover any overpayments to general unsecured creditors as a result of the filing of the aforementioned claims.

    1.   With respect to secured claims filed by creditors holding liens in real property surrendered pursuant to the Plan, each such secured creditor must file a proof of claim asserting its unsecured deficiency, if any, by no later than 90 days after any disposition, including a foreclosure sale. The proof of claim for any deficiency must be conspicuously identified as an "UNSECURED DEFICIENCY CLAIM." Attached to the proof of claim for the deficiency amount must be a detailed statement providing that the property was disposed of, the amount of the sale proceeds, a summary of costs incurred in connection with the disposition, and the unsecured deficiency balance remaining. This proof of claim must be filed even though a previous secured or unsecured claim was asserted prior to the disposition of the property. The failure to timely file a deficiency claim shall preclude the secured creditor from receiving further distributions under the Plan and such secured creditor's claim shall be subject to discharge.

    2.   With respect to secured claims filed by creditors holding liens in personal property surrendered pursuant to the Plan and non-debtor counterparties whose executory contracts or unexpired leases are rejected under the Plan, each such secured creditor or non-debtor counterparty must file a claim asserting its unsecured deficiency or rejection damages, if any, by no later than 180 days after entry of the order confirming the Plan. The proof of claim for any deficiency or rejection damages must be conspicuously identified on the proof of claim as an "UNSECURED DEFICIENCY CLAIM" or a "REJECTION DAMAGES CLAIM," as applicable. Attached to the proof of claim for the deficiency or rejection damages must be a detailed statement providing, if applicable, the date the property was disposed of, the rejection damages, the amount of any sale proceeds, a summary of costs incurred in connection therewith, and the unsecured deficiency balance remaining. This proof of claim must be filed even though a previous secured or unsecured claim was asserted prior to the surrender, rejection, or disposition of the property or rejection of the executory contract or unexpired lease. The failure to timely file a deficiency

or rejection damages claim means that such creditor or non-debtor counterparty shall be precluded from receiving further distributions under the Plan and such claim shall be subject to discharge.

3. A claimant treated as holding a wholly unsecured claim pursuant to paragraph III.C.1.f shall file a proof of claim within the time prescribed in Fed. R. Bankr. P. 3002(c), and any such claimant who does not file a proof of claim is not entitled to receive a distribution under the Plan. If such claimant files a secured proof of claim, the Trustee is authorized to treat such claimant as holding an unsecured claim.

H. TRUSTEE POST-CONFIRMATION DISBURSEMENT.

1. **Priority of Payments:** Unless otherwise specifically stated in the Plan, the following categories of claims will be paid in the following order (on a pro-rata basis within each category):

   a. unpaid court filing fees, regardless of any Plan provision to the contrary;

   b. trustee administrative fee;

   c. allowed DSO claims paid through the Plan;

   d. attorney fees and expenses, as allowed by an Order of the Court, subordinated to monthly continuing claims payments covered under 11 U.S.C. § 1322(b)(2);

   e. continuing, long-term, nonmodifiable allowed claims[xiii];

   f. other allowed secured claims (including arrears) and allowed claims arising from assumed executory contracts or unexpired leases (including any cure) with respect to which (i) the last payment will become due within the term of the Plan; and (ii) the Plan provides for equal monthly payments;

   g. arrears on continuing claims and other secured claims for which the Plan does not specify equal monthly payments;

   h. allowed priority unsecured claims; and

   i. allowed general unsecured claims.

2. **Post-Petition Mortgage Payments:** If the Plan directs the Trustee to make any post-petition mortgage payment, the Trustee may:

   a. modify the on-going mortgage payment upon receiving a notice pursuant to Fed. R. Bankr. P. 3002.1(b);

   b. increase the Plan payment by the amount of any mortgage payment increase plus additional trustee commission for any mortgage increase;

   c. amend a wage order or ACH payment amount for such increase with notice to the employer or ACH payor, Debtor(s) and the attorney for the Debtor(s); and

   d. adjust the post-petition mortgage or land contract payment date, or the date through which any arrears or cure is calculated, as needed to conform to any proof of claim filed by the mortgagee or land contract vendor.

3. **Initial Disbursement Date:** Except as otherwise stated in this Plan, a payment designated as equal monthly payments on secured claims, executory contracts/unexpired leases, priority unsecured claims, attorney fees, and tax escrow accruals shall be deemed to commence the first day of the month following the month of the petition date.

I. **TAX RETURNS.** All tax returns due prior to the petition date have been filed, except: _____.

J. **DEBTOR(S) ENGAGED IN BUSINESS.**

1. Any Debtor who is self-employed and incurs trade credit in the production of income shall comply with 11 U.S.C. § 1304 regarding operation of the business and any order regarding the continuation of a business operation entered in this case;

2. Any Debtor who, directly or indirectly, holds a controlling interest in a limited liability company, partnership or other corporation that incurs trade credit in the production of income, or who is otherwise in control of such an entity, shall cause the entity to comply with 11 U.S.C. 1304(c) and any order regarding continuation of a business operation entered in this case as if the Debtor were "engaged in business" within the meaning of that section;

[xii] Claims in this category include non-modifiable claims, including allowed secured claims, on which the last payment is due after the term of the Plan, and for which the Plan provides for a set monthly payment (subject to adjustment as set forth below). This category includes residential mortgage obligations, land contract obligations, and other long term, non-modifiable obligations under assumed executory contracts/unexpired leases.

8- As updated on 11-23-16

3. The duties listed in 11 U.S.C. § 1304(c) are imposed on any Debtor described in this Paragraph IV.J, and are incorporated herein by reference.

K. **EFFECT OF ADDITIONAL ATTORNEY FEES BEYOND THE NO LOOK FEE.** Any attorney fees and expenses beyond the no-look fee shall be paid as administrative expenses and shall not be paid out of the base previously disbursed to general unsecured creditors. The Trustee shall not recover funds disbursed to general unsecured creditors to satisfy any administrative expenses awarded to the attorney for the Debtor(s).

L. **PLAN REFUNDS.** The Trustee may agree to reasonable refunds to the Debtor(s) from the funds paid to the Trustee. The Plan duration may be extended to repay all such refunds. The trustee may require the Debtor(s) to file an amendment to the Plan.

M. **TRUSTEE'S AVOIDANCE POWERS.** The Debtor(s) acknowledges that the Trustee has discretion to utilize certain powers under Chapter 5 of the Bankruptcy Code. Notwithstanding any other language in this Plan, no lien shall be involuntarily avoided unless an adversary proceeding is filed, except that judicial liens may be avoided pursuant to 11 U.S.C. § 522(f) in connection with confirmation of the Plan upon proper notice. The Debtor(s) may not commence any avoidance action without court authorization or written consent of the Trustee. The Debtor(s) acknowledge(s) that any avoidance actions are preserved for the benefit of the estate pursuant to 11 U.S.C. § 551.

N. **LIEN RETENTION.** With respect to each allowed secured claim provided for by the Plan, the holder of such claims shall retain the lien securing such claim until the earlier of (i) the underlying debt determined under applicable non-bankruptcy law is paid in full, or (ii) entry of the discharge; provided, however, that entry of the discharge shall not release a lien that secures a claim subject to treatment under 11 U.S.C. § 1322(a)(5). Upon the occurrence of (i) or (ii) above, the holder shall release its lien and provide written evidence of the same to the Debtor(s) within 30 days after (i) or (ii) above. Notwithstanding the foregoing, if this case of the Debtor(s) under Chapter 13 is dismissed or converted without completion of the Plan, the holder of such claim shall retain its lien to the extent recognized by applicable non-bankruptcy law.

O. **MODIFICATION OF THE AUTOMATIC STAY.** Upon the filing of a motion for relief from the automatic stay, the Trustee shall suspend disbursement of funds to that creditor but shall hold said funds until further order of the Court. Upon entry of an order modifying the automatic stay and unless otherwise provided for in such order, the Trustee shall not disburse held or on-going payments to that creditor on that claim, until creditor files an amended claim or Debtor(s) file(s) an amended Plan directing the Trustee how to pay creditor's claim. Such amended proof of claim or Plan amendment shall be filed within 120 days after entry of the order modifying the automatic stay. An amended claim filed by such creditor shall be afforded the same secured status as provided for under the Plan. If a creditor fails to file an amended claim or Debtor(s) fail(s) to file an amended Plan directing the Trustee how to pay creditor's claim within 120 days of the entry of the order modifying the automatic stay, any held amounts shall be released for the benefit of the other creditors in accordance with the confirmed Plan and Trustee shall cease holding any future funds for on-going payments on such claim unless otherwise ordered by the Court. However, if a creditor files a claim after the order modifying the automatic stay and the confirmed Plan directed that such creditor was to be paid directly by Debtor(s) on such claim, such claim will not be paid by the Trustee.

P. **NOTICE OF FEES, EXPENSES AND CHARGES PURSUANT TO FED. R. BANKR. P. 3002.1.** The claim evidenced by notice of fees, expenses and charges pursuant to Fed. R. Bankr. P. 3002.1 will be treated as a separate debt or claim consistent with treatment of the underlying claim provided for under the Plan.

Q. **NON-APPLICABILITY OF FED. R. BANKR. P. 3002.1.** The requirements and provisions of Fed. R. Bankr. P. 3002.1 shall not apply to the Trustee in any chapter 13 case where the Plan as confirmed surrenders property to the creditor as provided in 11 U.S.C. § 1325(a)(5)(C) or proposes that Debtor(s) pay the creditor directly or to any claim as to which the automatic stay is modified for purposes of allowing the secured creditor to exercise its rights and remedies pursuant to applicable non-bankruptcy law.

R. **NONSTANDARD PROVISIONS.** Nonstandard provisions must be set forth below. A nonstandard provision is a provision not otherwise included in this Model Plan or deviating from it. Nonstandard provisions set out elsewhere in this Plan are ineffective and void. The following Plan provisions will be effective only if there is a check in the box "Included" in the Preamble.

BY FILING THIS DOCUMENT, THE ATTORNEY FOR THE DEBTOR(S) OR DEBTOR(S) THEMSELVES, IF NOT REPRESENTED BY AN ATTORNEY, ALSO CERTIFY(IES) THAT THE WORDING AND ORDER OF THE PROVISIONS IN THIS CHAPTER 13 PLAN ARE IDENTICAL TO THOSE CONTAINED IN THE APPROVED MODEL PLAN PURSUANT TO LOCAL BANKRUPTCY RULE 3015(d) FOR THE WESTERN DISTRICT OF MICHIGAN BANKRUPTCY COURT, OTHER THAN ANY NONSTANDARD PROVISIONS INCLUDED IN PARAGRAPH IV.R.

Date: _____   _____
                                                    , Debtor

Date: _____   _____
                                                    , Debtor

Date: _____   _____
                                          , Counsel for the Debtor(s)

10- As updated on 11-23-16

[Effective February 1, 2002. Amended effective February 1, 2007; March 21, 2012; November 23, 2016.]

Exhibit 9   U.S. BANKRUPTCY COURT

EXHIBIT 9.   DEBTOR'S MOTION TO DEFER ENTRY OF DISCHARGE

UNITED STATES BANKRUPTCY COURT
FOR THE WESTERN DISTRICT OF MICHIGAN

In re:

Case Number: _____
Date of Filing: _____
Chapter 7

_____ Debtor(s)

DEBTOR'S MOTION TO DEFER ENTRY OF DISCHARGE

Pursuant to Fed. R. Bankr. P. 4004(c)(2), the undersigned requests that this Court issue an order deferring entry of a Discharge pursuant to 11 U.S.C. § 727 for:

☐   For 30 days after entry of the Order approving Debtor's Motion to Defer Entry of Discharge.

☐   Until _____.

Date:_____   _____
                          Debtor/Debtor's Attorney

Date:_____   _____
                          Joint Debtor (if any)/Attorney

ORDER

☐   Denied.
☐   Granted.

Date:_____   _____
                          Daniel M. LaVille, Clerk of Court

[Effective February 1, 2002. Amended effective February 1, 2007.]

EXHIBIT 10. DEBTOR'S CERTIFICATION REGARDING DOMESTIC SUPPORT OBLIGATIONS

UNITED STATES BANKRUPTCY COURT
WESTERN DISTRICT OF MICHIGAN

_____

In re:

                                                Case No.
                                                Chapter 13

               Debtor.   Hon. _____
_____/

DEBTOR'S CERTIFICATION REGARDING DOMESTIC SUPPORT OBLIGATIONS

The debtor in the above-referenced matter certifies as follows:

Debtor   **Spouse**

☐   ☐   I have not been required by a judicial or administrative order, or by statute, to pay any Domestic Support Obligation as defined in 11 U.S.C. § 101(14A), either before this proceeding was filed, or at any time after the date of filing.

- OR –

Debtor   **Spouse**

☐   ☐   I have paid all amounts that I am required to pay under any judicial or administrative order, or statute, for a Domestic Support Obligation as defined in 11 U.S.C.§ 101(14A), including all amounts that came due after the petition was filed and pre-petition arrears to the extent provided for in the plan.

       I declare under penalty of perjury that the information provided in this Certificate is true and correct.

Dated:_____   _____
                                                  Debtor

Dated:_____   _____
                                             Joint Debtor (if applicable)

[Effective February 1, 2002. Amended effective February 1, 2007.]

EXHIBIT 11. NOTICE OF RIGHT TO DEMAND HEARING, ABANDONMENT OF PROPERTY, AND ORDER DISALLOWING SECURED CLAIMS

UNITED STATES BANKRUPTCY COURT
FOR THE WESTERN DISTRICT OF MICHIGAN

IN RE: _____

                            Case No.: _____

_____ Debtor(s)/

NOTICE OF RIGHT TO DEMAND HEARING, ABANDONMENT OF PROPERTY, AND ORDER DISALLOWING SECURED CLAIMS

The undersigned Trustee intends to abandon the property listed below which is either burdensome or of inconsequential value to the estate:

IN ACCORDANCE with Section 554, the above property will be deemed abandoned on the fifteenth (15th) day after the date of service shown below, unless a written objection to said abandonment and request for hearing thereon is filed with the U. S. Bankruptcy Court, Western District of Michigan, One Division Ave., N, Room 200, Grand Rapids, Michigan 49503 prior to said date. In the event such an objection and request for hearing is filed, a date and place of hearing will be set and further notice given to interested parties.

IT IS REQUESTED that a copy of this notice be served upon all parties in interest listed in the court records of this case.

                                  _____
                                  Trustee

IT IS HEREBY ORDERED that if no objection to the abandonment is filed as provided above, without further order of this court, any secured claim now filed claiming a security interest in the above property is disallowed because of the abandonment. Such secured creditors will have thirty (30) days from the date of service indicated below to file a proof of claim as an unsecured creditor, provided such creditor is entitled to assert a claim for the unpaid balance following repossession of the security, or such creditor may file its estimated deficiency claim within the aforesaid time subject to amendment prior to closing of the estate showing exact deficiency balance due.

                                  _____
                                  Daniel M. LaVille, Clerk of Court

Served upon all creditors and interested parties listed on case matrix by: _____

Date served: _____

[Effective December, 2009.]

EXHIBIT 12. DECLARATION RE: ELECTRONIC FILING

Revised: 12/09

UNITED STATES BANKRUPTCY COURT
WESTERN DISTRICT OF MICHIGAN

In Re:

Bankruptcy Case No.: _____

_____ Debtor(s)/

DECLARATION RE: ELECTRONIC FILING

PART I – DECLARATION OF PETITIONER:

I _____ and _____, the undersigned debtor(s), corporate officer, partner, or member, hereby declare under penalty of perjury that the information I have given or will give my attorney and the information provided in the electronically filed petition, statements and schedules is true and correct. **I declare under penalty of perjury that the Social Security Number(s) indicated below, as electronically transmitted with my petition, is(are) true and correct.** I consent to my attorney sending my petition, this declaration, statements and schedules and any future amendments of these documents to the United States Bankruptcy Court, United State Trustee and Panel Trustee. I understand that the **DECLARATION RE: ELECTRONIC FILING** is to be filed with the Clerk after the petition has been filed electronically but, in any event, no later than 7 business days after the petition has been filed. I understand that failure to file the signed original of the **DECLARATION** will cause my case to be dismissed without further notice.

[If petitioner is an individual whose debts are primarily consumer debts and has chosen to file under chapter 7] I am aware that I may proceed under chapter 7, 11, 12 or 13 of Title 11, United States Code, understand the relief available under each such chapter, and choose to proceed under chapter 7. I request relief in accordance with the chapter specified in the petition.

[If petitioner is a corporation, partnership or limited liability entity] I declare under penalty of perjury that the information provided in this petition is true and correct, and that I have been authorized to file this petition on behalf of he debtor. The debtor requests relief in accordance with the chapter specified in this petition.

Dated: _____   _____ _____
                            Debtor   **Joint Debtor**

                            Soc. Sec. No.: _____   Soc. Sec. No.: _____

Dated: _____   _____
                            Authorized Corporate Officer, Partner or Member

PART II – DECLARATION OF ATTORNEY:

I declare under penalty of perjury that I have reviewed the above debtor's(s') petition, schedules, statements and that the information is complete and correct to the best of my knowledge. The debtor(s) signed the Declaration before I submitted the petition, schedules and statements. I will retain all petition, schedules, statements, amendments, and pleadings filed with the court which contain the debtor's(s') original signature(s). I will give the debtor(s) a copy of all pleadings and information to be filed with, or received from, the United States Bankruptcy Court, and have complied with all other requirements of this Court. I have informed the individual petition that (he and/or she) may proceed under chapter 7, 11, 12 or 13 of Title 11, United States Code, and have explained the relief available under each such chapter. This declaration is based upon all information of which I have knowledge.

Dated: _____   Signed: _____
                            Attorney for Debtor(s), Michigan Bar No.
                            Attorney Address/E:mail Address
                            Attorney Phone No./Fax No.

(FILE ORIGINAL WITH COURT. DO NOT FILE ELECTRONICALLY)

[Effective December, 2009.]

SELECTED ADMINISTRATIVE ORDERS AND NOTICES
ADMINISTRATIVE ORDER 2004–01. CORRECTIONS OF ADMINISTRATIVE ERRORS

The Court recognizes that conversion to Case Management/Electronic Case Filing (CM/ECF) is a complex undertaking that will be prone to occasional administrative errors. Accordingly, the Court wishes to vest the Clerk of the Court and the Clerk's deputies with the authority to correct docketing errors now and in the future.

NOW, THEREFORE, IT IS ORDERED that the Clerk of the Court and the Clerk's deputies are authorized to correct administrative docketing errors, including but not limited to reopening of incorrectly closed cases, setting aside of incorrectly entered discharges, etc. until further order of this Court. IT IS FURTHER ORDERED that any party may seek a review of the actions of the Clerk in a particular case upon motion filed for good cause shown.

[Dated: January 20, 2004.]

ADMINISTRATIVE ORDER 2004–02. IN THE MATTER OF CASE MANAGEMENT/ELECTRONIC CASE FILING

Pursuant to Federal Rules of Bankruptcy Procedure 5005(a)(2), 7005 and 9029, and Local Bankruptcy Rule 5005–1(b),

IT IS HEREBY ORDERED that the *Administrative Procedures for the Electronic Filing Signing, Verification and Service of Documents* dated 12 January 2004, and attached hereto as an exhibit*, are adopted for use in all cases and proceedings in the United States Bankruptcy Court for the Western District of Michigan. Amendments to this Order or the Administrative Procedures may be entered periodically as authorized by the Court.

IT IS FURTHER ORDERED that the electronic filing of a document in accordance with the Administrative Procedures constitutes the filing of the document for all purposes of the Federal Rules of Bankruptcy Procedure and the local rules of this court, and constitutes the entry of the document on the docket by the Clerk under Fed.R.Bankr.P. 5003.

IT IS FURTHER ORDERED that the electronic filing of a petition, pleading, motion, proof of claim or other paper by a registered participant in the Electronic Filing System shall constitute the signature of that individual for all purposes, including those under Fed.R.Bankr.P. 9001 and 28 U.S.C. § 1746, and shall have the same force and effect as if the individual had affixed that individual's signature on a paper copy of the document being filed.

[Dated: February 3, 2004.]

* [**Publisher's Note:** The "Administrative Procedures for the Electronic Filing, Signing, Verification and Service of Documents" are set out following the Selected Administrative Orders and Notices.]

ADMINISTRATIVE ORDER 2004–03. IN THE MATTER OF CASE MANAGEMENT/ELECTRONIC CASE FILING

On February 3, 2004, the judges of this Court adopted Administrative Procedures for the Electronic Filing, Signing, Verification and Service of Documents dated January 12, 2004. Experience has shown that an amendment to those procedures is required.

Now, therefore, IT IS ORDERED that Section II(E)(4) of those Administrative Procedures shall read as follows:

II(E)(4): A copy containing an original signature of a party or individual other than that of the filing user must be retained for a period of 5 years after the closing of the case and all time periods for appeals have expired, unless the Court orders a different period. This retention period does not affect or replace any other periods required by other applicable laws or rules. Upon request of the court, the filing user must provide original documents for review. (new material underlined)

[Dated: April 29, 2004.]

ADMINISTRATIVE ORDER 2004–04.   IN THE MATTER OF
CASE MANAGEMENT/ELECTRONIC CASE FILING

To further enhance the court's conversion from paper files to electronic files the court has reviewed the existing local bankruptcy rules dated February 1, 2002, and has decided to make changes.

Accordingly, IT IS ORDERED that Local Bankruptcy Rules 2014(a)(7), 2016(a)(6), 3015(f)(2) and 9013(d)(3) are amended to strike existing language which requires the filing of an affidavit ("an affidavit that no objection has been filed" and "an affidavit of no response") and replace that language with the requirement of filing "a certificate stating that no timely response or request for hearing has been filed."

These revisions shall take effect immediately to insure the efficient transition into electronic case filing. The clerk is directed to post this order on the bulletin board of the clerk's office and on the court's web site with a request for public comment, if any, to be filed with the court on or before July 1, 2004.

[Dated: April 29, 2004.]

ADMINISTRATIVE ORDER 2004–06.   IN THE MATTER
OF MANDATORY ELECTRONIC CASE FILING

THE COURT FINDS that:

Federal Rules of Bankruptcy Procedure 5005(a)(2), 7005, 9029, and Local Bankruptcy Rule 5005–1(b) authorize this Court to establish practices and procedures for filing, signing, maintaining and verifying pleadings and papers by electronic means: and

On February 3, 2004, by Administrative Order 2004–2, the Court established Administrative Procedures for the Electronic Filing, Signing, Verification and Service of Documents, and authorized that amendments thereto may be entered periodically;

NOW, THEREFORE, IT IS ORDERED as follows:

Effective **January 1, 2005**, all petitions, pleadings and other papers filed in all cases and proceedings, whether pending or new, shall be filed electronically according to the procedures established by the Court. Petitions, pleadings and/or other papers filed by conventional means (via paper), shall be rejected by the Court pursuant to guidelines references in L.B.R. 5005–2. Exceptions to electronic filing are as follows:

1. Parties without legal representation (pro se parties) may continue to file all pleadings and other papers by conventional means.

2. Creditors who are not registered Electronic Case Filing users may continue to file all documents by conventional means.

3. Internet Failure—Filers experiencing Internet failure may submit their pleading and/or document on diskette or CD in pdf format along with a "Motion for Leave to File Conventionally".

4. All documents set forth in section III of the Electronic Case Filing Administrative Procedures Manual, as may be amended from time to time, may be filed conventionally, unless specifically authorized by the Court.

5. Petitions, pleadings and/or other papers file by conventional means which are accompanied by a Motion for Leave to File Conventionally as to why they are unable to file electronically with a proposed order.

[Dated: July 14, 2004.]

ADMINISTRATIVE ORDER 2005–01.   IN RE: DEBTORS WHO FILE A SUBSEQUENT
BANKRUPTCY CHAPTER 11, 12 OR 13 CASE WITHIN TWO YEARS OF A
PRIOR BANKRUPTCY CASE FILING

The United States Bankruptcy Court for the Western District of Michigan has previously adopted a policy whereby a debtor (or joint debtors) who files for bankruptcy relief, and then files a subsequent chapter 11, 12 or 13 case, shall have the same judge hear both cases. However, because of the adoption of new electronic case filing procedures, all bankruptcy cases, including those involving repeat filers, are now automatically assigned by blind computer draw, to the judges who hold court in a particular city. After full discussion at a court administration meeting, the judges unanimously determined to modify the blind assignment of cases by instructing the Clerk of the Court, and the deputy clerks, to reassign to the initial judge subsequent Chapter 11, 12 or 13 cases that are filed by the same debtor (or joint debtors). The judges agreed that this Administrative Order should be entered and published on the Website of the United States Bankruptcy Court for the Western District of Michigan.

NOW, THEREFORE, IT IS HEREBY ORDERED that, in those instances when a debtor (or joint debtors) has filed a bankruptcy case which has been assigned to a particular judge, and the debtor (or joint debtors) subsequently files another Chapter 11, 12 or 13 case within two (2) years of closing of the prior case, the Clerk of the Court, or a deputy clerk, shall immediately reassign the subsequent case to the bankruptcy judge who was assigned to preside over the prior bankruptcy case.

IT IS FURTHER ORDERED, notwithstanding the above general provision, the Clerk of the Court, or a deputy clerk, shall not reassign a subsequently filed Chapter 11, 12 or 13 case involving a debtor (or joint debtors) in the following circumstances:

1. In an instance when the prior judge was assigned to a particular city but is no longer responsible for holding court in that city, i.e., Lansing, Kalamazoo, Traverse City or Marquette; or

2. When the current judge, who is handling a subsequently filed Chapter 11, 12 or 13 case, advises the Clerk of the Court, in writing, that the current judge desires to continue to preside over the subsequent case.

IT IS FURTHER ORDERED that this Administrative Order shall be posted at the Grand Rapids and Marquette offices of the Clerk of the Court, posted outside of each courtroom door in all geographical locations that court is now held, and published on the Website maintained by the United States Bankruptcy Court for the Western District of Michigan.

[Dated: January 14, 2005.]

ADMINISTRATIVE ORDER 2005–02. IN RE: CLERK'S AUTHORITY TO ADDRESS MOTION FOR LEAVE TO FILE PAPERS CONVENTIONALLY

On July 14, 2004, by Administrative Order 2004–06, this Court established mandatory electronic case filing effective January 1, 2005. Exceptions to electronic case filing were established in that order which included, among others, the ability of an attorney to file a Motion for Leave to File Conventionally under unique circumstances.

NOW, THEREFORE, IT IS ORDERED that the Clerk of the Court and the Clerk's deputies are authorized to issue orders which address instances where pleadings are filed conventionally.

IT IS FURTHER ORDERED that any party may seek review of the actions of the Clerk in a particular case upon motion filed for good cause shown.

[Dated: January 27, 2005.]

ADMINISTRATIVE ORDER 2005–07. IN RE: FILING OF PAYMENT ADVICES PURSUANT TO 11 U.S.C. § 521(a)(1)(B)(iv)

IT IS HEREBY ORDERED, effective as to cases filed on or after December 1, 2005, that copies of all payment advices or other evidence of payment received within 60 days before the date of the filing of the debtor's petition from any employer of the debtor:

1) shall not be filed with the court unless otherwise ordered;

2) shall be provided to the case trustee no later than ten (10) business days prior to the initial date scheduled for the first meeting of creditors; and

3) shall likewise be provided to any creditor who timely requests copies of said payment advices or other evidence of payment directly from the debtor or debtor's counsel.

[Dated: November 28, 2005.]

ADMINISTRATIVE ORDER 2005–08.   IN RE: PRO HAC VICE ADMISSION POLICY

The Judges of the United States Bankruptcy Court for the Western District of Michigan ("Bankruptcy Judges") hereby establish the following policy and procedures for admission of attorneys pro hac vice in the Bankruptcy Court:

1.   All attorneys licensed to practice law in the State of Michigan must apply for admission to practice before the United States District Court for the Western District of Michigan and may *not* apply for pro hac vice admission.

2.   All attorneys licensed to practice in a state other than Michigan and who maintain a regular office within the State of Michigan must apply for admission to practice before the United States District Court for the Western District of Michigan and may *not* apply for pro hac vice admission.

3.   Licensed attorneys not subject to

   a.   An attorney may move for permission to appear and be heard in one specific base case and the contested matters and/or adversary proceedings arising therein;

   b.   The motion shall state the attorney's full name, business address, telephone number, e-mail address, and the state in which the attorney is licensed to practice;

   c.   The motion shall identify the other federal (bankruptcy, district, and/or circuit) courts in which the attorney is licensed to practice;

   d.   The motion shall verify that the attorney shall be bound by all rules, practices, and ethics that are applicable to those other attorneys admitted to practice before the United States District Court for the Western District of Michigan.

4.   Upon entry of an order by the Bankruptcy Court granting a motion to appear pro hac vice, the attorney admitted shall pay a pro hac vice admission fee payable to the United States District Court for the Western District of Michigan in the amount of $35.00. Said payment shall be remitted by check or money order within ten (10) days of the entry of the order. The admission fee shall be tendered to the Clerk of the Court, United States District Court for the Western District of Michigan, who shall cause the fee to be promptly forwarded to the Clerk of the Court, United States District Court for the Western District of Michigan. On the check or money order shall be noted "pro hac vice admission fee" with the name of the case and the case number.

5.   Failure to pay the pro hac vice admission fee shall result in revocation of the admission order and further result in the attorney being denied the privilege to appear and be heard in connection with the base case and all contested matters and/or adversary proceedings arising therein.

[Dated: December 20, 2005.]

ADMINISTRATIVE ORDER 2007–02.   IN RE: USE OF
COURTROOM ELECTRONIC EQUIPMENT

Counsel who intend to use any electronic equipment in the courtroom during a hearing or a trial are directed to familiarize themselves with the court's equipment. Accordingly, counsel shall contact the Automation Department of this United States Bankruptcy Court Clerk's office at (616) 456–2693 and ask for an appropriate time for training prior to the date of the court appearance.

Counsel who fail to comply with this order face the imposition of sanctions which include, but are not limited to, the cost to repair any of the court's technical equipment damaged by counsel's use.

[Dated: June 25, 2007.]

ADMINISTRATIVE ORDER 2008–01.   IN RE: RESCISSION
OF INTERIM BANKRUPTCY RULES

The Court adopted, in 2005, interim rules in response to the Bankruptcy Abuse Prevention and Consumer Protection Act of 2005. *See*, Administrative Order 2005–04 dated September 28, 2005 and amended on October 19, 2005. However, with the exception of Rule 5012 (Communication and Cooperation with Foreign Courts and Foreign Representatives), the Interim Rules will no longer be necessary when new Federal Rules of Bankruptcy Procedure become effective on December 1, 2008.

Therefore, the Court orders that all of the Interim Rules other than Interim Rule 5012 adopted by Administrative Order 2005–04 will be deemed repealed effective December 1, 2008.

[Dated: September 17, 2008.]

Interim Rule 5012.   Communication and Cooperation With Foreign Courts and Foreign Representatives

Except for communications for scheduling and administrative purposes, the court in any case commenced by a foreign representative shall give at least 20 days' notice of its intent to communicate with a foreign court or a foreign representative.   The notice shall identify the subject of the anticipated communication and shall be given in the manner provided by Rule 2002(q).   Any entity that wishes to participate in the communication shall notify the court of its intention not later than 5 days before the scheduled communication.

ADMINISTRATIVE ORDER 2008–02.   IN RE: CLERK'S AUTHORITY— REDACTION OF PERSONAL IDENTIFIERS

Federal Rule of Bankruptcy Procedure 9037(a) provides that neither an electronic nor paper filing made with the court may include:

1.   an individual's social security number or taxpayer identification number other than the last four digits;

2.   an individual's birth date other than the year of the individual's birth;

3.   the identification of an individual (except for the debtor) who is known to be or is identified as a minor other than by that individual's initials; or

4.   a financial account number other than the last four digits.

Moreover, the Clerk from time to time during the performance of his duties may discover either electronic or paper filings that are in violation of Rule 9037(a).

Therefore, the Court orders that the authority given by LBR 5003(a) to the Clerk to sign orders and notices without further direction of the Court is expanded to include the authority to redact electronic or paper filings in violation of Rule 9037(a) so as to conform with that rule.   However, the Clerk is under no duty to exercise this authority other than as the opportunity may present itself during the performance of his regular duties on behalf of the Court.   Nor is the Clerk under any duty to in fact make the redaction even should the opportunity present itself.

If, though, the Clerk does choose to exercise this authority, the redacted document shall replace the original document as the filing that appears for viewing in the Court's CM/ECF system. However, the Clerk shall still maintain with the Court's non-public records a paper copy of the original filing.

[Dated: September 17, 2008.]

ADMINISTRATIVE ORDER 2009–2.   IN RE: RULE 2016 STATEMENTS

Pursuant to its authority under 11 U.S.C. § 110 and 329, the court intends to monitor more closely the fees that individual Chapter 7 debtors pay to their bankruptcy petition preparers and attorneys, and therefore has decided to require debtors' counsel and petition preparers to file the disclosures under Fed. R. Bankr. P. 2016(b) and (c) as separate docket entries, rather than as part of the petitions or schedules.

NOW, THEREFORE, IT IS HEREBY ORDERED that effective October 1, 2009 the statement required by Fed. R. Bankr. P. 2016(b) or (c) shall be filed as a separate docket entry in every Chapter 7 case involving an individual debtor or debtors, and the Clerk shall implement reasonable measures to accomplish the purpose of this Administrative Order.

[Dated: October 1, 2009.]

ADMINISTRATIVE ORDER 2010–3. IN RE: ADOPTION OF REVISIONS TO INTERIM BANKRUPTCY RULE 1007–1

With the concurrence of all of the judges of this court, revisions to Interim Bankruptcy Rule 1007–1 (attached hereto) are adopted by this court effective December 1, 2010.

The intent of these revisions is to conform the existing Interim Bankruptcy Rule 1007–1, adopted by this court on December 18, 2008, to the Federal Rules of Bankruptcy Procedure, as amended, effective December 1, 2010.

[Dated: November 1, 2010.]

Interim Rule 1007–I.[1] Lists, Schedules, Statements, and Other Documents; Time Limits; Expiration of Temporary Means Testing Exclusion[2]

* * * * *

(b) Schedules, Statements, and Other Documents Required.

* * * * *

(4) *Unless either*: (A) § 707(b)(2)(D)(i) applies, or (B) § 707(b)(2)(D)(ii) applies and the exclusion from means testing granted therein extends beyond the period specified by Rule 1017(e), an individual debtor in a chapter 7 case shall file a statement of current monthly income prepared as prescribed by the appropriate Official Form, and, if the current monthly income exceeds the median family income for the applicable state and household size, the information, including calculations, required by § 707(b), prepared as prescribed by the appropriate Official Form.

* * * * *

(c) Time Limits. In a voluntary case, the schedules, statements, and other documents required by subdivision (b)(1), (4), (5), and (6) shall be filed with the petition or within 14 days thereafter, except as otherwise provided in subdivisions (d), (e), (f), (h), and (n) of this rule. In an involuntary case, the list in subdivision (a)(2), and the schedules, statements, and other documents required by subdivision (b)(1) shall be filed by the debtor within 14 days of the entry of the order for relief. In a voluntary case, the documents required by paragraphs (A), (C), and (D) of subdivision (b)(3) shall be filed with the petition. Unless the court orders otherwise, a debtor who has filed a statement under subdivision (b)(3)(B), shall file the documents required by subdivision (b)(3)(A) within 14 days of the order for relief. In a chapter 7 case, the debtor shall file the statement required by subdivision (b)(7) within 60 days after the first date set for the meeting of creditors under § 341 of the Code, and in a chapter 11 or 13 case no later than the date when the last payment was made by the debtor as required by the plan or the filing of a motion for a discharge under § 1141(d)(5)(B) or § 1328(b) of the Code. The court may, at any time and in its discretion, enlarge the time to file the statement required by subdivision (b)(7). The debtor shall file the statement required by subdivision (b)(8) no earlier than the date of the last payment made under the plan or the date of the filing of a motion for a discharge under §§ 1141(d)(5)(B), 1228(b), or 1328(b) of the Code. Lists, schedules, statements, and other documents filed prior to the conversion of a case to another chapter shall be deemed filed in the converted case unless the court directs otherwise. Except as provided in § 1116(3), any extension of time to file schedules, statements, and other documents required under this rule may be granted only on motion for cause shown and on notice to the United States trustee, any committee elected under § 705 or appointed under § 1102 of the Code, trustee, examiner, or other party as the court may direct. Notice of an extension shall be given to the United States trustee and to any committee, trustee, or other party as the court may direct.

* * * * *

(n) Time Limits for, and Notice to, Debtors Temporarily Excluded from Means Testing.

(1) An individual debtor who is temporarily excluded from means testing pursuant to § 707(b)(2)(D)(ii) of the Code shall file any statement and calculations required by subdivision (b)(4) no later than 14 days after the expiration of the temporary exclusion if the expiration occurs within the time specified by Rule 1017(e) for filing a motion pursuant to § 707(b)(2).

(2) If the temporary exclusion from means testing under § 707(b)(2)(D)(ii) terminates due to the circumstances specified in subdivision (n)(1), and if the debtor has not previously filed a statement

and calculations required by subdivision (b)(4), the clerk shall promptly notify the debtor that the required statement and calculations must be filed within the time specified in subdivision (n)(1).

[Dated: December 1, 2010.]

¹ Interim Rule 1007–I was adopted by the bankruptcy courts to implement the National Guard and Reservists Debt Relief Act of 2008, Public Law No: 110–438. The Act, which provides a temporary exclusion from the application of the means test for certain members of the National Guard and reserve components of the Armed Forces, applies to bankruptcy cases commenced in the three-year period beginning December 19, 2008.

² Incorporates (1) time amendments to Rule 1007 which took effect on December 1, 2009, and (2) an amendment, effective December 1, 2010, which extended the time to file the statement of completion of a course in personal financial management in a chapter 7 case filed by an individual debtor.

COMMITTEE NOTE

This rule is amended to take account of the enactment of the National Guard and Reservists Debt Relief Act of 2008, which amended § 707(b)(2)(D) of the Code to provide a temporary exclusion from the application of the means test for certain members of the National Guard and reserve components of the Armed Forces. This exclusion applies to qualifying debtors while they remain on active duty or are performing a homeland defense activity, and for a period of 540 days thereafter. For some debtors initially covered by the exclusion, the protection from means testing will expire while their chapter 7 cases are pending, and at a point when a timely motion to dismiss under § 707(b)(2) can still be filed. Under the amended rule, these debtors are required to file the statement and calculations required by subdivision (b)(4) no later than 14 days after the expiration of their exclusion.

Subdivisions (b)(4) and (c) are amended to relieve debtors qualifying for an exclusion under § 707(b)(2)(D)(ii) from the obligation to file a statement of current monthly income and required calculations within the time period specified in subdivision (c).

Subdivision (n)(1) is added to specify the time for filing of the information required by subdivision (b)(4) by a debtor who initially qualifies for the means test exclusion under § 707(b)(2)(D)(ii), but whose exclusion expires during the time that a motion to dismiss under § 707(b)(2) may still be made under Rule 1017(e). If, upon the expiration of the temporary exclusion, a debtor has not already filed the required statement and calculations, subdivision (n)(2) directs the clerk to provide prompt notice to the debtor of the time for filing as set forth in subdivision (n)(1).

ADMINISTRATIVE ORDER 2013–2. IN RE: DEFERRAL OF MOTION FEES FOR SECTION 363(f) SALES

On December 1, 2013 a new motion fee of $176.00 will be assessed upon the filing of a motion to sell property of the estate free and clear of liens and other interests under 11 U.S.C. § 363(f). The court recognizes that some estates may not have funds available at the time of the filing such a motion to pay the new fee, and that there is currently little procedural guidance addressing the deferral or waiver of the fee.

The court anticipates that the Judicial Conference of the United States (the "Conference") or the Administrative Office of the United States Courts (the "Administrative Office") may soon issue guidance regarding the collection, deferral, or waiver of the new motion fee but, until then, interim guidance to the Clerk and the bar is necessary and appropriate under LBR 9029(b). Therefore, in connection with the new motion fee the court will borrow the procedures governing the collection, deferral, and waiver of fees imposed for commencing adversary proceedings as described in Part G of the Bankruptcy Fee Compendium III, May 1, 2013 Edition (the "Fee Compendium"). The court further finds that the interim approach memorialized in this General Order is not inconsistent with the policies of the Conference. *Cf.* 28 U.S.C. § 1930(f)(3).

NOW, THEREFORE, IT IS ORDERED that trustees and debtors in possession without adequate estate funds may file motions to sell "free and clear" under § 363(f) and request to defer the fee until a time in which the estate realizes sufficient funds to pay the fee, in accordance with the procedures described in the Fee Compendium (Part G—Fees for Filing Adversary Proceedings).

IT IS FURTHER ORDERED that the court will treat the electronic checking of "defer" in the CM/ECF event codes as the registered filer's affirmative representation, subject to Fed. R. Bankr. P. 9011, that there are no funds available in the estate to pay the motion fee at the time of filing.

IT IS FURTHER ORDERED that upon the estate's realization of sufficient funds, the fee shall be paid as soon as practicable, and in other cases the fee shall be collected, or not, in accordance with the Conference or Administrative Office policy described in Part G of the Fee Compendium.

IT IS FURTHER ORDERED that this General Order shall govern the collection, deferral or waiver of the new motion fee until the earlier of (1) the issuance of formal guidance from the Conference or the Administrative Office, (2) the effective date of a local rule of this court addressing the issues, or (3) further order of the court.

[Dated: November 27, 2013.]

ADMINISTRATIVE ORDER 2014–4. IN RE: PROOF OF SERVICE ON MATRIX

Pursuant to Rule 9029(b) of the Local Bankruptcy Rules for the Western District of Michigan (collectively, the "LBR"), the Court has determined that an administrative order should be entered as an interim rule setting forth requirements for service on the creditor mailing matrix.

NOW, THEREFORE, IT IS HEREBY ORDERED that:

1.   Effective September 10, 2014 as to all service made on or after September 10, 2014, and unless the court orders otherwise, when the Bankruptcy Code, the Federal Rules of Bankruptcy Procedure, the LBR or other applicable law requires that service be effectuated on the creditor mailing matrix, the serving party shall attach to the certificate of service a copy of the actual creditor mailing matrix relied upon for service (the "Matrix").

2.   The Matrix shall be current and dated as of the date reflected on the certificate of service.

3.   The Matrix shall include the date stamp indicating the date upon which the Matrix was generated and shall not otherwise be materially modified; provided, however, that the serving party may redact duplicative parties in interest with the same name and address so as to avoid unnecessary expense.

4.   In the event that the certificate of service that attaches the Matrix does not substantially conform to this Administrative Order, the Clerk is authorized to strike the certificate of service as defective, and in that case shall send a notice to the serving party: (i) advising that the certificate has been stricken; (ii) providing a time within which to cure the defect: and (iii) advising that the certificate will be considered filed as of the date originally filed if it is amended to correct the defect, and filed, within the time prescribed.

5.   The Clerk may take any other action reasonably necessary to ensure compliance with this Administrative Order.

[Dated: September 9, 2014.]

ADMINISTRATIVE ORDER 2014–5. IN RE: SUSPENSION OF LBR 3016(c)

Pursuant to Rule 9029(b) of the Local Bankruptcy Rules for the Western District of Michigan (collectively, the "LBR"), the Court has determined to enter an administrative order, on an interim basis, suspending the application of LBR 3016(c) regarding the chapter 13 trustees' fees.

The application of LBR 3016(c) may be inconsistent with the governing statute and the timing of the collection of the trustees' fee. *Compare* LBR 3016(c) (authorizing chapter 13 trustee to collect fee *"at the time of distribution to the creditor"*) with 28 U.S.C. § 586(e)(2) (chapter 13 trustee "shall collect such percentage fee *from all payments received* by such [trustee] under plans . . ."). To avoid inconsistency and uncertainty, the Court has determined to defer to the statute by suspending the local rule. Fed. R. Bankr. P. 9029 (requiring local bankruptcy rules to be consistent with Acts of Congress).

NOW, THEREFORE, IT IS HEREBY ORDERED that, effective as of September 10, 2014, LBR 3016(c) is SUSPENDED and without effect, pending further order of the Court.

[Dated: September 9, 2014.]

ADMINISTRATIVE ORDER 2016–2. IN RE: DEPOSIT AND INVESTMENT OF REGISTRY FUNDS AND INTERPLEADER FUNDS TAX ADMINISTRATION COMPLIANCE

ORDER REGARDING DEPOSIT AND INVESTMENT OF REGISTRY FUNDS

As the Court has determined that it is necessary to adopt local procedures to ensure uniformity in the deposit, investment, and tax administration of funds in the Court's Registry,

IT IS ORDERED that the following shall govern the receipt, deposit, and investment of registry funds:

I. Receipt of Funds.

A. No money shall be sent to the Court or its officers for deposit in the Court's registry without a court order signed by the presiding judge in the case or proceeding.

B. The party making the deposit or transferring funds to the Court's registry shall serve the order permitting the deposit or transfer on the Clerk of Court.

C. Unless provided for elsewhere in this Order, all monies ordered to be paid to the Court or received by its officers in any case pending or adjudicated shall be deposited with the Treasurer of the United States in the name and to the credit of this Court pursuant to 28 U.S.C. § 2041 through depositories designated by the Treasury to accept such deposits on its behalf.

II. Investment of Registry Funds.

A. Where, by order of the Court, funds on deposit with the Court are to be placed in some form of interest-bearing account or invested in a court-approved, interest-bearing instrument in accordance with Rule 67 of the Federal Rules of Civil Procedure, the Court Registry Investment System ("CRIS"), administered by the Administrative Office of the United States Courts under 28 U.S.C. § 2045, shall be the only investment mechanism authorized.

B. Interpleader funds deposited under 28 U.S.C. § 1335 meet the IRS definition of a "Disputed Ownership Fund" (DOF), a taxable entity that requires tax administration. Unless otherwise ordered by the court, interpleader funds shall be deposited in the DOF established within the CRIS and administered by the Administrative Office of the United States Courts, which shall be responsible for meeting all DOF tax administration requirements. The Director of Administrative Office of the United States Courts is designated as custodian for all CRIS funds. The Director or the Director's designee shall perform the duties of custodian. Funds held in the CRIS remain subject to the control and jurisdiction of the Court.

C. Money from each case deposited in the CRIS shall be "pooled" together with those on deposit with Treasury to the credit of other courts in the CRIS and used to purchase Government Account Series securities through the Bureau of Public Debt, which will be held at Treasury, in an account in the name and to the credit of the Director of Administrative Office of the United States Courts. The pooled funds will be invested in accordance with the principles of the CRIS Investment Policy as approved by the Registry Monitoring Group.

D. An account will be established in the CRIS Liquidity Fund titled in the name of the case giving rise to the deposit invested in the fund. Income generated from fund investments will be distributed to each case based on the ratio each account's principal and earnings has to the aggregate principal and income total in the fund after the CRIS fee has been applied. Reports showing the interest earned and the principal amounts contributed in each case will be prepared and distributed to each court participating in the CRIS and made available to litigants and/or their counsel.

E. For each interpleader case, an account shall be established in the CRIS Disputed Ownership Fund, titled in the name of the case giving rise to the deposit invested in the fund. Income generated from fund investments will be distributed to each case after the DOF fee has been applied and tax withholdings have been deducted from the fund. Reports showing the interest earned and the principal amounts contributed in each case will be available through the FedInvest/CMS application for each court participating in the CRIS and made available to litigants and/or their counsel. On appointment of an administrator authorized to incur expenses on behalf of the DOF in a case, the case DOF funds should be transferred to another investment account as directed by court order.

III. Fees and Taxes.

A. The custodian is authorized and directed by this Order to deduct the CRIS fee of an annualized 10 basis points on assets on deposit for all CRIS funds, excluding the case funds held in the DOF, for the management of investments in the CRIS. According to the Court's Miscellaneous Fee Schedule, the CRIS fee is assessed from interest earnings to the pool before a pro rata distribution of earnings is made to court cases.

B. The custodian is authorized and directed by this Order to deduct the DOF fee of an annualized 20 basis points on assets on deposit in the DOF for management of investments and tax administration. According to the Court's Miscellaneous Fee Schedule, the DOF fee is assessed from interest earnings to the pool before a pro rata distribution of earnings is made to court cases. The custodian is further authorized and directed by this Order to withhold and pay federal taxes due on behalf of the DOF.

IV. Transition From Former Investment Procedure.

A. The Clerk of Court is further directed to develop a systematic method of redemption of all existing investments and their transfer to the CRIS.

B. Deposits to the CRIS DOF will not be transferred from any existing CRIS Funds. Only new deposits pursuant to 28 U.S.C. § 1335 from the effective date of this order will be placed in the CRIS DOF.

C. Parties not wishing to transfer certain existing registry deposits into the CRIS may seek leave to transfer them to the litigants or their designees on proper motion and approval of the judge assigned to the specific case.

D. This Order supersedes and abrogates all prior orders of this Court regarding the deposit and investment of registry funds, including General Order 2011–1.

E. This Order is generally effective September 14, 2016, but the DOF provisions will become effective the date the CRIS DOF begins to accept deposits.

[Dated: September 14, 2016.]

ELECTRONIC CASE FILING
ADMINISTRATIVE PROCEDURES FOR THE ELECTRONIC FILING, SIGNING, VERIFICATION AND SERVICE OF DOCUMENTS
I. REGISTRATION FOR THE ELECTRONIC CASE FILING SYSTEM

A. Designation of Cases. All cases filed in the Western District of Michigan, regardless of when a case was originally filed, are deemed to be assigned to the Case Management/Electronic Case Filing System (hereafter System) unless otherwise indicated by the Court.

B. Logins & Passwords.

1. Any attorney admitted to practice in the Western District of Michigan (including those admitted pro hac vice), United States Trustees, panel trustees, and others with court approval may register to participate in electronic case filing. Registration will permit the Filing User to retrieve and file pleadings and other documents. An attorney/participant's login & password, issued by the Court, constitutes the participant's signature on any document or pleading submitted electronically through the System.

2. *Filing User* is defined as the attorney of record or the actual party in interest, if not represented by counsel, who electronically transmits any pleading or document to the Court.

C. Registration.

1. An official registration form (See Court's Web site) must be submitted for each Filing User. A full participant user, with the exception of the US Trustee and Panel Trustees, must pay all applicable filing and/or motion fees via the Internet Credit Card module.

2. All registration forms are to be returned to:

United States Bankruptcy Court
P.O. Box 3310
Grand Rapids, MI 49501
Attn.: CM/ECF Project Team

3. After completion of training with the Clerk's Office, each registering Filing User will be assigned a login & password for the System. Only one login & password will be assigned for each attorney or authorized filer. Each Filing User will receive an internet e-mail message after his/her password has been assigned to ensure that the filer's internet e-mail address has been entered correctly into the System. Failure of any user to abide by established Court guidelines and procedures for filing electronically, may result in the revocation of user access.

4. A Filing User may change the assigned password. In the event a Filing User believes that the security of an existing password may have been compromised, he/she shall immediately change that password and notify the Clerk's office. If a user forgets password information, the Clerk's Office will assign a new password.

5. Registration as a Filing User constitutes (1) waiver of the right to receive notice by first class mail and consent to receive notice electronically; and (2) waiver of the right to service by personal service or first class mail and consent to electronic service, except with regard to service of a summons and complaint under Federal Rule of Bankruptcy Procedure 7004. Waiver of service and notice by first class mail applies to notice of the entry of the order or judgment under Fed. R. Bankr. P. 9022.

6. If any information on the registration changes, i.e., mailing address, e-mail address, etc., it is the Filing User's responsibility to log onto the system and make the appropriate changes by accessing the "Utility" menu and selecting "Maintain Your ECF Account" (see Court's Web site). It is not the Court's responsibility to re-send or investigate returned e-mails not properly maintained by the Filing Users.

7. Once registered, a Filing User may withdraw from participation in the System by providing the Clerk's Office with written notice of such withdrawal. Upon receipt of the written notice, the Clerk's Office will immediately cancel the Filing User's password and delete the user from any applicable electronic service list. An attorney's withdrawal from participation in the System does not constitute withdrawal from representation in any pending case. A withdrawing attorney must notify

all parties/attorneys who have appeared in a pending case that they can no longer be served electronically and must be served conventionally.

D.   Limited Use Participants.

1.   Attorneys and creditor representatives may obtain a "Limited Use Password" for access to the System by submitting a Limited Participant ECF User form (see Court's Web site). Access to the System is currently restricted to the filing of the following documents:

    a. Creditor Request for Notices

    b. Proofs of Claim

    c. Withdrawals or Transfers of Claim

    d. Reaffirmation Agreements

2.   Attorneys or creditor representatives wishing to obtain Limited Use access to the System must complete a Limited Use registration form. Upon completion of any applicable training, registrants will receive a limited use login and password. The use of this login and password are governed by the provision of paragraph I(C). Only attorney representatives will be permitted to receive e-mail notification; Creditor representatives are required to waive such notice. The Court will maintain all user account information for Limited Use participants. Participants are required to immediately notify the Court of any change(s) and/or corrections(s) to their mailing address or other pertinent information.

3.   Documents filed by a Limited Use participant are governed by all provisions of these administrative procedures. If a Limited User participant files a proof of claim electronically, all attachments, security interests or evidences of indebtedness required to be attached under the Fed. Rules of Bankr. Procedure shall be attached electronically to the proof of claim.

II.   ELECTRONIC FILING AND SERVICE OF DOCUMENTS

A.   Filing Electronically.

1.   Except as provided for in paragraph III(A) below, all pleadings and documents required to be filed with the Court in connection with a case assigned to the System shall be electronically filed.

2.   Documents that are associated with a pleading shall be prepared as separate documents, but should be electronically filed together as attachments to the main pleading, i.e.: certificates of service, affidavits, supporting briefs, proposed orders, etc., shall be filed as attachments to the motion, complaint or other pleading to which it relates. See III(A)(3) regarding exhibits.

3.   The Clerk's Office shall not maintain a paper court file in any case, except as otherwise provided by this Administrative Procedure or local Court policy. The official court record shall be an electronic file maintained on the Court's file server. The Court may dispose of any paper documents after scanning and docketing.

B.   Service.

1.   Whenever a pleading or other paper is filed, a "Notice of Electronic Filing" will be automatically generated by the System via electronic means at the time of docketing.

2.   The Filing User must serve pleadings or documents upon all persons entitled to notice or service in accordance with applicable rules. If the recipient is a registered participant in the System, service of the "Notice of Electronic Filing" shall be the equivalent of service of the pleading or other paper (other than a summons and complaint) by first class mail, postage prepaid, provided, however, that the three-day extension prescribed in Fed. R. Bankr. P. 9006(f) shall not apply when service is made through the System.

C.   Section 341(a) Meeting of Creditors. The attorney for the debtor shall bring to the Section 341(a) meeting of creditors, the electronically filed petition, schedules, lists and statement of affairs bearing the original signatures of the debtor(s).

D.   Timeliness.

1.   Filing of documents electronically does not alter the filing deadline for that pleading. Except where the presiding Judge specifically requires an earlier filing time, filing must be completed before midnight local time (Eastern Standard Time or Eastern Daylight Time, whichever is applicable at the time of filing) where the Court is located in order to be considered timely filed that day.

2. A document is deemed filed at the date and time reflected on the "Notice of Electronic Filing" from the Court.

3. A filer whose document is made untimely as the result of a technical failure of the court's System, may seek appropriate relief from the Court.

E. Signatures.

1. Petitions, lists, schedules and statements, amendments, pleadings, affidavits and other documents which must contain original signatures or which require verification under FRBP 1008 or an unsworn declaration as provided in 28 U.S.C. § 1746, shall be filed electronically by filing users registered in the System.

2. *Debtor's Declaration Re: Electronic Filing.* When the original petition is filed electronically, the attorney for the debtor(s) shall file in paper form, the originally executed "Declaration Re: Electronic Filing" (see Court's Web site) with the Court within five (5) business days of the electronic filing. The Court will retain the original Declaration. Failure to file the Declaration Re: Electronic Filing as prescribed, shall result in dismissal of the proceeding without prejudice, without further notice of the Court.

3. *Debtor's Statement of Social Security Number (Official Form B21).* Effective December 1, 2003, a completed Official Form B21 (Statement of Social Security Number) is required to be submitted to the Court containing the full 9–digit social security number(s) and original signature(s) of the Debtor(s). If the debtor does not have a Social Security number, the debtor shall submit the Statement of Social Security Number with that information. Failure to submit this form within 15 days from the date of the Notice to File Statement of Social Security Numbers shall result in dismissal of the proceeding without prejudice, without further notice of the Court. The full social security number(s) of the debtor(s) shall not be included in the PDF image of the electronically filed petition.

4. A copy containing an original signature* must be retained by the filing user for a period of 5 years after the closing of the case and all time periods for appeals have expired, unless the Court orders a different period. This retention period does not affect or replace any other periods required by other applicable laws or rules. Upon request of the Court, the filing user must provide original documents for review.

5. The pleading or other document electronically filed shall indicate the signature as "/S/ name", unless the document has been scanned and shows the original signature.

6. In the case of a stipulation or other document to be signed by two or more persons, the following procedure shall be used:

a. The filer shall initially confirm that the content of the document is acceptable to all persons required to sign the document and shall obtain the actual signature(s) of all parties on the document.

b. The filer shall then file the document electronically, indicating the signatures by "/S/ name".

c. The filer shall retain the hard copy of the document containing the original signatures in accordance with paragraph II(E)(3).

F. Special Documents.

1. *Creditor Mailing Matrix.* The creditor matrix shall be prepared in accordance with the "Creditor Matrix Styleguide". The creditor mailing matrix will accompany an electronically filed bankruptcy petition. The matrix shall be filed as an ASCII Text (.txt) file and uploaded immediately after the petition is filed. If an amendment is filed which adds creditors, then an amended matrix shall also be prepared as a .txt file for uploading which contains only the names and addresses of those creditors being added to the proceeding.

2. *Virtual Documents.* Virtual documents are certain documents (including some orders) which are frequently utilized by trustees, Office of the U.S. Trustee and the Court of which the text does not substantially vary from case to case. A virtual document consists entirely of the text contained in the docket entry and is not embodied in any other document. The docket entry for the virtual document shall be fully effective despite the absence of a hard document. Examples of a virtual document are a Trustee's Report of No Distribution, Trustee's Report of Plan Completion, Order Confirming Chapter 13 Plan, Trustee's report after conclusion/adjournment of the § 341(a) meeting of creditors and the Trustee's Request to Defer Payment of Filing Fee.

G. Fees Payable to the Clerk.

1.   Registered filers shall pay all applicable filing/motion fees through the U.S. Treasury Internet credit card program. It is the filers responsibility to maintain a credit limit adequate to cover all filing/motion fees due.

The filer may select "Pay Now" or "Continue Filling" on the payment screen. If "Continue Filing" has been selected, so as to pay multiple fees with a single payment, the payment for all fees due shall be made by the close of each business day.

Installment payments of filing fees are not permitted on the System. Filing fees must be paid in full at the time of filing, or at the close of each business day if the "Continue Fling" option is selected, or as provided through the debtor's Chapter 13 plan, if applicable.

2.   Any transaction declined by the credit card issuer for any reason must be paid to the Court in cash or by check or money order by the close of business on the next business day. The cardholder has the responsibility to notify the Clerk's Office of any transaction which is declined.

H. Orders. The Clerk's Office will electronically file all orders, notices and other court-produced documents into the System.

Any order filed electronically by the Court with the Judge's signature reflected as "/S/Judge's Name", has the same force and effect as if the Judge had affixed an original signature to a paper copy of the order and it had been entered on the docket in a conventional manner.

Any ministerial order filed electronically by the Clerk with the Clerk's signature reflected as "/S/Daniel M. LaVille, Clerk of Court", has the same force and effect as if the Clerk had affixed an original signature to a paper copy of the order and it had been entered on the docket in a conventional manner.

Proposed Orders—The Clerk is authorized to establish detailed procedures and requirements regarding the electronic filing of orders. Such procedures and requirements may be contained in guidelines, notices, user guides, etc., posted on the Court's website and available in the Clerk's office.

I. Entry and Correction of Docket Entries.

1.   The person electronically filing a pleading or other document will be responsible for designating a docket entry for the document by using one of the event categories prescribed by the Court.

2.   Once a document has been electronically filed, corrections will be made only by the Clerk's Office. The System will not permit filers to make changes to the document(s) or docket entry filed in error once the transaction has been entered. The filer will be advised by the Clerk's office if the document needs to be *re-filed*.

J. Exhibits/Attachments Other Than Exhibits for Hearings and Trials. Unless the Court permits conventional filing, all documents referenced as exhibits or attachments shall be submitted in electronic format. An exhibit to an electronic filing shall include only excerpts of the referenced document that is directly germane to the matter under consideration by the Court. Excerpted material must be clearly identified as such. A party filing excerpts of a document under this provision does so without prejudice to the right to file timely additional excerpts or the complete document. The exhibit in its' entirety must be available in the courtroom at any hearing pertaining to the matter.

III.   EXCEPTIONS TO ELECTRONIC FILING

Pleadings and documents must be filed via the Internet with the following exceptions: trial exhibits, original transcripts, documents filed by pro se parties, documents filed under seal, Debtor's Statement of Social Security Number and Debtor's Declaration Re: Electronic Filing

A. Alternate Procedures.

1.   *Documents Filed Under Seal.* The motion to file document(s) under seal shall be filed electronically. The actual document(s) under seal shall be prepared in paper form and submitted to the Court with the order granting the motion once the order has been entered.

2.   *Trial Exhibits.* Trial exhibits shall be submitted conventionally. The Court will not scan trial exhibits unless the Court determines that doing so will assist in managing the trial.

3.   *Proofs of Claim.* Claims may be filed conventionally by non-registered users. Claims submitted conventionally will be entered and scanned in their entirety into the System by the Court.

4. *Debtor's Statement of Social Security Number (Official Form B21).* See II(E)(3).

5. *Debtor's Declaration Re: Electronic Filing.* See II(E)(2).

IV. ELECTRONIC FILING PROTOCOLS

A. Format. All Documents, except the creditor mailing matrix or amended mailing matrix, shall be submitted in a PDF file. The creditor mailing matrix must be filed in .txt format.

B. Size of Documents. Document files must be no larger than 2 megabytes (MB) in size, or approximately 35 pages of text in standard word processing format, converted into PDF using Adobe Acrobat software or through other software. Scanning a document into PDF will result in a much larger file size. The transmission of a large document as a single file may not be successful due to security constraints on the length of time taken by an electronic filing. Large-sized documents should be broken down into sections and filed as consecutively number attachments pursuant to Court policy.

C. The Clerk is authorized to establish detailed procedures and requirements regarding the electronic filing of documents. Such procedures and requirements may be contained in guidelines, notices, user guides, etc., posted on the Court's website and available in the Clerk's office.

V. CONVENTIONAL FILING PROTOCOL

A. Quality. Documents must be printed in a format capable of producing a quality image when scanned by the Court.

B. Size. All documents, including exhibits and attachments, must be on standard letter size (8.5″ x 11″). The filing party is responsible for reducing larger documents to the standard size; or for copying smaller size documents onto standard size paper.

C. Assembly. Documents shall be submitted bound only by binder clips or clamps. Documents shall not be bound by staples, prong fasteners or standard paper clips. Documents may not contain tabs. Exhibits may be marked by including a separation sheet marked with the exhibit letter or number; or by noting the exhibit letter or number at the bottom of the first page of the exhibit.

D. Length. Documents which exceed 35 pages must be separated into 2 or more parts. Multiple parts of a separated document shall be identified in accordance with established guidelines.

E. Number of Copies. Only the original document need be presented for filing, with the exception of trial exhibits and legal briefs—two complete sets are to be filed with the Court. If the filing party would like file-stamped copies returned, then those copies must be submitted along with a self-addressed stamped envelope. Additional copies will not be returned if not accompanied with a self-addressed stamped envelope.

F. Return of Paper Documents. The official record consists of the electronic images of documents stored in the Court's System. The Court may dispose of paper documents after scanning and docketing.

G. Mailing Matrix. Only a pro se debtor who did not receive assistance from a bankruptcy petition preparer may file a creditor mailing matrix in paper format.

VI. TECHNICAL FAILURES

A Filing User who is unable to effect a filing through the Internet due to a technical failure should document the incident and report the occurrence the Clerk's office. A Filing User whose filing is made untimely as the result of a technical failure may seek appropriate relief from the Court. Known system outages will be posted on our web site if possible. Problems on the filer's end will not constitute a technical failure under these procedures nor excuse an untimely filing. (i.e., problems with phone lines, Internet Service Provider (ISP), hardware or software, etc.) A filer who cannot file a document electronically because of a problem on the filer's end, must file the document conventionally or contact the Clerk's Office for permission to file the document provisionally via FAX (See LBR 5005–1)

VII. PUBLIC ACCESS TO THE SYSTEM

A. Internet Access.

Non-ECF Participants. Any person or organization may access the System by establishing an account with the PACER Service Center. Registration may be made online at http://pacer.psc.uscourts.gov or by calling 1–800–676–6856. All applicable fees would apply.

ECF Participants. Registered users in the System will receive one free look at the document in the case through the hyperlink included in the Notice of Electronic Filing. In addition to receiving a login and password for filing documents through the System, all registered ECF participants must also establish an account with the PACER Service Center (see above) All other applicable fees would apply.

B. Access at Court. During regular business hours, electronic access to documents and case information is available at each of the Courthouses for the Western District of Michigan (Grand Rapids and Marquette). There are no fees for viewing the electronic documents at the Clerk's Office. Charges for copies of electronic and paper documents are described in the Electronic Public Access Fee Schedule (28 U.S.C. § 1930)

VIII. PRIVACY

A. In compliance with the policy of the Judicial Conference of the United States, and the E–Government Act of 2002, and in order to promote electronic access to case files while also protecting personal privacy and other legitimate interests, parties shall refrain from including, or shall partially redact where inclusion is necessary, the following personal data identifiers from all documents and pleadings filed with the court, including exhibits thereto, whether filed electronically or in paper, unless otherwise ordered by the Court or required by statute, the Federal Rules of Bankruptcy Procedure or the Official Bankruptcy Forms.

1. Social Security Numbers—If an individual's social security number must be included in a pleading, only the last four digits of that number should be used.

2. Names of minor children—If the involvement of a minor child must be mentioned, only the initials of that child should be used. On Schedule I of the Official Bankruptcy Form 6, list relationship and age of the debtor's dependents (i.e.: son, age 6)

3. Dates of Birth—If an individual's date of birth must be included in a pleading, only the year should be used. On Schedule I of Official Bankruptcy Form 6, list the age of each of the debtor's dependents.

4. Financial Account Numbers—If financial account numbers are relevant, only the last four digits should be used. On Schedules D, E & F of the Official Bankruptcy Form 6, debtors, if they so choose, may include their full account numbers to assist the trustee and creditors.

B. In compliance with the E–Government Act of 2002, a party wishing to file a document containing the personal identifiers listed above may file an unredacted document under seal. The court will consider a request to file an unredacted document under seal by ex-parte motion, although the court may require the filing party to give notice and an opportunity to request a hearing, or may set the matter hearing. The unredacted document shall be retained by the court as part of the record. The party shall file a redacted copy for the public file.

C. The responsibility for redacting these personal identifiers rests solely with counsel and the parties. The Clerk will not review each document for compliance with this rule.

[Amended effective December 1, 2016.]

* [**Publisher's Note:** *See* Administrative Order 2004–3, dated April 29, 2004, *ante.*]

POLICY—TRANSCRIPTS OF COURT PROCEEDINGS

At its September 2007 session, the Judicial Conference adopted a policy regarding electronic availability of transcripts of court proceedings. Earlier, at its September 2003 session (JCUS, SEP 03, pp. 16, 17), the Judicial Conference approved procedures (revised at its March 2007 session) to implement the Judiciary's privacy policy (now reflected in Federal Rule of Bankruptcy Procedure 9037) as it applies to electronic availability of transcripts.

This policy applies only to transcripts of this court's proceedings made available remotely via CM/ECF and PACER. It does not change any other local rule or policy with respect to sealing or redaction of court records for any other purpose.

A. Filing and Electronic Availability of Transcripts.

1. Transcripts of court proceedings filed with the court by the court reporter or transcriber will be available for viewing, downloading or printing only through CM/ECF. Notice of the filing to persons who attended the transcribed proceeding shall be by CM/ECF except with respect to those participants who are not CM/ECF filers.

2. Except as provided in this paragraph, the filed transcript will not be available for viewing for 90 calendar days after filing. The exceptions are:

(a) The filed transcript may be viewed electronically from a public terminal at the Clerk's Office.

(b) If the transcript is purchased from the court reporter or transcriber by an attorney of record, then the transcript will be available for remote electronic viewing and use by that attorney.

3. Under no circumstance may the filed transcript be printed or downloaded from the Court's CM/ECF system during the 90–day restriction period.

4. The Clerk's Office shall include in the docket entry of all transcripts filed with the court pursuant to this policy the following notation:

"Availability of this transcript for viewing, downloading and printing is subject to a 90–day restriction as provided in this Court's administrative Order No. 08–03."

B. Notice of Intent to Request Redaction.
Any person who wishes to redact from a transcript those personal identifiers noted in Fed.R.Bankr.P. 9037(a) must file a "Notice of Intent to Request Redaction" with the clerk and serve a copy of the notice on the transcriber within seven (7) calendar days of the filing of the transcript.

C. Request for Redaction Under Rule 9037(a).

1. A party filing a notice pursuant to paragraph B above has then until twenty-one (21) calendar days after the transcript was filed to file a Request for Redaction that sets forth the Rule 9037 personal identifiers, where they appear in the transcript by page and line, and how they are to be redacted. The Request for Redaction must also be simultaneously served upon the court reporter or transcriber.

For purposes of this paragraph, Rule 9037 personal identifiers mean:

- social security numbers;
- financial account numbers;
- dates of birth;
- names of minor children; and
- home addresses

If a person wishes to redact information other than Rule 9037(a) personal identifiers, then that person must file a motion for protective order under subpart (d) of that rule. The subject transcript will not be available for unrestricted viewing, downloading or printing until that motion is ruled upon notwithstanding paragraph D of this administrative order.

The responsibility for redacting personal identifiers rests solely with counsel and the parties. Neither the Clerk nor the court reporter or transcriber is responsible for reviewing transcripts for compliance with this policy.

2. If a Request for Redaction is both proper and timely, then the court reporter or transcriber shall have thirty-one (31) calendar days from the filing of the transcript to make the requested redactions and to file the redacted transcript with the court. The redacted transcript will then become the version of the transcript available for electronic viewing. As for the original transcript, the Clerk's Office shall keep the same for viewing at its public terminal or for reviewing remotely by any attorney of record who purchased the original transcript from the court reporter or transcriber unless the Court orders the original transcript to be placed under seal.

D. Unrestricted Electronic Viewing, Downloading, and Printing.
The original transcript filed will be available for unrestricted remote electronic viewing and printing and for printing from the Court Clerk's public terminal upon the expiration of the 90–day restriction period if no proper and

timely Request for Redaction is filed. Similarly, the redacted transcript will be available for unrestricted remote electronic viewing and printing and for printing from the Court Clerk's public terminal upon the expiration of the 90–day restriction period if a proper and timely Request for Redaction is made.

E. PACER Charges. Charges for access through PACER apply during and after the 90–day restriction period. Charges are not capped at 30 pages. The user will incur PACER charges each time the transcript is accessed even though he or she may have purchased it from the transcriber and obtained remote access through CM/ECF. **A free copy of the electronic transcript is not available via remote access.** After purchasing the transcript from the transcriber, an attorney can receive the original and any redacted transcript in both paper and electronic format.

F. Effective Date. This order applies to all transcripts of court proceedings filed after **September 26, 2008.**

RULES OF PROCEDURE OF THE
JUDICIAL PANEL ON
MULTIDISTRICT LITIGATION

Renumbered and Amended Effective November 2, 1998

Including Amendments Effective
October 4, 2016

I. RULES FOR MULTIDISTRICT LITIGATION
UNDER 28 U.S.C. § 1407

RULE 1.1 DEFINITIONS

(a) "Panel" means the members of the United States Judicial Panel on Multidistrict Litigation appointed by the Chief Justice of the United States pursuant to 28 U.S.C. § 1407.

(b) "Chair" means the Chair of the Panel appointed by the Chief Justice of the United States pursuant to Section 1407, or the member of the Panel properly designated to act as Chair.

(c) "Clerk of the Panel" means the official that the Panel appoints to that position. The Clerk of the Panel shall perform such duties that the Panel or the Panel Executive delegates.

(d) "Electronic Case Filing (ECF)" refers to the Panel's automated system that receives and stores documents filed in electronic form. All attorneys filing pleadings with the Panel must do so using ECF. All pro se individuals are non-ECF users, unless the Panel orders otherwise.

(e) "MDL" means a multidistrict litigation docket which the Panel is either considering or has created by transferring cases to a transferee district for coordinated or consolidated pretrial proceedings pursuant to Section 1407.

(f) "Panel Executive" means the official appointed to act as the Panel's Chief Executive and Legal Officer. The Panel Executive may appoint, with the approval of the Panel, necessary deputies, clerical assistants and other employees to perform or assist in the performance of the duties of the Panel Executive. The Panel Executive, with the approval of the Panel, may make such delegations of authority as are necessary for the Panel's efficient operation.

(g) "Pleadings" means all papers, motions, responses, or replies of any kind filed with the Panel, including exhibits attached thereto, as well as all orders and notices that the Panel issues.

(h) "Tag-along action" refers to a civil action pending in a district court which involves common questions of fact with either (1) actions on a pending motion to transfer to create an MDL or (2) actions previously transferred to an existing MDL, and which the Panel would consider transferring under Section 1407.

(i) "Transferee district" is the federal district court to which the Panel transfers an action pursuant to Section 1407, for inclusion in an MDL.

(j) "Transferor district" is the federal district court where an action was pending prior to its transfer pursuant to Section 1407, for inclusion in an MDL, and where the Panel may remand that action at or before the conclusion of pretrial proceedings.

[Former Rule 1 adopted May 3, 1993, effective July 1, 1993. Renumbered Rule 1.1 September 1, 1998, effective November 2, 1998. Amended September 8, 2010, effective October 4, 2010.]

RULE 2.1 RULES AND PRACTICE

(a) Customary Practice. The Panel's customary practice shall govern, unless otherwise fixed by statute or these Rules.

(b) Failure to Comply With Rules. When a pleading does not comply with these Rules, the Clerk of the Panel may advise counsel of the deficiencies and set a date for full compliance. If counsel does not fully comply within the established time, the Clerk of the Panel shall file the non-complying pleading, but the Chair may thereafter order it stricken.

(c) Admission to Practice Before the Panel. Every member in good standing of the Bar of any district court of the United States is entitled to practice before the Panel, provided, however, that he or she has established and maintains a CM/ECF account with any United States federal court. Any attorney of record in any action transferred under Section 1407 may continue to represent his or her client in any district court of the United States to which such action is transferred. Parties are not required to obtain local counsel.

(d) Pendency of Motion or Conditional Order. The pendency of a motion, order to show cause, conditional transfer order or conditional remand order before the Panel pursuant to 28 U.S.C. § 1407 does not affect or suspend orders and pretrial proceedings in any pending federal district court action and does not limit the pretrial jurisdiction of that court. An order to transfer or remand pursuant to 28 U.S.C. § 1407 shall be effective only upon its filing with the clerk of the transferee district court.

(e) Reassignment. If for any reason the transferee judge is unable to continue those responsibilities, the Panel shall make the reassignment of a new transferee judge.

[Former Rule 5 adopted May 3, 1993, effective July 1, 1993. Renumbered Rule 1.2 September 1, 1998, effective November 2, 1998. Former Rule 4 adopted May 3, 1993, effective July 1, 1993. Renumbered Rule 1.3 and amended September 1, 1998, effective November 2, 1998. Former Rule 6 adopted May 3, 1993, effective July 1, 1993. Renumbered Rule 1.4 September 1, 1998, effective November 2, 1998. Former Rule 18 adopted May 3, 1993, effective July 1, 1993. Renumbered Rule 1.5 September 1, 1998, effective November 2, 1998. Former Rules 1.2, 1.3, 1.4, and 1.5 redesignated and amended September 8, 2010, effective October 4, 2010.]

RULE 3.1 ELECTRONIC RECORDS AND FILES; COPY FEES

(a) Electronic Record. Effective October 4, 2010, the official Panel record shall be the electronic file maintained on the Panel's servers. This record includes, but is not limited to, Panel pleadings, documents filed in paper and then scanned and made part of the electronic record, and Panel orders and notices filed. The official record also includes any documents or exhibits that may be impractical to scan. These documents and exhibits shall be kept in the Panel offices.

(b) Maintaining Records. Records and files generated prior to October 4, 2010, may be (i) maintained at the Panel offices, (ii) temporarily or permanently removed to such places at such times as the Clerk of the Panel or the Chair shall direct, or (iii) transferred whenever appropriate to the Federal Records Center.

(c) Fees. The Clerk of the Panel may charge fees for duplicating records and files, as prescribed by the Judicial Conference of the United States.

[Former Rule 2 adopted May 3, 1993, effective July 1, 1993. Renumbered Rule 5.1 and amended September 1, 1998, effective November 2, 1998. Former Rule 5.1 redesignated and amended September 8, 2010, effective October 4, 2010.]

RULE 3.2 ECF USERS: FILING REQUIREMENTS

(a) Form of Pleadings. This Rule applies to pleadings that ECF users file with the Panel.

(i) Each pleading shall bear the heading "Before the United States Judicial Panel on Multidistrict Litigation," the identification "MDL No.____" and the descriptive title designated by the Panel. If the Panel has not yet designated a title, counsel shall use an appropriate description.

(ii) The final page of each pleading shall contain the name, address, telephone number, fax number and email address of the attorney or party designated to receive service of pleadings in the case, and the name of each party represented.

(iii) Each brief submitted with a motion and any response to it shall not exceed 20 pages, exclusive of exhibits. Each reply shall not exceed 10 pages and shall address arguments raised in the response(s). Absent exceptional circumstances and those set forth in Rule 6.1(d), the Panel will not grant motions to exceed page limits.

(iv) Each pleading shall be typed in size 12 point font (for both text and footnotes), double spaced (text only), in a letter size document (8½ × 11 inch) with sequentially numbered pages.

(v) Each exhibit shall be separately numbered and clearly identified.

(vi) Proposed Panel orders shall not be submitted.

(b) Place of Filing. Counsel shall sign and verify all pleadings electronically in accordance with these Rules and the Panel's Administrative Policies and Procedures for Electronic Case Filing found at www.jpml.uscourts.gov. A pleading filed electronically constitutes a written document for the purpose of these Rules and the Federal Rules of Civil Procedure and is deemed the electronically signed original thereof. All pleadings, except by pro se litigants, shall conform with this Rule beginning on October 4, 2010.

(i)* Pleadings shall not be transmitted directly to any Panel member.

(c) **Attorney Registration.** Only attorneys identified, or to be identified, pursuant to Rule 4.1, shall file pleadings. Each of these attorneys must register as a Panel CM/ECF user through www.jpml.uscourts.gov. Registration/possession of a CM/ECF account with any United States federal court shall be deemed consent to receive electronic service of all Panel orders and notices as well as electronic service of pleadings from other parties before the Panel.

(d) **Courtesy Copy of Specified Pleadings.** Counsel shall serve the Clerk of the Panel, for delivery within 1 business day of filing, with a courtesy paper copy of any of the following pleadings: (i) a motion to transfer and its supporting brief; (ii) a response to a show cause order; (iii) a motion to vacate a conditional transfer order or a conditional remand order; and (iv) any response, reply, supplemental information or interested party response related to the pleadings listed in (i), (ii) and (iii). No courtesy copies of any other pleadings are required. Courtesy copies of pleadings totaling 10 pages or less (including any attachments) may be faxed to the Panel. The courtesy copy shall include all exhibits, shall be clearly marked "Courtesy Copy–Do Not File," shall contain the CM/ECF pleading number (if known), and shall be mailed or delivered to:

> Clerk of the Panel
> United States Judicial Panel on Multidistrict Litigation
> Thurgood Marshall Federal Judiciary Building
> One Columbus Circle, NE, Room G–255, North Lobby
> Washington, DC 20002–8041

(e) **Privacy Protections.** The privacy protections contained in Rule 5.2 of the Federal Rules of Civil Procedure shall apply to all Panel filings.

[Former Rule 3 adopted May 3, 1993, effective July 1, 1993. Renumbered Rule 5.11 and amended September 1, 1998, effective November 2, 1998; renumbered Rule 5.1.1 and amended March 25, 2010, effective April 1, 2010. Former Rule 7 adopted May 3, 1993, effective July 1, 1993. Renumbered Rule 5.12 and amended September 1, 1998, effective November 2, 1998. Amended April 2, 2001, effective April 2, 2001; paragraph (a) suspended in part by Order filed April 19, 2005; renumbered Rule 5.1.2 and amended March 25, 2010, effective April 1, 2010. Former Rule 9 adopted May 3, 1993, effective July 1, 1993. Renumbered Rule 7.1 and amended September 1, 1998, effective November 2, 1998. Amended April 2, 2001, effective April 2, 2001. Former Rules 5.1.1, 5.1.2, and 7.1 redesignated in part and amended September 8, 2010, effective October 4, 2010. Amended effective July 6, 2011; October 4, 2016.]

* [**Publisher's Note:** So in original. No subdivision (ii) promulgated.]

RULE 3.3   NON–ECF USERS: FILING REQUIREMENTS

(a) **Definition of Non–ECF Users.** Non–ECF users are all pro se individuals, unless the Panel orders otherwise. This Rule shall apply to all motions, responses and replies that non-ECF users file with the Panel.

(b) **Form of Pleadings.** Unless otherwise set forth in this Rule, the provisions of Rule 3.2 shall apply to non-ECF users.

(i) Each pleading shall be flat and unfolded; plainly written or typed in size 12 point font (for both text and footnotes), double spaced (text only), and printed single-sided on letter size (8 ½ × 11 inch) white paper with sequentially numbered pages; and fastened at the top-left corner without side binding or front or back covers.

(ii) Each exhibit shall be separately numbered and clearly identified. Any exhibits exceeding a cumulative total of 50 pages shall be bound separately.

(c) **Place of Filing.** File an original and one copy of all pleadings with the Clerk of the Panel by mailing or delivering to:

> Clerk of the Panel
> United States Judicial Panel on Multidistrict Litigation
> Thurgood Marshall Federal Judiciary Building
> One Columbus Circle, NE,
> Room G–255, North Lobby
> Washington, DC 20002–8041

(i) Pleadings not exceeding a total of 10 pages, including exhibits, may be faxed to the Panel office.

(ii) The Clerk of the Panel shall endorse the date for filing on all pleadings submitted for filing.

[Former Rule 3 adopted May 3, 1993, effective July 1, 1993. Renumbered Rule 5.11 and amended September 1, 1998, effective November 2, 1998; renumbered Rule 5.1.1 and amended March 25, 2010, effective April 1, 2010. Former Rule 7 adopted May 3, 1993, effective July 1, 1993. Renumbered Rule 5.12 and amended September 1, 1998, effective November 2, 1998. Amended April 2, 2001, effective April 2, 2001; paragraph (a) suspended in part by Order filed April 19, 2005; renumbered Rule 5.1.2 and amended March 25, 2010, effective April 1, 2010. Former Rule 9 adopted May 3, 1993, effective July 1, 1993. Renumbered Rule 7.1 and amended September 1, 1998, effective November 2, 1998. Amended April 2, 2001, effective April 2, 2001. Former Rules 5.1.1, 5.1.2, and 7.1 redesignated in part and amended September 8, 2010, effective October 4, 2010.]

RULE 4.1   SERVICE OF PLEADINGS

(a) **Proof of Service.** The Panel's notice of electronic filing shall constitute service of pleadings. Registration/possession by counsel of a CM/ECF account with any United States federal court shall be deemed consent to receive electronic service of all pleadings. All pleadings shall contain a proof of service on all other parties in all involved actions. The proof of service shall indicate the name and manner of service. If a party is not represented by counsel, the proof of service shall indicate the name of the party and the party's last known address. The proof of service shall indicate why any person named as a party in a constituent complaint was not served with the Section 1407 pleading.

(b) **Service Upon Transferor Court.** The proof of service pertaining to motions for a transfer or remand pursuant to 28 U.S.C. § 1407 shall certify that counsel has transmitted a copy of the motion for filing to the clerk of each district court where an affected action is pending.

(c) **Notice of Appearance.** Within 14 days after the issuance of a (i) notice of filing of a motion to initiate transfer under Rule 6.2, (ii) notice of filed opposition to a CTO under Rule 7.1, (iii) a show cause order under Rules* 8.1, (iv) notice of filed opposition to a CRO under Rule 10.2, or (v) notice of filing of a motion to remand under Rule 10.3, each party or designated attorney as required hereinafter shall file a Notice of Appearance notifying the Clerk of the Panel of the name, address and email address of the attorney designated to file and receive service of all pleadings. Each party shall designate only one attorney. Any party not represented by counsel shall be served by mailing such pleadings to the party's last known address. Except in extraordinary circumstances, the Panel will not grant requests for an extension of time to file the Notice of Appearance.

(d) Liaison Counsel. If the transferee district court appoints liaison counsel, this Rule shall be satisfied by serving each party in each affected action and all liaison counsel. Liaison counsel shall receive copies of all Panel orders concerning their particular litigation and shall be responsible for distribution to the parties for whom he or she serves as liaison counsel.

[Former Rule 8 adopted May 3, 1993, effective July 1, 1993. Renumbered Rule 5.2 and amended September 1, 1998, effective November 2, 1998; March 26, 2009, effective December 1, 2009. Former Rule 5.2 redesignated and amended September 8, 2010, effective October 4, 2010. Technical revisions effective July 6, 2011.]

* [Publisher's Note: So in original.]

RULE 5.1 CORPORATE DISCLOSURE STATEMENT

(a) Requirements. A nongovernmental corporate party must file a disclosure statement that: (1) identifies any parent corporation and any publicly held corporation owning 10% or more of its stock; or (2) states that there is no such corporation.

(b) Deadline. A party shall file the corporate disclosure statement within 14 days after issuance of a notice of the filing of a motion to transfer or remand, an order to show cause, or a motion to vacate a conditional transfer order or a conditional remand order.

(c) Updating. Each party must update its corporate disclosure statement to reflect any change in the information therein (i) until the matter before the Panel is decided, and (ii) within 14 days after issuance of a notice of the filing of any subsequent motion to transfer or remand, order to show cause, or motion to vacate a conditional transfer order or a conditional remand order in that docket.

[Former Rule 2 adopted May 3, 1993, effective July 1, 1993. Renumbered Rule 5.1 and amended September 1, 1998, effective November 2, 1998. Former Rule 5.3 redesignated and amended September 8, 2010, effective October 4, 2010. Amended effective July 6, 2011.]

RULE 5.1.3 FILING OF PAPERS: COMPUTER GENERATED DISK REQUIRED [DELETED SEPT. 8, 2010, EFF. OCT. 4, 2010]

[Added May 22, 2000, effective June 1, 2000. And amended July 30, 2007, effective July 30, 2007; renumbered Rule 5.1.3 and amended March 25, 2010, effective April 1, 2010. Deleted September 8, 2010, effective October 4, 2010.]

RULE 6.1 MOTION PRACTICE

(a) Application. This Rule governs all motions requesting Panel action generally. More specific provisions may apply to motions to transfer (Rule 6.2), miscellaneous motions (Rule 6.3), conditional transfer orders (Rule 7.1), show cause orders (Rule 8.1), conditional remand orders (Rule 10.2) and motions to remand (Rule 10.3).

(b) Form of Motions. All motions shall briefly describe the action or relief sought and shall include:

(i) a brief which concisely states the background of the litigation and movant's factual and legal contentions;

(ii) a numbered schedule providing

(A) the complete name of each action involved, listing the full name of each party included as such on the district court's docket sheet, not shortened by the use of references such as "et al." or "etc.";

(B) the district court and division where each action is pending;

(C) the civil action number of each action; and

(D) the name of the judge assigned each action, if known;

(iii) a proof of service providing

(A) a service list listing the full name of each party included on the district court's docket sheet and the complaint, including opt-in plaintiffs not listed on the docket sheet; and

(B) in actions where there are 25 or more plaintiffs listed on the docket sheet, list the first named plaintiff with the reference "et al." if all the plaintiffs are represented by the same attorney(s);

(iv) a copy of all complaints and docket sheets for all actions listed on the Schedule; and

(v) exhibits, if any, identified by number or letter and a descriptive title.

(c) Responses and Joinders. Any other party may file a response within 21 days after filing of a motion. Failure to respond to a motion shall be treated as that party's acquiescence to it. A joinder in a motion shall not add any action to that motion.

(d) Replies. The movant may file a reply within 7 days after the lapse of the time period for filing a response. Where a movant is replying to more than one response in opposition, the movant may file a consolidated reply with a limit of 20 pages.

(e) Alteration of Time Periods. The Clerk of the Panel has the discretion to shorten or enlarge the time periods set forth in this Rule as necessary.

(f) Notification of Developments. Counsel shall promptly notify the Clerk of the Panel of any development that would partially or completely moot any Panel matter.

[Former Rule 10 adopted May 3, 1993, effective July 1, 1993. Renumbered Rule 7.2 and amended September 1, 1998, effective November 2, 1998. Amended April 2, 2001, effective April 2, 2001; March 26, 2009, December 1, 2009. Former Rule 7.2 redesignated in part and amended September 8, 2010, effective October 4, 2010.]

RULE 6.2 MOTIONS TO TRANSFER FOR COORDINATED OR CONSOLIDATED PRETRIAL PROCEEDINGS

(a) Initiation of Transfer. A party to an action may initiate proceedings to transfer under Section 1407 by filing a motion in accordance with these Rules. A copy of the motion shall be filed in each district court where the motion affects a pending action.

(b) Notice of Filing of Motion to Transfer. Upon receipt of a motion, the Clerk of the Panel shall issue a "Notice of Filing of Motion to Transfer" to the service list recipients. The Notice shall contain the following: the filing date of the motion, caption, MDL docket number, briefing schedule and pertinent Panel policies. After a motion is filed, the Clerk of the Panel shall consider any other pleading to be a response unless the pleading adds an action. The Clerk of the Panel may designate such a pleading as a motion, and distribute a briefing schedule applicable to all or some of the parties, as appropriate.

(c) Notice of Appearance. Within 14 days of issuance of a "Notice of the Filing of a Motion to Transfer," each party or designated attorney shall file a Notice of Appearance in accordance with Rule 4.1(c).

(d) Notice of Potential Tag-along Actions. Any party or counsel in a new group of actions under consideration for transfer under Section 1407 shall promptly notify the Clerk of the Panel of any potential tag-along actions in which that party is also named or in which that counsel appears.

(e) Interested Party Responses. Any party or counsel in one or more potential tag-along actions as well as amicus curiae may file a response to a pending motion to transfer. Such a pleading shall be deemed an Interested Party Response.

(f) Amendment to a Motion. Before amending a motion to transfer, a party shall first contact the Clerk of the Panel to ascertain whether such amendment is feasible and permissible considering the Panel's hearing schedule. Any such amendment shall be entitled "Amendment to Motion for Transfer," and shall clearly and specifically identify and describe the nature of the amendment.

(i) Where the amended motion includes new civil actions, the amending party shall file a "Schedule of Additional Actions" and a revised Proof of Service.

(ii) The Proof of Service shall state (A) that all new counsel have been served with a copy of the amendment and all previously-filed motion papers, and (B) that all counsel previously served with the original motion have been served with a copy of the amendment.

(iii) The Clerk of the Panel may designate the amendment with a different denomination (*e.g.*, a notice of potential tag-along action(s)) and treatment.

(h) Oral Argument*. The Panel shall schedule oral arguments as needed and as set forth in Rule 11.1.

[Former Rule 10 adopted May 3, 1993, effective July 1, 1993. Renumbered Rule 7.2 and amended September 1, 1998, effective November 2, 1998. Amended April 2, 2001, effective April 2, 2001; March 26, 2009, December 1, 2009. Former Rule 15 adopted May 3, 1993, effective July 1, 1993. Renumbered Rule 6.2 and amended September 1, 1998, effective November 2, 1998. Former Rule 7.2 redesignated in part and amended September 8, 2010, effective October 4, 2010. Technical revisions effective July 6, 2011.]

* **[Publisher's Note:** So in original.]

RULE 6.3 MOTIONS FOR MISCELLANEOUS RELIEF

(a) Definition. Motions for miscellaneous relief include, but are not limited to, requests for extensions of time, exemption from ECF requirements, page limit extensions, or expedited consideration of any motion.

(b) Panel Action. The Panel, through the Clerk, may act upon any motion for miscellaneous relief, at any time, without waiting for a response. A motion for extension of time to file a pleading or perform an act under these Rules must state specifically the revised date sought and must be filed before the deadline for filing the pleading or performing the act. Any party aggrieved by the Clerk of the Panel's action may file objections for consideration. Absent exceptional circumstances, the Panel will not grant any extensions of time to file a notice of opposition to either a conditional transfer order or a conditional remand order.

[Former Rule 15 adopted May 3, 1993, effective July 1, 1993. Renumbered Rule 6.2 and amended September 1, 1998, effective November 2, 1998. Former Rule 6.2 redesignated and amended September 8, 2010, effective October 4, 2010.]

RULE 7.1 CONDITIONAL TRANSFER ORDERS (CTO) FOR TAG–ALONG ACTIONS

(a) Notice of Potential Tag-along Actions. Any party or counsel in actions previously transferred under Section 1407 shall promptly notify the Clerk of the Panel of any potential tag-along actions in which that party is also named or in which that counsel appears. The Panel has several options: (i) filing a CTO under Rule 7.1, (ii) filing a show cause order under Rule 8.1, or (iii) declining to act (Rule 7.1(b)(i)).

(b) Initiation of CTO. Upon learning of the pendency of a potential tag-along action, the Clerk of the Panel may enter a conditional order transferring that action to the previously designated transferee district court for the reasons expressed in the Panel's previous opinions and orders. The Clerk of the Panel shall serve this order on each party to the litigation but shall not send the order to the clerk of the transferee district court until 7 days after its entry.

(i)* If the Clerk of the Panel determines that a potential tag-along action is not appropriate for inclusion in an MDL proceeding and does not enter a CTO, an involved party may move for its transfer pursuant to Rule 6.1.

(c) Notice of Opposition to CTO. Any party opposing the transfer shall file a notice of opposition with the Clerk of the Panel within the 7–day period. In such event, the Clerk of the Panel shall not transmit the transfer order to the clerk of the transferee district court, but shall notify the parties of the briefing schedule.

(d) Failure to Respond. Failure to respond to a CTO shall be treated as that party's acquiescence to it.

(e) Notice of Appearance. Within 14 days after the issuance of a "Notice of Filed Opposition" to a CTO, each opposing party or designated attorney shall file a Notice of Appearance in accordance with Rule 4.1(c).

(f) Motion to Vacate CTO. Within 14 days of the filing of its notice of opposition, the party opposing transfer shall file a motion to vacate the CTO and brief in support thereof. The Clerk of the Panel shall set the motion for the next appropriate hearing session. Failure to file and serve a motion and brief shall be treated as withdrawal of the opposition and the Clerk of the Panel shall forthwith transmit the order to the clerk of the transferee district court.

(g) Notification of Developments. Parties to an action subject to a CTO shall notify the Clerk of the Panel if that action is no longer pending in its transferor district court.

(h) Effective Date of CTO. CTOs are effective when filed with the clerk of the transferee district court.

[Former Rule 12 adopted May 3, 1993, effective July 1, 1993. Renumbered Rule 7.4 and amended September 1, 1998, effective November 2, 1998. Amended April 2, 2001, effective April 2, 2001; March 26, 2009, December 1, 2009. Former Rule 7.4 redesignated and amended September 8, 2010, effective October 4, 2010. Technical revisions effective July 6, 2011.]

* **[Publisher's Note:** So in original. No subdivision (ii) promulgated.]

RULE 7.2   MISCELLANEOUS PROVISIONS CONCERNING TAG–ALONG ACTIONS

(a) Potential Tag-alongs in Transferee Court. Potential tag-along actions filed in the transferee district do not require Panel action. A party should request assignment of such actions to the Section 1407 transferee judge in accordance with applicable local rules.

(b) Failure to Serve. Failure to serve one or more of the defendants in a potential tag-along action with the complaint and summons as required by Rule 4 of the Federal Rules of Civil Procedure does not preclude transfer of such action under Section 1407. Such failure, however, may constitute grounds for denying the proposed transfer where prejudice can be shown. The failure of the Clerk of the Panel to serve a CTO on all plaintiffs or defendants or their counsel may constitute grounds for the Clerk to reinstate the CTO or for the aggrieved party to seek § 1407(c) remand.

[Former Rule 13 adopted May 3, 1993, effective July 1, 1993. Renumbered Rule 7.5 and amended September 1, 1998, effective November 2, 1998. Amended April 2, 2001, effective April 2, 2001. Former Rule 7.5 redesignated and amended September 8, 2010, effective October 4, 2010. Amended effective July 6, 2011.]

RULE 8.1   SHOW CAUSE ORDERS

(a) Entry of Show Cause Order. When transfer of multidistrict litigation is being considered on the initiative of the Panel pursuant to 28 U.S.C. § 1407(c)(i), the Clerk of the Panel may enter an order directing the parties to show cause why a certain civil action or actions should not be transferred for coordinated or consolidated pretrial proceedings. Any party shall also promptly notify the Clerk of the Panel whenever they learn of any other federal district court actions which are similar to those which the show cause order encompasses.

(b) Notice of Appearance. Within 14 days of the issuance of an order to show cause, each party or designated attorney shall file a Notice of Appearance in accordance with Rule 4.1(c).

(c) Responses. Unless otherwise provided by order, any party may file a response within 21 days of the filing of the show cause order. Failure to respond to a show cause order shall be treated as that party's acquiescence to the Panel action.

(d) Replies. Within 7 days after the lapse of the time period for filing a response, any party may file a reply.

(e) Notification of Developments. Counsel shall promptly notify the Clerk of the Panel of any development that would partially or completely moot any matter subject to a show cause order.

[Former Rule 7.3 adopted May 3, 1993, effective July 1, 1993. Renumbered Rule 7.3 and amended September 1, 1998, effective November 2, 1998; March 26, 2009, effective December 1, 2009. Former Rule 7.3 redesignated and amended September 8, 2010, effective October 4, 2010.]

RULE 9.1   TRANSFER OF FILES; NOTIFICATION REQUIREMENTS

(a) Notice to Transferee Court Clerk. The Clerk of the Panel, via a notice of electronic filing, will notify the clerk of the transferee district whenever a Panel transfer order should be filed in the transferee district court. Upon receipt of an electronically certified copy of a Panel transfer order from the clerk of the transferee district, the clerk of the transferor district shall transmit the record of each transferred action to the transferee district and then, unless Rule 9.1(b) applies, close the transferred action in the transferor district.

(b) Retention of Claims. If the transfer order provides for the separation and simultaneous remand of any claim, cross-claim, counterclaim, or third-party claim, the clerk of the transferor district shall retain jurisdiction over any such claim and shall not close the action.

(c) Notice to Clerk of Panel. The clerk of the transferee district shall promptly provide the Clerk of the Panel with the civil action numbers assigned to all transferred actions and the identity of liaison counsel, if or when designated. The clerk of the transferee district shall also promptly notify the Clerk of the Panel of any dispositive ruling that terminates a transferred action.

[Former Rule 19 adopted May 3, 1993, effective July 1, 1993. Renumbered Rule 1.6 and amended September 1, 1998, effective November 2, 1998. Former Rule 1.6 redesignated in part and amended September 8, 2010, effective October 4, 2010.]

RULE 10.1   TERMINATION AND REMAND

(a) Termination. Where the transferee district court terminates an action by valid order, including but not limited to summary judgment, judgment of dismissal and judgment upon stipulation, the transferee district court clerk shall transmit a copy of that order to the Clerk of the Panel. The terminated action shall not be remanded to the transferor court and the transferee court shall retain the original files and records unless the transferee judge or the Panel directs otherwise.

(b) Initiation of Remand. Typically, the transferee judge recommends remand of an action, or a part of it, to the transferor court at any time by filing a suggestion of remand with the Panel. However, the Panel may remand an action or any separable claim, cross-claim, counterclaim or third-party claim within it, upon

(i) the transferee court's suggestion of remand,

(ii) the Panel's own initiative by entry of an order to show cause, a conditional remand order or other appropriate order, or

(iii) motion of any party.

[Former Rule 14 adopted May 3, 1993, effective July 1, 1993. Renumbered Rule 7.6 and amended September 1, 1998, effective November 2, 1998. Amended April 2, 2001, effective April 2, 2001; March 26, 2009, effective December 1, 2009. Former Rule 7.6 redesignated in part and amended September 8, 2010, effective October 4, 2010.]

RULE 10.2   CONDITIONAL REMAND ORDERS (CRO)

(a) Entering a CRO. Upon the suggestion of the transferee judge or the Panel's own initiative, the Clerk of the Panel shall enter a conditional order remanding the action or actions to the transferor district court. The Clerk of the Panel shall serve this order on each party to the litigation but shall not send the order to the clerk of the transferee district court for 7 days from the entry thereof.

(i)* The Panel may, on its own initiative, also enter an order that the parties show cause why a matter should not be remanded. Rule 8.1 applies to responses and replies with respect to such a show cause order.

(b) Notice of Opposition. Any party opposing the CRO shall file a notice of opposition with the Clerk of the Panel within the 7–day period. In such event, the Clerk of the Panel shall not transmit the remand order to the clerk of the transferee district court and shall notify the parties of the briefing schedule.

(c) Failure to Respond. Failure to respond to a CRO shall be treated as that party's acquiescence to it.

(d) Notice of Appearance. Within 14 days after the issuance of a "Notice of Filed Opposition" to a CRO, each opposing party or designated attorney shall file a Notice of Appearance in accordance with Rule 4.1(c).

(e) Motion to Vacate CRO. Within 14 days of the filing of its notice of opposition, the party opposing remand shall file a motion to vacate the CRO and brief in support thereof. The Clerk of the Panel shall set the motion for the next appropriate Panel hearing session. Failure to file and serve a motion and brief shall be treated as a withdrawal of the opposition and the Clerk of the Panel shall forthwith transmit the order to the clerk of the transferee district court.

(f) Effective Date of CRO. CROs are not effective until filed with the clerk of the transferee district court.

[Former Rule 14 adopted May 3, 1993, effective July 1, 1993. Renumbered Rule 7.6 and amended September 1, 1998, effective November 2, 1998. Amended April 2, 2001, effective April 2, 2001; March 26, 2009, effective December 1, 2009. Former Rule 7.6 redesignated in part and amended September 8, 2010, effective October 4, 2010. Technical revisions effective July 6, 2011.]

* **[Publisher's Note:** So in original. No subdivision (ii) promulgated.]

RULE 10.3   MOTION TO REMAND

(a) Requirements of the Motion. If the Clerk of the Panel does not enter a CRO, a party may file a motion to remand to the transferor court pursuant to these Rules. Because the Panel is reluctant to order a remand absent the suggestion of the transferee judge, the motion must include:

(i) An affidavit reciting whether the movant has requested a suggestion of remand and the judge's response, whether the parties have completed common discovery and other pretrial proceedings, and whether the parties have complied with all transferee court orders.

(ii) A copy of the transferee district court's final pretrial order, if entered.

(b) Filing Copy of Motion. Counsel shall file a copy of the motion to remand in the affected transferee district court.

(c) Notice of Appearance. Within 14 days of the issuance of a "Notice of Filing" of a motion to remand, each party or designated attorney shall file a Notice of Appearance in accordance with Rule 4.1(c).

[Former Rule 14 adopted May 3, 1993, effective July 1, 1993. Renumbered Rule 7.6 and amended September 1, 1998, effective November 2, 1998. Amended April 2, 2001, effective April 2, 2001; March 26, 2009, effective December 1, 2009. Former Rule 7.6 redesignated in part and amended September 8, 2010, effective October 4, 2010. Technical revisions effective July 6, 2011.]

RULE 10.4   TRANSFER OF FILES ON REMAND

(a) Designating the Record. Upon receipt of an order to remand from the Clerk of the Panel, the parties shall furnish forthwith to the transferee district clerk a stipulation or designation of the contents of the record or part thereof to be remanded.

(b) Transfer of Files. Upon receipt of an order to remand from the Clerk of the Panel, the transferee district shall transmit to the clerk of the transferor district the following concerning each remanded action:

(i) a copy of the individual docket sheet for each action remanded;

(ii) a copy of the master docket sheet, if applicable;

(iii) the entire file for each action remanded, as originally received from the transferor district and augmented as set out in this Rule;

(iv) a copy of the final pretrial order, if applicable; and

(v) a "record on remand" as designated by the parties in accordance with 10.4(a).

[Former Rule 19 adopted May 3, 1993, effective July 1, 1993. Renumbered Rule 1.6 and amended September 1, 1998, effective November 2, 1998. Former Rule 1.6 redesignated in part and amended September 8, 2010, effective October 4, 2010.]

RULE 11.1   HEARING SESSIONS AND ORAL ARGUMENT

(a) Schedule. The Panel shall schedule sessions for oral argument and consideration of other matters as desirable or necessary. The Chair shall determine the time, place and agenda for each hearing session. The Clerk of the Panel shall give appropriate notice to counsel for all parties. The Panel may continue its consideration of any scheduled matters.

(b) Oral Argument Statement. Any party affected by a motion may file a separate statement setting forth reasons why oral argument should, or need not, be heard. Such statements shall be captioned "Reasons Why Oral Argument Should [Need Not] Be Heard" and shall be limited to 2 pages.

(i)* The parties affected by a motion to transfer may agree to waive oral argument. The Panel will take this into consideration in determining the need for oral argument.

(c) Hearing Session. The Panel shall not consider transfer or remand of any action pending in a federal district court when any party timely opposes such transfer or remand without first holding a hearing session for the presentation of oral argument. The Panel may dispense with oral argument if it determines that:

(i) the dispositive issue(s) have been authoritatively decided; or

(ii) the facts and legal arguments are adequately presented and oral argument would not significantly aid the decisional process.

Unless otherwise ordered, the Panel shall consider all other matters, such as a motion for reconsideration, upon the basis of the pleadings.

(d) Notification of Oral Argument. The Panel shall promptly notify counsel of those matters in which oral argument is scheduled, as well as those matters that the Panel will consider on the pleadings. The Clerk of the Panel shall require counsel to file and serve notice of their intent to either

make or waive oral argument. Failure to do so shall be deemed a waiver of oral argument. If counsel does not attend oral argument, the matter shall not be rescheduled and that party's position shall be treated as submitted for decision on the basis of the pleadings filed.

(i) Absent Panel approval and for good cause shown, only those parties to actions who have filed a motion or written response to a motion or order shall be permitted to present oral argument.

(ii) The Panel will not receive oral testimony except upon notice, motion and an order expressly providing for it.

(e) Duty to Confer. Counsel in an action set for oral argument shall confer separately prior to that argument for the purpose of organizing their arguments and selecting representatives to present all views without duplication. Oral argument is a means for counsel to emphasize the key points of their arguments, and to update the Panel on any events since the conclusion of briefing.

(f) Time Limit for Oral Argument. Barring exceptional circumstances, the Panel shall allot a maximum of 20 minutes for oral argument in each matter. The time shall be divided among those with varying viewpoints. Counsel for the moving party or parties shall generally be heard first.

[Former Rule 16 adopted May 3, 1998, effective July 1, 1993. Renumbered Rule 16.1 and amended September 1, 1998, effective November 2, 1998. Amended April 2, 2001, effective April 2, 2001. Former Rule 16.1 redesignated and amended September 8, 2010, effective October 4, 2010.]

* [**Publisher's Note:** So in original. No subdivision (ii) promulgated.]

RULES 12 TO 15. [RESERVED]

II. RULES FOR MULTICIRCUIT PETITIONS FOR REVIEW UNDER 28 U.S.C. § 2112(a)(3)

RULE 25.1 DEFINITIONS

The Panel promulgates these Rules pursuant to its authority under 28 U.S.C. § 2112(a)(3) to provide a means for the random selection of one circuit court of appeals to hear consolidated petitions for review of agency decisions.

An "Agency" means an agency, board, commission or officer of the United States government, that has received two or more petitions for review in a circuit court of appeals to enjoin, set aside, suspend, modify or otherwise review or enforce an action.

[Former Rule 20 adopted May 3, 1993, effective July 1, 1993. Renumbered Rule 25.1 and amended September 1, 1998, effective November 2, 1998. Amended September 8, 2010, effective October 4, 2010.]

RULE 25.2 FILING OF NOTICES

(a) Submitting Notice. An affected agency shall submit a notice of multicircuit petitions for review pursuant to 28 U.S.C. § 2112(a)(3) to the Clerk of the Panel by electronic means in the manner these Rules require and in accordance with the Panel's Administrative Policies and Procedures for Electronic

Case Filing, except that the portion of Rule 3.2(d) requiring a courtesy copy is suspended in its entirety.

(b) Accompaniments to Notices. All notices of multicircuit petitions for review shall include:

(i) a copy of each involved petition for review as the petition for review is defined in 28 U.S.C. § 2112(a)(2);

(ii) a schedule giving

(A) the date of the relevant agency order;

(B) the case name of each petition for review involved;

(C) the circuit court of appeals in which each petition for review is pending;

(D) the appellate docket number of each petition for review;

(E) the date of filing by the court of appeals of each petition for review; and

(F) the date of receipt by the agency of each petition for review; and

(iii) proof of service (*see* Rule 25.3).

(c) Scope of Notice. All notices of multicircuit petitions for review shall embrace exclusively petitions for review filed in the courts of appeals within 10 days after issuance of an agency order and received by the affected agency from the petitioners within that 10–day period.

(d) Filing at the Panel. The Clerk of the Panel shall file the notice of multicircuit petitions for review and endorse thereon the date of filing.

(e) Filing With Each Circuit Clerk. The affected agency shall file copies of notices of multicircuit petitions for review with the clerk of each circuit court of appeals in which a petition for review is pending.

[Former Rule 21 adopted May 3, 1993, effective July 1, 1993. Renumbered Rule 25.2 and amended September 1, 1998, effective November 2, 1998. Amended September 8, 2010, effective October 4, 2010. Technical revisions effective July 6, 2011.]

RULE 25.3 SERVICE OF NOTICES

(a) Proof of Service. Notices of multicircuit petitions for review shall include proof of service on all other parties in the petitions for review included in the notice. Rule 25 of the Federal Rules of Appellate Procedure governs service and proof of service. The proof of service shall state the name, address and email address of each person served and shall indicate the party represented by each and the manner in which service was accomplished on each party. If a party is not represented by counsel, the proof of service shall indicate the name of the party and his or her last known address. The affected party shall submit proof of service for filing with the Clerk of the Panel and shall send copies thereof to each person included within the proof of service.

(b) Service on Clerk of Circuit. The proof of service pertaining to notices of multicircuit petitions for review shall certify the affected party has mailed or delivered copies of the notices to the clerk of each circuit court of appeals in which a petition for review is pending that is included in the notice. The Clerk shall file the notice with the circuit court.

[Former Rule 22 adopted May 3, 1993, effective July 1, 1993. Renumbered Rule 25.3 September 1, 1998, effective November 2, 1998. Amended September 8, 2010, effective October 4, 2010.]

RULE 25.4 FORM OF NOTICES; PLACE OF FILING

(a) Unless otherwise provided here, Rule 3.2 governs the form of a notice of multicircuit petitions for review. Each notice shall bear the heading "Notice to the United States Judicial Panel on Multidistrict Litigation of Multicircuit Petitions for Review," followed by a brief caption identifying the involved agency, the relevant agency order, and the date of the order.

(b) Rule 3.2(b) and (c) govern the manner of filing a notice of multicircuit petitions for review.

[Former Rule 23 adopted May 3, 1993, effective July 1, 1993. Renumbered Rule 25.4 and amended September 1, 1998, effective November 2, 1998. Amended September 8, 2010, effective October 4, 2010.]

RULE 25.5 RANDOM SELECTION

(a) Selection Process. Upon filing a notice of multicircuit petitions for review, the Clerk of the Panel shall randomly select a circuit court of appeals from a drum containing an entry for each circuit wherein a constituent petition for review is pending. Multiple petitions for review pending in a single circuit shall be allotted only a single entry in the drum. A designated deputy other than the random selector shall witness the random selection. Thereafter, an order on behalf of the Panel shall be issued, signed by the random selector and the witness,

    (i) consolidating the petitions for review in the court of appeals for the circuit that was randomly selected; and

    (ii) designating that circuit as the one in which the record is to be filed pursuant to Rules 16 and 17 of the Federal Rules of Appellate Procedure.

(b) Effective Date. A consolidation of petitions for review shall be effective when the Clerk of the Panel enters the consolidation order.

[Former Rule 24 adopted May 3, 1993, effective July 1, 1993. Renumbered Rule 17.1 September 1, 1998, effective November 2, 1998. Former Rule 17.1 redesignated and amended September 8, 2010, effective October 4, 2010.]

RULE 25.6 SERVICE OF PANEL CONSOLIDATION ORDER

(a) The Clerk of the Panel shall serve the Panel's consolidation order on the affected agency through the individual or individuals, as identified in Rule 25.2(a), who submitted the notice of multicircuit petitions for review on behalf of the agency.

(b) That individual or individuals, or anyone else designated by the agency, shall promptly serve the Panel's consolidation order on all other parties in all petitions for review included in the Panel's consolidation order, and shall promptly submit a proof of that service to the Clerk of the Panel. Rule 25.3 governs service.

(c) The Clerk of the Panel shall serve the Panel's consolidation order on the clerks of all circuit courts of appeals that were among the candidates for the Panel's random selection.

[Former Rule 25 adopted May 3, 1993, effective July 1, 1993. Renumbered Rule 25.5 and amended September 1, 1998, effective November 2, 1998. Former Rule 25.5 redesignated and amended September 8, 2010, effective October 4, 2010.]

III. CONVERSION TABLE

New to Old:

New Rule / Previous Rule		New Rule / Previous Rule	
1.1	1.1	9.1	1.6
2.1	1.2, 1.3, 1.4, 1.5	10.1	7.6
3.1	5.1	10.2	7.6
3.2	5.1.1, 5.1.2, 7.1	10.3	7.6
3.3	5.1.1, 5.1.2, 7.1	10.4	1.6
4.1	5.2	11.1	16.1
5.1	5.3	25.1	25.1
6.1	7.2	25.2	25.1, 25.2
6.2	7.2	25.3	25.3
6.3	6.2	25.4	25.1, 25.4
7.1	7.4	25.5	17.1
7.2	7.5	25.6	25.5
8.1	7.3		

Old to New:

Previous Rule / New Rule		Previous Rule / New Rule	
1.1	1.1	7.1	3.2, 3.3
1.2	2.1	7.2	6.1
1.3	2.1	7.3	8.1
1.4	2.1	7.4	7.1
1.5	2.1	7.5	7.2
1.6	10.4	7.6	10.1
5.1	3.1	16.1	11.1
5.1.1	3.2, 3.3	17.1	25.5
5.1.2	3.2, 3.3	25.1	25.1, 25.2, 25.4
5.1.3	-	25.2	25.2
5.2	4.1	25.3	25.3
5.3	5.1	25.4	25.4
6.2	6.3	25.5	25.6

[October 2010.]

ELECTRONIC CASE FILING ADMINISTRATIVE POLICIES AND PROCEDURES

1. DEFINITIONS.

1.1 **"ELECTRONIC FILING SYSTEM"** (ECF) refers to the United States Judicial Panel on Multidistrict Litigation's (the Panel's) automated system that receives and stores documents filed in electronic form. The program is part of the CM/ECF (Case Management/Electronic Case Files) software which was developed for the Federal Judiciary by the Administrative Office of the United States Courts.

1.2 **"CLERK OF THE PANEL"** means the official appointed by the Panel to act as Clerk of the Panel and shall include those deputized by the Clerk of the Panel to perform or assist in the performance of the duties of the Clerk of the Panel.

1.3 **"FILING USER"** is an individual who has a Panel-issued login and password to file documents electronically. In accordance with Rule 1.4 of the Rules of Procedure of the United States Judicial Panel on Multidistrict Litigation (the Panel Rules), every member in good standing of the Bar of any district court of the United States is entitled to practice before the Judicial Panel on Multidistrict Litigation.

1.4 **"NOTICE OF ELECTRONIC FILING"** (NEF) is a notice automatically generated by the Electronic Filing System at the time a document is filed with the system, setting forth the time of filing, the date the document is entered on the docket, the name of the party and attorney filing the document, the type of document, the text of the docket entry, the name of the party and/or attorney receiving the notice, and an electronic link (hyperlink) to the filed document, which allows recipients to retrieve the document automatically. A document shall not be considered filed for the purposes of the Panel's Rules until the filing party receives a system generated Notice of Electronic Filing with a hyperlink to the electronically filed document.

1.5 **"PACER"** (**Public Access to Court Electronic Records**) is an automated system that allows an individual to view, print and download Panel docket information over the Internet.

1.6 **"PDF"** (**Portable Document Format**). A document file created with a word processor, or a paper document which has been scanned, must be converted to portable document format to be filed electronically with the Panel. Converted files contain the extension ".pdf".

1.7 **"TECHNICAL FAILURE"** is defined as a failure of Panel owned/leased hardware, software, and/or telecommunications facility which results in the inability of a Filing User to submit a filing electronically. Technical failure does not include malfunctioning of a Filing User's equipment.

2. SCOPE OF ELECTRONIC FILING.

(a) All multidistrict litigation matters (MDLs) brought before the Panel under 28 U.S.C. § 1407 shall be assigned to the Electronic Filing System. Effective October 1, 2010, all MDLs, proceedings, motions, memoranda of law and other pleadings or documents filed with the Panel in new and existing dockets must be filed using CM/ECF unless otherwise specified herein.

(b) The filing of all MDL papers shall be accomplished electronically under procedures outlined in the Panel's CM/ECF User Manual.

(c) A party proceeding pro se shall not file electronically, unless otherwise permitted by the Panel. Pro se filers shall file paper originals of all documents. The clerk's office will scan these original documents into the JPML's electronic system, unless otherwise sealed.

3. ELIGIBILITY, REGISTRATION, PASSWORDS.

(a) Any attorney admitted to the Bar of any United States district court is eligible to practice before the Panel. Unless otherwise exempt as set forth herein, to become a Filing User, an attorney must register as a Filing User by completing the prescribed registration form and submitting it to the Clerk of the Panel.

(b) Registration as a Filing User constitutes consent to electronic service of all documents filed with or issued by the Panel in accordance with the Panel Rules.

(c) By submitting the online registration form, the Filing Users certify that they have read and are familiar with the Panel Rules and these administrative policies and procedures governing electronic filing and the method of training in the System used prior to becoming a Filing User. Filing users must also have a PACER account. An individual may register more than one Internet email address. The clerk's office will email the login and password to the attorney.

(d) Once the registration is processed by the clerk, the Filing User shall protect the security of the User password and immediately notify the clerk if the Filing User learns that the password has been compromised. Filing Users may be subject to sanctions for failure to comply with this provision. After registering, attorneys may change their passwords. If an attorney comes to believe that the security of an existing password has been compromised and that a threat to the System exists, the attorney must change his or her password immediately.

(e) Exemptions from mandatory electronic filing may be granted upon submission of a written request to the clerk. The written request shall include a supporting affidavit showing a substantial undue hardship. Final authority to grant such request is vested in the Clerk of the Panel or his/her designee.

(f)(1) Each attorney is responsible for keeping his/her contact information up to date. If an attorney is leaving a law firm and is the attorney of record on an existing case and representation in the case will remain with the law firm, withdrawal and substitution of counsel must be made prior to the attorney's termination in the law firm, for the following reason:

The attorney leaving the firm has an email address with the law firm he or she is leaving on record with the Panel. This email address may be disabled by the law firm as soon as the attorney terminates his/her employment. The electronic notices in CM/ECF will continue to go to the terminated attorney's email address at the former firm. If the email address is disabled at the law firm, the attorney will not receive the electronic notice. If a withdrawal/substitution of counsel has not been filed prior to the attorney leaving the firm, the law firm should not disable the email account of the attorney leaving the firm until another attorney in the firm enters his/her appearance. The law firm should designate someone in the firm to check this email account for CM/ECF notices until substitution of counsel has been filed with the Panel.

(2) If the attorney leaving the firm is taking active cases from the firm, the attorney needs to change his/her email address as soon as possible, otherwise the attorney will not receive electronic notices from CM/ECF. The email will continue to be sent to the former law firm's email address still on record. Procedures for changing an email address may be found in the Panel's CM/ECF User Manual.

4. ELECTRONIC FILING AND SERVICE OF DOCUMENTS.

(a) Electronic transmission of a document to the Electronic Filing System in accordance with these procedures, together with the transmission of a (System) Notice of Electronic Filing from the Panel with a hyperlink to the electronically filed document, constitutes filing of the document for all purposes of the Panel Rules of Procedure.

(b) Emailing a document to the clerk's office does not constitute filing the document. A document shall not be considered filed until the System generates a Notice of Electronic Filing (NEF) with a hyperlink to the electronically filed document.

(c) Before filing a scanned document with the court, a Filing User must verify its legibility.

(d) When a document has been filed electronically, the official record of that document is the electronic recording as stored by the Panel and the filing party is bound by the document as filed. A document filed electronically is deemed filed on the date and time stated on the Notice of Electronic Filing (NEF) from the Panel.

(e) Filing a document electronically does not alter the filing deadline for that document. Filing must be completed before midnight, **EASTERN TIME**, in order to be considered timely filed that day. However, if time of day is of the essence, the Clerk of the Panel may order a document filed by a certain time.

(f) Upon the filing of a document, a docket entry will be created using the information provided by the Filing User. The clerk will, where necessary and appropriate, modify the docket entry description to comply with quality control standards. In the event a Filing User electronically files a document in the wrong MDL or associated civil action, or the incorrect PDF document is attached, the Clerk of the Panel, or his/her designee, shall be authorized to strike the document from the record. A notice of the action striking a document from the record shall be served on all parties in the case.

(g) By participating in the electronic filing process, the parties consent to the electronic service of all documents, and shall make available electronic mail addresses for service. Upon the filing of a document by a Filing User, a Notice of Electronic Filing (NEF), with a hyperlink to the electronic document and an email message will be automatically generated by the electronic filing system, and sent via electronic mail to the email addresses of all parties who have registered in the MDL. In addition to receiving email notifications of filing activity, the Filing User is strongly encouraged to sign on to the electronic filing system at regular intervals to check the docket in his/her MDL and/or civil action.

(h) If the filing of an electronically submitted document requires leave of the Panel, such as a request to file out-of-time, the attorney shall attach the proposed document as an attachment to the motion requesting leave to file. If the Clerk of the Panel grants the motion, the document will be electronically filed without further action by the Filing User.

(i) A certificate of service must be included with all documents filed electronically. Such certificate shall indicate that service was accomplished pursuant to the Panel's electronic filing procedures. Service by electronic mail shall constitute service pursuant to Panel Rule 5.2.

A party who is not a registered CM/ECF participant with any United States federal court is entitled to a paper copy of any electronically filed pleading, document, or order pursuant to Panel Rule 5.1.1.(b). The filing party must therefore provide the non-registered attorney or party, including a terminated party or attorney, if appropriate, with the pleading, document, or order pursuant to Panel Rule 5.2. Under the Rule, they can be served with a paper copy of the electronically filed document, or they can consent in writing to service by any other method, including other forms of electronic service such as fax or direct email.

The following is a suggested certificate of service for electronic filing:

CERTIFICATE OF SERVICE

On [Date], I electronically filed this document through the CM/ECF system, which will send a notice of electronic filing to: [Attorney Name (attach list if necessary)]; and I [mailed] [hand delivered] [faxed] this document and the notice of electronic filing to: [Attorney/Party Name], [Address], [Parties Represented], [Civil Action(s)] (attach list if necessary).

> /s/ [typed name of attorney]
> Attorney's name
> Law Firm Name (if applicable)
> Address
> Phone Number
> Fax Number
> Attorney's Email address
> Attorney for:

5. ENTRY OF PANEL DOCUMENTS.

(a) A document entered or issued by the Panel will be filed in accordance with these procedures and such filing shall constitute entry on the docket kept by the Clerk.

(b) All signed orders will be electronically filed or entered. An order containing the electronic signature of a Panel Judge or the Clerk of the Panel shall have the same force and effect as if the Panel Judge or Clerk of the Panel had affixed a signature to a paper copy of the order and the order had been entered on the docket in a conventional manner.

(c) Orders may also be issued as "text-only" entries on the docket, without an attached document. Such orders are official and binding.

6. NOTICE OF PANEL ORDERS AND NOTICES.

Immediately upon the entry of an order or notice by the Panel, the clerk will transmit to Filing Users in affected cases in the MDL, in electronic form, a Notice of Electronic Filing (NEF), with a hyperlink to the electronic document. Electronic transmission of the NEF, along with a hyperlink to the electronic document, constitutes the notice required by Panel Rule 5.2. The clerk must give notice in paper form to a pro se party or an attorney who is not a Filing User to the extent notice is required.

7. ATTACHMENTS AND EXHIBITS.

Documents referenced as exhibits or attachments shall be filed in accordance with these administrative policies and procedures and the Panel's CM/ECF User Manual, unless otherwise ordered by the Panel. A Filing User shall submit as exhibits or attachments only those excerpts of the referenced documents that are directly germane to the matter under consideration by the Panel. Excerpted material must be clearly and prominently identified as such. Filing Users who file excerpts of documents as exhibits or attachments under these procedures do so without prejudice to their right to file timely additional excerpts or the complete document. Responding parties may timely file additional excerpts or the complete document that they believe are directly germane. The Panel may require parties to file additional excerpts or the complete document.

8. SEALED DOCUMENTS.

To ensure proper storage of a document, a document subject to a sealing order must be filed with the Panel on paper in a sealed envelope marked "sealed", citing thereon the MDL docket number and title and the associated case caption and case number; or by attaching thereto a paper copy of the Panel's order sealing the document or a copy of the NEF citing the entry of the court's order sealing the document. The clerk may require the document to be accompanied by a disk or CD–ROM containing the document in .pdf format. Only a motion to file a document under seal may be filed electronically, unless prohibited by law. The order of the Panel authorizing the filing of documents under seal may be filed electronically, unless prohibited by law or otherwise directed by the Panel. If a document is filed under seal pursuant to the E–Government Act of 2002, the filing party is nevertheless required to file a redacted copy for the public record along with the unredacted sealed document.

9. SPECIAL FILING REQUIREMENTS AND EXCEPTIONS.

9.1 Special Filing Requirements

The documents listed below shall be presented for filing on paper. The clerk may require the document be accompanied by a disk or CD–ROM containing the document in .pdf format:

> Sealed

> MDL dockets involving Qui Tam Cases (under seal)

9.2 Exceptions

All documents shall be filed electronically unless otherwise ordered by the Panel or specifically exempt herein.

10. RETENTION REQUIREMENTS.

(a) A document that is electronically filed and requires an original signature other than that of the Filing User must be maintained in paper form by counsel and/or the firm representing the party on whose behalf the document was filed until one year after all periods for appeals expire. On request of the Panel, said counsel must provide the original document for review.

(b) The clerk's office may choose to discard certain documents brought to the clerk's office for filing in paper form after those documents are scanned and uploaded to the System (to include pro se filings). Therefore, counsel and pro se filers shall provide the Panel with a copy of the original documents with intrinsic value for scanning and maintain the original signature in accordance with 10(a).

11. SIGNATURES.

(a) The user login and password required to submit documents to the Electronic Filing System serve as the Filing User signature on all electronic documents filed with the court. They serve as a signature for purposes of the Panel Rules and any other purpose for which a signature is required in connection with proceedings before the Panel.

(b) Each document filed electronically must indicate in the caption that it has been electronically filed. An electronically filed document must include a signature block in compliance with Panel Rule 7.1(e), and must set forth the name, address, telephone number, fax number, and email address. In addition, the name of the Filing User under whose login and password the document is submitted must be preceded by an "/s/" and typed in the space where the signature would otherwise appear. No Filing User or other person may knowingly permit or cause to permit a Filing User password to be used by anyone other than an authorized agent of the Filing User.

(c) A document requiring signatures of more than one party must be filed either by:

(1) electronically filing a scanned document containing all necessary signatures; or

(2) representing the consent of the other parties on the document; or

(3) identifying on the document the party whose signature is required and by the submission of a notice of endorsement by the other parties no later than three (3) business days after filing; or

(4) any other manner approved by the Panel.

(d) A non-filing signatory or party who disputes the authenticity of an electronically filed document with a non-attorney signature, or the authenticity of the signature on that document; or the authenticity of an electronically filed document containing multiple signatures or the authenticity of the signature themselves, must file an objection to the document within fourteen (14) days of service of the document.

(e) Any party challenging the authenticity of an electronically filed document or the attorney's signature on that document must file an objection to the document within fourteen (14) days of service of the document.

(f) If a party wishes to challenge the authenticity of an electronically filed document or signature after the fourteen (14) day period, the party shall file a motion to seek a ruling from the Panel.

12.   SERVICE OF DOCUMENTS BY ELECTRONIC MEANS.

12.1   Service

12.1.1   Filing User

Upon the electronic filing of a pleading or other document, the Panel's Electronic Case Filing System will automatically generate and send a Notice of Electronic Filing (NEF) to all Filing Users associated with that MDL and/or associated cases, along with a hyperlink to the electronic document. Transmission of the Notice of Electronic Filing with a hyperlink to the electronic document constitutes service of the filed document.

The NEF must include the time of filing, the date the document was entered on the docket, the name of the party and attorney filing the document, the type of document, the text of the docket entry, and an electronic link (hyperlink) to the filed document, allowing anyone receiving the notice by email to retrieve the document automatically. If the Filing User becomes aware that the NEF was not transmitted successfully to a party, or that the notice is deficient, *i.e.*, the electronic link to the document is defective, the filer shall serve the electronically filed document by email, hand, facsimile, or by first-class mail postage prepaid immediately upon notification of the NEF deficiency.

12.1.2   Individual who is not a Filing User

A non-registered participant is entitled to receive a paper copy of any electronically filed document from the party making such filing. Service of such paper copy must be made according to the Panel Rules.

13.   TECHNICAL FAILURES.

(a) If the site is unable to accept filings continuously or intermittently for more than one (1) hour occurring after 12:00 noon Eastern Time that day, the Clerk of the Panel shall deem the Panel's Electronic Case Filing web site to be subject to a technical failure.

(b) If a Filing User experiences a technical failure as defined herein, the Filing User may submit the document to the Clerk of the Panel, provided that the document is accompanied by a certification, signed by the Filing User, that the Filing User has attempted to file the document electronically at least twice, with those unsuccessful attempts occurring at least one (1) hour apart after 12:00 noon Eastern Time that day. The Clerk may require the document to be accompanied by a disk or CD–ROM which contains the document in .pdf format.

(c) The initial point of contact for a Filing User experiencing technical difficulty filing a document electronically will be the Panel's CM/ECF Help Desk at the numbers listed on the Panel's web site and in the CM/ECF User Manual.

(d) A Filing User who suffers prejudice as a result of a technical failure as defined herein or a Filing User who cannot file a time-sensitive document electronically due to unforeseen technical difficulties, such as the malfunctioning of a Filing User's equipment, may seek relief from the Clerk of the Panel.

14. PUBLIC ACCESS.

14.1 (a) A person may receive information from the Electronic Filing System at the Panel's Internet site by obtaining a PACER login and password. A person who has PACER access may retrieve docket sheets and documents (unless otherwise sealed or restricted) in MDL dockets and associated civil cases. Any case or document under seal shall not be available electronically or through any other means.

(b) If a case or document has been restricted, a PACER user may retrieve the docket sheet over the Internet, but only a Filing User who is counsel of record may retrieve restricted documents electronically. However, a restricted case or document will be available for viewing by the public at the clerk's office.

(c) Electronic access to electronic docket sheets and all documents filed in the System, unless sealed, is available to the public for viewing at no charge during regular business hours at the clerk's office. A copy fee for an electronic reproduction is required in accordance with 28 U.S.C. § 1932.

(d) Conventional copies and certified copies of electronically filed documents may be purchased at the clerk's office. The fee for copying and certifying will be in accordance with 28 U.S.C. § 1932.

14.2 Sensitive Information

Since the public may access certain case information over the Internet through the Panel's Electronic Filing System, sensitive information should not be included in any document filed with the court unless such inclusion is necessary and relevant. In accordance with these Administrative Policies and Procedures, if sensitive information must be included, certain personal and identifying information such as Social Security numbers, financial account numbers, dates of birth and names of minor children shall be redacted from the pleading, whether it is filed electronically or on paper.

The Panel recognizes that parties may need to include in the record a document containing information such as driver's license number; medical records, treatment and diagnosis; employment history; individual financial information; and proprietary or trade secret information.

To avoid unnecessary disclosure of private, personal or financial information, a party may:

(a) **RESTRICTED MDL DOCKETS OR DOCUMENTS.**

File a "Motion to Seal" or "Motion to Seal Document". The motion must state the reason and show good cause for restricting remote access to the case. If the motion is granted, remote access to documents will be limited to Filing Users who are counsel of record. However, the MDL docket sheet and/or documents will be available for viewing by the public at the clerk's office.

(b) **EXHIBITS.**

File an exhibit containing private, personal or financial information as an attachment to a pleading entitled "Notice of Filing Restricted Exhibit". The notice and the attached exhibit shall be filed as a separate docket entry, rather than as an attachment to the pleading supported by the exhibit. Remote public access to the notice and exhibit will be limited to Filing Users who are counsel of record. The notice and exhibit will, however, be available for viewing by the public at the clerk's office.

(c) **DOCUMENTS UNDER SEAL.**

(1) File a redacted copy of a pleading or exhibit containing private, personal or financial information, whether electronically or on paper, while concurrently filing an unredacted copy under seal. This document shall be retained by the Panel as part of the record.

OR

(2) File a reference list under seal. The reference list shall contain the complete personal data identifier(s) and the redacted identifier(s) used in its (their) place in the filing. All references in the case to the redacted identifier(s) included in the reference list will be construed to refer to the corresponding complete identifier. The reference list must be filed under seal, and may be amended as of right. It shall be retained by the Panel as part of the record.

(d) **MOTION TO SEAL.**

File a motion to seal the document or MDL associated case. The motion must state the reason and show good cause for sealing the document or MDL associated case. If the motion to seal is granted, the document or case under seal will not be available electronically or through any other means.

It is the sole responsibility of counsel and the parties to ensure that all documents filed with the Panel comply with these Administrative Policies and Procedures, regarding public access to electronic case files. The Clerk will not review any document for redaction.

Counsel are strongly urged to share this information with all clients so that an informed decision about the inclusion, redaction, and/or exclusion of certain materials may be made.

[Effective May 2010.]

FEDERAL COURTS MISCELLANEOUS FEE SCHEDULES

COURT OF APPEALS FEE SCHEDULE

(Effective December 1, 2016)

The fees included in the Court of Appeals Miscellaneous Fee Schedule[1] are to be charged for services provided by the courts of appeals, including relevant services[2] provided by the bankruptcy appellate panels established under 28 U.S.C. § 158(b)(1).

- The United States should not be charged fees under this schedule, except as prescribed in Items 2, 4, and 5 when the information requested is available through remote electronic access.

- Federal agencies or programs that are funded from judiciary appropriations (agencies, organizations, and individuals providing services authorized by the Criminal Justice Act, 18 U.S.C. § 3006A, and bankruptcy administrators) should not be charged any fees under this schedule.

(1) For docketing a case on appeal or review, or docketing any other proceeding, $500.

- Each party filing a notice of appeal pays a separate fee to the district court, but parties filing a joint notice of appeal pay only one fee.

- There is no docketing fee for an application for an interlocutory appeal under 28 U.S.C. § 1292(b) or other petition for permission to appeal under Fed. R. App. P. 5, unless the appeal is allowed.

- There is no docketing fee for a direct bankruptcy appeal or a direct bankruptcy cross appeal, when the fee has been collected by the bankruptcy court in accordance with item 14 of the Bankruptcy Court Miscellaneous Fee Schedule.

- This fee is collected in addition to the statutory fee of $5 that is collected under 28 U.S.C. § 1917.

(2) For conducting a search of the court of appeals or bankruptcy appellate panel records, $31 per name or item searched. This fee applies to services rendered on behalf of the United States if the information requested is available through remote electronic access.

(3) For certification of any document, $11.

(4) For reproducing any document, $.50 per page. This fee applies to services rendered on behalf of the United States if the document requested is available through remote electronic access.

(5) For reproducing recordings of proceedings, regardless of the medium, $31, including the cost of materials. This fee applies to services rendered on behalf of the United States if the recording is available through remote electronic access.

(6) For reproducing the record in any appeal in which the court of appeals does not require an appendix pursuant to Fed. R. App. P.30(f), (or, in appeals before a bankruptcy appellate panel, pursuant to Fed. R. Bankr. P. 8018(e)), $86.

(7) For retrieval of one box of records from a Federal Records Center, National Archives, or other storage location removed from the place of business of the court, $64. For retrievals involving multiple boxes, $39 for each additional box. For electronic retrievals, $10 plus any charges assessed by the Federal Records Center, National Archives, or other storage location removed from the place of business of the courts.

(8) For any payment returned or denied for insufficient funds, $53.

(9) For copies of opinions, a fee commensurate with the cost of printing, as fixed by each court of appeals.

(10) For copies of the local rules of court, a fee commensurate with the cost of distributing the copies. The court may also distribute copies of the local rules without charge.

(11) For filing:

- Any separate or joint notice of appeal or application for appeal from the bankruptcy appellate panel, $5;

- A notice of the allowance of an appeal from the bankruptcy appellate panel, $5.

(12) For counsel's requested use of the court's videoconferencing equipment in connection with each oral argument, the court may charge and collect a fee of $200 per remote location.

(13) For original admission of attorney to practice, including a certificate of admission, $181. For a duplicate certificate of admission or certificate of good standing, $19.

1 Issued in accordance with 28 U.S.C. § 1913.

2 Item 13 does not apply to bankruptcy appellate panels.

DISTRICT COURT FEE SCHEDULE

(Effective December 1, 2016)

The fees included in the District Court Miscellaneous Fee Schedule[1] are to be charged for services provided by the district courts.

- The United States should not be charged fees under this schedule, with the exception of those specifically prescribed in Items 2, 4 and 5, when the information requested is available through remote electronic access.

- Federal agencies or programs that are funded from judiciary appropriations (agencies, organizations, and individuals providing services authorized by the Criminal Justice Act, 18 U.S.C. § 3006 and bankruptcy administrators) should not be charged any fees under this schedule.

1. For filing any document that is not related to a pending case or proceeding, $47.

2. For conducting a search of the district court records, $31 per name or item searched. This fee applies to services rendered on behalf of the United States if the information requested is available through electronic access.

3. For certification of any document, $11. For exemplification of any document, $22.

4. For reproducing any record or paper, $.50 per page. This fee shall apply to paper copies made from either: (1) original documents; or (2) microfiche or microfilm reproductions of the original records. This fee shall apply to services rendered on behalf of the United States if the record or paper requested is available through electronic access.

5. For reproduction of an audio recording of a court proceeding, $31. This fee applies to services rendered on behalf of the United States, if the recording is available electronically.

6. For each microfiche sheet of film or microfilm jacket copy of any court record, where available, $6.

7. For retrieval of one box of records from a Federal Records Center, National Archives, or other storage location removed from the place of business of the court, $64. For retrievals involving multiple boxes, $39 for each additional box. For electronic retrievals, $10 plus any charges assessed by the Federal Records Center, National Archives, or other storage location removed from the place of business of the courts.

8. For any payment returned or denied for insufficient funds, $53.

9. For an appeal to a district judge from a judgment of conviction by a magistrate judge in a misdemeanor case, $38.

10. For original admission of attorneys to practice, $181 each, including a certificate of admission. For a duplicate certificate of admission or certificate of good standing, $19.

11. The court may charge and collect fees commensurate with the cost of providing copies of the local rules of court. The court may also distribute copies of the local rules without charge.

12.

- For handling registry funds deposited with and held by the court, the clerk shall assess a charge from interest earnings, in accordance with the detailed fee schedule issued by the Director of the Administrative Office of the United States Courts.

- For management of registry funds invested through the Court Registry Investment System, a fee at an annual rate of 10 basis points of assets on deposit shall be assessed from interest earnings, excluding registry funds from disputed ownership interpleader cases deposited under 28 U.S.C. § 1335 and held in a Court Registry Investment System Disputed Ownership Fund.

- For management of funds deposited under 28 U.S.C. § 1335 and invested in a Disputed Ownership Fund through the Court Registry Investment System, a fee at an annual rate of 20 basis points of assets on deposit shall be assessed from interest earnings.

- The Director of the Administrative Office has the authority to waive these fees for cause.

13. For filing an action brought under Title III of the Cuban Liberty and Democratic Solidarity (LIBERTAD) Act of 1996, P.L. 104–114, 110 Stat. § 785 (1996), $6,548. (This fee is in addition to the

filing fee prescribed in 28 U.S.C. § 1914(a) for instituting any civil action other than a writ of habeas corpus.)

14. Administrative fee for filing a civil action, suit, or proceeding in a district court, $50. This fee does not apply to applications for a writ of habeas corpus or to persons granted in forma pauperis status under 28 U.S.C. § 1915.

15. Processing fee for a petty offense charged on a federal violation notice, $30.

1 Issued in accordance with 28 U.S.C. § 1914.

BANKRUPTCY COURT MISCELLANEOUS FEE SCHEDULE

(Effective December 1, 2016)

The fees included in the Bankruptcy Court Miscellaneous Fee Schedule[1] are to be charged for services provided by the bankruptcy courts.

- The United States should not be charged fees under this schedule, with the exception of those specifically prescribed in Items 1, 3 and 5 when the information requested is available through remote electronic access.

- Federal agencies or programs that are funded from judiciary appropriations (agencies, organizations, and individuals providing services authorized by the Criminal Justice Act, 18 U.S.C. § 3006A, and bankruptcy administrators) should not be charged any fees under this schedule.

1. For reproducing any document, $.50 per page. This fee applies to services rendered on behalf of the United States if the document requested is available through electronic access.

2. For certification of any document, $11.

   For exemplification of any document, $22.

3. For reproduction of an audio recording of a court proceeding, $31. This fee applies to services rendered on behalf of the United States if the recording is available electronically.

4. For filing an amendment to the debtor's schedules of creditors, lists of creditors, or mailing list, $31, except:

- The bankruptcy judge may, for good cause, waive the charge in any case.

- This fee must not be charged if -

  - the amendment is to change the address of a creditor or an attorney for a creditor listed on the schedules; or

  - the amendment is to add the name and address of an attorney for a creditor listed on the schedules.

5. For conducting a search of the bankruptcy court records, $31 per name or item searched. This fee applies to services rendered on behalf of the United States if the information requested is available through electronic access.

6. For filing a complaint, $350, except:

- If the trustee or debtor-in-possession files the complaint, the fee must be paid only by the estate, to the extent there is an estate.

- This fee must not be charged if -

  - the debtor is the plaintiff; or

  - a child support creditor or representative files the complaint and submits the form required by § 304(g) of the Bankruptcy Reform Act of 1994.

7. For filing any document that is not related to a pending case or proceeding, $47.

8. Administrative fee:

- For filing a petition under Chapter 7, 12, or 13, $75.

- For filing a petition under Chapter 9, 11, or 15, $550.

- When a motion to divide a joint case under Chapter 7, 12, or 13 is filed, $75

- When a motion to divide a joint case under Chapter 11 is filed, $550.

9. For payment to trustees pursuant to 11 U.S.C. § 330(b)(2), a $15 fee applies in the following circumstances:

- For filing a petition under Chapter 7.

- For filing a notice of conversion to a Chapter 7 case.

- For filing a motion to convert a case to a Chapter 7 case.

- For filing a motion to divide a joint Chapter 7 case.

- For filing a motion to reopen a Chapter 7 case.

10. In addition to any fees imposed under Item 9, above, the following fees must be collected:

- For filing a motion to convert a Chapter 12 case to a Chapter 7 case or a notice of conversion pursuant to 11 U.S.C. § 1208(a), $45.

- For filing a motion to convert a Chapter 13 case to a Chapter 7 case or a notice of conversion pursuant to 11 U.S.C. § 1307(a), $10.

The fee amounts in this item are derived from the fees prescribed in 28 U.S.C. § 1930(a).

If the trustee files the motion to convert, the fee is payable only from the estate that exists prior to conversion.

If the filing fee for the chapter to which the case is requested to be converted is less than the fee paid at the commencement of the case, no refund may be provided.

11. For filing a motion to reopen, the following fees apply:

- For filing a motion to reopen a Chapter 7 case, $245.

- For filing a motion to reopen a Chapter 9 case, $1167.

- For filing a motion to reopen a Chapter 11 case, $1167.

- For filing a motion to reopen a Chapter 12 case, $200.

- For filing a motion to reopen a Chapter 13 case, $235.

- For filing a motion to reopen a Chapter 15 case, $1167.

The fee amounts in this item are derived from the fees prescribed in 28 U.S.C. § 1930(a).

The reopening fee must be charged when a case has been closed without a discharge being entered.

The court may waive this fee under appropriate circumstances or may defer payment of the fee from trustees pending discovery of additional assets. If payment is deferred, the fee should be waived if no additional assets are discovered.

The reopening fee must not be charged in the following situations:

- to permit a party to file a complaint to obtain a determination under Rule 4007(b); or

- when a debtor files a motion to reopen a case based upon an alleged violation of the terms of the discharge under 11 U.S.C. § 524; or

- when the reopening is to correct an administrative error.

- to redact a record already filed in a case, pursuant to Fed. R. Bankr. P. 9037, if redaction is the only reason for reopening.

12. For retrieval of one box of records from a Federal Records Center, National Archives, or other storage location removed from the place of business of the court, $64. For retrievals involving multiple boxes, $39 for each additional box. For electronic retrievals, $10 plus any charges assessed by the Federal Records Center, National Archives, or other storage location removed from the place of business of the courts.

13. For any payment returned or denied for insufficient funds, $53.

14. For filing an appeal or cross appeal from a judgment, order, or decree, $293.

This fee is collected in addition to the statutory fee of $5 that is collected under 28 U.S.C. § 1930(c) when a notice of appeal is filed.

Parties filing a joint notice of appeal should pay only one fee.

If a trustee or debtor-in-possession is the appellant, the fee must be paid only by the estate, to the extent there is an estate.

Upon notice from the court of appeals that a direct appeal or direct cross-appeal has been authorized, an additional fee of $207 must be collected.

15. For filing a case under Chapter 15 of the Bankruptcy Code, $1167.

This fee is derived from and equal to the fee prescribed in 28 U.S.C. § 1930(a)(3) for filing a case commenced under Chapter 11 of Title 11.

16.   The court may charge and collect fees commensurate with the cost of providing copies of the local rules of court. The court may also distribute copies of the local rules without charge.

17.

- For handling registry funds deposited with and held by the court, the clerk shall assess a charge from interest earnings, in accordance with the detailed fee schedule issued by the Director of the Administrative Office of the United States Courts.

- For management of registry funds invested through the Court Registry Investment System, a fee at an annual rate of 10 basis points of assets on deposit shall be assessed from interest earnings, excluding registry funds from disputed ownership interpleader cases deposited under 28 U.S.C. § 1335 and held in a Court Registry Investment System Disputed Ownership Fund.

- For management of funds deposited under 28 U.S.C. § 1335 and invested in a Disputed Ownership Fund through the Court Registry Investment System, a fee at an annual rate of 20 basis points of assets on deposit shall be assessed from interest earnings.

- The Director of the Administrative Office has the authority to waive these fees for cause.

18.   For a motion filed by the debtor to divide a joint case filed under 11 U.S.C. § 302, the following fees apply:

- For filing a motion to divide a joint Chapter 7 case, $245.

- For filing a motion to divide a joint Chapter 11 case, $1167.

- For filing a motion to divide a joint Chapter 12 case, $200.

- For filing a motion to divide a joint Chapter 13 case, $235.

These fees are derived from and equal to the filing fees prescribed in 28 U.S.C. § 1930(a).

19.   For filing the following motions, $181:

- To terminate, annul, modify or condition the automatic stay;

- To compel abandonment of property of the estate pursuant to Rule 6007(b) of the Federal Rules of Bankruptcy Procedure;

- To withdraw the reference of a case or proceeding under 28 U.S.C. § 157(d); or

- To sell property of the estate free and clear of liens under 11 U.S.C. § 363(f).

This fee must not be collected in the following situations:

- For a motion for relief from the co-debtor stay;

- For a stipulation for court approval of an agreement for relief from a stay; or

- For a motion filed by a child support creditor or its representative, if the form required by § 304(g) of the Bankruptcy Reform Act of 1994 is filed.

20.   For filing a transfer of claim, $25 per claim transferred.

21.   For filing a motion to redact a record, $25 per affected case. The court may waive this fee under appropriate circumstances.

1 Issued in accordance with 28 U.S.C. § 1930.

JUDICIAL PANEL ON MULTIDISTRICT LITIGATION FEE SCHEDULE

(Effective December 1, 2016)

Following are fees to be charged for services to be performed by the clerk of the Judicial Panel on Multidistrict Litigation. No fees are to be charged for services rendered on behalf of the United States, with the exception of those specifically prescribed in items 1 and 3. No fees under this schedule shall be charged to federal agencies or programs which are funded from judiciary appropriations, including, but not limited to, agencies, organizations, and individuals providing services authorized by the Criminal Justice Act, 18 U.S.C. § 3006A.

(1) For every search of the records of the court conducted by the clerk of the court or a deputy clerk, $31 per name or item searched. This fee shall apply to services rendered on behalf of the United States if the information requested is available through electronic access.

(2) For certification of any document or paper, whether the certification is made directly on the document or by separate instrument, $11.

(3) For reproducing any record or paper, $.50 per page. This fee shall apply to paper copies made from either: (1) original documents; or (2) microfiche or microfilm reproductions of the original records. This fee shall apply to services rendered on behalf of the United States if the record or paper requested is available through electronic access.

(4) For retrieval of one box of records from a Federal Records Center, National Archives, or other storage location removed from the place of business of the court, $64. For retrievals involving multiple boxes, $39 for each additional box. For electronic retrievals, $10 plus any charges assessed by the Federal Records Center, National Archives, or other storage location removed from the place of business of the courts.

(5) For any payment returned or denied for insufficient funds, $53.

ELECTRONIC PUBLIC ACCESS FEE SCHEDULE

(Issued in accordance with 28 U.S.C. §§ 1913, 1914, 1926, 1930, 1932)

(Effective April 1, 2017)

The fees included in the Electronic Public Access Fee Schedule are to be charged for providing electronic public access to court records.

Fees for Public Access to Court Electronic Records (PACER)

1. Except as provided below, for electronic access to any case document, docket sheet, or case-specific report via PACER: $0.10 per page, not to exceed the fee for thirty pages.

2. For electronic access to transcripts and non-case specific reports via PACER (such as reports obtained from the PACER Case Locator or docket activity reports): $0.10 per page.

3. For electronic access to an audio file of a court hearing via PACER: $2.40 per audio file.

Fees for Courthouse Electronic Access

4. For printing copies of any record or document accessed electronically at a public terminal in a courthouse: $0.10 per page.

PACER Service Center Fees

5. For every search of court records conducted by the PACER Service Center, $30 per name or item searched.

6. For the PACER Service Center to reproduce on paper any record pertaining to a PACER account, if this information is remotely available through electronic access: $0.50 per page.

7. For any payment returned or denied for insufficient funds, $53.

Free Access and Exemptions

8. Automatic Fee Exemptions:

- No fee is owed for electronic access to court data or audio files via PACER until an account holder accrues charges of more than $15.00 in a quarterly billing cycle.

- Parties in a case (including *pro se* litigants) and attorneys of record receive one free electronic copy, via the notice of electronic filing or notice of docket activity, of all documents filed electronically, if receipt is required by law or directed by the filer.

- No fee is charged for access to judicial opinions.

- No fee is charged for viewing case information or documents at courthouse public access terminals.

- No fee is charged for Chapter 13 bankruptcy trustees to download quarterly (i.e., once every 90 days) a list of the trustee's cases from the PACER Case Locator.

9. Discretionary Fee Exemptions:

- Courts may exempt certain persons or classes of persons from payment of the user access fee. Examples of individuals and groups that a court may consider exempting include: indigents, bankruptcy case trustees, pro bono attorneys, pro bono alternative dispute resolution neutrals, Section 501(c)(3) not-for-profit organizations, and individual researchers associated with educational institutions. Courts should not, however, exempt individuals or groups that have the ability to pay the statutorily established access fee. Examples of individuals and groups that a court should not exempt include: local, state or federal government agencies, members of the media, privately paid attorneys or others who have the ability to pay the fee.

- In considering granting an exemption, courts must find:

  - that those seeking an exemption have demonstrated that an exemption is necessary in order to avoid unreasonable burdens and to promote public access to information;

  - that individual researchers requesting an exemption have shown that the defined research project is intended for scholarly research, that it is limited in scope, and that it is not intended for redistribution on the internet or for commercial purposes.

- If the court grants an exemption:
  - the user receiving the exemption must agree not to sell the data obtained as a result, and must not transfer any data obtained as the result of a fee exemption, unless expressly authorized by the court; and
  - the exemption should be granted for a definite period of time, should be limited in scope, and may be revoked at the discretion of the court granting the exemption.
- Courts may provide local court information at no cost (e.g., local rules, court forms, news items, court calendars, and other information) to benefit the public.

Applicability to the United States and State and Local Governments

10.   Unless otherwise authorized by the Judicial Conference, these fees must be charged to the United States, except to federal agencies or programs that are funded from judiciary appropriations (including, but not limited to, agencies, organizations, and individuals providing services authorized by the Criminal Justice Act [18 U.S.C. § 3006A], and bankruptcy administrators).

11.   The fee for printing copies of any record or document accessed electronically at a public terminal ($0.10 per page) described in (4) above does not apply to services rendered on behalf of the United States if the record requested is not remotely available through electronic access.

12.   The fee for local, state, and federal government entities, shall be $0.08 per page until April 1, 2015, after which time, the fee shall be $0.10 per page.

JUDICIAL CONFERENCE POLICY NOTES

The Electronic Public Access (EPA) fee and its exemptions are directly related to the requirement that the judiciary charge user-based fees for the development and maintenance of electronic public access services. The fee schedule provides examples of users that may not be able to afford reasonable user fees (such as indigents, bankruptcy case trustees, individual researchers associated with educational institutions, 501(c)(3) not-for-profit organizations, and court-appointed pro bono attorneys), but requires those seeking an exemption to demonstrate that an exemption is limited in scope and is necessary in order to avoid an unreasonable burden. In addition, the fee schedule includes examples of other entities that courts should not exempt from the fee (such as local, state or federal government agencies, members of the media, and attorneys). The goal is to provide courts with guidance in evaluating a requestor's ability to pay the fee.

Judicial Conference policy also limits exemptions in other ways. First, it requires exempted users to agree not to sell the data they receive through an exemption (unless expressly authorized by the court). This prohibition is not intended to bar a quote or reference to information received as a result of a fee exemption in a scholarly or other similar work. Second, it permits courts to grant exemptions for a definite period of time, to limit the scope of the exemptions, and to revoke exemptions. Third, it cautions that exemptions should be granted as the exception, not the rule, and prohibits courts from exempting all users from EPA fees.